Clinical Handbook of Marriage and Couples Interventions

Clinical Handbook of Marriage and Couples Interventions

Edited by

W. Kim Halford

*School of Applied Psychology,
Griffith University, Nathan,
Queensland, Australia*

and

Howard J. Markman

*Department of Psychology,
University of Denver,
Denver, Colorado, USA*

Foreword by **Kurt Hahlweg**, *University of Braunschweig, Germany*

JOHN WILEY & SONS

Chichester · New York · Weinheim · Brisbane · Singapore · Toronto

Other Wiley Editorial Offices

John Wiley & Sons, Inc., 605 Third Avenue,
New York, NY 10158-0012, USA

VCH Verlagsgesellschaft mbH,
Pappelallee 3, 0-69469 Weinheim, Germany

Jacaranda Wiley Ltd, 33 Park Road, Milton,
Queensland 4064, Australia

John Wiley & Sons (Asia) Pte Ltd, 2 Clementi Loop #02-01,
Jin Xing Distripark, Singapore 129809

John Wiley & Sons (Canada) Ltd, 22 Worcester Road,
Rexdale, Ontario M9W ILI, Canada

Library of Congress Cataloging-in-Publication Data

Clinical handbook of marriage and couples interventions / [edited by]
    W. Kim Halford and Howard J. Markman; foreword by Kurt Hehlweg.
        p.   cm.
    Includes bibliographical references.
    ISBN 0-471-95519-1 (cloth)
    1. Marital psychotherapy—Handbooks, manuals, etc. I. Halford, W. Kim.
II. Markman, Howard, 1950–
RC488.5.C586   1997
616.89′156—dc20   96-24024
                                                                                                CIP

British Library Cataloguing in Publication Data

A catalogue record for this book is available from the British Library

ISBN 0-471-95519-1

Typeset in 10/12pt Times by Best-set Typesetter Ltd., Hong Kong
Printed and bound in Great Britain by Bookcraft (Bath) Ltd, Midsomer Norton, Somerset
This book is printed on acid-free paper responsibly manufactured from sustainable forestation, for which at least two trees are planted for each one used for paper production.

To my family for their ongoing support—HJM

To Barbara, my partner in life—WKH

Contents

About the Editors

Dr W. Kim Halford is Professor of Clinical Psychology and Head of the School of Applied Psychology at Griffith University in Nathan, Queensland, Australia. He is an internationally known expert on couples research and therapy, and has written extensively in the area of the influence of cognitive factors on couple interaction and couple therapy, and the prevention of relationship problems. He maintains an active practice in couples work, and has presented his research into couples work in North America, Western Europe and throughout Australasia.

Dr Howard J. Markman is Professor of Clinical Psychology and Director of the Center for Marital and Family Studies in the Department of Psychology at the University of Denver, in Denver, Colorado, USA. Professor Markman is an internationally recognized expert in the prevention of couples problems, and has been a pioneer in the empirical evaluation of these programs. He has published widely on the prediction and prevention of marital and family distress, and has presented the results of his research throughout Western Europe, North America and Australasia.

Contributors

Arellano, Charleanea, PhD, *Department of Psychology, Colorado State University, Fort Collins, CO, USA*

Baris, Mitchell A., PhD, *Private Practice, Suite 501, 1919 14th Street, Boulder, CO 80302, USA*

Bates, Leonard, *Department of Psychology, Indiana University, Bloomington, IN 47405-1301, USA*

Baucom, Donald H., PhD, *Department of Psychology, University of North Carolina, Davie Hall, CS #3270, Chapel Hill, NC 27599, USA*

Beach, Steven, PhD, *Department of Psychology, University of Georgia, Athens, GA 30602-3013, USA*

Behrens, Brett C., MCP, *Department of Psychiatry, University of Queensland, Mental Health Building, Royal Brisbane Hospital, Herston, Queensland 4029, Australia*

Bennun, Ian, PhD, *Department of Psychology, University of Exeter, Washington Singer Laboratories, Perry Road, Exeter EX4 4QG, UK*

Bouma, Ruth, MCP, *School of Applied Psychology, Griffith University, Nathan, Queensland 4111, Australia*

Bradbury, Thomas N., PhD, *Department of Psychology, University of California at Los Angeles, Los Angeles, CA, USA*

Chao, Christine M., PhD, *Private Practice; and Department of Psychology, University of Denver, Denver, CO 80208, Denver, USA*

Cordova, Allan D., *Department of Psychology, University of Denver, CO 80208, USA*

Daiuto, Anthony, *Department of Psychology, University of North Carolina, Chapel Hill, NC 27599, USA*

Davis, Elizabeth, PhD, *Oregon Research Institute, 1715 Franklin Boulevard, Eugene, OR 97403-1983, USA*

Dickson, Frances C., PhD, *Department of Human Communications, University of Denver, Denver, CO 80208, USA*

Epstein, Norman H., PhD, *Department of Family Studies, University of Maryland, College Park, MD 20742, USA*

Flanagan, Anna Smalley, MA, *Department of Psychology, University of Denver, Denver, CO 80208, USA*

Floyd, Frank J., PhD, *Department of Psychology, University of North Carolina, Davie Hall, CS #3270, Chapel Hill, NC 27599-3270, USA*

Fraenkel, Peter, PhD, *Ackerman Institute for Family Therapy, 149 East 78th Street, New York, NY 10021; and Department of Psychiatry, New York University, New York, NY, USA*

Furman, Wyndol, PhD, *Department of Psychology, University of Denver, Denver, CO 80208, USA*

Garrity, Carla B., PhD, *Private Practice, Suite 207, 5290 East Yale Circle, Denver, CO 80222, USA*

Glass, Shirley P., PhD, *Private Practice, 4 Caveswood Lane, Owing Mills, MD 21117, USA*

Guerney, Bernard, PhD, *Department of Human Development, Pennsylvania State University, College Park, PH; and 1190 Renwood Lane, North Bethesda, MD 20852, USA*

Halford, W. Kim, PhD, *School of Applied Psychology, Griffith University, Nathan, Queensland 4111, Australia*

Haynes, Stephen N., PhD, *Department of Psychology, University of Hawaii, Honolulu, Hawaii, USA*

Heyman, Richard E., PhD, *Department of Psychology, State University of New York at Stony Brook, New York, NY 11794-2500, USA*

Holtzworth-Munroe, Amy, PhD, *Department of Psychology, Indiana University, Bloomington, IN 47405-1301, USA*

Hosman, Clemens, *Nymachin University, The Netherlands*

Hops, Hyman, PhD, *Oregon Research Institute, 1715 Franklin Boulevard, Eugene, OR 97403-1983, USA*

Jones, Arthur C., PhD, *Department of Psychology, University of Denver, Denver, CO 80208, USA*

Julien, Danielle, PhD, *Department of Psychology, University of Quebec at Montreal C.P. 8888, Succ. "A", Montreal, PQ H3C 3P8, Canada*

Kelly, Adrian, MCP, *Department of Psychiatry, University of Queensland, Office 3, 1st Floor, Edith Cavell Building, Royal Brisbane Hospital, Herston, Queensland 4006, Australia*

Kelly, Shalonda, MA, *Department of Psychology, University of Michigan, East Lansing, MI, USA*

Lindahl, Kristin M., PhD, *Department of Psychology, University of Miami, PO Box 248185, Miamè, FL 33124-2070, USA*

Malik, Neena M., MA, *Department of Psychology, University of Miami, PO Box 248185, Miami, Florida 33124-2070, USA*

Markie-Dadds, Carol, MCP, *Department of Psychology, University of Queensland, St Lucia, Queensland 4072, Australia*

Markman, Howard J., PhD, *Professor of Psychology and Director, Center for Marital and Family Studies, Universtiy of Denver, Denver, CO 80208, USA*

Neidig, Peter H., PhD, *Department of Psychology, State University of New York at Stony Brook, New York, NY 11794-2500, USA*

Nicholson, Jan M., PhD, *School of Public Health, Queensland University of Technology, Kelvin Grove, Queensland 4059, Australia*

Noller, Patricia, PhD, *Department of Psychology, University of Queensland, St Lucia, Queensland 4072, Australia*

O'Farrell, Timothy J., PhD, *Department of Psychiatry, Harvard University Medical School, and Veterans' Affairs Medical Center, 940 Belmont Street MA 02401, USA*

Osgarby, Susan, BA, *School of Applied Psychology, Griffith University, Nathan, Queensland 4111, Australia*

Perry, Barbara Anne, PhD, *Private Practice, Eugene, OR; and Department of Psychology, University of Oregon, Eugene, OR 97403, USA*

Rotunda, Robert J., *Harvard Families in Addiction Program, Department of Psychiatry, Harvard University Medical School, Veterans' Affairs Medical Center, Brockton, MA 02401, USA*

Sanders, Matthew R., PhD, *Department of Psychology, University of Queensland, St Lucia, Queensland 4072, Australia*

Sandin, Elizabeth, MA, *Department of Psychology, Indiana University, Bloomington, IN 47405-1301, USA*

Schmaling, Karen B., PhD, *Department of Psychiatry and Behavioral Sciences, XD-45, University of Washington Medical School, Suite 306, 4225 Roosevelt Way NE, Seattle, WA 98105, USA*

Sher, Tamara G., PhD, *Department of Psychology, Illinois Institute of Technology, Chicago, IL, USA*

Smutzler, Natalie, *Department of Psychology, Indiana University, Bloomington, IN 47405-1301, USA*

Snyder, Douglas K., PhD, *Department of Psychology, Texas A & M University, College Station, USA*

Spence, Susan H., PhD, *Department of Psychology, University of Queensland, St Lucia, Queensland 4072, Australia*

Thompson, Briony M., PhD, *School of Psychology, Griffith University, Nathan, Queensland 4111, Australia*

Turgeon, Lyse, *Centre de Recherche Fernand Seguin, Hospital La Fontaine, Montreal, Quebec, Canada*

Van Wideneflt, Brigit, PhD, *Department of Psychology, University of North Carolina, Box 802, Chapel Hill, NC 27519, USA*

Weiss, Robert L., PhD, *Department of Psychology, University of Oregon, Eugene, OR 97403; 5338 Tahsili Street, Eugene, OR 97403, USA*

Whisman, Mark A., PhD, *Department of Psychology, Yale University, PO Box 208205, New Haven, CT 06520-8205, USA*

Wright, Thomas L., PhD, *Department of Psychology, Catholic University of America, Washington, DC 20064, USA*

Foreword

This is the most comprehensive publication on research and therapy with marriage and couples relationships yet published. Under the editorship of Kim Halford and Howard Markman, two outstanding researchers and clinicians in the marital field, the book is the collective work of authors from three continents: North America, Australia and Europe. All the authors share a belief in the importance of couple relationships in the lives and well-being of the citizens of the diverse cultures and countries in which those authors reside. Furthermore, all authors share a commitment to a scientist–practitioner approach to understanding couples' relationships, and developing and evaluating interventions to promote healthier and more satisfying relationships.

Kim Halford and Howard Markman have guided the focus of the book so that it distils the crucial elements about what we know about couples relationships, with particular emphasis on how to intervene to promote more satisfying relationships. For practitioners it is an overview of research, therapy and prevention programs which is directly relevant to their clinical practice. The content of the book addresses itself to clinical issues often neglected in other publications on couples therapy. For example, there are specific chapters on how to manage relationship problems when only one partner presents for therapy, and how to respond to the impact of an extra-marital affair on the presenting relationship.

The scope of the book is broad. Section I provides a clear overview of the nature of healthy, satisfying and stable couples relationships. This section addresses the behavioral, cognitive and affective elements of relationship interactions. Chapters in this section also address the issues of relationship violence, sex and gender differences. One of the strengths of the book is its attention to cultural diversity as it impacts upon couple relationships. In this first section there is an initial chapter on this theme, addressing in particular the socio-cultural influences on couples, and the nature of relationships which combine partners from different cultures.

Section II addresses the dynamic, changing nature of relationships. The first chapter in this section is a review of the influence of childhood, adolescent and young adult experiences upon subsequent couple relationships. This is followed by reviews of how relationships change over time, with a particular focus on the impact of changing life circumstances, children and aging.

Section III is a consideration of the impact of personal and environmental influences on couple relationships. This section addresses the effects of work, individual adjustment, and physical health on marriage. In each chapter specific implications of the research findings for assessment and intervention are described.

The largest part of the book, Section IV is on intervention. Chapters in this section include detailed descriptions on how to conduct assessment cognitive–behavioral and systemic interventions with maritally distressed couples. In clinical practice couples often present with co-existing relationship and individual problems. In this book clinical guidelines for managing these complex cases are given, with chapters on depression, alcohol abuse, spouse abuse, and children's problems. There also is a chapter on divorce mediation. The chapter on mediation underscores that staying together is not always the best option for distressed couples, and the competent couples therapist needs knowledge and skills in mediation. There also is a chapter specifically on the prevention of relationship problems, which emphasizes the editors' commitment to the need to address relationships problems at a much broader level than just those couples who present for marital therapy.

The final section of the book, Section V has two chapters on evaluating and improving interventions to assist couples. Together these chapters provide an excellent overview of the limitation of what we now know, and what further research is needed. I think the publication of this new and exciting volume will help bridge the gap between research and clinical practice in couples therapy.

Kurt Hahlweg, PhD
University of Braunschweig, Germany

Preface

We believe in good marriage. We believe that partners usually benefit from living in a committed, loving long-term relationship. We also believe that children usually benefit from being raised in a family based around a positive parental relationship. On almost any index of health, well-being or happiness, people in happy marriages are, on average, better off than other groups in society.

The majority of couples who marry are satisfied with their relationships. In most Western countries the majority of couples who marry stay together for life (the one exception to this is the United States of America, in which just over half of marriages end in divorce; however, even in the USA, *nearly* half of all marriages are life-long). And the overwhelming majority of married people say they are glad they are married.

The good news about marriage is that most people want to be married and, when marriage works, it is a very satisfying experience. The bad news about marriage is that a vary large number of people who enter marriage find the relationship is unsatisfying. Unhappy marriages have severe negative effects on the partners and their offspring. Really unhappy marriages often are associated with severe psychological problems in partners and offspring. In the most severe cases unhappy marriages are associated with abuse, violence and even murder.

Imagine gathering together a large crowd of hundreds of engaged couples, which in a sense we have done through our research. If, like us, you spent hundreds of hours chatting and watching these couples, you would find that at this point almost all the couples seem to be in love. The partners would tell you of their commitment to their partners and their relationships. Almost every person would be hoping that their marriage would be life-long.

Now wait. Wait 5 or 10 years. Then gather together your crowd of couples again. The majority of couples will still be together, will still be in love, will still be committed to the relationship. But quite a lot of couples will not be together, they will have divorced. Other couples who are together will be very distressed about their relationship. They will report lots of conflict and unhappiness.

We are fascinated by the different outcomes in marriage. As people and as psychologists, we are curious about many questions about marriages. Can we tell which of our engaged couples are destined to remain satisfied, and which are destined to become distressed? What predicts marital outcome: the couple's individual personalities, their beliefs about marriage, their cultural background, their style of communication, or what? What influences the characteristics people bring to a marriage? For example, where do partners learn about what to expect of marriage, and how to be a partner? What happens between the happiness during engagement and the distress later on? The answers to these questions, and more, are in our book.

Both of us are clinical psychologists. Our interest in marriage goes beyond academic curiosity. We are interested in trying to help people have satisfying marriages. That interest leads us to another set of questions. Can we prevent marital problems? Once a marriage is distressed can we help the couple to regain their past relationship satisfaction? When marriage and individual problems overlap, which they often do , how should we help with this complex of problems?

This book grew out of our mutual interest in trying to understand and promote happy, satisfying marriages. In 1992 we jointly convened a meeting of marital researchers in Brisbane, Australia. That meeting affirmed our view that available research provides important answers to at least some of the questions we are interested in. We set out to produce this book as a comprehensive guide to what is known about marriage. Our primary goal was to guide practitioners on how to understand, assess, prevent and change unhappy marriages. We were very fortunate to be able to gather together a wonderful set of contributors who present the current state of the art as they understand it. We thank them for their hard work, and for coping with the logistics of editing a book with over 50 authors dotted around the globe.

The field of marital research has occupied our attention individually and collectively for well over a decade. Our ongoing commitment is due, in large part, to the intrinsic interest of marriage as a topic. In addition we have been very fortunate to share our passionate interest in marriage with many valued students over the years. In particular, we want to thank the following for working with us and teaching us at least as much as we ever taught them: Charleanea Arellano, Adriana Balaguer, Brett Behrens, Susan Blumberg, Ruth Bouma, Mari Clements, Paul Howes, Adrian Kelly, Doug Leber, Kristin Lindahl, Sue Osgarby, Lydia Prado and Jenn Scott. Our interest in marriage has been fired and renewed by a network of valued colleagues and friends in Europe, Australasia and North America. Over the years we have written, talked, listened and debated with these people, and learned much form them. For all the fond memories of impassioned debates in exotic locations, and valued contributions to knowledge of marriage, we thank all our colleagues. In particular we thank Don Baucom, Steve Beach, Fran Dickson, Frank Floyd, John Gottman, Kurt Hahlweg, Rick Heyman, Amy Holtzworth-Munroe, Hy Hops, Neil Jacobson, Danielle Julien, Jan Nicholson, Pat Noller, Cliff Notarius, Dan O'Leary, Barbara Perry, Matt Sanders, Sue Spence, Scott Stanley, Brigit van Widenfelt, Dina Vivian, and Bob Weiss. Each of these people has done much more than being a colleague; thank you to each and all of them for the friendships and support.

We would also like to thank the countless couples and families who have shared their lives with us as participants in research, and as clients in our clinical practice. Without their investment, commitment and willingness to share, the new knowledge and insights presented in this book would not have been possible.

Throughout the book, we present clinical vignettes and case histories to illustrate some of the major patterns and findings from couples research and couples therapy. The identities of the couples involved have been altered in order to maintain anonymity and confidentiality. Often a case history represents composites of elements from several different couples or families. In addition, the challenges and experiences of our couples and families are often similar to others; indeed, when reading the case histories of another author, many times we are reminded of case histories from our own research or clinical practices. These case histories, combined with the new findings, techniques and programs for couples and families, make us very optimistic about the future of marriage. We feel strongly that it will be possible for couples to work out the problems they are facing, as well as for young couples who are just establishing relationships to create happy, satisfying unions.

Finally, we want to thank the people at Wiley for taking our vision and making it into a book.

Kim Halford
Howard Markman

Section I

The Nature of Healthy Marriage

Chapter 1

The Concept of a Healthy Marriage

W. Kim Halford*, Adrian Kelly and Howard J. Markman[†]**
*School of Applied Psychology, Griffith University, Nathan, and
**Department of Psychiatry, University of Queensland, Herston,
Queensland, Australia; and [†]Department of Psychology,
University of Denver, Denver, CO, USA*

[Our life together] has been great . . . fantastic. Couldn't have been better. Look at this jewel I still have. Pretty, smart and sexy (husband talking about his 52 years of marriage; Dickson, 1995).

. . . I think we have had a good life, I am very happy, but there have been very, not many times, several times when it's hard, you can't always see eye to eye on everything . . . but we enjoy each other's company . . . We can be sitting here reading and I'll say you know what I just thought of and he'll say, "I was just thinking of about that". It's weird (wife talking about her marriage of over 50 years; Dickson, 1995).

I don't recommend it [marital breakdown] to anybody. The breakdown of a marriage is obviously a dreadful thing and unfortunately causes great unhappiness and consternation and everything else inevitably. Obviously, I would much rather it hadn't happened, and I'm sure my wife would have felt the same . . . It's a deeply regrettable thing to happen, but it does happen and unfortunately in this case it has happened. It's the last possible thing I ever wanted to happen. I mean, I'm not a total idiot (Prince Charles on his reactions to his separation from Princess Diana, quoted in the *Sydney Sunday Times*, July 3, 1994).

Marriage is, for most people, the most intimate relationship they voluntarily enter. As the above quotes illustrate, marriage can be both the best of times, and the worst of times. When relationships work, they can be the most meaningful aspect of life. A strong satisfying relationship provides a centre of belonging to the partners' lives and a buffer against life's hardships. When relationships fail, they produce misery beyond expectation.

The scientific study of marriage has revealed a great deal about how relation-

Clinical Handbook of Marriage and Couples Interventions. Edited by W. Kim Halford and Howard J. Markman.
© 1997 John Wiley & Sons Ltd.

ships succeed or fail over time. Furthermore, this scientific information has been used to develop a number of successful programs to help troubled couples repair broken marriages, and to help happy couples remain happy. In this *Handbook* we bring together the work of many contributors to this scientific knowledge and provide a resource for professionals who work with couples.

THE SIGNIFICANCE OF MARRIAGE

Almost all people become involved in intimate couple relationships at some point in their lives, regardless of country and culture (DeGuilbert-Lantione & Monnier, 1992; McDonald, 1995). In Western countries over 90% of the population marry by age 50 years (McDonald, 1995). Even amongst those who chose not to marry, the vast majority engage in "marriage-like" relationships by living together in committed couple relationships (McDonald, 1995). Regardless of whether couples are formally married or not, societal expectations of couple relationships are high. Couple relationships are portrayed in television, film and print media as providing life-long companionship, romance, support, sexual fulfilment, commitment and individual well-being.

Although there is clearly a down side to couple relationships, negative relationship experiences do little to discourage people about the value of committed couple relationships. About 75% of divorcees remarry within 3 years of the end of their first marriage (Furstenberg & Spanier, 1984; Glick, 1984; Martin & Bumpass, 1989). Intimate couple relationships continue to be viewed as the best forum for meeting individual needs for affection, companionship, loyalty and emotional and sexual intimacy, even amongst those people who have experienced prior relationships as unsatisfactory.

THE NATURE OF RELATIONSHIP DISTRESS

Almost all couples who marry report high levels of relationship satisfaction early in their relationship (Markman & Hahlweg, 1993). However, for many couples these initially high levels of satisfaction erode over time. For many couples the erosion of satisfaction leads them to seek divorce. About 45% of Australian marriages, 55% of American marriages, 42% of English marriages and 37% of German marriages end in divorce (De Guilbert-Lantoine & Monnier, 1992; McDonald, 1995). For other couples the erosion of satisfaction is associated with significant relationship distress, but for various reasons the couples opt to remain together.

A lot is known about what couples do that is associated with sustained relationship satisfaction. One well identified characteristic of marital satisfaction is high rates of positivity in marital interaction. Happy couples spend more time together, do more mutually enjoyable things together, and behave more positively toward one another, than do unhappily married couples (Weiss, Hops &

Patterson, 1973). Furthermore, relative to unhappy couples, happy couples are more likely to respond positively even when their partner is being negative to them (Jacobson, Folette & McDonald, 1982). Weiss (1984) suggests the sharing of positivity in happy couples is analogous to making deposits in a bank account; over time a level of credit is established in the relationship account. The established relationship credit allows the partners not to reciprocate negativity. In contrast, the unhappy couple, having engaged in many fewer positive exchanges, have a relationship account which has little or no credit. Consequently, unhappy couples tend to reciprocate negativity.

A second well identified characteristic of marital distress is ineffective communication and management of conflict. When discussing problem issues, maritally distressed couples criticise each other and fail to listen actively to each other (Halford, Hahlweg & Dunne, 1990; Jacobson et al., 1985; Weiss & Heyman, 1990). Distressed couples also tend to withdraw from each other, and not to engage in positive problem-solving behaviours (Christensen & Shenk, 1991). For example, when discussing problem issues, distressed couples tend not to suggest possible solutions to problems, often refuse to discuss issues, or physically withdraw from interactions by going to another room or leaving the house. These unhelpful patterns of communication often result in problem issues not being resolved (Halford et al., 1992). In distressed couples there often are repeated conflicts about the same topic, conflicts which do not produce any positive change in the relationship.

A third characteristic of marital distress is that unhappy couples think about their partners in negative ways compared to happy couples. Maritally distressed people often selectively attend to their partner's negative behaviour, and attribute such negative behaviours to stable, blameworthy and global personality traits (Eidelson & Epstein, 1982; Floyd & Markman, 1983). For example, in a distressed relationship, a partner arriving home late may be perceived as "a generally selfish person who doesn't care about the family". In a satisfied relationship the same behaviour might be attributed to "someone who is struggling to keep up with a heavy load at work". In unhappy couples, negative thoughts about the partner predict future behaviour within the same interaction better than past behaviour (Halford & Sanders, 1990). In other words, distressed partners respond to their subjective perceptions of marital interactions, perceptions which are often biased.

A fourth, and final, characteristic of marital distress we wish to describe is negative relationship schemata. Over time people develop generalized perceptions of their partners and relationships (relationship beliefs). The relationship beliefs, or schemata, that partners in happy couples develop are characterized by shared, positive perceptions of the relationship and its history (Buehlman, Gottmann & Katz, 1992; Osgarby & Halford, 1996a). In unhappy couples the partners' schemata are characterized by negative sentiment about the relationship and its history. All couples tend to perceive and remember relationship events in ways consistent with their schemata (Osgarby & Halford, 1996b). In other words, happy couples selectively perceive and remember relationship interactions as positive. Unhappy couples selectively perceive and remember relationship interactions as negative.

Are the identified characteristics of distressed marriages the causes or effects or relationship problems? It seems unlikely that any of these characteristics are just the effects of marital distress, as each characteristic has been shown prospectively to predict relationship deterioration. Low rates of relationship positivity prospectively predict deteriorating relationship satisfaction (Karney & Bradbury, 1995). Assessed communication skills in couples whilst discussing conflictual topics in their relationship also predict subsequent relationship satisfaction and divorce risk (Gottman 1993; Markman & Hahlweg, 1993). Negative cognitions about the partner antedate relationship distress and prospectively predict decline in relationship satisfaction (Bradbury & Fincham, 1990; Buehlman, Gottman & Katz, 1992; Markman, 1981). Finally, relationship beliefs and schemata in engaged couples prospectively predict relationship satisfaction and divorce risk (Olson & Fowers, 1986; Olson & Larsen, 1989).

THE EFFECTS OF RELATIONSHIP DISTRESS

In mutually satisfying, long-term couple relationships each partner is buffered against the negative effects of life stresses. In distressed relationships, each partner is vulnerable and suffers more in response to life stresses. For example, maritally satisfied parents of severely disabled children report less depression and more positive family relations than their maritally distressed counterparts (Floyd & Zmich, 1991). People in satisfying marriages cope better with the stress of sudden, unexpected unemployment than people without that relationship (Gore, 1978).

Marital distress is associated with individual psychopathology in the partners. For example, people presenting for marital therapy report high levels of substance abuse (Halford & Osgarby, 1993), and people presenting for alcohol dependency treatment report high levels of marital distress (Blankfield & Maritz, 1990). Depression, especially in women, and anxiety disorders, especially in men, are both strongly correlated with marital distress (Halford & Bouma, this volume).

The association of individual psychopathology and relationship distress is not just the individual problems causing marital problems. Marital distress is often a precipitant of problem drinking (Maisto et al., 1988), and increases the chance of relapse in recently treated alcoholics (Haver, 1989). Similarly, prolonged marital conflict is the most frequently reported event preceding the onset of depression in women (Paykel et al., 1989) and is associated with poor prognosis for depression (Rousanville et al., 1979).

Interspousal violence is frequent in distressed relationships, and has serious physical and psychological sequelae, particularly for women (Cascardi, Langhinrichsen & Vivian, 1992). The risk of physical violence is accentuated where alcohol abuse is present in one or both partners (O'Farrell & Murphy,

1995). Marital distress and aggression impacts in a major way upon children. In particular, severe interparental conflict is associated with high rates of childhood behaviour problems, and maladjustment (Grych & Fincham, 1990; Sanders, Nicholson & Floyd, this volume).

Unhappy marriages also are associated with poor individual physical health in the partners, whilst happy marriages are associated with good individual health. The association between relationship satisfaction and individual heath is unlikely to be due to a unidirectional causal link, but probably is due to bidirectional influences (for a comprehensive review, see Burman & Margolin, 1992). There are several mechanisms by which marital distress can impact upon physical health. Marital interaction mediates certain health related behaviours, such as smoking and alcohol consumption, which may impact upon health. Distressed marital interaction also has direct physiological effects which can impact upon health. For example, distressed marital interaction is associated with immunosuppression (Kiecolt-Glaser et al., 1987, 1988), which can increase vulnerability to infectious and other diseases. The quality of marital interaction mediates the adherence to treatment regimens in people with established health problems, and this also can impact upon outcome (Schmaling & Sher, this volume). Finally, supportive and rewarding couple relationships act as a buffer against stressful life events, and this can reduce the negative health impacts of severe stressors (Burman & Margolin, 1992).

THE NATURE OF HEALTHY, LONG-TERM RELATIONSHIPS

We noted earlier that almost all couples at the beginning of committed relationships are highly satisfied with their relationships, but only some couples sustain that high initial satisfaction. We also noted that, relative to the couples who experience relationship satisfaction erosion, the couples that remain happy are characterized by doing more mutually pleasurable activies together, having better communication and conflict management skills, thinking more positively about their partners, and having more positive relationship schemata.

The characteristics of couples who sustain long-term satisfied relationships are not the same characteristics which determine initial attraction or commitment to relationships, a phenomenon we term the short-term/long-term disjunction dilemma. An example of the disjunction dilemma is that assessed communication skills in engaged couples are unrelated to their relationship satisfaction or commitment at the time, although these same skills prospectively predict relationship satisfaction 5 years later (Markman & Hahlweg, 1993). A second example of the disjunction dilemma is the relationship schemata of engaged couples. Relationship schemata do not correlate significantly with engaged couples' ratings of relationship satisfaction at the time, but these same schemata prospectively predict long-term relationship satisfaction and risk of divorce (Olson & Fowers, 1986; Olson & Larson, 1989).

The disjunction dilemma probably is due to several factors. Firstly, partners' initial attraction is related strongly to physical attraction and having highly pleasurable activities. In couples where these factors occur, an extreme positive bias in partner perception develops so that negative partner behaviour is overlooked or minimized. If relationships develop into long-term commitment, the intensity of physical attraction and the level of time together usually wanes. (This is probably fortunate for the future of the species. The intense romantic experience of being entirely besotted with your partner, thinking of little else and walking into walls in a dream-like state is wonderful in short bursts; in the longer term this romantic preoccupation makes it hard to attend to mundane but necessary tasks such as eating, doing the washing, holding down a job or driving safely.) As more realistic perceptions develop, the human failings of our partners become evident.

A second aspect of the disjunction dilemma is that relationship behaviours which promote short-term satisfaction may impede sustained, long-term satisfaction. For example, a very attentive partner may initially be seen as romantic and committed, but later the same behaviours may be seen as possessive and smothering. Behaviour initially seen as outgoing fun at parties becomes drunken buffoonery, spontaneity becomes chaotic disorganization, and charming eccentricities become irritating habits.

A key characteristic of long-term couple relationships is that they adapt to changing life circumstances. The couple who meet in their 20s, enjoy attending parties together, and share enthusiasm for high-energy outdoor sports, are unlikely to sustain the same lifestyle as a married couple with young children 10 years later. The relationship will need to adapt if the partners are to experience sustained relationship satisfaction. Thus, whilst common activities and physical attraction may bring the couple together, the ability to communicate effectively, to resolve conflict and to continue to develop new shared activities over time are likely to determine whether the couple stay satisfied with the relationship.

On the basis of these research findings and discussion, we define a healthy long-term couple relationship as:

> A developing set of interactions between partners which promotes the individual well-being of each partner and their offspring, assists each partner to adapt to life stresses, engenders a conjoint sense of emotional and sexual intimacy between the partners, and which promotes the long-term sustainment of the relationship within the cultural context in which the partners live.

This definition contains an implicit value statement that relationship longevity is an important component of a healthy relationship. Most people entering marriage hope their relationship will be life-long. Partners able to sustain a long-term, mutually satisfying relationship usually are better off than those without such a relationship. Furthermore, long-lasting, satisfying relationships do confer to partners an intimacy built upon shared history, an intimacy which is highly valued by those couples who experience life together (Dickson, 1995).

Sometimes changing partners is inaccurately seen as a solution to relationship dissatisfaction; second and subsequent marriages have higher rates of distress and divorce than primary marriages (McDonald, 1995). We have seen many clients who believed that changing partners would solve their relationship problems, only to find the same problems in subsequent relationships. For example, the second author saw a distressed couple in which one partner had received several promotions while the partner's career had stagnated over many years. The couple began to find differences in each other's role expectations, their social circles and their life goals. The upwardly mobile partner reported having an affair with a work colleague, reporting that they shared much in common and wanted the same things out of life. While changing partners might provide someone who is more similar, this approach would ignore that fact that the first couple felt similar in interests and goals at one time. The partner change option ignores the process by which the original couple drifted apart, and by ignoring this process the departing partner might simply repeat the same mistakes with a new partner. So, changing partners is not a universal fix for overcoming relationship distress.

We are *not* advocating that it always is desirable for couples to stay together for life. There are many examples from our clinical experiences in which couples have stayed together in mutual misery when they may have done much better apart. Whilst divorce often is distressing, many people report feeling much better after divorce. We *are* advocating that satisfying marriage potentially is a very powerful positive force in many people's lives. Sometimes changing partners helps someone to develop a positive, long-lasting relationship; sometimes changing partners transfers existing problems from an old to a new relationship.

THE CONTENTS OF THIS BOOK

This book is intended to guide practitioners who work with relationships. The book consists of five sections. In the first section of the book (Chapters 1–7) the authors describe the nature of healthy couple relationships. The behavioural and cognitive elements of relationship interaction are reviewed, and how these relate to the health of the couple's relationship. The coverage includes analysis of sexual aspects of relationship satisfaction. There also is a chapter specifically on the very important topic of relationship violence. Issues of gender and culture, and how they influence the nature of relationship functioning, are also considered.

The second section of the book (Chapters 8–11) is a review of the developmental processes influencing relationship satisfaction and stability. Issues considered here include the effects of individual past experiences, lifespan developmental changes, children and ageing on relationships. In particular, the authors review how opportunities to share positive couple activities, communication and conflict management, and cognitions and schemata about relationships are shaped by these various factors. Our primary goal as editors in working with the authors was to explicate the implications of existing knowledge for assessment and intervention with couple relationships.

The third section of the book addresses the often neglected individual and environmental influences on relationships. Chapters in this section are addressed to the reciprocal relationship between couple relationships and the individual partner's work, physical and mental heath.

The fourth, and largest, section of the book (Chapters 15–25) provides detailed descriptions of how to conduct a wide variety of interventions to change couple relationships. This section begins with a chapter on how to assess couples presenting with relationship distress. A series of nine chapters describe how to conduct various forms of couples therapy and interventions to prevent relationship distress. The chapters in this section deal with many difficult clinical issues, such as couples work when only one partner presents, working with couples in which one partner has a serious individual psychological problem, dealing with relationship aggression, working with couples who have significant parenting and relationship problems, dealing with affairs in couple relationships work, and divorce mediation. Detailed descriptions and case examples of state-of-the-art technology for assisting couples currently in, or at risk of developing, dysfunctional couple relationships are provided.

In the final section of the book (Chapters 26 and 27) there is an analysis of how effective current couples interventions are, and what can be done to make relationship interventions more effective. This analysis includes consideration of how couples therapy can be used as an adjunctive treatment for individual problems, and public health perspectives on how healthy marriages might be promoted. We conclude in the final Chapter by suggesting future directions for research.

REFERENCES

Blankfield, A. & Maritz, J.S. (1990). Female alcoholics. IV. Admission problems and patterns. *Acta Psychiatrica Scandinavica*, **82**, 445–450.

Bradbury, T.N. & Fincham, F.D. (1990). Attributions in marriage: a review and critique. *Psychological Bulletin*, **107**, 3–33.

Buehlman, K.T., Gottmann, J.M. & Katz, L.F. (1992). How a couple views their past predicts their future: predicting divorce from an oral history. *Journal of Family Psychology*, **5**, 295–318.

Burman, B. & Margolin, G. (1992). Analysis of the association between marital relationships and health problems: an interactional perspective. *Psychological Bulletin*, **112**, 39–63.

Cascardi, M., Langhinrichsen, J. & Vivian, D. (1992). Marital aggression: impact, injury, and health correlates for husbands and wives. *Archiver of Internal Medicine*, **152**, 1178–1184.

Christensen, A. & Shenk, J.L. (1991). Communication, conflict, and psychological distance in non-distressed, clinic, and divorcing couples. *Journal of Consulting and Clinical Psychology*, **59**, 458–463.

De Guilbert-Lantoine, C. & Monnier, A. (1992). La conjoncture demognishique: l'Europe et les pays developpes d'Outre-Mer. *Population*, July–Angust.

Dickson, F.C. (1995). The best is yet to be: research on long-lasting marriages. In J.T. Wood & S. Duck (eds), *Under-studied Relationships: Off the Beaten Track* (pp. 22–50). Thousand Oaks, CA: Sage.

Eidelson, R.J. & Epstein, N. (1982). Cognition and relationship maladjustment: development of a measure of dysfunctional relationship beliefs. *Journal of Consulting and Clinical Psychology*, **50**, 715–720.

Floyd, F.J. & Markman, H.J. (1983). Observational biases in spouse observation: toward a cognitive–behavioral model of marriage. *Journal of Consulting and Clinical Psychology*, **51**, 450–457.

Floyd, F.J. & Zmich, D.E. (1991). Marriage and the parenting partnership: perceptions and interactions of parents with mentally retarded and typically developing children. *Child Development*, **62**, 1434–1448.

Furstenberg, F. & Spanier, G. (1984). *Recycling the family: remarriage after divorce*. Thousand Oaks, CA: Sage.

Glick, P.C. (1984). Marriage, divorce, and living arrangements. *Journal of Family Issues*, **5**, 7–26.

Gottman, J.M. (1993). The roles of conflict engagement, escalation, and avoidance in marital interaction: a logitudinal view of five types of couples. *Journal of Consulting and Clinical Psychology*, **61**, 6–15.

Gore, S. (1978). The effect of social support in moderating the health consequences of unemployment. *Journal of Health and Social Behaviour*, **19**, 157–165.

Grych, J.H. & Fincham, F.D. (1990). Marital conflict and children's adjustment: a cognitive–contextual framework. *Psychological Bulletin*, **108**, 267–290.

Halford, W.K., Gravestock, F., Lowe, R. & Scheldt, S. (1992). Toward a behavioural ecology of stressful marital interactions. *Behavioral Assessent*, **13**, 135–148.

Halford, W.K., Hahlweg, K. & Dunne, M. (1990). The cross-cultural consistency of marital communication associated with marital distress. *Journal or Marriage and the Family*, **52**, 109–122.

Halford, W.K. & Osgarby, S. (1993). Alcohol abuse in clients presenting with marital problems. *Journal of Family Psychology*, **6**, 1–11.

Halford, W.K. & Sanders, M.R. (1990). The relationship of cognition and behaviour during marital interaction. *Journal of Social and Clinical Psychology*, **9**, 489–510.

Haver, B. (1989). Female alcoholics. II. Factors associated with psycho-social outcome 3–10 years after treatment. *Acta Psychiatrica Scandinavica*, **74**, 597–604.

Jacobson, N.S., Follette, W.C. & McDonald, D.W. (1982). Reactivity to positive and negative behaviour in distressed and non-distressed married couples. *Journal of Consulting and Clinical Psychology*, **50**, 706–714.

Jacobson, N.S., McDonald, D.W., Follette, W.C. & Berley, R.A. (1985). Attribution processes in distressed and non-distressed married couples. *Cognitive Therapy and Research*, **9**, 35–50.

Karney, B.R. & Bradbury, T.N. (1995). The longitudinal course of marital quality and stability: a review of theory, method and research. *Psychological Bulletin*, **118**, 3–34.

Kiecolt-Glaser, J.K., Fisher, L.D., Ogrocki, B.S., Stout, J.C., Speicher, C.E. & Glaser, R. (1987). Marital quality, marital disruption and immune function. *Psychosomatic Medicine*, **49**, 13–33.

Kiecolt-Glaser, J.K., Kennedy, S., Malkoff, S., Fisher, L., Speicher, C.E. & Glaser, R. (1988). Marital discord and immunity in males. *Psychosomatic Medicine*, **50**, 213–229.

Maisto, S.A., O'Farrell, T.J., Connors, G.J., McKay, J.R. & Pelcovits, M. (1988). Alcoholics' attributions of factors affecting their relapse to drinking and reasons for terminating relapse episodes. *Addictive Behaviors*, **13**, 79–82.

Markman, H.J. (1981). The prediction of marital success: a five-year follow-up study. *Journal of Consulting and Clinical Psychology*, **49**, 700–702.

Markman, H.J. & Hahlweg, K. (1993). The prediction and prevention of marital distress: an international perspective. *Clinical Psychology Review*, **13**, 29–43.

Martin, T.C. & Bumpass, L.L. (1989). Recent trends in marital disruption. *Demography*, **26**, 37–51.

McDonald, P. (1995). *Families in Australia*. Melbourne: Australian Institute of Family Studies.

O'Farrell, T.J. & Murphy, C.M. (1995). Marital violence before and after alcoholism treatment. *Journal of Consulting and Clinical Psychology*, **63**, 256–262.

Olson, D.H. & Fowers, B.J. (1986). Predicting marital success with PREPARE: a predictive validity study. *Journal of Marital and Family Therapy*, **12**, 403–413.

Olson, D.H. & Larsen, A.S. (1989). Predicting marital satisfaction using PREPARE: a replication study. *Journal of Marital and Family Therapy*, **15**, 311–322.

Osgarby, S.M. & Halford, W.K. (1996a). Positive intimacy skills in maritally distressed and non-distressed couples. Submitted for publication.

Osgarby, S.M. & Halford, W.K. (1996b). Memories, memories: memory biases in the recall of relationship events in maritally distressed and non-distressed couples. Submitted for publication.

Paykel, E.S., Myers, J.K., Dienelt, M.N., Klerman, G.L., Lindenthal, J.J. & Pepper, M.P. (1989). Life events and depression: a controlled study. *Archives of General Psychiatry*, **21**, 753–760.

Rousanville, B.J., Weissman, M.M., Prusoff, B.A. & Herceg-Baron, R.L. (1979). Marital disputes and treatment outcome in depressed women. *Comprehensive Psychiatry*, **20**, 483–490.

Weiss, R.L. (1984). Cognitive and strategic interventions in behavioral marital therapy. In K. Hahlweg & N.S. Jacobson (eds), *Marital Interaction: Analysis and Modification* (pp 337–355). New York: Guilford.

Weiss, R.L. & Heyman, R.E. (1990). Observation of marital interaction. In F.D. Fincham & T.N. Bradbury (eds), *The Psychology of Marriage* (pp. 87–118). New York: Guilford.

Weiss, R.L., Hops, H. & Patterson, G.R. (1973). A framework for conceptualizing marital conflict: a technology for offering it, some data for evaluating it. In L.D. Hardy & E.L. Marsh (eds), *Behaviour Change: Methodology, Concepts and Practice* (pp. 309–342). Champaign, IL: Research Press.

Chapter 2

A Clinical-Research Overview of Couples Interactions

Robert L. Weiss* and Richard E. Heyman**

*Departments of Psychology, University of Oregon, Eugene, OR, and **State University of New York, Stony Brook, NY, USA

Couples therapy offers unique challenges to those interested in developing theories of marital adjustment and to those marital therapists seeking to assist couples in distress. Typically, theories of marital adjustment focus on either the individual (emphasizing personality factors) or on the couple's interaction (emphasizing process factors). In practice, clinicians tend to view marital adjustment as the expression of personalities. In recent years behavioral approaches to marital therapy have greatly influenced thinking about marital adjustment. Theory and research identified with this tradition relies heavily on observations of marital interactions. In this chapter we will draw upon research within the behavioral orientation that helps explain the nature of distressed and satisfying intimate relationships. Specifically, we will focus on some of the useful, replicated facts spawned from this tradition, that marital therapists might find helpful. As is often the case, theory-driven research does not map neatly onto clinical practice. In some cases the research has generated more questions than it has answered, and applications seem ever more distant. Our aim in this review is to highlight whatever we can that may be potentially useful clinically, while being ever-careful not to claim greater clinical utility than is warrented. Additionally, our aim is to provide a concise summary of recent developments to those clinicians who are unable to study the original reports. In our earlier reviews of marital distress and behavioral observation (Weiss & Heyman, 1990a; 1990b) we examined the contributions of behavioral theory and research from a more academic point of view. This chapter is an updated and clinically oriented review of the developments in this literature.

The format we have adopted is to first define an issue of clinical relevance and then list whatever research findings may be germane to each issue. In the first

Clinical Handbook of Marriage and Couples Interventions. Edited by W. Kim Halford and Howard J. Markman.

section below we discuss how some self-report appoaches to marital assessment may contribute to a better conceptual understanding of marital accommodation and grievances. The second section reviews results from studies that utilize behavioral observations. This approach relies heavily on using how couples interact as a basis from which to build a theory of marital distress as well as to suggest possible interventions. The two major sections of the chapter thus focus on what couples say and what they do.

SELF-REPORT ASSESSMENT APPROACHES

Self-report has been a mainstay of all forms of assessment, no doubt because of economy, face-validity and ease of making group comparisons, and self-report often provides clients with a voice. These advantages have not been lost on marital researchers wishing to develop constructs relevant to therapists. In this section we review some of the constructs this approach has generated and their implementation in practice.

Marital Satisfaction

Although "marital satisfaction" stands as the premier construct in this area (certainly the putative goal of marital therapy), it is nonetheless unusual among variables selected for scientific scrutiny. As with any highly subjective state (e.g. "happiness") we must ask, "Do maritally satisfied people behave in ways that differentiates them from others?" What behaviors characterize marital satisfaction? In this approach we rely on individuals' testimony (e.g. "All things considered, I am happily marred"). As with all forms of self-report, we rely on reported subjective comfort or discomfort. Yet, unlike other so-called "clinical entities" (cf. DSM-IV) there are few, if any, behaviors seen by others that differentiate degrees of marital satisfaction. That is, marital distress does not intrude into the public's awareness as do other serious forms of psychopathology (e.g. bizarre mannerisms, phobic symptoms).

Assessment based on self-report can be complicated: self-report can be direct; persons observe and report on their own sentiments through narrative, free-form response statements (e.g. responding to, "What strengths do you see in your relationship?"). Or self-report can elicit categorical responses to standardized questions ("Do you and your partner disagree about finances: Very Often ... Sometimes ... Never"). In one sense self-reports are actual samples of the ways partners are presumed to express themselves in their relationship. In another sense these reports presume to be symptoms or indicants of broader relationship (dys)functioning. It is less important whether the respondents actually engage in the reported behaviors than it is that they choose to answer in a particular manner. These different assessment functions merely restate the familiar sample vs. sign distinction in assessment theory.

Behavioral approaches to close relationships tend to rely on self-reports as samples of what people feel and do. The assumption is that what people say (on self-report measures) largely reflects what they actually feel and what they are most likely to do in response to those feelings. Yet, it is generally recognized in clinical work that verbal report and subsequent actions are not often the same, a theme we develop later. Clinically useful self-report assessment devices do in fact sample observable consequences of relationship interactions. For example, non-distressed couples (as defined by the Locke–Wallace or Dyadic Adjustment Scales) behave differently in laboratory problem-solving interactions (e.g. Weiss & Heyman, 1990a). Thus, a combination of self-report and behavioral observation is necessary to establish the utility of our constructs.

Marital theorists and researchers alike have often noted that the construct of global marital satisfaction embodies two different components (cf. Heyman, Sayers & Bellack, 1994), namely an evaluative, sentiment or attitudinal component, and a performance-based, adjustment or skills-based component. The relation between these two major components is like that between knowledge as product and knowledge as knowing. Thus, in the earliest of the behavioral studies (cf. Wills, Weiss & Patterson, 1974) the aim was to define the association between reported daily (global) marital satisfaction (knowledge) and the reporting of behavioral, relationship events that occurred each day (knowing). The question was, do relationship events (e.g. affectional and instrumental exchanges), which spouses record as either "pleasing" or "displeasing," affect the evaluative (sentiment) component (i.e. reported marital satisfaction)? On a simple additive model, the more frequently daily pleasing events occur, the higher the level of reported satisfaction (likewise, the more frequently the number of negative or displeasing events occur, the lower the level of satisfaction). The additive model represents the strong empirical view which assumes that events "register" as data, and that events are the basis for one's knowledge of satisfaction.

Based on this, and many subsequent studies, the main conclusions seem to be:

1. Daily marital events appear only in a limited sense to be the basis for reported marital satisfaction.
2. Negative events (those experienced as displeasing) are more highly related to marital dissatisfaction than pleasing events are to satisfaction.
3. Satisfaction and dissatisfaction are not just opposites of one another. The absence of dissatisfaction is not satisfaction.
4. Not only is there relatively little overlap (to the extent of only 25% of the shared variance) between knowledge and knowing (thus reported satisfaction tends to be somewhat independent of what partners say they experienced), but the amount of agreement between reporting partners is quite low. Clearly, events are not "seen" as the same.
5. Attempts to isolate classes of events that account for satisfaction variance (i.e. more highly impact marital satisfaction) have shown that "feeling-based" or positive affectional events may be more salient contributors. But recent work by Johnson & O'Leary (1996) suggests that even when spouses

use a customized list of items to track daily events—those they identify as particularly important to their relationship—there is not a substantial amount of improvement in explaining satisfaction variance.

These findings do not lend great support to the strong empirical model decribed above. Why isn't there a closer correspondence between spouses' statements of their feelings about one another (the evaluative component) and what they report doing with one another (the skills component)? Perhaps we have failed to sample adequately the domain of marital events. This seems unlikely since the usual method (the Spouse Observation Checklist; Weiss & Perry, 1983) covers some 480 items! Perhaps couples really do not track events as behavioral psychologists think they should. This slippage between event occurrence and evaluation has led to the notion of a bank account model, suggesting that not every withdrawal (negative exchange) must be covered with an immediate deposit (positive exchange) (Gottman, 1979). At the heart of the issue is the concept of reciprocity: do well-adjusted couples reciprocate their exchanges in a *quid pro quo* fashion? Must each expression of affection be responded to immediately and in kind?

6. Research has shown that marital *quid pro quo*, temporally close tit-for-tat-exchanges, is, if anything, characteristic of marital dissatisfaction. That close reciprocity (opposite of the bank account model) is not what one wishes to instill in couples seeking relationship improvement.

This apparent disjunction between knowledge and knowing led to the "sentiment override" hypothesis (Weiss, 1980); when carried to extremes, the bank account model suggests that highly positive or highly negative sentiment overrides, as it were, the events that actually were exchanged (but here too, as noted above, spouses may not agree in their perceptions of what behaviors "are actually exchanged"). Thus, if partner A acts in a manner intended to be positive, but partner B is guilty of negative sentiment override, B would not "record" the event appropriately (i.e. as intended by A). Sentiment operates as a filter within the knowing process. One recent finding consistent with the reasoning of sentiment override is reported by Flowers et al. (1994). Although others have reported high correlations between marital satisfaction and marital *conventionalization* (i.e. the tendency to endorse unrealistically positive statements about one's partner) Flowers et al. found that the correlation holds only for those reporting high levels of marital satisfaction. Although supporting only the positive side of the sentiment override hypothesis, their study does not directly address the cognition–behavior relationship.

One clinical implication of findings from this line of research is that merely inducing partners to behave positively toward one another is unlikely to impact the sentiment or evaluative side of the equation. Skills training that is seen as coming from the outside (i.e. representing the therapist's interest) may be efficacious in the short term, but unless something is done to directly involve the sentiment component of "satisfaction" the longer-range gain is doubtful. We address possible ways for implementing change procedures after we have considered some of the other self-report assessments.

At this stage of our knowledge it seems that between the two components of marital satisfaction identified above, we know less about the impact of the skill component than we do about the sentiment component. The literature often suggests an illogical conclusion: marital health is the absence of marital distress. This seems to suggest that in order to be well adjusted couples should *not* say and do what distressed couples say and do. Since aspirin cures headaches, we cannot conclude that the lack of aspirin causes headaches. *Marital harmony is not just the absence of whatever it is that dissatisfied couples do.*

Some of the most interesting cases, from an assessment point of view, are seen with those couples who make very different presentations between their initial conjoint interviews and their self-report assessments. Their interview performance can be either better or worse than the material gleaned from the self-reported assessment. A couple may appear on assessment to be "statistically divorced", yet fail to make that degree of upset obvious in their interviews. Or, a couple may present themselves during the interview as inches away from a destructive divorce, yet show considerable evidence of marital strengths on their assessment devices.

There are a number of self-report assessment approaches that bear on the aspects of marital satisfaction we have been discussing; the Dyadic Adjustment (DAS: Spanier, 1976) and the Marital Satisfaction Inventory (MSI: Snyder, Lachar & Wills, 1988) are two among those available. Three instruments have been studied within the behavioral area and have considerable face and criterion validity:

(a)   The *Areas of Change Questionnaire* (ACQ: Weiss, Hops & Patterson, 1973; Margolin, Talovic & Weinstein, 1983) is a two part, 34-item questionnaire, based on the simple theory that the more a spouse wants the other to be different, the greater the dissatisfaction with that spouse. In its original format the ACQ is a self-report measure of changes one desires the other to make. (A second section records one's awareness of changes the partner wants the respondent to make.) The ACQ focuses on what each wants the other to change.

(b)   The *Marital Status Inventory* (MSI: Weiss & Cerreto, 1980) is a 14-item True–False questionnaire that describes steps along the way to divorce, culminating in actually filing for divorce. The more steps one has taken to dissolve a relationship the greater the presumed dissatisfaction with that relationship. (The MSI is not a direct measure of dissatisfaction because one may be prevented otherwise from taking steps toward dissolution.)

(c)   The *Communications Pattern Questionnaire* (CPQ: Sullway & Christensen, 1983) assess patterns of demand-withdrawal. The CPQ has been studied extensively by Christensen and associates (Christensen & Heavey, 1990; Heavey, Layne & Christensen, 1993) and it assesses how partners jointly cope with conflict (e.g. by each person either pursuing or withdrawing). Couples are asked to indicate whether a particular response pattern (e.g. Wife Demand–Husband Withdraw) typifies their pattern of dealing with conflict.

7. Studies have confirmed an association between magnitude of desired change and reported marital satisfaction/adjustment using various self-report measures (e.g. Heyman, Sayers & Bellack, 1994). In general, women seek more change from their husbands than men seek from their wives, and distressed, compared to non-distressed, couples indicate desiring significantly more change on each of the 34 items of the ACQ (Margolin, Talovic & Weinstein, 1983). The magnitude of desired change is responsive to behavioral marital therapy (i.e. after therapy fewer changes are desired).

8. The steps to divorce (MSI) measure has been shown to predict subsequent marital distress and particularly to predict depressive symptomatology some months after initial testing (Beach & Forehand, 1989; see also Crane, Soderquist & Gardner, 1995; Heyman, O'Leary & Jouriles, 1995).

9. Overall, demand–withdrawal patterns of coping are negatively associated with reported marital satisfaction. Although there first appeared to be an overriding gender effect, portraying women in the "demander" role and men in the "withdrawer" role, this pattern is moderated by whose issue is at stake: when it is the male's issues the gender effect is greatly reduced; male withdrawal and female demand are both less. In still another study, Klinetob et al. (1993) found a complete reversal of the pattern when it was the male's issue and couples were afforded greater choice in selecting issues. Additional work by Klinetob, Smith & House (1994), using a 6-month longitudinal design, disclosed that poor marital satisfaction was a precursor of the demand–withdraw pattern rather than the other way around.

Each of the three self-report devices reviewed thus far are clinically useful for assessing the status of a relationship. The ACQ and the CPQ map fairly directly onto what dissatisfied couples do in their attempts to change the other person. Many intervention tactics have been developed based on what research has shown to be typical of distressed relationships. These have been applied almost uniformly to couples seeking help. However, Halford, Sanders & Behrens (1993, 1994) have been critical of what we would call the "chicken soup" strategy of intervention. Chicken soup seems to make people feel better, and in some instances may even facilitate heal-ing. Can we assume that whatever the magic ingredient in chicken soup, it will work for all other conditions? Halford et al. argue that it may be reasonable to teach communication training to couples who have destruc-tive communication patterns, but in point of fact these communication "skills" probably are not used by these couples in real-life encounters. Even more likely, those couples who are not expressing marital distress do not use the skills we teach (also, see below our questioning of the standard observational context). In a word, the absence of paraphrasing skills does not lead to distress.

In a move to further customize marital assessment and intervention, Halford modified the instructions for the ACQ in a way that focuses on self-regulation (see Weiss & Halford, 1996). (In fact, his approach serves as a template for modifying other self-report forms as well.) In addition to stating desired changes in the partner, each person is asked to assess the change they desire in their own behaviors (i.e. among the 34 items presented in the ACQ). In addition to asking for desired change from one's partner (e.g. "I want my partner to express his/her emotions more clearly") the respondent would also rate the amount of change desired in his or herself (e.g. "I want to express my emotions more clearly").

Similarly, the demand–withdrawal pattern assessed by the CPQ could focus on what each person does to keep the dysfunctional coping strategy alive. Each partner is invited to assess their own reaction to (a) failure to get a desired result and (b) being pursued. Thus, what had been a focus on the shortcomings of the other becomes a focus on one's own reactions and abilities to adopt alternative responses.

In still another approach to the role of cognition in marriage, Fincham (1994) notes the robust (replicated) association between various measures of (causal and responsibility) attributions and marital satisfaction. Simply put, those spouses who, given the opportunity, attribute negative (relationship) causes to partner behaviors, are themselves more likely to be in distressed relationships. At first blush we may ask whether this association is trivial, since dissatisfaction yields dissatisfaction (because the same self-report methodology is involved, the semantic association is even more likely). Fincham careful and systematically addressed these "alternative" explanations and concluded that the association is more than artificial. Longitudinal studies have indicated that, indeed, the presence of negative attributions (time 1) predict decreased marital satisfaction at time 2, suggesting a strong causal link.

10. Cognitive contents, specifically causal and responsibility attributions, have been related to measures of marital satisfaction. Potential third variables have been considered and their effects are largely minimal. Despite what had been a promising line of research (i.e. the efficacy of congitive variables) there is no convincing evidence that adding a cognitive module to behavioral couples' therapy actually improves outcome (cf. Halford, Sanders & Behrens, 1993, 1994; Weiss & Halford, 1996).

The take-home message from this selective review of self-report assessments and their related studies is that marital therapists can and should use systematic assessment before launching into couples' therapy. We have identified different aspects of marital satisfaction, noting particularly how self-report and action are not isomorphic. Discrepancies between and among various tests and interview behaviors are important to note for therapy planning. The postive impact of partner behavior may be more limited than previously thought, suggesting that a focus on self-regulation may be far more important to effecting change than merely providing skills training. We reach a similar conclusion when we consider the findings from observation studies.

BEHAVIORAL OBSERVATION OF MARITAL INTERACTIONS

In this section we review highlights of research on behavioral observations of marital interaction. Because there is a heavy emphasis on technique in this area we will discuss more fully the role context plays in this line of research.

Standard Marital Observation Paradigm

Almost all of the studies cited in this section follow standard procedures: couples report to the laboratory, usually a suite of offices in a university psychology department. They complete an inventory listing common areas of disagreement in marriages (e.g. money, sex, in-laws) as a means of identifying their most high-conflict topics. Some studies follow Gottman's (1979) procedure, whereby the researcher carefully interviews the couple as to what the exact conflict is about (e.g. he spends too much money, his mother is intrusive about disciplining the children), thereby enhancing the reality of the upcoming conflict interaction (i.e. the object of observation). Other researchers simply instruct the couple to discuss the problem topic, and leave it up to the couple themselves to define the specifics. In either case, the researcher tells the couple that they are to discuss the problem for a set amount of time (uaually 10–15 minutes) and attempt to reach a resolution. Finally, the instructions usually include a suggestion that the couple try to act much they would at home. The researcher leaves the couple alone to begin their discussion and the videotaping begins.

The following is a transcript excerpt of a recently videotaped laboratory observation of Joseph, age 45 years, and Ann, 30 years, who presented at the Stony Brook Marital Therapy Clinic for marital therapy. They also participated in an observational study.

> Joseph: I acted like a prince to you. No?
> Ann: No, you haven't acted like a prince.
> J: A prince! No man has ever treated you like I have . . .
> A: Joseph, it's not true . . .
> J: . . . and dealt with the crap that you dished out.
> A: I don't see how you can say that you are a prince when you go out and work for yourself and day after day I have to plead for money from you for me and the baby. A box of diapers a month isn't enough. I feel so cheated.
> J: That's your feelings!

A: I'm feeling this way because that's the way you treat me!

J: You felt that way before the baby. I'm not going to be used.

A: I'm not going to be used. You said that you wouldn't have sex with me if I had the diaphragm in me, so I took it out. I'm not going to be made a fool of.

J: Nobody twisted your arm.

A: You allowed this to happen, and look at the way you treat me. How much could you have cared about me?

J: I did care about you. But you make it tough to like you. Very tough.

A: Well, that's the way I feel about you.

J: You make it very tough.

A: Especially because you don't give.

J: (*Leaning forward, teeth clenched*) I don't fucking have it to give!!

A: I call you up because I'm on welfare and the baby doesn't have diapers . . .

J: Do you want me to sell everything I have and live in a hole?

A: I'm embarrassed to have known you.

J: If you acted like a normal human being these things wouldn't happen.

Upon hearing about this procedure for the first time, most people's first reaction is, "Since these participants are being videotaped, there is no way that they would act like they would at home". For several reasons this laboratory procedure does indeed produce naturalistic interactions. First, the couples themselves report that the interactions are reminiscent of their typical interactions (e.g. Margolin, John & Gleberman, 1988). Second, watching the videotapes quickly disabuses skeptics of beliefs that people will not behave in their typical nasty ways while being videotaped. Interactions range from calm, even playful discussions (e.g. "Okay, in the count of three, let's each say how many children we want") to bitter screaming matches. Furthermore, spouses seem to habituate quickly to the video cameras. In a similar vein to the excerpt above, interactions at one of the authors' labs (REH) in suburban Long Island, New York, included a wife telling her husband "Why would I want to have sex with you? You're not my friend, you are more like my enemy!"; yet another woman exposed her bare breast for several seconds prior to nursing their infant during their conflict interaction. Americans typically do not say or do such things except behind closed doors! But as the transcript above indicates, spouses simply are not as self-conscious while being taped as outsiders might guess. (Empirical support for this point can be found in Christensen & Hazard, 1983; Jacob et al., 1994). Third, an intriguing study by Vincent et al. (1979) indicates that even when couples are instructed by the researcher to "fake good" or "fake bad," observers can still reliably discern happy from unhappy couples. Unhappy couples leak negative affect even when they are trying to behave as if they are happy. Thus, even if typical interaction samples researchers have collected are not quite as negative as they are at home, they are still strong enough to detect important differences. Finally, studies that have compared home and laboratory observations of couples have found substantial similarities, with laboratory discussions overall being less negative (Gottman, 1979). Thus, if anything, laboratory observations *understate* the differences between couples.

Established Findings

1. Distressed Couples' Behavior is More Hostile

By far the most robust finding of marital observation work is that distressed couples are more hostile than non-distressed couples. Although blatantly obvious, nonetheless research has been informative in several ways. First, it has been shown that couples have demonstrable differences in the way they act overtly when arguing; marital distress cannot be attributed solely to personality, upbringing, previous relationship history or other commonsense theories of marital harmony. Second, research has elaborated on which kinds of negative behaviors distinguish distressed from non-distressed couples, including criticism, hostility, excuses, denial of responsibility, withdrawal and complaints about the other's personality (see Weiss & Heyman, 1990b, for a more complete review). Finally, by establishing the ecological validity of the observational paradigm, this most basic and predictable level of finding has allowed researchers to make discoveries that their grandmothers might not necessarily have predicted. We consider possible limitations of this paradigm below.

Clinical implications

Although we cannot say whether marital distress causes high levels of hostility, or whether high levels of hostility cause marital distress (or even whether some third factor, like incompatibility or neuroticism, causes both), high levels of hostility are the primary presenting problem for marital therapy (e.g. O'Leary, Neidig & Heyman, 1995). As clinicians we should be familiar with behaviors that are normative and those associated with distress. The obvious clinical corollary is that most therapies attempt to reduce the level of overt hostility and hostile withdrawal.

2. Distressed Couples Exhibit Distinctive Patterns of Hostility

Although what people do when interacting is important (e.g. the base-rate analyses just described), how interactions unfold across time is possibly more important in understanding marital distress (e.g. Margolin & Wampold, 1981). In many areas of animal behavior, from the courting behavior of birds to the escalation of marital conflict, the patterning of behavior is critical; "... a defining characteristic of interaction is that it unfolds in time" (Bakeman & Gottman, 1986, p. 1). Furthermore, Gottman & Roy (1990, p. 1) contend that "the dimension of time is so central to conceptualizing social interaction that its use will lead us to think of interaction itself as temporal form". By studying sequences, observational researchers have unearthed a variety of fascinating findings.

Most marital studies that use methods for sequential analysis test whether one spouse's behavior follows the other spouse's behavior at a higher rate than expected by chance (i.e. as would be expected given specific base-rate frequencies). For example, does the wife's blame follow the husband's blame more frequently than the frequency expected from her base-rate level of blame? There are two forms of significant linkage between behaviors. First, compared to chance, the antecedent behavior can increase the likelihood of the consequent behavior. This is described as an escalation effect. Second, the antecedent behavior can decrease the likelihood of the consequent behavior. This is a suppression effect. Distessed couples, compared with non-distressed couples, exhibit a sequence of higher levels of hostility followed by hostility. This pattern, labeled by researchers as "negative escalation" includes patterns labeled as "blame → blame", "confront → confront", "confront → defend", "complain → defend", "complain → complain", "displeasure → displeasure" (see Weiss & Heyman, 1990b). Although reciprocation of positive behaviors has been found for both distressed and non-distressed couples, Filsinger & Thoma (1988) reported that positive reciprocity was predictive of relationship dissolution at 1.5-, 2.5- and 5-year follow-ups.

Researchers (e.g. Gottman, 1979, 1994) have interpreted these findings to indicate that responses of distressed couples are more "locked in" to one another. If one distressed spouse behaves with hostility, the other responds in kind, generating a loop of negativity that is very difficult to break. Negativity is like a black hole for distressed couples; along these lines, Gottman (1994) has referred to negativity as an "absorbing sate" for distressed couples. This matches nicely the clinical reports of distressed couples when they say that they can argue over anything, large or small, and that their fights escalate from disagreement to heated battle very quickly. Non-distressed couples do not respond in as predictable a manner, so they are able to break out of negativity cycles very quickly (e.g. hostility → hostility → accept responsibility → constructive problem discussion). Distressed couples' tit-for-tat pattern appears to be predictive of relationship failure even when positive behaviors are exchanged. Thus, understanding the temporal form of interaction appears to be very important.

Clinical implications

As a standard procedure of clinical assessment, we watch for the patterns, identified above, as couples discuss at least one problem for 10 minutes without our intervention (i.e. we merely observe their communication). Does the level of anger escalate? What happens when it does? Do they enter repetitive negative loops? Do they acknowledge afterwards that what occurred in session is what "always happens" when they discuss problems? Do they label the other person or the communication process as the problem? Since most forms of marital therapy include training in communication skills, being familiar with the basics of communication processes is very useful if one is to recognize communication faults and, importantly, be able to set appropriate treatment goals (e.g. teaching spouses how to monitor and exit negative loops rather than admonishing them not to behave with hostility).

3. Satisfied Couples "Edit" Their Thoughts during Conflict, Thus Avoiding Negative Escalation Loops

Two studies have attempted to examine "editing"—the ability to recognize a negative partner behavior yet not respond in kind (i.e. do respond with a non-negative behavior). Gottman, Markman & Notarius (1977) defined editing as a listener displaying negative affect but then following that state non-negatively in the next speaker turn. They found that non-distressed wives were the only ones who edited. Notarius et al. (1989) used a more complicated methodology that combined spouses' own ratings of their intent and impact with ratings from observers. They defined editing more precisely: if both observers and the listening spouse viewed the first behavior as negative, editing occurred whenever that (listening) spouse next replied in a non-negative manner. Not surprisingly, when defined this way, few spouses edited. However, whereas non-distressed spouses and distressed husbands edited 15% of the time, distressed wives edited only 1% of the time. Thus, as noted later, wives appear to play a key role in affect regulation, although despite much theorizing little research has been done to explore why.

Clinical implications

Editing is a rather high-level behavior. It requires self-control, an eye toward long-term goals (e.g. relationship harmony) rather than short-term retaliation, and the cognitive flexibility to come up with alternative attributions (via cognitive–behavioral therapy), experience the other's underlying emotions (via emotion-focused therapy), or ability to understand the historical scripts underlying the partner's hostility (via insight-oriented therapies). On the other hand, simply bottling up upset will typically result in a bit of editing followed by an explosion once the "editing threshold" has been crossed. Editing somewhat, but letting the other person know some of your upset, may be critical to relationship well-being (see the finding above). Some behaviors have positive short-term, but detrimental-long term, effects on marital adjustment (see below). Editing will almost certainly be the product of some of the above-mentioned required subskills, rather than a target in and of itself.

4. Non-distressed Couples Exhibit More Positive Behaviors during Conflicts

Satisfied couples use a variety of constructive behaviors during videotaped disagreements. These include significantly higher levels of approval/caring, empathy, humor, problem solutions, smiling, involvement and positive non-verbal behaviors. When they do complain, the complaint tends to be focused on the partner's behavior rather than his or her personality (see Weiss & Heyman, 1990b, for a more complete review). Gottman (1994) has described the ability of non-distressed couples to use metacommunication to "repair" errant features of their communication (e.g. W: "You're interrupting me." H: "I'm sorry. Go ahead."). Distressed couples appear to turn such possible repair moments into further negativity (e.g. W: "You're interrupting me." H: "Look who's talking; you interrupt me constantly.").

Clinical implications

Although the finding that non-distressed couples display more positive behaviors appears to be yet another instance of discovering the obvious, it has, nonetheless, many clinical implications. First and foremost, couples who are caught in negative loops (see 2, above) only monitor incoming negatives, whereas successful couples will more accurately monitor the process of their interaction. A large part of making sure that the process is constructive is to use metacommunication to get the conversation back on track. Furthermore, when the problem, not your partner or his/her personality, is the problem, it is possible to use humor, empathy and other positive behaviors to come up with an agreeable solution. Successful interventions almost always result in the couples becoming more aware of the negative and positive behaviors they use, an ability to monitor the communication process, correct it when negative loops begin to occur, and begin breaking negative loops with demonstrations of caring (empathy, listening, etc.).

5. Abrasive Marital Interaction Is Linked to Negative Health Outcomes

It has long been known that discordant marriages are associated with mental and physical health problems (see Bloom, Asher & White, 1978; Coyne & DeLongis, 1986; Burman & Margolin, 1992). Only recently, with the blossoming of psychoneuroimmunology, have the mechanisms for these effects been elucidated (e.g. Kiecolt-Glaser et al. 1994). Kiecolt-Glaser and colleagues have established a compelling series of related studies that explore these links. The first studies (Kiecolt-Glaser et al., 1987, 1988) found that separated/divorced women and men, when compared to married controls, have poorer immune responses on a number of marker variables (e.g. Epstein–Barr herpes virus (EBV) titers; helper t-cells). Among the married group, poor marital quality was associated with lowered immune functioning (e.g. high EBV titers; lower suppressor cell percentages).

With such strong circumstantial evidence, Kiecolt-Glaser embarked on a longitudinal study that first featured the collection of blood during marital interactions, thus allowing for a more direct test of the physiological effects of marital conflict. Ninety newly-married couples, recruited from marriage records, spent 24 hours in an Ohio hospital with catheters in their arms, allowing researchers to draw blood throughout the day. Two hours into their stay they participated in the standard marital conflict paradigm, arguing about 2–3 problems for 30 minutes.

The interactions were coded, and the sample was divided into those with high and low levels of hostility during the conflicts. In a series of papers (Kiecolt-Glaser et al., 1993, 1994, 1996) derived from the larger study, they reported the following: (a) on a vast array of markers, couples high in negativity showed significantly more compromised immune responses than those low on negativity; (b) high-negative couples displayed significantly elevated blood pressure that remained elevated long after the conflict discussion; (c) wives' immunology was more severely impacted than was husbands', and the effects were more persistent for wives; (d) a wife: hostility → husband: withdraw sequence was associated with the wife's increased production of stress hormones (norepinephrine, cortisol); (e) wives' positive behaviors were associated with their decreased levels of epinephrine and prolactin); (f) husbands' behavior was not associated with physiological changes.

In additional to providing critical information about the psychoneuro-immunological pathways linking marital conflict and compromised health, Kiecolt-Glaser's work has substantial theoretical impact. Gottman (1994; Gottman & Levenson, 1988) has put forth an elaborated theory that holds that men are more physiologically impacted by conflict and therefore withdraw to modulate their physiological distress. He draws on evolutionary theories, as well as health data and physiological responses, such as heart rate, during laboratory discussions. Women, in Gottman's model, are not affected as much by conflict and therefore they are more able to maintain high levels of hostility as conflicts unfold. Kiecolt-Glaser's findings directly refute Gottman's theory; according to her results it is *women* who clearly are more heavily impacted by conflict than men. As will be discussed below, the differences in men's withdrawal and women's hostility is probably more rooted in power and role inequities than in physiology (Vivian & Heyman, 1994). Unfortunately, Gottman's (1994) recent comprehensive treatise on marriage selectively presents only one piece of preliminary data from Kiecolt-Glaser's work as support for his theory. The issue has yet to be resolved.

Clinical implications

In clinical practice, it is tempting to rally both spouses around the idea that "All of this hostility at home is taking an incredible toll on each of you. Anything would be healthier than this". Data indicating the considerable physical toll that marital distress exacts can be useful in this regard. For spouses experiencing health problems (including mental health issues), the therapist can empathize with them and explain the necessity for the relationship to help, rather than harm, their well-being. For those who are not experiencing physical health problems, this finding can be used as an example of what may happen if things do not turn around. While obviously not a tactic to use with all couples, the impact of marriage on physical health can be useful leverage at times.

6. Physically Aggressive Couples are Even More Hostile than Other Distressed Couples

A burgeoning area of research compares the observed interactions of physically aggressive couples and non-aggressive couples (including non-distressed couples). Aggressive spouses display more overall hostility than non-aggressive couples (Burman, Margolin & John, 1993; Burman, John & Margolin, 1992; Cordova et al., 1993; Heyman, 1992; Margolin, John & Gleberman, 1988; Margolin, John & O'Brien, 1989). Aggressive couples are more likely to show negative escalation patterns (Burman, John & Margolin, 1992; Burman, Margolin & John, 1993; Cordova et al., 1993; Heyman, 1992; Morrel, Metzger & Murphy, 1994; Vivian & Heyman, 1994; Vivian et al., 1987). Furthermore, abused wives clearly engage in high levels of verbal hostility and reciprocity, contrary to the clinical descriptions of battered women (e.g. Walker, 1979). Although complaints arising from disempowerment appear to be a strong contributor to such negativity (see the discussion of Vivian's work below), the results converge on a picture of high degrees of mutual verbal combat (with few attempts at placating) in the marriages of moderately to severely abusive couples.

Of interest for further exploration is the negative reinforcement effect of hostility. Burman, Margolin & John (1993) and Heyman (1992) found aggressive husbands' hostility reduced the likelihood of their wives' emitting non-hostile dysphoric affect (a pattern found in some depressive marriages, see below). Heyman (1992) also found evidence for a H: withdrawal $\rightarrow$ W: hostility suppression effect and a W: hostility $\rightarrow$ H: withdrawal suppression effect, indicating that husbands' withdrawal effectively turned off their wives' hostility, and *vice versa*. Because both theoretical (e.g. Patterson, 1982) and clinical accounts indicate that couples act in negative ways to turn off the negativity of the partner, such patterns are of great interest. Cordova et al. (1993) found no evidence of a suppression effect, perhaps because their severely abusive couples were so consistent in their contingently hostile responses. Further studies are necessary before we can draw solid conclusions about negative reinforcement in aggressive couples.

Clinical implications

Although abuse in couples is discussed in other chapters in this volume, it is useful to note here that the majority of distressed couples report some physical aggression during the past year. Although there are probably different subgroups of aggressive couples (e.g. Vivian & Langhinrichsen-Rohling, 1995), most aggressive couples presenting for marital therapy report communication, not aggression, as their main problem (O'Leary, Vivian & Malone, 1992). Although therapists should routinely screen all couples for aggression, this is especially important in couples with high degrees of tit-for-tat hostility. For a discussion about how to treat aggressive couples and the issues involved in treating them, see Heyman & Neidig, this volume; Vivian & Heyman, 1996.

7. Behaviors in Depressed Couples Do Not Differ from Other Distressed Couples

Suppression effects, similar to those just discussed, were initially found for couples with a depressed wife (Biglan et al., 1985). Specifically, W: dysphoric affect → H: hostility and H: hostility → W: dysphoric affect suppression effects were found. This led to a great deal of excitement that a negative reinforcement cycle for hostility and depression had been observed. Biglan et al. did not include a non-depressed/distressed group; thus, one could not attribute the findings to depression and not mere marital distress. Two replications (Nelson & Beach, 1990; Schmaling & Jacobson, 1990) that included a distressed but not depressed group failed to find any unique effects for depression. Nelson & Beach concluded that suppression of hostility by dysphoric affect was correlated with the length of marital discord, not to the diagnosis of depression. Thus, hostility ↔ dysphoric affect sequences may be of interest in studying distressed couples, but these sequences are not unique to depressed couples. Perry (1993) also failed to find sequential effects in a sample of depressed men (as compared with a sample of non-depressed men) interacting with their wives.

Clinical implications

Given the high degree of overlap between marital distress and depression (e.g. Beach, Sandeen & O'Leary, 1990), clinicians should routinely assess and monitor depression and depressive symptomatology. If depression is a concern, understanding whether it preceded or followed the souring of the marriage is critical. Further, understanding (and observing) how depressive behavior may be reinforced (for example, by shutting down the partner's hostility) can be useful in planning interventions.

8. Male Withdrawal from Conflict Is Detrimental to Marital Health

Schaap (1984) reported that among distressed Dutch couples there were increased levels of W: blame → H: acquiesce. This was one of the first observational studies to confirm a widespread cultural belief that women press for change and men withdraw. A recent explosion of observational studies on this topic has demonstrated compelling evidence that this pattern is associated with distress (Christensen & Heavey, 1990; Gottman & Krokoff, 1989; Harvey, Heavey & Christensen, 1993). Unfortunately, most researchers have adopted Christensen's (1988) label "demand → withdrawal", which (unintentionally) implies a shrewish wife demanding changes, instead of the more typical overwhelmed and disempowered wife asking (with accompanying negative voice tone) for change in an equitable direction (Christensen, 1988; Vivian & Heyman, 1994). In fact, Roberts & Krokoff (1990), while finding that, overall, affective tone accounted for 50% of the variance in marital satisfaction, discovered that the H: withdrawal → W: hostility pattern added an additional 20%. Note that the key pattern was the husband's initiation of withdrawal, not withdrawal as a response (which was also tested). Thus, it appears more appropriate to call the sequence "withdrawal → hostility," or perhaps the bidirectional "withdrawal ↔ hostility."

Finally, the context of withdrawal is probably a critical, albeit underexplored, factor. Smith, Vivian & O'Leary (1991) found that premarital withdrawal correlated negatively with marital adjustment at 18 and 30 months of marriage. These longitudinal negative effects were similar to the controversial (see below) results of Gottman & Krokoff (1989), who reported that withdrawal had short-term payoffs but long-term detriments. However, Smith, Vivian & O'Leary (1991) reported that the effects of withdrawal were not all negative; high levels of both positivity and withdrawal were associated with gains in marital adjustment at 30 months. Thus, withdrawal may only be associated with marital discord as part of an overall pattern of negativity and stalemate (see the discussion of Gottman's three types of stable marriages, below, for a similar conclusion).

Clinical implications

Withdrawal is a behavior that is easier to assess in the therapy office than in the observational laboratory. Attaching recording wires to spouses, shutting them in a room and instructing them to talk tends to discourage their typical withdrawal behaviors! In natural settings withdrawal behaviors include leaving the room, watching TV, or occupying themselves in some other way. Thus, much information about withdrawal will occur in the verbal modality, but not in other observational modalities that may be better at assessing typical patterns of dealing with problems. As mentioned above, understanding the antecedents and consequences of withdrawal (e.g. do they come back to the problem, or hope that it will go away on its own?) is critical. Withdrawal can be a form of editing, or a positive, escalation-limiting time-out. It can also prevent resolution of virtually any difficulty, and can be a powerful provocation to the spouse. Understanding the clinical context and meaning of the behavior is critical.

Disputed Findings

1. It Doesn't Matter What You Argue About, It's the Way You Argue

Markman (e.g. Notarius & Markman, 1993) has been a prime advocate for the position that it is not what couples argue about, it is the way they argue that discriminates distressed and non-distressed couples. In brief, Markman marshals the following evidence to support his position: (a) all couples report problems on inventories; (b) couples trained in communication skills at premarriage have more satisfying marriages and vastly lower levels of divorce than control couples (e.g. Markman et al., 1993); (c) the vast literature, discussed above, documenting differences in communication behaviors between distressed and non-distressed couples (see also Markman, Stanley & Blumberg, 1995).

Vivian (e.g. Vivian, Heyman & Langhinrichsen-Rohling, 1995) has criticized such arguments as being "gender-neutral". In short, Vivian argues that behavior can only be understood in context, and that traditional coding systems ignore the fact that all marital behavior occurs in a gender context. Thus, coding systems that only code the form of the behavior (e.g. a wife is coded with "hostility", the husband with neutral problem statements) without understanding the context (e.g. the wife does 90% of the housework and wants a more equitable arrangement, the husband saying that he understands the problem but simply has no time to help). As a marital violence researcher, Vivian (1991) has argued that since power inequities and control (typically along patriarchal, gender lines) are believed to be the critical factors in aggressive marriages, coding systems that ignore what couples are talking about are missing the complete story.

Vivian et al. (1995) have compared results from a traditional behavioral coding system and a new thematic coding system. They found that on the behavioral level wives were more hostile, offered more negative attributions for the partner's behavior, and emitted less acceptance codes than their husbands. However, when coded thematically, the picture of the "hostile wife" changed: during the conflicts, wives were more likely than husbands to develop themes of desiring more affection/togetherness, equity about responsibilities, and public support from the partner. Husbands were more likely to display themes related to resisting change and needing to prevail or control. Furthermore, when the authors examined the interactions based on group status (community control couples vs. clinic couples), they found that clinic wives sought more respect/empowerment than did husbands or community spouses. These differences were, according to their hypotheses, especially pronounced in clinic wives who reported being hit during conflicts in the last year.

Jacobson (1991) has argued that behavioral marital therapy is not truly behavioral because it is not based on a functional analytic model. Vivian and Heyman have become convinced of a similar point with behavioral observational coding systems: to ignore context is to be decidedly unbehavioral. What couples are talking about is a critical contextual variable in understanding the way they talk. To know what people are discussing but not know how they discussing it is to know very little; yet to know couples are discussing something (e.g. the wife is very hostile, the husband neutral) but not know what they are discussing is also to know very little (e.g. the wife is doing all the household work and is seeking equity, the husband is refusing change). Vivian and Heyman have combined their topographical and thematic coding systems to offer both vantage points. Replication of these findings is of course in order, but it seems that the researchers must move beyond the traditional uses of traditional coding systems. This idea exploded into a recent controversy discussed below.

Clinical implications

We do not recommend a skills-only approach to marital therapy. It is important to know how people argue, of course, but it is also necessary to know what they argue about, and to understand that often there are gender-based reasons why they are arguing about it.

2. Negativity May Not Be All Negative

Only in scientific disciplines could debates erupt over whether negative behavior is negative. Commonsense explanations would, of course, recognize that negative behavior is negative (except, of course, when the same behavior was not viewed as negative; then it wouldn't be!). By forcing themselves to operationalize (define) what behaviors would be considered to be negative, scientists do not have the luxury of slippery commonsense definitions. Thus, "disagree" traditionally has been considered a negative behavior. Never mind that no right-minded clinician would seek to outlaw all disagreement! The empirical papers that discussed the notion that perhaps negativity in marriage is a "misnomer" (see a special issue of *Behavioral Assessment*; Weiss & Sher, 1991) found that under some circumstances, disagreement and withdrawal are predictive of positive outcomes. The problem may be that the traditional modes of observational inquiry label each behavior as belonging to a particular class for all couples under all conditions. Furthermore, labels like "negative" often lump behaviors such as put-downs with neutral disagreements. Further work must be done contextualizing negativity, answering what kinds of negativity for what kinds of couples under what circumstances is negative. Gottman's (1994) latest work, discussed below, attempts to address such questions.

Clinical implications

This somewhat silly but important controversy points out the gap between research and clinical practice. What is an obvious, commonsense issue to clinicians is not as clear-cut to researchers. Defining negativity is a bit like the US Supreme Court's definition of pornography: "I know it when I see it". Inflexible rules (e.g. ignoring context and subtle shades of meaning) lead to definitions that are unworkable. Of greatest implication, therefore, is the social construction of the meaning of all behaviors, but especially negative behaviors. Some behaviors (like physical aggression) are clinically definable as almost always negative; most other behaviors require generating a mutual understanding between the clinician and the spouses as to what is going to be considered negative.

3. Some Behaviors Have Positive Short-term, but Detrimental Long-term, Effects on Marital Adjustment

Although the statistical issues are far beyond the scope of this review, Gottman & Krokoff (1989) published a highly influential paper that purportedly showed that some behaviors (like men's withdrawal) had a short-term payoff for marital adjustment, but resulted in deterioration in marital adjustment across time. Gottman (1990, 1994) has used this finding as a central component in his theory-building. Critics (Mueser, 1989; Smith, Vivian & O'Leary, 1991; Woody & Castanzo, 1990) have argued that Gottman & Krokoff's design capitalized on "regression to the mean"—in part, the statistical principle that participants with extreme scores tend to score less extreme on subsequent test administrations. Although Gottman & Krokoff (1989) have cogently defended their analyses, we find the opposing arguments to be compelling. Replications using a study design different from that of Gottman & Krokoff are needed to settle this controversy.

Clinical implications

The finding that short-term, constructive conflict may lead to long-term harmony has a commonsense appeal. While its use in normalizing conflict is helpful, the empirical backing for this belief is still somewhat shaky.

New Findings

1. There Are Different Types of Stably Married Couples, But Only One Kind of Unhappy Couple

Gottman (1993, 1994) has used very complicated statistical methods to derive four typologies of couples in his quest to predict divorce. His conclusions are relatively simple, however. On the stable side: "*Marriages come in three discrete adaptations, and there are no in-between adaptations that are stable over time*" (Gottman, 1994, p. 185). These three types are labeled: validators (high levels of neutral problem discussions, positive behaviors, active listening); volatile (high levels of negatives and high levels of positives, intensely emotional); and conflict-minimizing (low levels of both negatives and positives and higher levels of emotional distance). All three types maintain positive:negative behavior ratios of at least 5:1. On the divorce-prone side: "*What is dysfunctional is the response to one's partner with criticism, disgust, contempt, defensiveness and stonewalling*" (Gottman, 1994, p. 185). Gottman presents findings that point toward hostile/detached and purely hostile couples. See Gottman (1994) for a complete description of the groups, the advantages and disadvantages of each one, and the clinical implications.

Fitzpatrick (1988) has also presented a three-group typology of functioning marriages. Gottman presents links to the substantial overlap of his groups and Fitzpatrick's typology of traditionals (validators), independents (volitiles), and separates (conflict-minimizers). Although further work using these typologies is necessary, it is heartening that both well-developed theories appear to converge substantially.

Critique of Standard Marital Observational Paradigm

1. Distressed Couples Discuss "Hotter" Problems than Non-distressed Couples. Is Observed Behavior a Function of Distress or Simply Anger Level Elicited During the Discussion?

Although it has occasionally been raised (e.g. Cordova et al., 1993), there is a major flaw in the logic of the standard observational paradigm. The logic goes something like this: if distressed and non-distressed couples argue about their top problems, and if there are observed differences in behavior, then these differences can be ascribed to their group status. Because correlation does not equate to causality, researchers cannot claim whether the distress caused the communication problems or whether the communication problems caused the distress (although Markman's studies of communication faults predating and predicting relationship decline is persuasive evidence for the latter). Still a third variable cannot be ruled out. That is, the top problems for distressed couples are far "hotter" than the top problems for non-distressed couples. When non-distressed couples are at their angriest, they often show the same kinds of behaviors as distressed couples (e.g. yelling, hostility loops, name-calling). They do not, however, tend to show these behaviors in the laboratory. In other words, distressed couples frequently and publicly show their worst (but probably not the worst of their worst!), whereas non-distressed couples rarely show their worst in the laboratory.

This point becomes especially telling in marital therapy. Does anyone talk the way that marital therapists try to make distressed couples talk? Wife: "I felt hurt and concerned when you stayed out all night. I would appreciate a call to let me know that you are safe". Husband: "I understand that you feel hurt and concerned. Why don't we brainstorm all of the possible solutions?" And even if they did, aren't we comparing people who are discussing a mild (albeit their worst) problem with those discussing a severe problem? Although problem severity and communication skillfulness are probably hopelessly confounded, one must interpret all communication studies with a grain of salt. The critical question, to us, is, "In what ways do successful couples manage life's difficulties so that they minimize and repair damage due to hostility?" Laboratory observations of volunteer couples provide important, although certainly not exhaustive, insights into this question. Exemplary research programs worthy of readers' further investigation on this topic are: (a) the cognitive–behavioral investigations of Bradbury & Fincham (1991); (b) the behavioral observational work of Gottman (1994); (c) the longitudinal studies of Markman (e.g. Markman et al., 1993); and (d) the social information processing studies of Holtzworth-Munroe (1992). The theories of the first two research teams will be discussed below.

2. Too Little Attention Is Paid to Whose Problem Is Being Discussed

Margolin, Talovic & Weinstein (1983) found that women reported more areas where they wanted change in their marriages and a greater degree of change requested in those areas. The accepted wisdom, both from clinicians and researchers, is that the wife is the "barometer" of the relationship (Floyd & Markman, 1983). Why then, do researchers pay so little attention to who is asking for the change in the problem being discussed?

This issue came to the fore when Christensen & Heavey (1990; Heavey, Layne & Christensen, 1993) compared spouses' behaviors when discussing a wife's problem and a husband's problem. They reported that demand/withdrawal behaviors differed significantly depending on whose issue it was. Thus, by picking one or two issues, researchers may not get a representative sample of conflict behaviors. This is a nuisance variable that should be controlled for in future studies (i.e. all couples discuss a wife's topic; all couples discuss a husband's topic; or all couples discuss one of each).

3. Stability of Findings—Is 10 Minutes Enough?

A similar problem is that the length of time observed, 10–15 minutes, has been reified. In the closely related field of family observation studies (e.g. Patterson, 1982), observations are typically done several times, for longer periods, over the course of several weeks. The published consistency data (e.g. Haynes, Follingstad & Sullivan, 1979; Weider & Weiss, 1980) has provided support for concordance across observations, but not overwhelming concordance. A symposium at a recent convention of the Association for the Advancement of Behavior Therapy (Eddy, 1993) heard researchers from a variety of marital/family observational laboratories empirically address the issue of "How much data is enough?" While no definitive standards were offered, all agreed that 10 minutes of data would not be enough data for stable results. We (Heyman, Eddy & Weiss, 1993) recommend that, to be fully confident of their results, researchers obtain at least two samples and emphasize only findings that were replicated between the two samples. If the husband and wife issue suggestion (above) were adopted, this would necessitate the collection of four behavioral samples. Although this might be unwieldy in some studies, it would greatly increase the confidence in the findings reported.

Theory-building in the Marital Observation Field

Bradbury & Fincham's (1991) contextual model describes the basic cognitive–behavioral model of marriage. Spouses bring to any interaction thoughts and feelings (pre-interaction appraisals) and personalities (distal context). When one person behaves, the other person processes the information (proximal context) and responds. Whilst having tremendous value as a descriptive, heuristic model, it does a better job of organizing findings than explaining them or sparking novel research questions.

Gottman has recently presented a similar model, but one that is more integrative and explanatory. While that is a strength, it also is a risk, as it has more chance of being wrong than a model like the one Bradbury & Fincham proposed.

Gottman's (1994) recent model borrows from physics and attempts to integrate psychophysiology, affect, behavior, cognition, couple typologies and change over time. While exciting, reading and understanding it is not for the faint of heart! Readers are encouraged to read and struggle with the theory for themselves, since it is the most well developed theory of marriage yet and summarizing it is not easy.

Gottman describes two levels of processing behavior: p-space and q-space. p-Space is the overt behavioral level (conveniently represented by the ratio of positive to negative behaviors unfolding across time). q-Space is the subjective sense of well-being in the relationship (this distinction between the overt behavior and the underlying thematic content is similar to Vivian's work, described below, which was in part derived from Gottman's earlier work on hidden agendas). When the ratio of positive to negative behaviors dips below a threshold, the q-space variable flips from a positive to a negative state (e.g. "I think he's acting selfishly"). Obviously, negative q-space cognitions, when held strongly enough, will begin to affect overt behavior. If this pattern continues, the behavioral interactions between the spouses will continue to detriorate. When q-space remains negative for a long time, it can become p-space (e.g. fights over the selfish motivation of the partner, tracking the partner's selfishness); q-space then jumps to a higher level of abstraction (e.g. "He's a selfish person"). This process can iterate several times (eventually to "His selfish nature is making this relationship unsalvageable"). Gottman also integrates couple typologies (validating, volatile, avoidant or hostile). Overall levels of negativity (p-space) and perceptions (q-space) are embedded within a context of critical behavioral processes (being flooded by the spouse's hostility) and cognitions (e.g. negative attributions). These in turn may result in increased distance and isolation, usually motivated by a desire to reduce unpleasant physiological arousal and psychological hurt. These processes interact with a rethinking of the viability of the whole marriage, and even to recast the entire history of the marriage (e.g. "Maybe we weren't happy before"). Left unchecked, spouses increase their steps toward dissolution and eventually divorce.

SUMMARY AND CONCLUSIONS

Two points stand out from our review: (a) the broader context of marital interaction provides the clinical theorist and researcher with a window through which to develop an empirically-based approach to rehabilitation of couple distress; and (b) although we seem to have made many false starts, there is now ample evidence to encourage clinicians to incorporate findings from this literature into their practices. Although the focus of this chapter has been on clinical research findings related to basic issues of assessment, including observational techniques with marital interactions, our hope is that through this very functional empirical approach we have added to the clinical understanding of couples. We have hinted at the attempts—far and few between!—to construct theory in this area. The progression in theory-building seems to have moved slowly from establishing some fairly basic, low-level, empirical generalizations, to ever more complex construals of adult intimacy, it successes and failures.

In our attempt to be even-handed, we have reviewed both self-report and the more complex forms of behavioral observation as methods of assessment. Perhaps most noteworthy in the self-report literature is the relative disjunction between reported satisfaction and underlying (supporting) behaviors. Yet, other constructs measured by self-report seem to have reasonable concurrent and predictive validity. Those most promising reflect fairly directly samples of couple behavior.

Behavioral observation of couple interactions has been the hallmark of current clinical empirical research in the marital area. We summarize procedures and discuss in detail how findings are dependent on the methods themselves. Among the promising leads on this area are the links to stress endocrine functioning, and Gottman's proposal for a typology of marriages based on a numerous observational studies. Finally, we are encouraged by what must be seen as gaining a greater appreciation for the texture of relationships, by relating the typography of interactions to important (but heretofore overlooked) contextual factors. What makes this entire enterprise especially deserving of our attention is that information about couple's interactions is presented in testable propositions, and these remain viable only until they are supplanted by newer evidence.

REFERENCES

Bakeman, R. & Gottman, J.M. (1986). *Observing Interaction: an Introduction to Sequential Analysis*. New York: Cambridge.

Beach, S.R.H. & Forehand, R. (1989). Marital relationship variables predict symptoms of depression and anxiety: a two-year prospective design. Paper presented to the Association for the Advancement of Behavior Therapy. Washington, DC, November.

Beach, S.R.H., Sandeen, E.E. & O'Leary, K.D. (1990). *Depression in Marriage*. New York: Guilford.

Biglan, A., Hops, H., Sherman, L., Friedman, L.S., Arthur, J. & Osteen, V. (1985). Problem-solving interactions of depressed women and their husbands. *Behavior Therapy*, **16**, 431–451.

Bloom, B., Asher, S.J. & White, S.W. (1978). Marital disruption as a stressor: a review and analysis. *Psychological Bulletin*, **85**, 867–894.

Bradbury, T.N. & Fincham, F.D. (1991). A contextual model for advancing the study of marital interaction. In G.J.O. Fletcher & F.D. Fincham (eds), *Cognition in Close Relationships* (pp. 127–147). Hillsdale, NJ: Erlbaum.

Burman, B. & Margolin, G. (1992). Analysis of the association between marital relationships and health problems: an interactional perspective. *Psychological Bulletin*, **112**, 39–63.

Burman, B., John, R.S. & Margolin, G. (1992). Observed patterns of conflict in violent, non-violent, and non-distressed couples. *Behavioral Assessment*, **14**, 15–37.

Burman, B., Margolin, G. & John, R.S. (1993). America's angriest home videos: behavioral contingencies observed in home reenactments of marital conflict. *Journal of Consulting and Clinical Psychology*, **61**, 40–50.

Christensen, A. (1988). Dysfunctional interaction patterns in couples. In P. Noller & M.A. Fitzpatrick (eds), *Perspectives on Marital Interaction* (pp. 31–52). Philadelphia: Multilingual Matters.

Christensen, A. & Hazzard, A. (1983). Reactive effects during naturalistic observation of families. *Behavioral Assessment*, **5**, 349–362.

Christensen, A. & Heavey, C.L. (1990). Gender and social structure in the demand/withdraw pattern of marital conflict. *Journal of Personality and Social Psychology*, **59**, 73–81.

Cordova, J.V., Jacobson, N.S., Gottman, J.M., Rushe, R. & Cox, G. (1993). Negative reciprocity and communication in couples with a violent husband. *Journal of Abnormal Psychology*, **102**, 559–564.

Coyne, J.C. & DeLongis, A. (1986). The role of social relationships in adaptation. *Journal of Consulting and Clinical Psychology*, **54**, 454–460.

Crane, D.R., Soderquist, J.N. & Gardner M.D. (1995). Gender differences in cognitive and behavioral steps toward divorce. *American Journal of Family Therapy*, **23**, 99–105.

Eddy, J.M. (Chair) (1993). State-of-the-art Observational Methodology: Issues in the Diversity and Temporal Stability of Couple, Parent and Child Behavior. Symposium conducted at the 27th Annual Convention of the Association for the Advancement of Behavior Therapy, Atlanta, GA, November.

Fincham, F.D. (1994). Cognition in marriage: current status and future challenges. *Applied and Preventive Psychology*, **3**, 185–189.

Fitzpatrick, M.A. (1988). *Between Husband and Wife: Communication in Marriage*. Beverly Hills: Sage.

Filsinger, E.E. & Thoma, S.J. (1988). Behavioral antecedents of relationship stability and adjustment: a five-year longitudinal study. *Journal of Marriage and the Family*, **50**, 785–795.

Flowers, B.J., Applegate, B., Olson, D.H. & Pomerantz, B. (1994). Marital conventionalization as a measure of marital satisfaction: a confirmatory factor analysis. *Journal of Family Psychology*, **8**, 98–103.

Floyd, F.J. & Markman, H.J. (1983). Observational biases in spouse observation: toward a cognitive/behavioral model of marriage. *Journal of Consulting and Clinical Psychology*, **51**, 450–457.

Gottman, J.M. (1979). *Marital Interaction: Experimental Investigations*. New York: Academic Press.

Gottman, J.M. (1990). How marriages change. In G.R. Patterson (ed.), *Depression and Aggression in Family Interaction* (pp. 75–102). Hillsdale, NJ: Erlbaum.

Gottman, J.M. (1993). The roles of conflict engagement, escalation, and avoidance in marital interaction: a longitudinal view of five types of couples. *Journal of Consulting and Clinical Psychology*, **61**, 6–15.

Gottman, J.M. (1994). *What Predicts Divorce*. Hillsdale, NJ: Erlbaum.

Gottman, J.M. & Krokoff, L.J. (1989). Marital interaction and marital satisfaction: a longitudinal view. *Journal of Consulting and Clinical Psychology*, **57**, 47–52.

Gottman, J.M. & Levenson, R.W. (1988). The social psychophysiology of marriage. In P. Noller & M.A. Fitzpatrick (eds), *Perspectives on Marital Interaction* (pp. 182–200). Philadelphia: Multilingual Matters.

Gottman, J.M., Markman, H.J. & Notarius, C.I. (1977). The topography of marital conflict: a sequential analysis of verbal and non-verbal behavior. *Journal of Marriage and the Family*, **39**, 461–477.

Gottman, J.M. & Roy, A. (1990). *Sequential Analysis*. New York: Cambridge University Press.

Halford, W.K., Sanders, M.R. & Behrens, B.C. (1993). A comparison of the generalization of behavioural marital therapy and enhanced behavioural marital therapy. *Journal of Consulting and Clinical Psychology*, **61**, 51–60.

Halford, W.K., Sanders, M.R. & Behrens, B.C. (1994). Self-regulation in behavioral couples therapy. *Behavior Therapy*, **25**, 431–452.

Heavey, C.L., Layne, C. & Christensen, A. (1993). Gender and conflict structure in marital interaction: a replication and extension. Special section: couples and couple therapy. *Journal of Consulting and Clinical Psychology*, **61**, 16–27.

Haynes, S.N., Follingstad, D.R. & Sullivan, J.C. (1979). Assessment of marital satisfaction and interaction. *Journal of Consulting and Clinical Psychology*, **47**, 789–791.

Heyman, R.E. (1992). Cognitive and Behavioral Differences between Physically Abusive and Non-abusive Early Married Couples. Unpublished doctoral dissertation. University of Oregon, Eugene, OR.

Heyman, R.E., Eddy, J.M. & Weiss, R.L. (1993). The stability of marital behavior across problem solving tasks: base-rate and sequential analytic studies. In J.M. Eddy (Chair), State-of-the-art Observational Methodology: Issues in the Diversity and Temporal Stability of Couple, Parent and Child Behavior. Symposium conducted at the 27th Annual Convention of the Association for the Advancement of Behavior Therapy, Atlanta, GA, November.

Heyman, R.E., Sayers, S.L. & Bellack, A.S. (1994). Global marital satisfaction versus marital adjustment: an empirical comparison of three measures. *Journal of Family Psychology*, **8**, 432–446.

Heyman, R.E., O'Leary, K.D. & Jouriles, E.N. (1995). Alcohol and aggressive personality styles: potentiators of serious physical aggression against wives? *Journal of Family Psychology*, **9**, 44–57.

Holtzworth-Munroe, A. (1992). Social skill deficits in maritally violent men: interpreting the data using a social information processing model. *Clinical Psychology Review*, **12**, 605–617.

Jacob, T., Tennenbaum, D., Seilhamer, R.A., Bargiel, K. & Sharon, T. (1994). Reactivity effects during naturalistic observation of distressed and non-distressed families. *Journal of Family Psychology*, **8**, 354–363.

Jacobson, N.S. (1991). To be or not to be behavioral when working with couples: what does it mean? *Journal of Family Psychology*, **4**, 436–445.

Johnson, P.I. & O'Leary, D.K. (1996). The behavioral components of marital satisfaction: an individualized assessment approach. *Journal of Consulting and Clinical Psychology*, **64**, 417–423.

Kiecolt-Glaser, J.K., Fisher, L.D., Ogrocki, P., Stout, J.C., Speicher, C.E. & Glaser, R. (1987). Marital quality, marital disruption, and immune function. *Psychosomatic Medicine*, **49**, 13–34.

Kiecolt-Glaser, J.K., Kennedy, S., Malkoff, S., Fisher, L., Speicher, C.E. & Glaser, R. (1988). Marital discord and immunity in males. *Psychosomatic Medicine*, **50**, 213–229.

Kiecolt-Glaser, J.K., Malarkey, W.B., Cacioppo, J.T. & Glaser, R. (1994). Stressful personal relationships: immune and endocrine function. In R. Glaser & J.K. Kiecolt-Glaser (eds), *Handbook of Stress and Immunity* (pp. 321–339). San Diego, CA: Academic Press.

Kiecolt-Glaser, J.K., Malarkey, W.B., Chee, M.A., Newton, T., Cacioppo, J.T., Mao, Y. & Glaser, R. (1993). Negative behavior during marital conflict is associated with immunological down-regulation. *Psychosomatic Medicine*, **55**, 395–409.

Kiecolt-Glaser, J.K., Newton, T., Cacioppo, J.T., MacCallum, R.C., Glaser, R. & Malarkey, W.B. (1996). Marital conflict and endocrine function: are men really more physiologically affected than women? *Journal of Consulting and Clinical Psychology*, **64**, 324–332.

Klinetob, N.A., Smith, D.A., House, V.L., deFijter, S., Niekro, D. & Noms, R. (1993). Demand and withdraw in marital communication: or is it demand/withdraw? Poster presented to 27th Annual Convention of the Association for Advancement of Behavior Therapy, Atlanta, GA, November.

Klinetob, N.A., Smith, D.A. & House, V.L. (1994). Longitudinal association between demand/withdraw and marital adjustment. Poster presented to 28th Annual Convention of the Association for Advancement of Behavior Therapy, San Diego, CA, November.

Margolin, G., Talovic, S. & Weinstein, C.D. (1993). Areas of Change Questionnaire: a practical approach to marital assessment. *Journal of Consulting and Clinical Psychology*, **51**, 944–955.

Margolin, G., John, R.S. & O'Brien, M. (1989). Sequential affective patterns as a function of marital conflict style. *Journal of Social and Clinical Psychology*, **8**, 45–61.

Margolin, G., John, R.S. & Gleberman, L. (1988). Affective responses to conflictual discussion in violent and non-violent couples. *Journal of Consulting and Clinical Psychology*, **56**, 24–33.

Margolin, G. & Wampold, B.E. (1981). Sequential analysis of conflict and accord in distressed and non-distressed marital partners. *Journal of Consulting and Clinical Psychology*, **49**, 554–567.

Markman, H.J., Renick, M.J., Floyd, F.J., Stanley, S.M. & Clements, M. (1993). Preventing marital distress through communication and conflict management training: a 4- and 5-year follow-up. *Journal of Consulting and Clinical Psychology*, **61**, 70–77.

Markman, H.J., Stanley, S.M. & Blumberg, S.L. (1995). *Fighting for Your Marriage*. San Francisco: Jossey-Bass.

Mueser, K.T. (1989). Negative communication may not facilitate marital satisfaction: a comment on Gottman and Krokoff (1989). Unpublished manuscript, Eastern Pennsylvania Psychiatric Institute, Philadelphia.

Morrel, T.M., Metzger, M.A. & Murphy, C.M. (1994). Lag sequential and multivariate time-series analysis of marital interactions (unpublished paper).

Nelson, G.M. & Beach, S.R.H. (1990). Sequential interaction in depression: effects of depressive behavior on spousal aggression, *Behavior Therapy*, **21**, 167–182.

Notarius, C.I. & Markman, H.J. (1993). *We Can Work It Out*. New York: Putman.

Notarius, C.I., Benson, P.R., Sloane, D., Vanzetti, N.A. & Hornyak L.M. (1989). *Behavioral Assessment*, **11**, 39–64.

O'Leary, K.D., Neidig, P.H. & Heyman, R.E. (1995). Assessment and treatment of partner abuse: a synopsis for the legal profession. *Albany Law Review*, **58**, 1215–1234.

O'Leary, K.D., Vivian, D. & Malone, J. (1992). Assessment of physical aggression against women in marriage: the need for multimodal assessment. *Behavioral Assessment*, **14**, 15–37.

Patterson, G.R. (1982). *Coercive Family Process*. Eugene, OR: Castalia.

Perry, B.A. (1993). Marital Problem-solving Interactions of Depressed Males. Unpublished doctoral dissertation. University of Oregon, Eugene.

Roberts, L.J. & Krokoff, L.J. (1990). A time-series analysis of withdrawal, hostility, and displeasure. *Journal of Marriage and the Family*, **52**, 95–105.

Schaap, C. (1984). A comparison of the interaction of distressed and non-distressed married couples in a laboratory situation: literature survey, methodological issues, and an empirical investigation. In K. Hahlweg & N.S. Jacobson (eds), *Marital Interaction: Analysis and Modification* (pp. 133–158). New York: Guilford.

Schmaling, K.B. & Jacobson, N.S. (1990). Marital interaction and depression. *Journal of Abnormal Psychology*, **99**, 229–236.

Smith, D.A., Vivian, D. & O'Leary, K.D. (1990). Longitudinal prediction of marital discord from premarital expressions of affect. *Journal of Consulting and Clinical Psychology*, **58**, 790–798.

Smith, D.A., Vivian, D. & O'Leary, K.D. (1991). The misnomer proposition: a critical reappraisal of the longitudinal status of "negativity" in marital communication. *Behavioral Assessment*, **13**, 7–24.

Snyder, D.K., Lachar, D. & Wills, R.M. (1988). Computer-based interpretation of the Marital Satisfaction Inventory: use in treatment planning. *Journal of Marital and Family Therapy*, **14**, 397–409.

Spanier, G.B. (1976). Measuring dyadic adjustment: new scales for assessing the quality of marriage and similar dyads. *Journal of Marriage and the Family*, **38**, 15–28.

Sullaway, M. & Christensen, A. (1983). Assessment of dysfunctional interaction patterns in couples. *Journal of Marriage and the Family*, 653–660.

Vincent, J.P., Friedman, L.C., Nugent, J. & Messerly, L. (1979). Demand characteristics in observations of marital interaction. *Journal of Consulting and Clinical Psychology*, **47**, 557–566.

Vivian, D. & Heyman, R.E. (in press). Is there a place for conjoint treatment of marital violence? *In Session.*

Vivian, D. (1991). Gender sensitivity in couples' communication: a preliminary proposal for a global multilevel coding system. Paper presented at the Indiana University conference for research on Clinical Problems—Marital Violence: Theoretical and Empirical Perspectives, Bloomington, IN, May.

Vivian, D. & Heyman, R. (1994). Aggression against wives: mutual verbal combat "in context". In V.M. Follette (Chair), Gender Issues in Couples Research. Symposium conducted at the 28th Annual Convention of the Association for the Advancement of Behavior Therapy, San Diego, CA, November.

Vivian, D., Heyman, R.E. & Langhinrichsen-Rohling, J. (1995). Topographical and contextual analyses of the marital interactions of aggressive, non-aggressive, and nondistressed couples. Manuscript submitted for publication.

Vivian, D., Smith, D.A., Sandeen, E.E. & O'Leary, D.K. (1987). Problem-solving skills and emotional styles of physically aggressive maritally discordant. Paper presented at the 21st Annual Convention of the Association for the Advancement of Behavior Therapy, Boston, November.

Walker, L.E. (1979). *The Battered Woman.* New York: Harper & Row.

Weiss, R.L. (1980). Strategic behavioral marital therapy: toward a model for assessment and intervention. In J.P. Vincent (ed.), *Advances in Family Intervention, Assessment and Theory*, Vol. 1 (pp. 229–271). Greenwich, CT: AI.

Weiss, R.L. & Cerreto, M.C. (1980). The Marital Status Inventory: development of a measure of dissolution potential. *The American Journal of Family Therapy*, **8**, 80–86.

Weiss, R.L. & Halford, W.K. (1996). Managing couples therapy. In V. van Hasselt & M. Hersen (eds), *Sourcebook of Psychological Treatment Manuals for Adult Disorders* (pp. 489–537). New York: Plenum.

Weiss, R.L. & Heyman, R.E. (1990a). Marital distress. In A. Bellack & M. Hersen (eds), *International Handbook of Behavior Modification* (pp. 475–501). New York: Plenum.

Weiss, R.L. & Heyman, R.E. (1990b). Observation of marital interaction. In F.D. Fincham & T.N. Bradbury (eds), *The Psychology of Marriage: Basic Issues and Applications* (pp. 87–117). New York: Guilford.

Weiss, R.L., Hops, H. & Patterson, G.R. (1973). A framework for conceptualizing, some data for evaluating it. In L.D. Handy & E.L. Mash (eds), *Behavior Change: Methodology Concepts and Practice* (pp. 309–342). Champaign, IL: Research Press.

Weiss, R.L. & Perry, B.A. (1983). The Spouse Observation Checklist. In E.E. Filsinger (ed.), *A Source Book of Marriage and Family Assessment* (pp. 65–84). Beverly Hills: Sage.

Weiss, R.L. & Sher, T.G. (1991). Negative communication in marital intraction: a misnomer? *Behavioral Assessment*, **13** (1: Special Issue).

Wieder, G.B. & Weiss, R.L. (1980). Generalizability theory and the coding of marital interactions. *Journal of Consulting and Clinical Psychology*, **48**, 469–477.

Wills, T.A., Weiss, R.L. & Patterson, G.R. (1974). A behavioral analysis of the determinants of marital satisfaction. *Journal of Consulting and Clinical Psychology*, **42**, 802–811.

Woody, E.Z. & Costanzo, P. (1990). Does marital agony precede marital ecstasy? A comment on Gottman and Krokoff's "Marital Interaction and Satisfaction: a Longitudinal View". *Journal of Consulting and Clinical Psychology*, **58**, 499–501.

Chapter 3

Cognitive and Affective Processes in Marriage

Patricia Noller*, Steven Beach** and Susan Osgarby[†]
Departments of Psychology, * University of Queensland, St Lucia,
Queensland, Australia; ** University of Georgia, Athens, GA, USA;
and [†] Griffith University, Nathan, Queensland, Australia

Rachael and Peter, like many other couples today, are continually arguing over the household chores. Although Peter is willing to help around the house by regularly doing the ironing and running the vacuum cleaner over the carpet, he thinks that Rachael could be more grateful that he does so much for her, and feels let down. For Rachael's part, however, any suggestion that Peter is "helping her" brings with it the implication that the housework actually belongs to her, and she feels very angry. "After all," she argues, "doesn't the housework belong to both of us, and shouldn't we be working together as a team, with equal responsibility, to get the housework done?"

This situation illustrates how cognitive and affective processes work in everyday marital situations that many couples face. Rachael and Peter see the housework quite differently. To put it another way, their cognitive processing around the issue of housework is very different. From Peter's perspective, the housework is really Rachael's responsibility and his willingness to help out is a sign of his caring for Rachael and she should be grateful. From Rachael's perspective, the housework belongs to both of them and when Peter helps out, he is merely fulfilling his part as a responsible member of the household. To thank him would imply that it's really her job.

Given their very different cognitions about the issue of housework, Rachael and Peter also have very different emotional reactions. Peter feels let down when Rachael isn't grateful, and Rachael feels angry when he suggests that she should be. Peter and Rachael may, through talking about this issue, come to reframe the housework issue in a way that will be satisfactory to both of them. Alternatively,

Clinical Handbook of Marriage and Couples Interventions. Edited by W. Kim Halford and Howard J. Markman.
© 1997 John Wiley & Sons Ltd.

Rachael may come to see Peter's approach to the housework as his way of "putting her down" or "keeping her in her place" and may see this behavior as occurring more and more in their relationship. Peter, on the other hand, may feel misunderstood and unappreciated and come to see this lack of appreciation as pervasive in their relationship. Either way, this example illustrates the power of affective and cognitive processes in marriage. It also illustrates the ways in which affective and cognitive processes are closely related.

Bradbury & Fincham (1987) point out that research on close relationships has generally focused on either affect or cognition in isolation, encouraging an artificial distinction between these two processes in marital functioning. To counteract this artificial separation, they have developed a detailed model in which affect and cognition interact in distressed couples to produce selective attention and recall of negative relationship events, which in turn are associated with high negative arousal and reduced capacity for effective problem-solving (Bradbury & Fincham, 1987, 1990, 1991). They argue that the frequency of negative affect and behavior found in distressed couples is due, in part, to differences in the cognitive processing of spouse behavior. In distressed couples, negative spouse behavior is viewed as global, enduring and intentional, and therefore negative behavior is made highly meaningful and relevant to the self. As self-relevant information is processed more fully, it becomes more memorable (Bradbury & Fincham, 1987). In this way, distressed couples are likely to develop elaborate and negative cognitive representations of the partner, in general, and also are likely to associate the partner with negative events, and to have negative memories about the relationship. In contrast, non-distressed couples will discount negative partner behavior by attributing it to specific, situational and unstable factors, and are thus less likely to spend a lot of time on this type of cognitive processing.

Figure 3.1, adapted form Bradbury & Fincham (1990) provides an example of how the processes involved in Bradbury & Fincham's (1987) model work. The figure shows what happens when the wife sends a message to her husband (path A). Note that this figure presents the model only as it relates to the wife. There is also a corresponding set of components for the husband. According to the model, the husband's behavior is followed by primary processing on the part of the wife, as shown by path B. She may also engage in a similar process for her own behavior (path C) that initially gave rise to her husband's response via path A. During primary processing, she attends to and extracts information from her husband's input. Two alternative paths are possible after primary processing.

To the extent that the wife perceives her husband's behavior to be low in negativity, expected and not self-relevant, she is likely to respond behaviorally without any further processing (path H). Her cognitive processing is likely to be outside her immediate awareness. In contrast, if she perceives her husband's behavior to be high in negativity, unexpected and self-relevant, she is likely to engage in secondary processing and to make an attribution for her husband's behavior (path D). (We see this process at work in the illustration about Rachael and Peter.) She may then behave in a way that is influenced by this attribution (path G). The outcome of primary processing and the nature of attributions made

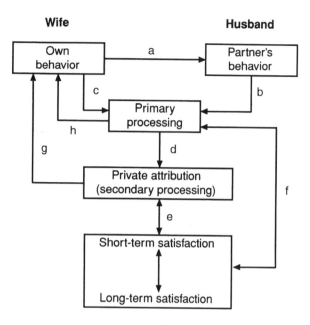

Figure 3.1 A framework relating attributions, behavior and marital satisfaction (from Bradbury & Fincham, 1990, with permission)

as a result of secondary processing are expected to affect, and be affected by, the couples's overall marital satisfaction. Path F provides the link between primary processing and marital satisfaction, and path E provides the link between secondary processing and marital satisfaction.

Bradbury & Fincham's model does away with the distinction between affect and cognition, seeing them both as aspects of internal mental processing. Primary processing involves paying attention to the relevant stimulus and forming a representation of it, especially in terms of whether it is negative or positive, expected or unexpected, and self-relevant or not. This process is similar to what Lazarus & Smith (1988) call appraisals. According to Lazarus & Smith, if appraisal of a situation has direct implications for one's well-being, emotion will result. For example, because Rachael and Peter have had numerous arguments about his contribution to household chores, Rachael now becomes instantly angry if she detects any indication that Peter is not enthusiastic and happy while vacuuming the carpet.

Secondary processing is then likely to occur when the stimulus is considered to be negative, unexpected and self-relevant, and is likely to involve an attributional search to identify a cause of the behavior or stimulus and to assign responsibility for it. Imagine a second marital situation where Rachael's husband Peter is late coming home from work and has not called to say that he will be late. If, as part of the primary processing or appraisal process, Rachael decides that this situation is just another example of his lack of concern and consideration for her, then her secondary processing will probably involve her thinking about the other times when he has been inconsiderate in this way, as well as other evidence for his lack of concern. Her view of her partner and their relationship will become progressively negative, as will her reactions to Peter when he arrives home from work.

Lazarus, Smith and their colleagues (Smith et al., 1993) showed that appraisals are more closely related to emotion than attributions, and account for more of the variance in emotion than attributions. In fact, these researchers found that once appraisals were taken into account, attributions added very little to the prediction of emotion. In addition, they found that appraisal mediated between attributions and emotions. They suggest, as do Bradbury & Fincham with their constructs of primary and secondary processing, that appraisals precede attributions, although they were not able to establish temporal order with their methodology. Perhaps studying these issues in the context of real relationships and actual interactions may increase our understanding of the order in which these various processes occur.

Bradbury & Fincham (1987) include two contextual variables in their framework: the distal context and the proximal context. The distal context for marital interactions includes each spouse's stable personality characteristics (such as Peter's tendency to get involved in work activities and forget to let Rachael know what is happening, and Rachael's tendency to put the worst possible construction on his behavior), and the couple's evaluation of the quality of their relationship. The distal context may also include aspects of their relationship history, such as what happened the last time (or the many times) they tried to deal with this issue, and recent events, such as the argument they had earlier in the day, as well as their overall level of satisfaction with their relationship. The proximal context includes what is actually happening in the current interaction, such as their transient thoughts and feelings, including their emotional reactions and attributions of the partner's intention in the current interaction. These two contexts both affect the interaction and are affected by it.

Bradbury & Fincham's framework provides a useful way of integrating the marital research to date. It offers a tentative explanation for the links between the various elements (each partner's behavior, each partner's response to that behavior) through affective and cognitive processing (at both the primary and secondary level) and the contexts (both distal and proximal) in which they interact.

AFFECT

Structure of Affect

Discussions of affect in marriage, whether focused on expressed emotion or self-report of experienced emotion, should be guided by the strong likelihood that affective experience in marriage is characterized by two primary dimensions (cf.

Beach & Fincham, 1994), although there is some disagreement about what these dimensions should be. Some researchers would argue for using a pleasant–unpleasant dimension, along with an arousal dimension (Russell, 1980), whereas others would argue for separate dimensions of positive and negative affect (Clark & Watson, 1991). Decisions about which set of dimensions to use should be guided by their utility in a given context. In either case, however, it would seem to be more informative for researchers and clinicians to ask spouses to express their feelings about their partner along at least two primary dimensions, rather than just assessing a unidimensional satisfaction or adjustment dimension. By using two dimensions, researchers may move closer to capturing clinically important differences between couples, and provide an empirically sound way of developing a typology of discordant couples.

Due to its heuristic value across a wide range of potential applications we would suggest adoption in the marital area of Watson & Tellegen's (1985) model, where positive affect and negative affect define separate dimensions of affective experience. It is important to note, however, that we are not wanting to imply that the arousal dimension is not relevant. Indeed, for some purposes, focusing on the two dimensions of arousal and degree of pleasantness/unpleasantness may be more useful. Relationships can be destroyed both by negativity that is high in arousal (high levels of anger, conflict and even violence) and by negativity that is low in arousal (lack of caring, disinterest, distance). For this reason, it may be useful to construe emotion in terms of arousal in some contexts. For example, we know that some relationships are high on both positivity and negativity (Fitzpatrick, 1988), but where spouses are also high on arousal, the relationship is likely to be volatile and even unstable. The emotional intensity of the relationship is likely to depend on what Kelley (1983) calls interdependence or level of involvement in the relationship, or what Rusbult (1987) calls investment or the resources an individual has put into the relationship (such as affection, disclosure, energy, gifts, time). Those who are strongly involved in their relationships are more likely to voice their concerns and fight for those relationships.

The primary ways that affect has been explored in marriage is through the study of (a) self-reported affect, (b) non-verbal communication, and (c) physiological responses during conflict.

Self-reported Affect

Self-reported affect has generally been studied in the context of particular interactions, or in diary studies. Gaelick, Bodenhausen & Wyer (1985) and Noller & Ruzzene (1991) videotaped couples during discussion of a conflict, and then had spouses report on the affect they were experiencing during that interaction. Gaelick, Bodenhausen & Wyer showed that spouses reciprocated the emotion (love or hostility) they thought their partner was conveying and saw their partners as reciprocating their own affect. Because spouses were not as accurate at decoding partners' expressions of love as they were at decoding their hostility, the negative emotion was more likely to be reciprocated. Thus, one reason that spouses tend to reciprocate negative, but not positive, interaction is that they have problems in accurately encoding or decoding positive affect. The findings from Noller's (1984) study of marital misunderstandings suggests that the encoding of positive messages, particularly by husbands, is likely to be contributing to this problem.

In a diary study, Kirchler (1988, 1989) had spouses answer questions about their own and their partner's affect at randomly selected times each day over a period of several weeks. Those in satisfying relationships reported more positive affect when their partner was present rather than absent, and were better able than other spouses to assess their partner's current needs. In addition, spouses were better able to assess their partner's current mood state when they were in agreement than when they were in conflict. Noller & Ruzzene (1991) similarly showed that distressed spouses particularly have more problems in accurately identifying the affect experienced by their partners during conflict episodes, and seem to lack rapport with their partners.

Guthrie & Noller (1988) studied communication in married couples in three different affective situations: when angry with the partner, when depressed about the relationship and when feeling affectionate. Spouses low in marital adjustment were less accurate than other spouses at perceiving their partner's intentions, and attributed more negative intentions to the partner than did those high in marital adjustment for both the depression and the affection situations.

These findings suggest that clinicians working with married couples need to be aware of likely problems in understanding each other's affect and intentions. For example, a husband who thinks that his wife is angry with him for being late, when she was really anxious about his safety, is likely to respond in ways that make the situation worse, rather than better. Hence, checking out that couples have understood the other's emotion and/or intention correctly may be an important skill to teach couples in programs of prevention, enrichment and therapy.

Non-verbal Communication

Non-verbal communication has been studied in terms of accuracy (or how well spouses are able to understand one another's non-verbal behaviours) (Gottman & Porterfield, 1981; Noller, 1984) and also through the observation of behavior (e.g. Gottman, Markman & Notarius, 1977; Noller, 1984; see Weiss & Heyman, 1990, for a review). We will not discuss observation in this chapter, since it is dealt with in the chapter by Weiss and Heyman (this volume).

Accuracy

Gottman & Porterfield (1981) and Noller (1984) used a standard content paradigm to examine non-verbal accuracy (or the decoding of positive, neutral and negative affect) in married couples. The results of both studies indicated that the endoding and decoding of husbands is more crucial to marital satisfaction than that of wives. In a follow-up study, Noller (1984) showed that spouses in distressed marriages seem to have a performance deficit, and are unable to use the skills with their partners that they use with strangers. Gottman & Porterfield (1981) similarly found evidence for a decoding deficit in husbands that was specific to their relationship with their wives. Noller & Ruzzene (1991) further showed that husbands who attribute negative intentions to their partners are less likely to decode the partner's non-verbal messages accurately. Perhaps the high negativity in the conflict situation interferes with the husband's ability to decode non-verbal messages from his wife accurately.

Physiological Responding

The finding that affect, particularly negative affect, is integral in distinguishing distressed and non-distressed couples, led Gottman & Levenson (e.g. Gottman & Levenson, 1985; Levenson & Gottman, 1985) to conduct a detailed analysis of negative affect in marital interaction from a physiological perspective. From these data, they calculated the interrelatedness of the husband and wife in terms of their physiological responding, and found that the greater their marital distress, the higher the "physiological linkage" between them. In other words, they assessed the extent to which, when one of them became highly aroused physiologically, the partner did also, increasing the likelihood that they would both react negatively. Of the variance in marital satisfaction, 60% was accounted for by this linkage variable. Following-up these couples 3 years later, the researchers found that the physiological reactions of couples in the original study were able to predict their later marital satisfaction. They concluded that physiological linkage is an index of negative affect reciprocity, reflecting the spouses' negative expectations of conflict interactions and their consequent predisposition to engage in such negative interactions.

This finding that distressed couples show high levels of negative behaviors and negative affect reciprocity, that often are accompanied by high physiological arousal, led to the hypothesis that this state of arousal, and being in the negative behavioral escalation process, is highly aversive. Consistent with this hypothesis, maritally distressed individuals, and particularly husbands, often attempt to escape from such interactions and avoid discussion of conflictual topics (Christensen & Shenk, 1991). It is argued that this pattern of escape and avoidance of these negative escalation traps reduces the chance of conflict resolution and thereby maintains relationship dissatisfaction.

Gottman & Levenson (1988) expounded a theory of gender differences in marital interaction in terms of differences between husbands and wives in their ability to function in the context of high negative affect. While men are able to play a reconciling role during low levels of marital conflict, they are likely to withdraw in situations of high conflict. Gottman & Levenson argue that this withdrawal is related to the high level of physiological responding of husbands, particularly those in unhappy marriages, in situations involving marital conflict. This withdrawal by husbands may set up what has become known as the demand–withdraw pattern of interaction in which wives nag and demand in order to get changes in the relationship, and husbands withdraw and refuse to discuss the issue (Christensen, 1988; Christensen & Heavey, 1990).

Depression and Marriage

Both marital discord and depression are negative affective states, and there is a correlation between level of marital satisfaction and depression which increases in magnitude over the first few years of marriage (e.g. Beach & O'Leary, 1993; Schaefer & Burnett, 1987). How does negative affect in marriage come to be increasingly linked with depression over time?

Of particular relevance for answering this question is the considerable stability in levels of positive and negative affect over time (Schuerger, Zarrella & Hotz, 1989). The trait-like nature of affective experience has been captured by the terms "negative affectivity" (NA) and "positive affectivity" (PA) which produce moderate to high stability coefficients over different time periods (Schuerger, Zarrella & Hotz, 1989). Persons high in NA are prone to experience anxiety and tension, but also anger, feelings of rejection and sadness. In addition, they may be more reactive to stimuli that induce negative affect (Larsen & Ketelaar, 1991) and are likely to be self-critical and introspective and to dwell on their own mistakes. Conversely, persons high in PA are prone to experience well-being, but also social dominance, energy and adventurousness (Clark & Watson, 1991) and may be more responsive to stimuli that induce positive affect (Larsen & Ketelaar, 1991). Elevated PA is also related to interest in social interaction, sex and achievement.

Given the apparent relevance of greater anger and feelings of rejection (NA) or greater interest in social interaction and sex (PA) for marital interaction, it seems reasonable to posit a relation between the dimensions of NA or PA on the one hand, and feelings toward the partner or marital behavior on the other. Supporting this speculation, O'Leary & Smith (1991) note that neuroticism (or alternatively NA) is related longitudinally to poor marital adjustment. However, they note that the mechanisms involved are not well understood and require theoretical and empirical attention. Similarly, Markman et al. (1987) note that psychopathology of husbands appears more consequential overall for the longitudinal prediction of marital satisfaction, but that level of depressive symptomatology (high NA, low PA) premaritally in either husbands or wives is the single best "individual pathology" predictor of lower marital satisfaction longitudinally.

More recently, Beach & O'Leary (1993) reported that elevated depressive symptomatology premaritally predicted a subsequent decline in marital satisfaction. Conversely, low marital satisfaction early in marriage predicted later higher levels of depressive symptomatology, particularly for persons with a dysphoric affective style (Beach & O'Leary, 1993). Accordingly, it appears that marital health and level of depressive symptomatology are related in important ways, with some persons being at greater risk than others both to develop marital discord and also to respond to marital discord with increases in depressive symptomatology.

Positive Affect

Although the association between poor conflict management and marital distress seems well established, it is unlikely that mere absence of conflict would be sufficient condition for maintaining marital satisfaction. Indeed, maritally satisfied couples typically report the occurrence of much higher rates of positive behavior in day-to-day interactions with their partners than do distressed couples (Broderick & O'Leary, 1986). In addition, recent work demonstrated that the development of a sense of shared positive marital history is an important predictor of long-term marital satisfaction (Buehlman, Gottman & Katz, 1992). Furthermore, content analysis of responses from long-term happily married couples about how they keep their relationships satisfying shows they also focus on the role of positive affect (Osgarby & Halford, 1996a). In this study, 78% of couples identified positive intimate behaviors as crucial to sustained relationship satisfaction, while only 11% of responses identified management of conflict as crucial. Examples of identified positive behaviors included spending enjoyable time together and expressing intimacy through verbal communication.

Despite the reports of couples about the importance they attached to positive affect, few studies have been able to identify positive intimate behaviors during interactions which are observed to covary with marital satisfaction. For example, when Halford & Sanders (1990) asked couples to discuss the previous day's activities in a relaxed setting, differences between distressed and non-distressed couples related primarily to higher rates of negative behavior in the distressed couples, with few differences in positive behavior. Similarly, reviews of observed interactions of distressed and non-distressed couples consistently find negative behaviors to be a better discriminator of marital distress than positive behaviors (Weiss & Heyman, 1990). This effect may reflect the nature of the observational tasks used, rather than a lack of influence of interactional behaviors on marital satisfacton. In relevant research, couples typically were asked to discuss conflictual topics, which seems unlikely to elicit or assess positive intimacy skills. On the other hand, when couples were asked to discuss a non-conflictual topic, and to provide social support about a problem the spouse was experiencing, marital satisfaction correlated with positive, prosocial behavior (Julien & Markman, 1991; Julien, 1992).

Osgarby and Halford (1996b) developed a task designed to directly assess couples' positive intimacy skills. It involved each partner identifying a very positive experience in their relationship history, and then the partners discussing its significance with each other. As expected, this task resulted in maritally happy couples showing higher rates of positive behaviors (both speaker and listener skills), higher rates of positive affect arousal and higher rates of positive cognitions than distressed couples. The happy couples also demonstrated significantly higher levels of what was called conversational meshing than distressed couples. Conversational meshing was defined as a series of communication behaviors where couples positively presented a conjoint story about a relationship event.

COGNITION

Differences between distressed and non-distressed couples have been documented across a wide range of cognitive phenomena. Baucom and his colleagues (e.g. Baucom & Epstein, 1990) identify five main types of cognitive processes that appear to play an important role in the development and maintenance of poor adjustment in marriage. These five categories are: selective attention (a perceptual process); assumptions and beliefs; standards of behavior; expectancies; and attributions about why events occur. There are other cognitive variables that are also relevant, such as working models, implicit rules and self-evaluation maintenance processes. We include working models under assumptions and beliefs, rules with standards (assuming that standards and rules are closely related), and deal with self-evaluation maintenance processes in a separate section. We will also examine areas of cognitive processes that have received little attention to date: goal structures, self-correction and self-regulation in marriage, and memory processes. Some of these cognitive variables are more likely to apply to the distal context, (e.g. attributions about causes of problems, working models, expectations and standards, beliefs), whereas others will apply to the proximal context (e.g. attributions of intention in the immediate situation).

Selective Attention

Differences have consistently been shown in the perceptual processes of happily and unhappily married couples in terms of how much they agree about relationship events, as well as in terms of the extent to which their perceptions of relationship events are similar to those of an outside observer. Couples in distressed relationships tend to have lower levels of agreement about relationship events (Christensen, Sullaway & King, 1983) and to have more negative biases, compared with objective observers, in their perceptions of their spouses' communication.

The literature on the decoding of non-verbal behavior in marriage is also relevant here, with happy couples better able to receive the message being sent by the partner, without distorting it (Gottman & Porterfield, 1981, Noller, 1984). Further, the evidence from Noller & Ruzzene (1991) that spouses, particularly husbands, were more likely to misinterpret their partner's affect if they attributed a negative intention to him/her, suggests that these misperceptions may be driven by other cognitive processes such as attributions.

Assumptions and Beliefs

In this section we will look at three main types of assumptions and beliefs: working models of relationships (as exemplified in adult attachment theory— Collins & Read, 1994; Hazan & Shaver, 1987), "rational" beliefs about such aspects of marriage as intimacy and closeness, sex roles, love and commitment; and what Epstein & Eidelson (1981) call "irrational" beliefs about marriage.

Working Models

According to Bowlby (1973), on the basis of early attachment experiences with primary caregivers, individuals develop working models of relationships which affect the ways they relate to others throughout life. Early work by Ainsworth and her colleagues (Ainsworth et al., 1978) pointed to three different attachment styles in children (secure, avoidant and anxious-ambivalent). Hazan & Shaver (1987) explored the relevance of these attachment styles to adults' romantic relationships. The concept of working models of attachment in adults and their effects on romantic relationships has particularly been explored by Collins & Read (1994). These working models are seen as affecting such core aspects of relationships as trust and intimacy.

Feeney, Noller & Callan (1994) explored the effects of attachment style on relationship satisfaction in a sample of newly-married couples (1–2 years). Attachment style was assessed using continuous measures of the two factors that are crucial to measuring attachment style: anxiety over abandonment and comfort with closeness (Feeney, Noller & Callan, 1994; Simpson, 1990). Communication quality as assessed by diary reports was positively related to comfort with closeness for husbands, and negatively related to anxiety over abandonment for wives. In addition, anxiety over abandonment was a strong predictor of behavior patterns during conflict for both husbands and wives. Anxious wives reported higher levels of conflict and more domination than other wives, as well as more coercion, more use of demand–withdraw and less mutual discussion. Anxious husbands reported more coercion, more demand–withdraw and less mutual discussion.

Attachment style also affected decoding accuracy which was assessed using a standard content task (Feeney, Noller & Callan, 1994). Wives high in comfort with closeness were better decoders of neutral and negative messages. Husbands high in anxiety were poorer decoders of all three types of messages after almost 2 years of marriage. There was also evidence in these studies that anxiety over abandonment was strongly related to marital satisfaction for both husbands and wives, and that comfort with closeness was related to satisfaction for husbands only.

Feeney, Noller & Callan (1994) explored the links between communication (quality, patterns during conflict, decoding accuracy), attachment style and relationship satisfaction. They found different patterns for husbands and wives. For wives there were moderately strong concurrent relations among the three sets of variables, and their later satisfaction was not predicted by attachment style. For husbands, not only was their communication and relationship satisfaction predicted by their attachment security, but there were reciprocal relations between attachment and communication patterns and between attachment and relationship satisfaction.

Beliefs about Marriage

Little work has been carried out on the beliefs that people hold about marriage. In her work on developing a typology of marriages and an instrument for categorizing individuals and couples into types, Fitzpatrick (1988) includes two ideological dimensions: Ideology of Traditionalism and Ideology of Uncertainty and Change. She argues that the values that individuals hold concerning marriage and family life affect both interactions with the spouse and judgments about the outcomes of those interactions. Spouses high on traditionalism tend to place greater emphasis on stability than on satisfaction in marriage, and to hold conventional values on relationships (e.g. that a woman should change her name when she marries). Spouses high on uncertainty and change tend to emphasize the excitement of spontaneity and relational uncertainty, as against predictability and stability.

Noller, Dixon & Limerick (1989) developed a broader set of beliefs about marriage. The 50 beliefs that were included in the questionnaire were reduced to four factors: the mutual supportiveness factor involved an emphasis on caring, sharing and open communication ("A good marriage is one where both partners are willing to give and take"); the sex roles factor included items about who should take what roles in a marriage, including leadership, paid work and caring for children, and was scored in the direction of male dominance ("It is better for the marriage if the husband takes the lead in making decisions"); the lack of institutional commitment factor included beliefs about commitment and independence in marriage ("Marriage is not necessarily a life commitment"); and the interpersonal commitment factor included beliefs about love, trust and happiness ("A marriage is a success if both partners care about and love each other").

Married men and women were more likely to agree with traditional male-dominance-oriented beliefs than were single men and women. Those with Protestant affiliations agreed more with the traditional sex role belief statements than did those with no religious beliefs, with Catholics falling between the other two groups. There was no difference between Catholics and Protestants on the lack of institutional commitment factor, but those with no religion scored lower on this factor. These findings suggest that core belief systems also have an effect on what couples believe is appropriate behavior in marriage (Markman, Stanley & Blumberg, 1994).

Irrational Beliefs

Irrational beliefs about marriage (e.g. Eidelson & Epstein, 1982) have also been shown to discriminate between couples in healthy marriages and those in distressed relationships. Distressed couples are more likely to believe that any form of disagreement is destructive, that their spouses should intuitively understand their ideas and feelings, and that their partners cannot possibly change. They also tend to be very perfectionist in their approach to sexual performance, and to believe that relational problems are rooted in fundamental differences between the sexes. Such beliefs are likely to affect directly the extent to which couples try to deal with differences and effect change, and are also likely to be linked to unrealistic standards and expectations of partner behavior.

Standards

According to Baucom et al. (1989), standards involve a person's ideas about the way relationships should be (and hence, how partners should behave). These standards may be irrational and unlikely to be met by any real-life partner (e.g. my partner should be able to read my mind and know what I need), or they may be quite functional (e.g. we should talk about things that are troubling us). Standards are problematic when they become extreme or are rigidly held, or when they have a negative effect on people's lives or relationships (Baucom et al., 1989).

Standards are also likely to lead to rules for relationships. Argyle & Henderson (1985) explored the rules of marriage and found that, in general, the same rules applied to both husbands and wives, although the order of importance was not always the same. The most important rules were about providing emotional support, sharing news of success, being faithful, creating a harmonious atmosphere in the home, respecting the partner's privacy, keeping confidences, using first names, engaging in sexual activity with the partner, giving birthday cards and presents, and standing up for the partner in his/her absence.

Jones & Gallois (1989) explored the implicit rules that spouses have about how to behave in a conflict. They found that rules mentioned by both partners were generally about avoiding material costs and maintaining intimacy. Specifically, these rules were about being positive, being considerate, doing things that help resolve conflicts, expressing feelings and attitudes, and being rational.

Expectancies

Expectancies can be categorized as either outcome expectancies (expectations about the consequences of certain behaviors) or efficacy expectations (beliefs about the likelihood that particular activities can be successfully carried out: Bandura, 1977; Weiss, 1984a,b). There is little work in the area of expectancies, but we do know that efficacy expectations relate positively to marital satisfaction (Fincham & Bradbury, 1989) and also to a number of correlates of marital satisfaction such as rates of positive behavior (Weiss, 1984a) and relationship attributions (Fincham & Bradbury, 1989).

Levenson & Gottman (1985) explain their finding that physiological arousal measured before a conflict interaction predicted marital satisfaction 3 years later in terms of the expectations of the interactants about the conflict. Presumably, those who had negative outcome expectancies (expected that they would have an interaction that was highly aversive and destructive to their relationship) would have higher physiological arousal, as would those who had negative efficacy expectancies (believed that they would be unable to resolve the conflict success-fully). Thus, high levels of emotional arousal are likely to be fueled by negative expectations. A vicious cycle involving both affect and cognition is likely to be set up, increasing the probability of a deterioration in marital satisfaction and even divorce.

Weiss (1984a) showed that spouses' expectations for their interactions with their partners predicted both their interpretations of events in their relationship and their responses to those events. Weiss has argued, in fact, that spouses are often not responding to the actual behaviors occurring in a particular interaction, but rather to "some affective–cognitive representation of one another that sets the 'value' of any particular bit of behavior" (1984b, p. 338). Weiss (1980) labeled this type of process as "sentiment override". Sentiment, or the overriding evalu-ation of the partner, may be positive, in which case the partner's behavior is likely to be seen through "rose-colored spectacles", or negative, in which case the partner's behavior will be interpreted in a negative light. Weiss (1984a) has further suggested that the reason that couples use their familiarity with one another in interpreting relationship events is that they believe that their knowl-edge of the other is perfect. Imagine Rachael saying to Peter, "Don't tell me what you meant! After all, I have been married to you for 10 years and I know exactly what you meant". Noller & Venardos (1986) found that spouses in unhappy marriages were particularly likely to think they had correctly interpreted the partner when their interpretation was wrong.

It is important to recognize the implications of negative sentiment override for change in the relationship. If the partner's response is mainly governed by nega-tive expectations, then attempts to change behavior are likely to go unrecognized by the partner and are very unlikely to be reinforced. In this situation, achieving constructive changes in behavior becomes very difficult. Therapists may need to work specifically on challenging the negative expectations and help spouses recognize and reinforce the partner's sincere attempts to change behavior.

Attributions

There is now a broad literature linking attributional style and marital discord. In addition to the many cross-sectional investigations demonstrating a link between attributional style and marital discord (see Bradbury & Fincham, 1990 for a complete review) there are now several longitudinal investigations consistent with the hypothesis that attributions cause marital distress (Fincham & Bradbury, 1987). There are also several studies showing an impact of attributional style on spouses' behavior toward one another (e.g. Fincham & Bradbury, 1988; Sillars, 1985), including the occurrence of violent behavior (Byrne & Arias, in press; Holtzworth-Munroe & Hutchinson, 1993). In addition, recent work has shown that attributions for partner behavior can predict subsequent marital interaction even after shared variance with marital satisfaction has been controlled (Bradbury & Fincham, 1992). The implications of this body of work are well summarized by the Attribution-efficacy Model of Conflict (Fincham & Bradbury, 1987).

The attribution-efficacy model highlights three stages in the process of attributing blame to the partner. First, an attribution that locates the cause of an event in the partner must be made before any blame can be assigned. Judging that cause to be stable and global (consistent over time and situation) will also ultimately influence blame. Second, inferences about responsibility are also considered critical in determining blame. That is, causal attributions are held to provide the basis for responsibity attributions, which in turn provide the basis for the assignment of blame (and subsequent negative behavior). The utility of this sort of ordering of attributional components has received initial support in the marital literature (Fincham & Bradbury, 1987, 1992).

It appears that early in a relationship, partners begin to form stable attributions regarding their relationship conflict. Once discordant, couples appear to be quite willing to attribute blame to one another and to do so with a high level of certainty (Noller & Ruzzene, 1991). Noller & Ruzzene found that distressed spouses, especially wives, tended to see problem-related behavior as pervasive and unlikely to change and partner behavior as selfish and blameworthy, and that they approached problem discussions from that perspective. For spouses who make more negative responsibility attributions, the propensity for negative interaction will be intensified. On the other hand, making more benign attributions of responsibility for their conflict should lead to spouses having healthier patterns of interaction over time. One contributor to the problems of Rachael and Peter discussed earlier is her tendency to attribute Peter's failure to call when he is running late to his lack of love and concern for her. Approaching problems from this perspective is only going to add to their distress.

Although some claim that we do not really know whether spontaneous cognitive responses in the natural environment are similar in quantity or quality to those obtained in research, Weiner (1985) does provide some indication of the situations in which attributions occur in real life. Attributional activity seems most likely to be elicited by unexpected events and failure to attain a goal. In close relationships like marriage, attributional activity should be particularly elicited by unexpected behavior on the part of the spouse, as well as the spouse's failure to behave in ways that increase the likelihood of the couple's or partner's goals being achieved. It is also possible in marriage that attributions from particular events are carried into other situations, so that there is a "permanent" attribution for behavior that is expected because it has happened before.

Clearly, the study of attributions in marriage has proved fruitful in elaborating our understanding of marital processes and particularly those processes related to marital distress. In broad brush, it has supported the value of considering the ways couples construe partner behavior as one component of a fuller understanding of dyadic interaction. That is, models accounting for marital satisfaction and distress cannot focus exclusively on topographical descriptions of interaction, but must include information about how spouses process those interactions.

Self-evaluation Maintenance Processes (SEM)

In the SEM model (Beach, Mendolia & Tesser, 1992) it is assumed that persons are typically motivated to maintain a positive self-evaluation and that self-evaluation is determined, in part, by two antagonistic process: reflection and comparison. The dynamics of comparison and reflection processes have been extensively examined in the social psychological literature. The comparison process is one in which self-evaluation is threatened by the outstanding accomplishments of a close other (cf. Suls & Wills, 1991). Examples of negative comparison are also quite common, as when one spouse feels threatened because he or she sees the partner as smarter or more verbal, or because the partner makes more money. Importantly, when positive self-evaluation is threatened, one common self-protective strategy is to reduce closeness in order to reduce the intensity of the threat to self-evaluation (Wood & Taylor, 1991).

The reflection process is one in which self-evaluation is bolstered by the outstanding accomplishments of a close other (cf. Cialdini et al., 1976). Examples of this process are frequent, as when one spouse takes pride in the other's accomplishments and basks in the reflected glory of a partner's fame, attractiveness or standing in the community.

Since the better performance of a close other can bolster self-evaluation (via reflection) or threaten that evaluation (via comparison), we need to understand how these processes are regulated, and what leads to comparison processes, rather than reflection processes, coming into play. The critical variable seems to be the relevance of the particular characteristic to oneself. The relevance of another's performance is high if the performance is on a dimension for which the self has personal aspirations, and if the other's performance is not so much better or worse than one's own as to preclude comparisons. The more relevant the other's performance to the self, the greater the importance of the comparison process relative to the reflection process (Tesser, 1988).

In sum, the SEM model has three basic parameters: closeness, relevance (or importance), and performance; and these parameters are all assumed to interact with each other and be important in determining reactions to interpersonal situations in which one person can be seen as outperforming the other. When people are outperformed by close others in areas low in importance to themselves, they report positive feelings and pride in the other; when they are outperformed by close others in areas high in importance to themselves they show negative emotions (Tesser, Millar & Moore, 1988). When situations resulting in negative effects on self-evaluation arise, people will alter their closeness to the spouse, and even change their self-definition to make the final outcome more positive for their self-evaluation. Self-evaluation maintenance processes, then, appear to be involved in many interpersonal transactions, and it appears that people are motivated to configure their interpersonal environments so that these processes result in positive outcomes.

To have a better intuitive feel for SEM processes in marriage, we might consider again the relationship between Rachael and Peter, who are continually arguing about chores. At the outset of the chapter we discussed this problem in terms of the differing cognitions and affective experiences of each partner. However, the SEM framework offers a somewhat different perspective. From an SEM perspective the couple is experiencing a problem due, in part, to the success of recent societal changes that have broken down traditional gender barriers. These changes have allowed couples today to experience greater overlap in areas of self-relevance than was previously the case.

If both Rachael and Peter consider their careers to be self-defining and neither considers maintenance of the household to be self-defining, then they may have set themselves on a collision course with basic SEM processes. As one of them does better in career success, it may well pose a problem of negative comparison for the other. If one of them does better or more with regard to household maintenance, it will provide an opportunity for the other to feel good, but no opportunity for the self to feel good. Over time, a lack of differentiation in areas of relevance could lead Peter and Rachael to view each other more negatively, perhaps influencing attributions for negative behavior and increasing negative feelings. At a minimum, Rachael and Peter have a head start on developing problems in their relationship, and may have difficulty working together to solve those problems.

Rachael and Peter may have started out feeling very much in love; however, as each threatens the other with feelings of failure and provides the other with few opportunities for reflection, those feelings might be expected to change. As Rachael demands that Peter shoulder more responsibility for housework, Peter may find himself focusing on the negative implications for his work performance. As he explodes angrily that he is already doing more than his fair share, he may add that he has work to do, or he may mention or think about some other highly self-relevant activity. His explosive response may have more to do with defending himself against a perceived threat to his work performance than any specific aversion to housework.

At the same time, Rachael also finds her work performance highly self-relevant. Indeed, her resentment of Peter may grow especially strong if she happens to think of how his lack of involvement negatively affects her own career. Rachael and Peter may berate each other about lack of involvment in housework and perhaps explore their feelings together. Yet, they may never notice the dramatic impact of work stress in precipitating their arguments or may never understand how work stress is connected to their arguments. Perhaps worse for the couple, they may find themselves unable to enjoy the other's successes, finding that such successes only make matters worse between them. In brief, they may find themselves caught in a series of rapidly escalating arguments that seem to come out of nowhere and take on a life of their own.

The Extended SEM Model

Early research on the SEM model did not include a component which weighted the actor's investment in the other. Affective reactions to the situation were predicted entirely on the basis of the subject's own experience of positive comparison. Clearly, however, this conceptualization is an over-simplification of what is likely to be involved when our focus is on dyadic functioning. In a marriage, the actor can ignore his/her effect on the partner only at some cost to the relationship (Brickman & Bulman, 1977). Accordingly, the SEM model has been expanded to propose that partners in committed relationships respond empathetically to their spouse's outcomes. The extended model therefore predicts that in many cases a spouse's benefit from positive comparison or reflection may be offset by the knowledge that the partner is suffering negative comparison or failing to benefit from positive reflection. Thus, the perceived outcome for the partner's self-evaluation is important, as well as the outcome for one's own self-evaluation maintenance.

Beach & Tesser (1993) found that, as predicted, greater satisfaction was reported when a relatively higher percentage of agreements occurred in areas for which there were potential reflection and comparison benefits to be had by the self. In addition, greater satisfaction was reported when the partner was also perceived as having greater opportunity for reflection and comparison benefits.

Taken together, available work suggests that SEM processes may have a substantial influence on marital behavior and that SEM manipulations may be sufficient to produce changes in communication behavior of the sort typically associated with dysfunctional relationships. In particular, spouses seem strongly motivated to minimize negative comparison for self and partner, and they tend to be happier with their relationships if reflection and comparison needs for each partner are satisfied. In addition, following a negative comparison experience, spouses are more likely to be negative and more likely to try to dominate their partner. Accordingly, it would appear that understanding the role of marital relationships in satisfying self-evaluation maintenance needs may be important in fully understanding marital distress, and the role of cognitive processes in maintaining that distress.

Goals, Self-correction and Self-regulation in Marriage

The goals that spouses have for an interaction are likely to affect that interaction. For example, Christensen (1988) found that the roles individuals played in demand–withdraw interaction depends on whether they are trying to achieve autonomy or closeness. Those who were trying to achieve closeness (generally females) were more likely to play the demanding role, whereas those who were trying to achieve independence (generally males) were more likely to adopt the role of withdrawer.

In another study, Christensen & Heavey (1990) looked at whether whose issue (husband's or wife's) was being discussed affected which spouse adopted the demanding and withdrawing roles. When the issue being discussed was raised by the wife, the classic wife-demand/husband-withdraw pattern was most common (that is, wife demanding and husband withdrawing). These researchers also found, however, that both husbands and wives were more likely to demand on issues they, themselves, had raised and more likely to withdraw on issues raised by the partner. These findings could be interpreted to mean that spouses are demanding when their goal is to achieve change (in the partner, that is) and more likely to withdraw when their goal is to avoid change. One possible motivation for the demand–withdraw pattern in its classic form could be the husband's desire to exert power over the wife by avoiding change and maintaining the *status quo*, a *status quo* with which she is not happy (Noller, 1993).

In the context of marital interaction it seems likely that widely varying goal structures could guide spousal behavior and, indeed, goal structures could shift from one occasion to another and diverge between partners. So, for example, in the context of a marital disagreement, either or both spouses might have the goal of avoiding rejection, inflicting punishment on the partner, or working toward a mutually agreeable solution. Depending on the extent to which each partner's goal facilitates the goal attainment of the other, goal conflict or goal compatibility may emerge. Hence it is important in understanding couple behavior to determine whether the partners are working toward compatible goals or whether they are working at cross-purposes (Read & Miller, 1989).

Especially in the case of spouses who are working at cross-purposes, the potential for vicious cycles seems clear, as is indicated by the earlier illustration from the work of Christensen and his colleagues. As one spouse succeeds in moving the interaction closer to his/her desired goal state (e.g. of more independence in the relationship), the partner is likely to be moved further away from her/his goal (e.g. of more closeness). But, when the partner recognizes her/his movement away from the desired goal state, redoubled efforts on her/his part to "correct" the situation are likely. Unfortunately, through the same process, any successful attempts on her/his part to "correct" the situation will result in redoubled efforts by the first spouse to resist. As spouses in such a situation exchange behaviors, one might expect a continuing process of escalation (Notarius & Markman, 1993). As this analysis suggests, any discussion of self-regulation in marital dyads must simultaneously consider the patterns of interdependence in the marriage. Couples who are highly interdependent are likely to be more prone to such escalation than couples who are more distant, since, by definition, each spouse's behavior has more implications for his/her partner (Kelley, 1983).

The origin and nature of goal structures is also of importance to the discussion of self-regulation in marriage. Goal structures sometimes may be primed prior to an interaction by unrelated experiences, and may sometimes influence behavior without awareness. Indeed, it seems likely that in many cases multiple goals are simultaneously operative in a given interaction (cf. Miller & Read, 1991). However, for at least some marital interaction, it may be conscious and intentional goals that are important. Indeed, a percentage of the problematic behaviors that spouses direct toward each other appear to reflect relatively voluntary responses and many of the behaviors that therapists suggest to couples are readily available and voluntary.

Halford, Sanders & Behrens (1994) outline a self-regulation approach to marital therapy where spouses are encouraged to move from a partner-blaming perspective to a self-regulation perspective which emphasizes the need for partners to take responsibility for their own behavior, to select their own goals for behavior change and their own standards for that behavior. The focus in this approach is on partners identifying the changes they can make to their own behavior in order to improve their relationships. At the same time, partners are discouraged from demanding change from their partners. More research needs to be carried out on this self-regulatory approach to explore the possibility that clients can be empowered to produce changes in their own relationships through changes in their own behavior.

Memory Processes

While much is known about cognitive "content", several problems remain in the assessment of cognitions, including the extent to which assessment strategies mirror the cognitive processes that occur in the day-to-day lives of couples, and the importance of the actual manner in which information about cognitions is obtained. For example, Holtzworth-Munroe & Jacobson (1985) found that direct and indirect methods of assessing attributions resulted in fairly different findings, with the two sets of data only modestly correlated. Self-report instruments currently in use rely on verbally mediated reports of the cognitions each spouse associates with particular marital events (Baucom & Sayers, 1987), based on the assumption that subjects have access to the cognitive processes that underlie their conscious thoughts and actions.

Much of the current literature is based on a trait conceptualization of cognitive processes. However, it has been shown that a couple's cognitions about their relationship are highly variable and do not demonstrate the consistency suggested by the trait model (Jacobson, Follette & McDonald, 1982). Research based on these trait conceptualizations has assumed, rather than demonstrated, that general beliefs or global attributions actually affect the on-line cognitions occurring during a couple's interactions (Fincham, Bradbury & Scott, 1990). Given that cognitive behavior therapists have recently been stressing the need to modify situationally specific cognitions (such as Rachael's belief about why Peter forgets to call her when he is running late), rather than general cognitive traits, more emphasis may need to be given to understanding the processing of cognitions.

Much of the previous research into marital cognitions is based on the dubious assumption that phenomenological experience is sufficient to understand cognition. This assumption is highly questionable as people do not have access to the great majority of cognitive processes that underlie conscious thought, even though they become aware of a few of the products of these processes (Neisser, 1967). For nearly a decade now, Bradbury & Fincham (1987, 1990, 1991) have been arguing for greater attention to be paid to the non-conscious construction of marital relationship experiences, and have been recommending the inclusion of the information-processing approaches of cognitive science in the study of marital cognitions, rather than relying on self-report measures. They argue that the central function of cognition in marriage is to understand past and present relationship events, and to predict and guide future relationship behaviors (Bradbury & Fincham, 1991). Implicit in this view is the importance of studying couples' memory for relationship events by assessing partners' cognitive constructions of previously occurring interactions.

Osgarby & Halford (1995c) recently concluded a study where they investigated how married couples process information about their partners and about their interactions. They examined the accessibility of cognitive information and the consistency of this information over time, and found significant evidence of differences in cognitive processing between happily married and distressed couples. More specifically, accessibility was measured by asking partners to identify the maximum possible positive and negative partner descriptors in a given time. Using measures of response latency and response quantity, they found that maritally distressed couples were less able to access positive partner information and more able to access negative partner information than happily married couples.

Consistency of information across time was assessed in two ways. Firstly, partners' self-reports of affective state obtained immediately after problem-solving and positive reminiscence discussions were compared with their recall of these affective states a week later. Secondly, partners' diary records of positive and negative couple interactions were compared with their recall of this same information after a week. While happily married couples accurately recalled the extent of negative interaction they recorded during the week, they significantly over-estimated the amount of positive interaction they had recorded. This accurate recall of relationship negativity and positive bias for relationship positivity suggests the operation of positive sentiment override in the way happy couples remember relationship information. In contrast, distressed couples showed a significantly different memory pattern by recalling more negative interaction, and less positive interaction, than they had originally recorded. This pattern is consistent with negative sentiment override processing, as it contained negative biases in couples' recall of both relationship negativity (negativity inflation) and relationship positivity (positivity minimisation).

For Rachael and Peter, these findings suggest that they may both have richer, more fully developed mental pictures of each other as "bad", and less elaborate schemata of each other as "good". Alternatively, they may have easier access to the "bad" picture than to the "good" one. The findings also suggest that their arguments about who does what around the house become magnified over time, and that the smiles and caring gestures happening in between times are forgotten. While the specific mechanism for change is unclear, their original mental pictures of what happened between them is altered by subsequent cognitive activity.

Previous cognitive research has led to the inclusion of cognitive restructuring strategies in programs of behavioral marital therapy (Baucom & Epstein, 1990). However, inclusion of cognitive restructuring has failed to enhance the overall efficacy of the original therapy practices (Jacobson, 1992). The additional cognitive strategies have been based on rational verbal attempts to change faulty cognitions in distressed couples, and to modify "what" distressed spouses thought. Concepts such as negative memory bias (Osgarby & Halford, 1995c) suggest encoding, representational, storage and retrieval processes that interfere with functional and satisfying marital interaction, and suggest the need for therapy to help distressed couples modify how they are processing their partner's positive and negative behavior.

The behavioral and cognitive strategies for promotion of positive intimacy skills, outlined previously in the chapter, are also relevant here. Additionally, if one of the aims of therapy is to alter "how" partners react cognitively to the negativity of the other, strategies that alter primary and secondary process reactions with some form of perceptual retraining would appear relevant. For example, if Peter can be guided during exposure to Rachael's criticisms, sarcasm and angry outbursts (real, videotaped or imaginary) without responding in the way he usually does (arguing back, sulking or walking away), his dysfunctional automatic primary process responses may gradually be weakened, on-line negative attributional processes may be modified, and more positive relationship schemata may result.

In summary, our discussion of cognitive processes has highlighted a number of important issues related to affect and cognition in marriage. Firstly, there seems no doubt that affective and cognitive processes are closely intertwined. Some cognitive processes such as attributions seem to affect our emotional states. In other situations, emotions may affect our cognitive processes, as when our emotional state affects what we remember or what we pay attention to. Secondly, it seems clear that both affective and cognitive processes have an impact on marital satisfaction. For example, cognitive processes such as unrealistic beliefs, expectations and standards, attachment styles (working models of relationships) and goals affect relationship functioning and relationship satisfaction. Relieving marital distress, then, would seem to involve increasing partners' self-control over the positive and negative cognitive and affective processes in their relationships and thus helping them to develop healthier patterns of interaction.

Clinical Implications

Helping couples like Peter and Rachael increase their marital satisfaction involves two major aims: improving their ability to manage conflict and negativity in their relationship, and building skills of positive relationship intimacy. While cognitive-behavioral marital therapy has provided many ways to help couples break the negative cycles of behavior, affect and cognition in which they are trapped (Jacobson & Margolin, 1979; Stuart, 1980; Notarius & Markman, 1993), less energy has been expended in defining strategies for promoting intimacy and positive interaction. In order to improve their relationship, Peter and Rachael need behavioral techniques for building positive relationship interaction, and cognitive techniques for creating positive sentiment override in the way they process each other's behavior.

Appropriate behavioral therapy strategies would involve using tasks aimed at helping Peter and Rachael individually to assess, increase and monitor their positive relationship behavior. For example, self-evaluation strategies using checklists of positive intimacy skills, where Peter and Rachael rate their own individual use of specific positive behaviors at regular intervals. Similarly, self-monitoring techniques would involve Peter and Rachael in recording information about the frequency, type and setting of their own daily positive behavior, using positive intimacy diaries. Such self-assessment would make Peter and Rachael's positive behavior more accessible and salient, and hence more amenable to change.

Following these self-assessment procedures, Peter and Rachael could be encouraged to set goals involving specific behavioral standards for increased intimacy, including ways of increasing companionship, mutual support, verbal intimacy and consideration for each other. This process can include a range of tasks such as selecting things to do together from a menu of rewarding activities, and setting aside specific love days where Peter and Rachael focus on how, when, where and what they can do to make each other feel special and loved. Additionally, therapists can help couples through guiding and practicing positive behavior in the session, by facilitating positive reminiscences, and by setting up positively-biased discussions, rather than continually focusing on rehearsing communication skills with predominantly conflictual topics.

Cognitive strategies for increasing relationship intimacy should be aimed at the entire range of cognitive variables important in relationship satisfaction. Firstly, there is a need to build Peter and Rachael's awareness of their own contributions to the relationship problems through therapist questioning designed to provide specific direction for positive self-directed change. For example, "What are some things that you do now, or could do in the future, to show Peter that you do care for him?", or "In what way would you like to be different in your relationship with Rachael?". Secondly, therapists can include in their program perceptual retraining activities such as "Catch each other being nice!". This activity involves Peter and Rachael being asked to identify one behavior performed by the other that made them feel loved and special, while at the same time to show one small example of caring towards the other, at least once during the coming week. These types of activities will increase Peter and Rachael's awareness of positive partner behavior.

A third therapist strategy involves using cognitive restructuring tasks, where Peter and Rachael identify negative relationship schemata such as "Rachael will never be happy with our relationship. No matter what I do, it will never be good enough", and "Peter is always putting me down and just doesn't care about me any more", and guide them to evaluate rationally the reality of these negative scripts. Fourthly, imaginative rehearsal of positive self-reactions can be used by the therapist. This strategy involves Peter and Rachael individually discussing with the therapist, and mentally replaying, how they would have preferred to act during earlier negative interactions. Finally, other cognitive strategies, potentially useful for therapist, counteract the negative memory biases in couples like Peter and Rachael. For example, positive memory enhancement strategies where they set aside daily time to individually review and reflect on examples of positive interactions between them.

SUMMARY: AFFECTIVE AND COGNITIVE PROCESSES IN MARRIAGE

The forgoing review of the literature has highlighted the differences in cognitive and affective processing between those in healthy marital relationships and those in distressed destructive relationships. In concluding, we will summarize the destructive relationship cycles which seem to characterize unhealthy or distressed relationships, and then contrast those with the behaviors more common in happily married couples.

Distressed spouses have problems in interpreting accurately one another's affect and intentions. In general, they tend to see their partner's intention and affect as more negative than it actually is. They are then more likely to reciprocate the negative affect from their partner, which leads to escalation of negativity and to aversive and destructive incidents. If these incidents are frequent, the partners are likely to develop negative expectations for conflict interaction. These negative expectations are likely to lead to high levels of physiological arousal (and consequent escalation of the conflict), along with a tendency to avoid dealing with conflict whenever possible.

The tendency to avoid is more likely to be characteristic of husbands, and may lead to wives becoming more and more demanding in their attempts to have issues dealt with. Husbands in these relationships are also likely to have learned that avoiding conflict has a power aspect to it as well—they can avoid having to deal with the changes that their partners are wanting and can maintain the *status quo*. These negative processes are likely to be fueled by negative biases that distort perceptions of partner behavior and intentions, by insecurity about the relationship that lead to destructive behaviors, by unrealistic and destructive beliefs about marriage, and by attributional processes that focus on blaming the partner and seeing negative behavior as a consequence of stable and global partner characteristics, rather than related to the context. They are also likely to be fueled by a lack of positive relationship interactions which would serve to provide protection against the influence of inevitable relationship conflict. Over time, partners in this type of relationship are likely to develop conflicting goals for their relationship, to become unsympathetic to one another's feelings and attitudes, to become rigid and inflexible in their interpretations of each other's behaviors and intentions, and to develop negative ways of interacting which make it virtually impossible to deal constructively with issues in their relationship.

In contrast, partners in healthy relationships are likely to be more accurate in their understanding of each other's intentions and affect and feel confident in expressing their feelings and attitudes to one another. They are able to deal with negative affect from the partner without reciprocating it, and are also able to reciprocate positive affect. These couples are more likely than other couples to deal with the issues in their relationships and to have developed constructive ways of dealing with each other's complaints, leading to the resolution of the problem. As a result, they expect to be able to resolve their issues and to do so in a positive and helpful way. Their interactions are characterized by a willingness to listen and to try to understand the partner's position, as well as a willingness to negotiate about possible solutions. These couples are characterized by an aware-ness of their shared relationship history, by shared goals, by constructive belief systems that recognize the need for flexibility in rules and standards, by attribu-tion patterns that recognize the situational factors that may have an impact on partner behavior, and by a willingness to take responsibility for and change their own behavior when necessary.

Thus, research has provided a clear picture of the differences between distressed and non-distressed couples. However, the challenge presented by Bradbury & Fincham's (1987) call to utilize an information-processing frame-work in order to better integrate the various threads of research in the marital area remains largely unmet. Indeed, it seems likely that the next step forward in understanding marital distress will result from greater attention to the rich and varied literature on basic information processing and its application to marriage.

REFERENCES

Ainsworth, M.D.S., Blehar, M.C., Waters, E. & Wall, S. (1978). *Patterns of Attachment: A Psychological Study of the Strange Situation*. Hillsdale, NJ: Erlbaum.

Argyle, M. & Henderson, M. (1985). *The Anatomy of Relationships*. Harmondsworth: Penguin.

Bandura, A. (1977). *Social Learning Theory*. Englewood Cliffs, NJ: Prentice-Hall.

Baucom, D.H. & Epstein, N. (1990). *Cognitive–Behavioural Marital Therapy*. New York: Brunner/Mazel.

Baucom, D.H., Epstein, N., Sayers, S. & Sher, T.G. (1989). The role of cognitions in marital relationships: definitional, methodological, and conceptual issues. *Journal of Consulting and Clinical Psychology*, **57**, 31–38.

Baucom, D. & Sayers, S.L. (1987). Attributional style and attributional patterns among married couples. Paper presented at the 21st Annual Convention of the Association for the Advancement of Behavior Therapy, Boston, MA, November.

Beach, S.R.H. & Fincham, F.D. (1994). Towards an integrated model of negative affectivity in marriage. In S.M. Johnson & L.S. Greenberg (eds), *The Heart of the Matter: Perspectives on Emotion in Marital Therapy* (pp. 227–255). New York: Brunner/Mazel.

Beach, S.R.H. & O'Leary, K.D. (1993). Dysphoria and marital discord: are dysphoric individuals at risk for marital maladjustment? *Journal of Marital and Family Therapy*, **19**, 355–368.

Beach, S.R.H., Mendolia, M. & Tesser, A. (1992). Self-protective processes at work in marital satisfaction and marital interaction. Paper presented at the 26th Annual Convention of the Association for the Advancement of Behavior Therapy, Boston, MA, November.

Beach, S.R.H. & Tesser, A. (1993). Decision-making power and marital satisfaction: a self-evaluation maintenance perspective. *Journal of Social and Clinical Psychology*, **12**, 471–494.

Bowlby, J. (1973). *Attachment and Loss: Vol. 2, Separation: Anxiety and Anger.* New York: Basic Books.

Bradbury, T.N. & Fincham, F.D. (1987). Affect and cognition in close relationships: toward an integrative model. *Cognition and Emotion*, **1**, 59–87.

Bradbury, T.N. & Fincham, F.D. (1990). Attributions in marriage: review and critique. *Psychological Bulletin*, **107**, 3–33.

Bradbury, T.N. & Fincham, F.D. (1991). A contextual model for advancing the study of marriage. In G.J.O. Fletcher & F.D. Fincham (eds), *Cognition in Close Relationships* (pp. 127–147). Hillsdale, NJ: Erlbaum.

Bradbury, T.N. & Fincham, F.D. (1992). Attributions and behavior in marital interaction. *Journal of Personality and Social Psychology*, **63**, 613–628.

Brickman, P. & Bulman, R.J. (1977). Pleasure and pain in social comparison. In J.M. Suls & R.L. Miller (eds), *Social Comparison Process: Theoretical and Empirical Perspectives* (pp. 149–189). Washington DC: Academic Press.

Broderick, J.E. & O'Leary, K.D. (1986). Contributions of affect, attitude and behavior to marital satisfaction. *Journal of Consulting and Clinical Psychology*, **54**, 514–517.

Buehlman, K.T., Gottman, J.M. & Katz, L. (1992). How a couple views their past predicts their future: predicting divorce from an oral history interview. *Journal of Family Psychology*, **5**, 295–318.

Byrne, C.A. & Arias, I. (in press). Marital satisfaction and marital violence: moderating effects of attributional processes. *Journal of Family Psychology*.

Christensen, A. (1988). Dysfunctional interaction patterns in couples. In P. Noller & M.A. Fitzpatrick (eds), *Perspectives on Marital Interaction* (pp. 31–52). Clevedon & Philadelphia: Multilingal Matters.

Christensen, A. & Heavey, C.L. (1990). Gender and social structure in the demand/withdraw pattern of marital conflict. *Journal of Personality and Social Psychology*, **59**, 73–81.

Christensen, A. & Shenk, J.L. (1991). Communication, conflict and psychological distance in non-distressed, clinic and divorcing couples. *Journal of Consulting and Clinical Psychology*, **59**, 458–463.

Christensen, A., Sullaway, M. & King, C.E. (1983). Systematic error in behavioral reports of dyadic interaction: egocentric bias and content effects. *Behavioral Assessment*, **5**, 129–140.

Cialdini, R.B., Borden, R.J., Thorne, A., Walker, M.R., Freeman, S. & Sloan, L.R. (1976). Basking in reflected glory: three (football) field studies. *Journal of Personality and Social Psychology*, **34**, 366–375.

Clark, L.A. & Watson, D. (1991). General affective dispositions in physical and psychological health. In C.R. Snyder & D.R. Forsyth (eds), *Handbook of Social and Clinical Psychology* (pp. 221–245). New York: Pergamon.

Collins, N.S. & Read, S.J. (1994). Cognitive representations of attachment: the structure and function of working models. *Advances in Personal Relationships*, **5**, 53–90.

Eidelson, R.J. & Epstein, N. (1982). Cognition and relationship maladjustment: development of a measure of dysfunctional relationship beliefs. *Journal of Consulting and Clinical Psychology*, **50**, 715–720.

Epstein, N. & Eidelson, R.J. (1981). Unrealistic beliefs of clinical couples: their relationship to expectations, goals and satisfaction. *American Journal of Family Therapy*, **9**, 13–22.

Feeney, J.A., Noller, P. & Callan, V.J. (1994). Attachment style, communication and satisfaction in the early years of marriage. *Advances in Personal Relationships*, **5**, 269–308.

Fincham, F.D. & Bradbury, T.N. (1987). The impact of attributions in marriage: a longitudinal analysis. *Journal of Personality and Social Psychology*, **53**, 510–517.

Fincham, F.D. & Bradbury, T.N. (1988). The impact of attributions in marriage: empirical and conceptual foundations. *British Journal of Clinical Psychology*, **27**, 77–90.

Fincham, F.D. & Bradbury, T.N. (1989). The impact of attributions in marriage: an experimental analysis. *Journal of Social and Personal Relationships*, **6**, 69–86.

Fincham, F.D. & Bradbury, T.N. (1992). Assessing attributions in marriage: the relationship attribution measure. *Journal of Personality and Social Psychology*, **62**, 457–468.

Fincham, F.D., Bradbury, T.N. & Scott, C.K. (1990). Cognition in marriage. In F.D. Fincham & T.N. Bradbury (eds), *The Psychology of Marriage: Basic Issues and Applications* (pp. 118–149). New York: Guilford.

Fitzpatrick, M.A. (1988). *Between Husbands and Wives*. Newbury Park: Sage.

Gaelick, L., Bodenhausen, G. & Wyer, R.S. (1985). Emotional communication in close relationships. *Journal of Personality and Social Psychology*, **49**, 1246–1265.

Gottman, J.M. & Levenson, R.W. (1985). A valid procedure for obtaining self report of affect in marital interaction. *Journal of Consulting and Clinical Psychology*, **53**, 151–160.

Gottman, J.M. & Levenson, R.W. (1988). The social psychophysiology of marriage. In P. Noller & M.A. Fitzpatrick (eds), *Perspectives on Marital Interaction* (pp. 182–200). Clevedon & Philadelphia: Multilingual Matters.

Gottman, J.M., Markman, H. & Notarius, C.I. (1977). The topography of marital conflict: a sequential analysis of verbal and non-verbal behavior. *Journal of Marriage and the Family*, **39**, 461–477.

Gottman, J.M. & Porterfield, A.L. (1981). Communicative competence in the non-verbal behavior of married couples. *Journal of Marriage and the Family*, **43**, 817–824.

Guthrie, D.M. & Noller, P. (1988). Spouses' perceptions of one another in emotional situations. In P. Noller & M.A. Fitzpatrick (eds), *Perspectives on Marital Interaction* (pp. 153–181). Clevedon & Philadelphia: Multilingual Matters.

Halford, W.K. & Sanders, M. (1990). The relationship of cognition and behavior during marital interaction. *Journal of Social and Clinical Psychology*, **9**, 489–510.

Halford, W.K., Sanders, M.R. & Behrens, B.C. (1994). Self-regulation in behavioral couples therapy. *Behavior Therapy*, **25**, 431–452.

Hazan, C. & Shaver, P.R. (1987). Romantic love conceptualized as an attachment process. *Journal of Personality and Social Psychology*, **52**, 511–524.

Holtzworth-Munroe, A. & Hutchinson, G. (1993). Attributing negative intent to wife behavior: the attributions of maritally violent versus non-violent men. *Journal of Abnormal Psychology*, **102**, 206–211.

Holtzworth-Munroe, A. & Jacobson, N.S. (1985). Causal attributions of married couples: when do they search for causes? What do they conclude when they do? *Journal of Personality and Social Psychology*, **48**, 1398–1412.

Jacobson, N.S. (1992). Behavioural couple therapy: a new beginning. *Behaviour Therapy*, **23**, 493–506.

Jacobson, N.S., Follette, W.C. & McDonald, D.W. (1982). Reactivity to positive and negative behavior in distressed and non-distressed couples. *Journal of Consulting and Clinical Psychology*, **49**, 269–277.

Jacobson, N. & Margolin, G. (1979). *Marital Therapy: Strategies Based on Social Learning Principles*. New York: Brunner-Mazel.

Jones, E. & Gallois, C. (1989). Spouses' impressions of rules for communication in public and private marital conflicts. *Journal of Marriage and the Family*, **51**, 957–967.

Julien, D. (1992). Expanding marital adjustment theories: what if marriage was fun? Paper presented at the Fourth World Congress on Behavior Therapy, Gold Coast, Australia, July.

Julien, D. & Markman, H.J. (1991). Social support networks as determinants of individual and marital outcomes. *Journal of Social and Personal Relationships*, **8**, 549–568.

Kelley, H.H. (1983). Love and commitment. In H.H. Kelley, E. Berscheid, A. Christensen, J.H. Harvey, T.L. Huston, G. Levinger, E. McClintock, L.A. Peplau & D. Peterson (1983). *Close Relationships* (pp. 265–314). New York: Freeman.

Kirchler, E. (1988). Marital happiness and interaction in everyday surroundings: a time-sample diary approach for couples. *Journal of Social and Personal Relationships*, **5**, 375–382.

Kirchler, E. (1989). Everyday life experiences at home: an interaction diary approach to assess marital relationships. *Journal of Family Psychology*, **2**, 311–336.

Larsen, R.J. & Ketelaar, T. (1991). Personality and susceptibility to positive and negative emotional states. *Journal of Personality and Social Psychology*, **61**, 132–140.

Lazarus, R. & Smith, C. (1988). Knowledge and appraisal in the cognition–emotion relationship. *Cognition and Emotion*, **2**, 281–300.

Levenson, R.W. & Gottman, J.M. (1985). Physiological and affective predictors of change in relationship satisfaction. *Journal of Personality and Social Psychology*, **49**, 85–94.

Markman, H.J., Duncan, S.W., Storaasli, R.D. & Howes, P.W. (1987). The prediction of marital distress: a longitudinal investigation. In K. Hahlweg & M. Goldstein (eds), *Understanding Major Mental Disorder: the Contribution of Family Interaction Research* (pp. 266–289). New York: Family Process Press.

Markman, H.J., Stanley, S. & Blumberg, S. (1994). *Fighting for Your Marriage: Positive Steps for Preventing Divorce and Preserving a Lasting Love*. San Francisco: Jossey-Bass.

Miller, L.C. & Read, S.J. (1991). On the coherence of mental models of persons and relationships: a knowledge structure approach. In G.J.O. Fletcher & F.D. Fincham (eds), *Cognition in Close Relationships* (pp. 69–99). Hillsdale, NJ: Erlbaum.

Neisser, U. (1967). *Cognitive Psychology*. New York: Appleton.

Noller, P. (1984). *Non-verbal Communication and Marital Interaction*. Oxford: Pergamon.

Noller, P. (1993). Gender and emotional communication in marriage: different cultures or differential social power? *Journal of Language and Social Psychology*, **12**, 92–112.

Noller, P., Dixon, K. & Limerick, T. (1989). Beliefs about marriage. In J.P. Forgas & J.M. Innes (eds), *Recent Advances in Social Psychology: an International Perspective* (pp. 53–62). Amsterdam Elsevier North Holland.

Noller, P. & Ruzzene, M. (1991). The effects of cognition and affect on marital communication. In Fletcher, G. & Fincham, F.D. (eds), *Cognition in Close Relationships* (pp. 203–233). New York: Erlbaum.

Noller, P. & Venardos, C. (1986). Communication awareness in married couples. *Journal of Social and Personal Relationships*, **3**, 31–42.

Notarius, C.I. & Markman, H. (1993). *We Can Work It Out*. New York: Putnam.

O'Leary, K.D. & Smith, D.A. (1991). Martital interactions. *Annual Review of Psychology*, **42**, 191–212.

Osgarby, S.M. & Halford, W.K. (1996a). Positive intimacy skills: what's love got to do with it? Manuscript in preparation, Psychiatry Department, The University of Queensland.

Osgarby, S.M. & Halford, W.K. (1996b). Being positive does matter: behaviour, cognition, affect and physiology of couples during problem-solving and positive reminiscence discussions. Manuscript in preparation, Psychiatry Department, The University of Queensland.

Osgarby, S.M. & Halford, W.K. (1995c). Do you remember? Couple's access and recall of information about their partners and their relationship interactions. Manuscript in preparation, Psychiatry Department, The University of Queensland.

Read, S.J. & Miller, L.C. (1989). Interpersonalism: toward a goal-based theory of persons in relationships. In L. Pervin (ed.), *Goal Concepts in Personality and Social Psychology* (pp. 413–472). Hillsdale, NJ: Erlbaum.

Rusbult, C. (1987). Responses to dissatisfaction in close relationships: the Exit-Voice-Loyalty-Neglect Model. In D. Perlman & S. Duck (eds), *Intimate Relationships: Development, Dynamics and Deterioration* (pp. 209–237). Newbury Park: Sage.

Russell, J.A. (1980). A circumplex model of affect. *Journal of Personality and Social Psychology*, **39**, 1161–1178.

Schaefer, E.S. & Burnett, C.K. (1987). Stability and predictability of quality of women's marital relationships and demoralization. *Journal of Personality and Social Psychology*, **53**, 1129–1136.

Schuerger, J.M., Zarrella, K.L. & Hotz, A.S. (1989). Factors that influence the temporal stability of personality by questionnaire. *Journal of Personality and Social Psychology*, **56**, 777–783.

Sillars, A.L. (1985). Interpersonal perception in relationships. In W. Ickes (ed.), *Compatible and Incompatible Relationships* (pp. 277–305). New York: Springer-Verlag.

Simpson, J. (1990). Influence of attachment styles on romantic relationships. *Journal of Personality and Social Psychology*, **59**, 971–980.

Smith, C.A., Haynes, K.N., Lazarus, R.S. & Pope, L.K. (1993). In search of the "hot" cognitions: attributions, appraisals and their relation to emotion. *Journal of Personality and Social Psychology*, **65**, 916–929.

Stuart, R. (1980). *Helping Couples Change*. New York: Guilford.

Suls, J. & Wills, T.A. (1991). *Social Comparison: Contemporary Theory and Research*. Hillsdale, NJ: Erlbaum.

Tesser, A. (1988). Toward a self-evaluation maintenance model of social behavior. In L. Berkowitz (ed.), *Advances in Experimental Social Psychology*, **21**, 181–227.

Tesser, A., Millar, M. & Moore, J. (1988). Some affective consequences of social comparison and reflection processes: the pain and pleasure of being close. *Journal of Personality and Social Psychology*, **54**, 49–61.

Watson, D. & Tellegen, A. (1985). Toward the structure of affect. *Psychological Bulletin*, **98**, 219–235.

Weiner, B. (1985). "Spontaneous" causal thinking. *Psychological Bulletin*, **97**, 74–84.

Weiss, R.L. (1980). Strategic behavioral marital therapy: toward a model for assessment and intervention. In J.P. Vincent (ed.), *Advances in Family Intervention*, Vol. 1 (pp. 229–271). Greenwich, CT: JAI Press.

Weiss, R.L. (1984a). Cognitive and behavioral measures of marital interaction. In K. Hahlweg & N.S. Jacobson (eds), *Marital Interaction: Analysis and Modification* (pp. 232–252). New York: Guilford.

Weiss, R.L. (1984b). Cognitive and strategic interventions in behavioral marital therapy. In K. Hahlweg & N.S. Jacobson (eds), *Marital Interaction: Analysis and Modification* (pp. 337–355). New York: Guilford.

Weiss, R.L. & Heyman, R.E. (1990). Observation of marital interaction. In F.D. Fincham & T.N. Bradbury (eds), *The Psychology of Marriage* (pp. 87–117). New York: Guilford.

Wood, J.V. & Taylor, K.L. (1991). Serving self-relevant goals through social comparison. In J. Suls & T.A. Wills (eds), *Social Comparison: Contemporary Theory and Research* (pp. 23–49) Hillsdale, NJ: Erlbaum.

Chapter 4

Sex and Relationships

Susan H. Spence
Department of Psychology, University of Queensland,
St Lucia, Queensland, Australia

THE RELATIONSHIP BETWEEN SEXUAL AND GENERAL RELATIONSHIP SATISFACTION

It comes as no surprise to find that there is a strong relationship between sexual and marital satisfaction (e.g. Clark & Wallin, 1965; Frank, Anderson & Rubinstein, 1979; Schenk, Pfrang & Raushe, 1983). Couples who report high overall satisfaction with their relationship typically report more frequent and more satisfying sexual relationships. Similarly, a very high proportion of couples seeking help for marital problems report dissatisfaction with their sex lives. For example, Hahlweg, Schindler & Revenstorf (1982) reported that around 50% of their marital therapy couples also reported sexual problems. Similarly, around 75% of couples seeking help for sexual difficulties also experience marital problems (Sager, 1974). Furthermore, marital distress is a significant predictor of outcome in the treatment of sexual problems (Zimmer, 1987).

Given the strong relationship between sexual and marital satisfaction, it is surprising that historically the two areas have developed relatively independently. Traditionally, therapists specialized in either marital or sexual therapies, rather than taking an integrative approach. It is only recently that couple therapists have stressed the importance of focusing on both the general and sexual aspects of relationships. This means that relationship therapists need to have a thorough understanding of the determinants of marital and sexual satisfaction and difficulties. This shift towards the integration of sexual and marital therapies is reflected in the current literature (e.g. Atwood & Dershowitz, 1992; Mobarak, Tamerin & Tamerin, 1986; Schnarch, 1991; Spence, 1991; Weeks & Hof, 1987).

Clinical Handbook of Marriage and Couples Interventions. Edited by W. Kim Halford and Howard J. Markman.
© 1997 John Wiley & Sons Ltd.

In many respects, sexual functioning and general marital satisfaction are determined by the same factors. Both are strongly influenced by the communication and intimacy skills of the couple, in addition to feelings about and attitudes towards the partner (McCabe, 1994; Noller & White, 1990). Furthermore, the sexual and general marital aspects of the couple's relationship are likely to influence each other. It is suggested here that a satisfactory sexual relationship is likely to enhance the general quality of the couple's relationship. Similarly, positive feelings about the relationship generally are likely to facilitate successful sexual relations.

There are numerous factors that influence the quantity and quality of sexual interactions between partners. The focus of this chapter is not on sexual dysfunctions in the clinical sense, but rather on the degree to which the couple find their sexual relationship satisfactory and enjoyable. For some couples, one or other of the partners may experience considerable dissatisfaction with their sexual relationship and yet neither individual could be classified as meeting the criteria for a psychosexual disorder. For example, sexual dissatisfaction may reflect marked differences between the partners in their desired frequency or preferred type of sexual activity. Others may report boredom associated with a long term-relationship, or may report occasional sexual difficulties that are not sufficiently persistent to meet any clinical diagnosis and yet present a considerable source of distress for the couple. The following section provides a brief outline of some of the most common difficulties that emerge in sexual relationships.

TYPES OF SEXUAL DIFFICULTIES

Sexual responding can be viewed as a series of integrated components involving sexual desire, arousal and orgasm. These components can then, in turn, be considered from physiological and psychological perspectives. Thus, sexual behaviour includes not just biological changes, but also the subjective feelings that relate to desire, arousal and orgasm. Superimposed upon these subjective experiences is the overall perception of satisfaction with the sexual relationship.

Sexual problems can manifest themselves in many different ways. For some couples, each biological stage of desire, arousal and orgasm may be unimpaired and yet sexual activities rarely take place, or leave one or both partners without a feeling of satisfaction with the sexual relationship. For other couples, sexual difficulties occur with one or both partners in relation to sexual desire, arousal and/or orgasm. Although sexual difficulties may be specific to either desire, arousal or orgasm, in practice these stages are so intricately interwoven that sexual difficulties tend to impact upon all three aspects of sexual responding. To complicate matters further, sexual difficulties are often experienced in both members of a partnership. For example, problems of excessively rapid ejaculation in the male partner may lead gradually to a decrease in arousal and desire in the female.

The following summary of psychosexual problems follows the structure of the

American Psychiatric Association's (1994) *Diagnostic and Statistical Manual of Mental Disorders* (DSM IV). Although this provides a useful framework, I reiterate that for many couples sexual difficulties are not sufficiently frequent or severe to meet diagnostic criteria. Thus, what follows refers to sexual difficulties or problems rather than clinically diagnosed disorders. During assessment, it is important to consider the degree to which the problem is of psychological origin or a general medical condition, lifelong or acquired, and generalized or situational. Acquired problems are distinguished from lifelong dysfunction in that the individual has experienced a period of time in which the problem was not present. The terms "generalized" or "situational" refer to the degree to which the difficulty occurs across all situations and with all sexual partners.

Problems Relating to Sexual Desire

Hypoactive Sexual Desire

The presenting pattern of low sexual desire varies considerably, but typically involves complaints of lack of interest in sex, lack of sexual fantasy, low frequency of sexual activity or a tolerance of sex to keep the partner happy. Low levels of sexual desire are relatively common, with around 16% of men and 25% of women reporting that disinterest in sex constitutes a problem for them (Nathan, 1986).

Sexual Aversion

Whereas lack of sexual desire is typified by disinterest in sex, sexual aversion problems involve strong feelings of fear and/or disgust, and avoidance of sexual activity with a partner. In practice, the problem may be specific to certain sexual activities. For example, some clients complain of an intense feeling of revulsion concerning semen and avoid any activities in which semen is involved. For others, the problem may be generalized to all forms of sexual contact.

Problems Relating to Sexual Arousal

Female Sexual Arousal Problems

For women, problems of sexual arousal reflect difficulty in attaining or maintaining sexual arousal responses, such as lubrication and vaginal swelling. These physiological symptoms are typically accompanied by lack of subjective feelings of sexual arousal and absence of pleasure during sexual activity. Occasionally, women may present with problems in either the physiological or subjective feelings aspects of sexual arousal, but in practice these components are usually related. It is difficult to determine the exact prevalence of sexual arousal problems in women, given the strong overlap between sexual desire and arousal components of responding. Given the high prevalence of lack of sexual desire, it is also likely that sexual arousal problems are relatively common.

Male Erectile Difficulties

This problem involves difficulty in attaining or maintaining an erection or a lack of subjective sense of excitement and pleasure during sexual activity. Estimates of the prevalence of such problems suggest that between 6 and 20% of adult males report recurrent erectile difficulties (Nathan, 1986; Spector & Carey, 1990). The prevalence is much higher if occasional erectile difficulty is examined, suggesting that it is extremely common for men to have erectile difficulty at some point in their lives.

Problems Relating to Orgasm

Female Orgasmic Difficulties

Orgasm difficulties are very common amongst women in the general population. Around 70–80% of women have problems experiencing orgasm from vaginal stimulation alone; however, it is much less common (around 5–15%) for a woman never to have experienced orgasm in any situation (Kaplan, 1983; Nathan, 1986). For some women, difficulty in experiencing orgasm is part of an overall picture, including inadequate sexual arousal. Difficulties in experiencing orgasm may present in different forms, with the most common type being difficulty in experiencing orgasm during intercourse. Other cases may present with difficulty in experiencing orgasm during some situations but not in others. For example, the woman may not experience orgasm during partner stimulation and yet experience orgasm relatively easily from self-stimulation. A further group of referrals include those women who have never or very rarely experienced orgasm from any form of stimulation.

Male Orgasmic Delay

Difficulty in experiencing orgasm is relatively less common in males than females, with delayed ejaculation occurring in around 3–4% of men below the age of 65 years (Nathan, 1986). Total absence of orgasm is relatively rare, being found in less than 0.2% of adult males. Such problems occur most frequently during vaginal penetration and are less likely to occur during oral or self-stimulation.

Premature Ejaculation

There is much debate about what constitutes a reasonable time for a male to maintain an erection during sexual stimulation before ejaculation occurs. In deciding whether a problem exists, it is important to take into account factors such as the intensity and novelty of the sexual stimulation. Given the marked variation in definitions of premature ejaculation, surprisingly consistent results have been found for the point prevalence of this problem, with between 18–38% of adult males reporting premature ejaculation (Nathan, 1986; Spector & Carey, 1990).

Sexual Pain Problems

Dyspareunia

Dysareunia involves recurrent or persistent genital pain occurring before, during or after intercourse and can be of psychological or medical aetiology. In practice it is relatively difficult to demonstrate that psychological factors account for dyspareunia. Perhaps rather questionably, psychological causes tend to be assumed if medical examinations do not reveal a biological cause. Fortunately, psychogenic dyspareunia appears to be relatively rare, although there is a lack of clear data from epidemiological studies.

Vaginismus

Vaginismus refers to involuntary spasm of the muscles of the outer region of the vagina, which may generalize to include the muscles of the inner thigh. This response may be so extreme as to make intercourse impossible or extremely difficult. The stimuli that trigger the muscle spasm vary, but may include anticipated or actual attempts at intercourse, vaginal medical examination and tampon insertion. The behavioural manifestations of vaginismus may range from total avoidance of any situation in which vaginal penetration is likely to occur, to tolerance of intercourse with discomfort and fear. From a physiological perspective, symptoms may include lack of lubrication and signs of fear, such as sweating, shaking or hyperventilation. The emotional and cognitive features of vaginismus typically include intense feelings of fear and anxiety and fearful thoughts about the consequences of penetration.

A strong relationship exists between vaginismus and pain. The muscle tightness and lack of lubrication may result in painful intercourse which, in turn, serves to confirm and enhance the vaginismus response. Reliable estimates of the prevalence of vaginismus are lacking, but transient episodes of vaginismus appear to be relatively prevalent, whereas severe and persistent problems are much less frequent.

DETERMINANTS OF SEXUAL RESPONDING AND SEXUAL SATISFACTION

The sexual behaviour of the couple, and the level of satisfaction with the sexual relationship, is determined by a complex interplay between biological and psychosocial influences. It would be remiss not to mention here some of the major factors that determine how we respond sexually. If either or both members of a partnership are dissatisfied with their sexual relationship, then it is important for the therapist to examine likely factors that could be accounting for the difficulties. This requires a basic understanding of biological, as well as psychosocial, determinants. Once biological causes have been excluded or dealt with medically, the therapist is then in a position to focus on the psychosocial influences.

Biological Causes of Sexual Problems

There is a wide range of biological factors that may affect sexual functioning. Although sexual difficulties are often a reflection of general difficulties within the relationship, it is important for couple therapists to have an adequate understanding of the biological determinants of sexual functioning. In some cases, sexual difficulties may result from biological causes and relationship difficulties may be the result of repeated sexual difficulties, rather than *vice versa*. Thus, if you discover that one or other partner is experiencing a clinically significant sexual problem, it is advisable to refer the client for a thorough medical examination. The processes of sexual arousal and orgasm are influenced by a whole host of neurological, hormonal and vascular factors. A detailed description of these is beyond the scope of this chapter, but the reader is referred to texts such as Lincoln (1992), O'Donohue & Geer (1994) or Spence (1991). In addition to a full medical examination, there are some biological influences that can be quickly checked out by the non-medical practitioner. Generally speaking, there are certain characteristics of sexual functioning that are suggestive of biological causes. A biological aetiology is unlikely if a person is sexually functional in some situations but not others. For example, if the problem is restricted to a certain partner or partners, or specific types of sexual activity (e.g. partner- but not self-stimulation), medical causes are unlikely. Similarly, biological aetiology of erectile difficulty is unlikely if a male experiences nocturnal and early morning erections, but has erectile problems during attempted intercourse with his partner. Although patterns such as these suggest that psychogenic rather than biogenic causes are present, the possibility of some biological contributions cannot be discounted. Thus, a strong case is made for a medical check-up before commencement of a psychologically-based treatment of a clinically significant sexual problem. The following section briefly summarizes the main sources of biological influence over sexual responding.

Any illness or injury which influences the neurological processes that regulate the physiological responses of arousal and orgasm at cortical, spinal cord or peripheral levels has the potential to disrupt sexual functioning. Direct physical injury to central neural pathways (e.g. spinal injuries, tumours, multiple sclerosis, cerebrovascular accidents), and diseases or injury to local neural pathways (e.g. neuropathy resulting from diabetes mellitus), may produce disorders of arousal and/or orgasm in males and females. Similary, any illness or surgical procedure which interferes with the vasocongestive response of sexual arousal may inhibit this aspect of sexual responding. In males, deficits in the penile arterial blood supply or excessive drainage of blood may result in inadequate pressure, thereby limiting the degree of erection. Local thrombotic diseases, vascular deterioration (e.g. resulting from diabetes mellitus), some forms of vascular reconstructive surgery and certain types of medication may be implicated here. Similar disorders in women may impair the lubrication–swelling phase.

A range of tumours, congenital defects, infections and physical injuries may disrupt the hormonal/endocrine system with subsequent impact upon sexual behaviour. Hypopituitarism, Cushing's syndrome, testicular tumours, ovarian tumours, castration, hepatic cirrhosis leading to testicular atrophy, and congenital defects are examples of disorders which may affect the endocrine system so as to impair sexual functioning.

Physical injury, inflammation or infection of the genital structures may interfere with sexual functioning, either through direct interference or through the resulting pain. Such problems include structural defects (e.g. clitoral adhesions or poor episiotomies in women, and excessively tight foreskins or marked penile curvature in males) and infections (e.g. urethritis, cystitis, prostatitis and sexually transmitted infections).

Sexual functioning may also be disrupted by a wide range of chemical substances, the exact nature of which will depend on the biological action of the chemical involved. Any drug which effects the neural, endocrine or vascular systems involved in sexual functioning may impair sexual responding. Particular attention must therefore be paid during assessment to any substance used by the client, whether it be prescribed medication, illicit drugs or alcohol. An excellent detailed review of the effects of drugs on sexual functioning is provided by Boller & Frank (1982). The primary drugs that should be examined during assessment include alcohol and other sedatives antihypertensives, antipsychotic agents, monor tranquillizers, antidepressants, oral contraceptives and illicit substances.

Finally, it is important to consider the impact of ageing upon sexual functioning. Although changes in sexual responding take place with age, sexual dysfunction is not part of the normal ageing process. The majority of people are capable of sexual activity, sexual desire, arousal and orgasm throughout their lives, as long as they remain in good physical health. Nevertheless, subtle changes in sexual responding typically occur as a normal part of ageing, which may be misinterpreted as an indication of sexual dysfunction and produce performance anxiety in the older person if not understood. Furthermore, there are numerous myths and maladaptive beliefs about the sex lives of older people which may interfere with sexual responding. For example, there are widespread beliefs within many societies that older people are sexually inactive or sexually incapable and do not desire sexual relationships (Spence, 1992). It is important that therapists and older people are aware of the normal changes which are associated with ageing and the many myths which influence sexual behaviour in the elderly. Menopause warrants a separate consideration in that this process may produce specific difficulties for some women, particularly if lubrication is affected.

Psychosocial Influences upon the Couple's Sexual Relationship

Assuming that medical examination and your own quick screen rule out biogenic causes, then it is important to investigate some of the important psychosocial influences upon sexual satisfaction. It is here that there is considerable overlap between the determinants of sexual and marital satisfaction. Let us look first at those factors that influence both the general and sexual aspects of the relationship, and then examine those variables that are more specific to sexual problems.

Couple Communication and Intimacy Skills

Communication skills play a vital role in determining the quality of both the sexual and general aspects of relationships. Numerous skills have been identified as being important determinants of sexual and marital satisfaction. Roughly speaking, these can be categorized into intimacy and conflict resolution skills. Couples need to be able to express affection, resolve conflicts, solve problems, disclose personal information, share their feelings, express their wants and needs, make requests of their partner, give praise and positive feedback, and give constructive, critical feedback. These skills are just as important for successful sexual interactions as they are in other aspects of the relationship. Much has been written in the literature about intimacy and there are many definitions. Some of the common elements in these definitions include the ability to reveal and share personal feelings, to trust the partner with very personal information, and to express feelings of affection (Talmadge & Talmadge, 1986). Inevitably, intimacy involves taking risks, in making oneself open to violations of trust. A further consequence of intimacy is an increase in the degree of dependency of partners upon each other. Talmadge & Talmadge (1986) pointed out that intimacy is fundamental to both marital and sexual satisfaction. These authors also emphasized the reciprocal influence of one partner's intimacy expression upon the sexual behaviour of the other partner. If one partner is highly intimately and emotionally expressive, this is likely to enhance feelings and expressions of intimacy in their spouse, and also enhance sexual desire. Indeed, Talmadge & Talmadge (1986) suggested that low sexual desire is often a reflection of lack of marital intimacy.

Family Circumstance and Life Events

There is a variety of situational variables that influence couples' sexual relationships. One of the strongest factors here is the presence of young children in the family. Perhaps not surprisingly, young children seem to have a dampening effect upon their parents' frequency of sexual activity and satisfaction with the sexual relationship (Donnelly, 1993). Sexual activity and satisfaction also tends to de-cline with increasing length of the couple's relationship, perhaps as familiarity and loss of novelty with the partner leads to loss of excitement. Pressures relating to work finances, commuting and housework may also negatively influence the sexual relationship (Greenblat, 1983). Negative life events, such as family con-flict, loss of employment, death of a family member, excessive work demands, unwanted pregnancies, abortion, sexual abuse or childbirth may also trigger sexual difficulties.

Psychological Well-being

Problems such as anxiety, depression and fatigue may all have a debilitating effect of the couple's relationship generally and have a particularly strong impact upon sexual functioning (Zimmer, 1987). Zimmer suggested that a reciprocal relationship exists between negative affective states, marital difficulties and sexual problems. In particular, he suggested that negative thoughts about the self, partner and the relationship, which typically occur in psychological distress, are strongly associated with the quality of both the general and sexual aspects of the relationship. Furthermore, as the marital and sexual relationship deteriorates, this may have a further negative impact upon the emotional state of the partner(s). Thus, it is important that symptoms of psychopathology are assessed and dealt with, if marital and sexual therapies are to be effective.

Attitudes, Beliefs and Thoughts

Thoughts, attitudes and beliefs about various aspects of the partner, the relation-ship and sexuality may have a considerable influence over the level of marital and sexual satisfaction. In the sexual domain, people hold beliefs and attitudes relat-ing to the acceptability of particular sexual activities, sex roles and the role of orgasm, spontaneity, passion, physical affection and mutual orgasm in a sexual relationship. A range of irrational or maladaptive attitudes and beliefs concern-ing such topics have been identified in relation to sexual difficulties (Baker & De Silva, 1988, Sanders & Cairns, 1987, Zilbergeld, 1995). Maladaptive attitudes, beliefs and thoughts are not only proposed to play an important role in the development of sexual problems but also in the continuation of sexual difficulties. For example, Masters & Johnson (1970) placed considerable emphasis on thoughts of fear of failure and focusing on one's performance rather than on pleasure ("spectatoring"). A detailed outline of the role of maladaptive attitudes and thoughts in the determination of sexual problems is provided by Spence (1991).

It is therefore important to explore the client's specific thoughts during differ-ent stages of sexual encounters and those beliefs and attitudes which tend to govern his/her behaviour. This may pinpoint maladaptive cognitions and beliefs which are impairing sexual responsiveness and which may become the focus of a cognitive therapy component during intervention.

The influence of gender roles warrants a specific mention here as the research findings are interesting. Some studies have suggested that greater sexual satisfaction is associated with more flexible gender role behaviour (Zimmer, 1987) and higher scores on androgyny (Safir et al., 1982). It is interesting, therefore, to find that higher levels of sexual activity are found amongst couples where the partners adhere to very traditional gender roles and religious fundamentalism (Scanzoni et al., 1989). It is important to note, however, that there is a difference between sexual satisfaction and frequency of sexual activity. It is feasible that strict adherence to traditional gender roles may lead to higher levels of sexual activity that is not particularly satisfying for one or other of the partners.

Family of origin influences have also been highlighted as playing an important role in the development of sexual attitudes and behaviour. Factors such as the level of intimacy expression within the family origin, discussion of sexual matters, gender roles, parental power and discipline strategies are all suggested to impact upon later sexual development (Atwood & Dershowitz, 1992). Indeed, Atwood & Dershowitz (1992) suggested that resolving family-of-origin issues forms a significant part of integrated marital and sexual therapy.

Emotional Reactions

A wide range of emotions such as anger, guilt, disgust, fear or shame may interfere with sexual functioning, and are also likely to influence the relationship in general. In particular, emotions and thoughts with regard to each other during sex should be given particular attention. Clearly, if partners feel angry and frustrated with each other, then this is likely to influence their behaviour towards each other, both generally and sexually. Interestingly, the concepts of romantic love, feelings of passion, physical attraction and trust have received little attention in the empirical research relating to sexual and marital therapy (Roberts, 1992). Roberts pointed out that couples typically marry because of romantic love and sexual attraction, and frequently divorce when these feelings cease to exist. Nevertheless, very little is known about valid ways of measuring, increasing and maintaining romantic love and sexual attraction. Until more empirically-based models, assessment measures and intervention strategies are developed in this area, we need to proceed using therapist intuition. Obviously, the emotional reactions of each partner need to be given careful consideration during assessment and treatment.

Sexual Knowledge and Sexual Skills

Knowledge of sexual anatomy and sexual techniques is important in enabling individuals to provide their partners and themselves with appropriate sexual stimulation (Derogatis & Meyer, 1979). It is insufficient, however, to be knowledgeable about sexual matters and techniques at a cognitive level if this knowledge cannot be put into practice. Each person needs to be able to stimulate his/her partner appropriately, and to achieve positions during sex from which both partners can obtain the greatest amount of arousal and pleasure.

Sexual Preference

Individuals vary in their preference for a particular type of sexual partner or sexual activity. Assessment should therefore explore this area by examining the content of sexual fantasies, targets of sexual desire and arousal and content of any erotic material used. For some individuals, erotic preferences may not be for traditional hetero- or homosexual activities but may be for some type of anomalous stimulus such as voyeuristic, sado-masochistic or transvestite situations (Freund & Blanchard, 1981).

Use of Erotic Material and Fantasy

Exposure to erotic stimuli, such as pictures, literature and videotapes, is highly effective in generating sexual arousal for most individuals and can be used as a therapy component (Gillan, 1977). Similarly, fantasy, in the form of visual imagery or verbal rehearsal, can be used as a technique to increase sexual arousal in clients for whom this is a therapy goal (Heiman. LoPiccolo & LoPiccolo, 1988). The couple's current use of fantasy and erotic materials (and their attitudes towards such stimuli) should be considered during assessment, as it may be feasible to use these components within therapy if sexual arousal levels are low.

THE ASSESSMENT OF SEXUAL FUNCTIONING

If we accept that difficulties in the general and sexual aspects of relationships are closely interrelated, and frequently found to coexist, then it is important that sexual functioning is routinely assessed in couples who present with marital problems. Sexual difficulties may range from dissatisfaction with the quantity and nature of sexual activities, to clinically significant psychosexual disorders. A combination of interview and questionnaire measures can be used to identify psychosexual difficulties, and to specify the nature and determinants of the problem.

Given the obvious importance of sexual functioning within the couple's relationship, it is surprising that many couple therapists are somewhat reluctant to approach this issue with their clients. Perhaps the best way to overcome this reluctance is to ensure that some form of screening for sexual difficulties is included in the assessment of all couples, as a matter of routine, within both self-report questionnaires (see below) and the interview.

Interview Content

There are several techniques that can be used to help couple therapists to overcome their reservations about asking clients about their sexual relationship. The first is to normalize the issue of sexual difficulties. For example, the interviewer can use statements such as, "We find that many of the couples coming in to the clinic also are finding some problems together sexually. . . . are there any things that you would like to improve in your sexual relationship?" Once the issue has been raised, the interviewer may proceed to ask each partner about possible sources of sexual dissatisfaction, concerning desired changes in frequency of sexual activity and whether they find sex enjoyable. After examining the general aspects of the sexual relationship, the interview may progress to more specific questions about sexual desire, arousal or orgasm problems. Clients do not typically become distressed or severely embarrassed about such questions if they are presented in a calm, clear, matter-of-fact, professional manner. Any discomfort can be quickly alleviated by reassurance that this type of questioning is routine and important. A quick illustration about the kinds of therapy problems that can arise if relevant sexual issues are not dealt with generally is helpful to the couple.

In some cases, it may be helpful to interview the couple separately, particularly if it is clear that either individual is highly reticent about disclosing sexual information in front of his/her partner. If time permits, it is preferable to conduct a brief screen for sexual difficulties, first with both partners present, followed by an individual interview with each person to obtain more specific information abut sexual functioning.

In some instances, couples report that they do not engage in sexual activity, or do so only rarely. Not all couples view this as a problem, and some report being satisfied with a sex-free relationship. Donnelly (1993), in a large-scale study, found that 16% of couples reported being sexually inactive in the month prior to the survey. Thus, sexually inactive marriages are relatively common. Although Donnelly (1993) also found an association between marital discord and sexual inactivity, it is unlikely that all sexually inactive couples had marital problems. Therefore, we need to bear in mind that sexual inactivity in itself may not be a problem unless it is viewed as such by one or other of the partners. In some instances, however, the couple may not view sexual inactivity as a problem and yet the results of the assessment suggest that lack of sexual interactions may be contributing to conflict in other areas of the relationship. Where this is the case, the therapist may wish to discuss this possibility with the couple to determine whether they would like to try an experiment. This would involve increasing sexual activity over a set period to determine whether it had a positive impact on the relationship more generally. Some systemic family therapists might question this suggestion in that avoidance of sexual activity has been proposed to play a functional role for some couples (Atwood & Dershowitz, 1992). If sexual inactivity is protecting the couple from other problems in their relationship, then instigation of sexual activity may bring out previously masked difficulties. For example, recommencing a sexual relationship may serve to highlight deficits in intimacy, communication and problem-solving skills, that previously had been dealt with by avoiding situations in which these skills are important.

If either partner reports dissatisfaction with the sexual relationship, the nature of the problem needs to be clarified. The assessor needs to identify exactly what each partner does overtly, how he or she responds physiologically, and what thoughts and emotions are experienced at different stages of sexual activity. In some instances sexual dissatisfaction is a reflection of unrealistic expectations on the part of the client(s) which would be best dealt with by giving them appropriate information and reassurance. In others, problems may be identified at one or more of the main stages of sexual activity, namely desire, arousal or orgasm.

If sexual difficulties are identified, the interview should proceed to examine the biological and psychosocial factors outlined above. A detailed guide to cognitive–behavioural interviewing for psychosexual difficulties is provided by Spence (1991) and Wilson, Spence & Kavanagh (1989). Referral for medical examination is suggested if problems of arousal or orgasm are identified.

Self-report Assessment Measures

A variety of self-report measures are available to assist in the assessment of sexual difficulties. These range from quick, screening instruments, to those that examine specific areas, and finally to complex questionnaire batteries that cover many aspects of sexual functioning. Several measures are available for investigating the possible presence of sexual difficulties amongst couples who initially present with general relationship problems. These include the sexual dissatisfaction scale of the Marital Satisfaction Inventory (Snyder, 1981) and the Golombok–Rust Inventory of Sexual Satisfaction (GRISS; Rust & Golombok, 1986). The GRISS is a short, 28-item self-report instrument, with separate versions for males and females. Scales concerning dissatisfaction, avoidance, non-sensuality, infrequency, vaginismus, anorgasmia, impotence and premature ejaculation are produced and the validity of these scales has been confirmed through factor analysis.

In terms of the assessment of satisfaction with the sexual relationship, the most well known measure is probably the Sexual Interaction Inventory (SII; LoPiccolo & Steger, 1974). The SII has been reported to have acceptable reliability and to discriminate between sexually dysfunctional and non-dysfunctional couples (LoPiccolo & Steger, 1974). Another method useful in screening couples to identify problems of sexual adjustment is the Self-evaluation of Sexual Behaviour and Gratification questionnaire (SSBG; Lift, 1981), which assesses sexual activities, duration of sex play, frequency of sexual intercourse and satisfaction with frequency.

Other measures focus on more specific aspects of the sexual relationship, such as the frequency or type of sexual activity. For example, the Bentler Scale (Bentler, 1967; 1968) assess the frequency of occurrence of 21 heterosexual behaviours. Separate versions are available for males and females. These scales do not assess whether the activities were satisfactory for those involved, or whether any sexual problems occurred. The Experience scale of the Derogatis Sexual Functioning Inventory (Derogatis, 1975), outlined below, and the Heterosexual Behaviour Inventory (Robinson & Annon, 1975) are alternative methods for assessing the nature of sexual activities.

In some cases, it will be useful to obtain information about the affective and cognitive components of sexual functioning. The Sexual Arousal Inventory (SAI; Hoon, Hoon & Wincze, 1976) is frequently used to assess arousal in women. This involves a list of 28 sexual activities for which clients must rate the degree to which arousal is affected adversely or positively. Its psychometric properties are reported to be good (Anderson et al., 1989). Factor analysis revealed five factors assessing erotica and masturbation, body caressing, seductive activities, oral–genital and genital stimulation and intercourse situations, thus supporting the construct validity of the questionnaire. A similar scale is available for men (Annon, 1975).

Sexual anxiety has been assessed in several research studies. For example, Spence (1985) reported the use of a modified version of the Bentler Scale (Bentler, 1967; 1968) to assess sexual anxiety amongst women with orgasmic difficulties. Patterson & O'Gorman (1986) developed an instrument for assessing anxiety in sexual situations.

A useful measure of sexual knowledge and attitudes is the Sexual Knowledge and Attitude Test (SKAT; Lief & Reed, 1972), which assesses participation in a wide range of sexual activities and also explores the client's attitudes and knowledge in relation to various aspects of sex. This measure has been widely researched and standardized, albeit with a student population. The SKAT provides measures of attitudes to heterosexual relations, sexual myths, abortion and masturbation. The Attitude scale of the Derogatis Sexual Functioning Inventory (Derogatis, 1975) assesses liberal vs. conservative beliefs concerning sexual behaviour. In addition, considerable information concerning attitudes towards various aspects of sex may be revealed during the interview. A detailed description of the assessment of sexual attitudes, beliefs and cognitions can be found in Spence (1991).

The measures outlined above tend to focus on specific aspects of sexual functioning, and may be used selectively where appropriate. Some therapists may prefer to use more extensive assessment batteries which, although time-consuming to administer, cover many different aspects of sexual behaviour. One of the most extensive instruments for the assessment of sexual issues is the Derogatis Sexual Functioning Inventory (Derogatis, 1975). This inventory assesses current sexual functioning in 10 primary content areas, namely sexual information, sexual experience, desire/drive, sexual attitudes, affect/emotions, symptoms of psychopathology, gender-role definition, fantasy, body image and sexual satisfaction.

Finally, valuable information may be obtained by having clients complete various self-monitoring tasks. There are many aspects of sexual responding that couples can be asked to observe and record, such as frequency of certain activities, antecedents and consequences of target behaviours, and emotions or specific thoughts before, during and after specified events.

INTEGRATING PSYCHOSEXUAL THERAPY AS A COMPONENT OF COUPLE THERAPY

Two main points emerge from this chapter so far. First, it is likely that sexual difficulties will exist for many couples presenting with general relationship problems. Second, given the strong mutual influence of sexual and marital satisfaction, there is a strong case for enhancing the quality of the sexual relationship in maritally distressed couples, even when no specific sexual difficulties exist. As Dumka (1992) pointed out, positive sexual experiences provide a valuable forum for the occurrence of enjoyable, shared experiences that serve a bonding or attachment function. Thus, the benefits gained through enhancement of sexual satisfaction are likely to carry over to produce a positive impact upon general relationship satisfaction. Thus, the assessment process should routinely screen for sexual difficulties and enhancement of sexual satisfaction should be integrated as a component of couple therapy.

It is beyond the scope of the present chapter to provide a detailed description of sex therapy techniques. Readers are referred to more comprehensive texts, such as Masters & Johnson (1970); Hawton (1985); Kaplan (1974, 1983, 1987); Spence (1991); Wincze & Carey (1991). Indeed, I suggest that all couple therapists should have a thorough grasp of the literature relating to aetiology, assessment and treatment of psychosexual problems. There seems to be little point in conducting a detailed couple therapy program if sexual difficulties are not dealt with.

Fortunately, many of the techniques of sex therapy have much in common with couple therapy. Both approaches place a major emphasis on enhancement of communication and intimacy skills, increasing enjoyable, shared experiences, and increasing positive affect towards the partner. Thus, it is relatively easy to produce an integrated sex/marital therapy approach.

Sexual Enhancement Techniques

For many couples, sexual activity has ceased to be an enjoyable or satisfying experience. Sex may occur infrequently; one or other partner may have little desire to have sex and may find it hard to become aroused. Such problems are extremely common, even amongst non-distressed couples. This has led to the development of many sexual enhancement programs (e.g. Barbach, 1982; LoPiccolo & Miller, 1975; Mayer, 1990). Before we examine methods of sexual enhancement, it is worth spending some time to examine why many couples shift from high-frequency, enjoyable sexual activities to a point at which they have little interest or enjoyment sexually.

In the early stages of the relationship, sexual activity with a new partner is a novel experience, usually accompanied by strong feelings of romantic love.

Sexual desire is strong, there is usually plenty of opportunity for private time alone and thus sexual activity occurs frequently. Many authors have written about the strong correlation between sexual desire and romantic love. There are poems, songs, books, and films, in addition to more academic treatises on the subject. As time progresses, several processes typically occur. Repeated exposure to sexual activities with the same partner results in loss of novelty and development of stereotyped sexual habits, with the resulting reduction in high levels of desire. For most couples, this period is accompanied by a shift in life circumstances. It is a time of high levels of input into career development, increasing financial commitments, pregnancies and childbirths. Sanders & Cairn (1987) summarize this process succinctly; they state, "Their quality time together generally suffers first. Sexual intimacy is assigned a low priority. Sex may have to be regulated to times when the couple is likely to be fatigued, irritable and least able to enjoy intimacy" (p. 90).

As couples begin to reduce their sexual activity and find it less enjoyable, they lose a major source of reinforcement for the positive feelings between each other. Ultimately, a vicious cycle may develop whereby loss of sexual intimacy results in loss of positive feelings, which further reduces the desire for sexual activities and so on. For some partners, sexual activity in the absence of desire and arousal becomes an aversive experience, to be avoided. Some authors have suggested that the sexual forum may become an arena in which many of the couples' general relationship problems are acted out (Atwood & Dershowitz, 1992; Atwood & Weinstein, 1989). Withdrawal from sex may become tangled up amongst issues of power and control, lack of trust, problems in intimacy expression, expressions of anger, punishment and so on. Thus it is obvious that, in therapy, both sexual and general relationship issues must be dealt with.

Sexual enhancement techniques have been developed from various theoretical backgrounds. Attachment theorists have emphasized the need for continuing, positive sexual experiences as a means of enhancing and maintaining couple attachment (Roberts, 1992). In contrast, a learning theory position would suggest that the pairing of positive experiences with the presence of the partner results in the partner acquiring secondary reinforcement properties. From a different perspective, communication theorists have focused on sexual experiences as a forum in which to develop communication skills (Tullman et al., 1981).

Interestingly, there is much overlap between the sexual enhancement methods arising from these different theoretical backgrounds. There is much to be learned from reading works based on systemic-family, experiential, attachment, cognitive and behavioural approaches. Some valuable therapeutic skills can be acquired from the different clinical orientations. The common elements of the various approaches to sexual enhancement can be summarized as aiming get the couple to achieve the following:

- Increase their knowledge about sexual responding and techniques.
- Increase positive non-sexual experiences.
- Identify positive sexual experiences from their past.

- Recall original feelings of sexual desire and arousal.
- Reinstigate private, undisturbed time for sexual activities.
- Focus on their partner's positive, rather than negative, features.
- Enhance positive affect relating to their partner, the self and sexual activities.
- Increase communication skills, generally and in relation to sexual interactions.
- Increase intimacy expression.
- Develop feelings of trust and commitment.
- Relax during sexual experiences.
- Provide periods of non-demanding pleasuring of each other, sexually and non-sexually.
- Learn about the partner's desires, fantasies, pleasures (sexual and non-sexual).
- Increase sexual skills in relation to giving and receiving pleasure.
- Increase sexual arousal through exposure to sexual stimuli (e.g. erotica and fantasy).
- Challenge and restructure maladaptive beliefs and thoughts regarding sex roles, the self, the partner, the relationship and sexual performance.
- Develop a collaborative set in which any problems are viewed as relating to the couple, rather than either individual.

There are an enormous number of sexual enhancement methods. The following methods reflect those used by the author in clinical practice and can be adapted to fit the educational, cultural and personal characteristics of different couples. The therapist plays an important part in determining when couples are ready for each exercise. There is a marked lack of empirical evidence to support or disqualify the use of specific methods in the enhancement of sexual functioning. Most approaches to increasing sexual satisfaction make use of multi-component interventions. Thus, it is difficult to determine the relative benefits of many of the specific techniques described here. What follows is therefore based on clinical experience of the author and the writings of other therapists, rather than empirically-based, treatment outcome evaluations.

Sensate Focus Activities

The Sensate Focus exercises described by Masters & Johnson (1970) are particularly helpful in developing sexual intimacy and communication skills, reducing anxiety about sexual contact, and learning how to give and receive sexual pleasure. It is easy to incorporate these tasks into couple therapy, particularly within the context of communication skills training. Typically, the exercises commence with non-genital contact (Sensate Focus 1), and proceed to genital massage (Sensate Focus 2) once non-genital massage can be conducted with pleasure and without anxiety. Throughout the assignments, the emphasis is on sensuality, rather than sexuality, in order to reduce performance demands. Frequently, sexual arousal is produced and the couple proceed to orgasm or intercourse activities. In some instances, a ban on intercourse may be specified, where performance demands and fears are evident. Where this is less of an issue, the couple are free to go on to regular sexual activities. The Sensate Focus Handouts (Tables 4.1 and 4.2) are adapted from Spence (1991).

Sensate Focus exercises are valuable in the treatment of most forms of sexual problem and in sexual enhancement programs. In addition, there are several other basic approaches that are common elements of sexual enhancement. These include increasing sexual knowledge, techniques for elevating sexual arousal and restructuring maladaptive attitudes and thoughts.

Table 4.1 Sensate Focus I: non-genital pleasuring

The aim of this exercise is to help you to really enjoy physical contact with your partner and to learn more about the types of touch and contact that your partner likes. Hopefully, the exercise will allow both of you to feel more relaxed and to become aware of and concentrate on pleasurable feelings. You should also find that the tasks help you to build up better communication with your partner. Even more importantly, Sensate Focus should be enjoyable for both of you.

The expression of physical affection and giving of pleasure through physical contact does not necessarily mean that touch has to involve your sexual parts (genitals). The sensations experienced in all parts of your body are important and it is possible to give and to receive pleasure through touch that is not sexual and does not involve the genitals. There are many different types of touch that can provide pleasant feelings, such as stroking, caressing, kissing, licking, massaging, fondling and tickling, just to mention a few. Different people find different forms of touch pleasurable at different times. It is important to be able to communicate with your partner so that he or she can use the type of touch that you would most enjoy at a particular time. It is also important that you are aware of the pleasant feelings that touch can provide and be able to concentrate on these feelings without feeling tense, embarrassed or distracted by other things.

We suggest that you practice the Sensate Focus 1 exercises at a time when you are both feeling relaxed, comfortable and not too tired. Some people prefer not to wear any clothes, while others find it better to keep their under-clothes on. It is up to you to decide what you wear, but you will need to remove some clothing for back rubs or leg massages. It is best to pick a warm, comfortable place, at a time when you won't be disturbed. Perhaps you could take the telephone off the hook. Some couples tell us that they find it helpful to create a romantic and relaxed atmosphere by dimming the lights, playing some soft music and perhaps having a glass of wine first. Remember that right from the start the aim is not to be sexual, but to enjoy the pleasurable feelings.

We suggest that you take it in turns to give and to receive pleasure. It is a good idea to decide in advance who is going to take the first turn in being the "receiver" and who is going to be the "giver". You might feel rather embarrassed about this, so perhaps you could toss a coin in order to decide. Try and work out beforehand when will be a good time to practice the exercises and then really make an effort to stick to this plan. Once you get started it will seem much easier. The person who is giving pleasure should try to explore different types of touch, in order to learn more about the type of contact that their partner finds pleasurable. The "giver" needs to concentrate on their partner's reaction and should not try to receive pleasure him- or herself at this point. Try to experiment with different types of touch, perhaps using massage oils or talcum powders, on different parts of the body. The face, neck, shoulders, back, stomach, arms and legs can be explored, remembering to avoid any touching of the breasts or sexual areas.

Table 4.1 *(continued)*

The person who is receiving pleasure should just relax and concentrate on enjoying the experience. It is important to give information to your partner about how you are feeling . . . about the type of touch that you find pleasurable and the parts of your body where you enjoy being touched. If your partner uses some form of contact that you do not find pleasurable, it is important to communicate this too, but very sensitively. Your partner will be trying very hard to give you pleasure and it is important that they do not feel hurt or embarrassed when they do not succeed. Always try to give your feedback in a positive way. You can show your pleasure by actually saying that you find something enjoyable, such as "oh, I really like it when you stroke me there". If you need to communicate something that you do not like, and yet want to keep it positive, you could say . . . "I think I preferred it when you massaged my shoulders . . . I thought that felt wonderful . . . could you do it again, please?". You can also communicate your likes and dislikes to your partner by actually guiding his or her hands and showing your partner what to do. Gradually, you will find these exercises easier to do and we realize that you may find them difficult at first . . . but please try really hard to make them work.

After you have had your first turn at being the giver or receiver for about 10 minutes, it is time to change over. We suggest that you take it in turns as to who will be first to be the giver each time you practise these exercises. Then, try to make each session last about 40 minutes and you should both have two chances at being the giver and two chances at being the receiver. Occasionally, you may feel tempted to break the rules and move on to include sexual areas of the body or even to take part in sexual intercourse. Please try not to do this, as it goes against the whole aim of the exercises. The aim is *not* to become sexually aroused but to allow you to practise these exercises in a relaxed way, where you do not feel at all pressured to take part in sexual activities. You should feel free to give and to receive pleasure without any sexual involvement.

Increasing Sexual Knowledge

A significant component in the enhancement of sexual functioning is an increase in knowledge about sexual responding and techniques. Obviously, the degree to which this is important will vary for different clients, according to the deficits in sexual knowledge identified during assessment. The major areas to be covered include sexual anatomy, the human sexual response and techniques for self and partner stimulation. The methods used to increase knowledge may include direct information from the therapist, discussion with the partner, reading material, films, guidance by the partner and observation of the partner. Some useful reading material for clients include *Men and Sex* by Zilbergeld (1995), *Woman's Experience of Sex* by Sheila Kitzinger (1985), Alex Comfort's *The New Joy of Sex* (1994) and *Becoming a Sexual Person* by R.T. Francoeur (1991).

Increasing Sexual Arousal through Use of Fantasy

Some clients find imagery very difficult and it may be necessary to begin fantasy training with non-sexual images, in order to increase control over imagery content. Non-sexual images are also more acceptable to those clients who have

Table 4.2 Sensate Focus II: genital pleasuring

This exercise is a continuation of Sensate Focus I. You are again asked to take it in turns to give and to receive pleasure, but this time you may include the touching of sexual areas of the body. The aim is to concentrate upon pleasurable feelings, rather than trying to become sexually aroused. At first, we suggest that you do not try to reach orgasm or ejaculation or have sexual intercourse during the exercises, even if you begin to feel sexually aroused.

The main aim of Sensate Focus 2 is to be sensual rather than sexual. The exercises should help you to feel relaxed about being touched by your partner, to be able to concentrate on feelings of pleasure and to allow your partner to know more about the type of touch that you find pleasurable. In the same way, your partner will become more aware of pleasurable feelings and you will learn more about the best ways to provide pleasurable sensations. As a couple, you should also become better at communicating about physical contact.

As before, we suggest that you organize a time in advance when you know that you will not be disturbed and where you can be comfortable and relaxed. Try not to pick times when you are likely to be tired, irritable or stressed. It is very important to set aside the time to practise your exercises, as it is very easy to come up with a variety of excuses which may stop you from doing them. Decide beforehand who is going to have the first turn at giving pleasure and who is to be the receiver. Make sure that you choose a warm comfortable place, and again you might like to use the dim lights and relaxing music to set the scene. Some couples have found it helpful to practise the exercises in the bath for part of the time.

The person who is giving pleasure should usually begin by using a variety of different types of touch and contact to the parts of the body covered in Sensate Focus 1, before gradually including the sexual areas (including the breasts). The aim is still to try different types of touch, such as stroking, caressing, kissing, licking or massaging over different parts of the body, in order to give pleasure to your partner and to discover the type of contact that he or she finds enjoyable. You may like to try different movements or different strengths and speeds of movement, all the time concentrating on your partner's response. Your partner has been asked to let you know what is pleasurable. Listen carefully to what your partner says and try to follow his or her suggestions. Occasionally, your partner may actually take your hand and guide it in order to show you the type of touch that is most enjoyable. If this happens, please do not try to resist, but relax and allow your partner to show you a particular form of touch. Remember that certain parts of the penis and clitoris may be very sensitive and you should try to vary your touching to include different parts of the body, rather than concentrating only on the sexual areas.

The person who is receiving pleasure should relax and concentrate on the enjoyable sensations. There is no need for you to do anything, other than enjoying the experience and communicating to your partner the type of touch that you are finding pleasurable. Try to relax when your sexual parts are being touched and concentrate on the nice feelings, rather than attempting to become sexually aroused. Try not to think about the sexual parts of your body as being different from the rest of your body, so that you can concentrate on sensual body feelings, rather than sexual ones. At this point we would like you to start to guide your partner's hands and show him or her the type of touch that gives you most pleasure. Your partner will be expecting you to do this, so do not feel worried about doing so.

Generally, we suggest that each of you spends around 10 minutes as the "giver" before swapping over to be the receiver. You may prefer to change over sooner than this if either of you is becoming tired. Ideally, each of you should have at least two turns at being the receiver and giver during the session. Gradually you will find that the communication between you and your partner becomes easier and you will both have learned to enjoy sensual feelings and to know the type of touch that each of you finds most pleasurable.

negative attitudes towards the use of fantasy. Initially, imagery may focus on simple objects, with attention being drawn to colour, shape and size. For example, the client may be asked to image a series of shapes, perhaps beginning with a red triangle, then a blue square, which gradually move together until the square is positioned below the triangle. Attention to bodily sensations is obviously important in sexual fantasies, hence it is important to train imagery which includes a focus on bodily sensations. Relaxing scenes, such as being at the beach, may be used to encourage clients to focus on imagery sensations such as what they can see, hear, touch and feel emotionally during the scene. Clients may also be able to describe non-sexual images of their own. Common examples include water scenes and snow scenes.

Once the client is able to produce realistic, non-sexual images and is able to experience the emotions and sensations associated with the scene, then training progresses to include a non-sexual massage example. Subsequently, the image may progress to a sensual massage and feelings of mild sexual arousal may be described. In the therapy sessions, it is suggested that the therapist focuses on very mild sexual situations, given that these are initially spoken aloud by the therapist. This avoids any ethical dilemmas concerning strong sexual fantasy talk by the therapist and the clients may practise the imagery scenes on their own at home.

During subsequent clinic-based practice, the client is asked to describe a situation that would trigger mild levels of sexual arousal. Details about the scene are given to the therapist so that he or she may describe the scene realistically. The scene is therefore individualized to the client. Instructions are given to concentrate upon the bodily sensations produced, to imagine really being present in the scene and to push out any intrusive thoughts. Each scene may then be practised at home, initially with audio-taped therapist guidance if the client is still having difficulties retaining the image under self-management. Again, it is not suggested that the therapist tape-record strong sexual fantasy instructions, as this task may be left to the client.

Use of Erotic Materials to Increase Sexual Arousal

The use of erotic material forms an important part of the sexual repertoire of many non-dysfunctional couples, serving to enhance arousal levels and to bring an element of variation into their sexual activities. Exposure to erotic stimuli such as tapes, literature, pictures or films is therefore a valuable method of enhancing sexual arousal in couples for whom low sexual desire or arousal is a problem (e.g. Gillan, 1977; Heiman, LoPiccolo & LoPiccolo, 1988; Spence, 1991). Before proceeding, it is important to note here that the materials used should be clearly erotic and sensual, rather than pornographic, and should not include stimuli involving violence or degradation of others.

Individuals will vary according to the type of erotic material that they find sexually arousing. Some people respond more to written material and pictures, others to movies, and some to audiotaped materials. There is an enormous range of materials that are publicly available, particularly in videotaped and magazine format. You may find it helpful to develop a resource list of materials that can be obtained easily in your locality. It is sometimes difficult to find erotic material that is particularly suited to women. Some examples of women's erotic literature that you may wish to include on your resource list include:

- *Little Birds: Erotica* by Anais Nin (1979).
- *Diary of Anais Nin* by Anais Nin (1966).
- *My Secret Garden* by Nancy Friday (1975).
- *Forbidden Flowers* by Nancy Friday (1994).

Cognitive Restructuring of Interfering Sexual Thoughts and Attitudes

Given the important role of attitudes and thoughts in determining sexual responding and satisfaction, cognitive restructuring procedures play a significant part in enhancing sexual functioning (Treat, 1987). One of the first steps in this component is to illustrate the role of cognitive influences by drawing the couple's attention to some of the most common myths and maladaptive thoughts that relate to sexual functioning. These typically relate to male–female roles in sex (what REAL men do and NICE girls don't!), and thoughts relating to performance and failure. Many of the major myths are outlined by Zilbergeld (1995) and Spence (1991). In addition, the major types of faulty thinking described by Beck et al. (1979) and Ellis (1958) can be described. These include overgeneralizations, e.g. "I will always be like this. I will never be able to reach orgasm"; all-or-none thinking, e.g. "Because our sexual relationship is poor, our whole relationship is a disaster"; magnifying negatives and disqualifying positives, e.g. "Having difficulty in keeping my erection is absolutely terrible"; and personalizations, e.g. "Because my partner has difficulty reaching orgasm, she can't find me attractive. She can't love me".

Weeks (1987) proposed that sexual desire and arousal are often inhibited by a focus on the negative characteristics of the self, partner and the relationship, with the exclusion of attention to positive characteristics. However, rather than attempt to challenge the accuracy or logicality of these negative thoughts, Weeks (1987) stressed the need to train clients to focus on positive features and to use positive self-talk. Thus, if negative thoughts concerning the partner's bad habits or one's own deficits are actually true, these do not need to be challenged, but rather the clients are asked to focus their attention on positive characteristics of the self, partner or the relationship.

Various methods may be used to identify maladaptive or negative thoughts and attitudes. In many instances these arise spontaneously during therapy sessions and the therapist should be on the constant lookout for their occurrence. Response to assessment questionnaires may also be a valuable source of information. Self-monitoring provides a useful means of obtaining information about the occurrence of negative, maladaptive thoughts in specific situations. For example, recording of actual thoughts before, during and after Sensate Focus exercises may provide a valuable source of data for cognitive restructuring sessions.

Once the individuals are aware of their cognitive distortions and can identify when they occur, the therapist is in a position to commence the teaching of cognitive challenging skills. Detailed descriptions of cognitive challenging methods are provided by Beck et al. (1979) and Fennel (1989). The aim is to teach clients to identify evidence to dispute the rationality or accuracy of their thoughts, and to replace them with more logical interpretations of events. In addition to reducing maladaptive thinking in terms of specific thoughts, cognitive therapy also aims to alter maladaptive styles of thinking in the sense of attitudes and beliefs.

Zilbergeld (1995) briefly describes a cognitive challenging approach which he terms "debunking male sexual mythology". McCarthy (1984) also mentions the use of cognitive therapy procedures in order to bring about attitudinal change, but neither of these authors provides specific guidelines for the conduct of cognitive therapy in relation to sexual problems.

Enhancement of Intimacy Skills

There are many techniques for increasing intimacy expression. Many of these are common to sexual and general relationship issues. Basic exercises include simple sentence completion tasks that each partner completes privately and then discusses. It is advisable to suggest that blaming or critical comments relating to their partner are avoided. Examples of sentence completion questions include:

I feel happy when . . .
I feel sad when . . .

and so on for . . . guilty, afraid, angry, disgusted, shocked, surprised, anxious, embarrassed.

A similar exercise is to ask each partner to describe a particular moment from his/her life:

My most sad experience was when . . .
My most happy experience was when . . .

and so on for . . . guilty, afraid, angry, disgusted, shocked, suppressed, anxious, embarrassed.

Couples can also be asked to make a list of five things that they most like about their partner. Each partner then reads out the list aloud.

In addition to basic exercises, the therapist plays a valuable role in discussing the nature of intimacy, trust and commitment. Each partner's fears and difficulties in these areas can then be explored. It is also important to discuss the preferred level of intimacy of each partner. Some individuals have considerable concern that engaging in high levels of intimacy will open them up to risk of being hurt, or will remove their ability to be independent. These issues need careful discussion. Methods need to be developed whereby each partner feels comfortable with his/her level of shared intimacy without losing his/her individuality or a desirable level of independence. Further and more complex tasks relating to verbal and non-verbal expressions of intimacy can then be set as appropriate for each couple.

Sexual Disclosure Task

A further task for the development of sexual intimacy involves disclosure of personal feelings, thoughts and attitudes relating to sexual matters. Again, a sentence completion method can be used in which each person writes down their response and later reads it aloud to their partner. Some possible example of open ended statements include:

My favourite sexual activity is . . . .
One sexual activity I have always wanted to do but never liked to ask for is . . . . .
When I get really sexually aroused I am thinking to myself . . . .
My biggest fear when we are having sex is . . . .
The most sexually arousing thing that my partner does to me is . . . .
The place that I most like to make love is . . . .
The best time my partner and I had sex was when . . . .
The thing I like doing most to give my partner sexual pleasure is . . . .
I think masturbation is . . . .

The sensate focus exercises are also a valuable means of developing sexual intimacy skills.

Discussion of Fantasies

One method of increasing sexual intimacy expression is to ask each partner to describe or write down his/her sexual fantasies that involve the partner. These fantasies should only include activities that would not be distasteful or harmful to the partner, or anyone else. It is then up to the partner to decide whether or not they wish to take part in making this fantasy a reality. The therapist must make it clear that there is no pressure on the partner to be involved in any acting-out process.

Sexual Role-plays

Couples may be set a task of jointly developing a script for a role-play scenario which they then act out in private. These scripts are very personal to each couple and some may find such a suggestion very embarrassing. Thus, it is important that the couple make their own suggestions about possible scenarios, rather than being influenced by the therapist. For example, one couple decided to roleplay two strangers who meet for the first time. They arranged to meet each other in a hotel bar for a role-played blind date and went on to stay the night at the hotel.

Role-play scenarios such as this one can be a useful means of regenerating some of the early feelings relating to novelty in the sexual relationship. The therapist will need to place some limits upon the acceptable content of role-plays, to ensure that both partners feel happy with the role that they are playing. Content relating to physical or emotional abuse should be discouraged.

Discussion of Sexual Information

There is a wide variety of literature relating to sexuality that couples can be given to read together and discuss. Dumka (1992) described a method in which each partner takes it in turn to read aloud a section from a book or article relating to sexual issues, while the other partner listens. After reading for around 10 minutes, the couple discuss the content and ask each other questions about their thoughts and attitudes about the material. This process serves a valuable role, not only in increasing sexual knowledge but also in desensitizing couples to talking about sexual matters. It also provides valuable material for discussion with the therapist in subsequent sessions. Interfering thoughts and beliefs are likely to be highlighted during this task and can form the content for cognitive restructuring with the therapist.

Reinstigating Early Sexual Feelings

Roberts (1992) emphasized the value of regenerating feelings from the early, romantic stages of the relationship. Couples are asked to describe their early feelings of passion and desire, and to identify shared activities that they used to engage in. They are then asked to reinstigate these activities where possible. Roberts described an experiential approach to the development of attachment between the partners. He stressed the importance of fundamental emotional experiences in the development and maintenance of attachment between partners, and proposed that verbal or cognitive mediation therapies are unlikely to be effective if the couple do not feel the emotions that underlie attachment. Thus, the couple are instructed to engage in activities that generate feelings of romantic love and sexual attraction. These could also include reviewing old photographs, visiting places or engaging in activities relating to their courtship phase. Roberts encourages couples to develop romantic habits that are repeatable and can be incorporated into their ongoing relationship. For example, a couple who used to go to the movies frequently during their courtship but has ceased to do so could be asked to reinstigate this activity.

DEALING WITH SPECIFIC PSYCHOSEXUAL DYSFUNCTIONS

The emphasis in this chapter has been on the enhancement of sexual functioning in couples with relatively mild sexual difficulties, or who can benefit from general approaches for increasing sexual desire and arousal. For some clients, however, psychosexual difficulties may be such that more specific sex therapy techniques are required. It is beyond the brief of this chapter to provide a detailed description of these techniques. Readers are advised to consult the many sex therapy texts available. General sex therapy texts include O'Donohue & Geer (1994), Wincze & Carey (1991), Lincoln (1992) and Spence (1991), to mention just a few. Those that deal with specific aspects of sexual difficulties include:

- Premature ejaculation: Kaplan (1989).
- Female orgasmic difficulties: Heiman LoPiccolo & LoPiccolo (1988).
- Erectile problems: Rosen & Leiblum (1992).
- Sexual desire problems: Leiblum & Rosen (1988).

Brief Case Illustration

The following example is designed to illustrate how attention to sexual issues may form an important component of couple therapy. Space does not permit a detailed case description and many of the more complex issues will necessarily appear simplified. James and Sharon initially presented with mild levels of marital discord. They were both in their late 30s and had been married for 11 years, having met at University. Both were in full-time employment and were high-income earners in the financial sector. They had three children.

As is the case with many referrals, there were many additional issues for which some individual therapy was required. Both partners had a history of depression, with ongoing presenting features, thus intervention involved a cognitive–behavioural approach to dealing with this aspect (Beck et al., 1979). Assessment also revealed that much of the couple's current conflict centred around parent management problems, and the behavioural difficulties of the three children. Therefore, part of the intervention focused on teaching parenting skills (Forehand & McMahon, 1981). This was highly successful in reducing the children's behavioural problems and in reducing conflict between the parents.

I will not describe in detail here the content of the marital intervention, as these matters are covered in detail elsewhere in this book. Suffice it to say, both partners initially reported mild marital dissatisfaction. The main areas of discontent concerned lack of time spent together, disagreements about household responsibilities, difficulty in discussing and resolving problems, and lack of sexual activity. The interview revealed that both individuals worked extremely hard and were generally tired by the end of the day. Sharon also reported feeling resentful that most of the housework and child care responsibilities fell on her, even though she was also working full-time. The children attended school or preschool and Sharon held the main responsibility for delivering and collecting the children, cooking the meals and cleaning the house. In turn, James felt highly stressed about his financial responsibilities in relation to his company. The couple had no support from extended family and little recreational time together. However, assessment did highlight some considerable strengths. Both partners were highly motivated to work on their relationship, they found each other very sexually attractive, they liked each other, and had the money to buy in help to manage some of the family tasks that were exhausting them.

Couple therapy involved teaching communication skills, increasing mutually enjoyable experiences, and problem-solving sessions to deal with the family management problems. The solutions chosen included employment of a cleaner and an after-school person to collect the children, and James agreed to cook dinner on two evenings per week and to tidy the kitchen after evening meals. Both James and Sharon were highly compliant with therapy tasks, but it was clear that additional therapist input was required to deal with the lack of sexual contact. Even though the couple were no longer so tired and irritable with each other, their sexual relationship had not automatically improved in line with the gains in other aspects of their relationship.

An in-depth assessment of their sexual functioning revealed some important issues. Both James and Sharon reported that they had initially had an excellent sexual relationship, with frequent sexual activity, both experiencing orgasm, and no specific difficulties. However, sexual activity had gradually decreased in frequency since the birth, 4 years ago, of their youngest child. Since that time, they rarely had privacy and quiet time together and when suitable occasions arose, both partners had felt too tired to engage in sex. Attempts to initiate sex by James were typically rejected, and their infrequent sexual activities were described as rather boring and unexciting. Gradually, James had ceased to initiate sex for fear of further rejections and neither partner felt particularly interested in mutual sexual activities. This did not reflect a total disinterest in sex, however, as both James and Sharon engaged in self-stimulation when they were alone. Indeed, James reported daily masturbation and Sharon reported masturbating once or twice per week. Further investigation revealed that James' frequent masturbation was a significant source of discomfort to Sharon. She described feeling extremely threatened by James using erotic pictures of other women to facilitate his masturbatory activities. This concern carried over into her sexual interactions with James, in which she had recurring thoughts that he was fantasizing about other women rather than focusing his attention on her. It also became clear that Sharon was finding it increasingly difficult to experience orgasm and was now rehearsing a series of negative self-statements during sexual interactions, such as, "I am not going to be able to orgasm. There is something wrong with me. If I don't orgasm, James will think that I don't feel the same way about him any more". These cognitions fitted clearly into the performance demand/spectatoring type of thoughts described by Masters & Johnson (1970). In turn, James reported a series of maladaptive thoughts that were inhibiting his sexual responding. These related to role demands and fear of failure, such as, "It is always me who has to make the first move, but when I do Sharon always says 'No'. There is no point in trying because it never works out. I guess that she doesn't find me attractive any more".

Several therapy techniques were included in the intervention. After the assessment phase, the couple were presented with a formulation in which their current difficulties were described as being relatively common amongst couples in long-term relationships, particularly those with young children. A model was drawn up that outlined the roles played by lack of privacy/opportunity, fatigue, general relationship dissatisfaction, lack of reinforcement following sexual attempts, and maladaptive thoughts concerning performance, failure, the self, partner and the relationship, culminating in lack of sexual interest and activity. The strengths of the couple were also emphasized, particularly the positive feelings that they had for each other, sexual attraction, a previously enjoyable sexual relationship, and positive gains already being made in the general relationship. Intervention focused on:

1. Reinstigating early sexual feelings through description of early sexual activities and feelings of passion and desire.
2. Increasing opportunities for sexual contact (reducing fatigue, creating opportunities for undisturbed private time, e.g. a weekend away from the children).
3. Reducing performance demands, increasing sexual communication skills, focusing on intimate pleasure, affection-giving and sensuality through sensate focus exercises (see above).
4. Turn-taking in responsibility for initiating sexual activities.
5. Reducing the frequency of masturbatory activities (while normalizing them) so as to channel sexual desire into couple activities.
6. Reducing interfering, maladaptive thoughts (through discussion, education, reduction of performance demands and cognitive restructuring methods). This section also involved monitoring and recording of thoughts that occurred before, during and after home tasks.
7. Increasing triggers for sexual desire and arousal through use of erotic material (literature, videotapes and magazines) in association with later genital sensate focus sessions.
8. Methods to further enhance sexual excitement, knowledge and skills, e.g. discussion of sexual fantasies, development of their own sexual role-plays, reading literature and practising activities such as those outlined in Alex Comfort's *The New Joy of Sex* (1994).

The couple was very compliant with all homework tasks, and made rapid progress through the programme. Sensate focus exercises followed on from the teaching of general communication skills, and were reported to be highly effective in producing relaxed, sensual experiences. Once these exercises were combined with methods to enhance sexual arousal, the couple rapidly progressed to sexually focused activities, including intercourse and oral sex. Recording of thoughts related to the various home tasks produced valuable information for cognitive restructuring, and maladaptive, interfering thoughts rapidly diminished.

At this point, the couple organized a weekend away, which was their first weekend alone for 11 years. This was highly enjoyable and the couple made long-term plans to ensure that they set aside private time for themselves in the future.

By the end of the intervention, both partners reported their sexual relationship to be very satisfactory and enjoyable. Sexual activities were taking place around twice per week, with both partners experiencing high levels of sexual arousal and orgasm. Booster sessions were conducted at 3- and 6-month follow-ups. At 3-month follow-up therapy benefits were maintained, but there was some decline in their sexual relationship at 6-month follow-up. At this follow-up, the couple reported periods of 2–3 weeks without sexual contact, during which neither partner felt interested or energetic enough to instigate sexual activity. Following a booster session, to reiterate the main points of therapy, the couple drew up a plan for enhancement of their sexual relationship over the following 3-month period. This included setting aside a special time each week for undisturbed privacy, during which each individual focused on giving pleasure to their partner. This time need not necessarily become sexual, and could be used for a sensual massage, reading or watching erotic material, listening to music or simply lying together in a cuddle. It was not, however, to be used for problem-solving.

Obviously, there are many couples for whom the presenting sexual difficulties are more complex than those reported here. This case example was selected to illustrate the integration of sex and couple therapies, using a cognitive–behavioural approach. The follow-up is still ongoing and the challenge for the therapist is now to teach the couple to monitor their relationship in order to identify patterns of behaviour that indicate the need to reinstigate the pro-gramme. In an attempt to prevent relapse, the booster sessions are now focusing on ways to integrate the components of therapy into the couple's everyday relationship. For example, one aim is to ensure that turn-taking for initiation of sexual activities, sensate focus exercises, and setting aside private time becomes a regular feature of James and Sharon's relationship. The couple have also been instructed to monitor the frequency of their sexual activity, and we have set a warning signal (of 6 weeks with no sexual contact) that will trigger reintroduction of the programme. Hopefully, these efforts will be successful in preventing fur-ther relapse.

SUMMARY AND CONCLUSION

This chapter stressed the close interconnections between satisfaction with the sexual and general aspects of couple relationships. A high proportion of couples presenting with what they describe as marital problems are likely to experience difficulties in their sexual relationship. Similarly, couples presenting for sex therapy frequently exhibit difficulties in other areas of their relationship. Many of the skills that are important for successful sexual functioning are the same skills that are important for marital satisfaction generally. Communication, intimacy and problem-solving skills are fundamental to both aspects of the relationship. Thus, there is a strong case for including sexual enhancement techniques as a component of couple therapy. This case is strengthened by the suggestion that positive sexual experiences are important for enhancing and maintaining relationship attachment and bonding between partners (or whatever forms the cognitive–behavioural components of what is commonly called "romantic love").

This chapter also provided an outline of the various ways in which sexual difficulties can be manifested and described those biological and psychosocial factors that most commonly influence sexual functioning. It was suggested that couple therapists should have a thorough understanding of the nature, aetiology, assessment and treatment of sexual difficulties. The chapter provided a summary of techniques and measures that are helpful in the assessment of sexual functioning.

Finally, this chapter provided examples of some of the techniques that can be used to improve sexual functioning. Sexual enhancement programs have developed from a variety of theoretical backgrounds, but there is much overlap in the content of these interventions. To date, there is a marked lack of empirical research to determine the relative contribution of specific components of sexual enhancement programs. Studies are needed that evaluate the relative effectiveness of various sexual enhancement techniques and their contribution to the effectiveness of couple therapy.

REFERENCES

American Psychiatric Association (1994). *Diagnostic and Statistical Manual of Mental Disorders*, 4th edn. Washington, DC: American Psychiatric Association.

Andersen, B.L., Broffitt, B., Karlson, J.A. & Turnquist, D.C. (1989). A psychometric analysis of the Sexual Arousability Index. *Journal of Consulting and Clinical Psychology*, **57**, 123–130.

Annon, J.S. (1975). *The Sexual Pleasure Inventory*. Honolulu: Enabling Systems.

Atwood, J.D. & Dershowitz, S. (1992). Constructing a sex and marital therapy frame: ways to help couples deconstruct sexual problems. *Journal of Sex and Marital Therapy*, **18**, 196–219.

Atwood, J.D. & Weinstein, E. (1989). The couple relationship as the focus of sex therapy: the integration of sex therapy ideas and techniques of marital and family therapy. *Australian and New Zealand Journal of Family Therapy*, **10**, 161–168.

Baker, C.D. & De Silva, P. (1988). The relationship between male sexual dysfunction and belief in Zilbergeld's Myths: an empirical investigation. *Sexual and Marital Therapy*, **3**, 229–239.

Barbach, L. (1982). *For Each Other: Sharing Sexual Intimacy*. New York: Doubleday.

Beck, A.T., Rush, A.J., Shaw, B.G. & Emery, G. (1979). *Cognitive Therapy of Depression*. New York: Wiley.

Bentler, P.M. (1967). Heterosexual behaviour assessment—I. Males. *Behaviour Research and Therapy*, **5**, 21–25.

Bentler, P.M. (1968). Heterosexual behaviour assessment—II. Females. *Behaviour Research and Therapy*, **6**, 27–30.

Boller, F. & Frank, E. (1982). *Sexual Dysfunction in Neurological Disorders: Diagnosis, Management and Rehabilitation*. New York: Raven.

Clark, A. & Wallin, P. (1965). Women's sexual responsiveness and the duration and quality of their marriage. *American Journal of Sociology*, **71**, 187–196.

Comfort, A. (1994). *The New Joy of Sex*. London: Mitchell Beazley.

Derogatis, L.R. (1975). *Derogatis Sexual Functioning Inventory*. Baltimore: Clinical Psychometrics Research.

Derogatis, L.R. & Meyer, J.K. (1979). A psychological profile of the sexual dysfunctions. *Archives of Sexual Behaviour*, **8**, 210–223.

Donnelly, D.A. (1993). Sexually inactive marriages. *Journal of Sex Research*, **30**, 171–179.

Dumka, L.E. (1992). Increasing the pleasure bond: sexual enhancement in marital therapy. *Journal of Family Psychotherapy*, **3**, 1–18.

Ellis, A. (1958). Rational psychotherapy. *Journal of Genetic Psychology*, **59**, 35–49.

Fennell, M.J.V. (1989). Depression. In K. Hawton, P.M. Salkovskis, J. Kirk & D.M. Clark (eds), *Cognitive Behaviour Therapy for Psychiatric Problems: a Practical Guide* (pp. 169–234). Oxford: Oxford University Press.

Forehand, R.L. & McMahon, R.J. (1981). *Helping the Non-compliant Child: a Clinician's Guide to Parent Training*. New York: Guilford.

Francoeur, R.T. (1991). *Becoming a Sexual Person*. New York: MacMillan.

Frank, E., Anderson, C. & Rubinstein, D. (1979). Marital role strain and sexual satisfaction. *Journal of Consulting and Clinical Psychology*, **47**, 1096–1103.

Freund, K. & Blanchard, R. (1981). Assessment of sexual dysfunction and deviation. In M. Hersen & A.S. Bellack (eds), *Behavioral Assessment: a Practical Handbook* (pp. 427–455). New York: Pergamon.

Friday, N. (1975). *My Secret Garden: Women's Secret Fantasies*. London: Quartet.

Friday, N. (1994). *Forbidden Flowers: More Women's Sexual Fantasies*. London: Arrow.

Gillan. P.W. (1977). Stimulation therapy for sexual dysfunction. In E.R. Wheeler (ed.), *Progress in Sexology* (pp. 137–151). New York: Plenum.

Greenblat, C. (1983). The salience of sexuality in the early years of marriage. *Journal of Marriage and the Family*, **45**, 277–288.

Hahlweg, K., Schindler, L. & Revenstorf, D. (1982). *Partnerschafts Probleme: Diagose und Therapie*. Berlin: Springer.

Hawton. K. (1985). *Sex Therapy: a Practical Guide*. Oxford: Oxford University Press.

Heiman, J., LoPiccolo, L. & LoPiccolo, J. (1988). *Becoming Orgasmic: a Sexual Growth Programme for Women* (revised and expanded edn). New York: Prentice Hall.

Hoon, E.F., Hoon, P.W. & Wincze, J.P. (1976). An inventory for the measurement of female sexual arousability. The SAI. *Archives of Sexual Behaviour*, **5**, 291–301.

Kaplan, H.S. (1974). *The New Sex Therapy: Active Treatment of Sexual Dysfunction*. New York: Brunner/Mazel.

Kaplan, H.S. (1983). *The Evaluation of Sexual Disorders: Psychological and Medical Aspects*. New York: Brunner/Mazel.

Kaplan, H.S. (1987). *The Illustrated Manual of Sex Therapy*. New York: Brunner/Mazel.

Kaplan, H.S. (1989). *How to Overcome Premature Ejaculation*. New York: Brunner/Mazel.

Kitzinger, S. (1985). *Woman's Experience of Sex*. Harmondsworth: Penguin.

Leiblum, S.R. & Rosen, R.C. (1988) *Sexual Desire Disorders*. New York: Guilford.

Lief, H.I. (1981). Self-evaluation of sexual behaviour and gratification. In H.I. Lief (ed.), *Sexual Problems in Medical Practice* (pp. 206–231). Monroe, WI: American Medical Association.

Lief, H.I. & Reed, D.M. (1972). *Sexual Knowledge and Attitude Test (SKAT)*, 2nd edn. University of Pennsylvania: Centre for the Study of Sex Education in Medicine.

Lincoln, R. (1992). *Psychosexual Medicine*. London: Chapman & Hall.

LoPiccolo, J. & Miller, V.H. (1975). A program for enhancing the sexual relationship of normal couples. *The Counseling Psychologist*. **5**, 41–45.

LoPiccolo, J. & Steger, J.C. (1974). The Sexual Interaction Inventory: a new instrument for assessment of sexual dysfunction. *Archive of Sexual Behaviour*, **3**, 585–595.

Masters, W.H. & Johnson, V.E. (1970). *Human Sexual Inadequacy*. Boston: Little, Brown.

Mayer, A. (1990). *How to Stay Lovers While Raising Your Children: a Burned-out Parents' Guide to Sex*. Los Angeles, CA: Price Stern Sloan.

McCabe, M.P. (1994). The influence of the quality of relationship on sexual dysfunction. *Australian Journal of Marriage and Family*, **15**, 2–8.

McCarthy, B. (1984). Strategies and techniques for the treatment of inhibited sexual desire. *Journal of Sex and Marital Therapy*, **10**, 97–104.

Mobarak, A., Tamerin, J. & Tamerin, N. (1986). Sex therapy: an adjunct in the treatment of marital discord. *Journal of Sex and Marital Therapy*, **12**, 229–238.

Nathan, S.G. (1986). The epidemiology of the DSM-III psychosexual dysfunctions. *Journal of Sex and Marital Therapy*, **12**, 267–281.

Nin, A. (1979). *Little Birds: Erotica*. New York: Harcourt Brace Jovanovich.

Nin, A. (1966). *The Diary of Anais Nin*. London: P. Owen.

Noller, P. & White, A. (1990). The validity of the Communication Patterns Questionnaire. *Psychological Assessment*, **2**, 478–482.

O'Donohue, W. & Geer, J.H. (1994). *Handbook of Sexual Dysfunctions: Assessment and Treatment*. Boston: Allyn & Bacon.

Patterson, D.G. & O'Gorman, E.C. (1986). The SOMA—a questionnaire measure of sexual anxiety. *British Journal of Psychiatry*, **149**, 63–67.

Robinson, C.H. & Annon, J.S. (1975). *The Heterosexual Behaviour Inventory*. Honolulu: Enabling Systems.

Rosen, R.C. & Leiblum, S.R. (1992). *Erectile Disorder: Assessment and Treatment*. New York: Guilford.

Rust, J. & Golombok, S. (1986). The GRISS: a psychometric instrument for the assessment of sexual dysfunction. *Archives of Sexual Behaviour*, **15**, 157–165.

Roberts, T.W. (1992). Sexual attraction and romantic love: forgotten variables in marital therapy. *Journal of Marital and Family Therapy*, **18**, 357–364.

Safir, M.P., Peres, Y., Lichtenstein, M., Hoch, Z. & Shepherd, J. (1982). Psychological androgyny and sexual adequacy. *Journal of Sex and Marital Therapy*, **8**, 228–240.

Sager, C.J. (1974). Sexual dysfunctions and marital discord. In H.S. Kaplan (ed.), *The New Sex Therapy* (pp. 501–518). New York: Brunner/Mazel.

Sanders, G.L. & Cairns, K.V. (1987). Loss of sexual spontaneity. *Medical Aspects of Human Sexuality*, **21**, 37–43.

Scanzoni, J., Donnelly, D., Dwyer, J. & Mulle, V. (1989). Exploring psychological well-being and relationship commitment among varied living arrangements. Unpublished manuscript.

Schenk, J., Pfrang, H. & Raushe, A. (1983). Personality traits versus the quality of the marital relationship as the determinant of marital sexuality. *Archives of Sexual Behaviour*, **12**, 31–42.

Schnarch, D.M. (1991). *Constructing the Sexual Crucible: an Integration of Sexual and Marital Therapy*. New York: Jacaranda Wiley.

Snyder, D.K. (1981). *The Marital Satisfaction Inventory Manual*. CA: Western Psychological Services.

Spector, I.P. & Carey, M.P. (1990). Incidence and prevalence of the sexual dysfunctions: a critical review of the empirical literature. *Archives of Sexual Behaviour*, **19**, 389–408.

Spence, S.H. (1985). Group versus individual treatment of primary and secondary female orgasmic dysfunction. *Behaviour Research and Therapy*, **23**, 539–548.

Spence, S.H. (1991). *Psychosexual Therapy: a Cognitive–Behavioural Approach*. London: Chapman & Hall.

Spence, S.H. (1992). Psychosexual dysfunction in the elderly. *Behaviour Change*, **9**, 55–64.

Talmadge, L.D. & Talmadge, W.C. (1986). Relational sexuality: an understanding of low sexual desire. *Journal of Sex and Marital Therapy*, **12**, 3–21.

Treat, S.R. (1987). Enhancing a couple's sexual relationship. In G.R. Weeks & L. Hof (eds), *Integrating Sex and Marital Therapy: a Clinician's Guide* (pp. 57–81). New York: Brunner/Mazel.

Tullman, G.M., Gilner, F.H., Kolodny, R.C., Dornbush, R.L. & Tullman, G.D. (1981). The pre- and post-therapy measurement of communication skills of couples undergoing sex therapy at the Masters and Johnson Institute. *Archives of Sexual Behaviour*, **10**, 95–109.

Weeks, G.R. (1987). Systematic treatment of inhibited sexual desire. In G.R. Weeks & L. Hof (eds), *Integrating Sex and Marital Therapy: a Clinician's Guide* (pp. 183–201). New York: Brunner/Mazel.

Weeks, G.R. & Hof, L. (1987). *Integrating Sex and Marital Therapy: a Clinical Guide* (pp. 183–201). New York: Brunner/Mazel.

Wilson, P.H., Spence, S.H. & Kavanagh, D.J. (1989). *Cognitive–Behavioural Interviewing for Adult Disorders: a Practical Handbook*. London: Routledge.

Wincze, J.P. & Carey, M.P. (1991). *Sexual Dysfunction: a Guide for Assessment and Treatment*. New York: Guilford.

Zilbergeld, B. (1995). *Men and Sex*. London: Harper Collins.

Zimmer, D. (1987). Does marital therapy enhance the effectiveness of treatment for sexual dysfunction? *Journal of Sex and Marital Therapy*, **13**, 193–209.

Chapter 5

Gender Issues in Heterosexual, Gay and Lesbian Couples

Danielle Julien*, Charleanea Arellano** and Lyse Turgeon[†]
Departments of Psychology, * University of Quebec at Montreal, Montreal, Canada, and ** Colorado State University, Fort Collins, Co, USA; and [†] Centre de Recherche Fernand Seguin, Hospital L.H. La Fontaine, Montreal, Canada

> Maxwell wants to be left alone, and Samantha wants attention; so he leaves her alone, and she gives him attention (D. Tannen).

Husbands and wives communicate differently. Clinicians and investigators of marital adjustment have found pronounced sex-related[1] differences, especially during times of highly emotional discussions of marital problems. Wives are more likely than husbands to detect marital problems, begin conflictual discussions, and engage in and pursue such discussions (e.g. Rands, 1988). Husbands, on the other hand, withdraw when confronted with marital conflict issues (e.g. Jacobson, 1983). The most robust findings of sex-related differences revealed in observational marital research have been wives' higher level of demands and expression of negative affect (Schapp, 1984), and husbands' withdrawal from wives' hostility during conflict discussions (e.g. Christensen, 1987; Krokoff, 1987; Margolin & Wampold, 1981; Notarius & Markman, 1989; Roberts & Krokoff, 1990).

---

[1] In this chapter, the term *sex-related* will be used to describe findings comparing people grouped into male and female categories (Eagly, 1995). It does not give priority to biological or social causes. The term *gender* will refer to the social meaning assigned to male and female categories. The term *gender role* will be used to describe one's affiliation to maleness and femaleness in terms of overt expression of behaviors and attitudes, and the term *social role* will refer to one's patterns of behaviors defined by the occupations in which one is engaged on a daily basis (e.g. role of worker, parent, housekeeper).

Clinical Handbook of Marriage and Couples Interventions. Edited by W. Kim Halford and Howard J. Markman.
© 1997 John Wiley & Sons Ltd.

This chapter reviews the hypotheses that have been put forward to organize the findings on sex-related differences in marriage. It examines the empirical evidence for those hypotheses and explores how some of those hypotheses fare in light of recent findings on gay and lesbian couples' communication. Comparing opposite-sex patterns with same-sex patterns in intimate relationships may help understanding of the relative contribution of sex and culture to partners' behavioral differences in communication. Implications for assessment and intervention are addressed for each set of findings reviewed.

SEX-RELATED DIFFERENCES IN THE DEMAND–WITHDRAWAL PATTERN

Historically, the demand–withdrawal pattern seems to be at least as old as the information that pioneers in marital research have collected using American couples' self-reports (e.g. Komarovsky, 1962; Rubin, 1983; Terman et al., 1938). Husbands in those early studies consistently complained their wives were too aggressive, whereas the wives complained their husbands did not want to talk. Contemporary studies assessing the demand–withdrawal pattern using questionnaires revealed similar findings, e.g. Christensen's Communication Patterns Questionnaire (Christensen, 1988).

We can illustrate the core finding using the following dialogue between Paula and Jeff, presented in Markman, Stanley & Blumberg (1994, p. 21). Both were concerned that the tension in their relationship was starting to affect their daughter Tanya:

Paula: When are we going to talk about how you're handling your anger?
Jeff: Can't this wait? I have to get these taxes done.
Paula: I've brought this up at least five times already. No, it can't wait!
Jeff: [*Tensing*] What's to talk about, anyway? It's none of your business.
Paula: [*Frustrated and looking right at Jeff*] Tanya is my business. I'm afraid that you may lose your temper and hurt her, and you won't do a damn thing to learn to deal better with your anger.
Jeff: [*Turning away and looking at the window*] I love Tanya. There's no problem here [*leaving the room as he talks*].
Paula: [*Very angry now, following Jeff into the next room*] You have to get some help. You can't just stick your head in the sand.
Jeff: I'm not going to discuss anything with you when you are like this.
Paula: Like what? It doesn't matter if I am calm or frustrated—you won't talk to me about anything important. Tanya is having problems and you have to face that.
Jeff: [*Quiet, tense, fidgeting*].
Paula: Well?
Jeff: [*Going to the closet and grabbing sweater*] I'm going out to have a drink and get some peace and quiet.
Paula: [*Voice raised, angry*] Talk to me, now. I'm tired of you leaving when we're talking about something important.
Jeff: [*Looking away from Paula and walking toward the door*] I'm not talking, you are. Actually, you're yelling. See you later.

This communication pattern is more difficult to observe in a laboratory setting than to assess with self-descriptions of marital discussions at home (Markman, Silvern & Clements, 1993). That may be because husbands, many of whom can leave the room at home, cannot withdraw from the video camera in a laboratory situation. They can, however, deviate from the subject, shut down, stonewall, look away, or turn their backs. Observational studies have provided consistent findings documenting wives' hostility and husbands' withdrawal, whether they used micro measures of hostility and withdrawal (e.g. stonewalling: Gottman, 1994; fidgeting: Turgeon et al., 1992; irrelevant comments and absence of responses: Schapp, 1982) or global observations of behavior patterns over large segments of marital discussions (Christensen & Heavey, 1990; Julien, Markman & Lindahl, 1989).

When researchers looked at the temporal connections between wives' demands and husbands' withdrawal, several studies found that husbands' withdrawal increases the likelihood of wives' hostility (Roberts & Krokoff, 1990; Sayers et al., 1991). As seen in the clinical example, Jeff's avoidance of conflict discussions seems to trigger Paula's push for talking. Alternately, husbands are more likely to withdraw after their wives have been hostile in the sense that they become more defensive, use more denial and increase somatic activities (e.g. fidgeting behaviors; Turgeon et al., 1992). Therefore, the demand–withdrawal dysfunction is a specific pattern of negative escalation during marital discussions.

The key role that the demand–withdrawal pattern plays in the development of marital distress is supported by accumulating evidence. For instance, over a 3-year period marital dissatisfaction declined most when, at year 1, husbands emotionally withdrew and wives pursued hostile confrontation (Levenson & Gottman, 1985). Similarly, a 12-year longitudinal study of marriage showed that the wives' demand–husbands' withdrawal pattern became increasingly salient as marital distress developed over time (Markman, 1994). A recent study using self-reports of conflict resolution styles also found that this pattern predicted dissatisfaction over a 2-year period (Kurdek, 1995).

We do not know yet whether the expression of marital distress through such clear sex-linked differences is specific to Western cultures (Markman & Kraft, 1989), or are generalized to other cultures as well. Although the contribution of the demand–withdrawal pattern to the development of marital distress in the Western culture seems to be established, the roots of this pattern are still elusive. Several researchers have already reviewed, discussed and interpreted the issues (e.g. Baucom et al., 1990; Christensen, 1988; Gottman & Carrère, 1994; Schapp, 1982; Noller, 1993; Notarius & Pellegreni, 1987). These researchers generally conclude that gender differences in the demand–withdrawal pattern are due to the greater physiological reactivity of men to conflict situations, the differential socialization of men and women, and the differential power assigned to males and females in the industrial technological societies.

Understanding the causes of husband's and wives' differences has implications regarding assessment and intervention with couples. For instance, if sex-related differences in the demand–withdrawal pattern are biologically based, this might limit the scope of possible behavior changes in husbands and wives when helping them to get along together. That could direct intervention toward spouses' acceptance of their biological differences. Evidence for socially-based differences between husbands and wives, on the other hand, may broaden the repertoire of behaviors that could be changed or learned. Although most researchers acknowledge that biology interacts with culture in producing sex-related differences, some researchers have favored theories that insisted more on biological constraints (Gottman & Levenson, 1988), whereas others have focused on the socialization of a sex-differentiated culture (e.g. Noller, 1993), or the unequal distribution of power between the sexes (e.g. Jacobson, 1983).

SEX-RELATED BEHAVIORAL DIFFERENCES AND PHYSIOLOGICAL REACTIONS TO EMOTIONAL STRESS

According to the Gottman & Levenson (1988) hypothesis, husbands' withdraw because they experience high levels of physiological arousal during marital confrontations, levels which they feel are strongly aversive. High levels of arousal during marital conflict would be one instance of males' biological predisposition to show stronger autonomic response than females when under stress. Avoidance behavior reduces such high-arousal discomfort. Gottman & Levenson further posit that women pursue confrontation instead of withdrawing because they are less physiologically aroused during marital arguments.

To determine whether this hypothesis is true, we need to show: (a) that there are physiological differences in males' and females' response during high emotional marital discussion; (b) that the physiological responses during emotional stress are synchronized with behavior (i.e. the timings of high arousal in husbands are synchronized with the timings of withdrawal behaviors); and (c) that the latter association accounts for marital distress.

In their review of research on stress reactivity, Gottman & Levenson (1988) cite studies showing experimental stressors create higher cardiovascular arousal in men than in women. However, other comprehensive reviews indicate an equally high number of studies showing women having higher reactions than men, or that they do not differ from men (Polefrone & Manuck, 1987). Most neuroendocrine studies have shown men to have higher levels of epinephrine than women under conditions of stress (Malarkey et al., 1994; Polefrone & Manuck, 1987). Thus, evidence for a sex difference in stress responses is mixed, but we cannot rule out that neuroendocrine differences may predispose males and females to behave differently when coping with emotional stress.

Whether marital conflict discussions, in particular, trigger different autonomic reactions in husbands and wives has also been investigated. One study has shown that men listening to their wives' complaints had greater skin conductance than women listening to their husbands (Notarius & Johnson, 1982). Yet, Gottman & Levenson (1988) and Malarkey et al. (1994) did not find husbands' cardiovascular reactions during marital discussions were stronger than their wives'. However, Gottman & Levenson did find distressed husbands and wives to be more aroused than non-distressed spouses. Moreover, the more synchronized the spouses' levels of arousal were, the greater was their marital dissatisfaction. In addition, high arousal of both spouses before and during marital discussion was associated with increased marital dissatisfaction over a 3-year period (Levenson & Gottman, 1983). Emde (1991) also observed higher heart rates in both distressed husbands and wives than in non-distressed spouses during baseline and marital discussions. She also found higher systolic and diastolic blood pressures in distressed males than in non-distressed males. Again, however, the husbands did not react more strongly than wives. And in one study, wives actually exhibited greater cardiac reactivity than husbands (Gottman & Levenson, 1992).

Therefore, the hypothesis that husbands have higher cardiovascular reactions than wives during a stressful marital discussion has no support. By contrast, most studies have been highly consistent in showing that, regardless of sex, maritally distressed spouses have higher levels of cardiovascular reactions than non-distressed spouses.

It has been suggested that even though husbands and wives have comparable levels of arousal during conflict, arousal is less aversive for women than for men, either because women do not perceive their arousal or because they tolerate it (Levenson, Carstensen & Gottman, 1994). This would motivate husband's withdrawal and wives' pursuit of hostility. In a study of arousal during marital conflict, the authors observed that husbands' subjective on-line assessment of discomfort while watching their videotaped discussions was better synchronized with their concurrent physiological responses than wives' assessment. The authors speculated that women have difficulties perceiving visceral changes because they have been socialized to rely on external social cues to assess how they feel; whereas men have learned to focus on their autonomic reactions and withdraw contingently upon those perceptions. However, no studies have yet demonstrated whether the timing of physiological responses is synchronous with the timing of withdrawal reactions; that is, we do not know whether males' avoidance behaviors are concurrent to or contingent upon a rise in arousal. Other antecedent or concurrent factors may predispose both sexes to behave differently during high conflict, as we will see in the remainder of this chapter. Because the arousal–withdrawal connection remains speculative, its contribution to marital distress also remains speculative.

SEX-RELATED BEHAVIORAL DIFFERENCES BETWEEN MALES AND FEMALES LIVING IN SAME-SEX AND OPPOSITE-SEX COUPLES

To shed light on whether the demand/withdrawal pattern is specific to male–female interactions or characterizes any relationships, investigating same-sex relationships would be revealing. If it is true that males are more reactive than females to conflict in intimate relationships, and if it is true that these gender differences in stress reactions motivate males to withdraw from conflict and enable females to tolerate negative affect and pursue conflict discussions, then we should observe quiet and reconciling styles of conflict discussions among gay couples, and much confrontation among lesbian couples (Gottman, 1994). In this regard, researchers have begun to investigate negative affect management in same-sex couples, with special reference to the female demand/male withdrawal pattern.

Two recent observational studies have compared distressed and non-distressed heterosexual, gay and lesbian partners during a relationship conflict discussion (Arellano, 1993; Julien et al., 1995b). Both studies examined levels of conflict–hostility–demand behaviors, and levels of withdrawal behaviors. When data were analysed on the basis of sex, Arellano's observational findings did not show differences between gays and lesbians in the ways they communicated or handled negative affect. Gay individuals, for example, did not indicate a greater tendency than lesbians to distance themselves from potential conflicts, neither did lesbian females demonstrate a stronger propensity than gays toward pursuit of confrontation. In their observational study of communication patterns in 150 heterosexual, gay and lesbian couples, Julien et al. (1995b) found also that heterosexual and gay individuals did not withdraw more than heterosexual and lesbian females. Therefore, both studies suggest withdrawal reactions are not sex-linked behaviors, at least as it could be observed in a laboratory setting. In addition, both studies showed that distressed partners, regardless of sex, had higher levels of withdrawal and higher levels of hostility than the non-distressed partners. In the Julien et al. (1995b) observational study, and in Arellano's (1993) self-reports study, levels of these behaviors were not linked to partners' sexual orientation. So, those behaviors that have been pinpointed as components of distress in heterosexual marriages remain key components of relationship distress, regardless of the sex composition of the dyads.

In their comparison of heterosexual, gay and lesbian partners' behaviors, Julien et al. found that heterosexual wives were much more hostile and confronting than all the other partners (husbands, gays and lesbians). The findings suggest that some characteristics associated with heterosexual couples are more important than biological sex in accounting for females' negativity. For example, wives have different socialization than husbands and these differences may potentiate high conflict, as any social difference does (e.g. different cultures, different social classes, different religions). That may be less true of gay and lesbian couples in which the two partners have higher probabilities of having similar socialization backgrounds, as we will discuss later in this chapter. Wives' higher levels of hostility may also result from a clash between the maintenance of traditional allocation of responsibilities in marriage, and the increasing changes of women's responsibilities in the workplace. Thus, as compared with the particular issues that heterosexual partners may be currently facing, same-sex couples may have different patterns of roles. This question is further developed in the next section.

Overall, the only strong empirical evidence that has emerged from research focusing on the effects of biological constraints on communication is that relationship distress, and not sex, is the variable most consistently associated with autonomic arousal. As far as cardiovascular reactions have been assessed in heterosexual males, husbands do not react differently than wives, and if distressed heterosexual couples tend to exhibit dysfunction through the demand–withdrawal patterns, there is no evidence that autonomic reactivity motivates such a dysfunctional pattern. Research with same-sex couples also has failed to show that gay males use quiet and reconciling styles of conflict discussions, or that lesbians exhibit more confrontation. No physiological data have yet been collected with same-sex couples.

Given the current state of knowledge regarding the biological constraints on communication, the implications for assessment and intervention are that there is too little ground for designing couples interventions based on sex-linked differences in biological reactions during intimate communication. On the other hand, assessment may focus on determining connections between high levels of arousal and destructive communication patterns. Given the generally high levels of arousal in distressed partners during conflict discussions, a general recommendation would be to help partners to become more aware of their high levels of arousal, and to learn strategies for lowering their reactions, before engaging in any discussions related to a marital conflict (e.g. Markman, Stanley & Blumberg, 1994). For example, the use of relaxation techniques or of ground rules for setting times for conflict discussion within safer, low-heat contexts, is an essential step for enabling partners to listen to each other and engage in the further steps of relationship problem-solving (Markman, Stanley & Blumberg, 1994).

It should be noted that there is considerable debate about other biological constraints on communication behavior. For instance, research on temperament and emotion have suggested a genetic heritability factor in determining individual differences in negative affect expressivity and gender-stereotypic traits, independent of biological sex (for reviews, see Goldsmith, 1993; Brody, 1993). Some research also has shown that gender-role orientation explains part of the variance in physiological responses to stress (Polefrone & Manuck, 1987). There is also a need for examining the sociocultural contexts of husbands' and wives' individual differences in their behavioral reactions to marital stress.

LEARNING TO DEMAND AND WITHDRAW: THE SOCIALIZATION OF RESPONSES TO RELATIONSHIP CONFLICT

Sex-differentiated socialization forms a major component of our understanding of sex-related differences in marital interaction. Even though some researchers favor theories based on biological constraints, researchers generally agree that social forces shape and maintain gender differences in expressions of affect, behavioral responses to emotional stress and responses to others' emotions (for reviews, see Brody & Hall, 1993; Maccoby, 1990; Manstead, 1992). From a functionalist point of view, emotion-related behaviors are shaped to serve adaptive purposes. Thus, the husbands'/wives' differences in emotional expression and communication are likely to be rooted in adaptation to their different social goals (Brody, 1993). In the past, socialization agents (parents, sex-segregated peer groups, schools, mass media, etc.) reinforced different behaviors for males and females in order to equip them for their traditional social roles. Although changes toward more commonalities between men's and women's social goals are visible, men are still expected to acquire the necessary resources to support their families. Socialization, therefore, prepares males for this "breadwinner" role by reinforcing and modeling behaviors that are perceived as important for mastering and gaining access to necessary resources. Among some of these behaviors are competitiveness, assertiveness, autonomy, self-confidence, instrumentality and the tendency not to express intimate feelings (e.g. Maccoby, 1990).

Females, on the other hand, are socialized in ways that foster their abilities to maintain the emotional aspects of family life. Studies on the socialization of emotions suggest that expression of feelings through words and facial expressions are encouraged in girls and discouraged in boys, and some researchers even argue that girls' earlier development of language may foster the verbal mode of emotional expression in girls and make them more accountable to others for internal feelings (Brody, 1993). Boys' later development of language would allow consolidation of non-verbal modes of expressing emotions (physiological, behavioral acting-out). Brody's hypothesis is in line with Tannen's (1990) argument that men and women come from different sociolinguistic subcultures which have different rules for engaging in conversation. In this view, males and females have difficulties resolving their conflicts because there are misunderstandings that come from their differences in the use of language (see Noller, 1993). Brody's hypothesis is also consistent with the fact that across the life-cycle, women are seen as the socio-emotional specialists and connecting agents of the family. Thus, nurturance, emotional expressivity, verbal exploration of emotions, and warmth are behavioral repertoires that are reinforced and modeled for females (Noller, 1993).

While complementarity between females' and males' socialization may provide benefits for opposite-sex couples in their negotiation of traditional roles in marriage, it may be at the root of marital problems as well. That is, women, on the one hand, who have learned to value emotional connections, to explore the facets of emotions with language and maintain social contacts through talking, will use that repertoire with husbands. Men, on the other hand, who have learned to maintain independence, and to resort to action and competition, and who have learned that negative affect can be detrimental to goal achievement, may distance themselves from interactions which require emotional exploration. A wife's attempt at connecting may be threatening to her husband's sense of autonomy, and a husband's attempt to disconnect from his wife may be threatening to his wife's needs. Thus, each partner may be approaching the relationship with the very behaviors that are threatening to the other, thus setting the stage for increased negative escalation and marital distress (Noller, 1993; Tannen, 1990; White, 1989). Vivian & Heyman (in press) also argue that communication Nohlems in violent marriages often are the unintended outcomes of gender-based struggles.

One issue of potential importance, on which there is little data but much speculation, is the possibility of gender differences in experiencing intimacy. In line with the above interpretations, Markman & Kraft (1989) have suggested that women often experience intimacy by verbal self-disclosure of affect, whereas men experience intimacy by sharing activities together. It is argued that both methods of experiencing intimacy are legitimate forms of closeness, but that the differences in socialization in experiences of intimacy may make it difficult for heterosexual couples to develop common senses of intimacy.

However, the communication differences between husbands and wives are not necessarily universally specific to men and women, as has been suggested already by studies of same-sex couples (Arellano, 1993). There is also accumulating evidence that gender role is associated with the expression of affect, regardless of biological sex. For example, Brody & Hall (1993) reviewed several studies outside the marital field and found that more feminine individuals, as defined by self-reports of stereotypic traits (e.g. nurturance), report more emotional expressiveness, more negative affect intensity, and more intimate self-disclosure than masculine individuals, regardless of biological sex. Likewise, observational studies have shown that people high in feminine traits are better encoders of non-verbal cues (Zuckerman et al., 1982). Studies that have compared the relative contribution of sex and gender roles to emotional expressiveness suggest gender roles contribute to more variations in emotional expressions than biological sex (Brody, Hay & Wandewater, 1990). Yet, it is still possible for gender traits to be genetically inherited, regardless of sex (Brody, 1993).

Gender Roles in Heterosexual Couples and Marital Conflict Management

Researchers in the marital field also have investigated the links between gender role and negative affect management. They generally expect that husbands' and wives' differences in expressiveness and instrumentality (i.e. some of the skills of gender-related attitudes) would account for their differences in marital communication.

Several studies have found that masculinity and feminity traits are associated with marital adjustment (e.g. Baucom & Aiken, 1984; Baucom et al., 1990; Burger & Jacobson, 1979; Kurdek & Schmitt, 1986; Markman, Silvern & Clements, 1993). However, no consistent patterns have emerged. In different studies partners high in feminine, masculine or both (androgynous) traits, reported higher marital adjustment than the partners with other patterns (e.g. Baucom & Aiken, 1984; Markman, Silvern & Clements, 1993; Peterson et al., 1989). In other studies, partners high in feminine traits reported lower marital adjustment (e.g. Sayers & Baucom, 1991). One study found husbands' and wives' masculinity traits were associated with marital adjustment in opposite directions (Markman, Silvern & Clements, 1993).

Likewise, studies on the links between gender role traits and communication behaviors have not produced a coherent set of findings. For instance, in some studies, feminine and androgynous husbands and wives had higher levels of self-reported negative communication (Yelsma & Brown, 1985) and higher levels of observed negative behaviors (Sayers & Baucom, 1991) than masculine and undifferentiated spouses. Opposite to those findings, other studies found that feminine husbands exhibited less negative behaviors than the other types, and only husbands and wives low in feminine and masculine traits were likely to complain about their spouses' demands and withdrawal (Markman, Silvern & Clements, 1993). Thus, very little consensus has emerged concerning the contribution of gender traits to demand and withdrawal behaviors. To some extent, the use of different measures of gender traits, different measures of behaviors, and the use of samples of couples homogeneously low (Sayers & Baucom, 1991) or high (Markman, Silvern & Clements, 1993) on scales of marital satisfaction may explain the difficulties of arriving at a coherent picture. However, because the findings outside the marital field have been so consistent, the marital field would benefit from a programmatic effort at understanding the contribution of gender traits to demand and withdrawal behaviors, and to relationship satisfaction.

Gender Roles in Gays and Lesbians

Many researchers operate from the premise that gays and lesbians conform to the respective masculine and feminine gender identity. Researchers' predispositions follow as a consequence of society's expectations about traditional gender roles for males and females, and because little is known about gender roles in gays and lesbians. In addition, the lack of role models for gays and lesbians may make it less likely that they will adopt unconventional gender roles. However, current clinical literature suggests that gays and lesbians do not universally adhere to conventional male and female roles (Brown & Zimmer, 1986; Peplau & Cochran, 1990). The few studies that have investigated gender roles among gays and lesbians have supported role flexibility. Gays and lesbians are more likely than heterosexuals to describe themselves in terms of characteristics of the same gender as well as the opposite gender (Brown & Zimmer, 1986; Kurdek, 1987). For example, lesbians describe themselves as more instrumental than do heterosexual women, and gays describe themselves as more emotionally expressive than do heterosexual men (Spence & Helmreich, 1978). Likewise, emotional intimacy, a characteristic generally linked to femininity, has been found to be more important to gay men than to heterosexual men (Schwabish, 1990). Given the above findings, one wonders how strongly related gender roles are to communication behaviors and relationship satisfaction among same-sex couples?

Gender Roles in Gay and Lesbian Couples and Relationships Conflict Management

In a study of the association between gender traits and communication in gay and lesbian couples, feminine lesbian and gay partners exhibited the highest levels of conflict behaviors, such as hostility and confrontation (Arellano, 1993). Those findings are consistent with findings in heterosexual couples that adherence to feminine traits is associated with higher rates of conflict engagement (Sayers & Baucom, 1991; Yelsma & Brown, 1985). Moreover, lesbians ascribing to a feminine gender role were more likely to show high levels of dominance, denial of problems, invalidation and low problem-solving than partners high in masculine or androgynous traits. Gay feminine males did not show these tendencies, which suggests that sex moderates the association between feminine traits and negative behaviors. For both gays and lesbians, masculine traits were not associated with withdrawal.

Do lesbian couples have greater difficulties managing conflict when both partners are high in feminine traits, than when they both are high in masculine traits or opposite traits? Arellano (1993) examined gay and lesbian couples' behaviors as a function of the couples' combination of gender roles. Interestingly, she found that gay and lesbian couples, where one partner ascribed to a feminine and the other to a masculine gender role, exhibited higher levels of negative behaviors than couples in which partners ascribed to any other combination of gender roles. Moreover, the effect of the feminine/masculine combination was stronger in lesbian couples than in gay couples. Lesbians' self-reports of communication skills were consistent with these observations: feminine/masculine lesbian couples reported the highest levels of destructive communication and conflict management, and the lowest levels of constructive skills. They also reported the lowest levels of relationship satisfaction and relationship efficacy, and the highest levels of problem intensity, verbal and physical aggression.

It is possible that two lesbians, because they are women, each expect that her partner will be the perfect nurturer and provide emotional support, which a traditional husband may not be able to supply. However, given that one of the partners ascribes to a traditionally masculine gender identity, she may not be skilled at providing emotional nurturance to her partner. Thus, as in heterosexual couples, the partner with a feminine gender identity may push for emotional nurturance whereas her partner, who ascribes to a masculine gender identity, may react by pulling away, which may set into motion the demand/withdrawal pattern leading to negative escalation.

These findings are important because they suggest that opposite gender roles in a couple (and not their respective roles), are likely to lead to difficulties with communication and conflict management. Alternatively, couples sharing some commonalities in gender role (androgynous/feminine, androgynous/masculine, feminine/feminine, etc.) may have a greater facility for understanding each other and communicating.

It is important to note that the feminine/masculine gay couples in Arellano's study were less negative than the feminine/masculine lesbian couples. Thus, it may be that the associations between feminine traits, conflict behaviors and satisfaction may be different for males and females, although replications are necessary for firm conclusions.

Unfortunately, gender role was not measured in the second study comparing heterosexual, gay and lesbian couples (Julien et at., 1995b). However, the authors did examine the couples' patterns of communication. They assessed expressed anger within the couple, and the higher score was used to define a partner as hostile-dominant in his/her couple. The level of withdrawal of the other partner to the hostile-dominant person was used to define the couple's withdrawal tendency. Hostile/hostile, withdrawal/withdrawal, and withdrawal/hostile patterns were defined in a similar way, always choosing the within-couple higher score on the first component to identify the dominant, and using the reaction score of their partner to complete the pattern. Thus, in the heterosexual group, some husbands were the hostile-dominant person in their couple whereas some wives were the withdrawal-dominant person.

Comparisons of the three groups of couples showed no differences in the hostile/withdrawal, withdrawal/withdrawal, or hostile/hostile patterns in the heterosexual, gay and lesbian groups. These three patterns were insensitive to the sex composition of the dyads. It is important to note that all the patterns were more intense in the distressed couples within each sexual orientation, again confirming that people dissatisfied with their relationship exhibit higher levels of negative behaviors than their satisfied controls, whatever their sexual orientation.

However, a different picture emerged with the withdrawal/hostile pattern. Although the intensity of withdrawal was about the same in heterosexual withdrawal-dominants than in the gay withdrawal-dominants, the hostility responses of the partners were much stronger in the heterosexual group than in the gay group. In addition, the lesbian withdrawal-dominants withdrew less than the heterosexual and gay withdrawal-dominants, and their lesbian partners' responses were less hostile than the partners' in the two other groups. Therefore, the findings indicated that the partners reacted differently to withdrawal, whether they reacted to somebody of the same sex or somebody from the opposite sex, the reaction being the strongest when partners react to somebody of the opposite sex. This is consistent with Brody's (1993) work showing that the expression of emotions vary with the sex of the person who is the object of the feelings. It is possible that two male partners culturally share a common understanding of the self-protective motives of conflict avoidance, whereas opposite-sex partners do not share as much cultural background. That could explain why withdrawal from conflict discussion by one partner did not trigger as strong emotional reactions in the other partner as it did in heterosexual couples. A similar interpretation could be made of lesbians, although the lower levels of hostility to withdrawal among lesbians could as well be explained by the fact that the dominant-withdrawal lesbians did not retreat from conflict discussion as much as the heterosexual and gay withdrawal-dominants did.

Overall, what is the general picture emerging from the comparative studies between heterosexual, gay and lesbian couples, and what do they tell us about gender issues? First, not only do dissatisfied partners seem to lack the basic communication skills for managing their differences, but partners in distressed couples also show more rigidly gender-stereotypic behaviors, and less commonalities in their emotional expressions and behaviors, than the non-distressed couples. So far, this appears to hold true for both same- and opposite-sex couples. Therefore, individuals who ascribe to a traditionally rigid masculine or feminine gender role may be at higher risk for having distressed relationships, especially if their partners ascribe to opposite traits. This appears to hold true for males, as well as for females. We need to assess how much, in the long run, rigidity in gender role contributes to the development of relationship distress.

The findings presented above also suggest that, regardless of couples' levels of satisfaction, difficulties in communicating may arise whenever one encounters unfamiliar reactions, such as habits learned through socialization. Differences in communication are likely to be found in any couple, whatever its sex composition. However, because of the strong association between sex and gender traits in the history of socialization, heterosexual men and women may be more likely to engage in marriage as strangers.

Regarding the implications for assessment and intervention, we suggest that the assessment of gender role traits of the partners may be a useful step and a useful tool for intervening with couples. Assessing the degree of flexibility/rigidity in each partner within the couple may be done by using the California Psychological Inventory (CPI: Baucom, 1976). Likewise, interventions regarding gender roles may focus on helping partners to develop better flexibility. A first step may be to make partners aware of their gender traits rigidity and how it impacts on the relationship, such as the many ways it shapes their communication when they face relationship conflicts. Then, in a second step, it may be helpful to teach partners the skills that are associated with gender traits that they do not exhibit, and to make them aware of how the new skills modify their capacity to address relationship conflicts constructively.

DEMANDING AND WITHDRAWING: THE SOCIAL ROLES AND SOCIAL STATUS OF MEN AND WOMEN

According to social roles theories, the reason men and women have received different gender role socialization lies in the complementarity of their social roles in the Western culture, which assigns productive work and domestic-family-care work predominantly on the basis of sex (Bernard, 1982; Eagly, 1987). Despite much discussion of the demand–withdrawal pattern in relation to gender roles socialization, we know very little regarding the potential contribution of work responsibilities to the demand–withdrawal communication pattern.

An interesting set of findings suggests that current social roles, that is the types of occupations in which men and women are engaged on a daily basis, shape their affective experiences, which in turn generalizes to their intimate relationships. For instance, a few studies by Brody and her colleagues (Brody, 1993) have shown that men and women who had traditionally female occupations (e.g. nurse, teacher) and men who had more traditionally female household work (child care, cooking, laundry) reported more nervousness and fear of people than men and women doing fewer of these tasks. However, women performing traditionally male work showed the lowest levels of nervousness and fear. Another study revealed that husbands and wives who interacted more with their children as- cribed to more feminine traits and talked more as a couple than husbands and wives who interacted less with their children (Risman, 1987). If the influence of daily occupations on the affective experience generalizes to other settings, then it may well be that wives' high levels of expressiveness, and men's control over their emotions, stem as much from their current daily experiences within and outside the family as from their past socialization. For instance, wives dealing with infants' and toddlers' cries and affective outbursts several times a day and night could explain part of their tolerance for negative affect during marital discussion. Alternatively, husbands dealing daily with emotional control in the work setting may be less prepared to cope with emotional outbursts at home. Should husbands and wives change their respective roles, then different sets of relational skills could emerge.

In their study of couples' transition to parenthood, Cowan & Cowan (1988) showed that during the first year following the birth of a child, all couples shared less of the individual tasks and shifted toward a more gender-stereotypic and segregated allocation of tasks. In their studies with violent couples, Vivian & Heyman (in press) observed that gender-segregated allocations of tasks is often the matter over which the spouses fight. Whether an increased rigidity in gender- stereotyped daily roles determines the increasing salience of the demand– withdrawal pattern as marriage develops over time is still open to scrutiny (Markman, 1994). We have good reasons to suspect that a rigid division of social roles within the family creates problems when one partner is temporarily absent, ill or incapacitated, because the other spouse may find it particularly difficult to develop skills in areas which had been exclusively under the control of the absent or incapacitated spouse (e.g. household management, finances, cooking). If the occupational role influences the emotional functioning in the couple, then en- couraging social role flexibility would favor commonalities of experiences be- tween the partners, enhance their companionship and help them to adapt better to changes of conditions over time. We need to know more about potential longitudinal changes in patterns of couples' interaction over the lifespan of the marriage.

It is noteworthy that almost all of the research undertaken with heterosexual couples, including all the work cited in this chapter, is based on samples of people typically in their 30s with young primary and pre-school children. Whether the same demand/withdrawal pattern would be evident in couples with much older children, in dual-career families, in retired couples, and in various other points of the family life-cycle is unknown. For example, the higher levels of hostility found in heterosexual wives as compared to heterosexual men, gays and lesbians may be motivated by the particular burdens of heterosexual wives during the childbearing years. Childbearing is not as pervasive among same-sex couples, even though an increasing number of same-sex couples are currently having or adopting children (Patterson, 1992). A more contextual, lifespan development approach to couples' communication would tell us whether couples' life-cycle changes impact the process of their disagreements.

Equity and the Demand–Withdrawal Pattern

Women want more changes in their couples than men do, and that may be at the root of their higher levels of hostility (Christensen & Heavey, 1990; Heavey, Layne & Christensen, 1993; Margolin et al., 1983). Although researchers have focused on wives' frustrations concerning emotional communication, content analyses of marital conflict discussions in the laboratory have shown that, if some of the discussions bear complaints about lack of emotional closeness, many of them relate to husbands' investment in domestic responsibilities and child and family care and activities (Julien et al., 1995a). To what extent are the women's desires for husbands' changes determinant of the couples' demand–withdrawal pattern?

One study examined whether the demand/withdrawal pattern was more intense when the couples discussed a change wanted by wives, as compared to a change wanted by husbands (Christensen & Heavey, 1990). In line with previous studies of husbands' withdrawal from marital conflict, husbands withdrew more than wives in both situations. As expected, however, the wives' demand–husbands' withdrawal pattern was greater when the wives asked for changes than when husbands wanted the changes. As other authors have suggested, the different social status of men and women and the power differences between the sexes may contribute to the stereotypic pattern of conflict management in marriages (Christensen, 1988; Heavey, Layne & Christensen, 1993; Murphy & Meyer, 1991; Jacobson, 1983; 1989; Raush et al., 1974). Those authors speculated that husbands, who have better access to economic resources and have greater advantage in marriage than wives, may have nothing to gain from discussion with their wives. Avoiding negotiating with the wives may be more beneficial because their advantageous marital situation is not disrupted. On the other hand, for wives who are in a position of weakness, resorting to discussions, demands, complaints and pushes for changes may be the only ways to protect and enhance their position.

The contribution of marital power to the demand–withdrawal pattern has been assessed in a sample of 132 heterosexual couples (Turgeon, 1995). Power was measured on a decision-making scale for different areas of marital life (e.g. domestic work, financial decisions, children's education) and by spouses' levels of dependencies on each other, sacrifices for each other, perceived control over discussions, etc. The author expected that inequity in favor of husbands would be associated with husbands' withdrawal. Opposite to predictions, husbands' withdrawal was associated with inequity favoring the wives, not the husbands. Therefore, the idea that some husbands may withdraw because they do not want to disrupt an advantageous situation was not supported. Perhaps they may want to avoid a painful process from which they have nothing to gain. Therefore, husbands' withdrawal may be more complex than the above interpretation, as it could also be a helplessness reaction. In Turgeon's study, the two spouses reported that wives were more likely than husbands to win conflict discussions, wives reported having more control over their husbands than the other way around and being less dependent on the marital relationship than their husbands, even though most of the wives were to some extent economically dependent on their husbands. Further studies on the association between marital equity and demand–withdrawal may benefit from redefining marital power on the basis of emotional resources besides economic and status resources.

Overall, the above review suggests that segregated social roles may exacerbate communication difficulties, although little data has been collected on the impact of couples' inequity on couples' communication. For assessing partners' differences in social roles and inequity, we recommend the use of the Household Tasks Questionnaire (Krausz, 1986) and the Decision-making Scale (Harvey 1985). Intervention regarding social roles may focus on helping partners develop better flexibility. As in the case of gender traits, it may be helpful to make partners cognizant of the risk their relationship incurs by having segregated occupations, and to help them acquire occupational flexibility that would increase their capacity to relate to each other's emotional daily experiences and facilitate adaptation to potential changes in the family life-cycle.

CONCLUSION

Why sex-related differences exist in marital communication has emerged as a complicated question. Researchers have advanced a set of hypotheses used to organize the findings here, and the empirical evidence for those hypotheses has been examined.

Overall, the only strong empirical evidence that has emerged from research focusing on the effects of biological constraints on communication is that relationship distress, and not sex, is the variable that is most consistently associated with autonomic arousal. No physiological data have yet been collected with same-sex couples. Research suggests there are individual differences in cardiovascular stress reactions, and potentially there are genetically-based gender traits in emotional expression independent of sex. Given the current limitation in research on the physiological bases of men's and women's differences in communication, there is insufficient ground for designing couples interventions based on sex-based differences in biological reactions to relationship stress. In contrast, research on the biological constraints consistently showed high levels of arousal in both distressed husbands and wives during conflict discussions. We have recommended assessing arousal during communication in order to teach couples to pay attention to initial cues of arousal before they get too aroused to solve problems constructively. Intervention may help partners lower their cardio-vascular reactions before engaging in any discussions related to a marital conflict (e.g. Markman, Stanley & Blumberg, 1994). This could be accomplished, for example, by use of relaxation techniques or agreed-upon rules for setting conflict discussion times. These measures ensure that couples will discuss issues within safer, low-heat contexts, which is an essential first step for enabling them to reduce levels of anger and defensiveness. Only then may partners be ready to listen to each other and engage in further steps of relationship problem-solving.

Pronounced gender roles may increase the risk of communication problems in intimate relationships, as demonstrated by comparing opposite-sex with same-sex communication patterns, and by comparing opposite-gender-trait patterns with same-gender-trait patterns. This is true of any dyad, whatever its sex compo-sition. Some research also suggests that partners' social roles impact their emo-tional experience, and we have good reasons to believe that non-overlapping social roles create additional sources of misunderstanding in couples. The fact that heterosexual partners have a higher likelihood for being socialized differ-ently, and have current social roles that often do not overlap, may explain why the demand–withdrawal pattern has such a high prevalence in heterosexual cou-ples. It appears that heterosexual partners may have more grounds than same-sex couples for misunderstanding. Nevertheless, the pattern was also strong among same-sex couples, particularly lesbians. Partners high in opposite gender traits or partners who have non-overlapping social roles have to relate to unfamiliar situations and contexts as well as unfamiliar emotional reactions. Therefore, these partners are more like cultural strangers.

From a prevention and intervention point of view, we think that couples who are made aware that diverging gender traits and diverging social roles put them at higher risk for communication problems may come to understand the social and situational roots of their communication problems. This would decrease blame following these exchanges, and widen couples' perspectives on their rela-tionship problems. For instance, a couple in which the wife is planning to quit her job temporarily for child care could be made aware that their temporary diver-gent path might augment their differences and difficulties in relating to each other. They would understand that, under those circumstances, they may have to work harder on their relationship than when they both were invested in employ-ment, so that they do not inadvertently widen stylistic differences and exacerbate marital difficulties. That is, they need to prevent backsliding into rigid social roles if they want to be empathetic with each other's daily, segregated, emotional experiences.

Whether cognitive–behavioral therapy can be applied to the issues of gay and lesbian couples is an implicit question in much of the material reviewed. It is difficult to give a definite answer at this stage because of the lack of cognitively-oriented research on these couples. However, since cognitions are an integral part of intimate relationships, there is no reason to assume that cognitive dysfunctions do not impede communication in these couples. Because the associations between negative cognitions and marital distress seem to be stronger for wives than husbands, it is possible, though speculative, that negative cognitions impact differently on lesbian and gay relationships, or couples in which there is much contrast in gender-related traits.

We need to emphasize again that a further understanding of gender issues in couples' relationships would largely benefit from more context-sensitive research on couples' communication. Many of our earlier assumptions concerning sex-linked differences have been challenged with our observation of communication on same-sex couples. Those couples taught us that partners' expressiveness differences matter, and partners' different life contexts matter, not their sex.

REFERENCES

Arellano, C.M. (1993). The Role of Gender in Handling Negative Affect in Same-sex Couples. Unpublished doctoral dissertation, University of Denver, Colorado.

Baucom, D.H. (1976). Independant masculinity and feminity scales on the California Psychological Inventory. *Journal of Consulting and Clinical Psychology*, **40**, 876.

Baucom, D.H. & Aiken, P.A. (1984). Sex role identity, marital satisfaction and response to behavioral marital therapy. *Journal of Consulting and Clinical Psychology*, **52**, 438–444.

Baucom, D.H., Notarius, C.I., Burnett, C.K. & Haefner, P. (1990). Gender differences and sex-role identity in marriage. In T.D. Fincham & T.N. Bradbury (eds), *The Psychology of Marriage: Basic Issues and Applications* (pp. 150–171). New York: Guilford.

Bernard, J. (1982). *The Future of Marriage*. New Haven, CT: Yale University Press.

Brody, L.R. (1993). On understanding gender differences in the expression of emotion. In S.L. Ablon, D. Brown, E.J. Khantzian & J.E. Mack (eds), *Human Feelings* (pp. 87–121). Hillsdale, NJ: Analytic Press.

Brody, L.R., Hay, D. & Vanderwater, E. (1990). Gender, gender role identity and children's reported feelings toward the same and opposite sex. *Sex Roles*, **3**, 363–387.

Brody, L.R. & Hall, J.A. (1993). Gender and emotion. In M. Lewis & J.M. Haviland (eds), *Handbook of Emotions* (pp. 447–460). New York: Guildford.

Brown, L.S. & Zimmer, D. (1986). An introduction to therapy issues of lesbian and gay male couples. In N. Jacobson & A. Gurman (eds), *Clinical Handbook of Marital Therapy* (pp. 451–468). New York: Guilford.

Burger, A.L. & Jacobson, N.S. (1979). The relationship between sex role characteristics, couple satisfaction, and couple problem-solving skills. *American Journal of Family Therapy*, **7**, 52–60.

Christensen, A. (1987). Detection of conflict patterns in couples. In K. Hahlweg & M.J. Goldstein (eds), *Understanding Major Mental Disorder: the Contribution of Family Interaction Research* (pp. 250–265). New York: Family Process Press.

Christensen, A. (1988). Dysfunctional interaction patterns in couples. In P. Noller & M.A. Fitzpatrick (eds), *Perspectives on Marital Imteraction* (pp. 31–52). Clevedon: Multilingual Matters.

Christensen, A. & Heavey, C.L. (1990). Gender and social structure in the demand/ withdraw pattern of marital conflict. *Journal of Personality and Social Psychology*, **59**, 73–81.

Cowan, P.A. & Cowan, C. (1988). Changes in marriage during the transition to parent- hood: must we blame the baby? In M.L. Hoffman (ed.), *The Transition to Parenthood* (pp. 114–154). Cambridge: Cambridge University Press.

Eagly, A.H. (1995). The science and politics of comparing women and men. *American Psychologist*, **50**, 145–158.

Eagly, A.H. (1987). *Sex Differences in Social Behavior: a Social-role Interpretation.* Hillsdale, NJ: Erlbaum.

Emde, J.E. (1991). Marital Communication and Stress. Unpublished doctoral dissertation. University of Denver, Colorado.

Goldsmith, H.H. (1993). Temperament: variability in developing emotion systems. In M. Lewis & J.M. Haviland (eds), *Handbook of Emotions* (pp. 353–364). New York: Guilford.

Gottman, J.M. (1994). *What Predicts Divorce?* Hillsdale, NJ: Erlbaum.

Gottman, J.M. & Levenson, R.W. (1988). The social psychophysiology of marriage. In P. Noller & M.A. Fitzpatrick (eds), *Perspectives on Marital Interaction* (pp. 182–200). Clevedon: Multilingual Matters.

Gottman, J.M. & Levenson, R.W. (1992). Marital processes predictive of later dissolution: behavior, physiology, and health. *Journal of Personality and Social Psychology*, **63**, 221–233.

Gottman, J.M. & Carrère, S. (1994). Why can't men and women get along? In D.J. Canary & L. Stafford (eds), *Communication and Relational Maintenance* (pp. 203–229). San Diego, CA: Academic Press.

Harvey, L.K (1985). Power in Marriage: the Dynamics of Married Living. Unpublished doctoral dissertation, Florida State University.

Heavey, C.L. Layne, C. & Christensen, A.C. (1993). Gender and conflict structure in marital interaction: a replication and extension. *Journal of Consulting and Clinical Psychology*, **61**, 16–27.

Jacobson, N.S. (1983). Beyond empiricism: the politics of marital therapy. *American Journal of Family Therapy*, **11**, 11–24.

Jacobson, N.S. (1989). The politics of intimacy. *Behavior Therapist*, **12**, 29–32.

Julien, D., Gagnon, I., Hamelin, M. & Bélanger, I. (1995a). A comparison of conflict issues in gay, lesbian and heterosexual couples, Unpublished manuscript.

Julien, D., Markman, H.J. & Lindahl, K. (1989). A comparison of global and microanalytic coding systems: implications for future trends in studying interaction. *Behavioral Assessment*, **11**, 81–100.

Julien, D., Pizzamiglio, M.T., Chartrand, E. & Bégin, J. (1995b). An observational study of communication in gay, lesbian and heterosexual couples. Manuscript submitted for publication.

Komarovsky, M. (1962). *Blue Collar Marriage.* New York: Random House.

Krausz, S.L. (1986). Sex roles within marriage. *Social Work*, **31**, 457–464.

Krokoff, L.J. (1987). The correlates of negative affect in marriage: an exploratory study of gender differences. *Journal of Family Issues*, **8**, 111–135.

Kurdek, L.A. (1987). Sex role self schema and psychological adjustment in coupled homosexual and heterosexual men and women. *Sex Roles*, **17**(9/10), 549–562.

Kurdek, L.A. (1995). Predicting change in marital satisfaction from husbands' and wives' conflict resolution styles. *Journal of Marriage and the Family*, **57**(1), 153–164.

Kurdek, L.A. & Schmitt, J.P. (1986). Early development of relationship quality in hetero- sexual married, heterosexual cohabitating, gay, and lesbian couples. *Developmental Psychology*, **22**, 305–309.

Levenson, R.W., Carstensen, L.L. & Gottman, J.M. (1994). The influence of age and gender on affect, psysiology, and their interrelations: a study of long-term marriages. *Journal of Personality and Social Psychology*, **67**, 56–68.

Levenson, R.W. & Gottman, J.M. (1983). Marital interaction: physiological linkage and affective exchange. *Journal of Personality and Social Psychology*, **45**, 587–597.

Levenson, R.W. & Gottman, J.M. (1985). Physiological and affective predictors of change in relationship satisfaction. *Journal of Personality and Social Psychology*, **49**, 85–94.

Maccoby, E.E. (1990). Gender and relationships. *American Psychologist*, **45**, 513–520.

Malarkey, W.B., Kiecolt-Glaser, J.K., Pearl, D. & Glaser, R. (1994). Hostile behavior during marital conflict alters pituitary and adrenal hormones. *Psychosomatic Medicine*, **56**(1), 41–51.

Manstead, A.S.R. (1992). Gender differences in emotion. In A. Gale & M.W. Eysenck (eds), *Handbook of Individual Differences: Biological Perspectives* (pp. 355–387). Chichester, UK: Wiley.

Margolin, G., Fernandez, V., Talovic, S. & Onorato, R. (1983). Sex role considerations and behavioral marital therapy: equal does not mean identical. *Journal of Marital and Family Therapy*, **9**, 131–145.

Margolin, G. & Wampold, B.E. (1981). Sequential analysis of conflict and accord in distressed and non-distressed marital partners. *Journal of Consulting and Clinical Psychology*, **49**, 554–567.

Markman, H.J. (1994). Men and women in relationships: implications from a prevention perspective. In V.M. Follette (Chair), *Gender Issues in Couples Research*. Symposium conducted at the 28th Annual Convention of the Association for the Advancement of Behavior Therapy, San Diego, CA, November.

Markman, H.J. & Kraft, S.A. (1989). Men and women in marriage: dealing with gender differences in marital therapy. *Behavior Therapist*, **12**, 51–56.

Markman, H.J., Silvern, L. & Clements, M. (1993). Men and women dealing with conflict in heterosexual relationships. *The Journal of Social Issues*, **49**, 107.

Markman, H.J., Stanley, S. & Blumberg, S. (1994). *Fighting for Your Marriage*. San Francisco: Jossey-Bass.

Murphy, C.M. & Meyer, S.L. (1991). Gender, power, and violence in marriage. *Behavior Therapist*, **14**, 95–100.

Noller, P. (1993). Gender and emotional communication in marriage. *Journal of Language and Social Psychology*, **12**, 132–154.

Notarius, C.I. & Johnson, J.S. (1982). Emotional expression in husbands and wives. *Journal of Marriage and the Family*, **44**, 483–489.

Notarius, C. & Markman, H. (1989). Coding marital interaction: a sampling and discussion of current issues. *Behavioral Assessment*, **11**, 1–11.

Notarius, C.I. & Pellegrini, D.S. (1987). Differences between husbands and wives: implications for understanding of marital discord. In K. Hahlweg & M.J. Goldstein (eds), *Understanding Major Mental Disorders: the Contribution of Family Interaction Research* (pp. 231–249). New York: Family Process Press.

Patterson, C.J. (1992). Children of lesbian and gay parents. *Child Development*, **65**, 1025–1042.

Peplau, A.A. & Cochran, S.D. (1990). A relational perspective on homosexuality. In D.P. McWhirter, S.A. Sanders & J.M. Reinish (eds), *Homosexuality/Heterosexuality: Concepts of Sexual Orientation* (pp. 321–349). New York: Oxford University Press.

Peterson, C.D., Baucom, D.H., Elliot, M.J. & Farr, P.A. (1989). The relationship between sex role identity and marital adjustment. *Sex Roles*, **21**, 775–788.

Polefrone, J.M & Manuck, S.B. (1987). Gender differences in cardiovascular and neuroendocrine response to stressors. In R.C. Barnett, L. Biener & G.K. Baruch (eds), *Gender and Stress* (pp. 13–38). New York: Free Press.

Rands, M. (1988). Changes in social behaviors following marital separation and divorce. In R.M. Molardo (ed.), *Families as Social Network* (pp. 127–146). Newbury Park (CA): Sage.

Raush, H.L., Barry, W.A., Hertel, R.K. & Swain, M.E. (1974). *Communication, Conflict and Marriage*. San Francisco: Jossey Bass.

Risman, B.J. (1987). Intimate relationships from a micro-structural perspective: men who mother. *Gender and Society*, **1**, 6–32.

Roberts, L.J. & Krokoff, L.J. (1990). A time-series analysis of withdrawal, hostility, and displeasure in satisfied and dissatisfied marriages. *Journal of Marriage and the Family*, **52**, 95–105.

Rubin, L.B. (1983). *Intimate Strangers*. New York: Harper & Row.

Sayers, S.L. & Baucom, D.H. (1991). Role of feminity and masculinity in distressed couples' communication. *Journal of Personality and Social Psychology*, **61**, 641–647.

Sayers, S.L., Baucom, D.H., Sher, T.G., Weiss, R.L. & Heyman, R.E. (1991). Constructive engagement, behavioral marital therapy, and changes in marital satisfaction. *Behavioral Assessment*, **13**, 25–49.

Schaap, C. (1982). *Communication and Adjustment in Marriage*. Lisse, Pays-Bas: Swets et Zeitlinger.

Schaap, C. (1984). A comparison of the interaction of distressed and non-distressed married couples in a laboratory situation: literature survey, methodological issues, and an empirical investigation. In K. Hahlweg & N.S. Jacobson (eds), *Marital Interaction: Analysis and Modification* (pp. 133–158). New York: Guilford.

Schwabish, R.M. (1990). Power and Intimacy Motives of Males in Same-sex and Opposite-sex Dating Couples. Unpublished doctoral dissertation, Hofstra University.

Spence, J.T. & Helmreich, R.L. (1978). *Masculinity and Femininity*. Austin: University of Texas Press.

Tannen, D. (1990). *You Just Don't Understand*. New York: Morrow.

Terman, L.M., Buttenweiser, P., Ferguson, L.W., Johnson, W.B. & Wilson, D.P. (1938). *Psychological Factors in Marital Happiness*. New York: McGraw-Hill.

Turgeon, L. (1995). Le rôle du pouvoir conjugal dans le conflit de demande/retrait, l'ajustement dyadique et la satisfaction conjugale des hommes et des femmes [Marital Power, Demand/Withdrawal Pattern, and Marital Adjustment]. Unpublished doctoral dissertation, University of Laval, Quebec City, Canada.

Turgeon, L., Julien, D., Desmarais, D., Chartrand, E. & Bégin, J. (1992). Observation of the demand/withdraw pattern of interaction in distressed and non-distressed couples. Poster session presented at the 26th Annual Convention of the Association for the Advancement of Behavior Therapy, Boston, MA, November.

White, B.B. (1989). Gender differences in marital communication patterns. *Family Process*, **28**, 89.

Yelsma, P. & Brown, C.T. (1985). Gender roles, biological sex, and predisposition to conflict management. *Sex Roles*, **12**, 731–747.

Yogev, S. (1981). Do professional women have egalitarian relationships? *Journal of Marriage and the Family*, **43**, 865–871.

Zuckerman, M., DeFrank, R.S., Spiegel, N.H. & Larrance, D.T. (1982). Masculinity–feminity and encoding of non-verbal cues. *Journal of Personality and Social Psychology*, **42**, 548–556.

Vivian, D. & Heyman, R.E. (in press). Is there a place for conjoint treatment of couple violence? *In Session: Psychotherapy in Practice*.

Chapter 6

Husband Violence: Basic Facts and Clinical Implications

Amy Holtzworth-Munroe, Natalie Smutzler,
Leonard Bates and Elizabeth Sandin
Department of Psychology, Indiana University,
Bloomington, IN, USA

We begin this chapter with an example of a case that a marital therapist might confront. Ellen originally called requesting couples therapy but expressed many reservations, both about whether she could convince her husband to come in to therapy and about whether they should stay together. After several phone calls, she finally arranged an appointment which both spouses did attend. They were both in their early 30s, had been married 4 years (a second marriage for Ken) and had one child together (Ken had three children from his previous marriage who were living with their mother in another state). Ken was unemployed, while Ellen worked at a local fast food restaurant.

Their recent problems involved Ken's extreme jealousy of Ellen and fights following his accusations of her infidelity. He would accuse her of having affairs, which she denied vigorously. In addition, since losing his job, he had begun to monitor her activities—driving her to and from work, going shopping with her, and sitting in the restaurant where she worked so he could observe her interactions with customers and co-workers. Her complaints about his behavior had resulted in two physical fights. In one he had called her degrading names (e.g. "bitch", "whore") and thrown things around the room, scaring her tremendously and breaking various items. In the other, he had pulled out a knife and waved it around, making vague threats that someone would die if she didn't "stop fooling around". In that incident, she had taken her child and left, staying with her parents until he convinced her, a few days later, that he was sorry and would

Clinical Handbook of Marriage and Couples Interventions. Edited by W. Kim Halford and Howard J. Markman.
© 1997 John Wiley & Sons Ltd.

change; he pleaded that he loved her and couldn't live without her. This incident had occurred about 1 month before Ellen had called the therapist; since then, no violence had occurred.

Given the recent crisis, the therapist extended the first session to complete additional assessment of relevant issues. She found out that Ken had a history of violence against female partners and that his first marriage had ended in part due to his violence. In addition, Ken was currently engaging in a wide variety of psychologically abusive behaviors. He sometimes became drunk, which escalated these behaviors. He admitted to "anger" problems and was experiencing general psychological distress (e.g. depression, anxiety). Both Ellen and Ken said that Ken had never been violent toward their child, although the boy had probably witnessed some of their verbal fights. Recently, Ellen had been quite frightened of Ken's behaviors and was not sure that she wanted the relationship to continue.

How should a marital therapist conceptualize the case of Ellen and Ken? Is Ken's use of violence a couples issue or an individual problem? Is conjoint marital therapy appropriate? How is his use of other controlling and abusive tactics related to his use of violence? How do the current stressors in his life (e.g. unemployment) and his other psychological problems (e.g. substance abuse) relate to his use of violence? What is the impact of his aggression on Ellen and their child? Why has Ellen stayed with Ken? We will be addressing such issues in this chapter.

INTRODUCTION

As illustrated by the case of Ellen and Ken, husband violence is a serious problem. While battered women advocates have been actively working in this area since the 1970s, only recently has marital violence received attention from researchers and clinicians. As a result, many clinicians never received training in the assessment or treatment of marital violence and know little about this problem. For example, consider a study by Hansen, Harway & Cervantes (1991). They mailed over 300 marital and family therapists one of two case descriptions of couples seeking therapy; these were actual cases that involved husband violence. However, when asked to provide their case conceptualization and treatment plans, very few of the therapists identified violence or battering as a problem, and even fewer indicated that lethality was a concern, despite the fact that one of the cases ended in the husband's murder of the wife.

We believe that it is time to introduce clinicians to the problem of husband violence. Thus, this chapter was written to serve as a brief overview of what is known about husband violence and some of the resulting clinical implications. Most importantly, we hope that reading this chapter will help clinicians to be alert to the possible occurrence of husband violence in the lives of their clients. Our review of the empirical data and the conclusions we reach are derived from three more detailed reviews—Holtzworth-Munroe Bates, Smutzler & Sandin (in press), and Holtzworth-Munroe, Smutzler & Bates (in press). In this chapter, we cite a few relevant references for the points and conclusions we make; however, we refer the reader to our three detailed review papers for a more thorough citation of the available research.

PREVALENCE OF HUSBAND VIOLENCE

The most widely cited studies of the prevalence of husband violence have been conducted in the USA, and these are reviewed here. However, we wish to point out that these figures may not be directly generalizable to other cultures. Indeed, relative to other countries, the USA is very violent (e.g. higher rates of homicide); thus, the prevalence rates reviewed here may be higher than those reported in other countries.

In the USA, two nationally representative surveys conducted by Straus and his colleagues provide the most comprehensive estimates of the prevalence of husband violence. The first survey, conducted in 1975, involved face-to-face interviews with over 2000 married or cohabiting couples (Straus, Gelles & Steinmetz, 1980); the second survey, conducted in 1985, involved phone interviews with approximately 3500 couples (Straus & Gelles, 1986). Across both studies, it can be estimated that each year, one out of every eight men will be physically aggressive (e.g. grab, push, slap) toward his wife and 1.5–2 million women will be severely assaulted by their husbands.

Two studies have demonstrated that, in the USA, physical aggression (i.e. not usually severe violence) is also prevalent before marriage. In one study, McLaughlin, Leonard & Senchak (1992) questioned 625 couples applying for a marriage license. In the other, O'Leary et al. (1989) recruited 272 couples from the community and assessed them 1 month prior to marriage. Extrapolating from both these studies, it can be estimated that approximately one-third of men have used physical aggression toward their female partners in the year prior to marriage.

Of particular importance to the readers of this volume, recent US research has demonstrated that husband physical aggression is relatively common among couples seeking marital therapy. Holtzworth-Munroe et al. (1992) found that approximately 50% of couples seeking marital therapy, at various clinics in different parts of the country, reported husband physical aggression in their relationship. In a study of 132 couples attending a university marital therapy clinic, O'Leary, Vivian & Malone (1992) also found high rates of physical aggression, but only when they specifically asked couples about aggression. Only 6% of women and 1.6% of husbands spontaneously reported physical aggression as a major problem in their relationship. However, 44% of wives and 46% of husbands indicated that physical aggression had occurred when questioned during a personal interview, and this rate increased to 53% when information was gathered with a behavioral checklist of violent behaviors.

Once introduced in a relationship, it appears that physical aggression may continue. In the first longitudinal study of this topic, O'Leary et al. (1989) reassessed the couples in their study after marriage. They found that the past occurrence of physical aggression was a good predictor of future aggression; if a partner had been violent at one point in time, there was a 46–72% probability that s/he would also report having used violence at the next assessment. Similarly, Feld & Straus (1989) found that 42% of couples who had experienced one or two severe husband assaults at one time reported continuing husband violence a year later; this figure rose to 67% among couples who had reported three or more severe husband assaults at the first assessment.

Clinical Implications of the Prevalence Data

It is quite clear that physical aggression in marriage is a widespread phenomenon in the general population, among newlyweds, and among couples seeking marital therapy. Thus, therapists must be alert to this possibility and consider it in every case they see. The O'Leary, Vivian & Malone (1992) data also make it clear that a therapist can not assume that couples will spontaneously report the occurrence of marital violence. Rather, clinicians must directly assess for physical aggression. The O'Leary, Vivian & Malone (1992) findings also suggest that, when so doing, it is best to separate spouses and to ask detailed behavioral questions.

To do so, it will probably be more productive to ask about the occurrence of particular aggressive behaviors (e.g. pushing, slapping) than to ask general questions that label these behaviors in socially undesirable ways (e.g. "Have you ever been violent or abusive?"). In our experience, it is a rare couple who will identify themselves as "violent" or "battered" or "abusive" when questions are phrased in this manner. However, it is also not uncommon for these same couples to admit that they have "pushed" or "grabbed" or "slapped" one another when questions are focused on such specific behaviors.

Related to this, clinicians should consider using a behavioral checklist such as the Conflict Tactics Scale (CTS; Straus, 1979) to assess the occurrence of violence; the CTS does not ask about "violence" or "abuse" but rather about the occurrence of specific behaviors (e.g. pushed, grabbed, slapped). The CTS is the most widely used measure of marital violence; it was used in most of the studies reviewed above. The CTS was designed to assess behavior during marital conflict and lists approximately 20 behaviors, beginning with non-violent items (e.g. "discussed the issue calmly") and progressing to physically aggressive items (e.g. from "pushed/grabbed/shoved" to "used a knife or gun"). Each spouse indicates whether either partner has ever engaged in any of the listed behaviors and, if so, how frequently the behaviors have occurred in the past year.

Finally, it is important to note that once physical aggression is introduced into a marriage, the couple is at risk for further aggression. This is why therapists can not assume, neither should they allow their clients to convince them, that "it was a one-time thing—it won't happen again". Rather, therapists should explain to couples that we don't yet know how to predict which couples will cease their use of physical aggression vs. which couples will continue, or even escalate, their violence. Since we don't know how to predict this, but we do know that past physical aggression is the best predictor of future physical aggression, any couple who has experienced physical aggression should be asked to view the aggression as a serious problem in need of attention during therapy.

DIFFERING CONSEQUENCES OF HUSBAND VS. WIFE VIOLENCE

Prevalence data clearly demonstrate that both husbands and wives engage in physical aggression (e.g. O'Leary et al., 1989; Straus & Gelles, 1986). Similarly, most couples seeking marital therapy will likely report that both spouses have used physical aggression. We believe that violence on the part of either spouse is unacceptable and potentially dangerous. Indeed, husbands are sometimes injured, or even killed, by their wives; in addition, wives who use physical aggression toward their husbands may be at risk for also using physical aggression toward their children. Thus, clinicians can not ignore or minimize the occurrence of wife violence and must address this problem in treatment. However, as reviewed in Holtzworth-Munroe, Smutzler & Bates (in press), recent studies conclusively demonstrate that husband and wife violence are not equivalent.

First, husband violence results in more negative consequences than wife violence. Specifically, husband violence is more likely than wife violence to lead to physical injuries and negative psychological consequences in its victims. Women are more likely, in fact about twice as likely, to experience every level (i.e. mild, moderate, severe) of physical injury than men, even among couples in which both spouses are violent. In addition, in experiencing spousal violence, wives are more likely than men to suffer lowered self-esteem, depression and stress, and to report that spousal aggression had more of a negative psychological impact.

Second, husband and wife violence appear to differ in function and purpose. For example, men are more likely than women to report that their violence was used to control their partners, while women are more likely to report that their violence was committed in self-defense or for retaliation or expressive purposes (e.g. Hamberger, Lohr & Bonge, 1994). Also, Jacobson et al. (1994) found that husband and wife violence differed in that husband violence escalated in response to a wide variety of partner behaviors and, once begun, no partner behaviors successfully suppressed husband violence; the same was not true for wife violence.

Clinical Implications of Data on the Differing Consequences of Husband and Wife Violence

No violence is acceptable in relationships. Thus, both partners must be helped to stop their use of physical aggression. Indeed, when we see couples in which only the wife has used physical aggression, we still view violence as a problem and address it in therapy. However, the data also indicate that husband violence differs from wife violence. Thus, husbands should not be allowed to attribute their violence to their wives or to deflect attention from their use of violence by cross-complaining about wife aggression.

Clinicians should carefully assess the consequences of any physical aggression (husband or wife) that has occurred in a couple's relationship. In particular, physical injuries must be assessed, so that the level of violence occurring can be understood. In general, it is recommended that clinicians separate spouses to discuss the consequences of violence, so that spouses, particularly wives, will feel freer to be honest. A more thorough discussion of assessment issues is offered in Holtzworth-Munroe, Beatty & Anglin (1995).

When working with couples, we usually make it clear that no violence, on the part of either spouse, is acceptable. We let couples know that we are concerned with both partners' safety, and we recommend that both spouses learn methods for decreasing the risk of violence. However, we also recommend that clinicians be clear in their own minds that husband violence is a greater problem than wife violence and track the occurrence of husband violence and its consequences quite carefully.

PSYCHOLOGICAL ABUSE

While this chapter primarily addresses husband physical aggression, researchers and clinicians also have begun to recognize the potential importance of psychological abuse (see review in Holtzworth-Munroe, Smutzler & Sandin, in press). In general, psychological abuse is defined as non-physical behaviors that "represent an attempt to control, dominate, or gain power over one's partner" (Murphy & Cascardi, 1993; p. 90). Researchers have begun to delineate different types of psychological abuse. For example, Rodenburg & Fantuzzo (1993) assessed a broad range of behaviors including: sexual abuse (e.g. "forced you to do un-wanted sexual acts"); psychological abuse (e.g. "harassed you over the telephone"); and verbal abuse (e.g. "told you that you were stupid"). Shepard & Campbell (1992) assessed such varied behaviors as: isolation (e.g. "tried to keep you from something you wanted to do, like going out with friends"); threats (e.g. "used your children to threaten you, for example, said he would leave town with the children"); use of male privilege (e.g. "refused to do housework or childcare"); and economic control (e.g. "prevented you from having money for your own use"). Tolman (1989) found that the items on his measure (the Psychological Maltreatment of Women Inventory) loaded onto two factors—emotional-verbal abuse (e.g. "yelled and screamed at you") and dominance-isolation (e.g. "monitored your time and made you account for where you were").

Reviewing available data on the prevalence of psychological aggression, Murphy & Cascardi (1993) examined studies using CTS psychological aggression items (i.e. insulted or swore at your partner; did or said something to spite partner; stomped out of room, house or yard; sulked or refused to talk about an issue). The percentage of couples reporting the occurrence of these behaviors was 89–97% for couples seeking marital therapy (Barling et al., 1987), 67–87% for engaged couples (Barling et al., 1987), and 33–58% for participants in the Straus et al. national survey (Stets, 1990). These high percentages suggest that such behaviors may be normative in our culture, occurring in a wide variety of couples, including couples who have not used physical violence. Such figures raise the question of when these types of behaviors should be called "abusive".

It is often assumed that they are abusive when used within the context of a physically aggressive relationship. Consistent with this notion, husband-to-wife psychological abuse is highly prevalent among couples experiencing husband violence. Follingstad et al. (1990) found that 99% of the women in her sample who had been victims of physical abuse had also experienced emotional abuse from their husband. Other researchers, studying women at a battered women's shelter, found a correlation of 0.86 between physical abuse and psychological abuse measures (Hudson & McIntosh, 1981).

Not only does psychological abuse often accompany physical aggression but it usually occurs more frequently than physical aggression. Perhaps because of its frequency, the available data suggest that psychological aggression is very damaging, at least among battered women (e.g. Walker, 1979). For example, Follingstad et al. (1990) found that almost three-quarters of the women in her sample believed that husband emotional abuse had a more severe negative impact on them than husband physical aggression.

Research also suggests that psychological aggression is a risk marker, and perhaps a precursor, of husband violence. For example, in their longitudinal study of almost 300 newly-married couples, Murphy & O'Leary (1989) found that husbands' use of psychological aggression at 18 months after marriage significantly predicted husband physical aggression at 30 months after marriage.

Clinical Implications of Data on Psychological Abuse

The available data suggest that therapists should assess for the presence of psychological abuse in all marital therapy cases. Among couples who have not experienced physical aggression, the psychological abuse may be a risk factor for the onset of violence, and among couples already experiencing husband violence, it is almost certain that psychological aggression is also occurring. For all couples, the psychological abuse may be occurring frequently and may have a very negative impact.

Currently, at least seven measures have been used to assess psychological abuse and aggression: the Conflict Tactics Scale (CTS: Straus, 1979); the Index of Spouse Abuse Scale (ISAS; Hudson & McIntosh, 1981); the Wife Abuse Inventory (WAI: Lewis, 1985); the Spouse-specific Assertiveness Scale (SSAS; O'Leary & Curley, 1986); the Psychological Maltreatment of Women Inventory (PMWI; Tolman, 1989); the Abusive Behavior Inventory (ABI; Shepard & Campbell, 1992); and the Measure of Wife Abuse (MWA; Rodenburg &

Fantuzzo, 1993). For more information on each of these measures, the reader is referred to Murphy & Cascardi (1993). Unfortunately, none of the currently available measures has been widely adopted by marital violence researchers or clinicians. In addition, we do not recommend use of the CTS solely, since all of the CTS psychological abuse items apparently measure only emotional-verbal abuse, rather than other forms of psychological abuse (Tolman, 1989).

SOCIODEMOGRAPHIC CORRELATES OF HUSBAND VIOLENCE

As reviewed in Holtzworth-Munroe, Smutzler & Bates (in press), certain sociodemographic variables correlate with husband violence. First, age is negatively correlated with prevalence of husband violence—couples in their 20s and early 30s are at the highest risk and may be twice as likely as older couples to use physical aggression. Second, there is a negative relationship between socioeconomic status and husband violence. Couples in poorer, working class or blue-collar groups are more likely to experience husband aggression than couples in upper class or white-collar groups. Similarly, husband unemployment is a risk factor for marital violence. Third, the available data suggest that husband violence is more prevalent among minority groups (e.g. African-Americans and Latinos) than among Whites. However, these group differences often disappear when group differences in age and socio-economic status are controlled. In addition, more sophisticated research has demonstrated that there is large variability in rates of husband violence across different ethnic groups (e.g. Kaufman Kantor, Jasinski & Aldarondo, 1994, found that Cuban-Americans are virtually nonviolent while Puerto Rican men engaged in high levels of marital violence). Fourth, couples who are cohabitating are at greater risk, indeed double the risk, for husband violence than couples who are married (e.g. Stets & Straus, 1990).

Clinical Implications of Sociodemographic Correlates

Clinicians should be especially alert to the occurrence of violence among groups at risk for husband aggression—young men, unemployed men from lower socioeconomic groups, men cohabiting with their partners and, possibly, men from ethnic minority groups. Clinicians working with such groups should seek out training for dealing with husband violence. However, clinicians should also remain aware of the fact that husband physical aggression can occur in any group (e.g. older, wealthier, married); thus, marital violence should still be assessed among all couples.

In addition, therapists need to know that the relationship between these variables and husband violence has generally been explained with models of stress and negative life events. In other words, the sociodemographic correlates of husband violence reflect stressors (e.g. lower income, racism) and a lack of coping resources to deal with stressors that increase the risk of aggression. Thus, helping couples to decrease the stressors in their lives and to increase their resources may be useful, in addition to teaching them that violence is not an appropriate or acceptable response to stress.

HOW MARITALLY VIOLENT MEN DIFFER FROM NON-VIOLENT HUSBANDS

In their earlier review of the available research, Hotaling & Sugarman (1986) concluded that: "Men's violence is men's behavior. As such, it is not surprising that the more fruitful efforts to explain this behavior have focused on male characteristics" (p. 120). In most cases, the variables to be reviewed have been proposed as potential causes of marital violence. However, given the cross-sectional nature of much of this research, at the current time it is impossible to tell if such variables actually precede violence or whether they are the consequences of violence. This review is derived from Holtzworth-Munroe, Bates et al. (in press).

Psychopathology, Psychological Symptoms and Personality Disorders

The available data clearly indicate that, as a group, violent men evidence more psychological symptoms than do their non-violent counterparts (for references see Holtzworth-Munroe, Bates et al., in press). Relative to non-violent men, batterers score higher on measures of Axis I symptomatology, including depression; they have related psychological problems such as lower self-esteem. In addition, relative to their non-violent counterparts, violent husbands are more likely to evidence personality disorders, including antisocial tendencies and borderline personality organization.

Consistent with their tendency to borderline personality traits, violent men are sometimes found to be more preoccupied with, and overly dependent upon, their wives. Based on such findings, some researchers have theorized that violent men are very emotionally and interpersonally needy and that they use violence to prevent a spouse from leaving or as a result of intense anger arising from frustrated attachment needs (e.g. Dutton, 1995).

Researchers have consistently found that, relative to non-violent men, violent husbands experience high levels of anger and hostility. This is true not only on questionnaire measures of general anger and hostility, but also in response to simulated marital conflicts and during actual marital problem discussions with their wives. In addition, longitudinal data suggests that husbands' premarriage scores on an aggression scale (i.e. tendency to act angrily, argumentatively, and vengefully) predict later husband psychological aggression toward wives which, in turn, predicts later husband physical aggression (O'Leary, Malone & Tyree, 1994).

Researchers consistently find a positive relationship between marital violence and alcohol problems. Violent men usually have more alcohol problems, in both clinical (e.g. Stith & Farley, 1993) and community samples (e.g. Kaufman Kantor & Straus, 1987; Leonard & Blane, 1992). In addition, rates of husband violence are high among men in treatment for alcoholism (O'Farrell & Murphy, 1995).

Assertiveness, Communication and Problem-solving Skills

It has been proposed that maritally violent men lack social skills (e.g. Holtzworth-Munroe, 1992), primarily communication and assertiveness skills, so that they may resort to violence when they are unable to resolve marital conflicts successfully using other, more constructive, methods. Researchers examining this notion using questionnaire measures of *general* assertiveness have found mixed results (e.g. O'Leary & Curley, 1986). However, more consistent results are found when researchers examine deficits in *spouse-specific* assertiveness (i.e. assertiveness with one's partner)—violent husbands have difficulty relative to non-violent men (e.g. Rosenbaum & O'Leary, 1981). In recent work, researchers have begun to find that the skill deficits of violent husbands are particularly evident in *certain types of marital situations*, including conflicts in which the husband feels rejected by his wife or is jealous (e.g. Holtzworth-Munroe & Anglin, 1991).

Cognitions

Researchers have examined a variety of cognitions held by violent vs. non-violent men, based on the notion that the beliefs and attitudes men hold may be related to their use of physical aggression (see review in Holtzworth-Munroe, Bates et al., in press). It is assumed that a *positive attitude toward violence* will increase the risk of violence, and the available data do link men's positive attitudes toward violence to their use of physical aggression against female partners. It has also been hypothesized that holding *traditional sex-role expectations* regarding the acceptable behavior of women would increase the probability that a man would engage in spousal aggression. However, the data on this proposed link is mixed and inconclusive. In the only study of men's *relationship standards and assumptions* (i.e. the ways they think relationships should be), violent and non-violent men did not differ (Holtzworth-Munroe & Stuart, 1994).

Researchers have also studied the attributions offered by violent men. Holtzworth-Munroe (1992) hypothesized that a husband's *attributing negative intentions to wife behavior* would increase the risk of husband aggression, since a husband could then view his violence as a justified retaliation. Consistent with this notion, it has been demonstrated that maritally violent men were more likely than non-violent husbands to attribute negative intentions to their wives for her negative behavior in hypothetical marital conflicts (Holtzworth-Munroe & Hutchinson, 1993). In addition, the available data demonstrate that husbands frequently *blame their wives or external factors for their own violence*. Such attributions may serve to excuse or justify a man's violent actions.

Husband Violence as a Means to Assert Power

It has been hypothesized that husbands use violence to assert power and control over their wives. This issue has been researched using a wide variety of indices of power, as reviewed in Holtzworth-Munroe, Bates et al. (in press). Studies directly assessing husband's *desire for power* have produced mixed findings. However, research regarding husbands' *feelings of powerlessness* suggests that violent husbands may view themselves as powerless, implying that they use violence to regain a sense of control. In addition, some researchers have proposed that violent husbands actually do *lack various resources* (i.e. socio-economic status, communication skills—see review above). Other researchers have investigated *imbalances of resources and power between spouses*. Indeed, across these studies, it appears that a relative imbalance of decision-making power, favoring either the husband or wife, is related to marital violence, as is couple dissatisfaction with their decision-making balance. For example, Coleman & Straus (1990) found that male-dominated relationships had the highest conflict and the lowest consensus, and egalitarian relationships had the lowest conflict and highest consensus; however, no matter what the power relationship, the higher the level of consensus regarding that arrangement, the lower the level of conflict.

Stress

When stress is conceptualized at a broader, sociodemographic level (e.g. low income), the data demonstrate that stressors are related to husband violence (see review above). In addition, the available data demonstrate a relationship between marital stress (e.g. marital dissatisfaction) and husband violence (see review below). However, research findings are less clear when one examines the relationship between narrower, individual-level stressors (e.g. work stress, negative life events that are not marital) and husband violence (see Holtzworth-Munroe, Bates et al., 1995, for a thorough review). Sometimes, a relationship between a stressor (e.g. work stress) and husband violence is demonstrated (e.g. Barling & Rosenbaum, 1986); however, sometimes this link is not found (e.g. Pan, Neidig & O'Leary, 1994). Indeed, it is generally not believed that stress leads directly to violence, but rather that various factors exacerbate or buffer the relationship between stress and marital violence.

Family of Origin

Many researchers have examined the proposed link between family-of-origin violence and a man's use of violence against his own wife (i.e. the inter-generational theory of the cycle of violence). Most have done so by comparing violent and non-violent men's retrospective reports of violence in their childhood homes. No standardized measures have been used and a variety of types of violence (e.g. witnessing parental violence, experiencing child abuse) have been assessed. Despite such methodological weaknesses, the data generally lead to the conclusion that growing up in a violent home is a risk marker for husband violence (e.g. Sugarman & Hotaling, 1989; Kalmuss, 1984; see Holtzworth-Munroe, Bates et al., in press, for a review).

Clinical Implications of Data Regarding Maritally Violent Men

Clearly, maritally violent men may evidence a broad range of psychopathology. We recommend that therapists assess for Axis I psychopathology and related symptoms. For example, most researchers have used the Beck Depression Inventory (BDI; Beck et al., 1961) to assess for depression and the Buss–Durkee Hostility Scale (BDHI; Buss & Durkee, 1957) or Multidimensional Anger Inventory (MAI; Siegel, 1986) to assess for anger and hostility. We also recommend that therapists assess for personality disorder; the Millon Clinical Multiaxial Inventory (MCMI; Millon, 1983) is most commonly used in the research, although Dutton has also begun using the Borderline Personality Organization questionnaire (Oldham et al., 1985) to examine this particular type of personality disturbance.

In addition, it will be crucial for therapists to assess for the presence of alcohol and substance abuse problems among violent husbands. Measures of alcohol-related problems (e.g. the Michigan Alcoholism Screening Test, MAST; Selzer, Vinokur & Van Rooijen, 1975) and questions about the quantity and frequency of drinking are most commonly used. While no empirical research has been conducted to test this clinical assumption, it is generally recommended that men initially receive treatment for substance abuse before beginning treatment addressing their use of aggression.

The findings regarding the lack of communication and assertion skills among violent husbands suggests that once they have learned *not* to resort to violence to solve marital conflicts, aggressive husbands may not know what else to do. Similarly, the data relating couples' dissatisfaction with decision-making to husband violence is relevant. Both findings suggest that training in communication skills may eventually be necessary, as discussed in more detail in the chapter by Heyman & Neidig (this volume).

Data regarding men's cognitions suggest that cognitive processes need to be examined in therapy. In particular, cognitions that support or justify the use of violence (e.g. acceptance of violence, blaming one's violence on others, assuming that one's wife acted with hostile intent) must be addressed. The data regarding non-marital stressors suggest that men should not be allowed to attribute their use of violence to stress in their lives.

The family-of-origin data demonstrate a relationship between having grown up in a violent home and using physical aggression is one's own marriage. This connection allows the clinicians to make several useful points. For example, it suggests that, due to poor role modeling, men have "learned" to use violence to solve marital disputes; a logical corollary is that men can now "learn" not to use violence and that therapy will provide such training. In addition, some men can be motivated to stop their violence by being asked to remember the impact that parental violence had on them as children.

This brief review makes it clear that clinicians should be alert to a wide variety of possible correlates of husband violence and should consider assessing any, or all, of these variables among the men they see in therapy who are maritally violent. However, as outlined in the next section, it may be less important to look for broad correlates of husband violence than to consider how variables cluster together, allowing a meaningful theoretical understanding of particular types of violent husbands.

SUBTYPES OF MARITALLY VIOLENT MEN

Researchers have begun to demonstrate that samples of maritally violent men are heterogeneous, varying along many theoretically important dimensions. In Holtzworth-Munroe & Stuart (1994) we reviewed previous batterer typologies, and in Stuart & Holtzworth-Munroe (1995) we discussed the clinical implications of these typologies. Based on our review, we observed that violent husbands can be classified along three descriptive dimensions: (a) severity of marital physical aggression and related (e.g. psychological) aggression; (b) generality of violence (i.e. family only or extra-familial violence); and (c) psychopathology or personality disorders (i.e. minimal psychopathology vs. general dysphoria and borderline characteristics vs. antisocial personality disorder and psychopathy). Using these dimensions we proposed that three subtypes of batterers will emerge in future research.

Family-only batterers engage in the least severe marital violence, and their violence is generally restricted to their family. These men evidence little or no psychopathology. They have the most stable and satisfactory marital relationships. They also have the most liberal sex-role attitudes, generally do not have positive attitudes toward violence, and express the most remorse about their own violence. However, relative to non-violent men, they do have some communication skills deficits and some anger problems and are more likely to have experienced violence in their family of origin. Their violence may result from a combination of stress and marital stress, such that on some occasions their anger and lack of skills leads them to use physical aggression in marital conflicts. However, their lack of psychopathology, their positive attitudes toward women and their wives, and their negative attitudes about violence may keep their aggression from escalating. We hypothesize that these men are the most likely to be seen in marital therapy clinics. They may be the most likely to benefit from the available batterer treatment programs, which are generally rather short and involve anger management and communication skills training. They also are the most likely to benefit from conjoint marital therapy.

Dysphoric/borderline batterers engage in moderate to severe wife abuse. Their violence is primarily confined to the wife, although some extra-familial violence may be evident. This group is the most dysphoric, psychologically distressed and emotionally volatile. Men in this group may evidence borderline and schizoidal personality characteristics and may have problems with alcohol abuse; they have difficulty controlling their explosive anger. They may be highly dependent upon, and obsessively jealous of, their wives. They may have very negative attitudes toward women. Writing about this group, Dutton (1995) has suggested that their past traumatic experiences (e.g. abuse in family of origin) may lead to their intense anger and attachment needs, which when frustrated result in violence. We hypothesized that these men are likely to need more intensive psychotherapy and that marital therapy may not be appropriate, at least initially, given the fear their wives are likely to experience and the controlling function their violence has served. Given their psychological problems (e.g. dependency), some preliminary evidence suggests that these men may benefit from psychodynamic therapy approaches (e.g. Saunders, 1995).

Generally violent/antisocial batterers engage in moderate to severe marital violence. These men engage in the most extra-familial aggression and have the most extensive history of related criminal behavior and legal involvement. They are likely to have problems with substance abuse. These batterers are the most likely to have an antisocial personality disorder/psychopathy. They were exposed to the highest levels of family-of-origin aggression and were the most likely to have been involved in deviant peer groups and activities as youths. Their marital relationships are generally poor. They have conservative sex-role attitudes, feel little remorse about their violence, and view violence as acceptable. Their marital violence may simply be part of their general use of violence and their pattern of antisocial, criminal behavior. We have hypothesized that traditional psychotherapeutic interventions are the least likely to help these men. Perhaps legal and criminal justice interventions would be more useful.

Clinical Implications of Batterer Typologies

Available batterer treatment programs have not been designed to accommodate variability among clients; rather, standardized programs are uniformly applied to all men. Informally, however, researchers and clinicians have discussed relevant dimensions in making therapeutic decisions. For example, most agree that couples experiencing severe or frequent husband violence should not be seen in conjoint therapy. As another example, clinicians often express their frustration at working with batterers who have a criminal record and/or severe substance abuse problems. Beyond this type of speculation, little has been done to match individual batterers to treatments tailored for their needs. Similarly, our ideas have not yet withstood empirical testing and thus should be viewed only as hypotheses. Thus, at this time, we can only recommend that clinicians be sensitive to variability among batterers and begin to consider how to match treatment modalities and components to different types of violent husbands.

BATTERED VS. NON-BATTERED WOMEN

The application of diagnostic labels to battered women is controversial. Diagnostic labels are often applied in a manner which focus on the "shortcomings" of these women, implying that they are responsible for their own victimization (e.g. "masochism" or "self-defeating personality"). However, we believe that making therapists aware of the symptoms suffered by battered women should increase the chances that they will consider the possibility of marital violence in their female clients' lives, rather than treating these symptoms with standard psychotherapy. Thus, in this section we review what is known about the prevalence of various psychological symptoms among battered women (for a more thorough review, see Holtzworth-Munroe, Smutzler & Sandin, in press).

It should be stated that researchers and clinicians increasingly agree that the symptoms of battered women should be viewed as the *result* or *consequence* of abuse. However, given the cross-sectional nature of the available research, this assumption can not be proven at this time. Indeed, it is interesting that while researchers generally assume that the male correlates of husband violence are causally related to violence, they also usually assume that the female correlates of husband violence are consequences of the violence suffered. While definitive demonstration of this awaits future research (e.g. longitudinal studies), recently gathered data does provide tentative support for this assumption. For example, as reviewed below, researchers have begun to demonstrate that the severity of abuse experienced by a woman is related to the level of her psychological symptoms, suggesting a direct link between experiencing husband violence and developing psychological problems.

As reviewed in Holtzworth-Munroe, Smutzler & Sandin (in press), battered women, having experienced the trauma of husband violence, are at high risk for Post-traumatic Stress Disorder (PTSD), with such symptoms as hyperarousal, avoidance responses, numbing of general responsiveness, re-experiencing of the trauma, sleep and eating disorders, and recurrent nightmares. Indeed, across studies, it appears that PTSD may be diagnosed in one- to two-thirds of battered women (e.g. Gleason, 1993; Houskamp & Foy, 1991). Researchers also have found that the severity of exposure to violence, as well as the recency of the abuse, may be positively related to PTSD symptomatology (e.g. Astin, Lawrence & Foy, 1993). In addition, social support and positive life events occurring since the battering may be negatively correlated with PTSD symptoms, whereas negative life events and stressors (i.e. poverty) may be positively related to the level of PTSD severity (e.g. Astin, Lawrence & Foy, 1993).

Battered women also are at high risk for depression. Across studies, researchers find that approximately 50% of battered women report depressive symptoms (e.g. Andrews, 1995; Cascardi & O'Leary, 1992). Similarly, the majority of studies suggest that battered women have lower self-esteem than non-battered women (e.g. Aguilar & Nightingale, 1994; Cascardi & O'Leary, 1992).

Researchers have found that battered women lack problem solving (e.g. Launius & Lindquist, 1988) and coping skills (e.g. Finn, 1985), relative to non-battered women. Such skills can be viewed as potential mediators of the effects of violence; for example, battered women with good coping and problem-solving skills might be expected to show fewer negative psychological effects from battering than women without such skills.

Researchers have studied the cognitions of battered women based on the belief that how a woman thinks—about the violence, her relationship, and herself—may influence the steps she is able to take to deal with the violence in her life (see review in Holtzworth-Munroe, Smutzler & Sandin, in press). Researchers have found that the majority of battered women do not blame themselves for their husband's violence, but that many attribute the cause of the violence to their relationship (e.g. lack of agreement between spouses). In addition, abused women often assume that the violence will not occur again (see review by Holtzworth-Munroe, 1988). However, one study suggested that battered women who do make internal and stable attributions of blame (i.e. characterological self-blame) for husband violence are more likely than other battered women to suffer persistent depression after the violent relationship ends (Andrews & Brewin, 1990). Researchers have also investigated the relationship between traditional sex role beliefs of women and marital abuse, but the findings in this area are mixed and contradictory.

Clinical Implications of Data on Battered Women

The available data make it clear that battered women are at risk for a variety of psychological problems resulting from the violence they have experienced. In particular, they are at risk for PTSD and depression; clinicians should consider assessing for both problems among the battered women they see. As noted above, the Beck Depression Inventory might be used to screen for depressive symptoms. In addition, a few measures of PTSD are available, including the Structured Clinical Interview (SCID; Spitzer & Williams, 1985), the PTSD Symptom Checklist (Foy et al., 1984), and the Impact of Events Scale (Horowitz, Wilner & Alavarez, 1979).

In addition, the data on coping and problem-solving skills suggest that clinicians will need to work with battered women to help them identify resources to cope with their situation. Finally, clinicians should address women's attributions for the violence, explaining that the violence may continue without intervention and that each spouse is responsible for his/her own violent behaviors. Given that self-blame may be a risk factor for depression among battered women, women should be helped to move beyond these types of attributions and to consider other causes of the violence.

WHY BATTERED WOMEN STAY

This is perhaps the most frequently asked question in the area of husband violence. However, it may be a false question, since researchers actually find that a large percentage of battered women do leave their partners, although it may require more than one separation before women permanently terminate their abusive relationships. Okun (1986) summarizes this point:

> The process of separating and recohabitating by battered women is not an endless back-and-forth shuttle in static equilibrium, but a progressive process toward change in the violent relationship, including the termination of that relationship (p. 118).

In addition, as reviewed in Holtzworth-Munroe, Smutzler & Sandin (in press), there are many reasonable explanations for why a woman would not leave. First, it may not be safe for her to leave. For example, Saltzman & Mercy (1993) found that women who have terminated their relationship are still at risk for homicide by their former male partner. Second, several researchers have demonstrated that economic dependence is related to a woman's decision; women who have their own means of support are more likely to leave an abusive relationship. Third, it has been suggested that a woman may decide to leave a relationship based on:

> a sudden change in the relative level of violence. Women who suddenly realize that battering may be fatal may reject rationalizations in order to save their lives (Ferraro and Johnson, 1983; p. 331).

Fourth, it has been noted that many people, not just abused women, find it difficult to leave bad marriages; thus, staying in an abusive relationship may not be a "deviant" response. Summarizing some of these findings in his review of the literature, Strube (1988) concluded:

> These studies paint a picture of women who lack the economic means to leave an abusive relationship, are willing to tolerate abuse so long as it does not become too severe or involve the children, and who appear to be very committed to making their relationship last (p. 240).

Interestingly, researchers often act as though the woman is the only person participating in the process. For example, investigators rarely consider how help obtained by women may impact the choice of remaining or leaving the relationship. Similarly, researchers rarely consider the batterer's influence over his partner's decision to return to the relationship, despite the fact that the few existing findings suggest that batterers are active participants in this decision, attempting to persuade their wives to return to them.

Clinical Implications of Research on Why Women Stay

Most marital therapists need to be sensitive to the question of whether or not a battered woman wants to end her marriage; she should be given the safety and latitude to make this decision without undue pressure from either the batterer or the therapist. Thus, clinicians must be sensitive to the forces that may operate to keep a woman in a violent relationship and to the need for her to decide for herself about the relationship, based upon what is best for her and her children, not based upon fear or batterer persuasion. In individual interviews, therapists should ask each partner about their feelings regarding continuing in the relationship, the level of their commitment, and what steps have been taken toward relationship dissolution. Battered women who want to end their relationship should be given appropriate referrals (i.e. to legal services and services for battered women) to begin that process.

VIOLENT VS. NON-VIOLENT COUPLES

As reviewed in Holtzworth-Munroe, Smutzler & Bates (in press), researchers have recently begun to examine how violent and non-violent couples differ in various relationship processes. They have primarily studied marital communication patterns, comparing the marital interactions of violent and non-violent couples, and the relationship between marital violence and marital distress.

Marital Communication Patterns

Recently, researchers have compared the videotaped marital interactions of violent and non-violent couples discussing problems in their relationship. The two primary studies in this area, published at the time of this review, were conducted by Margolin, Burman and their colleagues (Margolin, John & Gleberman, 1988; Margolin, John & O'Brien, 1989; Margolin, Burman & John, 1989; Burman, John & Margolin, 1992; Burman, Margolin & John, 1993) and by Jacobson, Cordova and their colleagues (Cordova et al., 1993; Jacobson et al., 1994).

The Margolin group found that couples experiencing husband physical aggression were more negative than comparison couples; in particular, physically aggressive husbands expressed more offensive negative behaviors, more negative voice tone, and more hostile behaviors than verbally aggressive or withdrawing husbands. Physically aggressive couples were more likely than comparison couples to engage in reciprocal patterns of hostile affect in which angry/

contemptuous behavior by one partner increased the likelihood of the same behavior in the other partner. The Jacobson group similarly found that violent/ distressed couples showed a greater tendency to engage in negative reciprocity patterns than distressed/non-violent or happily married couples, and that violent couples displayed more aversive negative behavior, anger, contempt and belligerence.

Researchers have also studied communication by comparing violent and non-violent couples' self-reported descriptions of marital interactions. Doing so, Margolin and her colleagues found that aggressive couples engage in a negative reciprocity pattern. Lloyd (1990) similarly found that, relative to non-violent couples, violent/distressed couples reported using more verbal attacks, anger and withdrawal. Jacobson and his colleagues found gender differences in marital violence. While abused wives stated that they used violence only in response to husband violence or emotional abuse, violent men used violence in reaction to a wide variety of wife behaviors; moreover, once husband violence began, no wife behaviors could suppress the aggressive attack, and women were more fearful than men.

Clinical Implications of Communication Data

Examining either self-report or observational data, it appears that violent couples display high levels of anger, contempt, and belligerence. In addition, violent couples seem unable to exit negative interaction cycles once they begin. While both spouses in physically aggressive relationships engage in angry and hostile behavior, the data suggest that it is particularly important to focus on violent husbands.

These findings suggest that, at some point, communication skills training may be useful for violent couples. However, given the level of anger and hostility expressed by violent couples (particularly husbands) during marital discussions, along with the fear experienced by wives and the evident gender differences in power (e.g. Jacobson et al.'s (1994) findings), we do not recommend the introduction of communication training until the husband has been taught to control his behavior when angry. In other words, if the wife fears husband violence, then communication can not take place in a fair and egalitarian fashion—the wife can not be a full and equal partner in negotiating relationship change. Thus, therapists should first address husband violence, teaching anger management and other non-violent methods of dealing with anger, before beginning traditional communication and problem-solving training.

Marital Distress, Dissatisfaction, and Conflict

Across a large number of studies, researchers have consistently demonstrated a strong positive relationship between marital dissatisfaction/distress and husband violence. However, our review of the literature (see Holtzworth-Munroe,

Smutzler & Bates, 1995) also led us to offer several qualifiers to this general conclusion. First, not all couples experiencing physical aggression are maritally distressed. Second, marital distress may predict violence only in interaction with other variables. For example, husbands' alcohol use or hostility may only be related to husband violence among men who are maritally dissatisfied (e.g. Leonard & Senchak, 1993). Third, longitudinal data suggest that, among newly-married couples, declines in marital satisfaction may be a consequence, rather than a precursor, of husband physical aggression (e.g. Heyman, O'Leary & Jouriles, 1995). Fourth, longitudinal data also suggest that marital dissatisfaction may not directly predict husbands' use of physical aggression. Instead, marital dissatisfaction may predict husband psychological aggression which, in turn, predicts husbands' use of physical aggression (e.g. O'Leary, Malone & Tyree, 1994).

Clinical Implications of Data on Marital Dissatisfaction

Most couples seen by marital therapists are experiencing marital dissatisfaction and distress. Thus, these couples are at high risk for husband physical aggression and, as discussed above, therapists should routinely assess for the occurrence of physical aggression. However, husband violence can occur in non-distressed relationships also; thus, therapists working with relatively happy couples (e.g. marital prevention or enrichment programs) should also assess for physical aggression and address this problem in their programs. In addition, the data make it clear that therapists can not assume that as a couple's marital distress decreases over the course of therapy, their use of physical aggression will also decrease or end. Instead, physical aggression must be directly addressed.

EFFECTS OF MARITAL VIOLENCE ON CHILDREN

As noted in Holtzworth-Munroe, Smutzler & Sandin (in press), a series of research reviews on the effects of marital conflict and marital violence on children have been written (Davies & Cummings, 1994; Grych & Fincham, 1990; Markman & Leonard, 1985; Rutter, 1994; Reid & Crisafulli, 1990; Emery, 1982; McDonald & Jouriles, 1991; Rosenberg, 1987; Jaffe, Wolfe & Wilson, 1990; Emery, 1989; Fantuzzo & Lindquist, 1989; Rosenberg & Rossman, 1990). Previous reviewers have concluded that children from maritally violent homes suffer from a variety of problems, including externalizing (e.g. acting out) and internalizing (e.g. depression) behavior problems, along with impaired functioning in areas such as social competence and social problem-solving.

While marital violence has a generally detrimental impact on children, variables may mediate the specific effects. One set of factors that may mediate the effects of interparental violence include *dimensions of the interparental conflict*. Reviewers agree that negative outcomes for children are primarily explained by exposure to overt interparental conflict rather than marital distress or divorce. In addition, intense conflict, such as physical aggression, has a greater impact upon children than milder conflict. Similarly, the frequency of interparental conflict leads to increasingly negative outcomes for children. As a final example, the way in which interparental conflicts are resolved is a mediator of children's reactions to parental conflict—children are less upset by conflicts that are successfully resolved.

In addition, *child-related* factors may mediate responses to marital violence. For example, the gender of the child may make a difference—there is a tendency for boys to evidence more externalizing problems than girls. In addition, the child's age may affect the consequences of marital violence, although the available data do not allow definitive conclusions to be drawn about specific ages.

When considering the link between marital violence and children's problems, one must also consider the *related stressors* that often exist in maritally violent homes. For example, children, perhaps boys especially, in maritally violent homes are at risk for being abused themselves. In addition, as discussed above, maternal depression is a frequent consequence for battered women which may affect parental functioning. As a final example, one must remember that marital violence often occurs in homes with such sociodemographic stressors as low socio-economic status.

A number of mechanisms have been proposed to explain the association between marital conflict and children's behavior problems. A primary mechanism discussed is *modeling*, in which children directly learn aggressive behavior and the attitude that violence is appropriate. Alternatively, parental aggression may serve as a *stressor* that results in behavior problems for the child, especially when compounded by other stressors. In addition, the child's *cognitive and emotional processing* of the marital violence may mediate responses to marital aggression. For example, behavior problems may be an effect of increased negative emotional arousal from exposure to spousal abuse. In violent homes there is also a *deterioration of parent–child relations* (e.g. child abuse, substance-abusing father, depressed mother).

On the other hand, researchers have suggested that some factors may serve as buffers mitigating the negative repercussions of marital violence. According to Jaffe, Wolfe & Wilson (1990):

> In a review of the stressors of childhood, Garmezy (1983) found that the protective factors of the children could be divided into three categories: (a) dispositional attributes of the child (e.g. ability to adjust to new situations); (b) support within the family system (e.g. good relationship with one parent); and (c) support figures outside the family system (e.g. peers, relatives) (p. 73).

Clinical Implications of Data on the Impact of Marital Violence on Children

When a therapist finds that a couple has engaged in physical aggression toward on another, she/he must consider the consequences of that aggression on any children in the home. First, the possibility of child abuse should be considered and discussed, while alerting the couple of the therapist's legal obligation to report any suspected child abuse to legal authorities. Second, the parents should be informed of the fact that their marital conflict may be having detrimental effects on the children. Such information may help motivate the couple to recognize their violence as a problem and to agree to a no violence contract in therapy. In addition, such information can begin a discussion of any problems the couple is having with their children. Based on this discussion, the therapist can begin to assess whether the couple needs to address child issues in therapy (e.g. parent training, family therapy).

CASE EXAMPLE

In this section, we provide a brief case example (modified to protect client identity) to illustrate some of the issues raised in this chapter. Nancy and Mark were a Caucasian couple in their mid-twenties. Mark was seeking a graduate degree in science, and Nancy worked as a receptionist in another university department. They were not married but had been living together for 4 years; they had no children. They were seeking couples therapy because of poor communication, increased fighting and a lack of enjoyable time together, particularly since Mark had begun graduate school in the past year. They primarily complained about increasing difficulty in solving either minor or major disagreements and about "major arguments". Both spouses expressed a desire to work on their problems before they got worse, both felt committed to the relationship, and both discussed a future together (e.g. having children).

Since at least half of couples entering couples therapy have experienced husband physical aggression, the therapist considered the fact that Nancy and Mark may have had physical fights. Their relationship also involved several other risk factors for husband violence, including their young age, their communication problems, relationship distress, recent stressors, and the fact that they were cohabitating. However, as is often the case, neither spouse spontaneously complained of physical aggression. Thus, the therapist decided to assess directly for physical aggression.

When asked to describe their "worst fight", they mentioned a recent incident in which Nancy had tried to leave the room, Mark had held her (by the arms), she had slapped him, and he had then pushed her down on the bed before running out of the room. Further questioning, along with completion of the CTS, revealed another similar incident that had also occurred in the past year. The couple was disturbed by these incidents and Mark felt badly about his behavior; Nancy reported that she was not frightened of Mark since she knew he "wouldn't go any further". Thus, through a careful assessment involving both the CTS and interviews, the therapist was able to establish the severity and frequency of the violence, along with its consequences. Both Nancy's lack of fear and Mark's remorse were potentially good prognostic indicators.

The therapist sent each spouse home with a packet of standardized question-naire measures to complete. Upon receiving these back from the couple and scoring them, the therapist found that both spouses reported some depressive symptoms, neither had alcohol or drug abuse problems, and neither evidenced major psychopathology or personality disorders. Neither reported major prob-lems with anger. Their relationship satisfaction was in the distressed range but did not indicate extreme dissatisfaction. They reported that they both engaged in some psychologically abusive behaviors, generally the more commonly occurring behaviors (e.g. namecalling, swearing) rather than the more controlling or domi-nating types of behaviors (e.g. monitoring partner's whereabouts, telling the partner who they can and can not see). While Mark had once seen his father push his mother, neither was aware of any other family of origin violence. They both reported a fair amount of stress connected to Mark's graduate school (e.g. financial stress, lack of time together), and both agreed that their problems dated to Mark's returning to school.

Given these data, the therapist tentatively hypothesized that this was a couple whose violence had emerged in a context of stress (e.g. Mark's graduate school and resulting marital stress and dissatisfaction). She began to think of Mark as a "family-only" violent husband rather than as a man with a history of aggression and related psychological problems.

Despite this conceptualization, she let the couple know that she was quite concerned about their use of physical aggression and that stopping it must be the first goal of therapy. While somewhat surprised, the couple agreed to this goal. Thus, the therapist proposed that they begin a "two-pronged approach" (Holtzworth-Munroe, Beatty & Anglin, 1995), working on both anger manage-ment (e.g. time out), to stop the physical aggression, and communication/prob-lem-solving, to teach the couple more productive ways of resolving conflicts. The therapist made it clear that further violence would not be acceptable and would lead to a re-examination of the therapy contract, with possible referrals to a men's group for Mark and to a women's group for Nancy. The couple agreed and therapy began.

CONCLUSIONS

This chapter was written to introduce clinicians, particularly marital therapists, to the problem of husband violence. We first reviewed information regarding the prevalence of husband violence and introduced the reader to the related problem of psychological abuse. We then highlighted findings from the empirical litera-ture comparing violent and non-violent husbands and identifying subtypes of violent men. We then switched our focus to the wives in violent relationships, examining available data regarding the psychological difficulties experienced by battered women; we also addressed the often misinformed question of why battered women stay with their abusers. Next, we examined recent research comparing couples experiencing husband violence to non-violent couples, focusing on difference in marital communication and the role of marital distress. We ended by reviewing data regarding the impact of marital violence on children.

Throughout the chapter, we drew clinical implications from the available data, making suggestions for therapists based upon what is known about husband violence. However, we wish to end with a cautionary note, informing the reader that these clinical implications have not been empirically tested. While they are derived from what is known about husband violence, it can not be assumed that they have been tested or demonstrated to be effective. Indeed, we recommend that future researchers more directly test various methods of intervening with husband violence. In the meantime, we hope that by informing clinicians about this problem, they will use common sense and intervene in ways that will address the problem of husband violence, helping their clients to lead violence-free lives.

REFERENCES

Aguilar, R.J. & Nightingale, N.N. (1994). The impact of specific battering experiences on the self-esteem of abused women. *Journal of Family Violence*, **9**(1), 81–95.

Andrews, B. (1995). Bodily shame as a mediator between abusive experiences and depression. *Journal Abnormal Psychology*, **104**, 277–285.

Andrews, B. & Brewin, C.R. (1990). Attributions for marital violence: a study of antecedents and consequences. *Journal of Marriage and the Family*, **52**, 757–767.

Astin, M.C., Lawrence, K.J. & Foy, D.W. (1993). Post-traumatic stress disorder among battered women: risk and resiliency factors. *Violence and Victims*, **8**, 17–27.

Barling, J., O'Leary, K.D., Jouriles, E.N., Vivian, D. & MacEwen, K.E. (1987). Factor similarity of the Conflict Tactics Scales across samples, spouses, and sites: issues and implications. *Journal of Family Violence*, **2**, 37–54.

Barling, J. & Rosenbaum, A. (1986). Work stressors and wife abuse. *Journal of Applied Psychology*, **71**, 346–348.

Beck, A., Ward, C., Mendelson, M., Mock, J. & Erbaugh, J. (1961). An inventory for measuring depression. *Archives of General Psychiatry*, **4**, 561–571.

Burman, B., John, R.S. & Margolin, G. (1992). Observed patterns of conflict in violent, non-violent, and non-distressed couples. *Behavioral Assessment*, **14**, 15–37.

Burman, B., Margolin, G. & John, R.S. (1993). America's angriest home videos: behavioral contingencies observed in home re-enactments of marital conflict. *Journal of Counseling and Clinical Psychology*, **61**, 28–39.

Buss, A. & Durkee, A. (1957). An inventory for assessing different kinds of hostility. *Journal of Consulting Psychology*, **2**, 343–349.

Cascardi, M. & O'Leary, K.D. (1992). Depressive symptomatology, self-esteem, and self-blame in battered women. *Journal of Family Violence*, **7**, 249–259.

Coleman, D.H. & Straus, M.A. (1990). Marital power, conflict and violence in a nationally representative sample of american couples. In M.A. Straus & R.J. Gelles (eds), *Physical Violence in American Families: Risk Factors and Adaptations to Violence in 8145 Families* (pp. 287–304). New Brunswick, NJ: Transaction.

Cordova, J.V., Jacobson, N.S., Gottman, J.M., Rushe, R. & Cox, G. (1993). Negative reciprocity and communication in couples with a violent husband. *Journal of Abnormal Psychology*, **102**, 559–564.

Davies, P.T. & Cummings, E.M. (1994). Marital conflict and child adjustment: an emotional security hypothesis. *Psychological Bulletin*, **116**, 387–411.

Dutton, D.G. (1995). Intimate abusiveness. *Clinical Psychology: Science and Practice*, **2**, 207–224.

Emery, R.E. (1982). Interparental conflict and the children of discord and divorce. *Psychological Bulletin*, **92**, 310–330.

Emery, R.E. (1989). Family Violence. *American Psychologist*, **44**, 321–328.

Fantuzzo, J.W. & Lindquist, C.U. (1989). The effects of observing conjugal violence on children: a review and analysis of research methodology. *Journal of Family Violence*, **4**, 77–94.

Feld, S.L. & Straus, M.A. (1989). Escalation and desistance of wife assault in marriage. *Criminology*, **27**, 141–161.

Ferraro, K.J. & Johnson, J.M. (1983). How women experience battering: the process of victimization. *Social Problems*, **30**, 325–339.

Finn, J. (1995). The stresses and coping behavior of battered women. *Social Casework: The Journal of Contemporary Social Work*, **66**, 341–349.

Follingstad, D.R., Rutledge, L.L., Berg, B.J., Hause, E.S. & Polek, D.S. (1990). The role of emotional abuse in physically abusive relationships. *Journal of Family Violence*, **5**, 107–120.

Foy, D.W., Sipprelle, R.C., Rueger, D.B. & Carroll, E.M. (1984). Etiology of post-traumatic stress disorder in Vietnam veterans: analysis of premilitary, military, and combat exposure influences. *Journal of Consulting and Clinical Psychology*, **52**, 79–87.

Garmezy, N. (1983). Stressors of childhood. In N. Garmezy & M. Rutter (eds), *Stress, Coping, and Development in Children* (pp. 43–84). New York: McGraw-Hill.

Gleason, W.J. (1993). Mental disorders in battered women: an empirical study. *Violence and Victims*, **8**, 53–66.

Grych, J.H. & Fincham, F.D. (1990). Marital conflict and children's adjustment: a cognitive–contextual framework. *Psychological Bulletin*, **108**, 267–290.

Hamberger, L.K., Lohr, J.M. & Bonge, D. (1994). The intended function of domestic violence is different for arrested male and female perpetrators. *Family Violence and Sexual Assault*, **10**, 40–44.

Hansen, M., Harway, M. & Cervantes, N. (1991). Therapist's perceptions of severity in cases of family violence. *Violence and Victims*, **6**, 225–234.

Heyman, R.E., O'Leary, K.D. & Jouriles, E.N. (1995). Alcohol and aggressive personality styles: potentiators of serious physical aggression against wives? *Journal of Family Psychology*, **9**, 44–57.

Holtzworth-Munroe, A. (1988). Causal attributions in marital violence: theoretical and methodological issues. *Clinical Psychology Review*, **8**, 331–344.

Holtzworth-Munroe, A. (1992). Social skill deficits in maritally violent men: interpreting the data using a social information processing model. *Clinical Psychology Review*, **12**, 605–617.

Holtzworth-Munroe, A. & Anglin, K. (1991). The competency of responses given by maritally violent versus non-violent men to problematic marital situations. *Violence and Victims*, **6**, 257–269.

Holtzworth-Munroe, A., Bates, L.E., Smutzler, N. & Sandin, E. (in press). A brief review of the research on husband violence. Part I: Maritally violent versus non-violent men. *Aggression and violent behavior*.

Holtzworth-Munroe, A., Beatty, S.B. & Anglin, K. (1995). The assessment and treatment of marital violence: an introduction for the marital therapist. In N.S. Jacobson & A.S. Gurman (eds), *Clinical Handbook of Couple Therapy*, 2nd edn (pp. 317–339). New York: Guilford.

Holtzworth-Munroe, A. & Hutchinson, G. (1993). Attributing negative intent to wife behavior: the attributions of maritally violent versus non-violent men. *Journal of Abnormal Psychology*, **102**, 206–211.

Holtzworth-Munroe, A., Smutzler, N. & Bates, L.E. (in press). A brief review of the research on husband violence. Part III: Sociodemographic factors, relationship factors, and differing consequences of husband and wife violence. *Aggression and violent behavior*.

Holtzworth-Munroe, A., Smutzler, N. & Sandin, E. (in press). A brief review of the research on husband violence. Part II: The psychological effects of husband violence on battered women and their children. *Aggression and violent behavior.*

Holtzworth-Munroe, A. & Stuart, G.L. (1994). Typologies of male batterers: three subtypes and the differences among them. *Psychological Bulletin,* **116**, 476–497.

Holtzworth-Munroe, A., Waltz, J., Jacobson, N., Monaco, V., Fehrenbach, •• & Gottman, J. (1992). Recruiting non-violent men as control subjects for research on marital violence; how easity can it be done? *Violence and Victims,* **7**, 79–88.

Horowitz, M.J., Wilner, N. & Alvarez, W. (1979). Impact of event scale: a measure of subject stress. *Psychosomatic Medicine,* **41**, 209–218.

Hotaling, G. & Sugarman, D. (1986). An analysis of risk markers in husband to wife violence: the current state of knowledge. *Violence and Victims,* **1**, 101–124.

Houskamp, B.M. & Foy, D.W. (1991). The assessment of post-traumatic stress disorder in battered women. *Journal of Interpersonal Violence,* **6**, 367–375.

Hudson, W.W. & Mcintosh, S. (1981). The assessment of spouse abuse: two quantifiable dimensions. *Journal of Marriage and the Family,* **43**, 873–885.

Jacobson, N.S., Gottman, J.M., Waltz, J., Rushe, R., Babcock, J. & Holtzworth-Munroe, A. (1994). Affect, verbal content, and psychophysiology and the argument of couples with a violent husband. *Journal of Counseling and Clinical Psychology,* **62**, 982–988.

Jaffe, P.G., Wolfe, D.A. & Wilson, S.K. (1990). *Children of Battered Women.* Newbury Park: Sage.

Kalmuss, D. (1984). Intergenerational transmission of marital aggression. *Journal of Marriage and the Family,* **46**, 11–19.

Kaufman Kantor, G., Jasinski, J.L. & Aldarondo, E. (1994). Sociocultural status and incidence of marital violence in hispanic families. *Violence and Victims,* **9**, 207–222.

Kaufman Kantor, G. & Straus, M.A. (1987). The "drunken bum" theory of wife beating. *Social Problems,* **34**, 213–230.

Launius, M.H. & Lindquist, C.U. (1988). Learned helplessness, external locus of control, and passivity in battered women. *Journal of Interpersonal Violence,* **3**, 307–318.

Leonard, K. & Blane, H. (1992). Alcohol and marital aggression in a national sample of young men. *Journal of Interpersonal Violence,* **7**, 19–30.

Leonard, K.E. & Senchak, M. (1993). Alcohol and premarital aggression among newlywed couples. *Journal of Studies on Alcohol,* **11**, 96–108.

Lewis, B.Y. (1985). The wife abuse inventory: a screening device for the identification of abused women. *Social Work,* **30**, 32–35.

Lloyd, S.A. (1990). Conflict types and strategies in violent marriages. *Journal of Family Violence,* **5**, 269–284.

Margolin, G., Burman, B. & John, R.S. (1989). Home observations of married couples re-enacting naturalistic conflicts. *Behavioral Assessment,* **11**, 101–118.

Margolin, G., John, R.S. & Gleberman, L. (1988). Affective responses to conflictual discussions in violent and non-violent couples. *Journal of Consulting and Clinical Psychology,* **56**, 24–33.

Margolin, G., John, R.S. & O'Brien, M. (1989). Sequential affective partners as a function of marital conflict style. *Journal of Social and Clinical Psychology,* **8**, 45–61.

Markman, H.J. & Leonard, D.J. (1985). Marital discord and children at risk. In W.K. Frankenburg (ed.), *Early Identification of Children at Risk* (pp. 59–77). New York: Plenum.

McDonald, R. & Jouriles, E.N. (1991). Marital aggression and child behavior problems: research findings, mechanisms, and intervention strategies. *The Behavior Therapist,* **June**, 189–192.

McLaughlin, I., Leonard, K. & Senchak, M. (1992). Prevalence and distribution of pre-marital aggression among couples applying for a marriage license. *Journal of Family Violence,* **7**, 309–319.

Millon, T. (1983). *Millon Clinical Multiaxial Inventory, Manual*. Minneapolis, MN: Interpretive Scoring Systems.

Murphy, C. & Cascardi, M. (1993). Psychological aggression and abuse in marriage. In R.L. Hampton, T.P. Gollotta, G.R. Adams, E.H. Potter & R.P. Weissberg (eds), *Family Violence: Prevention and Treatment* (pp. 86–112). Sage: Newbury Park.

Murphy, C.M. & O'Leary, K.D. (1989). Psychological aggression predicts physical aggression in early marriage. *Journal of Consulting and Clinical Psychology*, **57**, 579–582.

Okun, L. (1986). *Woman Abuse: Facts Replacing Myths*. Albany: SUNY Press.

Oldham, J., Clarkin, J., Applebaum, A., Carr, A., Kernberg, P., Lotterman, A. & Hass, G. (1985). A self-report instrument for borderline personality organization. In T.H. McGlashan (ed.), *The Borderline: Current Empirical Research* (pp. 1–18); The Progress in Psychiatry Series. Washington, DC: American Psychiatric Association.

O'Farrell, T.J. & Murphy, C.M. (1995). Marital violence before and after alcoholism treatment. *Journal of Consulting and Clinical Psychology*, **63**, 256–262.

O'Leary, K., Barling, J., Arias, I., Rosenbaum, A., Malone, J. & Tyree, A. (1989). Prevalence and stability of physical aggression between spouses: a longitudinal analysis. *Journal of Consulting and Clinical Psychology*, **57**, 263–268.

O'Leary, K.D. & Curley, A.D. (1986). Assertion and family violence: correlates of spouse abuse. *Journal of Marital and Family Therapy*, **12**, 281–289.

O'Leary, K.D., Malone, J. & Tyree, A. (1994). Physical aggression in early marriage: prerelationship and relationship effects. *Journal of Consulting and Clinical Psychology*, **62**, 594–602.

O'Leary, D., Vivian, D. & Malone, J. (1992). Assessment of physical aggression against women in marriage: the need for multimodal assessment. *Behavioral Assessment*, **14**, 5–14.

Pan, H., Neidig, P. & O'Leary, D. (1994). Predicting mild and severe husband-to-wife physical aggression. *Journal of Consulting and Clinical Psychology*, **62**, 975–981.

Reid, W.J. & Crisafulli, A. (1990). Marital discord and child behavior problems: a meta-analysis. *Journal of Abnormal Child Psychology*, **18**, 105–117.

Rodenburg, F. & Fantuzzo, J. (1993). The measure of wife abuse: steps toward the development of a comprehensive assessment technique. *Journal of Family Violence*, **8**, 203–228.

Rosenbaum, A. & O'Leary, K.D. (1981). Children: the unintended victims of marital violence. *American Journal of Orthopsychiatry*, **51**, 692–699.

Rosenberg, M.S. (1987). Children of battered women: the effects of witnessing violence on their social problem-solving abilities. *The Behavior Therapist*, **4**, 85–89.

Rosenberg, M.S. & Rossman, B.B.R. (1990). The child witness to marital violence. In R.T. Ammerman & M. Hersen (eds), *Treatment of Family Violence: A Sourcebook* (pp. 183–210). New York: Wiley.

Rutter, M. (1994). Family discord and conduct disorder: cause, consequence, or correlate? *Journal of Family Psychology*, **8**, 170–186.

Saltzman, L.E. & Mercy, J.A. (1993). Assaults between intimates: the range of relationships involved. In A.V. Wilson (ed.), *Homicide: The Victim/Offender Connection*; Eastern Kentucky University: Anderson Publishing Co.

Saunders, D.G. (1995). Matching domestic violence offender types to treatment methods: evidence from an experimental comparison of two treatments. Paper presented at the 4th International Family Violence Research Conference, Durham, NH, July.

Selzer, M.L., Vinokur, A. & van Rooijen, L. (1975). A self-administered short Michigan Alcoholism Screening Test (SMAST). *Journal of Studies on Alcohol*, **36**, 117–126.

Shepard, M.F. & Campbell, J.A. (1992). The abusive behavior inventory: a measure of psychological and physical abuse. *Journal of Interpersonal Violence*, **7**, 291–305.

Siegel, J. (1986). The multidimensional anger inventory. *Journal of Personality and Social Psychology*, **51**, 191–200.

Spitzer, R. & Williams, J.B.S. (1985). *Instruction Manual for the Structured Clinical Interview for DSM-III-R (SCID)*. New York: New York State Psychiatric Institute.

Stets, J.E. (1990). Verbal and physical aggression in marriage. *Journal of Marriage and the Family*, **52**, 501–514.

Stets, J.E. & Straus, M.A. (1990). Gender differences in reporting marital violence and its medical and psychological consequences. In M.A. Straus & R.J. Gelles (eds), *Physical Violence in American Families: Risk Factors and Adaptation to Violence in 8145 Families* (pp. 151–166). New Brunswick, NJ: Transaction.

Stith, S.M. & Farley, S.C. (1993). A predictive model of male spousal violence. *Journal of Family Violence*, **8**, 183–201.

Straus, M.A. (1979). Measuring intrafamily conflict and violence: the Conflicts Tactics (CT) Scale. *Journal of Marriage and the Family*, **41**, 75–88.

Straus, M.A. & Gelles, R.J. (1986). Societal change and change in family violence from 1975 to 1985 as revealed by two national surveys. *Journal of Marriage and the Family*, **48**, 465–479.

Straus, M.A., Gelles, R.J. & Steinmetz, S.K. (1980). *Behind Closed Doors: Violence in the American Family*. Garden City, NJ: Doubleday.

Strube, M.J. (1988). The decision to leave an abusive relationship: empirical evidence and theoretical issues. *Psychological Bulletin*, **104**, 236–250.

Stuart, G.L. & Holtzworth-Munroe, A. (1995). Identifying subtypes of maritally violent men: descriptive dimensions, correlates and causes of violence, and treatment implications. In S.M. Stith & M.A. Straus (eds), *Understanding Partner Violence: Prevalence, Consequences, and Solutions*.

Sugarman, D.B. & Hotaling, G.T. (1989). Violent men in intimate relationships: an analysis of risk markers. *Journal of Applied Social Psychology*, **19**, 1034–1048.

Tolman, R.M. (1989). The development of a measure of psychological maltreatment of women by their male partners. *Violence and Victims*, **4**, 159–177.

Walker, L.E. (1979). *The Battered Woman*. New York: Harper & Row.

Chapter 7

Racial, Ethnic and Cultural Issues in Couples Therapy

Arthur C. Jones* and Christine M. Chao**
*Department of Psychology, University of Denver, and
**Private Practice, Denver, CO, USA

Issues of race, ethnicity and culture have received increased attention by practicing clinicians in recent years, and there has been a corresponding proliferation in clinically-oriented writings addressed to these issues, particularly in the USA (e.g. Boyd-Franklin, 1989; Comas-Díaz & Greene, 1994; Gibbs & Huang, 1989; McGoldrick, Pearce & Giordano, 1982; Pinderhughes, 1989; Sue & Sue, 1990; Vargas & Koss-Chioino, 1992). In the specific arena of couples therapy, however, there has been a relative paucity of clinically-oriented scholarship. With the exception of a study by Ho (1990), most of the published work on culture and couples therapy has been limited to brief discussions of relatively circumscribed treatment issues. For example, there have been discussions of such issues as marital therapy with Ethiopian immigrants (Ben-David, 1993), the problems accompanying Black–White and other kinds of ethnic intermarriage (Davidson, 1992; McGoldrick & Preto, 1984; Pope, 1986), the issues arising in Jewish out-marriage (Gleckman & Streicher, 1990), the general dynamics of marriage across ethnic, national or religious boundaries (Clulow, 1993), and specific cultural considerations in strategic marital therapy (Ross, 1987). In contrast, the current chapter addresses a wide variety of racial, ethnic and cultural issues that are relevant to clinical work with couples, issues that previously have not been discussed together in one source. We also provide a sketch of significant treatment considerations and strategies. While space limitations preclude the kind of in-depth exploration that is still lacking in the clinical literature, we hope to provide practicing clinicians with at least a basic orientation to major clinical issues. We also hope that our chapter will motivate clinicians to continue to expand their own understandings and approaches. To this end, we have at-

Clinical Handbook of Marriage and Couples Interventions. Edited by W. Kim Halford and Howard J. Markman.
© 1997 John Wiley & Sons Ltd.

tempted to include references to key articles and books to which clinicians can refer for more comprehensive discussions of many of the issues we have touched on only briefly in our chapter.

WORKING DEFINITIONS: KEY CONCEPTS FOR THERAPISTS

The terms *race*, *ethnicity* and *culture* have been used inconsistently and sometimes interchangeably in the clinical literature. We want to outline our own working definitions of these and a few other terms so that our usage throughout the chapter will be clear.

Ethnicity is perhaps the most difficult to define. We like the definition offered by Monica McGoldrick (McGoldrick, Pearce & Giordano, 1982, p. 4), who describes ethnicity as "a sense of commonality transmitted over generations by the family and reinforced by the surrounding community. It is more than race, religion or national and geographic origin. It involves conscious and unconscious processes that fulfill a deep psychological need for identity and historical continuity".

Sometimes ethnicity overlaps with race (as in North Americans of African descent), sometimes with religion (as in certain adherents of the Jewish faith) and sometimes with nationality (as in such countries as Poland and Italy). However, these associations with race, religion and nationality are certainly not universal, as illustrated by the recent widely publicized ethnic strife in Rwanda and in the nation states comprising the former Yugoslavia, where racially homogeneous groups are nonetheless sharply divided by ethnic differences with intense and complicated histories. The defining marker for ethnicity is the idea of a group of people who consider themselves strongly connected by shared history, experiences and values, usually going back several generations.

Ethnic identities can change over time, across generations or even within a single generation, often in response to shifting social prejudices and oppressions (Bhavnani & Phoenix, 1994). People can also traverse multiple ethnic identities within a relatively short timespan. A woman born in India, for example, may think of herself as "Indian" in her home country, "Black" while living in London, and "woman of color" when she migrates to the USA (Mohanty, 1995). Relationships between partners in an intimate relationship may therefore undergo sequential changes as a function of the ethnic identities that both partners adopt in the various specific environments in which they live and work.

Culture, in our usage, is a set of attitudes, behavior and values that constitute the bonds that tie members of a particular ethnic group together. In other words, culture is the psychological and interpersonal currency through which members of an ethnic group interact. When operating within one's own ethnic community, culture is usually unconscious and simply taken for granted. For example, a Japanese man living in Japan may take for granted the expectation that affection is not displayed openly in public, even between spouses. However, the same man may become uncomfortably conscious of his cultural assumptions when he becomes involved in a dating relationship with a American with a different set of expectations, who falsely interprets her partner's reticence in public as an indication of lack of interest in the relationship.

Acculturation is the process by which a person migrating to a new geographic location assumes the values and behavioral patterns of the new culture. The process of acculturation is often quite complex and multi-layered. Acculturation issues play a major role in many intimate relationships.

Race is a set of phenotypic markers by which people are categorized by the larger society. Physical appearance features (including especially skin color, eye shape and hair texture) have typically constituted the defining markers of a particular racial group. However, the assignment of people to racial categories is influenced strongly by social and power issues (Pinderhughes, 1989). One example is the case of "mixed race" individuals, who are often forced into one or another racial category, neither of which reflects accurately their biological heritage (Camper, 1994; Chao, 1995b; Root, 1992, 1995; Russell, Wilson & Hall, 1992). Until very recently, for instance, the "one drop" rule was applied to North Americans with any trace of black heritage. That is, if a person had even "one drop" of black blood (i.e. if any black biological relative could be identified, no matter how remote), the person was considered to be black (Russell, Wilson & Hall, 1992). Obviously this makes no sense biologically, but it illustrates the strong social meanings and stigmas that often accompany racial categorization.

Race and *racial identity* frequently become synonymous with *ethnicity* and *ethnic identity*, because individuals with certain physical appearance features share a common experience of social oppression and therefore have a history of living together in isolated communities where originally non-existent ethnic ties have been developed and nurtured over long periods or time. The most dramatic example is the ethnically diverse African peoples who were enslaved involuntarily in North America in the seventeenth, eighteenth and nineteenth centuries. Their common experience in slavery was on factor that contributed to the emergence of a new ethnic community of people, known today as African-Americans, with a distinctive and cohesive culture (Jones, 1993; Levine, 1977; Stuckey, 1987).

In addition to race, culture and ethnicity, *power* is also an important concept, since economic and social power are frequently distributed according to ethnic and racial membership (Pinderhughes, 1989). Gender and sexual orientation are also status markers: Heterosexual women, lesbians and gay men have distinctively lower social status in most Western societies than heterosexual men (Collins, 1990; Greene & Herek, 1994). Other important status markers include age, socio-economic class and religious affiliation (Pharr, 1988). In order to be healthy psychologically, members of low-status groups must develop effective strategies for coping with experiences of *external oppression* (i.e. personal, cultural and institutional forms of prejudice and discrimination) (Jones, 1991; Pinderhughes, 1989).

The above defined terms denote key issues that should become a part of the working knowledge of any therapist engaged in work with couples. As Monica McGoldrick points out in the introduction to her classic book on ethnicity in family therapy (McGoldrick, Pearce & Giordano, 1982), ethnic and cultural issues are often active even for couples and families who are not from clearly "ethnic" background. McGoldrick argues that this is especially true in the USA, where many people who are racially White are influenced strongly (albeit sometimes unconsciously) by ethnic values and beliefs from a country (or countries) of origin that have been passed down through several generations in a quiet but nonetheless influential way.

COMMON BARRIERS AND IMPEDIMENTS TO HEALTHY RELATIONSHIPS

Although ethnic and cultural dynamics certainly have the potential to enrich intimate relationships, there are many ways in which these issues can create serious problems for couples who are unaware of or unprepared for their influence. Three common problems are: (a) discrepant levels and kinds of ethnic identifications; (b) ignorance or denial (in one or both partners of the significant impact of ethnic/cultural differences and/or external oppression); and (c) discrepant ideas about coping with external oppression. We should mention that we view these kinds of impediments as operative in a wide variety of circumstances in which cultural issues can be salient, including: international relationships (Cahill, 1990; Clulow, 1993), interethnic or interracial relationships (Clulow, 1993; Crohn, 1995; Davidson, 1992; Ho, 1990; Mathabane & Mathabane, 1992; McGoldrick & Preto, 1984; Pope, 1986; Reddy, 1994; Richard, 1991), interfaith relationships (Clulow, 1993; Cowan & Cowan, 1987; Crohn, 1995; Gleckman & Streicher, 1990; Spickard, 1989), arranged marriages (Blood, 1967), mail-order relationships and marriage (Cahill, 1990; Glodave & Onizuka, 1994), and relationships within a single ethnic community (Billingsley, 1992; Boyd-Franklin, 1989; Willie, 1985). As we discuss barriers and impediments to healthy relationships and, later, supports for healthy relationships, we will try to give some examples that cut across some of these varied kinds of cultural and intercultural relationship circumstances.

Mismatched Ethnic Identifications and Acculturation Conflicts

Partners in intimate relationships sometimes differ greatly in the intensity and quality of their ethnic identifications, even when they have a common ethnic or racial heritage. This issue is easily missed by couples therapists if they are unaware of the complex process of ethnic identity development, especially in people who are members of oppressed or marginalized groups (Bernal & Knight, 1993; Cross, 1991; Helms, 1990; Phinney, 1995).

Fernando and Gloria were a Mexican-American married couple seen in therapy. A great deal of unresolved anger had existed in the relationship for several years. Much of the therapy consisted of helping the couple to identify sore spots in their daily interactions, particularly with respect to Gloria's experience of being overburdened with household responsibilities and Fernando's feeling of being unappreciated for his attempts to address his wife's concerns. While working on these issues seemed to result in considerable improvement in both partners' satisfaction with the relationship, a certain, amount of mild but persistent tension remained, and neither partner could identify the source of the tension.

At the beginning of one session, Fernando talked nervously about the fact that Gloria rarely seemed available for lunch with him because she was always going out with her "gringgo" (White American) co-workers at the government office where she worked as a manager. The therapist asked Fernando if he had feelings about Gloria's seeming ease with "gringos". This led to a first-ever discussion between Fernando and Gloria about their different levels of comfort with Whites. Although both were third-generation Mexican-Americans, and shared many similar values (emphasizing the importance of education, hard work and financial success), Fernando felt that an essential component of "success" was maintaining pride in Mexican heritage, which included finding ways to associate socially and professionally with other Americans of Mexican descent. While Gloria had always mouthed agreement with this value, in fact (as she admitted for the first time) she felt more comfortable with White friends and co-workers than she did with Mexican-Americans. Finally, she was able to say that she perceived identification with "that old country" as an interference in her attempts to "fit in" at her office and in their ethnically mixed neighborhood.

This conversation opened up a new and much more difficult direction of work in the therapy. While the tension in the relationship was somewhat diminished after a few sessions, it was by no means resolved. Nonetheless, the couple elected to terminate therapy, insisting that they felt confident of their ability to continue to resolve conflicts on their own. It was clear to the therapist, however, that the couple's continuing struggle around ethnic identity was still a potentially volatile issue, and he encourage then to return to therapy if they found themselves repeatedly frustrated in their talks with each other. Shortly after the last session, however, Gloria was transferred to a job in a different city and the couple was forced to move. Although they promised to keep in touch, the therapist did not hear from them and therefore was unable to determine if the ethnic identification issue was ever successfully resolved.

Ethnic identity is rarely problematic psychologically when one's self-identification is congruent with the cultural norms of family, friends, and associated. When there is a mismatch, however, there are few issues with more potential to create conflict and distress, especially if the mismatch occurs between intimate partners. As illustrated in the above case example, the problem is often exacerbated by the fact that ethnic identification differences can be subtle and (sometimes) unconscious as well. In situations where ethnic identifications are markedly different between partners, as in the case of some international and mixed-race marriages, the obvious and overt cultural clashes that ensue may paradoxically be less problematic in some cases because partners *expect* these conflicts to occur and are therefore more prepared to deal with them (Reddy, 1994).

Therapists who are involved in marital distress prevention programs, or other forms of intervention with couples in which cultural/ethnic mismatch issues are prominent, may want to incorporate at least one session in which couples are prepared for conflicts which may emerge when the partners differ in their ethnic identifications. The session(s) could also include some practice in conflict resolution centered around cultural issues. Such preparation may contribute significantly to the prevention of entrenched long-term relationship difficulties involving cultural clashes.

Closely related to the issue of mismatched identifications is the issue of differing processes of acculturation experienced by one or both partners in a couple. The issue of acculturation is very complex. In the past, it was common to think of acculturation in a bimodal fashion; one either was *or* was not acculturated, and the results were either negative *or* positive. One had achieved in the society and thus was "melted down" into the pot, *or* was not acculturated and therefore marginalized and neurotic. After many years of clinical experience, it is now clear to us that acculturation is on a continuum, and that it is more accurate to speak of degrees of ease in being bi-cultural in a variety of life spheres. As a therapist, one needs to know where each partner is on the continuum in these various spheres. Sometimes one's work as a therapist involves helping members of the couple to navigate more easily and consciously along this continuum. The work also may involve dealing with difficult gender/power issues. The following two vignettes illustrate vividly some of the complex, multilayered dynamics of acculturation. Space limitations preclude a detailed analysis of these vignettes. However, it should be clear that if these couples were in therapy, the therapist would need to facilitate a discussion of the various layers and contexts of acculturation, helping the couples to negotiate a satisfactory way of relating to one another that is acceptable to both partners. The negotiation process would also require the therapist to be sensitive to the differing, multilayered gender role expectations held by the male and female partners in each couple:

> A first-generation Chinese-American couple moves to a large Mid-western American city, where the husband attends graduate school and the wife works as an administrative assistant on the campus where her husband attends school. After living in the USA for a year, the wife's parents, who are Chinese diplomats, also move to the USA. Over time, increased marital conflict develops because of the husband's resentment of his wife's differing ways of behaving towards him and her father. For example, when he and his wife are visiting in her parents's home, the wife fixes tea for her father. In contrast, she never fixes tea for her husband. Moreover, she was recently involved in a major incident at work in which she refused to fix coffee for her boss, insisting that this was not in her job description. From the husband's perspective his wife's failure to fix him tea could be "excused" if she were consistent in all of her relationships with men. However, her insistence on denying him this marital privilege while at the same time being over-solicitous (from his point of view) with her father is not acceptable. He also views the recent incident on her job as totally shameful. He feels that his wife should either act completely Chinese (fixing coffee or tea for her boss as well as all the males in the extended family) *or* she should be completely American (fixing tea or coffee for neither). The wife views herself as in the process of becoming more American, but she also loves and respects her father and is aware that he would not understand any "strange"

American behavior on her part in relation to him. On the other hand, her friendships with female American co-workers have taught her to value the experience of being a "liberated" woman.

In a second couple, the husband is African-American and his wife was born in Japan, where they met shortly after World War II. They had lived in the USA since shortly after their marriage. One source of contention surfaced when the wife started to take night courses to obtain an advanced degree, which they had both decided would be beneficial. Both their children were now in their teens and the wife wanted to explore options for a better income, which would benefit the whole family. Her husband was very supportive and encouraging, but on the nights she had classes he would bring home bags of fast food hamburgers and French fries, and he and the children would eat them in the living room while watching television shows. The husband enjoined the children not to say anything to their mother because they all knew that she regarded fast food as an unhealthy, extravagant expense. She also felt that the living room was not the proper place for meals. Before long, the wife began to express doubts about continuing with school. Of course the secret meals had not remained secret for very long. The wife had suffered many deprivations in Japan during and after World War II. She had not spoken of these hard times in any great detail because she felt that to do so would be selfish and individualistic, especially in light of the fact that she had relatives who had perished in Hiroshima. What she did express was a petulant annoyance at what she labeled "American waste and extravagance". She was an impeccable homemaker and in this arena she felt sure of herself. Outside the home she was conscious of her accented English and the fact that she still made grammatical mistakes. Furthermore, she had not told her parents, who were back in Japan, about her enrollment in school, for fear they would criticize her and tell her she was not being a dutiful wife.

Ignorance or Denial of Difficult Ethnic/Cultural/Racial Issues

For people who are members of socially oppressed groups, the development of a psychological strategy for dealing with experiences of oppression is critical. Furthermore, each person has to work out some satisfactory balance between resistance to oppression, identification with one's culture of origin, and competence in navigating one's way in the majority culture, all within the context of a unique personal history (Jones, 1985, 1989). As a therapist, one must come to understand how each partner in the relationship has worked this out and to what degree problematic areas continue to exert their influence. This process of individual adaptation is even more complex in an intimate relationship, where partners have to develop both an individual adaptation strategy and a satisfactory way of dealing with each other's differences. Ignorance about, or denial of, difficult racial and cultural issues on the part of one of both partners very often contributes to significant relationship difficulties.

Joy and Carl, who had recently become engaged to be married, consulted a therapist because they found themselves embroiled in daily arguments about seemingly trivial issues, such as choices of social activities (movies, parties, etc.). Carl, who was a White American, was attracted to Joy, who was of mixed White and Black American heritage. Joy was very much like him in her interests and values.

The event that finally brought the couple into therapy was their receipt of an invitation to attend a wedding between a White man and woman, to be held in Birmingham, Alabama. Joy was worried about how she and Carl would be treated as an interracial couple if they attended the wedding in Birmingham, a city with a long history of overt hatred and discrimination against Black Americans. Carl regarded Joy's worries as "silly", since most of the (White) people attending the wedding would be friends of Joy and Carl. Joy was incensed at what she perceived as surprising ignorance and naïvety on Carl's part.

Over the first few therapy sessions it became very clear that despite Joy's seeming ease in interacting with Whites, she was acutely conscious of her mixed race identity and very fearful about situations (in both Black and White communities) involving the potential for being treated negatively because of her racial background. It was clear that Carl had expected race to be a non-factor in his relationship with Joy. As it became apparent that this could not be so, the conflict in the relationship rose to intolerable levels and Joy elected to end the engagement.

Many members of socially oppressed and marginalized groups are able to live full and adaptive lives, but not without conscious attention to such issues as ethnic identification and racism (Jones, 1985, 1989; Pinderhughes, 1989). When these issues are denied or actively avoided, by one or both partners in an intimate relationship, it frequently has serious negative consequences for the relationship. In the case of Carl and Joy, Carl was obviously in denial about the potential impact on their relationship of race and racism. However, it was also clear that Joy still had considerable work to do in establishing some level of comfort with her own ethnic identification issues. It was no accident that Carl had not understood Joy's feelings about race. In their relatively long courtship period, Joy had never discussed it with him. Conversely, Carl had never thought to ask Joy about race. Race and its implications were areas about which both felt uncomfortable. Therapists should be aware that this kind of psychological discomfort and avoidance is a common occurrence in societies where there is considerable oppression based on historical circumstances (e.g. the USA with its long history of slavery, discrimination against Blacks and oppression of its indigenous peoples; the UK and other European countries with their history of colonial exploitation; Australia with its history of mistreatment of its indigenous peoples).

Differences in Strategies for Coping with External Oppression

Even when neither partner actively denies or avoids racial and cultural issues, differences between intimate partners in their preferred strategy for coping with experiences of prejudice and discrimination can contribute substantially to relationship distress.

Joseph and Patricia were a Nigerian couple living in the USA with their two young children while Joseph was pursuing a graduate degree in business. They sought couples therapy following an argument during which Joseph had struck Patricia physically. The argument had begun late on a Saturday evening when Joseph had decided to cancel his presence at a family dinner to work on a school project. Patricia had confronted Joseph openly (something she had not done before) about his repeated decisions to emphasize school work over family life. Joseph was so shocked in reaction to his wife's confrontation (which, incidentally, was a violation of traditional Nigerian norms concerning husband–wife interactions) that he slapped her in the face (something he had never done before). Joseph was immediately sullen and remorseful and agreed to Patricia's suggestion that they seek marital therapy.

Very quickly during the first few sessions of therapy, as the therapist explored each partner's feelings about being away from home and living in a different culture, the salient issue emerged: Joseph was considering strongly the possibility of living in the USA on a permanent basis. However, in the year since he and Patricia had moved to the USA, he had become acutely aware of the intense climate of racial discrimination against people with Black racial heritage, including native Africans. He had decided that to cope with this reality, he would have to be twice as competent professionally as his White colleagues. This meant, for him, that he would also have to excel in his graduate program in business. In turn, this meant that he would have to sacrifice time and attention devoted to family life.

Patricia was not so keen on the idea of living in the USA, but was willing to consider it because her husband seemed to want it so much. However, she disagreed vehemently with Joseph's strategy for coping with American racism. From her point of view, one's family and intimate friends are the most effective counter to attacks on personal and professional integrity. She felt that Joseph's decision to neglect family in favor of work was therefore self-defeating. She said that she was quite willing to work on being more understanding of Joseph's anxieties about professional success if he would listen to what she was saying about the importance of family life; perhaps they could reach some compromise, she felt.

Joseph was adamant about the validity of his coping strategy and intensely determined to be the very best business professional he could be, even if it meant neglecting his relationship with his wife and children. He said (convincingly) that he now understood that it was important for a wife to be able to challenge her husband if there was something she felt strongly about. But although he made attempts to see things from Patricia's point of view, he became increasingly frustrated as the therapy progressed and he finally announced in the middle of one session that he was not going to continue the therapy. He stormed out of the office and yelled, "If you are not willing to understand the nature of racism in America, then, as much as it may hurt me, we will have to get a divorce".

The therapist was unsuccessful (even on the telephone a week after the session) in getting Joseph to reconsider his decision to terminate his involvement in therapy. Six months later, Patricia phoned to report tearfully that she and Joseph were getting a divorce. She returned the next week to begin individual therapy.

There were obviously a number of issues underlying the the inability of Joseph and Patricia to resolve their relationship difficulties. Not the least of these was Joseph's strong feelings about Patricia's violation of the traditional Nigerian male-dominance model of relationships. However, it was clear that the pressures and anxieties accompanying acclimation to a new culture, combined with Joseph's increasing awareness of the reality of racism in the USA, made it difficult for him to consider alternative strategies for coping with these pressures. Ultimately, the couple's failure to come to some mutually agreed approach to these issues resulted in a failed relationship. Failures like this reinforce the need to build into prevention programs (and into the very first few sessions of conventional therapy) some consideration, where appropriate, of the difficult acculturation issues a couple is likely to be dealing with. The essential intervention strategy is to assist the couple in labeling and anticipating conflicts that will arise as a part of the acculturation process. This may help to defuse the "sting" of such conflicts as they surface during the therapy process.

COMPLEX CULTURAL DYNAMICS WITHIN MARRIAGE: KEY DYNAMICS

We have outlined above some of the common ethnic and cultural factors that can serve as barriers to a healthy relationship. What are common ingredients that *support* a healthy relationship? We'd like to begin our approach to this issue with an exploration of a number of relationship situations in which cultural issues are salient. At the end of our discussion we will present an outline of some of the critical factors we believe to be important in supporting the healthy development of these kinds of relationships. As a heuristic aid, we will use the interethnic relationship story of Leonard Bernstein's (1957, 1985) *West Side Story* as a focal point of our discussion.

Each of us embodies cultural heritage in a variety of ways, some of which are often unconscious (McGoldrick, Pearce & Giordano, 1982). Culture presents a giant grid to which is attached all manner of things: how we speak, how we dress, how we eat and what we eat, the external identity we show to the world and the intimate identity with which we interact with our partner; how we conduct our marriages and funerals, how we name and raise our children, the professions we enter and where we live. When two people agree to be in relationship there is a kind of twisting and turning that takes place between each "cultural grid" as partners try to seek where they mesh, where they clash, what parts of their grid they will try to forget, let slip to the background, or try and cut off completely. This process has the psychological potential to be destructively explosive or to bring partners together in a transformative appreciation of the unique aspects each person brings to the relationship.

In the American musical *West Side Story* (Bernstein, 1957, 1985), María, newly arrived from Puerto Rico, is bitterly and repeatedly told:

> Forget that boy and find another,
> One of your own kind!
> One of your own kind!
>
> A boy like that will give you sorrow,
> You'll meet another boy tomorrow,
> One of your own kind!
> Stick to your own kind!

Here, however, the cultural grid is not strong enough to keep María, who is in love, from crossing ethnic boundaries that are epitomized by rival gangs fighting over "territory" in the streets of the West Side of New York City. The Sharks are newly arrived Puerto Rican immigrants. The Jets are White European Americans whose forebears were probably in America only a scant generation more than their rivals. Tony is a former member of the Jets. (Of course, each gang is a "family" embodying its own culture, race and ethnicity.)

West Side Story ends in tragedy, with María holding Tony as he dies. But what if Tony had lived and gotten married to María? His love song declares, "I've just met a girl named María, and suddenly that name will never be the same to me". The truth to that line encompasses the fact that María is *not the same* as Tony and any future relationship will have to include Tony's awareness and understanding of the reality of María's culture and his understanding of how his own culture will factor into their relationship. Racially, both María and Tony are White/Caucasian (although Maria is *ethnically* Puerto Rican, she is *racially* White; see "Working Definitions" at the beginning of the chapter), but their different ethnicities put them and their families poles apart. Or *do* they?

If María and Tony were in couples therapy, there are a number of issues they would have to explore with their therapist in order to increase the probability that their relationship would succeed: what are their similarities and differences and how are these dynamically experienced by Tony and María and the current culture of their place, time and country? Although we are not told anything about Tony's ethnic roots, perhaps he is a second generation Italian whose father, like María's, immigrated to the (mainland) USA. Perhaps both fathers do not speak English as their first language. Do Tony and María realize that unless María learns to speak unaccented English, many people will take away 20 or more IQ points from their estimation of her intelligence as soon as she opens her mouth? Looking back on the experiences of his father, perhaps Tony will have great empathy for his brother-in-law Bernardo, and realize that it was easier for María to obtain a job as a seamstress in a bridal shop than it will be for Bernardo to be hired in any job. Countries like the USA have always had an easier time giving jobs to its women of color, be they native-born, immigrant or refugee, than giving jobs to men of color (Collins, 1990; Pinderhughes, 1989). A sometimes unconscious and often not so unconscious fear of minority men gaining power frequently operates to ensure a "glass ceiling" is in place, even in upper-level jobs (Cose, 1993). Again, witness the significantly greater number of women of color compared to men of color who are visible in the national limelight of network television news broadcasting in the USA.

One also wonders what kind of wedding ceremony Tony and María will have: secular, religious, with a priest, a minister? What names will they give their children, what holidays will they celebrate, in what religion will they raise their children and what will be cooked for dinner and by whom? What is their conception of the role of husband and wife? How are disagreements and hurt feelings brought up and negotiated? Finally, one must add to this the interaction of socioeconomic status. It would be an interesting and revealing exercise to take María and Tony and, holding one person constant, vary the race, ethnicity and socioeconomic status of the other person. We could then list the issues that a therapist might want to explore with the couple if they came for marital therapy.

One can imagine any two sets of cultural or ethnic origins for María and Tony and what those origins would mean for them and for a therapist who would see them in therapy. It should be clear that in each case it would be critical for the therapist to be open to learning about their cultural differences and similarities and the ways in which these issues interact with the unique personal stories of each of the partners. For example:

What if María Were a Mail-order Bride from the Philippines?

In this scenario Tony would sing, "I just wrote to a girl named María". He would have picked María's picture from a "catalog" he had purchased featuring mainly pictures of Asian women desperate to correspond with American men and hoping the end result will be a long-distance courtship that will end in matrimony and a plane ticket to the USA (Glodave & Onizuka, 1994). The catalog would have endorsements such as:

> . . . I had a dream 20 years ago to meet and marry an Asian lady when I got tired of finding my American wife watching TV when I returned home. . . . the house in disarray, no dinner started. I divorced my American wife . . . met and . . . married the Asian lady of my dreams. . . . (Asian women) believe that husbands should be the head of the family. They do not believe in women's liberation. . . . Most of them are not materialistic; they are easy to please. When it comes to sex, they are not demonstrative; however, they are uninhibited. . . . They love to do things to make their husbands happy.

In this scenario Tony would probably be 15–20 years older than María. He would probably be divorced, lonely and with a history of emotionally disastrous relationships with American women. He probably has never had a relationship with an American-born woman of Asian ancestry. He fantasizes that he has met some combination of "geisha", "China doll" or "exotic oriental" who will conform to every stereotype ever conceived by Western society.

Women who put their pictures in such catalogs also hold a number of fantasies about the American man with whom they correspond. One element which is not a fantasy is the poverty they hope to escape. Often they have little formal education and fewer job opportunities. Some come from broken homes and some come from large, poor families where they migrate to cities and come to "hang out" around US military bases. If they come to the USA and marry a citizen, there is the possibility of sending for some family members or sending money home, thus fulfilling obligations of filial piety (Chao, 1992). Many of these women have already endured so much hardship that marriage to someone much older, ever at the risk of loss of country, culture, family and friends seems a small sacrifice (Glodava & Onizuka, 1994).

Problems occur when the fantasies that operate for both husband and wife evaporate and reality sets in. She hasn't married an American "Prince Charming" and he hasn't wed the Asian equivalent of the Playboy Bunny. Behind the fantasies is no real knowledge of each other's culture, no real commitment, no real understanding of one's own psychological make-up or one's partner. In situations like these a seemingly insignificant incident can often lead to emotional and physical abuse.

Women who are caught in such marriages seldom reach out for help. They fear their husbands, who often threaten to deport them. They do not want to endure the shame and "loss of face" of a failed marriage. Culturally they have been taught to never go outside the family with problems. However, they have no family in their new country and therefore no place to go for help. If María, the mail-order bride and her husband Tony do come in for therapy, a reasonable goal might be to find a way for them to strip away their mutual fantasies to determine if there is in fact a true relationship that can be developed. If not, the therapist may be most helpful by assisting them in achieving an amicable separation.

CRITICAL FACTORS IN THE DEVELOPMENT OF HEALTHY RELATIONSHIPS

Recognition of the contribution that cultural factors play in a relationship can at times be daunting, as in the many "Tony and María" scenarios sketched above. What makes working with ethnically and raciatly mixed couples rewarding is the capacity for the individuals to become aware of their own and the other's cultural variations. Some couples can create something new, a relationship which can handle the tensions and respect the unique difference each person brings to the relationship.

The two partners in every intimate relationship, regardless of race, ethnic background, religious background, socio-economic class or gender, bring to the relationship their own unique psychological "culture" and as such, each must struggle with forging a relationship and coming the terms with how they will share resources, time and space; how they will make decisions concerning where to live, with whom to socialize, how to interact with their respective families of origin, how to spend leisure time, and how to allocate chores. In addition, a major issue (which we have left out of our discussion because of space limitations and because of the circumscribed focus of this *Handbook*) is the nurturing and raising or children, which also cannot be separated from culture (Gibbs & Huang, 1989; Vargas & Koss-Chioino, 1992).

We want to discuss three important culturally-related factors which we believe contribute to the development of healthy relationships: (a) a conscious awareness by both partners of the role which culture plays in relationships; (b) the ability of both partners to experience ethnic and cultural energies as an expansion rather than a threat to the self; and (c) the paradoxical ability of both partners to develop their own uniqueness because of the other partner's different cultural background.

Conscious Awareness of Cultural Issues

The supports for healthy marriage, the forging of a relationship and the building of a working partnership all require an active stance and a conscious awareness on the part of both intimate partners. A realization of the dynamic process that culture plays over and above its specific content is probably the cornerstone for constructing a viable relationship.

Partners need to construct common bonds that incorporate but transcend racial, cultural and ethnic issues and differences. This is important even for couples with similar ethnic and cultural backgrounds. Here we see the significance of the development of shared meaning, or a shared spiritual understanding, that goes deeper than specific religions or cultures. Of course, this is easier said than done, because in the process of relationship formation all sorts of old fears, old hurts, old assumptions and feelings will be dredged up.

> An African-American couple achieved a deeper understanding of each other and what was important to them after a long, drawn-out argument that had its genesis in "hair". Both executives in major corporations, the husband was born and raised in the Southern USA in a small, rural town that was predominately black. He felt he had escaped an impoverished background by being quiet, unassuming and twice as smart as everybody else. His wife came from a large cosmopolitan city in the North-eastern USA. She decided that she would stop "straightening" her hair, wear it long and let it naturally "lock" into a style known as "dreadlocks". After receiving no comments from her husband about this change, the wife confronted him and they launched into an intense discussion. There was a company dinner coming up and the husband was worried that with his wife in attendance, his bosses and colleagues, who were all white and 95% male, would label him as too radical. As he admitted these thoughts, he also said he felt very guilty about even having them and he worried that his wife would think he was an "Uncle Tom", catering to a corporate image that was rigidly monolithic. His wife admitted that she had always thought he was too accommodating and naive, especially when it came to White people. The couple began to talk about different styles in coping with racism, and came to discuss how their differences were rooted in personal and family history as well as their experiences of living in different regions of the USA.
>
> As they talked, the wife agreed that she had never really allowed herself to be cognizant of the stress under which her husband functioned. Finally, both began to talk about whether their jobs were seducing them with promises of entrance into a higher class standing while whittling away at values they held deeply in their souls. Issues of class, struggling with racism and the values they found in African-American culture that had nurtured them both now became topics of shared conversation which they felt was richer and deeper, though not without disagreements. They went to the dinner; the wife's hair was in her new natural style and she wore an African-inspired evening gown. Her husband wore a conservative tuxedo but had asked his wife to pick out a kente cloth (fabric from the Ashanti people of Ghana) to drape over his shoulder. She did, but then told him they would have to talk about gender roles, as her schedule left her no time to buy his clothes!

Experience of Cultural Energies as an Expansion of the Self

The above case also illustrates what we see as a second factor that contributes to the development of healthy relationships, namely the ability to experience ethnic and cultural energies as an expansion rather than a threat to the self. What we mean by cultural energies are the rich *inner* dynamics of various cultures, each of which can be characterized as having a unique *essence*. In African-American culture, for example, there is a long history of the use of spirituality, music, dance and various forms of oral and physical expression to provide support in dealing with life difficulties, as well as a channel for maintaining a strong sense of self-esteem, which actively contradicts the negative definitions of self that come from the outside (Jones, 1993; Levine, 1977). In her decision to sport dreadlocks (and her influence on her husband to wear the kente cloth), the wife in the above case was drawing on this African-American cultural essence. If you could put words to what her body was communicating, it would be something like, "Think what you may about me, but I *know* who I am, I *know* that I look good, and I *feel* great about that!" And as she and her husband engaged in dialogue about the experience of both their families in dealing with and overcoming obstacles, they also began to reflect consciously on what had helped them to "keep on keeping on", a phrase that they both had taken for granted but that both had heard in church. Though denominationally different, they both had attended black churches and realized they had been deeply rooted in a supportive and loving community that expanded their already extended family (Boyd-Franklin, 1989).

In African-American culture, the cultural energy or essence that embodies the heart of the culture is reflected most dramatically in its varied musical genres. Ferdinand Jones (1995), who has had a "love affair with jazz as long as I can remember", writes of the meaning that jazz holds for African-Americans and sees its genesis not as an accident but as coming out of the long history of experiences of Africans first brought to America enslaved. Particularly, he asserts that African-American culture embodies a psychology and esthetic of "challenge" that evolved and continues to evolve so that psychologically, emotionally, spiritually and even physically, black people could survive. Jazz, in this sense, is much more than music. It reflects the very essence of a culture in which music has always served as the vehicle of expression for a number of unique African-American sensibilities, beginning with the music created by early Africans who were first enslaved in the eighteenth and nineteenth centuries (Jones, 1993).

A cultural artifact, custom, institution, ritual or holiday can be static and devoid of significance. Alternately, it can be a rich source of meaning that can help psychologically ground and energize a person, and expand a sense of both personal identity and a larger identity as a member of the collective body of humans. For some South-east Asian refugees who have come to the USA, the decision about whether or not to erect an ancestor altar has had significant psychological ramifications. For example, some families become deeply divided, with those who feel they must leave "old ways" behind and others who feel that not erecting an altar would further exacerbate a long string of losses they have had to endure (Chao, 1992, 1995a)

> In another case, a Korean woman declared that she no longer cared what her partner or her fellow apartment dwellers would think; she needed to cook some pungent kimchee and fill the kitchen with the smell of garlic, cabbage and hot pepper. She was tired of people speaking the wrong language, not looking like her, and eating strange food. She needed kimchee not just as a condiment but as food for her soul.

Development of Uniqueness in Response to Differences

Finally, a third dynamic that contributes to a healthy partnership occurs most often in interethnic, interfaith or international couples, but can also be present in couples with seemingly similar ethnic, religious or national roots. This involves the paradoxical challenge to develop one's own uniqueness precisely because of the other partner's different background. Couples who access this dynamic are aware that you can't lean on your partner to slide by, or expect your partner to deal with the meaning of the various racial, ethnic, or religious issues in your own life. For example, Maureen Reddy (1994), who is of Irish ancestry and is married to an African-American, writes of her growing realization of what it means to be the recipient of the privilege of whiteness. She also describes the active fight against racial and gender oppression that must be undertaken in a White feminist community. These aspects of development of Reddy's own White racial identity (Helms, 1990) evolved during her relationship with her African-American partner.

The Korean woman in the earlier example realized that her reluctance to cook a Korean dish symbolized her trying to fit into American culture as a "model minority" and not make waves. She began to think about and discuss with her partner what it meant to be a Korean, immigrant woman in a lesbian relationship with a woman who was not Korean and also not out of the closet. These strong differences with her partner contributed strongly to her own ethnic identity development process.

CONCLUSIONS

The African-American jazz drummer Max Roach is quoted as saying:

> The world of organized sound is a boundless palette. On that palette you have classical European music, you have Charlie Parker . . . the music of the East, African music . . . the Middle East, electronic music. Some people think that what they are doing way over here in one corner is the end of all organized sound. That's like saying the Earth is the end of the universe (cited in Rose, 1994, p. 80).

Roach made his comment in response to the rampant ethnocentricity he experiences coming from Western-trained musicians who see classical music as superior to, rather than simply different from, other world music forms, However, his remarks have great symbolic relevance to our psychological theories, to ourselves as therapists who treat couples, and to the couples themselves. Race, culture and ethnicity are part and parcel of ourselves and our clients and we are all located on a "boundless palette". Too often in our training of therapists and our construction of theories of therapy we get caught "way over . . . in one corner" and have as our reference group White heterosexual Christian men with Western European ethnic roots.

In addressing therapists, we offer these closing points. First, we can all locate ourselves on the palette in terms of our race, culture(s) and ethnic background(s). Acknowledging this and becoming consciously aware of the social, political and psychological implications of this are essential to our competence as therapists (Bhavnani & Phoenix, 1994). If we don't recognize and deal with these issues in ourselves we cannot expect our clients to do so. We should also realize that a "boundless palette" can at times be intimidating! It seems to be a human tendency to want to use only a few colors and melodies and to stay safely tucked away in "one corner". Mental health professionals seem to have a predilection for doing this, but we do so at our peril and at the risk of diminishing our world and the world of our clients. When we transcend our fears and explore the variety of cultural perspectives open to us, it can boost our clinical competence, and provide a very satisfying experience besides (Jones, 1994).

This all said, we must also realize that we can't become experts in every cultural configuration. This also means letting go of the "hubris" that our psychological theories or particular school of thought explain everything. We have to let our clients teach us about the colors of their palette. Concomitantly, however, it is our responsibility to become aware of what is on the palette. We have to read the poems, the plays and the literature of many cultural traditions; our own and others. We have to try different kinds of music and look at all sorts of art work. We also have to become aware of issues of power, oppression and privilege, through active study and personal work (Bhavnani & Phoenix, 1994; Collins, 1990; Pharr, 1988; Pinderhughes, 1989). If we can do this and thus actively allow culture, race and ethnicity to be included in our work with couples, then we lessen our chances of mistakenly believing that "the earth is the end of the universe".

One thread which runs through our discussion is a value we both hold which undergirds our approach to treatment. This is the assumption that relationships function best when couples work to achieve open communication, shared power, and some sense of personal satisfaction in their relationships. This is of course a value which is itself culture-bound. There are any number of cross-cultural clinical situations in which these values are challenged (e.g. the circumstance of arranged marriage, where duty to family and community is often assumed to be more important than the personal satisfaction of the members of the couple). A substantive exploration of this issue of values could easily command a chapter of its own. Let us simply say here that we believe that this issue of therapist vs. client values is not limited to cross-cultural work. It presents itself in a myriad clinical situations. We hope, in the clinical examples we have provided, that we have given at least a sketch of the way that we attempt in our work to balance our own values against empathy and respect for clients' values and experiences, including the difficult task of assessing the changing values that clients often struggle with in connection to their own development as individuals and couples, particularly when issues of acculturation are involved.

It should be clear from our broad survey of racial, ethnic and cultural issues in couples therapy that this is a enormous topic; our presentation merely scratches the surface of a number of significant areas of concern for therapists seeking to be culturally competent. However, we hope we have provided practicing therapists with a point of orientation, some important food for thought, and some key readings for further study. The actual work of therapy with ethnically and culturally diverse couples will, of course, be the best teacher of this material. We hope that our chapter has provided a helpful orientating guide to the specifically cultural aspects of that practice.

REFERENCES

Ben-David, A. (1993). Culture and gender in marital therapy with Ethiopian immigrants: a conversation in metaphors. *Contemporary Family Therapy: An International Journal*, **15**, 327–339.

Bernal, M.E. & Knight, G.P. (1993). *Ethnic Identity: Formation and Transmission Among Hispanics and Other Minortites*. Albany: State University of New York Press.

Bhavnani, K. & Phoenix, A. (1994). *Shifting Identities, Shifting Racisms: a Feminism and Psychology Reader*. London: Sage.

Billingsley, A. (1992). *Climbing Jacob's Ladder: the Enduring Leguacy of African-American Families*. New York: Simon & Schuster.

Blood, R.O. (1967). *Love Match and Arranged Marriage: a Tokyo–Detroit Comaprison*. New York: Free Press.

Boyd-Franklin, N. (1989). *Black Families in Therapy: a Multisystems Approach*. New York: Guilford.

Cahill, D. (1990). *Intermarriages in International Contexts*. Quezon City, Philippines: Scalabrini Migration Center.

Camper, C. (1994). *Miscegenation Blues: Voices of Mixed Race Women*. Toronto: Sister Vision Press.

Chao, C.M. (1992). The inner heart: therapy with South-east Asian families. In L. Vargas & J. Koss-Chioino (eds), *Working with Culture: Psychological Interventions with Ethnic Minority Children and Adolescents* (pp. 157–181). San Francisco: Jossey-Bass.

Chao, C.M. (1995a). Ancestors and ancestor altars. *Asian Week*, February 10.

Chao, C.M. (1995b). A bridge over troubled waters: being Eurasian in the U.S. of A. In J. Adleman & G.M. Enguídanos-Clark (eds), *Racism in the Lives of Women: Testimony, Theory, and Guides to Anti-racist Practice*. San Francisco: Haworth.

Clulow, C. (1993). Marriage across frontiers: national, ethnic and religious differences in partnership. *Sexual and Marital Therapy*, **8**, 81–87.

Collins, P. (1990). *Black Feminist Thought: Knowledge, Consciousness and the Politics of Empowerment*. London: HarperCollins.

Comas-Díaz, L. & Greene, B. (1994). *Women of Color: Integrating Ethnic and Gender Identities in Psychotherapy*. New York: Guilford.

Cose, E. (1993). *Rage of a Privileged Class*. New York: HarperCollins.

Cowan, P. & Cowan, R. (1987). *Mixed Blessings: Marriage Between Jews and Christians*. New York: Doubleday.

Crohn, J. (1995). *Mixed Matches: How to Create Successful Interracial, Interethnic and Interfaith Relationships*. New York: Fawcett Columbine.

Cross, W.E. Jr (1991). *Shades of Black: Diversity in African-American Identity*. Philadelphia: Temple University Press.

Davidson, J.R. (1992). Theories about Black–White interracial marriage: a clinical perspective. *Journal of Multicultural Counseling and Development*, **20**, 150–157.

Gibbs, J.T. & Huang, L.N. (1989). *Children of Color: Psychological Intervention with Minority Youth*. San Francisco: Jossey-Bass.

Gleckman, A. & Streicher, P.J. (1990). The potential for difficulties with Jewish intermarriage: interventions and implications for the mental health counselor. *Journal of Mental Health Counseling*, **12**, 480–494.

Glodava, M. & Onizuka, R. (1994). *Mail-order Brides: Women for Sale*. Fort Collins: Alaken.

Greene, B. & Herek, G. (eds) (1994). *Lesbian and Gay Psychology: Theory, Research and Clinical Applications*. Thousand Oaks, CA: Sage.

Helms, J.E. (1990). *Black and White Racial Identity: Theory, Research and Practice*. Westport, CT: Praeger.

Ho, M.K. (1990). *Intermarried Couples in Therapy*. Springfield, IL: Charles C. Thomas.

Jones, A.C. (1985). Psychological functioning in Black Americans: a conceptual guide for use in psychotherapy. *Psychotherapy*, **22**, 363–369.

Jones, A.C. (1989). Psychological functioning in African American adults: some Elaborations on a model, with clinical applications. In R.L. Jones (ed.), *Black Adult Development and Aging* (pp. 297–307). Berkeley, CA: Cobb & Henry.

Jones, A.C. (1993). *Wade in the Water: The Wisdom of the Spirituals*. New York: Orbis Boods.

Jones, A.C. (1994). Cultural competence: from fear to opportunity. *The Child, Youth, and Family Services Quarterly*, **17**, 16–19.

Jones, F. (1995). *Jelly Rolling: Commentary of Jazz in African-American Culture*. Unpublished manuscript.

Jones, J.M. (1991). Racism: a cultural analysis of the problem. In R.L. Jones (ed.), *Black Psychology* (pp. 609–636). Berkeley, CA: Cobb & Henry.

Levine, L. (1977). *Black Culture and Black Consciousness*. New York: Oxford University Press.

Mathabane, M. & Mathabane, G. (1992). *Love in Black and White: the Triumph of Love Over Prejudice and Taboo*. New York: Harper Collins.

McGoldrick, M., Pearce, J. & Giordano, J. (eds) (1992). *Ethnicity and Family Therapy*. New York: Guilford.

McGoldrick, M., Pearce, J. & Giordano, J. (eds) (1982). *Ethnicity and Family Therapy*. New York: Guilford.

McGoldrick, M. & Preto, N.G. (1984). Ethnic intermarriage: implications for therapy. *Family Process*, **23**, 347–364.

Mohanty, C. (1995). Presentation on ethnicity, gender and social oppression; faculty meeting of the Union Institute, Cincinnati, Ohio, February 25.

Pharr, S. (1988). The common elements of oppressions. In *Homophobia: a Weapon of Sexism* (pp. 53–64). Inverness, CA: Chardon Press.

Phinney, J.S. (1995). Ethnic identity and self esteem: a review and integration. In A.M. Padilla (ed.), *Hispanic Psychology: Critical Issues in Theory and Research* (pp. 57–70). Thousand Oaks, CA: Sage, California.

Pinderhughes, E. (1989). *Understanding Race, Ethnicity and Power: the Key to Efficacy in Clinical Practice*. New York: Free Press.

Pope, B.R. (1986). Black men in interracial relationships: psychological and therapeutic issues. *Journal of Multicultural Counseling and Development*, **14**, 10–16.

Reddy, M.T. (1994). *Crossing the Color Line: Race, Parenting and Culture*. New Brunswick: Rutgers University Press.

Richard, M.A. (1991). *Ethnic Groups and Marital Choices: Ethnic History and Marital Assimilation in Canada, 1871 and 1971.* Vancouver: UBC Press.

Root, M.P.P. (1992). *Racially Mixed People in America.* Newbury Park, CA: Sage.

Root, M.P.P. (1995). *The Multiracial Experience: Racial Borders as the New Frontier.* Thousand Oaks, CA: Sage.

Rose, T. (1994). *Black Noise: Rap Music and Black Culture in Contemporary America.* Hanover, NH: Wesleyan University Press.

Ross, J.L. (1987). Cultural tensions in strategic marital therapy. *Contemporary Family Therapy: an International Journal*, **9**, 188–201.

Russell, K., Willson, M. & Hall, R. (1992). *The Color Complex: the Politics of Skin Color Among African Americans.* New York: Harcourt Brace Jovanovich.

Spickard, P.R. (1989). *Mixed Blood: Intermarriage and Ethnic Identity in Twentieth-Century America.* Madison: University of Wisconsin Press.

Stuckey, S. (1987). *Slave Culture.* New York: Oxford University Press.

Sue, D.W. & Sue, D. (1990). *Counseling the Culturally Different.* New York: Wiley.

Vargas, L. & Koss-Chioino, J. (eds) (1992). *Working With Culture: Psychological Interventions with Ethnic Minority Children and Adolescents.* San Francisco: Jossey-Bass.

Wang, L. (1994). Marriage and family therapy with people from China. *Contemporary Family Therapy: an International Journal*, **16**, 25–37.

Willie, C.V. (1985). *Black and White Families: a Study in Complementarity.* Bayside, New York: General Hall.

Section II

Developmental Influences on Marriage

Chapter 8

The Influence of Earlier Relationships on Marriage: an Attachment Perspective

Wyndol Furman and Anna Smalley Flanagan
Department of Psychology, University of Denver,
Denver, CO, USA

Most of us think that the person we marry is someone very special—someone unlike all those others we had dated before. At the time we get married, we often describe the relationship as so different—so intimate, open and wonderful. Yet, is this really the case? Is our partner "one of a kind"? Is the relationship "completely different" from the ones that came before? Or is the relationship similar to our past romantic relationships? Might it even bear some resemblance to the relationships we have had with our parents? Is there any truth to the adage that men marry their mothers, and women their fathers? Was Freud (1949) right when he asserted that the mother is the "prototype of all later love-relations" (p. 70)?

In this chapter we address these questions by examining how the characteristics of marriages may be affected by one's past experiences in close relationships. First, we present a brief overview of attachment theory, the conceptual framework which guides our approach to these questions. We then consider how different attachment styles and working models may influence marriages. We show that these attachment views are relatively stable over time and are characteristic of earlier romantic relationships. We next consider the origin of these individual differences by examining the role friendships, early parent–child relationships and marital partners may play. Finally, we discuss the implications for the practicing clinician.

The chapter focuses on how earlier relationships may affect the quality of the couple relationship. Earlier relationships also influence marriages in other ways.

Clinical Handbook of Marriage and Couples Interventions. Edited by W. Kim Halford and Howard
J. Markman.
© 1997 John Wiley & Sons Ltd.

For example, early family and peer relationships affect personality, psychosocial adjustment and mental health, all of which may influence marriage. Additionally, our early experiences may affect our expectations regarding the roles of husband and wife as well as the number of children desired and how they are to be parented. Although these are important influences, we emphasize the impact on the couple's interactions and the quality of their relationship. Finally, we restrict our focus to heterosexual relationships. We believe that an attachment perspective could be applied to gay and lesbian couples, but the relevant empirical work has not been conducted yet.

ATTACHMENT THEORY

John Bowlby (1969/1982) developed attachment theory as a way to account for people's tendency to form strong affectional bonds to particular others. Strongly influenced by ethological theory, he proposed that humans, like many other animals, have an innate bias to become attached. The attachment behavioral system has the set goal of proximity to a caretaker at times of threat. When there are threatening stimuli, the child seeks out the attachment figure. When things appear safer, she/he may use the figure as a secure base from which to explore the environment. The attachment system functions to protect the child from danger and increases the likelihood of survival.

Essentially all infants become attached to a caregiver or caregivers, but the nature of the attachment varies. Such differences are apparent in infants' behavior in the Strange Situation procedure, which presents the infant with a series of increasingly stressful separations from the caregiver (Ainsworth, Bell & Stayton, 1971). The nature of the attachment is particularly reflected in the infant's reunion behavior and whether she/he seeks contact from the caregiver, is comforted by that proximity, and is able to resume exploration of the novel environment in the caregiver's presence.

Ainsworth, Bell & Stayton (1971) identified one secure pattern and two insecure (avoidant and anxious–ambivalent) patterns of infant attachment that are linked to the parent's caretaking behavior. *Secure* children show pleasure upon the parent's return and are able to resume exploration quickly. They have experienced sensitive care and appropriately rely on the parent to meet their needs. *Avoidant* children appear self-contained; they are not distressed when the parent leaves and do not seek contact or interaction when the parent returns. It appears that they expect their overtures to be rebuffed, as they have had a history of parental rejection. *Anxious–ambivalent* children resist separation and are hard to soothe upon reunion. The parent has typically been inconsistent in caregiving, and it appears that the infant fears his/her needs will not be met unless they are expressed forcefully (and perhaps not even then).

More recently, Main & Solomon (1986) identified a fourth pattern of infant attachment—the disorganized pattern. Disorganized children show movements or expressions that are incomplete, inconsistent, confusing or temporally disorganized. They may seek proximity at one moment and then quickly avoid the parent or resist the parent's overtures. These infants seem to view the parent as frightening, making them uncertain which behaviors should be expressed toward the parent (Main & Hesse, 1990). This pattern is relatively rare in normative samples but quite common in high-risk or maltreated samples (Carlson et al., 1989).

Initially, the type of attachment is a property of a particular infant–caregiver relationship, but it becomes increasingly a property of the child him/herself (Bowlby, 1988). Children develop mental representations or working models of the attachment relationship, others and the self (Bowlby, 1973). These models are shaped by their attachment experiences. For example, secure children may view their caretakers as available and responsive and view themselves as worthy of such care. In contrast, insecure children may see the caretaker as unavailable and unresponsive and think that they are unworthy of such care. By internalizing such expectations, the child creates a basis on which to approach the relationship with the caretaker. Moreover, the working models shape expectations and attitudes about subsequent relationships. In fact, a later section in the chapter discusses how these experiences are predictive of the characteristics of later relationships.

Although the majority of research has focused on childhood, Bowlby (1979) believed that attachment behavior characterized humans "from the cradle to the grave" (p. 129). In recent years, researchers have applied attachment theory to adult relationships.

Adult Romantic Attachment Theory

Hazan & Shaver (1987) proposed that adult romantic relationships can be conceptualized as attachment relationships. They pointed out a number of similarities between infant–caregiver attachment and adult romantic love (Shaver, Hazan & Bradshaw, 1988). For example, distress at separation and proximity-seeking when frightened or sick are attachment behaviors displayed both by children toward their caregivers and by adults toward their romantic partners. Furthermore, both the parent and the romantic partner provide care and protection (a safe haven) and a secure base from which to approach the world.

At the same time, Shaver & Hazan acknowledge several notable differences between adult love and infant attachment. Specifically, adult love involves sexual behavior and reciprocal caregiving, two components that are non-existent in infant–caregiver attachment. Thus, they conceptualize adult romantic love as the integration of three behavioral systems—attachment, caregiving and sexuality (Shaver, Hazan & Bradshaw, 1988). Elsewhere, we have proposed that an affiliative behavioral system is also involved (Furman & Wehner, 1994). The addition of this fourth system is needed to account for the similarities between friendships and romantic relationships as well as for the influence of peer relationships on development.

Not only did Shaver & Hazan (1988) think that adult love relationships were attachment relationships, but they proposed that certain primary love styles—secure, avoidant and anxious–ambivalent—parallel the previously mentioned infant attachment patterns. *Secure* individuals are comfortable depending upon others and having others depend upon them. They find it easy to get close to others and do not worry too much about rejection or getting too close. *Avoidant* individuals are uncomfortable being close to others. They do not trust them and do not like to depend on them. *Anxious–ambivalent* adults often want to be closer than others would like. They worry that their partners do not love them or will not stay with them.

Bartholomew (1990) further distinguished between two forms of avoidance: (a) a fearful type in which the person desires intimate contact but avoids such relationships because of a fear of rejection; and (b) a dismissing type in which the person denies attachment needs and sees him/herself as fully adequate and self-sufficient. Although this distinction may prove useful, we have raised serious questions about the conceptual and empirical basis of this work and thus do not discuss it here (Furman & Gollob, 1995).

Measuring Adult Attachment

Today, many investigators are studying marriages and other romantic relationships from an attachment perspective. They have approached the topic using several distinct methods. Originally, Hazan & Shaver (1987) presented people with paragraphs describing the three attachment styles and asked people to choose the one that best described themselves in their most important romantic relationship. Other investigators have developed multi-item questionnaires for assessing these styles (e.g. Brennan & Shaver, 1995; Collins & Read, 1990; Feeney, Noller & Hanrahan, 1994; Simpson, 1990; Wehner, 1992). Such measures commonly assess either the three Hazan & Shaver styles or two underlying factors—secure vs. insecure, and anxious–ambivalent (preoccupied) vs. avoidant (dismissing) (Shaver & Hazan, 1993). Although normative information does not exist on any of the preceding measures, a clinician could readily use one as an index of self-perceptions of attachment style.

A different set of investigators has relied on interview techniques. In particular, Main and her colleagues developed the Adult Attachment Interview (AAI), which principally focuses on childhood experiences with parents and how these experiences affect one's current functioning (George, Kaplan & Main, 1985). The interview is coded for both inferred childhood relationships and current states of mind regarding attachment (i.e. current working models). Individuals are classified into four categories based on their states of mind. *Secure–Autonomous* individuals value attachment relationships and regard attachment-related experiences as influential. They are able to describe their experiences coherently and recognize the impact the relationships have had on them. *Dismissing* individuals attempt to limit the influence of attachment relationships and experiences. They may have few memories or may idealize the experiences as a way to defend against the parental rejection they may have experienced. *Preoccupied* individuals are confused or preoccupied with the relationships. They are often angry, conflicted, or passive. *Unresolved* individuals are currently experiencing a disorganized response to a death or traumatic experience. Secure–autonomous models are the most common in normative populations, but the majority of individuals in clinical populations have insecure models of parents (van IJzendoorn & Bakermans-Kranenburg, 1996).

Recently, Owens & Crowell (1993) have developed a similar interview, the Current Relationship Interview (CRI), for describing attachment relationships between steadily dating, engaged or married couples. Individuals are classified into categories that closely resemble the ones described above.

Although the self-report and interview categories may sound similar, attachment classifications using the two methodologies have been found to be unrelated in four samples (Borman-Spurrell et al., 1993; Crowell et al., 1993). People who are classified into a particular category on the basis of a self-report are not the same people as those who are classified into that category on the basis of an interview. Accordingly, in the chapter, we distinguish conscious attachment *styles* that can be assessed by self-report measures from internalized, often unconscious, *working models* or states of mind that may be assessed by interviews (Furman & Wehner, 1994). Taken together, styles and models are referred to as *views* in our terminology.

Our focus is on romantic attachments, but we will also examine parents when we consider the precursors of romantic attachments. As we shall see, views of romantic relationships and parents are related to, but also distinct from, each other.

ATTACHMENT IN MARRIAGE

For most adults, a spouse or long-term partner serves as the key attachment figure. The way one relates to a partner, however, varies by attachment style.

Relationship Satisfaction

In general, self-report measures of romantic attachment style seem related to marital satisfaction. Security or comfort with closeness tends to be associated with higher marital satisfaction (Feeney, 1994; Feeney, Noller & Callan, 1994; Fuller & Fincham, 1995). One's own anxiety over abandonment, a feature of the anxious–ambivalent style, is related to lower satisfaction for both husbands and wives (Feeney, 1994; Feeney, Noller & Callan, 1994). Anxious–ambivalents may be less satisfied than avoidants, but this difference may be misleading. Avoidants may rate their marriages as more satisfying because they have lower expectations regarding intimacy or are defensive regarding the quality of their relationships.

Relationship Stability

Secures are less likely to get divorced or separated (Hazan & Shaver, 1987; Kirkpatrick & Hazan, 1994). Interestingly, anxious–ambivalent husbands get married more quickly than secure or avoidant men (Senchak & Leonard, 1992). They may view marriage as a way to lessen their fears of abandonment and reassure themselves that they are loved.

Perceptions of Relationships and Patterns of Interaction

In addition to satisfaction and stability, patterns of communication within marriages vary for people reporting different attachment styles. For husbands, comfort with closeness is significantly related to their reports of involvement, self-disclosure and satisfaction with communication (Feeney, Noller & Callan, 1994). For wives, anxiety over abandonment is negatively related to involvement and satisfaction with communication (Feeney, Noller & Callan, 1994). One's own security is positively related to one's ability to rely on the partner when disclosing a personal loss or disappointment (Kobak & Hazan, 1991). It seems important that both partners feel comfortable relying on the other, as intimacy is greater when both are secure than when one or both are insecure (Senchak & Leonard, 1992).

The partners' dimensions of attachment are also associated with communication quality. Wives whose husbands are comfortable with closeness are more satisfied with the communication within the marriage, and husbands whose wives are anxious about being abandoned are less involved in the interactions (Feeney, Noller & Callan, 1994).

Wives' anxiety over abandonment is positively related to their own high ratings of conflict (Feeney, Noller & Callan, 1994), suggesting insecure attachment styles may be associated with higher levels of conflict within the marriage. In addition to the quantity of conflict, the quality of the conflict appears to differ among those reporting different romantic attachment styles. Wives who are more secure are less rejecting, and husbands who see their wives as available display less rejection and more support in a problem-solving interaction (Kobak & Hazan, 1991).

These differences may be due to the fact that when secure individuals approach problem-solving discussions, they tend to experience more positive affect and less anxiety than insecure individuals (Fuller & Fincham, 1995). These predispositions may set the tone for the subsequent interaction and influence the resolution strategies.

In fact, specific conflict resolution strategies are related to attachment dimensions. Secure couples report less withdrawal and verbal aggression than secure–insecure or insecure–insecure couples (Senchak & Leonard, 1992). Resolution of conflict may be more difficult for insecures because avoidant individuals would be expected to circumvent or dismiss the conflict, and anxious–ambivalent partners would be expected to dwell on the conflict and hold a grudge. For husbands and wives, comfort with closeness is positively related to mutuality and negatively related to coercion, destructive process and post-conflict distress, whereas anxiety over abandonment is related to greater use of the negative strategies (Feeney, 1994). In sum, security is linked with open, constructive communication during conflict, whereas insecurity is linked with avoidance, aggression and withdrawal.

DATING AND PREMARITAL RELATIONSHIPS

In the previous section, we showed that the characteristics of marriages are associated with attachment style. These styles can be seen in earlier romantic experiences as well. Specifically, in this section we show that romantic attachment styles are stable and that secure and insecure individuals have different dating and premarital experiences.

Stability of Attachment Styles

Attachment styles appear moderately stable over both short- and long-term time periods. In samples of dating and married individuals, stability of attachment style, as measured by the Hazan & Shaver self-report paragraphs, has been estimated at 80% over 4 months (Keelan, Dion & Dion, 1994), 65% over 2 years (Fuller & Fincham, 1995) and 70% over 4 years (Kirkpatrick & Hazan, 1994). The stability of romantic attachment models is moderately high over an 18-month period (Crowell et al., 1995).

As would be expected theoretically, changes in styles occur with certain relationship experiences. Specifically, break-ups lead some secures to switch to insecure, whereas some avoidants become secure when they become involved in a new relationship (Kirkpatrick & Hazan, 1994). The stability in styles, however, is not solely a function of whether one is in the same relationship, as changes in relationships are more common than changes in styles (Kirkpatrick & Hazan, 1994). Additionally, perceptions of support—a related construct—are quite stable over a year, even when individuals have new partners (Connolly, Furman & Konarski, 1995).

Relationship Satisfaction

Individuals with secure styles characterize their dating and premarital relationships as more positive and more satisfying than insecure people (Brennan & Shaver, 1995; Levy & Davis, 1988; Pistole, 1989; Simpson, 1990). The least satisfied are insecure individuals adhering to traditional gender-based stereotypes, i.e. avoidant men and anxious–ambivalent women (Collins & Read, 1990;

Kirkpatrick & Davis, 1994). By preferring emotionally distant and less committed relationships, avoidant men may find close relationships less satisfying. Similarly, anxious–ambivalent women are highly dependent on their partners and seek high levels of intimacy which may lead them to be disappointed in their relationships.

Satisfaction is also related to the dating partner's attachment style. In general, women are less satisfied with avoidant men, perhaps because such partners are prone to dismiss the importance of the relationship (Collins & Read, 1990; Simpson, 1990). On the other hand, men who have anxious–ambivalent partners are less satisfied (Collins & Read, 1990; Kirkpatrick & Davis, 1994; Simpson, 1990). These men may feel threatened by the demanding and possessive nature of anxious–ambivalent women.

Regardless of their own romantic attachment style, individuals respond more positively to hypothetical partners who are characterized as secure than to those characterized as insecure, especially those described as avoidant (Pietromonaco & Carnelley, 1994). The preference for secures may be because individuals imagine having greater conflict or tension in relationships with avoidant or preoccupied (anxious–ambivalent) partners.

Who pairs with whom? Secure people are prone to date another secure individual (Brennan & Shaver, 1995; Collins & Read, 1990; Kirkpatrick & Davis, 1994) and are prone to marry another secure (Feeney, 1994; Senchak & Leonard, 1992). It could be because the relationship that developed is shaped by attachment styles and *vice versa*. It is not clear why the moderate concordance in couples' attachment styles exists. It could be that individuals are attracted to others with similar styles, although some work discussed subsequently suggests that initial attraction is not a major factor (Owens, 1994; Owens et al., 1995). Similarity, availability and infatuation may play a bigger role in determining whom one is initially interested in, whereas attachment processes may be more important to the maintenance of a relationship, especially a long-term one.

Pairs comprising two avoidants or two anxious–ambivalents are uncommon, perhaps because a similarly insecure partner would violate the expectations held by the individual (Brennan & Shaver, 1995; Kirkpatrick & Davis, 1994). Specifically, an avoidant person would expect his/her romantic partner to exhibit demanding, clingy behavior, but another avoidant would not do this. Similarly, an anxious–ambivalent partner would not expect his/her partner to shy away from intimacy, but another anxious–ambivalent would be likely to shy away. The fact that a similarly insecure person would not meet their expectations may make these relationships unlikely to occur.

Relationship Stability

People with insecure styles are less likely to have an ongoing romantic relationship (Kirkpatrick & Davis, 1994). The picture is more complicated, however, if a steady or serious dating relationship has developed. Among the men, the anxious–ambivalents are most likely to have the relationship end within a couple years; among the women, the avoidants are most likely to have it end (Kirkpatrick & Davis, 1994). Avoidant men and anxious–ambivalent women's relationships are at least as long-lasting as the secures' relationships, even though they are the *least* satisfied with their relationships. Though the anxious–ambivalent women's relationships may be as lengthy, they seem to have an "on-again, off-again" pattern, breaking up with the partner and then re-establishing the relationship (Kirkpatrick & Hazan, 1994). Avoidant men's relationships may continue because they are typically paired with anxious–ambivalent or secure women (Kirkpatrick & Davis, 1994). In any case, the findings underscore the difference between stability and satisfaction, a distinction with which marital therapists are familiar.

Individual differences also occur in reactions to relationship dissolution. Those with anxious–ambivalent styles display higher levels of protest and despair following break-ups (Fraley & Davis, 1994). This finding is consistent with the idea that anxious–ambivalents place overwhelming emphasis on preserving relationships because of a deep fear of rejection. Highly avoidant men experience significantly less emotional distress about dissolution, even when length of relationship and relationship satisfaction are partialled out (Simpson, 1990). Avoidants may be prone to suppress strong emotions and engage in defensive behaviors in order to keep the attachment system relatively deactivated (Fraley & Davis, 1994).

Perceptions of Relationships and Patterns of Interaction

As the literature on satisfaction and stability would suggest, the three romantic attachment styles are associated with different perceptions of romantic relationships (Feeney & Noller, 1990, 1991; Hazan & Shaver, 1987; Simpson, 1990). Individuals characterized by secure romantic attachment describe more trust, closeness, interdependence and commitment in their relationships and feel a relative absence of jealousy and fear of intimacy. In contrast, avoidants describe fears of intimacy and less satisfaction in their experiences. Anxious–ambivalent romantic attachment is associated with emotional highs and lows, extreme jealousy, and obsession with and heavy reliance on the partner.

Patterns of communication also differ. Secure individuals and those with secure partners rate the general level of communication in the relationship as higher (Collins & Read, 1990). They report greater self-disclosure to their romantic partners and say they are more responsive to the other's self-disclosure (Collins & Read, 1990; Mikulincer & Nachsohn, 1991). Secures' perceptions are reflected in their interactions. When they are feeling anxious, secures seek more support from their partners than avoidants, and secure partners provide more support than avoidant partners (Simpson, Rholes & Nelligan, 1992). Compared with avoidants, secures exchange more physical contact, discuss their anxiety more, and respond with more reassuring and supportive comments. These findings are consistent with the idea that secure people desire intimacy and closeness in the romantic relationship.

Differences also exist in conflict resolution. Those with secure styles are more likely to use mutually-focused conflict strategies, such as compromising, than are those with insecure styles (Levy & Davis, 1988; Pistole, 1989). Secures appear to take into account both their own and their partner's needs when arriving at a solution to a conflict. Anxious–ambivalent individuals are significantly more likely to use the individually-focused strategy of obliging the partner than are avoidants (Pistole, 1989).

Ratings of avoidant styles are positively associated with a willingness to engage in uncommitted sexual relations, whereas secure ratings are negatively associated with this behavior (Brennan & Shaver, 1995). Such findings suggest that the avoidant attachment style may be associated with having affairs, but this has not been examined yet.

Dating violence and its relation to attachment views has only begun to be studied. Some preliminary work suggests that women who have been sexually victimized have more preoccupied (anxious–ambivalent) romantic styles (Flanagan, 1995). It is possible that individuals coping with past or present violent romantic experiences may have an unresolved or disorganized response to such trauma, but this idea needs empirical confirmation.

Adolescent Romantic Relationships

Despite their seeming importance, adolescent romantic relationships have received little attention from social scientists. We believe that romantic views develop over the course of romantic relationships (Furman & Wehner, 1994). In other words, adolescents are learning how to interact with romantic partners and what they can or should expect from them. In early dating relationships, the affiliation and sexual systems are more salient than attachment and caregiving, but the latter increase in importance with experience and as relationships become longer (Feiring, 1993).

Even though the adolescent relationships are different from subsequent ones, adolescents' relational styles are associated with perceptions of intimacy, conflict management and emotion regulation (Wehner, 1992). Specifically, secure styles are related to self-disclosure, expressing emotions, and addressing and resolving difficulties. Dismissing (avoidant) styles are associated with being rational (vs. emotional) and denying conflict. Preoccupied (anxious–ambivalent) styles are related to being dissatisfied with the degree of intimacy, being emotionally confused, and holding a grudge.

Secure romantic styles are also positively associated with more frequent and more satisfying dating, whereas insecure styles are negatively associated with these dating patterns. Secure romantic styles are positively related to the frequency of engaging in affectional sexual behavior (e.g. kissing, necking, light petting), whereas dismissing styles are negatively related. Higher preoccupied ratings are associated with engaging in light and heavy petting more quickly, but not more frequently. It appears that preoccupied individuals may use sex to hold onto someone, rather than as a form of expressing affection. Whether adolescents engaged in intercourse or not is primarily related to moral and religious views, and not to relational views.

In sum, the work on adolescent and young adults' romantic relationships is consistent with attachment theory and the work on marriages. Most of it is, however, correlational: thus, the causal links have not been isolated. The research is also based on self-report measures of attachment styles. In one study of engaged couples, individuals with secure models of romantic relationships reported more commitment and less conflict than those with insecure ones (Owens, 1994). Aside from this study, however, little is known about the role of working models in these relationships.

LINKS AMONG RELATIONSHIPS

In the previous sections, we have shown that romantic attachment styles and models are associated with characteristics of marital and premarital relationships. However, these studies do not actually demonstrate that early attachment experiences affect romantic relationships. After all, our measures of romantic attachment styles and models are largely based on how people describe these romantic relationships. Thus, up to this point, we have just shown that conscious or unconscious characterizations of these relationships are associated with other features of these relationships.

The desideratum is a longitudinal demonstration that examines whether childhood attachment is predictive of adult romantic attachment and characteristics of the marital relationship. Unfortunately, such a study does not yet exist. Longitudinal projects are underway, but the children have not yet grown up and become married. In the meantime, we must resort to two sources of indirect evidence. First, we show that early attachment is predictive of subsequent peer relationships in childhood and preadolescence. Second, we show that adolescents' and adults' views of their parent–child and romantic relationships are related.

Attachment and Childhood Peer Relations

Secure infant attachment relationships with mothers are associated with positive peer relationships subsequently. For example, children who were securely attached to mothers as infants interact more positively and competently with peers when they are toddlers than do those who were insecurely attached (Lieberman, 1977; Pastor, 1981; Pierrehumber et at., 1989; Waters, Wippman & Sroufe, 1979). Similar differences exist in subsequent relationships with preschool friends (Sroufe, 1983; Youngblade & Belsky, 1992). In some cases, however, the findings for preschool friends have been stronger for girls than for boys (Fagot &

Kavanagh, 1990; LaFreniere & Sroufe, 1985). Toddlers (Jacobson & Wille, 1986) and preschoolers (LaFreniere & Sroufe, 1985) who were classified as secure infants also elicit more positive responses from peers than do insecure children. The lower peer competence of insecure preschoolers appears to manifest itself in peer victimization, as avoidant children are most likely to be victimizers and anxious–ambivalent children to be victims (Troy & Sroufe, 1987).

Early parent–child attachment is also predictive of school-age relationships. Preadolescents who were secure infants are more likely to form friendships at a summer camp and are more involved and effective in the camp's peer groups (Elicker, Englund & Sroufe, 1992). They are more socially competent and interpersonally sensitive.

Although these results are encouraging, it should be noted that attachment status has been found to be unrelated to other psychosocial variables examined in these same studies. The failure to find effects could reflect measurement problems in some instances, but we need further work to understand what early attachment status does and does not predict. In addition, the investigators usually have combined all types of insecures into one group and compared them with secures. Further work is needed to differentiate the consequences of anxious–ambivalent, avoidant, and disorganized attachment.

Additionally, most of the longitudinal work has examined how *infant* attachment status is associated with subsequent relationships and psychosocial adjustment. One should not infer, however, that attachment theorists believe that only infant attachment status is important or that attachment status is essentially fixed by the end of the first year of life. The emphasis on infancy stemmed in part from having a powerful assessment tool in the Strange Situation. As age-appropriate measures have developed, investigators have begun to examine security of attachment in the preschool years (Greenberg, Cicchetti & Cummings, 1990) and in adolescence (Hilburn-Cobbs, 1995; Kobak, Sudler & Gamble, 1991).

Continuity and Discontinuity

Bowlby (1973, 1980) and contemporary attachment theorists recognize that both past and current circumstances are important determinants of behavior (Sroufe, 1988). Consistent with these ideas, indices of early and more recent adjustment have each been found to contribute uniquely to the prediction of subsequent adjustment. For example, when predicting adaptation to a summer camp, security of attachment in the second year of life and elementary school adjustment each provide an increment in explanatory power above that provided by the other (Sroufe, Egeland & Kreutzer, 1990).

Past and current attachment are typically related. After all, working models are expected to shape one's expectations of others and lead one to behave toward others in manners consistent with prior relationship experiences. Thus, working models are self-perpetuating or stable (*ceteris paribus*). In consistent environments, security of attachment is relatively stable from 1 to 6 years of age (Main,

Kaplan & Cassidy, 1985; Wartner et al., 1994). In fact, infant attachment classifications are predictive of corresponding classifications obtained from Adult Attachment Interviews gathered in late adolescence and early adulthood (Waters et al., 1995).

At the same time, security of attachment and working models are likely to change if the experiences with parents change. Negative experiences are associated with subsequent insecure attachments, whereas improvements in life circumstances are associated with a change in the direction of security. For example, an infant's change from secure to insecure attachment is associated with maternal reports of more stressful events, whereas change from insecure to secure attachment is associated with lower maternal stressful-events scores (Vaughn et al., 1979). Similarly, the correspondence between infant and adult attachment classification is less if the individual had experienced attachment-related negative life events, such as parental death or divorce, parental psychiatric disorders, a life-threatening illness of parent or child, or abuse (Waters et al., 1995). Thus, some of the discontinuity is lawful, as attachment views appear responsive to contextual circumstances.

Adults' Views and Recollections of Parents

Although we do not yet have direct evidence of the links between childhood attachment and adult romantic attachment, some work has examined the links between adults' views of parents and their views of romantic partners. Treboux et al. (1994) gathered Adult Attachment Interviews (assessing working models of parents) and Current Relationship Interviews (assessing models of romantic partners) from a sample of college students. Secure–insecure classifications on the two interviews were significantly related for men and women. In a similar study of engaged couples, men's classifications on the AAI and CRI were significantly related, and women's tended to be (Owens, 1994; Owens et al., 1995). Additionally, men's ratings of parental love and rejection were related to their ratings of the love and rejection experienced in the romantic relationship. Men's ratings of parents were also related to their fiancées' reports of the love and rejection the men displayed. The weaker ties for women between the AAI and CRI may be because women were more likely to have had intimate relationships with various friends, and such relationships may have influenced their models of couple relationships.

Not only are working models of parental and romantic relationships related, but relational styles for the two are as well (Furman & Wehner, 1993, 1994). Such links have been found in early adulthood and to some degree in middle adolescence. Perhaps the concordance becomes stronger as individuals acquire more experience in romantic relationships, particularly longer-term relationships in which attachment becomes more salient.

Models of parents are related to characteristics of current romantic relationships. For engaged men and women, individuals with insecure models of parents rate themselves as more jealous and tend to see their fiancé(e)s as more jealous than did those with secure models. In fact, if either person is insecure, issues of jealousy seem to arise (O'Connor et al., 1995). The engaged women with insecure parental models also report that their financés are more verbally and physically aggressive than do secure women.

Preliminary evidence suggests that views of parents may also be related to patterns of interactions in marriage. Specifically, observed marital interactions are more positive and less conflictual when the husband has a secure working model of parents; the security of the wife's model does not seem related (Cohn et al., 1992).

Young adults' retrospective accounts of their childhood relationships with their parents are also associated with their current romantic attachment style. Compared to insecures, secures report having had warmer relationships with their parents. In general, avoidants characterize their parents as having been rejecting, and anxious–ambivalents view their parents as having been unsupportive or unavailable (Feeney & Noller, 1990; Hazan & Shaver, 1987). Descriptions of the mother's behavior (Carnelley & Janoff-Bulman, 1992) and of the opposite-sex parent (Collins & Read, 1990) have been found to be particularly related to current romantic attachment style.

The Role of Friendships

Up to this point, we have focused on the seeming links between relationships with parents and those with romantic partners. Peer relations, particularly close friendships, may also play a critical role in shaping romantic relationships (Furman & Wehner, 1994). After all, romantic relationships are egalitarian ones which originate in the context of the peer group. Adolescent romantic relationships often develop with peers who are part of one's network, and such relationships are more likely to occur within larger networks of opposite-sex peers (Connolly, Furman & Konarski, 1995). Additionally, characteristics such as collaboration, co-construction, reciprocity and symmetrical interchanges are central features of romantic relationships that seem unlikely to have emerged from the early asymmetrical interactions with parents. We believe that parent–child relationships lay the basic foundation for the ability to be close to and intimate with another, but that peer relationships, particularly friendships, play a critical role in the development of the ability to be intimate in a reciprocal and mutual fashion (Furman & Wehner, 1994).

Consistent with these ideas, significant relations exist between general romantic relationship and friendship styles in both middle and late adolescence (Furman & Wehner, 1993, 1994). Furthermore, late adolescents who exhibit safe-haven and secure-base behavior with their best friends, and who communicate with them, are more likely to exhibit similar behaviors with their dating partners; working models of friendships and romantic relationships are also related

(Treboux et al., 1994). Not only are concurrent relations with friends and romantic partners associated, but also friendships are predictive of subsequent romantic relationships. Specifically, social support in adolescent close friendships is predictive of support in romantic relationships a year later, and a similar pattern is found for negative interactions (Connolly, Furman & Konarski, 1995). On the other hand, the characteristics of romantic relationships are not predictive of those of subsequent friendships. In sum, it appears that friendships provide a foundation of egalitarian intimacy which is carried forward into romantic relationships.

The Role of the Partner

Although romantic relationships seem to be linked to earlier relationships with parents and friends, important differences remain. First, it goes without saying that we do not interact the same way with parents, friends, dating partners and spouses. The characteristics of these four types of relationships are markedly different. Sexuality, the distribution of power, and the voluntary or involuntary nature of the ties all play major roles in shaping the nature of these relationships. Moreover, even though links exist among the different types of relationships, the magnitude of these relations is moderate at best. Thus, it appears that people have somewhat different styles and models for different types of relationships (Furman & Wehner, 1994).

One reason may be because the other person in each relationship is different, and they too shape the nature of the relationships (Furman, 1984). Working models not only assimilate new experiences to existing expectations, but also they accommodate to the experiences with the current attachment figures (Bowlby, 1973). In fact, Bowlby thought that a supportive marital partner and therapy were two of the more likely ways in which insecure working models could change in adulthood.

The role of the partner is well illustrated by recent results from the Stony Brook Relationship Project. Both members of engaged couples were administered the AAI and the CRI (Owens, 1994; Owens et al., 1995). As noted earlier, secure–insecure classifications on the two measures were significantly related for men and tended to be for women. Moreover, the concordance was high between the partners' working models of their relationship (as assessed by the CRI). This concordance does not seem to result from assortative mating, as the partners' working models of parents are not related (cf. van IJzendoorn & Bakermans-Kranenburg, 1996). The partner's model of parents was, however, predictive of one's own model of the romantic relationship. If both the partner and oneself had insecure models of parents, the chance that the focal person had a secure model of the couple relationship was only 20%, whereas if both had secure models, the chance increased to 77%. The difference was even greater when one considers the partner's model of the relationship as well. If all three (partner's AAI, own

AAI, and partner's CRI) were insecure, the chance that one's model of the couple relationship was secure was only 13%; if all three were secure, the chance improved to 96%—an impressive difference.

Unfortunately, if one member of a couple had a secure model of parents and the other an insecure model, both individuals were more likely to have insecure models of their romantic relationship than secure ones. In other words, the insecure partner's detrimental effect on the couple's romantic working models outweighed the secure partner's possible ameliorative effect. Taken together, these findings illustrate that security is influenced by prior relational experiences (past circumstances) and the experiences with the partner (present circumstances).

IMPLICATIONS FOR THE CLINICIAN

From Freud onward, clinicians have argued that earlier relationships have an impact on marriages. For many years, that assertion had been based on clinical observations, but our review shows that empirical findings are beginning to support these observations. Admittedly, we are still missing some key pieces of information, particularly a direct demonstration that attachment in childhood is predictive of attachment in marriage. In fact, relatively few longitudinal studies exist concerning attachment processes and romantic relationships in adolescence or adulthood. The specifics of when there is or is not continuity, and of the nature of such carryover, need to be fleshed out considerably. Additionally, investigators studying attachment to parents have relied on observations and interviews, whereas those studying romantic attachment have typically used self-report measures. Unfortunately, the different methods seem to assess different constructs (working models vs. styles), making it difficult to integrate findings across fields. Accordingly, it may be best to label our ideas as working hypotheses for clinicians to test in their work with couples. Nevertheless, the empirical literature has some interesting implications for both assessment and treatment.

Assessment Implications

An attachment perspective has implications for both what we ask and how we ask it. We would want to gather information about the use of the other as an attachment figure and whether she/he serves as a caregiver, especially at times of distress. Do the individuals rely on each other as a safe haven and secure base? What do they do when they are upset or distressed? When they are sick? Separated from each other? How does the partner respond? How are feelings of jealousy and rejection managed? How open is the communication and how are emotions expressed? How are conflicts resolved? What values are placed on intimacy and autonomy? Of course, most marital therapists know that these domains are important facets of marital functioning. An attachment perspective, however, provides a conceptual framework for organizing this material. Specifically, it suggests an etiology, delineates the functions served by adaptive and seemingly maladaptive patterns of behavior, offers a typology of individual differences, and specifies mechanisms of continuity and the means of change.

One would also want to gather information about attachment-related phenomena in other relationships. If the couple has been married for many years and it is the first marriage or lasting significant relationship for both, a history of romantic relationships is not as important, as their romantic views are likely to be reflected in and based on their experiences in the current relationship. For other couples, the nature of past romantic relationships may give clues about their current romantic views. Often, people have had a wide range of experiences in different romantic relationships which can make it tricky to glean the critical patterns. We would focus on the ones they perceive to be important or significant, as such relationships may be more likely to reflect their relational views. (Of course, it is sometimes interesting to note which relationships are not mentioned.) Relationships which people still think about or which they still regret ending warrant attention. Lengthy relationships are typically more important, as they are more likely to be attachment relationships. More recent relationships may give clearer clues about current working models or styles, especially as such views are shaped with experience. In fact, it is important to remember that most of us have probably had a relationship we subsequently regretted. Passion can readily get one into one-sided or exploitative relationships, especially when one is young. Our experience suggests that making a "mistake" is not important, but being able to coherently discuss it or learn from it is.

An assessment of relationships would also include friendships and family of origin. Current peer and parental relationships are important, as there may be someone else serving as a key attachment figure. And of course, a central thesis of this chapter is that past experiences in intimate relationships shape our relational views in marriage. The experiences *per se*, though, are not as important as the manner in which the person currently thinks about them. Following the onset of the cognitive stage of formal operations in adolescence, working models can be reworked (Main, Kaplan & Cassidy, 1985). In fact, some individuals ("earned secures") manage to develop secure models of attachment despite having had rejecting, negligent, role-reversing or abusive parents (Main & Goldwyn, 1985/ 1994).

The emphasis on the manner in which one thinks or talks about something leads quite naturally to the question of how one gathers assessment information. Earlier, we reported that self-report and interview measures are not very related. All clinicians know that a person's own report may not be accurate, but there is more to this point than that. One of the contributions of the Adult Attachment Interview classification system is its emphasis on individuals' coherency—i.e. whether they seem truthful and have evidence for their assertions, whether their comments are of appropriate length (succinct, yet complete), whether their answers are relevant, and whether their answers are clear (Main & Goldwyn, 1985/ 1994). Comparing abstract descriptors with specific memories or examples is a particularly good way to assess coherency. The emphasis on coherence also means that adverse experiences, such as the ones earned secures have had, may not be that worrisome if the person is able to discuss them coherently. The real problems are those areas that are not described coherently. Thus, the lesson is to attend to how it is said at least as much as to what is said.

Treatment Implications

As noted earlier, attachment theory's emphasis on communication patterns, emotional expression, intimacy and conflict regulation are certainly consistent with contemporary approaches to marital problems. Bowlby's (1988) idea of the therapist as a secure base also fits well with the recent emphasis on the therapeutic alliance as a change mechanism (Horvath & Luborsky, 1993). Attachment theory contributes to the marital therapy field by providing a framework for understanding what the meaning of a marital problem is, from whence it may have originated, and how it can be changed. For example, if someone is withdrawn and not very disclosive with a partner, it may reflect an avoidant pattern of compulsive self-reliance that stems from past experiences of being rejected when turning to others. Thus, an attachment-oriented therapist focuses on understanding the underlying meaning of interactions, especially when perceptions or expectations seem distorted or rooted in the past.

With couples (or individuals), we often use a sequential approach. In the beginning phases of therapy, we typically use behavioral or other structural approaches to change patterns of interaction. As other chapters in this volume indicate (e.g. Epstein, Baucom & Daiuto), these approaches are often effective and sufficient. If so, the case has been treated successfully and efficiently. If therapeutic progress has been limited, we begin to determine what bases might underlie the lack of change or resistance to change. We may begin to explore why a couple may have difficulty carrying out different therapeutic exercises. We examine the clients' perceptions, expectations or interpretations of their interactions to determine if they have construed such encounters in a distorted manner. Often the problems the couples are experiencing reflect problems in the underlying models of attachment. For example, our compulsively self-reliant person may very well understand a "homework assignment" involving intimate disclosure but, at an internalized level, believes that any expression of feeling would be rebuffed or ridiculed. Such a working model may have stemmed from earlier experiences with parents. That is, some problems may not be problems in the marital relationship *per se* (at least in origin) but may be problems that individuals have brought into the relationship.

How common is it for views of earlier relationships to carry over into or adversely affect a couple's relationship? Our review of the literature suggests that views of marriages and other relationships are related, but distinct. The intertwining may be greater, however, in adult clinical populations where preoccupied and unresolved models of parents are overrepresented (van IJzendoorn & Bakermans-Kranenburg, 1996). When such insecure working models are present, the patterns of communication are hindered through defensive exclusion of information; accordingly, the working models are less likely to reflect the current relationship accurately (Bowlby, 1988). Such distorted models of the current relationship are likely to have a detrimental effect on the marriage.

When working models seem implicated in the marital problems, we may want to help the clients address the unfinished business with parents and in effect rework their models of parents. We would also want to help them differentiate the current attachment relationship from past ones. The examination of past working models is not just intended to help individuals understand who they are and how they got to be that way, but also to empower them and help them learn that they can be different in their present relationships. Such work is also valuable to their partners (who of course would bring in their own issues), as they benefit by learning what issues are relationship issues and what issues are their partner's own issues to address.

And of course, the partner can play a critical role in the therapeutic process by learning how to serve as a secure base or safe haven, and thus helping promote change in working models. Conversely, the partner can serve as a major impediment in any change as prior working models, even though they may be secure, are dependent upon the specific relationship and the characteristics of the partner.

The practitioner may use a wide range of techniques for examining and modifying underlying working models. Cognitive–behavioral therapists may see striking parallels between the concept of working models and Aaron Beck's concept of schemas (see Beck et al., 1979; Wright & Beck, 1994). In fact, Beck's concept of schemas was derived from Bowlby and the neo-Freudians. Beck's techniques of Socratic questioning, imagery, role-play and thought-recording could all be used as means of identifying relationship models/schemas. Similarly, his techniques of examining the evidence for a schema, listing its advantages and disadvantages, generating alternative schemas, and cognitive rehearsal could be used for altering such cognitions (see Wright & Beck, 1994). The structured assignments used by behavioral marital therapists can also be fruitful if they are not just used as a means of changing overt behavior but as a forum for exploring and examining the couple's working models.

As part of their emotionally focused therapy, Greenberg & Johnson (1988) developed a series of techniques for accessing emotional experiences. These methods can be used to identify and alter the unexpressed emotions that are likely to reflect unconscious working models. For example, overt anger may actually reflect a fear that the partner may not be responsive to the person's needs. Finally, although they have not been sufficiently tested empirically, the techniques of systemic and strategic couples' therapies, as well as attachment therapy, also seem like promising approaches for treating cases in which underlying working models seem to be implicated (see Fraenkel, this volume; Guidano & Liotti, 1983).

SUMMARY

In the present chapter, we have argued that past experiences in close relationships may influence marital relationships. Specifically, views of attachment are related to relationship satisfaction, stability and patterns of interaction. Attachment styles and working models are relatively stable over time and are characteristic of earlier romantic relationships. Parents, close friends and past and present partners each seem to help shape the nature of these attachment views. As clinicians, we need to assess these views of relationships and address them in our therapeutic work. By taking into account the role of earlier relationships, we may be better able to foster change and promote healthy relationships.

Acknowledgement

Appreciation is expressed to Stephen Shirk for his comments on an earlier version of this chapter.

REFERENCES

Ainsworth, M.D.S., Bell, S.M.V. & Stayton, D.J. (1971). Individual differences in Strange-Situation behaviour of one-year-olds. In H. Schaffer (ed.), *The Origins of Human Social Relations* (pp. 17–57). New York: Academic Press.

Bartholomew, K. (1990). Avoidance of intimacy: an attachment perspective. *Journal of Social and Personal Relationships*, **7**, 147–178.

Beck, A.T., Rush, A.J., Shaw, B.F. & Emery, G. (1979). *Cognitive Therapy of Depression: a Treatment Manual*. New York: Guilford.

Borman-Spurrell, E., Allen, J.P., Hauser, S.T., Carter, A. & Coie-Detke, H. (1993). *Assessing Adult Attachment: a Comparison of Interview-based and Self-report Methods*. Manuscript under review.

Bowlby, J. (1969/1982). *Attachment and Loss: Vol. 1, Attachment*. New York: Basic Books.

Bowlby, J. (1973). *Attachment and Loss: Vol. 2, Separation*. New York: Basic Books.

Bowlby, J. (1979). *The Making and Breaking of Affectional Bonds*. London: Tavistock.

Bowlby, J. (1980). *Attachment and Loss: Vol. 3, Loss, Sadness and Depression*. New York: Basic Books.

Bowlby, J. (1988). *A Secure Base: Parent–Child Attachment and Healthy Human Development*. New York: Basic Books.

Brennan, K.A. & Shaver, P.R. (1995). Dimensions of adult attachment, affect regulation, and romantic relationship functioning. *Personality and Social Psychology Bulletin*, **21**, 267–283.

Carlson, V., Cicchetti, D., Barnett, D. & Braunwald, K. (1989). Disorganized/disoriented attachment relationships in maltreated infants. *Developmental Psychology*, **25**, 525–531.

Carnelley, K.B. & Janoff-Bulman, R. (1992). Optimism about love relationships: general vs. specific lessons from one's personal experiences. *Journal of Social and Personal Relationships*, **9**, 5–20.

Cohn, D.A., Silver, D.H., Cowan, C.P., Cowan, P.A. & Pearson, J. (1992). Working models of childhood attachment and couple relationships. *Journal of Family Issues*, **13**, 432–449.

Collins, N.L. & Read, S.J. (1990). Adult attachment, working models, and relationship quality in dating couples. *Journal of Personality and Social Psychology*, **58**, 644–663.

Connolly, J., Furman, W. & Konarski, R. (1995). The role of social networks in the emergence of romantic relationships in adolescence. Paper presented at the Society for Research in Child Development, Indianapolis, IN, March.

Crowell, J.A., Holtzworth-Munroe, A.H., Treboux, D., Waters, E., Stuart, G.L. & Hutchinson, G. (1993). Assessing working models: a comparison of the Adult Attachment Interview with self-report measures of attachment relationships. Manuscript under review.

Crowell, J., Treboux, D., Owens, G. & Pan, H. (1995). Is it true that the longer you're together the more you think alike? Examining two hypotheses of attachment theory. Paper presented at the Society for Research in Child Development, Indianapolis, IN, March.

Elicker, J., Englund, M. & Sroufe, L.A. (1992). Predicting peer competence and peer relationships in childhood from early parent–child relationships. In R.D. Parke & G.W. Ladd (eds), *Family–Peer Relationships: Modes of Linkage* (pp. 77–106). Hillsdale, NJ: Erlbaum.

Eagot, B.I. & Kavanagh, K. (1990). The prediction of antisocial behavior from avoidant attachment classifications. *Child Development*, **61**, 864–873.

Feeney, J.A. (1994). Attachment style, communication patterns, and satisfaction across the life cycle of marriage. *Personal Relationships*, **1**, 333–348.

Feeney, J.A. & Noller, P. (1990). Attachment style as a predictor of adult romantic relationships. *Journal of Personality and Social Psychology*, **58**, 281–291.

Feeney, J.A. & Noller, P. (1991). Attachment style and verbal descriptions of romantic partners. *Journal of Social and Personal Relationships*, **8**, 187–215.

Feeney, J.A., Noller, P. & Callan, V.J. (1994). Attachment style, communication and satisfaction in the early years of marriage. In K. Bartholomew & D. Perlman (eds), *Advances in Personal Relationships: Attachment Processes in Adulthood*, Vol. 5 (pp. 269–308). New York: Jessica Kingsley.

Feeney, J.A., Noller, P. & Hanrahan, M. (1994). Assessing adult attachment. In M.B. Sperling & W.H. Berman (eds), *Attachment in Adults: Clinical and Developmental Perspectives* (pp. 128–154). New York: Guilford.

Feiring, C. (1993). Developing concepts of romance from 15 to 18 years. Paper presented at the Society for Research in Child Development, New Orleans, LA, March.

Flanagan, A.S. (1995). Sexual victimization and perceptions of close relationships. Paper presented at the Society for Research in Child Development, Indianapolis, IN, April.

Fraley, R.C. & Davis, K.E. (1994). Unrequited love and relationship dissolution: an attachment theory perspective. Unpublished manuscript.

Freud, S. (1949). *An Outline of Psychoanalysis*. New York: Norton.

Fuller, T.L. & Fincham, F.D. (1995). Attachment style in married couples: relation to current marital functioning, stability over time, and method of assessment. *Personal Relationships*, **2**, 17–34.

Furman, W. (1984). Issues in the assessment of social skills of normal and handicapped children. In T. Field, M. Siegal & J. Roopnarine (eds), *Friendships of Normal and Handicapped Children* (pp. 3–30). New York: Ablex.

Furman, W. & Gollob, H.F. (1995). A re-examination of Bartholomew's two dimensional theory of attachment. Manuscript submitted for publication.

Furman, W. & Wehner, E. (1993). Adolescent romantic relationships: a developmental perspective. Paper presented at Society for Research in Child Development, New Orleans, LA, March.

Furman, W. & Wehner, E.A. (1994). Romantic views: toward a theory of adolescent romantic relationships. In R. Montemayor, G.R. Adams & T.P. Gullota (eds), *Advances in Adolescent Development: Personal Relationships During Adolescence*, Vol. 6 (pp. 168–195). Thousand Oaks, CA: Sage.

George, C., Kaplan, N. & Main, M. (1985). An adult attachment interview. Unpublished manuscript, University of California at Berkeley.

Greenberg, L.S. & Johnson, S.M. (1988). *Emotionally Focused Therapy for Couples*. New York: Guilford.

Greenberg, M.T., Cicchetti, D. & Cummings, E.M. (eds) (1990). *Attachment in the Preschool Years: Theory, Research, and Intervention*. Chicago: University of Chicago Press.

Guidano, V. & Liotti, G. (eds) (1983). *Cognitive Processes and Emotional Disorders*. New York: Guilford.

Hazan, C. & Shaver, P. (1987). Romantic love conceptualized as an attachment process. *Journal of Personality and Social Psychology*, **52**, 511–524.

Hilburn-Cobbs, C.L. (1995). Classification of attachment behavior in early adolescence: an observational methodology. Paper presented at the Society for Research in Child Development, Indianapolis, IN, March.

Horvath, A.O. & Luborsky, L. (1993). The role of the therapeutic alliance in psychotherapy. *Journal of Consulting and Clinical Psychology*, **61**, 561–573.

Jacobson, J.L. & Wille, D.E. (1986). The influence of attachment pattern on developmental changes in peer interaction from the toddler to the preschool period. *Child Development*, **57**, 338–347.

Keelan, J.P., Dion, K.L. & Dion, K.K. (1994). Attachment style and heterosexual relationships among young adults: a short-term panel study. *Journal of Social and Personal Relationships*, **11**, 201–214.

Kirkpatrick, L.A. & Davis, K.E. (1994). Attachment style, gender, and relationship stability: a longitudinal analysis. *Journal of Personality and Social Psychology*, **66**, 502–512.

Kirkpatrick, L.A. & Hazan, C. (1994). Attachment styles and close relationships: a four-year prospective study. *Personal Relationships*, **1**, 123–142.

Kobak, R.R. & Hazan, C. (1991). Attachment in marriage: effects of security and accuracy of working models. *Journal of Personality and Social Psychology*, **60**, 861–869.

Kobak, R.R., Sudler, N. & Gamble, W. (1991). Attachment and depressive symptoms during adolescence: a developmental pathways analysis. *Development and Psychopathology*, **3**, 461–474.

LaFreniere, P.J. & Sroufe, L.A. (1985). Profiles of peer competence in the preschool: interrelations between measures, influence of social ecology, and relation to attachment history. *Developmental Psychology*, **21**, 56–69.

Levy, M.B. & Davis, K.E. (1988). Lovestyles and attachment styles compared: their relations to each other and to various relationship characteristics. *Journal of Social and Personal Relationships*, **5**, 439–471.

Lieberman, A.F. (1977). Preschoolers' competence with a peer: relations with attachment and peer experience. *Child Development*, **48**, 1277–1287.

Main, M. & Goldwyn, R. (1985/1994). Adult attachment scoring and classification systems. Unpublished manuscript, University of California at Berkeley.

Main, M. & Hesse, E. (1990). Parents' unresolved traumatic experiences are related to infans disorganized attachment status: is frightened and/or frightening parental behavior the linking mechanism? In M.T. Greenberg, D. Cicchetti & E.M. Cummings (eds), *Attachment in the Preschool Years: Theory, Research, and Intervention* (pp. 161–182). Chicago: University of Chicago Press.

Main, M., Kaplan, N. & Cassidy, J. (1985). Security in infancy, childhood and adulthood: a move to the level of representation. In I. Bretherton & E. Waters (eds), *Growing Points of Attachment Theory and Research*. Monographs of the Society for Research in Child Development. Chicago: University of Chicago Press.

Main, M. & Solomon, J. (1986). Discovery of a new, insecure–disorganized/disoriented attachment pattern. In T.B. Brazelton & M. Yogman (eds), *Affective Development in Infancy* (pp. 95–124). Norwood: Ablex.

Mikulincer, M. & Nachsonn, O. (1991). Attachment styles and patterns of self-disclosure. *Journal of Personality and Social Psychology*, **61**, 321–331.

O'Connor, E., Pan, H., Water, E. & Posada, G. (1995). Attachment classification, romantic jealousy, and aggression in couples. Paper presented at the Society for Research in Child Development, Indianapolis, IN, April.

Owens, G. (1994). Correspondence between Engaged Couples' Mental Representations of their Attachments to Parents and Romantic Partners. Unpublished doctoral dissertation, SUNY at Stony Brook.

Owens, G. & Crowell, J. (1993). Current Relationship Interview Scoring System. Unpublished manual, SUNY at Stony Brook.

Owens, G., Crowell, J.A., Treboux, D., O'Connor, E. & Pan, H. (1995). Multiple vs. single working models of attachment: relations between models of child–parent relationships and later romantic relationships. Paper presented at the Society for Research in Child Development, Indianapolis, IN, April.

Pastor, D.L. (1981). The quality of mother–infant attachment and its relationship to toddlers' initial sociability with peers. *Developmental Psychology*, **17**, 326–335.

Pierrehumbert, B., Iannotti, R.J., Cummings, E.M. & Zahn-Waxler, C. (1989). Social functioning with mother and peers at 2 and 5 years: the influence of attachment. *International Journal of Behavioral Development*, **12**, 85–100.

Pietromonaco, P.R. & Carnelley, K.B. (1994). Gender and working models of attachment: consequences for perceptions of self and romantic retationships. *Personal Relationships*, **1**, 63–82.

Pistole, M.C. (1989). Attachment in adult romantic relationships: style of conflict resolution and relationship satisfaction. *Journal of Social and Personal Relationships*, **6**, 505–510.

Senchak, M. & Leonard, K.E. (1992). Attachment styles and marital adjustment among newlywed couples. *Journal of Social and Personal Relationships*, **9**, 51–64.

Shaver, P. & Hazan, C. (1988). A biased overview of the study of love. *Journal of Social and Personal Relationships*, **5**, 473–501.

Shaver, P.R. & Hazan, C. (1993). Adult romantic attachment: theory and evidence. In D. Perlman & W. Jones (eds), *Advances in Personal Relationships: Attachment Processes in Adulthood*, Vol. 4 (pp. 29–70). London: Jessica Kingsley.

Shaver, P., Hazan, C. & Bradshaw, D. (1988). Love as attachment: the integration of three behavioral systems. In R.J. Sternberg & M.L. Barnes (eds), *The Psychology of Love*. New Haven, CT: Yale University Press.

Simpson, J.A. (1990). Influence of attachment styles on romantic relationships. *Journal of Personality and Social Psychology*, **59**, 971–980.

Simpson, J.A., Rholes, W.S. & Nelligan, J.S. (1992). Support seeking and support giving within couples in an anxiety-provoking situation: the role of attachment styles. *Journal of Personality and Social Psychology*, **62**, 434–446.

Sroufe, L.A. (1983). Infant–caregiver attachment and patterns of adaptation in preschool: the roots of maladaptation and competence. In M. Perlmutter (ed.), *Minnesota Symposia in Child Psychology*, Vol. 16 (pp. 41–81). Hillsdale, NJ: Erlbaum.

Sroufe, L.A. (1988). The role of infant–caregiver attachment in development. In J. Belsky & T. Nezworski (eds), *Clinical Implications of Attachment* (pp. 18–38). Hillsdale, NJ: Erlbaum.

Sroufe, L.A., Egeland, B. & Kreutzer, T. (1990). The fate of early experience following developmental change: longitudinal approaches to individual adaptation in childhood. *Child Development*, **61**, 1363–1373.

Treboux, D., Crowell, J.A., Owens, G. & Pan, H.S. (1994). Attachment behaviors and working models: relations to best friendships and romantic relationships. Paper presented at the Society for Research on Adolescence, San Diego, CA, February.

Troy, M. & Sroufe, L.A. (1987). Victimization among preschoolers: the role of attachment relationship history. *Journal of the American Academy of Child Psychiatry*, **26**, 166–172.

van IJzendoorn, M.H. & Bakermans-Kranenburg, M.J. (1996). Attachment representations in mothers, fathers, adolescents, and clinical groups: a meta-analytic search for normative data. *Journal of Consulting and Clinical Psychology*, **64**, 8–21.

Vaughn, B., Egeland, B., Sroufe, L.A. & Waters, E. (1979). Individual differences in infant–mother attachment at twelve and eighteen months: stability and change in families under stress. *Child Development*, **50**, 971–975.

Wartner, U.G., Grossman, K., Fremmer-Bombik, E. & Suess, G. (1994). Attachment patterns at age six in South Germany: predictability from infancy and implications for preschool behavior. *Child Development*, **65**, 1014–1027.

Waters, E., Treboux, D., Crowell, J., Merrick, S. & Albersheim, L. (1995). From the Strange Situation to the Adult Attachment Interview: a 20-year longitudinal study of attachment security in infancy and early adulthood. Paper presented at the Society for Research in Child Development, Indianapolis, IN, April.

Waters, E., Wippman, J. & Sroufe, L.A. (1979). Attachment, positive affect, and competence in the peer group: two studies in construct validation. *Child Development*, **50**, 821–829.

Wehner, E.A. (1992). Adolescent Romantic Relationships: Attachment, Caregiving, Affiliation, and Sex. Unpublished dissertation, University of Denver.

Wright, J.H. & Beck, A.T. (1994). Cognitive therapy. In R.E. Hales, S.C. Yudofsky & J.A. Talbott (eds), *The American Psychiatric Press Textbook of Psychiatry*, 2nd edn (pp. 1083–1114). Washington, DC: American Psychiatric Press.

Youngblade, L.M. & Belsky, J. (1992). Parent–child antecedents of 5-year-olds' close friendships: a longitudinal analysis. *Developmental Psychology*, **28**, 700–713.

Chapter 9

The Developmental Course of Couples' Relationships

Kristin M. Lindahl*, Neena M. Malik* and Thomas N. Bradbury**
*Departments of Psychology, *University of Miami, Miami, FL; and ** University of California, Los Angeles, CA, USA*

With the divorce rate hovering around 50% for the past couple of decades (Cherlin, 1981), a better understanding of how marriages unfold over time is needed. How is it that while virtually all couples report feeling happy and committed as newlyweds, many unions ultimately result in separation and divorce, or in intact, but unfulfilling and bitter, relationships? What happens to couples' relationships as they make the transition to parenthood, or when children leave the home? An appreciation of the developmental course of marriage is critical for both researchers and clinicians working with couples of families. It is now well established that marital conflict has significant negative consequences for spouses as well as their children (e.g. Emery, 1988; Gottman & Katz, 1989; Howes & Markman, 1989). Much of the current research is focused on the marital processes or mechanisms that put couples at risk for separation or divorce or, conversely, that help couples create a solid foundation for building a lasting relationship. The present chapter examines the factors that are predictive of marital success, stability, and dissolution, as well as how couples weather important transitions in the family life cycle. As the research in these areas is discussed, implications for clinical assessment and intervention will be highlighted.

FACTORS THAT PREDICT MARITAL QUALITY OVER TIME

Until quite recently, the bulk of research on the longitudinal course of marriage has focused on specific factors predictive of marital outcomes, rather than the

Clinical Handbook of Marriage and Couples Interventions. Edited by W. Kim Halford and Howard J. Markman.

processes or mechanisms associated with marital stability and quality[1]. In a recent meta-analytic review of 115 longitudinal studies of marriage, Karney & Bradbury (1995) found sexual satisfaction and positive behaviors to be the best predictors of both marital stability and satisfaction over time. Similar to other studies, they found small to modest effect sizes for the effect of marital satisfaction on marital stability (aggregate rs for marital and sexual satisfaction ranged from 0.06 to 0.42). Thus, while marital dissatisfaction is considered one fo the strongest predictors of marital instability, it is limited in the amount of variance for which it can account. Certain individual factors (such as psychological adjustment and similarity of expectations for marriage) also were found to be predictive of marital satisfaction. However, in the absence of studies that examine the interrelations among independent variables, drawing conclusions regarding the relative contributions of different classes of variables in predicting marital stability and satisfaction is difficult. Many studies provide evidence that several factors, such as income, employment, and education, are weak but significant predictors of marital outcomes (see discussion of demographic variables below).

Factors such as employment and income might be just as important in the marital outcome equation as marital and sexual satisfaction, but they may exert their influence through mediating processes. For example, a couple may present in therapy with a seemingly stable marriage, where both partners report general satisfaction with their partnership but have specific areas of conflict, such as recurrent arguments about money. Initially, it may be difficult to understand what has precipitated the need for intervention, particularly if the couple appears able to support themselves and pay for therapy. Upon further interviewing, however, it may become clear that the couple negotiates many issues well but is stuck in a serious power struggle over who makes financial decisions in the marriage, and that the more educated or older spouse seems to feel entitled to make all decisions. Thus, money in and of itself is less the issue than is the couple's ability to manage deeper relationship issues that may be related to finances, such as respect of each other's opinions and equality in decision-making.

Other predictors of marital stability and quality have been found by examining in the laboratory what clinicians have done in their offices for decades: the processes associated with how spouses interact with one another. The paradigm generally used is to observe partners discussing and working to solve a relationship problem. As one might suspect, positive behaviors such as supportiveness, effective communication, and caring behaviors tend to be associated with marital

---

[1] In general, few gender differences are found in the literature on predictors of marital quality, such that the variables predictive of husbands' outcomes are also predictive of wives' outcomes and are in the same direction and of similar magnitude. Thus, results are presented jointly for males and females. Few data exist, however, regarding differences (and similarities) predictive of marital outcomes across cultures and various ethnic groups. Particularly lacking are longitudinal studies with non-Western couples. Throughout the chapter, when possible, cross-cultural data will be integrated into the discussion of research and the clinical implications of data on marital processes associated with marital outcomes.

success (e.g. stability, satisfaction, and overall quality of relationships), while negative behaviors such as reciprocity of negative affect and destructive communication tend to be associated with negative marital outcomes (e.g. distress and/ or divorce).

One longitudinal study that has examined specific factors and behavioral processes predictive of marital stability and quality is the Denver Family Development Project (see Markman, 1981; Markman et al., 1993; Lindahl, Clements & Markman, in press). This study followed couples for 10 years, starting before couples were married and then charting the first decade of marriage. In this sample, marital satisfaction generally declined over the early years of marriage, before plateauing approximately 3 years after the first premarital assessment (i.e. after approximately 3 years of marriage). After this point, marital satisfaction appeared to stabilize and no further significant declines have been noted at subsequent follow-ups. It is important to note that while significant drops in satisfaction were noted over the first several years of marriage, most couples remained in the non-distressed range of functioning. Over time, approximately 20% of the sample divorced, thus permitting a look at which premarital variables were most predictive of marital dissolution. Among the best discriminators of couples who later divorced, in comparison to those who stayed together, were husbands' emotional invalidation and negativity, wives' emotional invalidation and lack of problem-solving skills, and wives' younger age at marriage.

The above results suggest that what is important in a relationship is not so much the presence of conflict, as all relationships encounter some degree of disagreement, but the processes by which negative affect is regulated in the marriage and conflict is resolved. When assessing the stability of a couple's relationship in therapy, the Denver study indicates that if a couple enters therapy where the husband makes hostile, derogatory, and destructive comments to his wife, the wife seems to have difficulty contributing to the solution of problems, and both spouses seem to be insensitive to the emotional needs and responses of the other, their relationship is likely to be in a fragile and vulnerable state. Providing partners with skills to listen, attend and respond to each other's needs, as well as providing a structure for partners to speak to each other and solve problems constructively, will be essential goals for clinicians to reduce the risk of relationship break-up for these couples.

While relatively few studies examine simultaneously the predictors of marital quality and stability, those investigations have generally found that variables predictive of marital quality also predict marital stability and exert their effects in the same direction. One exception is length of marriage, which correlates negatively with satisfaction but positively with stability. While the duration of a marital relationship is inversely related to marital quality (for example, relationships tend to become less satisfying over time), longer marriages are also less likely to dissolve and hence become more stable (Karney & Bradbury, 1995). Thus, while stability and quality are clearly related phenomena, they represent qualitatively different outcomes and need to be considered as distinct. However, the distinction between these two constructs, and the factors differentially related to them, have not always been carefully articulated or examined in the empirical literature. In addition, while most people know and have worked with couples who are highly distressed or unhappy in their relationships and yet have been married for a long period of time, researchers have only recently started to develop theories that explain how this situation occurs (see the "Theoretical Models of the Course of Marriage" section of this chapter). One of the most important clinical implications of this work will be to guide couples more effectively toward developing healthier and better relationships, not just longer-lasting ones.

Demographic Variables Predictive of Marital Outcomes

Several demographic variables have been shown to predict marital stability and satisfaction. Greater age at marriage has been shown in several studies to be associated with increased marital stability (e.g. Kuh & Maclean, 1990; Rockwell, Elder & Ross, 1979; Sears, 1977). However, as Karney & Bradbury (1995) point out, the effect of age is confounded with duration of marriage, and the unique importance of age has yet to be determined. Socio-economic status has also been associated with marital outcome, with couples with less education and less income being at higher risk for poorer quality marriages and divorce (Elder & Caspi, 1988; Kurdek, 1993; Teachman & Polonko, 1990). Relatedly, employment and income have shown to predict marital outcomes, although the results depend on whether husbands' or wives' data are considered. Whereas husbands' employment and income tend to be positively related to marital outcomes, wives' employment tends to be related negatively (Greenstein, 1990). As Karney & Bradbury have discussed, it cannot yet be determined whether a dual income merely makes divorce easier to contemplate or whether marriages in which the wife has achieved some level of financial independence become less satisfying.

Aside from employment status and income level, relatively few factors outside the marital system have been studied longitudinally. One other domain that has received attention is stress. Stressful life experiences and general levels of stress have been shown to be related to lower marital stability and less marital satisfaction. For example, experiencing stress at work appears to lead to relatively negative marital interactions at home (Bolger et al., 1989). When husbands perceive higher levels of economic strain in their lives, they tend to be more hostile and less positive with their spouses (Conger et al., 1990). Lastly, studies of air traffic controllers indicate that higher daily workloads are linked with spouses' reports of greater negativity in their interactions (Repetti, 1989).

It is a matter of debate whether the demographic variable of premarital cohabitation increases the risk for poorer marital quality or relationship dissolution Although several studies have demonstrated a positive relation between living together prior to marriage and later separation and divorce (Newcomb, 1986), more recent studies and re-analyses of existing data suggest that the effect of premarital cohabitation is eliminated when controlling for the length of the relationship (Teachman & Polonko, 1990). In other words, cohabitors and non-cohabitors do not appear to differ in their rates of divorce or level of dissatisfaction when relationship duration is measured from the very beginning of the relationship instead of the date of legal union.

Behavioral Predictors of Marital Outcomes

Behavioral variables are among the most the most widely studied longitudinal correlates of marital stability and quality and are, from a clinical perspective, aspects of couples' relationships most amenable to intervention and change. In their analysis, Karney & Bradbury (1995) grouped the over 50 behavioral variables that have been studied into five main categories: positive behavior, negative behavior, avoidance, positive reciprocity, and negative reciprocity. Although the number of studies examining the marital processes or interaction patterns that are predictive of divorce is small, most of these studies find a positive association between partners' negativity and divorce. On the other hand, numerous studies have tried to predict marital quality from behavioral variables. A vast majority of the studies have found negativity to be associated with drops in satisfaction (e.g. Huston & Vangelisti, 1991; Levenson & Gottman, 1985; Lindahl, Clements & Markman, in press). The relationship between negative behaviors and marital dissatisfaction is not a straightforward one, however, and can be affected by other factors. For example, in a 2 year study of newlyweds, Huston & Chorost (1994) found that the deleterious impact of negativity on marital satisfaction could be reduced to some extent by the level of positivity in couples' exchanges. More specifically, they found evidence for a buffering effect of positive behaviors, such that the decline in wives' satisfaction associated with husbands' negativity was less great when husbands exhibited relatively high levels of affectional expression.

On the other hand, a few studies have found evidence for the counter-intuitive finding that negative interactions are actually associated with increases in marital satisfaction over time. For example, Heavey, Layne & Christensen (1993) reported husbands' negativity and demands to be predictive of wives' later satisfaction. Similarly, Gottman & Krokoff (1989) found that husbands' and wives' negative communication during a couples' problem discussion was positively correlated with marital satisfaction 1 year later. Although interpretation of these data is seriously constrained by various statistical considerations (e.g. Woody & Costanzo, 1990), it has been hypothesized that the expressions of disagreements or negative feelings may, when occurring within a positive context, force couples to confront and deal with their differences (Gottman & Krokoff, 1989).

The effect of negativity on marital quality likely depends on both the larger interpersonal context within which it is embedded and the characteristics of a couple's conflict, such as the frequency, intensity, and duration of the conflict, as well as the degree to which problems are resolved. Expressions of positive affect and caring seem, to some extent, to counter-balance the effects of behaviors that are otherwise potentially destructive. One implication for these findings is that, when a positive and supportive context is provided for a couple's expression of disagreement (such as typically occurs in the relative safety of a clinician's office), difficulties can be aired and resolved in a manner that may increase satisfaction with the marriage. Although some debate exists in the field on how negativity affects marriage, it is clear that few would argue that negative behaviors, such as insults, yelling, and intense negative affect, are good for marriage. What is good for marriage, however, is the opportunity in the relationship to air negative feelings. It is critical for healthy relationships that grievances and complaints are openly discussed; it is equally critical, as noted in the Denver study, that these discussions take place in a safe and constructive manner.

Marital Typologies

Relying primarily on behavioral indices, several attempts have been made to describe types of marriages that endure over time. In a 4-year longitudinal study of couple types, designed to predict which couples were most at risk for distress and instability, Gottman (1993b) described five types of couples. He found evidence for three types of stable couples: volatile, validating, and conflict-avoiding, which approximate to the three types of happy couples originally proposed by Fitzpatrick (1988): independents, traditionals, and separates, respectively. Two types of unstable couples (couples who later separated or divorced) were identified: hostile and hostile-detached.

Of the low-risk-for-divorce couples, volatile couples were rated as being the most emotionally expressive and tended to escalate frequently, seeming to believe in airing their feelings openly and completely about all issues, no matter how small. However, this escalation was balanced by high levels of affection, humor, and caring which, as noted above, tend to be associated with relatively high levels of positive marital satisfaction. Based on the data, volatile couples are likely to be those whom others describe as fighting often but passionate, and as partners who appear to have a strong and intimate connection. Validating couples displayed an intermediate level of emotional expressiveness, showing moderate levels of positive and negative affect. These are the couples whose relationships seem to progress smoothly and calmly, where passion may not be as evident as the level of comfort that partners have with each other. Conflict-avoiding couples were the least expressive of emotion of any sort, positive or negative. These couples tended to avoid bringing up or dealing with conflictual issues, seeming to prefer to agree to disagree. In such couples, partners may appear to get along well and have few, if any, rancorous disagreements, but the intimacy observed in volatile and validating couples may be attenuated somewhat in conflict-avoiding couples.

Research shows that the three stable couple types have more positive than negative behaviors and cannot be distinguished from each other on the ratio of positive to negative behaviors. As can be noted from this brief description (see

Gottman, 1993b, for further information), just because couples are unlikely to divorce does not mean that they are similar in their methods of handling conflict, although partners do appear on the whole to be more positive than negative with one another.

Unstable marriages (couples typed as hostile or hostile-detached) evidenced slightly fewer positive than negative behaviors (positive: negative ratio of 0.8:1), and their conversations were generally quite negative. Extrapolating from the data, hostile couples may be those who are in constant conflict with each other and often make angry, unkind comments toward one another. The anger partners feel toward each other may appear to be just under the surface and easily provoked, although partners may not appear to be angry and bitter individuals in other contexts. Hostile-detached couples may appear more bitter and resigned with each other than consistently angry; partners may be observed to make sarcastic, disrespectful side-comments about each other rather than often engaging directly in conflict.

THEORETICAL MODELS OF THE COURSE OF MARRIAGE

Relatively few longitudinal studies of marriage have been theory-driven. As a consequence, over the past several decades, the marital research field has become broader (targeting an ever-widening array of variables) but not deeper, thus failing to advance a more thorough explanation of the longitudinal course of marriage (Karney & Bradbury, 1995). For a review of the behavioral, social exchange, crisis, and attachment theories of marriage and the research that supports them, the reader is referred to Karney & Bradbury's article. The present chapter focuses on two promising new models that offer integrative explanations of marital change, Gottman's Cascade Toward Dissolution and Karney & Bradbury's Vulnerability–Stress–Adaptation model. These two models were chosen for review because of their ability to identify the marital processes or mechanisms that are associated with marital dissolution and to describe specific pathways that lead couples toward either marital dissolution or marital stability.

The Cascade toward Dissolution Model

John Gottman (1993a; 1993b; 1994) has introduced a balance theory of marriage to inform and integrate work done in the field of marital relationships. He theorizes that there is a continuum between marital quality and divorce, such that couples who divorce usually remain unhappily married for some time before seriously considering ending the relationship, then actually separate and divorce. In his work he uses an observational coding system, the RCISS (Rapid Couples Interaction Scoring System), to assign couples to "regulated" and "non-regulated" groups based on the behaviors they display in problem-solving discussions. Regulated couples have positive speaker slopes, meaning that when the amount of negativity in a couple's interaction is subtracted from the amount of coded positivity, the balance favors positivity (as noted in the case of the three types of stable couples discussed in Gottman, 1993b, above). In contrast, the balance of positive and negative behaviors does not favor positivity in non-regulated, hostile or hostile-detached, couples. Regulated and non-regulated couples show distinct trajectories toward stability or dissolution, with longitudinal data indicating that non-regulated couples are more likely to be unhappily married and more likely to consider terminating the marriage. It is the balance between positivity and negativity that Gottman considers to be key in predicting which couples are most at risk for discord and instability in their relationships. Evaluating the rate at which couples communicate positively and negatively with one another may be a useful tool for clinicians in both assessing a couple's relationship health and planning areas for intervention.

As other researchers have suggested, Gottman (1993a; 1994) found that some negative behaviors are more predictive of marital dissatisfaction and dissolution than others. For example, global levels of anger or conflict were not been found to be very good predictors of marital quality or stability over time. However, husbands' defensiveness, contempt, and withdrawal, and wives' criticism, defensiveness, and contempt were associated with greater risk for divorce. Using structural equation modeling, Gottman found these variables to be related to one another in a predictable fashion. More specifically, he described the results as supporting a "process cascade in which criticism leads to contempt, which leads to defensiveness, which leads to stonewalling (Gottman, 1993a, p. 62)." Stonewalling, defined as withdrawal from the interaction, was found to be more characteristic of males, although present in the behavior of both genders.

In addition to the process (behavioral) cascade, Gottman found evidence for a perceptual cascade called a "distance and isolation cascade", which was also predictive of marital dissolution in his studies. The distance and isolation cascade begins with flooding, which occurs when a spouse perceives the partner's negative emotions to be unexpected, intense, overwhelming, and disorganizing, such that the spouse will resort to any behavior to end the interaction. In the case of distressed couples, once a spouse feels flooded by the partner's negative emotional response, he/she begins to distort ambiguous cues in the direction of seeing them as threatening or frustrating, and attributes the behaviors to the personality of the partner as opposed to the situation in which the partners find themselves. With this component of the model, Gottman draws from existing research on spouses' maladaptive attributions, which are known to co-vary with marital distress, co-vary with negative behavior in marital interaction, and predict declines in marital satisfaction (see Bradbury & Fincham, 1990, for a review).

Particularly important for clinicians to note in assessing whether or not a couple has begun engagement in the distance and isolation cascade is whether one partner begins to see the other's behaviors as stable, global, and internal characteristics, rather than as temporary actions arising from conflictual moments in the context of a marital disagreement. These attributions are difficult to disconfirm and often lead to feelings of defensiveness. Feelings of distance and isolation appear to follow, with spouses perceiving their marital problems as severe and easier to work out on one's own rather than together. When feeling this way, couples often create parallel lives for themselves, with ensuing feelings of loneliness (Gottman, 1993a).

The possibility of divorce is great when a couple reaches this stage of disaffection and distance in the relationship. In order to help partners return to a point at which they can function as a team, Gottman proposes three components of "minimal marital therapy". These three components are often employed in couples' therapy and include learning how to present issues and criticisms non-defensively and non-provocatively, validation and non-defensive listening, and editing negative responses. Several therapeutic approaches have employed these skills with distressed couples; clinical experience would suggest, however, that these tools, in and of themselves, are unlikely to be sufficient for couples in which partners have strong, global, negative attributions about each other. For example, for those couples entrenched in the distance and isolation cascade, these behavioral communication skills are unlikely to affect the negative cognitions and strong negative emotions that maintain distance between partners. For these couples, "minimal marital therapy" will have to be supplemented by other strategies. These would include the clinician actively engaging partners in challenging their own faulty cognitions about each other, and providing structure and anger management techniques to couples (e.g. time out procedures and relaxation techniques), so that they will be able to engage the communication skills discussed by Gottman in the most productive manner.

Gottman's model is a valuable step in the right direction, because it discusses potential mechanisms explaining how an initially satisfying and stable marriage might become unhappy and unstable over time. However, as is the case with other behavioral and social exchange models, this model tends to minimize the importance of personality variables, life events, and family/relationship history. In addition, although Gottman clearly articulates links between the constructs of marital quality (such as negative and positive behaviors) and stability, he fails to articulate different predictors of the two constructs. In their Vulnerability–Stress–Adaptation model of marriage, Karney & Bradbury (1995) integrate elements of behavioral, attachment, and crisis theories in an effort to formulate a comprehensive model with which to explain the development of quality and stability in marriage.

The Vulnerability–Stress–Adaptation Model

In brief, Karney & Bradbury (1995) postulate that marital outcomes are most directly a consequence of adaptive processes, or the ways individuals and couples contend with differences of opinion and individual or marital difficulties and transitions. Adaptive processes refer to communication between partners, attributions partners make about each other, and partners' ability to provide support and understanding to each other (Karney & Bradbury, 1995). This element of their model represents an expanded version of traditional behavioral and social-learning approaches to marriage, where the focus is primarily on marital problem-solving. Karney & Bradbury expand the traditional approach further by arguing that adaptive processes are shaped by: (a) the personal strengths and weaknesses (or enduring vulnerabilities) that spouses bring to marriage, such as stable demographic, historical, personality and experiential factors; and (b) the stressful events, developmental transitions and chronic or acute circumstances that spouses and couples encounter. The Vulnerability–Stress–Adaptation model suggests that marital outcomes will emerge from the interaction of the three domains of adaptive processes, enduring vulnerabilities and stressful events. For example, couples who are relatively poor at contending with the stressful situations they encounter may have satisfying relationships if they encounter few such situations and if they possess few enduring vulnerabilities. In contrast, even couples who are quite capable at resolving personal and interpersonal problems can have poor marital outcomes, if they must contend with many such problems, and if their personal resources for doing so are limited.

This framework builds upon the tenets of social exchange theory by arguing that when a couple's capacity to adapt to challenges flexibly is poor, the costs of the relationship are perceived as high and the rewards perceived as low. When these perceptions are present, partners are more likely to experience dissatisfaction, conflict and/or emotional distance in their relationships. Similar to Gottman's theory, Karney & Bradbury suggest that once marital quality has eroded, the relationship is at greater risk for instability and dissolution.

One of the most appealing aspects of Karney & Bradbury's (1995) model is that it provides a variety of areas in which both individual and marital therapy may be utilized effectively to prevent and/or treat marital decline. Clinicians constantly encounter couples who are highly motivated to improve their relationships, but once certain aspects of their lives are revealed, it is apparent that the problems between partners have deep, historical roots. For example, cultural differences from families of origin may dictate that for one spouse, the raising of one's voice constitutes insulting, disrespectful behavior, while for the other spouse, yelling is a normative, acceptable manner in which to express emotions. These differences may affect the adaptive capability of the couple to manage differences and stressful events. According to the Vulnerability–Stress–Adaptation model, as long as each partner has few personal weaknesses and the couple encounters few highly stressful events, their relationship is likely to succeed. However, if added to this cultural, communication difference is a history of victimization on the part if one spouse, this may constitute an enduring vulnerability that may adversely impact the couple's ability to handle delicate issues such as sexuality, power and respect in the relationship. For a couple such as this, where adaptive processes and personal strength are compromised, the Vulnerability–Stress–Adaptation model suggests that their relationship is fragile and in need of intervention on multiple levels.

Summary

The study of marriage has become relatively advanced in its ability to identify the factors that predict marital outcomes, in terms of both marital quality and stability. Behavioral factors, including highly negative and destructive communication patterns indicative of an inability to adequately resolve problems, have proven to be among the strongest predictors of both dissatisfaction and divorce. Conversely, positive behaviors, such as affection, caring and support, predict marital satisfaction and stability. As noted above, data suggest that it is not the mere presence of negativity in a relationship in and of itself that affects longevity, but rather how couples negotiate difficulties and regulate their negative feelings that serve to either protect and strengthen or erode relationships. Less clear in the literature, however, is how aspects of marital quality, including behaviors and perceptions of satisfaction, develop over time in relationships, and exactly how marital quality as a construct relates to relationship stability. Karney & Bradbury (1995) in particular offer a comprehensive theoretical model explaining the relations between the constructs. As part of their model, Karney & Bradbury hypothesize that how couples are able to adapt to life transitions affects both marital stability and quality. Although the literature on developmental milestones in marriage rarely discusses how stability and quality are related, numerous studies have taken place examining both outcomes at various transitional stages in the family life-cycle.

DEVELOPMENTAL MILESTONES IN THE FAMILY LIFE-CYCLE: EFFECTS ON MARITAL STABILITY AND QUALITY

A number of developmental milestones in relationship and family life have been identified, and the effects of such normative changes on marital stability and quality over time have been assessed (see Belsky, 1990; Feeney, Peterson & Noller, 1994). In general, researchers have examined four primary developmental milestones: (a) the transition from dating or cohabiting to marriage; (b) the transition to first-time parenthood; (c) parenting of adolescent-aged children; and (d) the "empty nest", or the period after which the youngest child leaves home. Most of the investigations into family milestones have focused on the transition to parenthood (e.g. Belsky & Rovine, 1990; Hock et al., 1995; Kurdek, 1993; Lindahl, Clements & Markman, in press; MacDermid, Huston & McHale, 1990; Wallace & Gotlib, 1990, to name only a few), although a few studies have been conducted examining the other transitions (see Belsky, 1990).

It is most likely that these four transitional periods in relationship and family history exist across cultures, although it must be stated from the outset that family developmental milestones are likely to have different meanings for marriages in various parts of the world. For example, in many non-Western cultures, family units tend to include extended family members, particularly grandparents. These family members may act as a buffer against many of the stresses associated with transitions across the family life cycle, by providing couples with instrumental support (e.g. assistance with child-rearing and household chores), emotional support and advice in managing marital conflicts, and guidance for the complexities of raising children. Families in industrialized, Western cultures tend to be confined to the nuclear unit. Thus, partners tend to have only each other to rely on to cope with life changes and fulfill emotional needs. In addition, there are some cultures, primarily those that are agriculturally-based, wherein children (particularly sons) may never leave the home of their parents, such that an "empty nest" period is never present. Finally, other important markers of family development may exist, including the arrival of spouses' own parents in the home after children have moved on to their own families. Although it has not been a subject of empirical study, in Western cultures where advances in medicine have markedly increased the life-span, the occurrence of parenting one's own parents increasingly has become more common and likely has a profound impact on marital adjustment in the later years of life.

Unfortunately, most of the data available to discuss the development of relationships across family transitions come from studies of Anglo populations in the USA. The present section reviews the empirical literature that provides, with these populations, a description of how couple relationships adapt to the normative changes in family life. When available, cross-cultural data are included. Correlates of both stability and quality of relationships will be discussed.

The Transition to Marriage

Approximately nine out of ten individuals in the USA marry (Ahlburg & DeVita, 1992), and it is likely that these numbers are similar across Western cultures. As has been well documented in a number of studies predicting divorce (e.g. Gottman, 1994), however, the decision to marry in and of itself cannot ensure that a relationship necessarily will be stable. With regard to quality of relationships, research has documented that couples tend to be at their happiest during the premarital and newlywed phases of relationships, with evidence of some declines in satisfaction over the next several years, in couples both with and without children (Huston, McHale & Crouter, 1986; MacDermid, Huston & McHale, 1990; Markman & Hahlweg, 1993).

In one of the few longitudinal studies describing couples at the transition to marriage, the Denver Family Development Project found that at the premarriage stage, aspects of couples' observed communication behavior were related to relationship satisfaction and predicted later marital distress and divorce (Markman, 1984; Markman & Hahlweg, 1993; Markman, Jamieson & Floyd, 1983; Lindahl, Clements & Markman, in press). Markman and his colleagues found that at premarriage, a number of husband and wife communication behaviors, such as negativity, poor problem-solving skills and emotional invalidation, led to poor prognosis for couples, in terms of relationship stability and satisfaction (see above section discussing the Denver Family Development Project).

While it is not known whether, in the USA, various ethnic groups differ in the quality of their relationships or levels of marital satisfaction in the newlywed period, it appears that African-American men and women and Hispanic women are far more reluctant to marry than are their Anglo counterparts (South, 1993), and that African-American couples tend to be less happy in marriage in general than Anglos (Broman, 1993). Although marriage generally is considered a protective factor against many life difficulties, in terms of both physical and mental health (see Zick & Smith, 1991), fewer benefits may be associated with marriage for those who are not part of the dominant group in Western cultures (please see the Jones & Chao chapter on socio-cultural issues and healthy relationships, this volume, for more information on this important issue). At least in part, reluctance to marry may indicate a concern with taking on family responsibilities when such responsibilities are perceived as difficult to meet. In societies that provide ethnic minorities with fewer opportunities for economic and educational advancement, people of color may see marriage less as a protection against stressful life events and more as an undertaking that includes a set of responsibilities that are difficult to meet. Thus, if ambivalence is present from the outset, there may be important ramifications for marital stability and quality across the family life-cycle.

The Transition to Parenthood

The shifts in lifestyle and priorities that accompany the birth of a first child are profound and, according to most research, have a significant impact on marriage. By far, the preponderance of empirical information on developmental milestones in marriage comes from studies at the transition to parenthood. With regard to marital stability, data are fairly consistent in indicating that couples with children tend to have lower divorce rates than couples without children (see Belsky, 1990). Many studies examining various mechanisms of change related to the transition to parenthood have stressed the need to examine multiple, multi-systemic indices of how marriages weather this change (e.g. Belsky & Rovine, 1990; Levy-Shiff, 1994). Toward that end, studies have found that several variables are related to the addition of a child, such as shifts to more traditional division of labor roles for mothers and fathers, and a decrease in the amount of time couples spend on companionate activities with one another (Kurdek, 1993; MacDermid, Huston & McHale, 1990; Wallace & Gotlib, 1990). In addition, although occasionally investigations fail to find marital quality differences between groups of first-time parents and non-parents at the same point in relationship time (e.g. MacDermid, Huston & McHale, 1990), most studies (both cross-sectional and longitudinal) indicate a fairly reliable decrease in self-reported marital quality following the birth of a first child (see Belsky, 1990).

A widely accepted notion has been that the association between marital quality and age of children is a curvilinear one, such that accompanying the birth of a first child is a marked decline in marital quality, which continues for several years, levels off, and than begins to rise again, presumably when children leave home and spouses are able to spend more time together again. This theory, however, has been a source of some controversy, given that not all data indicating declines in marital quality fit the curvilinear model (see Belsky, 1990, for a comprehensive review). Data on the quality of the marital relationship at the transition to parenthood are complicated by the fact that different measures of marital quality, from rate of interaction to satisfaction, have been used, a variety of self-report measures have been used to assess each area of functioning, and few studies have combined questionnaire with observational methods. Questions then arise concerning the nature of any decline in marital quality, and whether the same processes account for decreased marital functioning across couples (Belsky & Rovine, 1990; Kurdek, 1993).

Data gathered thus far on spousal relationships at the transition to parenthood have not discovered a single underlying process of disruption. Several promising mechanisms, however, have been proposed. For example, Belsky & Rovine (1990) derived a set of variables that classified transition to parenthood couples into those whose relationships improved moderately and those whose relationships declined in marital quality. They examined 128 Anglo couples from the last trimester of pregnancy to 3 years after the birth of a child and were able to classify couples into those that experienced either improvement or decline based on self-reported demographic, personality, and marital variables, such as level of education, interpersonal sensitivity, and the degree to which each marriage was perceived either as a romance, a partnership, or a friendship. Those marriages adversely affected at the transition to parenthood appeared to have, for example, less income, less education, fewer years of marriage before childbirth, and younger partners who were less interpersonally sensitive and had lower self-esteem before the birth of the child. In addition, couples with declines in marital quality appeared to perceive their relationships more as romances than partnerships or friendships before the birth of their child, perhaps indicating unrealistic expectations for the relationship in the face of parenthood (Belsky & Rovine, 1990). Furthermore, particularly for wives, reports of child temperament were able to improve prediction of improvement or decline (Belsky & Rovine, 1990). Because young couples tend to be fairly satisfied with their relationships and rarely present in therapy prior to having children, clinicians do not often have the opportunity to intervene with young couples. If couples do come to therapy before having children, however, exploring the perceptions and expectations each partner holds about the nature of the relationship, and preparing them for the need to work as team-mates and not just romantic partners, is likely to be an important intervention in shoring up a marriage prior to childbirth.

In a multi-ethnic sample of married couples in Israel important for both its cross-cultural significance and use of multiple research methods, Levy-Shiff (1994) examined predictors of marital functioning across the transition to parenthood (pregnancy to the 9th month of childhood). While she found that marital satisfaction generally declined from the last trimester of pregnancy to 9 months post-partum, different predictors at many levels of analysis appeared to be associated with changes, both positive and negative, for men and women. For both mothers and fathers, marital quality increased in relation to fathers' involvement with their children and fathers' perceptions of themselves as caring and nurturing. Mothers who reported declines in marital quality also perceived their children as difficult, described themselves as highly impulsive, and felt strongly about the role of work in their lives. Fathers' reports of marital quality declined as mothers' involvement with children increased, perhaps because less time was available for companionate activities, as noted in other studies (see Levy-Shiff, 1994), or perhaps because fathers felt excluded from the mother–child dyad.

Levy-Shiff found that Western women spent less time with their children than did non-Western women, and non-Western men spent less time in child care than did Western men. Despite this finding, Levy-Shiff also discovered that non-Western women were less likely to report declines in marital quality. Alternate hypotheses for these data are either that these women are less likely to honestly report difficulty on psychological questionnaires, or that, based on the assumption that non-Western families are more traditional, non-Western families place a higher value on motherhood and afford it more status. Thus, Levy-Shiff hypothesizes, less ambiguity exists in roles, and the transitional period to parenting is fraught with far fewer areas for conflict and re-adjustment in non-Western families. The Belsky & Rovine (1990) and Levy-Shiff (1994) data, although suffering from some limitations, such as the reliance on self-reports (Belsky & Rovine) or the lack of pre-pregnancy marital data (both studies), suggest that multiple determinants of marital quality may exist longitudinally, with the addition of a child into the family impacting only indirectly on the marriage.

Another potential mechanism for understanding the nature of decline in marital quality over the transition to parenthood is the interplay between individual partners' sex-role beliefs and both partners' gender-based behaviors. Several studies have examined perceptions of sex-roles for women and men longitudinally (e.g. Bradbury, Campbell & Fincham, 1995), including over the transition to parenthood (Hock et al., 1995; MacDermid, Huston & McHale, 1990). In one of the few studies examining the transition to parenthood in both married and non-married couples, Hock et al. (1995) assessed the extent to which sex-role beliefs affected relationship satisfaction (as well as maternal depression). In this short-term longitudinal study, Hock and her colleagues found that fathers' endorsement of more traditional sex roles for themselves and their partners during pregnancy had a small but significant negative association with satisfaction with the relationship when their babies were 9 months old (Hock et al., 1995). It is possible that fathers who are more traditional in terms of sex-role orientation tend to withdraw somewhat from parenting behaviors, which may in turn impact how much mothers feel they are being supported and assisted with the new task of child-rearing.

Examining the associations among sex role traditionalism and marital quality more broadly, MacDermid, Huston & McHale (1990) found that, regardless of whether or not they experienced having a baby, couples over the first two-and-a-half years of marriage became somewhat more traditional in their role orientations and division of family tasks. Neither role orientation nor division of labor in and of itself predicted change in marital quality for couples. The data from MacDermid and colleagues indicate that declines in marital adjustment at the transition to parenthood are not necessarily related to sex roles *per se*. Instead, the transition to parenthood is a time when family tasks increase. At this time, if discrepancies between role orientations and role-related behavior exist (thus certain expectations regarding spousal behavior are violated), couple relationships may suffer. Violated expectations (in a negative direction) are often sources of discord in spousal relationships, which may be heightened at periods of stress and transition.

As noted in Karney & Bradbury's Vulnerability–Stress–Adaptation model (1995), stressful life events, such as the addition of a child into the couple relationship, are part of only one of the three domains of functioning that interact to determine marital stability and quality. The degree to which having a child will impact marital functioning, as can be extrapolated from the above data base, depends on multiple factors, with most of the data focusing on variables that can be categorized into the domains of adaptive processes and stressful events. Clearly, issues related to individual strengths and weaknesses, or individual historical events and experiences, such as the manner in which one was parented, will also have an impact on how a spouse will function as a new parent.

The Transition to Adolescence

Compared to the large number of studies conducted that examine the impact of a new baby on marriage, little research has examined how marriages weather the shift of children from school age to the often stormy adolescent period. Based on a search of the literature, it appears that there is a general lack of data on how the transition to adolescence is related to marital quality, and virtually no studies exist regarding this transitional period and its impact on marital stability. This lack of empirical data is likely to stem from the fact that research clearly is more difficult at this period, as adolescence, for better or worse, can be a relatively drawn-out transition, whereas the birth of a child is a discrete developmental transition in the family life-cycle. Clinical experience suggests that, despite a lack of research data on the subject, the period in which the oldest child becomes a teenager often potentiates may previously hidden family and marital difficulties, such as differences in discipline, ideas about levels of independence of growing children, and communication about issues such as sexuality, responsibility and even who makes decisions about use of the family car.

Belsky (1990) reviewed the only two longitudinal studies of the transition to adolescence, which found very little to suggest that marital quality is affected by the transition of an offspring from childhood to adolescence. Menaghan (1983) examined families for whom the oldest child was becoming a teenager and the youngest child was entering school. Menaghan found that at this period of family upheaval and reorganization, declines in marital satisfaction were related to equity imbalances in the relationship.

The Transition to the "Empty Nest"

As is true in the transition to adolescence, few studies have longitudinally examined what couple relationships look like through the stage in which the last child leaves home, in terms of either stability or relationship quality. Presumably, if couples have managed to stay together until this point in the family life-cycle, their relationships likely will last through the transition to the "empty nest". Indeed, cross-sectional data indicate that at this point in marriage there are fewer threats to stability, at least in part because of observed increases in marital quality (see the Dickson chapter on aging and marriage, this volume, for further information). Feeney, Peterson & Noller (1994) found that, as with couples in the child-rearing stage of marriage, spouses at the transition to having independent adult children report higher satisfaction when fairness and equal contributions by spouses in the partnership exist. Similar results were also obtained by Menaghan (1983).

Summary

Available data on the stability and quality of couple relationships at various developmental milestones in family life indicate that, indeed, there are some effects of the processes of transition and adaptation on marital functioning. Although scarce, data on marital stability indicate that, while marriage in and of itself is not a predictor of couple longevity (although some would argue that married couples break up less than non-married couples), the addition of a child appears to strengthen the couple relationship bond (see Belsky, 1990). Why that finding exists, or whether it means that couples then stay together only for the sake of children, remains a question. The extensive data on marital quality at the transition to parenthood indicates that children in and of themselves do not inextricably hurt marriage. If at the transition to parenthood personal or economic resources are scarce, or expectations about how labor will be divided are violated, among other factors, problems may arise in couple relationships. Some data also indicate that a child's temperament may affect the marriage. In general, however, data on marital quality at the transition to parenthood suggest that the impact of first-time children on the couple relationship is small, albeit fairly consistent (Belsky, 1990). As noted above, clinicians dealing with couples at this transition have the difficult task of examining multiple aspects of the marriage, the individual partners, and also the context of social support for the couple at the transition to parenthood, as having children potentiates changes in the couple relationship that may give rise to difficulties that may or may not have already existed to some degree. This potentiation of problems may particularly occur at this transition, as the added responsibility of a child by necessity requires more interdependence of partners.

As children grow and become more independent, it appears that fewer effects of children on marriage exist, and that greater independence of children, if having any impact, leads to increased marital quality. It must be noted, however, that research on the question of how older children affect marriage is quite difficult to conduct and has yet to answer the question in a longitudinal fashion. One of the most interesting gaps in the literature is the failure to measure issues in quality of family relationships as a whole, in addition to the marital relationship, as well as the extent to which the couple relationship becomes of subordinate importance in the family. It is possible that, although partners may respond to questions about their marriage in such a way that indicates some decline in quality of the couple relationship, these declines may be balanced by indications of satisfaction and quality of family relationships more generally.

CONCLUDING REMARKS

While notable strides have been made recently in our understanding of how marriages change over time and the forces that propel them to change, this is clearly an area in which more work is needed. It appears that the field is poised to reach for this new level of maturity. To increase our sophistication in explaining the developmental course of marriage, several goals for the field are recommended.

First, more theory-driven longitudinal research that looks at the same couples over multiple transitions in the family life-cycle will be necessary if we are to deepen our understanding of what happens to relationships over time. Second, while several factors that are predictive of marital stability are also predictive of marital quality, this is not always the case. Models that can differentially predict these two critical outcomes are needed, particularly if, as clinicians, we are to target effectively areas of relationships that require intervention. Bolstering a couple's skills, such that they are likely to stay together longer, will serve little purpose unless we are able also to improve partners' sense of happiness and fulfillment. Third, most studies have looked at direct, linear effects, rather than testing for possible mediating and moderating relationships. Until the associations among predictors are explored more carefully, we must be cautious in making statements about how various factors are related to marital outcomes.

Finally, research examining the longitudinal predictors of marital quality has almost uniformly assessed either marital satisfaction or marital stability as the outcome variable of interest. Very rarely have other possibilities been considered, such as marital and family cohesiveness, intimacy, and even the extent to which a relationship is seen as a contributing force and symbol of stability and strength in a community. Given the ideal that marriages constitute a basic and significant building block of society, it is important to begin to measure the impact of marriages on communities. As therapists, it is critical that we continue to utilize clinical and empirical resources in an effort to strengthen marriages and, by extension, communities.

REFERENCES

Ahlburg, D.A. & DeVita, C.J. (1992). New realities of the American family. *Population Bulletin*, **47**(2), 1–43.

Belsky, J. (1990). Children in marriage. In F.D. Fincham & T. Bradbury (eds), *The Psychology of Marriage: Basic Issues and Applications* (pp. 172–200). New York: Guilford.

Belsky, J. & Rovine, M. (1990). Patterns of marital change across the transition to parenthood: pregnancy to three years postpartum. *Journal of Marriage and the Family*, **52**, 5–19.

Bolger, N., DeLongis, A., Kessler R.C. & Wethington, E. (1989). The contagion of stress across multiple roles. *Journal of Marriage and the Family*, **51**, 175–183.

Bradbury, T.N., Campbell, S.M. & Fincham, F.D. (1995). Longitudinal and behavioral analysis of masculinity and femininity in marriage. *Journal of Personality and Social Psychology*, **68**, 328–341.

Bradbury, T.N. & Fincham, F.D. (1990). Attributions in marriage: review and critique. *Psychological Bulletin*, **104**, 3–33.

Broman, C.L. (1993). Race differences in marital well-being. *Journal of Marriage and the Family*, **55**, 724–732.

Cherlin, A. (1981). *Marriage, Divorce, and Remarriage*. Cambridge, MA: Harvard University Press.

Conger, R.D., Elder, G.H., Lorenz, F.O., Conger, K.J., Simons, R.L., Whitbeck, L.B., Huck, S. & Melby, J.N. (1990). Linking economic hardship to marital quality and instability. *Journal of Marriage and the Family*, **52**, 643–656.

Elder, G.H. & Caspi, A. (1988). Economic stress in lives: developmental perspectives. *Journal of Social Issues*, **44**, 25–45.

Emery, R.E. (1988). *Marriage, Divorce, and Children's Adjustment*. Newbury Park, CA: Sage.

Feeney, J., Peterson, C. & Noller, P. (1994). Equity and marital satisfaction over the life cycle. *Personal Relationships*, **1**, 83–99.

Fitzpatrick, M.A. (1988). *Between Husbands and Wives: Communication in Marriage*. Newbury Park, CA: Sage.

Gottman, J.M. (1993a). A theory of marital dissolution and stability. *Journal of Family Psychology*, **7**, 57–75.

Gottman, J.M. (1993b). The roles of conflict engagement, escalation, or avoidance in marital interaction: a longitudinal view of five types of couples. *Journal of Consulting and Clinical Psychology*, **61**, 6–15.

Gottman, J.M. (1994). *What Predicts Divorce? The Relationship Between Marital Processes and Marital Outcomes*. Hillsdale, NJ: Erlbaum.

Gottman, J.M. & Katz, L. (1989). Effects of marital discord on young children's peer interaction and health. *Developmental Psychology*, **25**, 373–381.

Gottman, J.M. & Krokoff, L.J. (1989). Marital interaction and satisfaction: a longitudinal view. *Journal of Consulting and Clinical Psychology*, **57**, 47–52.

Greenstein, T.N. (1990). Occupation and divorce. *Journal of Family Issues*, **6**, 347–357.

Heavey, C.L., Layne, C. & Christensen, A. (1993). Gender and conflict structure in marital interaction: a replication and extension. *Journal of Consulting and Clinical Psychology*, **61**, 16–27.

Hock, E., Schirtzinger, M.B., Lutz, W.J. & Widaman, K. (1995). Maternal depressive symptomatology over the transition to parenthood: assessing the influence of marital satisfaction and marital sex role traditionalism. *Journal of Family Psychology*, **9**, 79–88.

Howes, P. & Markman, H.J. (1989). Marital quality and child functioning: a longitudinal investigation. *Child Development*, **60**, 1044–1051.

Huston, T.L. & Chorost, A.F. (1994). Behavioral buffers on the effect of negativity on marital satisfaction: a longitudinal study. *Personal Relationships*, **1**, 223–239.

Huston, T.L., McHale, S.M. & Crouter, A. (1986). When the honeymoon's over: changes in the marriage relationship over the first year. In R. Gilmour & S. Duck (eds), *The Emerging Field of Personal Relationships*. Hillsdale, NJ: Erlbaum.

Huston, T.L. & Vangelisti, A.M. (1991). Socio-emotional behavior and satisfaction in marital relationships: a longitudinal study. *Journal of Personality and Social Psychology*, **61**, 721–733.

Karney, B.R. & Bradbury, T.N. (1995). The longitudinal course of marital quality and stability: a review of theory, method, and research. *Psychological Bulletin*, **118**, 3–34.

Krokoff, L.J., Gottman, J.M. & Roy, A.K. (1988). Blue-collar and white-collar marital interaction and communication orientation. *Journal of Social and Personal Relationships*, **5**, 201–221.

Kuh, D. & Maclean, M. (1990). Women's childhood experience of parental separation and their subsequent health and socioeconomic status in adulthood. *Journal of Biosocial Science*, **22**, 121–135.

Kurdek, L.A. (1993). Nature and prediction of changes in marital quality for first-time parent and non-parent husbands and wives. *Journal of Family Psychology*, **6**, 255–263.

Levenson, R. & Gottman, J.M. (1985). Physiological and affective predictors of change in relationship satisfaction. *Journal of Personality and Social Psychology*, **49**, 85–94.

Levy-Shiff, R. (1994). Individual and contextual correlates of marital change across the transition to parenthood. *Developmental Psychology*, **30**, 591–601.

Lindahl, K.M., Clements, M. & Markman, H.J. (in press). The development of marriage: a nine-year perspective. In T.N. Bradbury (ed.), *The Developmental Course of Marital Dysfunction*. Cambridge: Cambridge University Press.

MacDermid, S.M., Huston, T.L. & McHale, S.M. (1990). Changes in marriage associated with the transition to parenthood: individual differences as a function of sex-role attitudes and changes in the division of household labor. *Journal of Marriage and the Family*, **52**, 475–486.

Markman, H.J. (1981). The prediction of marital distress: a five-year follow-up. *Journal of Consulting and Clinical Psychology*, **49**, 760–762.

Markman, H.J., Jamieson, K.J. & Floyd, F.J. (1983). The assessment and modification of premarital relationships: preliminary findings on the etiology and prevention of marital distress. In J. Vincent (ed.), *Advances in Family Intervention, Assessment, and Theory*, Vol. 3 (pp. 41–90). Greenwich, CT: JAI Press.

Markman, H.J. & Hahlweg, K. (1993). The prediction and prevention of marital distress: an international perspective. *Clinical Psychology Review*, **13**, 29–43.

Markman, H.J., Renick, M.J., Floyd, F.I., Stanley, S.M. & Clements, M. (1993). Preventing marital distress through communication and conflict management training: a four- and five-year follow-up study. *Journal of Consulting and Clinical Psychology*, **61**, 70–74.

Menaghan, E. (1983). Marital stress and family transitions: a panel analysis. *Journal of Marriage and the Family*, **45**, 371–386.

Newcomb, M.D. (1986). Cohabitation, marriage, and divorce among adolescents and young adults. *Journal of Social and Personal Relationships*, **3**, 473–494.

Repetti, R.L. (1989). Effects of daily workload on subsequent behavior during marital interaction: the roles of social withdrawal and spouse support. *Journal of Personality and Social Psychology*, **57**, 651–659.

Rockwell, R.C., Elder, G.H. & Ross, D.J. (1979). Psychological patterns in marital timing and divorce. *Social Psychology Quarterly*, **42**, 399–404.

Sears, R.R. (1977). Sources of life satisfactions of the Terman gifted men. *American Psychologist*, **32**, 119–128.

South, S.J. (1993). Racial and ethnic differences in the desire to marry. *Journal of Marriage and the Family*, **55**, 357–370.

Teachman, J.D. & Polonko, K.A. (1990). Cohabitation and marital stability in the United States. *Social Forces*, **69**, 207–220.

Wallace, P.M. & Gotlib, I.H. (1990). Marital adjustment during the transition to parenthood: stability and predictors of change. *Journal of Marriage and the Family*, **52**, 21–29.

Woody, E.Z. & Costanzo, P.R. (1990). Does marital agony precede marital ecstasy? A comment on Gottman & Krokoff's "Marital interaction and satisfaction: a longitudinal view". *Journal of Consulting and Clinical Psychology*, **58**, 499–501.

Zick, C.D. & Smith, K.R. (1991). Marital transitions, poverty, and gender differences in mortality. *Journal of Marriage and the Family*, **53**, 327–336.

Chapter 10

Couples' Relationships and Children

Matthew R. Sanders*, Jan M. Nicholson** and Frank J. Floyd[†]
** Department of Psychology, University of Queensland,
St Lucia; and ** School of Public Health,
Queensland University of Technology,
Kelvin Grove Queensland, Australia;
and [†] Department of Psychology,
University of North Carolina, Chapel Hill, NC, USA*

Parenthood is a popular institution, with the majority (90%) of married couples having children (Houseknecht, 1987). Although couples have children later, and the number of couples who remain childless throughout their marriage has increased, for most couples having children is a natural and normal part of the adult life cycle. The transition to parenthood can be both a challenging and an extremely rewarding experience. The developmental literature highlights the dual function of the parental role. Parenting ensures the care, protection and education of the next generation. Parenting also contributes to an adult's own personal growth and development by enhancing competence and sense of identity. Marital partners are forced to reassess their priorities and, particularly for women, to temporarily delay career aspirations. They must become effective problem-solvers, advocates and better financial managers to simply cope with the demands of everyday living.

Although having children reduces the overall risk of marital breakdown (at least for a couple's first marriage), it is not a guarantee of marital harmony (Fergusson, Horwood & Lloyd, 1990). As parenthood is demanding and stressful, it can threaten the individual psychological well-being of individual marital partners as well as a couple's relationship.

Any examination of the association between marriage and children's adjust-

Clinical Handbook of Marriage and Couples Interventions. Edited by W. Kim Halford and Howard J. Markman.

ment must recognize the impact of important social changes in recent
decades that have affected family life and a couple's experience of parenthood.
These social changes include the high divorce rate, increasing acceptance of
non-marital cohabitation and ex-nuptial births, more readily available and
reliable methods of birth control, and greater involvement of married women
in both the full-time and part-time work force (Ochiltree, 1990). In Australia
in 1992, the majority of dependent children and young people still live at home
with both biological parents. However, a sizeable minority live in other
family constellations (14.9% live in a single-parent family and 5.4% live in a
step-family (Australian Bureau of Statistics, 1994)). This increasing diversity of
family structures demands that different types of family arrangements must be
understood in their own right. More specifically the association between a couple's relationship and their children's adjustment must be understood with the
expectation that the form of couple and family relationship experienced by the
child may change several times during childhood (Fergusson, Horwood &
Dimond, 1985).

There is a complex interrelationship between marital and parent–child relationships. The nature of this association may change over time as a result of
marriage breakdown and repartnering, and is best viewed as bi-directional and
dynamic, evolving over time, and being affected by a host of contextual factors
(Grych & Fincham, 1990).

The specific nature of the association between a couple's relationship and their
parenting experiences depends on a host of distal and proximal factors, including
child factors (e.g. the child's age, developmental level, temperament, behavioural
characteristics and health), individual parent factors (e.g. partners' views on
child-rearing, expectancies about parental roles, parenting skills and knowledge,
the mental health status of marital partners), couple factors (e.g. how couples
manage conflict in their relationships, their own parental modelling experiences
and histories of parental divorce), and external social factors impinging on marriage, such as the availability of social support, the couple's ongoing relationships
with their own parents and parents-in-law, and the couple's socio-economic
status.

Even though parenting issues are a frequent topic of conflict in couples
presenting for marital therapy, basic research on the interdependence of
marital and child adjustment problems needs to be drawn on more explicitly
in both the assessment of marital functioning, and in the treatment of conjoint
child and marital problems. This chapter provides an overview of the literature
on the relationship between marriage, parenting and child adjustment, and
aims to pinpoint implications for marital assessment and therapy. We review
the literature from two complementary perspectives: the effects of children
on marriage, and the effects of marriage on children. As marital breakdown followed by subsequent remarriage is common, we also discuss the
effects of remarriage on children and how children influence the quality of
remarried relationships. Finally, possible directions for future research are
discussed.

THE EFFECTS OF CHILDREN ON MARRIAGE

Children and Marital Stress

Traditionally, marital researchers and therapists have focused on the presence of children as a source of stress that negatively impacts upon the marital relationship. Support for this premise comes from a wide array of data on marital satisfaction and stability. Studies show that childless couples report higher levels of marital satisfaction than couples married for similar lengths of time who have become parents (e.g. Belsky & Pensky, 1988). Although it is a common colloquialism that children can "hold a marriage together", and indeed some couples remain together "for the sake of the children", it is equally likely that child-related stressors will undermine marital stability. Couples with children are only slightly more likely than childless couples to achieve long-term marital stability (Waite & Lillard, 1991). Further, single women with children have a lower probability of remarriage, and take longer to remarry after divorce than divorced women without children. The fact that women are usually the custodial parents following divorce accounts for their lower rates of remarriage and longer periods between marriages than men. Upon remarriage, negotiating relationships with children and stepchildren is perhaps the most significant challenge that threatens the well-being of the new marital relationship (Brand & Clingempeel, 1987).

The number and spacing of children also may affect marital adjustment. Earlier research suggested that marital satisfaction was lower for couples with many children spaced closely together than for couples with fewer children who were less densely spaced (Clausen & Clausen, 1973). However, because this trend was not consistently noted, the effects of child density may depend on other characteristics of the couples and the situation. For example, high density was negatively related to marital satisfaction for university students, but not for other samples of subjects, which may reflect the fact that parenting is particularly incompatible with the other demands of college life (Rollins & Galligan, 1978). Christensen (1968) proposes that the impact of child density depends on the couple's expectations about family size, and is negatively related to marital satisfaction only when it violates those expectations.

The most frequently cited evidence for the stress of children on marriage is cross-sectional data showing that marital satisfaction follows a U-shaped pattern, with the initial decline corresponding to the birth of the first child, and an increase occurring at the time that the children begin leaving home (e.g. Rollins & Feldman, 1970). Despite challenges, this has been a remarkably robust finding. For example, Spanier, Lewis & Cole (1975) questioned the apparent rise in marital functioning in the later years of marriage, but subsequent research has verified the presence of a significant curvilinear trend (Anderson, Russell & Schumm, 1983; Rollins & Galligan, 1978). Also, there are mixed findings about whether the decline in marital satisfaction during the early years of marriage, which has been attributed to the transition to parenthood, also occurs for childless couples over the same time period. McHale & Huston (1985) failed to find differences between couples who became parents vs. those who remained child-less during their first year of marriage. However, Cowan & Cowan's research (Cowan et al., 1985) does show more significant declines in marital satisfaction from before to after childbirth as compared with a matched sample of childless couples. Further, dozens of short-term longitudinal studies demonstrate that the event of childbirth is the precipitant of this decline (see Belsky & Pensky, 1988, for a review).

Limitations of Research on Child Stress Effects

There are some important caveats to consider in interpreting these data on the negative effects of children on marriage across the lifespan. Rollins & Galligan (1978) note that, despite the consistency of the findings regarding a U-shaped function, only 4–8% of marital satisfaction is associated with life-cycle stages. Thus, the bulk of individual differences in marital satisfaction cannot be attributed to the mere presence or absence of children. Additionally, they note that the research suggesting life-cycle effects is based on cross-sectional and short-term longitudinal data. This evidence makes it impossible to determine whether changes in satisfaction are actually caused by child effects, whether they are due to changes in the nature of the marital relationship itself over time, or whether they are caused by other events associated with adult development (e.g. career changes). They concede that child effects are suggested by evidence from older childless couples showing that qualitative aspects of marriage (e.g. communication, conflict management) and marital satisfaction resemble those of young childless couples. However, couples who delay having children, or choose not to have children, are probably a select and non-random sample in terms of their marital relationships.

Belsky & Pensky (1988) make a similar point about the course of long-term marital relationships, and argue that children may merely accentuate the changes that occur for couples with the passage of time. The few longitudinal studies that have used childless couples as controls (e.g. McHale & Huston, 1985; White & Booth, 1985) provide suggestive evidence that these couples show similar, though weaker, changes across time as couples who become parents. Further, in their longitudinal research with couples during the transition to parenthood, Cowan & Cowan (1988) found that the best predictor of marital quality after the birth of the child was the quality of the relationship beforehand. Although the transition to parenthood is a marker event for a general decline in marital satisfaction, couples show remarkable stability in their rank ordering for marital quality across this time (Belsky & Pensky, 1988).

Additionally, couples themselves may not perceive becoming a parent as a negative event. For example, Hoffman & Manis (1978) report interview data from their national sample of couples in which the wife was under 40. By using an open-ended response format, this research provides a view of what factors couples themselves see as salient. Consistent with studies using questionnaires, the couples in this study also reported a drop in marital satisfaction after the birth of the first child. However, the couples generally described the effects of children in positive ways. For example, they noted that the children brought them closer by giving them a shared task, increasing interdependence, creating a common goal, and providing shared joys. Negative effects were acknowledged, but to a lesser extent. These included, for example, having less time together as a couple, and having disagreements about child-rearing. Interestingly, childless couples who speculated about the potential impact of children on their marriages indicated that they feared that negative effects would predominate, but the couples with children tended to report more positive than negative effects. Similarly, perhaps research has over-emphasized negative effects and ignored the positive effects of children on couples' relationships.

The Hoffman & Manis (1978) study also sheds light on why declines in marital satisfaction during the child-rearing years may not threaten the general well being of most couples. Although their sample predominantly had young children, the data on marital adjustment were analysed according to family life-cycle stage, based on the ages of the youngest and oldest children. The results suggested that declines in marital satisfaction may be paired with declines in the salience of marriage to the individuals, with the goal of having a happy family life becoming more important than marital closeness during the parenting years. Couples with young children (under six) were more likely to note that both the positive and negative effects of children impacted on the marriage rather than on other domains of their lives. That is, marital closeness was a more important goal for these couples than it was at later stages of the family life cycle. Later, having a happy family life was the primary interest of the parents. Women tended to report that marital closeness became more salient again when the children became older and the couple approached the launching stage, coinciding with the point where marital satisfaction increases once again.

Nonetheless, with these qualifications in mind, it remains a reliable finding that the sum of all positive and negative effects of parenthood on the well-being of parents is balanced slightly toward the negative direction. Further, in their review of this research McLanahan & Adams (1987) conclude that among various measures of psychological well-being, the greatest impact of parenthood is felt in decreased marital happiness and greater worries, and that the negative effects have been increasing for the past 20 years and will continue to increase with the greater participation of women in the work force and increasing conflicts over gender-related family roles.

MECHANISMS BY WHICH CHILDREN INFLUENCE MARRIAGE

Raising children affects the development and well-being of parents through various pathways, including effects on individual development, emotional adjustment, social roles and economic well-being. For marriage, the most direct effects are those mediated through parenting experiences. Although this point may seem obvious, it is rarely made explicit by researchers, theorists and marital therapists. Nevertheless, the literature suggests several mechanisms for the influence of parenting on marriage.

Role Strain

One mechanism involves the build-up of demands and subsequent stress on the spouses associated with their parenting roles. Rollins & Galligan (1978) describe these effects in their model of family career transitions. Using work by Nye & Berardo (1973) and others, they propose that the effects of children and family size on marriage are accounted for by role accumulation associated with parenthood, which leads to role strain that disrupts the spouses' ability to enact marital roles that maintain satisfaction. They further argue that because so little of the variance in marital satisfaction is accounted for by family transitions, couples must learn strategies to avoid role strain. For example, one strategy may involve using family activities (e.g. involvement in children's recreational, sporting or artistic activities) to serve marital and parenting roles simultaneously.

Role Accumulation

A logical alternative to this role strain formulation posits that parenthood should have positive or negative effects depending upon whether it is associated with the accumulation of gratifying roles for the spouses. Role accumulation is presumed to be positive because it gives the individual alternative sources of gratification, so that well-being is not dependent upon success in a limited set of roles. This perspective is consistent with notions that parenthood can compensate for a bad marriage, or for limited career success. However, if parenting is so demanding that it obstructs other roles, such as outside employment for mothers, it decreases role accumulation and makes the person vulnerable to parenting stress. In support of this framework, a seminal study by Luckey & Bain (1970) revealed that couples low in marital satisfaction reported that children were the only source of joint satisfaction for them. Other research suggests that couples may increase their investment in parenting when marital difficulties arise (Brody, Pellegrini & Sigel, 1986). However, consistent with the role strain hypothesis, McLanahan & Adams' (1987) review suggests that role accumulation is more often associated with lower psychological well-being for parents.

Traditionalism

A third mechanism may be associated with the fact that gender roles become more traditional after the birth of a child, and appear to remain that way until children reach adolescence (e.g. Belsky, Lang & Rovine, 1985; Cowan & Cowan, 1988; Hoffman & Manis, 1978). Although sex-role attitudes also may vary to conform to the demands of parenting (Abrahams, Feldman & Nash, 1978), nonetheless, the more traditional roles are associated with greater conservatism in marital roles and less marital power for wives. This gender imbalance may account for why decreases in marital satisfaction are more reliably demonstrated for women as opposed to men (e.g. Belsky, 1990).

Parenting Alliance

A useful formulation for explaining both the positive and negative effects of children on marriage is the concept of the parenting alliance (e.g. Cohen & Weissman, 1984). This approach proposes that the couple's relationship as parents is itself a separate component of marital quality. Thus, for new parents, the new demands of parenting create new arenas for the couple working as a team, where they may either succeed or fail. Although at the time of the transition to parenthood, couples may initially complain that parenting disrupts marital roles (e.g. Cowan & Cowan, 1988), shortly afterwards and throughout the childhood years the major source of child-related stress for marriage appears to be disagreements about parenting (e.g. Hoffman & Manis, 1978). That is, instead of parenting disrupting existing marital roles, positive and negative experiences as a parenting team may be one among many shared couple experiences that determine how couples perceive the quality of their marital relationship. Parenting difficulties cause strain and discord for the marital partners, or conversely, parenting successes and accomplishments enhance the sense of closeness and happiness of the partners.

Gable, Belsky & Crnic (1992) offer a similar formulation in describing how marital quality affects child development. They contend that the parenting alliance is the central mediator by which marital problems disrupt child-rearing, or by which marital strengths benefit the child's well-being. Although research on the parenting alliance is sparse, initial studies document that it is related to, yet distinct from, other features of marital quality and that it is a predictor of a sense of competence in the parenting role (e.g. Floyd & Zmich, 1991, Frank et al., 1986). In their longitudinal study of couples during the transition to parenthood, Cowan & Cowan (1988) report that causal modelling of changes over time suggests that couples first experience stress in their roles as parents, and that this stress then negatively impacts upon marital satisfaction and personal well-being. Hopefully, future research will identify the factors that lead to the development of a positive parenting alliance, and will elucidate how the alliance can help to prevent declines in marital quality.

SPECIFIC EFFECTS OF CHILDREN AT VARIOUS LIFE-CYCLE STAGES

The question of the specific effects of children and parenting on the marital relationship has been most thoroughly studied at the point at which couples make the transition to parenthood, i.e. at the birth of the first child. In their review of both cross-sectional and longitudinal research on this period, Belsky & Pensky (1988) identify three areas of change in couples' relationships. As noted above, the birth of the first child marks the point at which the division of labour in the home becomes more traditional for couples, primarily because women assume the major responsibility for child care and household management. Second, as a result of the added burden for both partners, leisure activities for couples sharply decline, and joint activities tend to involve parenting or household chores rather than earlier forms of recreation. Third, the expression of affection tends to decrease between parents at a faster rate than between couples who do not have children.

Cowan & Cowan (1988) contend that spouses alter their sense of self by reducing the salience of "wife" or "husband" as an aspect of the self in order to make room for "mother" and "father" roles. Presumably, adopting a traditional division of labour, increasing family responsibilities while reducing couple activities, and reducing positive affectionate expressions are all be-havioural manifestations that either precede or follow from this cognitive shift. Cowan & Cowan (1988) also add to the list of potential stressors on marriage the fact that relationships with the couples' own parents may develop greater tension during this period, and that the couple experience changes in friendship networks and decreases in social support during the first year after childbirth. Importantly, all of these changes are paired with increasing conflict between the partners over child-related issues. The inability to resolve this con-flict effectively may be the most significant cause of deterioration in the marital relationship.

Relatively little research documents how children affect marriage at later points in the family life-cycle. Although conflicts about child-rearing may persist for some couples during the period of raising young children (e.g. Jouriles et al., 1991), others may adopt a division of labour that suc-cessfully avoids such conflicts (e.g. Floyd & Zmich, 1991). During the period of parenting adolescents, Hoffman & Manis' (1978) subjects reported that the negative impact of children involved worries about the safety and well-being of adolescents, rather than the effects of the child on marriage. However, they did note that teenagers curtailed the privacy of the couple more than did younger children. Also, Steinberg & Silverberg (1987) found that parents who had relatively distant relationships with their same-sex adolescents showed relatively greater declines in marital satisfaction over a 2-year period. Later, the point at which the children leave home sig-nals the return to a couple focus in the relationship, and greater attention to each other's individual needs (e.g. Menaghan, 1983). Indeed, com-panionship appears to be the primary component of marital satisfaction for older adults, although relationships with children continue to influence overall satisfaction with life in retirement (Floyd et al., 1992; Haynes et al., 1992).

EFFECTS OF CHILD DISABILITY OR HANDICAP ON MARRIAGE

The birth of a child with mental retardation or disability, or the later identification of a disability, is a period of acute crisis for couples (e.g. Klaus & Kennell, 1976). Additionally, episodes of emotional turmoil can recur throughout the child's lifetime as developmental milestones are missed or chronic medical conditions exacerbate (e.g. Wikler, 1986). The role tension hypothesis suggests that the added burden of caring for a child with special needs will exert particular stress on the marriage of the parents. However, there has been ongoing controversy in the research literature about these effects (Crnic, Friedrich & Greenberg, 1983). For example, Gath's (1977) data suggest substantial marital disruption for parents of young children with Down's syndrome. However, in Farber's seminal studies of family adaptation to mental retardation (e.g. Farber, 1959), he concluded that little marital disruption is directly linked to the birth or presence of the child with the handicap. Similarly, Korn, Chess & Fernandez (1978) examined families of children with congenital rubella and found that severe marital distress directly associated with the child's disabilities occurred in only 4% of their sample.

Other individual differences may make couples more or less vulnerable to experiencing negative outcomes. For example, marital distress may result when the spouses blame each other for the child's disability, or marital closeness may be enhanced when the couple join together to support an ill or needy child (e.g. Howard, 1978). There may also be life-cycle changes over the course of the child's development. Although some parents seem to accept long-term care of adult children with mental retardation as a positive role when they move into the later stages of life (Seltzer & Krauss, 1989), Howard (1978) reports that some mothers of physically handicapped children began to distance from the caretaking role during the child's adolescence, and re-emphasized marital closeness, similar to mothers of non-handicapped children.

Similar to findings about the effects of the transition to parenthood for parents of typically developing children, most couples who experience significant marital disruption showed signs of marital strain before the birth of a disabled child (Benson & Gross 1989). Further, marital satisfaction and the quality of the parenting alliance are among the most significant predictors of personal well-being and family adjustment for couples raising children with handicaps (Floyd & Zmich, 1991; Friedrich & Friedrich, 1981).

ROLE OF CHILD FOCUS IN THE TREATMENT OF MARITAL DISTRESS

Given the importance of parenting experiences and the parenting alliance as influences on marital quality, surprisingly little attention has focused on treating parenting problems in the context of marital therapy. Indeed, the literatures on marital therapy and on parenting interventions have been relatively independent. When a couple presents with parenting difficulties, therapists are encouraged to first diagnose the problem as primarily a marital problem or a parenting issue, and then implement the appropriate course of marital or parenting intervention. It is rarely acknowledged that these two components may be inextricably linked, or that therapists should be experienced in treating both types of problems simultaneously. No major studies of the effectiveness of marital therapy has focused on outcomes for the couples' relationship as parents, their parenting experiences, or the adjustment of the children. In general, the treatment literature has failed to recognize the need for a larger family system focus in treating marital problems.

There is, however, research showing that preventive interventions focused on parenting experiences may have positive effects on marital adjustment. For example, Markman & Kadushin (1986) showed that Lamaze training for first-time parents was associated with less severe declines in marital adjustment following childbirth as compared to couples who did not participate in Lamaze classes. A more comprehensive approach, directly addressing parenting stress, has been developed by the Cowans (e.g. Cowan & Cowan, 1988). They devised a couples' group intervention for couples going through the transition to parenthood that was designed to provide support and guidance about marital strains associated with this period, and to improve marital communication and conflict resolution concerning parenting issues. The couples who completed the intervention showed lesser declines in marital satisfaction following childbirth, and were less likely to divorce 2 and 3 years later than couples in a no-treatment group.

IMPACT OF COUPLES' RELATIONSHIPS ON CHILDREN

Healthy couple relationships may protect the well-being of family members and help to maintain quality family relationships. A positive, affectionate marital relationship predicts low levels of child and adolescent conduct problems, and provides a buffer for adults and children against a variety of stressors. However, many couples' relationships are characterized by frequent disagreement, dissatisfaction, or conflict. This section examines the impact of parents' relationships and relationship transitions on children.

Parental marital distress and interparental conflict are associated with significant concurrent and future adjustment problems for children (Emery, 1982; Grych & Fincham, 1990; Howes & Markman, 1989; Loeber & Stouthamer-Loeber, 1986). A dose–response relationship exists between child adjustment and the severity of marital distress. Children who are exposed to conflict which is more frequent, more intense, and which is overt rather than covert, tend to display more adjustment problems (Emery, 1982; Grych & Fincham, 1990; Reid & Crisafulli, 1990). These problems may take the form of externalizing problems (e.g. oppositional or conduct problems) or internalizing problems (e.g. anxiety, depression, somatic complaints) (Grych & Fincham, 1990). Importantly, reductions in the levels of conflict children are exposed to can lead to improved adjustment. Children from homes where parental separation results in reduced exposure to conflict tend to fare better than children who remain in intact high-conflict homes (Emery, 1982; Hetherington, Cox & Cox, 1982; Wallerstein & Kelly, 1980).

Inter-parental disagreements *per se* do not appear to impact on child adjustment. Provided that disagreements do not lead to aggressiveness or hostility, parents can hold quite differing views from each other with no negative effects on children. For example, children of parents who frequently disagree with each other but seek compromises show relatively few behavioural ill-effects (Camara & Resnick, 1989). In comparison, in families where fathers are verbally attacking during disagreements, children show elevated conduct problems (Camara & Resnick, 1989).

Significant numbers of children in Western countries experience family transitions resulting from parents moving in and out of couple relationships (Fergusson, Horwood & Dimond, 1985). There is considerable evidence from large, methodologically sound studies that family transitions (e.g. parental divorce and remarriage) are associated with poor child adjustment (Grych & Fincham, 1990; Lawton & Sanders, 1994). Compared with peers from intact families, children from divorced families and step-families have higher rates of externalizing and internalizing behaviour disorders, school achievement and discipline problems, peer relationship difficulties, and poorer physical health (e.g. Dawson, 1991; Fergusson, Dimond & Horwood, 1986; Hetherington, Cox & Cox, 1985; Peterson & Zill, 1986; Wadsworth et al., 1983). In addition, parental remarriage appears to be associated with adolescent disengagement from the family, increased risk-taking, and early drop-out from formal education (Lawton & Sanders, 1994). Superficially, the problems experienced by children from step-families appear similar to those observed for children from divorced, single-parent families. However, children from step-families tend to show more conduct problems than children from single-parent families, especially for girls and in the early stages of remarriage (Amato & Ochiltree, 1987; Fergusson, Dimond & Horwood, 1986; Hetherington, Cox & Cox, 1985; Peterson & Zill, 1986).

Family transitions may have a cumulative effect on children. Compared with their peers from stable families, children who experience more frequent life changes and family transitions fare more poorly in a variety of areas (Capaldi & Patterson, 1991). However, there can be considerable individual variation in adjustment to family transitions. A number of children do not show significant impairment, and others thrive in post-divorce or post-remarriage families (Barber & Eccles, 1992; Camara & Resnick, 1989).

Mechanisms by which Couples' Relationships and Family Transitions Impact on Children

Predisposing Factors

The impact of couples' relationships on children varies with a number of child characteristics. Children of all ages are at risk of negative adjustment to interparental conflict and family transitions. However, the way that problems are manifested varies with age and often involves areas of functioning which are currently presenting developmental challenges (Allison & Furstenberg, 1989; Wallerstein & Kelly, 1980). For example, toddlers may display heightened separation anxiety, while adolescents may engage in risk-taking behaviours. Adjustment problems following parental divorce appear to be greater for *younger* children, and may be associated with the child's limited ability to understand the changes occurring in the family environment. In contrast, after parental remarriage adjustment problems appear to be greater for *older* children and adolescents. The addition of a new authority figure in the form of a step-parent may be difficult for older children who are in the developmental stage of striving to gain autonomy and independence from the family (Hetherington, 1989; Pink & Wampler, 1985).

Child adjustment to parents' relationships is also related to the gender of the child. At high levels of interparental conflict boys and girls appear to respond in a similar fashion, with an increased risk of both externalizing and internalizing problems (Grych & Fincham, 1990). However, when children are exposed to marital disharmony which does not contain a high degree of interparental conflict, boys and girls may differ in the nature of their responses. For boys, moderate levels of parental marital disharmony is associated with increased rates of externalizing problems, while for girls this is associated with increased rates of internalizing problems (Grych & Fincham,1990).

Male gender has also been traditionally regarded as associated with a greater risk for externalizing problems following parental divorce, while internalizing problems have been regarded as more characteristic of girls post-divorce (Hetherington, Stanley-Hagan & Anderson, 1989). However, gender of child appears to interact with gender custodial parent and parent's remarriage status in determining post-divorce outcomes. Residing with the opposite-gender parent is associated with greater conduct problems, less prosocial behaviour and poorer self-esteem (Camara & Resnick, 1989; Hetherington, Cox & Cox, 1982; Warshak & Santrock, 1983), while residing with the same-gender parent appears to disrupt children's interactions with opposite-gender peers (Camara & Resnick, 1989). As most children live with their mothers after divorce, this is associated with an increased risk of behavioural problems for boys, and disrupted interactions with males for girls (Hetherington, Cox & Cox, 1982; Wallerstein & Corbin, 1989).

There has been considerable concern that parental divorce may have serious delayed effects for girls (Wallerstein & Corbin, 1989). Girls from divorced families may be at increased risk of deteriorated relationships with parents, problematic intimate relationships and role disruptions in adulthood (Gabardi & Rosen, 1992; Kinnaird & Gerrard, 1986; Wallerstein & Corbin, 1989). However, these conclusions have been challenged on the basis of significant methodological flaws. A recent longitudinal study of young people who were adolescents at the time of their parents' divorce found no evidence of long-term maladjustment. Ten years after their parents divorced, these young men and women were largely indistinguishable from their peers from non-divorced families in terms of anxiety, depression and self-esteem (Dunlop & Burns, 1995).

Research indicates that boys tend to benefit from parental remarriage after divorce while girls suffer. Boys may show some short-term deteriorations in behaviour, but in the long term, boys in stable step-families have fewer behaviour problems than boys in single-mother families (Hetherington, Cox & Cox, 1985). Girls from step-families have higher rates of behaviour problems than girls from intact or single-parent families, regardless of duration of remarriage (Bray, 1988, Fergusson, Dimond & Horwood, 1986; Hetherington, Cox & Cox, 1985; Peterson & Zill, 1986). The causes of these gender differences in child adjustment to family transitions may lie in changes which occur to parenting and family relationships, which are considered next.

Mediating Factors

Several factors mediate the impact of distressed and disrupted couple relationships on children. These include the direct effects of conflict and stressful life changes on children and indirect effects due to changes in parenting, family relationships and parental mood.

Impact of conflict and stress

Poor child adjustment to marital distress and to parental relationship transitions may be partly accounted for by exposure to conflict and multiple stressors. Conflict is highly distressing for children of all ages. It has been hypothesized that the way that a child reacts to stress and conflict varies according to the child's predisposition (Grych & Fincham, 1990). Children who are predisposed to externalizing behaviour problems (e.g. boys and children with a history of aggression) are likely to show behavioural deterioration when exposed to conflict, while other children (e.g. girls) may be more likely to display emotional distress. However, interparental conflict also provides children with a model of aggression, and this may increase the risk for all children of aggressive behaviour problems. Additionally, interparental conflict is often associated with parental emotional withdrawal and use of ineffective disciplinary strategies (Fauber et al., 1990), which in turn impact on children's adjustment.

One factor which may buffer children from the potential stressors and losses associated with divorce is ongoing contact between the child and the non-custodial parent. However, the benefit of this contact is moderated by the extent to which the child is exposed to further conflict, parental psychopathology and poor parenting. Divorce does not necessarily reduce the tensions between parents, and many children find themselves caught in the middle of battles over access and financial arrangements. Children may be asked to relay messages between parents, and many children report feeling pressured to take sides in their parents' arguments. Research confirms the negative impact of such situations on children (e.g. Amato, 1993a; Johnston, Kline & Tschann, 1989). A variety of strategies may be introduced to reduce children's exposure to conflict between divorced parents (e.g. the development of clear rules regarding pick-up and drop-off of children for access visits; negotiating for the hand-over of children to occur at the home of a neutral third party). Divorce mediation for reducing conflict between ex-spouses and for developing appropriate shared parenting plans is discussed in greater detail in a subsequent chapter (Baris & Garrity, this volume). Unfortunately, children in some families are exposed to considerable ongoing conflict (often combined with parental psychopathology) and access visits may need to be restricted, supervised or terminated.

Subsequent family transitions such as parental repartnering or remarriage may bring an escalation of conflict between ex-spouses. Remarriage also exposes many children to new conflicts within the family home. Parenting issues are a common source of conflict in step-families, and there is some evidence that step-families face daily problems which are more complex and more persistent than other families (Lawton & Sanders, 1994). The level of relationship conflict that children are exposed to in remarried families impacts on their adjustment to the family. Research indicates that high rates of conflict (between ex-spouses or between the remarried couple) are associated with clinically significant child behaviour problems (Nicholson, 1996). Thus, family transitions such as repartnering may signify a time when couples (the divorced couple or the new repartnered couple) have need of mediation or relationship therapy to help with negotiating parenting plans, resolving family problems and reducing conflict.

In addition to the conflict which accompanies family transitions, children and adults experience a number of potentially stressful changes to their family environment. From the child's perspective these may include changes to the composition of the family household, such as losing a parent or gaining a step-parent and step-siblings. The child's relationship with the custodial parent will change, frequently for the worse. The parent's ability to spend time with his/her child may be reduced following divorce by the pressures of trying to support the family alone, and following remarriage by the demands of the parent's developing relationship with his or her new partner. Additionally, children's roles and status in the family changes with relationship transitions. It has been well documented that after divorce children generally assume greater roles and responsibilities around the home (McDonald, 1986; Weiss, 1979). Following remarriage, further changes occur, with the step-parent and step-siblings likely to take over some roles previously held by the child, and the child may experience a loss of status in the family (Hetherington, 1989). In addition, relationship transitions frequently cause families to move house, with consequent disruptions in the child's educational, social and recreational activities. Empirical evidence links negative divorce-related changes and disrupted household routines to poor child adjustment (Amato, 1993b; Sandler, Wolchik & Braver, 1988; Stolberg et al., 1987). Interventions for parents undergoing transitions should aim to help parents maintain a stable and secure environment for their children.

Disrupted parenting

The effect of couples' relationship problems on parenting is an important factor in determining children's adjustment (Fauber et al., 1990; Jouriles, Pfiffner & O'Leary, 1988; Miller et al., 1993; Webster-Stratton, 1989). Coercive, irritable, inconsistent parenting has repeatedly been associated with the development of child behaviour problems, especially conduct problems and especially for boys (Loeber, 1990). Ineffective parenting is common among couples experiencing relationship distress, or relationship transitions such as divorce and remarriage (Hetherington, 1987; Vuchinich et al., 1991). Characteristic parenting patterns among such couples include: parental withdrawal from the child; increased parental negativity; greater inconsistency; and use of coercive discipline strategies. Interparental conflict is also associated with an increase in parental irritability and anger, some of which is likely to be directed toward children. In addition, marital distress is frequently associated with parental depression, which further limits the parents' ability to be consistent and responsive to their children's needs (Patterson, De Baryshe & Ramsey, 1989). Unfortunately, these parenting patterns occur at a time when children are emotionally vulnerable and acutely aware of any negativity or perceived rejection by parents.

Parenting disruptions which accompany couples' relationship transitions may be time-limited. Longitudinal research indicates that divorced parents become less coercive, more consistent and more responsive over time, and that these changes are associated with improved child behaviour (Hetherington, 1987). There is some evidence that remarriage-related disruptions to parenting are short-lived, and that by 2–6 years into the remarriage, parents use more responsive, effective parenting strategies (Amato, 1987; Hetherington, Stanley-Hagan & Anderson, 1989; Vuchinich et al., 1991).

Child gender appears to be related to the parenting practices employed during parental relationship transitions. Boys in single-mother families are at greater risk than girls of experiencing coercive parenting. This problem may be resolved by repartnering, where the addition of a stepfather to the family counters the poor parenting practices of single mothers with sons (Hetherington, 1987; Hetherington, Cox & Cox, 1982). However, girls appear to fare relatively poorly with parental remarriage, possibly as a result of the step-parent usurping the position and relationship the daughter had previously formed with the single parent.

Parenting in a step-family is complex and fraught with pitfalls. The couple's ability to manage cooperative parenting impacts on both the child's adjustment and the quality of the couple's relationship. Child adjustment in step-families is related to the level of step-parent involvement in parenting, the extent to which the biological parent provides support for the step-parent, and the duration of the remarriage relationship. Greater early involvement of the step-parent, especially in combination with withdrawal or chaotic discipline from the biological parent, is related to poorer child adjustment and couple conflict (Bray, 1988). Couple relationship problems and child behaviour problems are also likely to arise in families where the biological parent fails to support or actively undermines the step-parent's parenting.

These findings highlight the importance of parent–child interactions and parenting practices during periods of relationship conflict or transition. There is obvious potential for incorporating parent training approaches into interventions for distressed or transitioning couples. Behavioural parent training has a high degree of success for changing parental behaviour and child behaviour, especially if problems are caught in the early stages (Kazdin, 1987). In addition, there is growing evidence that behavioural parent training combined with couples interventions can successfully improve child outcomes for distressed couples and couples in step-families (Dadds, Schwartz & Sanders, 1987; Nicholson & Sanders, 1994). These interventions may be more likely to be successful if delivered in the early stages of a transition with the aim of minimizing the duration of disrupted parenting to which the child is exposed. Alternatively, programs which are preventive and help parents to avoid changes to parenting during forthcoming transitions may have the greatest potential for reducing negative outcomes for children.

Parental psychopathology

Couple relationship problems are associated with elevated psychopathology, especially depression (Halford & Bouma, this volume). Depression is independently related to poor child adjustment, in both intact and divorced families (Capaldi & Patterson, 1991; Kalter et al., 1989; Orvaschel, Walsh-Allis & Ye, 1988). This association may be due to disrupted parenting practices and parents' negatively-biased perceptions of children's behaviour (Brody & Forehand, 1988). It has been suggested that irritability, distractibility and lack of concentration contribute to inconsistent and coercive parenting for mildly depressed parents, while reduced energy levels further impair the parenting abilities of more severely depressed parents (Forehand et al., 1990). Depression is also common amongst parents in the immediate post-divorce phase, and may be prevalent amongst step-parents.

Research indicates that supplementary intervention strategies (such as cognitive–behavioural mood management) may be required for successfully improving the parenting skills of depressed mothers (McFarland & Sanders, 1992). Thus, in addition to assessing the parenting skills of couples experiencing relationship stress and transitions, therapists should routinely assess parental mood disorder and modify interventions accordingly.

Intervention Research Examining Couples' Relationships and Children

A variety of interventions have been developed for couples with children who are undergoing relationship distress or relationship transitions. The efficacy of these interventions and their core components are briefly reviewed.

Interparental Conflict and Children

Controlled clinical research is this area is practically non-existent. We were unable to locate any studies which looked at the modification of marital interventions to address issues of child adjustment. One study has been conducted which looks at the treatment of concurrent relationship distress in the context of referral for child conduct behaviour problems. This intervention combined positive parenting strategies with brief marital communication and conflict management skills training (Dadds, Schwartz & Sanders, 1987). Compared with standard parent training, the enhanced group showed better child and parent outcomes. This research indicates the potential of interventions which target both couples' relationship skills and parenting skills. Recommendations for intervention in this context are detailed in a subsequent chapter (Sanders, Markie-Dadds & Nicholson, this volume).

Parental Divorce and Children

Interventions which aim to impact on children's post-divorce adjustment are summarized in Table 10.1. Programs designed to ameliorate the negative impact of divorce may take the form of: (a) child-focused interventions which aim to help children deal effectively with divorce-related changes; (b) parent-focused programs which address parent adjustment and interactional factors that mediate the impact of divorce on children; and (c) systems-focused interventions such as divorce mediation (Baris & Garrity, this volume), which in part aim to lessen children's exposure to conflict and stressful events (Grych & Fincham, 1992; Stolberg & Walsh, 1988).

Divorce intervention programs show considerable promise. They address factors implicated in the development of child problems, and have often been enthusiastically adopted in the community. Unfortunately, evidence of program efficacy is very limited and few systematic evaluations have been undertaken. The research which has been conducted indicates that divorce interventions are generally positively evaluated by participants. However, programs which focus solely on parental adjustment show little evidence of impacting on child outcomes (Stolberg & Walsh, 1988).

Divorce intervention research remains in its infancy (Grych & Fincham, 1992). There is a great need for controlled outcome research to guide the development of appropriate programs. Well-designed divorce intervention programs have the

Table 10.1 Interventions for child behaviour and adjustment problems associated with parental divorce

Type of intervention	Etiological factors addressed	Effectiveness
Child-focused programs *Aims:* to help children deal with emotions, thoughts and practical problems associated with divorce	Impact of conflict on child	*Evaluation:* few systematic evaluations have been undertaken. Two programs resulted in improvements on some measures for teacher, parent and child self-report, including measures of overall child adjustment, anxiety and self-competence (Alpert-Gillis, Pedro-Carroll & Cowen, 1989; Garvin, Leber & Kalter, 1991; Pedro-Carroll & Cowen, 1985), with improvements evident at 6 months (Garvin, Leber & Kalter, 1991)
	Social support	
Format: educational and therapeutic group programs, often based in school settings. Strategies may include role-plays, story-telling, problem-solving, use of play and creative activities	Individual child factors (potential utility for identifying at-risk children)	*Limitations:* include lack of assessment of impact on mediating factors or comparison of alternative structural and process factors. Longer-term maintenance is unknown
Parent-focused programs		
Parenting Skills Focused		
Aims: to improve parent management of problem child behaviour and maintain parent–child relationships	Disrupted parenting	*Evaluation:* little known about efficacy of programs. Parenting skills intervention associated with improvements in parenting, parent–child relationships, and parent adjustment. Inconsistent effects on child adjustment. No impact on non-custodial parent–child relationships or interparental conflict (Wolchik et al., 1993). Parent adjustment intervention has been associated with short-term reductions in adult psychological symptoms, with lower symptoms and higher life satisfaction
	Parent distress, depression	
Format: group educational, using strategies such as active skills training	Parent coping	
	Other parental problems or psychopathology	

Parent Adjustment Focused

Aims: to promote parent well-being and coping with divorce-related changes

Format: educational, focusing on common stages and changes associated with divorce, social support and planning for the future

evident 4 years later (Bloom et al., 1985). May have little/no impact on child adjustment (Stolberg & Walsh, 1988)

Limitations: include lack of assessment of impact on mediating factors, or comparison of alternative structural and process factors

Systems-focused programs

Divorce Mediation

Aims: to reduce conflict, promote cooperation, and improve satisfaction with divorce outcome for couples

Format: individual mediator per couple, does not address psychological, emotional issues

- Stressful life events
- Family disruption
- Economic factors
- Conflict between parents
- Social support

Evaluation: limited. Associated with faster resolution of disputes, less subsequent litigation, improved satisfaction with outcome for men but not for women (Emery & Wyer, 1987)

Limitations: unknown impact on parental emotional or psychological adjustment, or on child adjustment. No evidence of improved financial outcome for custodial parent or reduction in interspousal conflict over child-rearing (Emery, Hatthess & Wyer, 1991) potential for impacting significantly on the well-being of a large portion of the community, with major long-term consequences. However, until further research is undertaken, the efficacy of these interventions remains unclear. Clinical strategies for divorce mediation are discussed in greater detail by Baris & Garrity (this volume).

Parental Remarriage and Children

A growing number of clinical interventions are available for step-families wishing to enhance family relationships, prevent remarriage breakdown or receive help with specific problems (Bielenberg, 1991; Mandell & Birenzweig, 1990; Nicholson & Sanders, 1994; Nadler, 1983). A number of clinicians have published clinical for therapists working with troubled step-families (e.g. Messinger & Walker, 1981; Visher & Visher, 1989, 1991). Educational and self-help materials, including leaders' manuals, audio-visual aids and handouts,

Table 10.2   Common features of stepfamily intervention programs

Typical format
  Group
  Educational, some include skills training
  Session duration $1\frac{1}{2}$–$2\frac{1}{2}$ hours
Target group
  5–6 Currently remarried/repartnered couples
  Most programs do not include children, some have concurrent child groups
Content
Common stepfamily problems
  Myths and expectations
  Grief and losses
  Differences from intact families
Child's perspective
  Developmental issues
  Loyalty conflicts, fears, rivalries
  Changes in family roles
Discipline and role of step-parent
  Expectations and parenting history
  Common problems/mistakes in parenting
  Conflict over parenting, undermining partner
Communication
  Effective communication skills
  Problem-solving skills
  Family decision-making processes
Development and maintenance of family relationships
  Importance of the couple relationship
  Planning couple activities, private time, etc.
  Maintaining/developing quality interactions with children
  Establishing new family activities and traditions

are available from general bookshops and specialist associations (such as the Step-family Association Of America) for therapists or lay people who are interested in conducting group programs for step-family members. Common features of interventions offered for step-families are summarized in Table 10.2.

Unfortunately, there is little quality research examining the efficacy of interventions for step-families (Lawton & Sanders, 1994). In a notable exception, Nicholson & Sanders (Lawton & Sanders, 1993; Nicholson & Sanders, 1994) have developed and comprehensively assessed the impact of an empirically-designed intervention program for remarried couples. The program aimed to improve both child and adult functioning, in the context of referral for child behaviour problems. Evaluations revealed that compared to waiting list control families, families receiving the intervention, either as a self-help package or in a therapist-delivered format, showed improved functioning on a variety of measures of child, couple, and family functioning. Clinical strategies for this intervention are described in greater detail by Sanders, Markie-Dadds & Nicholson (this volume).

Implications for Intervention with Couples

The preceding discussion has summarized the principle evidence linking couples' relationship quality and relationship transitions to the well-being of children. The discussion indicates a clear need for the well-being of children to be assessed and considered in the design of interventions for couples.

Interventions for couples experiencing relationship distress or in transition should include an educative component to help couples to predict and understand the behaviour of their children better. In distressed families where conflict between couples is intense, education about the impact this behaviour has on the children may facilitate couples' attempts to control their anger better. Couples may be more motivated to avoid conflict if they understand how this affects their children. While it may not be possible to get both parents to make the child's well-being a priority in their divorce settlement, if at least one parent has this goal, this may go some way toward reducing the amount of conflict to which the child is exposed.

Education alone may be insufficient to bring about significant change in some families. Active skills-training interventions may be required for families with multiple problems, high levels of conflict or concurrent child and adult pathology. Conflict management, stress reduction and positive parenting have been identified as potential intervention strategies for parents experiencing relationship distress or undergoing relationship transitions. In addition, parents moving into post-divorce single-parent families and step-families may need skills for cooperative parenting and for mobilizing social supports and resources. Where individual psychopathology is evident, this also needs to be addressed.

CONCLUSION

In summary, there is clear evidence that for all couples their relationships with children play an important role in determining the quality of family relationships, regardless of family structure. The transition to parenthood heralds a series of important adjustments that couples must make in order to protect and enhance their marital relationship. When parenthood takes place under disadvantageous circumstances, such as with unplanned teenage parenthood, unwanted pregnancy, lack of parenting knowledge and skill, poverty or low social support, this transition may be experienced as stressful and may negatively impact on the couple's relationship. These problems are compounded if a child is physically or intellectually disabled or has a chronic illness.

Although much has been learned about the relationship between marriage and children, there are many significant gaps in our knowledge. Much of the research in this area has focused on white Caucasian legally married couples. Couples participating in marital research generally are skewed towards better educated, higher socio-economic status families. Many of the conclusions derived from this research may not generalize to other ethnic groups or families from lower socio-economic groups. Adopted children and the families of gay and lesbian couples have been relatively neglected.

A particularly vulnerable group of children are those who have experienced a high degree of relationship instability of their parents. For example, children growing up with single parents who have multiple temporary partners, or parental figures who enter and then depart from a child's life, may increase the child's risk of developing behavioural and emotional problems. This same child may also have access visits to a father with similar relationship instability. Although repartnering takes place for the majority of divorced couples, the unpredictable relationship environment of a child's parent needs to be considered. Parents of these children rarely present for couples therapy, although their children may present through the school system or courts due to significant disruptive and antisocial behaviour. The presence of children in a first marriage increases its stability, but it does not guarantee marital quality. Indeed, in the case of second marriages, the presence of children increases the likelihood of relationship breakdown.

There are several important clinical implications that arise from our analysis of the relationship between marriage and children. In couples presenting with a marital problem who have children, it is important for the clinicians to determine the type of family structure that the couple live in (intact two-parent, step-parent) and the custody and living arrangements in place for children from prior relationships. The functional relationship between marital difficulties, parenting problems, and child adjustment problems needs to be assessed specifically. Some useful tools for the assessment of parenting difficulties are outlined by Sanders, Markie-Dadds & Nicholson, this volume). Apart from recognizing the common co-occurrence of difficulties in both the marital and parenting domains, there is the need to assess the possible detrimental effects on children of living in a highly conflicted or unstable family situation (Fantuzzo et al., 1991). As most marital therapists do not assess directly the adjustment of children when they assess marital conflict, decision rules are needed to guide marital therapists about when to assess children directly. This issue is addressed elsewhere in this volume. The co-occurrence of marital and child problems does not necessarily mean they are causally related. For example, both sets of problems have multiple determinants independent of the couple's relationship. If a child problem improves without specific intervention as a function of changes in the couple's relationship, there are several possible explanations for such changes. Improved marital harmony may reduce daily conflict between parents, which reduces stress and tension the child experiences at home. Alternatively, improvement in the marriage may improve a parent's mood, irritability, tolerance or consistency with children. Another possibility is that changes in each domain are independent and the child's improvement may be related to unplanned changes at school (change of teacher, more remedial help). Teasing out the causal determinants of concurrent marital and child problems is complex. Unfortunately, little systematic attention has been directed to these issues in the marital therapy field. Given the evidence that the experience of parental divorce is related to premarital communication skills, which in turn predict future marital breakdown, a child's experience of marital conflict prior to, during and following parental divorce needs to be major focus of research attention.

There are many unanswered questions concerning the relationship between parental marriage and children's adjustment. Some possible directions for future research include the development and evaluation of theory-driven intervention components designed to address those aspects of the couple's parent–child relationships that directly affect the couple's relationship (e.g. the expression of affection in front of children, the couple's respective roles in disciplining children; see Lawton & Sanders (1994) for a discussion of treatment components needed in intervention programs with step-families).

Research is needed to determine whether the effects of marital therapy are enhanced for couples experiencing problems with children, if there is a concurrent focus on both marital and parenting issues, compared to either focus alone. The specific effects of such interventions need to be determined on both the marital relationship and children's behaviour, adjustment and their views of their parent's marital relationship. This question has been addressed in one study (Dadds, Schwartz & Sanders, 1987) in the context of managing behaviour problems in children where there is concurrent marital distress. The combined child and marital intervention was superior to a child-focused intervention alone on measures of disruptive child behaviour and parent behaviour.

The goals of behavioural marital therapy are reasonably clear when the couple presents for relationship difficulties. However, it is not at all clear what strategies should be pursued when marital conflict occurs in the presence of significant child management problems. Referral elsewhere can sometimes be an option for management of the child's problem; however, the development of a coordinated, consistent approach between agencies can be problematic, particularly outside major metropolitan areas with fewer specialist mental health services. The treatment of the child's problem may require the couple to work cohesively to implement a parenting strategy at home.

There are other clinical issues that are important in working with step-families. These include how to manage specific therapeutic process issues such as: which family members to include in treatment; how to deal with the step-parent's uncertain status in the parenting role; and what strength of intervention to use at different points in the family life-cycle. For example, couples contemplating remarriage may benefit more from brief preventively focused marital and parenting interventions early in their relationship, than after the couple have moved into together and have experienced problems. These issues are discussed in more detail by Sanders, Markie Dadds & Nicholson (this volume).

Acknowledgements

This work was partly supported by the National Health and Medical Research Council of Australia (Grants 920182 and 954213). The second author published under the name Jan M. Lawton until 1994.

REFERENCES

Allison, P.D. & Furstenberg, F.F. Jr (1989). How marital dissolution affects children: variations by age and sex. *Developmental Psychology*, **25**, 540–549.

Alpert-Gillis, L.J., Pedro-Carroll, J.L. & Cowen, E.L. (1989). The Children of Divorce Intervention Program: development, implementation, and evaluation of a program for young urban children. *Journal of Consulting and Clinical Psychology*, **57**, 583–589.

Amato, P.R. (1987). *Children in Australian Families: the Growth of Competence*. Melbourne: Prentice Hall.

Amato, P.R. (1993a). Contact with non-custodial fathers and children's well-being. *Family Matters*, **36**, 32–34.

Amato, P.R. (1993b). Children's adjustment to divorce: theories, hypotheses, and empirical support. *Journal of Marriage and the Family*, **55**, 23–38.

Amato, P.R. & Ochiltree, G. (1987). Child and adolescent competence in intact, one-parent, and step-families: an Australian study. *Journal of Divorce*, **10**, 75–96.

Anderson, A., Russell, C. & Schumm, W. (1983). Perceived marital quality and family life cycle categories: a further analysis. *Journal of Marriage and the Family*, **45**, 127–139.

Australian Bureau of Statistics (1994). *Focus on Families: Demographics and Family Formation*, Catalogue No. 4420.0. Canberra: Australian Bureau of Statistics.

Barber, B.L. & Eccles, J.S. (1992). Long-term influence of divorce and single parenting on adolescent family- and work-related values, behaviors, and aspirations. *Psychological Bulletin*, **111**, 108–126.

Belsky, J. (1990). Children and marriage. In F.D. Fincham & T.N. Bradbury (eds), *The Psychology of Marriage: Basic Issues and Applications* (pp. 172–200). New York: Guilford.

Belsky, J., Lang, M. & Rovine, M. (1985). Stability and change in marriage across the transition to parenthood: a second study. *Journal of Marriage and the Family*, **47**, 855–866.

Belsky, J. & Pensky, E. (1988). Marital change across the transition to parenthood. *Marriage and Family Review*, **12**, 133–156.

Benson, B.A. & Gross, A.M. (1989). The effect of a congenitally handicapped child upon the marital dyad: a review of the literature. *Clinical Psychology Review*, **9**, 747–758.

Bielenberg, L.T. (1991). A task-centered preventive group approach to create cohesion in the new stepfamily: a preliminary evaluation. *Research on Social Work Practice*, **1**, 416–433.

Bloom, B.L., Hodges, W.F., Kern, M.B. & McFaddin, S.C. (1985). A preventive intervention program for the newly separated: final evaluations. *American Journal of Orthopsychiatry*, **55**, 9–26.

Brand, E. & Clingempeel, W.G. (1987). Interdependencies of marital and step-parent–step-child relationships and children's psychological adjustment: research findings and clinical implications. *Family Relations*, **36**, 140–145.

Bray, J.H. (1988). Children's development during early remarriage. In E.M. Hetherington & J.D. Arasteh (eds), *Impact of Divorce, Single Parenting and Step-parenting on Children* (pp. 279–298). Hillsdale, NJ: Erlbaum.

Brody, G.H., Pellegrini, A.D. & Sigel, I.E. (1986). Marital quality and mother–child and father–child interactions with school-aged children. *Developmental Psychology*, **22**, 291–296.

Brody, G.H. & Forehand, R. (1988). Multiple determinants of parenting: research findings and implications for the divorce process. In E.M. Hetherington & J.D. Arasteh (eds), *Impact of Divorce, Single Parenting, and Step-parenting on Children* (pp. 117–133). Hillsdale, NJ: Erlbaum.

Camara, K.A. & Resnick, G. (1989). Styles of conflict resolution and cooperation between divorced parents: effects on child behaviour and adjustment. *Journal of Orthopsychiatry*, **59**, 560–575.

Capaldi, D.M. & Patterson, G.R. (1991). Relation of parental transitions to boys' adjustment problems: I. A linear hypothesis. II. Mothers at risk for transitions and unskilled parenting. *Developmental Psychology*, **27**, 489–504.

Christensen, H.T. (1968). Children in the family: relationship of number and spacing to marital success. *Journal of Marriage and the Family*, **30**, 283–285.

Clausen, J.A. & Clausen, S.R. (1973). The effects of family size on parents and children, In J.T. Fawcett (ed.), *Psychological Perspectives on Population*. New York: Basic Books.

Cohen, R.S. & Weissman, S.H. (1984). The parenting alliance. In R.S. Cohen & S.H. Weissman (eds), *Parenthood: a Psychodynamic Perspective* (pp. 33–49). New York: Guilford.

Cowan, C., Cowan, P., Heming, G., Garrett, E., Coysh, W., Curtis-Boles, H. & Boles, A. (1985). Transitions to parenthood: his, hers and theirs. *Journal of Family Issues*, **6**, 451–482.

Cowan, P.A. & Cowan, C.P. (1988). Changes in marriage during the transition to parenthood: must we blame the baby? In G.Y. Michaels & W.A. Goldberg (eds), *The Transition to Parenthood: Current Theory and Research*. Cambridge: Cambridge University Press.

Crnic, K., Friedrich, W. & Greenberg, M. (1983). Adaptation of families with mentally retarded children: a model of stress, coping, and family ecology. *American Journal of Mental Deficiency*, **88**, 125–138.

Dadds, M.R., Schwartz, S. & Sanders, M.R. (1987). Marital discord and treatment outcome in the treatment of childhood conduct disorders. *Journal of Consulting & Clinical Psychology*, **55**, 396–403.

Dawson, D. (1991). Family structure and children's health and well-being: data from the 1988 National Health Interview Survey on child health. *Journal of Marriage and the Family*, **53**, 573–584.

Dunlop, R. & Burns, A. (1995). The sleeper effect—myth or reality. *Journal of Marriage and the Family*, **57**, 375–386.

Emery, R.E. (1982). Interparental conflict and the children of discord and divorce. *Psychological Bulletin*, **92**, 310–330.

Emery, R.E., Matthews, S. & Wyer, M.M. (1991). Child custody mediation and litigation: further evidence on the differing views of mothers and fathers. *Journal of Consulting and Clinical Psychology*, **59**, 410–418.

Emery, R.E. & Wyer, M.M. (1987). Child custody evaluation and litigation: an experimental evaluation of the experience of parents. *Journal of Consulting and Clinical Psychology*, **55**, 179–186.

Fantuzzo, J.W., DePaota, L.M., Lambert, L., Martino T, et al. (1991). Effects of interparental violence on the psychological adjustment and competencies of young children. *Journal of Consulting and Clinical Psychology*, **59**(2), 258–265.

Farber, B. (1959). Effects of a severely mentally retarded child on family integration. *Monographs of the Society for Research in Child Development*, **24**(2, Series No. 71).

Fauber, R., Forehand, R., Thomas, A.M. & Wierson, M. (1990). A mediational model of the impact of marital conflict on adolescent adjustment in intact and divorced families: the role of disrupted parenting. *Child Development*, **61**, 1112–1123.

Fergusson, D.M., Dimond, M.E. & Horwood, L.J. (1986). Childhood family placement history and behaviour problems in 6-years-old children. *Journal of Child Psychiatry*, **27**, 213–226.

Fergusson, D.M., Horwood, L.J. & Dimond, M.E. (1985). A survival analysis of childhood family history. *Journal of Marriage and the Family*, **47**, 287–295.

Fergusson, D.M., Horwood, L.J. & Lloyd, M. (1990). The effect of preschool children on family stability. *Journal of Marriage and the Family*, **52**, 531–538.

Floyd, F.J., Haynes, S.N., Doll, E.R., Winemiller, D., Lemsky, C., Burgy, T.M., Werle, M. & Heilman, N. (1992). Assessing retirement satisfaction and perceptions of retirement experiences. *Psychology and Aging*, **7**, 609–621.

Floyd, F.J. & Zmich, D.E. (1991). Marriage and the parenting partnership: perceptions and interactions of parents with mentally retarded and typically developing children. *Child Development*, **62**, 1434–1448.

Forehand, R., Thomas, A.M., Wierson, M., Brody, G. & Fauber, R. (1990). Role of maternal functioning and parenting skills in adolescent functioning following parental divorce. *Journal of Abnormal Psychology*, **99**, 278–283.

Frank, S.J., Hole, C.B., Jacobson, S., Justkowski, R. & Huyck, M. (1986). Psychological predictors of parents' sense of confidence and control and self versus child-focused gratifications. *Developmental Psychology*, **22**, 348–355.

Friedrich, W.N. & Friedrich, W.L. (1981). Comparison of psychosocial assets of parents with a handicapped child and their normal controls. *American Journal of Mental Deficiency*, **85**, 551–553.

Gabardi, L. & Rosen, L.A. (1992). Intimate relationships: college students from divorced and intact families. *Journal of Divorce and Remarriage*, **18**(3–4), 25–56.

Gable, S., Belsky, J. & Crnic, K. (1992). Marriage, parenting, and child development: progress and prospects. *Journal of Family Psychology*, **5**, 276–294.

Garvin, V., Leber, D. & Kalter, N. (1991). Children of divorce: predictors of change following preventive intervention. *American Journal of Orthopsychiatry*, **61**, 438–447.

Gath, A. (1977). The impact of an abnormal child upon the parents. *British Journal of Psychiatry*, **130**, 405–410.

Grych, J.H. & Fincham, F.D. (1990). Marital conflict and children's adjustment: a cognitive-contextual framework. *Psychological Bulletin*, **108**, 267–290.

Grych, J.H. & Fincham, F.D. (1992). Interventions for children of divorce: toward greater integration of research and action. *Psychological Bulletin*, **111**, 434–454.

Haynes, S.N., Floyd, F.J., Lemsky, C., Rogers, E., Winemiller, D., Heilman, N., Werle, M.,

Murphy, T. & Cardone, L. (1992). The Marital Satisfaction Questionnaire for Older Persons. *Psychological Assessment*, **4**, 473–482.

Hetherington, E.M. (1987). Family relations six years after divorce. In K. Pasley & M. Ihinger-Tallman (eds), Remarriage and Step-parenting: Current Research and Theory (pp. 185–205). New York: Guilford.

Hetherington, E.M. (1989). Coping with family transitions: winners, losers, and survivors. *Child Development*, **60**, 1–14.

Hetherington, E.M., Cox, M. & Cox, R. (1982). Effects of divorce on parents and young children. In M. Lamb (ed.), *Non-traditional Families: Parenting and Child Development* (pp. 233–288). Hillsdale, NJ: Erlbaum.

Hetherington, E.M., Cox, M. & Cox, R. (1985). Long-term effects of divorce and re-marriage on the adjustment of children. *Journal of the American Academy of Child Psychiatry*, **24**, 518–530.

Hetherington, E.M., Stanley-Hagan, M. & Anderson, E.R. (1989). Marital transitions: a child's perspective. *American Psychologist*, **44**, 303–312.

Hoffman, L. & Manis, J. (1978). Influences of children on marital interaction and parental satisfactions and dissatisfactions. In R. Lerner & G. Spanier (eds), *Child Influences on Marital and Family Interaction: a Life-span Perspective* (pp. 165–213). New York: Academic Press.

Houseknecht, S.K. (1987). Voluntary childlessness. In M.B. Sussman & S.K. Steinmetz (eds), *Handbook of Marriage and the Family*. New York: Plenum.

Howard, J. (1978). The influence of children's developmental dysfunctions on marital quality and family interaction. In R. Lerner & G. Spanier (eds), *Child Influences on Marital and Family Interaction: a Life-span Perspective* (pp. 275–298). New York: Academic Press.

Howes, P. & Markman, H.J. (1989). Marital quality and child functioning: a longitudinal investigation. *Child Development*, **60**, 1044–1051.

Johnston, J.R., Kline, M. & Tschann, J.M. (1989). Ongoing post divorce conflict: effects on children of joint custody and frequent access. *American Journal of Orthopsychiatry*, **59**, 576–592.

Jouriles, E.N., Pfiffner, L.J. & O'Leary, S.G. (1988). Martial conflict, parenting and tod-dler conduct problems. *Journal of Abnormal Child Psychology*, **16**, 197–206.

Jouriles, E.N., Murphy, C.M., Farriss, A.M., Smith, D.A., Richters, J.E. & Waters, E. (1991). Marital adjustment, parental disagreements about child rearing, and behavior problems in boys: increasing the specificity of the marital assessment. *Child Development*, **62**, 1424–1433.

Kalter, N., Kloner, A., Schreier, S. & Okla, K. (1989). Predictors of children's postdivorce adjustment. *Journal of Orthopsychiatry*, **59**, 605–618.

Kazdin, A.E. (1987). Treatment of antisocial behavior disorders in children: current status and future directions. *Psychological Bulletin*, **102**, 187–203.

Kinnaird, K.L. & Gerrard, M. (1986). Premarital sexual behaviour and attitudes toward marriage and divorce among young women as a function of their mother's marital status. *Journal of Marriage and the Family*, **48**, 757–765.

Klaus, M. & Kennell, J. (1976). *Maternal–Infant Bonding*. St Louis, MO: C.V. Mosby.

Korn, S., Chess, S. & Fernandez, P. (1978). The impact of children's physical handicaps on marital quality and family interaction. In R. Lerner & G. Spanier (eds), *Child Influ-ences on Marital and Family Interaction: a Life-span Perspective* (pp. 299–326). New York: Academic Press.

Lawton, J.M. & Sanders, M.R. (1993). A controlled evaluation of behavioral family intervention for children with disruptive behaviour problems in stepfamilies. Paper presented at the Association for the Advancement of Behaviour Therapy Annual Convention, Atlanta USA, 18–21 November.

Lawton, J.M. & Sanders, M.R. (1994). Designing effective behavioral family interventions for stepfamilies. *Clinical Psychology Review*, **14**, 463–496.

Loeber, R. (1990) Development and risk factors of juvenile antisocial behaviour and delinquency. *Clinical Psychology Review*, **10**, 1–41.

Loeber, R. & Stouthamer-Loeber, M. (1986). Family factors as correlates and predictors of juvenile conduct problems and delinquency. In M. Tonry & N. Morris (eds), *Crime and Justice: an Annual Review of Research*, Vol. 7 (pp. 29–149). Chicago: University of Chicago Press.

Luckey, E.B. & Bain, J.K. (1970). Children: a factor in marital satisfaction. *Journal of Marriage and the Family*, **28**, 43–44.

Mandell, D. & Birenzweig, E. (1990). Step-families: a model for group work with remarried Couples and their children. *Journal of Divorce and Remarriage*, **14**(1), 29–41.

Markman, H.J. & Kadushin, F.S. (1986). Preventive effects of Lamaze training for first-time parents: a short-term longitudinal study. *Journal of Consulting and Clinical Psychology*, **54**, 872–874.

McDonald, P. (ed.) (1986). *Settling Up: Property and Income Distribution on Divorce in Australia*. Sydney: Australian Institute of Family Studies & Prentice-Hall.

McFarland, M. & Sanders, M.R. (1992). On the relationship between depressed maternal cognitions, interaction patterns, and child behaviour problems. Paper presented at the Fourth World Congress on Behaviour Therapy, Gold Coast, Australia, 4–8 July.

McHale, S. & Huston, T. (1985). The effect of the transition to parenthood on the marriage relationship. *Journal of Family Issues*, **6**, 409–434.

McLanahan, S. & Adams, J. (1987). Parenthood and psychological well-being. *Annual Review of Immunology*, **5**, 237–257.

Menaghan, E. (1983). Marital stress and family transitions: a panel analysis. *Journal of Marriage and the Family*, **45**, 371–386.

Messinger, L. & Walker, K.N. (1981). From marriage breakdown to remarriage: parental tasks and therapeutic guidelines. *American Journal of Orthopsychiatry*, **51**, 429–438.

Miller, N.B., Cowan, P.A., Pape Cowan, C., Hetherington, E.M. & Clingempeel, W.G. (1993). Externalizing in preschoolers and early adolescents: a cross-study replication of a family model. *Developmental Psychology*, **29**, 3–18.

Nadler, J.H. (1983). Effecting change in stepfamilies: a psychodynamic/behavioral group approach. *American Journal of Psychotherapy*, **37**, 100–112.

Nicholson, J.M. (1996). Child Behaviour Problems in Stepfamilies: Assessment and Intervention. PhD thesis, University of Queensland, Brisbane, Australia.

Nicholson, J.M. & Sanders, M.R. (1994). Helping troubled stepfamilies: programs for parents and step-parents. Paper presented at the International Year of the Family Conference, Adelaide, 20–23 November.

Nye, F.I. & Berardo, F.M. (1973). *The Family: Its Structure and Interaction*. New York: Macmillan.

Ochiltree, G. (1990). *Children in Australian Families*. Melbourne: Langman Cheshire.

Orvaschel, H., Walsh-Allis, G. & Ye, W. (1988). Psychopathology in children of parents with recurrent depression. *Journal of Abnormal Child Psychology*, **16**, 17–28.

Patterson, G.R., De Baryshe, B.D. & Ramsey, E. (1989). A developmental perspective on antisocial behaviour. *American Psychologist*, **44**, 329–335.

Pedro-Carroll, J.L. & Cowen, E.L. (1985). The Children of Divorce Intervention Program: an investigation of the efficacy of a school-based prevention program. *Journal of Consulting and Clinical Psychology*, **53**, 603–611.

Peterson, J.L. & Zill, N. (1986). Marital disruption, parent–child relationships, and behaviour problems in children. *Journal of Marriage and the Family*, **48**, 295–307.

Pink, J.E.T. & Wampler, K.S. (1985). Problem areas in stepfamilies: cohesion, adaptability, and the stepfather–adolescent relationship. *Family Relations*, **34**, 327–335.

Reid, W.J. & Crisafulli, A. (1990). Marital discord and child behaviour problems: a meta-analysis. *Journal of Abnormal Child Psychology*, **18**, 105–117.

Rollins, B.C. & Feldman, H. (1970). Marital satisfaction over the life cycle. *Journal of Marriage and the Family*, **32**, 20–28.

Rollins, B.C. & Galligan, R. (1978). The developing child and marital satisfaction of parents. In R. Lerner & G. Spanier (eds), *Child Influences on Marital and Family Interaction: a Life-span Perspective* (pp. 71–105). New York: Academic Press.

Sandler, I.N., Wolchik, S.A. & Braver, S.L. (1988). The stressors of children's post-divorce environments. In S.A. Wolchik & P. Karoly (eds), *Children of Divorce: Empirical Perspectives on Adjustment* (pp. 111–143). New York: Gardner.

Seltzer, M.M. & Krauss, M.W. (1989). Aging parents with mentally retarded children: family risk factors and sources of support. *American Journal on Mental Retardation*, **94**, 303–312.

Spanier, G.B., Lewis, R.A. & Cole, C.L. (1975). Marital adjustment over the family life: the issue of curvilinearity. *Journal of Marriage and the Family*, **31**, 263–286.

Steinberg, L. & Silverberg, S. (1987). Influences on marital satisfaction during the middle stages of the family life cycle. *Journal of Marriage and the Family*, **49**, 751–760.

Stolberg, A.L., Camplair, C.W., Currier, K. & Wells, M.J. (1987). Individual, familial and environmental determinants of children's post-divorce adjustment and maladjustment. *Journal of Divorce*, **11**(1), 51–70.

Stolberg, A.L. & Walsh, P. (1988). A review of treatment methods for children of divorce. In S.A. Wolchik & P. Karoly (eds), *Children of Divorce: Empirical Perspective on Adjustment* (pp. 299–321). New York: Gardner.

Visher, E.B. & Visher, J.S. (1989). Parenting coalitions after remarriage: dynamics and therapeutic guidelines. *Family Relations*, **38**, 65–70.

Visher, J.S. & Visher, E.B. (1991). Therapy with stepfamily couples. *Psychiatric Annals*, **21**, 462–465.

Vuchinich, S., Hetherington, E.M., Vuchinich, R.A. & Clingempeel, W.G. (1991). Parent–child interaction and gender differences in early adolescents' adaptation to stepfamilies. *Developmental Psychology*, **27**, 618–626.

Wadsworth, J., Burnell, I., Taylor, B. & Butler, N. (1983). Family type and accidents in preschool children. *Epidemiology and Community Health*, **37**, 100–104.

Waite, L.J. & Lillard, L.A. (1991). Children and marital disruption. *American Journal of Sociology*, **96**, 930–953.

Wallerstein, J.S. & Corbin, S.B. (1989). Daughters of divorce: report from a ten-year follow-up. *Journal of Orthopsychiatry*, **59**, 593–604.

Wallerstein, J.S. & Kelly, J.B. (1980). *Surviving the Break-up: How Children and Parents Cope with Divorce*. New York: Baisic Books.

Warshak, R.A. & Santrock, J.W. (1983). The impact of divorce in father-custody and mother-custody homes. In L.A. Kurdek (ed.), *Children and Divorce* (pp. 29–46). San Francisco: Jossey-Bass.

Webster-Stratton, C. (1989). The relationship of marital support, conflict, and divorce to parent perceptions, behaviors, and childhood conduct problems. *Journal of Marriage and the Family*, **51**, 417–430.

Weiss, R.S. (1979). Growing up a little faster: the experience of growing up in a single-parent household. *Journal of Social Issues*, **35**, 97–111.

White, L. & Booth, A. (1985). The transition to parenthood and marital quality. *Journal of Family Issues*, **7**, 131–147.

Wikler, L.M. (1986). Periodic stresses of families of older mentally retarded children: an exploratory study. *American Journal of Mental Deficiency*, **90**, 703–706.

Wolchik, S.A., West, S.G., Westover, S. & Sandler, I.N. (1993). The Children of Divorce Parenting Intervention: outcome evaluation of an empirically based program. *American Journal of Community Psychology*, **21**, 293–331.

Chapter 11

Aging and Marriage: Understanding the Long-term, Later-life Marriage

Fran C. Dickson
Department of Human Communication Studies,
University of Denver, Denver, CO, USA

H: And there hasn't been anything going on for the last, what, two, three, years. And there isn't going to be.

W: Well, if there is, it does and that's the way it is.

H: I've had three dance partners since then and it's been all dance and not anything else, and it's been strictly dancing which I need and love . . . And we've been getting along better, I think she doesn't agree with me, getting along better the last year or two, almost better than we have our entire lives.

W: Yes, he's become aware too, I've noticed that, like if I'm having company, he'll set the table, you know and . . .

H: I've been doing that for years.

W: No, honey, when I had your mother's big birthday party, when you were involved with that woman. . . .

H: Maybe I was mowing hay or something . . .

W: No, you were with that woman.

H: Well, when I was dancing all the time . . .

W: But you promised, too, you were going to help around the house.

H: That was twenty-five years ago.

W: Yeah, but when you were involved it was different, you didn't even see the grandkids or kids start to walk and . . .

H: Well, a couple of, a couple of years I got busy, I'll agree.

W: Yeah, and before, I could sense, because he'd be so belligerent or something and that wasn't his nature, and I always felt he was being torn by what he's supposed to do, a churchgoing lad, instead of talking and trying to solve our problems so he'd be happy. Um, I'd say one thing, I think one reason our marriage survived, and it's been very difficult for him too, you can't imagine how awful it was and to cope with, uh, and it's been rough, um, but had it been

Clinical Handbook of Marriage and Couples Interventions. Edited by W. Kim Halford and Howard J. Markman.
© 1997 John Wiley & Sons Ltd.

very easy to get a divorce back then as it is today, I think we probably would
have, but somehow. . . .

H: It's just as easy today.

W: No, because the first time I was gonna divorce you with that woman you
were with, I was going to Las Vegas because it was too complicated here, um,
it would just take too long. You know, when our second daughter was a
baby . . .

This is an example of a couple married for 54 years discussing their early marital
problems in the context of their present relationship (Dickson, 1995). As you can
see from this dialogue, the couple has not resolved the issue of marital infidelity
on the husband's part. The couple is discussing an event that started 25 years ago
and still appears to be a problem. During this dialogue, the wife is becoming more
sarcastic and angry, while the husband is becoming more withdrawn. Both couple
members agree that they had problems, that still haunt them today; however,
neither of them will discuss the possibility of seeking out help for this marital
problem.

The purpose of this chapter is to review the existing literature on long-term,
later-life marriages and discuss concerns that clinicians may have when treating
couples in their later years. Long-term marriage is typically defined as couples
that have been married for over 50 years to the same spouse. Small amounts of
research focus on couples married over 45 years. Couples in the later years of
their marriage rarely seek marital therapy. More typically, marital problems are
addressed when they are connected to other health-related issues such as heart
disease, diabetes, cancer, or Alzheimer's disease. A more detailed review of how
health issues impact marriage are discussed in the Schmaling & Sher chapter (this
volume). However, this chapter attempts to increase understanding of the communication dynamics among later-life couples who are healthy, focusing on
improving wellness instead of dealing with illness by reviewing a number of issues
that impact the later-life couples, such as retirement, conflict and expression of
emotion.

A fact of life is that people are living longer. Our increased longevity is
impacting the life-cycle and the definition of relationships. For example, one out
of five couples are now celebrating their fiftieth wedding anniversary. Although
the length of marriages is increasing, the research on later-life couples is not.
Much of what we know about the dynamics of marriage is based on couples in the
early or middle years of marriage. Very little research is conducted on couples
involved in long-lasting, later-life marriage. Much of the existing research that
touches on the issue of marriage in later life actually focuses on the loss of the
spouse and bereavement instead of exploring the dynamics of existing long-
lasting marriages.

Most of the research discussed in this chapter is based on research conducted
on later-life couples living in the USA, Canada and UK. Presently, very little
research exists that explores the communication dynamics of later-life couples
from the Middle East or Asian countries. We can only speculate on how existing
research will generalize to other cultures.

MARITAL SATISFACTION AMONG LATER-LIFE COUPLES

Much of the existing literature states that in the later years of life married couples tend to be at their highest level of marital satisfaction. It is believed that after the children leave home marital satisfaction increases (Rollins & Feldman, 1970; Steere, 1981). For example, Sillars et al. (1992) found that older couples' communication commonly demonstrates communal themes such as togetherness and interaction. The longer the couple has been together, the more communal themes emerge in their communication. In addition, Sillars et al. (1992) found that older couples were more interdependent and conventional than their younger counterparts.

It is generally believed that marriage is more positive and beneficial for men than for women (Bloom, Asher & White, 1978). The research among later-life adults does not paint much of a different picture. In general, older husbands benefit more from marriage than their wives (Brehm, 1992). Men typically receive more help from their spouses and are more satisfied with the marital relationship (Keith & Schafer, 1985). Married men appear to have a smoother, more positive post-retirement experience than those who are widowed or single (Cole, 1984). The older marriage, in general, is a good source of social support and good way to avoid loneliness (Huych & Hoyer, 1982). Although the later-life marriage appears to be a happy marriage, the meaning of happiness and satisfaction may change over time.

Traditional measures of marital happiness emphasize the importance of the level of agreement as a dimension of happiness (Locke & Wallace, 1959; Spanier, 1976). This emphasis can inflate marriage happiness score for long-term, later-life couples since they have been together so long, they typically have a high degree of agreement on major life issues. It is possible that they agree on a number of issues but are still unhappy in their marriage. Therefore, caution needs to be exercised when interpreting marital satisfaction scores for long-term later-life couples. One might predict that overall measures of relationship happiness are more weakly associated with levels of disagreement in later-life couples than younger and middle-aged couples. Other measures, such as dyadic adjustment scales, might be more useful in measuring satisfaction among later-life couples than other-aged couples; however, researchers need to develop normative data on other measures of marital satisfaction among later-life couples before these kinds of statements can be empirically tested. In addition, researchers and therapists need to recognize that later-life couples are in a unique circumstance that creates particular challenges for relationship maintenance and satisfaction.

COHORT EFFECTS AND LATER-LIFE COUPLES

While exploring the dynamics of later-life couples, we cannot ignore the influence of context on the formation and maintenance of the intimate relationship. In

North America, the Great Depression and World War II had significant impact on the way these American couples defined and set up their relationships. For example, research has indicated that it is typical for later-life couples to overcome financial difficulties fairly easily, due to their Depression experience (Dickson, 1995). It was common for these couples to be happy with less money because they had already survived the Depression, which taught them to be satisfied with less personally and financially. It is not known if these patterns generalized to long-term, later-life couples in countries that did not experience the Depression.

World War II also had a strong impact on later-life couples. As a result of the War, many American couples spent their courtship and early stages of marriage communicating through letters. Some couples were married when men were on furlough, and then lived apart for great lengths of time. In other cases, couples courted through letter-writing, decided to marry through letter-writing, and even were apart after marriage, experiencing the early stages of marriage through letter-writing (Dickson, 1995). The lack of proximal interaction during the early stages of the relationship and marriage seem to have shaped long-term expectations for the relationship. As was the case for the Depression, these later-life couples have learned to be happy with less (Dickson, 1995).

Understanding the impact that the Depression and World War II had on these couples is very important. These two historical events have shaped the way this cohort experiences life and intimacy. They matured in a time when roles were clearly defined, accepted and acted out. The changing roles in our society today may be confusing for many later-life couples. Some may try to incorporate contemporary roles and styles into their intimate relationships and have a great deal of difficulty in doing so. The more contemporary understanding and experience are just not there.

COMMUNICATION AND RETIREMENT AMONG LATER-LIFE COUPLES

Retirement is a time of both celebration and readjustment for later-life couples. Typically, it is the husband who is retiring and it is common for many wives to go to work when the husband has retired. Retirement brings on much anticipation for these couples. Many dream of reconnecting with their spouse, traveling, spending time with family members and exploring personal interests and hobbies. For example, in a recent study, retired couples reported the joy in having spontaneity when deciding leisure activities and comfort with the increased time spent with their spouses (Dickson, 1995). Although retired couples may fulfill their dreams and hopes during retirement, many are faced with the difficulty of redefining and readjusting their relationships.

Typically, retirement is a time when older couples can re-establish their patterns of separateness or connectedness (Orthner, 1975). Research (Keith, Powers & Goudy, 1981) has indicated that many wives have a more difficult time adjusting to their husbands' participation in the home than husbands have adjusting to being home. The husbands' presence in the home creates some tension for the wives, who typically view the home as their territory. Wives report having mixed feelings about having their retired husbands around the house more often (Cole, 1984). Keating & Cole (1980) found that after retirement there is no increase in the level of communication, contrary to what one might expect. However, an early study found that retired couples enjoy the opportunity of sharing feelings and developing their relationship through participation in mutual interests (Stinnett, Carter & Montgomery, 1972). In a recent study one couple, married for 54 years, reported that they enjoyed refinishing furniture together and while they would work on projects they would discuss many different personal topics and issues (Dickson & Thompson, 1995). They believed, as others did, that working on projects together provided them with an opportunity to share an activity as well as share their feelings.

While retirement offers couples more opportunities to re-establish their relationship with each other and offers more time for recreation, it can create financial strains for the couple. The U.S. Bureau of the Census (1990) identified that older adults that fall below the poverty line were more likely to be widowed women, living along. It can be concluded, then, that at least in the USA, married later-life adults are at less risk for serious financial difficulties than single later-life adults living alone. This does not mean that retirement requires no life-style adjustments due to changes in financial situation. Discussions around money issues can create conflict for later-life couples, just as it does for younger or middle-aged couples. The difference is that later-life couples typically have no hope of increasing their financial status as do younger couples. Later-life couples report the fear of losing their autonomy (Hansson & Carpenter, 1994) which may result from having to rely financially on other family members. Loss of independence and autonomy can be associated with depression among later-life adults (Hansson & Carpenter, 1994). Later in this chapter the implications of depression within later-life marriages is discussed.

Some recent literature has focused on the connection between marital satisfaction and retirement. For example, Higginbottom, Barling and Kelloway (1993) explored the relationship among retirement satisfaction, marital satisfaction, and depressing. They found that those who were not satisfied with their retirement experience were more likely to have symptoms of depression. In addition, those who experienced depressive symptoms were more likely to have lower marital satisfaction. Research indicates that retirement satisfaction predicts depressive symptoms, and depressive symptoms predict marital satisfaction (Higginbottom, Barling & Kelloway, 1993). Findings such as these highlight the importance of understanding the retirement process and depression, and how both retirement and depression may impact marital quality.

COMMUNICATION BETWEEN LATER-LIFE COUPLES

Marital research tends to focus on exploration of communication and conflict as a primary area of intervention for non-distressed and distressed couples (Notarius & Markman, 1994). But when exploring conflict among later-life couples, it is also important to acknowledge what we know about emotional behavior among older adults.

Typically, it was believed that later-life adults' emotions are flat, rigid and dampened (Looft, 1972). However, there is more recent evidence to suggest that later-life adults tend to gain more control over their emotions as they age (Lawton et al., 1992). Carstensen, Gottman & Levenson (1995) found that when resolving conflict, older couples tend to express less emotional negativity and are more affectionate than are middle-aged couples. Zietlow & Sillars (1988) found that happy older couples tend to be less expressive than is typical for married couples today. However, they did find that emotional quality differed as a function of the importance of the topic of discussion to the couple. For example, in discussing unimportant topics, the couple tended to be polite to each other, whereas for topics that were highly important to the couple, they tended to be far more confrontive and showed greater negativity. Overall, it is believed that older couples are more affectionate with each other than are middle-aged couples (Levenson, Carstensen & Gottman, 1993). An unusual example of this emerged from a study of long-term, later-life couples (Dickson & Thompson, 1995). One of the couple members became blind in later life; however, the couple still looked at each other with loving looks and expressions, even through one was not sighted. This couple also had a great deal of hand holding and touching during the interview process, which was common among the later-life couples. One can speculate on why later-life couples are perceived and report being more affectionate and polite with each other than middle-aged couples. A possibility is that time together has mellowed them and they have learned how to treat each other with respect and dignity as they move through life together.

The sources and topics of conflict tend to be different for later-life couples when compared to middle-aged couples. Levenson, Carstensen & Gottman (1995) found that the five most salient topics of conflict for later-life couples are (rank-ordered in terms of importance): communication, recreation, money, children and sex. The rankings for middle-aged couples are: children, money, communication, recreation, and sex. For couples in their later years children no longer appear to be the most salient topic of conflict because the children are now adults. Communication becomes the greatest source of conflict for later-life couples. This can be an indication that the couple is spending more time together, as well as attempting to redefine and establish their relationship. Problems with communication can make this process more difficult, if not impossible. However, it needs to be noted that this study (Levenson, Carstensen & Gottman, 1995) found that when comparing later-life couples to middle-aged couples, later-life couples demonstrated less potential for conflict and greater potential for pleasure.

Although the sources of conflict may appear to be different for later-life couples compared to middle-aged couples, Ekerdt & Vinick (1991) found that the types and amount of marital complaints among retired and non-retired couples were no different. Both retired and non-retired married couples complained about the same things when discussing their marital partners. This study implies that the retirement process may not change the kinds of complaints and problems that married people experience.

When exploring the sequence of interaction among unhappy older couples, it was found that they were less likely to escalate negative affect in a conflict situation (Carstensen, Gottman & Levenson, 1995), having "learned to leave well enough alone" (p. 146). However, from a therapeutic standpoint, this kind of behavior may appear to be withdrawal or a lack of interest or involvement in the relationship. Another interesting finding that emerged from this study is that older unhappy couples were less likely to engage in negative start-ups in interaction sequences when compared to middle-aged couples. In other words, it is more typical to see negative patterns of exchange with middle-aged unhappy couples than older unhappy couples.

Overall, the discussions among middle-aged married couples were far more emotional than the discussions among older couples. How to interpret this lack of negative emotionality is the real question that faces the therapist. One should not confuse the lack of negative emotionality with the inability to express emotion in other situations. As noted earlier, later-life adults are able and willing to express positive emotionality and affection. It appears that in the face of conflict, later-life adults are less willing to express negative emotion. In addition, it may be typical for older couples to refuse to engage in conflict, leaving major points of contention unresolved. A concern for a therapist might be whether the couple members are just not invested in the relationship or if they just do not have the skills to engage in conflict constructively, and therefore, they avoid it.

Dickson (1995) conducted a study on couples married for more than 50 years, and developed a typology of later-life couples based on the quality and characteristics of their mutual storytelling. This project characterized couples as: (a) *connected couples*, who have high levels of marital satisfaction, participate in mutual storytelling, communicate with a great deal of politeness; respect, and understanding to their spouses, and even have incidences when they can read each others minds; and (b) *functional separates*, who engage in individual storytelling, focus more on the self than the couple, participate in separate recreational activities, and communicate with a great deal of respect and politeness. These functional separate couples report moderate to high levels of marital satisfaction, although they have appeared to negotiate comfortable levels of distant intimacy within their relationships. They are highly committed to each other and care a great deal about each other but appear to be independent of each other. A third characterization is that of (c) *dysfunctional separates*, who have maintained an unhappy marriage for more than 50 years. These couples participate in individual storytelling; disagree on characteristics of the stories they are telling; appear to have very different marital experiences; communicate in a distant, cold manner with their spouses; contradict each other; participate in separate recreational activities; and demonstrate a great deal of sadness and sometimes anger when discussing the marital relationship.

Dickson (1995) also identified reasons for how and why these couples were able to maintain a marriage for more than 50 years. The happy couples tended to have four common characteristics: (a) happily married later-life couples report that during their years together they have developed a mutual family vision, which usually takes the form of a plan or mutual desire that the couple develop on how they would like their life together to be; (b) these couples report that they put their spouse before all other activities, people or things, making their spouse the most important person in their lives; (c) they treat each other with respect, politeness, and kindness; finally, (d) these couples have learned how to manage comfortable levels of intimacy and distance in their marriage.

The dynamics are quite different for the unhappy later-life couples. These couples tend to have four common characteristics: (a) they report that while they were unhappy for many years in their marriage, divorce was not an option—it was common for women to report this more than the men; (b) many of these couples were highly religious and believed that you marry for life; (c) the women felt that they had financial security in their marriage and would not be able to obtain employment or financial security if they were divorced; (d) these couples also maintained high levels of emotional and physical distance, at least in the later years of their marriage. One characteristic of this distance is that these couples did not have high levels of conflict, even though they had high levels of unhappiness (Dickson, 1995).

Dickson's (1995) project on later-life, long-term marriages helps us to understand that there are various types of later-life marriages among older adults. The typical stereotype is of an older, loving. "cute" couple, when in fact there can be distance and dissatisfaction within the long-term marriage. Many times the outsider's view of the marriage can be very different from the reality. Therapists need to move away from stereotypes of later-life couples and focus on the different dynamics that can exist among older couples. For example, if a functional separate couple is in therapy, it might be inappropriate to structure a situation that might challenge the comfortable levels of distance and closeness that the couple has negotiated over time.

EXPRESSION OF EMOTION IN LATER-LIFE COUPLES

Much of the research on older adults states that as adults age the capacity to express emotion lessens. However, recently there has been a body of research that has challenged this way of thinking. Research has found that older and younger adults demonstrate difference in describing the intensity of their subjective emotional experience (Levenson et al., 1991). Another interesting finding is that older adults appear to have stronger self-regulation skills but report more moderation when expressing emotional responses (Lawton et al., 1992). Older people also have been found to be poorer decoders of emotional expression and are difficult to decode by others (Malatesta et al., 1987).

How does this information translate into the therapeutic setting for later-life couples? First, most of the existing research has been conducted on individual later-life adults, and very little research has been conducted on later-life couples.

Therefore, we need to translate what we know about the individual to what can be applied to the couple. One such study has found that later-life couples tend to be less emotionally negative and more affectionate than middle-aged couples when discussing marital problems (Carstensen, Gottman & Levenson, 1995). However, Carstenson, Gottman & Levenson (1995) also found that later-life wives were more affectively negative than their husbands and that husbands were more defensive than their wives. The greatest amount of negative affect exchange was found among the unhappy marriages with both middle-age and later-life couples.

Some studies have also found that older wives become more assertive and instrumental, whereas their husbands become more affiliative and expressive in later years (Grunebaum, 1979; Gutmann, 1977; Levinson, 1978). However, other studies have found that both males and females become more expressive as they grow older (Lowenthal & Robinson, 1976; Troll, 1982). Another interesting finding among later-life men and women is that husbands become more gentle and tender with old age, whereas the wives tend to experience this tenderness as their husbands becoming "clingy" (Troll, Miller & Atchley, 1979).

In summary, the research on the expression of emotion among later-life adults presents perplexing and possible contradictory information. From the therapeutic point of view, it is critical that the affective dimension associated with marital problems be acknowledged and handled productively. Emphasizing the decoding capacities of later-life couples may be an important step in setting up a successful marital therapy program. It is also important to acknowledge the differences in the expression of emotion among later-life husbands and wives within the therapeutic setting.

INTERVENTION PROGRAMS FOR LATER-LIFE COUPLES

It is apparent that later-life couples have unique circumstances that may make relationship maintenance and satisfaction difficult tasks for couples to achieve. There are a number of existing communication training and intervention programs for couples in their beginning and middle years that provide them with skills necessary to maintain relationship happiness and stability. However, no such programs exist that focus on later-life couples.

Before discussing what does exist, it needs to be noted that later-life adults may have more negative attitudes about couples therapy and intervention programs then other couples. Dickson (1995) found that when later-life couples were discussing their relationship, at times they did discuss attitudes and experiences about therapy. For example, one couple discussed the husband's frequent infidelity during their marriage. During the periods of the affairs it was typical for the wife to become depressed and suicidal. At one point she did decide to see a psychiatrist, who said that it was common for husbands to have affairs when their wives were pregnant or had young children, as she did. This experience was her first and only encounter with a psychiatrist, which occurred in the early 1960s, and had a negative impact on this woman's perceptions of the mental health community in general. Later in life this woman realized the lack of empathy that this doctor had for her situation; however, at the time it resulted in her feeling completely alone and isolated, making a bad situation worse. This wife reported later, when the doctor had finally passed away, that a great thing had happened to women who had ever seen him as a therapist.

Another couple reported a great deal of emotional distance between them occurred after the death of a baby. It appeared that the husband poured himself into his activities and building of their new home, while the wife reported a high level of depression and stress dealing with the other children in the family. She eventually turned to her minister and church for help, while the husband refused to deal with the loss in any public fashion. While losing a child was not a typical experience for couples participating in this study, the way in which the couple dealt with the loss was typical. It was common for a couple member, usually the wife, to seek out help for problems from people affiliated with their religious organization, not the mental health community.

These experiences, and others reported by couples, highlight the negative attitude that later-life adults may have about seeking therapy. This woman's experience is really atypical since it was not common for couples or individuals to seek therapy in general. Problems were viewed as personal and it was thought they should be kept in the home, which many couples reported doing. Therefore, if later-life couples do show up in a therapeutic setting, the therapist should be aware that negative attitudes about therapy possibly exist and that establishing a trusting environment for the couple to discuss their problems is of critical importance. In addition, intervention programs need to acknowledge the attitudes later-life couples may have about seeking communication training for problems in their marriage.

Communication research and theory has provided conceptual and empirical foundations for the development, implementation and evaluation of communication-based intervention programs for couples. Several well-known programs do exist. There are two separate major traditions in the family and couples' intervention area that have recently diverged, spiraled and grown apart, not unlike a DNA helix. The first of these traditions is represented by the pioneering work of Bernard Guerney (1977) at Pennsylvania State University and Miller, Nunally & Wackman (1975) at the University of Minnesota and now based in Denver, Colorado.

Guerney's program, called Relationship Enhancement, has its roots in basic communication principles, and it stresses the importance of expressive speaking and active listening. Relationship Enhancement recognizes the need for people to be validated and understood in intimate relationships, whether they be marital relationships, parent–child relationships, couples who are seeking treatment, or those taking advantage of educationally-based prevention programs. The Minnesota Couples' Communication Program, now simply called Couples' Communication, overlaps substantially the Relationship Enhancement approach to understanding and validation but has a strong component focusing on intrapersonal awareness.

The second major tradition is the behavioral/social learning tradition from psychology, broadly based in behavioral social exchange and social learning theories for relationships (see Weiss & Heyman, 1990, for review). Programs in this tradition had their start in the late 1960s with the pioneering efforts of Richard Stuart (1969) and Arnold Lazarus (1968) and with the publication of a book summarizing the theory, tools and techniques utilized (Jacobson & Margolin, 1979). This form of intervention for couples is among the most well researched and the most popular in the marital and couples therapy field. A more recent offshoot of this is behavioral family therapy for families with a member who has serious psychorathology (Falloon, 1988).

The Prevention and Relationship Enhancement Program (PREP) is an example of an empirically-based approach to the prevention and treatment of marital distress (Markman, Stanley & Blumberg, 1994). This program focuses on couples intervention because it combines the two pioneering traditions reviewed above with a clear empirical and conceptual basis stemming from research and theory on communication with couples. Early research revealed that the quality of the partner's communication discriminated between distressed and non-distressed couples (Gottman, Markman & Notarius, 1977; Markman, 1979, 1981, 1984). These studies and others laid the foundation for skills and types of interventions that are put forth in this program.

The focus and research foundation of PREP is on couples in the early and middle years of marriage. A major gap in the marriage and intervention literature concerns the characteristics and issues of the older couple. Presently, there are not many programs that focus on the needs of families with older members or later-life couples (Symer, Zarit & Quall, 1990). As a family grows older, a number of new stressors become apparent (Stephens et al., 1990) that create a need for different kinds of support and intervention programs.

There are a few programs in the country today that focus on communication needs of later-life couples and families. The programs that exist typically focus on caregiver enhancement and respite programs (Zarit, 1990), coping with death and dying (Shamis, 1985) and preventing elderly abuse (Hawkins & Traxler, 1988). Programs such as these attempt to alleviate the stress associated with older family members in general. Other programs that exist tend to operate out of, or are associated with, a hospital or medical facility. These programs focus on facilitating the couples' life changes that are associated with a particular illness such as diabetes, heart disease or cancer. None emphasizes the communication needs of later-life couples.

As our population ages there needs to be an awareness of the later-life adult's needs, and more of a focus on the treatment of later-life adults. Of the existing interventions and treatments for later-life adults, most focus on the individual, not the couple. Much of the research on therapy for later-life adults has found that traditional treatments used for younger populations also work well for the older patient in therapy. Horowitz et al., 1984; Pinkston & Linsk, 1984; Thompson, Gallagher & Breckenridge, 1987).

Much of the existing research on later-life adults in a therapeutic setting stresses the incidence of depression among this special population. It is estimated that about 20% of later-life adults suffer from depression (Blazer, Hughes & George, 1989; Fry, 1989). Depressive episodes in later-life adults tend to be more severe and to have more acute onset than depression in young adults, and more often are associated with biological causes. Major life events tend to play a small role in triggering the depressive episodes of the later-life adult (Gold, Goodwin & Chrousos, 1988). Depression among one or both of the later-life couple members may contribute to marital distress. Hansson & Carpenter (1994) believe that relationship enhancement training among later-life adults may be critical in treating and alleviating depression. Working to improve the communication skills for the later-life couple can also help them manage their depression.

In terms of treating the individual, a number of intervention programs exist that focus on the development and maintenance of social skills. Typically these programs emphasize assertiveness training and skills necessary for meeting new people. A number of programs exist that have adapted assertiveness training to meet the needs of an older population (e.g. Engels, 1991; Symer et al., 1990). Franzke (1987) developed an assertiveness training program for later-life adults that also emphasized self-concept issues. Other types of existing programs deal with social skills training and programs that attempt to improve communication between institutionalized older adults and their families and friends (Shulman & Mandel, 1988).

CONCLUSION

Understanding the later-life couple's communication dynamics and the issues relevant to this specific age group can lead to an effective treatment program that can meet the unique needs of later-life couples. The majority of the existing intervention programs and assessment techniques are designed to focus on the needs of young and middle-aged couples. In the past, researchers and therapists have assumed that these strategies can be applied to later-life adults; however, the generalizability of these materials to later-life adults has never been tested. In addition, a limited number of therapists have experienced the same major life transitions and events, such as World War II, as later-life couples. Consequently, few active therapists have the ability to understand the impact of these large events and their implications on individual lives. Therefore, it is important for therapists to educate themselves on the unique life circumstances of the later-life adult, in order to be better able to empathize with the stresses, pains and pleasures experienced by later-life adults.

Therapists should also recognize that cultural differences and values can impact the communication dynamics among later-life couples. Eastern and

Western cultures have very different views of their elderly populations. These views can affect the way in which these couples age and the kinds of marital concerns that exist. The Jones and Chao chapter (this volume) discusses cross-cultural influences on relationships, particularly among Asian relationships. That chapter can shed some light on the issue of cultural differences in couples communication.

Later life presents new challenges for the couple and can be a time of great readjustment. Therapeutic interventions that specialize in the needs of later-life couples may facilitate a smoother transition into this phase of life.

REFERENCES

Blazer, D.G., Hughes, D.C. & George, L.K. (1989). Age and impaired subjective support: predictors of depression symptoms at one-year follow-up. *Journal of Nervous and Mental Disease*, **180**(3), 172–178.

Bloom, B.L., Asher, S.J. & White, S.W. (1978). Marital disruption as a stressor: a review and analysis. *Psychological bulletin*, **85**, 867–894.

Brehm, S. (1992). *Intimate Relationships*. New York: McGraw Hill.

Carstensen, L.L., Gottman, J.M. & Levenson, R.W. (1995). Emotional behavior in long-term marriage. *Psychology and Aging*, **10**, 140–149.

Cole, C.L. (1984). Marital quality in later life. In W.H. Quinn & G.H. Hughston (eds), *Independent Aging: Family and Social Support Perspectives* (pp. 72–90). Maryland: Aspen Systems Corporation.

Dickson, F.C. (1995). The best is yet to be: research on long-lasting relationships. In J.T. Wood & S. Duck (eds), *Understanding Relationship Processes: Off the Beaten Track* (pp. 22–50). Beverly Hills, CA: Sage.

Dickson, F.C. & Thompson, J.L. (1995). A typology of couples' communication among long-term, later-life couples. Under review for publication.

Ekerdt, D.J. & Vinick, B.H. (1991). Marital complaints in husband-working and husband-retired couples. *Research on Aging*, **13**(3), 364–382.

Engels, M.L. (1991). The promotion of positive social interaction through social skills training. In P.A. Wisocki (ed.), *Handbook of Clinical Therapy with the Elderly Client: Applied Clinical Psychology* (pp. 182–202). New York: Plenum.

Falloon, I.R. (1988). *Handbook of Behavior Family Therapy*. New York: Guilford.

Franzke, A.W. (1987). The effects of assertiveness training on older adult. *The Gerontologist*, **27**, 13–16.

Fry, P.S. (1989). Perceptions of vulnerability and control in old age: a critical reconstruction. In P.S. Fry (ed.), *Psychological Perspectives of Helplessness and Control in the Elderly* (pp. 1–39). Amsterdam: North Holland.

Gold, P.W., Goodwin, F.K. & Chrousos, G.P. (1988). Clinical and biochemical manifestations of depression: relation to the neurobiology of stress. *New England Journal of Medicine*, **319**, 413–420.

Grunebaum, H. (1979). Middle age and marriage-affiliative men and assertive women. *American Journal of Family Therapy*, **7**(3), 46–50.

Guerney, B.G. (1977). *Relationship Enhancement*. San Francisco: Jossey-Bass.

Gutmann, D.L. (1977). The cross cultural perspective: notes toward a comparative psychology of aging. In J.E. Birren & K.W. Schaie (eds), *Handbook for the Psychology of Aging*. New York: Van Nostrand Reinhold.

Hansson, R.O. & Carpenter, B.N. (1994). *Relationships in Old Age*. New York: Guilford.

Hawkins, R. & Traxler, A. (1988). Elder abuse and communication. In C.W. Carmichael, C.H. Botan & R. Hawkins (eds), *Human Communication and the Aging Process*. Aospect Heights, IL: Waveland Press.

Huych, M.H. & Hoyer, W.J. (1982). *Adult Development and Aging*. Belmont, CA: Wadsworth.

Higginbottom, S.F., Barling, J. & Kelloway, E.K. (1993). Linking retirement experiences and marital satisfaction: a mediational model. *Psychology and Aging*, **8**(4), 508–516.

Horowitz, L.M., Marmar, C., Weiss, D.S., DeWitt, K.N. & Rosenbaum, R. (1984). Brief psychotherapy of grief reactions. *Archives of General Psychiatry*, **41**, 439–448.

Jacobson, N.S. & Margolin, G. (1979). *Marital Therapy*. New York: Brunner/Mazel.

Keating, N.C. & Cole, P. (1980). What do I do with him 24 hours a day? Changes in the housewife role after retirement. *Gerontologist*, **20**, 84–89.

Keith, P.M. & Schafer, R.B. (1985). Equity, role strains, and depression among middle-aged and older men and women. In W.A. Peterson & J. Quadagno (eds), *Social Bonds in Later Life: Aging and Interdependence*. Beverly Hills, CA: Sage.

Keith, P.M., Powas, E. & Goudy, W. (1981). Older men in employment and retired families: well-being and involvement in household activities. *Alternative Lifestyles*, **4**, 228–241.

Lawton, M.P., Kleban, M.H., Rajagopal, D. & Dean, J. (1992). Dimensions of affective experience in three age groups. *Psychology and Aging*, **7**, 171–184.

Lazarus, A. (1968). Behavior therapy and marriage counseling. *Journal of the American Society of Psychosomatic Dental Medicine*, **15**, 49–56.

Levenson, R.W., Carstensen, L.L., Friesen, W.W. & Ekman, P. (1991). Emotion, physiology, and expression in old age. *Psychology and Aging*, **6**, 28–35.

Levenson, R.W., Carstensen, L.L. & Gottman, J.M. (1995). Long-term marriages: age, gender, and satisfaction. *Psychology and Aging*, **8**, 301–313.

Levinson, D. (1978). *The Seasons of a Man's Life*. New York: Knopf.

Locke, H.J. & Wallace, K.M. (1959). Short-term marital adjustment and prediction tests: their reliability and validity. *Journal of Marriage and the Family*, **21**, 251–255.

Looft, W.R. (1972). Egocentrism and social interaction across the life span. *Psychological Bulletin*, **78**, 73–92.

Lowenthal, M.F. & Robinson, B. (1976). Social networks and isolation. In R.H. Binstock & E. Shanas (eds), *Handbook of Aging and the Social Science*. New York: Van Nostrand Reinhold.

Malatesta, C.Z., Izard, C.E., Culver, C. & Nicholic, M. (1987). Emotion communication skills in young, middle-aged, and older women. *Psychology and Aging*, **2**, 193–203.

Markman, H.J. (1979). The application of a behavioral model of marriage in predicting relationship satisfaction of couples planning marriage. *Journal of Consulting and Clinical Psychology*, **4**, 743–749.

Markman, H.J. (1981). Prediction of marital distress: a five-year follow-up. *Journal of Consulting and Clinical Psychology*, **49**, 760–762.

Markman, H.J. (1984). The longitudinal study of couples' interactions: implications for understanding and predicting the development of marital distress. In K. Hahlweg & N. Jacobson (eds), *Marital Interaction: Analysis and Modification* (pp. 253–281). New York: Guilford.

Markman, H.J., Stanley, S.M. & Blumberg, S.L. (1995). *Fighting for Your Marriage: Positive Steps for Presenting Divorce and Preserving a Lasting Love*. San Francisco, CA: Jossey-Bass.

Miller, S., Nunally, E. & Wackman, D. (1975). *Alive and Aware*. Minneapolis, MN: Interpersonal Communication Program.

Notarius, C. & Markman, H.J. (1994). *We Can Work It Out: How to Solve Conflict, Save Your Marriage, and Strengthen Your Love for Each Other*. New York: Berkeley.

Pinkston, E.M. & Linsk, N.L. (1984). Behavioral family intervention with the impaired elderly. *The Gerontologist*, **29**, 576–583.

Orthner, D. (1975). Leisure activity patterns and marital satisfaction over the marital career. *Journal of Marriage and the Family*, **37**, 91–102.

Rollins, B.C. & Feldman, H. (1970). Marital satisfaction over the family life cycle. *Journal of Marriage and the Family*, **32**, 20–28.

Shamis, H.S. (1985). Hospice: interdependence of the dying with their community. In W.A. Peterson & J. Quadaqno (eds), *Social Bonds in Later Life: Aging and Interdependence*. Beverly Hills CA: Sage.

Shulman, M.D. & Mandel, E. (1988). Communication training of relatives and friends of institutional elderly persons. *The Gerontologist*, **28**, 797–799.

Sillars, A.L., Burggraf, C.S., Yost, S. & Zietlow, P.H. (1992). Conversational themes and marital relationship definition: quantitative and qualitative investigations. *Human Communication Research*, **19**, 124–154.

Symer, M.A., Zarit, S.H. & Quall, S.H. (1990). Psychological intervention with the aging individual. In J.E. Birren & K.W. Schaie (eds), *Handbook of the Psychology of Aging* (pp. 375–403). San Diego: Academic Press.

Spanier, G.B. (1976). Measuring dyadic adjustment: new scales for assessing the quality of marriage and similar dyads. *Journal of Marriage and the Family*, **38**, 15–28.

Steere, G.H. (1981). The family and the elderly. In F.J. Berghorn & D.E. Schafter (eds), *The Dynamics of Aging* (pp. 289–309). Boulder, CO: Westview.

Stephens, M.A., Crowther, J.H., Hobfoll, S.E. & Tennenbaum, D.L. (1990). *Stress and Coping in Later-life Families*. Washington, DC: Hemisphere.

Stinnett, N.J., Carter, L.M. & Montgomery, J.E. (1972). Older Persons' perceptions of their marriage. *Journal of Marriage and the Family*, **34**, 665–670.

Stuart, R.B. (1969). Operant-interpersonal treatment for marital discord. *Journal of Consulting and Clinical Psychology*, **33**, 657–682.

Thompson, L.W., Gallagher, J.M. & Breckenridge, J.S. (1987). Comparative effectiveness of psychotherapies for depressed elders. *Journal of Consulting and Clinical Psychology*, **55**, 385–390.

Troll, L.E. (1982). *Continuations: Adult Development and Aging*. Monterey, CA: Brooks/Cole.

Troll, L.E., Miller, S.J. & Atchley, R.C. (1979). *Families in Later Life*. Belmont, CA: Wadsworth.

U.S. Bureau of the Census (1990). *1990 Decennial Census of the United States*. Washington, DC: U.S. Government Printing Office.

Weiss, R.L. & Heyman, R.E. (1990). Observation of marital interaction. In F. Fincham & T. Bradbury (eds), *The Psychology of Marriage* (pp. 87–117). New York: Guilford.

Zarit, S.H. (1990). Interventions with frail elders and their families: are they effective and why? In M.A. Stephens, J.H. Crowther, S.E. Hobfoll & D.L. Tennenbaum (eds), *Stress and Coping in Later-life Families* (pp. 241–265). Washington, DC: Hemisphere.

Zietlow, P.H. & Sillars, A.L. (1988). Life-stage differences in communication during marital conflicts. *Journal of Social and Personal Relationships*, **5**, 223–245.

Section III

Personal and Environmental Influences on Marriage

Chapter 12

Couples and the Work–Family Interface

Briony M. Thompson
School of Applied Psychology, Griffith University,
Nathan, Queensland, Australia

Dean Humboldt, an executive, blames his long working hours on a poor marriage: "One reason I got involved in a lot of activities was that I got a lot of positive feedback from them. The reason I spent so much time outside the home was that I felt my time was valued and my input rewarded, and I didn't feel that at home". Dean's ex-wife claims that his inattentiveness to his family, and making work a top priority, was a major source of their difficulties. The perceptions of Dean Humboldt and his ex-wife are reported by Kofodimos (1990) in her interview study of male executives, and the difficulties they have balancing work and family life. The work-committed male executive is a stereotypical example of someone who experiences difficulties in close personal relationships. However, the role demands, social and reward systems, expectations and time constraints of the work role impact on all men and women.

Burke & Greenglass (1987) argued that work would be expected to have a major impact on family for five reasons. Firstly, much work is relatively absorptive, i.e. it makes substantial demands in terms of commitment and performance and may even involve other family members, as in the case of career wives (Strickland, 1992). Secondly, the timing of work (hours and schedules) constrains family interaction and the meeting of family demands. Thirdly, rewards and resources available through work e.g. income and prestige) can impact on the relative power of family members. Work also has a cultural dimension, influencing values and self-perceptions. These values in turn can impact on family and couple processes such as child-rearing practices. Lastly, the social–psychological dimension of work (e.g. emotional climate) can arouse feelings which result in negative or positive spillover and affect family dynamics (Lambert, 1990).

Clinical Handbook of Marriage and Couples Interventions. Edited by W. Kim Halford and Howard J. Markman.
© 1997 John Wiley & Sons Ltd.

Kanter (1977) describes a commonly held view of what she calls "the myth of separate worlds", i.e. that work and family are independent aspects of an individual's life that can be conceptualized as separate systems and managed by organizational practices as if there is no interdependency. A review by Burke & Greenglass (1987) documents substantial evidence to refute this myth. An individual's functioning in work and family is affected by his/her experience in the other. For example, Barnett & Marshall (1992) found that job-related stress exacerbated the relationship between poor partner role quality and psychological distress in men.

This chapter is a review of key models for conceptualizing the work–family interface and an analysis of how work impacts on couple relationships. Work can impact in both positive (enhancing) and negative ways but, given the clinical emphasis of this book, my focus will be on the contribution of work–family conflict to difficulties couples experience in their relationships. Issues of gender, work patterns and individual attributes as correlates of work–family conflict are examined. Strategies for counselling couples where work–family issues are relevant are suggested.

THEORETICAL MODELS OF THE WORK–FAMILY INTERFACE

The interface between work and family has been conceptualized in a number of ways; however, the common theme has been an analysis of roles. In an analogous manner to research on the relationship of work and leisure (Kabanoff, 1980), processes linking work and family have been conceptualized as processes of role segmentation (i.e. they do not affect each other), compensation (i.e. lack of satisfaction in one area leads to attempts to compensate in the other) and spillover (i.e. effects spill over from one area to the other). Each of these models may be useful for understanding the work–family interface for some couples. For example, the segmentation model may hold for some groups such as blue collar workers, whilst compensation may occur when work is inherently dissatisfying (Lambert, 1990). Also some workers seek, and find it easier, to get their needs met in the work domain than in intimate relationships. Spillover can occur in both positive (e.g. job achievements induce positive mood states which carry into the family arena) and negative forms (as when job stress induces negative mood states and lower tolerance for frustration). As Lambert (1990) notes, attempts to determine a single model or process which best represents all variants of the work–family interface are naive. Most couples will experience some elements of all three processes of segmentation, compensation and spillover and they may occur simultaneously.

Much research on the work–family interface focuses on work–family conflict. This is a specific form of inter-role spillover in which the demands and role expectations of one role (work) make it more difficult to meet the demands and expectations of another role (family). Whilst most early research conceptualized work–family conflict as a unitary phenomenon, Gutek, Searle & Klepa (1991) conceptualized work–family conflict as having two components: family interference with work (FIW), and work interference with family (WIF). Their respondents reported more WIF than FIW, and showed some interesting gender differences: the correlations between the two forms of conflict were marginally stronger for men, and the correlation between hours in paid work and WIF was significant for men, but not for women, suggesting that men and women experience the work–family interface differently.

Work and family roles need not necessarily lead to role conflict. O'Driscoll (1996) examined processes of role enhancement where multiple roles energize individuals, and provide them with resources which result in more satisfaction in work and family roles. For example, women having more roles experience better psychological health (Rodin & Ickovics, 1990), and men with working wives benefit from increased family income, increased independence of the spouse, increased marital satisfaction and more companionship (Higgins & Duxbury, 1992). Similarly, time spent in parenting and community work correlates with increased job satisfaction and organizational commitment (Kirchmeyer, 1992).

The focus of this chapter will be on work–family conflict, on the assumption that couples who find their multiple roles enhancing, are less likely to be distressed. Work–family conflict is associated with job dissatisfaction, decreased life satisfaction, symptoms of physical and psychological ill health, and decreased marital and family satisfaction (Parasuraman, Greenhaus & Granrose, 1992). Work–family conflict impacts negatively on couple functioning for a number of reasons. Firstly, increased stress levels as a result of difficulty in balancing work and family roles gives individuals less emotional energy to invest in the relationship, and increases conflict. Individuals who experience more fatigue and communication can become more task-oriented, and lack intimacy. Finally, some individuals experience significant spillover of time demands from work to family. For example, long working hours can intrude into leisure time, and working at home limits time for couple activity. Thus, time, energy and opportunity to deal with couple issues are constrained. In addition, where couples do suffer marital distress, work-related stress and demands (e.g. for frequent travelling) could exacerbate distress.

In spite of extensive research on work and family roles, the process of investment in these roles is poorly understood (Lobel, 1991). In particular we do not understand why it is that some people invest highly in the work role at the expense of the partner role, and under what circumstances that could be detrimental to couple functioning. One model for understanding the role investment process is the utilitarian model, which assumes role investments are made on the basis of role rewards and costs. However, this model is inadequate in explaining people's role investments. Individuals continue to invest heavily in roles even in the absence of favourable reward–cost ratios (Lobel, 1991). For example, some women with young children continue a pattern of commitment to their career even when they have adequate financial support from a partner, are paying high costs for childcare, and are experiencing high levels of fatigue and stress in attempting to meet incompatible role demands.

A social identity approach to role investments conceptualizes work and family role investments as being consistent with the individual's self concepts arising from the groups with which those individuals identify. If the role of lawyer (a work role) is salient to the woman described in the previous paragraph, she may continue with work roles even at an economic and personal cost. A woman who invests highly in work and family roles may suffer more role conflict than a woman with the same role demands who invests highly in the family role but has a low investment in the work role. In the latter case her priorities are clearer, and are sex-role consistent.

Lambert (1990) proposes a research agenda investigating the relative contribution of the utilitarian and social identity models to understanding work and family role investments. With respect to couple functioning, research should address questions such as: how do couples negotiate role investments?; how do self perceptions get modified, if at all, in the process of that negotiation? How do role investments, their rewards and costs, and role salience, relate to role satisfactions and the distribution of power within the couple?

RESEARCH ON THE WORK–FAMILY INTERFACE

Work–Family Conflict and Marital Satisfaction

Work–family conflict does predict family distress. Frone, Russell & Cooper (1992) found work–family conflict to be related to family distress for blue collar workers. In a study of dual career couples, Higgins, Duxbury & Irving (1992) found a lower quality of family life was associated with higher levels of work–family conflict, and that work conflict spilled over to the family. Men in dual career marriages are more susceptible to negative spillover from work to family (Higgins & Duxbury, 1992).

Marital satisfaction is significantly negatively correlated with work stress for men and women (Bedeian, Burke & Moffat, 1988). Furthermore, work stress impacts on marital satisfaction via work–family conflict. For men and women, work–family conflict is more important as a predictor of marital satisfaction than is parental demands. The causal mechanisms for this are unclear. High involvement in work may discourage involvement in marriage, or work–family conflict may make it more difficult to act in a nurturant manner towards one's spouse.

Studies of spillover effects from work to home predominantly assess the impact of husbands' work environment on their wives. Higher occupational demands experienced by men are correlated with dissatisfaction and distress in wives (Burke, Weir & Duwors, 1980). For example, police officers experiencing high stress are likely to be more angry, uninvolved in family matters and have unsatisfactory marriages (Jackson & Malasch, 1982). In addition, work stress may affect the physical health and even life expectancy of partners (Haynes, Eaker & Feinleib, 1983).

Jones & Fletcher (1993) investigated the family effects of occupational stress transmission by looking at the relationships between an individual's psychological health and both their own and their partner's job stress. Men's reported job stress was correlated with their wives' anxiety and depression, but wives' job stress was not correlated with husband's psychological health. Thus, transmission of occupational stress does occur but it seems to be primarily from men to women. Perhaps male work stressors exert a dominant effect on many couple's mood and the psychological health of the partners. Women's roles as caregivers may sensitize them to male work stress. Dunne & Mullins (1989) found that wives of working couples maintain higher physiological arousal at the weekend than husbands, and this may be partly due to transmission of stress.

So work–family conflict produces a negative spillover effect to the partner, and lower marital satisfaction. Some caution must be exercised in assuming a causal influence. Many studies are correlational. It may be that certain individuals are more predisposed to experience stress in both work and family arenas, and these individuals may also report less satisfactory relationships. In support of the possibility that individual characteristics determine work satisfaction, recent research has suggested a predisposition toward stable job satisfaction across jobs, independent of the objective characteristics of the job (Gerhart, 1987).

However, there is evidence that negative spillover effects from work do vary according to the nature of the work. This evidence is reviewed in the next section.

Nature of the Work

As Burke & Greenglass (1987) noted, time and scheduling conflicts are a major source of work–family conflict. In particular, shift work requires the family and worker to adjust to schedules that are different from society's usual pattern. As much of society's activities are organized around the usual pattern, this is particularly stressful. Shift work often leads to disturbances of sleep, psychological symptoms and interference with social life (Toterdell et al., 1995).

Work-related separations, particularly frequent separations, can erode the marital bond (Vormbrock, 1993). Strong emotional reactions to routine separations are common: the "abandoned" partner tends to feel angry, whereas the partner away from home is likely to feel guilt. Repeated separations, as experienced by truck drivers, appear to erode marital relationships, and the husband may come to be seen as peripheral to the family (Hollowell, 1968). Marital separation and divorce are more common in couples experiencing routine work-related separations (Vormbrock, 1993). Relocation may also involve psychological costs to employees and their families (Munton, 1990), especially where periods of separation occur.

Loss of work also impacts upon couples' relationships. Unemployment is a highly stressful life event which affects the whole family system (Shliebnner &

Peregoy, 1994). Wives of unemployed men suffer emotional distress, with husbands' psychological reactions to unemployment predicting wives' responses (Liem & Liem, 1988). Separations and divorces among unemployed people occurs much more often than in employed families, suggesting that unemployment is a significant threat to the marital relationship (Liem & Liem, 1988). At the same time, the marital relationship is an important source of social support, buffering the stress of unemployment (Gore, 1978). However, marital support deteriorates as the unemployment continues and is reflected in lower family cohesion and more family conflict (Liem & Liem, 1988). Economic distress exacerbates this problem (Kong, Perrucci & Perrucci, 1993).

Most research on working patterns has focused on the experience of men and their partners. Little is known about the impact of women's working patterns on their partners, with the exception of research investigating the impact of having a working wife on men's psychological health and marital satisfaction. Burke & Greenglass (1987) reviewed the literature on wives' employment and husbands' well-being, concluding that that husbands' mental health may be adversely affected by wives' employment, and that where this occurred, the most likely explanation was that husbands of working wives felt more inadequate as breadwinners. More recently, Parasuraman et al. (1989) found that men with working wives reported lower job satisfaction and life satisfaction. However, wives' employment accounted for only a small proportion of variance in the satisfaction measures. A major study which included men and women at all occupational levels found that men's level of satisfaction with their personal lives did not vary according to the work status of their wives (Wolcott & Glezer, 1995). Research is needed to investigate personal and situational characteristics which may mediate the impact of partners' work roles on marital and life satisfaction.

Gender and the Work–Family Interface

Gender differences in the experience of the work–family interface have been widely researched, but the results are often inconsistent (Duxbury & Higgins, 1991). There is evidence that men and women do experience and manage the work–family interface differently. Women in dual-career marriages encounter more role overload than their husbands, and feel more dissatisfied with time available for family activities. This dissatisfaction increases with the number of children (Falkenberg & Monachello, 1990). Women also experience more simultaneous, rather than sequential, role demands than men, creating higher levels of role conflict (Hall, 1972) and they spend more hours in combined work and family activity than men (Pleck, 1985). Clearly, even in the dual-career couple who work similar hours, at similar jobs and have a similar level of professional training, it cannot be assumed that each gender experiences the work–family interface in the same way. For example, strong career aspirations are negatively correlated with work–family role conflict for men and positively correlated for women (Holohan & Gilbert, 1979).

Female gynaecologists work significantly fewer hours than male gynaecologists, and the women's work hours are more responsive to family influences than men's (Weisman & Teitlebaum, 1987). Gutek, Searle & Klepa (1991) found that women reported more work interference with family than did men working the same hours. They suggest that time spent in a sex-role-consistent domain is perceived as less of a burden. The implications for couples are that even in an egalitarian marriage women experience more work–family conflict, and feel more pressure to meet family demands. This is consistent with findings that professional women in egalitarian marriages still feel obligation to meet domestic responsibilities (Yogev, 1981) and usually retain ultimate responsibility for domestic tasks (Falkenberg & Monachello, 1990). Women's role orientations may contribute to role overload, and hence frustration, fatigue and anxiety. Husbands, who are less susceptible to role overload, may have difficulties understanding wives' fatigue, and may be hurt or angry if their wives lose interest in sex (Sekaran, 1986).

A theoretical framework used to conceptualize gender differences in the experience of work–family interface is that of asymmetrically permeable boundaries (Pleck, 1977). He argued that for men, work conflict is more likely to spill into the family domain (as, consistent with their sex role, it is acceptable for men's work to interfere with family roles). For women, the direction of interference is more likely to be family interference with work, as it is consistent with their traditional role. There is mixed support for this model (Duxbury & Higgins, 1991).

A note of caution needs to be sounded regarding the generalizability of the research to non-professional couples. Most studies of couples in which both partners work have examined dual-career professional couples, and it should be recognized that the findings for this group may not necessarily apply to non-career working couples (Falkenberg & Monatello, 1990). Falkenberg & Monatello argued that women in dual-income, as opposed to dual-career, families would be more susceptible to work–family conflict. Their argument was that the former women are more likely to be engaging in work behaviours that are incompatible with a role central to their self concept (home-maker), and also be more likely to carry the burden of home responsibilities. There is a dearth of research comparing career and non-career women, and also a dearth of research on the impact of self concept or identity on work–family conflict. However, it may be that where a work role is central to a woman's self concept and her partner supports that role, the couple more easily manages the work–family interface, and the woman experiences less role overload.

In summary, women are particularly susceptible to stress related to work and family roles. Counselling strategies need to recognize gender issues.

Individual Attributes

There is very little research on how characteristics of individuals affect their experience of work–family conflict (Falkenberg & Monatello, 1990), yet it seems reasonable to assume that personality, attitudes and values are likely to influence how an individual perceives, manages and experiences the work–family interface. Personality traits such as negative affectivity and external locus of control are related to reports of job stressors and job strains (Spector & O'Connell, 1994), and may predispose individuals to negative work experiences which spill over into the family domain. Personality characteristics may also affect how an individual experiences work–family conflict, and their use of more or less successful coping strategies.

Low self-esteem is consistently correlated with conflict between self, spouse and professional roles (Holohan & Gilbert, 1979). For both men and women, low self-esteem is correlated with high levels of work–family role conflict. Individuals with higher levels of self-esteem may perceive roles to be less conflicting because they manage the roles more competently, evaluate themselves less negatively when conflicts do occur, and are more resistant to negative evaluations from colleagues and family. Alternatively, the experience of successfully integrating roles may contribute to a sense of self-worth.

Type A work-related attitudes and behaviours of men have been researched extensively with respect to their impact on marital satisfaction. Burke & Greenglass (1987) reviewed that research and concluded that the wives of Type A men experience less marital satisfaction, fewer positive marital behaviours, and more negative impact of their husbands' jobs on personal, home and family life than do wives of Type B men. Marital adjustment is particularly poor in the case of a Type A man married to a Type B wife. However, if power motivation is more typical of the Type A man, then such men may also be more likely to marry Type B women than Type A women, as women who have high career aspirations of their own are perceived as threatening (Burke & Greenglass, 1987).

Initially research on Type A characteristics assumed a unidimensional construct; however, recent research recognizes two major dimensions— impatience–irritability and achievement striving (Spector & O'Connell, 1994). Spector & O'Connell found impatience to be positively correlated with experiencing conflict at work and symptoms of ill health. Achievement was positively associated with workload, but not correlated with conflict at work or health symptoms. Hence caution should be exercised in interpreting research on Type A personality and marital satisfaction since irritability–impatience may impact more negatively on spouse interactions than achievement striving. Most research has not differentiated these dimensions. However, on the assumption that behaviours spill over from one context to another, both dimensions may relate to reported family dissatisfactions when husbands/fathers use interaction patterns that are successful at work, such as lecturing, blaming, demanding and criticizing, in a family setting (Burke & Weir, 1977). The kinds of emotion management required for successful performance in many work roles occupied by men may also be inconsistent with the types of emotion management required in family and intimate relationships (Wharton & Erikson, 1993). This would suggest that men who are successful in terms of work roles, and who achieve highly in organizational cultures that encourage competition, conflict and political behaviour, may be at risk of marital problems. Whether or not the same expectations could be held of women who have a similar work orientation is not known.

INTERVENTIONS

In this section, interventions which may be used to facilitate couple functioning by enabling individuals to better manage the work–family interface will be suggested. The term "intervention" rather than "therapy" is used, since a couple's capacity to manage the work–family interface is at least partially dependent on structural variables such as supportive organizational practices, childcare and economic constraints. Organizational practices and policies, such as job design, flexitime, participation in decision-making, culture and support services impact on employee stress (Barling, 1994; Hughes & Galinsky, 1994). Consequently, counsellors may wish to adopt the role of family advocate, or assist couples to identify strategies to improve and better use organizational and community resources, in addition to providing therapy to couples.

The counselling needs of couples in two-career marriages have been neglected, but with the increasing numbers of such marriages (Pendleton, Poloma & Garland, 1982), and complexity of problems and lifestyle (Sekaran, 1986), it is likely that increasing numbers of couples in two-career marriages will seek assistance in resolving issues. Counselling couples who experience this lifestyle needs recognition of the particular problems that this pattern may precipitate. Therefore in this section, counselling needs of such couples will serve as the framework for discussion of interventions. It should be noted that couples in dual-earner marriages are likely to experience similar factors related to dissatisfactions, although gender issues (assuming more traditional roles) may lead to different tensions and different coping styles (Falkenberg & Monachello, 1990). In the case of a couple in a single-earner marriage, the following frameworks would also be useful to guide interventions in the case where work–family conflict is apparent.

Sekaran (1986) and Falkenberg & Monachello (1990) suggest that a role dilemma framework is useful for exploring issues that couples need to address in the area of work–family conflict. For example, the extent to which couples have unrealistic estimates of the demands made by children may make it difficult to manage conflict between work and parent roles. Partners also may feel tension between how each would like to define their roles and their felt needs. In addition, role overload is a problem experienced by many women, and needs addressing in terms of exploring assumptions about what roles are appropriate, the standard to which they are performed, and stresses in the role system. For example, there may be different expectations by a woman and her partner as to the way that parenting roles should be performed, and what behaviours demonstrate commitment to family roles.

Sekaran (1986) suggests that there are five common role dilemmas which can lead to relationship dissatisfactions. The first dilemma is role overload, which often is linked to gender issues. A second dilemma is identity issues, which are also linked to gender-role expectations, but particularly need addressing when self concept and self identity are not clear. The third role dilemma is role cycling, in which demands occurring at particular points in the life-cycle elicit particular role conflicts. For example, many career-oriented women experience tension and distress in trying to meet family and work roles simultaneously when they have young children, and they often lower their career ambitions. These women may resent partners who have not also lowered their career ambitions, and this issue needs to be addressed. Scarcity of time may lead couples to minimize contact with friends and family, resulting in small social support networks (network dilemmas). Finally, couples experience stress due to adopting roles which are discrepant with traditional values (dilemmas caused by environmental sanctions). For example, men who take responsibilities for children may be negatively perceived by colleagues, and feel the need to "cover up" family-related activities (Hall, 1972). Women may be sensitive to suggestions of inadequate mothering and be particularly vulnerable if their self-esteem is low. They may also experience conflicting expectations from role senders.

There are a number of instruments which can assist in diagnosis and assessment of work–family conflict and the dilemmas associated with that conflict. Key measures are presented in Table 12.1 which enable identification of coping strategies, values, role salience, self image, career salience, marriage type and career type. These scales can serve as a useful basis on which to examine individual beliefs and attitudes, especially if both partners fill in the scales and the results are used to clarify areas of misperception. For example, Pendleton, Poloma & Garland's (1982) dual-career family scales designed for women allow identification of key issues in work–family conflict to be addressed by the couple. Based on these addressed needs, a number of interventions are useful which can address work–family conflict.

1. *Developing effective work and family coping strategies.* A crucial issue in resolving work–family conflict is that of developing effective coping strategies for both work and family roles. Researchers have identified a number of coping strategies (Gilbert & Holohan, 1982; Gray, 1983; Hall, 1972; Wiersma, 1994) which may be explored with the couple. Hall (1972) found two types of coping: (a) altering the expectations of role senders (e.g. renegotiating work roles with a boss to build in flexibility); (b) altering one's own role expectations and behaviour (e.g. changing one's perception of what a good parent is) are associated with greater satisfaction in women. On the other hand, attempting to fulfil all role demands is associated with lower satisfaction. Gilbert & Holohan (1982) found gender differences in the use of three coping strategies: (a) cognitive appraisal and understanding of the problem; (b) stress management strategies; and (c) action aimed at altering the source of stress. High effective copers rated strategies of perspective-taking and recognition of societal influence as more true of themselves, and rated strat-

Table 12.1 Scales for the measurement of work–family conflict

Authors	Scale	Subscales	Comments
Amatea et al. (1986)	Life Role Salience Scales (LRSS)	Eight scales (Five items each): 1. Occupation role reward value 2. Occupational role commitment 3. Parental role value 4. Parental role commitment 5. Marital role reward value 6. Marital role commitment 7. Home care role reward value 8. Home care role commitment	These scales are designed to measure work and family role expectations of both men and women. They would serve as a useful focus for identifying assumptions about roles, and the relative importance of roles. The instrument was developed on undergraduate students and on married couples currently balancing work and family roles, thus suggesting applicability to couples early in their relationship and careers, and couples with established roles. Statistical analysis supports the hypothesis that these eight scales represent independent dimensions
Frone, Russell & Cooper (1992)	Work–family conflict	Two Subscales (with two items each): 1. WIF (work interference with family) 2. FIW (family interference with work)	A short scale useful for research purposes
Holohan & Gilbert (1979)	Inter-role conflict	Items for two scales: 1. Job and parent role conflict 2. Job and spouse role conflict are reported in Frone & Rice (1987) Each scale contains four items.	Respondents are asked to indicate how much conflict would be generated by a number of situations of potential role conflict, e.g.: "1. Feeling it is more important for your spouse to succeed vs. feeling it is more important for you to succeed in your work". These scales would be useful to diagnose differences in perceptions of role conflict by the couple

Table 12.1 (continued)

Authors	Scale	Subscales	Comments
Karambya & Reilly (1992)	Work Restructuring	One scale: sever items	Assess how conflicts between work and family roles are resolved. Respondents are asked if they use specific activities to restructure (yes/no), and if yes, why? Would be useful to guide couples in examining how they manage role conflicts
Pendleton, Poloma & Garland (1980)	Dual Career Family Scales	Six subscales: 1. Marriage type (six items) 2. Domestic responsibility (three items) 3. Satisfaction (three items) 4. Self-image (four items) 5. Career salience (eight items) 6. Career line (seven items)	These scales were developed on dual-career wives, but could be adapted for use by couples. The Marriage Type subscale assesses the degree to which the couple is egalitarian. Domestic Responsibility assesses perceived responsibilities assumed by the woman. Satisfaction with the roles of wife, mother and career woman are assessed by the Satisfaction Scale. Self-image assesses how the woman perceives herself as a wife and mother, and Career Salience assesses the extent to which the career role is as important as family roles. Career Line measures a woman's perception of her potential career involvement. These scales would be useful to assist examination of the importance of various roles and how priorities are assigned
Pendleton, Poloma & Garland (1982)	Dual Career Family Scales	Six Subscales: 1. Family and career interface (six items) 2. Personal satisfaction with trend-setting (four items) 3. Career support of the traditional wife–mother role (six items)	An extension of previous work by Pendleton, Poloma & Garland (1980), these scales were developed on professional women in dual- career families. Each subscale ordered by Guttm ananalyses; can give the clinician guidance as to priority areas needing to be addressed. Examples of counselling strategies used in this ordering are provided

		4. Trend-breaking role of the career woman (four items) 5. Trend-maintenance of the domestic role (five items) 6. Compensatory factors (three items)	
Thomas & Ganster (1995)	Work Family Conflict Scale	24 Items; 16 items from a & scale developed by Bohen & Viveros-Long (1981); eight items from Kopelman, Greenhaus & Connelly (1983)	Specifically assesses perceived conflicts between work and family roles. Useful to explore specific pressure points (e.g. not finding enough time for self and children, and work schedule interference with family). Also assesses feelings (e.g. feeling ordered, rushed)
	Control Scale	14 Items	Measures perceptions of degree of control over work and family areas that have been shown in research to contribute to work–family conflict (e.g. the extent to which time off can be arranged, choice of working schedules and child care). Could be useful to facilitate discussion of options and strategies
Wiersma (1994)	Categories of Work–home Role Conflict	1. Domestic chores 2. Maintaining social relations 3. Role cycling 4. Competition 5. Social pressure 6. Job mobility	The items were developed on the basis of an analysis of critical incidents, and reflect behavioural strategies used to cope with work and home role demands. They provide a useful basis for exploring the coping strategies couples use, and would aid in goal-setting

egies of time out and depression as less true of themselves, than low effective copers. So counsellors could facilitate exploration of coping strategies used by the couple, in particular assessing effectiveness, other options and the extent to which each person's coping strategies mesh with his/her partner's.

2. *Changing attributions.* Couples in relationship distress are likely to make attributions regarding their partners' negative behaviour, and often fail to recognize the extent to which the environment is affecting behaviour (Noller, Beach & Osgarby, this volume 1966). For example one couple, Jenny and Brian, typify the issues confronted by a young couple with their first child and who make unhelpful attributions. Both partners had been highly career-oriented until the birth of their first child. At that time Jenny temporarily withdrew from her career. At the same time Brian's career became more demanding, and he now works long hours. Jenny is suffering fatigue and resenting Brian, who appears to her uninvolved with his family. Her requests for him to take more family responsibility are perceived by Brian as nagging and he feels she can't manage the baby. His response to work pressures, typical at the establishment stage of his career, are interpreted by her as lack of interest and support. Her difficulties, typical of a mother with a young child, are perceived by him as inadequacies, and he resents her demands when he is working to establish a sound financial base for the family.

Couples therapy needs to identify the situational dilemmas each faces, and this can help each partner to develop more benign attributions. In addition, the counsellor would need to recognize that Jenny has lost a valued work role, which can be reflected in feelings of inadequacy and low self-esteem. Couples should be helped to realize that feelings of inadequacy, guilt and frustration are a normal response to such role pressures. This couple would benefit from exploring their assumptions and expectations of work and family roles, and assisted to see how the attributions they are making exacerbate dissatisfaction and conflict.

Discussion should centre around role expectations in the couple, and role clarification and negotiation could be useful. Yogev (1981) suggested that a major factor in wives' marital adjustment is the extent to which the family can accommodate wives' employment. Having a supportive husband who is willing to make career sacrifices, and who shares similar values and beliefs about women's employment, is essential. Exploration of all options, of which one may be agreements about turntaking in having one's career a priority, is required.

3. *Planning for family demands.* Yogev (1981) notes that a good predictor of marital adjustment in professional women is childlessness; couples may need assistance to work through issues regarding size of family and spacing of children, develop a more realistic assessment of likely demands, and obtain practical assistance in identifying resources such as child care and care for sick children, which would enable better management of children's demands.

4. *Developing support networks.* The couple may need to develop strategies to expand support networks (friends, family and caretakers), and to deal with

feelings of guilt at not being able to meet all demands (for example, from elderly relatives).

5. *Managing stress and work demands.* If either partner is experiencing work-related stress, resulting in negative spillover from work to family, techniques of stress management may assist by increasing the capacity to cope with stress. Another strategy would be to teach time management techniques, such as goal setting and prioritizing, which could have more direct effects on the capacity to manage work demands. An exploration of work roles may identify problems such as unwillingness to delegate (characteristic of Type A managers), which inhibit effective solving of the problem of work overload. In the case of Jenny and Brian, Brian could be helped to review his work role with the aim of freeing up some time to spend with Jenny and his daughter.

6. *Resolving power issues.* In dual-career couples, unresolved issues of power are particularly problematic. As O'Neil, Fishman & Kinsella-Shaw (1987) argue, traditionally men have exercised overt power in families, and women may develop covert power bases that control the spouse role and family dynamics. In two-career families, blurring of career and family roles make decision-making and control of resources more difficult, as in the case of determining career priorities and expenditure. Men giving up power may feel resentful, and women gaining power may feel less feminine. Issues of power dynamics are particularly likely to come into play during career transitions that threaten established dynamics, e.g. in the case of a woman receiving a promotion when her male partner is frustrated by lack of advancement. Marriages in which wives earn more than husbands are particularly at risk. So an assessment of power dynamics, and an exploration of feelings about power in the relationship, is a useful aspect of counselling.

CONCLUSIONS

Research on work–family conflict has identified key issues relevant to assisting couples. Work can have a negative impact on couple functioning. Occupational stress can be transmitted from one partner to another, particularly men to women, and this can influence the mood of the couple and the psychological and physical health of both partners. Some couples may be more predisposed to marital dissatisfaction associated with work–family conflict due to personal attributes of one partner, such as Type A personality in men. Men and women experience the work–family interface differently, and women generally are more susceptible to stress and role overload. A gender role analysis suggests that issues of power in dual-career couples are likely to be problematic. Finally, organizational policies and practices, such as flexible working hours and participative decision-making, do reduce stress. The problems created by work–family conflict need addressing at individual, couple and organizational levels.

REFERENCES

Amatea, E.S., Cross, E.G., Clark, J.E. & Bobby, C.L. (1986). Assessing the work and family role expectations of career oriented men and women: the life role salience scales. *Journal of Marriage and the Family*, **48**, 831–838.

Barling, J. (1994). Work and family: in search of more effective workplace interventions. In C.L. Cooper & R.M. Rousseau (eds), *Trends in Organisational Behaviour*, Vol. 1 (pp. 63–73). Chichester: Wiley.

Barnett, R.C. & Marshall, N.L. (1992). Men's job and partner roles: spillover effects and psychological distress. *Sex Roles*, **27**, 455–472.

Bedian, A.G., Burke, R.J. & Moffat, R.G. (1988). Outcomes of work–family conflict among married male and female professionals. *Journal of Management*, **14**, 475–491

Bohen, H.H. & Viveros-Long, A. (1981). *Balancing Jobs and Family Life*. Philadelphia, PA: Temple University Press.

Burke, R.J. & Greenglass, E.R. (1987). Work and family. In C.L. Cooper and I.T. Robinson (eds), *International Review of Industrial and Organizational Psychology* (pp. 273–320). Chichester: Wiley.

Burke, R.J. & Weir, T. (1977). Why good managers make lousy fathers. *Canadian Business*, **50**, 51–54.

Burke, R.J., Weir, T. & Duwors, R.E. (1980). Work demands on administrators and spouse well-being. *Human Relations*, **33**, 253–278.

Dunne, E.A. & Mullins, P.M. (1989). Sex differences in psychological and psychophysiological arousal patterns: a study of working couples. *Work and Stress*, **3**, 261–268.

Duxbury, L.E. & Higgins, C.A. (1991). Gender differences in work–family conflict. *Journal of Applied Psychology*, **76**, 60–74.

Falkenberg, L. & Monachello, M. (1990). Dual-career and dual-income families: do they have different needs? *Journal of Business Ethics*, **9**, 339–351.

Frone, M.R. & Rice, R.W. (1987). Work–family conflict: the effect of job and family involvement. *Journal of Occupational Behaviour*, **8**, 45–53.

Frone, M.R., Russell, M. & Cooper, M.L. (1992). Antecedents and outcomes of work–family conflict: testing a model of the work–family interface. *Journal of Applied Psychology*, **77**, 65–78.

Gerhart, B. (1987). How important are dispositional factors as determinants of job satisfaction? Implications for job design and other personnel programs. *Journal of Applied Psychology*, **72**, 366–373.

Gilbert, L.A. & Holohan, C.K. (1982). Conflicts between student/professional, parental and self-development roles: a comparison of high and low effective copers. *Human Relations*, **35**, 635–648.

Gray, J.D. (1983). The married professional woman: an examination of her role conflicts and coping strategies. *Psychology of Women Quarterly*, **7**, 235–243.

Gore, S. (1978). The effect of social support in moderating the health consequences of unemployment. *Journal of Health and Social Behaviour*, **19**, 157–165.

Gutek, B.A., Searle, S. & Klepa, L. (1991). Rational versus gender role explanations for work–family conflict. *Journal of Applied Psychology*, **76**, 560–568.

Hall, D.T. (1972). A model of coping with role conflict: the role behavior of college educated women. *Administrative Science Quarterly*, **4**, 471–486.

Haynes, S.G., Eaker, E.D. & Feinleib, M. (1983). Spouse behaviour and coronary heart disease in men: prospective results from the Framingham heart study. *American Journal of Epidemiology*, **118**, 1–21.

Higgins, C.A. & Duxbury, L.E. (1992). Work–family conflict: a comparison of dual career men and traditional men. *Journal of Organizational Behavior*, **13**, 389–411.

Higgins, C.A., Duxbury, L.E. & Irving, R.H. (1992). Work–family conflict in the dual career family. *Organizational Behavior and Human Decision Processes*, **51**, 51–75.

Holohan, C.K. & Gilbert, L.A. (1979). Conflict between major life roles: women and men in dual career couples. *Human Relations*, **32**, 451–467.

Hollowell, P.G. (1968). *The Lorry Driver*. New York: Humanities Press.

Hughes, D. & Galinsky, E.G. (1994). Work experiences and marital interactions: elaborating the complexity of work. *Journal of Organizational Behavior*, **15**, 423–438.

Jackson, S.E. & Malasch, C. (1982). After-effects of job related stress: families as victims. *Journal of Occupational Behaviour*, **3**, 63–77.

Jones, F. & Fletcher, B.C. (1993). An empirical study of occupational stress transmission in working couples. *Human Relations*, **40**, 881–903.

Kabanoff, B. (1980). Work and non-work: a review of models, methods and findings. *Psychological Bulletin*, **88**, 60–77.

Kanter, R.M. (1977). *Work and Family in the United States: a Critical Review and Agenda for Research and Policy*. New York: Russell Sage.

Karambya, R. & Reilly, A.H. (1992). Dual earner couples: attitudes and actions in restructuring work for family. *Journal of Organizational Behavior*, **13**, 585–601.

Kirchmeyer, C. (1992). Non-work participation and work attitudes: a test of scarcity versus expansion models of personal resources. *Human Relations*, **45**, 775–795.

Kofodimos, J.R. (1990). Why executives lose their balance. *Organizational Dynamics*, **19**, 58–73.

Kong, F., Perrucci, C.G. & Perrucci, R. (1993). The impact of unemployment and economic stress on social support. *Community Mental Health Journal*, **29**, 205–221.

Kopelman, R.E., Greenhaus, J.H. & Connelly, T.F. (1983). A model of work, family and inter-role conflict: a construct validation study. *Organizational Behavior and Human Performance*, **32**, 198–215.

Lambert, S. (1990). Processes linking work and family: a critical review and research agenda. *Human Relations*, **43**, 239–257.

Liem, R. & Liem, J.H. (1988). Psychological effects of unemployment on workers and their families. *Journal of Social Issues*, **44**, 87–105.

Lobel, S.A. (1991). Allocation of investment in work and family roles: alternative theories and implications for research. *Academy of Management Review*, **16**, 507–521.

Munton, A.G. (1990). Job relocation, stress and the family. *Journal of Organizational Behavior*, **11**, 401–406.

Noller, P., Beach, S. & Osgarby, S. (1996). Cognitive and affective processes in marriage. In this volume.

O'Driscoll, M.P. (1996). The interface between job and off-job roles: enhancement and conflict. In C.L. Cooper & I.T. Robertson (eds), *International Review of Industrial and Organizational Psychology* (pp. 279–306). Chichester: Wiley.

O'Neil, J.M., Fishman, D.M. & Kinsella-Shaw, M. (1987). Dual-career couples' career transitions and normative dilemmas: a preliminary assessment model. *The Counseling Psychologist*, **15**, 50–96.

Parasuraman, S., Greenhaus, J.H. & Granrose, C.S. (1992). Role stressors, social support, and well-being among two career couples. *Journal of Organizational Behavior*, **13**, 339–356.

Parasuruman, S., Greenhaus, J., Rabinowitz, S., Bedeian, A.G. & Mossholder K.W. (1989). Work and family variables as mediators of the relationship between wives' employment and husband's well-being. *Academy of Management Journal*, **32**, 185–201.

Pendleton, B.F., Poloma, M.M. & Garland, T.N. (1980). Scales for the investigation of the dual-career family. *Journal of Marriage and the Family*, **May**, 269–276.

Pendleton, B.F., Poloma, M.M. & Garland, T.N. (1982). An approach to quantifying the needs of dual-career families. *Human Relations*, **35**, 69–82.

Pleck, J.H. (1977). The work–family role system. *Social Problems*, **24**, 417–428.

Pleck, J.H. (1985). *Working Wives/Working Husbands*. Beverly Hills, CA: Sage.

Rodin, J. & Ickovics, J.R. (1990). Women's health: review and research agenda as we approach the 21st century. *American Psychologist*, **45**, 1018–1034.

Schliebner, C.T. & Peregoy, J.J. (1994). Unemployment effects on the family and child: interventions for counsellors. *Journal of Counselling and Development*, **72**, 368–372.

Sekaran, U. (1986). *Dual Career Families*. San Francisco, CA: Jossey Bass.

Spector, P.E. & O'Connell, B.J. (1994). The contribution of personality traits, negative affectivity, locus of control and Type A to the subsequent reports of job stressors and job strains. *Journal of Occupational and Organizational Psychology*, **67**, 1–11.

Strickland, W.J. (1992). A typology of career wife roles. *Human Relations*, **45**, 797–811.

Thomas, L.T. & Ganster, D.C. (1995). Impact of family supportive work variables on work–family conflict and strain: a control perspective. *Journal of Applied Psychology*, **80**, 6–15.

Toterdell, P., Spelten, E., Smith, L., Barton, J. & Folkard, S. (1995). Recovery from work shifts: how long does it take? *Journal of Applied Psychology*, **80**, 43–57.

Vormbrock, J.K. (1993). Attachment theory as applied to wartime and job-related separation. *Psychological Bulletin*, **114**, 122–144.

Wharton, A.S. & Erikson, R.J. (1993). Managing emotions on the job and at home: understanding the consequences of multiple emotional roles. *Academy of Management Review*, **18**, 457–486.

Wiersma, U.J. (1994). A taxonomy of behavioural strategies for coping with work–home role conflict. *Human Relations*, **47**, 211–276.

Weisman, C.S. & Teitlebaum, M.A. (1987). The work–family role system and physician productivity. *Journal of Health and Social Behavior*, **28**, 247–257.

Wolcott, I. & Glezer, H. (1995). *Work and Family Life: Achieving the Integration*. Melbourne, Australia: Australian Institute of Family Studies.

Yogev, S. (1981). Do professional women have egalitarian marital relationships? *Journal of Marriage and the Family*, **November**, 865–871.

Chapter 13

Individual Psychopathology and Marital Distress

W. Kim Halford and Ruth Bouma
*School of Applied Psychology, Griffith University,
Nathan, Queensland, Australia*

Tricia presented to one of us (WKH) very distressed about her marriage to Lee, and her financial position. She reported that her husband had been on a week-long gambling binge in which he had lost about $700. Both Lee and Tricia were on illness benefits, Tricia because of ongoing problems with cancer of the bone in her arm which prevented her from working, and Lee because of bipolar disorder. The gambling loss was considerable to them, particularly as both were in their late 50s and were planning for retirement. Tricia and Lee had been married for 10 years. Lee has a 15-year history of bipolar disorder. When taking his medication and controlling his drinking Tricia described Lee as a gentle, caring and fun companion. When he was drinking and not on medication she said he was impulsive, irritable and unreliable. She felt desperate about his latest gambling binge, and believed his psychological disorder needed better management if they were to have any chance in their marriage. When Lee was seen he described his drinking and refusal to take medication as resulting from his feeling stressed by the demands from Tricia to get a job; he felt he could not manage working as this often made him have a psychotic relapse. Lee felt they had a long-standing relationship problem in poor communication and conflict management. How should we begin to understand the problem of Lee and Tricia?

Given that marriage is the most intimate relationship for most adults, it is not surprising that significant individual psychological disorders both influence, and are influenced by, the marital relationship. Despite the obviousness of this statement it is striking how many marital therapists ignore individual problems when analysing a couple's relationship. Conversely, those who predominantly treat individual problems often overlook the importance of the relationship context

Clinical Handbook of Marriage and Couples Interventions. Edited by W. Kim Halford and Howard J. Markman.
© 1997 John Wiley & Sons Ltd.

within which psychological disorder exists. In the first half of this chapter we analyse the association of marital and individual problems, and review the evidence on effects of interventions with couples in which one partner has significant psychological disorder. The second half of the chapter is focused upon the implications of the evidence for the assessment and treatment of coexisting individual and couples problems.

ASSOCIATION OF INDIVIDUAL PSYCHOPATHOLOGY AND RELATIONSHIP PROBLEMS

There is a well established association between marital status and individual psychopathology. In community samples married men and women are less likely to have a diagnosable psychiatric disorder than those who are separated or divorced (Bebbington, 1987a; Romans-Clarkson et al., 1988; Stansfield et al., 1991). Married people also have a lower rate of presentation to outpatient mental health services (Bachrach, 1975) and are less likely to be admitted to a psychiatric hospital (Bebbington, 1987b; Milazzo-Sayre, 1977). Epidemiological data such as these establish that the presence of marital problems severe enough to lead to divorce are correlated with the occurrence of psychiatric disorder, although this does not establish that any causal relationship exists.

It is inaccurate to conclude that simply being married conveys protection against psychological disorder. Couples in which there is ongoing marital difficulty have high rates of psychological disorder, particularly depression in wives (Beach, Arias & O'Leary, 1986; Beach & O'Leary, 1986; Waring et al., 1986) and alcohol abuse in husbands (Halford & Osgarby, 1993). Marital problems also are correlated with maladjustment in the couple's children, who evidence high rates of behaviour problems (Emery, Joyce & Fincham, 1987; Hetherington, Cox & Cox, 1985). On the other hand, being in a marriage rated as high in intimacy and satisfaction is associated with low risk for psychiatric disorder (Waring et al., 1986; Weiss & Aved, 1978; Weissman, 1987) and increased resistance to the negative effects of major stressors such as unemployment (Gore, 1978) or having a chronic illness (Goodenow, Reisine & Grady, 1990; Smith & Wallston, 1992).

There have been some suggestions that while marriage is associated with better mental health in men, this may not be true for women. Some authors even suggest that marriage may be harmful to the mental health of women (e.g. Hafner, 1986; Weissman & Klerman, 1987). Such generalizations are inaccurate and do not take into account of the quality of the marriage. Women in relationships within which they feel able to confide in their partner have much lower risk of psychiatric disorder than women without such a relationship (Brown & Harris, 1978). The consistent finding is that both men and women in satisfying marriages are at lower risk for psychiatric disorder than other segments of the population.

The association between marital distress and psychiatric disorder is not due just to marital problems causing psychological disorder. Individuals suffering from severe psychiatric disorder are less likely to develop a satisfying marriage. For example, patients diagnosed with schizophrenia or severe personality disorders are much less likely than the rest of the population to get married, and are much more likely to get divorced if they do marry (Mulder, 1991; Reich & Thompson, 1985). Neither is the association between marital problems and psychiatric disorder simply psychiatric disorder causing marital problems. For example, in cases of coexisting marital problems and depression the marital problems often antedate the onset of depression, even in individuals alleged to have endogenous depression (Birchnall & Kennard, 1983). Thus, a simple unidirectional model of causality is inadequate; marital distress and psychological disorder reciprocally influence each other. To further analyse the association of psychopathology and marital functioning, we now turn to the relationship of specific disorders to specific interactional processes between the couple.

Depression

A distressed couple relationships is a very strong predictor of the risk of developing depression, particularly for women. The relative risk for developing depression in unhappily married women is approximately 25 times that for happily married women (Weissman, 1987). However, the importance of marital distress as a risk factor for developing a disorder varies greatly across depressive disorders. Marital problems are strongly associated with risk for dysphemia, adjustment disorder with depressed mood, and episodes of non-psychotic major depression (Bachrach, 1975; Bebbington, 1987b; Department of Health and Social Security, 1985), but there is only a weak, though still statistically significant, association between psychotic depression and marital problems (Bebbington, 1987b).

A prolonged increase in marital arguments is the most frequent life event reported as preceding the onset of depression in married women (Paykel et al., 1969). Even when treatment produces an improvement in depressed mood there is limited effect on marital distress (Dobson, 1987; Klerman & Weissman, 1982; O'Leary & Beach, 1990), and the ongoing marital problems are associated with poor prognosis for the depression (Rousanville et al., 1979). Thus, marital distress impacts upon depression in a very important manner.

There are specific characteristics of the relationship of couples in which one partner is depressed. Depression most often is coexistent with marital discord in relationships characterized by emotional distance, and an uneven distribution of power between the partners (Hautzinger, Linden & Hoffman, 1982). In particular, women who have little power in the relationship are at high risk for developing depression. Brown & Harris (1978) reported that low levels of self-disclosure in the marital relationship are associated with increased risk of depression. Smolen, Spiegal & Martin (1986) assessed individuals' reports of the frequency of their partners' infringements of their personal rights and their ability to respond assertively to those infringements. High rates of infringement by the partner, when combined with low personal assertion, were associated with low marital satisfaction and depression in both male and female partners.

Most of the above data is based on self-report of marital interaction. Kowalik & Gotlib (1987) found that, relative to observers, depressed patients had a negative bias in the perceptions of their spouses' communications. Thus, self-report of marital interaction may be biased by depressed persons' negative cognitive set. Direct behavioural observation of the marital interaction of depressed persons circumvents some of the methodological difficulties associated with self-report assessments. Observational studies of marital interaction show that depressed people express dysphoric mood, self-derogation and negative well-being at higher rates than do non-depressed, maritally distressed individuals (Biglan et al., 1985; Hops et al., 1987; Hautzinger, Linden & Hoffman, 1982). Furthermore, the depressed partners show low rates of positive affect expression, and high rates of aggression, toward their spouses (Biglan et al., 1985; Hops et al., 1987). These findings highlight that depressed persons express their depression strongly within the relationship.

Depressive behaviours often serve to terminate aggression and elicit assistance from spouses (Biglan et al., 1985; Hops et al., 1987; Hautzinger, Linden & Hoffman, 1982; Schmaling & Jacobson, 1990). The finding about depression offsetting aggression is consistent with earlier research that depression often functions to offset negative responses from other people (Coyne, 1976). This is not to say that the depressed person deliberately expresses depression to terminate aggression. Rather, it seems that in the context of a lack of relationship power and unassertiveness, expressions of dysphoria may be the only response which offsets the spouse's aggression and criticism. In this manner depressive mood inadvertently may be maintained by the negative reinforcement of the offset of a partner's aggression, and possible positive reinforcement of sympathy and support.

The development of depression in the context of marital discord seems to be associated with gender roles. Radloff & Rae (1979) suggested that the high rate of depression in women can be related to the learned helplessness model of Seligman (1975). Women in Western culture have been suggested to have less control over their lives than men do, which has been alleged to increase the risk of feeling helpless and becoming depressed. Where the female partner is unassertive, the male partner is markedly aggressive, or where both these conditions exist, the marital difficulty could elicit a sense of helplessness in the female partner. Depression may develop in response to this learned helplessness, and could be maintained as a response which provides temporary respite from the control of the male partner.

It is interesting to note that males who are physically aggressive towards their partners seem to show similar characteristics to women who become depressed. The most outstanding similarities are that men who are physically aggressive often lack social skills to express their points of view assertively (Holzworth-Munroe, 1992), and also are less powerful in the relationship than their female partners (Babcock et al., 1993). Women who are depressed also are low in assertion and power (Hautzinger, Linden & Hoffman, 1982). It may be that gender roles, and differences in physical strength, mediate the different responses by men and women to a sense of powerlessness in their relationship: women more often become depressed whereas men tend to become aggressive.

In essence, the above research suggests that distressed marital interaction can interact with the characteristics of individual partners to inadvertently maintain depression. Characteristics of individuals which predispose them to develop depression can interact with the characteristics of their spouses and the couples' interactional styles to maintain depression. An important clinical implication of these findings is that, when a couple present with marital problems, depression should be assessed in the individual partners. Conversely, when the presenting concern of a married person is depression, then assessment of the marital relationship is needed.

Alcohol Abuse

There is a strong association between alcohol abuse and marital problems. While alcoholics are just as likely as the rest of the population to have been married (Steinglass, 1976), the separation and divorce rates are significantly higher (Nace, 1982). In fact for both male and female problem drinkers the divorce rates are higher than for any other psychological disorder. There is also a high incidence of alcohol abuse found in intact relationships of couples presenting with marital problems. For example, Halford & Osgarby (1993) found approximately one-third of their sample of couples presenting with marital problems reported alcohol abuse in the male partners, and over three-quarters of couples reported frequent disagreement about alcohol consumption.

Many of the problems reported by couples in which a partner is a problem drinker ("problem drinking couples") are similar to the problems reported by couples presenting with marital distress but without alcohol problems. Low relationship satisfaction (Zweben, 1986), frequent and intense arguments and poor sexual functioning (Blankfield & Maritz, 1990) have been reported by men presenting for alcoholism treatment and their partners. Observational studies of marital discussions of problem drinking couples have identified marked deficits in problem-solving and communication skills. More specifically, problem drinking couples are characterized by high rates of negative affect expression verbally and non-verbally, few supportive and constructive responses, and male withdrawal during conflictual discussions (Jacob & Leonard, 1992; Jacob et al., 1981). All of these characteristics are similar to the characteristics of couples presenting with marital distress (Weiss & Heyman, 1990).

Whilst the problems experienced by problem drinking couples resemble those of maritally distressed couples, research has identified some more specific alcohol-related characteristics of problem drinking couples in which it is the male who is the problem drinker. Whilst both partners in these couples report marital distress, the wives report significantly lower levels of marital satisfaction than their problem drinking husbands (O'Farrell & Birchler, 1987). This is in contrast to the low, but approximately equal, levels of marital distress reported by husbands and wives presenting for couples therapy. Much of the distress of wives of heavy-drinking men is accounted for by specific alcohol-related problems; the level of marital distress correlates with the extent that drinking interferes with the families everyday functioning (e.g. neglecting responsibilities, failing to participate in family activities, aggression; Zweben, 1986). Ongoing marital conflict also is associated with the development of depression and other adjustment problems in the non-drinking spouse (Billings & Moos, 1983). Furthermore, while spouse abuse is frequent in distressed relationships (Cascardi, Langhinrichsen & Vivian, 1992), the risk of physical violence has been consistently found to be greater where alcohol abuse is present in one or both partners (Halford & Osgarby, 1993; Kelly, Halford & Young, 1996).

There is much speculation in the literature as to whether the problems experienced in problem drinking (PD) relationships are the cause or the consequences of alcohol abuse (e.g. Steinglass, 1980; Wiseman, 1981; Frankenstein, Hay & Nathan, 1985). While the aetiological connections remain unclear, once both problem drinking and marital distress coexist, the two problems reciprocally influence each other (Kelly, Halford & Young, 1996). On the one hand, alcohol abuse contributes to marital discord through the many stresses it creates, including financial problems, job problems, embarrassing incidents, verbal and physical abuse, poor parenting and poor sexual functioning. Such stressors, along with repeated broken promises to change, lead to high levels of anger and mistrust by the non-drinking spouse and fewer positive activities shared with the problem drinker (O'Farrell & Bayog, 1986). On the other hand, the couple's relationship often contributes to the maintenance of problem drinking. For example, the drinking frequently becomes the focus of the couple's interactions. The non-drinking spouse attempts to reduce the partner's drinking through episodic use of aversive means such as criticizing, nagging and threatening (Thomas & Ager, 1993), while positive non-drinking behaviour goes virtually unnoticed. Such aversive techniques are largely ineffective, produce negative reactions in the problem drinker (most likely further alcohol abuse) and can perpetuate existing patterns of marital conflict (Thomas & Ager, 1993; O'Farrell, 1986). Overall, marital problems stimulate excessive drinking (Davis et al., 1974), precipitate relapse by abstinent alcoholics (Maisto et al., 1988) and are predictive of poor prognosis in alcohol treatment programmes (Billings & Moos, 1983; Vannicelli, Gingerich & Ryback, 1983). Clearly, the link between alcohol problems and relationship adjustment is a complex one. Given the frequent co-occurrence of alcohol and marital problems, it is desirable routinely to assess both alcohol and marital problems when either is the presenting problem.

Anxiety Disorders

Thus far we have concluded that there is a strong association between marital problems and depression, and between marital problems and alcohol problems. There also is an association between anxiety disorders and marital problems, but the association is complex and is moderated by the gender of the person with the disorder, the type of anxiety disorder, and whether the partner also has an anxiety disorder.

Most studies of the relationship between marital distress and anxiety disorders have been conducted on the marriages of women with phobias, agoraphobia or panic disorder. This may be attributable to the considerable speculation, largely from a systemic family perspective, that women's anxiety disorders often maintain the stability of a relationship with a dysfunctional male (e.g. Fry, 1962; Hafner, 1986). Available empirical evidence largely refutes the validity of this systemic hypothesis. Based on this systemic notion, one would predict that reductions in the allegedly relationship-maintaining anxiety symptoms would increase marital difficulties and dysfunctional behaviour by the male partner. However, resolution of women's anxiety problems tends to increase marital satisfaction and male partners' functioning (Lange & van Dyck, 1992; Cobb et al., 1984; Emmelkamp et al., 1992). These results suggest that, rather than enhancing dysfunctional relationships, anxiety disorders actually are associated with poorer relationship functioning.

Consistent with the interpretation that anxiety disorders are associated with marital distress, there are well replicated associations of agoraphobia, panic disorder, and obsessive-compulsive disorder with low marital satisfaction in clinical populations (Goldstein & Chambless, 1978; Emmelkamp, De Haan & Hoogduin, 1990; Hafner, 1986; Hoogduin et al., 1989; Lange & van Dyck, 1992; Kleiner & Marshall, 1987). However, these results are based almost exclusively on the self-reports of female patients in therapy. There are no studies involving partner's report of the marriage, or direct observation of marital interactions of anxious persons, and few studies of the marriages of anxious men. Furthermore, since all of these studies were conducted with those seeking therapy, the associations may be an artefact of the pathways to therapy. For example, suppose higher proportions of women with panic disorder and marital problems seek therapy than women with panic disorder but no marital problems (possibly because they lack support to cope with their panic disorder). This would lead to artefactual association of anxiety and marital problems in the assessed clinical population.

There are a few epidemiological studies of representative community samples which overcome the possible sampling bias effects of studies of clinical populations. One such study (McLeod, 1994) compared perceived marital quality among couples in which either one, both or neither spouse met criteria for one of three anxiety disorders. Relationships were found between anxiety disorders and marital functioning; however, the association varied according to the gender of the sufferer and whether the perceptions of the sufferer or the partner were assessed. Phobias in men were associated with low marital quality being reported by both the men and their wives, but the presence of phobias in women was not associated with the level of marital quality reported by the women or their husbands. Panic disorder in either men or women was associated with low marital quality reported by both the sufferer and his or her spouse. Women suffering from general anxiety disorder reported poor marital functioning, but their male partners did not. General anxiety disorder in men was not associated with poor marital functioning being reported by either spouse. Overall these results provide further evidence of an association of marital problems and anxiety, but also highlight the complexity of this relationship.

One possible explanation for the complexity of the anxiety–marital distress relationship is the impact of comorbid problems on marital quality in anxious patients. Depressive disorders and substance abuse are common in anxious patients (Weissman, 1990), and their link to poor marital functioning has been described earlier. Lange & van Dyck (1992) found significant correlations between marital distress and comorbid symptoms in agoraphobic women, such as depression, somatization, suspicion and feelings of insufficiency. In this sample correlations between specific agoraphobic symptoms, such as agoraphobic avoidance, and marital stress were low (Lange & van Dyck, 1992). However, it is unlikely that all the association between marital distress and anxiety is due to covariation with comorbid problems. Research with both clinical and community samples demonstrates an association between marital functioning and anxiety disorders even when controlling for the effects of comorbidity (McLeod, 1994).

The causal connections between anxiety disorders and marital problems are far from certain. There is some evidence that marital distress increases the risk of development of anxiety in vulnerable people. Ongoing marital conflict frequently precedes the onset of agoraphobic symptoms (Kleiner & Marshall, 1987; Lange & van Dyck, 1992) and general anxiety disorder (McLeod, 1994). Once established, anxiety symptoms may be exacerbated by marital distress. The onset of additional anxiety symptoms is more strongly predicted by self-reported marital quality than by existing anxiety disorders in people with general anxiety disorder (McLeod, 1994). The mechanisms by which marital interaction may exacerbate anxiety are unclear. It has been shown that the parents of anxious children often inadvertently prompt and reinforce anxious cognitions and behaviour in their offspring (Barrett et al., in press). Hafner (1986) speculated that a spouse's expressed negative beliefs about his/her anxious partner's ability to perform certain tasks might both undermine marital satisfaction and maintain anxiety symptoms, but this hypothesis has not been tested.

The limitations in functioning of someone with an anxiety disorder may lead to marital distress. Families of patients with general anxiety disorder and obsessive-compulsive disorder frequently report that anxiety disrupts family interactions and routines, restricts leisure, impacts negatively upon family finances and disrupts the marital relationship (Chakrabarti, Kulhara & Verma, 1993). The burden imposed upon spouses of anxiety sufferers is reported to be of at least similar magnitude to other severe limiting disorders such as depression (Chakrabarti, Kulhara & Verma, 1993).

The interaction of anxiety disorders and marital distress needs considerably more research. However, even at this point in our knowledge, it is possible to draw some conclusions on the clinical implications of the current evidence. The co-existence of marital dysfunction with anxiety disorders is common enough to warrant assessment of both problems when either is the presenting concern. Furthermore, given the high rate of covariation of anxiety with depression and alcohol problems, individuals presenting with anxiety disorders should be assessed for alcohol abuse and depression.

Psychoses

Partners living with someone with a psychotic disorder face numerous difficulties which can include coping with severely disturbed behaviour during periods of acute psychotic disturbance, disrupted household routines (e.g. as the result of night-time waking, irregular eating and self-care), awkward interpersonal behaviour, social withdrawal, and emotional unresponsiveness (Hatfield, 1987; Hooley et al., 1987). Given these problems, it is unsurprising that people with psychoses are less likely to get married than the rest of the population (Reich & Thompson, 1985), and that when they do marry their relationships are characterized by low relationship satisfaction (Hooley et al., 1987), and a high rate of separation and divorce (Reich & Thompson, 1985).

The marriages of people with psychoses have not been studied extensively, but the interactions between sufferers and their family of origin have been a major focus of research activity. We will review this latter field briefly and point to the implications for understanding the marriages of people with psychoses. A long-standing hypothesis states that family interaction is associated with the onset and course of psychotic disorders (Goldstein, 1988; Halford, 1994). Initially, some postulated that dysfunctional family processes could cause disorders such as schizophrenia (e.g. Bateson et al., 1956; Fromm-Reichmann, 1948). Hirsch & Leff (1975) reviewed a large volume of research evidence and concluded that deviant family interaction was neither necessary nor sufficient to cause psychotic disorders. More recent research suggests that a combination of genetic vulnerability to develop psychotic disorders, plus disturbed family interaction, are associated with high risk for developing severe psychiatric disorder (Goldstein, 1985; Tienari et al., 1987). However, the causal links between the onset of such disorders, genetic vulnerability and family interaction remain unclear.

A second hypothesis states that differences between families' responses to emerging psychotic symptoms mediate the course of psychotic disorders (Leff & Vaughn, 1985). Over the last 30 years research testing this hypothesis has been dominated by the construct of high Expressed Emotion (EE). High EE is a composite measure of family psychological environment focusing on criticism, hostility and emotional over-involvement, which is assessed via a semi-structured interview with a relative living with someone with severe psychiatric disorder (Leff & Vaughn, 1985). Reviews of the literature show that high EE is a well replicated predictor of relapse in schizophrenia (Halford, 1994; Kavanagh, 1992), and there is some evidence that high EE also predicts relapse in affective psychoses (Miklowitz et al., 1988). High EE predicts the course of disorders equally well when someone is living with a spouse as when the sufferer is living with their family of origin (Halford, 1991; Hooley, Orley & Teasdale, 1986).

Originally, high EE was conceptualized as a stable characteristic of families that caused poor outcome in patients vulnerable to psychotic disorders (e.g. Leff & Vaughn, 1985). More recent research shows that EE varies over time in response to a variety of factors, including the severity of psychiatric symptoms in the nominated patient (Stirling et al., 1993). There is a complex interaction over time between family interactional processes, the development of individual psychopathology, the broader cultural and social environment of the family, available mental health services, and the vulnerabilities of the person with the disorder (Birchwood et al., 1992; Falloon & Fadden, 1993; Halford, 1994, 1995; Neuchterlein, Snyder & Mintz, 1992).

There have been a number of recurrent criticisms of the EE construct, particularly that the construct is atheoretical and not linked to broader models of marital and family functioning, that the focus is on negative aspects of family interactional processes such as criticism, and that the EE construct ignores positive processes such as empathy and support (e.g. Halford, 1991; Koensberg & Handley, 1986; Lange, Schaap & Van Widenfelt, 1993). Furthermore, in the assessment of EE there is exclusive reliance upon inference of interactional processes from individual interviews, which may not elucidate critical interactional processes as well as direct observation (Halford, 1991).

Several studies in the last 10 years have utilized the observational procedures described by Weiss & Heyman (1990) to assess the family interaction of people with psychoses. High EE classified on the basis of interview was found to be associated with relatives making high rates of criticism and intrusiveness in face-to-face interactions with the person suffering from schizophrenia (Doane et al., 1981), and with patients also making high rates of criticisms and low rates of autonomous statements during those same interactions (Strachan et al., 1989). High EE also is associated with high rates of patient expression of subclinical psychopathology, and relatives being critical of those psychiatric symptoms (Rosenfarb et al., 1995). The finding that both patient and relative behaviours differed across EE status underscores that EE reflects family interaction processes, rather than characteristics of the relatives. Further supporting this viewpoint, Hahlweg et al. (1989) found that high EE family interactions were characterized by coercive escalation cycles during problem-solving interactions.

The observational studies reviewed above showed EE covaried with observable family interactional processes, but did not directly link these observed processes to patient outcome. Halford et al. (1996) used observed family interaction as a predictor of patient outcome in patients having their first hospital admission for a psychotic disorder. They found positive, supportive family inter-action processes between the patient and relative prospectively predicted better patient outcome across a variety of outcome indices, including low rates of relapse, fewer psychiatric symptoms and better patient quality of life, at follow-up. This prediction was independent of the patient's premorbid functioning, severity of psychopathology at hospital admission or psychiatric diagnosis. Fur-thermore, this prediction held whether the person was living with his/her spouse or with parent(s). Combined with other available data (e.g. Falloon & Fadden, 1993), these findings suggest that living within a supportive family environment, be that with a spouse or parent(s), offers significant advantage to the sufferer of a psychotic disorder.

COUPLE INTERVENTIONS

The use of couple interventions can form either the entire treatment or an element of treatment of individual psychopathology. In this section we will review the application of couples interventions with couples in which at least one partner is depressed, abuses alcohol, is anxious or has a psychotic disorder. Later chapters in the book provide detailed treatment outlines for the conjoint treat-ment of the most common of these coexisting problems: marital distress and depression (Hops, Perry & Davis, this volume), and alcohol and marital problems (O'Farrell & Rotunda, this volume).

Depression

As noted previously, people with co-existing marital problems and depression often do not respond well to traditional individual therapies for depression. Beach & O'Leary (1986) and Jacobson et al. (1991) both showed that Behav-ioural Marital Therapy (BMT) was highly effective in reducing both marital distress and depression where wives were depressed and the couples were mari-tally distressed. Individual cognitive therapy also was somewhat effective with these clients, but not as effective as BMT (Beach & O'Leary, 1986; Jacobson et al., 1991). Of particular interest was Jacobson's finding that, whilst both BMT and cognitive therapy were helpful, adding cognitive therapy to BMT did not enhance outcome. In Jacobson's study the treatment conditions were matched for total hours of therapy contact. As a consequence the combined condition received less BMT than the BMT alone condition, and this may explain why the combined treatment condition did not do as well.

The Jacobson et al. (1991) study highlights that couples therapy should not be used for all presentations for depression by married clients. For depressed clients where there was no marital distress, individual cognitive therapy was superior to BMT in its effect on depression. Even when marital problems and depression coexist there is a need to make careful judgements as to when couples therapy is most helpful. In couples where the individual depression is severe, the marital problems postdated the onset of depression, and neither partner attributes the cause of the depression to the marital problems, then marital therapy seems less effective than individual therapy (Jacobson et al., 1991). On the other hand, where the marital problems antedate the depression, the marital problems are severe, and the source of the depression is attributed by at least one of the partners to the marital problems, then marital therapy seems to be the treatment of choice (Jacobson et al., 1991). Thus, the decision to use a couples-based approach must be based upon a careful analysis of the interrelationship of the key problems.

There are at least two major limitations in the research on depression and marriage. First, depression in men has been largely ignored. Whilst depression is less common for men than women, it still is a major mental health problem in men (Robins et al., 1984). Depressed men show some differences to depressed women in their interactions with their spouses, with the men showing higher rates of irritability and anger (Perry, 1993). A second limitation is the failure to consider relationships in which both partners are depressed. There is a higher incidence of concordance in depression of marital partners (i.e. both partners are depressed) than would be expected by a chance distribution of depression (McLeod, 1994). These relationships with two depressed partners are character-ized by extremely low levels of relationship satisfaction (McLeod, 1994), but there are no studies of the interactions of couples in which both partners are depressed to clarify the interactional processes that may be associated with depression in both partners.

In summary, depression needs to be assessed routinely in both partners when marital problems are presented. Couples therapy appears to be the treatment of choice for coexisting depression in women and marital problems when the mari-tal problems antedate the depression, and when the partners see the salience of a couples intervention. The association of marital problems and men's depression needs further research.

Alcohol Abuse

There is a large body of literature attesting to the value of various forms of couples therapy in treatment of alcohol problems. The best established approach is the use of BMT to complement individual therapy in the treatment of alcohol abuse. In the case of people with heavy dependence on alcohol, there has been successful use of conjoint contracting to promote use of Antabuse (an oral drug which induces severe illness if alcohol is consumed) to establish sobriety (O'Farrell & Bayog, 1986). Once sobriety is established, conjoint BMT promotes both improvements in marital satisfaction and enhanced maintenance of drinking control (Bowers & Alredha, 1990; O'Farrell et al., 1992; O'Farrell, Cutter & Floyd, 1985). When BMT is combined with relapse prevention training there is even better maintenance of drinking control (O'Farrell et al., 1992). Further-more, there also is a substantial reduction in the prevalence of marital violence after BMT, at least in those couples with mild to moderate severity of violence (O'Farrell & Murphy, 1995).

A significant limitation of the possible impact of couples treatments for problem drinking is the frequent reluctance of the alcoholic to accept couples treatment (O'Farrell et al., 1986). This may be associated with the more general reluctance of many people who abuse alcohol to accept treatment. Wives of male problem drinkers often present to treatment agencies reporting that their partners refuse to seek treatment (Halford & Osgarby, 1993). The frequent unwillingness of the person abusing alcohol to accept help, with consequent strains on the relationship and individual distress, have prompted the development of therapies to assist the spouses of heavy drinkers. For example, Thomas & Ager (1993) and Sisson & Azrin (1986) both developed therapies aiming to help clients reduce the negative impacts of their partners' drinking. Both these programs were aimed at teaching women to manage stress associated with their husbands' drinking, and to encourage the men to seek individual therapy (Sisson & Azrin, 1986; Thomas & Ager, 1993). These programs do assist the women to reduce their individual distress, and there is some evidence that these approaches can increase the chance of the male drinker presenting for individual treatment (Halford et al., 1996; Sisson & Azrin, 1986; Thomas & Ager, 1993).

Some programs for the wives of male problem drinkers also were aimed at helping the women to influence the men to reduce drinking. For example, Sisson & Azrin (1986) described helping women identify high-risk settings for problem drinking, and suggesting that wives schedule activities incompatible with drinking for high risk times. Partners also have been encouraged to praise sobriety, and not to inadvertently reduce the negative consequences of drinking (e.g. by refusing to ring your partner's supervisor to say your partner is sick when he really has a hangover). Similar strategies were used by Halford et al. (1996). The only systematic evaluation of this approach was in the Halford study, which found that these strategies had little impact upon the drinker's alcohol consumption. It seemed that the spouse's behaviour had only limited effect on the drinking, or at least that women changing these behaviours had little effect in the absence of a commitment to change by the male drinkers.

Overall, individual work with the spouses of problem drinkers can be helpful for the presenting spouse, but seems to have little impact upon the problem drinking itself. When the drinker is involved, conjoint treatments are effective in establishing and helping maintain control over drinking. However, there are a number of limitations to existing knowledge. There is limited research into the effectiveness of a couples-based approach with female problem drinkers, with couples in which both partners are problem drinkers, and with relationships with histories of severe physical aggression.

Psychoses

Effective management of functional psychoses involves the integration of pharmacotherapy and psychological intervention (Halford, 1994). There is no evidence that couples therapy alone can modify the course of functional psychoses. However, interventions which produce change in the interactional processes within families can cause a dramatic improvement in the patient's well-being and the relative's sense of coping (Barraclough & Tarrier, 1992; Glick, 1992; Falloon & Coverdale, 1995). Whilst most of this data is based upon intervention with patients living with parents, there are striking parallels in the assessed difficulties of parents living with an adult offspring, and with someone living with a spouse, suffering from a psychotic disorder (Halford, 1991). Furthermore, the interventions seem just as effective with people living with spouses, as those living with parents (Glick, 1992).

The impetus for the development of family interventions (FI) was the EE research (Leff & Vaughn, 1985) which was reviewed earlier in the chapter. FI originally was intended to modify the family environment, conceptualized within the EE literature as a cause of patient relapse, and thereby improve patient outcome. The duration and content of FI programs vary widely and include different combinations of patient and relative education about the nature of psychiatric disorder and its management, support and discussion opportunities for the family, problem-solving and communication skills training, and cognitive restructuring of unhelpful beliefs and attributions family members hold about each other's behavior (Barraclough & Tarrier, 1992; Falloon & Coverdale, 1995; Halford & Hayes, 1991).

Controlled trials consistently show that FI reduces patient psychotic relapse (Falloon & Coverdale, 1995; Halford & Hayes, 1991), improves patient functioning between psychotic episodes (Falloon et al., 1985; Goldstein et al., 1978), decreases negativity of family communication (Doane et al., 1985) and decreases relative's sense of burden in caring for the person with a psychotic disorder (Falloon & Pederson, 1985). The diversity and complexity of FIs have made it difficult to establish the crucial components of FI (Halford & Hayes, 1991). The extent of decreases in observed family communication negativity is associated with the extent of reductions in relative burden (Falloon & Pederson, 1985) and extent of improvement in patient functioning (Doane et al., 1985). Furthermore FI which includes communication skills and problem-solving training is more effective than FI which does not include this component (Zastowny, Lehman, Cole & Kane, 1992). These data are consistent with the view that changes in family communication and interaction are the sources of improved outcome.

Given that the efficacy of FI is well replicated, the widespread adoption of FI for work with couples in which one spouse has a psychotic disorder is desirable. Several recently published papers highlight the challenge this dissemination provides to service providers (Brooker et al., 1993; Kavanagh et al., 1993; McFarlane et al., 1993). Even when provided with intensive in-service training, most mental health professionals fail to implement FI frequently or effectively (Kavanagh et al., 1993; McFarlane et al., 1993). It is only with intensive training followed by ongoing individual supervision of therapists that effective use of FI occurs (Brooker et al., 1993). We suspect that the combination of knowledge and skills in couples therapy, and knowledge and skills in management of psychotic disorders, is rare amongst mental health professionals. We hope this book will be useful in helping those without a background in couples and family work to develop the necessary knowledge. For readers with a background in couples therapy who want detailed therapy guidelines for working with sufferers of psychoses, we recommend the books by Barrowclough & Tarrier (1992), Clarkin, Haas & Glick (1988) and Falloon, Boyd & McGill (1984).

Anxiety Disorders

There has been no systematic evaluation of the use of BMT or other couples therapy in anxiety disorders. A number of studies have investigated the effect of "spouse-aided" treatment on agoraphobia. These spouse-aided treatments focused on the partner as a support person for individual treatment of the anxiety sufferer. Lange & van Dyck (1992), Cobb et al. (1984), and Emmelkamp et al. (1992) found involvement of the spouse in behaviour therapy made no significant difference to treatment outcome on agoraphobic symptoms or ratings of marital adjustment, but Barlow, O'Brien & Last (1984) found exposure therapy to be improved by spouse involvement. Couples did not have marital distress in the Cobb et al. (1984), Emmelkamp et al. (1992) or Lange & van Dyck (1992) studies, but did in the Barlow, O'Brien & Last (1984) study. It would appear that, as with depression, including the spouse in treatment will make little difference to the efficacy of individual therapy where there is no co-existing marital distress. Marital problems in people with agoraphobia predicts poor prognosis in the outcome of individual behavioural treatment (Bland & Hallum, 1981; Emmelkamp & van der Hout, 1983; Monteiro, Marks & Ramm, 1985), so further investigation of the use of couples therapy is warranted.

Spouse-aided therapy is no more effective than self-exposure in the treatment of obsessive-compulsive disorder, irrespective of the presence of marital distress (Emmelkamp & de Lange, 1983; Emmelkamp, de Haan & Hoogduin, 1990). This does not establish that the involvement of the spouse in treatment is superfluous. Spouse involvement in these studies did not include components of marital therapy, which may have a positive impact on outcome, particularly in those clients with co-existing marital distress.

Couple's therapy, in combination with individual cognitive behavioural therapy, may be helpful for many clients with anxiety disorders. In cases where the spouse holds beliefs that may influence the persistence of the partners' anxiety disorder, involving the spouse would seem a necessary prerequisite for treatment outcome. For example, in the instance of obsessive-compulsive disorder, changing the reactions of the spouse to the compulsive behaviour has been suggested to be crucial for successful outcome of treatment (Hoogduin & Duivenvoorden, 1988; Pauly & Vandereyken, 1990), particularly if the spouse is part of the compulsive ritual or avoidance behaviour (Lange, Schaap & van Widenfelt, 1993). Couple's treatment for anxiety disorders including BMT strategies, with a focus on behaviours of both spouses that may perpetuate the anxiety, warrants systematic evaluation.

IMPLICATIONS OF RESEARCH FOR ASSESSMENT AND THERAPY WITH COUPLES

Assessment

Problems to Screen For

Given the very strong covariation between individual and couple problems, it is important that clients presenting either individually or conjointly be screened for both individual and couple problems. In other words, people in committed relationships who nominate their presenting problems as an individual problem such as alcohol abuse, depression or anxiety, need to be screened for relationship problems. Conversely, couples who nominate relationship problems as their presenting concern also need to be screened for individual psychological disorder.

Given that there is a separate chapter in this book on assessment of relationship distress, we will not review measures for screening for marital problems in detail. However, we present in Table 13.1 a summary of key areas that need to be screened for, and an example of a measure for assessing each area. General relationship adjustment is important to assess, since poor adjustment is associated with poor prognosis in response to individual psychological treatment of many disorders, most notably alcohol abuse, depression and anxiety disorders. Screening for relationship aggression is important, because such aggression often is under-detected by those providing couples therapy (O'Leary & Vivian, 1990). When severe violence is detected it is critical to ensure that steps are taken to protect the victim(s) of violence (see Heyman & Neidig, this volume for more detail on this issue).

Table 13.1 Areas of marital functioning to screen individual presentations

Area to assess	Example measure	Significance of results
Relationship adjustment	Dyadic Adjustment Scale (DAS) (Spanier, 1976)	Poor adjustment predicts poor response to individual therapy, need to consider couples intervention
Divorce/separation potential	Marital Status Inventory (MSI) (Weiss & Cerreto, 1980)	High scores indicates high separation potential, need to consider separation mediation
Relationship aggression and violence	Conflict Tactics Scale (CTS) (Strauss, 1979)	Severe aggression leads safety of victim(s) to be priority

Even when relationship distress, steps toward divorce and aggression are not reported, partner involvement in therapy may assist the individual presenting with a psychological problem, the partner and the relationship. For example, many partners living with someone with a psychotic disorder may not report being maritally distressed (Hooley et al., 1987), but might still benefit from assistance delivered in a conjoint format. Information and supportive discussion on the nature of psychiatric disorder, the role of medication in managing psychoses, and managing day-to-day problems within the home precipitated by the person's psychiatric disorder, can improve patient functioning and reduce stress on the spouse (Falloon & Fadden, 1993; Halford, 1994).

When the key presenting problem is relationship distress, there are a wide variety of individual problems which may be influencing the partners' functioning. It is unrealistic to attempt to screen for all these possible disorders in detail. Based on the high prevalence of depression, alcohol abuse and anxiety disorders in conjunction with relationship distress, we suggest these disorders should be screened for routinely. Given the potentially profound impact of severe psychiatric disorder in relationships, we recommend that all marital therapists ask each partner individually if they have ever received psychological or psychiatric care in the past, as either an inpatient or an outpatient. The occurrence of such treatment does not contra-indicate couples therapy, but might necessitate attention to issues such as medication management as part of the therapy approach.

There are a number of possible instruments to screen for common individual problems. In Table 13.2 we list some useful measures for such screening. The selection of measures any clinician uses will be dependent, in part, upon the client population she or he serves. However, we feel the recommended measures have demonstrated reliability and validity and are sensitive to the individual problems most relevant to couple interactions.

Table 13.2 Measures for screening for individual psychopathology often co-existing with presenting marital distress

Measure	Authors	Brief description
Beck Depression Inventory (BDI)	Beck et al. (1961)	28-Item self-report measure of depression, with emphasis on cognitive symptoms
Canterbury Alcohol Screening Test (CAST)	Elvy & Wells (1984)	Self-report measure of alcohol abuse and alcohol-related problems
Depression, Anxiety, Stress Scale (DASS)	Lovibond & Lovibond (1995)	Self-report measure of depression, anxiety and stress
Khavari Alcohol Test (KAT)	Khavari & Faber (1978)	14 Items self- or partner-report measure of frequency, mean and maximum alcohol consumption
Symptom Checklist (SCL-90)	Derogatis Lipman & Coui (1973)	90-Item self-report measure of occurrence of psychiatric symptoms

Salience of Couple and Individual Assessments to the Partners

When people present for individual therapy they may not see the relevance of assessments of their relationships. Indeed such assessments might be seen as the therapist missing the client's view of the key issues of therapy. Conversely, a couple presenting for relationship problems may not see individual problems are relevant. For example, in a couple one of use saw (WKH) the man had a long history of difficulty with alcohol abuse. When asked about prior psychological treatment he became quite irritated and stated that was not relevant to therapy. Subsequently he reported he felt implicitly blamed for the relationship problems when asked to disclose his prior drinking problems. Failing to attend to the beliefs and expectations of the client(s) about what information is salient can undermine therapy at a very early stage. Consequently, we think it is very important for the therapist to make explicit the rationale for the assessments of *both* individual and relationship functioning.

If someone presents for individual therapy and is in a relationship, we routinely would ask a question along the lines of the following; "Given all the difficulties you have described, I would guess this has made a major impact on your life. What effect do you think these problems have had on your relationship?" Rarely do people say that problems severe enough to lead them to seek therapy have no impact upon their relationship at all. Once the issue of the relationship context is raised, asking clients to complete a few self-report questionnaires to provide extra information is rarely problematic.

In the case of a couple presenting for therapy we would always see each partner individually (see Weiss & Halford, 1995, for a detailed description of our assessment procedure). During the individual interviews we ask both partners if they believe that individual problems contribute to the relationship problems. We also ask if either partner has ever sought individual psychological or psychiatric assistance. Once the issue of individual functioning is raised, we also ask a question of the general form: "Having relationship problems can be very stressful, and hard to cope with. What effect do you think the relationship problems are having on you?" The individual assessment measures can be introduced as being part of a careful assessment of the effect of the relationship problems.

Developing a Collaborative Cognitive Set about Couples Therapy

A major challenge in couples therapy is to assist the couple to develop a collaborative cognitive set about the nature of their problems, a cognitive set which promotes therapeutic change (Baucom & Epstein, 1990; Weiss & Halford, 1995). In the context of coexisting individual and couple problems a variety of unhelpful beliefs can interfere with therapy. Such unhelpful beliefs can include: (a) one partner attributing all relationship difficulties to their partner's psychological disorder; (b) the partner with the psychological disorder attributing all blame for their disorder to the partner or the relationship; or (c) the patient with the disorder blaming him/herself for all relationship distress. Rarely in our experience are coexisting relationship and individual problems adequately understood in terms of simple unidirectional causality. Neither do such simple viewpoints help the partners to develop a common understanding about the nature of their problems, understanding which is consistent with both their experiences of the relationship.

The process of assessment can be used strategically to help partners to develop a shared understanding of how the individual's psychological disorder interacts with the relationship. Asking each partner to consider how the psychological disorder is expressed within the relationship (e.g. "How do you know when he is depressed?"; "What changes do you notice when she drinks?") and how this expression is responded to within the relationship context (e.g. "What do you think and do when he is depressed?"; "How do you react to her when she has been drinking?") can help both partners and the therapist develop an understanding of the critical processes.

Often clients are unable to describe how the individual and couple problems interact, and more extensive assessments are necessary. As an illustration of this process, monitoring where, when and under what circumstances one partner evidences their problem (e.g. drinks heavily, or expresses depression, or becomes anxious), and also monitoring what the immediate consequences of that behaviour are, can help identify what relationship processes may be part of the problem. For example, Genevieve and Max presented with marital difficulties and at intake both reported concern about Max's drinking. Max did not meet DSM-IV criteria for a clinical diagnosis of alcohol dependence. However, he was significantly overweight, which he attributed in part to his heavy beer drinking, he drank to intoxication once or twice per week, and had missed days of work through suffering hangovers after alcohol abuse. Genevieve reported feeling disgust toward Max for some days after she saw him intoxicated, and said she hated sleeping beside him when he drank heavily because he snored and smelled of alcohol. Max identified excessive drinking as a personal problem, and Max and Genevieve had agreed the drinking had impacted upon their marriage.

In order to better understand the drinking within the relationship context, each partner monitored Max's drinking on a daily basis for 2 weeks. A recurrent pattern was found that Max often drank when the couple were anticipating talking together; three times in that period it was about Genevieve's dissatisfaction with her current job. Max reported that he felt frustrated by Genevieve's frequent complaints about her work but her refusal, as he saw it, to take his advice on how to change jobs. Genevieve reported that she felt Max did not understand how unhappy she was, how trapped in her current job situation she felt, and the devastating effect she felt on her self-esteem when she had five job interviews without getting a job offer. Both partners reported that discussion about Genevieve's job reminded them of unsuccessful discussions they had from time to time about money management within their relationship.

From the above analysis they agreed that difficulties in communication about sensitive topics was a source of stress to both of them, and that each needed to develop their communication and conflict management skills. In addition, Max and Genevieve agreed that Max used alcohol as an attempt to control stress, and that this method of stress management was unhelpful to him at times. Max set himself the goal of trying to develop a broader range of options for managing stress, rather than relying on alcohol consumption. Genevieve concluded that she reacted to heavy drinking in Max by having a period of several days in which she was distant and expressed disgust toward Max in subtle ways. She concluded that this had not been effective in influencing Max's drinking, and may actually have exacerbated their relationship problems. The effect of assessment was to externalize the problems as something they could agree about, and work together to solve.

In summary, the process of assessment helps the couple and therapist to define a shared understanding of the interaction of individual and couple problems, and to develop agreed-upon goals for therapy. Perhaps the most difficult challenge to developing this shared understanding is when one partner is reluctant to attend therapy, and we turn our attention to this issue in the next section.

Engaging the Reluctant Partner

Judith presented reporting a long history of marital problems and excessive drinking by her husband Rick. She stated that she was not wanting to end the marriage, but felt she could not stand things as they were. Judith reported that Rick would "never agree to see a psychologist, or anything like that". Presentations such as Judith's, in which there is a mixture of individual and couple problems, only one partner is presenting and the other partner is believed to be reluctant to enter therapy, are quite common in clinical practice (Halford & Osgarby, 1993). Yet the published literature on marital therapy focuses almost exclusively on working with couples with both partners in therapy (for an exception to this, see Bennum, this volume).

Sometimes it is better not to attempt to engage the absent spouse. For example, in a study we recently conducted assisting women who reported excessive drinking by their partners, we had a number of presentations by women who reported significant fear of assault if their partners knew they were seeking assistance (Halford et al., 1996). In most instances the absent partner had a history of severe violence toward the presenting client, suggesting such fears were quite realistic.

The presenting client needs to decide whether he/she wants the reluctant partner involved with therapy. To assist the client to make that decision the therapist can help clarify the options and provide information. Based on our own work and the research of others, we believe that the chances of success in therapy with coexisting individual and couples problems generally is greater if both partners have at least some involvement with therapy (Halford et al., 1996; O'Farrell, 1993). In particular, there is no evidence that you can improve a distressed relationship, in which at least one partner has an individual problem, by seeing only one partner. So we aim to engage both partners except where there is a strong contra-indication, such as the risk of assault.

Often we find the presenting client reports that the absent partner would not attend. It is important to explore with the client the evidence for that assertion. Often the topic of attending therapy has not explicitly been raised, and an inference is made that therapy would not be attended. For example, when Alf first presented he reported that he and his partner had attended three sessions of marital therapy some years before. His wife refused to attend after the third session because "she thought it was all a waste of time, and was getting nowhere". From this Alf concluded she would never see a marital therapist again. However, when Alf did ask his partner Sheree to attend, she did come (interestingly, Sheree reported in her first session that she was prepared to give therapy a lot of effort, as she felt things between her and Alf were at a critical point now. She had felt that therapy was not really necessary 3 years earlier).

We routinely ask where, when, and under what circumstances the presenting client has said exactly what to the absent spouse about attending therapy. Rarely, in our experience, has the presenting client calmly and clearly asked their partner to come to therapy in a collaborative way. It is common for the issue of therapy only to be raised in the context of a heated argument. (Rarely, in our experience, do spouses respond well to a message such as, "You're crazy, you need to see a shrink" shouted in the middle of an argument.)

It can be helpful to work with the client to identify where, when and under what circumstances the spouse might be most responsive to an invitation to attend therapy. Also, helping the client to practice a form of words which extends a collaborative, positively framed invitation is important. For example, George presented concerned about his marriage to Rebecca. Rebecca had a long history of alcohol abuse and depression, and had attempted suicide twice in the past 5 years. George was concerned that Rebecca would become angry if he suggested therapy and this might precipitate her relapse back to drinking. Initially George said he had to "make Rebecca see reason, she has to change otherwise I have had it". The therapist noted the passion with which George expressed his desire to improve things with Rebecca. After extensive discussion, George decided to make a dinner for the two of them at home. At the end of the dinner, he resolved to tell his wife that he loved her deeply, and that he was proud of her for overcoming her drinking problems. He then wanted to say that he felt the last few years had been pretty difficult for both of them, and that their relationship had been at risk. (George had left for a few weeks some about 12 months earlier.) Finally, he decided he wanted to tell her that he wanted to work to make the relationship stronger, and he wanted the two of them to go to therapy to achieve that goal together.

It often is helpful for the therapist to extend an invitation to the absent partner to attend therapy. Routinely we would, with the permission of the presenting spouse, ring the non-presenting partner. There is a risk that the non-presenting partner may feel blamed for the presenting client's concerns. Consequently, we usually frame this initial contact as an invitation to provide information which would help with the therapy of the presenting client. Such an invitation is less threatening than a request to be part of therapy. Furthermore, we suggest it is premature to determine that spouse involvement is the best approach to therapy until assessment has been conducted with both partners.

Intervention

In this section we draw together the implications of the research we have reviewed earlier for intervention. Rather than restating the major empirical findings, we will simply present these as a series of unreferenced conclusions.

The Style of Couples Therapy

Across different individual problems, different styles of couples therapy have been used. At one end of the spectrum are interventions in which the individual with psychopathology is accompanied by their partner to therapy, but there is no specific utilization of interaction between the spouse and the partner as part of therapy. For example, in most of the work on anxiety disorders there has been the use of spouse-involvement with treatment. This usually has involved the spouse in gaining some information about the nature of anxiety disorders, and accompanying the spouse on various exposure-based treatment exercises. However, there has been little attempt specifically to train the spouse in different ways of interacting with the individual who has psychopathology. Furthermore, in the anxiety disorders this form of spouse involvement has been used without any modification taking account of the presence of the spouse, and has simply involved the spouse in attending individually focused treatment.

In a different approach to spouse involvement in individual treatment, cognitive–behavioural marital therapy has been incorporated as an element of treatment. For example, in the treatment of alcohol problems behavioural marital therapy is an effective adjunct to individual treatment which improves long-term maintenance of controlled drinking. Often the couples therapy needs modification to take account of the individual psychopathology, such as contracting between the spouses for adherence to use of Antabuse in the treatment of severe alcohol abuse. Similarly, in family psychoeducation with patients with psychotic disorders, traditional cognitive–behavioural marital therapy is used as an adjunct to chemotherapy and individual therapy. There is no evidence in either the alcohol or psychoses outcome literature that cognitive–behavioural couples therapy, or any other form of couples therapy, is a sufficient treatment for these disorders. However, couples therapy is a useful adjunct to individual treatment.

There are some individual psychological disorders for which cognitive–behavioural couples therapy can be used as the primary means of treatment. For women who are suffering from mild to moderate depression, who have coexisting marital distress and whose marital distress antedates their depression, then marital therapy seems to be the treatment of choice.

Sequencing Therapy Process: Which Problem First?

In instances where couples therapy and individual therapy are both to be incorporated into the therapy program, the therapist needs to decide how to sequence these different elements of therapy. It is possible to do either individual therapy first, couple's therapy first, or to run the two elements conjointly. In some instances the decison about sequencing may be relatively straight forward. There are some basic entry skills that people need to benefit from couples therapy, and individuals with significant psychopathology may lack these entry skills. More specifically, it seems unlikely that people will benefit from couples therapy if the individual's mental state is severely disturbed by an acute psychotic episode, or if their abuse of alcohol inhibits their ability to engage effectively in therapy. Similarly, if someone is so severely depressed that they have very low levels of activity and are minimally affectively responsive, then individual treatment probably needs to precede couples therapy.

Assuming that both individuals do have the entry skills to engage in couples therapy, then there are several other criteria by which the clients and therapist may negotiate the sequencing of therapy. First, attention should be paid to the salience of individual vs. couple problems to both partners. Second, the functional analysis suggesting the interrelationship of the variables should be taken into account. Third, those aspects of the complex problems which are most likely to be changed easily should be targeted first, as success initially will help to maintain engagement and commitment to therapy.

Duration of Therapy

Traditionally, couples therapy, as it is described in the research literature, lasts anything from 15 to 20 conjoint sessions. If individual therapy of a similar length is added to the conjoint therapy, then therapy becomes a very substantial expense and commitment for clients. For that reason, we advocate trying to deliver therapy at the minimum necessary therapeutic dose to achieve the desired result. Brief couples interventions may well be effective in helping people with individual psychological disorders. For example, Dadds, Schwartz & Sanders (1987) found that just three sessions of intensive couples therapy, focusing on supporting partners to be better parents, improved marital satisfaction and enhanced the effectiveness of behavioural parent training with children with conduct disorders. This effect was only evident for parents who were maritally distressed. In other words, the combination of traditional parent training and a very brief marital intervention was significantly helpful for these couples.

Brief marital interventions may be particularly effective if therapy is provided in the context of early detection of individual and relationship problems (Halford & Behrens, 1996). Recent work that we have undertaken (Halford, Osgarby & Kelly, in press) showed that brief interventions of just three sessions can be effective for couples with mild to moderate marital distress. The lengthy courses of therapy more typical of programs reported in the literature may discourage many people from seeking therapy till problems become severe. At the same time, there are couples who require very extensive intervention. Individuals with severe psychotic disorders are unlikely to benefit from brief one- or two-session interventions. In fact, the available data suggests that family interventions with people with schizophrenia need to run for a substantial period of time in order to produce sustained effects (Halford, 1994, 1995).

CONCLUSIONS

Throughout this chapter we have tried to identify some of the key themes emerging from the research on the interaction of individual psychopathology and couples relationships. It is clear that there is a strong relationship between individual distress and couple distress. This relationship is bidirectional, with individual problems impacting upon marital problems and *vice versa*. Guidelines derived from the research were presented to help clinicians decide when targeting individual problems, the couple's distress, or both, was likely to be helpful.

One theoretical implication of the research reviewed is in terms of how we conceptualize psychopathology. Traditionally, psychopathology has been described in terms of intra-individual processes. Standard diagnostic criteria define psychopathology largely in terms of internal subjective experiences, with some reference to behavioural manifestations at the individual level. The research reviewed in this chapter highlights how the subjective experiences and individual behaviours of psychopathology are shaped by, and impact upon, the interpersonal context in which abnormal behaviour occurs. To ignore that context, and only to assess psychopathology at the level of the individual, may be to miss the crucial elements of psychopathology. In other words, we believe that understanding of psychopathology will be enhanced by greater attention to how that psychopathology interacts with the relationship context. Attention to the relationships of our clients with individual problems also allows us to be more helpful to those clients.

REFERENCES

Babcock, J.C., Waltz, J., Jacobson, N.S. & Gottman, J.M. (1993). Power and violence: the relation between communication patterns, power discrepancies, and domestic violence. *Journal of Consulting and Clinical Psychology*, **61**, 40–50.

Bachrach, L.L. (1975). *Mental Health, Marital Status and Mental Disorders: an Analytic Review*. Washington, DC: US Government Publishing Office.

Barlow, D.H., O'Brien, G.T. & Last, C.G. (1984). Couples treatment of agoraphobia. *Behavior Therapy*, **15**, 51–58.

Barrett, P.M., Rapee, R.M., Dadds, M.R. & Ryan, S.M. (in press). Family enhancement of cognitive style in anxious and aggressive children: cognitive biases and the fear effect. *Journal of Abnormal Child Psychology*.

Barrowclough, C. & Tarrier, N. (1992). *Families Schizophrenic Patients: Cognitive–Behavioural Interventions*. London: Chapman & Hall.

Bateson, G., Jackson, D., Haley, J. & Weakland, J. (1956). Toward a theory of schizophrenia. *Behavioural Science*, **1**, 252–264.

Baucom, D.H. & Epstein, N. (1990). *Cognitive–Behavioral Marital Therapy*. New York: Brunner Mazel.

Beach, S.H.R., Arias, I. & O'Leary, K.D. (1986). The relationship of marital satisfaction and social support to depressive symptomatology. *Journal of Psychopathology and Behavioural Assessment*, **8**, 305–316.

Beach, S.R. & O'Leary, K.D. (1986). The treatment of depression occurring in the context of marital discord. *Behavior Therapy*, **17**, 43–49.

Bebbington, P.E. (1987a). Marital status and depression: a study of English national admission statistics. *Acta Psychiatrica Scandinavica*, **75**, 640–650.

Bebbington, P.E. (1987b). The social epidemiology of clinical depression. In A.S. Henderson & G. Burrows (eds), *Handbook of Studies on Social Psychiatry*. Melbourne: Blackwell.

Beck, A.T., Ward, C.H., Mendelson, M., Mock, J.E. & Erbaugh, J.K. (1961). An inventory for measurement of depression. *Archives of General Psychiatry*, **4**, 451–471.

Biglan, A., Hops, H., Sherman, L., Friedman, L., Arthur, J. & Osteen, V. (1985). Problem solving interactions of depressed women and their husbands. *Behavior Therapy*, **16**, 431–451.

Billings, A.G. & Moos, R.H. (1983). Psychosocial processes of recovery among alcoholics and their families: implications for clinicians and program evaluators. *Addictive Behavior*, **8**, 205–218.

Birchnall, J. & Kennard, J. (1983). Does marital maladjustment lead to mental illness? *Social Psychiatry*, **18**, 79–88.

Birchwood, M., Cochrane, R., Macmillan, F.M., Copastake, S., Kucharska, J. & Cariss, M. (1992). The influence of ethnicity and family structure on relapse in first-episode schizophrenia: a comparison of Asian, Afro-Caribean, and white patients. *British Journal of Psychiatry*, **161**, 783–790.

Bland, K. & Hallam, R.S. (1981). Relationship between response to graded exposure and marital satisfaction in agoraphobics. *Behaviour Research and Therapy*, **19**, 335–338.

Blankfield, A. & Maritz, J.S. (1990). Female alcoholics IV. Admission problems and patterns. *Acta Psychiatrica Scandinavica*, **82**, 445–450.

Bowers, T.G. & Alredha, M.R. (1990). A comparison of outcome with group/marital and standard individual therapies with alcoholics. *Journal of Studies on Alcohol*, **51**, 301–309.

Brooker, C., Tarrier, N., Barrowclough, C., Butterworth, A. & Goldberg, D. (1993). Training community psychiatric nurses for psychosocial intervention: report of a pilot study. *British Journal of Psychiatry*, **160**, 836–844.

Brown, G.W. & Harris, T. (1978). *Social Origins of Depression*. New York: Free Press.

Cascardi, M., Langhinrichsen, J. & Vivian, D. (1992). Marital aggression, impact, injury and health correlates for husbands and wives. *Archives of Internal Medicine*, **152**, 1178–1184.

Chakrabarti, S., Kulhara, P. & Verma, S.K. (1993). The pattern of burden in families of neurotic patients. *Social Psychiatry and Psychiatric Epidemiology*, **28**, 172–177.

Clarkin, J.F., Haas, G.L. & Glick, I.D. (eds) (1988). *Affective Disorder and the Family*. New York: Guilford.

Cobb, J.P., Mathews, A.A., Childs-Clarke, A. & Bowers, C.M. (1984). The spouse as a co-therapist in the treatment of agoraphobia. *British Journal of Psychiatry*, **144**, 282–287.

Coyne, J.C. (1976). Depression and the response of others. *Journal of Abnormal Psychology*, **89**, 186–193.

Dadds, M.R., Schwartz, S. & Sanders, M.R. (1987). Marital discord and treatment outcome in behavioral treatment of child conduct disorders. *Journal of Consulting and Clinical Psychology*, **55**, 396–403.

Davis, D.I., Berenson, D., Steinglass, P. & Davis, S. (1974). The adaptive consequences of drinking. *Psychiatry*, **37**, 209–215.

Department of Health and Social Security (1985). *Inpatient Statistics from the Mental Health Enquiry, 1982*. London: HMSO.

Derogatis, L., Lipman, R. & Coui, L. (1973). The SCL-90: an outpatient rating scale. *Psychopharmacology Bulletin*, **9**, 13–28.

Doane, J.A., Goldstein, M.J., Mikowitz, D.J. & Falloon, I.R.H. (1985). The impact of individual and family treatment on the affective climate of families of schizophrenics. *British Journal of Psychiatry*, **148**, 279–287.

Doane, J.A., West, K.L., Goldstein, M.J., Rodnick, E.H. & Jones, J.E. (1981). Parental communication deviance and affective style: predictors of subsequent schizophrenia spectrum disorders in vulnerable adolescents. *Archives of General Psychiatry*, **38**, 679–685.

Dobson, K.S. (1987). Marital and social adjustment in depressed and remarried women. *Journal of Clinical Psychology*, **43**, 261–265.

Elvy, G.A. & Wells, J.E. (1984). The Canterbury Alcoholism Screening Test (CAST): a detection instrument for use with hospitalised patients. *New Zealand Medical Journal*, **97**, 111–115.

Emery, R.E., Joyce, S.A. & Fincham, F.D. (1987). The assessment of child and marital problems. In K.D. O'Leary (ed.), *Assessment of Marital Discord* (pp. 223–262). Hillsdale, NJ: Erlbaum.

Emmelkamp, P.M.G., De Haan, E. & Hoogduin, C.A.I. (1990). Marital adjustment and obsessive-compulsive disorder. *British Journal of Psychiatry*, **156**, 55–60.

Emmelkamp, P.M.G. & de Lange, I. (1983). Spouse involvement in the treatment of obsessive-compulsive patients. *Behaviour Research and Therapy*, **21**, 341–346.

Emmelkamp, P.M.G., van Dyck, R., Bitter, M., Heins, R., Onstein, E.J. & Eisen, B. (1992). Spouse-aided therapy with agoraphobics. *British Journal of Psychiatry*, **160**, 51–56.

Emmelkamp, P.M.G. & van der Hout, A. (1983). Failure in treating agoraphobia. In E.B. Foa & P.M.G. Emmelkamp (eds), *Failures in Behavior Therapy*. New York: Wiley.

Falloon, I.R.H., Boyd, J.L. & McGill, C.W. (1984). *Family Care of Schizophrenia*. New York: Guilford.

Falloon, I.R.H., Boyd, J.L., McGill, C.W., Williamson, M., Razani, A., Moss, H.B., Guilderman, A.M. & Simpson, G.M. (1985). Family management in the prevention of morbidity of schizophrenia—clinical outcome of a two-year longitudinal study. *Archives of General Psychiatry*, **42**, 887–896.

Falloon, I.R.H. & Coverdale, J.H. (1995). Cognitive–behavioural family interventions for major mental disorders. *Behaviour Change*, **11**, 213–222.

Falloon, I.R.H. & Fadden, G. (1993). *Integrated Mental Health Care*. Cambridge: Cambridge University Press.

Falloon, I.R.H. & Pederson, J. (1985). Family management and the prevention of morbidity in schizophrenia: the adjustment of the family unit. *British Journal of Psychiatry*, **147**, 153–156.

Frankenstein, W., Hay, W.M. & Nathan, P.E. (1985). Effects of intoxication on alcoholics' marital communication and problem solving. *Journal of Studies on Alcohol*, **46**, 1–6.

Fromm-Reichmann, F. (1948). Notes on the development of treatment of schizophrenics by psychoanalytic psychotherapy. *Psychiatry*, **1**, 263–273.

Fry, W.F. Jr (1962). The marital context of an anxiety syndrome. *Family Process*, **1**, 245–252.

Glick, I.D. (1992). Medication and family therapy for schizophrenia and mood disorder. *Psychopharmacology Bulletin*, **28**, 223–225.

Goldstein, M.J. (1988). The family and psychopathology. *Annual Review of Psychology*, **39**, 283–299.

Goldstein, M.J. (1985). Family factors that antedate the onset of schizophrenia and related disorders. *Acta Psychiatrica Scandinavia*, **71**, 7–18.

Goldstein, A.J. & Chambless, D.L. (1978). A reanalysis of agoraphobia. *Behavior Therapy*, **9**, 47–59.

Goldstein, A.J., Rodnick, E.H., Evans, J.R., May, P.R. & Steinberg, M. (1978). Drug and family therapy in the aftercare treatment of acute schizophrenia. *Archives of General Psychiatry*, **35**, 1169–1177.

Goodenow, C., Reisine, S.T. & Grady, K.E. (1990). Quality of social support and associated social and psychological functioning in women with Rheumatoid Arthritis. *Health Psychology*, **9**, 266–284.

Gore, S. (1978). The effect of social support in moderating the health consequences of unemployment. *Journal of Health and Social Behavior*, **19**, 157–165.

Hafner, R.J. (1986). *Marriage and Mental Illness: a Sex-roles Perspective*. New York: Guilford.

Hahlweg, K., Goldstein, M.J., Neuchterlein, K.H., Magana, A., Mintz, J., Doane, J.A. & Snyder, K.S. (1989). Expressed emotion and patient–relative interaction in families of recent onset schizophrenia. *Journal of Consulting and Clinical Psychology*, **57**, 11–18.

Halford, W.K. (1995). Behaviour therapy and schizophrenia in context: challenges and opportunities provided within the changing mental health system. *Behaviour Change*, **12**, 41–50.

Halford, W.K. (1994). Familial factors in psychiatry. *Current Opinion in Psychiatry*, **7**, 186–191.

Halford, W.K. (1991). Beyond expressed emotion: behavioural assessment of family interaction associated with the course of schizophrenia. *Behavioural Assessment*, **13**, 99–123.

Halford, W.K. & Behrens, B.C. (1996). Prevention of marital difficulties. In P. Cotton & H.J. Jackson (eds), *Early Intervention and Preventive Mental Health Application of Clinical Psychology*. Brisbane: Australian Academic Press.

Halford, W.K. & Hayes, R.L. (1991). Psychological rehabilitation of chronic schizophrenic patients: recent findings on social skills training and family psychoeducation. *Clinical Psychology Review*, **11**, 23–44.

Halford, W.K. & Osgarby, S.M. (1993). Alcohol abuse in clients presenting with marital problems. *Journal of Family Psychology*, **6**, 1–11.

Halford, W.K., Osgarby, S.M. & Kelly, A. (in press). Brief behavioural couples therapy: a preliminary investigation. Cognitive and Behavioural Psychotherapy.

Halford, W.K., Price, J., Bouma, R.O., Kelly, A. & Young, R. (1995). The wives of untreated men misusing alcohol: their marriages and coping. Paper under review.

Halford, W.K., Steindel, S., Varghese, F. & Schweitzer, R.D. (1996). Observed family interaction and outcome in first admission psychoses. Paper submitted for publication.

Hatfield, A.B. (1987). Coping and adaption: a conceptual framework for understanding families. In A.B. Hatfield & H.D. Lefley (eds), *Families of the Mentally Ill* (pp. 60–84). New York: Guilford.

Hautzinger, M., Linden, N. & Hoffman, N. (1982). Distressed couples with and without a depressed partner: an analysis of their verbal interaction. *Journal of Behaviour Therapy and Experimental Psychiatry*, **13**, 307–314.

Hetherington, E.M., Cox, M. & Cox, R. (1985). Long-term effects of divorce and remarriage on the adjustment of children. *Journal of the American Academy of Child Psychiatry*, **24**, 518–530.

Heyman, R.E. & Neidig, P.H. (1996). Treatment of spouse abuse. In W.K. Halford & H.J. Markman (eds), *Clinical Handbook of Couple Relationship and Couples Intervention* (pp. 13–42). Chichester: Wiley.

Hirsch, S.R. & Leff, J.P. (1975). *Abnormalities in Families of Schizophrenics*. London: Oxford University press.

Holzworth-Munroe, A. (1992). Social skill deficits in maritally violent men: interpreting the data using a social information processing model. *Clinical Psychology Review*, **12**, 605–617.

Hoogduin, C.A.I. & Duivenvoorden, H.J. (1988). A decision model in the treatment of obsessive-compulsive neuroses. *British Journal of Psychiatry*, **152**, 516–521.

Hoogduin, C.A.I., Duivenvoorden, H.J., Schaap, C. et al. (1989). On the outpatient treatment of obsessive-compulsive disorder: outcome, prediction of outcome and follow-up. In P.M.G. Emmelkamp et al. (eds), *Annual Series of European Research in Behaviour Therapy, Vol. IV: Fresh Perspective on Anxiety Disorders*. Amsterdam: Swets.

Hooley, J.M., Orley, J. & Teasdale, J.D. (1986). Levels of expressed emotion and relapse in depressed patients. *British Journal of Psychiatry*, **148**, 642–647.

Hooley, J.M., Richters, J.E., Weintraub, S. & Neale, J.M. (1987). Psychopathology and marital distress: the positive side of positive symptoms. *Journal of Abnormal Psychology*, **96**, 27–33.

Hops, H., Biglan, A., Sherman, L., Arthur, J., Friedman, L. & Osteen, V. (1987). Home observations of family interactions of depressed women. *Journal of Consulting and Clinical Psychology*, **55**, 341–346.

Jacob, T. & Leonard, K. (1992). Sequential analysis of marital interactions involving alcoholic, depressed and non-distressed men. *Journal of Abnormal Psychology*, **101**, 647–656.

Jacob, T., Ritchey, D., Cvitkovic, J.E. & Blane, H.T. (1981). Communication styles of alcoholic and non-alcoholic families when drinking and not drinking. *Journal of Studies on Alcohol*, **42**, 466–482.

Jacobson, N.S., Dobson, K., Fruzetti, A.E., Schmaling, K.B. & Salusky, S. (1991). Marital therapy as treatment of depression. *Journal of Consulting and Clinical Psychology*, **59**, 547–557.

Kavanagh, D. (1992). Recent developments in expressed emotion and schizophrenia. *British Journal of Psychiatry*, **160**, 601–620.

Kavanagh, D., Clark, D., Piatowski, O., O'Halloran, P., Manicavasager, V., Rosen, A. & Tennant, C. (1993). Application of cognitive–behavioural family intervention for schizophrenia: what can the matter be? *Australian Psychologist*, **28**, 1–8.

Kelly, A., Halford, W.K. & Young, R. (1996). Alcohol and marital problems: assessment and treatment issues. Paper under review.

Khavari, K.A. & Farber, P.D. (1978). A profile instrument for the quantification and assessment of alcohol consumption. *Journal of Studies on Alcohol*, **39**, 1525–1539.

Kleiner, L. & Marshall, W.L. (1987). The role of interpersonal problems in the development of agoraphobia with panic attacks. *Journal of Anxiety Disorders*, **1**, 313–323.

Klerman, G.L. & Weissman, M.M. (1982). Interpersonal psychotherapy: theory and research. In A.J. Rush (ed.), *Short-term Psychotherapy for Depression: Behavioural, Interpersonal, Cognitive and Psychodynamic Approaches*. New York: Guilford.

Koensberg, K.W. & Handley, R. (1986). Expressed emotion: from predictive index to clinical construct. *American Journal of Psychiatry*, **143**, 1361–1373.

Kowalik, D.L. & Gotlib, I.H. (1987). Depression and marital interaction: concordance between intent and perception of communication. *Journal of Abnormal Psychology*, **43**, 127–134.

Lange, A., Schaap, G. & van Widenfelt, B. (1993). Family therapy and psychopathology: developments in research and approaches to treatment. *Journal of Family Therapy*, **15**, 113–146.

Lange, A. & van Dyck, R. (1992). The function of agoraphobia in the marital relationship: a research note. *Acta Psychiatrica Scandinavica*, **85**, 89–93.

Leff, J. & Vaughn, C. (1985). *Expressed Emotion in Families*. New York: Guilford.

Lovibond, S.H. & Lovibond, P.F. (1995). *Manual for the Depression Anxiety Stress Scale*. Sydney: The Psychology Foundation of Australia.

Maisto, S.A., O'Farrell, T.J., Connors, G.J., McKay, J.R., & Pelcovits, M. (1988). Alcoholics' attributions of factors affecting their relapse to drinking and reasons for terminating relapse episodes. *Addictive Behavior*, **13**, 79–82.

McFarlane, W.R., Dunne, E., Lukens, E., Newmark, M., McLaughlin-Toran, J., Deakins, S. & Horen, B. (1993). From research to clinical practice: dissemination of New York State's family psychoeducation project. *Hospital and Community Psychiatry*, **44**, 265–270.

McLeod, J.D. (1994). Anxiety disorders and marital quality. *Journal of Abnormal Psychology*, **103**, 767–776.

Miklowitz, D.J., Goldstein, M.J., Neuchterlein, K.H., Snyder, K.S. & Mintz, J. (1988). Family factors and the course of affective disorder. *Archives of General Psychiatry*, **45**, 225–231.

Milazzo-Sayre, L. (1977). *Admission Rates to State and County Psychiatric Hospitals by Age, Sex and Marital Status, 1975*. Washington: US Government Publishing Office.

Monteiro, W., Marks, I.M. & Ramm, E. (1985). Marital adjustment and treatment outcome in agoraphobia. *British Journal of Psychiatry*, **146**, 383–390.

Mulder, R.T. (1991). Personality disorders in New Zealand. *Acta Psychiatrica Scandinavica*, **84**, 197–202.

Nace, E.P. (1982). Therapeutic approaches to the alcoholic marriage. *Psychiatric Clinics of North America*, **5**, 543–561.

Neuchterlein, K.H., Snyder, K.S. & Mintz, J. (1992). Paths to relapse: possible transactional processes connecting patient illness onset, expressed emotion and psychotic relapse. *British Journal of Psychiatry*, **161**, 88–96.

O'Farrell, T.J. (1993). A behavioral marital therapy couples group program for alcoholics and their spouses. In T.J. O'Farrell (ed.), *Treating Alcohol Problems: Marital and Family Interventions*. New York: Guilford.

O'Farrell, T.J. & Bayog, R.D. (1986). Antabuse contracts for married alcoholics and their spouses: a method to maintain Antabuse ingestion and decrease conflict about drinking. *Journal of Substance Abuse Treatment*, **3**, 1–8.

O'Farrell, T.J. & Birchler, G.R. (1987). Marital relationships of alcoholic, conflicted, and non-conflicted couples. *Journal of Marital and Family Therapy*, **13**, 259–274.

O'Farrell, T.J., Choquette, K.A., Cutter, H.S.G., Brown, E.D. & McCourt, W.F. (1992). Behavioural marital therapy with and without additional couples relapse prevention sessions for alcoholics and their wives. *Journal of Studies on Alcohol*, **53**, 652–666.

O'Farrell, T.J., Cutter, H.S.G. & Floyd, F.J. (1985). Evaluating behavioral marital therapy for male alcoholics: effects on marital adjustment and communication from before to after treatment. *Behavior Therapy*, **16**, 147–167.

O'Farrell, T.J., Cutter, H.S.G., Choquette, K.A., Floyd, F.J. & Bayog, R.D. (1992). Behavioral marital therapy for male alcoholics: marital and drinking adjustment during the two years after treatment. *Behavior Therapy*, **23**, 529–549.

O'Farrell, T.J., Kleinke, C.L., Thompson, D.L. & Cutter, H.S.G. (1986). Differences between alcoholic couples accepting and rejecting an offer of outpatient marital therapy. *American Journal of Drug and Alcohol Abuse*, **12**, 285–294.

O'Farrell, T.J. & Murphy, C.M. (1995). Marital violence before and after alcoholism treatment. *Journal of Consulting and Clinical Psychology*, **63**, 256–262.

O'Leary, K.D. & Beach, S.R.H. (1990). Marital therapy: a viable treatment for depression and marital discord. *American Journal of Psychiatry*, **147**, 183–186.

O'Leary, K.D. & Vivian, D.A. (1990). Physical aggression in marriage. In F.D. Fincham & T.N. Bradbury (eds), *The Psychology of Marriage: Basic Issues and Applications* (pp. 323–348). New York: Guilford.

Pauly, F. & Vandereyken, W. (1990). Interactionele aspecten van dwangstoornissen (Interactional aspects of obsessive-compulsive disorders). *Directieve Therapie*, **10**, 131–148.

Paykel, E.S., Myers, J.K., Dienelt, M.N., Klerman, G.L., Lindenthal, J.J. & Pepper, M.P. (1969). Life events and depression: a controlled study. *Archives of General Psychiatry*, **21**, 753–760.

Perry, B. (1993). The Marital Problem-solving Interactions of Depressed Men. Unpublished doctoral thesis, Faculty of Education, University of Oregon.

Radloff, L.S. & Rae, D.S. (1979). Susceptibility and precipitating factors in depression: sex differences and similarities. *Journal of Abnormal Psychology*, **88**, 174–181.

Reich, J. & Thompson, W.D. (1985). Marital status of schizophrenic and alcoholic patients. *Journal of Nervous and Mental Disease*, **173**, 499–502.

Robins, L.N., Helzer, J.E., Weissman, H.M., Orvaschel, H., Gruenberg, Z., Burke, J.O. & Regier, D.A. (1984). Lifetime pevalence of specific Psychiatric disorders in three communities. *Archives of General Psychiatry*, **41**, 949–958.

Romans-Clarkson, S.E., Walton, V.A., Herbison, G.P. & Mullen, P.E. (1988). Marriage, motherhood and psychiatric morbidity in New Zealand. *Psychological Medicine*, **18**, 983–990.

Rosenfarb, I.S., Goldstein, M.J., Mintz, J. & Neuchterlein, K.H. (1995). Expressed emotion and subclinical psychopathology observable within the transactions between schizophrenic patients and their family members. *Journal of Abnormal Psychology*, **104**, 259–267.

Rousanville, B.J., Weissman, M.M., Prusoff, B.A. & Herceg-Baron, R.L. (1979). Marital disputes and treatment outcome in depressed women. *Comprehensive Psychiatry*, **20**, 483–490.

Schmaling, K.B. & Jacobson, N.S. (1990). Marital interaction and depression. *Journal of Abnormal Psychology*, **99**, 229–236.

Seligman, M.E.P. (1975). *Helplessness: On Depression, Development and Death*. San Francisco: Freeman.

Sisson, R.W. & Azrin, N.H. (1986). Family member involvement to initiate and promise treatment of problem drinkers. *Journal of Behavior Therapy and Experimental Psychiatry*, **17**, 15–21.

Smith, C.A. & Wallston, K.A. (1992). Adaptation in patients with chronic rheumatoid arthritis: application of a general model. *Health Psychology*, **11**, 151–162.

Smolen, R.C., Spiegal, D.A. & Martin, C.J. (1986). Patterns of marital interaction associated with marital dissatisfaction and depression. *Journal of Behaviour Therapy and Experimental Psychiatry*, **17**, 261–266.

Spanier, G.B. (1976). Measuring dyadic adjustment; new scales for assessing the quality of marriage and similar dyads. *Journal of Marriage and the Family*, **38**, 15–28.

Stansfield, S.A., Gallacher, J.E.J., Sharp, D.S. & Yarnell, J.W.J. (1991). Social factors and minor psychiatric disorder in middle-aged men: a validation study and a population survey. *Psychological Medicine*, **21**, 157–167.

Steinglass, P. (1976). Experimenting with family treatment approaches to alcoholism, 1950–1975. *Family Process*, **15**, 97–123.

Steinglass, P. (1980). A life history model of the alcoholic family. *Family Process*, **19**, 333–354.

Stirling, J., Tantam, D., Thomas, P., Newby, D., Montague, L., Ring, N. & Rowe, S. (1993). Expressed emotion and schizophrenia: the ontogeny of EE during an 18 month follow-up. *Psychological Medicine*, **23**, 771–778.

Strachan, A.M., Feingold, A., Goldstein, M.J., Miklowitz, D.J. & Neuchterlein, K. (1989). Is expressed emotion and index of a transactional process? 2. Patients' coping style. *Family Process*, **22**, 169–182.

Strauss, M.A. (1979). Measuring intrafamily conflict and violence: the conflict tactics scale. *Journal of Marriage and the Family*, **41**, 75–78.

Thomas, E.J. & Ager, R.D. (1993). Unilateral family therapy with spouses of uncooperative alcohol drinkers. In T.J. O'Farrell (ed.), *Treating Alcohol Problems: Marital and Family Interventions* (pp. 3–33). New York: Guilford.

Tienari, P., Sorri, A., Lahti, I., Naarala, M., Wahlberg, K., Moring, J. & Wynne, L.C. (1987). Genetic and psychosocial factors in schizophrenia: the Finnish adoptive family study. *Schizophrenia Bulletin*, **13**, 477–484.

Vannicelli, M., Gingerich, S. & Ryback, R. (1983). Family problems related to the treatment and outcome of alcoholic patients. *British Journal of Addiction*, **78**, 193–204.

Waring, E.M., Patton, D., Neron, C.A. & Linker, W. (1986). Types of marital intimacy and prevalence of emotional illness. *Canadian Journal of Psychiatry*, **31**, 720–725.

Weiss, R.L. & Aved, B.M. (1978). Marital satisfaction and depression as predictors of physical health status. *Journal of Consulting and Clinical Psychology*, **46**, 1379–1384.

Weiss, R.L. & Cerreto, M.S. (1980). The Marital Status Inventory: development of a measure of dissolution potential. *American Journal of Family Therapy*, **8**, 80–85.

Weiss, R.L. & Halford, W.K. (1995). Managing couples therapy. In V. Van Hasselt & M. Hersen (eds), *Sourcebook of Psychological Treatment Manuals for Adult Disorders*. New York: Plenum.

Weiss, R.L. & Heyman, R. (1990). Marital distress and therapy. In A.S. Bellack, M. Hersen & A. Kazdin (eds), *International Handbook of Behavior Modification*, 2nd edn (pp. 475–502). New York: Plenum.

Weissman, M.M. (1990). Epidemiology of panic disorder and agoraphobia. *Psychiatric Medicine*, **8**, 3–13.

Weissman, M.M. (1987). Advances in psychiatric epidemiology: rates and risk for major depression. *American Journal of Public Health*, **77**, 445–451.

Weissman, M.M. & Klerman, G.L. (1987). Sex differences and the epidemiology of depression. *Archives of General Psychiatry*, **135**, 459–462.

Wiseman, J. (1981). Sober comportment: patterns and perspectives on alcohol addiction. *Journal of Studies on Alcohol*, **42**, 106–126.

Zastowny, T.R., Lehman, A.F., Cole, R.C. & Kane, C. (1992). Family management of schizophrenia: a comparison of behavioural and supportive family treatment. *Psychiatric Quarterly*, **63**, 159–186.

Zweben, A. (1986). Problem drinking and marital adjustment. *Journal of Studies on Alcohol*, **47**, 167–172.

Chapter 14

Physical Health and Relationships

Karen B. Schmaling* and Tamara G. Sher**
Department of Psychiatry and Behavioral Sciences,
*University of Washington Medical School, Seattle, USA;
and ** Department of Psychology,
Illinois Institute of Technology, Chicago, IL, USA

A CLINICAL SCENARIO: KIM AND JAMIE

Kim and Jamie had been together for 10 years and have had a committed relationship for the last 7 years. Kim is 45 and Jamie is 51. They have no children and had never had any plans to include children in their family. They each have high profile jobs. Kim is a buyer for a large department store. Jamie is a university professor. Kim travels often and has long hours when in town, often leaving the house before dawn and not returning until late that evening. Jamie also works nights but has a more flexible schedule, preferring to sleep late and work later into the night as a result. Kim and Jamie value their time together because it is so hard to come by. They like to travel, visit with friends, and take advantage of the many cultural opportunities in their community. Their relationship is strong and egalitarian in terms of household responsibilities.

About 1 year ago, Kim was in a car accident. At the time of the accident, both Kim and the doctors who examined Kim following the accident described the injuries as mild (cuts and bruises) and had no reason to believe that there would be any lasting effects. However, about 1 month following the accident, Kim began complaining of fatigue, muscle soreness, headaches and back pain. The pain was intermittent in terms of intensity, ranging from mild to severe enough to keep Kim home from work and in bed for a few days at a time. Though both Kim and Jamie believed that Kim had a flu that was difficult to shake due to Kim's

Clinical Handbook of Marriage and Couples Interventions. Edited by W. Kim Halford and Howard J. Markman.
© 1997 John Wiley & Sons Ltd.

long hours and lack of attention to diet and exercise, they soon sought medical attention when the symptoms did not change after a month.

Doctor after doctor examined Kim and ran many diagnostic tests, including orthopedic, neurologic and psychiatric work-ups. All medical tests came back negative. The psychiatric evaluation labeled Kim as having a tendency for somatic complaints but otherwise normal. By this time, Kim was missing more and more work and was in danger of losing the job that had been so important in the past. Kim and Jamie worried about the effects of this job loss on their finances, Kim's self-esteem and their home. Kim's symptoms were not improving and the relationship between Kim and Jamie was worsening. They disagreed about which doctors to consult next, how to allocate their diminishing savings, and what to do in their free time. Kim seemed only to want to sleep, some days never getting dressed. Although Kim had been primarily responsible for the day-to-day maintenance of their home, lately, Jamie was picking up the slack, combining Kim's original chores with those that had always been Jamie's responsibility. They went out seldom, if ever, due to their inability to make plans because they could not know in advance if Kim would be "up" for socializing or leaving the house. They had not had sex since the symptoms began. Jamie did not want to initiate sexual activity because of the fear of rebuff. Kim did not have much of a sexual drive currently but would have liked the closeness of sexual contact. Kim did not initiate sex due to a fear that Jamie would then minimize Kim's physical symptoms—i.e. Kim was well enough for sex but not for household tasks.

Friends were at first very supportive of both Kim and Jamie. However, the longer the symptoms lasted, the less offers of help were made. After repeatedly having to cancel plans, Kim and Jamie stopped making them. Friends said that they understood but began calling the house less until the 'phone rarely rang. Jamie was finding it difficult to concentrate at work. Colleagues, although informed of the situation, became increasingly irritated at the time that Jamie was having to spend at home and the lack of responsiveness that was shown for departmental obligations.

As the symptoms persisted, the relationship became increasingly strained. Kim eventually was referred to a psychologist by the orthopedist. Although Kim first sought individual therapy, couples therapy was recommended following the first visit.

We will return to Kim and Jamie later in this chapter.

THE STATUS OF RESEARCH ON PHYSICAL HEALTH AND RELATIONSHIPS

Despite a lengthy history of productive research in relationship assessment and the treatment of relationship dissatisfaction (reviewed in other chapters in this volume), the role in significant relationships of physically ill persons has received little attention. For example, it is known that physical illness exerts stress upon intimate relationships and that relationship distress in turn has negative effects on many illness processes. What is surprising is that more research into the exact mechanisms behind these associations has not been conducted. Similarly, based on our clinical experience in medical settings, the inclusion of an intimate partner in the treatment plan of a medical patient is underutilized and rarely suggested in the patient's medical record.

In this chapter we will examine the association between physical illness and relationships. This review utilizes a biopsychosocial model of illness, with a specific emphasis on the intimate social environment of the patient. The term biopsychosocial implies that in order to understand illness and its treatment, we must understand the biological, psychological and social factors which are integrally involved in the health and disease process. This chapter will focus on more intimate social relationships and how they both impact and are impacted by illness. Where possible we will present relevant research findings and discuss the implications of these findings for the clinician working with medical patients and their partners. At other times, we present issues of relevance for this population and make conjectures based on our clinical experience as psychologists working in hospital settings.

Within the literature on couples and medical problems, three categories of relationship variables have been studied with regard to how they might impact upon illness or the disease process (Burman & Margolin, 1992): *relationship status* (e.g. married or single); *relationship quality* (e.g. degree of relationship satisfaction vs. distress); and *specific relationship behaviors* (e.g. hostile affect, critical verbalizations). Throughout this chapter, we will discuss how these relationship variables might affect the physical status of a partner both globally, in terms of overall health, and specifically, in terms of discrete diseases.

We propose a conceptual framework for understanding how dissatisfied intimate relationships and negative interpersonal behavior contribute to illhealth. The proposed model (Figure 14.1) is circular, suggesting that a person may enter the cycle at any point and that the remaining factors in the model will contribute to illness. (Similarly, the model implies that successful treatment of any of the components of the model will break the cycle.) The presence of relationship dissatisfaction or negative relationship behaviors is a common premorbid factor. The emotional reactions to relationship dissatisfaction create physiological changes (e.g. in autonomic tone, immune function) that may contribute to illness vulnerability, and in turn, worsening functional status and morbidity. Dysfunctional responses to the illness may include poor coping, poor compliance, or negative emotional reactions to the illness by the patient, while the patient's partner may engage in solicitous or other reinforcing responses to the patient's illness behavior, which in turn perpetuate relationship distress. Evidence to support this model follows.

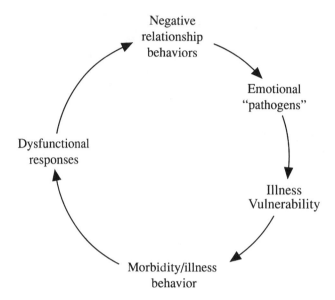

Figure 14.1 Cyclical relationship between negative interpersonal behavior and ill-health

HOW THE RELATIONSHIP AFFECTS PHYSICAL HEALTH

Relationship Status

In terms of simple marital status, irrespective of relationship quality, being un-married is a risk factor for physical illness, especially for men (Verbrugge, 1979; House, Robbins & Metzner, 1982; Reis et al., 1985). Epidemiological studies have demonstrated clear differences between married and unmarried people in mental and physical health, whereby those who are divorced or separated have poorer mental and physical health than comparable married, widowed or single adults (for a review, see Kiecolt-Glaser et al., 1988).

Relationship Satisfaction

Intuitively, since not all relationships are equally happy or supportive, it would be predicted that relationships do not buffer equally against physical illness. Yet some research has not supported this prediction (Haynes, Feinleib & Kannel 1980), and few studies have looked at relationship satisfaction (Burman & Margolin, 1992). More satisfied relationships appear to be associated with better immune function and less depression (reviewed below and in other chapters in this volume)—which would suggest that global relationship satisfaction is a moderating variable at best. More information is needed about the specific relationship behaviors that are associated with changes in the relevant illness-related outcome (e.g. physiology, symptom severity, medication use, etc.).

HOW PHYSICAL HEALTH AFFECTS RELATIONSHIPS

There are more than 31.5 million people in the USA who have chronic health conditions (U.S. Bureau of Census, 1993). The impact of these conditions on labor force participation, family responsibilities and personal well-being can only be conjectured. This section will focus on the relationship between chronic illness and the marital relationship.

Although the literature on the effects of physical illness upon relationships is not extensive, there are a number of consistent findings. First, it has been noted and demonstrated repeatedly that the onset of chronic illness such as coronary heart disease, cancer, rheumatoid arthritis and diabetes is often accompanied by adverse psychological reactions in both patients and spouses (Croog & Fitzgerald, 1978; Hegelson, 1993; Stern & Pascale, 1979; Thompson & Cordle, 1988). Interestingly, it has also been noted that the specific mechanisms which cause this distress have not been identified (Burman & Margolin, 1992; Helgeson, 1993). Additionally, previous investigations have determined that there are a number of very specific areas of the family relationship which are affected by a chronic illness. These include work, family roles and relationships, and life satisfaction (Hafstrom & Schram, 1984). Each of these has implications for the partner and the relationship.

Influence on Work

Chronic illness affects many aspects of a person's working life. These include income, labor force participation and household production activities (Hafstrom & Schram, 1984). Previous investigations have found that annual income was negatively related to health status, according to male respondents (Davis, 1972; Luft, 1975). Additionally, household responsibilities are affected by a chronic illness by either total household output or substitutions in responsibilities (Hafstrom & Schram, 1984). Empirical findings suggest that when a husband's health is poor, his housework time does not change (Parsons, 1979). However, when a wife's health is poor, she spends about $6^{1}/_{2}$ *more* hours on housework per week than do other wives (Hafstrom & Schram, 1984). This latter finding is explained in one of two ways: either these women spend more time on housework because they have more time to spend on it due to decreased labor force participation; or they spend more time because it takes them longer to do it than non-chronically ill women. Interestingly, with the exception of the amount of time the wife and husband spend together, wives with chronically ill husbands were least satisfied with husband's help around the house, although the husband's time involvement was no different from that of other husbands (Hafstrom & Schram, 1984). These changes, however, are often short-lived with the greatest shift occurring within the first 3 months of the onset of the illness (Helgeson, 1993).

Influence on Family Roles

When either a husband or wife has a chronic illness, their own and their spouse's family roles may be altered (Schulz & Tomkins, 1990). Following a heart attack, men have been shown to become more dependent upon their wives and this dependence has been linked to greater marital satisfaction for the patients and less marital satisfaction for the spouses (Michela, 1986). It has been argued that spouses may experience the patient's dependence as a burden, and feelings of burden have been shown to negatively affect the adjustment of caregiving (Coyne et al., 1987). Helgeson (1993) found that both cross-sectionally and prospectively, the most robust predictor of adjustment for patients and spouses was a responsibility shift. More specifically, she found that changes in household responsibilities are beneficial to patients during the initial stage of recovery but detrimental to patients during the later recovery stages. For the spouse, however, such changes were consistently related to poor adjustment, consistent with other research (e.g. Coyne & Smith, 1991).

Influence on the Marital Relationship

A chronic illness in one spouse affects not only the other spouse, but the marital relationship in general. Researchers have studied the effects of illness on both patients' and spouses' marital quality and have found both increases (e.g. Mayou, Foster & Williamson, 1978a,b), decreases (e.g. Williamson & Freer, 1986) and no change (Brown, Rawlinson & Hardin, 1982) in marital satisfaction subsequent to health problems. These inconsistencies have been explained as a function of type of illness as well as specific characteristics within an illness category, such as the intensity, severity or chronicity of the illness or the time since illness onset (Burman & Margolin, 1992).

Additionally, many authors have noted a general association between health problems and marital dissatisfaction (e.g. Burman & Margolin, 1992; Hafstrom & Schram, 1984; Renne, 1970; Siegel, 1986). Other investigations have compared distressed and non-distressed couples after the onset of health problems in order to assess factors that may relate to marital satisfaction, such as depression, stress and degree of impairment. Not surprisingly, couples who indicate higher levels of relationship dissatisfaction also express more stress (e.g. Croog & Fitzgerald, 1978). In these studies, degree of functional impairment is not necessarily related to relationship satisfaction (Brown, Rawlinson & Harding 1982; Williamson & Freer, 1986). However, Ahern, Adams & Follick (1985) found that self-reported impairment in social interactions predicted marital maladjustment, suggesting that type of functional impairment may be relevant (Burman & Margolin, 1992).

The interaction between depression, illness and marital quality is also unclear. Bouras, Vanger & Bridges (1986), in comparing rheumatoid arthritis patients, heart disease patients and depressed patients and spouses, found that marital dissatisfaction was greatest for depressed patients and their spouses and least for cardiac patients and spouses. They concluded that depression has a much greater impact upon marital life than does chronic physical illness, and that the more serious a physical illness (e.g. cardiac disease), the more considerate spouses may be with each other. However, among patients with chronic pain, Mohamed, Weisz & Waring (1978) found that depressed patients had higher marital satisfaction than patients who suffered from both pain and depression.

As Burman & Margolin (1992) conclude, although health problems presumably have an impact upon relationship quality, research has not identified consistent patterns. Future research is needed to address the association between health and relationship quality, as well as what differentiates couples with good postmorbid adjustment from those with poor postmorbid adjustment.

POSSIBLE CO-VARIATES OF THE ASSOCIATION BETWEEN PHYSICAL HEALTH AND RELATIONSHIPS

Children

The addition of children into a couple's life and the transition to parenthood have been found to be associated with decreases in relationship satisfaction (Cowan & Cowan, 1988), although the mechanism for this effect is unclear. Larger families use health services less (Andersen & Kasper, 1973). Rates of physical illness increase among working mothers as the number of children in the family increase (Hare & Shaw, 1965). Illnesses could increase among mothers secondary to: (a) increased exposure to pathogens via the children (e.g. if the child is in daycare); (b) the stress of increased responsibilities and burdens, which could result in; (c) poorer self-care behaviors or compliance.

Depression

Physical health and depression co-vary, in part because of the somatic nature of some depressive symptoms. Depression and marital status also co-vary. Weiss & Aved (1978) examined the relative predictive value of relationship satisfaction or depression on physical health separately for husbands and wives. A gender difference was found: relationship satisfaction was the best predictor of health status among the men, whereas depression was the best predictor of health status among women. However, relationship satisfaction accounted for an additional unique and significant portion of the variance in women's health status. The relative contributions of depression and relationship dissatisfaction to physical illness must be examined further.

HOW SIGNIFICANT RELATIONSHIPS AFFECT HEALTH BEHAVIORS

It has long been acknowledged that an individual patient's approach to such issues as the decision to seek medical care, the type of care that is sought, and compliance or non-compliance with treatment is influenced by individual (age, gender, educational level, etc.) and many non-individual factors (Mechanic, 1968). Non-individual factors that influence the process of medical care include socialization, cultural background, and modeling history. While a good deal of research has been done on families' reactions to children's illnesses, little research has been done on the effects of significant others on adult patients, which are of primary interest to this volume.

Compliance

Interventions involving self-care probably constitute the majority of medical treatment, compared to those in which the physician is the direct agent of change (e.g. surgical procedures). Examples of self-treatment interventions include taking medications and other behaviors, such as smoking cessation. Compliance is defined as the extent to which the patient's behavior is consistent with medical advice. Non-compliance with self-treatment is an enormous problem, especially for conditions that are not readily "felt" by the patient, such as hypertension, or for which the symptoms or other painful consequences are not immediate, e.g. disabling chronic obstructive pulmonary disease typically develops after decades of heavy cigarette smoking. For example, it has been estimated that only 16% of antihypertensive patients are adequately compliant with their medications within a year of diagnosis (NHLBI Working Group, 1982).

Past research has found high concordance between intimate partners in health-care and health-related behaviors such as physician visits, diet and compliance with prescribed treatments (see Becker, 1989, for a review). Similarly, the attitudes and expectations of the patient's partner have been found repeatedly to be powerful predictors of patient behavior and compliance or non-compliance. The concordance between partners in various aspects of health behavior could occur through a variety of mechanisms, including assortative mating among people with similar levels of interest in health, or reciprocal reinforcement for healthy behaviors. For example, the hypertensive man whose wife values a low-salt diet and regular exercise for herself, and expresses interest in his health and pleasure at lower blood pressure readings, is more likely to comply successfully with treatment recommendations than one whose wife complains that food is tasteless without more salt, that exercise takes away time that should be spent otherwise, and nags.

Partner-involved interventions to increase compliance with medical treatments have been studied in areas such as obesity and hypertension. In general, these studies have indicated that passive participation by patients' families (e.g. in an education program) does not promote patient behavior change; indeed, patient compliance appears to be inhibited by behaviors such as nagging and complaining by significant others. However, active participation by intimate others involving *positive* behaviors, e.g. expressing interest and positively reinforcing compliant behavior and progress, have been associated with treatment adherence and health improvement. These beneficial effects may become increasingly evident over time. Some outcome studies have found the superior effects of positive reinforcement by the partner to become evident only after several years' follow-up (e.g. Morisky et al., 1983).

Gruzd, Shear & Rodney (1986) examined predictors of failure to show up for appointments at a family medicine clinic. Marital status, i.e. being unmarried, was one of six significant predictors of appointment-keeping behavior. The other predictors were type of care, chronic illness, linguistic capability, mode of payment, and patient–physician sex differences. However, other studies have found no relationship between marital status and compliance (Linn, Linn & Stein, 1982).

Utilization of Health Care Services and Medical Decision-Making

Consultation with a professional health-care provider is often a distal step in a chain of responses to a perceived physical problem. The precursors of health-care seeking include perceptual processes; observation of the symptoms, and appraisal of various dimensions (e.g. threat, seriousness, control-ability). Most individuals treat themselves or follow the advice of significant others (or friends, co-workers, etc.) before consulting a medical doctor. In these early stages, it seems reasonable to imagine that significant others' responses may influence the patient strongly, and be associated with revised perceptions or behavior. The effects of significant others on health care behavior before the patient comes to the attention of a medical professional would be an important area for future research.

Few examples of the effects of marital status on medical decision-making exist. Among 206 breast cancer patients, 110 (53%) had the option of mastectomy or conservation (lumpectomy and radiation treatment). Marital satisfaction was not related to the treatment decision; however, women who elected for mastectomy reported more sexual problems and more emotional problems (depression, anxiety, etc.) than did those who chose conservation (Wolberg et al., 1987).

Adjustment and Coping

Intimate relationships can be a source of stress and vulnerability or a source of support, with buffering effects. Coping is defined as the collective set of behaviors in a person's repertoire that may be used in response to distress (physical or emotional). Coping styles include: emotion-focused, aimed at managing the distress; problem-focused, intended to reduce the stress causing the distress; and relationship-focused, with the goal of maintaining the integrity of the relationship above an individual's needs (Lazarus & Folkman, 1984; Coyne & Smith, 1991). Successful coping involves responding flexibly to varying problems and demands. A chronic health problem may require keeping active and distracted with positive self-statements or "cheerleading". An acute health problem may be best dealt with by actively seeking medical help and the use of acute distraction techniques (e.g. hypnosis).

One can easily imagine how a significant other could support or impede a patient's coping attempts; however, little research on this topic exists (Revenson, 1994). What constitutes support is in the eye of the beholder; well-intended partner behavior may impact negatively on the patient, especially among couples in distressed relationships (e.g. Fincham, Beach & Nelson, 1987).

The literature on non-intimate supportive relationships informs us regarding the striking impact that social support can have on health and illness. For example, Spiegel et al. (1989) found that patients with metastatic breast cancer who participated in supportive weekly group therapy reduced fatigue, anxiety and depression and, over a 10-year follow-up, survived twice as long as control group patients. These dramatic results suggest that social support is a potent method to reduce stress, improve mood, maintain activity levels, and perhaps boost immune system function, thereby affecting the disease process.

Treatments focused on improving coping may be particularly suited for chronic, variable or progressive conditions for which cure-seeking is unrealistic or unwarranted; rather, a flexible and adaptive approach is needed.

We wish to note that the majority of research on relationships in general, and certainly on relationships and health in particular, has utilized heterosexual couples. However, acquired immune deficiency syndrome (AIDS) has struck the gay community disproportionately in the USA. Improved coping could benefit AIDS sufferers by averting depression and improving physiological responding, which in turn are associated with enhanced immune function. Gay men are suffering multiple bereavements, to which there are cumulative negative emotional effects (Martin, 1988). Bereavements adversely affect the immune system (Schleifer et al., 1983), and the death of a partner has long been considered to be a particularly potent stressor. Conversely, more satisfaction with social support is associated with less depression among HIV-seropositive men (Hays, Turner & Coates, 1992), and depression, in turn, predicts lower CD4 counts and more AIDS-related symptoms (Burack et al., 1993; Lyketsos et al., 1993).

Health Promotion Behaviors

Little research has been done on the role of intimate partners in patients' health promotion behaviors such as exercise, limited use of caffeine and alcohol, cigarette and drug abstinence, safe sex, and good diet and sleep hygiene. As noted above in the section on Compliance, lifestyle and risk factor concordance between spouses has been found for specific behaviors, such as smoking (Venters et al., 1984), and more general risk factors, such as stress level (Haynes, Eaker & Feinleib, 1983). Also, partners follow each other in death sooner than is statistically expected (Parkes, Benjamin & Fitzgerald, 1969; Jones & Fletcher, 1992).

The treatment literature has shown that behavior change may be more successful when a partner is involved (cf. Mermelstein, Lichtenstein & McIntyre, 1983). The converse also applies: marital dissatisfaction and separation have been found to be associated with poor coping and increases in sickness-related absences from work, smoking and alcohol consumption (Hallberg & Mattsson, 1992).

THE PHYSIOLOGY OF MARITAL INTERACTION

There has been a significant body of literature which underscores the relationship between interpersonal variables and illness processes. Investigators have become interested not only in the relationship of marital status and health, but also that of marital quality and health and the specific physiological relationship between them. The importance of this type of study is that it calls into question the long-held belief that marital *status* is a more critical variable than marital *quality* in relation to health outcomes. That is, new evidence suggests that the simple presence of a spouse is not necessarily protective against disease; a troubled intimate relationship is itself a source of stress, while simultaneously limiting the partner's ability to seek support in other relationships (Coyne & DeLongis, 1986). For example, Renne (1970) found that unhappily married individuals reported poorer physical health than either happily married or divorced people of the same race, sex and age.

Recent physiological data provide evidence of multiple pathways through which marital relationships may influence health. For example, Kiecolt-Glaser et al. (1988) note that chronically abrasive marital relationships may have autonomic correlates, providing evidence of one mechanism through which health might be affected. Supporting this notion, Levenson & Gottman (1983, 1985) found that greater autonomic arousal among married couples was strongly predictive of a decline in marital satisfaction 3 years later. Additionally, they found that greater declines in marital satisfaction were strongly correlated with poorer health ratings at follow-up.

The relationship between immune functioning and marital quality has also been studied, based upon the notion that the link between personal relationships and immune function is one of the most robust findings in psychoneuro-immunology (Kiecolt-Glaser & Glaser, 1992). In one study of marital discord and immunity, Kiecolt-Glaser et al. (1988) obtained self-report data and blood samples from separated or divorced men and a matched sample of married men. They found that separated/divorced men were more subjectively distressed, lonelier and reported significantly more recent illness than did married men. Again, it should be noted that these men are different from traditionally grouped "single" men in that they, by definition, have experienced marital stress and strife. The divorced/separated men also had significantly poorer values on two functional indices of immunity but did not differ from married men on quantitative indices of immunity. Additionally, poorer relationship quality in the married group was significantly related to greater depression and global distress, greater loneliness, poorer response on one functional immunologic assay, and lower quantitative immunologic indices.

This same group of researchers has also demonstrated significant and deleterious endocrine system changes associated with hostile and negative behavior (Malarkey et al., 1994) despite using a sample of happily married newlyweds. This study adds to the profusion of negative health effects of dysfunctional intimate interactions, and underscores the need to examine the effects of specific interpersonal behaviors to identify potential relationship "pathogens".

Hypertension is another area of investigation between interpersonal variables and physical health. Blood pressure (BP) levels are known to vary considerably over the course of 24 hours; environmental stimuli can contribute to these changes (Ewart, Burnett & Taylor, 1983). As a result, investigators have examined the relationship between marital interactions and BP directly. Ewart et al. (1991) suggested that chronically distressed marital relationships might contribute to hypertension and atherogenesis. They found that a 10-minute marital problem-solving task produced clinically significant increases in BP among patients with essential hypertension. These BP increases were specifically associated with hostile marital interactions: neither supportive nor neutral behaviors produced significant changes. Again, however, these data do not answer the question of how social events alter BP.

A consistent and significant relationship between physiological processes and relationship behaviors has been found. Although the exact mechanisms of effect are still unidentified, researchers are closer to understanding the sensitivity of immunologic, endocrinologic and cardiovascular parameters to the social and hence marital environment. Clearly more research is needed in this very promising area of psychoneuroimmunology if we are to understand the balance between our health and our social lives.

THE ASSOCIATION BETWEEN PHYSICAL HEALTH AND RELATIONSHIPS FOR SPECIFIC DISEASE CLASSES

With the increasing understanding of the role that relationships play in the course of physical diseases and the impact of diseases upon relationship satisfaction, investigators are beginning to look at relationship variables in order to better understand specific physical conditions. Table 14.1 reviews a number of studies

Illness/disease class	Partner effects on morbidity	Couples' treatment and morbidity	Family relationships and morbidity	Effects of illness on relationships	Social support and morbidity
Chronic pain	Roy, 1985; Kerns et al., 1990, 1991; Romano et al., 1992	Moore & Chaney, 1985; Langelier & Gallegher, 1989; Saarijarvi et al., 1990; Saarijarvi, 1991	Shanfield, et al., 1979; Maruta et al., 1981; Hafstrom & Schram, 1984; Turk & Scholz, Flor, 1987	Flor, Turk & Scholz, 1987	
Cancer			Lichtman, Wood & Tayior, 1982; Fuller & Swenson, 1992; Weisman & Worden, 1977; Nayeri, Pitaro & Feldman, 1992	Baider & De-Nour, 1984, 1988; Baron et al., 1990	Dunkel-Schetter & Wortman, 1982; Chekryn, 1984; Gotay, 1984
Cardiac disease		Stern & Pascale, 1979; Radley & Green, 1986; Bar-On & Dreman, 1987; Waltz et al., 1988	Croog & Levine, 1977; Walz, 1986	Croog & Levine, 1977; Coyne & Smith, 1991; Fiske, Coyne & Smith, 1991	
Pulmonary and allergic disorders	Schmaling et al., 1996		Hermanns et al., 1989; Lane & Hobfoll, 1992; Ehlers et al., 1994		
Renal, endocrine and GI disorders	Reiss, Gonzales & Kramer, 1986	Steidl et al., 1980	Campbell, 1986; Chowanec & Binik, 1989	Steimer-Krause, Krause & Wagner, 1990	
Musculo skeletal and neurological disorders	Ward & Leigh, 1993		Wineman et al., 1993	Manne & Zautra, 1989, 1990	

which have examined relationship factors with regard to a specific disease. Because each study uses different outcome and predictor criteria, the Table is organized by type of illness and how it relates to the interpersonal environment. The Table is meant as a resource for the interested reader to pursue the research findings in more detail, as a generalized review of this area is beyond the scope of the current chapter. In Table 14.1, the first column of references (i.e. "Partner effects on morbidity") are studies that examined the effects of a close relationship on illness process or outcome. Research that addresses specific partner behaviors that increase or decrease pain reports or pain behavior by the patient are particularly numerous. The second column lists articles regarding the effects of couples-involved treatment on illness process and outcome. Studies that have examined the association between family relationships (i.e. those of the patient with non-spousal family members) and illness-related morbidity comprise the third column. Fourth, limited attempts have been made to examine how illness affects the patients' partners. Finally, some studies did not specifically examine intimate relationships but rather the more broadly defined variable of social support and its relationship with morbidity are included.

A review of the studies that utilized direct behavioral observation of patient–partner interactions is especially provocative. Across illnesses, negative interactions of patients with their significant other appear to be risk factors for poorer physical health. These data remind us of previous work that has found that critical or overinvolved significant others are predictive of relapse of emotional illnesses, including depressive disorders (Hooley, Orley & Teasdale, 1986) and schizophrenia (Vaughn et al., 1984). There is little evidence for illness-specific patterns of interaction, although the data have typically not been presented with this goal in mind. The work of Steimer-Krause, Krause & Wagner (1990) was a notable exception. The mechanism through which these negative interactions are associated with ill-health is unknown. Relationship stress may exert a direct deleterious effect on physical health; or the effect may be indirect, such as via impairment of the patient's ability to care for him/herself optimally, e.g. to be upset and forget to take medications, and so forth.

SUMMARY, TREATMENT IMPLICATIONS AND FUTURE DIRECTIONS

It is an exciting time to be investigating the area of physical health and intimate relationships. This "new partnership" presents us with much optimism regarding how fruitful an area it may be for our understanding of illness onset, course and recovery processes. It is our hope that other researchers will expand our understanding of the association between relationships and health and that clinicians can benefit from both current and future research findings. Additionally, other active areas of investigation, such as psychoneuroimmunology, are likely to augment the investigation of physical health and relationships a great deal.

At this time, our review suggests the following guidelines for potential interventions for couples where one person is ill: (a) there is a reciprocal relationship between health and relationship variables and improvement in one is likely to effect the other; (b) clinicians can benefit from the addition of a partner into a treatment plan, if not the treatment itself; (c) in order for treatments to be maximally effective, the needs of the partner must also be considered; and (d) psychological interventions can be geared to help couples cope with the effects of an illness on themselves, each other, and the relationship in general. To our knowledge, no assessment instruments exist that are meant for couples where one person is ill that are generally applicable to a variety of illnesses. We have used assessment procedures that have been well validated on distressed and non-distressed couples (see chapter by Floyd, Haynes & Kelly, this volume) and interpreted the results cautiously. For example, if both members of a couple rate high levels of disagreement in the area of recreational activities, it would be important to explore whether the disagreement is attributable to activity limitations that are secondary to the illness vs. other factors, such as a longstanding lack of shared interests. A somewhat better prognosis is probably associated with the former. A discussion of how areas of relationship strength and weakness have changed as a function of illness onset, worsening or improvement can also help elucidate the areas of relationship stress that appear to be most relevant to the illness. Partner-involved treatment is likely to be indicated for the majority of couples where one person is ill. The goal of the assessment process is to determine whether a couple has a satisfying or distressed relationship. In the former case therapy can focus on enhancing the couple's skills and bolstering ways in which the partner can support the patient in caring for him/herself; in the latter case, the therapist must first improve the couple's functioning in the relationship if at all possible. Couples therapy may be contraindicated among severely disturbed couples (e.g. couples who are physically abusive); the therapist's initial task becomes the identification of other sources of support for the patient apart from the partner.

Cognitive–behavioral couples therapy (CBCT) for distressed couples in well studied (see chapter by Epstein, Baucom & Jaiuto, this volume) but has been little used for couples in which one person has a physical illness. But many standard CBCT techniques are likely to be helpful to such couples, including communication training and problem-solving. Behavioral family management (BFM: Falloon, Boyd & McGill, 1984) is another useful treatment model that may be applied to couples living with an illness. BFM, in conjunction with medication, decreases relapse rates in serious mental illnesses such as schizophrenia and bipolar disorder. The components of BFM overlap partially with CBCT, e.g. communication and problem-solving training. BFM also emphasizes psychoeducation. Both the patient and partner can benefit from conjoint discussions of the illness, treatment approaches, common difficulties with the illness and its treatments, and the role of stress in the illness and hence the need for stress management.

Kim and Jamie Revisited

The problems facing Kim and Jamie include Kim's chronic pain, inactivity and probable depression, and the change and disruption in sexual activity, roles and instrumental tasks for both of them. Jamie appears to have been engaging in a type of relationship-focused coping known as "protective buffering" (Coyne & Smith, 1991), i.e. trying to shield Kim from concerns and worries by taking over. Yet this strategy may not be effective over the long term because Jamie's good will and patience *are* likely to erode. Couple-based treatment was clearly indicated.

A comprehensive cognitive–behavioral treatment (CBT) program for chronic pain may be found in Turk, Meichenbaum & Genest (1983). This includes an emphasis on the role of the significant other in CBT treatment of chronic pain. The treatments of chronic pain, depression, and relationship distress all emphasize *activity*, as well as expanding coping repertoires. Increasing certain forms of activity protects the patient from further deconditioning and disability, involves mastery experiences that are antidepressing, and infuses positive shared experiences into a relationship. For example, directing Kim and Jamie to take short walks together may work towards accomplishing all three goals. Jamie and Kim would likely benefit from a frank discussion of the roles of reinforcement, and coaching each how to avoid inadvertent reinforcement of Kim's condition.

Communication and problem-solving techniques would be useful for Jamie and Kim's situation (Schmaling, Fruzzetti & Jacobson, 1989). Working on clear and direct expression of feelings and wishes may counteract, for example, Kim's concern that Jamie would misinterpret Kim's desire for sexual activity. Furthermore, renegotiation of "who does what" and other goals through problem-solving discussions would be useful for both to feel that they can function again as an effective couple. Finally, Jamie and Kim would benefit from an emphasis in their treatment on renewing their sex life. It is likely that a series of exercises including increasing non-sexual affection and sexual enhancement techniques (e.g. Barbach, 1983) would suffice to help them be "back on track", since they had no previous history of sexual difficulties.

Future Directions

There is a great need for longitudinal studies of physical health and relationships to tease apart the relative contributions of each to the other, and to better determine the primacy of the effects of one on the other. Such effects may vary by disease. While the immediate consequences of certain interactional behaviors on physiology have been observed in the laboratory or clinic, there is a need to study these processes in the natural environment, and to examine longer-term effects of relationship variables and interactional behavior.

Some disease processes that seem intuitively to be influenced by the patient's relationship with a significant other have not been studied to our knowledge. Infertility without identifiable physical cause, and gastrointestinal problems such as pectic ulcer disease, are examples of illnesses that are likely influenced by stress and its effects (e.g. on the hypothalamic–pituitary–ovarian axis) but how they affect and are affected by significant relationships is unknown.

Predictors of responsiveness to relationship variables with physical sequelae need further study. Hostile interactions have been found to have more negative impact on immune function in women than men (Kiecolt-Glaser et al., 1993), but result in more rapid physiological (ANS) arousal and slower recovery for men than women (Gottman & Levenson, 1986). Men whose wives co-attended obesity classes lost *less* weight than those whose wives did not attend (Jeffrey et al., 1984). Conversely, supportive husband involvement has been found to be beneficial for wives' weight loss (Pearce, LeBow & Orchard, 1981). Further examination is needed of gender differences or other variables that may mediate a person's vulnerability to ill health in the face of relationship stress. We return again to the general literature on couple interaction to see how this could inform future research with couples in which one or both partners are physically ill. Past research has found that, among heterosexual couples, women are the emotional "barometers" for the relationship (Barry, 1970). In couples with one ill partner, perhaps the barometer will be the ill partner, regardless of gender, and perhaps different partner behaviors will be beneficial or deleterious with ill men vs. ill women. Compared with couples in satisfied relationships, couples with distressed relationships have been found to be *reactive*—that is, how a distressed couple evaluates the relationship at a given time is strongly affected by positive or negative events (e.g. an argument heralds the end of the relationship), whereas couples in satisfied relationships are not as affected by daily or hourly variation (Jacobson, Follette & MacDonald, 1982). Ill couples may be vulnerable like couples in unhappy relationships—will their health status be similarly reactive? Or will the status of the ill partner's health and/or his/her ability to cope with the illness be the barometer for the status of the relationship?

A better understanding is needed of the specific relationship factors that affect health vs. illness, and the mechanism by which relationship factors affect physical health. Until such specific associations and mechanisms are identified, or at least coherently hypothesized, relationship-based treatments will be of limited utility. Future research needs to determine which relationship variables have potent *negative* health consequences, and attempt to reverse those effects, e.g. by identifying which interaction patterns resulted in increased blood pressure and modifying those patterns (Ewart, Burnet & Taylor, 1983). But additionally, it is important to note which interaction patterns *enhance* health and wellness, and increase the presence of such behaviors in patients' lives. However, perhaps there are some couples for whom such interventions will be contraindicated. Or, perhaps some illnesses will not be affected by interpersonal factors (but we can't think of any!).

Systems theory researchers are noted for emphasizing the role of significant others in illness, and the examination of a unit of analysis that is larger than the patient (e.g. Minuchin, Rosman & Baker, 1978). It is unclear how much of the total variability in health can be accounted for by relationship-related issues. The accumulated evidence suggests that much benefit could come of further emphasis in this area. And while most of the research and treatment efforts have focused on traditional married couples, it should be noted that non-traditional significant others may play an influential role in a patient's health (extended family, co-workers, physician) and these relationships deserve similarly close examination.

REFERENCES

Ahern, D.K., Adams, A.E. & Follick, M.J. (1985). Emotional and marital disturbance in spouses of chronic low back pain patients. *Clinical Journal of Pain*, **1**, 69–74.

Andersen, R. & Kasper, J.D. (1973). The structural influence of family size on children's use of physician services. *Journal of Comparative Family Studies*, **4**, 116–129.

Baider, L. & De-Nour, A.K. (1988). Adjustment to cancer: who is the patient—the husband or the wife? *Israel Journal of Medical Sciences*, **24**, 631–636.

Baider, L. & De-Nour, A.K. (1984). Couples' reactions and adjustment to mastectomy *International Journal of Medical Psychiatry*, **14**, 265–276.

Barbach, L. (1983). *For Each Other*. New York: New American Library.

Bar-On, D. & Dreman, S. (1987). When spouses disagree: a predictor of cardiac rehabilitation. *Family Systems Medicine*, **5**, 228–237.

Baron, R.B., Cutrona, C.E., Hicklin, D., Russell, D.W. & Lubaroff, D.M. (1990). Social support and immune function among spouses of cancer patients. *Journal of Personality and Social Psychology*, **59**, 344–352.

Barry, W. (1970). Marriage research and conflict: an integrative review. *Psychological Bulletin*, **73**, 41–54.

Becker, L.A. (1989). Family systems and compliance with medical regimen. In C.N. Ramsey (ed.), *Family Systems in Medicine* (pp. 416–431). New York: Guilford.

Bouras, N., Vanger, P. & Bridges, P.K. (1986). Marital problems in chronically depressed and physically ill patients and their spouses. *Comprehensive Psychiatry*, **2**, 127–130.

Brown, J.S., Rawlinson, M.E. & Hardin, D.M. (1982). Family functioning and health status. *Journal of Family Issues*, **3**, 91–110.

Burack, J.H., Barrett, D.C., Stall, R.D., Chesney, M.A., Ekstrand, M.L. & Coates, T.J. (1993). Depressive symptoms and CD4 lymphocyte decline among HIV-infected men. *Journal of the American Medical Association*, **270**, 2568–2573.

Burman, B. & Margolin, G. (1992). Analysis of the association between marital relationships and health problems: an interactional perspective. *Psychological Bulletin*, **112**, 39–63.

Campbell, T.L. (1986). Families' impact on health: a critical review. *Family Systems Medicine*, **4**, 315–328.

Chekryn, J. (1984). Cancer recurrence: personal meaning, communication and marital adjustment. *Cancer Nursing*, **7**, 491–498.

Chowanec, G.D. & Binik, Y.K. (1989). End-stage renal disease and the marital dyad: an empirical investigation. *Social Science and Medicine*, **28**, 971–983.

Cowan, C.P. & Cowan, P.A. (1988). Who does what when partners become parents: implications for men, women, and marriage. *Marriage and Family Review*, **12**, 105–131.

Coyne, J.C. & DeLongis, A. (1986). Going beyond social support: the role of social relationships in adaptation. *Journal of Consulting and Clinical Psychology*, **54**, 454–460.

Coyne, J., Kessler, R., Tal, M., Turnbull, J., Wortman, C. & Greden, J. (1987). Living with a depressed person. *Journal of Consulting and Clinical Psychology*, **55**, 347–352.

Coyne, J.C. & Smith, D.A.F. (1991). Couples coping with a myocardial infarction: a contextual perspective on wives' distress. *Journal of Personality and Social Psyhology*, **61**, 404–412.

Croog, S.H. & Fitzgerald, E.F. (1978). Subjective stress and serious illness of a spouse: wives of heart patients. *Journal of Health and Social Behavior*, **19**, 166–178.

Croog, S.H. & Levine, S. (1977). *The Heart Patient Recovers: Social and Psychological Factors*. New York: Human Sciences.

Davis, J.M. (1972). Impact of health on earnings and labor market activity. *Monthly Labor Review*, **95**, 46–49.

Dunkel-Schetter, C.A. & Wortman, C.B. (1982). The interpersonal dynamics of cancer: problems in social relationships and their impact on the patient. In H.S. Friedman & M.R. DiMatteo (eds), *Interpersonal Issues in Health Care* (pp. 69–100). New York: Academic Press.

Ehlers, A., Osen, A., Wenninger, K. & Gieler, U. (1994). Atopic dermatitis and stress: possible role of negative communication with significant others. *International Journal of Behavioral Medicine*, **1**, 107–121.

Ewart, C.K., Burnet, K.F. & Taylor, C.B. (1983). Communication behaviors that affect blood pressure. *Behavior Modification*, **7**, 331–344.

Ewart, C.K., Taylor, C.B., Kraemer, H.C. et al. (1991). High blood pressure and marital discord: not being nasty matters more than being nice. *Health Psychology*, **10**, 155–163.

Falloon, I.R.H., Boyd, J.L. & McGill, C.W. (1984). *Family Care for Schizophrenia: a Problem-solving Approach to Mental Illness*. New York: Guilford.

Fincham, F.D., Beach S.R. & Nelson, G. (1987). Attribution processes in distressed and non-distressed couples: III. Causal and responsibility attributions for spouse behavior. *Cognitive Research & Therapy*, **11**, 71–86.

Flor, H., Turk, D.C. & Scholz, O.B. (1987). Impact of chronic pain on the spouse: marital, emotional and physical consequences. *Journal of Psychosomatic Research*, **31**, 63–71.

Fuller, S. & Swensen, C.H. (1992). Marital quality and quality of life among cancer patients and their spouses. *Journal of Psychosocial Oncology*, **10**, 41–56.

Gotay, C.C. (1984). The experience of cancer during early and advanced stages: the view of patients and their mates. *Social Science and Medicine*, **18**, 605–613.

Gottman, J.M. & Levenson, R.W. (1986). Assessing the role of emotion in marriage. *Behavioral Assessment*, **8**, 31–48.

Gruzd, D.C., Shear, C.L. & Rodney, W.M. (1986). Determinants of no-show appointment behavior: the utility of multivariate analysis. *Family Medicine*, **18**, 217–220.

Hafstrom, J.L. & Schram, V.R. (1984). Chronic illness in couples: selected characteristics, including wife's satisfaction with and perception of marital relationships. *Family Relations*, **33**, 195–203.

Hallberg, H. & Mattsson, B. (1992). Separation and distress—sickness absence and health screening in newly divorced middle-aged Swedish men. *Scandinavian Journal of Primary Health Care*, **10**, 91–97.

Hare, E.H. & Shaw, G.K. (1965). A study in family health: health in relation to family size. *British Journal of Psychiatry*, **111**, 461–466.

Haynes, S.G., Eaker, E. & Feinleib, M. (1983). Spouse behavior and coronary heart disease in men: prospective results from the Framingham Heart Study, Part I. *American Journal of Epidemiology*, **118**, 1–23.

Haynes, S.G., Feinleib, M. & Kannel, W.B. (1980). The relationship of psychosocial factors to coronary heart disease in the Framingham Heart Study: III. Eight-year incidence of coronary heart disease. *American Journal of Epidemiology*, **111**, 37–58.

Hays, R.B., Turner, H. & Coates, T.J. (1992). Social support, AIDS-related symptoms, and depression among gay men. *Journal of Consulting and Clinical Psychology*, **60**, 463–469.

Helgeson, V.S. (1993). The onset of chronic illness: its effect on the patient–spouse relationship. *Journal of Social and Clinical Psychology*, **12**, 406–428.

Hermanns, J., Florin, I., Dietrich, M., Lugt-Tappeser, H., Rieger, C. & Roth, W.T. (1989). Negative mother–child communication and bronchial asthma. *German Journal of Psychology*, **13**, 285–292.

Hooley, J.M., Orley, J. & Teasdale, J.D. (1986). Levels of expressed emotion and relapse in depressed patients. *British Journal of Psychiatry*, **148**, 642–647.

House, J.S., Robbins, C. & Metzner, H.L. (1982). The association of social relationships and activities with mortality: prospective evidence from the Tecumseh Community Health Study. *American Journal of Epidemiology*, **116**, 123–140.

Jacobson, N.S., Follette, W.C. & McDonald, D.W. (1982). Reactivity to positive and negative behavior in distressed and non-distressed married couples. *Journal of Consulting and Clinical Psychology*, **50**, 706–714.

Jeffrey, R.W., Bjornson-Benson, W.M., Rosenthal, B.S., Lindquist, R.A., Kurth, C.L. & Johnson, S.L. (1984). Correlates of weight loss and its maintenance over two years of follow-up among middle-aged men. *Preventive Medicine*, **13**, 155–168.

Jones, F. & Fletcher, B. (1992). Disease concordances amongst marital partners: not "way of life" or mortality data artifact. *Social Science and Medicine*, **35**, 1525–1533.

Kerns, R.D., Haythornthwaite, J., Southwick, S. & Giller, E.L. (1990). The role of marital interaction in chronic pain and depressive symptom severity. *Journal of Psychosomatic Research*, **34**, 401–408.

Kerns, R.D., Southwick, S., Giller, E.L. Haythornthwaite, J.A. et al. (1991). The relationship between reports of pain-related social interactions and expressions of pain and affective disorders. *Behavior Therapy*, **22**, 101–111.

Kiecolt-Glaser, J.K., Kennedy, S., Malkoff, S., Fisher, L., Speicher, C.E. & Glaser, R. (1988). Marital discord and immunity in males. *Psychosomatic Medicine*, **50**, 213–229.

Kiecolt-Glaser, J.K. & Glaser, R. (1992). Psychoneuroimmunology: can psychological interventions modulate immunity? *Journal of Consulting and Clinical Psychology*, **60**, 569–575.

Kiecolt-Glaser, J.K., Malarkey, W.B., Chee, M. & Newton, T. (1993). Negative behavior during marital conflict is associated with immunological down-regulation. *Psychosomatic Medicine*, **55**, 395–409.

Lane, C. & Hobfoll, S.E. (1992). How loss affects anger and alienates potential supporters. *Journal of Consulting and Clinical Psychology*, **60**, 935–942.

Langelier, R.P. & Gallagher, R.M. (1989). Outpatient treatment of chronic pain groups for couples. *Clinical Journal of Pain*, **5**, 227–231.

Lazarus, A.A. & Folkman, S. (1984). *Stress, Appraisal, and Coping*. New York: Guilford.

Levenson, R.W. & Gottman, J.M. (1983). Marital interaction: physiological linkage and affective exchange. *Journal of Personality and Social Psychology*, **45**, 587–597.

Levenson, R.W. & Gottman, J.M. (1985). Physiological and affective predictors of change in relationship satisfaction. *Journal of Personality and Social Psychology*, **49**, 85–94.

Lichtman, R.R., Wood, J.V. & Taylor, S.E. (1982). Close relationship after breast cancer. Paper presented at the Annual Meeting of the American Psychological Association, August, Washington, DC.

Linn, M.W., Linn, B.S. & Stein, S.R. (1982). Satisfaction with ambulatory care and compliance in older patients. *Medical Care*, **20**, 606–614.

Luft, H.S. (1975). The impact of poor health on earnings. *Review of Economics and Statistics*, **57**, 43–57.

Lyketsos, C.G., Hoover, D.R. Guccione, M., Senterfitt, W., Dew, M.A., Wesch, J. et al. (1993). Depressive symptoms as predictors of medical outcomes in HIV infection. *Journal of the American Medical Association*, **270**, 2563–2567.

Malarkey, W.B., Kiecolt-Glaser, J.K., Pearl, D. & Glaser, R. (1994). Hostile behavior during marital conflict alters pituitary and adrenal hormones. *Psychosomatic Medicine*, **56**, 41–51.

Manne, S.L. & Zautra, A.J. (1989). Spouse criticism and support: their association with coping and psychological adjustment among women with rheumatoid arthritis. *Journal of Personality and Social Psychology*, **56**, 608–617.

Manne, S.L. & Zautra, A.J. (1990) Couples coping with chronic illness: women with rheumatoid arthritis and their healthy husbands. *Journal of Behavioral Medicine*, **13**, 327–342.

Martin, J.L. (1988). Psychological consequences of AIDS-related bereavement among gay men. *Journal of Consulting and Clinical Psychology*, **56**, 856–862.

Maruta, T., Osborne, D., Swanson, W. & Halling, J.M. (1981). Chronic pain patients and spouses: marital and sexual adjustment. *Mayo Clinic Proceedings*, **51**, 307–310.

Mayou, R., Foster, A. & Williamson, B. (1978a). The psychological and social effects of myocardial infarction on wives. *British Medical Journal*, **1**, 699–701.

Mayou, R., Foster, A. & Williamson, B. (1978b). Psychosocial adjustment in patients one year after myocardial infarction. *Journal of Psychosomatic Research*, **22**, 447–453.

Mechanic, D. (1968). *Medical Sociology*. New York: Free Press.

Mermelstein, R.J., Lichtenstein, E. & McIntyre, K.O. (1983). Partner support and relapse in smoking cessation programs. *Journal of Consulting and Clinical Psychology*, **51**, 465–466.

Michela, J. (1986). Interpersonal and individual impacts of a husband's heart attack. In A. Baum & J.E. Singer (eds), *Handbook of Psychology and Health: Volume 5. Stress and coping* (pp. 255–301). Hillsdale, NJ: Erlbaum.

Minuchin, S., Rosman, B. & Baker, L. (1978). *Psychosomatic Families*. Cambridge: Harvard University Press.

Mohamed, S.N., Weisz, G.M. & Waring, E.M. (1978). The relationship of chronic pain to depression, marital and family dynamics. *Pain*, **5**, 282–292.

Moore, J.E. & Chaney, E.F. (1985). Outpatient group treatment of chronic pain: effects of spouse involvement. *Journal of Consulting and Clinical Psychology*, **53**, 326–334.

Morisky, D.E., Levine, D.M., Green, L.W., Shapiro, S., Russell, R.P. & Smith, C.R. (1983). Five year blood pressure control and mortality following health education for hypertensive patients. *American Journal of Public Health*, **73**, 153–162.

Nayeri, K., Pitaro, G. & Feldman, J.G. (1992). Marital status and stage at diagnosis in cancer. *New York State Journal of Medicine*, **92**, 8–11.

NHLBI Working Group (1982). Management of patient compliance in the treatment of hypertension. *Hypertension*, **4**, 415–423.

Parkes, C.M., Benjamin, B. & Fitzgerald, R. (1969). Broken heart: a statistical study of increased mortality among widows. *British Medical Journal*, **4**, 740–743.

Parsons, D.O. (1979). Health, family structure, and labor supply. *American Economic Review*, **67**, 703–712.

Pearce, J.W., LeBow, M.D. & Orchard, J. (1981). Role of spouse involvement in the behavioral treatment of overweight women. *Journal of Consulting and Clinical Psychology*, **49**, 236–244.

Radley, A. & Green, R. (1986). Bearing illness: study of couples where the husband awaits coronary graft surgery. *Social Science and Medicine*, **23**, 577–585.

Reis, H.T., Wheeler, L., Kernis, M.H., Spiegel, N. & Nezlek, J. (1985). On specificity in the impact of social participation on physical and psychological health. *Journal of Personality and Social Psychology*, **48**, 456–471.

Reiss, D., Gonzales, S. & Kramer, N. (1986). Family process, chronic illness, and death: on the weakness of strong bonds. *Archives of General Psychiatry*, **43**, 795–804.

Renne, K.S. (1970). Correlates of dissatisfaction in marriage. *Journal of Marriage and the Family*, **32**, 54–67.

Revenson, T.A. (1994). Social support and marital coping with chronic illness. *Annals of Behavioral Medicine*, **16**, 122–130.

Romano, J.M., Friedman, L.S., Hops, H., Turner, J.A. et al. (1992). Sequential analysis of chronic pain behaviors and spouse responses. *Journal of Consulting and Clinical Psychology*, **60**, 777–782.

Roy, R. (1985). Chronic pain and marital difficulties. *Health and Social Work*, **10**, 199–207.

Saarijarvi, S., Hyyppa, M.T., Lehtinen, V. & Alanen, E. (1990). Chronic low back pain: patient and spouse. *Journal of Psychosomatic Research*, **34**, 117–122.

Saarijarvi, S. (1991). A controlled study of couple therapy in chronic low back pain patients: effects on marital satisfaction, psychological distress and health attitudes. *Journal of Psychosomatic Research*, **35**, 671–677.

Schleifer, S.J., Keller, S.E., Camerino, M., Thornton, J.C. & Stein, M. (1983). Suppression of lymphocyte stimulation following bereavement. *Journal of the American Medical Association*, **250**, 374–377.

Schmaling, K.B., Fruzzetti, A.F. & Jacobson, N.S. (1989). Marital problems. In K. Hawton, P.M. Salkovskis, J. Kirk & D.M. Clark (eds), *Cognitive Behaviour Therapy for Psychiatric Problems: a Practical Guide*. Oxford: Oxford University Press.

Schmaling, K.B., Wamboldt, F.S., Telford, L., Newman, K.B., Hops, H. & Eddy, J.M. (1996). Interaction of asthmatics and their spouses: a preliminary study of individual differences. *Journal of Clinical Psychology in Medical Settings*, **3**, 211–218.

Schulz, R. & Thompkins, C.A. (1990). Life events and changes in social relationships: examples, mechanisms, and measurement. *Journal of Social and Clinical Psychology*, **9**, 69–77.

Shanfield, S.B., Heiman, E.M., Cope, N. & Jones, J.R. (1979). Pain and the marital relationship: psychiatric distress. *Pain*, **7**, 343–351.

Siegel, J.P. (1986). Marital dynamics of women with premenstrual tension syndrome. *Family Systems Medicine*, **4**, 358–366.

Spiegel, D., Bloom, J.R. Kraemer, H.C. & Gottheil, E. (1989). Effect of psychosocial treatment on survival of patients with metastatic breast cancer. *Lancet*, **2**, 888–891.

Steidl, J.H., Finkelstein, F.O., Wexler, J.P., Feigenbaum, H., Kitsen, J., Kliger, A.S. & Quinlan, D.M. (1980). Medical condition, adherence to treatment regimens, and family functioning: their interaction in patients receiving long-term dialysis treatment. *Archives of General Psychiatry*, **37**, 1025–1027.

Steimer-Krause, E., Krause, R. & Wagner, G. (1990). Interaction regulations used by schizophrenic and psychosomatic patients: studies on facial behavior in dyadic interactions. *Psychiatry*, **53**, 209–228.

Stern, M.J. & Pascale, L. (1979). Psychosocial adaptation to post-myocardial infarction: the spouse's dilemma. *Journal of Psychosomatic Research*, **23**, 83–87.

Thompson, D.R. & Cordle, C.J. (1988). Support of wives of myocardial infarction patients. *Journal of Advanced Nursing*, **13**, 223–228.

Turk, D.C., Meichenbaum, D. & Genest, M. (1983). *Pain and Behavioral Medicine: a Cognitive–Behavioral Perspective*. New York: Guilford.

US Bureau of the Census (1993). *Statistical Abstract of the United States*. Washington DC: Government Printing Office.

Vaughn, C.E., Snyder, K., Jones, S., Freeman, W.B. & Falloon, I.R.H. (1984). Family factors in schizophrenic relapse: a replication in California of British research on expressed emotion. *Archives of General Psychiatry*, **41**, 1169–1177.

Venters, M., Jacobs, D., Luepker, R., Maiman, L. & Gillum, R. (1984). Spouse concordance of smoking patterns: the Minnesota Heart Survey. *American Journal of Epidemiology*, **120**, 608–616.

Verbrugge, L. (1979). Marital status and health. *Journal of Marriage and the Family*, **41**, 267–285.

Walz, M. (1986). Marital context and post-infarction quality of life: is it social support or something more? *Social Science and Medicine*, **22**, 791–805.

Waltz, M., Badura, B., Pfaff, H. & Schott, T. (1988). Marriage and the psychological consequences of a heart attack: a longitudinal study of adaptation to chronic illness after 3 years. *Social Science and Medicine*, **27**, 149–158.

Ward, M.M. & Leigh, J.P. (1993). Marital status and the progression of functional disability in patients with rheumatoid arthritis. *Arthritis and Rheumatism*, **36**, 581–588.

Weiss, R.L. & Aved, B.M. (1978). Marital satisfaction and depression as predictors of physical health status. *Journal of Consulting and Clinical Psychology*, **46**, 1379–1384.

Weissnian, A.D. & Worden, J.W. (1976–77). The existential plight in cancer: significance of the first 100 days. *International Journal of Psychiatry in Medicine*, **1**(1), 1–15.

Williamson, S.E. & Freer, C.A. (1986). Aphasia: its effect on marital relationships. *Archives of Physical Medicine Rehabilitation*, **67**, 250–252.

Wineman, N.M., O'Brien, R.A., Nealon, N.R. & Kaskel, B. (1993). Congruence of uncertainty between individuals with multiple sclerosis and their spouses. *Journal of Neuroscience Nursing*, **25**, 356–361.

Wolberg, W.H., Tanner, M.A., Romaas, E.P., Trump, D.L. & Malec, J.F. (1987). Factors influencing options in primary breast cancer treatment. *Journal of Clinical Oncology*, **5**, 68–74.

Section IV

Assessment and Intervention with Couples

Chapter 15

Marital Assessment: a Dynamic Functional–Analytic Approach

Frank J. Floyd*, Stephen N. Haynes** and Shalonda Kelly[†]
*Departments of Psychology, * University of North Carolina,
Chapel Hill, NC; ** University of Hawaii, Honolulu, Hawaii; and
[†] Michigan State University, East Lansing, MI, USA*

The design and implementation of effective interventions for relationship problems requires first formulating an accurate working model of the causal mechanisms leading to distress for a couple. A working model of a couple is guided by the clinician's theoretical framework and knowledge about common causal mechanisms that affect marital relationships. The model also relies on careful assessment of the specific factors that elicit and maintain distress and dysfunction for a particular couple at a particular point in time. Accurate assessment requires having available reliable and valid measures of relevant domains of marital functioning. However, as experienced clinicians recognize (e.g. Baucom & Epstein, 1990; O'Leary, 1987), accurate *measurement* alone does not guarantee that we can *understand* the causes of marital problems and the treatment needs of couples in distress. In addition to measurement, clinical assessment involves an iterative decision-making process in which the clinician generates working hypotheses and tests causal models with specific treatment goals in mind (Cone, 1988).

Clinical assessment with couples can draw upon the principles and tools of causal modeling used in scientific research. Like researchers, clinicians can specify causal models of positive and negative functioning, then test these models by quantitative means. Such an approach involves the systematic integration of assessment data into a coherent and clinically useful model of the client. Principles of assessment can guide clinical judgments; they suggest methods of acquiring clinically useful, valid and accurate data, and they suggest a strategy for

Clinical Handbook of Marriage and Couples Interventions. Edited by W. Kim Halford and Howard J. Markman.
© 1997 John Wiley & Sons Ltd.

integrating these data into a useful conceptual scheme—a functional–analytic causal model.

The purpose of this chapter is to describe an approach to couples assessment that incorporates a functional–analytic causal modeling method with a lifespan developmental perspective. The emphasis on functional analysis advocates systematic assessment along with an idiographic and flexible approach to understanding and treating marital problems. The lifespan developmental perspective incorporates emerging knowledge about the effects of normative and non-normative life events on couples' relationships across the lifespan. The goals of the chapter are: (a) to summarize important principles and methods of assessment so that clinicians will seek the best data available on their clients; (b) to encourage a developmental perspective in marital assessment; and (c) to describe and illustrate functional–analytic causal models as a method of integrating valid assessment data and developmental considerations into a model of a client that facilitates treatment decisions.

The chapter presents a conceptual and procedural overview for dynamic, functional analysis of marital distress. We begin with an argument for the value of systematic assessment with couples, and then briefly summarize some well known, empirically validated and useful couples assessment instruments. Next, we elaborate on relevant principles of multimodal and multidimensional assessment, levels of inference, and measurement error. We review the model of the marital life-cycle and principles of lifespan development relevant to assessment with couples, use this model to explain the dynamic aspects of marital functioning, and discuss ways to measure them and integrate them into functional–analytic causal models. Finally, we summarize several key practical points about conducting developmentally sensitive, functional analyses of couples' relationships, and illustrate these points with a clinical example.

GOALS AND IMPORTANCE OF MARITAL ASSESSMENT

Clinical assessment goals for working with couples include: (a) specifying both problems and strengths for the couple; then (b) identifying variables that maintain and mediate problems and prevent couples from employing a new, more effective behavioral repertoire. In causal modeling terms, these steps identify relevant relationship outcomes, then identify relationship factors that account for significant amounts of variance in the outcomes. In addition, other assessment goals relate to manipulating causal variables in treatment. These involved: (c) specifying environmental resources that might affect treatment outcomes; (d) establishing treatment goals; and (e) identifying reinforcers that can be used in treatment to achieve these goals (Haynes et al., 1993).

With the exception of behaviorally oriented approaches, many forms of clinical practice forego systematic pretreatment assessment, and instead rely on the therapist's impressions gained from ongoing interactions with the client as an informal way of gathering data to guide clinical decisions. Such informal assessment is probably a useful and necessary practice for generating hypotheses about intervention needs. However, the failure to conduct more systematic assessments as well is probably a major reason for misguided and ineffective interventions (Nezu & Nezu, 1989; Turk & Salovey, 1988).

The need for formal assessment is particularly pronounced in the case of marital therapy for several reasons. First, the nature of marital relationships and causes of marital problems are impossible to discern from one vantage point, and multiple types and sources of data are needed to illuminate various domains of functioning and causal mechanisms. Second, couples who seek therapy are usually focused on their experience of relationship problems; they selectively attend to negative features of their partners and the relationship, and they formulate attributions of causality that incorporate global, stable and internal negative features of their partners (Bradbury & Fincham, 1990). Even if these formulations are partially accurate, they fail to take into account other contextual data necessary to understand the causes and impact of relationship problems, such as relationship strengths or functioning in other, non-problematic domains. Formal assessment can also yield data pertinent to developmental issues of which the couple is unaware.

OVERVIEW OF ASSESSMENT METHODS

Marital distress is a construct with multiple behavioral, cognitive, emotional and physiological components. Accordingly, many methods and instruments can be appropriate and useful for assessment. Table 15.1 lists a number of the most commonly used measures and the most promising new instruments. As shown in the table, the methods of assessment can include observation at home or in clinic settings (Weiss & Tolman, 1990), reports about behaviors of the spouse (Mead et al., 1990), assessment of cognition (Baucom & Epstein, 1990), interviews (Haynes & Chavez, 1983), and self-monitoring (Bornstein, Hamilton & Bornstein, 1986). The list is not exhaustive, and other methods and instruments directed at specific domains of marriage are discussed in separate chapters in this book and in many previously published books and articles (e.g. Margolin, Michelli & Jacobson, 1988; O'Leary, 1987).

Although we focus this chapter on how available measures can be used in conducting functional analyses with individual couples, it is also useful for initial screening purposes to administer a standard set of measures to couples when they first enter therapy. The goals of screening are to provide a standard set of criteria against which to judge the functioning of a particular couple, and to cover a broad range of issues and content areas in order to explore whether problems exist that are not described in the couple's presenting complaint. Administering measures to spouses either before an initial session (e.g. self-report inventories) or within the first few meetings (e.g. self- and spouse-monitoring) usually helps to raise consciousness about relationship functioning and encourages the spouses to

Table 15.1 Marital assessment instruments

Content area	Title and authors	Type of report	Description	Subscales[a]	Number of items	Response class[b]
Marital quality						
Marital satisfaction						
Overall	Dyadic Adjustment Scale (DAS; Spanier, 1976)	Self-report questionnaire	Indicates overall adjustment and frequencies of behaviors	Affection, Cohesion, Consensus, Satisfaction	32	B (A)
	Marital Satisfaction Inventory (MSI; Snyder, 1979)	Self-report questionnaire	Provides a global measure of satisfaction, and information on validity and facets of marital interaction, as well a norms and a profile sheet	Affective communication, Problem-solving, Time together, Finances, Sexual dissatisfaction, Childrearing, Dissatisfaction with children, Role-orientation, Family history of distress	280	A C
	Marital Satisfaction Questionnaire for Older Persons (Haynes, Floyd et al., 1992)	Self-report questionnaire	Measures aspects of marital satisfaction that are relevant for older persons	Satisfaction, Sex/Affection	24	B A
	Marital Status Inventory (MSI; Weiss & Perry, 1979)	Self-report questionnaire	Measures dissolution potential	None	14	C B
Marital history	Joint Narrative Storyboard (Veroff et al., 1993)	Interview	Clinically assesses eight parts of the history of the couple's relationship, can be coded according to affect, interactions or themes	Eight parts: Meeting, Getting interested, Planning marriage, Wedding, Post-wedding, Now, The future	None	B A C
	Oral History Interview (Buehlman, Gottman & Katz, 1992)	Interview	Clinically assesses the history of the couple's relationship	Two parts: History of relationship, Philosophy of marriage	12	B A C
	Outline of Marital History (Baucom & Epstein, 1990)	Interview	Clinically assesses the history of the couple's relationship	Four areas of interest: Initial encounter, Relationship development, Marriage, Relationship and personal difficulties	21	B (A) C

Domain	Instrument	Method	Description	Content/dimensions measured	No.	Code
Beliefs and attributions	Relationship Beliefs Inventory (RBI; Epstein & Eidelson, 1981)	Self-report questionnaire	Measures extent of five dysfunctional beliefs about intimate relationships	Disagreements are destructive, Mindreading is expected, Relationships cannot be changed, Sexual perfectionism is necessary, Gender differences cause conflict	40	C (A)
	Dyadic Attribution Inventory (DAI; Baucom & Epstein, 1990)	Self-report questionnaire	Measures each partner's attributions regarding hypothetical (+) and (−) events occurring in their relationship	(+)Me, (+)Partner, (+)Outside circumstances, (+)Stable, (+)Global, (+)Important, (+)Feeling, (−)Me, etc.[c]	24	C A
	Attribution Questionnaire (Fincham & O'Leary, 1983)	Self-report questionnaire	Measures each partner's attributions regarding hypothetical (+) and (−) events occurring in their relationship, and their resultant feelings and responses	Dimensions: Internal/external, Global/specific, Stable/unstable, Controllable/uncontrollable	12	C A B
	Partner Observational/Attitudinal Questionnaire (POAQ; Baucom & Epstein, 1990)	Self-report questionnaire	Measures each partner's attributions regarding actual marital events, and the degree of marital satisfaction in a 24-hour period	(+)Impact, (−)Impact, Neutral impact, Attributed to me, Attributed to partner, Attributed to outside circumstances, Global/specific, Stable/unstable[d]	102	C A B
	Marital Attitude Survey (MAS; Pretzer, Epstein & Fleming, 1985)	Self-report questionnaire	Assesses the specific content of attributions for current marital problems	Perceived ability to change, Expectancy of improvement, Attributed to own behavior, Attributed to own personality, Attributed to partner's behavior, Attributed to partner's personality, Attributed to partner's malicious intent, Attributed to partner's lack of love	74	C
Specific aspects of marital relationships	Commitment Inventory (CI; Stanley & Markman, 1992)	Self-report questionnaire	Assesses the personal dedication and constraint aspects of commitment to the relationship	Morality of divorce, Availability of partners, Social pressure, Structural investments, Relationship agenda, Meta-commitment, Couple identity, Primacy of relationship, Satisfaction with sacrifice, Alternative monitoring	60	C B A

Table 15.1   (continued)

Content area	Title and authors	Type of report	Description	Subscales[a]	Number of items	Response class[b]
	Trust Scale (Rempel, Holmes & Zanna, 1985)	Self-report questionnaire	Measures aspects of the subject's trust in the partner	Predictability, Dependability, Faith	26	B A (C)
	Personal Assessment of Intimacy in Relationships (PAIR; Schaefer & Olson, 1981)	Self-report questionnaire	Assesses each partner's perceived and desired levels of intimacy in six areas of the relationship, as well as marital conventionalization	Emotional, Social, Sexual, Intellectual, and Recreational Intimacy	36	B A
	Positive Feelings Questionnaire (PFQ; e.g. O'Leary, Fincham & Turkewitz, 1983)	Self-report questionnaire	Assesses the degree of positive affect that partners feel for one another	None	17	A
	Family Adaptability & Cohesion Scales III-Couple Version (FACES III; Noller, 1990)	Self-report questionnaire	Measures couple adaptability and cohesion, both actual and ideal	Adaptability, Cohesion	40	B (A)
Communication	Spouse Verbal Problems Checklist (VPC; Haynes, Chavez & Samuel, 1984)	Self-report questionnaire	Assesses the subject's perceptions of the spouse's communication problems	None—adapted from Carter & Thomas' (1973) categories of potentially problematic areas of verbal interaction	27	B
	Marital Interaction Coding System—Global (Weiss & Tolman, 1990)	Observational measure	Measures a 10-minute segment of the couple's interactions regarding a problem in their marriage	Conflict, Problem-solving, Validation, Invalidation, Facilitation, Withdrawal	None: takes 10 hours to train	B A
	Communication Skills Test (Floyd & Markman, 1984)	Observational measure	Measures the content and affect of spouses' verbal and non-verbal communication behaviors	None; rates behaviors from very positive to very negative	None	A B
	Primary Communication Inventory (Navran, 1967)	Self-report questionnaire	Measures frequency and character of spousal communication	None	25	B (C) (A)
	Marital Communication Inventory (Bienvenue, 1970)	Self-report questionnaire	Measures thoughts, feelings and attitudes about the communication process	Regard, Empathy, Self-disclosure, Discussion, Aversive communication, Conflict management	48	B A C
	Couples Interaction Scoring System (CISS; Gottman, 1979)	Observational measure	Measures content and affect in couple interactions	Has separate content and affect codes	None	B A
	Communication Patterns Questionnaire, Short Form (CPQSF; Christensen, 1988)	Self-report questionnaire	Assesses interaction patterns used by each partner when problems arise, during, and after discussions about relationship problems	Husband demand/wife withdraw, Wife demand/husband withdraw, Total demand/withdraw, Overall positive interaction	8	B
	Clinician Rating of Adult Communication (CRAC; Basco et al., 1991)	Interview and observational measure	Rates couples on 14 communication behaviors, derived from an interview and couple communication sample	Involvement, General communication skill, Problem-solving, Abusiveness, Attribution of blame	20	B (C)

Category	Instrument	Method	Description	Subscales	N	Codes
Sexual issues	Sexual Interaction Inventory (LoPiccolo & Steger, 1974)	Self-report questionnaire	Measures heterosexual and homosexual sexual functioning and satisfaction, by having partners respond to explicit drawings and two statements. Offers computer scoring	Each partner's Frequency, Self-acceptance, Pleasure, Partner perceptual accuracy, Mate acceptance and Total disagreement	17	B A C
	Sexual Arousability Inventory—Expanded (SAI-E; Chambless & Lipshitz, 1984)	Self-report questionnaire	Measures arousal and anxiety experienced during specific sexual behaviors, but only has female norms	Arousal Anxiety	56	B A
	Sex Questionnaire Scales (Zuckerman, 1973; Zuckerman, Tushup & Finner, 1976)	Self-report questionnaire	Measures cumulative heterosexual and homosexual experiences and attitudes, including varieties and frequencies, and has separate male and female versions	Heterosexual experience, Homosexual experience, Number of heterosexual partners, Number of homosexual partners, Orgasmic experience, Masturbation	30	B A
	Golombok Rust Inventory of Sexual Satisfaction (GRISS; Rust & Golombok, 1986)	Self-report questionnaire	Measures heterosexual sexual quality and functioning, and has both male and female forms	Males: Impotence, Premature ejaculation. Females: Anorgasmia, Vaginismus	28	B
Conflict/ problem areas	Marital Strengths and Weaknesses (Weiss & Perry, 1979)	Self-report questionnaire	Spouses provide behavioral descriptions of strengths and weaknesses of 6 out of 26 areas	None	24	B
	Enrich (e.g. Fowers & Olson, 1989)	Self-report on computer	Evaluates marital strengths and weaknesses along 10 dimensions, has a premarital form, and can also yield couple typologies, overall marital satisfaction, cohesion and adaptability	Personality issues, Communication, Conflict resolution, Financial management, Leisure activities, Sexual relationship, Children and parenting, Family and friends, Equalitarian roles, Religious orientation	125	A C B
	Conflict Tactics Scale (Straus, 1979)	Self-report questionnaire	Assesses the nature of physical and verbal violence in the home	Reasoning, Verbal aggression, Violence, Life-threatening violence	18	B
	Inventory of Marital Conflicts (IMC; Olson & Ryder, 1970)	Self-report questionnaire/ observational measure	Provides interaction data on the couples' decision-making processes and conflict resolution regarding prepared vignettes, coded for 29 categories	None	18	B C

Table 15.1 (continued)

Content area	Title and authors	Type of report	Description	Subscales[a]	Number of items	Response class[b]
Marital activities	Spouse Observation Checklist (SOC; Weiss, Hops & Patterson, 1973)	Self-monitoring questionnaire	Daily reports of satisfaction and summary evaluations of spouses' pleasing and displeasing activities in twelve areas	Affection, Parenting, Companionship, Communication, Consideration, Coupling, Employment/ Education, Finances, Household, Personal habits, Independence, Sex	408	B
	Comprehensive Areas of Change Questionnaire (Mead et al., 1990)	Self-report questionnaire	Assesses marital complaints in 29 areas of marital problems	Desired change, Perceived change, Perceptual accuracy, Total change	82	B
	Daily Checklist of Marital Activities (DCMA; Broderick & O'Leary, 1986)	Self-monitoring questionnaire	Provides daily measures of time spent with spouse, occurrence of and pleasure derived from various appetitive, instrumental and by-product activities, and overall satisfaction	Companionship, Affection, Consideration, Sex, Communication process, Coupling activities, Childcare, Household management, Finances, Employment and education, Personal habits, and Self-Spouse independence	109	B A
Parenting alliance	Parenting Alliance Inventory (PAI; Abidin & Brunner, 1995)	Self-report questionnaire	Measures the quality of the co-parenting relationship	None	20	B A C
	Family Experiences Questionnaire (FEQ; Frank et al., 1991)	Self-report questionnaire	Measures the quality of the co-parenting relationship, as well as parenting attitudes	Co-parenting subscales: General parenting alliance scale, Shared responsibilities, Denigrated spouse, Discipline conflicts, Positive problem-solving. Parenting Attitudes subscales: Confidence, Undercontrol, Overcontrol, Self-focused gratifications, Role-focused gratifications, Child-focused gratifications	132	B A C

[a] This term is used loosely to cover dimensions, factors, etc., where applicable.
[b] This refers to whether the instrument primarily measures affect, behaviors, cognition or some combination of the three. Parentheses are used to denote a response class that is used minimally in the scale.
[c] For each positive subscale listed, there is a corresponding negative subscale.
[d] This measure yields 15 scores; there are five attribution scores which are combined with three affect scores.

think more carefully about possible problem areas. This information will provide direction for further detailed functional assessment in relevant areas.

The marital therapy literature suggests a common set of domains that should be assessed with all couples. First, most experts (e.g. Baucom & Epstein, 1990; Jacobson & Margolin, 1979; Margolin, Michelli & Jacobson, 1988; O'Leary, 1987) recommend that screening batteries include a measure of general marital functioning, such as the Dyadic Adjustment Scale (DAS; Spanier, 1976) or the Marital Satisfaction Inventory (MSI; Synder, 1979), which evaluate spouses' satisfaction and impressions of couple functioning in numerous areas of married life. Second, negative behaviors that may cause difficulties and positive behaviors that may be lacking in the relationship can be assessed with a spouse-report behavioral rating scale such as the Areas of Change Questionnaire (AOC; Mead et al., 1990) or the Spouse Observation Checklist (SOC; Weiss, Hops & Patterson, 1973). Third, because communication problems frequently underlie or exacerbate other marital problems, self-reports and observations of couples' communication should be examined. Marital clinicians should become familiar with the communication skills assessed with any of several well-validated observational coding systems listed in Table 15.1. Evaluation of couples' communication behaviors during a brief analog marital problem discussion provides information about the patterns of exchanges and the communication skills deficits that contribute to the couples' problems (Margolin, Michelli & Jacobson, 1988). A self-report measure such as the Communication Patterns Questionnaire (CPQ; Christensen, 1988) can augment and clarify the observational data. Fourth, most clinicians also recommend conducting an interview with the couple focused on relationship history in order to understand the context and development of current problems. Suggested interview outlines are referenced in the table. Fifth, couples should be directly questioned about sexual problems and about marital violence because they are often reluctant to raise concerns spontaneously in these areas. Most self-report measures of general relationship functioning include items about sexual functioning and satisfaction; however, they do not address violence. Thus, specific questioning, possibly augmented with the Conflicts Tactics Scale (Straus, 1979), should explore the occurrence of past and recent violence in the relationship. Finally, cognitive factors such as unrealistic expectations for the relationship and distorted perceptions of the partner can be important sources of marital tensions (Baucom & Epstein, 1990). Table 15.1 lists some measures that tap common cognitive distortions in couples' relationships. Other cognitive distortions may be revealed by searching for discrepancies between self-reports from the husband and the wife, and discrepancies between self-reports and the clinician's observations.

PRINCIPLES OF ASSESSMENT

There are many principles of assessment that can guide the acquisition of valid data on couples needed for functional analyses. The following sections will address three of them: (a) multimodal, multidomain, multidimensional assessment; (b) level of inference and aggregated measures; and (c) errors in assessment.

Multiple Modes, Domains, Dimensions and Targets in the Assessment of Marital Distress

Multiple Modes and Domains

Marital distress can be characterized by multiple response modes, including affective and physiological responses (Bradbury & Fincham, 1987), cognitive responses (Arias & Beach, 1987) and behavioral responses (Weiss & Heyman, 1990). Additionally, marital problems can be manifested across multiple domains, or content areas, such as communication, sex or co-parenting. Response modes tend to co-vary. For example, subjective evaluations by couples of their communication during analog communication assessment tend to be significantly correlated with physiological and behavioral measures of their communication (Gottman & Levenson, 1985). However, the magnitude of correlations tend to be low to moderate, suggesting considerable discordance across modes of responding.

There are two important reasons for low levels of co-variation among the response modes of marital distress. First, different response modes may be affected by different causal variables and have different underlying mechanisms. For example, the physiological responses accompanying marital distress may be caused by conditioning experiences, such as when emotional arousal is paired with failed attempts at problem-solving. However, the negative verbal behaviors displayed by the spouses may be caused by negative reinforcement mechanisms because they are learned ways of reducing or avoiding aversive interactions. A second reason why response modes may show little co-variation is because they have dissimilar time-courses. The time-course of a variable refers to its temporal characteristics, such as rate and latency to onset (Haynes, Blaine & Meyer, 1995). Physiological, cognitive, and verbal responses to aversive dyadic exchanges may exhibit different latencies, and thus appear to be only moderately or weakly related. Similarly, different modes may show different time-courses in response to interventions, and thus therapy-generated change may appear discordant across response modes (e.g. a couple may quickly show improved communication but their feelings toward each other may change more slowly).

Differences in response modes and variation across content domains point to the necessity of multimodal assessment of marital distress, using multiple assessment strategies. The assessment of a male spouse's sexual dysfunction illustrates the importance of multimodal assessment (Haynes & Wu-Holt, 1995). Decisions about the best treatment for a client's erectile difficulties are facilitated by: (a) measures of subjective anxiety and distress associated with specific sexual situations and behaviors; (b) biothesiometry (vibratory sense of the penis); (c) arteriography and other physiological measures of blood flow and neurological integrity; (d) client reports of expectancies and self-efficacy thoughts; and (e) reports about sexual behaviors and sexually related interactions with his wife (Carey, Lantinga & Krauss, 1994). Important components and causal factors of the sexual dysfunction might be missed with an assessment strategy that focused only on anxiety, or only on possible biological dysfunctions. An assessment strategy with a restricted focus would reduce the chance that the intervention would focus on important variables that underlie the disorder. Furthermore, the effects of an intervention program can be more comprehensively evaluated with a multimodal assessment strategy that examines changes across response modes and content domains.

Multiple Dimensions

Each response mode can be characterized on multiple dimensions. For example, verbal exchanges between spouses can be measured by the mean daily rate, the degree of variability, and the conditional nature of spouses' verbal exchanges. Multiple dimensions of a response mode often demonstrate low magnitudes of co-variation (Jensen & Karoly, 1992), thus assessment of multiple dimensions may be necessary to discover which feature of the response is a relevant component of marital problems. Further, similar to response modes, causal, mediating and moderator variables can also have multiple dimensions. For example, social support, which has been implicated as a moderator of responses to environmental stressors (Cohen & Wills, 1985; Heitzmann & Kaplan, 1988), can be characterized on many dimensions, such as global ratings of perceived emotional support, frequency of positive social interaction, financial support from friends and family or informational support. Similarly, environmental stressors can be measured on multiple dimensions such as intensity, duration, controllability, psychological significance, cyclicity, predictability and proximity.

Differential Validity and Utility of Multiple Measures

Despite low-to-moderate magnitudes of co-variation, multiple measures of various response modes, across various domains and involving various dimensions of marital distress, can all be valid. For example, the frequency of self-monitored positive marital communication, the rates of positive and negative communication assessed by external observers, expectancies about future marital communications, and self-ratings of satisfaction with marital communication, can all be valid indicators of the "marital communication" domain. Each measure may validly tap the domain, although some of the measures may share relatively small amounts of variance while others are more highly related. Also, different response modes and different dimensions of each mode can be valid for different purposes or under different conditions. For example, current positive and negative communication patterns (e.g. agreements, interruptions, criticisms) may be more valid predictors of future marital status and satisfaction than of current marital satisfaction (Gottman & Krokoff, 1989).

Multiple Assessment Targets—a Systems Approach

Many variables that are highly correlated with, but external to, the construct of "marital distress" often serve as mediators or moderators of causal relationships for marital distress, or they co-vary with marital treatment outcome. The validity and utility of clinical judgments can be improved by focusing on these variables as additional assessment targets. Additional assessment targets that may facilitate clinical judgments include:

1. The side-effects of marital treatment, such as changes in parenting practices or work-related activities.
2. Behavior problems which may be co-variates of, or co-morbid with, marital distress (e.g. depression, substance abuse).
3. The generalization of treatment effects across situations and time (e.g. are newly learned communication skills used to address new marital problems?).
4. The independent variables in treatment implementation (e.g. do couples practice communication exercises at home?).
5. The personal and social resources of the client.
6. The life-cycle stages of the individuals and the family life-cycle stage of the couple.

Multiple targets of assessment are important because they help clinicians to estimate the impact, applicability and utility of a particular treatment strategy for a particular couple. Will a strategy that focuses on expectations and beliefs, one that focuses on teaching problem-solving strategies, or a combination of the two be the most effective intervention? Is family or marital therapy more useful with a case involving substance abuse? Should a spouse be treated for depressive symptoms prior to or concurrent with marital treatment? These judgments are affected by many factors other than the main effects of the treatment on the primary behavior problem. The assessor must also judge the effects of the treatment program on (a) other non-relationship behaviors and outcomes (e.g. depression symptoms, overall quality of life, feelings of self-esteem); (b) the client's behavior in other situations (e.g. work, socializing and parenting situations); and (c) other persons in the client's environment (e.g. children, family, friends).

Summary of Assessment Implications

The multimodal and multidimensional nature of behavior problems and causal variables have several important implications for the assessment of distressed married couples:

1. Measures of different response modes of behavior problems can all be valid and clinically useful (Weiss & Heyman, 1990). For example, the identification

of important cognitive factors for a distressed couple does not preclude the operation of important behavioral, affective and physiological factors. Cognitive, behavioral, affective and physiological models of marital distress should be viewed as complimentary, not competing.

2. Comprehensive assessment requires the measurement of multiple dimensions of behavior problems, client goals, and causal variables. A failure to measure multiple dimensions can result in insufficient data about a couple and erroneous clinical judgments about the characteristics of their distress, the causes of the distress, or the effects of marital therapy.

3. A systems approach should be assumed in marital assessment. Marital distress can significantly co-vary with other behavior problems and may be mediated by, and may affect, many other aspects of clients' personal and interpersonal functioning.

The Level of Inference and Aggregated Measures in Marital Assessment

The variables measured in marital assessment can differ along a dimension of "level of inference." The level of inference refers to the number of components subsumed by the variable. Behavior problems, client goals and causal variables can be construed and measured at higher or lower levels of inference (these are sometimes termed "molar" vs. "molecular" variables, "higher-order" vs. "lower-order" variables, or "global" vs. "specific" variables). For example, the variable "marital distress" is a higher-order variable that includes components such as dissatisfaction with affection, communication, shared values and perceived support. The component variable "dissatisfaction with communication" is more specific, but also includes more molecular components such as satisfaction with the frequency of communication, being "listened to", and the ability to solve marital problems, each of which in turn is composed of more specific components, and so on.

Both higher- and lower-order variables can be appropriate targets in marital assessment, and the most useful level of inference for variables targeted in an assessment depends on the purpose of the assessment. For brief screening or epidemiological survey purposes, measurement of a higher-order variable such as global "marital distress" might be sufficient. In contrast, if the purpose of the assessment is to identify specific areas of distress for a couple entering marital therapy, data on more specific variables, such as "communication satisfaction", "satisfaction with affection" or "satisfaction with child-rearing strategies" would be more useful. When designing a communication training program for a couple, data on even more molecular variables such as "rate of interruptions", "rate and type of supportive comments", "rate and quality of reflections" and "rate and timing of criticisms" would be most helpful.

Clinicians frequently err by measuring variables that are so molar they provide no direction for clinically relevant inferences. For example, a total score of 80 on the Dyadic Adjustment Scale (DAS) indicates a distressed marriage but does not indicate which aspects of the relationship contribute to distress. Similarly, an increase in the DAS score following treatment fails to identify specific treatment effects. It is also possible that several components of the aggregated molar variable can change in opposite ways (e.g. improved communication but lower perceived consensus) so that the overall aggregate score remains stable despite considerable change in the relationship. We suspect that this lack of clinical utility for global variables is the primary reason why clinicians become disenchanted with structured assessment and rely on less valid and reliable impressions gained from clinical interviews. Although lower-order variables are often more time-consuming, and thus more costly to measure, they have greater utility in clinical decision-making.

A study on the assessment of marital violence demonstrates how molar variables may not only fail to provide useful information, but also may provide misleading data. O'Leary, Vivian & Malone (1992) evaluated different methods of acquiring self-report data on marital violence from clients seeking marital therapy. The authors found that significantly different reports of physical violence in marriages were obtained from 132 couples seeking treatment at an outpatient marital therapy center, depending on how the information was solicited. When clients were asked to describe their "marital problems" in writing, 6% of wives reported that physical violence was a problem. When specifically asked about "physical violence" in structured interviews or questionnaires, 53% reported physical violence in their marriage. This discrepancy probably occurred because physical violence often was not considered "abusive" by wives in this study, and thus was not identified as a marital problem. Whether or not a violent behavior by the husband was considered "abusive" was influenced by the wife's perception of the harm done, whether she thought she triggered it, its frequency in the past, whether the husband apologized, and whether or not he was intoxicated. In effect, "perceived abuse" is a higher-level construct that is composed of multiple behaviors, causal attributions and beliefs; "physical violence" is only one component of the "abuse" construct. Asking about "abuse" or about "marital problems" may not provide accurate data on incidents of physical violence.

The dilemma for clinicans is that global variables such as marital satisfaction are often seen as the most "relevant" variables on which to show change, while molecular variables are actually the most relevant for developing causal models to guide treatment decisions. The dilemma is intensified by the fact that some complex constructs of interest, such as "love", "trust" and "alliances" probably cannot be understood as a linear combinations of molecular components (Floyd, 1989). Further, aggregated measures of multiple components tend to show better reliability and stability than the individual component measures (Haynes & Wu-Holt, 1995).

Summary and Marital Assessment Implications

This discussion of level of inference of measured variables has several implications for marital assessment:

1. Marital satisfaction inventories such as the DAS and the MSI are aggregate measures of the higher-order construct "marital distress". They have limited clinical utility because of their lack of specificity, but they provide a reliable criterion for evaluating treatment effectiveness. Also, examining the component scores may help to identify specific components for additional assessment.

2. Lower-level, less inferential, component measures often provide more specific, complete and accurate data on the phenomena of interest in clinical assessment. For this reason, they are especially important in pretreatment functional analyses (Haynes & O'Brien, 1990; Haynes et al., 1993). For example, if the clinician is interested in sexual dysfunctions, ask specific questions about successful and unsuccessful intercourse experiences, orgasm rates and specific methods of sexual stimulation, etc., rather than molar questions about "sexual difficulties".

Errors Associated with Assessment Methods and Instruments

Clinical judgments about couples are adversely affected by errors which are inherent in all assessment methods and instruments. For example, observational methods and self-monitoring often have powerful reactive effects (Gardner & Cole, 1988; Haynes & Horn, 1982). Data from interviews and self-report questionnaires are affected by memory impediments, differences in the interpretation of items, response biases, social desirability and falsification (La Greca, 1990). Similarly, different assessment instruments that target the same construct, such as questionnaires about marital distress and observational systems for coding marital interactions, sample different components and differ in their level of specificity, scoring formats, comprehensiveness and demand factors (Floyd, O'Farrell & Goldberg, 1987; Weiss & Heyman, 1990).

Marital Assessment Implications

The problem of multiple and idiosyncratic sources of measurement error further substantiates recommendations elaborated above: whenever possible, a multimethod and multi-instrument approach to marital assessment should be used. However, the aggregated validity associated with using multiple measures depends upon the validity of each of the instruments in the battery. Thus, adding an invalid measure to a valid measure can reduce the validity of a measurement strategy (Mash & Terdal, 1988; Ollendick & Hersen, 1993).

DYNAMIC ASSESSMENT OF MARITAL RELATIONSHIPS

In addition to heeding the principles of assessment described above, couples assessment should take into account dynamic features of marital relationships.

Over the course of a relationship, changes in the social environment, the structure of the family, and the individual pursuits of the spouses alter both content dimensions and response modes in marital relationships. The magnitude and direction of effects of causal and mediator variables can also change over time. In addition, within shorter time-frames, studies demonstrate daily and weekly changes in marital interactions (e.g. Price & Haynes, 1980; Robinson & Price, 1980) and other behavioral and environmental variables that can affect relationships (Haynes, 1992). Clearly, in order to develop an accurate causal model of couples' relationship problems it is necessary to account for the unstable and dynamic nature of relationships, including both long-term changes and short-term fluctuations.

Long-term Changes in Couples' Relationships: the Marital Life Cycle

Marital relationships show both continuity and flexibile change over time (e.g. Buehlman, Gottman & Katz, 1992; Raush et al., 1974). Although divorce is most likely within the first few years of marriage, it can also occur at any point, and couples can never be certain of stable marital happiness. Even for couples in "stable" relationships, the context and nature of marital relationships undergo substantial changes as the partners themselves mature, their family roles change with the arrival, development and departure of children, and work roles change and bring either economic advancement or decline. Such changes cause shifts in how relationships function and in the partners' goals and expectations for each other. Whereas long-standing patterns of relating may put couples at risk for marital dysfunction, it is the developmental shifts that are the proximal causes of problems.

To date, behavioral and cognitive–behavioral clinical approaches with couples have focused on relationship processes that appear to be relevant to couples at all stages of the life cycle, such as communication quality, problem-solving skills and attributional styles. Accordingly, assessment research has focused on understanding these dimensions of couples' relationships. Much less effort has been devoted to understanding specific content domains or issues (e.g. dealing with children, expectations about closeness) that may be specific to particular stages of the family life-cycle. With few exceptions, assessment instruments are not specifically designed to be sensitive to these developmental features of couples' relationships. Thus, available instruments are useful tools for measuring potentially relevant features of couples' relationships, but using such measures is only the first step toward developing functional causal models that incorporate relevant developmental information.

The marital life cycle model suggests both useful assessment principles and relevant content areas to consider in constructing causal models of marital distress for couples seeking treatment (Carter & McGoldrick, 1980, Duvall, 1977).

Although every marriage is unique, many characteristics of relationships undergo predictable changes as the couple progresses through the marital life-cycle, from courtship and early marriage, through parenthood, midlife and later life (Spanier, Lewis & Cole, 1975). Thus, marital assessment should consider a couple's current functioning in the context of its position along a trajectory of change. Additionally, understanding a couple's developmental goals is particularly important because these goals may induce change or influence its direction. For example, expectancies and goals for the future may serve as eliciting stimuli for change, while rigid standards and faulty assumptions may impede movement towards those goals (Baucom & Epstein, 1990).

The marital life-cycle model also focuses attention on transition periods, which are major shifts in functioning brought on by life events, including both normative events and non-normative stressors (Baltes, 1987). These events can affect couples negatively, either by altering successful ways of relating or by interfering with the acquisition of new skills. Although the event itself may be a somewhat distal and unalterable causal factor, examining the meaning of the event and the subsequent changes in the couple's ways of relating (the causal sequelae) provides clues to more proximal, and potentially alterable, causal mechanisms. Further, during transitions, behavior may appear chaotic, so that previous causal mechanisms no longer act in predictable ways. At the same time, transitional states may be sensitive periods (Bornstein, 1989), when behavior becomes highly reactive to new causal variables. Because transitions are, by definition, periods of instability, measurements at these times may be inherently unreliable because of the instability of functioning, and thus assessments should be constantly updated and causal models revised as needed.

The marital life-cycle model also alerts clinicians to domains of marital relationships and potential stressors that tend to be relevant to couples at different periods in their marriage. Knowing the issues and sources of stress salient at various life-cycle stages helps to guide the search for causal mechanisms in developing an idiographic functional model for each couple. Several other chapters in this volume provide detailed information about marital relationships at different life-cycle stages, and summarize key themes which are often relevant for couples at different points in their relationships. In Table 15.2 we summarize some of the assessment questions which may be particularly relevant for couples at different stages of the marital life cycle.

The enormous variability in the course and outcomes of couples' relationships, and the occurrence of transitions in and out of marriage for a substantial portion of the population, suggest that any stage formulation is a gross oversimplification of the dynamic ebb and flow of couples' relationships. Nevertheless, conceptualizing marriage in terms of life-cycle stages has heuristic value, it focuses us on change and the dynamics of marital relationships, and it is a convenient way to organize our knowledge about differences in marital relationships over time.

Table 15.2 Marital life-cycle stages: stage-relevant concerns for marital assessment

Premarital and early marital relationships
1. Are there problems associated with the development of commitment in the relationship? How are perceptions of relationship rewards, costs, investments and equity, as well as perceptions of alternatives, affecting commitment to the relationship for each spouse?
2. Are there difficulties associated with regulating closeness–distance or dependency–independence within the relationship? What are the spouses' expectations and standards in these domains? Is divorce in their families of origin causing catastrophic expectations or other fears about the marriage?
3. Are generally positive sentiments about the relationship distorting the spouses' recognition of relationship problems? Is there evidence of ineffective problem-solving or aversive interactions that may cause strain on the relationship now or in the future?
4. Is there evidence of physical violence or verbally abusive precursors to physical violence?

Transition to parenthood and early parenthood
1. Has the transition to parenthood caused the couple to adopt more traditional gender roles than previously? If so, has this upset the equity balance in the relationship (e.g. through greater home responsibilities for the wife, feelings of incompetence for the husband, loss of employment and job-related rewards for the wife)?
2. Have positive couple experiences declined since the birth of the child (e.g. couple leisure activities, sex and affection)?
3. Has the couple formed a positive, mutually supportive parenting alliance?

Midlife
1. Are marital problems related to midlife personal concerns with generativity vs. stagnation? For example, have concerns about generativity led to increased work involvement (in the form of seeking or obtaining promotion) by a spouse, or burn-out, frustration and depression?
2. Have changes in financial circumstances, either improvement or declines, caused conflict about financial decision-making, retirement planning or financial stress?
3. How is the couple affected by the increasing autonomy of their children? Have parent–child conflicts escalated as children move into adolescence? Are young-adult children meeting the parents' expectations for self-sufficiency or are they remaining financially and emotionally dependent on the parents?
4. Are there stressors from relationships with the older generation? Has the couple assumed caretaking responsibilities for aging parents? Has the recent death of a parent caused adjustment problems for a spouse that are affecting the marriage?
5. Are there stressors associated with health and physical changes (e.g. heart disease, menopause)?

Older Couples
1. Has launching children caused the couple to place greater demands on the marital relationship as a source of interpersonal rewards?
2. How has retirement affected the couple? Are they financially secure? Have they replaced work-related roles with rewarding activities? Has difficulty in managing increased leisure time caused strain on the marital relationship? Can the spouses act as motivators for each other in leading active lifestyles?
3. Does the couple need help in coping with health problems? Are unrealistic expectations about self or partner care causing a strain on the relationship? Are there fears about deteriorating health that the spouses are unable to discuss and resolve?

Short-term Change: Phase-space Functions and the Dynamic Aspects of Variables in Marital Assessment

Phase-space Functions

Short-term changes in marital relationships can be examined with the concept of a phase-space function. The values of a dynamic variable plotted over time represent the phase-space of that variable (Haynes, Blaine & Meyer, 1995). The "state" of the variable is its value at any point in time. The phase of the variable is its direction and rate of change at a measurement point. The value of the variable, along with its direction and rate of change is its phase-state (Peitgen, Jrgens & Saupe, 1992).

Figure 15.1 illustrates how the dynamic nature of variables has important implications for assessment. The figure depicts hypothetical phase-state functions of the variable "marital distress" for three persons in marital therapy. The vertical axis represents the magnitude of distress and the horizontal axis is time (in this case, days). The three functions depict a steady decline in marital distress for spouse A, a sharp increase from a low to a high level of distress for spouse B, and an initial slow increase followed by a stable level of distress for spouse C. Note that taking a single measurement at day 10 would indicate that each person's level (state) of distress is the same, but would fail to indicate that the distress is taking a different course (phase) for each spouse. Similarly, measuring each spouse only at day 16 would show differences in their state of distress, but would also fail to account for the phase differences. To understand the importance of

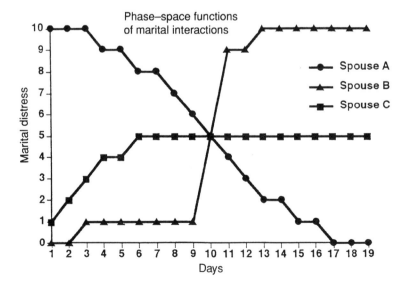

Figure 15.1 Phase–space functions of marital interactions for three persons of 19 days

phase-space functions, consider the inferences about treatment effects that would be based on a single post-treatment measurement at day 10. Although all clients experience the same level of distress, it seems that therapy has had a detrimental effect on clients B and C. Also, consider the inferential errors associated with correlating distress at day 10 with other variables, such as depression. The state scores for distress fail to accurately represent the different changes in distress for subjects across time.

Marital Assessment Implications

The dynamic nature of marital variables indicates that they should be measured frequently using a time-series assessment strategy during treatment (Mash & Hunsley, 1993). Frequent sampling captures the phase-state of variables, and also strengthens inferences about causal relationships because precedence between variables can be examined. For example, with a time-series assessment, we can determine whether depression affects subsequent marital interactions or whether marital interactions affect subsequent depression. The precedence of these variables has important implications for the focus of therapy (Beach, Sandeen & O'Leary, 1990). Additionally, biases that sometimes enter into retrospective reports of causal relationships (O'Leary, Malone & Tyree, 1994) are minimized with time-series strategies. Time-series assessment is applicable with all assessment methods, including questionnaires (e.g. weekly ratings of satisfaction with various domains of marriage), behavioral observation (e.g. in-session observations of problem-solving) and self-monitoring (e.g. daily self-monitoring of positive and negative exchanges). A key to designing an effective time-series measurement strategy is to capture the time-course of the variable so that the sampling rate is appropriate for the rate of change of the variable (Suen & Ary, 1989).

FUNCTIONAL ANALYSIS AND THE DESIGN OF INTERVENTIONS

A Focus on Causal Variables

Among the many situational and contextual factors that may influence a clinician's decisions about marital intervention strategies (Fincham & Bradbury, 1990; O'Leary, 1987), the variables that are presumed to cause the marital distress should be paramount. Causal variables are those variables that affect the dimensions (e.g. onset, frequency, duration, magnitude) of a client's behaviors. A focus on causal variables in assessment is based on the tenet that if the variables affecting a behavior are changed, the behavior will change. For example, on the basis of pretreatment assessment, a clinician may identify negative escalations during problem discussions, avoidance and abrupt termination of problem discussions, a low rate of positive exchanges and supportive comments, and discrepancies between each spouse's idea of a good marriage as important causal variables affecting their distress. The clinician might also rank these in terms of importance (i.e. estimate the magnitude of effect for each causal variable) to help guide the initial intervention focus. Presumably, the most important causal variables will show the greatest treatment effects when they are changed.

The analysis of causal relationships operating for a couple is complicated in several ways. First, as shown in Figure 15.2 (which is discussed more fully later), the causes of a behavior problem may involve complex permutations of multiple causal factors. Also, causal factors may differ across the parameters of distress (e.g. different factors may affect the onset of problems than affect the maintenance of problems), and may also differ across settings or circumstances which moderate the effects of causal relationships (e.g. whether or not the children are present). Finally, causal relationships can change over time, so that causal factors may gain or lose their potency and thus, distress may be controlled by different mechanisms.

Collecting information on multiple variables using multiple and valid assessment instruments can be an intimidating task. Integrating this information in a way that facilitates intervention design is even more intimidating. The functional–analytic, causal modeling approach provides a useful framework to help guide the clinician in these tasks.

Functional Analysis

The most important product of a pretreatment marital assessment is the functional analysis, which is a synthesis of a client's behavior problems and the variables that are correlated with and hypothesized to cause those behavior problems (Haynes & O'Brien, 1990). The functional analysis is a working model of a client's problem behaviors, goals, maintaining and mediating factors, and the interrelationships among these variables. An invalid functional analysis, one that contains erroneous causal variables, or omits important causal variables or behavior problems, mis-estimates the strength of relationships and reduces the chances of designing an optimally effective treatment program. Unfortunately, however, there is a dearth of published studies in which treatments are based on a functional analysis (Haynes et al., 1993).

Important functional relationships relevant to a client can be represented systematically in the form of a functional–analytic causal model (FACM). A FACM is a vector diagram of a functional analysis of an individual client (Haynes, 1994). FACMs symbolize and integrate variables and relationships among variables that are important for the design of intervention programs. FACMs are visual models of the clinician's assessment-based hypotheses about a couple's behavior problems and goals and the variables that affect them. The form and structure of FACMs are borrowed from traditional causal modeling (e.g. Asher, 1976) and vector geometry.

Ideally, the FACM incorporates seven types of information that can guide intervention with a couple:

1. The identification and specification of a client's behavior problems and goals (e.g. specific areas of marital distress).
2. A ranking of the relative importance of each behavior problem and goal.
3. An estimation of the form (e.g. causal/non-causal, direction) and strength of relationships among a client's multiple behavior problems and goals.
4. An estimation the sequelae of a client's behavior problems and goals.
5. The identification of the causal variables affecting a client's behavior problems and goals, with an emphasis on those that are controllable.
6. An estimation of the strength of causal relationships.
7. An estimation of the modifiability of causal variables.

Case Example of a Functional–Analytic Causal Model

Figure 15.2 presents a FACM of a distressed married couple in which self-injurious behavior by the wife was the presenting concern. The 36-year-old, professionally employed wife was originally seen in individual treatment for her ritualistic self-injury—she cut her arms with razor blades several times per month, for 10 years. The cutting was superficial and painless, usually 10–15 minor scrapes across her forearms. Marital therapy was indicated when the results of assessment suggested that marital altercations were a major trigger for these episodes and that both altercations and self-injurious behaviors had been increasing in recent months. The topics of these arguments varied, centering around financial issues, jealousy, the expression of affection, and their critical style of interacting.

Her most important treatment goal was the enhancement of her 4-year marriage; she also reported that marital distress was also associated with recently increasing episodes of depression (scoring between 15 and 25 on the Beck Depression Inventory) and binge drinking (increasing from once a month to about twice a week in recent months). Self-monitoring and clinical interview data indicated that cutting relaxed her physiologically, distracted her from negative ruminations about stressors in her life, and were often followed by solicitous and physically affectionate behavior by her husband. She reported a history of sexual abuse and different forms of self-injurious behaviors beginning from the age of 8 years (e.g. purposeful bicycle falls, purposeful exposure to poison ivy).

She and her husband were seen together, beginning with the third session. Her husband also indicated a strong interest in strengthening their marriage. He reported significant stresses at his job and periodic binge drinking in response to that stress and following marital altercations. Responses on the Conflict Tactics Scale from both indicated a tendency for critical, insulting verbal interactions. Their interactions during an analog communication exercise were congruent with these findings—they emitted a high rate of interruptions, disagreements and put-

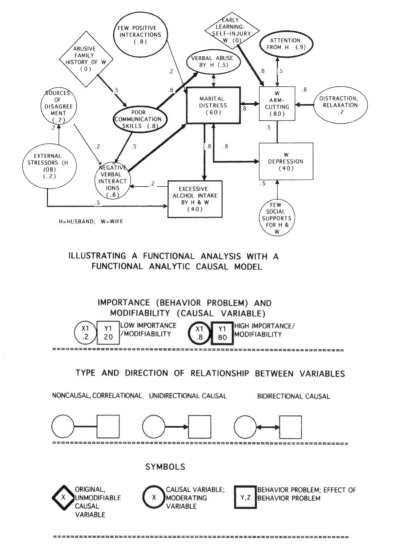

ILLUSTRATING A FUNCTIONAL ANALYSIS WITH A
FUNCTIONAL ANALYTIC CAUSAL MODEL

IMPORTANCE (BEHAVIOR PROBLEM) AND
MODIFIABILITY (CAUSAL VARIABLE)

TYPE AND DIRECTION OF RELATIONSHIP BETWEEN VARIABLES

NONCAUSAL, CORRELATIONAL   UNIDIRECTIONAL CAUSAL   BIDIRECTIONAL CAUSAL

SYMBOLS

STRENGTH OF RELATIONSHIP BETWEEN VARIABLES

INDICATED BY ARROW THICKNESS; MORE PRECISELY BY COEFFICIENTS

Figure 15.2 A functional analytic causal model (FACM) of a distressed marital couple.
The figure illustrates the relative importance of behavior problems, the modifiability of
causal variables, the strength and direction of causal relationships, the effects of behavior
problems, and an unmodifiable causal variable

downs, few positive communication behaviors, and a negative, escalating emotional tone.

The FACM in Figure 15.2 presents a relatively molar-level analysis of the married couple. Its purpose is to guide the therapist in making initial decisions about what factors should be the initial targets of intervention. The model suggests that marital distress is an important causal factor for the wife's self-cutting, depression and binge drinking and also for the husband's drinking. Although both persons had other sources of concern (e.g. job stressors), the marital relationship was the most significant source of concern and the major variable impairing their quality of life. This model also suggests what factors might contribute most strongly to the marital distress. A more specific FACM would be necessary if the therapist selected communication training as a treatment focus. The components of "Poor Communication Skills" would then have to be specified. These might include avoidance behaviors, patterns of escalation, attributions made during arguments, critical behaviors, the lack of supportive and problem-solving behaviors, personally attacking and historical comments.

Estimating the Magnitude of Effects

Functional analytic causal models allow the clinician to estimate the relative magnitude of effect that would result from focusing treatment on any of the causal variables in the model. The FACM can be used to provide a quantitative estimate of the *relative*, rank-ordered, aggregated effects on a client's behavior problems of intervening with each of the causal variables. The estimated magnitude of effect is based on the lower-level clinical judgments outlined on page 370: the modifiability of the causal variables, the strength and direction of the causal and noncausal relationships, and the importance of the behavior problems.

In the case presented in Figure 15.2, the clinician estimated that marital distress (0.8), early learning experiences with self-injury (0.8), and attention from her husband (0.5) were strong causal factors affecting her arm-cutting. However, marital distress is itself a designated problem and a function of several other causal variables. Early learning experiences cannot be modified (0), and the cognitive and physiological effects of her arm-cutting are also difficult to modify (0.2). Consequently, based on the clinical judgments illustrated in the FACM, the most cost-effective interventions would focus on the response of the husband, and many of the variables affecting the marital relationship (e.g., communication skills, negative interactions). For example, the expected magnitude of effect of focusing treatment efforts on "distraction/relaxation" would be: $0.2 \times 0.8 \times 80 = 12.8$ (plus collateral effects on marital distress, depression, and alcohol intake). This product attains significance only in relationship to the products from other paths: it allows the clinician to estimate the relative magnitude of effect associated with focusing treatment on any of the causal variables identified in the FACM.

The estimated impact of a particular treatment focus is also affected by the importance and effects of each behavior problem. For example, in this case, any therapy that reduced the frequency, magnitude and duration of the client's marital distress would also affect her alcohol intake, self-injury, and depression—thus enhancing the impact of modifying a causal variable such as negative verbal interactions. Specific instructions for the calculation of path coefficients can be found in Haynes (1994) and a computer program for calculating estimated treatment effects is available from the second author.

General Principles of FACMs with Married Couples

Several general principles of functional analyses of marital couples are illustrated in the FACM displayed in Figure 15.2:

1. A causal relationships can be bidirectional. In this case, marital distress tended to trigger self-cutting episodes which, in turn, increased marital distress.
2. The designation of "cause" and "problem" is often arbitrary and is frequently dictated by the salience of the behavior or by the referral question. In this case, if "cutting" had been less serious, we could have considered it a minor effect of marital distress, which would then become our major dependent variable.
3. Chains of events can lead to a behavior problem. In this case poor communication skills led to verbal abuse by husband, which increased marital distress and arm-cutting by the wife.
4. Causal relationships can differ dramatically in their strength, as illustrated by differences in the magnitudes of effect for causal variables on the problem behavior.
5. Causal variables differ in their clinical utility. In this case, a history of sex abuse was an important but uncontrollable causal factor. However, the poor communication skills that resulted from that family environment were important and modifiable.
6. Mediating variables can be an important therapy focus. This is particularly true when important causal variables cannot be directly modified.
7. A systems approach is important in marital assessment. Many factors, both inside and outside the marital relationship, and both contiguous and non-contiguous factors, can impinge on a couple.

SUMMARY AND CONCLUSIONS

The goal of this chapter was to increase awareness and sensitivity to dynamic processes and life-cycle issues that impinge on couples' relationships, and to present an approach for incorporating these issues into functional assessments of relationship distress and dysfunction. Although we outline a scheme for conducting FACMs with couples, research is needed to demonstrate that treatments which follow from careful FACMs are more effective than those in which assessment did not guide the intervention. Thus, in addition to providing guidance for clinicians, we hope that this chapter will spark greater research interest in marital development and the functional analysis of relationship distress.

Acknowledgement

Preparation of this chapter was supported by grants R01 HD24205 and K04 HD01023 from NICHD.

REFERENCES

Abidin, R.R. & Brunner, J.F. (1995). Development of a parenting alliance inventory. *Journal of Clinical Child Psychology*, **24**, 31–40.
Arias, I. & Beach, R.H. (1987). Assessment of social cognition in the context of marriage. In K.D. O'Leary (ed.), *Assessment of Marital Discord: an Integration for Research and Clinical Practice* (pp. 109–138). Hillsdale, NJ: Erlbaum.
Asher, H.B. (1976). *Causal Modeling*. Beverly Hills, CA: Sage.
Baltes, P.B. (1987). Theoretical propositions of life-span developmental psychology: on dynamics between growth and decline. *Developmental Psychology*, **23**, 611–626.
Baucom, D.H. & Epstein, N. (1990). *Cognitive–Behavioral Marital Therapy*. New York: Brunner/Mazel.
Basco, M.R., Birchler, G.R., Kalal, B., Talbott, R. & Slater, M.A. (1991). *Journal of Clinical Psychology*, **47**, 368–380.
Beach, S., Sandeen, E. & O'Leary, K.D. (1990). *Depression in Marriage*. New York: Guilford.
Bienvenue, M.J. (1970). Measurement of marital communication. *The Family Coordinator*, **19**, 26–31.
Bornstein, M.H. (1989). Sensitive periods in development: structural characteristics and causal interpretations. *Psychological Bulletin*, **105**, 179–197.
Bornstein, P.H., Hamilton, S.B. & Bornstein, M.T. (1986). Self-monitoring procedures. In A.R. Ciminero, C.S. Calhoun & H.E. Adams (eds), *Handbook of Behavioral Assessment*, 2nd edn (pp. 176–222). New York: Wiley.
Bradbury, T.N. & Fincham, F.D. (1987). Assessment of affect in marriage. In K.D. O'Leary (ed.), *Assessment of Marital Discord: an Integration for Research and Clinical Practice* (pp. 59–108). Hillsdale, NJ: Erlbaum.
Bradbury, T.N. & Fincham, F.D. (1990). Attributions in marriage: review and critique. *Psychological Bulletin*, **107**, 3–33.
Broderick, J.E. & O'Leary, K.D. (1986). Contributions of affect, attitude, and behavior to marital satisfaction. *Journal of Consulting and Clinical Psychology*, **54**, 514–517.
Buehlman, K.T., Gottman, J.M. & Katz, L.F. (1992). How a couple views their past predicts their future: predicting divorce from an oral history interview. *Journal of Family Psychology*, **5**, 295–318.
Carey, M.P., Lantinga, L.J. & Krauss, D.J. (1994). Male erective disorder. In M. Hersen & R.T. Ammerman (eds), *Handbook of Prescriptive Treatments for Adults* (pp. 347–367). New York: Plenum.

Carter, E.A. & McGoldrick, M. (1980). *The Family Life Cycle: a Framework for Family Therapy.* New York: Gardner Press.

Chambless, D.L. & Liptshitz, J.L. (1984). Self reported sexual anxiety and arousal: the Expanded Sexual Arousability Inventory. *Journal of Sex Research,* **20,** 241–254.

Christensen, A. (1988). Dysfunctional interactional patterns in couples. In P. Noller & M.A. Fitzpatrick (eds), *Perspectives on Marital Interaction* (pp. 31–52). Philadelphia, PA: Multilingual Matters.

Cohen, S. & Wills, T.A. (1985). Stress, social support, and the buffering hypothesis. *Psychological Bulletin,* **98,** 310–357.

Cone, J.D. (1988). Psychometric considerations and the multiple models of behavioral assessment. In A.S. Bellack & M. Hersen (eds), *Behavioral Assessment: a Practical Handbook,* 3rd edn (pp. 42–66). New York: Pergamon.

Duvall, E.M. (1977). *Family Development.* Chicago: J.B. Lippincott.

Epstein, N. & Eidelson, R.J. (1981). Unrealistic beliefs of clinical couples: their relationship to expectations, goals, and satisfaction. *American Journal of Family Therapy,* **9,** 13–22.

Fincham, F.D. & Bradbury, T.N. (eds) (1990). *The Psychology of Marriage: Basic Issues and Applications.* New York: Guilford.

Fincham, F.D. & O'Leary, K.D. (1983). Causal inferences for spouse behavior in maritally distressed and non-distressed couples. *Journal of Social and Clinical Psychology,* **1,** 42–57.

Floyd, F.J. (1989). Segmenting interactions: coding units for assessing marital and family behaviors. *Behavioral Assessment,* **11,** 13–29.

Floyd, F.J. & Markman, H.J. (1984). An economical observational measure of couples' communication skills. *Journal of Consulting and Clinical Psychology,* **52,** 97–103.

Floyd, F.J., O'Farrell, T.J. & Goldberg, M. (1987). Comparison of marital observational measures: the Marital Interaction Coding System and the Communication Skills Test. *Journal of Consulting and Clinical Psychology,* **55,** 423–429.

Fowers, B.J. & Olson, D.H. (1989). ENRICH marital inventory: a discriminant validity and cross-validation assessment. *Journal of Marital and Family Therapy,* **15,** 65–79.

Frank, S.J., Olmsted, C.L., Wagner, A.E., Laub, C.C., Freeark, K., Breitzer, G.M. & Peters, J.M. (1991). Child illness, the parenting alliance, and parenting stress. *Journal of Pediatric Psychology,* **16,** 361–371.

Gardner, W.I. & Cole, C.L. (1988). Self-monitoring procedures. In E.S. Shapiro & T.R. Kratochwill (eds), *Behavioral Assessment in Schools: Conceptual Foundations and Practical Applications* (pp. 206–246). New York: Guilford.

Gottman, J.M. (1979). *Marital Interaction: Experimental Investigations.* New York: Academic Press.

Gottman, J.M. & Krokoff, L.J. (1989). Marital interaction and satisfaction: a longitudinal view. *Journal of Consulting and Clinical Psychology,* **57,** 47–52.

Gottman, J.M. & Levenson, R.W. (1985). A valid procedure for obtaining self-report of affect in marital interaction. *Journal of Consulting and Clinical Psychology,* **53,** 151–160.

Haynes, S.N. (1992). *Models of Causality in Psychopathology: Toward Synthetic, Dynamic and Non-linear Models of Causality in Psychopathology.* Des Moines, IA: Ayllon & Bacon.

Haynes, S.N. (1994). Clinical judgment and the design of behavioral intervention programs: estimating the magnitudes of intervention effects. *Psicologia Conductual,* **2,** 165–184.

Haynes, S.N., Blaine, D. & Meyer, K. (1995). Dynamical models for psychological assessment: phase-space functions. *Psychological Assessment,* **7,** 17–24.

Haynes, S.N. & Chavez, R. (1983). The marital assessment interview. In E.E. Filsinger (ed.), *A Sourcebook of Marriage and Family Assessment* (pp. 116–152). Beverly Hills: Sage.

Haynes, S.N., Chavez, R.E. & Samuel, V. (1984). Assessment of marital communication and distress. *Behavioral Assessment*, **6**, 315–321.

Haynes, S.N., Floyd, F.J., Lemsky, C., Rogers, E., Winemiller, D., Heilman, N., Werle, M., Murphy, T. & Cardone, L. (1992). The Marital Satisfaction Questionnaire for Older Persons. *Psychological Assessment*, **4**, 473–482.

Haynes, S.N. & Wu-Holt, P. (1995). Methods of assessment in health psychology. In M.E. Simon (ed.), *Handbook of Health Psychology* (pp. 420–444). Madrid: Sigma.

Haynes, S.N. & Horn, W.F. (1982). Reactivity in behavioral observation: a review. *Behavioral Assessment*, **4**, 369–385.

Haynes, S.N., Uchigakiuchi, P., Meyer, K., Orimoto, Blaine, D. & O'Brien, W.O. (1993). Functional analytic causal models and the design of treatment programs: concepts and clinical applications with childhood behavior problems. *European Journal of Psychological Assessment*, **9**, 189–205.

Haynes, S.N. & O'Brien, W.O. (1990). The functional analysis in behavior therapy. *Clinical Psychology Review*, **10**, 649–668.

Heitzmann, C.A. & Kaplan, R.M. (1988). Assessment methods for measuring social support. *Health Psychology*, **7**, 75–109.

Jacobson, N.S. & Margolin, G. (1979). *Marital Therapy: Strategies Based on Social Learning and Behavior Exchange Principles*. New York: Brunner/Mazel.

Jensen, M.P. & Karoly, P. (1992). Self-report scales and procedures for assessing pain in adults. In D.C. Turk & R. Melzack (eds), *Handbook of Pain Assessment* (pp. 135–151). New York: Guilford.

La Greca, A.M. (1990). *Through the Eyes of the Child*. New York: Ayllon & Bacon.

LoPiccolo, J. & Steger, J.C. (1974). The Sexual Interaction Inventory: a new instrument for assessment of sexual dysfunction. *Archives of Sexual Behavior*, **3**, 585–595.

Margolin, G., Michelli, J. & Jacobson, N. (1988). Assessment of marital dysfunction. In A.S. Bellack & M. Hersen (eds), *Behavioral Assessment: a Practical Handbook*, 3rd edn (pp. 441–489). New York: Pergamon.

Mash, E.J. & Hunsley, J. (1993). Assessment considerations in the identification of failing psychotherapy: bringing the negatives out of the daskroom. *Psychological Assessment*, **5**, 292–301.

Mash, E.J. & Terdal, L.G. (1988). Behavioral assessment of child and family disturbance. In E.J. Mash & L.G. Terdal (eds). *Behavioral Assessment of Childhood Disorders* (pp. 3–65). New York: Guilford.

Mead, D.E., Vatcher, G.M., Wyne, B.A. & Roberts, S.L. (1990). The Comprehensive Areas of Change Questionnaire: assessing marital couples' presenting complaints. *American Journal of Family Therapy*, **18**, 65–79.

Navran, L. (1967). Communication and adjustment in marriage. *Family Process*, **6**, 173–184.

Nezu, A.M. & Nezu, C.M. (1989). *Clinical Decision Making in Behavior Therapy: a Problem Solving Perspective*. Champaign, IL: Research Press.

Noller, P. (1990). The couple version of the FACES III: validity and reliability. *Journal of Family Psychology*, **3**, 440–451.

O'Leary, K.D. (ed.) (1987). *Assessment of Marital Discord*. Hillsdale, NJ: Erlbaum.

O'Leary, K.D., Fincham, F. & Turkewitz, H. (1983). Assessment of positive feelings toward spouse. *Journal of Consulting and Clinical Psychology*, **51**, 949–951.

O'Leary, K.D., Malone, J. & Tyree, A. (1994). Physical aggression in early marriage: prerelationship and relationship effects. *Journal of Consulting and Clinical Psychology*, **62**, 594–602.

O'Leary, K.D., Vivian, D. & Malone, J. (1992). Assessment of physical aggression against women in marriage: the need for multimodal assessment. *Behavioral Assessment*, **14**, 5–14.

Ollendick, T.H. & Hersen, M. (1993). Child and adolescent behavioral assessment. In T.H. Ollendick & M. Hersen (eds), *Handbook of Child and Adolescent Assessment* (pp. 3–14). Boston, MA: Allyn & Bacon.

Olson, D.H. & Ryder, R.G. (1970). Inventory of Marital Conflicts (IMC): an experimental interaction procedure. *Journal of Marriage and the Family*, **32**, 443–448.

Peitgen, H-O, Jrgens, H. & Saupe, D. (1992). *Chaos and Fractals: New frontiers of Science*. New York: Springer-Verlag.

Pretzer, J.L., Epstein, N. & Fleming, B. (1985). The Marital Attitude Survey: a measure of dysfunctional attributions and expectancies. Unpublished manuscript.

Price, M.G. & Haynes, S.N. (1980). The effects of participant monitoring and feedback on marital satisfaction. *Behavior Therapy*, **11**, 134–139.

Raush, H.L., Barry, W.A., Hertel, R.K. & Swain, M.A. (1974). *Communication, Conflict, and Marriage*. San Francisco: Jossey-Bass.

Rempel, J.K., Holmes, J.G. & Zanna, M.P. (1985). Trust in close relationships. *Journal of Personality and Social Psychology*, **49**, 95–112.

Robinson, E.A. & Price, M.G. (1980). Pleasurable behavior in marital interaction: an observational study. *Journal of Consulting and Clinical Psychology*, **48**, 117–118.

Rust, J. & Golombok, S. (1986). The GRISS: a psychometric instrument for the assessment of sexual dysfunction. *Archives of Sexual Behavior*, **15**, 153–165.

Schaefer, M.T. & Olson, D. (1981). Assessing intimacy: the PAIR Inventory. *Journal of Marital and Family Therapy*, **7**, 47–60.

Snyder, D.K. (1979). Multidimensional assessment of marital satisfaction. *Journal of Marriage and the Family*, **41**, 813–823.

Spanier, G.B. (1976). Measuring dyadic adjustment: new scales for assessing the quality of marriage and similar dyads. *Journal of Marriage and the Family*, **38**, 15–28.

Spanier, G.B., Lewis, R.A. & Cole, C.L. (1975). Marital adjustment over the family life cycle: the issues of curvilinearity. *Journal of Marriage and the Family*, **37**, 263–275.

Stanley, S.M. & Markman, H.J. (1992). Assessing commitment in personal relationships. *Journal of Marriage and the Family*, **54**, 595–608.

Straus, M.A. (1979). Measuring intrafamily conflict and violence: the Conflict Tactics (CT) Scales. *Journal of Marriage and the Family*, **41**, 75–86.

Stull, D.E. (1988). A dyadic approach to predicting well-being in later life. *Research on Aging*, **10**, 81–101.

Suen, H.K. & Ary, D. (1989). Analyzing quantitative observation data. Hillsdale, NJ: Erlbaum.

Turk, D.C. & Salovey, P. (eds) (1988). *Reasoning, Inference, and Judgment in Clinical Psychology*. New York: Free Press.

Veroff, J., Sutherland, L., Chadiha, L. & Ortega, R.M. (1993). Newlyweds tell their stories: a narrative method for assessing marital experiences. *Journal of Social and Personal Relationships*, **10**, 437–457.

Weiss, R.L. & Heyman, R.E. (1990). Observation of marital interaction. In F.D. Fincham & T.N. Bradury (eds), *The Psychology of Marriage: Basic Issues and Applications* (pp. 87–117). New York: Guilford.

Weiss, R.L., Hops, H. & Patterson, R.L. (1973). A framework for conceptualizing marital conflict, a technology for altering it, some data for evaluating it. In L.A. Hamerlynck, L.C. Handy & E.J. Mash (eds), *Behavior Change: Methodology, Concepts and Practice* (pp. 203–233). Champaign, IL: Research Press.

Weiss, R.L. & Perry, B.A. (1979). *Assessment and Treatment of Marital Dysfunction*. Eugene, OR: University of Oregon & Oregon Marital Studies Program.

Weiss, R.L. & Tolman, A.O. (1990). The Marital Interaction Coding System—Global (MICS-G): a global companion to the MICS. *Behavioral Assessment*, **12**, 271–294.

Zuckerman, M. (1973). Scales and sexual experience for males and females. *Journal of Consulting and Clinical Psychology*, **41**, 27–29.

Zuckerman, M., Tushup, R. & Finner, S. (1976). Sexual attitudes and experience: attitude and personality correlates and changes produced by a course in sexuality. *Journal of Consulting & Clinical Psychology*, **44**, 7–19.

Chapter 16

Systems Approaches to Couple Therapy

Peter Fraenkel
Ackerman Institute for the Family, New York, NY, USA

There is an enormous variety of systems approaches to couple and family therapy. The approximately 40-year history of the field of couple and family therapy has been characterized by much debate among the proponents of these various approaches. As a result, the differences among the systemic approaches have generally been highlighted more than the similarities (Nichols & Schwartz, 1995), despite several attempts to develop syntheses of two or more systemic models, or overarching "metaframeworks" (Breunlin, Schwartz & Mackune-Karrer, 1992; Nichols, 1987; Schwartz, 1994; Todd, 1986).

In addition to differences among what are now often called the "traditional" systems theories—MRI (Mental Research Institute), structural, strategic, Milan-systemic, Bowenian, contextual, family of origin, and experiential—the growing popularity of social constructionist ideas since the early 1980s has led to a bevy of new perspectives and practices. Social constructionist theorists have questioned some of the fundamental premises of systems theory (Anderson & Goolishian, 1988), essentially seeking to redefine what is meant by a systemic orientation—in some cases, even going so far as to reject entirely the metaphor of families as "systems" (Paré, 1995). Thus, any attempt to bridge facilely the theoretical divides that separate systems approaches risks missing each one's important subtleties and distinctive flavors.

Nevertheless, there are many ideas that link these approaches, and where there are differences, these are often complementary rather than contradictory. However, this chapter does not profess to provide a new synthesis. Rather, the purpose of this chapter is to provide, in a small space, a concise description of the major principles and practices of *systems-oriented* couple therapy. The emphasis will be on the traditional systems approaches, which, despite the postmodern

Clinical Handbook of Marriage and Couples Interventions. Edited by W. Kim Halford and Howard J. Markman.
© 1997 John Wiley & Sons Ltd.

critiques lodged against them, appear to continue to flourish (Nichols & Schwartz, 1995). It begins with an historical overview, briefly discusses the major concepts of couple organization, development and dysfunction; moves to consider key aspects and issues of couple assessment; and then addresses principles and techniques of therapeutic intervention, illustrated by case vignettes.

HISTORICAL DEVELOPMENT

Systems approaches to couple therapy developed as part of the broader family therapy movement, and it is impossible to discuss the history of one apart from the other (see Nichols & Schwartz, 1995, for an excellent account of the field). Many of the early, seminal descriptions of core systemic ideas in family therapy—such as complementarity and symmetry in interaction (Bateson, 1972; Lederer & Jackson, 1968), the notion of underlying rules that structure interactions (Jackson, 1965) and feedback loops (Bateson, 1972)—centered on patterns observed in couples, or at least in dyads (Watzlawick, Beavin & Jackson, 1967). In addition, therapists who work from a multigenerational perspective with families often work directly with only the adult couple (Kerr & Bowen, 1988).

Thus, although couple therapy is often described as distinct from family therapy, with its own particular challenges (Jones, 1993), the two modalities draw from the same body of concepts and techniques. In practice, couple therapy is often one aspect or stage of a broader family therapy, which may have begun with a child as the identified client (Kaslow, 1988; see also Sanders, Nicholson & Floyd, this volume). Although the focus of this chapter will be on working systemically with the adult couple in the therapy room, the reader should realize that in any particular case, couple and family therapy may be intertwined. Indeed, it is a common belief among systemic therapists that much change in the couple can be accomplished in a family therapy in which a symptomatic child or other family member is the overt focus. In this view, the adult dyad is considered the core subunit of the family that largely establishes the family's range of acceptable patterns of interaction (Minuchin, 1974) and emotional expression (Satir, 1972; Whitaker & Keith, 1981), and that transmits patterns and beliefs from one generation to the next (Boszormenyi-Nagy, Grunebaum & Ulrich, 1973; Kerr & Bowen, 1988). The central role of this dyad in the family makes it an important fulcrum for change.

Systems approaches developed in large part as a reaction against the perceived limitations of therapies that attributed psychological and social dysfunction to problems lying solely within the individual, whether these were viewed as biological, psychodynamic or behavioral in nature. Up until the early 1980s, the systemic approaches focused largely on refining theoretical positions distinct from those that highlighted individual-based pathology. As a result, there was a focus on general concepts of family and couple organization, development, dysfunction, and treatment, with less attention paid to differences *among* families, or among family members.

Over the last 10 years there has been a growing appreciation within the field of the great diversity of family forms and norms of functioning predicated on ethnic, racial, cultural, religious, class, education, sexual orientation, regional and other differences among persons and families in Western societies (Falicov, 1988; Hardy, 1989). In addition, differences organized by gender—particularly around the distribution of power between the adult male and female partners—have become central concerns (Goldner, 1985, 1988; Hare-Mustin, 1986).

Another important development in systems approaches over the past 10 years has been a rapprochment with perspectives that recognize the role of factors within the individual in shaping his/her social interactions. The chapters by Halford, Kelly & Markman and Halford & Bouma, this volume, examine the various patterns of influence that may obtain between individual psychological disorder and health, and couple functioning. Whereas in the early systems formulations, individual pathology was often viewed as produced or maintained by problematic interactions, current research suggests that individual psychological disorders may also lead to relationship problems, and that the pattern of influence between the individual and the interactional is frequently bidirectional.

Although there are many interesting theoretical sequelae of these developments for systems thinking, one key practical implication for couple therapists is that they must broaden their purview beyond the interactions of the partners, and even beyond the couple's immediate social network, to include "internal" aspects of each partner as well as the multilayered social ecology within which the couple (and the therapist) lives. For instance, in a couple in which the female partner repeatedly sought increased commitment of time from the male partner and he repeatedly distanced her—an interaction that appeared at first glance to be a "pursuer–distancer" sequence organized along typical gender lines (discussed in detail later)—it was crucial to know that the woman was a socially isolated, severe epileptic who could not travel with her developmentally-delayed son by a previous marriage for long distances without someone else present, in case she had a seizure. The pursuer–distancer pattern was unlikely to end without attention to the woman's realistic medical concerns. As another example, in understanding the power struggles in a middle-class, college-educated African-American couple, it became important both to explore the man's experience of oppression and "invisibility" as a Black man in US society (Franklin, 1992)—as demonstrated by his sense of being passed over for promotions awarded to White colleagues, experiences of being ignored by sales clerks, and so on—as well as the woman's experiences of oppression on the basis of race *and* gender. Within this broader explanatory frame, the man was able to recognize that his attempts to have his wife "obey" him derived in part from his wish to have at least one person in the world show him unflagging respect, and that by insisting on this, he was unwittingly recreating within their relationship the oppressive forces of the society.

Given that the concept of the "system" relevant to an individual, couple or family has expanded, and that theoretical formulations of couple problems and change have become ever more diverse, it may be useful to identify the one core assumption at this juncture in the field's history that is shared by all those who work systemically, and which provides the central rationale for conjoint therapy. At the broadest level, it can be argued that all systems therapies agree on the idea that the problems of individuals always occur in *context*. An individual's problems are influenced by many elements of his/her context, and in turn, influence that context. Context includes most directly the persons that make up the individual's family (including the partner in the couple, as well as the couple's children and members of each partner's family of origin), but also includes friends, peer group, teachers, and others who hold an important position in the individual's life. On a broader level, the context of problems includes internalized *values and beliefs* about appropriate and inappropriate social behavior beliefs that are drawn from the dominant culture, as well as the subcultures to which the individual, couple or family belongs. The broader context of problems also includes the effects on the individual and the couple of the work setting and each partner's employment status (income, job stability, time requirements); the degree to which the socio-political environment affords privilege or oppression to the couple partners on the basis of their cultural affiliations and physical characteristics; the physical environment (housing, limitations of space, pollution); as well as the role played in people's lives by the "larger system" public institutions with which they are involved (e.g. schools, child welfare, child protective services, hospitals, and the various branches of law enforcement). Many of the chapters of the current volume highlight the growing base of empirical data that document the effects of these contextual variables on individual and couple functioning; thus, from this broad perspective, this entire book reflects a systemic viewpoint.

It is important to note that from a systems perspective, elements of the social context may either contribute to sustaining the problem, or may serve as untapped *resources* for change. In many cases, the key to the solution of a couple's problems lies in reconsidering and reapproaching elements previously viewed as part of the problem, and finding ways to transform them into part of the solution. A classic example is that of a young couple for whom the in-laws have become intrusive and controlling around the raising of the grandchildren; the solution may involve recruiting the parents into a role that is experienced as mutually beneficial, rather than the couple either attempting to force the parents away, or becoming resigned to experiencing the parents as an uncontrollable nuisance.

As will be discussed in greater detail, in inquiring about the nature of a couple's problems and range of possible solutions, it is important to consider how all aspects of the social context might be involved. Interventions may target change in the couple's interaction, in partners' beliefs and expectations about the relationship, or in the interface between the couple and some aspect of its broader context.

SYSTEMS CONCEPTS OF COUPLE ORGANIZATION, DEVELOPMENT AND DYSFUNCTION

In systems approaches, theory, assessment and intervention are inseparable. Murray Bowen, a founder of the field, often noted that it was more important for a trainee to learn to *think* systemically than to learn any particular techniques of assessment or intervention (Kerr & Bowen, 1988). And Mark Karpel (1994) has recently commented that "it makes little sense to launch into a discussion of 'how' to evaluate without first introducing 'what' is being evaluated" (p. 1). The following discussion of the basic concepts of systems theories is intended to equip the reader with a practical set of systemic "lenses" with which to view and think about couples, their problems and the possibilities for change.

Properties of Systems

Basic Definition of Systems

Many of the key ideas about the properties of systems were originally introduced to the study of couples and families by anthropologist Gregory Bateson and his colleagues in the 1950s, and were drawn from work on self-guided machines (the field of cybernetics), biological systems, information theory and anthropology. A system is defined as a set of elements that interact with each other regularly and in patterned ways over time. The characteristic patterns of a system organize the behavior of the constituent elements, such that the whole of the system becomes greater than the sum of the parts. In a couple, it is the patterns that develop between the partners, or between them and others in the system, that define and determine both the quality of the interaction as well as each partner's internal life and accessible range of behavior. The colloquial expression "You bring out the best in me" captures the positive side of the power of patterned interaction to define each partner.

Unfortunately, patterns may also draw out less adaptive, less useful aspects of each partner. On the broadest level, the systemic theory of couple dysfunction holds that problems are the result of overly rigid, limited interpersonal patterns, in which certain attributes of one or both partners become highlighted and other, more adaptive abilities are underutilized.

Circular Causality and Other Theories of Problem Maintenance

Most systems theories (MRI, structural, strategic, Milan-systemic, solution-oriented) hold that the causal links among elements in a pattern are circular or recursive, rather than linear. Linear causal thinking holds that an element A leads to a reaction in element B often and predictably enough that we would consider A to cause B. Circular causal thinking expands the "punctuation" (Bateson, 1972) of the observer's attention, so that B's reaction to A is found to elicit, or "cause", a reaction in A, which then again leads to the reaction in B. Each element's behavior provides "feedback" to the other, which stimulates a further reaction.

From this perspective, there is relatively little interest in how a couple's patterns originated. Whether the presenting problem is a symptom in one member or dissatisfaction with some aspect of the relationship, the focus is on how patterns are maintained in the present and what role each partner plays in the overall pattern.

There are two basic forms of circular pattern in couples: symmetrical and complementary (Bateson, 1972; Lederer & Jackson, 1968). A symmetrical pattern is one in which each partner contributes a similar type of behavior. (For the remainder of this chapter, consider the term "behavior" to include action, thought, feeling, and perception—any aspect of the individual's psychological and behavioral response.) A classic example is the "negative escalation", in which the partners trade increasingly negative remarks and behaviors, with each partner's reaction stimulating more of the same from the other partner. Researchers working from a cognitive–behavioral perspective have done much to substantiate empirically the characteristics and predictability of symmetrical circular patterns, showing that partners in distressed marriages become both affectively and physiologically linked to one another's responses (for review, see Gottman, 1994).

A complementary pattern is one in which each partner contributes a "different but mutually fitting behavior" to the interaction (Jones, 1993, p. 11). Each partner's behavior requires the other's in order to make sense and continue, and so each partner's contribution reinforces and is reinforced by that of the other partner. A classic type of problematic complementary pattern, often called the "overfunctioning—underfunctioning" pattern (Guerin et al., 1987), is when one partner consistently behaves more competently than the other—for instance, one partner always nurtures and protects the other, and the other's behavior is limited to acting in ways that require this nurturance and protection.

For example, in one couple, the woman came from a family of ten siblings, in which she was the youngest and was treated as the "baby". The family had immigrated to the USA from a Central American country when she was 15, requiring her to finish high school in English, of which she spoke little. Her struggle with the language and her general shyness reinforced her role as the family baby and increased her tendency to withdraw from opportunities to become more independent. Unlike several of her siblings who became doctors and lawyers, she did not go to college but instead remained at home, unemployed.

Her husband, on the other hand, was a third-generation Italian American, the oldest of two brothers, a successful lawyer, and had functioned in his own family as the "protector" of the parents. When he met her at a flea market that he and his parents ran (and at which her parents had a table of wares), he saw her as a "beautiful flower needing only to be watered". He courted her gently and romantically, which she enjoyed; guided her around the city; and helped her become more independent from her family, which she desired. After they married, he, according to both of them, "took care of her every need", but after a year became less attentive, eventually ignoring her almost completely, and made important decisions (such as purchasing a house in another location, further away from her family) without consulting her. She got a job as an office clerk, and became increasingly independent. He continued to ignore her, attending to his business, and she had an affair with a co-worker, a Spanish-speaking man whom she considered more of an "equal". According to the husband, the affair "woke him up": He attempted to return to taking care of her, but she now found his care cloying and infantilizing. The couple's struggle to continue the marriage, which was eventually successful, centered around the partners finding new ways of connecting that did not require him to overfunction and her to underfunction.

Another classic complementary pattern is the "pursuer–distancer" (mentioned in an example earlier), in which one partner attempts to increase intimacy or closeness (through dialogue or physical contact) while the other responds by withdrawing, leading the pursuer to intensify his or her efforts, resulting in more withdrawal by the distancer, and so on. Complementarity may also take the form of a kind of cognitive–emotional "division of labor", in which one partner plans and thinks about the future, while the other encourages having fun in the moment; or in which one partner takes a positive position about a matter of concern to the couple, while the other voices the negative position; and so on.

For example, in one couple in their mid-30s, the wife, a high-powered businesswoman, advocated having a baby soon (although she didn't know how she would fit it into her schedule), while the husband, an artist, always identified the possible drawbacks. As it turned out, she too had reservations, but feared sharing these with him lest he garner her statements for his arguments against; while he actually wanted to have a baby, but took the negative position as a way to reassure her so that she wouldn't feel inadequate each time another couple they knew announced a pregacy. Once they began an open dialogue about the issue, they became less polarized in their positions.

Symmetricality and complementarity in the behaviors of partners are not by definition problematic: indeed, well-functioning couples generally display a mix of patterns, some in which each partner contributes similar behaviors and some in which each partner's contribution balances the other's. Problems occur mainly when these patterns are rigid, limiting the couple's ability to meet changes and challenges. For example, a couple in which the wife generally initiates conversations about feelings, and the husband initiates problem-solving, may function quite well until faced with a situation in which the wife needs the husband to initiate feeling talk and in which problem-solving is not immediately appropriate, such as when the wife loses a beloved parent. Many of the problems of couples in which one or both partners adhere to traditional gender roles center around complementary patterns that may have worked for a time, but which are maladaptive given the couple's changed circumstances.

Not all systems theories ascribe to the notion of circular causality, at least as the sole explanation of couple problems. Some object to restricting understanding of a couple's problems to present patterns of interaction. For instance, by definition, intergenerational approaches (Boszormenyi-Nagy, Grunebaum & Ulrich, 1991; Kerr & Bowen, 1988), discussed in more detail later, do seek to understand the roots of a couple's present patterns in each partner's past family relationships. The Milan systemic school of therapy (Boscolo et al., 1987) attempted to combine attention to transmission of patterns across generations with notions of circularity by formulating hypotheses that included *intergenerational* circular patterns.

Other approaches, notably those based on social constructionism (including the increasingly popular narrative approach pioneered by White & Epston, 1990), eschew entirely the application of mechanistic notions of causality to human systems (Paré, 1995). Stated briefly, these approaches take as their first premise the notion that what we experience as "reality" is circumscribed by the language we use to describe our experience. Thus, these approaches view problems as sustained by the type of *language* (descriptions) used to define them, as well as by the *processes* of discourse or dialogue among persons about the problem, which "privilege" (give greater power to) some languages over others (Anderson & Goolishian, 1988; Paré, 1995; White, 1992). According to these approaches, problems are maintained when focused on, talked about in ways that emphasize their salience or importance to the exclusion of recognizing exceptions to the problem pattern, and when described in terms of language that implies little possibility of change. In simple terms, this view argues that it is how people think and talk about a problem that holds it in place.

From one perspective, these approaches have simply rediscovered and highlighted the role of cognitive processes long familiar to cognitive–behavioral psychologists, such as selective inattention and the confirmation bias (Baucom & Epstein, 1990), as well as the restrictive power of labeling (Sarbin & Mancuso, 1980). The emphasis is on understanding couple partners' *experiences*, with relatively little attention or explanatory power given to circular, repetitive patterns of interaction. Rather than observe or inquire about sequences of behavior between couple partners, the narrative therapist might be more likely to inquire, in a linear fashion, about the history of when the problem first got identified and named, who named it, and how the problem narrative increasingly came to define each partner's sense of him or herself and of the relationship. Narrative therapists generally hypothesize that couples are, in the words of White & Epston (1990), "recruited" into viewing themselves as having a problem by the power of persuasive perspectives (referred to as "voices" or "available narratives"), which are often provided by persons or institutions that hold the status of "experts" in the society.

For example, one couple became alarmed that their marriage was flawed after repeated exposure to pop psychology books and talk show programs suggesting that having sex less than three times a week was a sign of "intimacy problems". As it turned out, the couple experienced satisfying levels of intimacy through many other, non-sexual means. In another couple, a husband had been told by a previous therapist that he "had a chronic character disorder", leading him and his wife to assume that his "selfish" behavior in the relationship could not change. Detailed review of times when he had acted differently and more positively towards her, and she had responded enthusiastically, began a process in which these exceptions became more the rule, and his problematic behavior receded in frequency and salience.

Feminist family therapists have also critiqued the notion of circular causality, suggesting that it implies a kind of "no-fault" approach to couple problems, in which both partners are viewed as holding an equal role in sustaining problematic interactions and equal power to interrupt them (Jones, 1993). Feminists argue that whereas circularity is useful in explaining many couple patterns, it does not account well for situations in which one partner abuses power—as in relationships in which the man batters the woman (Goldner et al., 1990). Application of circular causal notions to such situations risks absolving abusive partners of moral responsibility. As Goldner (1985) writes, "The systemic *sine qua non* of circularity looks suspiciously like a hypersophisticated version of blaming the victim and rationalizing the *status quo*" (p. 333). The feminists' recognition of the differences in power between members of a couple and the reality of coercive force has been echoed on a larger systems scale by the multicultural perspective, which points to the impact of oppression on minority couples and families (Boyd-Franklin, 1993; Pinderhughes, 1989).

Despite specific criticisms of the notion of circular causality, the idea that members of the system may interact in repetitive, fairly predictable ways around problems and reciprocally influence each other remains one of the central concepts of most systems approaches. It may be that early approaches overextended the application of this concept, and that the field now can benefit from a more diverse conception of how problems occur—one that also allows for the impact of the past on the present, and that accepts the differential power of members of the couple or larger system to create and sustain problems.

Stability and Change

Another important property of systems is the tension between stability and change. In the early systems approaches based on mechanical cybernetics, the focus was on how systems preserved themselves (Watzlawick, Weakland & Fisch, 1974). The notion was that when a system was challenged to change by stimuli from within or without, the elements of the system interacted in ways that preserved the equilibrium, or "homeostasis". This premise was developed further, particularly by the strategic schools (Haley, 1987; Selvini Palazzoli et al., 1978b), in the notion that the symptoms of one family member serve a "function" in stabilizing a system in crisis. For example, as partner A's increased involvement in career leads to a change in the available amount of time and energy for couple activities, partner B might become symptomatic (depressed, anxious, alcoholic), requiring partner A to decrease the time spent in career and increase attention to partner B. Partner B's symptoms thus function so as to restore the balance of couple involvement that preceded partner A's increased career commitments, albeit at a cost to both partners and to the quality of the relationship.

It should be noted that this early view of an individual's symptoms as serving protective systemic functions has come under question—particularly by those in the psychoeducational movement who work with families in which one member has a chronic mental illness which, far from being sustained because of a homeostatic need of the family, is viewed as biologically based (Falloon, Boyd & McGill, 1985).

The concept of the homeostatic "closed" system was also criticized as not adequately explaining how systems grow and change. It was largely replaced by the notion of "open systems" (Davidson, 1983; Minuchin, 1974), in which the system is conceived as being in constant interaction with its broader context, transferring energy and information in and out, and is stimulated to grow by events occurring within the system as well as within the context. Thus, although the original concept of family homeostasis is considered outdated, the notion that couples and families strive to find a balance between change and continuity, or between novelty and familiarity, remains a guiding premise of systems approaches.

Couple Development: Life-cycle and Idiosyncratic Transitions

For the couple system, a major stimulus for change and development is provided by the challenges of life-cycle stages (Carter & McGoldrick, 1989), the content and timing of which are in turn largely defined by the particular culture(s) within which the couple is embedded (Falicov, 1988). In many societies across the world, couples evolve through the stages of "courtship" leading to marriage, or some commitment to life-long permanency of the relationship; bearing and raising young children; raising adolescents; launching the children to more independent living; and adjusting to couplehood in later life. There are many variations of these generic stages, some predicated on ethnic, class, racial and other differences; some on societal trends, such as the high divorce and remarriage rate in US society; some on the individual needs, wishes and capacities of particular couples, such as the decision to have or not have children, or the inability to do so because of fertility problems (Meyers et al., 1995); and some on social constraints provided by the society—for instance, the legal impossibility of homosexual marriages (in most states of the USA).

Whatever the precise set of stages experienced by particular couples, they will be challenged at each one to balance maintenance of established patterns with the need to grow and change. For instance, a number of studies have documented the challenges faced by couples experiencing the "transition to parenthood" (Bradt, 1989). Among other things, this event stimulates re-evaluation and often change in how the couple utilizes the resource of time (Fraenkel, 1994a). Partners usually must reallocate time amongst their various activities—time spent in leisure activities alone or with each other, in work and career pursuits, with friends and family—in order to parent. Couples that attempt to make this transition with little accommodation to the challenges of the stage may be thrown into a crisis that threatens the future of the marriage.

In addition to life-cycle transitions shared by many couples in a particular reference group, most couples experience "idiosyncratic" events that challenge them to adapt (Minuchin, 1974)—events such as loss of a job, illness of one or both partners, premature death of a parent (or child), forced or chosen migration, and so on. In responding to generic and idiosyncratic events and transitions, couples that can alter their patterns and access individual and shared resources tend to function better than those stuck in patterns with restricted range and flexibility.

Concepts of Couple Organization: Power and Connectedness

Another key feature of a system, human or otherwise, is its organization—the manner in which it is regularly patterned over time and space. In many of the traditional systems approaches, the term "rules" is used to denote the organizing action patterns that obtain across particular contents and contexts, as well as the underlying beliefs and expectations that guide interaction. Much of the work being done from a multicultural perspective delineates racial, ethnic and cultural group differences in terms of family organization (McGoldrick, 1993).

In contrast to these continuing efforts, social constructionist approaches have essentially abandoned the project of delineating typical features of couple and family organization, arguing in part that such normative descriptions cannot do justice to the great variability of family forms. At present, these approaches generally limit their conception of organization to the notion that the relevant group for addressing a couple or family problem is all persons who are "in conversation" about the problem—that is, all persons who share a language and meaning system about the problem (Anderson & Goolishian, 1988; Paré, 1995).

Although conceptions of organization vary widely across different systems theories, as a whole, these theories characterize the rules or understandings that underlie couple patterns primarily in terms of two interactional dimensions:

- Power, control, hierarchy
- Connectedness, togetherness, proximity, involvement, closeness, cohesion

In plain language, when observing the interactions of couples, and hearing them describe their interactions outside the therapy room, the systems-oriented therapist notes who is together with whom in which particular activities and contexts, how partners describe the quality of emotional connection between them and others, and who has the most control or power around particular activities, or in the relationship in general. At the most general level, couple problems involve struggles around the balance of power and degree of closeness, not only between the partners, but often between them and others in their lives.

Two of the most influential theories of family organization are those of structural family therapy (Colapinto, 1991; Fishman, 1993; Minuchin, 1974) and the intergenerational approaches, particularly Bowen theory (Kerr & Bowen, 1988). The core organizational concepts of these theories are described below.

The structural theory of family organization—which is also central to the strategic approaches of Haley (1987) and Madanes (1981)—holds that families are divided into subsystems, each defined by particular types of interactions, activities and functions. For instance, a two-parent family with children includes marital, parental, sibling and individual subsystems. Note that as a dyad, the adult partners in such a family are involved in two subsystems, the marital and parental. The specific roles and activities of each subsystem define them as different, although involving the same two people. Families with regular involvement of the parents of the adult partners include a number of other subsystems (adult parent–adult child subsystem; grandparent–grandchildren subsystem).

Subsystems are defined by "boundaries", a metaphoric term that denotes the rules, often unspoken, that specify who is and who is not a member of a subsystem. For instance, partners who take care not to talk in front of the children or in-laws about issues relating to them as spouses (for instance, sex, personal habits, friends) have established a certain type of boundary around the marital subsystem.

Boundaries are described as varying in "permeability" from highly exclusive to extremely open and fluid, depending on the ease with which others can enter and exit a subsystem. A multicultural perspective suggests that the clinician's assessment of the adaptiveness of a particular couple's boundaries needs to take into account the norms of the cultural group(s) to which the couple belongs— with degree of "belonging" being determined not only by which groups partners are born into, but the degree of identification each partner feels with those groups. For instance—speaking very generally—in some ethnic or racial groups, it is common for the boundary around the marital subsystem to be quite fluid, with parents, siblings and other relatives involved in the couple's important decisions and daily social life (Boyd-Franklin, 1989; McGoldrick, 1993). However, any *particular* couple may vary widely in the degree to which they feel comfortable with and live out the level of boundary permeability characteristic of the group(s) to which they belong.

A large number of couple difficulties can be viewed as centering on the regulation of boundaries around the parental, marital and other subsystems, as well as around the family as a whole. One partner may repeatedly act in a manner that contributes to an open boundary, while another attempts to enforce a more exclusive boundary. For example, a common issue encountered with parents of young children is that of when to begin to create "private time" when they cannot be interrupted by the children, except in the case of an emergency. Often this involves a quite concrete boundary issue—that of whether to lock the partners' bedroom door at certain times so that the couple can have uninterrupted sex.

Often, one partner is more in favor of this arrangement than is the other. These sorts of specific struggles over the permeability of the boundary around the marital subsystem may reveal previously unarticulated differences between each partner's desired level of intimacy.

As another example, one of the ways in which couples may attempt to distinguish themselves from their cultures of origin (and their families of origin) is by setting a different type of boundary than that which each partner experienced growing up. Such attempts to change the level of boundary permeability across generations may precipitate crisis and conflict. For example, one third-generation Italian-American couple I worked with broke with family tradition by moving out of the close-knit, working-class neighborhood in which both had been raised. This move, motivated by both partners' wish to "get some distance" from their families and their "old-fashioned ways", also represented their wish to affiliate more closely with what they felt was now their more relevant "culture"—that of young, professional couples.

In addition, partners may agree on the desired *permeability* of a system or subsystem boundary, but may disagree about *whom* to include within the system. For instance, in one couple I worked with in which the husband was of Iranian descent and the wife of Iraqi descent, he wished to include the in-laws in many decisions and activities, whereas she wanted to maintain distance from in-laws, and instead wished to form close, family-like relationships with other couples. Each saw their desired boundary as carrying on their particular ethnic traditions.

The issue of boundary regulation also interacts with that of adjusting to new life cycle stages and other transitions. Certain stages may be better negotiated by opening boundaries (for instance, taking in information from teachers and other parents when the child begins school) and others by closing them somewhat (for instance, when the couple needs a period of relative privacy in order to mourn the loss of a family member, or to come to terms with a chronic illness).

Within and between subsystems, relationships are described along a dimension of proximity or involvement with "enmeshment", or high degree of involvement and emotional closeness on one end, and "disengagement", or emotional distance, on the other. Although couples at either extreme on this dimension may function well for a long time, inflexibility around degree of closeness may lead to problems when the couple is challenged. For instance, one partner of an enmeshed dyad is given a job promotion (including a much-needed raise) that will entail taking occasional business trips, which threatens the couple's high degree of proximity, and results in one or the other partner becoming so anxious that the partner must turn down the promotion.

Couples and families are organized in terms of power hierarchies between and within the subsystems. Hierarchy is viewed as an essential aspect of the organization and optimal functioning of a system: lack of clarity about who is in charge of whom or what results in a breakdown of the system as a whole, because neither those higher or lower in the hierarchy know how to act (Haley, 1987).

One formulation of the way in which complementarity in power differences may serve to maintain problems (and that sheds a different light on the Bowenian concept of "overfunctioning" and "underfunctioning" partners) is that advanced by Cloe Madanes (1981), a leading strategic therapist. She argues that in couples in which one partner has a symptom—depression, alcohol abuse, anxiety— the interaction around the symptom defines "simultaneously their power and their weakness in relation to each other" (p. 30). She writes: "Typically, the symptomatic person is in an inferior position to the other spouse, who tries to help and change him; yet the symptomatic spouse is also in a superior position in that he refuses to be helped and to change" (p. 30). These patterns, which evolved because of the couple's inability to confront issues around the balance of power directly, become rigid because if the symptom abates, the non-symptomatic partner loses her status as superior (and powerful) and the sympto-matic partner loses his power, which he gained through helplessness. Of course, prior to working with such an interactional formulation, it is essential to consider other explanations for an individual's symptomatic behavior and the impact this may have on the couple's interaction (again, see chapter by Halford & Bouma, this volume).

Whereas the structural and strategic approaches assess functional and dys-functional aspects of the couple's here-and-now organization within the family and larger system, intergenerational theories (Boscolo et al., 1987; Kerr & Bowen, 1988; Boszormenyi-Nagy et al., 1991), focus on the manner in which the couple's problems around power and closeness represent a distillation and inten-sification of patterns drawn from each partner's family of origin. The focus of assessment in these approaches includes not only the couple and the current extended family, but at least the two previous generations, some members of which may be deceased.

Bowenian therapists conceptualize dyads as inherently unstable due to each partner's vacillation between a need for individuality and a need for togetherness (Kerr & Bowen, 1988). When one partner seeks more individuality or together-ness than the other, anxiety results. A wide variety of problem patterns may ensue from each partner's attempts to reduce anxiety. The "pursuer–distancer" is an example of such a pattern: as one partner attempts to lower anxiety about too much individuality by drawing closer and increasing intimacy, the other partner attempts to lower his or her anxiety about too much togetherness by withdraw-ing. Another common pattern is that of "pseudoharmony" (similar to the early influential notion of "pseudomutuality"; Wynne et al., 1958), in which partners tacitly "agree to disagree" and work to minimize conflict, sometimes at the expense of a sense of warmth or connectedness. From another (e.g., behavi oral) theoretical vantage point, Gottman (1994) has described these couples as "conflict-avoiders", and presents longitudinal data showing that these couples often stay married for many years. However, further data are needed to identify how such couples handle stressors that might require them more directly to handle strong emotions and solve problems.

Another process that may ensue in the couple's attempt to reduce anxiety about closeness is known as "triangulation". In a triangle, anxiety in the couple is reduced and contained through involving a third party: a child, parent, friend, drug, activity or therapist, to name a few possibilities. This allows the couple to redirect the conflict between them onto issues of managing the third party; alternatively, the third party may support one partner against the other (a pattern termed a "coalition" in structural-strategic theory), or may mediate between them.

Consistent with their intergenerational emphasis, Bowenian therapists hold that triangles can only be fully understood by considering the manner in which they replicate aspects of triangles in which the adult partners have participated in their respective families of origin. In this way, the current couple is organized by patterns of power and closeness extending backward and forward in time, much as a triangle in a geodesic dome is held in place by the other triangles to which it is connected.

According to Bowen theory, the degree to which the couple engages in problematic patterns depends on each partner's level of "differentiation". Differentiation includes an intrapsychic aspect—the ability to distinguish thought from emotion, and to base judgments and actions primarily on thought—as well as an interpersonal dimension—the ability to be in relationship with one's partner and members of one's family of origin without automatically responding to the implicit and explicit demands of those persons. The current couple's patterns of relationship are more likely to be organized by intergenerational triangles to the degree to which each partner is not well differentiated from his or her family of origin.

For example, in one couple I worked with, the husband, Jeff, was caught in the role of mediator in renewed conflict between his divorced parents, in which the father's retirement (NB: life-cycle change as precipitant) led him to decide to cut off alimony payments. The father had left the mother several years prior, complaining that she was not sufficiently emotionally supportive of him. Jeff's wife, Christine, had become closer to Jeff's father over the years than to his mother, and had felt shunned by the mother. When the conflict between Jeff's parents occurred, she found herself more supportive of the father. This deeply disturbed Jeff, who was more protective of his mother in this conflict, and led him to question the viability of his own marriage, stating that Christine did not "support him" well enough—the same reason his father had given for leaving his mother.

Feminist family therapists (Goldner, 1985; Hare-Mustin, 1986) have critiqued structural and Bowenian formulations of couple and family organization, arguing that these theories need to take account of the variable of gender. In particular, they argue that beliefs about the appropriate and inappropriate behaviors for men vs. women form an irreducible substrate in couple relationships, and greatly shape couples' patterns and problems around power and connectedness. For example, feminists hold that without considering gender, a structural therapist might assume that partners who parent effectively, and so have an appropriately hierarchical relationship towards their children, have a "healthy" family structure. However, the lens of gender might lead the therapist to inquire about differences in decision-making power between the partners, revealing that the husband enforces his position through subtle intimidation and threat. In other words, in assessing the functioning of a couple, the therapist needs to consider organization and power not only in terms of "generation" but also in terms of gender (Goldner, 1988).

Just as it is important not to assume *a priori* that a particular couple whose members are of a particular ethnicity, race, or cultural group perfectly fit even well-researched group descriptions or norms (McGoldrick, 1993), in viewing a particular couple through the lens of gender, it is important not to *assume a priori* the existence of power discrepancies between the male and female partner. This caution is particularly important now that feminism has had some impact on changing and loosening gender norms (Ellman & Taggart, 1993). Rather, the lens of gender (and of race, ethnicity, and culture) is best used as a source of possible hypotheses developed and tested during assessment.

ASSESSMENT

Overview

It is probably fair to say that for most systems-oriented clinicians, the interview is the sole modality of couple assessment and evaluation. Books and articles on systems-oriented couple assessment generally emphasize details of the interview, with little or no mention of standardized assessment instruments (Guerin et al., 1987; Haley, 1987; Karpel, 1994; Selvini Palazzoli et al., 1980). In addition, the results of a recent survey indicate that relatively few clinicians regularly use assessment instruments in their practice of marriage and family therapy (Boughner et al., 1994)—despite the availability of well over 1000 marriage and family assessment instruments and techniques, many of which measure constructs relevant to a systems approach (Filsinger, 1983; Fredman & Sherman, 1987; Grotevant & Carlson, 1989; Markman & Notarius, 1987; Jacob & Tennenbaum, 1988; Touliatos, Perlmutter & Straus, 1990).

Before outlining a general guide to couple evaluation through use of the clinical interview, I will mount an argument for the inclusion of standardized assessment instruments in couple evaluation.

Use of Standardized Assessment in Couple Therapy

The underuse of standardized instruments in systems-oriented couple evaluation appears to reflect a broader rift between researchers—who develop these instruments—and clinicians (Liddle, 1991; Sprenkle & Bischoff, 1995). The reasons for this rift and for the underuse of standardized instruments in clinical work are thought to be multifarious, including ideological differences between researchers and clinicians, especially in regard to the question of whether norms of couple or family functioning—which form the backbone of standardized instruments—can reveal anything of relevance about a *particular* couple or family.

Elsewhere, I have characterized this ideological split partly as one between nomothetic and idiographic thinking (Fraenkel, 1995a). A nomothetic approach seeks to understand patterns of adjustment, organization and dysfunction that obtain across different couples and families, whereas an idiographic approach seeks to appreciate the uniqueness of the individual case. I have argued that rather than remaining polarized, these two approaches would be better viewed as complementary and mutually informing. Knowledge of how many other couples respond to certain situations, experiences, or stimuli can assist in evaluating the meaning of the responses of a particular couple; and the responses of the particular couple can be used to revise and enlarge the knowledge base about couples in general.

Clinical assessment is the perfect arena for linking the nomothetic and idiographic perspectives. The unique contribution of standardized instruments (including here self-report questionnaires and projective instruments, behavior rating scales and observational coding systems) is that they can provide a ready means with which to compare a particular couple's issues and strengths on dimensions of interest to those of a range of other couples, especially where normative data have been collected. In addition, the obvious value of standardized assessments is that the theoretical constructs of interest are clearly operationalized. In contrast, because of the lack of clear, standardized operationalizations of key systemic constructs, clinicians often make judgments about the couple's "boundaries", degree of "enmeshment–disengagement", degree of "differentiation" and "triangulation" and the like, based on their particular, possibly idiosyncratic, definitions of these constructs. Clinicians also rely on their "internal norms", which are entirely dependent on range and level of experience and education, to place a particular couple on the theoretical dimensions of interest.

The logic involved in selecting *multiple* assessment instruments that provide subjective (self-report) *and* more "objective" or observational data, and that tap the different levels of the system (individual, dyadic, family as a whole, family in the larger system) has been detailed in numerous publications (Gurman & Kniskern, 1981; Gurman, Kniskern & Pinsof, 1986; Wynne, 1988). The philosophy of those on the cutting edge of couple assessment and outcome research has long been in line with the notion, more recently made popular by constructivist and social constructionist theorists and therapists, that ". . . there exists no single 'objective' reality, only multiple realities" (Gurman, Kniskern & Pinsof, 1986, p. 607).

However, a useful reminder from the social constructionist perspective is that the clinician using standardized instruments needs to remember not to view them as providing data that are better or "more true" than those provided by the couple through the interview. In this way of thinking, the clinician needs to avoid presenting the results of standardized assessment as the final, "scientific" word on the couple. A more collaborative approach involves presenting the data to the couple without interpretations or conclusions, noting that these data represent only one, limited type of information, and asking *the partners* to evaluate the degree to which these data reflect them or not. This more tentative stance towards the products of standardized assessment reflects both a respect for the idiographic uniqueness of each individual couple, as well as a more accurate understanding of the limits (e.g. regarding generalizability, reliability and validity) inherent in all nomothetic, scientifically-based methods.

A Brief Guide to the Clinical Interview

There are numerous published guides to interviewing couples and families, some of which attempt to be atheoretical (Karpel, 1994), and most of which are tailored to address a specific theory of therapy, such as structural–strategic (Haley, 1987) or problem-focused (Weber, McKeever & McDaniel, 1985); brief and solution-oriented (Walter & Peller, 1992); narrative (White & Epston, 1990); Milan-systemic (Selvini Palazzoli et al., 1980; Tomm, 1987); and Bowenian (Guerin et al., 1987). Space does not permit a recapitulation of the many interesting and important points covered in these excellent texts. Rather, I will present a more general orientation to useful principles for interviewing couples.

Interviewing as Hypothesis Testing

Effective interviewing of a particular couple (defined here to include both question-asking and observation) is guided by theory about couples in general. Although there are general issues to assess about couples regardless of one's theoretical approach (covered in detail in Karpel, 1994), many of the specific foci of a particular couple's evaluation will be guided by the theoretical orientation of the clinician, and by the presenting problems of the couple, rather than by a standard list of "systemic questions". Theory provides a set of generic hypotheses about couple functioning and dysfunction, which the therapist then uses as a guide to frame specific interview questions. The couple's responses to these questions serve as data that allow the therapist to confirm, modify or disconfirm the usefulness or "fit" of a particular hypothesis as an explanation of the couple's patterns and problems (Selvini Palazzoli et al., 1980). The following basic framework guides the interview in this process of hypothesis testing:

> These sorts of problems in couples are usually due to X, Y, and Z variables (specified by a particular systems theory). In what ways do *this* couple's statements and behavior (including reactions to therapist interventions) reflect X, Y, and Z variables? Do ideas from another theory provide further clarification of this couple's problems?

Rather than directly ask couple partners the theory-based or "hypothesis" question of interest, it is best to frame open-ended questions that will elicit narratives (accounts of unique or repeated events in their lives) that the clinician can then "comb" to support or modify hunches (Fraenkel, 1994b; see also Alexander, 1990, for an excellent description of this interviewing technique). When the clinician directly asks the hypothesis question, partners often provide only general opinions or "Yes/No" answers, rather than the important details of sequence that assist the clinician to ascertain the patterns of interaction and specific experiences that characterize problems as they happen in the life of the couple. Open-ended questioning typically begins with the phrase, "Tell me about a time when . . . ," and usually follows with the probe, "And then what happened?" to encourage the couple to describe details. For example, if the clinician wishes to explore the degree to which the couple works together as a parenting subsystem, rather than asking the hypothesis question—"Do you two normally work together as a parenting unit, or is one of you aligned with the child against the other?"—he or she might ask the couple, "Could you tell me about some times when your child misbehaved?" By eliciting a number of detailed vignettes about their parenting—including times that went well and times that did not, from each partner's perspective—the clinician is provided with raw data with which to test hypotheses about the degree to which the couple's approach to parenting represents a strength or a problem. In addition, by attending not only to the *content* of these narratives, but also to the partners' interactions with each other and with the clinician, the clinician can formulate hypotheses about the patterns of closeness and power between the partners.

TECHNIQUES OF CHANGE

General Principles of Intervention

There are numerous logistical issues and choice points in conducting systems-oriented couple therapy, not the least of which is deciding whether the couple is the appropriate unit to work with in treatment, or whether individual, family or group therapy might be preferable or used in combination with couples work. Space does not permit discussion of these issues: an excellent recent discussion of them can be found in a book by Mark Karpel (1994). Rather, the focus here will be on the link between systems theories and particular techniques of intervention.

Each of the specific systems approaches has its own intervention philosophy, language and body of techniques, and there are many important differences and debates among them (Fraenkel & Markman, in press; Nichols & Schwartz, 1995). However, these approaches do share several principles and practices: an emphasis on strengths, resources and health; attention to the formation and maintenance of the therapeutic system; a focus on pattern identification, interruption and substitution; redefinition of problems as a first step towards change; and an attempt to make therapy economical. These general principles will be discussed first, followed by a discussion of prominent specific techniques.

Emphasis on Strengths, Resources and Health

A guiding principle of systems approaches is that each partner, and the couple as a unit, operate from a base of health (rather than from a base of intrapsychic conflict or interpersonal dysfunction), and generally have the potentials and resources to solve their problems and achieve their personal and relationship goals. In the initial session, the therapist may express this resource orientation by asking about individual and shared interests and abilities (in career, hobbies) *prior* to discussing the presenting problem. An opening sentence might be, "Before we talk about the problems that have brought you here, I'd like to hear a bit about your life *apart* from these problems". Often, partners' interests and abilities provide metaphors that can be applied to change efforts.

For instance, one husband, an emotionally-reserved computer scientist uncomfortable talking with his wife about intimate feelings, warmed to the idea once it was explained in terms of informational "input" and "output". A successful businesswoman who felt stymied in her attempts to become accepted by the husband's mother and sister, despite his attempts to facilitate this, was asked how she would handle the situation if the in-laws were potential clients: she immediately found a solution. A couple in which both partners were architects despaired that the relationship was "fundamentally flawed": however, once attention was drawn to some of their strengths in handling a particularly stressful transition, they decided that their "foundation" was solid and that they needed only to "renovate and remodel". Through introducing metaphors from their areas of interest and expertise in discussions about problems, the therapist engages the "strong sides" of couple partners and helps to cast threatening topics in a more familiar language and way of thinking. In addition, by introducing metaphoric language about which *they* are the experts, the therapist subtly empowers the partners—they can correct the therapist's misuse of particular terms, educate the therapist about their areas of knowledge, and so on—an interaction which may result in the couple feeling less in a "one-down" position *vis-à-vis* the "expert" therapist and the process of therapy.

Resources continue to be emphasized through inquiring about and building on exceptions to the problem—identifying times when the couple successfully handled difficulties, times when the problem was less severe, entirely absent, and what part the couple played in these positive outcomes. Often, exploration of the early history of the relationship reveals forgotten sources of affection and pride that can stimulate hope. In addition, many of the therapist's "reframes" (discussed below) or other means of redefining problems lend a positive cast to aspects of the relationship previously viewed by the couple as negative.

Formation and Maintenance of the Therapeutic System

In order to intervene effectively with a couple, the therapist must first engage in activities that forge a connection with the couple in which the partners feel safe and respected as persons by the therapist, and in which they see the therapist as someone who can potentially be helpful to them. Minuchin (1974) coined the term "joining" to denote these activities of building the "therapeutic system". Joining techniques include acting as a courteous host, "tracking" (careful listening and paraphrasing of what each partner says), "maintenance" (offering support and validation), and "mimesis", subtly matching the couple's verbal and non-verbal style—for instance, speaking in a formal or informal style to match the style of the particular couple.

Although "joining" is a term specific to structural family therapy, all systems therapists emphasize the importance of developing and maintaining the therapeutic system—essentially, the systemic version of the "therapeutic alliance" (Pinsof & Catherall, 1986)—which is essential to all effective therapy, not only at the beginning but throughout.

Systems therapists also monitor the ways in which the couple "inducts" or "triangulates" them into particular roles—as a cheerleader, judge, common enemy, and so on (Colapinto, 1991). Depending on the particular systemic approach, the therapist might use this inducted role strategically, or might comment on how it replicates triangles in the couple's relationships with family and others. By adopting a general stance of "curiosity" (Cecchin, 1987)—an equal interest in each partner's perspective—the therapist can maintain a basic connection with each partner, even at times when he or she deliberately sides with one or the other in order to stimulate change (a technique known as "unbalancing", described below).

Focus on Pattern Identification, Interruption and Substitution

All systems approaches agree that change occurs through identifying and interrupting the rigid patterns of interaction and meaning that block access to the couple's resources, and by substituting new and more flexible patterns. In the words of Minuchin, "the therapist must introduce novelty" (Fraenkel, 1995b). Generally, the systems therapist assists the couple to initiate the smallest change that will make a positive difference in the experienced quality of the relationship, the assumption being that a small alteration in a pattern will become amplified by the system's natural, recursive "feedback" loops.

For example, with couples in which each partner complains that the other does not initiate affection, a useful first intervention is some variant of the "odd days–even days" prescription developed by the Milan strategic school (Selvini Palazzoli et al., 1978a), in which the therapist suggests that the partners alternate days in the week on which they will initiate some affectionate contact (with one day reserved for spontaneity). The same intervention can be adapted to interrupt standoffs around other issues—the doing of housework, handling the children, and so on.

When the couple follows through with the activity, it often helps them revive a sense of hopefulness, commitment and trust in one another that then fuels other changes. It also begins to substitute a more *symmetrical* pattern between the partners for the previous, problematic complementary pattern, in which one person overfunctioned and the other underfunctioned in a certain domain of couple activity. When the couple (or one partner) does not fully follow through with a suggested activity that both partners had agreed might be useful to them, this provides further information about the couple's patterns around the problem, and may lead to a more careful consideration of each partner's feelings, beliefs and expectations on the topic. This is an example of how intervention and assessment are inextricably linked.

Of course, it would be simplistic and insensitive to cultural and other differences among couples to assume that what all want and need is to become perfectly symmetrical in terms of partners' contributions to the relationship. However, it can be argued that the value and need for *fairness* in relationships is a common assumption of the "culture" of therapy (whether or not it is shared by all the cultures in which couples are embedded), and that the therapist will work to assist partners to find ways to treat each other more fairly and respectfully (Karpel, 1994). In some cases, this will translate into more symmetrical contributions by each partner, and in others into a different and more egalitarian complementarity. It is critical that the therapist try not to impose his/her particular preferences, but rather, work collaboratively with the couple to define what seems fair and just for each partner.

Redefinition of Problems as a First Step Towards Change

Novelty is introduced to the couple first by reformulating the presenting problem in a manner that is more amenable to change (Haley, 1987). In most cases, this means redescribing the problem so that it is no longer viewed as due to enduring character flaws in one or both partners, or as reflective of general deficits of the relationship, but rather as the result of specific beliefs, sequences of interactions or circumstances that can be altered. The particular content of the reformulation depends on the specific systems approach used, as well as the particular meaning of the problem to the couple. For instance, in a strategic approach, "depression" (for which medical/psychiatric etiologies have been ruled out) might be redescribed as one partner's "irresponsibility" (Madanes, 1981), which requires the other partner to be overly responsible. In a narrative approach (White & Epston, 1990), "depression" might be viewed as a constraining description of experience that draws its power from the influence and overuse in the culture of the prevailing psychiatric nomenclature, and the couple might be encouraged to find other, more transformable ways to describe this experience. In a structural approach, one partner's depression might be reframed as "loneliness", and addressed by finding ways to increase communication and affection between the partners. In a feminist approach, a woman's depression might be attributed to her frustration with her lack of power in the relationship, and measures might be taken to examine further and redress these power inequities. And in an approach sensitive to social forces of oppression, one lesbian partner's angry, brooding "depression" might be in part viewed as an expectable response to her repeated experiences of discrimination in the workplace based on her sexual orientation, and the partners might be encouraged to find ways to keep the impact of this discrimination from negatively influencing their relationship—possibly by connecting with support and legal action groups.

In addition, the therapist might work with the couple to develop a more complex redescription of the problem that combines features of several of these perspectives. As with offering suggested activities, it is important that the therapist not use his/her position as an expert to impose or insist on a particular redescription of problems (Jones, 1993). Rather, the therapist needs to offer new ideas tentatively, in the spirit of "trying out ways of thinking differently", and needs to engage the couple actively in considering and revising these ideas until all agree upon a useful redescription of the problem.

Therapy Should Be Economical

A guiding premise of systems approaches is that therapy should strive to be brief. The belief is that therapeutic brevity saves time, energy and money, and reduces the chance that the couple will become dependent on the therapist (Cade & O'Hanlon, 1993). In addition, by communicating the belief that therapy can be brief, the therapist may increase the couple's sense of hope and the energy partners direct toward change. Although the MRI, strategic, and solution-oriented approaches may emphasize brevity more than do others, even approaches that explore each partner's family history tend to do so in a more abbreviated and problem-focused manner than would occur in a typical psycho-analytic individual therapy. Research has generally supported the notion that systems approaches can result in clinically useful change in brief periods—between 1 and 20 sessions (for reviews, see Gurman, Kniskern & Pinsof, 1986; Sprenkle & Bischoff, 1995).

Specific Systems Techniques

One useful way to organize a brief synopsis on systemic intervention is to group the techniques in terms of time-frame focus. Certain techniques work mostly on directly changing present patterns; others focus on the relationship between the couple's present and each partner's past; and others change the present by turning attention towards the future. In a pragmatic, integrationist approach, the couple therapist can shift between these time frames when one frame fails to stimulate productive hypotheses and change.

Present-oriented Techniques

The early MRI and strategic approaches pioneered many of the standard present-oriented interventions. "Reframing" involves redescribing problem behavior so that its significance (both meaning and importance) changes; as its significance changes, the couple is freed to interact in new ways not defined by the problem. Reframes often locate meanings for the behavior opposite to those the couple had assumed, and often find something positive about a situation viewed previously as negative. For instance, persistent arguing, viewed by a couple as a sign of distance, might be reframed as a sign of passion and involvement, albeit expressed somewhat destructively; differences of opinion about how to spend money, decorate the home, or raise the children might be reframed as a potential richness of perspectives, in which each partner's ideas might serve to balance out the other's; and so on.

The key to effective and respectful reframing is that the reframe must be experienced as "true" by the couple: it must emphasize a neglected aspect of the problem pattern that, on consideration, the couple can also see. Otherwise, the couple may experience the reframe as irrelevant or even insulting. For instance, one type of reframe that gained widespread use but was later criticized for leading to negative reactions on the part of some families (Jones, 1993) was the positive connotation (Selvini Palazzoli et al., 1978b). In this technique, the therapist would suggest that there were positive intentions behind each family member's behavior, no matter how overtly destructive or pathological.

"Paradoxical directives" are related to reframes in that they introduce novelty by contradicting couples' assumptions about their problems, and about what to do with them. The two classic paradoxical directives are "prescribing the symptom" and "restraining change". In prescribing the symptom, the therapist suggests that the couple do *more* rather than less of the problem. In restraining change, the therapist suggests to partners beginning to change that they should slow down, not change too quickly, because they may not be prepared to face the consequences of eliminating their problem.

For instance, in the traditional use of these interventions, partners who complain of "uncontrollable" arguments about money might be told that their problem is that they don't ever argue long enough to get to the bottom of their disagreement, and that they should schedule three arguments during the next week, each for twice as long as they usually argue, beginning and ending precisely at certain preselected times. When the partners return the next week having not completed the task and instead, having argued less, the therapist might restrain change by suggesting that they really should keep arguing, because they might not yet have other ways to connect with each other. The intent of paradoxical directives is to redirect the couple's resistance to change into resistance of the therapist's directive to do more of the symptoms and *not* to change: by resisting the therapist, the couple changes. In addition, when the partners perform a symptom they described as 'uncontrollable", they realize that they can control and eliminate it.

As with the positive connotation, paradoxical directives have been criticized for their potential to insult couples. However, if delivered with humor in the context of a supportive therapeutic relationship, and developed with input from the couple, paradoxical directives can be well received and quite effective. For instance, I worked with one middle-aged couple that had become divided around how to handle their 29-year-old son, who had recently begun calling at unpredictable times to berate his parents about how they had raised him—blaming them, especially his mother Sally, for his current difficulties holding a job. The son, named Michael, would often end these diatribes with a request for money, which the parents often agreed to send, in order to placate him. Although by their description of raising Michael it did not appear that they had made any egregious errors, each phone call from Michael would send Sally into paroxysms of guilt. In a panic, she would express these feelings to her husband Larry, who would listen for a while but then become annoyed and withdraw, leading Sally to attempt to engage him further in guilty reflections about the past, leading him to withdraw, resulting in a classic "pursuer–distancer" pattern.

The partners agreed that they needed to take a more "united front" against Michael's accusations and requests (strengthening the boundary around the spousal and parental subsystems). They came up with the plan that Larry would comfort and support Sally after an upsetting phone call rather than withdrawing, and that they would then try to put Michael "out of (their) minds". Although this approach disrupted the pursuer–distancer pattern and led them to feel more like a team, both described continuing to feel "traumatized" and "thrown off guard" by Michael's unpredictable calls. In addition, both parents found themselves worrying that Michael might call at some point during the day.

I suggested that the problem was that they were trying to force themselves *not* to think about Michael, and that they might better prepare themselves for his surprise calls by purposefully thinking about him together each day. I engaged the couple to come up with an exercise they could do each morning and evening to think together about Michael. We came up with the plan that they would spend a half an hour each morning and evening chanting his name over and over, an exercise that they came to refer to as "Michaeling". This exercise—which the couple found absurd but agreed to do anyway—had an immediate and lasting effect, drawing the partners together, giving them a sense of control, and making them laugh each morning and evening about the problem with their son, rather than cowering in fear of his phone calls.

Another technique that was pioneered by the Milan group as an extension of paradox and positive connotation, but was then broadened in scope and application by others (Imber-Black, Roberts & Whiting, 1989) is that of "rituals". Rituals involve sequences of action, which may or may not include words, and which occur once or repeatedly (often at a set time and in a set place). Rituals are attributed a special, symbolic meaning, and elicit a sense of heightened experience for all participants. Therapists have used rituals to assist couples to make transitions through the life cycle, to reaffirm aspects of the relationship, to keep certain memories alive, or to let others go, as in rituals of forgiveness.

For example, the paradoxical directive of "Michaeling" used in the case of Sally and Larry (see above) was a ritual. I had also encouraged this couple to develop a ritual to perform each time Michael called, one that would strengthen the boundary around the spousal subsystem by representing the partners' wish to reaffirm their current life cycle stage as an older couple with children living out of the home. They came up with the idea of playing a Peggy Lee record and dancing together, followed by toasting their future.

Like those of the early MRI and strategic schools, structural family therapy techniques (Colapinto, 1991; Minuchin & Fishman, 1981) seek to change present patterns of power and closeness, but rely less on directives and tasks for couples to do between sessions, and more on changes initiated in the therapy room. "Enactments" involve asking the couple to demonstrate problem interactions (although couples will often spontaneously do so, needing no special invitation!), as well as to try new interactions suggested by the therapist, in which the usual patterns of proximity and power are blocked and new patterns are encouraged. Building "intensity" involves use of the "dramaturgical" elements of therapeutic communication to emphasize a reframe or other new ways of thinking about problems: gestures, qualities of speech (tone, volume and pace); mantra-like repetition of a phrase; metaphors or other powerful imagery; and changes in the physical proximity of the therapist to one or the other partner. The goal of enactments and intensity-building techniques is to create with the couple a memorable, novel experience in the therapy room that will stay with them between sessions and hopefully stimulate continued change.

For instance, in one couple, the husband was regarded as "depressed" and "ineffective" by both partners. As an example of his depression, he claimed that he was unable to initiate or complete household activities, yet continually complained about his wife's failure to do so (despite her actually handling 95% of the couple's chores). Only when his wife yelled at him several times would he complete some part of a chore. The couple appeared to be stuck in a complementary pattern in which the husband's under-responsibility and passivity stimulated the wife's over-responsibility and activity, which in turn allowed the husband to remain passive.

Examination of their expectations, including beliefs about gender and home responsibilities, as well as attempts at straightforward problem-solving discussions, had been ineffective in changing this pattern. In order to emphasize a novel way of thinking about the couple's pattern, each time the husband complained about his wife, I built intensity by slowly and repeatedly intoning to the husband, "How is it that you have trained your wife to be your trainer?" Occasionally, I also turned to the wife, stating, in a sympathetic tone, "How did he recruit you to be his trainer?" The intent of the intervention was to reframe the husband's passivity as activity and interpersonal power, and to encourage indirectly the wife to refuse to support his passivity. Once she recognized his "hidden" activity in organizing her behavior, the wife refused to complete the chores they had previously designated as his responsibility. The husband, who did not like the idea that his wife was training him, began to complete his chores, which started him in the direction of assuming greater competence both at home and at work.

In addition to building intensity to emphasize the reframe, this intervention made use of another structural technique, "unbalancing". In unbalancing, the therapist temporarily supports one partner's perspective or position more than the other's, in order to disrupt a problematic pattern of power inequality. In the example above, the wife's position was temporarily supported over the husband's in order to empower her to re-evaluate her willingness to fill in for him around the house.

The constraining effects of expert knowledge and other sources of problem definition constitutes the major focus of intervention in the narrative approach to therapy (Freedman & Combs, 1996; White & Epston, 1990). One of the core practices in this approach is called "externalizing" the problem. The goal of externalizing is to assist persons to separate their sense of themselves from their "problem-saturated" narratives, a process which then allows them to build on more positive narratives of success and competence. The steps of externalizing include: identifying all the ways in which the problem has affected couple partners' lives; identifying "unique outcomes", instances in which partners have acted in ways that defy the influence of the problem; redefining the problem, often by giving it a name that characterizes it as an entity separate from the person or persons said to "have it"; and expanding on unique outcomes to take further action against or in spite of the problem. Couple partners are then encouraged to incorporate these problem-defying instances into their individual and joint self descriptions.

For example, I worked with Sarah and Jim, a couple in their early 30s. Both partners had prior histories of drug and alcohol abuse. In addition, each reported extremely difficult childhoods with parents who had been verbally abusive, leading them each to feel extremely sensitive to criticism from one other. Their relationship was characterized by frequent escalations which, in their words, would lead Sarah to become "depressed and hopeless" and Jim to be "filled with archetypal rage". Although these escalations decreased somewhat as a result of learning and using communication and problem-solving skills, and identifying their unarticulated expectations and hidden issues (Markman, Stanley & Blumberg, 1994), the couple frequently lost the sense of "teamwork" necessary to initiate these cognitive–behavioral techniques.

I introduced them to the basic ideas of narrative therapy, obtained their agreement to try this approach, and engaged each partner in giving a name to the experience of being criticized. Sarah named her experience "Rotunda", and described the image of an enormously fat woman (which reminded her of her mother) who would sit on her and "crush" her in response to criticism. In turn, Jim captured the effects of criticism on him in the image of the "Dark Knight", which would spear a lance into him and raise him helplessly into the air, leaving him with intense feelings of shame. Each partner agreed to refer to these characters when feeling criticized by the other, rather than directly to complain that the partner was being critical—for instance, when Sarah felt Jim was being critical of her, she would say "I feel Rotunda coming!" Each agreed to stop criticizing once the character was invoked, and instead, to offer a comforting response that aimed to decrease the effects of these now externalized problems.

The results of this intervention were dramatically positive and sustained, and when therapy ended, both partners commented that they found themselves less sensitive to criticism from friends, colleagues and family members as well. In particular, Jim, who had believed his reactions to be "deeply rooted in the unconscious" and unlikely to change, expressed surprise that a technique that focused on here-and-now interactions could affect the way he felt about himself in general.

Past-oriented Techniques

A shift of focus from the details of the couple's present problem patterns to hypotheses about possible sources of the patterns in each partner's family-of-origin experiences can be useful in several ways:

1. *Reducing blame.*   As each partner becomes more aware of the historical roots of the other's sensitivities and behavior, blame is reattributed from the partner to unfortunate aspects of the partner's family of origin. As Gerson and colleagues write, "It is easier to become more accepting and respectful when a partner's behavior is seen not as out to thwart or frustrate, but as the product of previous life experiences and expectations" (Gerson et al., 1993, pp. 341–342). Additionally, blame of self and of the other is reduced as partners become aware of the family-of-origin sources of their *own* behavior. Each partner comes to take greater responsibility for unwittingly transmitting their particular family issues to the current relationship.
2. *Decreasing conflict intensity in the session.*   When partners are extremely angry and repeatedly escalate in the session, a shift away from direct discussion of their present problems to each partner's family history can decrease conflict intensity. The therapist can ask each partner to speak to her or him while the other listens, and may need actively to block the listening partner from interjecting in a non-productive manner. If escalations continue, the therapist may need to meet with one partner at a time or, if possible, have the partner listen from behind a one-way mirror (Gerson et al., 1993).
3. *Widening the frame to include beliefs and expectations.*   As was noted earlier, exploration of each partner's family of origin often reveals unacknowledged beliefs and expectations about power and connectedness that underlie current conflicts (Guerin et al., 1987; Jones, 1993). According to Bowen theory (Kerr & Bowen, 1988), persons often engage in "emotional cutoff" from their families in an attempt to free themselves from the pull of triangles and other disturbing past experiences; one manifestation of this cutoff may be to deny any relationship between one's current beliefs and those of one's parents. However, exploration of the family of origin can allow partners to identify ways in which they react to each other based on these hidden beliefs, despite their conscious attempts to distance themselves from these beliefs. In some cases, experiences from families of origin serve as direct models for current behavior; in others, partners consciously or unconsciously attempt to reverse the beliefs and values absorbed from their families (Gerson et al., 1993).

The major technique of intergenerational approaches is careful interviewing of each partner to bring about increased understanding of the links between past experiences and present beliefs and interactions. The underlying assumption is that increased recognition and understanding of these links will allow for change in the present patterns (Kerr & Bowen, 1988). Often, patterns linking past and present are summarized using a diagram called a genogram (McGoldrick & Gerson, 1985). The genogram typically includes basic facts (birth and death dates, salient educational, employment and medical/mental health history) about all members of each partner's family of origin going back at least two generations, and uses symbols to describe, in a shorthand manner, the kinship connections and quality of the relationships between all members. The clinician then reviews the genogram to identify triangles, emotional cutoffs, and other problematic patterns in family relationships, and looks for evidence of how these patterns have been transmitted across generations.

In some approaches to intergenerational therapy, three or more generations may be invited to join the couple in sessions (Boscolo et al., 1987); in others, couple members are "coached" to return to their respective families to work out old conflicts and forge more positive connections with parents and siblings (Guerin et al., 1987; Kerr & Bowen, 1988). By "differentiating" themselves from their respective families of origin, partners become better able to avoid transferring triangles and other patterns into their current relationship.

The following case vignette, presented in more detail elsewhere (Fraenkel & Markman, in press) illustrates the use of past-oriented techniques. Tim and Laura were a couple in their mid-30s. They reported having a generally satisfying marriage, except that Tim became cold, distant and rageful whenever Laura's rheumatoid arthritis required bedrest. In Laura's view, Tim became "selfish" during these periods: for instance, refusing to assist her to complete minor household chores. Tim agreed that his behavior was an over-reaction, but could not explain it beyond noting his feeling of "incredible resentment" about her illness. Both partners felt that this pattern was severe enough to threaten the future of the relationship.

Exploration of Tim's family of origin revealed that both his father and grandfather had been extremely bitter when their respective financial and career plans had been interrupted because of the need to assume sole responsibility for supporting their chronically-ill mothers. In addition, Tim's brother had been sick beginning as a child, and as a result received much more attention from the mother than had Tim. And Tim's father had been ill for the past 10 years and, in Tim's view, complained excessively as a means of gaining sympathy. Recognizing the family-of-origin sources of Tim's intense reactions to Laura's illness greatly reduced the tension in the couple. Tim then met with his father to reduce the emotional cutoff between them, and became more sympathetic to his father's and grandfather's experiences, which led him to feel less tied to repeating their ways of coping with illness.

Future-oriented Techniques

Some couple therapists have argued that a focus on the link between past and present problems, or on the details of the present problem pattern, impedes change (de Shazer, 1991). These solution-focused (de Shazer, 1991) or solution-oriented (Furman & Ahola, 1992) therapists generally eschew the previously-discussed theories of couple organization and dysfunction entirely. Instead, these therapists work with couples to locate what they want to be different in the immediate and more distant future, and how to make that happen (de Shazer, 1991; Furman & Ahola, 1992).

Some of the more distinctive future-oriented techniques include asking the partners to reflect on what about their relationship they wish to *preserve* or even *amplify* in the future (rather than focusing solely on what they wish to change); examining and highlighting "exceptions"—strategies that have already worked in handling their problems, as well as those that might work in the future (O'Hanlon & Weiner-Davis, 1989); and the "Miracle Question" (de Shazer, 1991), in which partners are asked to identify specific changes that would result if they woke up to find that their problems had magically disappeared overnight: "What would be different, how would you know?" The key to future-oriented techniques is to engage couples in generating detailed images of how life would be without their problems—images at least as detailed as their current, constraining descriptions of their lives *with* the problems. This specific, future-oriented imagery increases hope and serves as a plan that motivates and guides the couple in attempts to initiate change.

For example, Ben Furman (personal communication) describes the use of a future-oriented approach to assist couples to eliminate escalations. In sessions in which a couple repeatedly engages in bitter, acrimonious exchanges, Furman first asks the partners how they feel the interaction is going, and receives the expected answer—"Not well!" He then suggests that the rest of the session be spent planning how they would prefer to talk with each other in the next session. Encouraging them to identify the specifics of how each would speak with the other more productively and kindly allows the partners to see that they already know how to do so, and sets the stage for change.

Guidelines for Choosing Interventions: the "Therapeutic Palette"

Through the early 1980s, practitioners of systems approaches generally claimed allegiance to one school of therapy (structural, strategic, Bowenian) and tested the limits of their particular school's set of interventions (Nichols & Schwartz, 1995). One effect of the introduction of postmodern thinking into the field has been to loosen these allegiances, as practitioners have come to realize that no theory captures the whole "truth" about families. Attention has turned to the more pragmatic question of which approach works with which couple with which therapist in which moment of the therapy—"effectiveness", at least in the sense of what Pinsof (1988) has called "small outcomes": changes observed and experienced in the session or between sessions that appear linked to interventions. Unfortunately, at the present time the research literature does not generally provide confident guidance for the practitioner to select one systems approach over another for particular presenting problems (Lebow & Gurman, 1995; Piercy

& Sprenkle, 1990; Sprenkle & Bischoff, 1995). More importantly for those who wish to integrate the useful aspects of the different systemic approaches, process research has not advanced yet to the point of identifying clear directions for choosing one approach or technique over another at a particular juncture in therapy—for example, when it might be useful to shift from a structural or strategic approach to an intergenerational approach. In addition, there is still a relative lack of published, manualized couple therapy based on systems concepts. And some researcher–clinicians have noted that manualized treatments may not offer the complete answer in any case, as they "can limit exactly that kind of complex decision-making typical in more complex variants of family therapy" (Lebow & Gurman, 1995, p. 46).

One organizing heuristic for making such choices that I have found useful in practice and teaching is the notion of the "therapeutic palette". Metaphorically speaking, the various specific systemic approaches and their associated practices represent a range of "colors", none of which is in itself better or worse than any other. Rather, each approach is selected at a particular time based on the needs of the particular "artist" painting a particular "painting", and its usefulness is judged based on its effectiveness in developing the painting according to the artist's vision. In other words, all therapeutic approaches and techniques are potentially useful, and gain their value in the moment based on their effectiveness in reaching the goals of a therapy with a particular couple.

Three of the general principles discussed earlier guide the application of this metaphor in therapy: the need to balance joining and supporting the existing system with the need to introduce novelty; an attempt to make therapy economical; and a belief in accessing the existing health and resources of the couple. Briefly and in turn: the therapist selects an intervention mindful that some will fit better with a couple's existing ways of thinking about themselves and their problems. For instance, some couples come in ready for present and future-oriented action approaches, and others believe their problems can only be solved by reflection on the past. As part of joining and developing the therapeutic system, the therapist may choose to begin the therapy by intervening in a manner congenial to the couple's existing ways of conceptualizing problems and change, and may save other, more challenging interventions for when the couple seems more secure in the therapeutic relationship. Alternatively, the therapist might decide to offer from the outset an approach that contrasts with the couple's ways of thinking. The therapist's choice will be guided by his or her assessment of how much novelty the couple needs and can handle at a particular moment.

In terms of economy, one way to approach making therapy brief is to begin with present and future-oriented techniques, reserving the more time-consuming family-of-origin approaches for instances when these other techniques fail to stimulate sufficient change.

Accessing the couple's existing health and resources can be viewed as the superordinate principle of the three. The more readily the therapist enables couples to find solutions to their problems from within their own sets of experiences and accustomed ways of thinking, perceiving, feeling and acting, the less novelty need be introduced, and the briefer will be the therapy. In addition, this emphasis on discovering what couples already can do fits with a guiding ethic in the field that therapists need to be respectful of partners' beliefs, values, and capacities, and should avoid overly directive approaches when these are not called for.

Thus, a therapist might begin with less directive approaches, such as highlighting exceptions to the problem, eliciting hidden beliefs, and offering supportive, positive reframes. If these interventions lead to little change, the therapist might engage in more challenging strategic and structural techniques, such as paradoxical interventions and unbalancing.

Even when using more confrontational approaches, the therapist needs to be respectful and to maintain an overall sense of collaboration. To return to the art metaphor, therapy is a painting co-created by the therapist and the couple: the therapist should look for every opportunity to hand the couple the brush.

REFERENCES

Alexander, I.E. (1990). *Personology: Method and Content in Personality Assessment and Psychobiography*. Durham, NC: Duke University Press.

Anderson, H. & Goolishian, H.A. (1988). Human systems as linguistic systems: preliminary and evolving ideas about the implications for clinical theory. *Family Process*, **27**, 371–393.

Bateson, G. (1972). *Steps to an Ecology of Mind*. New York: Ballantine.

Baucom, D.H. & Epstein, N. (1990). *Cognitive–Behavioral Marital Therapy*. New York: Brunner/Mazel.

Boscolo, L., Cecchin, G., Hoffman, L. & Penn, P. (1987). *Milan Systemic Family Therapy*. New York: Basic Books.

Boszormenyi-Nagy, I., Grunebaum, J. & Ulrich, D. (1991). Contextual therapy. In A.S. Gurman & D.P. Kniskern (eds), *Handbook of Family Therapy*, Vol. 2 (pp. 200–238). New York: Brunner/Mazel.

Boughner, S.R., Hayes, S.F., Bubenzer, D.L. & West, J.D. (1994). Use of standardized assessment instruments by marital and family therapists: a survey. *Journal of Marital and Family Therapy*, **20**, 69–75.

Boyd-Franklin, N. (1989). *Black Families in Therapy: a Multisystems Approach*. New York: Guilford.

Boyd-Franklin, N. (1993). Race, class, and poverty. In F. Walsh (ed.), *Normal Family Processes*, 2nd edn (pp. 361–376). New York: Guilford.

Bradt, J.O. (1989). Becoming parents: families with young children. In B. Carter & M. McGoldrick (eds), *The Changing Family Life Cycle: a Framework for Family Therapy*, 2nd edn (pp. 235–254). Boston: Allyn & Bacon.

Breunlin, D., Schwartz, R. & MacKune-Karrer, B. (1992). *Metaframeworks: Transcending the Models of Family Therapy*. San Francisco: Jossey-Bass.

Cade, B. & O'Hanlon, W.H. (1993). *A Brief Guide to Brief Therapy*. New York: Norton.

Carter, B. & McGoldrick, M. (eds) (1989). *The Changing Family Life Cycle: a Framework for Family Therapy*, 2nd edn. Boston: Allyn & Bacon.

Cecchin, G. (1987). Hypothesizing, circularity, and neutrality revisited: an invitation to curiosity. *Family Process*, **26**, 405–413.

Colapinto, J. (1991). Structural family therapy. In A.S. Gurman & D.P. Kniskern (eds), *Handbook of Family Therapy*, Vol. 2 (pp. 417–443). New York: Brunner/Mazel.

Davidson, M. (1983). *Uncommon Sense*. Los Angeles: J.P. Tarcher.

de Shazer, S. (1991). *Putting Difference to Work*. New York: Norton.

Ellman, B. & Taggart, M. (1993). Changing gender norms. In F. Walsh (ed.), *Normal Family Processes*, 2nd edn (pp. 377–404). New York: Guilford.

Falicov, C. (1988). Learning to think culturally. In H.A. Liddle, D.C. Breunlin & R.C. Schwartz (eds), *Handbook of Family Therapy Training and Supervision* (pp. 335–357). New York: Guilford.

Falloon, I.R.H., Boyd, J.L. & McGill, C.W. (1985). *Family Care of Schizophrenia*. New York: Guilford.

Filsinger, E.E. (ed.) (1983). *Marriage and Family Assessment: a Sourcebook for Family Therapy*. Beverly Hills, CA: Sage.

Fishman, H.C. (1993). *Intensive Structural Therapy: Treating Families in their Social Context*. New York: Basic Books.

Fraenkel, P. (1994a). Time and rhythm in couples. *Family Process*, **33**, 37–51.

Fraenkel, P. (1994b). Principles of narrative interviewing. Unpublished manuscript, Ackerman Institute for Family Therapy, New York.

Fraenkel, P. (1995a). The nomothetic–idiographic distinction in family therapy. *Family Process*, **34**, 113–121.

Fraenkel, P. (1995b). Minuchin's maxims, filtered through simile. Paper submitted for publication.

Fraenkel, P. & Markman, H. (in press). The family therapies. In S.J. Lynn & J. Garske (eds), *Contemporary Psychotherapies: Models and Methods*, 3rd edn. Pacific Grove, CA: Brooks Cole.

Franklin, A.J. (1992). Therapy with African-American men. *Families in Society*, **7**, 350–355.

Fredman, N. & Sherman, R. (1987) *Handbook of Measurements for Marriage and Family Therapy*. New York: Brunner/Mazel.

Freedman, J. & Combs, G. (1996) *Narrative Therapy: The Social Construction of Preferred Realities*. New York: Norton.

Furman, B. & Ahola, T. (1992). *Solution Talk: Hosting Therapeutic Conversations*. New York: Norton.

Gerson, R., Hoffman, S., Sauls, M. & Ulrici, D. (1993). Family-of-origin frames in couples therapy. *Journal of Marital and Family Therapy*, **19**, 341–354.

Goldner, V. (1985). Feminism and family therapy. *Family Process*, **24**, 31–47.

Goldner, V. (1988). Generation and gender: normative and covert hierarchies. *Family Process*, **27**, 17–33.

Goldner, V., Penn, P., Sheinberg, M. & Walker, G. (1990). Love and violence: gender paradoxes in volatile attachments. *Family Process*, **29**, 343–364.

Gottman, J.M. (1994). *What Predicts Divorce? The Relationship Between Marital Process and Marital Outcomes*. Hillsdale, NJ: Erlbaum.

Grotevant, H.D. & Carlson, C.I. (1989). *Family Assessment: a Guide to Methods and Measures*. New York: Guilford.

Guerin, P.J., Fay, L.F., Burden, S.L. & Kautto, J.G. (1987). *The Evaluation and Treatment of Marital Conflict: a Four-stage Approach*. New York: Basic Books.

Gurman, A.S. & Kniskern, D.P. (1981). Family therapy outcome research: knowns and unknowns. In A.S. Gurman & D.P. Kniskern (eds), *Handbook of Family Therapy* (pp. 742–775). New York: Brunner/Mazel.

Gurman, A.S., Kniskern, D.P. & Pinsof, W.M. (1986). Research on the process and outcome of marital and family therapy. In S.L. Garfield & A.E. Bergin (eds), *Handbook of Psychotherapy and Behavior Change*, 3rd edn (pp. 565–624). New York: Wiley.

Haley, J. (1987). *Problem-solving Therapy*, 2nd edn. San Francisco: Jossey-Bass.

Hardy, K.V. (1989). The theoretical myth of sameness: a critical issue in family therapy training and treatment. In G.W. Saba, B.M. Karrer & K.V. Hardy (eds), *Minorities and Family Therapy*. New York: Haworth.

Hare-Mustin, R.T. (1986). The problem of gender in family therapy theory. *Family Process*, **26**, 15–27.

Imber-Black, E., Roberts, J. & Whiting, R. (1989). *Rituals in Families and Family Therapy*. New York: Norton.

Jackson, D.D. (1965). Family rules: marital *quid pro quo*. *Archives of General Psychiatry*, **12**, 589–594.

Jacob, T. & Tennenbaum, D.L. (1988). *Family Assessment: Rationale, Methods, and Future Directions*. New York: Plenum.

Jones, E. (1993). *Family Systems Therapy: Developments in the Milan-systemic Therapies*. Chichester: Wiley.

Karpel, M.A. (1994). *Evaluating Couples: a Handbook for Practitioners*. New York: Norton.

Kaslow, F.W. (ed.) (1988). *Couples Therapy in a Family Context: Perspective and Retrospective*. Rockville, MD: Aspen.

Kerr, M. & Bowen, M. (1988). *Family Evaluation*. New York: Norton.

Lebow, J.L. & Gurman, A.S. (1995). Research assessing couple and family therapy. *Annual Review of Psychology*, **46**, 27–57.

Lederer, W. & Jackson, D.D. (1968). *The Mirages of Marriage*. New York: Norton.

Liddle, H.A. (1991). Empirical values and the culture of family therapy. *Journal of Marital and Family Therapy*, **17**, 327–348.

Madanes, C. (1981). *Strategic Family Therapy*. San Francisco: Jossey-Bass.

Markman, H.J. & Nortarius, C.I. (1987). Coding marital and family interaction: current status. In T. Jacob (ed.), *Family Interaction and Psychopathology: Theories, Methods, and Findings*. New York: Plenum.

Markman, H.J., Stanley, S. & Blumberg, S.L. (1994). *Fighting for your Marriage*. San Francisco: Jossey-Bass.

McGoldrick, M. & Gerson, R. (1985). *Genograms in Family Assessment*. New York: Norton.

McGoldrick, M. (1993). Ethnicity, cultural diversity, and normality. In F. Walsh (ed.), *Normal Family Processes*, 2nd edn (pp. 331–360). New York: Guilford.

Meyers, M., Diamond, R., Kezur, D., Scharf, C., Weinshel, M. & Rait, D.S. (1995). An infertility primer for family therapists. Part I: Medical, social, and psychological dimensions. *Family Process*, **34**, 219–229.

Minuchin, S. (1974). *Families and Family Therapy*. Cambridge, MA: Harvard University Press.

Minuchin, S. & Fishman, H.C. (1981). *Family Therapy Techniques*. Cambridge, MA: Harvard University Press.

Nichols, M.P. (1987). *The Self in the System*. New York: Brunner/Mazel.

Nichols, M.P. & Schwartz, R.C. (1995). *Family Therapy: Concepts and Methods*, 3rd edn. Boston: Allyn and Bacon.

O'Hanlon, W.H. & Weiner-Davis, M. (1989). *In Search of Solutions: a New Direction in Psychotherapy*. New York: Norton.

Paré, D.A. (1995). Of families and other cultures: the shifting paradigm of family therapy. *Family Process*, **34**, 1–19.

Piercy, F.P. & Sprenkle, D.H. (1990). Marriage and family therapy: a decade review. *Journal of Marriage and the Family*, **52**, 1116–1126.

Pinderhughes, E. (1989). *Understanding Race, Ethnicity, and Power: the Key to Efficacy in Clinical Practice*. New York: Free Press.

Pinsof, W.M. (1988). Strategies for the study of family process. In L.C. Wynne (ed.), *The State of the Art in Family Therapy: Controversies and Recommendations* (pp. 159–174). New York: Family Process Press.

Pinsof, W.M. & Catherall, D.R. (1986). The integrative psychotherapy alliance: family, couple, and individual scales. *Journal of Marital and Family Therapy*, **12**, 137–151.

Sarbin, T.R. & Mancuso, J.C. (1980). *Schizophrenia: Medical Diagnosis or Moral Verdict?* New York: Pergamon.

Satir, V.M. (1972). *Peoplemaking*. Palo Alto, CA: Science and Behavior Books.

Schwartz, R.C. (1994). *Internal Family Systems Therapy*. New York: Guilford.

Selvini Palazzoli, M., Boscolo, L., Cecchin, G. & Prata, G. (1978a). A ritualized prescription in family therapy: odd days and even days. *Journal of Marriage and Family Counseling*, **4**, 3–9.

Selvini Palazzoli, M., Boscolo, L., Cecchin, G. & Prata, G. (1978b). *Paradox and Counterparadox*. New York: Jason Aronson.

Selvini Palazzoli, M., Boscolo, L., Cecchin, G. & Prata, G. (1980). Hypothesizing–circularity–neutrality: three guidelines for the conductor of the session. *Family Process*, **19**, 3–12.

Sprenkle, D.H. & Bischoff, R.J. (1995). Research in family therapy: trends, issues, and recommendations. In M.P. Nichols & R.C. Schwartz, *Family Therapy: Concepts and Methods*, 3rd edn (pp. 542–580). Boston: Allyn & Bacon.

Todd, T.C. (1986). Structural–strategic marital therapy. In N.S. Jacobson & A.S. Gurman (eds), *Clinical Handbook of Marital Therapy* (pp. 71–105). New York: Guilford.

Tomm, K. (1987). Interventive interviewing: Part I. Strategizing as a fourth guideline for the therapist. *Family Process*, **26**, 3–13.

Touliatos, J., Perlmutter, B. & Straus, M.A. (1990). *Handbook of Family Measurement Techniques*. Newbury Park: Sage.

Walter, J.L. & Peller, J.E. (1992). *Becoming Solution-focused in Brief Therapy*. New York: Brunner/Mazel.

Watzlawick, P., Beavin, J.H. & Jackson, D.D. (1967). *Pragmatics of Human Communication*. New York: Norton.

Watzlawick, P., Weakland, J. & Fisch, R. (1974). *Change: Principles of Problem Formation and Problem Resolution*. New York: Norton.

Weber, T., McKeever, J.E. & McDaniel, S.H. (1985). A beginner's guide to the problem-oriented first family interview. *Family Process*, **24**, 357–364.

Whitaker, C.A. & Keith, D.V. (1981). Symbolic–experiential family therapy. In A.S. Gurman & D.P. Kniskern (eds), *Handbook of Family Therapy* (pp. 187–225). New York: Brunner/Mazel.

White, M. (1992). Deconstruction and therapy. In D. Epston & M. White (eds), *Experience, Contradiction, Narrative, & Imagination: Selected Papers of David Epston and Michael White* (pp. 109–151). Adelaide, South Australia: Dulwich Centre Publications.

White, M. & Epston, D. (1990). *Narrative Means to Therapeutic Ends*. New York: Norton.

Wynne, L.C. (ed.) (1988). *The State of the Art in Family Therapy Research: Controversies and Recommendations*. New York: Family Process Press.

Wynne, L.C., Ryckoff, I., Day, J. & Hirsch, S.I. (1958). Pseudomutuality in the family relationships of schizophrenics. *Psychiatry*, **21**, 205–220.

Chapter 17

Cognitive–Behavioral Couples Therapy

Norman B. Epstein*, Donald H. Baucom**
and Anthony Daiuto**
*Department of Family Studies, University of Maryland,
College Park, MD; and ** Department of Psychology,
University of North Carolina, Chapel Hill, NC, USA

Cognitive–behavioral couples therapy (CBCT) has emerged as a major approach for the treatment of marital and couple distress, with growing empirical support for its effectiveness (cf. Baucom & Epstein, 1990). In this chapter, we discuss the CBCT approach to assessing and treating relationship distress. Prior to doing so, we introduce the individual and relationship variables that typically are the foci of our attention during work with a distressed couple. These include the behaviors, cognitions and emotions that characterize the partners and their pattern of functioning as a couple. In addition to these factors, which have traditionally been the foci of CBCT, we describe three major content themes (boundaries, power/control, and investment) associated with relationship distress that commonly arise in couples' behavioral, cognitive and affective responses to each other, and that have more recently been foci of our clinical and empirical work.

FACTORS IN MARITAL DISTRESS

Behavioral Factors

Fundamental to the practice of CBCT are social learning (Bandura, 1977) and social exchange (Thibaut & Kelley, 1959) models that postulate that an individual's behavior both influences and is influenced by his/her environment. When applied to the domain of marital relationships, these theories suggest that each

Clinical Handbook of Marriage and Couples Interventions. Edited by W. Kim Halford and Howard J. Markman.
© 1997 John Wiley & Sons Ltd.

spouse's behaviors influence the actions of the other, thus creating a reciprocal process of mutual causality in relationship interactions. CBCT typically focuses on two aspects of this process: (a) exchanges of positive and negative "non-communication" behaviors; and (b) communication skills that influence interaction processes. A detailed review of the empirical support for the importance of these types of behavior in relationship functioning is provided in the chapter by Weiss & Heyman, this volume, as well as in Baucom & Epstein (1990) and Weiss & Heyman (1990). There is considerable evidence to support the social exchange concept that an individual's satisfaction with a relationship depends on the rates of positive and negative "non-communication" behaviors experienced with the partner. For example, a number of studies (e.g. Birchler, Weiss & Vincent, 1975; Christensen & Nies, 1980; Jacobson, Follett & McDonald, 1982; Margolin, 1981; Wills, Weiss & Patterson, 1974) have shown that spouses' overall marital satisfaction and their daily reports of satisfaction both are correlated with their partners' daily frequencies of specific pleasing and displeasing affectional (e.g. giving a hug) and instrumental (e.g. working on a household chore) behaviors.

Similarly, because communication problems are the most commonly reported presenting complaint of distressed couples (Geiss & O'Leary, 1981), there is an extensive clinical and empirical literature addressing couples' communication skills from a behavioral perspective. Baucom & Epstein (1990) have proposed that there are two important foci of couples' communications, and that conversations can vary greatly depending on the purpose of the communication. One focus involves expressive and listening skills (involving the sharing of the two partners' thoughts and emotions), and the other involves the use of problem-solving skills for the identification and resolution of problems in the relationship.

Concerning expressive and listening skills, the ability to share important thoughts and feelings with another person is one of the distinguishing characteristics of intimate relationships. Yet, when couples seek treatment, they frequently note that the sharing of intimate thoughts and feelings has greatly decreased. Furthermore, spouses may differ in their ability and comfort with expressing different kinds of positive and negative emotions, such as affection, tenderness, anger and fear.

The lack of expression of certain emotions should not be interpreted automatically as a behavior skills deficit that simply needs to be practiced. There might be important cognitive factors (see discussion below) that inhibit a partner from expressing certain emotions. For example, one partner might hold a standard that a person should not "complain" to others while feeling down, because such complaining places a burden on the listener. Such a standard might inhibit a spouse from expressing dejection, worry or uncertainty to his/her partner. Thus, the CBCT approach to understanding and treating couples' communication problems views them in a broader context in which behavior, cognition and emotion continuously influence each other.

In addition to helping couples develop greater specificity and clarity (logic, organization, and verbal–nonverbal consistency) in their expressions of thoughts and emotions, CBCT emphasizes how messages are interpreted or "decoded" by the recipient. For example, there is evidence that distressed spouses selectively attend more to negative than to positive behaviors by their partners (e.g. Christensen, Sullaway & King, 1983).

Problem-solving skills can be used to address a wide range of issues in couples' relationships, from relatively minor daily decisions (e.g. how to spend weekend time) to major problems (e.g. serious conflicts about in-laws). Successful problem-solving is a process that involves: (a) defining the problem clearly in behavioral terms; (b) generating alternative solutions; (c) agreeing on a solution; and (d) implementing the solution (Baucom & Epstein, 1990; Epstein, Baucom & Rankin, 1993). A goal of CBCT is to substitute constructive problem-solving for the aversive control strategies (e.g. threat, punishment) and negative behavior exchanges that are common among distressed couples (Baucom & Epstein, 1990; Weiss & Heyman 1990, and this volume). Along with the specific problem-solving skills, couples are taught a variety of communication strategies that can assist them as they proceed through the problem-solving steps. These strategies fall into three major categories (see Baucom & Epstein, 1990, for a detailed description): (a) communications that assist in establishing one's own current desires, as well as one's role in previous interactions in the problem area, e.g. speaking for oneself and using "I" messages; acknowledging one's responsibility and role in the problem, rather than blaming one's partner; (b) communications to acknowledge one's partner, e.g. using eye contact to express listening and concern, reflecting back important thoughts and feelings that the partner has expressed; and (c) communications that can help maintain a focus on finding good solutions, e.g. focusing on the future progress rather than who may have been at fault in the past, avoiding becoming sidetracked onto tangential or unrelated issues.

Cognitive Factors

The importance of cognitive factors in relationship functioning lies in the fact that objectively observable behavioral events are often subjectively experienced quite differently by the partners. CBCT assumes that dysfunctional emotional and behavioral responses within the relationship are mediated, to some extent, by maladaptive cognitive processing. In our work with couples, we focus on five types of cognitions (Baucom & Epstein, 1990; Baucom et al., 1989; Epstein & Baucom, 1993) applicable to intimate relationships.

Assumptions are basic beliefs about the nature of intimate relationships and the behaviors of spouses. All individuals have developed such beliefs, based on a variety of life experiences observing or participating in relationships. Assumptions can be problematic when they are based on limited or inaccurate information and therefore are not representative of marriage in general, or a person's own marriage. Thus, if an individual grew up in a home in which any disagreement led to hostile, destructive arguments, he or she may assume that expression of disagreement is destructive to a relationship, and may be inhibited from discussing any relationship problems with his/her partner.

Standards are views that partners hold about the way that close relationships and intimate partners "should" be. Standards commonly serve positive functions in intimate relationships, such as providing partners with ethical guidelines for their conduct with each other (e.g. treating each other with respect, avoiding abusive behavior). However, difficulties between partners may arise if one or both partners hold extreme or unrealistic standards, or if they are dissatisfied with how their relationship standards are being met. Baucom et al. (1996) found that the degree to which an individual was satisfied with how his/her standards were being met in the marriage was a stronger predictor of marital adjustment than was the extremity of the standards or the discrepancy between the two partners' standards.

Selective attention refers to the process of focusing on only a subset of partner behaviors when cognitively processing the events occurring in one's relationship. Although this is adaptive to some extent, it can become problematic when attention is biased in some systematic way, perhaps by an inaccurate assumption, an unrealistic standard or the prevailing emotional climate in the relationship. Thus, if an individual assumes that people who love each other consistently express those feelings verbally, he/she may attend selectively to a partner's verbal expressions of love, failing to notice the partner's non-verbal behaviors (e.g. hugs, actions done as favors). Weiss (1980) described the process of "sentiment over-ride" in which an individual's perception of a partner's current behavior as positive or negative can be determined more by the person's overall positive or negative emotions toward the partner than by the quality of the partner's actions.

Attributions are the basic inferences that spouses make to explain partner behaviors and marital events. An extensive body of empirical literature (cf. Baucom & Epstein, 1990; Bradbury & Fincham, 1990; Noller, Beach & Osgarby, this volume) has documented that spouses' relationship distress is associated with their tendencies to make global and stable attributions for relationship problems, as well as their tendency to blame their partners. These attributions to negative partner traits have been labeled "distressed-maintaining" (Holzworth-Munroe & Jacobson, 1985) because they contribute to reciprocity in negative behavior exchanges between spouses (Bradbury & Fincham, 1992).

Expectancies are inferences that spouses make about future marital events and partner behaviors. When based on accurate observation of one's spouse over time, expectancies can contribute to a smooth meshing of the two individuals' behaviors. However, expectancies are likely to be maladaptive when they are based on inaccurate information or assumptions. For example, an individual who grew up in a family characterized by escalating arguments may have developed an assumption that people respond to any criticism with defensiveness. In subsequent relationships, the individual may predict such defensiveness and therefore may choose not to reveal any sources of dissatisfaction with others' behavior.

Affective Factors

Although much of the therapeutic work in CBCT is directly focused on behavioral and cognitive factors, an understanding of each partner's affective responses as both causes and consequences of behaviors and cognitions is critical to effective CBCT. We focus on four important affective factors in our assessment and treatment of couples:

First, the degree and timing of positive and negative emotions experienced by the spouses can serve as indicators of significant relationship events and guide therapists in exploring links between these emotions and the partner's cognitive and behavioral processes (Kelley et al., 1983). Specific emotions are often linked to salient cognitive themes and may motivate different behavioral responses in a predictable way, as when the attribution that one's partner is intentionally trying to be hurtful elicits anger and verbal attacks against the partner. Second, the partners' abilities to recognize their emotions and the causes of them is essential for clear communication. Spouses vary widely in their ability to clearly differentiate subtly distinct emotional states, or the internal and external events that cause them. Third, both deficits and excesses of emotional expressiveness are clinically significant, as is the degree of consistency between each individual's verbal and non-verbal messages (Stuart, 1980). Finally, the presence of intense emotional reactions (e.g. anxiety, anger, jealousy, depression) by one or both of the partners warrants clinical attention when they reflect serious relationship problems or interfere with adaptive behavioral and cognitive functioning (e.g. problem-solving and communication skills).

THEMATIC ISSUES IN COUPLE INTERACTIONS

The above factors represent the traditional targets of assessment and intervention in CBCT. In our ongoing work with distressed couples, however, we have focused on three thematic issues that partners inevitably confront at some point in an intimate relationship. These issues guide our conceptualization of a couple's pattern of functioning, unifying the partners' maladaptive behaviors, dysfunctional cognitions and negative emotions in a psychologically meaningful way that facilitates treatment planning.

The issue of boundaries refers to the degree of emotional and interpersonal distance or autonomy between the partners. Conflicts about boundaries can arise in couples' relationships in two major ways. First, even though two individuals have chosen to form an intimate relationship, the two partners may have different preferences concerning the amount of autonomy vs. sharing between them. For example, some couples experience conflict and distress because one partner enjoys spending time involved in individual activities more than the other does, or the members of the couple differ in the extent to which they express personal thoughts and feelings with the other person. Second, an individual partner may have an *internal* conflict between desires for autonomy and togetherness, where perceiving the self as moving in one direction leads to distress and an attempt to move in the other direction. Thus, members of some couples even appear to engage in alternating cycles of approaching and distancing from each other, as they respond to subjective distress from too great or too little of a boundary between them. Empirical and clinical reports suggest that better relationship adjustment is associated with the partners' ability to balance individual autonomy and togetherness (Argyle & Furnham, 1983; Fitzpatrick, 1988).

Power issues involve the degree of symmetry in the two partners' control over the relationship (Blumberg & Coleman, 1989; Stuart, 1980). Power in a couple's relationship can be viewed in terms of the *process* by which the partners attempt to influence decisions and events in the relationship and the *outcomes* of decisions and events. For example, each partner may use varying degrees of persuasive strategies (e.g. logical arguments, threats) in the process of trying to induce the other person's compliance. Power outcomes ultimately involve the degrees to which the two partners' preferences are reflected in the ways that the couple carry out the various functions in their life together, such as how money is spent and how they divide household tasks. In asymmetrical relationships, one partner exercises greater influence than the other over relationship processes and/or outcomes. Symmetrical relationships, characterized by balanced levels of influence and shared control over relationship functioning, have been found to be associated with higher levels of relationship satisfaction (Gray-Little & Burks, 1983).

Finally, investment involves the types and amount of contributions that the partners make to the relationship. Partners can give of themselves both in the affective realm (e.g. expressing caring and support for the partner) and instrumentally (e.g. spending time on household chores and parenting responsibilities). Studies (e.g. Ray, 1988; Rusbult, Zembrodt & Gunn, 1982) show that both types of investment are associated with positive relationship adjustment. Furthermore, there is evidence that spouses who attribute relationship problems to their partners having selfish motivation (as opposed to giving of themselves) experience greater marital distress (Bradbury & Fincham, 1990). Marital therapists commonly encounter couples in which the two members have conflicts and distress regarding the ways and degrees to which each person expresses investment in their relationship. Sometimes the source of the conflict is that one partner focuses on expressive acts and the other on instrumental acts as the mode of expressing investment, with one or both individuals unhappy with what the other is providing.

ASSESSMENT

In clinical practice, the assessment of the cognitive, affective and behavioral factors influencing the quality of a couple's relationship is based on three major sources: (a) conjoint and individual interviews of the two partners; (b) questionnaires; and (c) the therapist's direct observation of the couple's behavioral interactions. Given the mutual influences among the cognitive, affective and behavioral components of relationship functioning, we generally attempt to integrate our assessment of them by collecting information about all three simultaneously as we use each of the above three data sources. Consequently, this section describes an integrative assessment by interview, questionnaire and behavioral observation. It also is important to note that in clinical practice, assessment is not restricted to an initial period before clinical interventions are initiated; rather, assessment is ongoing throughout the course of therapy. Therapists commonly use a couple's responses to specific interventions as further data about the couple, at times modifying the treatment on the basis of the new information. Furthermore, as a couple becomes more comfortable with their therapist, they may reveal more personal information (e.g. regarding abuse or sexual problems) that they withheld earlier. Thus, we make systematic efforts to conduct assessment in our initial contacts with couples but also approach treatment planning as a flexible process that evolves as additional assessment occurs. The following is an overview of assessment in CBCT; for a more detailed description, see the text by Baucom & Epstein (1990).

Interviews

One of the early clinical decisions facing the couples therapist is whether, and how much, to interview the members of a couple individually vs. conjointly. Overall, we prefer to assess couples conjointly, in order to identify the mutual, circular influences that the two partners have on each other. However, even though individual interviews raise a number of significant clinical and ethical issues, such as confidentiality and the handling of secrets (e.g. Karpel, 1980; Margolin, 1986), there are situations in which we believe that meeting with each partner alone can be of value. First, when either or both partners exhibit a degree of individual psychopathology (e.g. clinical depression, a personality disorder) that appears to have a negative impact on the couple's relationship, an individual interview can be used to gather information on the person's past and current functioning, within and outside the marriage. Similarly, when our initial conjoint interview(s) with a couple suggest that one or both members experience affective responses (ranging from emotional detachment to high levels of emotion such as anger or anxiety) that are likely to interfere with conjoint therapy, individual interviews provide an opportunity to assess the determinants of these emotions and the potential for moderating them in the interest of constructive couple work. We attempt to avoid focusing on one partner as the "identified patient" by scheduling similar individual assessment interviews with both members of a couple.

Interview Assessment of Behavior

During their initial interview with a therapist, couples typically expect to describe the problems that have led them to seek professional assistance, but individual partners vary in the degree to which they provide specific examples of the behaviors involved in the problems, as compared with global descriptions. Consequently, when we ask the members of a couple to tell us what led them to contact us, we follow up any vague or general terms they use with queries concerning behavioral definitions of the problems. For example, if a husband states that his wife is "uncooperative when I try to get her to sit down and discuss our finances", the therapist might ask him to provide specific examples of how he asks her, how she responds, and how he behaves subsequently. He also would be asked about the context of the interaction (e.g. location, time of day, preceding events). Given that two partners' perceptions and memories of even recent, concrete events in their relationship can differ considerably (Christensen, Sullaway & King, 1983), the wife in this couple may provide a different description of the same incident. Consequently, rather than viewing these self-reports as objective data concerning the couple's behavioral interactions (unless the partners' reports of an event are very similar), we consider them to be "filtered" versions of events, influenced by each partner's selective attention or tendency to hold the other person responsible for problems in their relationship.

Although couples commonly focus on describing their problems during initial interviews, it is important to assess current strengths in their relationships as well, particularly when partners' distress may have been increased by their selective attention to problems. Identifying sources of positive interaction can help counteract negative selective attention (and the negative affect that tends to accompany it), and increasing these positive interactions can be an important goal for therapy. We typically ask couples to identify and situations in which they have more positive or constructive interactions, and to describe the sequence of those interactions in the same degree of detail that they used to tell us about their problematic interactions.

For example, a couple interviewed by one of us reported frequent arguments and a mutual feeling of alienation from each other. Their conflicts typically centered on how each spouse used time on a daily basis. On the one hand, the wife was unhappy with the degree to which her husband spent time at his job and working on household and yard projects, rather than spending more time with her and taking care of their 3-year-old daughter. On the other hand, the husband complained that his wife used time very inefficiently (e.g. spending long periods of time getting their daughter ready for bed; browsing slowly when shopping in stores; sitting and worrying about events at her job). Their two daily schedules were poorly meshed, such that they had little leisure time together. This problem was compounded by the fact that the couple did not feel comfortable leaving their child with babysitters (they had no relatives living nearby), and thus they rarely went out together as a couple. Consequently, there were few exchanges of affection and infrequent sex. Nevertheless, when the therapist inquired about instances of positive interaction, the couple described how, on their last wedding anniversary, they had made a special exception and left their daughter overnight with their close friends and had checked into a local hotel. They reported having a very enjoyable evening of dancing, sharing their favorite foods at dinner, and pleasurable sex. The therapist used this example to discuss with the couple the evidence that their conflict and distress appeared to be situation-specific, and that they clearly were still capable of enjoying themselves together. Even though it was not possible to make daily life like their anniversary celebration, the success of that experience provided valuable information for problem-solving discussions designed to make even small changes in their daily interactions that could capture the essence of what produced intimate feelings on that occasion.

Thus, within a social exchange framework, the couple is interviewed about the types and frequencies of their positive and negative interactions. This assessment includes questions about their typical daily schedules, focusing on how much time they spend together, under what conditions, and what activities they share. This aspect of the interview focuses on the "non-communication" behaviors in the relationship and is important in the design of interventions to increase positive exchanges and decrease negative ones.

In order to place the descriptions of current problems and strengths in a developmental context, the therapist also interviews the couple about their relationship history. Questions focus on how and where they met, what qualities attracted them to each other (and whether those are still present), what events led to their decision to get married (or form a committed relationship), what positive and negative events seemed to shape their relationship over time, when they first noticed the problems developing, and what solutions they have attempted to solve the problems. Baucom & Epstein (1990) provide a more detailed description of the history-taking interview. The partners' responses to these questions help the therapist to identify past events in the relationship (e.g. abuse, an affair) that may be influencing the couple's current functioning, to determine whether current interaction patterns are chronic or are responses to situational factors (e.g. the transition to parenthood), and to form hypotheses about whether partners' decreases in satisfaction over time were the result of changes in each other's behavior or changes in what each person experiences as pleasing or acceptable.

Asking the couple how they have attempted to resolve their problems can shed light on their problem-solving strategies and skills. For example, it is common to hear that partners have used various forms of coercion (e.g. verbal threats, criticism) to try to influence each other, or have withdrawn from each other in the face of apparent stalemates. Again, it is important to view these self-reports as the partners' subjective perceptions of their problem-solving behavior, which the therapist should supplement with direct observation (described below).

When the couple described above was interviewed about their relationship history, they described how they initially were very attracted to each other and spent a large amount of time together sharing activities, talking, and having very enjoyable sex. However, a combination of parenthood, home ownership, and increasing pressures from both partners' jobs led the couple to develop their current pattern of minimal time together. Tracking how developmental shifts in their interactions were correlated with changes in the quality of their communication (e.g. decreased sharing of feelings, especially concerning caring feelings for each other) contributed to a conceptualization of their problems, as well as to a treatment plan for counteracting the negative changes.

Interviews afford opportunites to gather a variety of other information about a couple's relationship, such as an assessment of each partner's commitment to the relationship and level of motivation for therapy, and life stresses (e.g. job, childrearing, in-law conflicts, physical illesses, substance abuse) affecting the partners' daily functioning. Although much of this information involves the partners' cognitions and emotions, it also it important to obtain behavioral descriptions of these issues. For example, when an individual says that he/she finds visits with the partner's parents stressful, the therapist should ask for details about the sequences of interactions among all of the involved parties, preferably with specific reference to a recent visit.

Interview Assessment of Cognition and Affect

The assessment of each partner's cognitions and emotions regarding their relationship is integrated with the assessment of behaviors during clinical interviews. Whenever asking about frequencies and patterns of behaviors, the therapist is prepared to probe for information about associated cognition and affect. At times couples spontaneously report such experiences, but often the therapist needs to elicit the material with questions that do not "lead" the interviewees. Sometimes a shift in a partner's verbal or non-verbal behavior during a session is a clue that an event in the interaction has triggered a cognition or emotion that should be explored. For example, as one partner is describing a recent argument the couple had, the therapist may notice that the other partner seems upset. After the former individual has had an opportunity to finish his/her description, the therapist can turn to the latter individual and say, "I noticed that while Jim was talking, you seemed to be feeling something. Would you be willing to describe it?" The therapist can use a series of follow-up questions to help the partner specify the cognitions (e.g. the perception, "Jim won't take *any* personal responsibility for our problems") and emotions (e.g. anger) that were elicited by hearing what the other person was saying. Further assessment of such cognitions and emotions can be conducted through systematic observation of a couple's interactions in planned behavioral tasks (described below).

In addition to identifying moment-to-moment cognitions and emotions that occur in the course of a session, the therapist can interview the members of a couple about their assumptions, standards and other cognitions concerning their relationship, especially when he/she has heard "hints" that particular cognitions are relevant to the couple's presenting complaints. For example, when members of a couple report that they often argue about the division of household responsibilities, the therapist can ask each partner to describe his/her personal standards about how such tasks should be handled. The therapist who interviewed the couple described above, who had grown apart as they faced parenthood, home ownership and increasing job demands, inquired about what each partner found upsetting regarding the other's use of time. The ensuing discussion revealed that the relationship themes of boundaries and investment were salient. The wife held a standard that spouses should exhibit their investment in their marriage by spending time expressing feelings and listening to each other's feelings, as well as by spending leisure time with each other. Her focus was on expressive invest-ment, whereas the husband expressed his standard that a responsible husband shows his investment in his marriage and family by earning a good living and making improvements to their house and yard. Furthermore, the wife attributed the husband's extensive time spent at work and on house projects to a boundary problem, expressing her concern about his involvement outside their marriage by referring to it as "his affair with his work". Thus, the interviewer was able to identify specific core themes in each partner's cognitions that became foci of therapeutic interventions.

Similarly, interviews afford an opportunity to assess the range and intensity of emotions that each partner experiences in the context of their relationship, as well as more broadly in his/her life. At times an individual will report experienc-ing considerable pleasure at work and with friends, in contrast to feelings of anger and sadness when with the partner, whereas sometimes an individual describes more global and chronic affect (e.g. depression). It is important for the therapist to probe for information about times and situations when a particular emotion has been present or absent, both within and outside the relationship.

Clinical interviews can be limited by the skills of the interviewer in seeking information that is sufficiently broad and deep concerning partners' cognitions and emotions. Consequently, it can be helpful to use an outline or other written guide (cf. Baucom & Epstein, 1990) as a reference when conducting assessment interviews with a couple. However, no structured guide can be a substitute for the interviewer's own ability to use a series of follow-up questions to help partners different specific cognitions and emotions that they experience.

Structured Observations of Couple Interaction

As described above, the data that members of couples provide during clinical interviews tend to be subjective reports, often concerning past events outside the therapy room. Given the potential biases in such reports, cognitive–behavioral therapists traditionally have stressed the importance of observing a couple's interactions first-hand. Even though couples may censor their behavior in the presence of therapists, there is considerable evidence that behavioral interactions in such controlled settings differentiate distressed from non-distressed couples (Weiss & Heyman, 1990).

Observation of Behavioral Interactions

In marital research studies, couples often are asked to engage in fairly brief (e.g. 15-minute) discussions in which their task is to try to resolve a problem that they have identified in their relationship. The interaction is videotaped and subse-

quently coded by trained raters, using a behavioral coding system such as the
Marital Interaction Coding System (MICS; Weiss & Summers, 1983), the Couples Interaction Scoring System (CISS; Gottman, 1979; Notarius & Markman,
1981) or the Kategoriensystem für Partnerschaftliche Interaktion (KPI; Hahlweg
et al., 1984). These act-by-act coding systems allow the identification of both
frequencies and sequences of behavior exchanges between members of a couple.
Although they have been valuable tools in marital research, they tend to be
cumbersome and expensive in clinical practice. However, Baucom & Epstein
(1990) have described how therapists can become familiar with coding systems
and use their categories as guides for assessing couples' interactions. For example, Baucom & Epstein's (1990) text includes a checklist version of Weiss &
Summers' (1983) Marital Interaction Coding System (MICS III), with which the
clinician rates the frequency with which couples exhibit each MICS category of
verbal and non-verbal behavior (e.g. problem description, complain, positive
solution, deny responsibility, interrupt, positive physical contact, smile, turn-off),
using a four-point scale ranging from "not at all" to "large amount". This approach is similar to the global version of the MICS developed by Weiss & Tolman
(1990), in which observers rate each member of a couple on major categories of
behavior (problem-solving, validation, facilitation, invalidation, conflict and
withdrawal) that he/she exhibits during a problem-solving discussion. Ratings are
made after every few minutes of interaction, using a six-point scale reflecting the
frequency and intensity of the behavior. Weiss & Tolman (1990) provide guidelines for identifying the verbal and non-verbal behaviors that comprise the six
major behavioral categories, and for making the global frequency/intensity ratings. For example, the conflict category includes verbal content such as complaints, criticism, negative mindreading (attributing negative characteristics to
the partner), put-downs, and negative commands, as well as non-verbal behaviors
such as hostile gestures, whining and vocal tone qualities reflecting anger, sarcasm or bitterness. When we ask a couple to allow us to observe their problem-
solving interaction, we explain that it is very helpful for us to have an opportunity
to see how they talk and work with each other. In a similar manner, we ask
couples to discuss their thoughts and feelings about a particular relationship
issue, and we observe their expressive and listening behaviors.

Observation of Cognitive and Affective Responses

As noted earlier, a therapist can monitor cues that partners are experiencing
thoughts and emotions about each other's behavior during clinical interviews,
and can explore these. In addition to waiting for these responses to occur spontaneously during interviews, the therapist can use structured couple discussions
to assess them. As described above, asking a couple to select a relationship issue
and engage in either a problem-solving discussion or a discussion where they
exchange their thoughts and emotions can elicit interactions that may be milder
than those that occur at home, but genuine responses commonly are elicited

nevertheless. In contrast to the clinical interview where one can interrupt the discussion to inquire about moment-to-moment cognitive and emotional responses, the therapist may allow the couple to talk without interruptions, thereby obtaining a more representative sample of their communications. Although subsequently asking each partner to recall his/her cognitions and emotions retrospectively risks some error, this limitation can be reduced by videotaping the interaction and replaying it for the couple.

Among the cognitive factors that are important to assess are assumptions and standards about communication and problem-solving (e.g. "I shouldn't have to tell my partner how to behave so that I feel loved. She should know"; "A good relationship shouldn't take all of this work of sitting down and discussing how to solve problems"). Also important are the attributions that partners make about each other during their discussions (e.g. "He is a selfish person who won't consider any solution that might benefit me"), their expectancies (e.g. "If I tell her that it would be painful if she left me, she'll use that as ammunition to control me") and instances of their selective attention (e.g. "He always interrupts me when I'm expressing my feelings").

Observation of a couple's discussions also provides a sample of each partner's emotional responses. For example, the therapist may observe evidence of sentiment override (Weiss, 1980), in which one person appears to become angry about things that the other says, even when the partner is expressing positive feelings about the relationship or is suggesting constructive solutions to a problem. For example, Walsh et al. (1993) found that within maritally distressed couples, if one spouse said anything about the partner (either a positive, neutral or negative comment), it increased the likelihood that the partner would respond with a negative. The therapist then can explore causes of the sentiment override, such as the person's memories of past negative experiences with the partner and a desire to protect oneself from future hurt. It also is important to determine whether the general sentiment reflects a broader affective issue for the individual (e.g. a mood or anxiety disorder) that may require some specific intervention in itself. The therapist also may observe a pattern in which a partner's specific emotional responses are associated with discussions of particular relationship themes (e.g. anger associated with conflicts between partners about appropriate boundaries between them) that should be foci of therapeutic efforts.

When observing a couple sharing their thoughts and emotions about a topic, the therapist also can observe the degree to which each partner appears to be able to recognize his/her emotions and their causes, as well as the skill with which the emotions are expressed. Some individuals have difficulty articulating specific emotional responses, and this deficit can become an important target for therapeutic interventions. As noted earlier, it is important to ask questions to determine whether a deficit in emotional expressiveness is due to a skill problem or reflects inhibition about expression based on cognitive factors.

Questionnaires

Whereas clinical interviews and structured observations allow varying degrees of latitude in probing for couples' idiosyncratic responses, questionnaires can be quite helpful by providing efficient and systematic coverage of behavioral, cognitive and affective components of a couple's interactions. Questionnaires also can elicit a wealth of information that can be explored in greater depth with interviews. There are numerous instruments that have been constructed to assess couples' relationships, and a comparative review of them is beyond the scope of this chapter. Consequently, the reader can consult general sources such as Jacob & Tennenbaum (1988), Touliatos, Perlmutter & Straus (1990), as well as marital texts such as Baucom & Epstein (1990) and O'Leary (1987). The following is a sample of questionnaires that assess behavioral cognitive and affective factors in couple relationships.

Questionnaires Assessing Behavioral Interactions

Several instruments have been used widely in CBCT to assess the behaviors that partners perceive in their relationships. Some measures focus on the exchanges of positive and negative non-communication behaviors, whereas others are devoted to the assessment of communication. For example, on the Areas of Change questionnaire (A-C; Weiss, Hops & Patterson, 1973), each partner reports the degree to which he/she wants the partner to make particular kinds of behavioral changes, in areas such as household tasks, finances, communication and sex. Rather than providing an index of what behaviors actually occur in the relationship, the A-C tends to reflect partners' perceptions and standards for behavior (Baucom & Epstein, 1990).

The Spouse Observation Checklist (SOC; Weiss & Perry, 1983) is an inventory of 408 specific behaviors that each partner is asked to complete, to describe positive and negative events occurring in their relationship during 24-hour periods. The items were developed to cover twelve important content areas, such as affection, companionship, communication and household management. Because there often are discrepancies between partners concerning the events that occurred, even when they report relatively concrete behaviors within a discrete time-frame (Christensen, Sullaway & King, 1983; Floyd & Markman, 1983; Jacobson & Moore, 1981), the therapist who uses instruments such as the SOC must take into account this subjectivity. It is important to explore discrepancies in couples' reports carefully and to try to identify the factors that produced them (e.g. inhibition about revealing negative behaviors).

Most questionnaires that assess couples' communication have tended to include fairly global items and result in a total score that indicates the overall quality of communication. Examples of such instruments are the Marital Communication Inventory (MCI; Bienvenu, 1970) and the Primary Communication Inventory (PCI; Navran, 1967). In contrast, items in Christensen's (1988) Communication Patterns Questionnaire (CPQ) ask the respondent about the frequencies of specific behavioral sequences, such as one partner making demands and the other then withdrawing. It has been our experience that instruments such as the CPQ are needed to elicit the level of specificity about behavioral interactions that is required for designing therapeutic interventions.

Questionnaire Measures of Cognition

There is a growing number of questionnaires designed to assess couples' assumptions, standards, attributions, expectancies and selective attention concerning their relationships. Eidelson & Epstein's (1982) Relationship Belief Inventory (RBI) has been used widely (e.g. Baucom & Epstein, 1990; Bradbury & Fincham, 1993; O'Leary, 1987), and it taps two standards (that partners should be able to mindread each other's thoughts and emotions; that individuals should be perfect sexual partners) and three assumptions (that disagreement is destructive to a relationship; that partners cannot change themselves or their relationship; that marital problems are due to innate gender differences). In spite of the utility of the RBI, we have developed a new questionnaire, the Inventory of Specific Relationship Standards (ISRS; Baucom et al., 1996) that is designed to survey partners' standards concerning boundaries, control/power and investment across twelve relationship content areas, such as affection, household tasks, communication of positive and negative feelings, finances and leisure time. The items have three parts, assessing: (a) the person's standard about how often his/her relationship should have a particular characteristic; (b) whether or not the individual is satisfied with how the standard is being met in the relationship; and (c) how upset he/she tends to be when the standard is not met. The ISRS is the first measure of couples' cognitions that has assessed the major relationship themes across content areas, and the initial reliability and validity data have been encouraging. In clinical practice, reviewing each partner's responses and initiating discussion about how the couple handles discrepancies between their standards has provided valuable information for treatment planning.

Several instruments have been produced that assess partners' attributions about their relationships, such as the Relationship Attribution Measure (RAM; Fincham & Bradbury, 1992), the Marital Attitude Survey (MAS; Pretzer, Epstein & Fleming, 1991) and the Dyadic Attribution Inventory (DAI; Baucom, Sayers & Duhe, 1989). Although some of these measures ask about attributions for hypothetical relationship events and others focus on attributions for actual events, overall they provide indices of the degree to which partners attribute positive and negative events to global vs. specific, internal vs. external, and stable vs. unstable causes, as well as to various types of partner motives (e.g. malicious intent, selfish motivation). Increasingly there has been attention paid to the content of couples' attributions, and our recent research has included work on a new instrument to assess attributions to boundary, control/power and investment issues (Carels et al., 1995).

To date, there has been less work on the development of questionnaires assessing expectancies and selective attention than has been devoted to assumptions, standards and attributions. Notarius & Vanzetti's (1983) Marital Agendas Protocol surveys partners' expectancies that problems in each of ten areas of their relationship (e.g. money, communication) will be resolved. Pretzer, Epstein & Fleming's (1991) Marital Attitude Survey has subscales assessing global expectancies that the couple can and will solve their relationship problems. Concerning the assessment of selective attention, as noted earlier, the Spouse Observation Checklist provides opportunites to identify discrepancies between two partner's perceptions about specific events that occurred in their relationship, and it thus can be used to explore possible biases in the two individuals' views of their interactions.

Questionnaires Assessing Affect

Although CBCT practitioners and researchers increasingly are paying attention to affective factors in couples' relationships, there is a relative dearth of questionnaires for assessing them. Baucom & Epstein (1990) review several global measures of marital satisfaction or adjustment and note that these do not differentiate various emotions (e.g. anger, sadness, anxiety) that may comprise individuals' relationship distress. In clinical practice, couples can be asked to use the Daily Record of Dysfunctional Thoughts (DRDT; Beck et al., 1979) to record pleasing and upsetting interactions with each other, along with associated emotions and thoughts. This measure can be useful in identifying the range, intensity and situational context of emotions that each partner experiences in the relationship. Neidig & Friedman (1984) have used a variation of the DRDT to have partners in abusive relationships keep logs of anger-inducing interactions.

INTERVENTION

As noted above, behaviors, cognitions and emotions are intimately related, and these interconnections provide much of the richness and challenge in addressing relationship distress. Thus, any assessment strategy has the potential to inform the clinician in all three of these domains. Similarly, although interventions typically have been developed with an emphasis on one of these arenas (i.e. various interventions are routinely labeled as either behavioral, cognitive or affective), most interventions likely impact all three realms of functioning. Understanding how an intervention aimed primarily at behavior can have major cognitive implications, for example, is critical if optimal treatment planning is to ensue. Thus, in the discussion of various intervention strategies, we will attempt to clarify how any given intervention can have implications for all three domains of functioning.

Although not a clear dichotomy, CBCT interventions also can be differentiated in terms of the amount of skills-training that is involved. To a great degree, CBCT has been conceptualized as a skills-oriented approach in which partners are taught new ways to relate, with a major emphasis on a variety of communications training techniques. At the same time, CBCT therapists often recommend that spouses engage more in certain types of behaviors (e.g. pleasing behaviors such as back rubs, taking walks together, etc.) that do not involve learning new skills. Instead, the emphasis is on altering the frequency and timing of specific behaviors that are likely to enhance the relationship without learning new skills in relating. Consequently, the interventions below will be differentiated in terms of skills-oriented vs. non-skills-oriented techniques.

Skills-oriented Interventions

Communications Training

As noted earlier, couples' communication difficulties tend to be of two major types: (a) problems with expressive and listening skills needed for the sharing of thoughts and feelings; and (b) deficits in problem-solving skills. Thus, one type of communications training that is helpful to couples involves teaching them or reminding them how to share thoughts and feelings with each other. We refer to this type of communications training as emotional expressiveness training (EET). Second, in order for the couple to deal with more pragmatic and at times mundane aspects of life, the couple needs to be able to make decisions and resolve differences effectively. Whereas effective problem-solving involves understanding the partners' thoughts and feelings, the goal still is somewhat different from EET. The primary goal of EET is to understand and be understood. This can contribute to a sense of increased intimacy between partners when they have been feeling distant, and it can serve as a major form of emotional support when one partner is distressed about some aspect of his/her personal life. Problem-solving has the explicit goal of reaching a decision, deciding how to handle some situation that the couple is confronting. Thus, problem-solving training seems particularly valuable when the couple's life is disorganized and many tasks are not being accomplished, or when the couple reports that the way that decisions are made and issues are discussed leads to distress or upset (e.g. one spouse dictates a solution, leaving the partner angry or feeling unimportant). In working with maritally distressed couples, we teach them these two different purposes for communicating, along with the skills needed to engage in each type of conversation.

We also note to couples the importance of making certain that both persons are having the same type of conversation: if one partner is distressed and is seeking support in the form of sharing thoughts and feelings and the partner responds by offering solutions in a problem-solving mode, then the couple is likely to experience frustration, often without even realizing why. At the same time, some individuals are able to articulate, "When I come to him distressed and upset with a problem, he always tries to solve it immediately. That usually is not what I want; I just want him to listen and understand what I'm upset about". Thus, couples are taught not only the specifics of EET and problem-solving, but they are taught to clarify for each other what they are seeking in the conversation.

Emotional Expressiveness Training (EET)

EET involves teaching couples a set of communication behaviors in which they share important thoughts and feelings; thus in a very basic way, this intervention focuses on behavior, cognitions and emotions. In EET, couples are taught that there are two roles: a speaker and a listener. Explicit sets of guidelines are provided elsewhere for both of these roles (Baucom & Epstein, 1990; Guerney, 1977). However, the basics involve having the speaker express his/her thoughts and feelings using "I" statements and moderating the impact of expressing negative feelings by including any positive feelings that are involved in the situation. The listener is taught to use appropriate non-verbal cues while the speaker is speaking (e.g. making eye contact, using head nods), and to reflect or summarize the speaker's most important thoughts and feelings when the speaker has finished speaking. At times couples comment on the awkwardness and artificiality of consistently reflecting each speaker's message. Hahlweg (1995) reported on the results of a prevention program to assist couples planning to marry. The findings indicated that couples learned the communication skills that they were taught, and a follow-up assessment revealed that the couples generally continued to use them. However, the couples were unlikely to use the specific skill of reflecting a partner's statement. Only 28% of spouses reported using this type of communication. Consequently, after teaching couples how to reflect, we provide them with a list of times when it is particularly important to reflect (e.g. if the partner is complaining about not feeling understood; if the listener is planning to offer a contrary perspective). They also are provided with alternatives to reflecting that demonstrate listening and respect for the speaker (e.g. the partner could reciprocate, demonstrating that he or she heard the message—"I'm so glad that you enjoyed it. I had a great time, too") (Baucom & Epstein, 1990).

As described earlier, spouses commonly differ in their expression of various positive and negative emotions (e.g. happiness vs. anger), and this variation may be influenced by cognitions such as standards about feeling expression, or expectancies about the consequences of revealing particular emotions to a spouse. Thus, therapeutic interventions must be individualized to each couple's needs. As with most behavioral interventions, this can be structured along a hierarchy from the emotions that members of a couple find less difficult to express to those that they find more difficult. It is important to explore the couple's standards and other cognitions about expressing emotions and attempt to alter them when they seem to be inappropriate.

For example, one newlywed wife held a standard that expressing negative feelings places undue burdens on others, i.e. that is it not appropriate to complain to others about one's personal problems. Based on this standard, she concluded that she should shield her husband from the distress she was experiencing concerning her mother's cancer. The couple sought therapy when they started to feel distant and disengaged even within the first year of their marriage. When the therapist and couple discussed the wife's standard about expressing negative feelings, she specified her belief that she should deal with her sadness without bringing it into their marriage. The husband responded by explaining that he was feeling distant from his wife not because he was sensing her sadness, but rather because he was feeling shut out and unable to share an important part of her life. He stated that he would not consider it "complaining" if his wife shared her upset about her mother's illness with him. The therapist then discussed how partners can serve as an important source of social support when one spouse is encountering the inherent complexities of life, and how facing such concerns together has the potential to strengthen the couple's relationship. The therapist and couple then discussed examples of differences between what each partner would experience as complaining vs. intimacy-enhancing expressions of negative feelings. The wife, who actually was quite adept at expressing emotions, was then willing to experiment with sharing her feelings about her mother's cancer with her husband on a much more frequent basis, and the husband's receptive responses gradually helped her modify her standard about expressing negative emotions.

Not only can the expression of emotion be influenced by other variables such as relationship standards, but adaptive expression of emotions also has the potential for altering cognitions and behaviors. Often spouses are displeased with their partners' behavior not just because it is inherently negative, but because of how the behavior is interpreted, that is, the attributions or explanations that spouses provide for each other's behavior. When couples do not communicate sufficiently, there is little opportunity to alter faulty or distorted attributions. Whereas spouses do not always fully accept their partners' explanations for their behavior, sharing thoughts and feelings about an important area of concern can provide an important forum for understanding each person's behavior in a new way. In the example above, the husband came to realize that his wife was remaining silent about her mother's cancer, not because she did not trust him or did not want his support, but rather because she was trying to protect their new marriage from the depressing effects of a major illness. Through their sharing of thoughts and feelings, she came to understand that his distance was not due to his sensing her dejection and trying to avoid it, but instead was due to feeling excluded. As noted above, behavior change followed once this new understanding had been achieved.

At times, sharing thoughts and feelings leads to immediate behavior change in the domain being discussed, as in this instance. Sharing thoughts and feelings also can have a more generalized effect on behavior. If as a result of these discussions, partners understand each other more fully and feel more "connected" and at times more intimate, then a number of behaviors not focal to the conversations might change as well. For example, partners at times complain of a low frequency of sexual interaction, resulting from feeling distant or disengaged. To the extent that sharing thoughts and feelings helps to create a sense of closeness, it has the potential to impact the couple's comfort and desire for sexual interaction, even when sexuality has not been the focus of the discussion. (Of course, many instances of infrequent sexual interaction are much more complex and require interventions focused more directly on sexual issues, as described in the chapter by Spence, this volume.)

Whereas sharing thoughts and feelings can lead to understanding and immediate behavior changes, on many occasions couples realize that they still need to resolve a difficult issue which they now understand more clearly. In order to resolve such differences, problem-solving skills are needed.

Problem-solving Training

Problem-solving has the explicit goal of reaching a solution or deciding how to address an area of concern. A number of volumes that provide extensive discussion of problem-solving have been written both for professionals (e.g. Baucom & Epstein, 1990; Bornstein & Bornstein, 1986; Jacobson & Margolin, 1979; Stuart, 1980) and for couples (Fincham, Fernandes & Humphreys, 1993; Markman, Stanley & Blumberg, 1994; Notarius & Markman, 1993). Whereas these various authors vary somewhat in the exact steps in problem-solving that they propose, most of them are consistent with steps that we have outlined previously (Baucom & Epstein, 1990): (a) clearly and specifically stating what the problem is; (b) discussing possible solutions; (c) deciding upon a specific solution that is acceptable to both partners; and (d) deciding upon a trial period to implement the solution, if it is a recurrent issue. These problem-solving steps are taught to couples by means of basic skill training procedures based on social learning principles. Typically the therapist provides the couple with a rationale for using effective problem-solving to resolve relationship conflicts, differentiates problem-solving from expressive communication, and outlines the sequence of problem-solving steps. The therapist's oral presentation of the steps can be enhanced by giving the couple written descriptions that they can use as a guide in sessions and at home (cf. Baucom & Epstein, 1990). Oral presentations and handouts also can be used to outline the types of general communication described earlier (e.g. expressive and listening skills) that tend to impede or facilitate problem-solving. The therapist also can model examples of how one can translate a problem into clear behavioral terms, generate possible solutions, etc. Based on prior assessment of the couple's unresolved issues and of possible limitations in their current use of problem-solving skills, the therapist then discusses with the couple ways in which improved problem-solving could benefit them.

The core of problem-solving training involves having the couple practice the steps during sessions, using real unresolved issues in their relationship. Typically, the therapist asks the partners to begin practicing the skills with fairly low-level conflict issues, so that their ability to stay on task is not impeded by the experience of strong emotions that are likely to be elicited by high-conflict topics. The therapist provides feedback and coaching to the couple as they rehearse the problem-solving skills and the associated general communication skills (e.g. verbal and non-verbal acknowledgements of one's partner). The therapist and couple commonly plan for the partners to practice at home the skills that they successfully enacted during sessions. When a couple is able to use problem-solving with relatively low level conflict issues, they move on to working on more difficult ones.

With the couple who had little shared time due to work, housework and childrearing responsibilities, the therapist initially focused the partners on identifying a specific situation that occurred on a daily basis and that interfered with their spending time alone together. The wife noted her distress concerning her husband's tendency to "disappear quickly" after dinner to work on house projects, and the husband replied in a fairly defensive manner that he saw the evenings as his only opportunity during a typical busy week to make progress on home improvements that both spouses desired. The therapist then asked the wife to re-state her complaint as a positive request for change that would please her, and she was able to define her goal as finding a way for them to spend more time together before bedtime. The therapist then coached the couple in brainstorming a variety of possible solutions (e.g. agreeing to drop some of the mutually desired home improvements; working together on some projects after their daughter was asleep), weighing the pros and cons of each solution, and selecting a solution to try during the next week.

To the extent that problem-solving leads to the couple's experience of working together productively to resolve issues in their marriage as well as implementing needed solutions, problem-solving has the potential to influence important cognitions and emotions. When spouses witness their partners compromising and implementing solutions, their expectancies or predictions about the future of the relationship can change due to this new information. As a series of issues are resolved and the relationship improves, their attributions for their partners' previous negative behavior might become more benign. For example, rather than viewing those behaviors as intentional or the result of character flaws on each other's part, the spouses may shift to attributions that emphasize a lack of communication skills or a previous lack of knowledge about how to work together as a team. Furthermore, as each spouse behaves more frequently in ways that please the partner, the partner's emotions toward the individual are likely to change in a positive direction. Thus, problem-solving has the potential to have impacts on a variety of behaviors, cognitions and emotions.

Cognitive Restructuring Techniques

In the above interventions, attempts to alter behavior through expressing emotions adapatively or through resolving problems also can serve the important function of altering how each spouse thinks about the partner and the relationship. Thus, behavioral changes can lead to cognitive changes. In addition, there are a number of interventions that can be employed to focus more directly on a spouse's cognitions (Baucom & Epstein, 1990). A detailed discussion of the range of cognitive interventions available is beyond the scope of this work, but some examples will serve to demonstrate how to focus more directly on spouses' cognitions.

As noted previously, spouses often are upset not only by a partner's actual behavior or lack of behavior, but also by the explanations that they give for the behavior, which give meaning to the behavior and often to the relationship. These explanations or attributions for a partner's behavior can at times lead to the need for attributional re-evaluation. Whereas negative attributions for a partner's behavior might seem destructive, and therapist does not automatically attempt to alter any negative attribution. At times, such attributions might be very realistic, and the partner making the attribution might need to take this explanation into account in deciding how or if to proceed with the relationship. For example, a wife might conclude that her husband is coming home late because he does not want to spend time with her and the children. Instead of immediately attempting to have the wife view this situation in a more positive light, the therapist might ask the husband to clarify for his wife why he comes home late. If indeed the husband notes that the aversive atmosphere at home does encourage him to stay at work later, then the couple needs to spend time discussing the home environment rather than attempting to alter her attribution.

On other occasions, one spouse's attributions appear to be distorted or at least open to other interpretations. On such occasions, focusing on these attributions might be important. For example, one wife concluded that her husband did not obtain erections when they were engaging in foreplay because he consciously decided to frustrate her sexually. The therapist then engaged in what would be called a logical analysis with the wife, exploring her understanding of sexual functioning and helping her decide whether she had reached a logical conclusion regarding his erectile dysfunction. This discussion included educational information from the therapist about human sexual functioning, plus asking the husband to describe what he was thinking and feeling when they engaged in foreplay. Together the therapist and couple discussed other possibilites for the husband's lack of erections, including the possibility that the anxiety he experienced about becoming vulnerable to his wife was a significant factor in his sexual difficulties. As in most instances, the wife did not immediately discard her previous attribution, but she became open to the possibility that other explanations were available and was willing to test out the anxiety hypothesis by attempting to make it safe for her husband to be vulnerable with her.

The husband in another couple we treated was very upset whenever his wife preferred to watch television rather than telling him about her day at work, and he reported that he attributed her behavior to a lack of interest in sharing her life with him. When he made this attribution, he often interrupted his wife's television watching and accused her of neglecting him, which tended to provoke an argument between them. When the therapist questioned the wife about the behavior that upset her husband, she reported that she found her job very stressful and that recounting her day's activities made her re-live unpleasant experiences, so she preferred to watch the news to help her forget about the day.

In therapy, the husband was coached in considering alternative explanations for his spouse's behavior, and the couple was coached in problem-solving alternative ways in which the wife could "unwind" without consistently retreating into solitary activities that reduced intimacy between the partners.

Other cognitions, such as relationship standards, are not always open to logical analysis. Many people's values are not based on logic *per se*, and attempting to show them that their standards are illogical is likely to be met with significant resistance. Instead, addressing unrealistic or extreme standards can be approached in a different manner that typically includes five steps. First, the existing standard needs to be clarified. Frequently, individuals have not clarified what their standards are, although they seem to operate according to some vague set of guidelines that define appropriate behavior. In order to evaluate and perhaps alter a standard, first it must be clarified. Second, once the standard is stated clearly, the pros and cons of that standard are discussed. The therapist explains that most often people adopt particular relationship standards for good reasons, based on their personal ethics and understanding of social behavior. At the same time, there are limitations to almost all standards, or ways in which a standard complicates life as well as providing guidelines for living. Thus, the therapist helps the individual list the pros and cons of his/her standard. Although it must be done carefully and with tact in order minimize the person's defensiveness, pros as well as cons regarding the standard can be offered by the other partner and therapist as well. Third, the therapist helps the spouse think of ways that the standard can be altered or modified to maintain many of its positive features, while attempting to decrease its negative impact. Simply moderating an extreme standard is much less threatening to an individual than attempting to have that person abandon the standard altogether. During this time, the couple often engages in EET to clarify how both persons would feel about this altered standard for behaving. Once the revised standard is articulated, step four can begin. The therapist asks the couple to problem-solve about how the new standard can be taken into account behaviorally in their relationship. That is, how will the couple attempt to incorporate this revised standard into the ways that they interact with each other? This might involve a number of problem-solving sessions if the standard has broad implications for the couple's functioning. Fifth, and finally, the couple and therapist discuss how the new solutions based on the altered standard are proceeding and whether the individual believes that he/she can continue to operate within this new context. Frequently, spouses are willing to try a new way of relating, but over time they find that they simply are not comfortable with this new set of interactions and that they have stretched their own values too far. This is important to know because the individual who is experimenting with a revised standard either will not maintain the behavior changes or will feel bad that he/she has operated outside of his/her value system.

These steps were followed in working with a couple in which the wife was involved in a medical residency training program. The husband believed that partners should spend almost all of their free time with each other, particularly given the small amount of time they had available due to his wife's heavy professional demands. This issue came to a head when he insisted that the couple take their young children in a van to her professional conference some distance away. Due to limited financial resources, the husband planned that he and the children would sleep in the van while she shared a hotel room with another resident. His wife felt embarrassed, humiliated, anxious and angry about the possibility of her family sleeping outside the convention in a van.

Once the husband's standard for togetherness was clarified, its pros and cons were discussed; not surprisingly, it was simple to assemble a list for both columns. The major task became thinking of how to alter this standard in a way that validated his desire for closeness and togetherness with his wife at a time in their lives when time was at a premium, without the wife feeling suffocated and even spied upon at times. The husband was able to alter his standard in a way that incorporated the need for each partner to have some time alone, as well as the value of spending time with friends and colleagues without the other partner present at all times. Then the couple began a series of problem-solving sessions to clarify how they would take this into account in their relationship. This included discussions of professional conferences, leisure time, visits with families of origin, etc. Finally, the couple made specific plans to enact the solutions that they devised, and the therapist subsequently explored with the couple whether the new solutions were meeting their needs for both autonomy and relatedness. In this instance, both persons felt positive about the changes that had occurred in their relationship, and the husband believed that he had become more attuned to the importance of clarifying his standards and whether they were contributing to their relationship difficulties, as well as his personal life. He reported that rather than creating an uncomfortable distance between them, the new approach to autonomy and relatedness reduced much of the tension in the marriage and increased the couple's intimacy.

As noted above, cognitive restructuring of relationship standards commonly involves focusing on behaviors and emotions to create the cognitive change. The partners are encouraged to express their thoughts and feelings about the original and modified standard. They also are asked to problem-solve about new ways of putting the revised standard into effect, and evaluating these behavior changes over time. If these attempts at cognitive restructuring are successful, then further emotional and behavioral changes are likely as well. If the individual finds that the partner now complies with his/her altered relationship standards (typically those that both persons consider acceptable), then he/she is likely to feel more positively towards the partner. Baucom et al. (1996) have found that when spouses conclude that their relationship standards have not been met to their satisfaction, there are a number of negative emotional and behavioral consequences. Similarly, when a person feels that his/her standards are being met, he/she is likely to behave in ways that meet his/her partner's own standards. Rankin et al. (1995) have found that spouses (particularly wives) exhibit behaviors that tend to be attentive to (consistent with) their partners' standards.

Non-skills-oriented Interventions

The discussion of the above interventions is not intended to be exhaustive of the skills-oriented approaches that are employed in working with distressed couples from a cognitive–behavioral perspective. However, it points out broad domains of interventions that therapists can employ. In addition to teaching couples to express thoughts and feelings, problem-solve, and evaluate their cognitions differently, often the therapist decides with the couple on a variety of additional interventions that require no new skills. These interventions tend to focus on the quantity and quality of the couple's behavioral interactions during daily life. As described earlier, there is considerable evidence that marital satisfaction is associated with the events that occur between partners on a daily basis.

For example, if the couple reports that they engage in few acts of caring and concern for each other, the therapist can suggest that they engage in an activity called "love days" or "caring days" that has been implemented in a variety of forms by couple therapists (e.g. Stuart, 1980). Generally, this involves asking each member of a couple to engage in a specified number of caring acts toward his or her partner, each day or each week, based on a list generated by that person, with or without input from the partner. The types of caring behaviors to be enacted are determined for each couple. For example, if an individual has been distressed that the partner participates minimally with household chores, the partner's caring days activities could center on this theme. If a spouse is concerned that the partner expresses little love and affection, either verbally or non-verbally, during the week, the partner might decide to find little ways to show he/she cares that are comfortable for both people (e.g. telephone calls, notes left under the pillow). Third, if one spouse complains of little alone time, the partner can think of things to do that will give the other some time alone (e.g. "You go upstairs and relax while I take care of the dishes tonight"). Thus, whereas these interventions can be as broad as "do five positive things that would make your partner happy this week", the therapist should also consider focusing the intervention on specific relationship themes in the conceptualization of the couple derived from the initial and ongoing assessment.

A frequent complaint of many couples is that as their life has become more complicated with children, civic and/or job demands, they spend little time with each other having fun. In social exchange terms, the spouses are engaging in a low rate of mutually pleasing "non-communication" behaviors. Thus, the couple and therapist might conclude that they need to increase their frequency of enjoyable "coupling" activities. Some couples are aware of what activities they enjoy together and merely need to work out a mechanism for ensuring the time together. This might involve their deciding to reserve and protect a special date night. For example, some couples who have marital therapy in the late afternoon or early evening decide to make therapy night their night out because they have already arranged for baby sitters (although this might be contraindicated if the couple has frequent intense arguments during therapy sessions). Other couples struggle to identify shared activities that they enjoy, and a variety of joint activity lists have been developed to help such couples generate alternatives (e.g. Baucom & Epstein, 1990; Gottman et al., 1976).

In addition to the above interventions that are aimed at increasing positive behaviors in a broad range of relationship spheres, other interventions have been developed for more focal targets. For example, for couples who report that their sex lives have become affected by the deterioration of their marital relationship, interventions with their sexual and sensual relationship typically are integrated within a more comprehensive treatment plan based on an understanding of the couple's functioning (see the chapter by Spence, this volume). Although at times intervention might begin with a focus on sexual concerns, often the therapist deals with these later in treatment, when the couple has developed more positive affective, cognitive and behavioral responses to each other. If the couple report residual anxiety and avoidance in the sexual arena, the therapist might help the couple begin a series of standard sensate focus exercises (Masters & Johnson, 1970) to help them become comfortable once again touching each other. The couple can use EET and problem-solving skills to address any difficulties that they experience as they progress through the steps in the sensate focus hierarchy.

At times, in order to assist a distressed couple, the therapist needs to develop new interventions that are based on sound psychological principles known to operate in relationships but also designed to address a particular couple's needs and personal styles. For example, the current authors describe elsewhere the development of new interventions to assist one couple who experienced sexual difficulties (Baucom, Epstein & Carels, 1992). This young couple spent a great deal of time together in joint activities and really enjoyed each other, but both of them became anxious when they related sexually, because of the vulnerability that they associated with such intimate experiences. They had much difficulty discussing sex, and on the infrequent occasions in which they did engage in intercourse, they rarely kissed because it felt too intimate. The therapist employed their love of games in devising a series of sensual exercises to desensitize them to sexual interaction and discussion. To help them become more comfortable using sexual terms and discussing sex, the therapist devised a game called "Sex Scrabble", in which every acceptable word had to have a clear sexual connotation that the player could describe if challenged. Likewise, to help them become more comfortable with kissing, the therapist described kissing as a form of non-verbal communication. The couple was then asked to play a game called "Read My Lips", in which each spouse was to guess the particular emotion that the partner was trying to communicate with a kiss. Within our cognitive–behavioral approach, these games were intended to develop new expectancies for both partners that engaging in verbal and non-verbal expressions of sexuality could be playful, enjoyable experiences, rather than sources of danger. On the one hand, it was important to guide them in a logical analysis of their original negative expectancies (e.g. examining any evidence bearing on their prediction that being vulnerable to each other sexually could lead to being hurt emotionally). On the other hand, it was their first-hand positive experiences of interacting in playful sexual ways that appeared to allow this couple to approach what previously had been anxiety-producing situations. Thus, although most of the non-skills-oriented interventions focus on behavior, they are intended to have cognitive and emotional impacts as well. In fact, almost no affectively neutral interventions are described in the cognitive–behavioral marital literature.

In addition, these behavioral interventions are intended and devised to have cognitive impact on the couple. Thus, although techniques for *quid pro quo* behavior exchange contracts have been devised that make each partner's behavior contingent on the other's behavior, these interventions are used less frequently at present, in part because of their presumed cognitive impact. If a husband believes that his wife has agreed to spend more time with him after dinner just so he will agree to clean the dishes, then the very behavior that he desired (increased time with his wife) might now be viewed negatively because of the attribution that he makes for her new behavior. Consequently, most of the procedures for encouraging behavior changes are arranged in ways that emphasize the partners' good will, positive motivation, and desire to improve the relationship, rather than what each individual stands to gain personally by cooperating with the spouse. Many behavior change interventions also are designed to alter a spouse's expectancy or prediction regarding the future of the marriage. Seeing one's partner change, decreasing negative behaviors and increasing positive interactions, can alter an individual's expectancy that there is hope for the marriage. This expectancy is important for obtaining maximum cooperation from both spouses during the intervention.

As can be seen, there are a wide variety of interventions available to the cognitive–behavioral marital therapist, depending on the couple's specific needs. Although for heuristic purposes these typically have been separated into behavioral, cognitive and emotional interventions, any intervention is likely to have impact on all three spheres of functioning. Understanding and anticipating these impacts is one of the great challenges for marital therapists at they devise a sequence of interventions to assist distressed couples. Although there are an endless number of factors that might be considered in developing treatment plans, elsewhere we have attempted to provide a set of factors to consider in developing an initial treatment plan, as well as guidelines for altering initial plans once intervention has begun (Baucom & Epstein, 1990).

RECENT DEVELOPMENTS AND FUTURE DIRECTIONS

Although there are a large number of treatment outcome investigations demonstrating the effectiveness of cognitive–behavioral marital therapy with distressed couples (see Baucom & Epstein, 1990; Hahlweg & Markman, 1988, for reviews), theorists, clinicians and researchers continue to advance the field in a number of directions. At least three major foci are likely to be incorporated into expanding models of cognitive–behavioral couples therapy in the future. First, increasing attention is being given to the individual in marital therapy. To a great degree, CBCT traditionally has considered the relationship to be the client, but now the individual is being considered in several ways that might make CBCT more effective in general or more applicable to specific populations. Second, in early descriptions of behavioral marital therapy, the emphasis was on producing behavior change. With the increased focus on cognitions in marriage, less emphasis is being placed on behavior change as the sole goal of couples therapy, and increased work in this area is continuing. Third, CBCT frequently has viewed the presenting complaints of distressed couples as discrete concerns involving low rates of positive behaviors and excesses of negative behaviors. However, little attention (especially research) has been paid to the major themes that typify marital distress. Incorporating these thematic elements into CBCT can help to organize clinicians' ways of thinking about specific couples and can address the meanings that upsetting and pleasing relationship events have for the persons involved.

The Individual within the Relationship

In terms of an increased emphasis on the individual within CBCT, at least three different but related developments are occurring. First, Halford, Sanders & Behrens (1994) have clarified how CBCT has placed emphasis on the relationship and emphasized the interactive nature of relationship distress. Whereas they do not attempt to negate these findings, they articulate how this has often resulted in de-emphasizing the individual's responsibility for improving the relationship. Thus, they provide a shift in emphasis that focuses on what each individual can and agrees to do to improve the relationship.

Second, increased attention has been given to how individual psychopathology is affected by and affects marital functioning. For example, Beach & O'Leary (1992) have demonstrated the CBCT is an effective intervention for both improving the marriage and alleviating depression among couples experiencing both concerns. In a recent meta-analysis, Daiuto & Baucom (1996) found that interventions that combine *in vivo* exposure with a focus on the couple's functioning are more effective than *in vivo* exposure alone in reducing agoraphobic symptoms at follow-up, and the more the relationship changes during treatment, the fewer the agoraphobic symptoms at follow-up. Thus, marital interventions can be effective treatments for individual problems, as well as for assisting in relationship functioning. Third, Rankin et al. (1995) found that couples were most satisfied in marital relationships that contributed to a sense of autonomy for each individual, as well as contributing to a sense of relatedness as a couple. Overall, CBCT has emphasized how each individual can contribute to the well-being of the marriage, but little emphasis has been give to how the marriage can contribute to the well-being of each individual. Thus, we propose that comprehensive interventions for couples should explore how the relationship contributes to each individual's personal growth.

Acceptance vs. Change

Whereas early models of marital functioning from a behavioral perspective emphasized behavior change, more recently investigators have suggested that at times cognitive change without behavior change is the focus of an intervention. Thus, if a spouse alters his/her attribution for a partner's behavior, he/she might now find that behavior to be much more acceptable and experience increased satisfaction without a change in the behavior. Jacobson & Christensen (see Christensen, Jacobson & Babcock, 1995) are in the process of developing and evaluating a series of interventions to help spouses accept certain aspects of their partners. Whether this is viewed as acceptance vs. change as Jacobson & Christensen conceptualize it, or cognitive vs. behavioral change as Baucom, Epstein & Rankin (1995) have suggested, there is an increased recognition that focusing solely on behavior change is a simplistic approach to working with couples. At present, evaluation of what the most effective ways to promote cognitive change or acceptance may be is still in the early stages.

Relationship Themes

To this point, CBCT has focused on the process of couple behavior exchanges and has not emphasized the major thematic concerns of couples that could serve to organize many of their specific presenting complaints. Recently, we have noted that there are several major dimensions of marital functioning that all couples must address, either explicitly or implicitly, and that serve as the source of many marital complaints. As described earlier, the three major dimensions on which we have focused are: (a) boundaries, or the ways in which members of couples operate as individuals vs. share with each other and function as a unit; (b) power/control, or the ways that couples make decisions and who has what say in final outcomes; and (c) investment, or the ways that couples contribute or give to the relationship both emotionally or instrumentally (Baucom, Epstein, Daiuto et al., 1996; Baucom, Epstein, Rankin & Burnett, 1996).

Our findings indicate that couples often attribute their marital conflicts to these dimensions and that dissatisfaction with how one's standards on these dimensions are met are correlated with a wide range of indices of marital distress. It is not unusual for therapists to comment when describing a couple that the partners are engaged in a power struggle, or that the major problem is that one spouse is less invested in the relationship than the other, or that the couple has become enmeshed because they have lost all sense of personal boundaries. Yet, CBCT literature has rarely discussed such issues or provided clinicians with suggestions on how to approach these issues employing standard or new CBCT interventions. Our own research has involved the development of measures of couples' cognitions that take boundary, power/control and investment issues into account, and we are in the process of refining CBCT interventions so that treatment plans can be tailored to the themes that are relevant for each couple. By organizing presenting complaints along these as well as other dimensions, hopefully we can develop more efficient and effective interventions to address couple functioning.

One of our client couples has provided good examples of all three of the above issues. Both members of the couple were in their late 20s, and it was the first marriage for both of them. They sought marital therapy after a year of marriage, when the wife told the husband that she was unsure she had made the right decision in marrying him, that she was not sure that she loved him enough, and that she might want to separate. Both spouses reported that they had been good friends before their relationship developed into a romantic one, and that they communicated well. They had been attracted to each other because of their similar religious and educational backgrounds, their shared interests and personal values, and their shared sense of humor. Although physical attraction had been a positive factor, it had been secondary to the other attracting characteristics.

During the initial assessment interview, the couple reported differences in the types of relationships that they experienced in their families of origin. Whereas the husband grew up in a family where the parents were (and continue to be) almost inseparable, and the emphasis was on cohesiveness among all family members, the wife came from a family where autonomy was modeled by her parents and strongly encouraged for herself and her siblings. In the couple's own relationship, the husband preferred that most leisure time be spent together, but the wife valued time by herself or with her own friends. Over time, as the husband became upset whenever his wife even talked about wanting time for herself, the wife felt increasingly "trapped" in their relationship. She also began to feel that she was being asked by her spouse to sacrifice her individual identity for the sake of marital cohesiveness. These thoughts tended to elicit as least mild anxious and depressed moods. In turn, the husband felt increasingly anxious as he sensed his spouse distancing from him, and when she told him about her thoughts of separation and divorce, he experienced panic symptoms. Although both partners' anxiety appeared to be situational, each described some history of generalized anxiety that predated their relationship.

Although space constraints preclude a full discussion of the characteristics of this couple and their dyadic patterns, several key points can be noted. First, the wife's concerns about apparent incompatibility between her personal needs and the survival of the marriage involved the issue of whether this couple could achieve a balance of autonomy and relatedness that was compatible with each person's individual needs. In fact, initially both spouses were concerned that the type of relationship that the other would desire was not one that he/she could also find satisfying.

Second, it appeared that each partner's tendency toward worry and anxiety affected the relationship, because the husband would catastrophize about danger in the wife's desire for autonomy, while the wife would catastrophize about implications of the husband's desire for togetherness. As circular pattern developed, in which the wife's anxiety about being trapped led her to attempt to create more distance between them, which elicited anxiety from the husband, who in turn sought more togetherness, and so on.

Third, the conflict about autonomy vs. relatedness involved the major relationship content theme of boundaries, and there was evidence that the spouses had developed personal standards about boundaries in close relationships on the basis of experiences in their families of origin. They also made negative attributions about the other's behavior, with the husband concluding that his wife wanted little intimacy with him, and the wife concluding that the husband wanted to restrict most of her freedom (i.e. their views of each other had become polarized, such that they perceived their intentions as opposite and incompatible).

Finally, although they genuinely liked each other and their in-laws, each tended to judge the other's style of personal relationships as unacceptable, and thus viewed their options as either inducing the other person to change his/her behavior, or remaining dissatisfied and perhaps divorcing. When they began couples therapy, neither partner seemed to consider the possibility of accepting their differences and finding ways to live happily within those limitations.

Consequently, our cognitive–behavioral work with the couple included: (a) exploration of each partner's degrees of striving for autonomy and relatedness (where each was coached in identifying some degree of each tendency in himself or herself, thereby counteracting their tendency to polarize their views of each other); (b) emotional expressiveness training to help them clarify the misinterpretations that they made bout each other's intentions; (c) problem-solving discussions focused on devising "experiments" with various autonomous and shared activities; (d) exploration and challenging of each partner's standards regarding boundaries in marital and family relationships, with an emphasis on their testing their own abilities to find satisfaction in a relationship with a spouse whose personal style is at least somewhat different from his/her own; and (e) conjoint work with both partners on developing cognitive and behavioral skills for coping with their own worry and anxiety. These interventions changed the couple's behavioral interaction pattern, their cognitions about each other, and their emotional responses to each other's behavior. For example, as the husband reduced his clinging behavior and was willing to cooperate with his wife having opportunities to spend more time with her friends, she in fact felt less trapped and less need to be apart from him. As the wife experimented with challenging her belief that her spouse's desire for togetherness was abnormal, rather than just different from her own preference, the husband was more open to making more plans with his own friends and spending time without her. Thus, our cognitive–behavioral approach addressed the complexities of the couple's relationship problems by focusing on the interplay among behaviors, cognitions and emotions, by taking both individual and relationship needs into account, by addressing core relationship themes, and by balancing behavior change efforts with facilitation of the partners' acceptance of some of each other's characteristics.

REFERENCES

Argyle, M. & Furham, A. (1983). Sources of satisfaction and conflict in long-term relationships. *Journal of Marriage and the Family*, **45**, 481–493.

Bandura, A. (1977). *Social Learning Theory*. Englewood Cliffs, NJ: Prentice-Hall.

Baucom, D.H. & Epstein, N. (1990). *Cognitive–Behavioral Marital Therapy*. New York: Brunner/Mazel.

Baucom, D.H., Epstein, N. & Carels, R. (1992). A cognitive–behavioral model of marital dysfunction and marital therapy. In S. Budman, M. Hoyt & S. Friedman (eds), *The First Session in Brief Therapy* (pp. 225–254). New York: Guilford.

Baucom, D.H., Epstein, N., Daiuto, A.D., Carels, R.A., Rankin, L.A. & Burnett, C.K. (in press). Cognitions in marriage: the relationship between standards and attributions. *Journal of Family Psychology*, **10**, 209–222.

Baucom, D.H., Epstein, N. & Rankin, L.A. (1995). Cognitive aspects of cognitive–behavioral marital therapy. In N.S. Jacobson & A.S. Gurman (eds), *Clinical Handbook of Couple Therapy* (pp. 65–90). New York: Guilford.

Baucom, D.H., Epstein, N., Rankin, L.A. & Burnett, C.K. (1996). Assessing relationship standards: the Inventory of Specific Relationship Standards. *Journal of Family Psychology*, **10**, 72–88.

Baucom, D.H., Epstein, N., Sayers, S. & Sher, T.G. (1989). The role of cognitions in marital relationships: definitional, methodological, and conceptual issues. *Journal of Consulting and Clinical Psychology*, **57**, 31–38.

Baucom, D.H., Sayers, S.L. & Duhe, A. (1989). Attributional style and attributional patterns among married couples. *Journal of Personality and Social Psychology*, **56**, 596–607.

Beach, S.R.H. & O'Leary, K.D. (1992). Treating depression in the context of marital discord: outcome and predictors of response of marital therapy versus cognitive therapy. *Behavior Therapy*, **23**, 507–528.

Beck, A.T., Rush, A.J., Shaw, B.F. & Emery, G. (1979). *Cognitive Therapy of Depression*. New York: Guilford.

Bienvenu, M.J. (1970). Measurement of marital communication. *The Family Coordinator*, **19**, 26–31.

Birchler, G.R., Weiss, R.L. & Vincent, J.P. (1975). Multimethod analysis of social reinforcement exchange between maritally distressed and non-distressed spouse and stranger dyads. *Journal of Personality and Social Psychology*, **31**, 349–360.

Blumberg, P.L. & Coleman, M.T. (1989). A theoretical look at the gender balance of power in the American couple. *Journal of Family Issues*, **10**, 225–250.

Bornstein, P.H. & Bornstein, M.T. (1986). *Marital Therapy: a Behavioral–Communications Approach*. New York: Pergamon.

Bradbury, T.N. & Fincham, F.D. (1990). Attributions in marriage: review and critique. *Psychological Bulletin*, **107**, 3–33.

Bradbury, T.N. & Fincham, F.D. (1992). Attributions and behavior in marital interaction. *Journal of Personality and Social Psychology*, **63**, 613–628.

Bradbury, T.N. & Fincham, F.D. (1993). Assessing dysfunctional cognition in marriage: a reconsideration of the Relationship Belief Inventory. *Psychological Assessment*, **5**, 92–101.

Carels, R.A., Daiuto, A.D., Baucom, D.H., Epstein, N., Rankin, L.A. & Burnett, C.K. (1995). Relationship dimensions of attributional processing: affective and behavioral correlates. Unpublished manuscript.

Christensen, A. (1988). Dysfunctional interaction patterns in couples. In P. Noller & M.A. Fitzpatrick (eds), *Perspective on Marital Interaction* (pp. 31–52). Clevedon, Avon, UK: Multilingual Matters.

Christensen, A., Jacobson, N.S. & Babcock, J.C. (1995). Integrative behavioral couple therapy. In N.S. Jacobson & A.S. Gurman (eds), *Clinical Handbook of Couples Therapy* (pp. 31–64). New York: Guilford.

Christensen, A. & Nies, D.C. (1980). The Spouse Observation Checklist: empirical analysis and critique. *American Journal of Family Therapy*, **8**, 69–79.

Christensen, A., Sullaway, M. & King, C. (1983). Systematic error in behavioral reports of dyadic interaction: egocentric bias and content effects. *Behavioral Assessment*, **5**, 131–142.

Daiuto, A.D. & Baucom, D.H. (1996). A meta-analytic evaluation of the interpersonal model of agoraphobia. Manuscript submitted for publication.

Eidelson, R.J. & Epstein, N. (1982). Cognition and relationship maladjustment: development of a measure of dysfunctional relationship beliefs. *Journal of Consulting and Clinical Psychology*, **50**, 715–720.

Epstein, N. & Baucom, D.H. (1993). Cognitive factors in marital disturbance. In K.S. Dobson & P.C. Kendall (eds), *Psychopathology and Cognition* (pp. 351–385). San Diego, CA: Academic Press.

Epstein, N., Baucom, D.H. & Rankin, L.A. (1993). Treatment of marital conflict: a cognitive–behavioral approach. *Clinical Psychology Review*, **13**, 45–57.

Fincham, F.D. & Bradbury, T.N. (1992). Assessing attributions in marriage: the Relationship Attribution Measure. *Journal of Personality and Social Psychology*, **62**, 457–468.

Fincham, F.D., Fernandes, L.O.L. & Humphreys, K. (1993). *Communicating in Relationships: a Guide for Couples and Professionals*. Champaign, IL: Research Press.

Fitzpatrick, M.A. (1988). *Between Husbands and Wives: Communication in Marriage*. Newbury Park, CA: Sage.

Floyd, F.J. & Markman, H.J. (1983). Observational biases in spouse observation: toward a cognitive–behavioral model of marriage. *Journal of Consulting and Clinical Psychology*, **51**, 450–457.

Geiss, S.K. & O'Leary, K.D. (1981). Therapist ratings of frequency and severity of marital problems: implications for research. *Journal of Marital and Family Therapy*, **7**, 515–520.

Gottman, J.M. (1979). *Marital Interaction: Experimental Investigations*. New York: Academic Press.

Gottman, J., Notarius, C., Gonso, J. & Markman, H.J. (1976). *A Couple's Guide to Communication*. Champaign, IL: Research Press.

Gray-Little, B. & Burks, N. (1983). Power and satisfaction in marriage: a review and critique. *Psychological Bulletin*, **93**, 513–538.

Guerney, B.G. Jr (1977). *Relationship Enhancement*. San Francisco: Jossey-Bass.

Hahlweg, K. (1995). The current status of behavioral marital therapy and prevention programs. Paper presented at the World Congress of Behavioral and Cognitive Therapies, Copenhagen, July.

Hahlweg, K. & Markman, H.J. (1988). Effectiveness of behavioral marital therapy: empirical status of behavioral techniques in preventing and alleviating marital distress. *Journal of Consulting and Clinical Psychology*, **56**, 440–447.

Hahlweg, K., Reisner, L., Kohli, G., Vollmer, M., Schindler, L. & Revenstorf, D. (1984). Development and validity of a new system to analyze interpersonal communication: kategoriensystem für Partnerschaftliche Interaktion. In K. Hahlweg & N.S. Jacobson (eds), *Marital Interaction: Analysis and Modification* (pp. 182–198). New York: Guilford.

Halford, W.K., Sanders, M.R. & Behrens, B.C. (1994). Self-regulation in behavioral couples' therapy. *Behavior Therapy*, **25**, 431–452.

Holtzworth-Munroe, A. & Jacobson, N.S. (1985). Causal attributions of married couples: when do they search for causes? What do they conclude when they do? *Journal of Personality and Social Psychology*, **48**, 1398–1412.

Jacob, T. & Tennenbaum, D.L. (1988). *Family Assessment: Rationale, Methods, and Future Directions*. New York: Plenum.

Jacobson, N.S., Follett, W.C. & McDonald, D.W. (1982). Reactivity to positive and negative behavior in distressed and nondistressed married couples. *Journal of Consulting and Clinical Psychology*, **50**, 706–714.

Jacobson, N.S. & Margolin, G. (1979). *Marital Therapy: Strategies Based on Social Learning and Behavior Exchange Principles*. New York: Brunner/Mazel.

Jacobson, N.S. & Moore, D. (1981). Spouses as observers of the events in their relationship. *Journal of Consulting and Clinical Psychology*, **49**, 269–277.

Karpel, M.A. (1980). Family secrets. *Family Process*, **19**, 295–306.

Kelley, H.H., Berscheid, E., Christensen, A., Harvey, J.H., Huston, T.L., Levinger, G., McClintock, E., Peplau, L.A. & Peterson, D.R. (1983). *Close Relationships*. New York: W.H. Freeman.

Margolin, G. (1981). Behavioral exchange in happy and unhappy marriages: a family cycle perspective. *Behavior Therapy*, **12**, 329–343.

Margolin, G. (1986). Ethical issues in marital therapy. In N.S. Jacobson & A.S. Gurman (eds), *Clinical Handbook of Marital Therapy* (pp. 621–638). New York: Guilford.

Markman, H., Stanley, S. & Blumberg, S. (1994). *Fighting for Your Marriage: Positive Steps for Preventing Divorce and Preserving a Lasting Love*. San Francisco: Jossey-Bass.

Masters, W.H. & Johnson, V.E. (1970). *Human Sexual Inadequacy*. Boston: Little, Brown.

Navran, L. (1967). Communication and adjustment in marriage. *Family Process*, **6**, 173–184.

Neidig, P.H. & Friedman, D.H. (1984). *Spouse Abuse: a Treatment Program for Couples*. Champaign, IL: Research Press.

Notarius, C.I. & Markman, H.J. (1981). The Couples Interaction Scoring System. In E.E. Filsinger & R.A. Lewis (eds), *Assessing Marriage: New Behavioral Approaches* (pp. 112–127). Beverly Hills, CA: Sage.

Notarius, C. & Markman, H. (1993). *We Can Work It Out: Making Sense of Marital Conflict*. New York: G.P. Putnam's Sons.

Notarius, C.I. & Vanzetti, N.A. (1983). The Marital Agendas Protocol. In E.E. Filsinger (ed.), *Marriage and Family Assessment: a Sourcebook for Family Therapy* (pp. 209–227). Beverly Hills, CA: Sage.

O'Leary, K.D. (ed.) (1987). *Assessment of Marital Discord: an Integration for Research and Clinical Practice*. Hillsdale, NJ: Erlbaum.

Pretzer, J., Epstein, N. & Fleming, B. (1991). The Marital Attitude Survey: a measure of dysfunctional attributions and expectancies. *Journal of Cognitive Psychotherapy*, **5**, 131–148.

Rankin, L.A., Burnett, C.K., Baucom, D.H. & Epstein, N. (1995). Autonomy and relatedness in marital functioning. Manuscript submitted for publication.

Ray, J.A. (1988). Marital satisfaction in dual-career couples. *Journal of Independent Social Work*, **3**, 39–55.

Rusbult, C.E., Zembrodt, I.M. & Gunn, L. (1982). Exit, voice. loyalty, and neglect: responses to dissatisfaction in romantic involvements. *Journal of Personality and Social Psychology*, **43**, 1230–1242.

Stuart, R.B. (1980). *Helping Couples Change: a Social Learning Approach to Marital Therapy*. New York: Guilford.

Thibaut, J.W. & Kelley, H.H. (1959). *The Social Psychology of Groups*. New York: Wiley.

Touliatos, J., Perlmutter, B.F. & Straus, M.A. (eds) (1990). *Handbook of Family Measurement Techniques*. Newbury Park, CA: Sage.

Walsh, V.L., Baucom, D.H., Tyler, S. & Sayers, S.L. (1993). Impact of message valence, focus, expressive style, and gender on communication patterns among maritally distressed couples. *Journal of Family Psychology*, **7**, 163–175.

Weiss, R.L. (1980). Strategic behavioral marital therapy: toward a model for assessment and intervention. In J.P. Vincent (ed.), *Advances in Family Intervention, Assessment and Theory*, Vol. 1 (pp. 229–271). Greenwich, CT: JAI Press.

Weiss, R.L. & Heyman, R.E. (1990). Observation of marital interaction. In F.D. Fincham & T.N. Bradbury (eds), *The Psychology of Marriage: Basic Issues and Applications* (pp. 87–117). New York: Guilford.

Weiss, R.L., Hops, H. & Patterson, G.R. (1973). A framework for conceptualizing marital conflict, a technology for altering it, some data for evaluating it. In L.A. Hamerlynck, L.C. Handy & E.J. Mash (eds), *Behavior Change: Methodology, Concepts and Practice* (pp. 309–342). Champaign, IL: Research Press.

Weiss, R.L. & Perry, B.A. (1983). The Spouse Observation Checklist: development and clinical applications. In E.E. Filsinger (ed.), *Marriage and Family Assessment: a Sourcebook for Family Therapy* (pp. 65–84). Beverly Hills, CA: Sage.

Weiss, R.L. & Summers, K.J. (1983). Marital Interaction Coding System—III. In E.E. Filsinger (ed.), *Marriage and Family Assessment: a Sourcebook for Family Therapy* (pp. 85–115). Beverly Hills, CA: Sage.

Weiss, R.L. & Tolman, A.O. (1990). The Marital Interaction Coding System—Global (MICS–G): a global companion to the MICS. *Behavioral Assessment*, **12**, 271–294.

Wills, T.A., Weiss, R.L. & Patterson, G.R. (1974). A behavioral analysis of the determinants of marital satisfaction. *Journal of Consulting and Clinical Psychology*, **42**, 802–811.

Chapter 18

Relationship Interventions with One Partner

Ian Bennun
*Department of Psychology, University of Exeter,
Exeter, Devon, UK*

The conjoint interview is a distinctive feature of contemporary couples therapy. Usually both partners attend together and are seen by either one or two therapists. Conjoint work can take other forms, such as a conjoint group where a group of couples meet together, or concurrent conjoint and individual sessions. In this form of treatment, conjoint sessions are interspersed with individual sessions for each partner. In this chapter I intend to discuss how it is possible to work unilaterally with just one partner or family member within a broad systemic framework.

Despite the controversies surrounding individual treatment for relationship problems, treating only one partner has always been recognized as a form of couples therapy. On occasions, couples request this form of intervention (Fibush, 1957) and in certain circumstances, the therapist may suggest individual rather than conjoint sessions. Partners who find sessions competitive or who may not be able to tolerate the stress of conjoint sessions are often more appropriately seen individually (Blanck, 1965; Nadelson, 1978). Indeed, Nadelson (1978) recommended individual sessions when one partner's previous unresolved conflicts are considered to interfere with and threaten the stability and functioning of the couple relationship. Similarly, Blanck (1965) has suggested that if the clinician detects areas in which frustration cannot be tolerated or where one partner's anxiety may become unmanageable, then it would be preferable to treat the partner alone. There are other presenting problems which may respond better to individual rather than conjoint sessions, including dependence–independence difficulties, problems in sustaining two-person relationships, couples presenting aggressive or violent behaviour, and where one partner has exceedingly low self-

Clinical Handbook of Marriage and Couples Interventions. Edited by W. Kim Halford and Howard J. Markman.

esteem while the other seemingly appears confident and competent (Bennun, 1985).

Attempting to resolve the question of the relative effectiveness of individual or unilateral treatment by looking to the empirical data does not offer clear clinical directives (Gurman & Kniskern, 1986; Wells & Gianetti, 1986a, 1986b). As is often the case, this debate has relied on questions of methodology rather than clinical interpretations of outcome. Gurman and his colleagues have repeatedly stated that individual sessions are the least effective of all the forms of couple therapy and that it produces negative/deterioration effects (Gurman, Kniskern & Pinsof, 1986).

These conclusions are based on incorrect assumptions rather than methodological or empirical issues. The negative/deterioration effects have been reported from case studies or uncontrolled studies where marital satisfaction was used as a measure of outcome following individual psychotherapy. The presenting problems were not necessarily linked to relationship distress, but the status of the relationship was used to assess treatment efficacy. While this may be perfectly acceptable, it does not demonstrate the adverse effects of marital therapy with one partner. If, however, the presenting problems were indeed relational, then the conclusions would be valid. In a controlled study, Bennun (1985a) found no significant difference between conjoint, group and one-partner treatment in couples presenting with marital distress.

This controversy is based, therefore, on the confusion surrounding the focus of treatment. There is a clear distinction between conjoint sessions for dyadic–interactional problems and conjoint sessions as a way of relieving individual psychopathology such as depression or anxiety. Similarly, it remains unclear whether the critiques have included the effects of individual psychotherapy on marital functioning (Hurwitz, 1967) or on the untreated partner (Kohl, 1962). Systemically oriented therapists would not be surprised that changes occurring as a result of treating one partner have an effect on spouses and are likely to predict these. Systems theory posits that a change in any one element of a system would have an effect on all the elements that comprise the system. So, if one partner presents with agoraphobic difficulties and improves during the course of individual treatment, his/her spouse may have to adjust to a more competent, effective and possibly more independent partner. It is not surprising, then, that individual therapy has been seen as a precursor to later conjoint sessions (also see Halford, Sanders & Behrens, 1994).

The description offered by Watters (1982) unfortunately may be the most accurate. He describes the somewhat arbitrary decisions that are sometimes taken when couple discord emerges during psychiatric and psychological consultations. If relationship issues are identified, and the practitioner considers interpersonal factors as a possible cause, then couples are referred for conjoint treatment. If underlying relationship issues are not uncovered and the clinician is not attuned to interpersonal factors, then the individual is treated alone.

REDISCOVERING THE INDIVIDUAL

An inevitable consequence of the rapid development of couple/family/systems therapy, is the apparent neglect of the individual within this context. A brief account of systems theory may help towards understanding why this may have occurred in contemporary psychotherapeutic treatments. The majority of couple and family therapists base their clinical approach upon a broad systems theory framework. The ideas behind systems theory, as formulated within the biological sciences, describe a relationship between mutually independent units. Systems are defined as a set of objects together, the relationship between them and their attributes. The couple therefore represents a functioning operational system in which the partners together determine its total functioning (for simplicity I refer to just the couple and not other generations). Each element (partner) is in a functional relationship with the other and is thus dependent on that relationship for determining his/her health and well-being. Intervening, then, with one element (e.g. individual therapy) will precipitate changes in both and their combined functioning. A change in one partner will lead to the system having to recalibrate or reorganize itself to deal with that change, be it positive or negative (see Bennun, 1988).

A woman presenting with panic attacks requested individual treatment. The collaborative client–therapist formulation suggested that there were interpersonal issues within the marriage that maintained the panic. The client described her husband as a well known and locally respected man who she felt undermined her in company to the extent that she feared being in social situations with him. She believed that she did not have anything worthwhile to contribute and he always dominated conversations. He did not ask her opinion and when in company, she was often ignored. She described being increasingly unconfident and less self-assured. As treatment progressed, she became more confident and began challenging her husband when he spoke for both of them. He in turn, had to take account of her positive changes to the extent that he had to alter his attitude towards her and the way they, as a couple, interacted with others. A different example involved the way a marital relationship had to adjust after one of the partners, who had been hospitalized for a long period, returned to the family.

This illustrates how couples are interrelated and interdependent, and also emphasizes the dependence that each partner/member has on the other, an already known precipitant of relationship distress. One therefore needs to temper the theory to take account of important psychological processes that enhance the individual without ignoring their position within the system. Systemic marital and family therapy should be seen as part of the range of treatment orientations rather than *the* established approach.

Walter (1989) describes systemic therapies as needing to be "mature" enough to integrate with other approaches without fear of losing their identity. He further sees, as one of the major implications, the need to resurrect individually oriented therapies. In making this case, decisions obviously need to be made as to when and why individual therapy is chosen in preference to family or couple treatment, and *vice versa*. The two approaches to therapy have different rules and norms; while both are effective, separating them arbitrarily may perpetuate the idea that they developed from conflicting realities, rather than from different ones. Historically, the distinction has been between the intrapsychic and the interactional, without any deliberate attempt to place each in a related context, especially when clinical need prevails. One obvious solution is to develop hybrid models/approaches, e.g. behavioural–systemic therapy, cognitive–behavioural–strategic therapy (Bennun, 1987); however these attempts at integration are based on therapeutic models which arguably have insufficient theoretical justification.

Carter & McGoldrick (1988) and Falicov (1988), as well as others who have written on the family life-cycle, describe how viewing the family as negotiating successive developmental stages can help clinicians understand the complexity of family life; however, these descriptions tend to neglect the essence of individuality in their analyses. The life-cycle is a dynamic analysis illustrating the simultaneous changes for both individuals and systems, yet it is the latter that usually attracts our attention and provides a framework for systemic therapy. There are methods for working with just one member of the partnership/family which can address both systemic and individual areas of change.

UNDERSTANDING NON-ATTENDANCE

Clinicians need to examine the previously ignored but complex situation when partners refuse to attend conjoint sessions. On one level, this suggests that the problem resides with(in) their spouse and they see no need to attend. There are reports describing the difficulties therapists have encountered in attempting to convene conjoint sessions (Stanton & Todd, 1981) and engaging husbands in couples therapy (Rice, 1978).

The literature on men and fathers in therapy is steadily growing. The initial emphasis was on men's influence on their children's development, but more recently it has focused on the personal experience of fatherhood and help-seeking (Lewis and O'Brien, 1987). The factors that characterize men who do not attend include those who have difficulties with self-disclosure, show an antipathy towards sharing personal problems and who have high expectations of receiving purposive advice from a "recognized expert" (Blackie & Clark, 1987). Unfortunately there is little systematic research on non-attending partners; what has been reported is a description of the potential treatment drop-out.

Marriage counselling agencies are familiar with the resistant spouse who refuses to attend therapy sessions. These spouses may be unaware of their partner's distress, may believe that they are not connected with it or fail to acknowledge their contribution to the discord. Moreover, they may be aware of what they believe are risks if they attend, e.g. disclosure, being challenged, having to consider change options, etc. In some circumstances, therapists can insist that couples attend together or attempt to intervene through contact with the attending partner alone. The therapist's aim should be to convene conjoint sessions where possible, rather than withhold or refuse treatment if one partner is unwilling to attend. Treatment methods are required that can be of benefit to distressed couples where convening conjoint sessions is unlikely. Insisting that an unwilling partner attend will accomplish little and low motivation for treatment will present as a major treatment obstacle. One possible consequence could be the development of a collusive alliance between the attending partner and therapist, such that the therapeutic relationship represents a "preferred marriage".

From the non-attending partner's perspective, understanding the decision not to attend is important when thinking about likely clinical outcomes. Two discussions, one empirical (Bennun, 1989) and one theoretical (Scott, 1973a; 1973b; Street, 1994) offer therapists some directives for working with one partner irrespective of their preferred treatment model. Bennun explored the extent to which family members' perceptions of the therapist were associated with clinical outcome. The results showed that these interpersonal perceptions did have a marked impact on outcome. If fathers/husbands perceive the therapist as competent and active in providing direct guidance, the likelihood of good outcome is increased. This pattern does not hold for mother/wife perceptions. Generally, men are more reluctant to attend for consultations and when they do, they often remain disengaged (Littlejohn & Bruggen, 1994). These results suggest that it may not be advisable to engage resistant and reluctant husbands initially, as they appear to be particularly influential in determining the outcome of treatment. If they can be recruited into the treatment regime through some other means, this is preferable to having them adversely effect the course of treatment.

Scott's work (1973a,b) developed from understanding some of the family processes when one member is hospitalized presenting with a severe psychiatric disorder. He noted how, within families, positive interactions are *closed* as family members find ways of avoiding positive or helpful interactions by focusing on the negative features of the disorder. Family members then perceive themselves as being unable to cope with their distressed relative, who may subsequently be removed to an institution for treatment. Scott described these family interactions as creating a *treatment barrier* which prevents constructive therapeutic work from taking place. He used the notion of *closure* to describe the way positive interactions cease and the family withdraw from being actively involved in treatment.

Both of these approaches are worth considering if therapists have to treat just one marital partner. The empirical literature suggests that the gender of the attending partner is important and if it is the husband, then certain aspects of the therapeutic relationship should receive specific attention. If the husband is not attending, then the way he is included should be within a framework that facilitates his involvement. The non-attending partner's perception of their spouse *viz-à-viz* closure must be assessed and ways of preventing this should be included in the treatment approach. Certainly some principles from the systemic approaches may be helpful in developing the treatment plan.

INTERVENING WITH ONE PARTNER

Before examining two models of working with just one partner or family member, it is worth considering how this unilateral approach can be used more generally in clinical practice. It is certainly appropriate to ask whether a case can be made to single out one partner in preference to seeing both together.

Within the couple context, treating just one partner should always remain an option. Frequently when psychological problems are viewed as part of a marital dynamic, both partners are routinely invited to attend. In a previous section, it was suggested that individual and interpersonal processes should be seen as co-existing and that systemic or conjoint enthusiasm should be lessened by remaining cognizant of individual dynamics and how these interact with dyadic processes. As a general statement, it should be accepted that change can come about through working with one partner alone. There are data to support this (Szapocznik, Kurtines & Spencer, 1984; Szapocznik et al., 1986; Bennun, 1985) and clearly there are clinical instances when this approach is appropriate.

It was also noted previously that certain clinical problems may respond more favourably to individual treatment. These individual sessions can also be used to help the attending partner tolerate the stress of later planned conjoint interviews. This may best be achieved through developing a positive therapeutic relationship and reducing the risk of the individual feeling exposed and vulnerable if or when his/her partner eventually attends. Beck (1989) suggests that therapists should respond to a partner's request to be seen alone, but that the reason for this request and its meaning should be explored. The individual session may help the partner clarify his/her position about the future of the relationship and it will help in exploring commitment and motivation. It will also provide the therapist with an opportunity to distinguish between individual and relationship concerns.

Clinicians need to be acutely aware of timing and not introduce or re-introduce the partner into conjoint sessions too soon. Often the content of the individual session includes the expression of fear that difficulties will be belittled or negated by the partner. Sometimes the conjoint session will be perceived as potentially too threatening and the individual may need time to consider whether he/she would prefer his/her partner to attend.

The case for this form of therapy can be made theoretically where particular couple or family interactions have undermined personal resources. Years of performing a role, for example as parent or partner in relation to another, may leave the person without a sense of self or a clear identity; including others in treatment may repeat that experience. While "rediscovering" the individual is an important treatment focus, the sessions may need to help an individual redefine rather than rediscover who they are, and then adjust to their present circumstances. The previously described example of the woman presenting with panic attacks is illustrative of this process. In essence, the person in the dysfunctional role needs to be extracted from it and be validated within the context of the therapeutic relationship. We hear too often, "I am just a housewife", without taking enough care to understand what lies behind these statements.

Working with one partner alone can also bring about changes in repetitive sequential interactions. In these interactions, the sequences and outcomes are more or less predictable, given previous experience. Behaviourally oriented therapists may wish to witness these interactions in order to bring about change, thereby opting for conjoint sessions. It is, of course, an empirical question whether the interactions that occur outside would be reliably transferred to the conjoint session. Structural therapists (e.g. Minuchin, 1974) would encourage the couple to enact the dysfunctional sequences, and then provide them with some alternatives. However, the degree of generalization from the session remains unclear, so the value of new learning will always be uncertain. An alternative approach, more similar to strategic methods (e.g. Madanes, 1981) would be to help one partner develop strategies that interrupt dysfunctional recurring patterns while not making these explicit to the partner. Repetitive sequences strengthen or reinforce systems, so the act of surprise or unpredictability could unbalance it and necessitate a change in the usual pattern of interaction. Strategic therapists aim to develop "tactics of change" but sometimes these are appropriately not shared with both partners so as to maximize their impact. In its most simplistic form, therapists may advise one person to act differently in a given situation and monitor the change from the usual pattern of events. A case where this worked successfully was with a couple where the wife presented with an eating disorder. Instead of the husband encouraging his wife to eat, which always ended in a row, he was advised to cook just for himself. The essential distinction between this and other approaches is the extent to which *both* partners are aware of the therapeutic intervention. The element of surprise or unpredictability, as illustrated with this example, can only be accomplished in a one-to-one session. If both partners attend, then the intervention is shared and would not have the same impact.

Another indicator for intervening with one partner is where the identifiable problem is both interpersonal and individual in nature. Here the therapy can have two foci, one individually oriented and one exploring how the system maintains it. Jealousy provides a useful illustration because it can be formulated in both individual and systemic terms. Jealousy experienced as an individual problem can be understood as a loss of self-esteem, rejection, feeling under threat and, at its most extreme, part of a paranoid psychosis. A partner experiencing morbid jealousy (Im, Wilner & Breit, 1983; Teismann, 1979) will characteristically express personal and interpersonal concerns. He/she will inevitably experience interactions which confirm his/her beliefs and which exacerbate the distress. The clinician can choose whether or not to treat conjointly, but still work with both individual and interactional issues in a concurrent way. If the therapist explores personal conflicts as hypothesized precursors to the current distress with the partner present, then the individual may find it difficult to participate for fear of appearing foolish in front of his/her spouse. Most people presenting with jealousy periodically admit to its irrational nature, and are more likely to do so in a self-defeating manner within conjoint sessions. In instances such as these, developing a trusting one-to-one relationship in order to explore the possible determinants of the difficulty would be preferable. When jealousy is present, therapists need to be cautious not to collude by establishing a counter-jealous relationship which can be used outside of the session with disastrous consequences.

A related consideration is where the system interacts in a way that maintains individual problems. In instances of jealousy, panic, agoraphobia and the like, there is always the question of "How rational am I being?" whereas in other instances this may not be so. Agoraphobia is an example where the clinical formulation could view it as an interpersonal problem, providing the dependent individual with a solution to threat or as perceived lack of safety (Bennun, 1986). Traditional views of agoraphobia see it as a fear of leaving home or of public/ open places. It is usually thought to be an individual problem, although conjoint treatments have been used. The interpersonal formulation suggests that agora-phobia can maintain a particular dyadic pattern. It may fulfil the husband's need for a weak, dependent wife or, alternatively, provide a means of not challenging the husband's power base within the relationship. Although these systemic for-mulations may be correct, the timing of dyadic interventions is crucial and indi-vidual work with both a systemic and individual focus may prove to be the most effective.

All of these factors need to be examined on a case-by-case basis before deciding on whether to use a unilateral approach. Conjoint sessions can have the same treatment foci as unilateral sessions, but the dangers of joining partners prematurely or not exploring individual issues seem to outweigh adopting a systemic approach to the conjoint session before the therapist has gained an adequate understanding of the presenting problem. Interpersonal factors are usually more obvious within conjoint approaches, whereas individual issues tend to remain masked until tactfully uncovered.

ONE-PERSON FAMILY THERAPY (OPFT)

Szapocznik and colleagues have developed and evaluated their method of family therapy where one member is a drug misuser (Szapocznik et al., 1983, 1986; Szapocznik, Kurtines & Spencer, 1984) and their methods can certainly be applied and expanded to other clinical presentations, including relationship discord.

In their first study, these authors presented data on 37 families in which one member was a drug-abusing adolescent. The families received either conjoint treatment or OPFT and the results supported the view that it was possible to achieve favourable outcomes in both treatment conditions. There was improve-ment in family functioning and symptomatology for both treatment groups using a variety of clinical outcome measures and these positive gains were maintained at follow-up. Indeed there was slightly greater efficacy in the one-person ap-proach in bringing about continued symptom reduction in the drug-abusing adolescent. The second study of 35 families replicated the initial findings but the one-person approach appeared to be somewhat better at sustaining improved functioning at follow-up.

OPFT aims to change repetitive dysfunctional interactions. All family members attend the initial session so as to obtain a picture of the family structure. The therapist then chooses the one person who, by virtue of his/her position in the family, is central to the most significant repetitive and complementary dysfunctional behaviours. Having identified the one person, the therapist tracks the family's interactional structure and then directs appropriate changes. The final step is to restructure the family interactions by altering the way that the one person participates in family functioning, examining both interpersonal and intrapersonal factors. This approach does depend on the therapist meeting the whole family initially and understanding its interaction style. This aspect of the assessment enables therapists to remain reality-oriented in their work. The conjoint interview is clearly an assessment interview to observe interactions within the family.

The choice of family member directly involved in the treatment approach depends on three factors: centrality in the family interactions, power and availability. Together these three combine to determine who has most control over family interactions. A positive collaborative therapeutic relationship is emphasized so that the therapist can direct change and monitor the family's interactions through the perception of the engaged family member. Because just one family member is present, only *analogue enactment* is possible, which refers to exploring how the individual has internalized his/her role in the family's interactions. The analogue, by definition, implies a construction of reality as perceived by the individual. As no others are present to confirm or disconfirm this reality, the therapist needs to maintain a reality-oriented perspective within treatment. The attending person therefore describes their view of interactional sequences instead of actually enacting them, which would otherwise allow the therapist to observe the interactions directly. In conducting the enactment analogue, emphasis is given to the role the individual adopts within the reported interactions. This needs to be clearly identified so that the complementary roles that occur within these exchanges can be identified.

The notion of complementarity is important and is based on the premise of systems theory outlined earlier, that in order for the system to maintain itself, the one person must complement the behaviour of the others. The complementary interaction can thus be divided in two, those of the one person and those of the rest of the family. When these are combined, the therapist can construct a map of the total family functioning and intervene through changing the one person's reported behaviour or perceptions. When these two parts of the interaction network are brought together to form the whole, the therapist can use the map to explore the relationship between the engaged person and their family/partner and their internalized complementary behaviours within the whole.

Case Illustration

A case example will illustrate how this complementarity is fundamental within OPFT and can be applied to couple relationships. Hilary and James were referred for couples therapy after she had been assessed at the local community mental health centre. She described a variety of somatic complaints which had previously been investigated by the family physician. On finding no physical causes for her clinical presentation, a psychological assessment was requested. During the interview, Hilary admitted to relationship problems and when both were invited for a conjoint session, James made it clear that he had no intention of attending further sessions as he believed this approach to be inappropriate. He did state that his wife could continue attending on her own if she wished.

At the outset, it was important to use this one session to observe how the couple interacted together and identify the complementary relationships within the marriage. It became apparent that one source of tension in the relationship was how the couple, as parents, were preparing themselves and their youngest daughter for her forthcoming move away from home to university. Important decisions needed to be finalized, which included finances, accommodation, the extent to which members of the extended family near to the university town would become involved and the frequency of visits at home. At the end of the session, all agreed that Hilary was closer to their daughter and that the issues raised were making the separation increasingly difficult. This had come to the notice of their daughter who was suggesting that she could choose a different college "to maintain the peace".

In the subsequent one-person sessions, the therapist tried to develop a therapeutic relationship that reflected an understanding of Hilary's feelings but at the same time was fair to James. The focus of the sessions was two-fold: exploring the affective processes of the couple's differing points of view, as well as getting clear details of the sequences of events and discussions when the couple made plans for their daughter. Hilary described a fear of isolation when her daughter left, as well as of being overwhelmed by her husband's family, who lived nearby. She had used her daughter "as a foil" in dealing with him, although he disputed the way she described his family.

These two components, Hilary's description of her interaction with James and her fear of being overwhelmed, were combined by the therapist to construct a map of the couple's interaction, noting these complementary processes. Through a positive therapeutic alliance with Hilary, the therapist identified the complementary behaviours and cognitions maintaining the difficulties and began directing changes through her. It was important to formulate the interaction of the two complementary aspects: the disagreements about dealing with their daughter's future and the perception of the strength of the extended family. The more the couple disagreed, the more Hilary described her fear at not being able to stand up to his relatives. Information to support this formulation was elicited using circular questioning (Selvini Palazzoli et al., 1980; Penn, 1982; Tomm, 1988) which provided much detail as well as indicators for introducing change. Hilary used the sessions to explore her fears following her daughter's departure, role playing how she would assert herself with her in-laws and get James to appreciate how she felt when in their company.

Circular questioning enables the therapist to test and expand clinical formulations. The questions are one of the fundamental techniques of systemic therapy and give therapists the opportunity of gaining information so that connections can be made between actions, beliefs and relationships. These questions can make explicit the belief systems that maintain distress or introduce the element of time by asking the participants to consider hypothetical questions about the future so that they can consider alternative options or choices. Selvini Palazzoli and colleagues define the process of circularity as being the therapist's capacity to investigate interpersonal processes on the basis of feedback in response to information obtained from the individual, couple or family. It involves using information gained from participants and feeding this back to them so that they can explore and modify current repetitive and/or dysfunctional beliefs, behaviours or attitudes. Some of the questions put to Hilary included: "Who in James' family do you think he has most difficulty standing up to?"; "Who are you most similar and different to in that family?"; and "Who else has the same fear of being overwhelmed?" The responses to these questions were then used to explore whether Hilary was the only one who felt overwhelmed by her in-laws and whether she could use the perceived alliances in order not to feel so isolated and threatened. Similarly, Hilary considered the different ways she and her husband would miss their daughter, who would adjust sooner and what or who would they use "as a foil" after she left?

Several techniques can be used with the analogue enactments, such as role play, using the therapist to construct complementary roles, an empty chair technique, sketching structural relationships and cognitive restructuring (for detail, see Szapocznik, Kurtines & Spencer, 1984). Although this method was developed for family work, it can be applied to dyadic relationships as it bears many of the hallmarks outlined in the previous discussion of the unilateral therapy principles, particularly the interface between the personal and interpersonal. Partners often internalize roles/behaviours that support repetitive couple interactions and this method illustrates how, through one person, change at both levels can be achieved. The therapist could convene an initial conjoint session and then continue to work with the attending partner. The engaged partner is usually identified through presenting symptoms or by exclusion, that is the spouse being unwilling to attend. Therapists often try to convince the non-attending partner to participate in treatment and waste valuable therapeutic time. Failing to engage the reluctant spouse and admitting to this failure after a few sessions could reflect the experience of the attending member and further exacerbate feelings of helplessness and impotence. As with most forms of one-partner couple therapy, inadvertently repeating with the therapist those interactions that occur within the dyad could undermine both future attendance, motivation and compliance.

INDIVIDUAL COUPLE THERAPY

As individual partners presenting at couples counselling agencies increases (Tyndall, 1985), so it has become necessary to reformulate conjoint procedures to accommodate individual consultations or referrals. Some therapists insist on convening conjoint sessions and are reluctant to do otherwise. Some of the reservations include gaining a biased account of the existing problem, becoming embroiled in couple secrets, the therapeutic relationship being used as a competing relationship and doubting whether dyadic change can be achieved through individual sessions. Over the last 10 years, a model has been developed that addresses these reservations. It has been used sometimes without convening an initial conjoint session, but it is always preferable to try and see both partners at the outset.

This individual couples therapy approach was evaluated in a controlled trial (Bennun, 1985a, 1985b). Fifty-seven couples were randomly assigned to either conjoint treatment, couples groups or treating just one partner. Outcome evaluations included blind pre–post independent assessments, as well as measures of marital satisfaction, sexual adjustment and an assessment of the couple's specific target problems. The results showed no significant differences between the three treatment conditions, suggesting that at the end of treatment, the individual modality was equally as effective as the other more established treatments in facilitating positive change. However, when the data were analysed with the view to exploring rates of change, the couples receiving conjoint treatment appeared to resolve their target problems more rapidly. This latter finding does not invalidate the approach; rather practitioners and researchers should explore ways of refining and developing the treatment of one partner alone.

There are three guiding principles within the approach: the dyadic–systemic focus, giving attention to the non-attending partner and exploring contributions to conflict. These are considered simultaneously during the sessions and, unlike the OPFT approach, it is less sequential in its delivery, relying more on the therapist's role in relation to the attending and non-attending partner.

The Dyadic–Systemic Focus

Intervention requires a balance between an individual and a dyadic focus. Relationships fulfil a variety of psychological and physical needs, both for the individual and the couple. When these needs are unfulfilled, the ensuing distress affects the individual, his/her partner and the relationship. This triad is often ignored if the focus is oriented purely towards the individual. Similarly, if the focus is predominantly on the relationship, the needs of the two persons within the relationship may go unrecognized.

The distinction between intrapersonal and interpersonal processes has already been noted. This approach attempts to maintain a balance rather than see these as two contradictory foci. By way of setting a treatment agenda, the dual focus needs to be made explicit at the initial assessment so that the non-attender is not "let off the hook" by subscribing to the view of "fixing her/him will improve our marriage". Just as the OPFT approach requires a conjoint assessment, the approach here too invites and encourages both partners to attend together for the first session. If the referral indicates that one partner may be reluctant to attend, this is acknowledged in the way that the couple are initially invited. It is therefore advisable to communicate the wish to see the couple conjointly first, indicating that it may not be necessary for the couple to attend together for subsequent sessions. Obviously if there is a willingness for both to participate fully, then the usual practice of conjoint therapy can proceed. However, therapists need to be cautious when the seemingly non-symptomatic partner willingly agrees to attend. While his/her motives may be honest, there is always the possibility that he/she wishes to attend as a gate-keeper, to ensure that certain information or detail is not included or disclosed during the treatment.

Whether or not both attend, the therapist needs to inform the individual or couple of their need to maintain the dual focus and orientate them to this as soon as possible. When unwilling partners declare their intention, it is important to convey that even in their absence, they will be part of the treatment. Accepting their resistance may increase the possibility of participation in any therapeutic directives or tasks as they emerge. Clinical experience has shown that when attending partners repeatedly share the details of the sessions with their spouses at home, the latter often have a change of mind and attitude and then agree to attend. It should be noted that the approach is not a subtle attempt to coax attendance, but rather to use, as productively as possible, their somewhat reduced participation in the treatment.

Essential to the dyadic–systemic focus is the way problems are defined and clinically formulated. This guides both the therapist and the attending partner to looking primarily at the relationship issues rather than at individual psychological problems. Should these arise from relationship issues, then they are obviously explored in appropriate way. If the therapist is working towards the resolution of a specific two-person problem, the treatment goal needs to be formulated in terms that include both partners. For example in the case of a woman with panic attacks, the dyadic perspective that the therapist adopts ensures that the presenting problem is understood both as panic and the extent that her partner contributes to it. This formulation/hypothesis can only be developed after a systematic assessment of the individual–couple situation.

It is inevitable that the partner will spend time during the sessions discussing personal difficulties and defocus the relationship; it is equally likely that the relationship will predominate to the exclusion of the individual. Although just one partner attends, the focus of treatment needs to be directed at relationship change and the psychological development of both partners.

The Non-attending Partner

The success of this approach to treatment rests on the therapist gaining the confidence of both partners; it is therefore important to consider the role of the non-attending partner. The initial conjoint session is the most appropriate opportunity to be specific about the non-attending partner's participation in treatment. During the conjoint session, the rationale of the treatment must be explained to both and the therapist must make explicit each partner's contribution to the process of therapy. This conjoint session may be the only occasion on which the couple are seen together, so in addition to observing how they interact, the ground-rules of therapy should be explained and negotiated. It should also be used to discuss presenting problems, develop therapeutic targets and consider the possible difficulties that may arise (e.g. reactance, relapse).

In order to maintain the collaborative set where both partners acknowledge the difficulties and see the need for change, some treatment expectations need to be stated. The attending partner should give the non-attending partner an account of the session, preferably on the same day that it takes place. It is useful to negotiate this early on so as to assess both partners' motivation. Secondly, if specific home assignments are joint tasks, the non-attending partner must be willing to co-operate. Thirdly, the therapist should receive feedback from the non-treated partner about the task or any other topic that he/she may wish to share. Both have a shared responsibility for creating change and the power relationships should not be reinforced through these artificial roles.

Contributions to Conflict

Working within this approach can result in therapists stepping out of their neutral role and joining with one partner in a treatment coalition. While efforts to avoid this are usually successful, a crucial factor in working with one partner is adherence to the systemic notion that conflict is the result of interaction and feedback and that one partner is not solely to blame. A fundamental premise in the individual couple therapy paradigm is to acknowledge that both partners contribute to the conflict and that both are responsible for its resolution. While couple therapy sessions often enable partners to express and discharge emotion, blame is never far behind. In the treatment with one partner, the blaming and scapegoating processes are usually more intense because the partner is not present to defend him/herself or offer a different point of view. In conjoint sessions, the opposing views often escalate the intensity of the sessions and the same is likely to occur during individual sessions. The therapist's neutral position counteracts the blaming and scapegoating and maintains the view that both partners contribute to the development and maintenance of marital distress. Therapists should not be side-tracked into deciding what proportion each partner is responsible for; rather they should be clear in communicating an understanding of the problem by presenting a systemic formulation that helps both partners identify their respective contributions to conflict.

In keeping with the dyadic–systemic focus, both partners' contributions to the presenting distress can be made explicit through the reformulation of problems with a specific two-person focus. A distressed couple, complicated by a wife's agoraphobia, should be seen in a way that goes beyond the fear of open spaces. The reformulation could include, if the assessment indicates it, fear of going out and the accompanying dependency, *as well as* the husband's supposedly strong protective self-perception, which he may be reluctant to relinquish. Hafner (1986) considers the origins of agoraphobia as being in the choice of partner. The particular choice enables the couple to hold this as their undeclared (unconscious) basis for their relationship. The husband will undermine his wife's attempts toward greater autonomy and she will not challenge his strength and autonomy. It would not be surprising to find that in this type of relationship the husband is unwilling to attend, so it would be necessary to challenge the wife's perception that she is responsible for causing the distress. The agoraphobic symptoms will often be strengthened by its apparent capacity to reduce interpersonal conflict. Processes such as these need to be uncovered through careful questioning and developing clinical hypotheses that account for both partners' involvement.

Case Illustration

Individual couple therapy is especially useful when therapy is provided in specialist residential units. Bryan was attending a 3-month residential course for those with little or no sight. This national centre accepts clients from all over the country and inevitably couples therapy is provided to the attender alone. Many residents have a variety of associated mental health problems and the disability often has marked effects on couple and family relationships. Those attending the course are usually assessed with an informant (spouse or parent) and return home for three or four weekends during the 3-month training period.

Bryan was a 48-year-old man who had been married for 12 years. His wife Julie had been married previously and had a 14-year-old son. Following the onset of deterioration in his sight 5 years previously, Bryan was admitted to a psychiatric hospital with a suggested diagnosis of schizophrenia. He had become disinhibited, had burned some of the kitchen fittings and was behaving in an aggressive manner. The admission lasted 3 weeks, during which time his condition stabilized. The only residual side-effect of the medication was that he felt that his memory had deteriorated.

During the conjoint assessment, Julie was very critical of her husband and clearly had unrealistic expectations of him, given both his mental health history and his visual impairment. Although she accepted that his residential stay was primarily to acquire skills for employment, she indicated that with his residual sight he should have been able to do more. Some of the care staff had gained the impression that Julie was remaining in the marriage because she felt "sorry" for her husband and could not leave him to fend for himself. Bryan occupied himself by looking after the animals on their smallholding. Both acknowledged that he had a good relationship with her son who helped his step-father a great deal in a facilitative way.

The extent to which Julie conveyed a critical negative attitude towards Bryan highlighted the potential closure process. She focused on the negative elements of his mental health and visual disability, suggesting little hope for change. One therapeutic task during this session was to limit the impact or reduce the effect of her behaviour and attitude and avoid the interactions creating the treatment barrier. This was achieved by exploring Julie's attitude towards disability, her fears of a second "failed" marriage, and how she blamed Bryan for his poor sight even though he had no control over it (sight loss through risky or dangerous pursuits would be an obvious reason for "blame").

The therapeutic aim for the first session was to observe the couple's interaction, address the possible closure processes and inform Julie what her role might be when Bryan returned home on weekend leave. The couple distress was formulated systemically: in an attempt to meet Julie's expectations, Bryan makes demands on himself which he is unable to achieve. This makes him feel worse, which further impaires his general ability. These issues were also placed in the context of Julie's fear of a second separation.

Julie needed unambiguous information about what could be expected from her husband, the nature and prognosis of his disabililties and help with clarifying ways of reducing the distress that surrounded their marriage. In considering the non-attending partner, the therapist sensitively shared the essence of the dyadic–systemic formulation, discussing with them their respective contribution to their relationship conflict. Furthermore, Julie was given advice on how to gain appropriate and relevant information about sight problems. Agreement was also obtained that during the weekend home visits, she would enquire about the psychological help her husband was receiving in general and the marital/relationship issues in particular. It was made explicit to both that they shared responsibility for creating change and that both might undermine the psychological benefits gained from the rehabilitation course.

The series of individual sessions explored both individual and relationship concerns. Bryan was aware that his sight would not improve and that he risked losing his "role in society". He feared the impact this would have on his mental health and ways of dealing with this in a preventative manner were explored. To the extent that he felt continually criticized, his attempts to overcome these self-esteem issues were being undermined. This was a topic which he wanted to share with Julie, and he was able to do so successfully on one of his weekends at home. Julie raised with him what she considered to be his "self-pity", which became a useful focus for change, having an impact on both intra- and interpersonal functioning.

At the end of the course, Julie wrote about how helpful the psychological treatment had been and how they had become much clearer about the way they were dealing with their difficulties. She reported feeling more optimistic and grateful that she was now aware how they "could change in order to deal with the obvious circumstances which would not change".

THE CHALLENGE OF WORKING INDIVIDUALLY

These two models of working with one marital partner address many of the reservations about one-person or individual couple therapy. Treating one partner does risk the attending partner presenting a biased account of the couple relationship and the distress. However, by insisting on a dyadic–systemic focus and encouraging the couple to acknowledge that they both contribute to the problem, the therapist can check the validity of the information received, as well as use the session as a means of providing and receiving feedback. On occasions, audio-recordings of sessions can be used to facilitate tasks/discussions at home.

The initial conjoint session gives the therapist the opportunity to meet the non-attending partner, especially when there are risks that the therapeutic relationship may compete with the couple relationship. All attempts to discourage this are valuable. Transference processes are inevitable in one-to-one therapeutic encounters, so all three participants need to be cognizant of the three sets of two-person relationships: therapist–attender; therapist–non-attender and the couple relationship.

Marital therapists and counselling agencies do not always have the opportunity of treating couples conjointly; once a partner refuses to attend, the decision to intervene through just the attending partner must be carefully considered. If a partner chooses to be seen alone, the therapist may need to explore how conjoint sessions can be convened, ensuring that the person seeking treatment does not feel threatened or anxious. However, therapists need to be cautious not to invite the non-attending partner too soon. There are some occasions which appear to suggest that individual sessions are indicated and the clinical assessment should address these at the outset. These can be divided into relationship, individual and intervention factors. If the relationship is described as not being supportive of the individual and is not considered sufficiently "nourishing" or safe, then experience suggests that partners should be seen separately, possibly with the view to subsequent conjoint sessions. Perceptions such as these need to be explored carefully and in some detail without the interference or interruption of a "contradicting partner". The lack of safety and support may be misattributed to the relationship and this needs to be clarified in the context of individual sessions. However, if both partners perceive their relationship as being unsafe or unfilfilling, then in all likelihood they would be willing to attend together.

Personal factors that contra-indicate conjoint sessions include those individuals who, at least initially, would be unlikely "to stand their ground" in what could potentially be competitive and hostile conjoint sessions. Such individuals may report being undecided about their commitment to the marriage, may present with low self-esteem or describe a history of difficulty in sustaining two-person relationships. Their fear of repeating a well-trodden, albeit destructive, path within the current relationship is more suitably worked through without their partners being present. This is often linked to fears of dependency; individuals who have experienced hurt in a previous relationship may fear becoming dependent on either another person or their relationship. The source of the fear or indeed their dependent needs is more appropriately considered within an individual context. As noted earlier, an assessment needs to be made about their presenting problem being both personal and interpersonal. Even though the primary focus may be on relationship improvement, it does not necessarily require both partners attending together.

Many authors have cautioned against individual work because of the risk of individuals disclosing "a secret" which they would not share conjointly. Occasionally, couple and family therapists receive information about their clients by means other than through the therapy sessions. Private telephone calls and correspondence or chance meetings with the therapists are the usual avenues that can be exploited to convey secret information. Individual couples therapy is an easy arena for the attending partners to reveal information that they do not want to share with their partners, and most often this places the therapist in a dilemma about dealing with this material. There are two quite different ways of dealing with this issue. The therapist can make it explicit at the outset that while the content of the session is confidential, the boundary of confidentiality extends to all those involved. It must be made clear that all material is available for sharing between the three participants. In this way, the dilemma is resolved by making clear to the attending partner that the therapist will not be bound by the secrecy if conjoint sessions occur at a later date.

A contrasting approach addresses the fear of collusion quite differently; what needs to be considered is the therapist's task and role. It is not as an arbitrator or judge, but rather is an effort to resolve relationship distress. If a secret is undermining the stability or future of a relationship, then refusing to have it disclosed or demanding to do so oneself, could undermine the therapist's purpose of helping couples *and individuals* resolve their difficulties. Too often secrets are considered as a paralysing influence on the therapist: in these situations the therapist too easily assumes the responsibility for colluding with the source of the distress. The individual partner must decide how revealing some or all of the detail may affect the relationship. The therapist is ill-advised to depart from a position of neutrality as an advocate for both individuals and the relationship. The notion of neutrality does not imply that the therapist should resist taking sides; rather it describes the therapist as a "naive enquirer" needing information in order to understand the individual's or couple's predicament. However, if violence or abuse is being disclosed, then the therapist may have a (statutory) responsibility to intervene more directly and step out of the neutral position.

Finally, having considered individual and relationship factors, the choice of the individual approach may be appropriate if particular types of interventions are being considered. These are usually developed from the strategic approach (e.g. Madanes, 1981; Todd, 1986) and would be less effective if both partners were present. They often introduce elements of surprise, are counter-intuitive and test the structure of the relationship by introducing "tactics" to break an existing impasse.

Couples therapy approaches that see just one partner represent a paradigmatic shift. In some respects, it illustrates that couples therapy has come the full circle, appreciating that there is a place for non-conjoint perspectives. The early psychoanalytic methods saw the conjoint session as interfering with the development of the transference relationship and argued against seeing both partners together. The next stage was characterized by the emergence of the various forms of conjoint and conjoint–group approaches, including systemic methods. Now again, the role of individual couples therapy is being considered as a viable treatment option. This "second generation" of individual approaches has incorporated systemic principles which makes it distinctive, but it does require constant refining and development. Major issues, including non-compliance, resistance, drop-out and engaging men as active participants, continue to require special attention.

REFERENCES

Beck, R. (1989). The individual interview in couples treatment. *Journal of Family Therapy*, **11**, 231–241.

Bennun, I. (1985a). Behavioural marital therapy: an outcome evaluation of conjoint, group and one-spouse treatment. *Scandinavian Journal of Behaviour Therapy*, **14**, 157–168.

Bennun, I. (1985b). Prediction and responsiveness in behavioural marital therapy. *Behavioural Psychotherapy*, **13**, 186–201.

Bennun, I. (1986). A composite formulation of agoraphobia. *American Journal of Psychotherapy*, **40**, 177–188.

Bennun, I. (1987). Behavioural marital therapy: a critique and appraisal of integrated models. *Behavioural Psychotherapy*, **15**, 1–15.

Bennun, I. (1988). Systems theory and family therapy. In E. Street & W. Dryden (eds), *Family Therapy in Britain* (pp. 3–22). Milton Keynes: Open University Press.

Bennun, I. (1989). Perceptions of the therapist in family therapy. *Journal of Family Therapy*, **11**, 243–255.

Blackie, S. & Clark, D. (1987). Men in marriage counselling. In C. Lewis & M. O'Brien (eds), *Re-assessing Fatherhood* (pp. 197–211). London: Sage.

Blanck, R. (1965). The case for individual treatment. *Social Casework*, **46**, 70–74.

Carter, E. & McGoldrick, M. (1988). *The Family Life-Cycle: a Framework for Family Therapy*. New York: Guilford.

Falicov, C. (1988). *Family Transitions*. New York: Guilford.

Fibush, E. (1957). The evaluation of marital interaction in the treatment of one partner. *Social Casework*, **38**, 303–307.

Gurman, A. & Kniskern, D. (1986). Commentary: individual marital therapy—have reports of your death been somewhat exaggerated? *Family Process*, **25**, 51–62.

Gurman, A., Kniskern, D. & Pinsof, W. (1986). Research on the process and outcome of marital and family therapy. In S. Garfield & A. Bergin (eds), *Handbook of Psychotherapy and Behaviour Change* (pp. 565–624). Chichester: Wiley.

Hafner, R. (1986). Marital therapy for agoraphobia. In N. Jacobson & A. Gurman (eds), *Clinical Handbook of Marital Therapy* (pp. 471–493). New York: Guilford.

Halford, W., Sanders, M. & Behrens, B. (1994). Self-regulation in behavioural couples' therapy. *Behaviour Therapy*, **25**, 431–452.

Hurwitz, N. (1967). Marital problems following psychotherapy with one spouse. *Journal of Consulting Psychology*, **31**, 38–47.

Im, W., Wilner, R. & Breit, M. (1983). Jealousy: interventions in couples therapy. *Family Process*, **22**, 211–219.

Kohl, R. (1962). Pathological reactions of marital partners to improvement of patients. *American Journal of Psychiatry*, **118**, 1036–1041.

Lewis, C. & O'Brien, M. (1987). *Re-assessing Fatherhood*. London: Sage.

Littlejohn, R. & Bruggen, P. (1994). Fathers past and present: their role in family therapy. *Current Opinion in Psychiatry*, **7**, 229–232.

Madanes, C. (1981). *Strategic Family Therapy*. London: Jossey-Bass.

Minuchin, S. (1974). *Families and Family Therapy*. Cambridge, MA: Harvard University Press.

Nadelson, C. (1978). Marital therapy from a psychoanalytic perspective. In T. Paolino & B. McCrady (eds), *Marriage and Marital Therapy* (pp. 89–164). New York: Brunner Mazel.

Penn, P. (1982). Circular questioning. *Family Process*, **21**, 267–280.

Rice, D. (1978). The male spouse in marital and family therapy. *The Counselling Psychologist*, **7**, 64–67.

Scott, R. (1973a). The treatment barrier: Part I. *British Journal of Medical Psychology*, **46**, 45–55.

Scott, R. (1973b). The treatment barrier: Part II. The patient as an unrecognised agent. *British Journal of Medical Psychology*, **46**, 57–67.

Selvini Palazzoli, M., Boscolo, L., Cecchin, G. & Prata, G. (1980). Hypothesizing, circularity and neutrality: three guidelines for the conductor of the session. *Family Process*, **19**, 3–12.

Stanton, D. & Todd, T. (1981). Engaging resistant families in treatment: principles and techniques in recruitment. *Family Process*, **20**, 261–293.

Street, E. (1994). A family systems approach to child–parent separation: developmental closure. *Journal of Family Therapy*, **16**, 347–365.

Szapocznik, J., Kurtines, W. & Spencer, F. (1984). One-person family therapy. In W. O'Connor & B. Lubin (eds), *Ecological Approaches to Clinical and Community Psychology* (pp. 335–355). New York: Wiley.

Szapocznik, J., Kurtines, W., Foote, F., Peres-Vidal, A. & Hervits, O. (1993). Conjoint versus one-person family therapy: some evidence for the effectiveness of conducting family therapy through one person. *Journal of Consulting and Clinical Psychology*, **51**, 889–899.

Szapocznik, J., Kurtines, W., Foote, F., Peres-Vidal, A. & Hervits, O. (1996). Conjoint versus one-person family therapy: some further evidence for the effectiveness of conducting family therapy through one person with drug-abusing adolescents. *Journal of Consulting and Clinical Psychology*, **54**, 395–397.

Teismann, M. (1979). Jealousy: systemic problem-solving therapy with couples. *Family Process*, **18**, 151–160.

Todd, T. (1986). Structural–strategic marital therapy. In N. Jacobson & A. Gurman (eds), *Clinical Handbook of Marital Therapy* (pp. 71–105). New York: Guilford.

Tomm, K. (1988). Interventive interviewing: Part III. Intending to ask lineal, circular, strategic or reflexive questions? *Family Process*, **27**, 1–15.

Tyndall, N. (1985). The work and impact of the national marriage guidance council. In W. Dryden (ed.), *Marital Therapy in Britain*, Vol. 1 (pp. 91–117). London: Harper and Row.

Walter, J. (1989). Not individual, not family. *Journal of Strategic and Systemic Therapies*, **8**, 70–77.

Watters, W. (1982). Conjoint couple therapy. *Canadian Journal of Psychiatry*, **27**, 91.

Wells, R. & Gianetti, V. (1986a). Individual marital therapy: a critical appraisal. *Family Process*, **25**, 43–51.

Wells, R. & Gianetti, V. (1986b). Rejoiner: whither marital therapy? *Family Process*, **25**, 62–65.

Chapter 19

Reconstructing Marriages after the Trauma of Infidelity

Shirley P. Glass* and Thomas L. Wright**
*Private Practice, Owing Mills, MD; and
**Department of Psychology, Catholic University of America,
Washington, DC, USA

Couples therapy following an extramarital disclosure can often be explosive and wearing in those difficult cases where one or both spouses are ambivalent, crises and relapses occur and affect is intense. Long-held assumptions about the meaning of the marriage, perceptions of the partner and views of oneself are shattered. The betrayed spouse is obsessed with uncovering lies, is hypervigilant for continued betrayal and alternates between numbness, rage and clinging behaviors. The involved spouse grieves for the lost dreams of the affair, believes that the marriage can never fully satisfy their needs, and fears that the betrayed spouse will never put this event in the past.

John, a betrayed husband, reviews all of the credit card statements and the telephone bills for further evidence of continuing infidelity. John can no longer listen to his favorite country and western radio station because the songs trigger flashbacks of the affair. When John initiates lovemaking with his wife, he is flooded with images of his wife and the other man in erotic scenarios. He states, "I don't know who my wife is anymore. I didn't think we had any problems except that she wasn't that interested in sex. I believed that she was a highly moral person who disapproved of lying and infidelity. How can I ever trust her again when she works late at the office?"

John's wife, Joan, is having difficulty ending the affair and is clearly ambivalent about making a full commitment to the marriage. She feels disloyal to her affair partner when she makes love with her husband. John's unrelenting suspiciousness is driving her further away. Joan says, "I feel terrible that John found out. I didn't mean to hurt him. I love him, but I'm not in love with him. I can't stand his constant inquisition about the sex, and I'm not going to report to him every five minutes when I'm out of the house. He'll never trust me or let me forget about this. I feel empty

Clinical Handbook of Marriage and Couples Interventions. Edited by W. Kim Halford and Howard J. Markman.
© 1997 John Wiley & Sons Ltd.

and hopeless without the other relationship. I don't know why I can't continue to have a friendship with my affair partner".

The discovery of infidelity is frequently the catalyst for initiating marital therapy. Surveys indicate that approximately 25% of couples initiating marital therapy present with the issue of extramarital sex (EMS) and 30% more will disclose EMS during the course of therapy (Greene, 1981; Humphrey, 1983a,b; Sprenkle & Weiss, 1978). In non-clinical samples, incidence of EMS ranges from 30% to 60% of the men, and from 20% to 50% of the women, with an even higher incidence among divorced and separated persons (Glass & Wright, 1977, 1985; Hunt, 1974; Petersen, 1983).

Our definition of extramarital involvement (EMI) is not solely contingent upon the traditional criteria of sexual intercourse but includes non-coital sexual intimacies and extramarital emotional involvement. Utilizing this extended definition of EMI, 60% of our clinical couples have been impacted by an EMI. Lawson (1988) reported "adulteries of the heart" in 40% of the British subjects she surveyed. We differentiated in an article by Peterson (1988) between platonic friendships and emotional affairs which can present a serious threat to the marriage and are characterized by *sexual chemistry, emotional intimacy* and elements of *secrecy* or deception. Spousal mistrust of a friendship may indicate pathological jealousy or could connote a valid concern where a sexual attraction and emotional sharing is intensifying behind a wall of secrecy.

Betrayed spouses often appear to be suffering from a post-traumatic reaction which includes: obsessive ruminating and repetition, hypervigilance and digging for details, accusatory suffering and flashbacks. We will present a relational trauma model for healing after the betrayal of infidelity which parallels the individualistic trauma literature, particularly that which focuses on survivors of abuse. Our clinical interventions have been derived from 12 years of co-therapy with couples and 20 years of empirical research on gender differences in marital and extramarital relationships.

OVERVIEW

This chapter will present common responses in betrayed spouses that characterize a traumatic reaction. Individualistic and relational variables which impact on the level of traumatization include basic assumptions about the marriage, the extent of the deception, the manner of discovery, and the individualistic vulnerabilities on both sides. Our interpersonal trauma model and its derivations will create a conceptual framework for the stages of traumatization, healing and recovery.

The first therapeutic task is to create a sense of safety in the therapeutic relationship and within the marital relationship. Detriangulating by opening windows between spouses and putting up walls with the extramarital partner is a crucial step. This initial phase of therapy establishes caring behaviors and constructive communication. Crisis intervention and affect management carefully titrates the expression of strong emotions with the need to control these feelings. Discussing the details of the betrayal should be delayed until the marital relationship has clearly strengthened and stabilized.

There are several stories which will be integrated into a meaningful whole: the story of the individuals, the story of the marriage, and the story of the affair. The narrative of the EMI will evolve as the process shifts from adversarial truth-seeking, to neutralized information-seeking, to an empathic search for deeper understanding. Requisite signs of healing include a stronger marriage, mutual empathy and responsibility, and acknowledgement of individualistic vulnerabilities. Healing which is delayed may be attributed to unfinished business, accusatory suffering, unresolved flashbacks or lingering pain and suspiciousness.

The important issues of confidentiality in secret affairs and approaches for dealing with an involved spouse's ambivalence will be addressed. The chapter will conclude with a discussion of what outcomes are associated with EMI among our therapy couples and in other research samples of non-clinical couples.

TRAUMATIC REACTIONS TO INFIDELITY

We have observed that the symptoms of many betrayed spouses are strikingly similar to the post-traumatic stress reactions of the victims of emotional, physical and sexual abuse. The symptoms of post-traumatic stress disorder, 309.81 in DSM-IV (American Psychiatric Association, 1994), cluster into three categories: (a) intrusion, which involves recounting and reexperiencing the trauma; (b) constriction, which is evidenced by avoidance and numbing behaviors; and (c) hyperarousal, which is characterized by physiologic arousal and extreme hypervigilance.

Lusterman (1995) has also proposed that post-traumatic stress reactions are associated with marital infidelity. Although Lusterman focuses on "protracted marital infidelity" as a precursor to traumatic reactions, we do not believe that length of infidelity is the critical feature. A one-night stand can be as traumatizing as a long-term affair if it shatters the beliefs of a betrayed spouse.

Janoff-Bulman (1992) asserts that traumatic reactions are associated with "shattered assumptions" regarding an individual's sense of safety in the world after a catastrophic event. She proposes that three fundamental assumptions held before the traumatic event are that, "The world is benevolent, the world is meaningful, and the self is worthy" (p. 6). We propose that basic marital assumptions commonly held before a crisis of infidelity are: (1) "We both value monogamy"; (2) "I can trust you"; (3) "You're honest with me"; (4) "We're committed to each other"; and (5) "I'm safe in this relationship".

Herman (1992) states that the damage is particularly severe when the traumatic events themselves involve the betrayal of important relationships. Even in open marriages we've treated, spouses were devastated by the betrayal of partners who breached their explicit contracts by getting emotionally involved with extramarital sexual partners or by engaging in undisclosed, extramarital sex. Although mistrust and intense affect may be present in both spouses surrounding an infidelity, it is the betrayed spouse who frequently exhibits the specific post-traumatic symptoms of hypervigilance, obsessive ruminating and flashbacks.

WHY SOME ARE MORE TRAUMATIZED THAN OTHERS

The severity of reactions differs greatly among betrayed spouses. Some appear to take it in their stride and others respond catastrophically. The apparently non-reactive spouse must be assessed for a numbing response before concluding that this is not a traumatic event.

Shattered Assumptions

The intensity of a betrayed spouse's traumatic reactions appears to be associated with the strength of his/her basic marital assumptions regarding a mutual commitment to monogamy prior to the disclosure of the infidelity. The disillusionment and loss of innocence prevent a return to the blind trust that existed prior to the event. One betrayed spouse said, "It'd be easier if you had died". Another betrayed spouse said, "I wish I had died last year when I was sick . . . before I learned the terrible truth about you".

The depth of traumatization is increased by the collapse of basic marital assumptions which created a sense of safety in the marriage. A betrayed husband said, "My wife was a virgin when we married, and she's always been a devoted wife and mother. I would have bet two million dollars that could not have been my wife coming out of a motel with another man". A betrayed wife said, "I don't know who this person is anymore. I can't believe that he's been cheating on me for over 20 years. He's religious and hates liars and never was that interested in sex". These preceding responses contrast sharply with a couple who were hurt and angry but not shocked because they were unfaithful to each other during the engagement. A tornado can be more catastrophic than a hurricane because there's no warning.

Individuals who seem to accept their partner's EMI with minimal distress may include a high potential for spousal infidelity in their basic marital assumptions. These expectations could arise from socio-cultural influences, personal experiences or knowledge of their partner's pre-existing extramarital attitudes and/or behaviors. Partners whose marital contracts include EMI do not experience feelings of betrayal and distress unless other specific marital assumptions are violated.

The Discovery of the Infidelity

The depth of trauma is associated with the manner of discovery and the extent of the deception. Our research and clinical observations do not support the systems-oriented view that the betrayed spouse must have some level of awareness and colludes in an extramarital triangle (Brown, 1991). Admittedly some partners welcome the decreased pressure for emotional or sexual intimacy which affairs create. Other partners deny the clues because of fears that the marriage would end if they acknowledged the infidelity. Research findings indicate that persons in well developed relationships demonstrate a truth bias resulting in greater judgments of truthfulness and lower detection of deception (Stiff, Kim & Ramesh, 1992). When involved persons are discreet, compartmentalize their extramarital relationships and maintain a loving relationship with their spouse, the infidelity may be totally unsuspected.

> Al and Alice had an exciting sexual relationship, enjoyed doing things together, and were warm and affectionate toward each other. While they were on vacation on a romantic tropical island, she accidentally walked in while he was engaged in an intimate telephone conversation with a female employee back home. Alice constantly obsesses about that moment of discovery and about their entire life together to find clues that she could have overlooked which would have prepared her for this shock.

Partners who are truly in the dark contrast sharply with those whose suspiciousness, growing mistrust and repeated denials by their partner create a state of paranoia that is only alleviated by discovery. Discovery may follow a period of confrontations and denial or may be totally unexpected. The spouse who hires a private investigator or checks the glove compartment for evidence will respond more angrily and less catastrophically than the unsuspecting spouse who gets a letter from "an interested party" or who discovers a sexually transmitted disease. Lawson (1988) found that the consequences were more negative for men whose wives discovered their infidelity compared to those who volunteered the information.

The betrayed spouse whose suspiciousness has been met by repeated denials may find disclosure a relief at first because their reality has been validated, but the pain and anger created by repeated lies and deception will make recovery more difficult. This is similar to a person who is concerned about obvious symptoms of a serious medical condition but is still stunned when the diagnosis is confirmed. Recovery requires exploring the assumptions which were destroyed by the discovery and recalling the vivid images associated with the moments of discovery.

Individualistic Issues

The level of traumatization is also associated with individualistic issues from past relationships. Persons with a history of trust issues and those with low self-esteem will have greater difficulty recovering. Dougherty & Ellis (1976) found that men with morbid jealousy had witnessed their mothers' extramarital sexual liaisons. Herman (1992) writes that, "Trauma forces the survivor to relive all [her] earlier struggles over autonomy, initiative, competence, identity and intimacy" (p. 54); "Traumatic life events, like other misfortunes, are especially merciless to those who are already troubled" (p. 60).

> Bobbi grew up in a home with a critical father and depressed, unavailable mother. Her husband, Bob, was the only person in her life she had ever trusted, and she felt safe and loved in the relationship. When he became involved with another woman she was devastated. He had many individualistic problems of his own which contributed to his affair, but she blamed her own unworthiness and regressed back to the little girl who felt neglected and unloved.

Continuing Threat

The traumatic reaction deepens when the threat continues. Traumatic reactions to the Los Angeles earthquake deepened with the aftershocks. The threat continues when the involved spouse continues a business or personal relationship with the affair partner, whereas a sense of safety develops when contact and availability is totally stopped. When the involved spouse is ambivalent and continues with an emotional or sexual attachment, the constant retraumatization will make healing more difficult if the affair finally ends.

OUR INTERPERSONAL TRAUMA MODEL AFTER DISCOVERY OF INFIDELITY

Our interpersonal trauma model is targeted for couples attempting to reconstruct their marriage after the discovery of infidelity. This model works when the involved spouse is willing to stop the EMI, and the betrayed spouse is willing to hang in while they rebuild the marriage and explore the meaning of the affair. A lasting commitment is contingent on creating a monogamous relationship which provides mutual satisfaction. Their marriage has been blown apart, and we want to reassemble the pieces in a new pattern which integrates and benefits from the new information.

Creating Safety and Hope in the Therapy

The central task of the first stage of recovery is establishment of safety (Herman, 1992). "This task takes precedence over all others, for no therapeutic work can possibly succeed if safety has not been adequately secured" (p. 159). Creating a sense of safety and hope in the therapy requires structure, validation and information.

Clarifying the Contract

If couples wish to reconstruct their relationship, we establish that their therapeutic contract is for marital therapy or reconciliation therapy (if they have been separated). We establish an open window between the marital partners and between the co-therapists, and we clarify that we will not collude in ongoing deception. We advise an initial period of twelve sessions, but for couples who are distressed and ambivalent, a commitment of four or six sessions is suggested. Committing to a specific number of sessions provides a sense of security in the therapy and in the marriage.

It is common for spouses to differ in the level of commitment and degree of ambivalence. After we listen to the presenting problems and their goals for therapy, we might determine that the appropriate therapeutic contract will be for ambivalence therapy or separation therapy. Confidentiality issues in ambivalence therapy and separation therapy which are negotiated with the couple are discussed later in this chapter.

Normalizing Traumatic Reactions to Betrayal of Infidelity

Normalizing symptoms is validating for both partners and aids the involved spouse to develop empathy for the betrayed spouse's pain.

We have found that presenting the PTSD diagnostic criteria is reassuring. Herman describes trauma victims who carried tattered copies of the symptom list which they referred to long after the initial debriefing. Our clients also have found it comforting to refer to the list of traumatic reactions. Lusterman (1992) gives couples his proposed sub-type of PTSD "subsequent to the discovery of protracted infidelity", which links PTSD symptoms with specific sequelae of betrayal. However, he cautions therapists that "from a standpoint of a diagnosable condition for third-party payment, a symptom-based diagnosis such as dysthymia, anxiety reaction or adjustment disorder with mixed features will suffice" (Lusterman, 1995, p. 264).

We discuss Janoff-Bulman's concept of shattered assumptions to address their feelings of disbelief, disorientation, and unreality. Exposure to their partner's duplicity destroys their sense of safety and shatters their basic assumptions of honesty and trust. We suggest that it will be possible eventually to construct new assumptions which incorporate all the events that have happened. Reconstructing safety and security in light of the betrayal is a major task early in the therapy and at this stage of the marriage.

Information promotes security by reassuring clients of the therapist's expertise and experience and helps clients to set more realistic and hopeful expectations for the therapeutic work. We tell about other couples who have built a stronger, more satisfying relationship after going through this process of reconstruction and disclosure. We predict progression and relapses in the early phase of therapy and particularly caution against setbacks after periods of closeness which evoke the vulnerability that existed prior to the disclosure. We outline our approach,

including the necessity for eventually discussing the affair. We recommend magazine articles and popular books on affairs to support our position, to provide a
background for understanding multiple causation, and to reinforce the potential
for surviving infidelity (Pittman, 1989, 1993; Subotnik & Harris, 1994).

Continuing dishonesty at the onset of therapy is fairly common. We validate
that deception is part of this territory; i.e. people who have affairs necessarily lie,
but this doesn't mean that they are generally liars. Deception can sometimes be
reframed as evidence of not wanting to dissolve the marriage or hurt the marital
partner. Misinterpretations or inappropriate projections caused by assumed similarity errors are addressed by presenting the findings on gender differences in
EMI.

Recreating Safety and Hope in the Marriage

"The traumatized person is the most vulnerable of all when the person to whom
they might ordinarily turn to for security is precisely the source of danger"
(Herman, 1992, p. 168). That is certainly the case in discovered EMI. Building
safety in the marriage requires the involved spouse to shift the walls and windows
so that the affair partner is on the outside and the betrayed spouse is now on the
inside; "stop and share" characterizes this shift. Building hope in the marriage is
fostered by encouraging positive interactions and mutual good will.

Reversing Walls and Windows to Detriangulate: Stop and Share

During an affair the involved spouse often discusses the marriage with the affair
partner, whereas the marital partner has a brick wall of secrecy, much like a one-
way mirror. Reversing these alliances detriangulates and establishes the marriage
as the primary relationship. Opening a window into the affair and putting up a
wall with the affair partner rebuilds trust. The *walls and window* image is a
powerful metaphor which couples find very meaningful (Glass & Wright, 1991).
The involved spouse is advised to *stop and share* in order to reverse the walls and
windows in the extramarital triangle.

In reconciliation or marital therapy, the involved spouse has to agree to stop
all contact with the affair partner. Stopping does not just mean sex: stopping
means no more coffee breaks or telephone calls. The betrayed spouse will not
feel safe enough to begin healing until all interpersonal contact with the affair
partner stops. This can be very difficult if the affair partner is a co-worker or
employee because of potential sexual harassment issues. When it is impossible to
avoid all contact, to stop means to refrain from any personal discussions with the
affair partner (particularly about the marriage or the therapy).

> When Al and Alice returned from their tropical vacation, he made a commitment to
> stop his relationship with his employee. Alice was not satisfied with just the termi-
> nation of the sexual relationship; she wanted the work relationship to be terminated,
> but Al considered the other woman a key employee to whom he felt a definite

loyalty. Every morning when Al left the house for work, Alice would start shaking and crying. This continued for 9 weeks, at which time the employee left to find another position. The recovery process was tedious and prolonged because the shock of discovery had been followed by 9 weeks of agony in which she felt clear and present danger.

The window must be open about unavoidable or ongoing contact with the affair partner. The involved spouse agrees to share any current encounters, and we advise them to *tell before they're asked*. This is counter-intuitive because the involved spouse prefers to avoid mentioning anything that is likely to be upsetting. We encourage the betrayed spouse to reinforce how much more trustbuilding it is to receive information voluntarily instead of through probing and investigation. Opening this window establishes loyalty and increases emotional intimacy in the marriage.

When John asked "Did you see *him* at the meeting today?" Joan answered tersely, "Yes." John responded, "Well, when were you planning to tell me?" He believed that he would not have learned the truth if he had not asked the question. Several weeks later, Joan volunteered the information that she had run into her former lover on the parking lot. She reported that she had said "Hello" but had cut him short when he asked how she was doing. John was reassured by her openness and honesty, and he let her know how much he appreciated her telling him something without his asking.

Promoting Positivity and Caring in the Couple

We begin to foster resources in the couple soon after we have heard and acknowledged the couple's presenting problems. Strong negative affect and an obsessive need to know may preclude focused work on caring for a while. We suggest that they avoid deep discussions at home and "dump their garbage" in our office while they work outside the therapy on building positives.

Fostering positive cognitions

Positive cognitions are fostered by affirming the couple's strengths through feedback about resources in their relationship, such as their co-parenting skills or good sex or common interests. Solution-oriented questions (Weiner-Davis, 1992) focus on a happier past or a hopeful future; for example, "What was it like when things felt good between you?" or, "If you woke up tomorrow morning and a miracle had happened, how would the relationship be?" Sharing recollections of their first date and courtship impressions and expectations can create a shared nostalgia and sense of bonding.

Our assessment package includes Stuart's "Caring Behaviors" form (1983) in which each person lists at the top of the form ten pleasing things about their partner. The couple alternates reading to each other, and we ask them to elaborate by giving an example or saying why that particular item is meaningful. They are often quite moved to hear how they are appreciated, and good will is enhanced. In the first or second session, we ask what caring they have received in the past week. After heavy sessions, we use ongoing caring checkups as emotional relief to lighten things up and send them out with a more positive affect.

Bullseye caring

After sharing Stuart's ten pleasing behaviors as discussed above, we play "The Newlywed Game" with the other two sections of the caring form. We ask them to compare what they believed that their partner wants more of with their partner's actual wish list. Caring efforts pay off better with "bullseye caring". A correct guess implies that they know what's in their partner's bullseye for caring, although "wrong" guesses are sometimes considered as good or better. The therapist can infer whether they place more value on instrumental, expressive or affectional caring. This exercise identifies miscommunication caused by inadequate asking or faulty listening. We help individuals who have a hard time asking for caring to strengthen their "I-want muscles".

Extra-marital involvement (EMI) rationales for caring behaviors

The flattering mirror in the affair which reflects admiration and respect is a clearly preferable alternative to the mirror in the marriage which reflects a tarnished image. Caring behaviors foster positive mirroring and opportunities for appreciation in the marriage. Caring promotes positive cycles in the marriage which were inherent in the affair. However, a remarkable and sudden shift to positive cycling might indicate over-reactivity and enmeshment, which could easily flip to negative cycling. Fostering caring also creates a way to equalize responsibility for enhancing the relationship and offers a way for each to be the best partner they know how to be without waiting for changes in the other. Resistance to caring may be a sign of ambivalence or of a hidden agenda to prove the marriage can't succeed.

Face-saving ways to overcome resistance to caring

When they say, "I don't feel anything yet", we say, "Do it first and feelings will follow". Behavior can precede feelings, and caring is a way to get emotionally involved. The more they invest in the relationship, the more they'll feel. If there is a lot of antagonism, we try to get a truce and we suggest, "Treat each other as nicely as you would treat a stranger this week". Another strategy is to ask them to "pretend" (Madanes, 1981) that everything is already the way they would like it to be.

If they are too alienated to consider giving or receiving "caring", we suggest that they concentrate instead on *respect and consideration*. When feminist women won't consider their husband's efforts at household tasks to be caring behaviors, we ask them what *sharing* behaviors they might have *noticed* during the past week that could be evidences of change. If the ambivalent spouse is afraid that any affectional behaviors could be misinterpreted as a commitment that they are not yet willing to make, they need permission to act on positive impulses. Teach both spouse not to overinterpret caring behaviors so they can act spontaneously on fleeting, warm feelings.

MANAGING AFFECT AND CRISIS INTERVENTION

Managing intense affect disrupts other early therapeutic agendas such as establishing caring behaviors and improving communication patterns. Matsakis (1992) delineates in her book, *I Can't Get Over It*, an *emotional stage* in which the traumatized individual experiences the feelings associated with the event. After the disclosure of an infidelity, expressions of rage, hopelessness, depression and anxiety are common. The betrayed spouse is enraged by the deception, hypervigilant for signs of further betrayal, distraught over the loss of the marriage as it existed, and anxious about the future. The involved spouse grieves for the loss of the unfulfilled romantic fantasies that the affair offered and is angered by the security-based demands of the betrayed spouse, which constrict autonomy.

Sleep deprivation will intensify the stress symptoms, so sleep patterns should be monitored. Either or both spouses may need to be referred for medication if their depressive and/or anxiety symptoms do not improve sufficiently. A lot of the early therapeutic work is crisis intervention, and suicidal ideation is common in both the betrayed and the involved spouses.

It may be necessary to see the couple more than once a week during this phase, alternating with individual and conjoint sessions. Lots of telephone calls are predictable. We suggest that they call to "dump" on our answering machines during the time between sessions if expressing their negative feelings to their partner would be destructive for the relationship.

Balance Expression and Inhibition of Affect

It is essential to validate that intense feelings are normal, but the need to express intense feelings must be balanced with the need not to let that expression get out of control. Everstine & Everstine (1993) caution against catharsis in the acute stage. Violence and unending tirades are not acceptable; couples are instructed in "time-out" and other anger management procedures (Bach & Wyden, 1970; Notarius & Markman, 1993).

Utilize Individual Sessions

Although conjoint sessions are the preferred format, affect management may be achieved in the early stages through individual sessions. The therapist can provide support and an opportunity to express negative emotions that the marital partners are not ready to accept. The involved spouse is often unable to endure his/her partner's unrelenting expression of pain and rage. The betrayed spouse may be unwilling to tolerate his/her partner's grief over loss of the affair or his/her partner's negative feelings about the marriage. Ambivalence about commitment to the marriage may be discussed more openly in individual sessions.

Although we each work with couples on our own, we feel that we have a distinct advantage when we do co-therapy with the difficult issues associated with EMI. We always have the option of separating during a conjoint session that gets too hot and working with the spouses individually. People express comfort with the male–female team and feel that they each have an advocate who understands them. Furthermore, we can confront earlier in the therapy, because one of us will counter-balance the confrontation with support. Since the presenting problem is a triangle, it is significantly easier to maintain balance when the therapeutic process does not replicate the presenting triangle.

Assess Suicidal and Homicidal Ideation

Homicidal threats, particularly toward the extramarital partner, should be evaluated carefully; duty to warn may supersede confidentiality in these uncommon cases. Suicidal ideation is more common and needs to be routinely assessed in both spouses. The therapist needs to guard against suicidal threats being used as emotional blackmail. It may be necessary to hospitalize the suicidal (or homicidal) spouse for his/her own protection and to relieve the other spouse of responsibility.

> Bob was concerned because Bobbi had threatened to jump from the third floor staircase when he refused to stop his contact with his extramarital partner. Bobbi told the therapist that this was just a gesture to show Bob how desperate she was, but she insisted that she did not want to die. She finally acknowledged that she could survive even if Bob left her. On the other hand, Bobbi expressed concern that Bob was suicidal because he kept talking about his life being over and there being no way out of his dilemma. Bob flatly denied that he was suicidal, became enraged over her "accusation" and stated once again that we were concerned about the wrong person.
>
> Two days later, Bob terminated the extramarital relationship. While driving home he had acute and intense suicidal feelings and could "taste the metal of the gun" in his mouth. He came home and admitted his suicidal feelings to Bobbi. In a conjoint session, he agreed to get all guns out of the house and to give Bobbi the bullets to store in a safety deposit box. Bob accepted the interpretation that Bobbi's suicidal gesture was a form of communication and a cry for help whereas his denial of suicidal ideation was potentially more dangerous.

Anticipate Crises and Relapses

Crises will be generated as new information emerges about previous deceptions, and as new incidents occur that further erode the trust. Relapses in the early stages are fairly common as part of the process of closure and weaning away from the extramarital affair. The transition from less openness and more lies to more openness and less lies is almost predictable.

Often as the couple is strengthening their bond, the lover precipitates a crisis. The lover may make harassing or self-disclosing phone calls to the betrayed spouse, pursue the continuation of the relationship with the involved spouse, or call the therapist and threaten suicide. We tell the couple that they cannot control this other person's behavior, but they can manage intrusions together by creating a *united front* for dealing with the affair partner. Calls can be screened with caller ID or answering machines, and many couples decide to change to an unlisted phone number. They may refuse contact, respond only when they are together, or share all information around any unavoidable encounters. Behavior rehearsals and role plays can be utilized to prepare for anticipated intrusions by the extramarital partner.

Crises also arise when a major life-cycle event such as a daughter's wedding or son's bar mitzvah occurs during this fragile state. Therapy can focus on concrete planning to get the couple through this highly pressured family event to set realistic expectations and limit sources of potential damage. Separations caused by business trips require focused preparation that addresses the security needs of the betrayed spouse.

MANAGING TRAUMATIC REACTIONS

Post-traumatic symptoms of intrusion, constriction and hyperarousal are common and should be validated. The symptoms of intrusion and hyperarousal may oscillate with symptoms of constriction. The therapist should encourage attempts at containment to counterbalance the prevailing reactions of intrusion and hyperarousal, and *vice versa*.

Suppressers vs. Sensitizers

In general, men prefer suppressive mechanisms and women are more likely to be sensitizers. Gender differences in response styles emerge after negative events such as life-threatening illnesses and create polarities within couples (Lichtman & Taylor, 1986). However, after the betrayal of infidelity, the polarity in response styles is mitigated by whether a spouse is viewed as the perpetrator or the victim of the EMI, regardless of gender. The involved spouse wants to bury the past and "get on with it", whereas the betrayed spouse usually has a need to discuss, analyze and ruminate. It may be an artifact of the clinical setting that we see a preponderance of betrayed sensitizers; betrayed suppressers apparently don't initiate therapy because they avoid dealing with it. Herman (1992) observes the perpetrator's attempt to suppress discussion:

In order to escape accountability . . . the perpetrator does everything . . . to promote forgetting. Secrecy and silence are the perpetrator's first line of defense. . . . one can expect to hear the same predictable apologies; it never happened; the victim lies; the victim exaggerates; the victim brought it upon herself; and in any case it is time to forget the past and move on (p. 8).

Intrusion

Intrusion comes from the indelible imprint of the betrayal. The traumatic images may be the moment of disclosure, the visualization of the imagined intimacies in the affair, or the recounting of the string of lies preceding the disclosure. The trauma is re-experienced in the form of dreams, flashbacks, intrusive memories or unrest created by anniversaries of the discovery or at being reminded about the betrayal by love songs and especially by TV talk shows.

Obsessive Ruminating

The betrayed spouse's obsessive rumination and compulsion to know all of the details of the affair is analogous to the *cognitive stage* described by Matsakis (1992). Much energy is invested in discovering the truth about earlier lies. It is common for the entire history of the marriage to be reviewed while grappling with the shattered assumptions.

The need to recapitulate and go over the minute details may test the therapist's patience (Everstine & Everstine, 1993) in addition to that of the marital partner. We validate their need to construct the story just as in any other trauma recovery or bereavement work. Brown (1991), who prefers to "redirect" the obsessive spouse, offers a contrasting view: "The obsession functions as a way of avoiding issues that the couple had not been willing to face earlier in the marriage. . . . Continued obsession is a guarantee that the marriage will end" (p. 78). We find that the obsessive features of this early stage generally abate as safety and openness are established in the marriage.

Normalizing and accepting the obsessional thoughts and behaviors will sometimes need to be balanced with therapeutic interventions that alleviate interference with daily life activities. We encourage the betrayed spouse to bring in his/her questions, and we file the lists with a promise to cover all of them later when the marriage is more secure. Writing down the questions provides an outlet for anxiety and allows them to let go temporarily. The therapist can assign structured worry times, encourage journaling, suggest "vacations" from thinking about the event, and provide imagery rehearsals for "switching the tape to another channel". Subotnik & Harris (1994) present a number of useful coping strategies in their book *Surviving Infidelity*.

Flashbacks

Initially, while the couple is vulnerable and working to establish safety, the therapist should advise the couple to avoid situations that could trigger flashbacks. Flashbacks can be predicted when cued by anniversary events and concrete reminders of the affair. For example, John becomes upset when he notices the leaves turning colors because autumn is the season when he discovered his wife's infidelity, and Alice dreads Thanksgiving this year because Al was mysteriously missing for part of the day last year. Other triggers for flashbacks may be distressing to both spouses because they occur spontaneously without warning; i.e. lovemaking scenes in movies may create vivid images of the illicit sex, or words spoken in another context, such as "loyalty", can trigger a whole train of intrusive thoughts.

"Flashback training" will reassure couples about the normality of flashbacks and provide them with skills to deal with flashbacks in relationship-enhancing ways. The betrayed spouse learns to share his/her distress without blaming or accusing, and the involved spouse learns to listen empathically without discounting or minimizing his/her partner's pain.

> When Frank had to work late, Fran became very anxious and panicky because it recalled the late nights when Frank was lying about his whereabouts. She called Frank and said, "I'm having a hard time tonight because I was flashing back to all the nights you were out late last year. I'm feeling very insecure." Frank responded, "I understand that this is hard for you, and I am really sorry that you're in so much pain, but I want you to know that I love you, and I am looking forward to coming home and cuddling with you".

Predicting situations that evoke flashbacks and doing behavioral rehearsals in therapy sessions will enable couples to handle intrusive thoughts and feelings together. Flashbacks can provide an opportunity to share the pain and emotionally join in a healing process. Flashbacks occur for a prolonged period of time but will diminish first in frequency, then in duration, and finally in intensity (Lusterman, 1992).

Constriction

Constriction, a less frequent reaction after disclosure, is fostered by perpetrators. Constriction is evidenced by avoidance behavior with a numbing of emotions and reduced interest in others and the outside world. In infidelity, numbing may appear as "head in the sand" as the spouse's behavior becomes more and more suspicious, but before the suspicions have been confirmed. We explain to persons who have a delayed reaction that, "First you numb, then you bleed". The betrayed spouse who expresses very little affect, asks no questions, and appears overly calm after disclosure may be experiencing numbing. Clinical judgment can determine whether this is an adaptive position or not.

> Georgia, a constricted wife who described feeling "nothing", asked no questions of her sexually addicted husband, George, after his compulsive sexual behaviors led to his arrest by the police. The risk of recurrence was high if there was no sharing of the *modus operandi*, so we started asking detailed questions ourselves. He revealed where and how he had "scanned" for pickups. Although Georgia developed physi-

ological symptoms of distress after first hearing George's animated description of his extramarital encounters, she realized that it was not wise to keep her head in the sand. He followed our suggestion to participate in a sexual addiction group, and he shared his new awarenesses with her. In conjoint sessions we monitored his fantasies, potential opportunities, and ongoing examples of how he was inhibiting his impulses to engage in promiscuous sex. As she eventually began to ask questions of her own, they worked together on relapse prevention.

Hyperarousal

Hyperarousal, the persistent expectation of danger, is evidenced physiologically by insomnia, agitation, irritability, anger outbursts, and startle responses. The loss of safety and security in the marital relationship creates a state of hypervigilance in the betrayed spouse, which is characterized by suspicion, jealousy and indefatigable inquiries concerning the whereabouts of the involved spouse. Hypervigilance typically lessens as security and comfort in the marriage increases. It is important to temper the following clinical interventions with a sensitivity to a prior history of excessive or morbid jealousy.

Teach Betrayed Spouse to Be a Detective

The therapist must be cautious about offering reassurance if the betrayed spouse is suspicious about ongoing contact with the affair partner. We have learned that the instincts of the betrayed spouse have been surprisingly accurate in detecting further signs of deception after the initial disclosure. On the other hand, the betrayed spouse can be excessively insecure and panicky when his/her partner is engaging in an activity which served as a cover for extramarital liaisons. However, persistent questioning is very destructive for the marriage, and information obtained under duress does not enhance trust. Walking in a detective's shoes is more constructive than donning the robes of an inquisitor.

> Ken became very anxious when Karen went to play tennis because she had often met with her affair partner when she was supposed to be playing tennis. Ken gave her the third degree after her tennis game, and Karen became very angry. Ken was advised to be a detective and "check it out" next time he was worried. When Karen went to a meeting that had also been a cover for her affairs, Ken drove to the location, saw her car there, and came home feeling more secure. When he told Karen what he had done, she was supportive because she knew that the only way he could trust her again was to learn that she was now telling him the truth.

Utilize the Therapist's "Deception Detector"

When our own "deception detector" goes off, we have found it easier and more effective to confront our own suspicions in a conjoint session than individually. Signs that are often associated with ongoing EMI are resistance to carrying out caring, discounting or minimizing partner's attempts to change and sustained idealization of extramarital partner, juxtaposed with hostility and lack of empathy toward the spouse. Refusal to discuss the EMI or anger about providing information about current whereabouts are further cues for lack of commitment to rebuilding marital trust and security.

A real dilemma occurs when information about continued betrayal is obtained in an individual session because the therapist must either collude in the secret, push the involved partner to disclose, or suspend conjoint sessions. It can feel empowering not to know the secrets, because we can confront without setting traps or betraying confidences. The therapist can say, "If I were your partner, I'd be wondering whether you're still involved because. . . .".

DEVELOPING CONSTRUCTIVE COMMUNICATION PATTERNS

Until a couple can talk easily about whose turn it is to do the laundry, they will not be able to discuss constructively the complex, painful issues surrounding the affair. Dysfunctional communication patterns in the couple can be observed and channeled into a positive process of expressive and receptive skills (Notarius & Markman, 1993). Conflict-avoidant spouses who turn to an affair after years of suppressed resentment (Brown, 1991) are typical of the "stonewallers" observed in communication research (Gottman, 1994). They are at risk for continued EMI unless they learn to express their preferences and disappointments to their marital partner. The betrayed spouse learns that reporting insecurities and flashbacks by using non-accusatory "I" messages reduces their partner's defensiveness.

When an involved spouse says, "I feel more accepted in the other relationship", the therapist can infer that the EMI provides more empathic listening than does the marriage. The aftermath of an affair intensifies obvious emotionally invalidating responses which need to be curtailed, such as judging, interrupting, contradicting and criticizing. Subtler forms of emotional invalidation, such as analyzing and interpreting, also need to be monitored and inhibited because they impede the development of mutual empathy.

EXPLORING THE CONTEXT FOR THE AFFAIR

Exploring individual issues, marital issues and the contextual background provides a multidimensional picture to understand areas of vulnerability related to EMI. Addressing individual issues in conjoint sessions will increase empathy, openness and intimacy between spouses. Marital therapy interventions address relationship factors which are linked to extramarital behaviors and attitudes. A review of life events in the 2-year period preceding the infidelity provides a context in which to understand the meaning of the trauma.

Both individualistic and relational considerations must be explored despite unidimensional explanations provided by the spouses. We have learned with much regret that the ignored aspect can emerge as a vulnerability for a subsequent EMI. Involved spouses who blame marital problems for their EMI may be denying their individual issues, and those who explain their EMI with an entirely individualistic perspective may be avoiding confrontation regarding marital problems. Prevailing gender differences in which men are more individualistic and women are more relationally oriented (Gilligan, 1982) are also found in EMI. Attitudes and values are the strongest influence on men's EMI, whereas marital dissatisfaction is the greatest predictor for women's EMI (Glass & Wright, 1992b).

The Story of the Individuals

Individualistic aspects include belief systems influenced by friends, co-workers, family of origin and personal experience with EMI. Psychological variables which are derived from clinical observations have little empirical support in the literature at this time.

Extramarital Attitudes and Values

We routinely assess extramarital attitudes and behaviors as part of our pre-counseling inventory (Glass, 1981). Men and women discriminate between extramarital justifications for sex, emotional intimacy and love. Sexual excitement is approved more as a reason by men, and falling in love is approved more by women (Glass & Wright, 1992b). Individuals with extramarital experience endorse more reasons, but these attitudes may either precede or follow EMI. We have observed that people who strongly endorse justifications but deny actual EMI may not be telling the truth on the questionnaire or they may be highly vulnerable to opportunities.

Extramarital behavior may be ego-syntonic or ego-dystonic; involved individuals with permissive attitudes differ from those who basically value monogamy. A remorseful spouse who empathizes with his/her partner's pain presents a better prognosis than the involved spouse who minimizes his/her partner's distress over the betrayal. A husband who had been repeatedly caught in elaborate deceptions told his wife, "If you make me leave, then *you* have to take responsibility for breaking up this family". Change was minimal and he eventually left his wife for his lover.

Attitudes and values are influenced by a social context such as observing and talking with friends and colleagues who have experienced extramarital relationships (Atwater, 1979; Buunk, 1980; Thompson, 1984) or a work environment which condones or offers opportunities for extramarital sex. Transgenerational patterns (Weil & Winter, 1993) and socio-cultural double standards can establish an expectation of extramarital sexual permissiveness or a strong reaction against those traditions.

Donna was horrified when her mother cheated on her father while he was away in the military. Donna's husband Don observed his father's amused response to discovering his wife's clandestine meeting with another man. When Don had an affair after several years of marriage, he tried to minimize the meaning of it, whereas Donna was extremely distraught.

Persons who are fundamentally monogamous frequently justify their EMI with a belief that they fell in love, tend to rewrite the marital history, and retrospectively deny loving their spouses. "Monogamous infidels" who cannot be in two relationships at the same time, withdraw from their spouses sexually and emotionally. They feel unfaithful to the lover when they are intimate with the spouse. Pittman & Wagers (1995) observed that people "justify their actions by deciding that they must have fallen out of love before the affair began" (p. 297).

Psychodynamic Aspects

Psychodynamic formulations (Strean, 1980) derive from clinical observations although there is no empirical data to support greater personality disorders among involved spouses. Our non-clinical data does support splitting of sex and affection by men in that 44% of the involved men had extramarital sexual intercourse without emotional involvement (Glass & Wright, 1985). Men who compartmentalize their sexuality perceive women in a "madonna–whore" dichotomy which negates the wife's erotic side, particularly after the birth of children.

After a passionate courtship and the birth of three children, Carl and Carla had a congenial sexual relationship which became a deferred priority in their busy schedules. Carl engaged in undisclosed, casual sex with seductive single women for many years before the discovery of an intense affair with a colleague. Carla found a sexually explicit greeting card which Carl had bought for his affair partner. When we asked Carl if he would send a card like that to Carla, he said, "Oh no! That wouldn't be appropriate. Although Carla said that she would enjoy getting that kind of card, Carl remained very reluctant to regard her in that light. The potential for continued EMI is high unless Carl can integrate his affectional and sexual feelings and perceive his wife as an erotic partner.

Individualistic Needs

Personal needs for excitement, escapism, romantic love or admiration create powerful incentives for EMI. The romantic projections, forbidden aspects and shared fantasies create an illusion and positive mirroring which are used to counter intrapsychic feelings of emptiness, depression and poor self image. Beach, Jouriles & O'Leary (1985) found greater depression in sexually involved spouses. Existential crises and personal losses which often precede the onset of an EMI must be resolved.

People who need to be "in love" are extremely susceptible to the romantic idealization that characterizes "Stage I" relationships (Goldstine et al., 1978);

they may exhibit parallel motivations in the rest of their lives in that they are attracted to "beginnings" but fade out in "the middles" of pursuits. "Falling in love" may be the only sensation intense enough to cross the emotional threshold of alexythymic persons who are unable to identify and describe their feelings. The person who says, "I love my spouse, but I'm not *in love* with him/her", might be comparing the romantic intensity, excitment and anxious attachment of an illicit, forbidden affair with the secure attachment of a long-term, stable marriage. Some involved spouses come to regard their romantic attachments as periods of "temporary insanity" (Pittman, 1989) after they disown their extramarital partners.

The individual who has engaged in multiple sexual encounters over an extended period of time may have a sexual addiction or may simply feel entitled to opportunities for casual sex. The addict, who is characterized by compulsivity, guilt, shame and feelings of worthlessness, appears unable to carry out internal resolutions to inhibit sexual promiscuity (Carnes, 1985) and will often need to engage in a self-help group for sexual addictions. In contrast, one survey respondent stated that a justification for extramarital relationships is that "I never refuse a gift". In cases of previous EMI, the current episode must be addressed as a pattern of behavior which will be disclosed and understood.

The Story of the Marriage

When EMI is associated with troubled marriages, it is not always clear whether the distress preceded or followed the disclosure of infidelity. Spanier & Margolis (1983) found that separating and divorced persons attributed their spouses' affairs to be the cause of marital problems, but their own affairs to be the result of marital difficulties. Examining the marital and sexual issues should not provide a justification for deception as there are many conflictual and unhappy marriages that maintain a monogamous contract. The therapist must maintain a delicate balance between addressing the deficits in the marriage that could create a vulnerability vs. a stance which "blames the victim" for the partner's betrayal.

Marital and Sexual Dissatisfaction

Clinicians who regard all affairs as a symptom of problems in the marital relationship (Brown, 1991; Rhodes, 1984) are disregarding empirical evidence that EMI does not always reflect an unhappy marriage. Hunt's findings (1969) are remarkably similar to our data in which high marital satisfaction was reported by 56% of involved men and 33% of involved women in our non-clinical sample. The most happily married of the involved persons are husbands whose EMI is primarily sexual (Glass & Wright, 1985). However, these men usually do not come for therapy until they finally "fall in love" with a sexual partner, or the promiscuity is revealed if the wife contracts a sexually transmitted disease.

Marital and sexual dissatisfaction are more predictive for wives' EMI, which usually entails a deep emotional involvement (Glass, 1981). We have found that women with "combined-type" involvements more often present for individual therapy. When they do come for conjoint therapy, they are reluctant to share information about their affair, and the affair is usually symptomatic of extreme alienation from the marital partner.

History of the Marriage

Constructing a marital lifeline with the couple is a constructive exercise which can tap into resources from courtship and the "good times". The initial attractions and expectations may be the very same attributes that are now causing dissatisfaction. Vulnerability for EMI may be linked to critical transitions such as parenting, and other relevant history such as abortions, miscarriages, infertility, illness of children and significant losses. Telling the stories of the marriage and the affair is part of the mourning and remembrance stage of healing (Herman, 1992).

Equity Issues

Although it is commonly believed that the involved spouse may not have been getting enough in the marriage, we have also observed that the involved spouse may not have been investing enough. It is easier for someone who never put much energy into the marriage to be open to an extramarital opportunity because one foot is already out the door. This is especially true for workaholics of either gender. The under-benefited spouses may be dissatisfied, but their commitment is greater because they've invested so much more. Many years later when they are burned out by unilateral giving, their embitterment may then lead to an EMI.

Our Equity Measure, "Who Does More?" (Glass & Wright, 1988) reveals more reciprocity perceived in the affair than in the marriage. If the involved spouse gives more in the affair than in the marriage, intense emotions are fostered by the greater investment of time and energy. Both over-benefited and under-benefited spouses are less happy than partners in equitable relationships (Walster, Traupmann & Walster, 1978). Therapists need to guard against being triangulated and putting the burden of change on one partner; it is important to develop more give-and-take, with special attention given to the spouse who does too much and the tangential partner who will only attach to the marriage as he/she devotes more initiative, time and energy.

Dysfunctional Patterns

Strengthening the marital bond requires shifting dysfunctional systems which are characterized by unhealthy hierarchies, power struggles, lack of intimacy or conflict-avoidance (Brown, 1991; Moultrop, 1990). Patterns of pursuing–distancing, nagging–procrastinating or blaming–placating couples can be shifted so the power and responsibility are more equitably distributed. The over-functioning spouse needs encouragement to inhibit and "let go", while the under-functioning spouse needs to be more engaged and assertive.

In marriages where the husband and wife interact like a parent–child dyad, the involved spouse may be rebelling against smothering, over-protecting or perceived dominance. On the other hand, the involved spouse may feel sexually inhibited with a partner who is seen as childlike and immature. Unfortunately, women who have rebelled against "parental" husbands by engaging in extramarital sex appeared to be extremely resistant to treatment and often ended up leaving the marriage.

BUILDING THE NARRATIVES OF THE AFFAIR: OPENING THE WINDOW

The healing process is incomplete until the involved spouse replaces the walls of secrecy and deception with an open window into the affair. Telling the story of the affair enables the couple to form a joint account of the traumatic events. Wigren (1994) states that creating narratives serves the vital psychological functions in trauma recovery of providing a connection between the past and the present, between the self and the other, and between cognitions and affect.

Setting the Stage

The marriage must provide a sense of safety and security before the discussion of the affair can be constructive. In the early phase, the involved spouse is likely to tell lies which cause a further erosion of trust, and the betrayed spouse is likely to be both fragile and attacking. Moreover, the involved spouse who is still ambivalent could be brutally honest and make unflattering comparisons between the lover and the marital partner. Herman (1992) asserts, "Though the single most common therapeutic error is avoidance of the traumatic material, probably the second most common error is premature or precipitate engagement in exploratory work, without sufficient attention to the tasks of establishing safety and securing a therapeutic alliance" (p. 172).

Motivations of both spouses should be explored in light of the question, "How will this information *help the healing process*?" The involved spouse may be motivated to share in order to alleviate guilt, to blame his/her partner for failing him/her, or to create openness in the marriage. Motivations for withholding information may be to avoid retaliation, to protect the affair partner, to protect the spouse from further pain, or to continue the extramarital behavior. We support a search for greater understanding but do not encourage agendas which focus on detecting lies or using information as a weapon. The bottom line is that the betrayed spouse's need to know is the determining factor for how much detail and understanding is necessary, but we control the timing and the process.

The Process of Disclosure

The process of disclosure must be guided in a shift from a truth-seeking inquisition, to information-seeking, to a healing exploration with understanding and mutual empathy as the goal. The content of disclosure, which addresses questions which have been deferred, provides an extraordinary opportunity to change the interactive patterns in the couple. Only information offered openly can counter the distrust created by lies and deception. The following case example exemplifies the gradual and healing process of disclosure.

Therapy was initiated after Maxine learned about Max's affair through an anonymous phone call. Maxine was enraged and distraught when they initiated conjoint therapy, and Max was apologetic but constrained in his willingness to share anything about his paramour. They agreed that if Max would stop all contact with his extramarital partner (Wendy), Maxine would not engage in any hostile acts toward her.

During the third therapy session, Max angrily reported having run into Wendy at the local gas station, where she had told him about a nasty, abusive letter she had received from Maxine. He was clearly protective of Wendy and not sympathetic toward Maxine. The female therapist said, "If I were your wife I might find it difficult to trust that this information was obtained at an accidental meeting. I might believe that you were still in contact with your affair partner". Max stood up and with great hostility said, "If you don't trust me, then this therapy is over". He eventually calmed down, and the session proceeded.

Six weeks later, Max said that he owed us an apology because the suspicions about him had been correct. However, he had now really severed his relationship with Wendy and was ready to share the truth. He went on to disclose that although he had originally stated that he had only had sex with Wendy three or four times, it was really hundreds of times over a 2-year period. Furthermore, he exposed his *modus operandi* by revealing that every day he had gone to Wendy's house before and after work by concealing his regular work hours. Maxine was greatly relieved that he was now confiding in her, and her need to harass the other woman was reduced.

Max agreed to Maxine's request that she be present when he made a final call to tell Wendy that he was committed to his marriage and wanted no further contact. The following day Max came home from work and told Maxine that Wendy had called him at work because she believed his call was made under duress. He convinced Wendy that the affair was truly over, and Maxine was assured by his willingness to voluntarily disclose this conversation. As Maxine learned to listen without interrupting or blaming, Max became more open about negative aspects of his EMI, such as Wendy's other involvements with married men, about her drug addiction, and the abortion to which Max had accompanied her.

As Max discussed his vulnerabilities, since this was not his first affair, his frustration over the issue of Maxine's constricted sexuality emerged. Maxine worked through an incident of sexual molestation by her piano teacher in the conjoint sessions. She was very emotional as she relived her fear and humiliation, and Max became empathic about her discomfort at being approached suddenly from behind. They successfully completed a program of gentle desensitization regarding her resistance to having her breasts fondled. They were clearly developing a sense of unity and intimacy while rebuilding mutual trust and empathy.

Truth-seeking with an Adversarial Process

The initial process between the spouses often feels like an interrogation between a district attorney and a criminal. It is wise to delay explosive questions and gory details of the affair until a more constructive process evolves, but it is unrealistic for the story to be completely inhibited. When the couple's process is too adversarial, the therapist can begin the initial questioning by modeling a calm non-threatening demeanor. It is best to select factual questions first, such as *who*, *what*, *where* and *when*, and save the *how* and *why* questions for later. We sometimes suggest that the betrayed spouse pretend he/she is behind a one-way mirror if his/her volatility would inhibit the tentative process of early disclosure. The betrayed spouse is given blank index cards to write down questions and comments while the therapist "lifts the lid a little" and does a sketch of the affair.

Information Seeking with a Neutral Process

The process is gradually shifted from a detective–criminal interrogation to a more neutral information-seeking process analogous to a journalistic interview. Initially, the involved spouse does not believe that revealing the truth will improve the relationship, so the betrayed spouse should be encouraged to give feedback regarding how hearing painful information creates hope. The couple should be prepared for the probability that additional previous lies will be uncovered during this process, but this is the most powerful tool to rebuild honesty in the relationship.

In the early stage of disclosure, we suggest that they *not* discuss the story of the affair at home but wait for the structure and safety provided by therapy. Later, they learn to table discussions that get too hot at home and bring them in as a joint therapy agenda. One sign of progress is when the agendas are created jointly, rather than by one spouse who unilaterally brings up issues week after week.

When the process becomes destructive during a session, we suggest a "Take Two", such as in the movies where scenes are filmed over and over again until they "get it right". Doing a "Take Two" gives the couple a chance to analyze their process, to create a prototype for dealing with conflict, and to cooperate in changing to a more productive exchange. Couples transfer this technique to discussions at home which are getting off track; one of them will suggest starting over and doing a "Take Two".

The therapist must create balance by facilitating openness in the involved spouse and inhibition by the betrayed spouse. Imbalance is apparent when it begins to look like there are two therapists interrogating or analyzing one identified patient. It takes time and positive experiences for the involved spouse to believe that honesty is beneficial and for the betrayed spouse to ask questions without setting traps and to listen calmly to the answers. Kluft (as cited in Herman, 1992) suggests "the Rule of Thirds" for telling the trauma story; i.e. do the "dirty work" in the first third of the session, intense exploration in the second third, and the last third is set aside to reorient and calm.

Seeking Deeper Understanding with an Empathic Process

An empathic process of disclosure develops positive patterns of shared intimacy and acceptance. Couples who discuss the painful issue of EMI with mutual understanding are creating an exceptional bond. Conversations are a shared experience of introspection, respect, sensitivity and free-flowing information that contrasts sharply with the earlier process, in which reactions were glib, clipped or hostile.

When they have a constructive process and can recognize and control destructive patterns, they gradually do more and more on their own. They lie in bed at night talking and holding each other. We were delighted when a betrayed husband reported that his wife had answered some questions that were "too personal" to discuss in therapy. Ochberg (1991) states that a goal of post-traumatic therapy is consensus regarding what happened in the past and optimism regarding the future capacity to cope.

> Harry and Harriet had seen several therapists over a period of 3 years during which there was continued betrayal by Harry. The couple separated, the affair ultimately ended, and the couple reconciled. Harriet was enraged because the only truthful information she had ever obtained was through her own detective work. Harry was very effusive in praise of his wife and expressed great remorse about his deceitful behaviors, but he was extremely reluctant to discuss the EMI. Now that he was back in the marriage, he wished to forget the past and begin with a fresh start.
>
> The process of disclosure began by "lifting the lid" and asking specific questions such as, "What restaurants did you go to?", so that Harriet could choose to either reclaim or avoid places he had visited with his lover. During an 8-month period, the amount of new information provided by Harry was sparse. Harriet brought in lists of questions she wanted answered. Some of the questions were traps to prove his honesty, some were complex questions of intent and meaning, and some questions were specific facts and details.
>
> We suggested that they place each question on a separate piece of paper inside a glass fishbowl. When Harry was in the mood to answer a question he would go to the fishbowl on his own and pull out questions until he found one that he could answer without too much discomfort. We instructed Harriet to accept his answers without a challenge and to acknowledge how the information was helpful to her.
>
> After a tediously slow start, Harry gradually realized that healing could never occur without honesty. We were amazed when they came for therapy and reported that they had spent the entire weekend in a hotel room, having all their food brought in while they went through every question in the fishbowl. Their pride and cohesiveness shone brightly as they began a trusting, bonded relationship.

The Content of Disclosure

Discussing the details of the affair helps to satiate the obsession of the betrayed spouse, demystifies the romantic idealization of the involved spouse, and exposes the *modus operandi*. When Al told Alice that he had left for work an hour earlier than necessary each day in order to visit his affair partner, he could no longer use that deception to provide time for carrying on an affair. The betrayed spouse won't be satisfied until the story he/she hears validates what he/she believes. Although it hurts that a spouse talked of love with the affair partner, the betrayed spouse who knows this at an intuitive level must hear it from his/her partner.

Thresholds and Vulnerabilities

Men and women exhibit different codes and pathways toward EMI (Glass & Wright, 1985, 1988). It is more common for men to begin with a sexual attraction, and for women to begin with an emotional involvement. When they cross the threshold into a combined-type involvement, they are treading in the domain with greater sanctions. Wives are more threatened by their husband's emotional involvement with another women, and men are more threatened by their wives' sexual involvement with another man (Buss, 1994; Francis, 1977). Therefore, women will minimize sexual involvement and men will diminish emotional attachment. The therapist can direct early discussions into more comfortable areas by first asking women about emotional involvement and men about sexual involvement.

The cognitions and behaviors which occurred as boundaries and thresholds were crossed on the journey into the extramarital relationship will reveal vulnerabilities and values. We ask, "How did you give yourself permission to go ahead with a secret lunch date? What were you anticipating?" People will discuss the thrill of the conquest, the excitement of the forbidden, satisfying a sense of curiosity, or the attraction of being admired or accepted. The betrayed spouse will often ask, "How could you do this to me?" The reality is that the involved spouse did not consider his/her partner at all, did not anticipate tragic consequences, or the pain that he/she could inflict at the time he/she made the decision to pursue the extramarital adventure.

For the entitled philanderer, a commitment to exclusivity can engender a sense of loss which symbolizes movement away from the duality of single life and family life. The *modus operandi* must be disclosed, fantasies and opportunities should be monitored on a sustained basis, with the individual work around these recalcitrant issues remaining open to the betrayed spouse.

If an EMI started as a friendship, how did it shift into an affair? When married persons confide in opposite-sex friends about problems in the marriage, they are revealing a vulnerability and potential availability at the same time that they are creating an intimacy in the friendship that can supersede the intimacy in the marriage.

Les was touched by his co-worker's tale of a distressed marriage, was flattered by her idealized comparisons between him and her husband, and saw himself as having the capacity to rescue this unhappy lady from her troubled life. Although he initially discussed his co-worker with his wife, Lisa, a wall of secrecy regarding lunch dates and weekend phone calls signalled a shift from friendship to an emotional affair.

The sexual chemistry intensified as they declared their intent to inhibit any actual sexual encounter. The first kiss was a greater leap across boundaries than was the journey from kissing to intercourse. Les was convinced that he was in love and began to detach emotionally and sexually from the marriage. Six months later he talked about the affair as an illusion as he recognized his love for his wife. His tendency to sexualize friendships and to rescue lost maidens signalled the necessity to erect distinct boundaries with unhappy, attractive women.

Assumed Similarity Errors

The betrayed spouse's attempt to understand the story of the affair is influenced by his/her own beliefs and experiences, which can be projected inappropriately onto his/her partner. Errors of assumed similarities interfere with acceptance of the story told by the involved spouse. Gender differences in type of EMI can create different perceptions in that women link sex and love, whereas men's affairs are primarily sexual (Glass & Wright, 1985). Wives are bewildered and incredulous when husbands insist that they never loved the other woman. On the other hand, husbands cannot believe wives who deny having intercourse while meeting secretly for a year in an affair with a deep emotional involvement. Normative education about gender differences can diffuse the polarity created by these assumed similarity errors.

New Roles

Long-term relationships limit the potential for development of new roles because the original roles that are adapted in an interpersonal system become stable and somewhat rigid. For example, the CEO of a large corporation continues to be regarded and teased in his family of origin as "the baby". Affairs offer an opportunity to experiment with different ways of being and provide opportunities for growth and change. New relationships allow people to be different, to be more assertive, or more frivolous, or more giving. The insensitive, detached husband is energized by his own empathy and devotion in the affair. The sexually disinterested wife is exhilarated by new-found passion and erotic fantasies in the affair.

We are not interested in direct comparisons between the betrayed spouse and the extramarital partner. Instead of comparing the marital partner with the affair partner, attention should be directed toward role comparisons of the involved spouse in the two relationships. We ask, "How were you different in the other relationship, and what did you experience about yourself in the other relationship that you would like to bring back to your marriage?" In order to avoid splitting and double lives, the various roles must be integrated and fostered in the marriage. The betrayed spouse may be threatened by the changes or may be embittered that the changes that occurred with somebody else were eagerly pursued but never possible in the marriage until now.

Attributions about the Affair Partner

The betrayed spouse has seen the affair partner as seductive and evil, whereas the involved spouse frequently idealizes the lover and can admit no flaws. Contrasting perceptions of the affair partner which cause splitting within the couple must be resolved. They need to balance their polarized attributions, with the betrayed spouse accepting some positive or human qualities and the involved spouse accepting some of the imperfections in the affair partner.

The betrayed spouse often blames the affair partner entirely for the EMI and is not willing to accept the active role taken by the involved spouse. The ways in which the involved spouse encouraged the beginning and the energy invested in keeping the affair going must be recounted. The potential for recurrence is diminished when responsibility for engaging in an extramarital relationship is attributed to the involved spouse.

> Al and Alice quarreled about their divergent perceptions of his affair partner, Zoe. Alice regarded Zoe as "a bitch and a manipulative slut who was out to get Al's money", whereas Al tended to glorify Zoe's competence, loyalty and sexual attractiveness. As Al revealed more and more about his relationship with Zoe, it became apparent to him that he could never have maintained a long-term relationship with Zoe because of her domineering ways. Alice, on the other hand, grew to understand that Zoe's constant praise and admiration and her sexual spontaneity reached Al in his vulnerable areas. They reached an impasse, however, because Al could not agree with Alice that Zoe had manipulated him. We suggested that they do a role reversal with Alice defending Zoe and Al citing the evidence for manipulation. Halfway through the role play, Al started to laugh because Alice was doing such a good job of imitating his stance. He said, "Boy, I sure sound hokey, don't I?" His acknowledging Alice's attribution marked a breakthrough in therapy.

MASTERY OF MEANING

The mastery stage of empowerment involves finding meaning in the trauma and developing a survivor rather than victim mentality (Matsakis, 1992). Understanding why an EMI occurred establishes the meaning of the affair for both the involved and the betrayed spouse. The couple will need to restructure their basic assumptions to assimilate the story of the betrayal as they construct new images and altered perceptions of their relationship, their partner and themselves. They will have to mourn the loss of dreams and illusions they held regarding the marriage or the affair. Their task is to weave the separate narratives of the individuals, the marriage and the affair into an integrated co-construction that explains who they are and how it happened. Herman (1992) states that the final stage of recovery is reconnecting with ordinary life.

Forget the Pain but Remember the Lesson

While they gradually let go of the pain, they do not want to forget the lessons learned. There is an increased clarity about appropriate thresholds in friendships, and they can discuss vulnerabilities and danger signals without defensiveness. They can recognize problems in the marriage that could threaten their commitment and deal with it in a united way. They learn that a child-centered marriage does not nurture their relationship, so they invest more in creating a couple-centered marriage which prioritizes setting aside some private times for themselves.

Forgiveness, Recommitment and Reclaiming Lost Territories

At this stage, couples are encouraged to develop their own rituals of forgiveness and recommitment. Getting rid of the offending bed, disinfecting the family automobile which was violated, or destroying souvenirs of the affair such as gifts, pictures, and other mementoes can be cleansing. Burning the love letters together symbolizes the ending of a traumatic era in their lives, although they must choose together whether to share the content or avoid the pain of reading the letters.

Couples who regard their wedding vows as having been shattered may need to go through a period of courtship and recommitment. A great deal of symbolism and comfort has been derived from renewing vows in an informal or formal ceremony or by exchanging new wedding rings.

> After their reconciliation, Mel and Marla invited their children and some close friends to a church service in which they renewed their vows. They picked the verses together, and Mel spent hours choosing the musical selections. They delayed having sexual intercourse until this meaningful ceremony had taken place and took a second honeymoon without their children as they began a new era of a "couple-centered" marriage.

Couples are encouraged to reclaim activities, dates and settings which painfully recall the affair. Anniversary events, such as last year's birthday which was ruined because of the affair, can be rewritten with a special celebration this year so that the memories will not be contaminated for the rest of their lives. If a particular convention was an excuse to meet secretly with the affair partner, it may be important for the couple to attend this year's convention and reclaim the territory. Failure to integrate these aspects of the affair into the marriage perpetuates the tendency to split parts of the self.

WHEN HEALING AND RECOVERY ARE DELAYED

Delayed healing may represent a relational issue that has not been resolved, continuing ambivalence by the involved spouse, or an individualistic issue by the betrayed spouse. Fear of recurrence is realistic and must be considered as an ongoing issue until a sense of safety and security has been established. Lingering pain and suspicion may result from a valid mistrust. Continuing ambivalence by the involved spouse increases the potential for additional betrayal.

Insecurity and obsessiveness may continue if the involved spouse has not returned emotionally to the marriage. A betrayed wife was decompensating because she didn't feel secure after cessation of her husband's infidelity. The husband appeared very concerned and caring to us, so we referred her for to a psychiatrist who placed her on medication. It was only much later, after they separated, that we learned that her husband's affair had continued the whole time.

Lingering pain and suspicion may persist as an individualistic issue despite the sincerity and best efforts of the involved spouse. Research by Dougherty & Ellis (1976) on men's pathological jealousy describes an inability to let go of a wife's betrayal if the mother's infidelity was witnessed by them in childhood. We have observed that women whose fathers were unfaithful think they have married someone different from their fathers whom they can trust implicitly. Their husband's infidelity opens up all the old wounds, and the projections from the past must be differentiated from the current betrayal. Furthermore, healing in the betrayed spouse may be delayed by other unresolved issues from family of origin, such as narcissistic vulnerability, concerns about attractiveness and esteem, and competition associated with sibling rivalry.

The betrayed spouse may hold onto the pain because he/she is afraid that returning to a normal life will diminish the significance of the betrayal. There is some validity to the perception that some individuals violate their vows, go through a little bit of hell, and repeat the pattern when they calculate the cost/benefit ratio. However, continuation of "accusatory suffering" after a couple has worked for many months through all of the stages of healing and recovery requires addressing the individualistic issues.

> "Accusatory suffering" is a victim's unconscious idea that full recovery would somehow exonerate the perpetrator from blame ... The victim *must* remain unhelped. To recover would be to dismantle the living memorial which accuses the perpetrator. This failure of recovery is the unhealed wound (Seagull & Seagull, 1991, p. 16).

Asking "What would it take for you to heal?" may uncover unfinished business or unresolved issues. A husband who refused his wife's request to give away the plant he received from his lover is still bonded with the affair partner. Several betrayed spouses finally let go when their partners agreed to tell their former lovers in a letter or phone call that they stayed in the marriage "for love" and not "for the sake of the children".

SIGNS OF HEALING: HOW DO I KNOW YOU WON'T BETRAY ME AGAIN?

An optimistic response to the question "How do I know you won't betray me again?" is contingent on the following signs of healing (Glass & Wright, 1992a):

1. *Vulnerabilities are understood.* They recognize and acknowledge danger signals of relational and individualistic vulnerabilities. A significant sign of healing is that they can refer to events related to the affair with calmness and sometimes with humor. The individual vulnerabilities of the involved spouse, such as curiosity, depression and need for excitement, are understood. We ask "How would your partner know that you're lying again?" The co-dependent spouse is aware of behaviors such as hiding his/her head in the sand or giving and giving without getting anything back, and change has occurred in these areas.

2. *They have a stronger marriage.* The marriage is stronger with improved caring, communication and conflict management. A strong marriage allows both partners to stretch and assume new roles. If they foster and nurture each other's growth they won't have to go outside. Since there is often more equity in the extramarital relationship than in the marriage, another measure of relationship health is the level of reciprocity.

    They understand the relational vulnerabilities, such as letting the children's demands get in the way of making time for the couple. Expressing appreciation allows the marriage to meet some of the needs for positive mirroring and acceptance which the affair supplied. Establishing emotional and sexual intimacy decreases vulnerability for an affair by creating both a strong friendship and an erotic bond between the marital partners.

3. *They have mutual empathy and joint responsibility.* Probably the best predictor of recovery and most important sign of healing is mutual empathy and responsibility. The involved spouse is empathic for the pain caused by the infidelity and assumes responsibility for the act of betrayal, even if problems in the marriage created the vulnerability for an affair. The betrayed spouse has also achieved a level of understanding and shares the responsibility for change.

4. *The walls and windows are shifted.* They make united decisions concerning fallout from the EMI such as intrusive phone calls, a request for AIDS testing, or the crisis of a pregnancy from the affair. They reclaim the lost territories and manage ongoing and future encounters with the affair partner together. The involved spouse may have to renounce the EMI partner before the healing process can be complete, but the betrayed spouse may need to accept that there were positive aspects in that other relationship.

5. *They have shared values.* The couple has a shared vision of monogamy and fidelity. The involved partner with more permissive attitudes is now fully committed to exclusivity because of the pain that his/her behavior has caused. He/She may also be motivated by the belief that another incident will end the marriage.

CONFIDENTIALITY AND SECRET COALITIONS

Whenever we present a workshop on extramarital relationships, the question we are most commonly asked is how to handle secret affairs. We do not keep secrets of an ongoing EMI if our contract is for reconciliation or marital therapy because we do not want to do *collusion therapy*. The issue of disclosing EMI which occurred in the past requires clinical judgment as to whether previous EMI is an essential part of the history and is connected to the presenting problem.

If our contract is for separation therapy, we will maintain confidentiality between the spouses and even between co-therapists, but these walls of secrecy are made explicit. During separation therapy, some couples choose to discuss the story of the affair and/or the present status of the affair. We will support whatever choice they make, and we are open about re-negotiating the contract as therapy proceeds.

Secret Affairs at Onset of Conjoint Therapy: Stop *or* Share

How to gather confidential information from each spouse at the beginning of conjoint therapy and what to do with the secrets after you get them are controversial issues. Therapists are divided according to whether they have a relational or an individualistic perspective. Some therapists hold individual sessions to learn secrets which they maintain while they work with the spouses individually and in conjoint sessions (Ables, 1982; Humphrey, 1983b). Kaslow (1993) states, "Much marital therapy seems to lack respect for the fact that the content of a secret belongs to the possessor and only he or she can decide to whom and when he/she wishes to disclose it". In contrast, Scharff (1978) and Jacobson & Margolin (1979) insist that the spouses reveal secret EMI before they do marital therapy. Pittman & Wagers (1995) state, "A secret in this context belongs not to anyone individual, and certainly not to the therapist, but to the marriage" (p. 308).

We gather confidential information about EMI in our pre-counseling inventory (Glass, 1981). Then, as part of our initial session, we meet separately with each spouse if they have reported any extramarital involvements. If the EMI is a secret, we inform the involved spouse that we do not collude in ongoing secret affairs (collusion therapy). An involved spouse who chooses to work with us will have to *stop OR share* information about the EMI. "Stop" means that the extramarital relationship is put on hold for a specific period of time and all contact with the affair partner stops while the couples therapy is ongoing. The involved spouse who is unable to stop the EMI must "share" the fact that he or she is involved in an EMI. We will not begin conjoint marital therapy with any involved spouse who refuses to *stop or share*. We suggest that involved spouses with secret EMI tell their partners that they don't want to work with us. This preserves confidentiality and avoids destructive agendas between the spouses that could occur if we openly refused to treat them.

Initially we don't simply trust that he/she will completely stop all contact, but his/her agreement to stop the affair establishes his/her intention and affirms our position that we will not collude in an ongoing secret affair. Some involved spouses terminate their secret affairs gradually rather than suddenly. As they invest energy in rebuilding the marriage, they become more able to wean themselves from the extramarital relationship. Once we have begun marital therapy, we are vigilant about signs of continuing deception, and we periodically confront the status of the "stopped" EMI in individual sessions. If the secret affair is not stopped, we have to redefine the contract. This could lead to suspending conjoint sessions, or to establishing walls around individual sessions if the unsuspecting spouse accepts that condition, or to terminating or referring out.

Ambivalence Therapy

The involved spouse who cannot commit to either partner or leave either partner must resolve the ambivalence and get off the fence. We will only contract for ambivalence therapy in conjoint sessions if the ambivalence concerning the extramarital triangle is made explicit. Where the walls and windows will be in ambivalence therapy needs to be negotiated with the couple. The betrayed spouse may be present when the involved spouse works on resolving the ambivalence by discussing the alternative outcomes with both relationships. Ambivalence therapy may be done in individual sessions of either spouse prefers to have a wall concerning what is going on with the affair partner. If there are walls between the spouses and between therapists, conjoint sessions are suspended, and both spouses are seen individually until the walls between the spouses and between the co-therapists are eliminated.

When the ambivalent spouse appears stuck and unable to make a decision, it may be that he/she actually wishes to maintain both relationships and continue in a double life. At some point this covert arrangement should be made overt in an effort to get the betrayed spouse to take some action. We believe that the worst outcome of ambivalence therapy is a stable triangle.

OUTCOME AT TERMINATION

Reconstructing marriages after the disclosure of infidelity is usually long-term therapy lasting 1–2 years. As the crisis abates, couples are at risk of slipping into old patterns that potentiated individualistic and relational vulnerabilities for an EMI. Furthermore, coping with the aftermath of pain and disillusionment can create new incentives for the affirmation of an EMI for either spouse. Termination should be gradual, with booster sessions and check-ups to maintain stability through anniversary events of the affair and new psychosocial stressors.

An analysis of 200 couples seen in marital therapy demonstrates that couples with EMI are more likely to separate or divorce than distressed couples without EMI. Twenty-five percent of our couples with EMI (disclosed or undisclosed) were separated at the end of therapy vs. 10% of couples without EMI. Among those couples with EMI who were together at the conclusion of therapy, 34% were considerably happier and non-distressed, 28% showed improvement but were still somewhat distressed or ambivalent, and 14% were unhappily together. In some situations divorce is a better outcome than continuing unhappiness or a stable triangle.

One predictor of separation among couples with EMI was a lower commitment to the therapy, as evidenced by coming for four sessions or less. Other differentiating characteristics of EMI couples who separated were: (a) either spouse engaged in an EMI early in the marriage; (b) the wife had experienced extramarital sexual intercourse, whereas husbands who engaged in primarily sexual involvements were unlikely to separate; (c) both the husband and the wife had engaged in an EMI; or (d) either spouse had a "combined-type" involvement, with an even higher likelihood of separation for "combined-type" wives than husbands. Other studies have also found that high divorce rates are associated with extramarital sex which occurs early in the marriage (Glass & Wright, 1977; Hunt, 1974; Lawson, 1988).

In general, the consequences are worse for the marriage when the wife has an EMI (Lawson, 1988). We have observed that women attribute their EMI to an unhappy marriage, are more emotionally attached to their affair partners, and are more unwilling to discuss their EMI with their husbands. Furthermore, betrayed husbands are more impatient and angrier than betrayed wives about spousal ambivalence during the early phase of rebuilding.

Although EMI contributes to marital separation and divorce, very few involved spouses end up with their affair partners. We share this information with involved spouses who are ambivalent about which relationship to commit to. In her British non-clinical sample, Lawson (1988) found that only 10% of those who left the marriage because of an EMI married the affair partner. By the time that Spanier & Margolis (1983) interviewed recently separated and divorced persons, 73% of the extramarital sexual relationships had ended. Affairs continued for 20% of the men and 33% of the women.

Our own expectations of honesty in therapy have shifted to cautious skepticism because we have discovered that some people deceived us about EMI which was exposed after termination. We have seen a wide range of outcomes for couples who returned to therapy to deal with a new EMI or a resumption of the former EMI. Those who were still expressing ambivalence when they stopped the prior therapy may be finally ready to clarify whether they want this marriage or are contemplating divorce. It is very disappointing when an individual gets involved in further EMI despite having appeared satisfied with his/her spouse and committed to the marriage. The potential for a positive outcome is enhanced when the recurrence is perceived as a more compelling signal of distress and motivation for change than the earlier EMI. We have been pleased to find couples many years later whose relationship has been stronger, more intimate and more committed since the healing and reconstruction that took place in the therapeutic experience or experiences.

REFERENCES

Ables, B.S. (1982). *Therapy for Couples*. San Francisco: Jossey Bass.

American Psychiatric Association (1994). *DSM-IV: Diagnostic and Statistical Manual of Mental Disorders*, 4th edn. Washington, DC: American Psychiatric Association.

Atwater, L. (1979). Getting involved: women's transition to first extramarital sex. *Alternative Lifestyles*, **1**(2), 33–68.

Bach, G.R. & Wyden, P. (1970). *The Intimate Enemy: How to Fight Fair in Love and Marriage*. New York: Avon Books.

Beach, S.R.H., Jouriles, E.N. & O'Leary, D. (1985). Extramarital sex: impact on depression and commitment in couples seeking marital therapy. *Journal of Sex & Marital Therapy*, **11**(2), 99–108.

Brown, E.M. (1991). *Patterns of Infidelity and Their Treatment*. New York: Brunner/Mazel.

Buunk, B. (1980). Extramarital sex in The Netherlands: motivation in social and marital context. *Alternative Lifestyles*, **3**, 11–39.

Buss, D. (1994). *The Evolution of Desire: Strategies of Human Mating*. New York: Basic Books.

Carnes, P. (1985). *Out of the Shadows: Understanding Sexual Addiction*. Minneapolis, MN: Compcare.

Dougherty, J.P. & Ellis, J. (1976). A new concept and finding in morbid jealousy. *American Journal of Psychiatry*, **133**(6), 679–683.

Everstine, D.S. & Everstine, L. (1993). *The Trauma Response: Treatment for Emotional Injury*. New York: W.W. Norton.

Francis, J.L. (1977). Toward the management of heterosexual jealousy. *Journal of Marriage and Family Counseling*, **3**, 61–69.

Gilligan, C. (1982). *In a Different Voice*. Cambridge, MA: Harvard University Press.

Glass, S.P. (1981). Sex differences in the relationship between satisfaction with various aspects of marriage and types of extramarital involvements (doctoral dissertation, Catholic University, 1980). *Dissertation Abstracts International*, **41**(10), 3889B.

Glass, S.P. & Wright, T.L. (1977). The relationship of extramarital sex, length of marriage, and sex differences on marital satisfaction and romanticism: Athanasiou's data reanalyzed. *Journal of Marriage and the Family*, **39**(4), 691–703.

Glass, S.P. & Wright, T.L. (1985). Sex differences in type of extramarital involvement and marital dissatisfaction. *Sex Roles*, **12**(9/10), 1101–1119.

Glass, S.P. & Wright, T.L. (1988). Clinical implications of research on extramarital involvement. In R. Brown & J. Field (eds), *Treatment of Sexual Problems in Individual and Couples Therapy*. New York: PMA.

Glass, S.P. & Wright, T.L. (1991). *Moving Walls and Windows to Resolve Extramarital Triangles*. Institute (#112) presented at meeting of American Association for Marriage and Family Therapy, Dallas, TX. Audiotape: Resource Link (1-800-241-7785).

Glass, S.P. & Wright, T.L. (1992a). "How do I know you won't betray me again?" Workshop (#314) presented at meeting of American Association for Marriage and Family Therapy, Miami, FL. Audiotape: Resource Link.

Glass, S.P. & Wright, T.L. (1992b). Justifications for extramarital involvement: the association between attitudes, behavior, and gender. *Journal of Sex Research*, **29**(3), 361–387.

Goldstine, D., Larner, K., Zuckerman, S. & Goldstine, H. (1978). *The Dance Away Lover*. New York: Ballantine.

Gottman, J. (1994). *Why Marriages Succeed or Fail*. New York: Simon & Schuster.

Greene, B.L. (1981). *A Clinical Approach to Marital Problems*. Springfield, IL: Charles C. Thomas.

Herman, J.L. (1992). *Trauma and Recovery*. New York: Basic Books.

Humphrey, F.G. (1983a). Extramarital relationships: Therapy issues for marriage and family therapists. Paper presented at meeting of American Association for Marriage and Family Therapy, Washington, DC.

Humphrey, F.G. (1983b). *Marital Therapy* (pp. 47–66). Englewood Cliffs, NJ: Prentice-Hall.

Hunt, M. (1969). *The Affair*. New York: World Publishing Company.

Hunt, M. (1974). *Sexual Behavior in the 1970s*. Chicago: Playboy Press.

Jacobson & Margolin (1979). *Marital Therapy: Strategies Based on Social Learning and Behaviour Exchange Principles*. New York: Brunner/Mazel.

Janoff-Bulman, R. (1992). *Shattered Assumptions: Towards a New Psychology of Trauma*. New York: Free Press.

Kaslow, F. (1993). Attractions and affairs: fabulous and fatal. *Journal of Family Psychotherapy*, **4**(4), 1–33.

Lawson, A. (1988). *Adultery*. New York: Basic Books.

Lichtman, R. & Taylor, S. (1986). Close relationships and the female cancer patient. In B.L. Anderson (ed.), *Women with Cancer: Psychological Perspectives* (pp. 257–288). New York: Springer-Verlag.

Lusterman, D. (1992). The Broderick Affair. Workshop presented at the annual meeting of the American Association of Marriage and Family Therapy, Miami, FL.

Lusterman, D. (1995). Treating marital infidelity. In R.H. Mikesell, D. Lusterman & S.H. McDaniel (eds), *Integrating Family Therapy: Handbook of Family Psychology and Systems Theory* (pp. 259–270). Washington, DC: American Psychological Association.

Madanes, C. (1981). *Strategic Family Therapy*. San Francisco: Jossey-Bass.

Matsakis, A. (1992). *I Can't Get Over It: a Handbook for Trauma Survivors*. Oakland, CA: New Harbiger.

Moultrop, D.J. (1990). *Husbands, Wives, and Lovers; the Emotional System of the Extramarital Affair*. New York: Guilford.

Notarius, C. & Markman, M. (1993). *We Can Work It Out: Making Sense of Marital Conflict*. New York: G.P. Putnam's Sons.

Ochberg, F.M. (1991). Post-traumatic therapy. *Psychotherapy: Theory/Research/Practice/Training*, **28**(1), 5–15.

Petersen, J.R. (1983). The Playboy readers' sex survey. *Playboy*, **30**(3), 90–92, 178–184.

Peterson, K. (1988, June 20). When platonic friendships get too close for comfort. *USA Today*, p. 6D.

Pittman, F. (1989). *Private Lies: the Betrayal of Infidelity*. New York: W.W. Norton.

Pittman, F. (1993). Beyond betrayal: life after infidelity. *Psychology Today*, **May/June**, 33–38, 78–82.

Pittman, F. & Wagers, T.P. (1995). Crises of infidelity. In N.S. Jacobson & A.S. Gurman (eds), *Clinical Handbook of Couples Therapy* (pp. 295–316). New York: Guilford.

Rhodes, S. (1984). Extramarital affairs: clinical issues in therapy. *Social Casework*, **November**, 541–546.

Scharff, D.E. (1978). Truth and consequences in sex and marital therapy: the revelation of secrets in the therapeutic setting. *Journal of Sex and Marital Therapy*, **4**, 37–51.

Seagull, E.G. & Seagull, A.A. (1991). Healing the wound that must not heal: psychotherapy with survivors of domestic violence. *Psychotherapy: Theory/Research/Practice/Training*, **28**, 16–20.

Spanier, G.B. & Margolis, R.L. (1983). Marital separation and extramarital sexual behavior. *Journal of Sex Research*, **19**, 23–48.

Sprenkle, D.J. & Weiss, D.L. (1978). Extramarital sexuality: implications for marital therapists. *Journal of Sex and Marital Therapy*, **4**, 279–291.

Stiff, J.B., Kim, H.J. & Ramesh, C.N. (1992). Truth biases and aroused suspicion in relational deception. *Communication Research*, **19**, 326–345.

Strean, H.S. (1980). *The Extramarital Affair*. New York: Free Press.

Stuart, R.B. (1983). *Couples Pre-counseling Inventory*. Champaign, IL: Research Press.

Subotnik, R. & Harris, G. (1994). *Surviving Infidelity*. Holbrook, MA: Bob Adams Press.

Thompson, A.P. (1984). Emotional and sexual components of extramarital relations. *Journal of Marriage and the Family*, **46**(1), 35–42.

Walster, E., Traupmann, J. & Walster, G.W. (1978). Equity and extramarital sexuality. *Archives of Sexual Behavior*, **7**(2), 127–141.

Weil, B.E. & Winter, R. (1993). *Adultery: the Forgivable Sin*. New York: Birch Lane Press.

Weiner-Davis, M. (1992). *Divorce Busting*. New York: Simon & Schuster.

Wigren, J. (1994). Narrative completion in the treatment of trauma. *Psychotherapy*, **31**(3), 415–423.

Chapter 20

Concurrent Interventions for Marital and Children's Problems

Matthew R. Sanders*, Carol Markie-Dadds*
and Jan M. Nicholson**
**Department of Psychology, University of Queensland, Brisbane,
Australia and **School of Public Health, Queensland University
of Technology, Kelvin Grove, Queensland, Australia*

A relationship between marital distress and behaviour problems in children has been well established (Amato & Keith, 1991; Emery, 1982, 1988; Grych & Fincham, 1990). In Chapter 10 we argued that the transition to parenthood can be demanding and a potential threat to both the individual well-being of marital partners and the couple's relationship (Sanders, Nicholson & Floyd, this volume). Given that parent and marital problems co-vary, it is not surprising that therapists frequently encounter concurrent marital and child-related problems in their clinical practice (Sanders & Dadds, 1993). Practitioners face a dilemma in determining which problem domain should receive intervention priority. Moreover, it can be challenging to integrate the therapeutic strategies employed for treating marital distress with those that are useful for treating child behaviour problems.

When marital and child problems are concurrent, the context of the referral is critical for determining the focus of the initial assessment and the intervention. To illustrate this point, when children are referred for behavioural or emotional problems, the parents' attention is likely to be specifically focused on helping their child. In this context, attempts by the clinician to explore possible marital conflict can be met with resistance (e.g. "We are here for our child, not our marriage"). This is particularly likely if: (a) parents have been pressured or coerced into seeking help for their child from an external agency (e.g. school); (b)

Clinical Handbook of Marriage and Couples Interventions. Edited by W. Kim Halford and Howard J. Markman.
© 1997 John Wiley & Sons Ltd.

there is a situational crisis (e.g. the child has been suspended from school); or (c) only one parent presents with a child. Clinicians must work tactfully to gain a mandate from parents to explore marital distress when the parents are seeking help for their child's behaviour.

Conversely, a couple presenting with primary concerns about their marital relationship can be resistant to the clinicians' attempts to examine child adjustment issues. Although parents are frequently concerned about the negative effects of marital conflict on their children, the main goal of couples seeking marital therapy is often the survival of their marriage. Again, the clinician must gain a mandate from the parents to explore child-related problems in the context of a presentation for marital distress. Moreover, there are important differences in how these problems are tackled, depending on the relationship between marital and child problems, the couple's immediate focus of concern and the couples' motivation to address each problem.

The relationship between marriage and child behaviour problems is dynamic and may change during the course of therapy. New child or marital problems may begin after the commencement of treatment. Hence, there is a need for continuous monitoring of both domains and, where necessary, adjustment to the treatment plan.

This chapter aims to examine the concurrent treatment of marital and child behaviour problems. We begin by examining the relationship between marital conflict and child behaviour problems when the referral context is for a marital problem and subsequently when the referral context is for a child behaviour problem. Different levels of adjunctive child-focused interventions are described, together with guidelines for the clinical management of marital distress through partner support interventions. Finally, we explore the specific difficulties clinicians encounter when dealing with remarried couples who have children from former relationships (i.e. step-families). We identify some critical process issues and consider possible directions for future clinical research.

MANAGING CHILDREN'S BEHAVIOUR PROBLEMS IN THE CONTEXT OF MARITAL REFERRALS

Couples presenting for marital therapy frequently experience difficulties with their children. A variety of behaviour problems and adjustment difficulties have been shown to be related to the presence of marital conflict (Sanders, Nicholson & Floyd, this volume), particularly conduct problems (Fantuzzo et al., 1991). Generally, the more severe the marital conflict the greater the negative effects on children. However, not all child problems are related to marital conflict. For example, there is little evidence linking marital conflict to childhood internalizing problems, such as recurrent abdominal pain syndromes, anxiety disorders or childhood depression.

Many children from maritally discordant homes have negative reactions to high levels of marital conflict. Child behaviour difficulties can be an important additional source of stress for parents and can exacerbate marital distress. Failure to resolve significant parenting and child management concerns can disrupt couples' therapy. For example, when children are noisy and disruptive and refuse to go to bed, couples can experience problems complying with homework tasks such as practising communication sessions. Nightly battles with children can lead to parents, particularly mothers, being exhausted and having little energy to put into their own intimacy needs. Communication problems over child-rearing issues, such as division of household and parenting responsibilities, disagreements over discipline techniques and the amount of time individual partners put into their parenting role, can be an important source of conflict.

To our knowledge there have been no controlled clinical trials evaluating the effects of marital therapy on children's behaviour problems (using adequate methodology with comprehensive multi-modal assessment of child behaviour and adjustment), when there has been a pre-existing child problem and when the focus of the referral has been the marriage, rather than the child. Consequently, the therapeutic guidelines suggested in this chapter are based on our clinical experience in managing such cases and on the use of child management procedures we have found helpful in treating behaviour problems in children.

MANAGING COUPLES' RELATIONSHIP PROBLEMS IN THE CONTEXT OF CHILD REFERRALS

There is conflicting evidence concerning the role of marital conflict in the treatment of children's disruptive behaviour (Dadds, Sanders & James, 1987; Sayger, Horne & Glaser, 1993). Some evidence shows that behavioural parent training for parents of children with disruptive behaviour can result in increases in marital satisfaction (e.g. Forehand et al., 1982), whereas others have argued that marital discord interferes with treatment outcome (e.g. Cole & Morrow, 1976; Kent & O'Leary, 1976). In a controlled factorial experiment, Dadds, Schwartz and Sanders (1987) found that maritally distressed couples with a problem child who received a brief marital communication skills program (partner support training) maintained treatment gains just as well as non-maritally distressed couples. However, maritally distressed couples who only received parent training, rather than a combined child-focused and brief marital intervention, tended to relapse by the 6-month follow-up. These findings suggest that specific attention to marital conflict is essential if treatment gains for the child are to be maintained.

The following section describes the concurrent treatment of marital and child behaviour problems, with special consideration given to the referral context.

Table 20.1 Commonly used measures of child behaviour problems and parenting

Measure	Description	Scores produced	Reference
Child behaviour and adjustment			
Child Behavior Checklist	An 118-item measure of behavioural and psychopathological symptoms, for preschool, school-age, or teenage children, in parent-report, teacher-report or youth self-report forms	In addition to several subscales, this measure can provide scores for total problem behaviours, externalizing or internalizing problems, and social competence	Achenbach & Edelbrock (1983)
Eyberg Child Behavior Inventory, and Sutter-Eyberg Student Behavior Inventory	These are 36-item measures of disruptive child behaviour for parents and teachers of children aged 2–16 years	(a) Intensity score—how often a problem behaviour occurs, (b) Problem Score—identifies specific behaviours that are current problems for parents	Eyberg & Robinson (1983); Funderburk & Eyberg (1989)
Parent Daily Report Checklist	Consists of 34 child problem behaviours that are rated by parents as present or absent over a 7-day period. Suitable for children aged 2–10 years	(a) Total Problem Score—number of behaviour problems present, (b) Targeted Problem Score—number of specific behaviours previously identified by parent as problematic	Chamberlain & Reid (1987)
Child Manifest Anxiety Scale—Revised	A 37-item self-report measure of child anxiety	Total anxiety score, with three narrow range factors, and a scale to detect possible confound from social desirability	Reynolds & Richmond, (1978)
Child Depression Inventory	A 27-item self-report measure of symptoms of child depression, suitable for children 8–17 years	Total depression score with individual items that examine suicidal ideology	Kovacs (1981)

Coopersmith Self-esteem Inventory	A 58-item self-report measure of child self-esteem for children 8 years and older	Total self-esteem, four sub-areas of self-esteem (general, academic, social, home), and a scale to detect possible confound from social desirability	Coopersmith (1981)
Parenting skills and competence			
The Parenting Scale	A 30-item measure of dysfunctional discipline practices in parents of children aged 18–48 months	Discipline styles: (a) Laxness (permissive discipline); (b) Overreactivity (displays of anger, meanness and irritability); (c) Verbosity (overly long verbal reprimands)	Arnold et al. (1993)
Parenting Sense of Competence Scale	A 17-item scale which taps efficacy and satisfaction dimensions of parenting self-esteem	(a) Efficacy score (competency, problem-solving ability and capability in parenting role), (b) Satisfaction Score (parenting frustration, anxiety and motivation)	Johnston & Mash (1989)
Parent Problem Checklist	A 16-item measure of interparental conflict which examines the parents' ability to cooperate and work together as a team in their parenting roles	Problem score—number of sources of parental disagreement	Dadds & Powell (1991)
Depression Anxiety Stress Scale (DASS)	A 42-item measure of three affective dimensions. Yields information on a broad range of symptoms of depression, anxiety and stress in adults	(a) Depression Score (b) Anxiety Score (c) Stress Score	Lovibond & Lovibond (1995)

THERAPEUTIC GUIDELINES FOR THE CONCURRENT TREATMENT OF MARITAL AND CHILD ADJUSTMENT PROBLEMS

Comprehensive Assessment of Family Functioning

A comprehensive assessment of family functioning involves obtaining interview, self-report, self-monitoring and behaviour observational data to assess marital functioning, children's adjustment and any parenting concerns. To minimize the effects of subjective bias and to account for different perspectives, it is essential that multiple informants are used. Several useful self-report measures for assessing child and family functioning are outlined in Table 20.1, and described in detail in Sanders and Dadds (1993). It is important not to overburden couples with assessment tasks. Each measure needs to be carefully explained and justified to each partner, otherwise compliance will be low. Assessment measures for special populations often lack empirical validation, and it may not be necessary to employ such tools. For example, we have found with step-families that adequate assessment data can be obtained from instruments described in Table 20.1, when supplemented with measures of marital functioning and careful interviewing.

In addition, observation data should be collected to supplement more subjective self-report measures. This is especially important since marital problems and depression often co-vary. Depressed parents may perceive their children as having more behaviour problems than is evident in teacher reports or by independent behavioural observation (Webster-Stratton & Hammond, 1988). Therefore, parental reports should not be taken at face value. Direct observation of family interaction may include a couple problem-solving discussion on a current "hot" relationship issue and a "hot" parenting topic, as well as a structured parent–child interaction task. A 15-minute structured parent–child interaction task may in-

Table 20.2 The clinical interview

Area of inquiry	Specific guidelines
1. Parents' main concerns about their child	Give each parent an opportunity to describe what the child is doing that causes concern. Encourage the parent to elaborate on the nature of the presenting complaint and place the problem described in its specific situational context. Establish the approximate frequency, intensity, duration and context within which each of the problems occurs. Clarify approximately when the problem first began. Establish whether both parents experience similar problems with the child
2. Other difficulties the child may have	Explore the presence or absence of other problems which may be logically related to the pattern of presenting complaints mentioned by the parent

Table 20.2 (*continued*)

Area of inquiry	Specific guidelines
3. History of the presenting complaint	Establish: (a) date of onset (when the problem first began); (b) chronological development of symptoms (how the problem has changed from the time when it first began to the present)
4. Topography of presenting problems	Clarify the dimensions of the problem behaviour by getting a best estimate of the frequency, duration or intensity of each behaviour of interest
5. History of mental health service	Establish: (a) the type of problem; (b) previous help sought
6. Family structure, stability and history	In families where parents have separated, divorced or remarried, history details should include: duration of current marital or cohabiting relationship, time since separation of child's parents, number of changes experienced in parent figures, residences and schools, current full-, half- and step-siblings in household on full-time or part-time basis
7. Family relationships and interaction	(a) Relationships between parents: determine the nature and degree of marital conflict that may exist in the family; (b) parent–child interaction: explore how each parent sees his/her own and the other's relationship with the child; (c) parents' expectations regarding child behaviour and family rules; (d) child's involvement in family decision-making; (e) parenting roles and expectations: in stepfamilies, it is important to assess the current role of the step-parent; parent and step-parent expectations of the step-parent's role; and parent and step-parent beliefs about parenting (especially discipline styles)
8. Extended family relationships and interaction	In families where the child's biological parents are separated or divorced, assess: (a) the relationship between biological parents (level of conflict, child's exposure to conflict, degree of communication over parenting); (b) the child's relationship with the non-custodial parent; and (c) support from or conflict with extended family
9. Developmental history	Stages to assess: (a) pregnancy, delivery, and neonatal period; (b) infancy; (c) toddlerhood; (d) preschool age; (e) middle childhood; (f) early adolescence
10. Educational history	Establish: (a) schools attended; (b) academic progress; (c) behaviour and peer relationships at school
11. Child's general health	Identify whether the child has any current major health problems, handicaps or disabilities
12. Therapeutic expectations	Determine the parents' expectations regarding the process and outcome of therapy. Clarify with each parent what specific changes they would like to see in their child's behaviour or adjustment

volve three elements. To start, the parent may be requested to engage the child in free play for approximately 5 minutes. For the next 5 minutes, the parent and child can try to complete a jigsaw puzzle or some other goal-directed activity that is appropriate to the child's developmental level. For the remainder of the observation, the parent can be asked to supervise the tidying-up of the toys. Sanders and Dadds (1993) provide more information on setting up and coding observational tasks. Direct observations provide measures of interactional negativity between parents and children, as well as couples' communication and problem-solving skills.

In the context of a marital referral, the initial interview with a couple should always explore the possibility of child behaviour and adjustment difficulties. A rationale for this inquiry can include the need to identify factors which may currently be a source of stress or conflict for the couple. When the initial interview suggests the presence of child behaviour problems, a more detailed assessment of the nature of these difficulties is warranted. Table 20.2 presents a summary of the areas to address when assessing child behaviour problems in an intake interview. In light of the large number of families who experience transitions such as remarriage and divorce, and the complex structure of many households, care should be taken to ensure that these areas are adequately assessed. As shown in Table 20.2, information should be collected regarding family history, stability, current household composition, and contact with extended family.

When child behaviour problems are the main source of referral, the clinician can explore how the couple's relationship has been affected by their child's behaviour. Prior to examining the marital relationship, it is imperative that the clinician has fully explored the parent's concerns about their child. This will ensure that the parents feel that their concerns have been listened to and adequately addressed. Subsequently, the clinician can explain how children's behaviour problems can put stress on family members and in particular the marital relationship. As a matter of course, self-report measures of marital functioning should be administered whenever a child presents for treatment.

Determining the Current Level of Distress Experienced by the Child

A thorough assessment will help determine the degree of distress experienced by the child and therefore assist in identifying the most appropriate form of intervention. This rating is related to judgements about the severity and chronicity of the child adjustment problems. The management of common everyday problems can be dealt with quite effectively by providing appropriate reading material and brief practical advice on how to implement specific management strategies (e.g. time out). However, when a child's problem is more severe, the provision of self-help material alone will be inadequate and more intensive child-focused treatment may be indicated (Sanders & Markie-Dadds, 1995). For example, if a child is clinically depressed or has attention deficit disorder, oppositional defiant disorder, conduct disorder or a chronic illness, then it is likely that the child will require a more intensive program.

Determining the Degree of Distress Experienced by the Couple

It is also important to determine the degree of relationship distress experienced by the couple. Other chapters provide some insight into the nature of couples' relationship problems. This section refers to relationship problems associated with children's disruptive behaviour. Parental distress about parenting may not be directly related to the severity of the child's problem behaviour, particularly if the mother is depressed as a result of marital conflict. There are several different sources of distress, potentially ranging from mild to severe, which can affect parenting. These include conflict between marital partners about child-rearing issues, conflict between one or both parents and the child, and conflict between marital partners over matters unrelated to the child.

Establishing a Relationship between Marital Problems and Child Behaviour Difficulties

Education about the nature of the presenting problem is an important component of any clinical intervention. The discussion of assessment findings provides an opportunity and an important context to put both child management and marital issues on the therapy agenda. Treatment efficacy may depend on the extent to which clients accept the rationale for therapy (Sanders & Lawton, 1993). A primary goal of reviewing assessment results with couples is to develop a shared perspective of the causes of the problems experienced. In the case of co-morbid child and marital problems, establishing a shared view of the relationship between these problems is critical for gaining a mandate to intervene in both couple and child areas of functioning.

During the review of assessment results all of the available assessment data addressing marital, parental and child functioning is summarized and presented. Discrepancies from various information sources need to be addressed. In addition, the review should provide parents with a social learning perspective for understanding the nature and causes of child behaviour problems. For non-traditional families, it can be helpful to present an overview of the impact of family transitions such as divorce and remarriage on children. Other topics which should be considered for discussion include factors which affect adults' ability to be available to, and consistent with, children. Child and family topics which should be considered for inclusion in the review are presented in Table 20.3.

Problems can sometimes arise during a review session when parents realize the impact of their behaviour on children. Care needs to be taken to present feedback in a way which emphasizes the interactional nature of family and marital problems, whilst not appearing to lay blame with one partner. This is especially

Table 20.3 Common causes of children's behaviour problems

Inherited or genetic factors
- Child temperament
- Early behaviour patterns

Social learning factors
- Accidental rewards for misbehaviour
- Coercive escalation cycles
- Modelling of inappropriate behaviour by parents, siblings and peers
- Poor instruction-giving
- Inconsistent or ineffective consequences for misbehaviour
- Use of angry or emotional messages
- Ignoring of prosocial behaviours

Factors associated with family transitions which impact on children
- Losses associated with transitions
- Fears of replacement or abandonment
- Changes in rules and expectations
- Changes in child's status in the household
- Loyalty conflicts between biological and step-parents
- Lack of cooperative, consistent parenting between biological and step-parents

Factors that impact on adults and their parenting behaviour
- Stressors (unemployment, financial, relationship)
- Marital problems
- Social isolation
- Conflict with extended family or ex-spouses
- Family change (relationship breakdown, birth of a new child, child leaving home)
- Depression or other psychological problems

important in families where there is a long-standing history of conflict over parenting. If one parent feels singled out, or perceives that the therapist is taking his/her partner's side, it is difficult to establish an adequate therapeutic relationship and that parent may be resistant to subsequent attempts at behaviour change. We have found it useful to present the causes of child behaviour problems from the point of view of the child. Most parents are eager to gain a professional opinion about what their child is experiencing. Presenting a behavioural perspective on parenting from the child's point of view can be less threatening than illustrating what each partner is specifically doing wrong.

Developing a Treatment Plan for Concurrent Marital and Child Behaviour Problems

Once it is clear that there are concurrent child and marital adjustment problems, a plan for intervention is needed. A shared perspective of the problems and their causes will facilitate this process. When there are multiple presenting problems, couples should be given several options regarding how best to pursue the issues (concurrently; sequentially; by referral, monitor and review; or by agreeing to a temporary moratorium on one issue whilst tackling the other). The timing and sequencing of child and marital interventions is important.

For marital referrals we generally advocate an initial focus on the couples' relationship. Where couples seek specific child behaviour management advice, this should be given. However, such guidance should not be perfunctory and must be based on a careful appraisal of the child's problem and the likelihood of success in pursuing each option. In general it is important initially to give parents tasks with which they are likely to have success. For example, self-monitoring of low-rate troublesome child behaviours, or discussion of household rules relating to the children, can be useful relatively low-threat activities. However, the marital therapist who avoids addressing critical parenting issues, or refers all child problems elsewhere, is missing an important opportunity to address a family problem in a cohesive, systematic and integrated fashion. Consequently, in our clinical work, clinicians are encouraged to obtain expertise in both child and marital problem domains.

In the context of a child referral, Dadds (1992) emphasizes the importance of initially having a moratorium on marital problems to focus the couples' attention on the needs of the child. Parents are asked if they can put their marital differences aside for a couple of weeks while they and the therapist work as a team to help the child. This approach ensures that the parents play an active role in determining the sequencing of interventions. Clinical experience suggests that most families will agree to this moratorium. However, when a couple cannot work together, the clinician needs to explore why. At times, a maritally-focused intervention may be needed before a child-focused program can be implemented successfully.

Integrating Marital and Child Foci

Many of the parenting skills that are related to successful relationships with children and the management of difficult behaviour are also relevant to marital relationships (e.g. praise and positive attention; provision of engaging and enjoyable activities; clear expectations and ground rules; avoidance of coercion and escalation traps; how we ask children to do things; use of non-violent discipline strategies; appropriate use of ignoring). Indeed, some partners can use these skills quite successfully with their children, or at work, but not within their marriage. Hence, when these skills are being taught, it is useful to point out, or better still have the parent point out, the possible applications of the same strategies in other situations, such as their marriage. Some parents can readily accept the idea that children need positive feedback to learn new skills, but have difficulty accepting this idea when applied to their marital partner. This discrepancy can be pointed out and the basis of the parents' views explored and, if necessary, challenged.

After the clinician has decided on the strength of intervention required to address the child's problem, the program is implemented, whereever possible linking the child-related homework tasks to similar activities the couple may undertake to improve their relationship. For example, quality time with a marital partner does not always mean time alone. There are many enjoyable family activities that all family members can share. Couples sometimes complain about family activities not being enjoyable because of constant disruptions and demands from children. However, behaviour management advice that specifically address problems that occur on outings or travelling in the car may be just the kind of intervention needed to enable all family members to find the outing rewarding.

Monitoring and Evaluation

It is important that all clinicians monitor the effects of their interventions. In the context of a marital referral, it is tempting simply to deal with parenting and child management issues as promptly as possible. To avoid a haphazard and potentially damaging intervention, adequate monitoring and follow-up is essential, particularly when significant psychopathology in the child is evident. Part of each session can be devoted to reviewing and trouble-shooting parenting and child management issues. However, it is important to note that discussion of the children can also become a convenient digression from discussing more threatening topics concerning the relationship. Where children are receiving services elsewhere some liaison with other treatment agencies involved with the child is highly desirable (after obtaining parental consent). This will help to avoid conflicting advice being given to parents.

The Intervention Program

Treatment procedures for marital therapy are presented in other chapters. The next section focuses on strategies for the treatment of child behaviour problems in the context of a marital referral. In the context of a child referral, an adjunctive intervention called Partner Support Training is used to help parents support one another in their parenting and to solve family problems. This powerful intervention is presented in the latter part of this section.

Recent evidence has shown that a variety of treatment options may be viable alternatives for the management of child behaviour problems (Sanders, 1995). Sanders and Markie-Dadds (1996) outlined five different levels of family intervention to tackle child behaviour problems, ranging from brief self-help programs to more intensive skills based programs that concurrently address child and marital difficulties. A parenting program known as Triple P (Positive Parenting Program) has evaluated each of these five levels of intervention with young children with conduct problems (Sanders & Markie-Dadds, 1995).

Interventions for Mild Child Adjustment Problems

In the context of a marital referral, brief child-focused interventions can be successfully integrated with couples issues, either within the same session as other issues are dealt with or separately. The provision of brief, reliable and effective information about children's development and how to tackle specific child-rearing problems can be effective for families experiencing mild child behaviour problems. For example, a brief parenting tip sheet can help parents manage some common behavioural and developmental problems.

Parents can be given more detailed written parenting information in the form of a parenting book such as *Every Parent: a Positive Approach to Children's Behaviour* (Sanders, 1992), and its companion workbook *Every Parent's Workbook: a Practical Guide to Children's Behaviour* (Sanders, Lynch & Markie-Dadds, 1994). Together, these books make up a 10-week self-help program for parents, with no practitioner contact. Each weekly session contains a series of set readings and suggested homework tasks for the parents to complete. Positive reports from families have shown this program to be a powerful intervention (Markie-Dadds & Sanders, 1994). This intervention is made more effective with the inclusion of regular follow-up contact (Connell, Sanders & Markie-Dadds, in press). These brief consultations provide minimal support to parents as a means of keeping them focused and motivated while they work through the program.

If necessary, the clinician can provide information in combination with active skills training to teach parents how to manage specific problems or problem behaviours in specific settings (e.g. bedtime and sleep problems, feeding difficulties, non-compliance or thumb-sucking). With narrowly focused interventions, the emphasis is on the management of a specific child behaviour rather than developing a broad range of child management skills. Training techniques such as instruction, modelling, rehearsal and feedback are used until parents reach an acceptable criterion level of performance on the skills being taught.

Interventions for Moderate to Severe Child Adjustment Problems

Intensive behavioural parent training is likely to be necessary for more severe child behaviour problems and is commonly used when the child's behaviour is the main source of the referral. This broadly focused intervention combines the provision of information with active skills training and support. However, this level of intervention teaches parents to apply parenting skills to a broad range of target behaviours in both home and community settings with the target child and all relevant siblings. This program incorporates several generalization enhancement strategies (e.g. training with sufficient exemplars and training loosely), to promote the transfer of parenting skills across settings, siblings and time. Active skills training methods include modelling, role-playing, feedback and the use of specific homework tasks. Active *in vivo* skill training with the parents and child is also conducted in the child's home on three or four occasions. The aim of the *in vivo* training is to provide parents with clear, specific and helpful information about their interactions with the target child and siblings. Parents are prompted to self-select goals to practise, are observed interacting with their child and implementing parenting skills, and subsequently receive feedback from the clinician (Sanders & Glynn, 1981; Sanders & Dadds, 1982). The strategies taught in intensive behavioural parent training are presented in Table 20.4. More detailed information on these strategies can be found in Sanders and Dadds (1993).

Table 20.4 Strategies taught in intensive parent training

Type of strategy	Description	Recommended age (years)	Applications
Increasing desired behaviour or teaching a new skill			
Spending quality time with children	Spending frequent, brief (0.5–3 min) uninterrupted time in child-preferred activities	All ages	Conveying interest and caring for the child: provides opportunities for children to self-disclose and practise conversational skills
Tuning in to desirable behaviour	Providing contingent positive attention following prosocial or other appropriate behaviour	All ages	Speaking in a pleasant voice; playing cooperatively, sharing, drawing pictures, reading, compliance
Giving plenty of physical affection	Providing contingent positive physical contact following desired child behaviour	All ages	Hugging, touching, cuddling, tickling, patting
Conversing with children	Having brief conversations with children about an activity or interest of the child	All ages	Vocabulary, conversational and social skills
Using incidental teaching	Using a series of graded prompts to respond to child-initiated language interactions	1–5	Language utterances, problem-solving cognitive ability
Setting a good example through modelling	Providing the child with a demonstration of desirable behaviour through the use of parental modelling	3–12	Using bathroom, washing hands, tying shoelaces, solving problems
Encouraging independence through "ask", "say", "do"	Using verbal, gestural and manual prompts to teach self-care skills	3–7	Self-care skills (brushing teeth, making bed, tidying up)
Providing engaging activities for children	Arranging the child's physical and social environment with persons, objects, materials and age-appropriate toys	All ages	Board games, paper, paints, pens, tapes, books, construction toys, balls

Table 20.4 (*continued*)

Type of strategy	Description	Recommended age (years)	Applications
Weakening or reducing problem behaviour			
Establishing ground rules	Involves negotiating in advance a set of fair, specific, and enforceable rules which apply in particular situations	4–12	Rules for watching TV, shopping trips, visiting relatives, going out in the car
Directed discussion	The repeated rehearsal of the correct behaviour contingent on rule-breaking	4–10	Leaving school bag on floor in kitchen, leaving a mess on the table
Good-behaviour charts	A simple token economy involving the provision of social attention and back-up rewards contingent on the absence of undesired behaviour or following the performance of desired alternative behaviour	3–9	Doing homework, playing cooperatively, speaking pleasantly when making requests, telling the truth, staying calm
Terminating instructions	A formal of verbal reprimand involving a description of the incorrect and correct alternative behaviour	2–8	Touching electrical outlets, dangerous play (e.g. pulling cat's tail), hitting baby, pulling another child's hair
Logical consequences	The provision of a specific consequences which involves either the removal of an activity from the child or the child from an activity	4–12	Leaving a bike or toys in the hall, leaving the computer turned on
Quiet time	Placing a child in chair or bean bag in the same environment as other family members for a specified time	1–5	Squealing, temper outbursts, whining, demanding, hitting, non-compliance
Time out	The removal of a child to an area away from other family members for a specified time period contingent on a problem behaviour	1–9	Swearing, stealing, aggressive behaviour, tantrums
Planned ignoring	Extinction—the withdrawal of attention while the problem behaviour continues	1–7	Answering back, protesting after providing a punishing consequence, crying and whining
Planned activities	Providing engaging activities in specific high-risk situations	All ages	Out-of-home disruptions (e.g. shopping trips, visiting, travelling in a car, bus, train)

Adjunctive Intervention for Promoting Partner Support

Once behavioural parent training has been completed, and usually significant improvements in the child's behaviour have occurred, Partner Support Training (PST) can commence. PST is a brief adjunctive intervention, designed to facilitate parent training through cooperative, supportive parenting (Dadds et al., 1987a,b). The intervention can be completed within three sessions and encourages parents to: (a) communicate on a daily basis over child-rearing matters; (b) provide support for one another to use the child management strategies; and (c) use problem-solving skills to resolve conflict in a mutually acceptable manner. Table 20.5 presents an overview of the three strategies taught in PST, namely casual conversations, partner support and problem-solving. Each of the components of PST is rehearsed with the parents in sessions until reasonable mastery is obtained by both parents.

In PST, parents are taught to make interested inquiries about each other's daily parenting experience, not to interfere with each other's discipline attempts, to provide constructive, non-judgemental feedback on parent–child interactions, and to use problem-solving discussions to resolve disagreements regarding parenting issues (Sanders & Dadds, 1993). These skills are particularly important when parents need to be consistent to change their child's behaviour, or when couples have conflicting views on parenting. For example, many couples in stepfamilies have a history of battling over parenting, with each attempting to compensate for the perceived failings of the other. Partner support training for these couples can result in considerable gains in both the child's behaviour and the couple's relationship satisfaction.

Casual conversations involve setting aside some time on a daily basis to talk about the children and child-rearing issues in a fairly informal way. Casual conversations serve to: (a) keep parents up-to-date about what is happening in the family; (b) provide parents with the opportunity to support one another; (c) enable parents to share positive parenting experiences; and (d) promote consistency between parents using positive parenting strategies. Parents can be encouraged to identify a typical home situation in which this strategy could be used and to practice the strategy within the session.

To increase the likelihood that casual conversations will be effective, parents should plan their discussions for a time when both are able to listen and take part in the conversation. It is not a good idea for a parent to "dump" on their partner as soon as they walk through the door. Parents should be prompted to stop discussions as soon as one or both partners feels uncomfortable. Subsequently, a problem-solving discussion can be scheduled to identify the problem, decide on a solution and implement the plan.

The provision of partner support for use when a child behaviour problem occurs helps parents be consistent in their use of the positive parenting strategies. Parental consistency is essential when trying to change a child's pattern of behaviour. Through supportive interactions, parents can work together to show their children that they are a united team which cannot be undermined. This compo-

Table 20.5 Therapeutic components of partner support training

Casual conversations	Partner support	Problem-solving discussions
Ask your partner about their day. Show you are listening and interested	Remain calm, speak in a calm voice	Agree on a convenient time and place to talk to each other about any problems currently occurring. It should be when you are both calm and will not be interrupted by the children
Ask how the children have behaved in your absence	Try not to interfere if your partner is dealing with the child. That is, don't come to the rescue by being the tough parent. The parent who gave the instruction to the child should see it through	
If there have been no problems, ask what the children have been doing and give positive feedback to your partner		Identify the problem behaviour as specifically as possible. Write down the problem as clearly as possible. Check that you both agree on what needs change. Deal with one problem at a time
If a problem occurred, ask for a clear description of what happened. Listen carefully and show that you are listening and interested	Help your partner if he/she asks or obviously needs it. For example, if your partner is looking after one child and the other children start to misbehave, you could help by taking the other children	
		Brainstorm together, thinking of as many solutions as possible. Write them down
Ask how you partner dealt with the situation. Again show that you are listening and interested	Back each other up by NOT giving contradictory instructions to the child	Discuss each solution, weighing its pros and cons, its likelihood of success, whether it is practical to use, and any problems that might arise
Offer to do something to help avoid the problem next time	Do NOT comment on your partner's behaviour until after the incident is over and you are more relaxed. Do NOT blame or criticize each other	Choose the best solution(s) by mutual agreement
If your partner had trouble handling the problem: (a) give positive feedback on any successful aspects of their attempt; (b) arrange a time for a problem-solving discussion	After the problem is over discuss it together in private and if necessary, arrange a problem-solving discussion	Plan a strategy for using the solution. Be specific, working out exactly what you will both do and say when the problem occurs
		Review how the solution is working by arranging another meeting

nent of PST focuses on the parent's ability to avoid starting, or to quickly resolve, an escalating conflict situation. If needed, parents can schedule a problem-solving discussion for later when they are both calm.

Couples can find it difficult to work together when they have differing views on how the family should operate, such as disagreements over what is unacceptable behaviour or about how children should be disciplined, or one parent may be tough while the other is soft. Parents who do not work together often end up undermining each other's efforts in the family. As a result their relationship with each other, and the quality of their family life, may suffer.

The therapist can work through the suggestions described in Table 20.5 with the parents and identify some common situations in which partner support skills could be used (e.g. whenever a child behaviour problem occurs and both parents are present; dinner time when Mum is feeding the children; bed time when Dad is putting the children to bed). Part of this process involves parents giving constructive feedback to their partner about the use of the child management strategies. For those couples who show deficits in positive communication skills, the therapist may need to highlight constructive communication styles and strategies for giving and receiving feedback.

To allow parents to deal with family problems without outside help, they are taught to hold problem-solving discussions. These discussions promote: (a) parental agreement on household rules and discipline strategies; (b) parents' ability to formulate specific plans for overcoming problems; and (c) discussion of problems when both parents are relaxed and able to concentrate. Problem-solving discussions provide a fair way of resolving problems and generally lead to creative solutions which satisfy both partners. This approach can be used to address a range of family problems from child management issues, to how to spend more time together as a couple, to choosing a new car.

When teaching parents problem-solving, the clinician can prompt the parents to choose a problem which does not have a high level of emotional involvement attached to it (a "cool to warm" topic), rather than an issue that one or both parents feels very strongly about (a "hot" topic). The problems that are best suited to this approach are those where there are a number of possible solutions. Subsequently, in a step-by-step fashion, the clinician can rehearse the problem-solving procedure with the parents by taking the role of facilitator and director of the discussion. The clinician's role is to keep the parents on task, to encourage both parents to contribute equally to the discussion, and to reinforce the parent's generation of creative solutions.

Process Issues

Often in the context of a child referral only one parent, usually the mother, attends the initial appointment. However, it is important to obtain the perspective of both parents, especially when marital problems are indicated. Fathers should therefore be encouraged to attend appointments. In our clinical experience, a personal invitation to the father via the telephone can be effective in involving fathers in the treatment process. Once permission from the mother has been obtained to contact the father, the clinician can express the opinion that they need the father, who is an expert in their family situation and their child's problem, to help. If a father chooses not to attend, the mother should not be denied access to treatment.

A trusting relationship between the parents and clinician is needed before the relationship between the child's problems, the parents' management strategies and any marital problems can be explored (Sanders & Dadds, 1993). During the initial interview, it is important for the clinician to establish relationships with the parents and children individually. Parents who feel their clinician blamed them for their child's problem, or did not listen to their perception of the problem, are likely to drop out of therapy.

Once a trusting relationship and a shared perspective of the problems has been established by the parents and clinician, the treatment phase can commence. Initially, with a child referral, the focus will be on solving the child's problem. During this time, marital issues that arise during the sessions should be acknowledge and noted for later discussion. As the child's behaviour improves the clinician can focus more on the marital relationship, using the examples collated during the early treatment phase.

Referral

If the child behaviour problem is severe and remains unresolved after intervention, the child should be referred to a child specialist for more intensive treatment and evaluation. Some marital therapists deal with child problems by referring parents to a parent training group after marital therapy is completed. This strategy is not always successful, simply because the ongoing distress of parenting an out-of-control child can prevent adequate focus on the marital concerns. Many of these problems are best dealt with concurrently rather than sequentially, with the degree of emphasis changing across consecutive sessions.

Summary

Mild child behaviour problems can be effectively treated with brief minimal interventions in the context of a marital referral. However, when the child's behaviour problems are severe or are the main source of referral, more intensive behavioural parent training procedures will be necessary. In the context of a child referral, partner support training can be a useful intervention as an adjunct to parent training for helping couples work together as a team. However, PST requires both spouses to participate. In addition, couples must agree to suspend dealing with any marital issues until they have learned some basic child-management skills. However, by focusing on the child's problem first, the likelihood of successfully intervening with the marital relationship is enhanced (Sanders & Dadds, 1993). The following section presents a treatment program for concurrent marital and child problems in step-families.

INTERVENTIONS IN THE CONTEXT OF PARENTAL REMARRIAGE

There has been little empirical research investigating the effectiveness of interventions for either child behaviour problems or couple's relationship problems in step-families (Lawton & Sanders, 1994; Sanders, Nicholson & Floyd, this volume). In a randomized controlled trial, Nicholson and Sanders (Lawton & Sanders, 1994; Nicholson & Sanders, 1994) examined the efficacy of a behavioural intervention combining parent training, partner support techniques, and strategies for enhancing family communication and family relationships. Compared to a wait list control group, the intervention was successful at producing reductions in child behaviour problems, with concomitant improvements in the couple's relationship for some families. However, a number of important differences exist between the conduct of interventions with nuclear families and step-families. Some of these differences are discussed next and illustrated with a case example.

Assessment

When couples who have children from a former relationship (i.e. step-families) present for therapy, regardless of the reason for presentation, it is important to assess both the couple's relationship and child adjustment. Remarried couples typically present for one of three problems: couple relationship problems, step-parent–child relationship problems, or child behavioural or adjustment problems. However, in our experience it is rare for problems to be limited to one of these areas. Typically, all three areas need to be addressed by an intervention.

Distressed couples in remarriages can be somewhat unusual in their presenting symptoms. We have commonly encountered couples who claim to be very satisfied in their couple relationship, but are considering separation. For these couples, distress may be concentrated around the step-parent–child relationship or parenting issues. Over time these problems erode the couple relationship, but a surprising number of remarried couples will report high levels of global relationship satisfaction, right up until the time at which they separate. In assessment with step-families it is therefore important to assess both global measures of relationship distress and also the steps the couple may have taken toward initiating a separation.

Intervention Components

With step-families, it can be difficult to determine whether to commence therapy with a primary focus on the couple or on parenting. Again, as a general rule of thumb, it is best to start with the presenting complaint, and integrate other aspects as therapy progresses. For example, for couples presenting with child behavioural problems or step-parent–child relationship problems we found that parent training followed by partner support and family relationship skills was effective (Lawton & Sanders, 1994; Nicholson & Sanders, 1994). For remarried couples presenting for relationship enhancement, we are currently evaluating an intervention which commences with a focus on couples' relationship skills, and then addresses broader parenting and family issues (Nicholson et al., 1995). With these couples we introduced the parenting focus by using parenting issues as topics for discussion when couples rehearsed their communication skills. We took care to ensure that low-conflict topics were selected initially, with couples tackling progressively more difficult topics as their conflict management skills progressed.

Family meetings has been one of the most positively evaluated aspects of programs we have conducted for couples from step-families. Family meetings provide a structured forum for democratic decision-making and family-based problem-solving (Dinkmeyer, McKay & McKay, 1987). Topics which can be covered at family meetings include reviewing children's achievements, planning future family activities, discussing rules and solving problems. Family meetings can be conducted formally with a set agenda, a chairperson and secretary. Decisions made at meetings are recorded and the outcome of any action is reviewed at the next meeting. Family meetings prompt parents and step-parents to communicate on a regular basis with their children. Family members are encouraged to share decision-making, and brain-storming can lead to creative solutions to family problems.

Parent training and couples interventions fail to address one area of family functioning which is important for step-families. Troubled step-families may require specific interventions for fostering family relationship. This is partly addressed through the positive parenting strategies which encourage parent–child interactions, and through couple's relationship enhancement skills. However, broader family relationships are not addressed well by these approaches. We have developed a set of techniques we call Planned Family Activities Training (PFAT; Lawton & Sanders, 1994) which aim to enhance the family environment by promoting positive interactions within the family. Family cohesion is fostered by increasing the number of "special" planned activities family members undertake together. Parents are encouraged to use problem-solving skills to plan new activities with their children. The strategies employed include: (a) planning regular family outings and activities which everyone can enjoy and participate in (e.g. trips to playgrounds, amusement parks, picnics, sporting activities, car trips, etc.); (b) gradual development of a set of "traditional" activities which are unique to the family (e.g. Friday night family dinners, family meetings for planning weekend activities, monthly games nights); and (c) provision of opportunities for step-parent and child to develop a positive relationship (e.g. step-parent helping child accomplish a new skill, attending a sports match together, working together on a project in the house or yard).

PFAT focuses attention on positive aspects of family development, prompting parents and step-parents to actively create a healthy family environment. These strategies require advanced skills from parents. Therefore, PFAT may not be effective until substantial changes are apparent in the child's behaviour or the couple's relationship.

Process Issues

When parent training strategies are employed with remarried couples, a number of important process issues need to be addressed. First, common assumptions about parenting roles may not be applicable to couples in step-families. Indeed, step-family members seeking therapy frequently complain of therapists using a nuclear family model of functioning (Lawton & Sanders, 1994). In parent training and PST it is easy for therapists to give the impression that optimal family functioning involves both parent and step-parent taking an active role in all aspects of child-rearing. In fact, this is contrary to the empirical research, which suggests that step-family dysfunction is likely when step-parents quickly assume active disciplinary roles (Hetherington, Arnett & Hollier, 1988). Therapy may be facilitated by the therapist's initiation of discussions about the step-parent's role in the family, and active encouragement for couples to use their growing problem-solving skills to negotiate and develop interaction patterns which best fit their family.

A second key process issue for conducting interventions with step-families concerns the accurate identification and handling of resistance. Couples can be reluctant to change their parenting approaches, especially if they are convinced that it is their partner's behaviour which is inappropriate. In this situation, early introduction of partner support techniques accompanied by clear negotiation of parenting roles may be critical to treatment outcome. The following example illustrates this problem.

Case Example

Ian and Margaret had been married for 3 years when they presented for therapy for relationship problems. The couple lived with Margaret's school-age children. During her time as a single parent, Margaret admitted that she had been some-what lax with discipline. However, as long as things got done sometime, she was not too concerned. Ian disapproved of the lack of rule enforcement. He believed that children should comply immediately with adult requests. Over time, this couple become progressively polarized in their parenting, with each trying to compensate for the other's perceived failings. Margaret believed that her children were getting too much discipline from Ian, so she backed off from this, and at times, reversed or undermined Ian's decisions. Ian, in turn, became progressively tougher with the children, feeling that "if he didn't do it, no one would". Both reported feeling frustrated and unsupported, and the children were resentful toward Ian.

During parent training this couple showed considerable resistance, which could have threatened the therapy process. Margaret was reluctant to adopt a stricter disciplinary approach when she perceived Ian as already too harsh with the children. Also Ian believed his strict approach needed to be maintained because of Margaret's lack of activity in this area. With this couple, it was necessary to negotiate a shared parenting approach, with both agreeing to give a little in order to work together. In the feedback of assessment results, it was important to illustrate the impact of the inconsistent parenting, while conveying an understanding of each partner's position. For Margaret, key behavioural goals were: to increase appropriate responding to problem behaviour from the children, express her support for Ian to the children, and not to criticise, argue or over-ride Ian's decisions. In turn, Ian agreed to stand back and let Margaret handle the discipline, and to focus on spending quality time with the children. Both agreed to hold regular reviews of parenting to ensure that the children's behaviour was being dealt with appropriately, and the couple were encouraged to use their growing communication and problem-solving skills to negotiate how to respond to problems.

CONCLUSION

This chapter demonstrates the critical importance of addressing parenting and child management problems in the context of marital therapy. It is tempting from this analysis to conclude that a family focus to intervention is always necessary in working with distressed couples with children. However, it is important to note that many couples make excellent progress on their marital relationship without intensive focus on parenting issues. The key is to demonstrate rather than assume a functional relationship between child and marital problems. This requires close attention to the day-to-day co-variation between marital stress and child problems, as well as parents' own view on the relationship between parenting problems and their marriage.

A major obstacle to successfully integrated marital and child interventions is that many marital therapists have not had adequate specialized training in the management of child behaviour problems. Similarly, too few child specialists have adequate training in marital therapy skills. Despite this limitation, some kinds of child problems respond well to relatively brief interventions (e.g. getting children to sleep in their own beds). The challenge is to develop empirically tested decision rules to help the clinician decide who should receive what intervention.

The complexity of the relationship between marital and child problems is complicated further by the changing patterns of family formation with divorce, co-parenting and repartnering becoming increasingly common. Within a single therapy situation, the possible number of relationship combinations can be very complex. For example, a couple may have children from both previous marriages, who are co-parented by former spouses and their new partners, who may also have children from previous relationships, as well as their own children from the current marriage.

There is some evidence to show that long-term outcomes are enhanced in cases where both child and marital problems exist when both areas are tackled within therapy. However, there are many unanswered questions that need to be addressed in future research. Research on the relationship between marital distress and child-focused treatment must begin reporting more extensive information about the dimensions of marital distress that may be critical to long-term effectiveness of child-focused treatment.

Selection of a suitable level of therapeutic intervention for families is an important consideration in therapy. Face-to-face therapy may be burdensome for some couples with large, young families or where both parents work. The optimal level of intervention may be determined by the skills family members display at initial contact. Families vary in their pre-existing skills, with some needing substantial therapist guidance while others respond well to minimal interventions. Our research suggests that self-help materials that are carefully designed along behavioural principles can provide effective alternatives to therapist-directed interventions for families who show moderate levels of distress (Lawton & Sanders, 1993; Markie-Dadds & Sanders, 1994). The disadvantages of self-help programs include the potential burden for parents living in chaotic households or for those with poor reading skills, and they are not recommended for couples experiencing severe problems, especially marital conflict.

Most studies have relied on measures of marital satisfaction such as the Locke–Wallace Marital Adjustment Test (Locke & Wallace, 1959). Other dimensions of marital distress relevant to children include the specific nature of the marital distress (i.e. to what extent it implicates the child, either directly or indirectly), whether the marital problem involves spousal violence (and if so the type and severity); and how far towards separation or divorce couples have reached (e.g. has either partner consulted a solicitor?). It would also be useful to know more about children's current coping repertoire for dealing with their parents' marital distress.

Acknowledgements

This work was partly supported by the National Health and Medical Research Council of Australia (Grants 920182, 954213, 940001). The third author published under the name Jan M. Lawton until 1994.

REFERENCES

Achenbach, T.M. & Edelbrock, C.S. (1983). *Manual for the Child Behavior Checklist and Revised Child Behaviour Profile.* Burlington, VT: Department of Psychiatry, University of Vermont.

Amato, P.R. & Keith, B. (1991). Separation from a parent during childhood and adult socio-economic attainment. *Social Forces,* **70**, 187–206.

Arnold, D.S., O'Leary, S.G., Wolff, L.S. & Acker, M.M. (1993). The Parenting Scale: a measure of dysfunctional parenting in discipline situations. *Psychological Assessment,* **5**, 137–144.

Chamberlain, P. & Reid, J.B. (1987). Parent observation and report of child symptoms. *Behavioural Assessment,* **9**, 97–109.

Cole, C. & Morrow, W.R. (1976). Refractory parent behaviours in behaviour modification training groups. *Psychotherapy: Theory, Research and Practice,* **13**, 162–169.

Connell, S., Sanders M.R. & Markie-Dodds, C. (in press). Self-directed behavioral family intervention for parents of oppositional children in rural and remote creas. *Behavior Modification.*

Coopersmith, S. (1981). *SEI—Self-esteem Inventories.* Palo Alto, CA: Consulting Psychologists Press.

Dadds, M.R. (1992). Concurrent treatment of marital and child behaviour problems in behavioural family therapy. *Behaviour Change,* **9**, 139–148.

Dadds, M.R. & Powell, M.B. (1991). The relationship of interparental conflict and global marital adjustment to aggression, anxiety, and immaturity in aggressive and non-clinic children. *Journal of Abnormal Child Psychology,* **19**, 553–567.

Dadds, M.R., Sanders, M.R. & James, J.E. (1987a). Enhancing generalization effects in parent training: the role of planned activities and social support. *Behavioural Psychotherapy,* **15**, 289–313.

Dadds, M.R., Schwartz, S. & Sanders, M.R. (1987b). Marital discord and treatment outcome in the treatment of childhood conduct disorders. *Journal of Consulting & Clinical Psychology,* **55**, 396–403.

Dinkmeyer, D., McKay, G.D. & McKay, J.L. (1987). *New Beginnings: Skills for Single Parents and Step-family Parents. Parent's manual.* Champaign, IL: Research Press.

Emery, R.E. (1982). Interparental conflict and the children of discord and divorce. *Psychological Bulletin,* **9**, 310–330.

Emery, R.E. (1988). Children in the divorce process. *Journal of Family Psychology,* **42**, 141–144.

Eyberg, S.M. & Robinson, E.A. (1983). Conduct problem behavior: standardization of a behavior rating scale with adolescents. *Journal of Clinical Child Psychology,* **12**, 347–354.

Grych, J.H. & Fincham, F.D. (1990). Marital conflict and children's adjustment. *Psychological Bulletin,* **108**, 267–290.

Fantuzzo, J.W., DePaola, L.M., Lambert, L., Martino, T. et al. (1991). Effects of interparental violence on the psychological adjustment and competencies of young children. *Journal of Consulting and Clinical Psychology,* **59**, 258–265.

Forehand, R., Griest, D.L., Wells, K. & McMahon, R.J. (1982). Side effects of parent counseling on marital satisfaction. *Journal of Counseling Psychology,* **29**, 104–107.

Funderburk, B.W. & Eyberg, S.M. (1989). Psychometric characteristics of the Sutter–Eyberg Student Behavior Inventory: a school behaviour rating scale for use with preschool children. *Behavioral Assessment,* **11**, 297–313.

Hetherington, E.M., Arnett, J.D. & Hollier, E.A. (1988). Adjustment of parents and children to remarriage. In S.A. Wolchik & P. Karoly (eds), *Children of Divorce: Empirical Perspectives on Adjustment* (pp. 67–107). New York: Gardner.

Johnston, C. & Mash, E.J. (1989). A measure of parenting satisfaction and efficacy. *Journal of Clinical Child Psychiatry*, **18**, 167–175.

Kent, R.N. & O'Leary, K.D. (1976). A controlled evaluation of behaviour modification with conduct problem children. *Journal of Consulting and Clinical Psychology*, **44**, 586–596.

Kovacs, M. (1981). Rating scales to assess depression in school-aged children. *Acta Paedopsychiatrica*, **46**, 305–315.

Lawton, J.M. & Sanders, M.R. (1993). A controlled evaluation of behavioural family intervention for children with disruptive behaviour problems in stepfamilies. Paper presented at the Association for the Advancement of Behaviour Therapy Annual Convention, Atlanta, USA, 18–21 November.

Lawton, J.M. & Sanders, M.R. (1994). Designing effective behavioural family interventions for stepfamilies. *Clinical Psychology Review*, **5**, 463–496.

Locke, H.J. & Wallace, K.M. (1959). Short-term marital adjustment and prediction tests: their reliability and validity. *Journal of Marriage and the Family*, **21**, 251–255.

Lovibond, P.F. & Lovibond, S.H. (1995). The structure of negative emotional states: comparison of the Depression Anxiety Stress Scales (DASS) with the Beck Depression and Anxiety Inventories. *Behaviour Research and Therapy*, **33**, 335–343.

Markie-Dadds, C. & Sanders, M.R. (1994). Self-directed interventions and the prevention of conduct problems. Paper presented at the 28th Annual Convention of the Association for the Advancement of Behavior Therapy, San Diego, USA, November.

Nicholson, J.M., Halford, W.K. & Sanders, M.R. (1995). *Stepfamilies Preparation Program*. School of Public Health, Queensland University of Technology.

Nicholson, J.M. & Sanders, M.R. (1994). Helping troubled step-families: Programs for parents and step-parents. Paper presented at the International Year of the Family Conference, Adelaide, Australia, 20–23 November.

Reynolds, C.R. & Richmond, B.O. (1978). What I Think and Feel: a revised measure of children's manifest anxiety. *Journal of Abnormal Child Psychology*, **6**, 271–280.

Sanders, M.R. (1996). Advances in behavioural family intervention with children. In T. Ollendick & R. Prinz (eds), *Advances in Clinical Child Psychology*, vol. 18 (pp. 283–330). New York: Plenum Press.

Sanders, M.R. (1992). *Every Parent: a Positive Guide to Children's Behaviour*. Sydney: Addison-Wesley.

Sanders, M.R. & Dadds, M.R. (1982). The effects of planned activities and child management training: an analysis of setting generality. *Behaviour Therapy*, **13**, 1–11.

Sanders, M.R. & Dadds, M.R. (1993). *Behavioral Family Intervention*. Needham Heights, MA: Allyn & Bacon.

Sanders, M.R. & Glynn, T. (1981). Training parents in behavioral self-management: an analysis of generalization and maintenance. *Journal of Applied Behavior Analysis*, **14**, 223–237.

Sanders, M.R., Lynch, M.E. & Markie-Dadds, C. (1994). *Every Parent's Workbook: a Positive Guide to Positive Parenting*. Brisbane: Australian Academic Press.

Sanders, M.R. & Lawton, J.M. (1993). Therapeutic process issues in the assessment of family problems: the guided participation model of information transfer. *Child and Family Behaviour Therapy*, **15**, 5–35.

Sanders, M.R. & Markie-Dadds, C. (1996). Triple P: a multilevel family intervention program for children with disruptive behaviour disorders. In P. Cotton & H. Jackson (eds), *Early Intervention and Preventive Mental Health Applications of Clinical Psychology* (pp. 59–85). Melbourne. Australian Psychological Society.

Sayger, T.V., Home, A.M. & Glaser, B.A. (1993). Marital satisfaction and social learning family therapy for child conduct problems: generalization of treatment effects. *Journal of Marital and Family Therapy*, **19**, 393–402.

Webster-Stratton, C. & Hammond, M. (1988). Maternal depression and its relationship to life stress, perceptions of child behaviour problems, parenting behaviours and child conduct problems. *Journal of Abnormal Child Psychology*, **16**, 299–315.

Chapter 21

Marital Discord and Depression

Hyman Hops*, Barbara Anne Perry** and Betsy Davis*
*Oregon Research Institute; and
**Private Practice, Eugene, OR, USA

MARITAL DISCORD AND DEPRESSION: TWO MAJOR SOCIAL PROBLEMS

Two separate indices of social distress, the prevalence of affective disorders and the rates of divorce, have captured our attention in the past two decades. Affective disorders, sometimes referred to as the "common cold" of mental health (e.g. Beach, Sandeen & O'Leary, 1990), have been shown to have lifetime prevalence rates ranging from 8.3%, as reported in the United States National Institute of Mental Health Epidemiologic Catchment Studies (ECA; Regier et al., 1988), to 19.3%, found in the more recent and methodologically improved National Comorbidity Study (NCS; Kessler et al., 1994). The NCS findings approximate the 20.9% found in the Oregon Adolescent Depression Project (Lewinsohn et al., 1993), indicating a fast-declining age of onset of depression, with lifetime rates among 14–18-year-old adolescents similar to those of adults. An examination of divorce rates over time (National Center for Health Statistics) shows the proportions of marriage ending in divorce escalating from 1970 (approximately 33%) to 1993 (approximately 50%), with some estimating a further increasing trend (e.g. Gottman, 1994).

When depression is examined within the context of marriage or committed relationships, both problems appear intensified. Approximately 50% of women who are maritally distressed are depressed and 50% of women who are depressed are maritally dissatisfied (see Beach, Sandeen & O'Leary, 1990). Other studies have found similar evidence of overlap for both men and women. O'Leary, Christian, and Mendell (1994), for example, found the odds of being depressed

Clinical Handbook of Marriage and Couples Interventions. Edited by W. Kim Halford and Howard J. Markman.

increased 10-fold in the presence of marital discord, regardless of gender. The extensive overlap between depression and marital discord has led some to speculate as to whether there is a causal influence between these two problematic situations. Although research to date is inconclusive on the specific direction of the proposed causality (e.g. Jacobson, Holtzworth-Munroe & Schmaling, 1989; Schmaling & Jacobson, 1990), the overlap does suggest there may be common aspects of both problems that lend themselves to common treatments. As we shall show, even in the absence of definitive knowledge of the causal links between marital discord and depression, in the presence of both, the direction of treatment focus is more clear-cut.

The purpose of the present chapter is to provide a general framework within which to approach the problem of co-existing depressive symptomatology and marital discord. The framework draws upon current theoretical models and the few available treatment outcome studies. Acknowledging that certain interactional patterns displayed in the microcosm of marriage are created and shaped by the large social environment, we will pinpoint developmental, historical and gender-role socialization factors that are likely to have an impact on the efficacy of certain treatment facets. A case study will also be presented in which the recognition of both depressive symptomatology and marital discord was essential to successful treatment. Finally, we will present some cautions on when conjoint therapy may be contraindicated, and some notions on future directions necessary for addressing the weaknesses of current assessment and intervention procedures.

THE TREATMENT OF MARITAL DISCORD AND DEPRESSION

The search for the most efficacious therapeutic approach to the treatment of co-existing marital discord and depression has focused on either intrapersonal models designed to address depressive disorders (e.g. Beck, 1983) or interpersonal variations designed to address marital relationship problems (e.g. Beach, Sandeen & O'Leary, 1990; Jacobson et al., 1991). While the causal links between marital discord and depression remain uncertain, research examining the superiority of one treatment approach over the other appears more conclusive.

Although few treatment outcome studies have been carried out, those that exist show consistently that treatment approaches focusing on the depressed individual in isolation may help to alleviate depressive symptoms but are of little help in changing either discordant marital interactions or the couple's views of the marital relationship or their partner (Beach & O'Leary, 1992; Jacobson et al., 1991; O'Leary & Beach, 1990). This may not be surprising if we consider that: (a) marital discord has been shown to be a common correlate of, and possible precursor to, major depressive episodes (e.g. Weissman, 1987); (b) marital relationships remain problematic even after the depressive episodes have ended (Weissman & Paykel, 1974); and (c) studies have linked the dysfunctional interaction patterns of depressed persons to the etiology and maintenance of marital dissatisfaction (Biglan et al., 1985; Biglan, Hops & Sherman, 1988). Research conducted over nearly three decades, regardless of its theoretical base, has consistently shown problematic social relationships among depressed individuals (e.g. Biglan et al., 1985; Coyne et al., 1987; Gotlib & Colby, 1987; Hops et al., 1987; Klerman et al., 1984; Lewinsohn & Shaw, 1969; Weissman & Paykel, 1974). Thus, it does not make sense from a treatment perspective to treat depressive symptoms as if they were completely independent of the marital relationship, given that the discord is likely to trigger increases in depressive symptomatology and the likelihood of a depressive relapse.

The most consistent finding of the few treatment studies conducted is that conjoint interventions, focusing on the enhancement of communication, intimacy and interpersonal interactions within the dyadic relationship, are the most efficacious route to both improvement in the marital relationship and alleviation of depressive symptomatology (Jacobson et al., 1991, 1993; Koerner, Prince & Jacobson, 1994; Beach & O'Leary, 1992; O'Leary & Beach, 1990)[1]. Why are therapies that involve the dyad more successful in addressing the co-existence of marital discord and depression than therapies designed solely for depression? As noted above, interpersonal difficulties are common characteristics of both depressive disorders and marital discord. A significant feature of successful ongoing relationships is the ability to accommodate to change in the partner's behavior over time. Stress increases if this accommodation is difficult. To reduce distress within the relationship, couples therapies focus on the spouses' abilities to change with their partners' wishes through accommodation, compromise and behavior change (Jacobson, 1992). If traditional therapies aimed at strengthening the marital relationship through behavior change (e.g. Jacobson & Margolin, 1979) can have a beneficial impact on dysfunctional interactional patterns related to marital distress, it is not surprising that these same therapies have been shown to be effective at treating depression, with its associated dysfunctional interactional styles within distressed couples (Jacobson et al., 1991; O'Leary & Beach, 1990). Further theoretical support for the inclusion of the spouse in the therapeutic process can be seen in the partially successful attempt to add a social component (Foley et al., 1989) to a traditional intrapersonal therapy for addressing depression alone (Klerman et al., 1984).

A SOCIAL–INTERACTIONAL DEVELOPMENTAL PERSPECTIVE

A parsimonious framework within which to integrate the findings of treatment studies regarding the complex interplay between marital discord and depression draws upon a social–interactional perspective (Cairns, 1979; Patterson, 1982)

---

[1] This conclusion should be tempered in that much of the work on couples therapy has not included severely depressed or hospitalized patients. Furthermore, recruiting willing spouses in a severely distressed population may prove more difficult as well. Thus, practitioners should be aware that the efficacy of behavioral marital intervention within this population has not been fully tested.

within a developmental framework. This theoretical perspective emphasizes the importance of behavior within a responsive social environment and suggests that the interactional patterns within salient contexts are key targets for change.

The marital relationship can be conceptualized as one of the most powerful interpersonal contexts that people can encounter. More specifically, marriage is entered into by individuals with singular interactional styles, as well as unique expectations and perceptions of the relationship and the quality and quantity of the partner's contributions (Koerner et al., 1994; Baucom, 1994). To the extent that these interpersonal behavior patterns, expectations and perceptions are incompatible, discord within the relationship is inevitable.

As mentioned above, the dysfunctional interactional patterns of depressed persons have been linked to the etiology and maintenance of marital dissatisfaction (e.g. Biglan et al., 1985; Nelson & Beach, 1990). Add to these findings research linking the stress of marital discord with depressive episodes (e.g. Weissman, 1987), and the complex interplay between the dysfunctional interactional patterns displayed by the depressed individual, and the discordant couple is understandable: so understandable, in fact, that to disregard the existence of one in the treatment of the other can only serve to weaken intervention efforts. This interplay can lead to a negative spiral of coercive and detrimental interactions (Patterson & Reid, 1970; Weiss, Hops & Patterson, 1973) that, if left unattended, destines the depressed individual to future episodes of depression and the marital relationship to further discord.

Gender Effects and Developmental Trajectories

What variables contribute to the incompatibility of interactional styles and thereby the negative spiral of dysfunctional interactions within marriage? Society itself may be responsible, in part, by socializing gender roles that predispose males and females to potentially conflictual interactional patterns (Maccoby, 1990), especially when placed within the context of the intimacy and intensity of marriage. Cultural expectations are presumed to work at the level of the family via the shaping of gender-specific behavior patterns very early on in an individual's life. Reviews of the developmental and clinical literature (e.g. Hops, Sherman & Biglan, 1990; Kavanagh & Hops, 1994) suggest that as a result of a differential social reinforcement history, males and females behave in ways that can be considered incompatible, with the behavior patterns becoming more divergent with increasing age. This incompatibility may lead to difficulties in heterosexual relationships under normal circumstances (see Maccoby, 1990) and exacerbate the difficulties under more stressful conditions. As a result, socialization practices produce women who are more sensitive to relationship issues, communicate more equitably, and respond to distress in ways that are more emotional and less aggressive or assertive. Men, on the other hand, are more aggressive and assertive, respond to stress with more instrumental, problem-solving behaviors and focus less on relationships compared to women.

Psychopathology may be conceptualized as gender-typic responses under highly stressful circumstances or the extreme effects of early shaping conditions (Hops, 1996; Kavanagh & Hops, 1994). As such, the socialization effects are consistent with the higher prevalence rates for depression among females and for more overt disorders, such as substance use or antisocial personality, among males during adolescence (Lewinsohn et al., 1993) and adulthood (Kessler et al., 1994). Previously, Hops (1992) delineated a number of skill deficits that are likely to exist in the repertoires of depressed adults. These include: (a) deficits in problem-solving and/or coping skills which severely limit their ability to manage stressful and/or aversive events; (b) the functional use of coercive tactics to ward off aversive behaviors of others; (c) limitations in affective repertoires, such as not being affectionate and expressing more sadness than joy in interactions with others; and (d) pessimism, irrational beliefs and negative views of the world. This pattern of responding is consistent with the view that women have been socialized to be less assertive and consequently more vulnerable and ineffective than men (Blechman, 1981; Radloff, 1975). While an unassertive depressive coping repertoire elicits more sympathetic responding and reduces aversive family interactions (Biglan, Hops & Sherman, 1988, 1989; Dumas, Gibson & Albin, 1989), empirical evidence shows that this is effective only in the short run (Biglan et al., 1985; Hops et al., 1987).

How do these socialized interactional patterns play out in the context of the therapeutic process? We will present a case study in which recognition of not only the patient's depression but also the potential of marital discord as a contributing factor was necessary to address the patient's needs fully. This case study highlights the importance of gender-socialization patterns and their incompatibility in creating and maintaining depressive symptomatology and marital discord. Specifically, it is a demonstration of gender differences in partners' reponses to increasing levels of frustration produced as the demands of family life change over time.

A CASE STUDY

Maddie sought help from her primary care physician for continuing symptoms of depression several months after the birth of twin girls. She had a history of depression at age 17 and again after the birth of her first child. Also, she indicated that at least three relatives had suffered from recurring bouts of depression. From a medical and historical perspective, there was enough information to suggest that a trial of anti-depressant medication was the logical first step in Maddie's treatment. However, after taking a prescribed antidepressant for about 3 weeks, she continued to feel as though she were at a "snapping point". Consequently, Maddie was referred to a mental health therapist by her primary care physician, and at the same time, was switched to a different anti-depressant.

Initial Assessment and Interview

Maddie came to the initial interview saying that she had put off seeking help because she felt she "was supposed to be able to handle [her] own problems". According to her responses on the Beck Depression Inventory (Beck et al., 1961), administered and discussed during the session, she was experiencing moderate symptoms of depression, including intense feelings of sadness and guilt, increasing irritability, problems with making decisions and extreme fatigue. An in-depth interview revealed no evidence of suicidal ideation or co-morbid psychopathology, but further evidence of depressive symptomatology such as irritability and self-denigrating thoughts. She experienced several "mini-rages" daily and frequently yelled at the children, causing her to question her parenting abilities.

Evidence of social isolation was also found. Her only out-of-the-house activity was a "twins club" meeting monthly, but she found them devoid of emotional support. Married 8 years to Mike, they lived with the 4-month-old twins, their 4-year-old daughter, and Mike's two older children, aged 10 and 12, from a previous relationship. The family had moved less than 2 years previously, leaving family and friends behind, and were finding it difficult to develop new friendships and activities. To make matters more stressful, Maddie discovered that she was "unexpectedly" pregnant with twin girls at about the same time she was accepted into a graduate degree program. Her pregnancy effectively delayed her re-entering school for at least a year and a half, and the birth of the twins required leaving her job, which had been a major source of gratification as well as a necessary source of income. She expressed how difficult it was being the primary caregiver for five children, and she complained that her husband seemed increasingly distant and unhelpful.

While Maddie struggled to care for the twins, she thought she would be "nagging" if she asked Mike to contribute to household duties. Wishing to avoid any overt conflict with her husband, she had never told him how unhappy, overwhelmed and lonely she was. She wanted more contact with him, but wanted him to make the first move to prove that he "really wanted" to be with her. On the rare occasions when they sat down together after the children were in bed, they usually shared a glass of wine or smoked marijuana to relax; however, one or both of them would fall asleep on the couch before going to bed.

Engaging the Partner

It became clear from the interview that, despite the likelihood of a biological base for Maddie's depressive mood, her social isolation and the lack of communication with her husband played a significant role in her feelings of frustration and irritability, and she readily agreed to ask Mike to join her at the next therapy session. Mike was offered, but declined, a prior individual session to allow him equal time to reveal his expectations for marriage, perceptions of Maddie's problems and commitment to the relationship.

The first joint session provided an opportunity for both Maddie and Mike to hear each other's perception of the situation. It also became clear that neither was aware of the other's view and both had entered an avoidant, non-productive interactive pattern. Since Mike had seen Maddie improve following her previous post-partum episode, he assumed that waiting this one out would also work. Consequently, he avoided interactions with her, spending most of the time with the two older children. He made some instrumental attempts to be helpful, such as taking care of the twins when he got home from work, to allow Maddie to rest. But this was not done at optimal times for either one. At that time of day, he preferred to be alone whereas Maddie was primed for adult interaction. Maddie had the opportunity to let Mike know how isolated and distraught she had become, and he acknowledged that caring for the twins was a chore. At the end of the session, both agreed that they wished they could resume their former happy relationship but they were not sure how they could accomplish that task.

Assessment of Marital Issues

Mike and Maddie were asked to complete and return a battery of instruments prior to their next joint meeting. These included the BDI; the Marital Status Inventory (MSI; Weiss & Cerreto, 1980), to determine the dissolution potential of the marriage; the Dyadic Adjustment Scale (DAS; Spanier, 1976), to assess the level of marital satisfaction; the Areas of Change Questionnaire (ACQ; Weiss & Birchler, 1975; Weiss, Hops & Patterson, 1973), to assess the partners' presenting complaints, their perceptions of one another's complaints, and the perceptual accuracy between actual and perceived complaints; and the Inventory of Rewarding Activities (IRA; Birchler & Weiss, 1977). They were also asked to write positive and negative comments about six different areas in their relationship (e.g. household management, affection and closeness, partner's work).

The assessment process was presented to the couple as an effective way to get a detailed picture of both the positive and negative aspects of their relationship and their strengths and weaknesses. This information would allow them, in consultation with the therapist, to design a course of therapy to fit their particular needs and goals.

As is typical of discordant couples, Maddie reported more distress than did Mike, although both were in the distressed range on the DAS (i.e. below 100). Similarly, not only did Maddie present a longer list of specific problem issues than did Mike, she was more accurate in her perception of Mike's desire for change than he was of hers.

Structuring the Assessment Feedback and Establishing Therapeutic Goals

The focus of the next session was to provide feedback to the couple based on the assessment and get the couple to agree on mutually acceptable therapeutic goals.

However, Mike's reluctance to pay for childcare appeared to jeopardize the therapeutic process. In fact, a previous session was cancelled because of a disagreement over this issue. As a result, blaming escalated. According to Maddie, Mike "obviously" did not care about her or the children. Not only was he a "skinflint" but he had "never" helped her with the children and "always" put his career above hers. Mike then began to list Maddie's faults and shortcomings. To prevent further conflict, the therapist changed the focus of the session to be more positive. Acknowledging the difficulties and frustrations, the therapist explained the likely downward spiral of negative interactions that increased their negative perceptions of each other. The therapist also explained that this "negative filter" tends to reinforce the view that their partner does not care, is a "jerk", won't do what they want, etc., by ignoring the more positive aspects of their partner's conduct. Moreover, as the partners become more frustrated and angry, their interaction becomes more negative, they engage in fewer satisfying activities together, further reinforcing their negative perceptions of each other. The therapist also pointed out that even events beyond their control (e.g. moving from friends and familiar activities, birth of twins, loss of job) impact upon their relationship and can be blamed on the partner. In summary, the therapist noted how the events of the past 2 years placed radically different demands on each one, forcing them to adopt more traditional roles, and draining their personal and financial resources. In this way, the therapist thwarted the blaming and name-calling for both members of the dyad.

Additionally, the therapist highlighted the potential strengths of the relationship and those of the individual members to provide some starting point for goal setting. Using the results of the assessment instruments, the therapist emphasized their commonalities, which showed how similar they were in their religious and educational background, their ideas abut childrearing, and the importance each placed on being active in the community. To encourage further movement and highlight their commitment to the relationship, the therapist noted that neither partner had given any indication of wanting to end the marriage. They had sought counseling primarily to improve the relationship, and they agreed, independently, on the major problem areas that needed attention. These were: handling family finances, sex/intimacy–togetherness, and dividing up household responsibilities. In addition, each had listed a broad range of joint activities they wanted to increase.

To end the session, the therapist sketched out a plan of action. First, Mike and Maddie needed to develop clear and effective communication skills. They tended to "mindread" the other, make many assumptions about the partner's wishes, and act on these without checking their accuracy. Second, they needed to develop strategies for enhancing the adult part of their relationship; virtually all of their time was spent on work, childrearing or household management. Maddie's and Mike's individually-conceived avoidant strategies exacerbated their problems and helped make the few positive exchanges in their relationship seem non-existent. Finally. they needed to learn effective ways to solve problems and negotiate conflict. When they accomplished those three major objectives, they could re-evaluate their relationship and decide whether to continue therapy.

Communication Skills Training

Sessions four and five focused on establishing clear and effective communication between Mike and Maddie. During therapy sessions, they were taught the standard set of skills, such as how to make pinpointed "I want . . ." statements, state clearly the intent of their remarks (e.g. whether they wanted to problem-solve or simply discuss their feelings about certain topics), paraphrase, and reflect the other's feeling statements. For homework, they were given practice assignments. Practice sessions typically started with less problematic issues until they mastered a skill, when they progressed to more difficult, emotionally laden topics.

It was an eye-opening experience for both partners. Maddie had no idea that Mike wanted to be much more involved with the twins but felt he would be encroaching on Maddie's "territory". Mike did not know that Maddie's silence at the end of the workday meant that she wanted him to help out with the twins. Both partners had been operating on assumptions they thought were valid instead of checking them out. Mike and Maddie had few problems with the communication skills exercises; both seemed pleased that they were actively working on their relationship, and Maddie's depressive symptoms appeared to have lessened.

Problem-solving, Negotiation and Increasing Relationship Benefits

An impasse and a slight regression was reached when the focus turned to "increasing relationship benefits". Although the use of communication skills had temporarily improved the relationship, it was, not surprisingly, insufficient. The "real world" continued to be stressful to Maddie. She was the one stuck at home, not improving professionally, whereas Mike was free to expand his pleasurable activities. She ruminated about this until negative thoughts about the relationship increased and she began withdrawing physically and emotionally from Mike, demonstrating a return to a depressive behavior pattern.

This seemed an apt time to introduce problem-solving and negotiation skills to see whether the couple could find some solution to specific issues. The relevant skills were introduced in the context of a change in the focus from quantity to quality. Yes, there were many things each of them wanted to do, alone, as a couple, and as a family; but, which things were most important at this stage of their relationship? Using this discussion, the therapist identified the necessary skills for prioritizing and carrying out their wishes—utilizing agenda-setting sessions, time-limited decision-making sessions, brainstorming and ways to evaluate potential problem solutions. Within this context, several agreements were made. Maddie had two major goals: (a) to exercise at a local spa three times a week; and (b) to take one graduate course at night. The solution to the first one was achieved quickly. Mike agreed that by leaving for work 45 minutes later three times a week, he could watch the children while Maddie attended an early morning aerobics class. Although he would arrive home later on those days, Maddie felt that the exercise would be more helpful to her mood and overall health and that she could handle the children on the evenings when Mike worked late.

A second agreement focused on Mike's realization that what he missed most was having time with Maddie to talk about work, politics and everyday matters. He missed having her as a sounding board and friend. The two of them acknowledged that the time they spent together after the children went to bed was wasted if they drank wine or smoked marijuana. The agreement ensured that the children would all be in bed by 9 p.m., the TV would be off, and they would talk quietly with each other for at least half an hour. They also decided that this would not be a time to bring up troublesome issues or attempt to problem-solve family matters.

Maddie's desire to take a graduate class opened up a difficult discussion regarding money. Mike believed that their limited income precluded its use for Maddie's tuition. Maddie reflected and agreed with Mike's financial concerns. In response to Mike's suggestion, Maddie agreed that it wasn't the credit for classes or getting her graduate degree that was important so much as her continued involvement in her professional field. With this in mind, they agreed to brainstorm less expensive ways for Maddie to remain connected to her work during the coming year.

Fading Therapist Involvement and Maintaining Gains

After continued progress, the couple decided to stop regular counseling sessions. At the therapist's suggestion, they discussed how they would recognize and respond to future difficulties in their relationship. They noted, on a worksheet, which skills they had learned that would be helpful in specific situations and which were most beneficial to them. These were sealed in an envelope, to be posted on their bedroom mirror with the instructions that either one could open the envelope "in the event our relationship feels shaky". Opening the envelope would initiate a joint review of the relationship's current strengths and weaknesses, leading to a decision to work on their own or re-enter therapy. Maddie and Mike consulted with Maddie's physician and decided that after 3 months, if everything still seemed to be going well, she would wean herself off her medication to see whether her positive mood could be maintained without an antidepressant.

Summary

Initially, Maddie's depressed mood appeared to be the result of a post-partum or biological depression; indeed, her own and her family history indicated that she was predisposed to depression and could be at risk for depressive episodes for the rest of her life. However, further examination of the current and historic context revealed that Maddie had suffered two major losses of reinforcers in a short period of time, combined with a substantial increase in stress. When she quit her job because of pregnancy and became overloaded with the twins' care, she lost not only a major avenue for her self-esteem but also her closest confidante, Mike. Having neither to bolster her morale, and with the increased stress in raising five children, she succumbed to a depressive spiral that increasingly reduced the number of pleasant activities in her life that brought her satisfaction. As she became more depressed and ruminative, she attributed more negative motives to Mike's behavior. Mike, too, made assumptions that contributed to the decline of their relationship satisfaction. By remaining uninvolved because he thought Maddie would snap out of her depression on her own, he fostered her feelings of isolation and her perception that he did not care about the relationship. As the breadwinner, it was easy for him to immerse himself in more pleasant activities by going to work, providing the family with income, and interacting solely with the older children.

The therapist helped the couple reframe the past 2 years as "external events" for which neither were to blame but the solution to which now required teamwork. As they learned to communicate better Maddie's overall mood improved, but thoughts of her stalled career were still a sticking point. Both realized that this would likely be an ongoing issue that they would have to address as the children got older and demands of parenting changed.

As illustrated here, one of the overriding goals of marital therapy is to teach the partners effective ways to express, as well as actively listen to, both negative and positive feelings, and to be able to specify what they want from their relationships rather than what they do not want. Clear communication was a necessary prerequisite for increasing the satisfying aspects of their lives and developing the problem-resolution skills for the myriad of issues that will appear from day-to-day.

The therapist's reframing of the issues and possible causes of the stressful events that led to the depression assisted in changing Maddie's depressogenic cognitions. More structured cognitive therapy procedures designed to change cognitive schemata may be necessary if reframing and the focus on interactional methods are ineffective. These would include procedures designed to identify, challenge and change negative thoughts and irrational beliefs, following the work of Beck and his colleagues (e.g. Beck et al., 1979) and Ellis & Harper (1961). Although depressogenic cognitions have been shown to be associated with depression, their etiologic role has not been clearly determined. However, successful interventions using cognitive methods have been demonstrated with adults (Dobson, 1989).

This couple demonstrated some of the sex-typical behavior patterns discussed earlier that made communication and resolution of the problem more difficult. Maddie displayed a number of behaviors, typical of depressed women, such as self-derogation ("It's my fault. I should be able to cope with this"), complaints and rumination. The effect on Mike was increased avoidance of both positive and negative interactions. In addition, as the assessment revealed, compared to Mike, Maddie had a long list of specific complaints. She was also more aware of the areas of change Mike desired in herself than he was of hers. Mike's solution to the entire problem was simpler; wait it out. These represent interactional styles more typical of each gender, but in the extreme, and under stressful circumstances, they become unproductive and dysfunctional.

CONTRAINDICATIONS FOR CONJOINT THERAPIES

Our treatment focus has centered on conjoint therapies within a social interactional framework that has shown much promise. There are, however, certain situations when working with both partners and focusing on the marital relationship is contraindicated. Perhaps the most obvious of these is when one partner is actively suicidal and stabilizing the depressed spouse must become the primary focus of intervention. Individualized therapy may range from intensive one-on-one sessions to crisis intervention, including the use of hospitalization. O'Leary, Sandeen & Beach (1987) found individual cognitive therapy to be more effective than conjoint therapy for such patients. As the spouse becomes less suicidal, it may be helpful to engage the other partner to provide emotional support or other behaviors that are helpful in reducing the likelihood of suicide attempts. However, the focus is clearly on the suicidal spouse, even though the partner may be included in sessions or in planning treatment strategies. It is the therapist's judgment call whether a depressed person can be helped better with or without his/her partner in these situations.

There is research to suggest that, in some instances, detrimental interactions in the relationship must be addressed first, before the spouse can assume any position in the therapeutic process of the depressed individual (Beach, Sandeen & O'Leary, 1990). In this instance, marital therapy may be necessary before the non-depressed spouse will be allowed by the depressed individual to participate in any individually-directed therapy. For example, some depressed patients are highly reluctant to disclose the contents of their ruminations, especially those that indicate hostility, to their partners. This is particularly true in those instances where marital discord and dysfunctional interactions are a well-established practice. Beach and his colleagues found that under these circumstances, once the dysfunctional marital interactions are addressed the depressive episode often recedes as well and further therapy for depression is not required.

Beach, Sandeen & O'Leary (1990) have outlined other criteria for determining whether marital therapy is appropriate for couples. In addition to ruling out suicidal ideations, the therapist must be assured that the depression is diagnosed as unipolar rather than bipolar and that the spouse does not display psychotic episodes or present with organic mood disorders. The features of such diagnoses certainly would hinder the patient's participation in any meaningful couple therapy without first addressing the individual psychopathology. In addition to ascertaining the psychopathologic state of the patient, the therapist should also be satisfied that marital discord has been firmly established before conjoint therapy is indicated. There has been some question as to the validity of a depressed person's ability to adequately self-report on the quality of his/her relationship. However, observational research indicates that there is enough concordance between observed conflict and self-report of marital discord to merit the use of self-report measures as an index of the overall quality of the marital relationship (Beach, Whisman & O'Leary, 1994).

If marital discord is evident in the relationship, the therapist must also determine whether or not depression antedates the marital problems. There is some evidence to suggest that actual or perceived temporal ordering of marital discord and depression plays a critical role in determining the appropriateness of traditional marital therapy as opposed to an individual cognitive therapy. O'Leary, Risso & Beach (1990) found that conjoint therapy was more successful for couples who perceive the marital distress as leading to the depressive episode, with individual therapy being more successful when depression is viewed as antedating the marital problems.

PROMISING APPROACHES

It is clear that the successful treatments that have been described here for dealing with depressed persons in the context of marital discord have, admittedly, failed with many couples as well. Jacobson (1992) has noted that a traditional behavioral marital approach works primarily for young, less traditional couples, those who are less severely distressed, those who are emotionally engaged or committed to the relationship, and couples who are more compatible in terms of their agreement on basic issues. We noted characteristics quite similar to these in the couple described in the case study. In order to make therapeutic interventions successful for a wider range of couples, it is obvious that improvements continue to be necessary.

Clearly, there are many couples who do not match this profile but are still maritally distressed and require treatment. Several approaches have been offered recently toward this goal. Jacobson, Christensen and colleagues offer an approach they call Integrative Behavior Couple Therapy (IBCT; Christensen, Jacobson & Babcock, 1991; Koerner, Prince & Jacobson, 1994) based on the notions of acceptance and commitment described by Hayes and Kohlenberg (Kohlenberg, Hayes & Tsai, 1993). The IBCT model appears more flexible and assumes differences in the couples interactional styles and preferences, some of which will be unchangeable. From a theoretical stance, IBCT does seem potentially useful for treatment of depression in women. In removing blame from conflict, it may counter women's tendency to blame themselves in self-denigrating ways. The common problem requires teamwork for a solution to be reached. Second, it attempts to create more intimacy during the session despite differences between the partners, and thus counters the usual coercive interactions. Third, it allows differences to exist as a necessary part of the relationship, providing opportunities for the couple to explore their differences and how they may attenuate or enhance the relationship.

A second approach which allows for dissimilarities to exist is the self-regulation model propounded by Halford, Sanders & Behrens (1994). They argue, similarly, that their model involves moving away from a partner-blaming mode to one that requires both partners to collaborate on finding solutions to problems. In offering less structure by the therapist, the focus is on reinforcing individual members to come up with their own solutions, as well. In relation to depression among a member of the dyad, Halford et al. argue that it is important to educate the other member about the possible implications of the pathology. As well, the self-regulation model requires that each partner identify his/her own behavior change that will work towards alleviation of the problem. They also note that the treatment may require individual as well as conjoint sessions.

Although promising, IBCT and the self-regulation model are new and have not been effectively tested as a treatment of depression within the context of marital discord. Further research is required to demonstrate their efficacy.

FUTURE CHALLENGES

Several other questions remain unanswered that also require further research. To begin with, almost all of the outcome studies conducted on maritally discordant couples with a depressed member have focused on women as the target. Thus, predictors of outcome can only speak to the effects for depressed women. We have made the argument here, that there are normal sex-typal behavior patterns displayed by women that bear a moderate relationship to that of depressed individuals generally. That women make up two-thirds of those with a depressive disorder necessarily confounds this relationship. Unfortunately, how depressed men behave, in and out of maritally discordant relationships, is still relatively unknown. It might be predicted that when depressed, men would tend to be more irritable and more aggressive, in keeping with expected socialization effects. However, the two available studies of husband–wife interaction indicate that different processes may be involved. Perry (1993) found that, during interactions with their wives, depressed men did not display more negative behavior, but withdrew more frequently during conflictual discussions. The male withdrawal pattern has been noted clinically as well as in research among distressed couples (see Gottman, 1994). Jacob & Leonard (1992) found less negative reciprocity, suggesting a suppressive effect similar to that found by Biglan et al. (1985) and Hops et al. (1987). Results from the two studies of depressed men noted a common characteristic, a generally lower responsiveness (Perry, 1993) and less contingent involvement by the wives (Jacob & Leonard, 1992), suggesting other interaction processes at work. Clearly, more research on the marital interactions of depressed men is needed.

The available data suggests that interventions may need to be more gender-specific. This is also consistent with Halford, Sanders & Behrens' (1994) recommendation that couple therapy provide ample opportunity to develop the specific skills necessary for individual partners to cope with the situation in which one member has a psychological disorder. That is, individuals within a dyad may need to learn specific skills to cope with the specific pathology of sex-specific behaviors of the other member. As noted by Beach, Smith & Fincham (1994), it is too soon to "accept the null hypothesis" that gender differences are unimportant in examining the etiology of depression among men and women (see Hops, 1996, for one perspective).

A second issue is the need to develop better measures of marital quality and interaction (Weiss & Heyman, 1990). For example, maritally discordant wives have been shown to score significantly lower than their husbands on measures of marital satisfaction, such as the DAS (Christian, O'Leary & Vivian, 1994). Thus, Beach, Sandeen & O'Leary (1990) used gender-adjusted criteria as indicants of marital discord (i.e. DAS of 100 or less for wives and DAS of less than 115 for husbands). Whether this is fruitful or not will require further examination and focus on the specific items or subscales within each measure.

Finally, improvements in therapeutic procedures must be viewed within the context of an ever-changing society. As social contexts evolve and socialization practices change, so will the form and function of couple relationships. Consequently, the continued evolution of intervention procedures to assist discordant couples, especially those with a depressed member, must be sensitive to current and historical contexts.

Acknowledgements

This manuscript was supported in part by grants from the National Institute of Mental Health (MH43311 and MH45188) and from the National Institute of Drug Abuse (DA03706). The authors also wish to acknowledge the contribution of Peggi Rodgers in the preparation of this manuscript.

REFERENCES

Baucom, D.H. (1994). Introduction to the special series, the person and marriage: attending to individual and dyadic concerns. *Behavior Therapy*, **25**, 341–344.

Beach, S.R.H. & O'Leary, K.D. (1992). Treating depression in the context of marital discord: outcome and predictors of response for marital therapy vs. cognitive therapy. *Behavior Therapy*, **23**, 507–528.

Beach, S.R.H., Sandeen, E.E. & O'Leary, K.D. (1990). *Depression in Marriage: a Model for Etiology and Treatment*. New York Guilford.

Beach, S.R.H., Smith, D.A. & Fincham, F.D. (1994). Marital interventions for depression:

empirical foundation and future prospects. *Applied & Preventive Psychology*, **3**, 233–250.

Beach, S.R.H., Whisman, M.A. & O'Leary, K.D. (1994). Marital therapy for depression: theoretical foundation, current status, and future directions. *Behavior Therapy*, **25**, 345–371.

Beck, A.T. (1983). Cognitive therapy of depression: new perspectives. In P.J. Clayton & J.E. Barrett (eds), *Treatment of Depression: Old Controversies and New Approaches* (pp. 265–290). New York: Raven.

Beck, A.T., Rush, A.J., Shaw, B.F. & Emery, G. (1979). *Cognitive Therapy of Depression*. New York: Guilford.

Beck, A., Ward, C., Mendelson, M., Mock, J. & Erbaugh, J. (1961). An inventory for measuring depression. *Archives of General Psychiatry*, **4**, 561–571.

Biglan, A., Hops, H. & Sherman, L. (1988). Coercive family processes and maternal depression. In Peters and McMahon (eds), *Social Learning and Systems Approaches to Marriage and the Family* (pp. 72–103). New York: Brunner/Mazel.

Biglan, A., Hops, H., Sherman, L., Friedman, L.S., Arthur, J. & Osteen, V. (1985). Problem-solving interactions of depressed women and their spouses. *Behavior Therapy*, **16**, 431–451.

Biglan, A., Rothlind, J., Hops, H. & Sherman, L. (1989). Impact of distressed and aggressive behavior. *Journal of Abnormal Psychology*, **98**, 218–228.

Birchler, G.R. & Weiss, R.L. (1977). Inventory of Rewarding Activities. Unpublished manuscript, University of Oregon, Marital Studies Program, Eugene, OR.

Blechman, E.A. (1981). Competence depression, and behavior modification with women. In M. Hersen, R.M. Eislser & P.M. Miller (eds), *Progress in Behavior Modification*, Vol. 12 (pp. 227–263). New York: Academic Press.

Cairns, R.B. (1979). *The Analysis of Social Interaction: Methods, Issues, and Illustrations*. Hillsdale, NJ: Erlbaum.

Christian, J.L., O'Leary, K.D. & Vivian, D. (1994). Depressive symptomatology in maritally discordant women and men: discrimination and prediction. *Journal of Family Psychology*.

Christensen, A., Jacobson, N.S. & Babcock, J. (1991). Integrative behavioral couple therapy. In N.S. Jacobson & A.S. Gurman (eds), *Clinical Handbook of Marital Therapy*, 2nd edn. New York: Guilford.

Coyne, J.C., Kessler, R.C., Tal, M., Turnbull, J., Wortman, C.B. & Greden, J.F. (1987). Living with a depressed person, *Journal of Consulting and Clinical Psychology*, **55**, 347–352.

Dobson, K.S. (1989). A meta-analysis of the efficacy of cognitive therapy for depression. *Journal of Consulting and Clinical Psychology*, **57**, 414–419.

Dumas, J.E., Gibson, J.A. & Albin, J.B. (1989). Behavioral correlates of maternal depressive symptomatology in conduct-disorder children. *Journal of Consulting* and Clinical Psychology, **57**, 516–521.

Ellis, A. & Harper, R.A. (1961). *A Guide to Rational Living*. Hollywood, CA: Wilshire.

Foley, S.H., Rounsaville, B.J., Weissman, M.M., Sholomaskas, D. & Chevron, E. (1989). Individual versus conjoint interpersonal therapy for depressed patients with marital disputes. *International Journal of Family Psychiatry*, **10**, 29–42.

Gotlib, I.H. & Colby, C.A. (1987). *Treatment of Depression: an Interpersonal Systems Approach*. New York: Pergamon.

Gottman, T.M. (1994). *What Predicts Divorce? The Relationship Between Marital Processes and Marital Outcomes*. New Jersey: Erlbaum.

Halford, W.K., Sanders, M.R. & Behrens, B.C. (1994). Self-regulation in behavioral couples therapy. *Behavior Therapy*, **25**, 431–452.

Hops, H. (1996). Intergenerational transmission of depressive symptoms: gender and developmental considerations. In C. Mundt, M. Goldstein, K. Hahlweg & P. Fiedler (eds), *Interpersonal Factors in the Origin and Course of Affective Disorders* (pp. 113–129). London: Royal College of Psychiatrists.

Hops, H. (1992). Parental depression and child behaviour problems: implications for behavioural family intervention. *Behaviour Change*, **9**, 126–138.

Hops, H., Sherman, L. & Biglan, A. (1990). Maternal depression, marital discord, and children's behavior: a developmental perspective. In G.R. Patterson (ed.), *Depression and Aggression in Family Interaction* (pp. 185–208). New York: Erlbaum.

Hops, H., Biglan, A., Sherman, L., Arthur, J., Friedman, L. & Osteen, V. (1987). Home observations of family interactions of depressed women. *Journal of Consulting and Clinical Psychology*, **55**, 341–346.

Jacob, T. & Leonard, K. (1992). Sequential analysis of marital interactions involving alcoholic, depressed, and non-distressed men. *Journal of Abnormal Psychology*, **101**, 647–656.

Jacobson, N.S. (1991). Behavioral versus insight-oriented marital therapy: labels can be misleading. *Journal of Consulting and Clinical Psychology*, **59**, 142–145.

Jacobson, N.S. (1992). Behavioral couple therapy: a new beginning. *Behavior Therapy*, **25**, 452–462.

Jacobson, N.S., Dobson, K., Fruzzetti, A.E., Schmaling, D.B. & Salusky, S. (1991). Marital therapy as a treatment for depression. *Journal of Consulting and Clinical Psychology*, **59**, 547–557.

Jacobson, N.S., Fruzzetti, A.E., Dobson, K., Whisman, M. & Hops, H. (1993). Couple therapy as a treatment for depression: II. The effect of relationship quality and therapy on depressive relapse. *Journal of Consulting and Clinical Psychology*, **61**, 516–519.

Jacobson, N.S., Holtzworth-Munroe, A. & Schmaling, K.B. (1989). Marital therapy and spouse involvement in the treatment of depression, agoraphobia, and alcoholism. *Journal of Consulting and Clinical Psychology*, **57**, 5–10.

Jacobson, N.S. & Margolin, G. (1979). *Marital Therapy: Strategies Based on Social Learning and Behavior Exchange Principles*. New York: Brunner/Mazel.

Kavanagh, K. & Hops, H. (1994). Good girls? Bad boys? Gender and development as contexts for diagnosis and treatment. In T.H. Ollendick & R.J. Prinz (eds), *Advances in Clinical Child Psychology*, **16**, 45–79. New York: Plenum.

Kessler, R.C., McGonagle, K.A., Zhao, S., Nelson, C.B., Hughes, M., Eshleman, S., Wittchen, H.-U. & Kendler, K.S. (1994). Lifetime and 12-month prevalence of DSM-III-R psychiatric disorders in the United States. *Archives of General Psychiatry*, **51**, 8–19.

Klerman, G.L., Weissman, M.M., Rounsaville, B.J. & Chevron, E.S. (1984). *Interpersonal Psychotherapy of Depression*. New York: Basic Books.

Koerner, K., Prince, S. & Jacobson, N.S. (1994). Enhancing the treatment and prevention of depression in women: the role of integrative behavioral couple therapy. *Behavior Therapy*, **25**, 373–390.

Kohlenberg, R.J., Hayes, S.C. & Tsai, M. (1993). Radical behavioral psychotherapy: two contemporary examples. *Clinical Psychology Review*, **13**(6), 579–592.

Lewinsohn, P.M. & Shaw, D.A. (1969). Feedback about interpersonal behavior as an agent of behavior change: a case study in the treatment of depression. *Psychotherapy and Psychosomatics*, **17**, 82–88.

Lewinsohn, P.M., Hops, H., Roberts, R.E., Seeley, J.R. & Andrews, J.A. (1993). Adolescent Psychopathology: I. Prevalence and incidence of depression and other DSM-III-R disorders in high school students. *Journal of Abnormal Psychology*, **102**(1), 133–144.

Lewinsohn, P.M., Rohde, P., Seeley, J.R. & Fischer, S.A. (1993). Age-cohort changes in the lifetime occurrence of depression and other mental disorders. *Journal of Abnormal Psychology*, **102**(1), 110–120.

Maccoby, E.E. (1990). Gender and relationships: a developmental approach. *American Psychologist*, **45**, 513–520.

Nelson, G.M. & Beach, S.R.H. (1990). Sequential interaction in depression: effects of depressive behavior on spousal aggression. *Behavior Therapy*, **12**, 167–182.

O'Leary, K.D. & Beach, S.R.H. (1990). Marital therapy: a viable treatment for depression and marital discord. *American Journal of Psychiatry*, **147**, 183–186.

O'Leary, K.D., Christian, J.L. & Mendell, N.R. (1994). A closer look at the link between marital discord and depressive symptomatology. *Journal of Social and Clinical Psychology*, **14**, 1–9.

O'Leary, K.D., Risso, L.P. & Beach, S.R.H. (1990). Attributions about the marital discord/depression link and therapy outcome. *Behavior Therapy*, **21**, 413–422.

O'Leary, K.D., Sandeen, E. & Beach, S.R.H. (1987). Treatment of suicidal, maritally discordant clients by marital therapy or cognitive therapy. Paper presented at the 21st Annual Meeting of the Association for Advancement of Behavior Therapy, Boston, MA.

Patterson, G.R. (1982). *Coercive Family Process*. Eugene, OR: Castalia.

Patterson, G.R. & Reid, J.B. (1970). Reciprocity and coercion: two facets of social systems. In C. Neuringer & J.L. Michael (eds), *Behavior Modification in Clinical Psychology*. New York: Appleton-Century-Crofts.

Perry, B.A. (1993). Marital Problem-solving Interactions of Depressed Males. Unpublished doctoral dissertation, University of Oregon, Eugene, OR.

Radloff, L. (1975). Sex differences in depression: the effects of occupation and marital status. *Sex Roles*, **1**, 249–265.

Regier, D.A., Boyd, J.H., Burke, J.D., Rae, D.S. et al. (1988). One-month prevalence of mental disorders in the United States: based on five epidemiologic catchment area sites. *Archives of General Psychiatry*, **45**(11), 977–986.

Schmaling, K.B. & Jacobson, N.S. (1990). Marital interaction and depression. *Journal of Abnormal Psychology*, **99**, 229–236.

Spanier, G.B. (1976). Measuring dyadic adjustment: new scales for assessing the quality of marriage and similar dyads. *Journal of Marriage and the Family*, **38**, 15–28.

Weiss, R.L. & Birchler, G.R. (1975). Areas of Change Questionnaire. Unpublished manuscript, University of Oregon, Marital Studies Program, Eugene, OR.

Weiss, R.L. & Cerreto, M.C. (1980). The Marital Status Inventory: development of a measure of dissolution potential. *American Journal of Family Therapy*, **8**(2), 80–85.

Weiss, R.L. & Heyman, R.E. (1990). Marital distress and therapy. In A.S. Bellack, M. Hersen & A . Kazdin (eds), *International Handbook of Behavior Modification*, 2nd edn. New York: Plenum.

Weiss, R.L., Hops, H. & Patterson, G.R. (1973). A framework for conceptualizing marital conflict: a technology for altering it, some data for evaluating it. In L.A. Hamerlynck, L.C. Handy & E.J. Mash (eds), *Behavior Change: Methodology, Concepts, and Practice*. Champaign, IL: Research Press.

Weissman, M.M. (1987). Advances in psychiatric epidemiology: rates and risks for major depression. *American Journal of Public Health*, **77**, 445–451.

Weissman, M.M. & Paykel, E.S. (1974). *The Depressed Woman: a Study of Social Relationships*. Chicago: University of Chicago Press.

Chapter 22

Couples Interventions and Alcohol Abuse

Timothy J. O'Farrell* and Robert J. Rotunda**
*Families and Addiction Program, Department of Psychiatry,
Harvard University Medical School; and ** Veterans' Affairs
Medical Center, Brockton and West Roxbury, MA, USA

THERAPY FOR COUPLES WITH AN ALCOHOLIC MEMBER

Jim and Millie were referred to our couples' treatment program when Jim was an inpatient in an alcoholism rehabilitation unit. The referring counselor felt our program might help the couple, who had been separated for the majority of the year before Jim entered the rehabilitation program, to decide whether Jim should return to live with his wife after leaving the rehabilitation. Jim and Millie were both in their late 40s. They had been married 24 years and had three children, a 23-year-old son living on his own and two teenage daughters at home. Jim was an unemployed manager and Millie worked full-time as a hairstylist. Jim's alcohol problem had started over 20 years earlier with excessive drinking at parties and during business activities associated with his work.

The couple had separated at Millie's insistence when Jim was fired from his job for drinking and arrested for the second time for drunken driving. Jim refused to get treatment and continued to drink very heavily on a daily basis after the initial separation. The family had experienced an emotional roller-coaster ride in response to his drinking and efforts to stop over the years. Jim's heavier drinking periods and almost chronic abdication of parental and spousal functions prompted an escalating cycle of mistrust, mutual hostility, blame, and resentment within the marriage, which in turn triggered more drinking and Jim's refusal to get help. Now, Millie told Jim she would consider giving their marriage "one last try" if he completed this rehabilitation program, established an aftercare plan that seemed reasonable, and remained abstinent.

Clinical Handbook of Marriage and Couples Interventions. Edited by W. Kim Halford and Howard J. Markman.
© 1997 John Wiley & Sons Ltd.

As the above example illustrates, couples with an alcoholic partner have usually traveled a tortuous road before seeking treatment. The pervasive negative impact of alcoholism on marriage, and the failure to find distinct pathological personality traits or interaction patterns among couples with an alcoholic member, have been among the factors that have accompanied the development of couples therapy and spouse-involved interventions for use with alcoholics and their partners. This chapter presents couples therapy and spouse-involved interventions for use with alcohol abusers and alcoholics during three broadly defined stages of recovery (Prochaska & DiClemente, 1983): (a) initial commitment to change—recognizing that a problem exists and deciding to do something about it; (b) the change itself—stopping abusive drinking and stabilizing this change for at least a few months; and (c) the long-term maintenance of change. O'Farrell (1993) provides more details on the therapy methods described in this chapter.

INITIATING CHANGE AND HELPING THE SPOUSE WHEN THE ALCOHOL ABUSER RESISTS TREATMENT

Few clinical scenarios are as frustrating for clinicians as when an alcoholic's family member presents in despair to ask for help in coping with the alcoholic's drinking and advice on how to engage the alcoholic who refuses treatment. When family members give their narrative of how the drinking has hurt them, therapists often have initial "gut" reactions which include feelings of vicarious helplessness and urgency to tell them to leave the relationship. However, these inclinations are usually not helpful, especially if the family is hopeful that, given the right circumstances, the drinker can change. Besides the importance of an empathic response to the client's plight, we employ two general guidelines when faced with this situation. First, it is essential that spouses and (if possible) children are informed that they are not responsible for and have not caused the drinking problem. Following from this premise is the assertion that they can not make the drinker change because they are not ultimately responsible or in control of the problem. In addition, we seek to empower the spouses and help them identify what is within their control. For instance, encouragement is given to "take care of yourself", and decide how much negativity they are willing to live with, and what they are not willing to tolerate. Referrals to self-help groups such as Al-Anon, and to other community resources, along with individual therapy, can help family members cope with the drinking.

Moreover, clinical wisdom and experience suggest it is useful to advise family members not to argue with the person who has been drinking in order to lessen the risk of violence and childrens' exposure to conflict. Counseling them to take advantage of "windows of motivation" the alcohol abuser may experience to enter treatment can be helpful as well (e.g. requesting the alcoholic get help when expressing remorse about drinking, or when talking with a physician during an emergency room visit).

Four approaches address the difficult and all-too-common case of the alcohol abuser who is not yet willing to stop drinking. Three of the approaches try to help the spouse to motivate the uncooperative, denying alcohol abuser to change his /her drinking. Community Reinforcement Training for Families is a program for teaching the non-alcoholic family member (usually the wife of a male problem drinker): (a) how to reduce physical abuse to herself; (b) how to encourage sobriety; (c) how to encourage seeking professional treatment; and (d) how to assist in that treatment (Sisson & Azrin, 1986, 1993). The Johnson Institute "Intervention" involves three to four educational and rehearsal sessions to prepare the spouse and other family members. During the intervention session itself, the spouse and other family members confront the alcohol abuser about his or her drinking and strongly encourage entry to an alcohol treatment program (Johnson, 1973; Liepman, 1993).

The Unilateral Family Therapy (UFT) approach assists the non-alcoholic spouse to strengthen his/her coping capabilities, to enhance family functioning, and to facilitate greater sobriety on the part of the alcohol abuser (Thomas & Ager, 1993). UFT provides a series of graded steps the spouse can use prior to confrontation. These steps may be successful in their own right or at least pave the way for a positive outcome to a UFT "programmed confrontation" experience, which is similar to the Johnson approach and adapted for use with an individual spouse. For example, a therapist using UFT first provides a treatment orientation which emphasizes the assumption that the non-alcoholic spouse is not to blame for the drinking, and the potential of the spouse to become a rehabilitative influence (Thomas & Ager, 1993). The spouse is educated about alcohol abuse and shown how to monitor the partner's alcohol consumption to assess the severity of the problem. Next, the spouse is encouraged to enhance the relationship by engaging in behaviors pleasing to the drinker during sober periods, and to refrain from enabling or trying to actively control the drinking. In general, the strategy is to reinforce sobriety and efforts to attain it so that later confrontive and non-confrontive interventions directed at convincing the alcoholic to enter treatment will have a greater likelihood of success.

A fourth and final approach is a group program for wives of treatment-resistant alcohol abusers (Dittrich, 1993). This program tries to help wives cope with their emotional distress and concentrate on their own motivations for change rather than trying to motivate the drinker to change. This approach borrows many concepts from Al-Anon, by far the most widely used source of support for family members troubled by a loved one's alcohol problem. Al-Anon advocates that family members detach themselves from the alcoholic's drinking in a loving way, accept that they are powerless to control the alcoholic, and seek support from other members of the Al-Anon program (Al-Anon Family Groups, 1981).

GOALS AND PREPARATION FOR COUPLES THERAPY WITH ALCOHOLICS

Goals

Once the alcohol abuser has decided to change his/her drinking, couples therapy has two basic objectives in order to stabilize short-term change in the alcohol problem and in the marriage relationship. The first goal is to reduce or eliminate abusive drinking and support the drinker's efforts to change. To this end, a high priority is changing alcohol-related interactional patterns (e.g. nagging about past drinking but ignoring current sober behavior). One can get abstinent alcohol abusers and their spouses to engage in behaviors more pleasing to each other, but if they continue talking about and focusing on past or "possible" future drinking, frequently such arguments lead to renewed drinking (Maisto et al., 1988). They then feel more discouraged about their relationship and the drinking than before, and are less likely to try pleasing each other again. The second goal involves altering general marital patterns to provide an atmosphere that is more conducive to sobriety. This involves helping the couple repair the often extensive relationship damage incurred during many years of conflict over alcohol, as well as helping them find solutions to relationship difficulties that may not be directly related to the alcohol problem. Finally, the couple must learn to confront and resolve relationship conflicts without the alcohol abuser resorting to drinking.

After the change in the alcohol problem has been stable for 3–6 months, the goals of marital therapy in contributing to long-term maintenance of change are to (a) help the couple prevent relapse to abusive drinking and (b) deal with marital issues frequently encountered during long-term recovery. Methods which therapists can use to reach each of these goals will be presented in detail after we consider the initial assessment and crisis intervention sessions that are so important if therapeutic goals are to be accomplished.

Assessment and Crisis Intervention

Our couples therapy begins when both partners present for a conjoint session. However, work may be required to engage the often reluctant non-alcoholic partner in treatment. We use a non-threatening, positive approach to obtain the alcoholic's permission to contact his/her spouse after an initial screening assessment is completed and rapport established. Common fears drinkers have about spouse contact, such as warnings from them that their partner is exceedingly angry and may not talk to the therapist, or fears that the therapist may advise the partner to consider separation, are predictable and immediately addressed. We then talk directly to the spouse by phone to engage them for a joint interview, if possible when we are in the presence of the alcoholic. It is critical that the spouse's perspective be assessed and understood by the therapist, who is careful not to be seen as an agent for the alcoholic.

During his treatment in an inpatient alcoholism rehabilitation program, Jim decided to make an all-out effort to stay sober so that he could "win back" the trust of his family. Although apprehensive about the referral to a marital therapy program at first, he began to think that involving Millie in his aftercare treatment would hasten reconciliation with her. However, when she was contacted by the therapist she expressed confusion and doubt in her decision to give him another chance. The therapist allowed her to vent, empathized with her anger at Jim, and explained that couples counselling might be an opportunity for both of them to figure out the future of the relationship. She eventually agreed to come to the rehabilitation unit to meet with the therapist and Jim for an initial consultation.

In the initial interview, the therapist needs to: (a) determine at what stage the drinker is in the process of changing his/her alcohol abuse; (b) assess whether there is a need for crisis intervention prior to a careful assessment; and (c) orient the couple to the assessment procedures. If the alcohol abuser already has initiated changes in the drinking or at least clearly recognizes that a problem exists and may want to change it, then proceeding with the assessment makes sense. If the alcohol abuser has not yet made a firm decision to change the drinking, then facilitating this decision becomes one of the goals of the assessment. It is very important to give priority to the drinking in the initial sessions. We generally attempt to establish at least a temporary contract of abstinence during the two to four assessment sessions. A minimal requirement is abstinence on the days of assessment sessions, and clients are informed that an alcohol breathalyzer test is a standard feature of all assessment sessions we conduct. An inquiry about the extent of drinking and urges to drink between sessions is a routine part of each assessment session. We also ask the couple to commit themselves, for the time period needed to complete the assessment, to stay living together, not to threaten separation or divorce, and to refrain from bringing up the past in anger at home.

The therapist evaluates whether any serious negative consequences are likely to occur if two to four assessment sessions are conducted before taking action on the presenting complaints. For example, crisis intervention is necessary for cases in which violence or divorce seem a likely result of delayed action or cases in which the drinker is ready to stop drinking but needs immediate hospitalization for detoxification. Often the usual assessment can be conducted after the crisis has been resolved. Other issues which also may present obstacles to assessment and require intervention are discussed in more detail below after considering assessment methods.

Assessment Targets and Procedures

A series of assessment issues or targets are investigated in progressively greater depth as the assessment progresses. In the initial session, the therapist's clinical interview should gather information about: (a) the client's drinking, especially recent quantity and frequency of drinking, whether the extent of physical dependence on alcohol requires detoxification to obtain abstinence during the assessment, what led to seeking help at this time and prior help-seeking efforts, and whether the drinker's and spouse's goal is to reduce the drinking or to abstain either temporarily or permanently; (b) drug use other than alcohol; (c) the stability of the marriage in terms of current planned or actual separation as well as any past separations; (d) recent violence and any fears of recurrence; (e) suicidal ideation or behavior for either the client or the spouse; and (f) the

Table 22.1 Targets and procedures in assessing alcoholic couples

Assessment target area	Instrument/procedure[a]
1. The alcoholic's drinking	
(a) Drinking history	
Frequency and quantity of drinking	Time-Line Follow-Back Drinking Interview (Sobell et al., 1985)
Drinking situations	Inventory of Drinking Situations (Annis, 1985)
Antecedents to drinking	Situational Confidence Questionnaire (Annis, 1982)
(b) Dependence syndrome	Alcohol Dependence Scale (Skinner & Allen, 1982)
Impaired control over drinking	
Increased tolerance	
Relief of withdrawal symptoms through drinking	
(c) Problems related to drinking	Michigan Alcoholism Screening Test (Selzer, 1971)
Biomedical (e.g. traumatic injury, liver disease, pancreatitis)	Laboratory test results (O'Farrell & Maisto, 1987)
Psychosocial (e.g. work, family, legal problems)	Structured interview (Sobell, 1979)
(d) Goal for drinking— reduction or abstinence (temporary/permanent)	Clinical interview
2. Marital stability	Marital Status Inventory (Weiss & Cerreto, 1980)
3. Marital violence	Conflict Tactics Scale (Straus, 1979)
4. Alcohol-related crises	Clinical interview
5. Marital relationship	
(a) Overall adjustment	Marital Adjustment Test (Locke & Wallace, 1959)
(b) Changes desired	Areas of Change Questionnaire (Margolin, Talovic & Weindrein, 1983)
(c) Sexual adjustment	Sexual Adjustment Questionnaire (O'Farrell, 1990)
(d) Communications skills	Videotaped sample of communication (Floyd, O'Farrell & Goldberg, 1987)

[a] References cited provide more information about each instrument. A clinical interview can also be used alone or in conjunction with these instruments to assess each area.

existence of alcohol-related or other crises that require immediate attention. Allowing 75–90 minutes for the initial session and including 5–10 minutes separately with each spouse alone provides sufficient time to gather the needed information and to learn of important material (e.g. plans for separation, fears of violence) that either spouse may be reluctant to share during the conjoint portion of the interview.

Our own practice makes use of a number of structured assessment instruments and procedures after the initial interview session to explore in greater detail the issues covered in the initial session (see Table 22.1 for more details.). We also explore the marital relationship in depth in these subsequent assessment sessions. We give special attention to the overall level of satisfaction experienced in the relationship, specific changes desired in the relationship, sexual adjustment, and level of communication skills, especially when talking about conflicts and problems. This additional assessment seeks to determine: (a) what changes are needed in marital and family life as well as other day-to-day activities in order to achieve and maintain the goal for the alcohol abuser's drinking; and (b) what marital changes are desired to increase marital satisfaction, if one assumes that the drinking goal will be achieved.

After the assessment information has been gathered, the couple and therapist meet for a feedback session. The therapist shares impressions of the nature and severity of the drinking and marital problems and invites the couple to respond to these impressions. This session allows therapists the opportunity to increase motivation for treatment by reviewing in a non-judgmental, matter-of-fact manner the negative consequences of the excessive drinking. A second goal of the feedback session is to decide whether or not the couple will begin couples therapy and prepare them for the couples therapy if that is the decision. Assuming the decision is to start couples therapy, the therapist usually emphasizes the value of such therapy in achieving sobriety and a more satisfying relationship, and tries to promote favorable therapeutic expectations. The therapist asks the husband and the wife to promise that they will live together for at least the initial course of therapy, not threaten divorce or separation during this period, and do their best to focus on the future and the present (but not the past) in the therapy sessions and at home. The therapist also asks the couple to agree to do weekly homework assignments as part of the therapy. Finally, the therapist gives an overview of the course of therapy and tells the couple in more detail about the content of the first few sessions.

Obstacles Frequently Encountered During Initial Sessions

Alcohol-related Crises

Despite their seeming suitability for couples therapy, many alcohol abusers and their spouses will present the therapist with substantial obtacles. Common problems encountered during assessment are pressing alcohol-related crises (e.g. actual, impending, or threatened loss of job or home, or major legal or financial problems) that preclude a serious and sustained couples therapy focus. The therapist can help the couple devise plans to deal with the crisis or refer them elsewhere for such help, often after establishing a behavioral contract about drinking and alcohol-related interactions (see below). Other assessment and therapy procedures can be started when the crisis has been resolved.

Potential for Violence

Many couples whose negative interactions escalate quickly have difficulty containing conflict between sessions and pose a potential for violence in some instances. Responses to initial interviews with the couple and with the spouses separately, and further inquiry during subsequent sessions, help identify many such violence-prone couples during the pretherapy assessment. Once identified, these couples have conflict containment as an explicit goal of their therapy from the outset. For couples with a history of domestic violence, it is important to determine whether the violence was limited to occasions when the alcohol abuser had been drinking. If so, then methods to deal with the alcohol abuse may relieve much of the couple's concern about violence. Nonetheless, an additional procedure described by Shapiro (1984) can be very useful in cases where violence still seems likely. This involves a written agreement that spouses are not to hit or threaten to hit each other, and that if they do, one of the spouses (named in the agreement) will leave the home and go to a designated place for 48–72 hours. A "time-out" agreement is another useful procedure for containing conflict. In this procedure, if either party gets uncomfortable that a discussion may be escalating, he/she says, "I'm getting uncomfortable. I want a 5-minute time-out". Spouses go to separate rooms and use slow deep breathing to calm themselves. Afterward, the couple may restart the discussion if both desire it. If either partner requests a second time-out, then the couple definitely must stop the discussion.

The Blaming Spouse

It usually is not helpful to interpret the non-alcoholic spouse's frequent conversations about past or possible future drinking as an attempt to punish the alcohol abuser or sabotage the drinker's recovery. Overtly disapproving of the spouse's blaming behavior also does not help. The therapist can emphathize with the spouse by sympathetically reframing the spouse's behavior as trying to protect the couple from further problems due to alcohol. From this perspective, the spouse's talk about drinking is intended to be sure the drinker: (a) knows fully the negative impact of the past drinking (and this is plausible, since often the drinker does not remember much of what happened); (b) is aware of the full extent of the problem so his/her motivation toward sobriety will be fortified; and (c) is prepared for situations that may lead to a relapse or a lapse in motivation. Once the spouse feels understood, he/she becomes more receptive to the therapist's suggestion that the spouse has been "doing the wrong thing for the right reason" and to suggestion about more constructive methods to achieve the same goal. The following shows what a clinician might say.

> It is understandable, Millie, that you feel so hurt and angry considering what has happened in the past. You have spent a lot of energy and worked pretty hard to protect the family and hold it together since Jim began drinking heavily. I know you want to make sure he realizes how much his drinking has hurt you and the family so he won't continue to drink. It's important for you now that he's sober that he understand this, so you're trying to make it clear to him in various ways, and maybe sometimes doing the wrong thing for the right reason. His sobriety means so much you probably have found yourself doing and saying things you normally wouldn't to motivate him to stop drinking. From what both of you have told me, it hasn't helped when you've tried to tell him your feelings about the past and how you've been affected by the drinking, and it has sometimes made things worse. Now we need to focus on ways both of you can work together toward recovery and still communicate directly and honestly with each other.

Typical Structure and Sequence of Therapy Sessions

Once assessment is complete and initial obstacles have been overcome, couples therapy to help stabilize short-term change in the alcohol problem and associated marital discord usually consists of 10–20 therapy sessions, each of which last 60–75 minutes. Sessions tend to be highly structured, with the therapist setting the agenda at the outset of each meeting. A typical session begins with an inquiry about any drinking, or urges to drink, that have occurred since the last session, including compliance with any sobriety contract (see below) that has been negotiated. It moves from a review of the homework assignment from the previous session to considering important events of the past week. Then the session considers new material, such as instruction in, and rehearsal of, skills to be practiced at home during the week. It ends with the assignment of homework and answering questions. Generally, the first few sessions focus on decreasing alcohol-related feelings and interactions and increasing positive exchanges. This decreases tension about alcohol (and the risk of abusive drinking) and builds good will. Both are necessary for dealing with marital problems and desired relationship changes in later sessions using communication and problem-solving skills training and behavior change agreements. The following section describes typical interventions used.

Once the alcohol problem has been under control for 3–6 months, the structure and content of marital therapy sessions often change as the emphasis of the therapy becomes maintaining gains and preventing relapse. This phase of therapy is described later in the chapter.

PRODUCING SHORT TERM DRINKING AND RELATIONSHIP CHANGES

Alcohol-focused Interventions

General Goals and Issues

After the alcohol abuser has decided to change his/her drinking, the spouse can be included in treatment designed to support the drinker in adhering to this difficult and stressful decision. The first purpose of such treatment is to establish a clear and specific agreement between the alcohol abuser and spouse about the goal for the drinking, and the role of each partner in achieving that goal. Behavioral contracting can be very useful for this purpose and is described further below.

Specifying other behavioral changes needed requires a careful review of individual situations and conditions. Possible exposure to alcoholic beverages and alcohol-related situations should be discussed. The couple should decide if the spouse will drink alcoholic beverages in the alcohol abuser's presence, whether alcoholic beverages will be kept and served at home, if the couple will attend social gatherings involving alcohol, and how to deal with these situations. Particular persons, gatherings or circumstances that are likely to be stressful should be identified. Couple interactions related to alcohol also need to be addressed, because arguments, tensions and negative feelings can precipitate more abusive drinking. Therapists need to discuss these patterns with the couple and suggest specific procedures to be used in difficult situations. The remainder of this section describes specific methods and examples of how to achieve the general goals just described.

Behavioral Contracting

Written behavioral contracts, although different in many specific aspects of the agreements, have a number of common elements that make them useful. The drinking behavior goal is made explicit. Specific behaviors that each spouse can do to help achieve this goal are also detailed. The contract provides alternative behaviors to negative interactions about drinking. Finally, and quite importantly, the agreement decreases the non-alcoholic spouse's anxiety and need to control the alcohol abuser and his/her drinking.

Structuring the spouse's and the alcoholic's role in the recovery process

Daniel Kivlahan and Elizabeth Shapiro (personal communication, May 18, 1984) have drinkers and their spouses engage in what they call a Sobriety Trust Contract, as depicted in Figure 22.1. Each day, at a specified time, the drinker initiates a brief discussion and reiterates his/her desire not to drink that day. Then the

SOBRIETY CONTRACT

In order to help _June_____ with her self-control and to bring peace of

mind to _Bill_____, her **partner**, _June_ and

_Bill_____, agree to the following arrangement:

June Responsibilities	_Bill_ Responsibilities
1. _June___ states her intention to stay sober that day to partner.	1. Records that he received this statement of intention on calendar provided.
2. Thanks _Bill_____ for listening.	2. Thanks _June___ for stating this intention to him/her.
3. If necessary, requests that _Bill_____ not mention past drinking or any fears about future drinking.	3. Does not mention past drinking or any fears about future drinking.

EARLY WARNING SYSTEM

If at any time the sobriety trust discussion does not take place for two days in a row,

_Bill or June___ should contact _Rob Rotunda, Ph. D._____ (phone
no: _(508) 583-4500 x3481_) immediately.

LENGTH OF CONTRACT

This agreement covers the time from today until _10_ / _6_ / _93_ . It cannot be changed

unless _June_____ and _Bill_____ discuss the changes in a face-to-face meeting
of at least 30 minutes.

Date: _4_ / _6_ / _93_   _June_____   _William_____
Dr. Rotunda, Ph. D.

Figure 22.1 Sample sobriety trust contract

alcohol abuser asks if the spouse has any questions or fears about possible drinking that day. The drinker answers the questions and attempts to reassure the spouse. The spouse is not to mention past drinking or any future possible drinking beyond that day. The couple agrees not to discuss drinking at other times, to keep the daily trust discussion very brief, and to end with a positive statement.

Two examples illustrate other types of contracts we have used. In the first case, a male alcohol abuser, who recognized he had an alcohol problem and had abstained for 3 months in the past year, was trying to engage in "social drinking". Periodically he would drink heavily for a period of 3–5 days, and three serious binges had occurred in the past 6 weeks. Each binge ended after an intense fight in which the husband became verbally abusive and the wife threatened to terminate their relationship. At a conjoint session with the wife, the following agreement was negotiated: (a) the husband's goal was at least 6 months' abstinence from alcohol; (b) if he drank before then, he would start daily Antabuse and continue it at least to the end of the 6-month period; (c) if the wife thought he had been drinking, she would remind the husband of their agreement and ask him to start the Antabuse; (d) if the husband refused, the wife would refrain from arguing or threats and leave their home until the husband had stopped drinking and started the Antabuse. Two weeks later, the husband drank and then voluntarily started the Antabuse. Both husband and wife were pleased that their customary intense argument was not necessary to terminate the drinking.

In the second case, a chronic alcohol abuser with serious liver cirrhosis reported good progress in outpatient sessions but complained that his wife was unfairly accusing him of drinking and that they were arguing about financial and other problems. At about the same time, liver function tests showed elevated liver enzymes, most likely indicating recent drinking. Couple sessions were begun and the following agreement was established: (a) each evening the husband would taken an alcohol breath test using a Mobile Breath Alcohol Tester ("Mobat; Sobell & Sobell, 1975) to verify that he had not been drinking that day: (b) the wife would refrain from accusations about current drinking or complaints about past drinking; (c) the daily Mobat review would continue until normal liver test results and no evidence of drinking were achieved for two consecutive months; (d) the couple would continue in conjoint sessions about their other relationship problems. Only two isolated instances occurred in which the Mobat indicated the husband had been drinking that day; and the couple conflicts were resolved satisfactorily in later sessions.

Participation in AA and Al-Anon self-help groups is often part of the behavioral contracts we negotiate with couples. As with any other behavior that is part of a "Sobriety Contract", as we call the various forms of behavior contracts we use, attendance at AA and Al-Anon meetings is reviewed at each therapy session.

Antabuse contracts to promote abstinence

Antabuse (disulfiram), a drug that produces extreme nausea and sickness when the person taking the drug ingests alcohol, is often used in treatment for persons with a goal of abstinence. However, Antabuse therapy often is not effective because the alcohol abuser discontinues the drug prematurely (O'Farrell, Allen & Litten, 1995). The Antabuse Contract or Disulfiram Assurance Plan, as depicted in Figure 22.2, is a procedure that has been used by a number of investigators (e.g. Azrin et al., 1982; O'Farrell, Cutter & Floyd, 1985). It is designed to

ANTABUSE CONTRACT

In order to help ___*Mike*___ with ⟨his/her⟩ own self-control and to bring peace of

mind to ___*Nancy*___ , ⟨his/her⟩ ___*wife*___ , ___*Mike*___ and

___*Nancy*___ agree to the following arrangement.

MIKE Responsibilities	***NANCY*** Responsibilities
1. ___*Mike*___ takes Antabuse each day.	1. Observes the Antabuse being taken and records that ___*Nancy*___ observed it on the calendar provided.
2. Thanks ___*Nancy*___ for observing the Antabuse.	2. Thanks ___*Mike*___ for taking the Antabuse and shows appreciation when ⟨he/she⟩ takes it.
3. If necessary, requests that ___*Nancy*___ not mention past drinking or any fears about future drinking.	3. Does not mention past drinking or any fears about future drinking.
4. Refills Antabuse prescription <u>before</u> it runs out.	4. Reminds when prescription needs refilling.

EARLY WARNING SYSTEM: If at any time Antabuse is not taken and observed for 2

days in a row, ___*Nancy or Mike*___ should contact ___*Jane Alter, M.S.W.*___

(Phone No: *(508) 583-4500* *X3481*) immediately.

LENGTH OF CONTRACT: This agreement covers the time from today until

___*8/17/93*___. It cannot be changed unless ___*Mike*___ and

___*Nancy*___ discuss the changes in a face-to-face meeting of at least 30 minutes.

Date: *4/6/93* ___*Nancy*___ ___*Mike*___

___*Jane*___

Figure 22.2 Sample Antabuse contract

maintain Antabuse ingestion and abstinence from alcohol and to decrease alcohol-related arguments and interactions between the drinker and his/her spouse. Before negotiating such a contract, the therapist should be sure that the drinker is willing and medically cleared to take Antabuse and that both the alcohol abuser and spouse have been fully informed and educated about the effects of the drug. In the Antabuse Contract, the drinker agrees to take

Antabuse each day while the spouse observes. The spouse, in turn, agrees to positively reinforce the drinker for taking the Antabuse, to record the observation on a calendar provided by the therapist, and not to mention past drinking or any fears about future drinking. Each spouse should view the agreement as a cooperative method for rebuilding lost trust and not as a coercive checking-up operation. Other articles (e.g. O'Farrell & Bayog, 1986) present more details on how to implement the Antabuse Contract and how to deal with common resistances to this procedure.

Reducing hazardous drinking

Peter Miller (1972) used contingency contracting with an excessive drinker and his wife to produce reduced consumption and fewer arguments about drinking. The couple signed a contract that required the husband to limit his drinking to between 1 and 3 drinks a day (in the presence of his wife before the evening meal) and the wife to refrain from negative verbal or non-verbal responses to her husband's drinking. Each partner agreed to pay the other $20 if he/she broke the agreement. Each spouse received a few fines during the first few weeks of the contract, but the infractions rapidly diminished when each partner learned that the contract would, in fact, be enforced. The alcohol abuser treated by Miller was employed, showed no medical damage from his excessive drinking, and the negative impact of his drinking was confined to the marital relationship. These factors suggested an attempt to reduce rather than eliminate the drinking. Therapists need to choose carefully in each individual case whether the goal of treatment should be moderation or total abstinence. Therapists should use available guidelines (Heather & Robertson, 1981, pp. 215–240) prior to implementing such a behavioral contracting procedure.

Decreasing Spouse Behaviors that Trigger or Enable Drinking

Noel & McCrady (1993) implemented procedures to decrease spouse behaviors that trigger or enable abusive drinking with a female alcohol abuser, Charlotte, and her husband, Tom. The couple identified behaviors by Tom that triggered drinking by Charlotte (e.g. drinking together after work, trying to stop her from drinking, arguing with her about drinking). Charlotte reacted by criticizing Tom until he left her alone and drinking still more. Moreover, Tom unwittingly reinforced Charlotte's drinking by protecting her from the consequences of her drinking (e.g. by helping her to bed when she was drunk, cleaning up after her when she drank). Noel & McCrady helped the couple find mutually comfortable and agreeable methods to reverse Tom's behavior that inadvertently had promoted Charlotte's drinking. Tom decided to give up drinking. He worked hard to change his feelings that he must protect Charlotte from the negative consequences of her drinking. The therapists also taught Tom to provide positive reinforcers (such as verbal acknowledgement, going to movies and other events together) only when Charlotte had not been drinking.

Dealing with Drinking During Treatment

Drinking episodes may occur during couples therapy. Outcomes are best if the therapist intervenes before the drinking goes on for too long a period. Having the drinker keep a daily record of urges to drink (and any drinking that occurs) and reviewing this record each session can help alert the therapist to the possible risk of a relapse. Between-session phone calls to prompt completion of homework assignments can also alert the therapist to precursors of a drinking episode or to drinking already in progress. Once drinking has occurred, the therapist should try to get the drinking stopped and to see the couple as soon as possible to use the relapse as a learning experience. At the couple session, the therapist must be extremely active in defusing hostile or depressive reactions to the drinking. The therapist should stress that drinking does not constitute total failure, that inconsistent progress is the rule rather than the exception. The therapist should help the couple decide what they need to do to feel sure that the drinking is over and will not continue in the coming week (e.g., restarting Antabuse, going to AA and Al-Anon together, reinstituting a Trust Contract, entering a detoxification ward). Finally, the therapist also should try to help the couple identify what couple conflict (or other antecedent) had led up to the relapse and generate alternative solutions other than drinking for similar future situations.

Interventions to Improve the Marital Relationship

After several months of work focusing on stabilizing Jim's recovery and gradually repairing his relationship with Millie, the couple decided to try living together again. Although this came none too soon for Jim, their teenage daughters had reservations when Millie allowed him to return home. Through continued abstinence reinforced by the couple's Sobriety Contract, trust was rebuilt and the couple's communication and negotiation skills improved as a result of their active participation in a behavioral marital therapy couples group program (O'Farrell, 1993a). Although they were aware of how fragile their renewed relationship was, they were able to address concerns of daily life better including issues of parenting, finances and adjustment to life without alcohol.

Once the alcohol abuser has decided to change his/her drinking and has begun successfully to control or abstain from drinking, the therapist can focus on improving the couple's relationship. Spouses often experience resentment about past abusive drinking and fear and distrust about the possible return of abusive drinking in the future. The drinker often experiences guilt and a desire for recognition of current improved drinking behavior. These feelings experienced by the drinker and the spouse often lead to an atmosphere of tension and unhappiness in the marriage. There are problems caused by drinking (e.g. bills, legal charges, embarrassing incidents) that still need to be resolved. There is often a backlog of other unresolved marital and family problems that the drinking obscured. These long-standing problems may seem to increase as drinking declines, when actually the problems are simply being recognized for the first time, now that alcohol cannot be used to excuse them. The couple frequently lacks the communication skills and mutual positive feelings needed to resolve these problems. As a result, many marriages are dissolved during the first 1 or 2 years of the alcohol abuser's recovery. In other cases, marital conflicts trigger relapse and a return to abusive drinking. Even in cases where the alcohol abuser has a basically sound marriage when he/she is not drinking abusively, the initiation of sobriety can produce temporary tension and role readjustment and provide the opportunity for stabilizing and enriching the marriage. For these reasons, many alcohol abusers can benefit from assistance to improve their marital relationship once changes in drinking have begun.

Two major goals of interventions focused on the drinker's marital relationship are: (a) to increase positive feeling, goodwill and commitment to the relationship; and (b) to resolve conflicts, problems and desires for change. Procedures useful in achieving these two goals will be covered separately, even though they often overlap in the course of actual therapy sessions. More detailed descriptions of the procedures are available elsewhere (O'Farrell, 1993a). The general sequence in teaching couples and families skills to increase positive interchanges and resolve conflicts and problems is: (a) therapist instruction and modeling; (b) the couple practicing under therapist supervision; (c) assignment for homework; and (d) review of homework with further practice.

Increasing Positive Interchanges

Increasing pleasing behaviors

A series of procedures can increase a couple's awareness of benefits from the relationship and the frequency with which spouses notice, acknowledge and initiate pleasing or caring behaviors on a daily basis. The therapist tells the couple that *caring behaviors* are "behaviors showing that you care for the other person", and assigns homework called "Catch Your Partner Doing Something Nice" to assist couples in *noticing* the daily caring behaviors in the marriage. This requires each spouse to record one caring behavior performed by the partner each day on sheets provided by the therapist (see Figure 22.3). The therapist should encourage each partner to take risks and to act lovingly toward the spouse rather than wait for the other to make the first move. Finally, the therapist can remind spouses that at the start of therapy they agreed to act differently (e.g. more lovingly) and then assess changes in feelings, rather than wait to feel more positively toward their partner before instituting changes in their own behavior.

Planning shared recreational and leisure activities

Many couples have discontinued or decreased shared leisure activities because in the past the drinker has frequently sought enjoyment only in situations involving alcohol and embarrassed the spouse by drinking too much. Reversing this trend is important because participation by the couple in social and recreational activi-

Check (✓) below if you
told your partner you liked
the behavior you wrote
down today.

"CATCH YOUR PARTNER DOING SOMETHING NICE"

NAME: _Mike_____   NAME OF PARTNER: _Nancy_____

DAY	DATE	PLEASING BEHAVIOR	
MON.	4/6	waited to have dinner with me because I had to stay late at work. Made me feel good.	✓
TUES.	4/7	told me she loved me.	✓
WED.	4/8	cooked a delicious Italian dinner and afterwards we had a very romantic evening.	✓
THUR.	4/9	was patient with me as I came home tired and moody from work.	✓
FRI.	4/10	enjoyed a walk together around the neighborhood.	✓
SAT.	4/11	woke me gently and rubbed my back.	✓
SUN.	4/12	helped me host an afternoon party with some friends of ours.	✓

Figure 22.3   Sample record sheet of daily caring behaviors

ties is associated with positive alcohol treatment outcome (Moos, Finney & Cronkite, 1990). Planning and engaging in shared rewarding activities can be very effective in re-establishing affective expression and other positive aspects of the relationship lost because of drinking.

Resolving Conflicts and Problems

Training in communication skills

Inadequate communication is a major problem for alcohol abusers and their spouses (O'Farrell & Birchler, 1987). Inability to resolve conflicts and problems can cause abusive drinking and severe marital tensions to recur (Maisto et al., 1988). Therapists can use instructions, modeling, prompting, behavioral rehearsal and feedback to teach couples and families how to communicate more effectively. Learning communication skills of listening and speaking, and how to use planned communication sessions, are essential prerequisites for problem-solving and negotiating desired behavior changes.

Behavior change agreements

Many alcohol abusers and their spouses need to learn positive methods to change their partner's behavior to replace the coercive strategies previously used. Many changes that spouses desire from their partners can be achieved through the aforementioned caring behaviors, rewarding activities, and communication and problem-solving skills. However, deeper, emotion-laden conflicts that have caused considerable hostility and coercive interaction for years are more resistant to change. Learning to make positive specific requests (PSR) and to negotiate and compromise are prerequisites that can lead to sound behavior-change agreements to resolve such issues.

Agreements can be a major focus of a number of therapy sessions. Couples negotiate written behavior-change agreements for the forthcoming week, often with very good effects on their relationship. During the sessions, the therapist reviews unkept agreements briefly, provides feedback about what went wrong, and suggests changes needed in the coming week. After completing agreements under therapist supervision, the couple uses a communication session at home to negotiate an agreement on their own and to bring it to the following session for review. A series of such assignments can provide a couple with the opportunity to develop skills in behavior change that they can use after the therapy ends. We encourage good-faith agreements in which each partner agrees to make his/her change independent of whether or not the spouse keeps the agreement and without monetary or other rewards or punishments. This approach stresses the need for each spouse freely and unilaterally to make the changes needed to improve the marital relationship.

MAINTAINING DRINKING AND RELATIONSHIP CHANGES

Preventing Relapse

Methods to ensure long-term maintenance of the changes in alcohol problems made through couples therapy are beginning to receive attention (McCrady, 1993; O'Farrell, 1993b). We use three general methods during the maintenance phase of treatment, defined somewhat arbitrarily as the phase that begins after at least 6 consecutive months of abstinence or consistent non-problem drinking have been achieved. First, the therapist must plan maintenance prior to the termination of the active treatment phase. We review the previous therapy sessions with the clients to determine which therapeutic interventions or behavior changes (e.g. Antabuse contract, communication sessions) have been most helpful. Then we plan how the couple can continue to engage in the desired new behaviors when needed (e.g. rehearsing how to cope with situations likely to interfere with the new behavior, rereading handouts from the therapy periodically, agreeing to periodic monitoring by the therapist). A second method is to anticipate what high-risk situations for relapse to abusive drinking may be likely to occur after treatment, and to discuss and rehearse possible coping strategies that the alcoholic and spouse can use to prevent relapse when confronted with such situations. A third method is to discuss and rehearse how to cope with a relapse when it occurs. Here, the techniques suggested by Marlatt & Gordon (1985) can be useful: allow a delay after the first drink; call the therapist; engage in realistic and rational thinking about the slip. A specific couple relapse-episode plan, written and reheased prior to ending active treatment, can be particularly useful. Early intervention at the beginning of a relapse episode is essential and must be stressed with the couple. Often, spouses wait until the drinking has reached dangerous levels again before acting. By then, much additional damage has been done to the marital relationship and to other aspects of the drinker's life.

We suggest continued contact with the couple via planned in-person and telephone follow-up sessions, at regular and then gradually increasing intervals, for 3–5 years after a stable pattern of recovery has been achieved. The therapist uses this ongoing contact to monitor progress, to assess compliance with planned maintenance procedures, and to evaluate the need for additional therapy sessions. The therapist must take responsibility for scheduling and reminding the couple of follow-up sessions and for placing agreed-upon phone calls so that continued contact can be maintained successfully. The therapist tells couples that the reason for continued contact is that alcohol abuse is a chronic health problem that requires active, aggressive, ongoing monitoring to prevent or to quickly treat relapses for at least 5 years after an initial period of stable recovery has been established. The follow-up contact also provides the opportunity to deal with marital issues that appear later.

Marital Issues in Long-term Recovery

Many alcohol abusers continue to experience significant marital difficulties after a period of stable recovery has been established. Although a wide variety of issues can present difficulties during long-term recovery, a number of concerns and life patterns predominate. These problem areas include: (a) role readjustment when the drinker tries to regain important marital and family roles lost through drinking; (b) sex and intimacy; and (c) parent–child relationships, especially communication and behavior management with adolescents. Finally, couples during the recovery process seem particularly vulnerable to stresses created by critical transitions in the family life cycle (e.g. children leaving home), external life change events (e.g. job loss), and/or developmental changes in any of the family members (e.g. mid-life crisis). These issues are by no means unique to couples with an alcohol-abusing member. However, the therapist has two additional responsibilities when such issues are presented by couples during long-term recovery. First, the therapist must determine whether a relapse is imminent so that necessary preventive interventions can be instituted immediately. Second, the therapist must: (a) determine each spouse's view of the relationship between the former alcohol problem and the current marital difficulties; and (b) carefully assess whether or not he/she shares the couple's view. The latter is important because couples often continue to attribute difficulties in their relationships to the previous alcohol problem, rather than to their current life situation.

A final problem encountered all too frequently is that even though the alcohol problem is under control, the marriage is no longer viable. We label this "successful sobriety and the bankrupt marriage" to the couples we work with and consider "breaking up without breaking out" a major accomplishment. Spouses may have grown apart, or one may be unwilling to set aside the past hurts. Whatever the reason, facing the emptiness and inevitable dissolution of the marriage often precipitates a dangerous crisis. If there has been a strong tendency to blame the drinker for relationship problems, there is a strong push to want the alcohol abuser to drink again to provide the reason for the marital break-up. The therapist can try to help the couple confront separation and divorce without requiring the alcohol abuser to fail again and be the scapegoat for the break-up. If the couple can separate without the alcohol abuser drinking, the alcohol abuser's future relationship with his/her children may be preserved, and both spouses may be able to obtain a realistic assessment of the basis for their divorce.

CLINICAL ISSUES IN APPLICATION

Many clinical issues have already been considered. Therapist and client characteristics associated with positive therapeutic outcomes deserve further consideration.

THERAPIST ATTRIBUTES AND BEHAVIORS NEEDED

Our clinical experience suggests that certain therapist attributes and behaviors are important for successful couples therapy with alcohol abusers. From the outset, the therapist must structure treatment so that control of the alcohol abuse is the first priority, before attempting to help the couple with other problems. Many of our clients have had previous unsuccessful experiences with therapists who saw the couple without dealing with the alcohol abuse. The hope that reduction in marital distress will lead to improvement in the drinking problem is rarely fulfilled. More typically, recurrent alcohol-related incidents undermine whatever gains have been made in the marital relationship.

Therapists must be able to deal effectively with strong anger in early sessions and at later times of crisis. The therapist can use empathic listening to help each member of the couple feel they have been heard and insist that only one person speaks at a time. Helping the couple defuse intense anger is important, since failure to do so often leads to a poor outcome (Gurman & Kniskern, 1978).

Therapists need to structure and take control of treatment sessions, especially the early assessment and therapy phase and at later times of crisis (e.g. episodes of drinking or intense couple conflict). Highly structured therapy sessions with a directive, active therapist are more effective than a less structured mode of therapy. Many therapists' errors involve difficulty establishing and maintaining control of the sessions and responding to the myriad forms of resistance and non-compliance presented by couples. Therapists must steer a middle course between lack of structure and being overly controlling and punitive in response to non-compliance. Therapists need to establish the rules of treatment and to acknowledge progress despite significant shortcomings.

Finally, therapists need to take a long-term view of the course of change—both the alcohol problem and associated marital distress may be helped substantially only by repeated efforts, including some failed attempts. Such a long-term view may help the therapist encounter relapse without becoming overly discouraged or engaging in blaming and recriminations with the alcohol abuser and spouse. The therapist also should maintain contact with the couple long after the problems apparently have stabilized. Leaving such contacts to the couple usually means no follow-up contacts occur until they are back in a major crisis again.

CLIENTS MOST LIKELY TO BENEFIT

Unfortunately, studies examining predictors of response to couples therapy with alcohol abusers are not yet available. However, clinical experience and studies of factors that predict acceptance and completion of couples therapy among alcoholics (Noel et al., 1987; O'Farrell, Kleinke & Cutter, 1986; Zweben, Pearlman & Li, 1983) provide some information on clients most likely to benefit from such treatment, since the clients must accept and stay in therapy to benefit. Clients most likely to accept and complete couples therapy have the following characteristics: (a) a high school education or better; (b) employed if able and desirous of working; (c) live together or, if separated, are willing to reconcile for the duration of the therapy; (d) older; (e) have more serious alcohol problems of longer duration; (f) enter therapy after a crisis, especially one that threatens the stability of the marriage; (g) spouse and other family members do not have serious alcohol problems; (h) alcohol abuser, spouse and other family members without serious psychopathology or drug abuse; and (i) absence of domestic violence that has caused serious injury or is potentially life-threatening. Further, evidence that the drinker is motivated to change and to take an active role in a psychologically-oriented treatment approach also suggests potential for benefiting from couples therapy. Such evidence includes contact with the treatment program personally initiated by the problem drinker and a history of successful participation in other outpatient counseling or self-help programs (as opposed to those only admitted to detoxification for relief of physical distress due to heavy drinking, without further active ongoing treatment participation). Compliance with the initial month of outpatient treatment, including abstinence, keeping scheduled appointments and completing any required assignments, are process measures that seem to predict likely benefit on a clinical basis.

These characteristics may sound like those of model clients who are likely to benefit from nearly any treatment method. However, clients do not have to fit these criteria for therapists to use the couples therapy methods described in this chapter. Rather the couples therapy methods have to be adapted for some of the more difficult cases—generally by going slower, individualizing the approach to a greater degree, and dealing with more varied and more frequent obstacles and resistances. Strategies for dealing with some of the more difficult cases (e.g. the separated alcohol abuser; the family with more than one alcohol-abusing member) have been presented elsewhere (O'Farrell, 1986).

OUTCOME RESEARCH

This overview of outcome research covers studies that included a comparison group of some type and at least some follow-up data. This review is organized according to the stage of the change to which the treatment in each study was directed.

STUDIES OF METHODS TO INITIATE CHANGE IN THE DRINKER AND HELP THE SPOUSE WHEN THE ALCOHOL ABUSER RESISTS TREATMENT

Unilateral Family Therapy (UFT) with the spouses of alcohol abusers has been evaluated in two studies. An initial pilot study (Thomas et al., 1987) randomly assigned 15 spouses of alcohol abusers to receive either immediate or delayed UFT and studied 10 other non-random comparison cases who dropped out after little or no treatment. From 13 (of 15) UFT-treated cases with usable data, eight drinkers (62%) had entered treatment and/or reduced drinking, whereas none of the 10 untreated cases with available data had done so (p = 0.02 by Fisher's Exact Test). Results also showed a decrease in spouses' emotional distress and increases in marital satisfaction after UFT. A second study (Thomas et al., 1993) randomly assigned spouses to either an immediate ($n = 27$) or delayed ($n = 28$) UFT treatment. An additional non-random, untreated comparison group consisted of 14 spouses. Results showed reductions after UFT in certain spouse behaviors, including enabling attempts to control the alcohol abuser's drinking, psychopathology and life distress, and improvements in marital adjustment and satisfaction. Treatment entry of the alcohol abuser was significantly higher immediately following spouse treatment than at comparable time periods for the delayed and untreated cases. The preliminary reports of these two studies (Thomas et al., 1987, 1993) present favorable outcomes for UFT. We need a more complete report of the findings of these two studies to evaluate the effectiveness of UFT more fully.

In their study of Community Reinforcement Training (CRT) for families, Sisson & Azrin (1986) randomly assigned 12 family members (mostly spouses) to either the CRT program or to a "traditional disease model program" of alcohol education, individual supportive counseling, and referral to Al-Anon. Six of seven alcohol abusers entered treatment after relatives had received CRT for a mean of 58.2 days and an average of 7.2 sessions. During the 5 months after their relative started CRT, the drinkers showed more than a 50% reduction in average consumption prior to treatment entry and nearly total abstinence in the 3 months after entering treatment. None of the five drinkers whose relatives received the traditional program (mean of 3.5 sessions) entered treatment and their drinking was not reduced during the 3 months for which outcome data were available. The impressive results, the small sample size, and the differential credibility and intensity of the CRT and comparison treatments argue strongly for a need to replicate the results.

Research support for the Johnson Institute Intervention approach comes from a demonstration project (Liepman, Nirenberg & Begin, 1989) in which less than 30% (7 of 24) of families given the Intervention training completed the confrontation. Of the seven drinkers who were confronted by their families and social networks, six (86%) entered treatment as compared with 17% of those not confronted. The confronted drinkers had longer periods of abstinence on average (11 months vs. 3 months) than those not confronted. Given the self-selected rather than random assignment to confronted and non-confronted groups, this study provides only very modest support for the Johnson Intervention. The low rate of performing the confrontation was unexpected. Only further study can determine the extent of this problem and the efficacy of the Johnson approach.

Dittrich & Trapold (1984) randomly assigned 23 wives of treatment-resistant alcohol abusers to an 8-week group therapy program with a primarily disease concept focus ($n = 10$) or a waiting-list control condition ($n = 13$). Results showed significant improvements in enabling behaviors, anxiety, and self-concept at the end of treatment for the experimental group relative to the waiting-list control; similar improvement occurred for those on the waiting list once they had completed treatment. Improvements were maintained at the 2- and 4-month follow-up. Outcomes during the 12 months after intake showed that 48% of the husbands had entered some form of treatment for their alcohol problem and 39% of the wives had either separated from or divorced their husband.

Al-Anon is by far the most widely used source of support for family members troubled by a loved one's alcohol problem. Although no controlled research is available concerning the effectiveness of Al-Anon, a small number of correlational studies have been done. Among wives of alcohol abusers, Al-Anon membership is associated with: (a) fewer ineffective ways (e.g. covering up for the drinker, nagging, trying to control the drinking) of coping with their husbands' drinking (Gorman & Rooney, 1979; Rychtarik et al., 1988); and (b) better abstinence rates for alcohol abusers whose wives are receiving outpatient counseling (Wright & Scott, 1978).

STUDIES OF METHODS TO STABILIZE CHANGES WHEN THE ALCOHOL ABUSER SEEKS HELP

Separate Concurrent Treatment of the Alcohol Abuser and the Spouse

Separate concurrent treatment for the alcohol abuser and family remains quite popular in clinical practice in the USA. The Hazelden 3–5-day residential psychoeducational program for spouses and family members of alcohol abusers is a well known example. Based on the 12-step Al-Anon program, the Hazelden family program advocates that family members should detach from the alcohol abuser and focus on themselves in order to help reduce their own emotional distress and improve their own coping. Although program evaluation reports have shown participants' satisfaction with various program elements, attitude changes targeted by the program, and Al-Anon involvement by about half (e.g. Laundergan & Williams, 1979), controlled studies are needed to provide support for the effectiveness of the Hazelden family program. This is important because many treatment agencies use such a psychoeducational disease model program as their "family program" component. In contrast with clinical practitioners, outcome researchers have paid little attention to separate and concurrent treatment for the alcohol abuser and family. Research of the last 20 years has concentrated on methods that involve the alcohol abuser and spouse together in treatment.

Non-behavioral Conjoint Treatment of the Alcohol Abuser and the Spouse

Building on earlier studies (Burton & Kaplan, 1968; Cadogan, 1973; Corder, Corder & Laidlaw, 1972), McCrady et al. (1979) evaluated the relative effectiveness of adding joint hospitalization and couples therapy to individual treatment for alcohol problems. Subjects were randomly assigned to: (a) individual involvement in which only the drinker attended group therapy; (b) couples involvement in which the drinker and spouse participated in an outpatient interactional couples therapy group in addition to concurrent individual treatment groups for each spouse; or (c) joint admission in which both partners were initially hospitalized and then participated in both the couples group therapy and individual therapy groups following discharge. At 6-month follow-up, findings indicated significant decreases in alcohol intake for both the couples involvement and joint admission treatment groups but not for the individual treatment group. All groups showed significant decreases in marital problems. Four-year follow-up data from the McCrady et al. (1979) joint hospitalization and couples therapy outcome study showed there were no longer any significant differences among the different treatment groups in the study on either marital or drinking adjustment (McCrady et al., 1982). The results of this study also showed a commonly observed pattern of decay in outcomes over time with more than 75% of the subjects showing improvement at 6-month follow-up but less than one-third functioning consistently well over the 4 years.

Zweben and colleagues (Zweben, Pearlman & Li, 1988) conducted the only controlled outcome study to date of a family systems approach to treating alcohol problems. The study randomly assigned 116 alcohol abusers to either: (a) eight sessions of Conjoint Therapy based on a communication–interactional approach, in which the presenting problem (alcohol abuse) was viewed from a systemic perspective as having adaptive or functional consequences for the couple; or (b) a single session of Advice Counselling which also involved the spouse. Results over an 18-month follow-up period indicated that couples in both Advice Counselling and Conjoint Therapy showed significant improvement on all marital adjustment and drinking-related outcome measures, but there were no significant between-group differences on any of the outcome measures. Thus, a single session of Advice Counselling was as effective as eight sessions of systems-based Conjoint Therapy. Zweben et al. noted that their subjects had only a moderate degree of alcohol-related difficulties and relatively non-distressed marital relationships and suggested that their findings may be limited to this specific client population.

Behavioral Conjoint Treatment of the Alcohol Abuser and the Spouse

Behavioral Contracting to Maintain Antabuse (Disulfiram) Ingestion

Azrin et al. (1982) randomly assigned alcohol abusing outpatients to one of three treatment groups: (a) traditional, self-initiated disulfiram treatment; (b) disulfiram assurance with a significant other, usually the spouse, observing and reinforcing the ingestion of the medication; and (c) disulfiram assurance plus a multifaceted behavior therapy program. At six-month follow-up, the behavior therapy plus disulfiram assurance group was almost fully abstinent, drinking on the average 0.4 days a month. The traditional group, in contrast, had stopped disulfiram and was drinking on the average 16.4 days a month. Follow-up results for the disulfiram assurance group as a whole were intermediate between the other two groups. However, for married alcohol abusers, disulfiram assurance alone was sufficient to produce almost total abstinence.

Keane et al. (1984) randomly assigned male alcohol abusers being discharged from a 4-week behaviorally-oriented inpatient alcohol treatment program to: (a) disulfiram prescription and contract with significant other, usually the wife, plus instructions for the wife to use positive reinforcement for contract compliance; (b) disulfiram prescription and contract with significant other; or (c) disulfiram prescription without contract. At 3-month follow-up, 84% of all subjects were still abstinent and taking disulfiram daily by collateral report, with no significant differences among treatment groups. A greater proportion of subjects in the contract groups had filled all three monthly prescriptions of disulfiram, but this difference did not significantly distinguish the groups.

The Azrin et al. (1982) and Keane et al. (1984) studies of spouse behavioral contracting to maintain disulfiram ingestion reach opposite conclusions about the usefulness of such procedures. A number of differences in the studies may explain the differing results. The Azrin et al. study was with applicants for outpatient treatment who received 5 weekly outpatient sessions, the spouse was not involved in the prescription-only condition, and data were gathered for 6 months follow-up. In the Keane et al. study, subjects started disulfiram after at least 4 weeks of inpatient treatment, the spouse and patient together received a videotape on the use of disulfiram and its effects in all conditions including the prescription-only group, and only 3 months' follow-up data were gathered. Given these differing results and the evidence from other studies showing that patients who stay on disulfiram have better alcohol treatment outcomes (Allen & Litten, 1992; O'Farrell et al., 1993), further research is needed.

Multifaceted Behavioral Couples Therapy

The Program for Alcoholic Couples Treatment (PACT) study

This study compared three types of behavioral spouse-involved treatment. McCrady and colleagues (McCrady et al., 1986) randomly assigned alcohol abusers and spouses to one of three outpatient behavioral treatments: (a) minimal spouse involvement (MSI), in which the spouse simply observed the alcohol abuser's individual therapy; (b) alcohol-focused spouse involvement (AFSI), which included teaching the spouse specific skills to deal with alcohol-related situations plus the MSI interventions; (c) alcohol behavioral marital therapy (ABMT), in which all skills taught in the MSI and AFSI conditions were included as well as BMT. Results at 6-month follow-up indicated that all subjects had decreased drinking and reported increased life satisfaction and suggested ABMT led to better treatment outcomes than the other spouse-involved therapies. Specifically, ABMT couples: (a) maintained their marital satisfaction after treatment better and tended to have more stable marriages than the other two groups; and (b) were more compliant with homework assign-ments, decreased the number of drinking days during treatment, and their post-treatment drinking increased more slowly than AFSI couples. Follow-up data through 18 months from the PACT study (McCrady et al., 1991) showed that patients who received marital therapy (i.e. ABMT group) had fewer marital separations and more improvement in marital satisfaction and subjective well-being than those who received individual alcohol-focused therapy only (MSI group) or individual plus spouse focus to change drinking (AFSI group). Furthermore, ABMT had better drinking outcomes at 18-month follow-up than MSI or AFSI.

The Counseling for Alcoholics' Marriages (CALM) Project study

In this initial Project CALM study, O'Farrell and colleagues (O'Farrell & Cutter, 1982; O'Farrell, Cutter & Floyd, 1985) investigated the effect of adding behavioral marital therapy (BMT) couples group treatment to individually-oriented outpatient treatment of married male alcohol abusers. Thirty-six couples, in which the husband had recently begun individual alcohol counseling that included an Antabuse prescription, were randomly assigned to a no-marital-treatment control group or to 10 weekly sessions of either a BMT (Antabuse Contract plus behavioral rehearsal of communication skills and marital agreements) or an interactional (largely verbal interaction and sharing of feelings and Antabuse without spouse involvement) couples group. Assessment of marital and drinking adjustment provided comparison data pre- and post-treatment and at two and six months follow-up. Results for marital adjustment showed the BMT couples: (a) improved from pre- to post-treatment on a variety of measures and remained significantly improved at follow-ups; (b) did better than control couples who did not improve on any measures; and (c) did better than interactional couples whose improvement from pre- to post-treatment on two measures was not sustained at follow-up. On drinking adjustment, alcohol abusers in all three treatments showed significant improvements that were sustained at follow-ups and BMT subjects did better than interactional subjects at post and at 2-month follow-up. O'Farrell and colleagues concluded that adding a BMT couples group to outpatient alcoholism counseling showed clear advantages for the alcohol abusers' marital relationships but no additional gains in drinking adjustment. The less positive results for the interactional couples group suggested that just talking about relationship problems without making specific changes may lead to conflict and drinking, and that the Antabuse Contract protected the BMT couples while they learned new skills to confront their problems without alcohol.

Two-year follow-up data from the initial Project CALM study (O'Farrell et al., 1992), known as CALM-1, showed that alcohol abusers and their wives who received BMT in addition to individual counseling remained significantly improved on marital and drinking adjustment throughout the 2 years. Although BMT remained superior to individual counseling alone on marital adjustment throughout much of the 2-year follow-up, the strength and the consistency of findings favoring BMT diminished as time after treatment increased. Similarly the superiority of BMT over the interactional group on marital outcomes faded as a function of time after treatment. On drinking, BMT remained superior to interactional for part of the first year after treatment, but by 24 months follow-up there were no differences between groups, all of which remained significantly improved from pretreatment levels. Finally, alcohol abusers with the most severe marital and drinking problems prior to treatment had the worst outcomes in the 2 years after treatment. Thus, CALM-1 study results showed that the addition of BMT to individual counseling produced: (a) marital (but not drinking) outcomes that were markedly superior to individual counseling alone during, and in the six months after, treatment, but that difference faded in strength and consistency by the end of the 2-year follow-up; and (b) BMT marital and drinking outcomes were modestly superior to the interactional couples therapy through 6-month follow-up, but there differences diminished rather quickly thereafter. These results suggested that a logical next step in research on BMT would involve an outcome study of treatment methods to maintain the gains produced by BMT, especially for drinking and related behaviors.

COUPLES RELAPSE PREVENTION SESSIONS

The CALM-1 results just described led to a CALM-2 study to evaluate the usefulness of couples relapse prevention (RP) sessions for maintaining changes in marital and drinking adjustment produced by short-term BMT couples groups. A couples-based maintenance intervention was used because, in earlier BMT research, events in the marriage and factors involving the spouse were the reasons most frequently cited by the alcohol abusers as the cause of relapse and as reasons for ending a relapse episode (Maisto et al., 1988). In this study, 59 couples with an alcohol-abusing husband, after participating weekly for 5 months in a BMT couples group program, were assigned randomly to receive or not receive 15 additional couples RP sessions over the next 12 months. Outcome measures were collected before and after BMT and at quarterly intervals for the $2\frac{1}{2}$ years after BMT. The CALM-2 study (O'Farrell et al., 1993, 1995) produced two major findings. First, results for the entire sample showed the additional RP sessions produced better outcomes during and for the 6–12 months after the end of RP. Specifically, alcohol abusers who received RP after BMT had more days abstinent and used the Antabuse Contract more than those who received BMT alone, with the superior RP drinking outcomes lasting through 18 months' follow-up (i.e. 6 months after the end of RP). Couples who received the additional RP also maintained their improved marriages longer (through 24 months' follow-up) than did their counterparts who received BMT only (through 12 months' follow-up). Second, for alcohol abusers with more severe marital and drinking problems, RP produced better marital and drinking outcomes throughout the 30-month follow-up period. Specifically, alcohol abusers with more severe marital problems at study entry had better marital adjustment, more abstinent days, and maintained relatively stable levels of abstinence, if they received the additional RP, while their counterparts who did not receive RP had poorer marital adjustment, fewer abstinent days, and showed a steep decline in abstinent days in the 30 months after BMT. Further, alcohol abusers with more severe alcohol problems at study entry used the Antabuse Contract more, and showed a less steep decline in use of the Antabuse Contract in the 30 months after BMT, if they received the additional RP than if they did not. Thus the CALM-2 study indicated that adding couples RP sessions in the year after BMT produced better marital and drinking outcomes than BMT alone. These better RP outcomes persisted through 18–24 months after BMT for the entire sample, and throughout the entire 30 months follow-up period after BMT for those with more severe marital and drinking problems. The better results cannot be attributed with certainty to the couples RP sessions since this CALM-2 study did not include control groups that received aftercare sessions without the spouse involved and without a specific RP focus.

The CALM-2 study also examined the mechanisms whereby BMT and RP produce change. We assume that BMT produces better outcomes because BMT increases marital relationship factors that are conducive to sobriety. These factors include social support for abstinence, relationship cohesion, and effective communication. BMT attempts to provide social support for abstinence so that the spouse reinforces behaviors leading toward abstinence (e.g. Antabuse) and refrains from punishing attempts at sobriety (e.g. by nagging about past or feared future drinking). Building relationship cohesion and positive activities together provides a less stressful family environment which reduces the risk of relapse. Teaching the couple effective communication and problem-solving skills provides coping skills for dealing with marital and environmental stressors. The CALM-2 study (O'Farrell et al., 1993, 1995) found that the additional RP produced greater continued use of behaviors targeted by BMT (e.g. the Antabuse Contract, shared recreational activities, constructive communication) than did BMT alone. Further, greater use of BMT-targeted behaviors was associated with better marital and drinking outcomes after BMT irrespective of the amount of aftercare received.

CONCLUSIONS AND FUTURE DIRECTIONS

Studies show that couples therapy and spouse-involved interventions can be used effectively to motivate an initial commitment to change in the alcohol abuser and help the spouse when the drinker is unwilling to seek help. Further, correlational research shows an association between spouse involvement in Al-Anon and more sobriety for the alcohol abuser and better coping for the spouse. These studies require replication since they generally have relatively small samples and present a variety of methodological concerns. Moreover, the most popular and frequently used methods—the Johnson Institute Intervention and Al-Anon—have little or no controlled research supporting their effectiveness. Conversely, methods that have at least some research support for their effectiveness—Community Reinforcement Training, Unilateral Family Therapy, Dittrich's groups therapy for spouses—are used infrequently, if at all.

Evidence continues to accumulate that couples therapy helps stabilize marital relationships and supports improvements in alcohol abusers' drinking during the 6–12 month period following treatment for alcohol problems. Couples therapy produces better results during this time period than methods that do not involve the spouse. Two conclusions can be drawn from this work on couples therapy to stabilize changes in drinking and relationships for the alcohol abuser who seeks help. First, the most promising method is a behavioral approach that combines both a focus on the drinking and drinking-related interactions, plus work on more general marital relationship issues. Second, reminiscent of concerns about methods to initiate change, the most popular, most influential and most frequently used methods—family systems and family disease models—have little or no research support for their effectiveness. Conversely, methods that have the strongest research support for their effectiveness—various behavioral couples therapy methods—enjoy little popularity and are used infrequently, if at all.

Studies of couples therapy to promote long-term recovery are relatively recent and consist solely of behavioral methods. Two studies suggest that BMT with both an alcohol and relationship focus may reduce marital and/or drinking deterioration during long-term recovery better than individually focused methods (McCrady et al., 1991; O'Farrell et al., 1992). An additional study supports the effectiveness of behavioral couples relapse prevention sessions (O'Farrell et al., 1993, 1995). Despite these recent positive beginnings, more research is needed to understand the potential of BMT in maintaining gains and preventing relapse.

Future directions for outcome research follow from this overview of couples therapy and spouse-involved interventions to initiate, stabilize and maintain changes in drinking and relationships among alcohol abusers and their spouses. First, narrowing the gap between research and practice is an important direction for future work. To narrow this gap, future work should replicate promising approaches, evaluate popular but untested methods, and apply research tested methods to clinical practice. Second, couples therapy research must expand its focus. To test the generalizability of current couples therapy research findings, we need studies with broader target populations that include women and minorities, and a wide range of clients from poorer prognosis cases with co-morbid psychopathology and drug problems (Fals-Stewart, Birchler & O'Farrell, 1996) to those with mild to moderate alcohol problems (Walitzer, Dermen & Connors, 1995). Expanded research questions will move beyond issues of effectiveness to questions about patient treatment-matching (Longabaugh et al., 1995) and the mechanisms whereby couples therapy produces change (McCrady, Epstein & Hirsch, 1995; O'Farrell et al., 1995). In addition, the positive effects observed with couples therapy should lead to efforts to evaluate the use of methods that involve members of the alcoholics' broader social network beyond the spouse (Longabaugh et al., 1993). Finally, outcome domains will go beyond statistical significance of comparisons between groups on measures of drinking and relationship adjustment. Future studies should evaluate the functioning of spouses and children and the clinical and societal significance of changes observed. Examples of the latter are recent studies showing: (a) reductions in domestic violence after BMT (O'Farrell & Murphy, 1995); and (b) cost savings from reduced alcohol-related health and legal system utilization after BMT that were more than five times the cost of delivering the BMT program (O'Farrell et al., 1996).

This chapter shows that couples therapy and spouse-involved interventions, particularly behavioral methods, are an effective treatment for alcohol problems. Future work will narrow the gap between research and practice and expand the focus of couples therapy and alcoholism research to consider family systems and 12-step family disease approaches. This future work, much of which is now in progress, will aid our efforts to help alcohol abusers and their spouses.

REFERENCES

Al-Anon Family Groups (1981). *This Is Al-Anon*. New York: Al-Anon.

Allen, J.P. & Litten, R.Z. (1992). Techniques to enhance compliance with disulfiram. *Alcoholism: Clinical and Experimental Research*, **16**, 1035–1041.

Annis, H.M. (1982). *Situational Confidence Questionnaire*. Toronto: Addiction Research Foundation.

Annis, H.M. (1985). *Inventory of Drinking Situations*. Toronto: Addiction Research Foundation.

Azrin, N.H., Sisson, R.W., Meyers, R. & Godley, M. (1982). Alcoholism treatment by disulfiram and community reinforcement therapy. *Journal of Behavior Therapy and Experimental Psychiatry*, **13**, 105–112.

Burton, G. & Kaplan, H.M. (1968). Group counseling in conflicted marriages where alcoholism is present: client's evaluation of effectiveness. *Journal of Marriage and the Family*, **30**, 74–79.

Cadogan, D.A. (1973). Marital group therapy in the treatment of alcoholism. *Quarterly Journal of Studies on Alcohol*, **34**, 1187–1194.

Corder, B.F., Corder, R.F. & Laidlaw, N.D. (1972). An intensive treatment program for alcoholics and their wives. *Quarterly Journal of Studies on Alcohol*, **33**, 1144–1146.

Dittrich, J.E. (1993). A group program for wives of treatment-resistant alcoholics. In T.J. O'Farrell (ed.), *Treating Alcohol Problems: Marital and Family Interventions* (pp. 78–114). New York: Guilford.

Dittrich, J.E. & Trapold, M.A. (1984). Wives of alcoholics: a treatment program and outcome study. *Bulletin of the Society of Psychologists in Addictive Behaviors*, **3**, 91–102.

Fals-Stewart, W., Birchler, G.R. & O'Farrell, T.J. (1996). The effect of behavioral couples therapy on treatment response and outcome among male drug abusers. *Journal of Consulting and Clinical Psychology*, in press.

Floyd, F.J., O'Farrell, T.J. & Goldberg, M. (1987). A comparison of marital observational measures: the Marital Interaction Coding System and the Communication Skills Test. *Journal of Consulting and Clinical Psychology*, **55**, 423–429.

Gorman, J.M. & Rooney, J.F. (1979). The influence of Al-Anon on the coping behavior of wives of alcoholics. *Journal of Studies on Alcohol*, **40**, 1030–1038.

Gurman, A.S. & Kniskern, D.P. (1978). Deterioration in marital and family therapy: empirical, clinical and conceptual issues. *Family Process*, **17**, 3–20.

Heather, N. & Robertson, I. (1981). *Controlled Drinking*. London: Methuen.

Johnson, V.A. (1973). *I'll Quit Tomorrow*. New York: Harper & Row.

Keane, T.M., Foy, D.W., Nunn, B. & Rychtarik, R.G. (1984). Spouse contracting to increase Antabuse compliance in alcoholic veterans. *Journal of Clinical Psychology*, **40**, 340–344.

Laundergan, J.C. & Williams, T. (1979). Hazelden: evaluation of a residential family program. *Alcohol Health and Research World*, **13**, 13–16.

Liepman, M.R. (1993). Using family member influence to motivate alcoholics to enter treatment: the Johnson Institute Intervention approach. In T.J. O'Farrell (ed.), *Treating Alcohol Problems: Marital and Family Interventions* (pp. 54–77). New York: Guilford.

Liepman, M.R., Nirenberg, T.D. & Begin, A.M. (1989). Evaluation of a program designed to help family and significant others to motivate resistant alcoholics into recovery. *American Journal of Drug and Alcohol Abuse*, **15**, 209–221.

Locke, H.J. & Wallace, K.M. (1959). Short marital adjustment and prediction test: their reliability and validity. *Journal of Marriage and Family Living*, **21**, 251–255.

Longabaugh, R., Beattie, M., Noel, N., Stout, R. & Malloy, P. (1993). The effect of social investment on treatment outcome. *Journal of Studies on Alcohol*, **54**, 465–478.

Longabaugh, R., Wirtz, P.W., Beattie, M., Noel, N. & Stout, R. (1995). Matching treatment focus to patient social investment and support: 18-month follow-up results. *Journal of Consulting and Clinical Psychology*, **63**, 296–307.

Maisto, S.A., O'Farrell, T.J., Connors, G.J., McKay, J. & Pelcovitz, M.A. (1988). Alcoholics' attributions of factors affecting their relapse to drinking and reasons for terminating relapse events. *Addictive Behaviors*, **13**, 79–82.

Margolin, G., Talovic, S. & Weinstein, C.D. (1983). Areas of Change Questionnaire: a practical approach to marital assessment. *Journal of Consulting and Clinical Psychology*, **51**, 920–931.

Marlatt, G.A. & Gordon, J. (1985). *Relapse Prevention: Maintenance Strategies in the Treatment of Addictive Behaviors*. New York: Guilford.

McCrady, B.S. (1993). Relapse prevention: a couples therapy perspective. In T.J. O'Farrell (ed.), *Treating Alcohol Problems: Marital and Family Interventions* (pp. 327–350). New York: Guilford.

McCrady, B.S., Epstein, E. & Hirsch, L. (1995). Testing hypothesized mediators of change in conjoint behavioral alcoholism treatment. In T.J. O'Farrell (Chair): Marital and Spouse-involved Therapy for Alcohol Problems: New Directions. Symposium conducted at the Annual Convention of the American Psychological Association, New York, August.

McCrady, B.S., Moreau, J., Paolino, T.J. Jr & Longabaugh, R. (1982). Joint hospitalization and couples therapy for alcoholism: a four-year follow-up. *Journal of Studies on Alcohol*, **43**, 1244–1250.

McCrady, B.S., Noel N.E., Abrams, D.B., Stout, R.L., Nelson, H.F. & Hay, W.N. (1986). Comparative effectiveness of three types of spouse involvement in outpatient behavioral alcoholism treatment. *Journal of Studies on Alcohol*, **47**, 459–467.

McCrady, B.S., Paolino, T.J. Jr, Longabaugh, R. & Rossi, J. (1979). Effects of joint hospital admission and couples treatment for hospitalized alcoholics: a pilot study. *Addictive Behaviors*, **4**, 155–165.

McCrady, B., Stout, R., Noel, N., Abrams, D. & Nelson, H. (1991). Comparative effectiveness of three types of spouse-involved alcohol treatment: outcomes 18 months after treatment. *British Journal of Addiction*, **86**, 1415–1424.

Miller, P.M. (1972). The use of behavioral contracting in the treatment of alcoholism: a case report. *Behavior Therapy*, **3**, 593–596.

Moos, R.H., Finney, J.W. & Cronkite, R.C. (1990). *Alcoholism Treatment: Context, Process, and Outcome*. New York: Oxford University Press.

Noel, N.E. & McCrady, B.S. (1993). Alcohol-focused spouse involvement with behavioral marital therapy. In T.J. O'Farrell (ed.), *Treating Alcohol Problems: Marital and Family Interventions* (pp. 210–235). New York: Guilford.

Noel, N.E., McCrady, B.S., Stout, R.L. & Nelson, H.F. (1987). Predictors of attrition from an outpatient alcoholism treatment program for aloholic couples. *Journal of Studies on Alcohol*, **48**, 229–235.

O'Farrell, T.J. (1990). Sexual functioning of male alcoholics. In R.L. Collins, K.E. Leonard, B.A. Miller, & J.S. Searles (eds), *Alcohol and the Family: Research and Clinical Perspectives* (pp. 244–272). New York: Guilford.

O'Farrell, T.J. (1986). Marital therapy in the treatment of alcoholism. In N.S. Jacobson & A.S. Gurman (eds), *Clinical Handbook of Marital Therapy* (pp. 513–535). New York: Guilford.

O'Farrell, T.J. (ed.) (1993). *Treating Alcohol Problems: Marital and Family Interventions*. New York: Guilford.

O'Farrell, T.J. (1993a). A behavioral marital therapy couples group program for alcoholics and their spouses. In T.J. O'Farrell (ed.) (1993). *Treating Alcohol Problems: Marital and Family Interventions* (pp. 170–209). New York: Guilford.

O'Farrell, T.J. (1993b). Couples relapse prevention sessions after a behavioral marital therapy couples group program. In T.J. O'Farrell (ed.), *Treating Alcohol Problems: Marital and Family Interventions* (pp. 305–326). New York: Guilford.

O'Farrell, T.J., Allen, J.P. & Litten, R.Z. (1995). Disulfiram (Antabuse) contracts in treatment of alcoholism. In J.D. Blaine & L. Onken (eds), *Integrating Behavior Therapies with Medications in the Treatment of Drug Dependence* (NIDA Research Monograph 150, pp. 65–91). Washington DC: National Institute on Drug Abuse.

O'Farrell, T.J. & Bayog, R.D. (1986). Antabuse contracts for married alcoholics and their spouses: a method to ensure Antabuse taking and decrease conflict about alcohol. *Journal of Substance Abuse Treatment*, **3**, 1–8.

O'Farrell, T.J. & Birchler, G.R. (1987). Marital relationships of alcoholic; conflicted and non-conflicted couples. *Journal of Marital and Family Therapy*, **13**, 259–274.

O'Farrell, T.J., Choquette, K.A., Cutter, H.S.G., Brown, E.D. & McCourt, W. (1995). Problem severity predicts outcomes of couples relapse prevention sessions. In T.J. O'Farrell (Chair), Marital and Family Therapy for Alcoholism and Drug Abuse: New Results from Controlled Outcome Studies. Symposium conducted at the International Conference on the Treatment of Addictive Behaviors, The Netherlands, June.

O'Farrell, T.J., Choquette, K.A., Cutter, H.S.G., Brown, E.D. & McCourt, W.F. (1993). Behavioral marital therapy with and without additional relapse prevention sessions for alcoholics and their wives. *Journal of Studies on Alcohol*, **54**, 652–668.

O'Farrell, T.J., Choquette, K.A., Cutter, H.S.G., Brown, E.D., Bayog, R., McCourt, W., Lowe, J., Chan, A. & Deneault, P. (1996). Cost–benefit and cost–effectiveness analyses of behavioral marital therapy with and without relapse prevention sessions for alcoholics and their spouses. *Behavior Therapy*, **27**, 7–24.

O'Farrell, T.J., & Cutter, H.S.G. (1982). Effect of adding a behavioral or an interactional couples group to individual outpatient Alcoholism counseling. In T.J. O'Farrell (Chair), Spouse-involved Treatment for Alcohol Abuse. Symposium conducted at the Sixteenth Annual Convention of the Association for the Advancement of Behavior Therapy, Los Angeles, November.

O'Farrell, T.J., Cutter, H.S.G., Choquette, K.A., Floyd, F.J. & Bayog, R.D. (1992). Behavioral marital therapy for male alcoholics: marital and drinking adjustment during the two years after treatment. *Behavior Therapy*, **23**, 529–549.

O'Farrell, T.J., Cutter, H.S.G. & Floyd, F.J. (1985). Evaluating behavioral marital therapy for male alcoholics: effects on marital adjustment and communication from before to after therapy. *Behavior Therapy*, **16**, 147–167.

O'Farrell, T.J., Kleinke, C. & Cutter, H.S.G. (1986). Differences between alcoholic couples accepting and rejecting an offer of outpatient marital therapy. *The American Journal of Drug and Alcohol Abuse*, **12**, 301–310.

O'Farrell, T.J. & Maisto, S.A. (1987). The utility of self-report and biological measures of alcohol consumption in alcoholism treatment outcome studies. *Advances in Behaviour Research and Therapy*, **9**, 91–125.

O'Farrell, T.J. & Murphy, C.M. (1995). Marital violence before and after alcoholism treatment. *Journal of Consulting and Clinical Psychology*, **63**, 256–262.

Prochaska, J.O. & DiClemente, C.C. (1983). Stages and processes of self-change of smoking: toward an integrative model of change. *Journal of Consulting and Clinical Psychology*, **51**, 390–395.

Rychtarik, R.G., Carstensen, L.L., Alford, G.S., Schlundt, D.G. & Scott, W.O. (1988).

Situational assessment of alcohol-related coping skills in wives of alcoholics. *Psychology of Addictive Behavior*, **2**, 66-73.

Selzer, M.L. (1971). The Michigan Alcoholism Screening Test: the quest for a new diagnostic instrument. *American Journal of Psychiatry*, **127**, 1653–1658.

Shapiro, R.J. (1984). Therapy with violent families. In S. Saunders, A. Anderson, C. Hart & G. Rubenstein (eds), *Violent Individuals and Families: a Handbook for Practitioners* (pp. 112–136). Springfield, IL: Charles C. Thomas.

Sisson, R.W. & Azrin, N.H. (1993). Community Reinforcement Training for families: a method to get alcoholics into treatment. In T.J. O'Farrell (ed.), *Treating Alcohol Problems: Marital and Family Interventions* (pp. 34–53). New York: Guilford.

Sisson, R.W. & Azrin, N.H. (1986). Family-member involvement to initiate and promote treatment of problem drinkers. *Journal of Behavior Therapy and Experimental Psychiatry*, **17**, 15–21.

Skinner, H.A. & Allen, B.A. (1982). Alcohol dependence syndrome: measurement and validation. *Journal of Abnormal Psychology*, **91**, 199–209.

Sobell, L.C. (1979). *Alcohol and Drug Treatment Outcome Evaluation Training Manual.* Nashville, TN: Dede Wallace Center Alcohol programs and Vanderbilt University.

Sobell, L.C., Sobell, M.B., Maisto, S.A., & Cooper, A.M. (1985). Time-line Follow-back Assessment Method. In D.J. Lettieri, M.A. Sayers & J.E. Nelson (eds), *Alcoholism Treatment Assessment Research Instruments,* NIAAA Treatment Handbook Series, Vol. 2. (DHHS Publication No. 85-1380, pp. 530–534). Washington, DC: National Institute on Alcohol Abuse and Alcoholism.

Straus, M.A. (1979). Measuring intrafamily conflict and violence: the Conflict Tactic (CT) scales. *Journal of Marriage and the Family*, **41**, 75–88.

Thomas, E.J. & Ager, R.D. (1993). Unilateral family therapy with spouses of uncooperative alcohol sbusers. In T.J. O'Farrell (ed.), *Treating Alcohol Problems: Marital and Family Interventions* (pp. 3–33). New York: Guilford.

Thomas, E.J., Santa, C.A., Bronson, C. & Oyserman, D. (1987). Unilateral family therapy with spouses of alcoholics. *Journal of Social Service Research*, **10**, 145–162.

Thomas, E.J., Yoshioka, M., Ager, R.D. & Adams, K.B. (1993). Experimental outcomes of spouse intervention to reach the uncooperative alcohol abuser: preliminary report. In K. Corcoran & J. Fischer (eds), *Measures for Clinical Practice: a Sourcebook*, 2nd edn. New York: Free Press.

Walitzer, K.S., Dermen, K.H. & Connors, G.J. (1995). Spouse involvement in treatment of male and female problem drinkers. In T.J. O'Farrall (Chair): Marital and Spouse-involved Therapy for Alcohol Problems: New Directions. Symposium conducted at the Annual Convention of the American Psychological Association, New York, August.

Weiss, R.L. & Cerreto, M.C. (1980). The Marital Status Inventory: development of a measure of dissolution potential. *American Journal of Family Therapy*, **8**, 80–85.

Wright, K.D. & Scott, T.B. (1978). The relationship of wives' treatment to the drinking status of alcoholics. *Journal of Studies on Alcohol*, **39**, 1577–1581.

Zweben, A., Pearlman, S. & Li, S. (1983). Reducing attrition from conjoint therapy with alcoholic couples. *Drug and Alcohol Dependence*, **11**, 321–331.

Zweben, A., Pearlman, S. & Li, S. (1988). A comparison of brief advice and conjoint therapy in the treatment of alcohol abuse: the results of the Marital Systems study. *British Journal of Addiction*, **83**, 899–916.

Chapter 23

Physical Aggression Couples Treatment

Richard E. Heyman and Peter H. Neidig
*Department of Psychology, State University of New York,
Stony Brook, NY, USA*

All marital therapists treat violent couples, whether they know it or not. Most couples presenting to a general marital therapy clinic are physically aggressive, although few define aggression as a problem (O'Leary, Vivian & Malone, 1992). Because few therapists assess for violence, most couples are treated for a variety of presenting problems without an explicit focus on stopping the aggression. At best this is poor clinical practice because it falsely presumes a level of safety necessary for couples to learn new ways of relating to each other. At worst it places clients (most often women) in physical jeopardy, exacerbates conflicts that result in violence, and implicitly condones intimidation and violence via the therapist's failure to identify and stop it.

The purpose of this chapter is to describe an empirically tested program for physical aggression: Physical Aggression Couples Treatment (PACT). It is critical to understand that PACT is not standard marital therapy. PACT states emphatically that its purpose is to eliminate violence in the home. Period. Because PACT principles assert that violence is a self-defeating attempt to effect relationship change, we believe that therapeutic efforts to reduce anger and to increase competence in relationship skills will reduce the risk for physical violence. The first half of PACT focuses on taking responsibility for one's own violence and on anger control skills. The second half focuses on couple issues (e.g. improving communication, renegotiating more equitable marriage contracts, jealousy). The purpose of the second half is to increase alternatives to violence and to decrease conflicts that may lead to violence. Thus, while there is some focus on relationship issues, it is done in service of the primary aim (violence abatement).

Clinical Handbook of Marriage and Couples Interventions. Edited by W. Kim Halford and Howard J. Markman.
© 1997 John Wiley & Sons Ltd.

This chapter will serve as a clinical guide to PACT and will be divided into six sections. First we will discuss the clinical assessment of couples who may be physically aggressive, including both screen-in and screen-out criteria for PACT. Second, we will provide a session by session overview of PACT. Third, we will discuss commonly expressed concerns about PACT. Fourth, we will consider the advantages and disadvantages of PACT as a treatment format. Fifth, PACT is typically conducted in groups. Arguments for and against both group and individual conjoint treatment will be presented, including suggestions for clinicians in adapting standard group PACT to a conjoint format. Finally, we will present the preliminary results from our ongoing study testing the effectiveness of PACT and will discuss future directions for PACT.

ASSESSMENT

Prevalence of Spouse Abuse in Marital Treatment Settings

O'Leary, Vivian & Malone (1992) conducted a multimodal assessment of husband-to-wife violence of 132 consecutive couples who presented for general marital therapy at the University of New York at Stony Brook's marital clinic. Only 1.5% of the husbands and 6.0% of the wives listed physical aggression as a presenting problem. However, 46% of the husbands and 44% of the wives (or 56% of the couples) indicated that "physical abuse" or "violence" was occurring when asked in an individual interview. Furthermore, 53% of the husbands and wives (or 67% of the couples) indicated on a questionnaire that at least one act of physical aggression had occurred in the previous year.

Furthermore, both "mild" and severe aggression should be taken seriously by clinicians. Although typically men and women engage in violent behaviors (e.g. Straus, Gelles & Steinmetz, 1980; Straus & Gelles, 1986), the physical and psychological impact on women is clearly more severe than it is on men. In a clinical sample of 93 couples, also from the Stony Brook clinic, 40% of the wives had received superficial bruises from their husband's violence during the past year, 17% reported serious bruises, and 13% reported broken bones, teeth or damage to sensory organs (Cascardi, Langhinrichsen & Vivian, 1992). The authors reported that women were as likely to report being injured from mild acts (e.g. pushing, grabbing, shoving, slapping) as from severe acts (e.g. hitting). This last finding should be interpreted with caution, because Cascardi et al. did not present separate analyses for women who were victimized solely by "mild" acts vs. victimized by both mild and severe acts. However, it does suggest that "mild" acts should not be ignored by the clinician. Moreover, wives rated the psychological impact of both mild and severe aggression as extremely negative.

Screening and Assessment

As stated earlier, recognizing physical aggression, even when it is not one of the problems a couple may spontaneously list, is crucial for marital therapists. Once this is accomplished, it is also critical for therapists to recognize who is *not* appropriate for PACT. For example, we are currently in the fourth year of a grant examining the effectiveness of PACT and gender-specific treatments (i.e. men's groups and women's groups) for marital violence. Couples must be willing to be randomly assigned to either of the treatments. To qualify for our program at Stony Brook, a wife must, in a separate interview: (a) say that she feels comfortable with conjoint treatment; (b) report that she is not fearful of speaking her mind in front of her husband; and (c) report that she has not needed to seek medical attention for injuries from husband violence; couples are also screened out if (d) the husband meets the Diagnostic and Statistical Manual (American Psychiatric Association, 1987) criteria for alcohol abuse or dependence; (e) the wife reports in a private interview that the husband has a drinking problem; (f) the couple is not married or is married but separated; or (g) group treatment for aggression would be contraindicated by normal clinical practice (e.g. psychotic or bipolar diagnosis with no medication; violent criminal past; screening clinician's concern for wife's safety). The interested reader is referred to Rosenbaum & O'Leary's (1986) excellent flow chart on the clinical decision-making process regarding aggressive couples who present for marital therapy.

As befits a large treatment study, spouses complete an extensive questionnaire battery and a detailed interview. The most critical components of pre-treatment assessment that should be conducted as a matter of course by all marital therapists at the intake are: (a) the Conflict Tactics Scale (Straus, 1979), a short measure of aggressive behaviors that can be supplemented with questions about injury, impact and intent (cf. Adapted Conflict Tactics Scale, Cascardi, Langhinrichsen & Vivian 1992); (b) a measure of psychological abuse, such as the Tolman Psychological Maltreatment Scale (Tolman, 1989—we use a 16-question subscale of the full measure); and (c) a measure of marital satisfaction or adjustment, such as the Relationship Satisfaction Questionnaire (Burns & Sayers, 1992; Heyman, Sayers & Bellack, 1994) or the Dyadic Adjustment Scale (Spanier, 1976). Questions about fear and aggression should be asked during the intake interview, as should screening questions for alcoholism, depression and PTSD.

Couples for whom PACT is not appropriate can be referred to gender-specific treatment. A detailed safety plan should be discussed with the wife, and numbers of abuse hotlines and shelters should be provided (see Rosenbaum & O'Leary, 1986).

Group Composition

Our clinical impression is that the greater the homogeneity of the group in life stages (e.g. years married, number and age of children), the greater the group cohesion. As will be discussed later, we have a 48% drop-out rate for those who attend at least one session. To maintain a critical mass, we schedule 8–10 couples to start a group. Typically, two couples who commit to starting a group never show up. With a starting size of 6–8 couples, we conclude the group with 3–4 couples left. Any fewer couples and the group runs the risk of disintegrating.

Table 23.1 Session-by-session summary of PACT

Session	Content
1	Introducing the program; recounting violent incident
2	Cycle of violence; discriminating different levels of anger
3	Discriminating different levels of anger (cont.); time out procedures
4	Cognitive–Behavioral (ABC) model of anger
5	Anger control techniques; challenging hot thoughts
6	Stress–Abuse connection; irrational beliefs
7	Midterm progress evaluation; review
8	Communication principles and skills; positive behaviors
9	Gender differences in communication; expressing feelings; empathy
10	Assertion vs. aggression; equality in rights and decision-making
11	Conflict escalation process; principles of conflict containment
12	Dirty fighting techniques
13	Sex; jealousy; expanding social support network
14	Wrap-up; maintaining gains; expressive vs. instrumental violence

TREATMENT (see Table 23.1)

Intrapersonal Sessions (1–7)

Our clinical belief is that spouses must learn to identify and manage their anger before it will be beneficial to focus on their marital conflicts. Thus, the first half of the program focuses on the following intrapersonal skills: (a) emphasizes self-responsibility for one's own conflict behaviors; (b) guides spouses though a heightened discrimination of their anger responses; (c) implements a contract for non-violent conflict management (i.e. time out); (d) teaches spouses how to identify and cope with anger-provoking cognitions; and (e) explores the effects of stress and Type-A personality behaviors on spouses' coping levels (see Table 23.1).

Session 1

The first session is in many respects the most important in the program. If the participants leave this session convinced that the program will be relevant to their needs and that the leader seems skillful and respectful of their feelings, then in many respects, the rest of the program seems to fall into place. If these objectives are not realized, at least to a minimal extent, the leader can look forward to contending with them until they are accomplished. The objectives of the first session are to: (a) establish the fact that the participants are there because of their past violent behavior; (b) foster a sense of personal responsibility for their own violent behavior; (c) reduce resistance and denial; (d) explain the objectives, structure and rationale of the program; and (e) encourage realistic grounds for optimism.

It is important in the initial portion of the first session to help participants feel at ease by anticipating what some of their questions and reservations are likely to be, and providing answers without requiring a high level of participation or self-disclosure. After the leaders spend some time in introducing themselves and distributing the Participant's Workbooks (Neidig, 1992), members are asked to introduce themselves by giving their name, the number of years they have been married, and the number and ages of any children. The leaders attempt to summarize the introductions by commenting on any similarities or patterns in group composition.

The group leaders then explain the principles for the group, making sure to answer any questions participants may have (and it is unusual for them not to have questions). The principles are as follows:

1. The primary goal of the program is to eliminate violence in the home.
2. Although anger and conflict are normal elements of family life, violence within the family is never justified.
3. We learn to be violent and we can learn to be non-violent. Violence is a choice.
4. Abusive behavior is a relationship issue in which each partner must be responsible for his/her own behavior. The consequences of violence are serious for all members of the family.
5. Abusiveness is a desperate, but self-defeating, effort to change the relationship.
6. Abusiveness tends to escalate in severity and frequency if not treated.

Following a review of the principles, the group leaders quickly provide an overview of the content to be covered, using the Table of Contents as a guide. The overview is important in conveying the logic of putting aside individual agendas and concerns until the appropriate portion of the curriculum has been reached. Repeating this requirement several times will probably be necessary as participants frequently want immediately to introduce complex, conflict-laden issues. Leaders should assure participants that these are legitimate concerns that will be addressed, and then explain again the logic of the sequential approach of the program.

The next order of business is to review and have participants sign a non-violence contract. The public declaration of an intention to be non-violent represents an important commitment. However, it is mostly a symbolic act, as almost all couples would be non-violent if all that was necessary was disavowing violence.

Following a short break, each couple is asked to describe their most recent episode of physical violence. The intentions of this portion of Session 1 are the following: (a) to establish the fact that it is the violent behavior that resulted in their selection for the program; (b) to highlight that the program's goal is the elimination of future incidents; (c) to share this common concern; (d) to assess and to reinforce their acceptance of personal responsibility for the violent behavior. Personal responsibility can be emphasized by asking questions such as "What do you think *you* did that made the situation worse?"

Although the description of a recent violent incident is the first step toward the critical acceptance of responsibility, subtle therapist behaviors make the difference between an effective launching of the group and an implosion. First, the therapists should decide during the break which couple is most likely to use the description exercise constructively. Those who are joking a lot or are highly resistant do not tend to get the exercise off to a good start. When the exercise begins well and is guided well by the leaders, the remaining couples pick up on this and the exercise flows smoothly. Second, the therapists should preface the exercise by saying that they expect that each person's account will be different from the partner's. It is not supposed to be a trial in which each person presents his/her case to try to convince the group of the partner's culpability. Each partner is asked to describe in detail his/her own (*not* his/her spouse's) contribution to the escalation of the conflict. Third, therapists should ask for details. The descriptions of the violence are usually vague (and typically self-serving in their vagueness), and the therapists should ask questions such as, "When you say one thing led to another, what *exactly* did you do?" Fourth, as will be shown in the following transcription of a first session, the therapists can increase the couples' motivation by relating their concerns to the material that will be covered in the group. Participants should leave the group thinking not only that they are in the right place, but also that the group is designed to help *their* problems.

Fifth, as will be seen below, the most common excuse for violence is a loss of control. We believe that there is no such thing as a violence reflex in the sense that there is a blink or a knee-jerk reflex. Violence always requires higher cortical activity and thus it represents a decision or choice. For those who avoid responsibility by claiming that they "lost control", leaders can sometimes point out the selective nature of their loss by asking why they did not kill the other: "If you were that angry, why didn't you pick up a bat and really let them have it?" If the loss was only partial (as, of course, it is), then they chose how much control to lose: "How much control did you choose to lose?"

Finally, although those with a serious alcohol problem are screened out of the group, the role of alcohol is sometimes raised. Alcohol may be an important predisposing factor; however, its role is often exaggerated to avoid accepting personal responsibility for violent behavior. Individuals rarely strike their bosses or police officers; rather, even when drunk, they are selective over how much control they "lose". Our position is that people do not hit because they have been drinking—they drink in order to hit. After careful questioning, individuals typically report that they were angry *before* they started drinking. For those who report that they cannot remember the violence, start at that point in the sequence where they are willing to recall and accept responsibility and begin to work forward. "How were you feeling when you decided to get drunk?"; "What did you think your reception would be like when you got home and how were you going to deal with it?"

The following excerpts provide a glimpse at this portion of the first session[1]. The first couple chosen, Bruce and Sheila, were selected because they had come to the first session of a previous group but, because of scheduling problems, were reassigned to this group. Sheila spoke first and described an incident in which she was very angry and argued with Bruce until he hit her to get her to stop. Then the therapist turned to Bruce:

Therapist	Bruce, how would you describe what happened?
Bruce	What she said. It happened like that. I'm calm at the beginning, and I reach a certain point, and I snap. And after that, all hell breaks loose. I did it today, not with my wife, but somebody provoked me on the road, in my car. Before that I was fine, but I went crazy. I snap.
Therapist	In thinking back over it, what do you think that you did that made the situation worse?
Bruce	It's a pattern in our marriage. She continually goes on and on, and it doesn't get anywhere with me. I'm never going to respond to that, with Sheila or anyone else. And she still doesn't see it. It winds up getting worse.
Therapist	It's interesting, Bruce, that you said that you "snap". But it also sounds like you can see it coming on, right? You said, "First I'm calm, and then eventually I snap", right?
Bruce	Yeah, steam starts building, literally.
Therapist	What you're describing is common for people entering our group. On one hand you say you "snap", but on the other hand, you recognize the build-up. "First I'm calm, then steam comes out of my ears, then I snap".
Sheila	Shouldn't he walk away in that situation?
Therapist	Right, that's exactly why each of you are here. We'll be making suggestions over the coming weeks about things that you should be doing to—. . . .
Sheila	Although sometimes when he walks away I follow.
Therapist	Right. So we're not going to suggest purely walking away. I don't want to get too far ahead, but we're going to suggest ways you can cool off the conflict, but then come back to it so that it's eventually resolved.

The therapist has suggested two ideas. First, cues of anger can be discriminated and therefore violent episodes do not come out of the blue. Second, there are techniques (i.e. time out) that will be covered that will meet their needs. The next couple, Dan and Rachel, had a similar theme to Bruce and Sheila. Because Rachel had called the police, their description brought legal repercussions into the discussion:

Leader	Let's move on to Dan and Rachel. Dan, could you describe your last violent incident?
Dan	I don't remember what it was about. She was banging shit around in the kitchen, and I just went into a rage. I went into the kitchen, threw her against the door, and grabbed her by the face.

[1] A video of a model first session is available from Behavioral Science Associates, POBox 87, Stony Brook, NY 11790, USA.

Leader   What did it mean to you that she was throwing stuff around the kitchen?
Dan   It just got under my skin.
Leader   Why? What were you thinking?
Dan   That's the whole thing. I don't remember what started it. I'm sitting on the couch. Bing, bang, boom, I'm in the kitchen. "Cut it out". I just smacked her. Like I said, I just got into a rage.
Leader   You told her to be quiet? So your goal was to eliminate the noise in the kitchen?
Dan   It was just stupid fight.
Leader   So you threw her up against the wall . . .
Dan   And I grabbed her by the face. Then the police came. They just asked me to leave. If they had wanted to arrest me, they would have had to call a back-up or something.
Leader   So they just told you to cool off.
Rachel   I could have had him arrested.

[Brief group discussion about mandatory arrest laws]

Leader   So Dan, thinking back, if you could change something you did, what would it be?
Dan   I just would have controlled my temper.
Leader   When would you have controlled it? When you stormed into the kitchen? When do you think it would have been the time to do that?
Dan   When I was in the living room. Before I even went into the kitchen.
Leader   Okay, so recognizing that it was starting to build then, and dealing with it before it the point where—. . . .
Dan   You know what, though? It's not like I could feel it coming.
Leader   In a few weeks I'll be interested if you have the same opinion. Because what you're describing is typical of people starting the group. But I've yet to meet a single person that by session four is not able to recognize it way in advance. Nobody teaches us to pay attention to these signals, but once you start paying attention, they're there loud and clear. But if you were good at recognizing your anger, the police wouldn't have had to been called that night.
Dan   Exactly.

Like Bruce, Dan is struggling with the acceptance of responsibility. He acknowledges that he should control his anger, but he and Bruce try to give themselves the excuse that they "snap". The therapist tries to normalize this struggle while still imparting hope that they *can* learn to control themselves.

The next couple, Karen and Matt, brought up the cognitive component of anger escalation:

Karen   Our last incident was last week. I had had a really hard week at work. Matt was home sick with like a 102°F fever. And as I was driving home on the expressway, I started to get really mad. I knew the house would be a mess when I got home, because he wouldn't have cleaned. If I were home, I would have cleaned, but I knew he wouldn't have so I was getting really mad. So I got home and the place was a mess and I lost it.
Leader   When you say you lost it, what exactly did you do?
Karen   I'd get mad at Matt and go into the bedroom and yell at him, and then I would leave. I'd sit in the living room thinking about how unfair it was that he didn't clean up, and I'd go in and yell at him some more. After I did this

Leader   a couple of times, I was so mad that he kept saying, "I'm sick, give me a
         break", that I took a big glass of water off the bed stand and threw it at
         him. Then he kicked me.
Leader   How do you think you made the situation worse?
Karen   The poor guy was sick and I couldn't get off of how unfair it was that he
         didn't clean. Maybe he should have cleaned. I would have, no matter how
         sick I was. But I needed to cool off instead of keep going in there and
         getting madder and madder each time.

The inquiry portion of the session should be concluded by reinforcing participants for their honesty, their ability to express this unpleasant and embarrassing content, and for any statements that implies a sense of personal responsibility and of regret. Assurances are given that this will be the last time in the program that they will have to repeat specifics concerning past violent behaviors.

The session is concluded on a positive note by saying that they are in the right place. That is, that they share some common experiences and problems and that the program is intended to provide assistance with such concerns. Participants are also told that the rest of the program will be much more positive in focus as it is devoted to growth, problem-solving and positive change.

As homework, participants are asked to complete a participant's contract, which includes provisions for non-violence, attending sessions, and homework compliance. They are also asked to complete a personal goals worksheet, which asks such questions as, "Why are you in this program?"; "Have you engaged in any conflict behaviors that you later regret?" "What do I want to get out of this program?" (personal goals).

Session 2

The second session sets an important precedent for how this and all future sessions will be conducted. A check-in procedure is instituted; it is intended as a brief update, and the group leaders must balance the need to understand and join with clients on one hand and the need to move on to new material on the other. By establishing both the purpose and the need for brevity in this session, fewer struggles occur in later sessions. We have found it helpful to write the three check-in questions on a blackboard or writing pad—the prompt makes it much easier to stay on task. The questions are, "Was there any violence this week?" (for obvious reasons); "What did you do right this week" (to aid in reinforcing and shaping appropriate behaviors); and "Were there any major changes this week?" (our clients often lead turbulent lives and it is important to be aware of significant changes or stressors).

Couples, especially in the first several weeks in the program, will often notice a large decrease in conflict. Just as with violent behavior, leaders should take care to elicit self-responsibility for non-violence.

Leader   Fred and Nancy, did you all have any violence this week?
Fred   No. No violence at all.
Nancy   We didn't even argue this week, if you can believe it.

Leader   What do you chalk that up to? What did you do right?
Fred   We were so busy this week, we hardly saw each other. I don't think we did
         anything.
Leader   But it seems like when things are going badly, you find time to fight. Last
         week you mentioned that you were working a lot of overtime, but you
         were fighting all the time.
Nancy   I tried to keep things in perspective. If he did something that bothered me,
         I just told myself to stay calm and not get mad about it.
Leader   That's great.

The primary goal of Session 2 is to introduce the systemic idea of mutual and circular causality of couple conflict. Both spouses are apt to believe that they are reacting to the other's provocative behavior, and that the responsibility for reducing conflict lies in the partner. By realizing that they are both provoking and being provoked, spouses understand that they must take responsibility for reducing their own conflict-escalating behaviors. This is the core construct on which the program is built. It is critical to reiterate, during the presentation of the model, the program principle that each partner is solely responsible for his aggression. Although each partner can take steps to reduce the likelihood of conflict escalation, no one provokes the other into violence.

Following a review of the goal's homework, we use the short film *Deck the Halls*[2] to provide a memorable stimulus for discussing both the context of aggression and the affective, behavioral and cognitive precipitants to abuse. To prepare the group for the film, the leaders briefly describe Walker's (1979) three-phase model of battering (tension building, abusive incident, remorse). In addition, the leaders suggest that anger is not an on/off phenomenon, but rather a continuous one. Following the film, the group discusses it, and the following points are developed:

1. *The relationship between stress and violence.* Violence does not occur randomly; rather, it tends to take place during times of high stress and conflict. Participants describe the stressors they witnessed in the film (e.g. job stress, rigid sex roles, alcohol).
2. *The cycle of violence.* Behaviors that delineate the tension-building, acute violence and remorse phases are discussed.
3. *The stages of conflict escalation.* Leaders draw on the board a conflict/anger chart ranging from 0 to 100. The scale is broken into three zones: the safety zone (anger levels of 0–40), the danger zone (40–70), and the violence zone (70–100). The discussion invariably establishes the fact that conflict escalates sequentially to the point of violence, and that spouses have ample warning of

---

[2] *Deck the Halls* is available from Select Media, 74 Varick Street, New York, NY 10013, USA. It is a 20-minute film depicting a middle class couple whose post-Christmas party stress erupts into wife battering. The film amply displays the affective, behavioral, cognitive and situational antecedents to the violence and thus helps all couples focus on a common analysis of these factors before then applying the behavioral model to their own violence antecedents.

the changes in their thinking, feeling and acting. The concept of "triggers" (behaviors that the aggressor believes are intolerable and that justify [to them] the escalation to physical violence) and "point of violence inevitability" (the point in the escalation cycle in which self-control is so eroded that the next provocative behavior will result in the choice of violence) are introduced and discussed.

4. *The circular model of causation.* A spirited discussion typically occurs when the discussion turns to who "caused" the violence. The position of the group leaders is that although each spouse is solely responsible for his/her own choice to use violence, both partners play a role in conflict escalation and either could have taken actions to reduce the likelihood of violence. Special care must be taken to avoid the implication that the woman in the film (or in the group) can prevent the violence by being non-conflictual; this is the very belief that aggressors (and at times, society as a whole) use to excuse violence. Rather, to reduce the risk of violence, *both* partners must accept the responsibility for managing their *own* anger and take steps to eliminate their *own* use of violence.

5. *Adequate coping and communication skills reduce the likelihood of violence.* It is important to introduce the idea that stressors do not have to be eliminated to reduce the risk of violence; instead, participants learning to put their feelings into words so that their partners can hear and try to understand them will again reduce their risk of violent escalation.

For homework, participants are then asked to apply the principles from the film discussion to their own situation, using a workbook exercise.

Session 3

The check-in begins the session. Typically, questions and comments regarding *Deck the Halls* have been simmering all week and participants want to comment about it. It may take most of the first half of the third session to review the concepts introduced in the second session and the extensive amount of homework. The group leaders chart on the chalkboard the thinking, acting and feeling cues participants have noticed in each of the three zones (safety, danger and violence). This typically requires extensive inquiry and coaching by the therapists, because ignoring these cues (or not noticing them at all) is a hallmark feature of aggressive couples.

Therapists should also be alert to the fact that many men equate "anger" with out-of-control rage and thus will report that they almost never get angry, and certainly could not report gradations of anger. Sometimes this is merely a matter of semantics. One man in a recent group finally grasped the idea and reported, "First, I'll get irritated. Then I'll get annoyed. If she keeps pushing it, I start getting really bothered, and then I start getting pissed off. If it keeps up, finally I get angry."

Once participants can recognize their own anger cues, they are ready for the first anger management strategy: time out. The six steps of time out are outlined for the group and discussed:

1. *Self-Watching.* Participants are asked to review the anger exercise described earlier and mark at what point they think time out should be called. Most couples pick a point in the low levels of the danger zone (e.g. 40). Some couples will not agree on a level, with one partner saying it should be called at 20 and the other at 50. This must be dealt with, because some spouses will tacitly reserve the right to refuse to abide by time out if they believe it has been called too early or for a tactical advantage.

2. *Signalling.* Ideally, time out should be clearly signaled. Each couple should be urged to choose a signal that feels comfortable for them; some couples use the "T" hand signal, some couples say, "I need to cool off". Although storming out of the room would obviously be preferable to violence, it is often seen as a provocation by the partner; an unambiguous signal is strongly suggested. Three other points are also worth noting: (a) the signal must be given in a non-aggressive manner; (b) each partner has the right to call time out whenever he/she believes the conversation to be deteriorating (whether he/she is him/herself angry or not); (c) a spouse calls time out for him/herself—one does not *send* his/her spouse on time out (as one would a child).

3. *Acknowledging.* One spouse calls time out and the other is obligated to acknowledge it. This is done for communication clarity; one does not have the choice of granting or not granting the time out.

4. *Detaching.* Ideally, spouses go to separate places to cool off. Driving while angry is discouraged. Because couples in our groups routinely fight in the car, we like to remind them that using time out is still possible and they showed mentally, rather than physically, detach.

5. *Anger control.* Each spouse attempts to reduce his/her level of anger. We suggest that each spouse attempt to find at least one part of the partner's point of view that they can identify with, and find at least one part of their own behavior that was making the conflict worse.

6. *Returning.* After a short period (which can be renewed), the person who called time out should reinitiate contact with the other. If the conflict escalates again, then the sequence can be repeated. A member of a recent group pointed out that a time out in sports does *not* mean that a team leaves the stadium, never to return; time out is called to regroup, and then play resumes.

Typically couples are drawn to the concept of tamping the escalation process, but typically some group members have reservations. The most common reservation is that; "Time out is fine, but it is a Band-aid and does not resolve our real problems". Obviously this is true, but the leader should emphasize that until the specter of violence is removed, true conflict resolution will be impossible. Second, spouses (usually men) who view conflict as a war will express concern that their partners will insult or degrade them and then call time out to avoid retaliation. By agreeing to time out they are giving the partner a tactical advantage. Although these members are typically the more difficult group members to work with, the leaders can emphasize that by participating in the program, both spouses have agreed that they want to make their conflicts less destructive. Exercising self-control by acknowledging time out, even in the face of unpleasant behaviors by their partners, is always going to be a victory for them. Third, when spouses begin to try to use time out, there invariably will be times when they felt so angry and so full of self-righteousness that they did not want to call time out (i.e. they wanted to continue to stoke their anger). When spouses give this as a reason for not calling time out, they are admitting that they chose to stay angry. Leaders should note the successes implicit in this "failure" (i.e. they are now self-watching and attributing anger to choice rather than to provocation) and try to shape them toward the eventual goal of time out.

Session 4

The check-in begins the session. Most of the time at least one couple will have called a time out successfully and is feeling positive about their new-found control over the conflict escalation process. The leaders should use this as an example, and the steps should be reviewed and reinforced. Anyone who did not call a time out should be encouraged to use it in the coming week, even if they are not having a substantial conflict (analogies to fire drills are useful in giving this assignment).

Session 4 is devoted to an introduction to a cognitive–behavioral model of anger and anger control. Affective, behavioral and cognitive anger cues, which were first explored in the previous session, are reviewed. Participants are then introduced to the idea that anger requires cognitive mediation. The model that participants typically have is that events cause their anger; the program's model is that events cause thoughts that cause anger (see Baucom & Epstein, 1990, for an account of the depth of the theoretical tradition and treatment implications of this model with couples). It is usually helpful to warm up the group to this model by presenting non-relationship-oriented examples, such as anger over being cut off in freeway traffic (e.g. "That jerk almost killed me" vs. "sometimes make dumb maneuvers too", or "Maybe there's an emergency"). Once participants understand the concept that anger requires active perceptions and interpretations of the environment, they begin to apply that to their relationship. A passage in the participants' workbook reads, "The fact is, there is only one person who can make you angry and that is you. Others may act in an unpleasant, provocative manner. They may even try to make you angry. However, you control your thinking and consequently, you control your anger."

The leader can more skillfully cover this material by weaving in three elements. First, we are trying to modify *escalating* levels of anger that lead to destructive interchanges. Anger is a normal, human emotion. Trying it to eliminate all anger would be silly and counterproductive. The goal, however, is to recognize that: (a) anger indicates that an issue is important; but (b) that as anger escalates, one must take steps to keep it from leading to harmful behavior.

Second, anger does become more automatic (i.e. overlearned) over time. Other examples of overlearned behavior, which initially require high levels of cognitive effort but later become automatic (e.g. finding a radio station while driving), can be discussed to make this phenomenon clearer. Nevertheless, anger control skills can still be employed to reduce anger, even if the rise in anger is quicker than it once was. Third, many spouses do not recognize that they have anger-arousing thoughts. The leader can let such participants know that not recognizing these thoughts is common, but that most people become aware of them once they start paying attention to their thinking during anger episodes. Like the approach typically taken in cognitive therapy, the leader should treat this proposed exercise as an experiment to test the influence of thoughts on emotion, rather than trying to force participants to accept the model.

Once participants understand the model, six principles are covered: (1) recognize the automatic, hot thoughts that cause your anger; (2) thinking can be seen as self-talk when we repeat certain sentences to ourselves—the sentences may be true or false, hot or cool; (3) when you get angry, your self-talk is hot; (4) the hot self-talk sentences fuel your anger; (5) you cannot get angry unless you repeat the hot sentences to yourself, and you will stay angry only as long as you keep thinking the hot statements; (6) when you stop thinking the hot self-talk, you will stop being angry.

Finally, six types of cognitive distortions are covered: labeling (e.g. "He's a lazy slob"); catastrophizing (e.g. "You ruined my whole day"); mind-reading (e.g. "She intentionally tried to embarrass me in front of my friends"); "should" statements (e.g. "She should shut up when I say I don't want to discuss it"); fortune-telling (e.g. "I know that when I get home she'll be on the warpath"); and vengeance ("I'll get even with him over this; it isn't over"). Participants are asked to complete an anger log during the coming week, which has them identify their hot thoughts and begin categorizing the types of distortions they are using.

Session 5

The check-in begins the session. The objective for this session is for participants to become increasingly familiar with the cognitive approach to anger control. The homework assignments involving anger are thoroughly reviewed. Examples of situations in which the participants experienced anger are again reviewed on the board in the situation–anger level–thoughts format until all members demonstrate an ability to recognize patterns of self-angering thoughts. It is important to focus on *individual* experiences of anger and not allow the discussion to devolve into a particular couple arguing over the correctness of their positions during this exercise. It is useful to remind participants that their hot thoughts represent *distortions* and, as such, each should try to give his/her spouse some slack in expressing these thoughts (i.e. that these distorted thoughts do not contain the "truth" or the person's complete feelings for the spouse).

Once participants recognize anger cues, they are typically very eager to begin modifying their anger responses. Four steps are presented: (a) recognize anger signs; (b) pause; (c) decide what to do; and (d) control thinking. By now all participants should be able to recognize their own anger signs. Because almost all participants have already complained about the automatic and reflexive nature of their anger arousal patterns, pausing is presented as a way to help buy them some time. Several pause techniques (i.e. counting to ten; repeating anger control reminders, deep breathing, and thought stopping) are quickly discussed.

More time is spent covering "deciding what to do"—short-term and long-term consequences of anger are presented. Is it not unusual for the participants to focus solely on the *detrimental* effects of anger. The leader must take care to emphasize that anger and violence had to be serving some function (e.g. making someone shut up or do things your way) for them or they would not have continued to do it. On the other hand, the leader parlays the focus on the harmful effects of anger into a commitment to decide to use non-violent means of expression.

Most of the session is spent on cognitive challenges to hot thoughts. Participants are asked to take examples of their hot thoughts and come up with cool thoughts. The workbook presents suggestions for each type of distortion: (a) labeling—describe the behavior, not the personality; (b) mind-reading—focus on the behavior and avoid speculations about motives and intentions—even if you are right most of the time, there are times when you are wrong and have an unnecessary fight; (c) fortune-telling—nobody knows what will happen in the future; (d) catastrophizing—quantify statements by saying how often or how undesirable something is; (e) "should" statements—do not translate preferences into demands or commands; (f) vengeance—do not dwell on thoughts of vengeance and getting even; recognize the wisdom of the saying, "He who seeks vengeance should first dig two graves".

As with all forms of cognitive therapy, the leader must emphasize that cool thoughts are not pollyanna-ish; cool thoughts do not try to make a bad situation good ("Isn't it wonderful how spontaneous he is when he leaves his dirty socks on the floor"). This is the most common form of confusion and resistance to this exercise. Rather, cool thoughts recognize the bad situation for what it is and do not make it worse. Thus, "I'll wring his neck when he gets home, that lazy bastard" can be challenged with the thought, "It really bothers me when he leaves his socks on the floor. When he gets home, I'll remind him of how important it is to me that they go in the hamper". The homework assignment extends the anger log assignment by including a column to record cool thoughts.

Session 6

Much of this session is spent solidifying the cognitive anger control strategies from the previous session. It is common during the check-in and homework review for a group member to say, as a recent participant did, "I have no problem identifying my hot thoughts. But what do you do if they're right?" Although Albert Ellis may get away with labeling such thoughts as "irrational", we are more likely to agree with the person that the thought seems to fit at the time, but then ask him/her some questions that help to recognize how maladaptive the thoughts are. Thus, quite a bit of work is still necessary before participants are as comfortable with their cool thoughts as they are with their hot ones. The leader also attempts to derive some of the underlying beliefs that guide their hot thoughts and bring them into open discussion. This is accomplished through the kind of Socratic questioning familiar to cognitive therapists.

The objective of the remainder of Session 6 is to explore the relationship between stress and violence and to introduce some stress management strategies. Participants fill out a short Type A personality style inventory and the Holmes and Rahe (1967) Social Readjustment Scale. Discussion points can include why such Type A traits as perfectionism, time urgency, competitiveness, etc., increase the likelihood of violence in the home. When reviewing the Holmes & Rahe scale, it is the rule that couples report an astounding number of significant stressors. After processing this with the group, participants complete an exercise that asks them what behaviors they and their spouses exhibit when stressed, how they would like their spouses to support them, and how they think they could support their spouses. This exercise can be used to reframe a spouse's potentially unpleasant behavior as symptomatic of stress and thus, not to be taken as personally as they may now take it. Another point that often surfaces is that what may be experienced by one partner as helpful during times of stress is not necessarily what is of most help to the other. Participants should leave this session with a newly energized commitment to turn *to* each other when stressed (i.e. "Us against the world") rather than to turn *on* each other (i.e. "It's your fault"). The anger log is assigned for homework, and is a part of every homework assignment for the remainder of the program.

Session 7

Session 7 is the mid-program self-evaluation and review. Participants take stock of what elements they've mastered and what remains to be accomplished. The leader should reinforce participants for the changes they have made and acknowledge how hard these changes are to make. Leaders should keep in mind that changes are always made by successive *approximations* of the target behavior and that *any* improvements should be reinforced. Few couples call textbook-perfect time outs during the duration of the program; leaders should be prepared to reinforce spouses for storming out of the room or even merely noticing hot thoughts, because only by reinforcing the intermediate behaviors can the leader hope to shape the target behavior. Leaders should troubleshoot any problematic areas and review material where appropriate.

Later Sessions (8–14)

Session 8

Session 8 is the session couples have been waiting for since week one. Finally we get to focus on our problems! The objective of this session is to introduce some basic principles of communication and to review some basic communication skills. Because most spouses have the skills to communicate effectively but tend not to use them when the marriage is distressed (e.g. Birchler, Weiss & Vincent, 1975), there is much discussion about the skills and the perceived impediments to using them, and little actual role-playing or skills rehersal (which is assigned for homework).

First, four communication principles are discussed; once each one is presented, then participants engage in a lively discussion applying the principle to their own situation. Principle I is that, "The message sent is not always the message received" (e.g. Gottman & Porterfield, 1981; Noller, 1980). Spouses often assume that just because they told their partners something, it was fully understood. Then, if there is a failure to comply, it is further assumed that this was the result of a deliberate effort to be difficult, rather than a misunderstanding. Principle II is that, "It is impossible not to communicate" (cf. Lederer & Jackson, 1968). All behavior, even silence, sends a message. Because "the message sent is not always the message received", non-verbal forms of behavior are particularly prone to misunderstandings. Principle III is that, "Every message has both content and feeling" (cf. Gottman, Markman & Notarius, 1977). Principle IV is that, "The feeling component (often non-verbal) is more important than the content" (e.g. Notarius, Benson, Sloan, Vanzetti & Hornyak, 1989). When there is a discrepancy between the content and the feeling, we usually pay more attention to the feeling and how it is said.

Following the discussion on communication principles, participants complete a worksheet asking them to grade themselves on various subskills in areas such as request-making, listening, validation, feeling talk, and negative and positive expression. A discussion of each subskill ensues, with a limited amount of time spent modeling and role-playing more challenging subskills. For homework, participants are asked to focus on three subskills and attempt to show improvement during the week.

The final segment of Session 8 is devoted to increasing positive interaction, a hallmark of behavioral couples therapy (e.g. Jacobson & Margolin, 1979; Weiss, Patterson & Hops, 1973). As with most discordant couples, participants often report that they derive little pleasure from their relationships. This directly reduces their marital satisfaction and indirectly makes compromise and conflict management less appealing. Increasing positive interactions is described as a mutual project involving two steps: (a) initiating a positive interaction; and (b) recognizing and rewarding the positive contributions of your partner. After group discussion, participants are asked to do at least two positive acts for their partner each day. Each partner tracks the things that they did and the things that they received.

Session 9

Following the check-in, any unfinished communication material from Session 8 is completed. Most groups will have a considerable amount of communication-related problems and questions that should be addressed. Modeling and role-playing, sometimes using couples who are more adroit at that skill, is appropriate.

The goal of the remainder of the session is to explore gender-related differences in the participants' communication skills. Areas such as asking permission, decision-making, request-making, talking about problems, and seeking and sharing information are discussed. Skillful leadership of this session involves several areas. First, this session is not supposed to be "The Battle of the Sexes"—it is common for the men and women to quickly bond into same-sex camps, defending their own way of doing things and minimizing the usefulness of the other's way. The leader should bring out the pros and cons of each style, with the goal being for the spouses to team together to use their different styles to maximize the advantages (and reduce the disadvantages). Second, it is common for participants to start speaking of the way "men" and "women" think and act, as if these behaviors were secondary sex characteristics. Left unchecked, this can easily become a gripe session, with the implicit message being, "We're men (or women). We're born communicating this way, so leave me alone if you don't like it". Fruitful discussions can arise about whether *all* men and *all* women are like this, and what role the participants' socialization experiences may have played in shaping their current styles. Thus, the leader should be careful to emphasize the point that functional communication behaviors are not immutable characteristics, but are behaviors that either sex can perform.

A related exercise covers the detection and communication of feelings. In the workbook, participants are presented with a list of 60 feelings and are asked to check off: (a) the feelings that they have experienced; and (b) those that they are able to express with their spouses. They then compare their lists. More often than not, this is an eye-opening experience for couples, especially for those in which one spouse is more reserved in expressing his/her emotions. Discussion can then begin on: (a) lowering impediments to expression and the eliciting of support; and (b) increasing the partner's empathy for the unexpressive spouse's internal experience. Another area for discussion is the difference between primary emotions (like sadness or anxiety) and secondary emotions (like anger) (cf. Greenberg & Johnson, 1988). Although this concept requires a bit of practice during the group, it can be a very powerful exercise, as wives say that they would respond much better to husbands' expressing hurt or disappointment rather than anger. This idea is also revisited in Session 13, when the emotion of jealousy is explored.

Session 10

The goal of Session 10 is to delineate the difference between assertion and aggression, and to renegotiate the marriage contract. During the early part of the session, we define assertion as standing up for your own rights without violating the rights of others, and aggression as enforcing your own rights without regard to the rights of others. Not surprisingly, this concept takes a bit of discussion and role-playing before it becomes clear to participants. Participants role-play, making *assertive* requests and *assertive* refusals.

The second half of the session has participants complete a "Marriage Bill of Rights" exercise, in which both partners respond to a list of behaviors (e.g. the right to be treated with respect; the right to express opinions; the right to come and go as you please) as: the husband only has this right; the wife only has this right; we both have this right; or, neither has this right. Although this straightforward exercise will not work miracles for highly controlling men, it does result in spirited groups, with couples agreeing with each other far more than they disagree. A similar exercise is conducted on decision-making rights.

Session 11

Now that participants have obtained a modest degree of anger control proficiency, have begun trying to unearth their communication skills, and are reconsidering their rights and responsibilities in the marriage, the next two sessions are aimed at consolidating these gains. The goal of Session 11 is to emphasize a "team" approach to conflict containment and resolution. See the chapter by Epstein, Baucom & Daiuto (this volume) for additional material on standard behavioral couples therapy approaches in this regard. For homework (in addition to the standing assignment of the anger log) participants attempt to use these skills at home the week to define, discuss and attempt to resolve a relationship problem.

Session 12

Session 12 continues to focus on conflict containment by having participants complete a workbook exercise, a long list of humorously presented "dirty fighting techniques" (e.g. blaming, using money, being sarcastic). Although entertaining, participants are sometimes rattled by how many of these techniques they employ. The typical result is a strengthened commitment to "play by the book", and the remainder of the session can be used to continue practicing conflict resolution.

Session 13

The goal of Session 13 is to bring up three interrelated topics: sex, social support networks and jealousy. Typically, the topics of trust and jealousy are both relevant and potentially difficult issues for the participants in the program to deal with. It is not at all uncommon for many of the members to have experienced real or imagined infidelities and for this to have been one of the precipitants for some of their most unpleasant and violent conflicts. It is for these reasons that it is important for the issue to be addressed, but in a constructive, non-confrontational and non-emotional manner. When discussed in this way, we have found that the participants are often quite relieved to find that they are able to apply the same problem-solving approach skills previously mastered to this most difficult area.

Sex and sex myths are covered first, using a workbook exercise. Once any particular areas of sexual problems or disagreements are dealt with, the topic of jealousy is introduced by completing the Support System Evaluation Exercise. This is used to introduce the following points. First, although married, individuals continue to require relationships with other people to meet a variety of legitimate needs. Second, one's spouse cannot be expected to provide all the functions. The challenge for a marital relationship is how to establish appropriate boundaries and how to talk about relationship rules in a way that the normal problems of jealousy and mistrust will be contained. Thus, the topic is framed as inevitable, normal, and not particularly different from any of the problem areas previously experienced.

Having established the point that marital relationships cannot be so exclusive that all other forms of relationships with others are avoided, the topic of jealousy is introduced. Leaders explain that jealousy involves a comparison of the satisfaction available in the marriage with the perceived satisfaction available from other relationships (cf. Thibaut & Kelley, 1959). This representation leads to several additional points about jealousy: first, it is an interpersonal, rather than an intrapersonal phenomenon, and as such, it is determined by the nature of the relationship between the two partners at any particular point in time. Thus, the jealous partner must take responsibility for his/her own contribution to the jealousy scenario, and not just focus on the "provocative" behavior. Second, because relationships are dynamic and constantly changing, one's threshold for jealousy (that is, one's resistance to potentially jealousy-eliciting situations) is also constantly changing. Third, when jealousy is experienced, there are two possible courses of action to take—positive, relationship-enhancing behaviors or negative, punitive and controlling actions. Finally, the negative course of action involves expressing secondary emotions (anger, vengeance, etc.) and the positive approach involves expressions of the primary emotions of insecurity and caring.

At this point, considerable time is devoted to discussing the possible consequences of these two approaches to dealing with situations in which one experiences jealousy. The probability that expressions of anger and control will be responded to, in turn, by expressions of resentment and anger ("You can't tell me what to do", etc.) is underscored by referring to past experiences with jealousy. Participants are invited to consider what the outcome would be if, in the next situation where they experienced insecurity leading to jealousy and mistrust, they were to share these feelings with statements such as, "When you were late getting home, I got worried and missed you"; "When you danced him at the club, I felt worried about us", etc.

Session 14

The goal of Session 14 is to recognize the achievements of the group, to anticipate the consequences of conflict, to make commitments for additional change, and to provide a forum for airing feelings about termination. First, a violence contingency contract is completed, in which participants list the concrete steps they will take should violence occur again. Second, the group completes and discusses a worksheet in which they rate their accomplishment of the program goals. It is common for participants to say that they are very pleased that they are no longer violent and are strongly committed to never being violent again; however, they say, our marital problems have not been totally resolved. Given the difficult population and the depth of their marital distress at intake, this should not be surprising. Participants should be lauded for the steps they have taken and for their realistic appraisal of their current state. Referrals can be given to those who want to pursue additional therapy. Some time is necessary to process the ambivalent feelings participants have about terminating; almost all completers said during post-treatment interviews that they wanted the group to be longer. In our outcome study, the last half of this session is spent completing a battery of measures and being interviewed by research assistants on their reaction to the program. We suggest that some outcome data be routinely collected at the end of Session 14, whether or not it is being used for formal outcome research.

Commonly Expressed Concerns about PACT

In this section we would like quickly to address several commonly expressed concerns about the wisdom of treating violent men in a couples modality.

1. *Conioint sessions put the wife at risk.* Although we were initially quite concerned about this possibility and continue to maintain a high level of vigilance, there does not seem to be any support in our treatment study for the concern that there is any higher risk of violence for those in conjoint, as opposed to gender-specific, treatment.

   Although episodes of physical aggression do occur during the course of couples treatment, wives report significantly ($p = 0.001$) fewer episodes during the 14 weeks of treatment than during the comparable time period immediately prior to treatment. The fact that aggression is reduced according to the wives' report during treatment suggests that the risk level is actually decreased while the couple is being seen in conjoint therapy. Aggression occurs at the same low rate in both the PACT and gender-specific groups.

   Theoretically, one could make the argument that separating couples would be more likely to heighten concerns about what family secrets had been divulged and whether the treatment was a threat to the relationship— issues known to precipitate violent conflicts for some couples. For example, we frequently have spouses in the gender-specific treatment groups who spy on each other's workbooks. Such arguments never occur in the PACT format.

2. *PACT's implicit message is that the wife is responsible for violence* (e.g.

Adams, 1988; Edleson, 1984; Ganley & Harris, 1978; Sato, 1991). As discussed earlier, the explicit message of the group is that violence is unacceptable, that there are always alternatives to violence, and that each spouse must take responsibility for his/her behaviors that lead conflicts in a destructive direction. We never imply that one spouse can provoke the other into violence, or that women should placate their husbands to avoid conflict. We reject the idea that blame is inherent in conjoint treatment and believe that accepting personal responsibility is actually enhanced by having both partners present.

3. *Wives will be too intimidated by the presence of their husbands to participate fully.* Subjects are asked if they would be at all fearful or intimidated by the presence of their spouses in the sessions, and those that respond affirmatively in this screening would be referred elsewhere for gender-specific treatment. Additionally, in conducting the sessions, care is taken not to press for a level of self-disclosure or of confrontation that might cause discomfort or subsequent conflicts. In fact, the sessions tend to be didactic in nature and emotionally neutral or positive in tone.

  The wives in PACT do not appear to be at all inhibited by the presence of their husbands. There does not appear to be a gender difference in the level of participation, except that wives do tend to be somewhat more verbal. Anyone who watched videotapes of our treatment sessions would be quickly disabused of the idea that women do not participate fully and intensely.

  In pre-treatment screening, participants were asked how fearful they would be about sharing their feelings if their partner were not in the group and if he/she were present in the treatment group. Women reported that they would be no more fearful if their husband were present (mean of 2.7 for both items on a 1 [not fearful]–5 [fearful] scale).

4. *Wives will be afraid to report aggression during or after the program.* Clearly, it is essential to have valid reporting of subsequent episodes of aggression to monitor progress and refine the treatment interventions. In fact, one major shortcoming of men's programs is men's tendency (if there is no means for checking the truthfulness of their self-reports) to state consistently during check-ins that they had a fine week with no episodes of aggression.

  It does seem reasonable to assume that reporting will be influenced by the perceived consequences. Thus, the leaders do everything they can to facilitate accurate reporting. Participants are assured that although we would hope that they will have no additional episodes of violence, we recognize that this is somewhat unrealistic. It takes time to acquire the skills necessary to accomplish non-violence and setbacks are likely.

  In fact, 35% of the couples report additional episodes during treatment. Again, the sharing of episodes by other participants seems to facilitate rather than inhibit self-disclosure. These reports seem to be volunteered by either gender. Regardless of which partner initially shares the information, we have not experienced situations in which the aggression was denied by the other partner, or was responded to with a sense of anger or betrayal. Subjects appear to be genuinely disappointed and embarrassed by their recidivism. This is interpreted as a positive signal that they have accepted the value of non-violence but have not yet been fully able to attain it.

Advantages and Disadvantages of PACT

There are five primary advantages of PACT over traditional gender-specific treatments. First, many physically aggressive couples are interested in marital therapy, not aggression treatment. PACT requires a focus on anger and violence before moving on to interpersonal skills, which is palatable to many aggressive couples who would flatly turn down gender-specific treatment. Second, an emphasis on personal responsibility in men's groups frequently encounters resistance such as, "But what about what my wife does?" In PACT, this is rarely heard (after the first session) because both spouses are encouraged to accept responsibility for their destructive conflict behaviors. Thus, we believe that increased personal responsibility is easier to achieve in PACT. Third, systemic intervention, such as time out, can be dangerous if both spouses are not informed. Withdrawal is a frequently cited provocation; time out without proper prior agreement between spouses may actually *increase* the likelihood of violent escalations. Prior agreement under therapeutic control is possible in PACT but not in gender-specific treatment. Fourth, monitoring of aggression is more easily accomplished when both spouses report. Men rarely deny violence in PACT, whereas they frequently do in gender-specific treatment. Fifth, little time is spent complaining about the partner in PACT. The "You'd hit her too if you had to live with her" argument is never heard.

Certainly, there are disadvantages that should be noted. First, although it rarely occurs, spouses can sometimes get angry with what the other says. The leaders can sometimes use these incidents as opportunities to employ the skills being worked on. At other times, therapists need to exercise good clinical judgment in defusing the situation and keeping both spouses safe. Second, spouses will sometimes want to use group time to "send messages" to their partner (i.e. wait until the group to uncork their anger about a problem). Third, PACT in its current incarnation is "gender-neutral"; that is, violence is violence. Little attention is paid to gender inequality, differential effects of violence, or the context in which spouses' anger is embedded. Although not appropriate for all couples, some couples could use more work on examining the inequalities of their implicit marriage contract. Fourth, the partner's presence can inhibit expression during the intrapersonal sessions. Hot thoughts represent participants at their worst; despite warnings before this exercise, we have rarely encountered problems where one spouse was offended by the other's hot thoughts. Fifth, PACT couples occasionally fight about group content (e.g. the proper way to take a time out; what the therapist meant by a certain comment).

Group PACT vs. Individualized PACT

The focus of our chapter thus far has been on running PACT in a group format. We have successfully used PACT with individual couples with only minor modifications. There are obvious advantages, such as being able to personalize the material more and moving at a pace tied to that couple's skill acquisition, not the needs of the group. Further work can be conducted on understanding the context of anger for that couple, especially when the context includes struggles over gender inequality. Obviously, such couples cannot benefit from the group process, vicarious learning, support, and the normalizing effect of going through treatment with others who share a problem.

Future directions in PACT

Several states in the USA have adopted legislation proscribing couples treatment when there is aggression. How this affects a treatment specifically for spouse abuse that nevertheless uses a conjoint format (i.e. PACT) is unclear. Obviously, therapists need to be aware of the legal and ethical regulations in their area. Spouse abuse is a highly political area and therapists considering employing PACT should familiarize themselves with the controversies in this field (e.g. Caesar & Hamburger, 1989; Gelles & Loseke, 1993; Yllo & Bograd, 1988).

Currently we are piloting a format that combines gender-specific treatment and PACT. Following two assessment sessions, spouses receive gender-specific treatment for 6 weeks. The men's treatment focuses on anger management and reduction of power and control beliefs and behaviors. The women's treatment addresses the top two individual presenting concerns (e.g. anger management, depression, post-traumatic stress disorder). Only when anger management skills have been successfully attained will the conjoint, interpersonal PACT sessions occur. Because of the logistical difficulties of groups, we are piloting this in an individualized format.

RESEARCH RESULTS FROM THE STONY BROOK DOMESTIC VIOLENCE TREATMENT PROGRAM

Treatment Outcome

As hypothesized, physical aggression (both mild and severe) at post-treatment was significantly reduced according to both husbands' and wives' reports. Both husbands and wives scored significantly higher on marital adjustment and on positive feelings about the spouse at post-treatment than at pre-treatment. They both scored significantly lower on dominance/isolation behaviors (i.e. psychological aggression) and on maladaptive beliefs (that spouses cannot change and that all disagreement is destructive). There were no differential effects for treatment modality (i.e. PACT vs. gender-specific).

At post-treatment, husbands reported significant increases in taking responsibility for their own aggression and significant decreases in placing responsibility for their own aggression on their wives. Wives significantly decreased taking responsibility for the husbands' aggression. There were no differential effects for treatment modality.

The initial findings from our 1-year follow-up are promising. Husbands' physical aggression (both mild and severe) at 1 year post-treatment was significantly reduced according to husbands' and wives' reports. Some relationship variables were also significantly improved: wives' marital adjustment and positive feelings about the relationship were significantly higher at the 1-year follow-up than at pre-treatment; husbands' maladaptive beliefs that all disagreement is destructive were significantly reduced. 2-Year follow-ups are currently underway.

In terms of consumer satisfaction, participants were very highly satisfied (average of 8 on a 9-point scale), with both treatments (e.g. how interesting the group was, relevance of the program, personality of the therapists, skills of the therapists, how much their concerns or goals were met by the program). Satisfaction continued to be high at 1 year follow-up, although those who received the couples group rated it significantly higher on the question about their feelings regarding "your interest and involvement in the program". Spouses at 1 year rated themselves and their spouses as slightly to moderately better (between 6 and 7 on a 9-point scale) at controlling anger, at self-control and accepting responsibility for their own actions, at their ability to contain conflict, and at their lessened use of verbal aggression. Spouses rated themselves moderately better (7 on a 9-point scale) at curtailing mild and severe physical aggression.

When asked at a post-treatment debriefing interview, 96% of subjects said that they would like the program to be longer. Sixty-seven per cent of those participants in the gender-specific group said that they would have liked additional couple sessions. Regarding psychological aggression, 20% of the gender-specific group ($n = 16$ couples) reported a cessation since treatment commenced, 20% reported no change during the program, and 60% reported improvement. In the PACT group ($n = 23$ couples) the figures were 13%, 30% and 56% respectively. Regarding physical aggression, 56% of gender-specific participants reported none since the group started, 19% reported no change, and 25% reported improvement. Sixty-five % of PACT participants reported a cessation of physical aggression, whereas 35% reported no change.

In summary, both groups appear to be successful in reducing physical aggression and in improving the marital quality of participants. Furthermore, some of these effects (including the effect on aggression) continue 1 year following treatment. Participants who complete the program appear to be pleased with the treatment they received, though most gender-specific participants would like to receive attention to their couple issues following 14 weeks of gender-specific treatment.

Prediction of Drop-out

Given the 48% drop-out rate in our volunteer sample, much of our recent efforts are in predicting drop-out. Heyman, Brown & O'Leary (1995) used the pretreatment communication samples to predict treatment drop-out. The best predictors of drop-out are wives' higher use of humor and husbands' lack of empathy (i.e. husbands' responding with hostility to wives' self-disclosure). Husbands' lack of empathy alone accounted for over 40% of the variance in drop-out. The percentage of correctly classified cases was 91.3%. Wives' use of humor was interpreted as a way to placate the husband or defuse the conflict, a behavior that is probably highly adaptive.

Brown & O'Leary (1995) examined relationship, demographic and aggression-related variables as predictors of completion. They predicted that severity of psychological aggression and physical aggression would be associated with treatment completion. Marital adjustment, relationship commitment and demographic variables (e.g. age, education) did not predict drop-out. Severe physical aggression was associated with treatment completion; conversely, severe psychological aggression was associated with drop-out. However, it was wives', not husbands', physical aggression that predicted treatment completion. Husbands' psychological aggression was significantly associated with treatment drop-out. Couples' own explanations for drop-out were also obtained. Eighty per cent of drop-outs reported that they discontinued treatment because the program's goals (violence cessation) and the couples' needs or goals (relationship enhancement) did not match.

In summary, results thus far indicate that husbands' lack of empathy and psychological aggression predict drop-out. Furthermore, if wives are not aggressive, the couple is more likely to drop out of treatment (regardless of modality). We believe that future treatments must assess for and attempt to address these factors at the earliest stage of contact with the couple to reduce the likelihood of dropout.

Posttraumatic Stress Disorder

Schlee, Heyman & O'Leary (1995) hypothesized that women in our study who were diagnosed with physical aggression-related PTSD (one-third of our sample) would be more likely to drop out and, if they completed, would benefit from treatment significantly less than women without PTSD. Although women diagnosed with PTSD were not more likely to drop out, women with PTSD avoidance symptoms (e.g. efforts to avoid thoughts, feelings or conversations associated with the abuse; efforts to avoid activities, places or people that elicit recollections of the abuse) were more likely to drop out than those without PTSD. Those with numbing symptoms (e.g. feeling detached restricted affect) were not more likely to drop out, regardless of PTSD diagnosis. Schlee, Heyman & O'Leary's hypothesis that completers with PTSD would show less improvement than non-PTSD completers was also not supported; both groups showed highly significant improvements on physical aggression, marital adjustment, depression and dominance/isolation by husband. Women with and without PTSD also reported reductions in fear of upsetting their husband and in fear that their husband would assault them again.

In summary, contrary to expectations, PTSD diagnostic status did not increase the likelihood of drop-out or make it more difficult to benefit from either PACT or gender-specific treatment. Women with avoidance symptoms are at risk for dropping out. Sensitive attention to these women's needs at the earliest point of contact with a treatment program may make it less likely for these women to drop out. Perhaps the content of our program (i.e. explicit focus on violence) and/or the group format made it too difficult or unappealing for these women to continue. If the therapist were made aware of the PTSD diagnostic status and attempted to ensure that the therapeutic bond was strong enough to weather the discussion of abuse (as in the Foa et al., 1991, protocol for treatment of PTSD in rape survivors), it may be possible to retain these participants.

Conclusion

Despite controversy, PACT is a treatment that appears to be safe and effective. It is not for couples with severe levels of violence. However, for couples with mild to moderate levels of violence and a strong preference to preserve their marriage, PACT may be the most palatable means to reduce violence.

Acknowledgement

This chapter was supported by National Institute of Mental Health Grant MH 4248804.

REFERENCES

Adams, D. (1988). Feminist perspectives on wife abuse. In K. Yllo & M. Bograd (eds), *Feminist Perspectives on Wife Abuse* (pp. 176–199). Beverly Hills, CA: Sage.

American Psychiatric Association (1987). *Diagnostic and Statistical Manual of Mental Disorders*, 3rd edn (revised). Washington, DC: American Psychiatric Association.

Baucom, D.H. & Epstein, N. (1990). *Cognitive–Behavioral Marital Therapy.* News York: Brunner/Mazel.

Birchler, G.R., Weiss, R.L. & Vincent, J.P. (1975). Multimethod analysis of social reinforcement and exchange between maritally distressed and non-distressed spouse and stranger dyads. *Journal of Personality and Social Psychology*, **31**, 349–360.

Brown, P.D. & O'Leary, K.D. (1995). Reasons for drop-out from couples therapy. Paper presented at the American Psychological Association Convention, New York, August.

Burns, D.D. & Sayers, S.L. (1992). Development and validation of a brief relationship satisfaction scale. Unpublished manuscript.

Caesar, P.L. & Hamberger, L.K. (eds) (1989). *Treating Men who Batter: Theory, Practice, and Programs.* New York: Springer.

Cascardi, M., Langhinrichsen, J. & Vivian, D. (1992). Marital aggression, impact, injury, and health correlates for husbands and wives. *Archives of Internal Medicine*, **152**, 1178–1184.

Edleson, J.L. (1984). Violence is the issue. A critique of Neidig's assumption. *Victimology*, **9**, 5.

Foa, E.B., Rothbaum, B.O., Riggs, D.S. & Murdock, T.B. (1991). Treatment of post-traumatic stress disorder in rape victims: a comparison between cognitive–behavioral procedures and counseling. *Journal of Consulting and Clinical Psychology*, **59**, 715–723.

Ganley, A.L. & Harris, L. (1978). Domestic violence: issues in designing and implementing programs for male batterers. Paper presented at the annual meeting of the American Psychological Association, Toronto, Canada, August.

Gelles, R.J. & Loseke, D.L. (eds) (1993). *Current Controversies on Family Violence*. Newbury Park, CA: Sage.

Gottman, J.M., Markman, H.J. & Notarius, C.I. (1977). The topography of marital conflict: a sequential analysis of verbal and non-verbal behavior. *Journal of Marriage and the Family*, **39**, 461–477.

Gottman, J.M. & Porterfield, A.L. (1981). Communicative competence in the non-verbal behavior of married couples. *Journal of Marriage and the Family*, **43**, 817–824.

Greenberg, L.S. & Johnson, S.M. (1988). *Emotionally Focused Therapy for Couples*. New York: Guilford.

Heyman, R.E., Brown, P.D. & O'Leary, K.D. (1995). Drop-out in spouse abuse treatment: role of couples communication. Paper presented at the American Psychological Association Convention. New York.

Heyman, R.E., Sayers, S.L. & Bellack, A.S. (1994). Global marital satisfaction vs. marital adjustment: an empirical comparison of three measures. *Journal of Family Psychology*, **8**, 432–446.

Holmes, T.H. & Rahe, R.H. (1967). The social readjustment rating scale. *Journal of Psychosomatic Research*, **11**, 213–218.

Jacobson, N.S. & Margolin, G. (1979). *Marital Therapy*. New York: Brunner/Mazel.

Lederer, W.J. & Jackson, D.D. (1968). *The Mirages of Marriage*. New York: Norton.

Neidig, P.H. (1992). Participants' Workbook for PACT. Unpublished manuscript, State University of New York at Stony Brook.

Noller, P. (1980). Misunderstandings in marital communication: a study of couples' non-verbal communication. *Journal of Personality and Social Psychology*, **39**, 1135–1148.

Notarius, C.I., Benson, P.R., Sloane, D., Vanzetti, N.A. & Hornyak, L.M. (1989). Exploring the interface between perception and behavior: an analysis of marital interaction in distressed and non-distressed couples. *Behavioral Assessment*, **11**, 39–64.

O'Leary, K.D., Vivian, D. & Malone, J. (1992). Assessment of physical aggression in marriage: the need for a multimodal method. *Behavioral Assessment*, **14**, 5–14.

Rosenbaum, A. & O'Leary, K.D. (1986). Treatment of marital violence. In N.S. Jacobson & A.S. Gurman (eds), *Clinical Handbook of Marital Therapy* (pp. 385–405). New York: Guilford.

Sato, R.A. (1991). Assessment of the appropriateness of conjoint treatment with battering couples. In J.P. Vincent (ed.), *Advances in Family Intervention, Assessment and Theory* (pp. 69–88). London: Jessica Kingsley.

Schlee, K.A., Heyman, R.E. & O'Leary, K.D. (1995). Treatment for abused women: are there differential treatment effects for women with PTSD? Paper presented at the 4th National Family Violence Conference, Durham, NH, July.

Spanier, G.B. (1976). Measuring dyadic adjustment: new scales for assessing the quality of marriage and similar dyads. *Journal of Marriage and the Family*, **38**, 15–28.

Straus, M.A. (1979). Measuring intrafamily conflict and violence: the Conflict Tactics (CT) Scale, *Journal of Marriage and the Family*, **41**, 75–78.

Straus, M.A. & Gelles, R.J. (1986). Societal change and change in family violence from

1975 to 1985 as revealed by two national surveys. *Journal of Marriage and the Family*, **48**, 465–479.

Straus, M.A., Gelles, R.J. & Steinmetz, S.K. (1980). *Behind Closed Doors: Violence in the American Family*. Garden City, NY: Anchor Books/Doubleday.

Thibaut, J.W. & Kelley, H.H. (1959). *The Social Psychology of Groups*. New York: Wiley.

Tolman, R. (1989). The development of a measure of psychological maltreatment of women by their male partners. *Violence and Victims*, **7**, 159–177.

Walker, L. (1979). *The Battered Woman*. New York: Harper & Row.

Weiss, R.L. Patterson, G.R. & Hops, H. (1973). A framework for conceptualizing marital conflict: a technology for altering it, some data for evaluating it. In L.D. Handy & E.L. Mash (eds) *Behavior Change: Methodology Concepts and Practice* (pp. 309–342). Champaign, IL: Research Press.

Yllo, K. & Bograd, M. (eds) (1988). *Feminist Perspectives on Wife Abuse*. Newbury Park, CA: Sage.

Chapter 24

Co-parenting Post-divorce: Helping Parents Negotiate and Maintain Low-conflict Separations

Mitchell A. Baris* and Carla B. Garrity**
Private Practice, *Boulder and **Denver, CO, USA

Marital therapy cannot assure that all couple relationships will survive. Sometimes the goal of therapy needs to shift from repairing the marital relationship to assisting a couple in separating without compounding the hurt. In this chapter, the stages involved in divorce planning will be explored, especially divorce planning that allows a couple to structure a low-conflict, cooperative separation. The chapter concludes with planning for the children of high-conflict parents or impaired parents, including parents who abuse or abduct children.

The number of children who live in one-parent families is growing at a consistent and dramatic rate. Estimates range from 35% to 55% within Western countries. The USA has the highest divorce rate, with recent studies finding that as many as 55% of American couples, 42% of English couples and 35% of Australian couples divorce. For the last 20 years, researchers have documented the difficulties faced by children of divorce, and most countries have enacted legal reforms and social policies to provide protection for these children of divorce. Only recently, however, have social scientists begun to consider the impact of marital conflict on children and to assess whether the post-divorce adjustment problems are the result of the divorce or of the exposure to the marital conflict prior to the divorce, or some combination of the two. Children from high-conflict home environments have been shown to be at increased risk for behavioral and emotional problems, for lower academic performance, and for dysfunctional social and interpersonal relationships with peers (Cummings & Davies, 1994).

Clinical Handbook of Marriage and Couples Interventions. Edited by W. Kim Halford and Howard J. Markman.
© 1997 John Wiley & Sons Ltd.

Some children living in families with high marital discord are further exposed to the dysfunctional effects of how parents attempt to cope with an unhappy marriage. Considerable evidence is available that demonstrates that marital conflict can result in depression, substance abuse, interspousal aggression, and even child abuse. The co-occurrence of multiple stressors can create a highly negative environment for the growth and development of children.

THE EFFECT OF MARITAL CONFLICT ON CHILDREN

Little research has been done on the length of time couples continue negative interactional patterns before reaching a decision to divorce. Certainly, most children of divorce have long histories of exposure to high levels of parental conflict before the divorce occurs. Some researchers (Block, Block & Gjerde, 1988) have found evidence of childrens' distress as long as 11 years prior to the divorce. A longitudinal study conducted in the UK in the 1970s followed a large group of children from age 7 to age 11. As is typically found, the children whose parents had divorced by age 11 were doing less well than those who remained in intact families. The surprise, however, was that when the earlier data were examined, these same children were in distress 4 years earlier while their families were still intact. For boys especially, the study found that the divorce *per se* did not appear to be as large a contributing factor as did the pre-divorce family environment (Cherlin et al., 1991). Interparental conflict within an intact family has been the focus of a number of recent studies (Fincham, Grych & Osbourne, 1994; Grych & Fincham, 1990). The link between parental anger and children's capacity to cope has been found to be complex and multi-determined. Some children demonstrate remarkable resilience and capacity to seek protective relationships outside of the family. These children demonstrate good interpersonal adjustment, self-esteem and coping in spite of living in a hostile family environment. Other children, however, appear to succumb to the conflict between their parents. Boys are most at risk to externalize and model their parents' ineffective problem-solving style by becoming aggressive with peers while girls are more likely to internalize their distress and to suffer from anxiety and depression. The processes by which marital conflict impacts children are complex and multi-determined; four factors are considered primary determinants: (a) modeling of an ineffective problem-solving style by the parents; (b) emotional dysregulation within the child as a result of living in a tension-filled home environment; (c) feeling responsible for the marital conflict; and (d) disruption of the relationship between each parent and the child. While most researchers agree that there is a definite link between marital conflict and child adjustment issues, more long-term studies are needed to fully understand the pathways by which these factors impact children. The age of the child, the resiliency within the child's personality, and the capacity to have or seek out protective influences are all important mitigating effects of living in a home filled with tension and hostility between the parents (Emery & Forehand, 1994).

Is divorce, therefore, the best solution for children exposed to high levels of marital conflict? The answer to this question might well be "yes," provided the divorce will reduce the level of hostility and conflict to which the children are exposed. Unfortunately, this is not always the case. Parental conflict can increase when a marriage is dissolved, and approximately 25% of all divorced couples continue moderately high to high levels of conflict for years following their divorce (Johnston & Campbell, 1988; Emery, 1988). What is clear is that children cannot thrive and develop in an environment of interparental hostility, be it within a marriage or outside of a marriage. Children of all ages respond with distress to interadult anger. Furthermore, children frequently adopt coping styles early in life that tend to set the stage for how they problem-solve and adapt to conflict throughout their lives. Boys are likely to adapt with increased aggressiveness, which they display with peers during childhood and with their own spouses during adulthood. Girls, on the other hand, are more likely to become withdrawn and anxious and to be ineffective problem-solvers during childhood and victims of domestic violence in their own marriages (Kate & Gottman, 1993; Jaffe, Wolfe & Wilson, 1990). Consequently, what the research does tell us is that long-term exposure to high levels of conflict between parents is unhealthy for children. It does not matter if it is within an intact family or a divorced family; unresolved high conflict is not in the best interest of children's emotional development. Therefore, if parents cannot manage their own anger, it is critical for the well-being of the children that alternative forms of conflict resolution and anger management be found through the marital therapist, divorce mediator or parenting coordinator.

THE DECISION TO DIVORCE

Some parents remain in a kind of limbo, unable to move in either direction, not able to repair the marital relationship or to decide to end it. They remain in an intimate relationship with high negativity and conflict. Ultimately, this can hurt all of the family members, the adults and the children. Some couples can move rapidly from working on being together to working on separating. Others will linger for months or even years defining and redefining their relationship but never containing the destructive conflict. They cannot decide to divorce, neither can they decide to remain married or even to move to a trial separation. During this time, the parents may move in and out of the house, in and out of communication with each other, and in and out of each other's lives.

A high degree of ambivalence is characteristic of this period. Some attempt to cope with this ambivalent phase in ways that are harmful; this might include substance abuse, spouse-battering or other erratic and impulsive means of coping. If a couple remains for a long period of time in this phase, the damage to the children may be profound and long-lasting. Parents stuck in this ambivalence will need help to focus their attention on the potential harm to their children and to contain the conflict for the sake of their children as well as themselves. It is at this stage that redefining goals, affirming the need to separate, and mediating a parenting plan might be the appropriate and humane intervention.

For example, Jill and Ray were unable to make the decision to leave each other. They had established a pattern of destructive anger and physical abuse with each other, each one the perpetrator of abuse on the other. Sadly, they had two young children, both preschoolers, who were witness to this repeated escalation of violence between their parents. No matter what measures were taken to help them contain their anger, including physical separation, they would continually re-approach each other and again allow their conflict to erupt. This ultimately resulted in criminal charges being filed and restraining orders being issued by the court, which both Jill and Ray continually violated. They remained ambivalent, some part of them convinced they could work through the difficulties of their relationship, and yet at other times feeling that they needed to live apart, that they would never survive each other physically or emotionally. Over time, this took an extremely negative toll, both on their safety and on the well-being of their children. The children became symptomatic. Their daughter became highly anxious, clingy and regressed. Their son developed aggressive symptoms at his preschool and verbalized to his parents his sense of depression, despair and helplessness over being unable to get his parents to disengage from their continual negative behavior.

THE ROLE OF THE PROFESSIONAL

Divorce mediation focuses on maintaining joint parenting so that the needs of the children are foremost and so that the children are protected from the conflict commonly generated between the ex-spouses during and following divorce. Marital therapies tend to focus on building areas of communication and intimacy. Divorce mediation, on the other hand, will need to work toward narrowing the focus of communication and limiting intimacy. A new relationship is restructured so that the couple may proceed in a dispassionate business-like partnership to make reasonable joint decisions for the children while limiting communication about their relationship as a couple. This process, therefore, establishes strict boundaries between the parents as individuals and ultimately contributes to the establishment of a sense of two separate families with the children.

A professional helping a couple to transform a marital relationship into a cooperative post-divorce parenting relationship is called on to perform more tasks than a traditional mediator. Many professional roles and unique skills must be combined to guide the parents toward a relationship that is built solely around the needs of the children without again opening old wounds and re-engaging the conflict remaining from the marital breakdown. Consequently, the term "parent coordination" will be used to define this means of divorce mediation. Ideally, the parenting coordinator is experienced in many different disciplines: dispute resolution, communication building, mediation techniques, relevant legal requirements of divorce planning for children (these will vary across jurisdictions), adult psychotherapy, child development and the phases of divorce adjustment in both children and adults. The focus the parenting coordinator must maintain during the mediation sessions is that of the children's protection and well-being. The client, therefore, is no longer the couple or the marital relationship; rather, the client is the relationship between the children and the parents. Protecting and preserving that relationship at as optimal, safe and conflict-free a level as possible is the goal of the coordinator.

Redefining the Roles of the Parents

Functioning post-divorce means shifting from a conflicted marital relationship to parenting cooperatively for the sake of the children. An important issue is the management of anger and negativity resulting from the sense of loss that may be present around the demise of the marriage. That means focusing communication on the children only and working to build and rebuild problem-solving skills around the children only. It may be necessary for the parenting coordinator to take an active role in directing the flow of communication. It is no longer uncovering and working on building intimacy so much as managing the extraneous issues that are inappropriate to the relationship at this point, like derogatory remarks about the other parent or bringing up issues of old hurts and old wounds. It is important that in the sessions, the new behavior that is going to prevail outside of the sessions is established and sustained. In this way, a structure is built by which the couple learns to define what areas are appropriate for communication and how to keep their problem-solving discussions focused on the children. Research is demonstrating that couples who have been in high conflict need to go through a period of emotional disengagement before they are able to co-parent cooperatively (Mnookin 1992). Often it helps to structure the communication itself for some period of time, even to the extent that all communication is in writing; on answering machines, voice mail, E-mail, fax or computer. This is advisable when open communication seems to lead invariably to negativity and an escalation of the conflict. It often needs to be stressed that such highly structured means of communication are usually necessary only for a specified period of time, until some healing and disengagement from the wounds inflicted within the relationship has taken place. For some couples, this may mean that the mediator or parent coordinator cannot see the two together as a couple. Rather the professional may need to work individually, seeing them separately for a period of time, or for several sessions or parts of sessions. This is especially true for couples where violence and intimidation have taken place.

Kristin and Gene had been extremely intimidating to each other. Gene had been violent with Kristin, which had prompted her to call the police on several occasions to restore calm to the process of exchanging the children. While Gene had been physically intimidating in the past, he denied responsibility and claimed he felt unjustly accused by Kristin. He walked into the joint mediation session looking over both shoulders, literally creeping along the wall of the office and was anxious, jumping out of his chair at times when in the presence of his ex-wife, fearing she would further accuse him unjustly. Kristin too was intimidated in the presence of Gene and felt unable to think creatively and openly in his presence. In a couple of mediation sessions, he vented his anger at Kristin for her audacity in winning a court battle which resulted in her having the children more that 50% of the time. Kristin clearly felt this was in the children's best interest. It was agreed that in order to mediate with any degree of effectiveness, it would be necessary to meet with the parents one at a time to hear out their issues, and finally to do brief follow-ups with each parent on the telephone. In this way the parents were able to carry on a conversation on specific issues and bring some of their issues to closure. This required multiple, brief telephone contacts; however, it allowed them to look at one issue of co-parenting at a time and to come to some conclusions which were written and mailed to both parents. It allowed the parents to process their thinking without being in the high-anxiety situation generated by being in the presence of the other parent.

Negotiating a Post-divorce Parenting Arrangement

Typically a divorce mediation session will begin with setting an agenda. At this time the goals are stated regarding co-parenting. Also identified are decisions regarding the children that need to be made. It is in this first phase of mediation that the parent coordinator will begin to work to narrow the agenda, structure communication, and make it clear that the ultimate goal is to create and define the co-parenting relationship where conflict is minimized. The goal of the mediation is a written parenting plan. This plan will contain a statement of decision-making and time-sharing arrangements which may be contained in the separation agreement. It may also set boundaries, establish communication skills, narrow the focus of the relationship, and provide for containing the conflict for the sake of the children. Frequently, it is those parents who most need structure who protest when it is imposed. These individuals will protest against surrendering control of the relationship that rigid adherence to clearly defined time-share schedules and controlled means of communication signifies. Nevertheless it is such structuring that will help the high-conflict couple to readjust and to formulate a cooperative relationship, which is the ultimate goal of the divorce mediation.

Sam and Nancy, a divorced couple, continually fought and argued with each other about their involvement with other relationships when their child, Mark, aged 10, was visiting at each household. The parents were suspicious that these new dating relationships had actually started before their marriage had ended. They had entered into a cycle of externalization and accusation for some time. The parents had agreed that they would not introduce any dating partner to Mark unless it was a long-term, committed relationship. Nevertheless, every time the parents got together, usually during the transitions of Mark, they accused each other of involving their casual dating partners. Each continually questioned Mark about the other parent's dating behavior. Mark, through his participation in the mediation, shared that it felt like an enormous burden was placed on him when Mom would have men spend the night at her house, because he knew Dad would ask him for information that would either hurt Dad or make him angry, either at Mark or at Mom. Mark did not want to be empowered in this way. In addition, Mark felt that when Mom questioned him about Dad's dating behavior, it confused his sense of loyalty. He wished that if Mom had questions about Dad's dating behavior she would ask Dad directly. When this situation was shared with Dad and with Mom, they were able to resolve to limit the accusations of each other in terms of whose extramarital relationships had caused the break-up of the marriage. They were able to build empathy for Mark and, in so doing, they were able to diminish the manifestation of this conflict.

The parenting coordinator helps the parents to build empathy for the children. Often in the therapeutic sessions, it will be necessary to bring the focus back to the children. When two angry parents are brought together, the focus of the conversation may drift into a rehashing of past problems in the couples' relationship. That needs to be limited and the focus needs to be brought back to the children and to how the children are feeling. It may be necessary to work initially with each of the parents to help in building understanding of what the child has been through and how that child experiences the divorce.

Judith Wallerstein (1991) proposes useful guidelines for telling the children of an impending divorce. Children are best informed when a firm decision has been made to proceed to divorce. If they are not told at the onset of the divorce/ separation process, parents run the risk that others are going to tell them. The children may feel they were left out, misled or deceived, and that their parents have been withholding information from them. It is important as well to have both parents involved in telling all the children together at the same time, at least initially. A short time later each child may need a developmentally appropriate explanation. Each parent must be made available individually and/or together to continue to address the children's questions and issues. It is helpful for the children to understand what is known vs. what is not known, even if all aspects of post-divorce plans have not been worked out. It is also important to stress to the children that neither parent is abandoning the children and to let the children know what changes might take place in the first year and what changes are likely to take place in ensuing years. For example, if the children are going to stay in the same house for another year, it is beneficial for them to understand that. If one parent moves out now and the other is planning to move out of the family's residence within the year, the children deserve this information so that they, too, may begin to prepare for such an adjustment.

Containing Conflict

A major differential between divorce mediation and marital therapy is continued containment of conflict. The parenting coordinator's goal is that of preventing conflict from spreading and escalating. The factors that contribute to conflict are going to vary for different couples. Depending upon what the causes of the conflict are, interventions will be planned accordingly. Some couples are able to rework a relationship rapidly. Some individuals and couples are well-functioning. They are able to minimize the damage that they do to each other in the process. But others take considerable time in terms of being able to rework their relationship, and some require a great deal of structuring over a long period of time to keep from re-enacting the negative parts of their former spousal relationship. Some of the factors that contribute to the development of long-term impasses following divorce may be issues as serious as substance abuse, physical or sexual abuse, psychopathology or impulse problems on the part of one or both parents. If these are present, then it is important to have adjunctive treatment components in addition to the divorce mediation. Some problems warrant individual therapy or different kinds of intervention programs to be able to provide a safe environment for the children while continuing to help the parents to be able to co-parent in a constructive way. Personality problems of the parents comprise more of a gray area, in terms of their implications for providing a safe environment for the children. Characterological acting out could be activated by the conflict or it could be a pervasive problem-solving and interactional style on the part of a parent. Often special kinds of interventions are necessary to deal with these kinds of issues.

For example, a young mother, Carolyn, felt that she was always the more appropriate parent and that she provided a special kind of nurturing that Bob would never be able to provide for their child. Therefore, she decided, their child should not have overnights with Dad. They had been divorced 2 years, when their child was 6 years old and still refusing overnights. Carolyn was asked initially to state out loud all that was wrong with Bob's parenting. She enumerated approximately 15 things. After she did that, these items were read back to her and she agreed that they were the sum total of the problems with Bob. We then agreed that if we worked on Bob's changing these 15 things, then she would feel comfortable in having him parent and participate with her as a more co-equal parent. At this point Carolyn rolled her eyes back and looked dismayed. Truly making all of these behavior changes on Bob's part would not fully reassure her. In working with her, Carolyn was asked to make specific suggestions as to what would remediate various problems that would come up. Sometimes her input was structured as asking her opinion or alternatives that were given to her, e.g. for option A or option B. She would select which course of action felt the best for her. It seemed that as long as Carolyn was able to make the selection or feel that she was driving the direction of the mediation that she was able to participate in time-share with the child. However, if she felt she was no longer in control then it would activate red flags and the conflict would escalate and she was once again reluctant to share their child's time with Bob.

Once again, the overall goal in divorce mediation is that of containing the conflict for the sake of the children while helping both parents to restructure their relationship into a cordial, more businesslike one, devoid of negative emotions and behaviors. There are some early warning signs that a parenting coordinator, or divorce mediator, can use to assist in predicting which families are going to experience the most difficulty with this process. Families at risk for high conflict are going to require structure, distance and disengagement from each other, and a time period of at least 2 years to heal. Recent research in the divorce field has identified some of the factors that are predictive of individuals likely to remain in protracted conflict. Johnston & Campbell (1988) provide a model for understanding the different levels of impasse that the family system can be caught in, such that healing and recovering are inhibited and conflict continues to be chronic and serious. One factor that is predictive of conflict is the extent of negativity within the marriage. When negative feelings have built over a long period of time, post-divorce conflict is likely to be intense. Assessing the history of the marriage, the length of the negativity and the factors involved in the decision to separate will help to predict this factor. Another factor predictive of long-term conflict is the extent to which either or both individual parents exhibit "vulnerability". Vulnerability can be defined as an individual's incapacity to manage the loss, grief and emotional pain generated by the end of the marriage. Certain individuals are predisposed to be more vulnerable to the painful aftermath generated by the demise of a marriage than others. Those who have the greatest degree of personal vulnerability are going to have the hardest time healing. For some, there may never be healing.

This vulnerability arises from experiences early in life. Difficulty coping with relationship issues often originated in the early childhood experiences of these individuals; sometimes, they represent failures in receiving adequate nurturing and protection within their families of origin. These unresolved issues become interwoven into a maladaptive personality style, which leaves the individual with a troublesome conflict resolution style. The severity of vulnerability table (Table 24.1) and the accompanying questions can be used as a guide toward identifying individuals prone to exhibit these characteristics. The table lists a number of variables along a continuum. These variables are not meant to indicate measurable behaviors in any psychometric sense. Rather, they are provided as a guide to the different features that might identify a tendency toward vulnerability.

For example, one mother, Alexandra, had suffered considerably in her own childhood and had a very stormy adolescence in which there was continual testing of her own parents. There was a great deal of uncertainty and mistrust as to whether her parents loved her and accepted her. Throughout her life she had had periods of closeness and then separation again from her own parents. This included several placements outside of her parents' home. She had acted out considerably in her own adolescence and when her daughter, Lisa, reached adolescence Alexandra projected suspiciousness and acting-out behaviors onto her. Lisa complained that she was unable to gain her mother's trust. Furthermore, the mother's self-esteem was so fragile that whenever Lisa would try to identify for her that there truly were communication issues in their relationship, Alexandra would externalize the responsibility and the blame to Dad's bad temper for all the family's problems. Alexandra's long-standing difficulties with

Table 24.1 Severity of vulnerability

Criteria	Mild traits			Ingrained personality structure		
• Will not experience pain, will not hurt, externalizes pain						
• Cannot accept their own role in the breakup of marriage—no capacity for insight						
• Cannot protect the children from the conflict. Little awareness of, or empathy for, impact conflict has on children						
• Degree of devaluing other parent						
• Level of intensity						
• Insatiable quality—nothing seems to resolve the conflict						
• Time-frame of conflict—how long at this level of intensity?						
• Pervasiveness across other social, emotional and occupational relationships						
• Active intensification of the conflict through recruitment of others						

Interview questions to accompany the above Table:
1. It must be hard for you to be here?
2. What will your ex-spouse bring up that is negative about you? What are your liabilities as a parent?
3. How does this divorce and conflict affect the children? (Listen for protection)
4. How did you explain it to the children? What do you withhold from them?
5. Any recent significant changes in your life?
6. How have you tried to allay the conflict before you came here?
7. (Note intensity of anger.) Externally directed anger: if it occurs, ask the parent to shift gears and talk about:
   (a) Children's strengths
   (b) What you enjoy sharing/doing together
   (c) What parts of child care are most enjoyable for you
8. How about the rest of your functioning? Who else helps/matters? Who are they? How do they help?
From Garrity & Baris, *Caught in the Middle*, Lexington Books, 1994, reproduced by permission.

her own self-esteem precluded her from being able to hear her daughter Lisa's pain and ultimately prevented her from establishing a trusting relationship with Lisa. Lisa ultimately acted out many of the very same conflicts that Alexandra had enacted within her own family of origin.

Another contributing factor in terms of identifying which individuals may struggle to restructure their relationship post-divorce are those who have a very high composite of injury. This injury arises from the length and degree of the negativity that has gone on throughout the marriage and into the divorce. It is comprised of the memories and the images of the actual hurtful acts committed. The composite of injury is how much hurt has been perpetrated back and forth between the couple. The third factor contributing to difficulty in healing and restructuring the relationship is the external social factor. This is defined by the extent the conflict has been spread to others. This may involve a reworking of the history of the relationship with new significant others in a negative cast. This may involve only a few close friends and family, or it may include wider circles of individuals including members of the community, the professionals involved with the children and family, or even the press and mass media. It is thus important to look at all of these factors, which comprise the actual injury that has been perpetrated. If for an individual or a couple there is high injury and high vulnerability, then the likelihood of requiring structure over a longer period of time is also greater. Conversely, if any of these factors is lower, then the prognosis for healing looks better, and will probably take place faster.

One other factor to which the divorce mediator wants to be attuned in predicting which couples will require high structure and active involvement for a period of time is the ages of the children that are involved. Children will handle the conflict differently at differing ages. An important factor to look for in younger children is the extent to which they are able to protect themselves from the parental conflict. Younger children generally require more protection as they cannot speak for themselves. But we also know that as children get older they begin to take sides in the conflict.

Parents may require intervention and support to understand that this is normal for children and that they can ease the pain of this process for their children if they do their best to contain their conflict. Children who are caught in heated conflict will seek to resolve it somehow. Children older than about 11 may resolve it by tending to take sides. An only child is more likely to be hurt because he/she is the sole arena in which the parents may enact their conflict. Having a sibling is usually a protective factor in divorce for children, and so parents need to keep this in mind when designing a time-share agreement in which they may or may not want to keep the siblings together. If conflict is high, then the presence of one or more siblings may be a protective factor for the children.

When Annie, now aged 15, was younger, her parents divorced in a highly contentious, angry, litigious divorce that lasted for many years of her childhood and continued into her adolescence. Despite the parents' attempts to mediate with each other, each would attempt to have Annie align with that parent against the other parent. Annie was able to cope when she was younger by asking that the parents minimize their access to her when she was at the home of the other parent. In other words, she did not want to receive any telephone calls from Mother when she was at Dad's house initially, and she did not want to hear from Dad when she was at Mother's. She wanted, in essence, to drive the positive relationship she had with each parent underground so far as the other parent was concerned. She felt that she could not show any affection or understanding for either parent in the presence of the other. This worked for Annie in her childhood. However, as she approached adolescence, she took an increasingly allied stance with her Mom against her Dad. The maintenance of a positive relationship became more and more untenable as Mom's demands for loyalty and more of Annie's time intensified. Annie voiced at age 12 that by the time she was 14 or older, she planned to discontinue visits with her Dad altogether. The divorce mediator, while not betraying Annie's confidence, needed to bring to the awareness of the parents the view that children such as Annie need to be able to maintain a relationship with both parents. Much of this was done in terms of educating Mom to existing outcome studies on children of divorce that seem to indicate that, by whatever method a parent is excluded from the child's life, the child is still left with the issues of feeling abandoned. This may have devastating consequences for the self-esteem of the child and beyond into his/her adulthood. Adults abused as children experience difficulties in feeling confident that they are lovable and worthy of positive relationships.

Establishing a Time-sharing Plan

The initial focus of the divorce mediation thus becomes setting up a reasonable time-share arrangement for the children, coordinating other issues around parenting functions for the children, and establishing a reasonably civil means of decision-making and communication between the parents. To set up the time-share arrangement for the children, there are developmental considerations to be understood for each child, as children of different ages have different developmental needs. They have a progression of psychological tasks to accomplish as they pass through the different chronological ages. It is very important that a time-share arrangement be able to accommodate the children's developmental needs for each age group (Baris and Garrity, 1988). Table 24.2 presents appropriate time-sharing arrangements for families who can cooperatively co-parent. These developmental factors must be balanced with the degree of conflict within the family, between the parents and between the parents and children.

Basically, the guidelines are to allow younger children more frequent renewal of the relationship with each of the parents to whom they are in the process of bonding and relationship-building. Infants and toddlers with well-functioning parents can visit each parent back and forth each day or every other day. Parenting functions for children of this age are largely to tend to basic needs. As children become older, and as they establish more long-term memory and verbal skills, they can begin to sustain longer and longer periods of visitation away from

Table 24.2 Developmental guidelines for time-sharing

	Infancy (0–12 months)	Toddler (12–30 months)	2½–5 years	6–8 years	9–12 years	13–18 years
Goal	To build attachment and security	Continue building sense of familiarity with visiting parent while not disrupting the attachment	Slow introduction of separation from primary caretaker Continue strengthening relationship with visiting parent	Maximize continuity with peers and community from both homes	Maximize continuity with peers and community from both homes Increased emphasis on child input into schedule	Maximize continuity with peers and community from both homes Adolescent development focus is to emancipate from both homes Communication between parents and adolescents is essential to pattern visitation based on balancing parental relationship with the adolescent's role in the community
Visitation	Short daytime visits No overnights	Gradually lengthen daytime visits to full day No overnights	Introduce longer visitation gradually throughout this stage to a maximum of a split week at age 5 Implement overnights—one per week initially, extend to a maximum of three per week by age 5	Gradually increase visitation to a split week: or one home-base with weekend visitation and midweek dinner or overnight	Gradually increase visitation to a split week or alternate weeks or 2 weeks: or continued home-base with weekend and midweek visitation	One home-base or two Adolescent input into schedule is essential

Adapted from Baris and Garrity 1988.

M.A. BARIS AND C.B. GARRITY

either parent. Children who are very young, particularly infants and preschoolers, require more frequent transitions between the parents. It becomes the task of the parent coordinator to structure the transitions such that the parents are not fighting and arguing at the times of these transitions, so that the children can be kept out of the interparental conflict. If the sight of the other parent incenses and incites that parent to anger, then they are to be kept out of sight of each other. It is most helpful for children if parents can at least say "Hello" to each other and acknowledge that the other exists. It is at the transition time itself when the parents are most vulnerable to fighting. The risk of the repetition of angry exchanges of words and behaviors at transitions is that children will develop a sense of responsibility for the fighting. As the children observe their parents fighting and arguing, the stress builds. One suggestion around making transitions easier is to have each parent deliver, rather than pick up the child, in transitioning between homes. This precludes parents encountering each other or waiting at the doorway for children who are not quite packed up and ready to leave the other home. Some parents are unable to encounter each other without active arguing and extreme tension. For these parents setting up a neutral transition point for the children is advisable. This could be a day-care home, or a public place like a library or shopping mall, to keep to a minimum the possibility that the parents are going to rekindle their arguments and begin to fight again. One couple who was very argumentative felt that the only safe place to exchange their children was at their local police station. That is an extreme example at best. More often a local shopping mall, a library or a school is a suitable place to transition children. As children get older, beyond their preschool years, they are able to transition themselves from the curbside or driveway into the home of the other parent. Again, deliveries rather than pick-ups are preferable because there is more leeway for the delivering parent to say good-bye to the children and to transition the children out of his/her home. With delivery, there is also the opportunity for the psychological message of "I sanction this time and relationship with the other parent".

Scott used to go to the home of Deena to pick up his two children, a boy aged 4 and a girl aged 5. He would stand inside the doorway of Deena's house while she was trying to get the children ready to leave with their Dad. Frequently the children would not be ready and Deena would have difficulty packing up the children and getting them out the door, while Scott would be standing in the doorway. It would create enormous tensions inside the home. Deena and the children would squabble and argue. The children would feel from time to time that they hadn't finished what they were doing and they weren't ready to go. It heightened their sense of conflict of loyalty to have Dad stand in the doorway while Mom tried to pack them up and usher them out. Transitions were taking longer and creating a fair amount of stress, as the parents might argue, and Deena felt her boundaries were intruded upon with Scott standing inside and "observing" and "judging" the dynamics of how she was dealing with the children. The transition became considerably easier when Deena was able to pack up the children and bring them to Scott's doorstep, where she was able to say good-bye to them at her house, deliver them to Scott, giving them the psychological as well as the explicit message that she wished for them to have a good time and that she approved of their being there. Then she could say a quick good-bye to them at Scott's door as he would be ready to receive them and engage them in activities.

It is very difficult for children to build a long-distance relationship with a parent from infancy to approximately age 8. These are the years in which bonding and relationship-building are taking place. If a child has built a solid relationship with a parent by the age 8 or 9, usually that relationship can be sustained even at a distance. The long-distance parent can maintain phone contact and the child can travel on an airplane alone to another city or another geographical location to be with that parent. It is therefore recommended that parents, if they are able to, negotiate a clause that states that each of them, if they wish to be involved with the child, will remain in the same geographical location until the child is 9 years old. Young children, or infants, require one parent visiting the geographical area of the other parent to maintain visitation. For example, if Mom has residence, then she will travel to the father's area of residence and then Dad will have the opportunity to meet with the infant at several intervals throughout the day, returning to the mother for renewal of the relationship with her. This can take place similarly with the father visiting the geographical location of the mother. The necessity for this diminishes as children grow older. It is difficult for children who are of preschool age, and even of elementary school age, to carry on a verbal relationship over the telephone. Parents are advised to settle for quick telephone conversations that are relevant to one or two thoughts or issues. Parents also can send notes and post cards, recorded messages on cassette tapes, story books, etc. to each other's areas. There are several good resource books that detail ideas for long-distance visitation, but no book is going to promote a relationship as effectively as parents residing in the same area. Young children require time spent together and the meeting of basic needs for a bond to build between parent and child.

Creating the Parenting Plan

A rule of thumb is that the higher the degree of conflict, the more ground rules and structured containment of conflict there needs to be in creating the co-parenting plan. The younger the children, the harder it will be to figure out how to support emotional disengagement and maintain physical distance between the parents as they exchange the children back and forth. The co-parenting checklist (Appendix I) suggests considerations to take into account in planning an agreement between parents (Garrity & Baris, 1994). It is helpful to have a co-parenting checklist to work with to make sure that no important area of decision-making has been left unaddressed. For some families such things as religious training may be a critically important part of their lives, and for other families that may be unimportant. For some families sharing holidays works out simply because one likes Christmas Eve and one likes Christmas Day, while for other families holidays may cause bitter disputes. The co-parenting checklist will guide the early discussions with the parents as to what to consider in planning for each family. The more thorough the parenting coordinator is, the more likely the conflict will be contained and the subsequent difficulties for the children averted. Aspects of such an agreement are going to vary depending on the ages of the children. For young children, a journal may be passed back and forth to describe illness, feeding and sleeping issues as well as medication issues. School age children often have homework as well as events or activities which require both homes to provide support and transportation. A co-parenting plan will need to include whether parents can jointly attend events. Parents in very high conflict often cannot comfortably attend events together because conflict is likely to erupt. Some children describe that it is anxiety-provoking for them and they are even more nervous performing at their event because they are afraid that their parents will break into an argument. Therefore, events may need to be pre-scheduled in terms of which parent has the greatest interest in that type of activity. For example, one parent might be more culturally-minded and would attend the cultural and artistic events, while the other might be more sports-minded. Some events may need to be attended by each parent alternately.

Adolescents pose a different set of issues in that they are sometimes very expert at moving between the two homes in such a way that they avoid accountability to either parent. They may be up to things that are truly not in their best interest, and neither Mom nor Dad knows about it because they flee from one house to the other. If there is no communication, nobody quite knows what is going on. Adolescents require limit setting. Sometimes adolescents in divorce situations have nobody setting very clear limits on them because both parents are struggling with their own adult issues and they might be eager to over-indulge the child in order to persuade the child to choose to spend time with them. These parents often believe they are gaining an edge by giving a lot of freedom, only to find, surprisingly, that their child is out in the world in a lot of trouble. The parenting coordinator may have to take responsibility for finding out what is going on between the two homes and informing the parents that they are being manipulated by their adolescent. The parenting coordinator may need to help support the parents in encouraging some consistent limit-setting.

It is helpful, too, to be able to conceptualize with a parent what being a single parent is like. Sometimes parents want to fall back into a position of shared responsibility when they can no longer sustain as a single parent. An example of this is the parent who relies on the other to pass them information about when the school events are, when the performances are, when the play-offs are going to be. The parent fails to take the initiative to develop a direct relationship with the teachers, the coaches, the instructors of the children. It is important that parents recognize that as a single parent there are many functions that they used to rely on the other parent for that they now will have to build and sustain on their own. In almost every instance this is an important point to stress. It helps the couple to disengage from dependency on each other. Another area to emphasize is the coordination of rules. There are surprisingly few rules that need to be coordinated between households. Sometimes parents will try to re-engage the other parent in an ongoing relationship by talking about the need to keep the rules consistent across two households. It is important that parents recognize that this is a likely set-up for them to remain negatively and unnecessarily involved with each other. It is also a source of confusion. For example, if a child is being punished or grounded in one home, it is not necessary for the other parent to carry out that parent's grounding. That sort of expectation leads to confusion, misunderstanding and blaming between the parents. It is important for parents to understand that children will respond favorably to internal consistency of rules within each household. The most helpful rules to coordinate are bedtimes and allowances for children.

Children can learn to go between two homes with very different sets of rules. At quite a young age, children can comprehend that there are different rules at different houses. It is a goal of the mediation process to help parents recognize that they cannot dictate to the other parent the rules in that parent's household. Except in cases of endangerment of children, what one parent does is truly not the other parent's concern. If one parent cares to feed fast food for every meal, that remains his/her decision. It may not be sound dietary practice, nor within the value structure of one of the parents, and that parent may want to comment, but there must be recognition that they can do little to change it. Parents must be assisted in the mediation process to see that they can truly set up two different households. Often parents have not thought this situation through ahead of time. They may have been so caught up in the angry animosity and negativity of the marital conflict from which they desperately desired escape that they have not focused on how single parenting will change their relationship to their children. Some parents need a period of trial separation to decide if they truly want to divorce, which a marital therapist may also suggest. But when such a separation is put into place, it should be with a lot of the parenting and financial ground rules that will be there if a final divorce is to take place. Fisher (1981) outlines the areas of agreement to be defined and adhered to for a specified period of time. After the trial separation parents can make a decision to reconcile or separate permanently. When parents waffle and move together and apart, together and apart, they cause their children a great deal of confusion.

Protecting the Children

Some children of divorcing parents will have a therapist or perhaps a guardian *ad litem* who has been appointed by the court to represent their interests and feelings. Some children of divorce, however, have no one to look out for their interests. Very young children, frightened children or children caught in high conflict may not be capable of examining, much less expressing, their feelings. Consequently, the decision as to whether to interview the children rests with the parenting coordinator. The following guidelines may prove helpful to parenting coordinators attempting to decide whether to meet the children or whether to initiate a referral to a professional trained in the area of child development and divorce conflict. Children typically need to be evaluated if any of the following exist:

1. They are showing symptoms of distress.
2. The parents disagree about the needs of the children.
3. The parents present widely differing views of their children's needs, behavior and the underlying causes of that behavior.
4. The children are asking to talk with someone in order to share their feelings or represent their own interests.
5. The children appear to be firmly aligned with one parent.
6. The children refuse to visit with one parent.

When the child has a therapist or is referred to a therapist, the parenting coordinator must be especially sensitive to not violating the special terms of that relationship. For many children caught in a high-conflict divorce, their therapist may be their only friend and ally who is neutral, who can hear their feelings and help them to accept and cope with their losses. If the therapist is brought into the arena of the conflict by making recommendations or decisions that might appear to favor one parent over the other, there is a danger that the disgruntled parent will either actively or covertly undermine the therapist. Ultimately, the children will be the losers, with no-one to share their feelings. Consequently, the parenting coordinator must take final responsibility for any such recommendation or arbitrated decision-making. Open communication between the coordinator and the child's therapist is essential for the children's needs and interests to have a forum, but actual changes in the implemention of visitation planning must rest with the coordinator.

Ongoing Role of the Parenting Coordinator

The parenting coordinator, therefore, assumes a unique professional role that is quite different from that which has been defined within the mental health or legal field in the past. The parenting coordinator must be multi-talented, with expertise in areas of divorce such as conflict management, adult psychopathology, child development, communication training and mediation. The primary mandate is that of protecting the children from the interparental conflict, assisting the parents in disengaging and parenting together to the extent that they are capable, and representing the children's rights to develop in a growth-promoting environment by finding and implementing strategies that maximize the children's wellbeing. The parenting coordinator may perform the role of mediator/arbitrator, or mediator/child therapist, depending on the professional's areas of skill and expertise. It may be necessary to bring in another arbitrator or clinical therapist, however, as the performance of all three roles is impossible for one professional to maintain.

The initial focus of the coordinator is toward the primary goal of emotional disengagement between the parents, as often the parents are well locked into a negative cycle with each other. An important focus of the coordinator is to state clearly that couples issues within the relationship are no longer going to be discussed in a couples format. Individual or group therapy may be recommended for those parents who come to the divorce mediation and want to talk about all of the areas of the marital relationship that they feel were not worked out or understood sufficiently. Some demand endless explanations. Even though they may have received such explanations, they will still come back and persist, "I don't understand why you left me". Some of these individuals are struggling with issues that are now defined as individual issues and that are no longer couples issues, and they should be kept out of the mediation and post-divorce co-parenting process. It is important to set a very restrictive agenda for mediation sessions and often the professional will be screening agenda items and classifying them as individual, rather than appropriate post-divorce couples issues. The guideline for determining appropriate issues for discussion and decision-making is to keep the focus very much on what the children's needs are and how the parents will minimize the expressions of tensions and conflict so as to minimize the stresses of the exchanges on the children. Cognitive and behavioral techniques are much more helpful than the psychodynamic techniques often utilized in marital therapy. Helping the couple to arrive at structured, behavioral solutions to define the terms of their co-parenting interrelating is most helpful. It is important to know that as couples make progress toward the goal of disengagement, then many of the rigid rules initially required around communication may be relaxed. As the parent coordinator remain involved with couples over time, they can begin to pare back in terms of the frequency of meetings, as two separate households working in parallel become established. But sometimes, for high-conflict couples, there will be a period of years of disengagement. Initially, the parent coordinator will work intensively to set up the co-parenting arrangements and then will work with decreasing frequency, sometimes as little as once or twice a year, just to help the couple plan changes and revisions in their regular school year time-share schedule, the holidays and the vacations.

Part of the function of the coordinator is educative, as well. Parents often need help to visualize and understand the elements that are going to contribute to successful co-parenting. Those elements are defined by minimizing the stresses on the children. It is helpful for the parents to recognize how they may inadvertantly place children in "loyalty binds". Children feel very much that they are part of each of their parents. When their parents are in open conflict with each other, children report that they feel they are being torn apart emotionally in the process. It is helpful for parents to recognize this, and to build empathy for the children's position. To do this, it is important for the parents to build a sense of respect for the positive assets of the other parent. It is important that parents encourage the children to love and to respect the other parent. If respect and trust do not exist, then it is important in the context of the divorce mediation to identify the area of difficulty and to determine the means by which the issue can be resolved. This may include psychotherapy, education or other avenues that will help restore a sense of respect and trust for the other parent. Areas of adjunctive treatment and resource-building may include help with substance abuse, controlling angry impulses, building parenting skills and empathy, or other issues. It is an important goal that each parent be able to make positive statements about the other parent's relationship with the child.

It may be reassuring to one parent to know that the other parent is getting help. At the least, they know somebody outside is monitoring or supervising the situation. Generally speaking, people are less likely to act out their conflict publicly in front of others. That is why transferring at public places is often a helpful technique. Similarly, the parenting coordinator staying involved, sometimes for the duration of the children's growing-up years, can be helpful. Just knowing that there is someone in the background remaining involved in the situation provides external monitoring for those who do not have adequate impulse control on their own. This is discussed in more detail in a later section on the abusive family.

In summary, there are three phases or aspects to the parenting coordinator's role. The first is assessing the needs of each individual family, based on the ages of the children and their subsequent developmental needs; the amount of woundedness and vulnerability; an understanding of the conflictual areas between a couple; and the degree to which the conflict has spread to new significant others, extended family, and other parts of the community. This phase may be viewed as that of assessment. The next phase is constructing the agreement between the parents, and the final phase is that of implementing the agreement. These phases may be handled sequentially or in a somewhat overlapping sequence, but all three must be considered and included. Phasing in portions of the new agreement, re-assessing and modifying it over time is generally indicated.

Implementing the Agreement

In implementing all aspects of the agreement, parents often need professional help around productive problem-solving and communication. Sometimes they cannot communicate effectively verbally and they may do well communicating by journal or temporarily through the parenting coordinator.

It is important to avoid putting children into the pressured position of having to decide who they want to live with or what their time-share schedule is going to be. Truly most children do not have an idea in terms of what is reasonable for them to sustain a meaningful post-divorce relationship with each parent. It is helpful if parents can work out a time-share arrangement that makes sense developmentally, while taking into account how much conflict there is in the parental relationship. In addition, a viable time-share schedule takes into account the lives, the work schedules, the availability of the parents, as well as their past functioning and participation as parents. It is helpful if the parents decide on a predictable time-share schedule and propose that to the children, letting them know that this is not set in stone, communicating that the parents together think that this is what is going to be most manageable for all members of the family, they are still open to hearing the children's input and that they would make adjustments accordingly at an appropriate time. It is suggested that the parents agree to try out a time-share schedule with the idea that it will be assessed, looked at and modified over time as it proves to be working or not working.

If there are retriggers and red flags that are going to re-engage the parents in conflict, then it is important to identify these to the parents. This understanding of the nature of their specific negative pattern of interaction will help them to avoid retriggering difficult situations. Some of these retriggers may involve maladaptive personality styles which one or both of the parents may bring to negotiating sessions. For example, those parents who are narcissistic may have a great deal of difficulty in terms of yielding ground. They may feel that if a ground rule is not adhered to that they have had input into designing, then they have been transgressed in some serious way, and they are likely to retaliate and escalate conflict. It is thus important to work with such parents to give them considerable input into the rules and guidelines agreed to, sometimes to limiting that parent's alternatives in asking them to suggest the options in terms of how any particular rule or visitation issue is going to be handled. These parents can endorse issues that emanate from themselves and will have a great deal of difficulty in adhering to rules that are set up by others, especially by the other parent. It is then important to discourage active or passive sabotaging behavior on the part of the ex-spouse. It is helpful to understand this conflict management approach when setting up the initial agreement as well as in terms of adhering to the agreement over time.

Other parents have a passive and dependent style and are "easily victimized". They are very prone to crumble under negative criticism from the other parent. As a parenting coordinator, it is important to recognize the "triggers" that are part of the rekindling of the conflict for these people. Knowing how easily humiliated they are and what some of the situations are that humiliate them will guide the parenting coordinator in designing a parenting agreement to keep such trigger situations from occurring. These parents will do well in skill-building or support groups or in their own individual therapy to help to define and fortify their own sense of boundaries. Often parents from this group have difficulty in establishing their boundaries, and it is easy to cross these lines and to draw them into a conflict. For instance, at drop-off or pick-up the more outwardly aggressive parent might say, "Can I talk to you for a minute?" and then the easily victimized parent is drawn into a conversation that turns very destructive in short order. This individual is wounded again, and the children have witnessed this. Whatever ground has been gained in terms of disengagement, has now been lost. Therefore, recognizing this style, these parents need help getting strong and saying, "No, thank you, I will not talk to you at the point of transitioning the children", or, "You can communicate what you want to in a letter". The professional can help parents to structure these ground rules initially and then help them over time to become proficient in knowing what their own triggers are and avoiding trigger situations. The parenting coordinator builds these ground rules as concrete behavioral strategies, but they are based on a psychodynamic understanding of each person's early history, wounds within the marriage and divorce, and present circumstances in life that might make them vulnerable. The parent coordinator thus understands the family psychodynamically, but does not use those techniques in insight-oriented treatment. Building cognitive strategies based on that understanding toward minimizing the conflict is the primary goal. As conflict remains minimized, the couple will heal, they will disengage, and the children will be protected from the harmful effects of the adult conflict.

Still other parents have a personality style where they feel in control when they are disappointing the expectations of those around them. It is important to take note that children must be protected from this kind of disappointment of expectations. The other parent will need support in terms of predicting this kind of behavior and staying disengaged from re-entering a battleground when an expectation is failed, violated, or not adhered to. This is the kind of parent that might promise to show up for an event or promise to do something with the children, such as shop for a birthday present for a party, and then fail to follow through. They likely had this destructive style in the marriage and they still are in the old pattern of disappointing their ex-spouse by not following through. They also, sadly, are disappointing their children at the same time. It is important for the children of these parents to understand that when an agreement is made, it is not a hard and fast agreement that they can absolutely count on, and to know that there might not be follow-through. This will help cushion the impact of the possible disappointment. The children need to build a realistic sense of what they can count on from such a parent.

Mediation has been thought of in the past as useful to help parents structure an initial agreement. In this model, however, the mediator, or parenting coordinator, remains available throughout the children's growing-up years. It may involve very limited on-going contact for some families, only perhaps at the beginning of the school year or the beginning of the summer months to plan around scheduling. It may well be around a life circumstance that has occurred— a former spouse has remarried, there has been a death, there has been a move, etc. For some families the role of the parenting coordinator will be very active for a long period of time to help manage the conflict and to keep the parents constructively disengaged and emotionally distant. About 25% of all families stay in heightened conflict for most of their children's growing-up years (Maccoby & Mnookin, 1992). The parenting coordinator needs to be available throughout those years to help to contain the conflict if the children are going to be protected.

Planning for the Abusive Family

For most children of divorce, the residence and visitation plan outlined in the final divorce decree is gradually adapted to and parents either cooperate in making modifications as circumstances warrant or professionals assist them in making adaptations. Sadly, for approximately 25% of all children of divorce, the planning of residence and visitation does not go smoothly (Maccoby & Mnookin, 1992). Many of these children face situations that pose grave risks to their subsequent development because they must either live in or visit an environment that represents a negative living situation. An abusive family is one in which there is a high risk of emotional or physical endangerment for the children. There are four primary high risk environments:

1. A parent with a history of perpetrating physical or sexual abuse to the children, ex-spouse, or others.
2. A parent with a substance abuse problem.
3. A parent with serious psychopathology.
4. A parent with an impulse discharge problem.

In all of these situations, protection of the children is the first and foremost concern. Visitation planning is more complex than the divorce mediation process described earlier. The parenting coordinator needs to plan visitation in a manner that assures the safety of the children and slowly builds to increased time as the offending parent clearly demonstrates a capacity to recover. Typically, visitation needs to be in a supervised setting while a careful assessment is conducted by a professional with expertise in the area of concern. Structure, distance and disengagement between the parent is essential for the protection of the children. Finally, the children frequently benefit from a therapist of their own to allow them the opportunity to work through the trauma, to realize that they are not to blame for one or both parent's difficulties and to represent the children's feelings in planning for the future.

Following the assessment phase, the parenting coordinator will need to predict the likelihood for recovery, which will in turn determine which pathway of visitation to consider (see Figure 24.1). It is important that the parenting coordinator, assisted by the evaluator of the offending parent, proceed slowly and in a stepwise fashion, always placing the children's safety as the primary determining factor in planning visitation. Understanding the prognosis for recovery and the time-frame within which recovery is likely is a critical dimension in visitation planning. Many factors must be balanced with the prognostic indicators: the child's safety from physical and emotional harm; the child's age; capacity to report a harmful environment and to seek safety; the fearfulness the child is experiencing; and the developmental level of the child.

Research findings indicate that well-trained clinicians can predict with some degree of accuracy the profiles of parents likely to recover. For example, parents

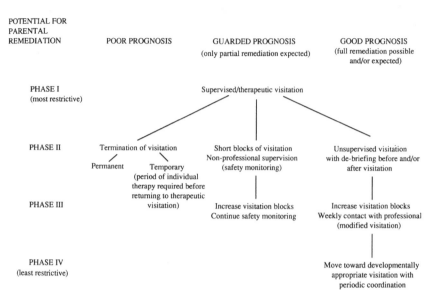

Figure 24.1   Visitation planning for the abusive family (from Garrity & Baris, 1995, with permission)

who have repeatedly physically or sexually abused their children are at high risk to continue that pattern of behavior and careful monitoring of the children is critical (Finkelhor, 1986). Approximately 50% of substance abusers will manage to remain substance-free over time, even with the assistance of a therapeutic program (Alterman et al., 1991). Domestic violence is often partially determined by an impulse control problem. Violence present over a long period of time within the marriage, be it by the wife or the husband, is far more likely to carry over into the post-separation stage than is violence that erupted only at the end of the marriage (Johnston & Campbell, 1993). Other impulse control problems due to serious character pathology are not usually treatable conditions and care must be taken to assure the children's continuing safety. Many of the parents in this latter category will maintain control of their impulses while in a highly structured and supervised setting, but will deteriorate when more normalized visitation is instituted. It is consequently critical that the pathways to recovery be individually assessed and carefully mapped out by the parenting coordinator so that the children's rights to safety are preserved at all times.

As therapeutic gains are made by the offending parent, less and less structured visitation time can be gradually instituted, as outlined in Figure 24.1. There is no one rule of thumb that can be applied to the multi-determined factors that are involved in providing safety in the abusive family. Coordination between the parenting coordinator, the children's therapist and the individual supervising the visitation is essential as graduated degrees of unsupervised visitation are initiated. An offending parent may go from strict supervision in an office or hospital setting to a period of monitoring following each visit, to a less supervised structure of monitoring on a weekly or monthly basis. Some parents may simply fail to ever recover sufficiently to maintain a safe environment for their children. If that is the determination made over time, then a "safety monitor" may be required until the children are old enough to take action to protect themselves. Safety monitors might be relatives, friends, and AA sponsor, or a volunteer from the Red Cross. Sadly, some parents never fully recover and represent an ongoing toxic environment for their children. Some of these parents eventually drop out of their children's lives and the children need the support of therapy to understand that they are lovable and desirable children who had a tragedy happen in their lives that was not their fault. Other parents continue to have an interest in visiting but constantly disappoint or hurt their children emotionally. For some of these children, limited but continued visitation on an infrequent basis is preferable to a complete suspension of visiting. However, children who show distress around visitation and appear not to be benefiting may need to have visitation suspended while the parent is encouraged to again work on his/her difficulties. When and if the parent has completed a therapeutic program, visitation can be resumed. Complete termination of visitation is a serious issue but one that may have to be considered for the well-being of the children. The harm done by visitation must be balanced against the harm engendered by the loss of a parent. Children who are distressed about visitation, who have a strong supportive network and who appear to have some understanding of their parent's pathology may be better off with a termination of visitation.

Parental child abduction is a very poorly researched area. Unofficial estimates are that 25 000–100 000 children are abducted by a non-custodial parent each year in the USA (Long, Forehand & Zogg, 1991; Forehand, Long & Zogg, 1990). Parental child-snatching is when a parent physically takes, restrains, and does not return a child under the age of 14 after a visit, keeping the child concealed so that the other parent does not know where the child is. Typically, this occurs within the first 2 years post-divorce in a very high-conflict divorce where a legal decision has been made against one parent. The parents most likely to snatch children are impulse-disordered parents in very high-conflict divorces who have just received a legal ruling that is not in their favor. They take matters into their own hands by abducting their child or children. Most parents do not plan this very carefully; rather, it is very impulse-discharged. They do not think about where they are going, how they are going to hide, or how they are going to support themselves. They just go suddenly and somewhat unpredictably. While more men tend to abduct children than women, it is important to understand that this data is skewed because more fathers lose custody of their children than mothers. Mothers who lose custody also are at risk to take their children. A few national projects in the USA have looked at solutions for this problem and basically they have found that neither traditional mediation nor the legal system are very helpful intervention methods. These are often families who are angry at the legal system, angry at the determination that has been made by the court, and unable to work within that system. Therefore, the parent coordination model might be a useful model for parents who tend to have this kind of difficulty. The impaired parent model of beginning visitation within a therapeutic setting, Stage One, assures that a parent likely to abduct can control his/her own impulses and establish better ways to problem-solve before moving into less restrictive visitation. Visitation can then be moved to Stage Two, provided that the parent coordinator sees growth in those aspects of the impulse-disordered parent.

TRANSITIONING FROM MARITAL THERAPY TO DIVORCE MEDIATION

When marital therapy fails, the professional working with the couple must decide whether to terminate with separate referrals for the husband and wife to new therapists or to move into the role of divorce mediator or parenting coordinator. Some marital therapists may suggest a trial separation prior to a firm decision to divorce. If so, the therapist may help the couple to conceptualize single parenting, the time period of the trial separation and the terms. Some couples may elect to continue meeting with the therapist as a couple during this time, others may not.

Transitioning roles means honest self-examination on the part of the therapist, an examination of one's own skills, and possible countertransference issues. Before moving into a new arena and focus of therapy, a professional must feel confident that he/she has the necessary skills. Equally important is that the therapist take time to reflect on the feelings regarding the failure of the marital therapy. If the therapist is carrying blame for the breakdown, is not certain that all avenues were tried or is clearly biased toward one partner and harboring anger toward the other, an outside referral may be the best avenue.

After examining one's own skills, reactions and feelings, the therapist must then assess with the couple the level of trust that still exists within the therapeutic relationship. If each individual within the couple can sustain trust, feels there is a benefit in that the therapist knows a great deal about their history, interactional style and communications, then a change of roles can be explored further. Sometimes one member of the couple may feel very angry at the therapist for not being successful at repairing the marriage, and may be unable to sustain trust and confidence.

Becoming a parenting coordinator is a significant change of roles, as a wide variety of skills are involved that many professionals trained only in marital therapy may not have. A parenting coordinator needs to have some knowledge of child development and child divorce issues, practical skills in communication and conflict resolution, anger containment and management, and finally behavioral and cognitive techniques that are solution-oriented rather than insight- or process-oriented. Crisis intervention might be necessary, as couples in the midst of divorce often get into heated conflict and demand decision-making at times such as weekends when children are in transit between homes. Many parents will need parent education as well. Functioning as a single parent means handling child-care tasks that the other parent may have managed when the couple lived together. Sorting out the stresses of the divorce on the children from the normal stresses of development may be an area in which the parenting coordinator needs to assist both parents.

Research in the field of marital therapy (Notarius & Markman, 1993) suggests that many couples seek help for their marriage as a last resort. In other words, the marriage is often seriously impaired when the couple's therapy process begins. One partner will be withdrawing and ready to terminate the relationship, but the couple seek therapy as a self-restorative effort primarily to affirm that all possible was tried and then in all good conscience they can end the marriage. It is, therefore, not surprising that many marital therapists are dealing with couples that are in a failed marriage even before they initiate marital therapy. It is also likely that the couple will realize that the problems within the marriage are insurmountable, or that the conflict is so intense and so frightening that the children are definitely being hurt. A marital therapist must ethically confront the issues of when it is in the best interests of everyone to terminate a marriage for the well-being of both the adults and the children. As explored in the introduction, high-conflict marriages hurt children and adults and must be balanced against the possibility of a reasonably cooperative divorce.

If abuse is present in the dynamics between a couple, or there is concern for the safety of either party or the children, a couple might need to be educated about safety issues and at least a trial separation recommended while they work on problem resolution styles and communication. A marital therapist with experience and awareness of divorce mediation can then assist the couple should they be able to reconcile, or should they make the decision to divorce. Having some knowledge and skills in divorce mediation means that the marital therapist can assist in keeping the children out of the conflict as the couple move toward repairing or terminating the marriage.

REFERENCES

Alterman, M., O'Brien, C., McClellan, C. & Thomas, L. (1991). Differential therapeutics for substance abuse. In R. Frances & S. Miller (eds), *The Clinical Textbook of Addictive Disorders*. New York: Guilford.

Baris, M. & Garrity, C. (1988). *Children of Divorce*. A Developmental Approach to Residence and Visitation. DeKalb, IL: Psytec.

Block, J., Block, J.H. & Gjerde, P.J. (1988). Parental functioning and the home environment in families of divorce: prospective and concurrent analyses. *Journal of the American Academy of Child and Adolescent Psychiatry*, **27**, 207–213.

Cherlin, A.J., Furstenberg, F.F., Chase-Lansdale, L., Kiernan, K.E., Robins, P.K., Morrison, D.R. & Teitler, J.O. (1991). Longitudinal studies of effects of divorce on children in Great Britain and the United States. *Science*, **251**, 1386–1389.

Cummings, E.M. & Davies, P. (1994). *Children and Marital Conflict*. New York: Guilford.

Emery, R.E. (1988). *Marriage Divorce and Children's Adjustment*. Newbury Park, CA: Sage.

Emery, R.E. & Forehand, R. (1994). Parental divorce and children's well-being: a focus on resilience. In R.J. Haggarty et al. (eds), *Stress Risk and Resilience in Children and Adolescents* (pp. 64–99). New York: Cambridge University Press.

Fincham, F.D., Grych, J.H. & Osborne, L.N. (1994). Does marital conflict cause child maladjustment? Directions and challenges for longitudinal research. *Journal of Family Psychology*, **8**, 128–140.

Finkelhor, D. (1986). *A Sourcebook on Child Sexual Abuse*. Newbury Park, CA: Sage.

Fisher, B. (1981). *Rebuilding: When Your Relationship Ends*. San Luis Obispo, CA: Impact.

Forehand, R., Long, N. & Zogg, C. (1990). Parental abduction: the problem and possible solution. In B. Lahey & A. Kardin (eds), *Advances in Clinical Psychology*, **12**, 113–137.

Garrity, C. & Baris, M. (1994). *Caught in the Middle*. Boston, MA: Lexington Books.

Garrity, C. & Baris, M. (1995). Custody and visitation issues in the abusive family. *Family Advocate*, Winter.

Grych, J. & Fincham, F. (1990). Marital conflict and children's adjustment: a cognitive–contextual framework. *Psychological Bulletin*, **108**, 267–290.

Jaffe, P., Wolfe, D. & Wilson, S. (1990). *Children of Battered Women*. Newbury Park, CA: Sage.

Johnston, J. & Campbell, L. (1988). *Impasses of Divorce*. New York: Free Press.

Johnston, J. & Campbell, L. (1993). Parent–child relationships in domestic violence families disputing custody. *Family Conciliation Courts Review*, **31**, 282–299.

Katz, L.F. & Gottman, J.M. (1993). Patterns of marital conflict predict children's internalizing and externalizing behaviors. *Developmental Psychology*, **29**, 940–950.

Long, N., Forehand, R. & Zogg, C. (1991). Preventing parental child abduction: analysis of a national project. *Clinical Pediatrics*, 549–554.

Maccoby, E. & Mnookin, R. (1992). *Dividing the Child*. Cambridge, MA: Harvard University Press.

Mnookin, R. (1992). Dividing the child: how professionals can help parents make decisions. Paper presented at 16th Annual Child Custody Conference, Keystone, Colorado.

Notarius, C. & Markman, H. (1993). *We Can Work It Out*. New York: G.P. Putnam's Sons.

Wallerstein, J. (1991). The long-term effects of divorce on children: a review. *Journal of American Academy of Child Psychiatry*, **30**, 349–360.

APPENDIX—CO-PARENTING CHECKLIST

In creating a parenting plan, the parenting coordinator is wise to be as specific as possible. Uncertainty fuels conflict for couples who are uncooperative. Each family situation is unique in the developmental needs of the children, the level of conflict, and the requirements for structure. The following checklist is to assist the coordinator in devising as clearly detailed a plan as possible. The checklist covers the main areas that typically need addressing for all families; the specifics within each area will vary from family to family.

Visitation Plan
- Daily, weekly, or long-distance time-share schedule.
- Drop-off/pick-up: where, time, how, who.
- Consideration of child's needs.
- Transportation between households: delivery or pick-up.
- Penalty for late drop-off or pick-up.
- Rescheduling: canceled visits rescheduled?
- Overnights: phasing in.
- Phasing in increased parental involvement.

- If visitation refusal is a problem, how will it be handled?
- Responsibility for sick children.

Trade-off or Last Minute Changes

- Is a right of refusal for babysitting to be accorded? A right of refusal means the other parent has first option for child care over and above a sitter for any length of time 4 hours or longer (a shorter length of time is an intrusion, a longer length of time is fine).
- Must ask in writing or verbally, not via the children. The other parent responds yes or no with the understanding that no explanation is expected or sought.
- Flexibility is a two-way process. For high-conflict parents, it is a good first step toward learning cooperative communication.

Phone Calls

- Typically not regulated but if a problem, it needs to be.
- Typically, child can initiate phone calls in private at any time.
- Parent-initiated calls: if problematic, need to be scheduled; specify how long, how often and when or whether allowed.

Toys and Belongings

- Two complete sets are best.
- Need guidelines for things moving between two households.
- Specify what travels and what cannot (e.g. expensive sports equipment).

Holiday Visitation

- Holidays supersede regularly scheduled visitation with no make-up expected; Christmas Eve, Christmas Day, New Year's Eve, New Year's Day, Spring Break, Easter, July 4th, Memorial Day, Labor Day, Halloween, Thanksgiving, President's Day, Passover, Rosh Hashanah and other holidays of significance and/or time off from school.
- Birthdays: children will celebrate two happily.
- Father's Day and Mother's Day.
- Alternative arrangements:
  1. Alternate odd/even years.
  2. Split holiday in mid-day.
  3. Monday holidays must be specified whether attached to weekend visitation.

Extracurricular Activities

- If you expect the other parent to support your choice, then you must seek his/her endorsement.
- Activities: who pays, provides transportation, and attends.
- Expensive equipment needs to be covered in financial agreement for clarity.

Religious Planning

- Religious training and/or education.
- Frequency of church or synagogue attendance.
- Observing religious holidays.
- Other religious issues.

Medical and Professional Appointments

- Emergency: either parent can initiate.
- Regularly scheduled doctor's and dentist's appointments.
- An effort is made to keep other parent informed of prescriptions, illness, but ultimate responsibility rests with each parent to maintain communication with professionals working with the children.
- Evaluations for special needs.

- Communication with professionals.
- Ability to obtain records.

Communication Plan
- Need a plan for communication between the parents for moderate to severe conflict.
- Telephone permitted: when, where?
- Appointments with coordinator.
- Notebook.
- Writing.

School
- Selection of school.
- Change of school.
- Access to teachers and conferences.
- Report cards.
- Back to school night.
- School events: attendance.
- Communication with school: responsibility of each parent.
- Projects of child—which parent helps?

Vacations
- Is out-of-state travel allowed?
- Is out-of-country travel allowed?
- How long: developmental considerations.
- Telephone contact with other parent.
- Sleeping arrangements while on vacation.
- Phone numbers left in case of emergency.
- Pre-planned vacations take precedence over regular visitation.

Financial Planning for Future
- College money.
- Special needs planning.

Grandparents and Other Relatives
- Extended family has access during child's regular visitation with that parent (typically not specified).

Endangerment
- Each agrees other is safe or a provision for safety is inserted.
- Relatives, friends and activities may need to be considered as well.

Boundaries or Rules at Other Household
- Basically neither parent may dictate to the other.
- If endangerment is an issue, parenting coordinator is to be contacted.
- Serious concerns about parental judgment are to be addressed to parenting coordinator.
- Is corporal punishment or other means of discipline an issue?
- Including friends or pets on visits.

Alternative Beliefs
- If one parent objects to the other's belief systems, then boundaries and ground rules will need to be specified via the parenting coordinator.
- One parent cannot set the rules for the other's household.

Significant Others and Dating
- If relationship is truly seen as committed, then a gradual introduction of the significant other is suggested. Both parents need to clarify their values with the children.

- Basically, one parent cannot dictate to the other his/her lifestyle.
- Better to limit the children's involvement in relationships with others until long-term commitments are made.

Special Needs Considerations
- Disability, physical or mental.
- Chronic medical conditions.
- Ethnic/cultural issues.

Parenting Coordinator
- Either parent has open access to the parenting coordinator for dispute resolution at any time for any issue.
- Define emergency procedures for unexpected flare-ups of the conflict.

Chapter 25

Prevention of
Relationship Problems

Brigit Van Widenfelt*, Howard J. Markman, Bernard Guerney[†],
Brett C. Behrens[‡] and Clemens Hosman*****
*Departments of Psychology, * University of North Carolina,
Chapel Hill, NC; ** University of Denver, CO, USA; and
***University of Nijmegen, The Netherlands; [†] Department of
Human Development, Pennsylvania State University, College
Park, PA, USA; [‡] Department of Psychiatry, University of
Queensland, St Lucia, Australia*

Prevention of relationship distress is an essential element of promoting better mental heath care (Bond & Wagner, 1988). Because having satisfying couple relationships is a central influence on mental health, prevention interventions offer possibilities for reducing the staggering social, emotional and economic costs related to relationship distress and dissolution (Coie et al., 1993). The current knowledge base on the determinants of healthy relationships is extensive, providing a solid empirical foundation for developing, implementing and evaluation preventive interventions. The purpose of this chapter is to review the growing literature on prevention and effectiveness of prevention programs and to suggest recommendations on how to improve the quality of preventive interventions.

This chapter is the result of an international collaboration across three continents: North America, Australia and Europe. The authors draw together research and their clinical experience across these continents. After clarifying several key concepts in prevention work, arguments in favor of prevention are presented. Next, a review is provided of current developments and implementation of prevention programs, including a description of selecting couples at risk for relationship distress and dissolution. Program elements are described with particular attention being given to two sample programs, the Prevention and

Clinical Handbook of Marriage and Couples Interventions. Edited by W. Kim Halford and Howard J. Markman.

Relationship Enhancement Program (Markman and associates), and Relationship Enhancement (Guerney and colleagues). These two programs are chosen as they represent the preventive research of the authors of this chapter, and at the same time offer two different approaches. Finally, we focus on a set of issues facing the prevention field, including implementation guidelines developed from the practical experience of the authors as researchers and clinicians, the costs of programs, recruitment and training issues, and suggested standards for research and evaluation of prevention programs.

CLARIFYING TERMS: PROMOTION VS. PREVENTION

The terms promotion and prevention are both used in this chapter and we will consider intervention efforts that have been developed from both promotion and prevention perspectives. Promotion efforts usually are directed at populations without definded risk, although there is considerable overlap with prevention efforts, which are primarily aimed at risk groups. We conceptualize promotion and prevention as lying on a continuum. Health *promotion* is a term that was originally popularized by the World Health Organization (WHO) in the 1980s. The term is defined as "the process of enabling individuals and communities to increase their control over the determinants of health, and thereby to improve their health" (de Leeuw, 1989). The concept of health promotion is characterized both by a focus on health instead of on illness, and on the control of and improvement of health by influencing the main determinants of health. In contrast to health promotion, in *prevention* the goal is to decrease the incidence or prevalence of specific disorders. Reasoning backwards, one searches for specific risk factors and develops interventions to influence those risk factors. Since several mental disorders could have risk factors in common, referred to as non-specific or generic risk factors, it is often cost-effective to target preventive interventions at influencing such non-specific risk factors (e.g. destructive family conflict). Even in such a case, however, the goal is still prevention. Thus, interventions that promote a healthy satisfying intimate relationship can be considered preventive as such interventions would modify disorders such as major depression (Coie et al., 1993).

The term *prevention* is usually further differentiated into primary, secondary and tertiary prevention. *Primary prevention* is aimed at (a) preventing the development of a disorder, and (b) promoting well-being with the purpose of preventing dysfunction (Cowen, 1983). For example, interventions targeted at currently satisfied couples would be the focus of primary preventive efforts. In contrast to primary prevention, secondary and tertiary prevention focus on existing dysfunction or distress. The aim of *secondary prevention* is to decrease the duration and severity of a disorder. Signs of the disorder or dysfunction are detected as early as possible and an intervention is offered. Intervening with couples that are showing early signs of relationship distress (i.e. based on questionnaire scores) would constitute secondary prevention (Cowen, 1983), *Tertiary prevention* encompasses treatment of an existing disorder which is intended to reduce current distress and prevent future problems. The focus of this chapter is on primary prevention of marital distress.

ARGUMENTS IN SUPPORT OF PREVENTION

Limitations of Couples Therapy

The goal of prevention, in contrast to that of therapy, is to lower the incidence of a disorder. A preventive intervention thus differs from a therapeutic intervention in that the goal is to *reduce the probability of new cases in the future*. The primary goal of prevention of relationship distress is to reduce relationship distress and dissolution, but also to prevent related future physical and emotional distress in the adult partners and their offspring.

One argument used in favor of prevention (vs. therapy) is the limited success of couples therapy. Cognitive–behavioral couples therapy (C–BCT) is one of the more successful forms of couples therapy, and is certainly the best researched. Although C–BCT has been found to be more effective than no therapy (Hahlweg & Markman, 1988), a substantial number of couples who have received C–BCT do not attain the levels of satisfaction reported by non-distressed couples. Thus, even after receiving C–BCT, many couples remain somewhat unsatisfied with their relationship (Hahlweg & Markman, 1988). Furthermore, after initial gains, relapse is quite common (Jacobson, Schmaling & Holtzworth-Munroe, 1987).

To address the limitations of C–BCT, researchers have done a number of recent studies focused on augmenting current C–BCT interventions with other treatment components, including more cognitive interventions (Baucom & Epstein, 1990), a greater focus on emotional expressiveness (Baucom, Sayers & Sher, 1990), affect exploration (Greenberg & Johnson, 1988; Snyder & Wills, 1989) and enhancing generalization of change (Behrens, Sanders & Halford, 1990; Halford, Gravestock, Lowe & Scheldt, 1992).

Despite the expected improvements to C–BCT from these various enhanced additions, treatment effects for augmented CBC–T have not been found (Baucom et al., 1990; Halford, Sanders & Behrens, 1993). In response to these disappointing results several new directions to improve the success of couples therapy have been suggested by researchers: increase greater acceptance of partner (vs. focusing only on changing behavior) (Jacobson, 1992), more insight-oriented therapy (Greenberg & Johnson, 1988) and more focus on individual self-regulatory or self-control procedures (Halford, Sanders & Behrens, 1994; Schaap, Hoogduin, Van Widenfelt & Streik, 1992).

Despite our guarded optimism about these new efforts (covered in detail in many chapters in this volume), in this chapter we want to discuss a complementary avenue of research—the investigation of the effect of promoting relationship health *before* couples become distressed. We suggest it is probably easier for couples with no or mild negative relationship patterns to enhance their interactions, and to feel efficacious in their relationships, than it is for couples who have more severe relationship problems to alter entrenched, negative interactional patterns. Thus, we may have more overall success in helping couples by focusing attention on keeping happy couples happy, rather than helping unhappy couples become happy. To date, no research has compared the efficacy of interventions with satisfied and dissatisfied couples.

One of the binds for obtaining money for evaluating prevention programs is that, given the limited funding for mental health research and treatment, investing more money in prevention can reduce resources for treatment. The long-term goal of preventive interventions is to reduce the number of people that need therapy. By decreasing the number of couples that need therapy, professionals could concentrate limited resources on a smaller number of couples who are distressed and in need. This is a worthy goal in itself as therapy is an extremely costly level of intervention, and is characterized by the most suffering. In other areas of health, investing in prevention tends to save treatment dollars spent later on. However, limited funding may leave little money for testing out the effects of prevention on reducing the need for therapy. Ideally, continued evaluations are needed of both preventive interventions for non-distressed or mildly distressed couples, and therapy for couples in advanced stages of relationship distress.

Reaching Couples who Do Not Seek Therapy

A second argument in favor of prevention is that therapy is available for only a small group in the population and as such it cannot lower the population incidence of a prevalent disorder such as relationship distress (Albee, 1990). Furthermore, the availability of psychotherapy is largely restricted to the middle and upper class, yet almost all social and emotional disorders are most prevalent among the poor (Albee, 1990). Thus therapy is least available to those who need it the most.

Most couples experiencing relationship distress do not seek professional help; the reasons for this failure to seek help are unclear (Bradbury & Fincham, 1990). Some couples may fear that treatment may do more harm than good, or that therapy will not work, or that the therapist will intrude into their priate lives. There are strong barriers for seeking any sort of therapy, and many people may not seek couples therapy for fear of becoming stigmatized as mentally ill. Thus, as noted by Halford (1994), people are "voting with their feet" regarding couples therapy.

Prevention, with its stress on education rather than treatment, and on wellness instead of illness, may be less likely to provoke these kind of fears. Certainly there are many more couples who attend relationship preparation programs than present for couples therapy (Halford & Behrens, 1996). Prevention efforts may reduce the barriers to receiving professional help to enhance couple relationships, thus it is likely that more couples will be reached.

Costs of Treatment vs. Prevention and Promotion

Implementing prevention and promotion efforts in the early stages of relationship distress probably is more cost-efficient than to implement a therapeutic intervention after distress has set in. Given the fact that psychopathology often results from severe ongoing marital distress, couples therapists need to be highly trained in individual as well as couples therapy. Intervening with non-distressed couples may require less training, as psychopathology is less common than when treating distressed couples. Specifically, prevention programs may be able to be delivered by para-professionals, such as clergy and community workers of various levels of training. Furthermore, prevention programs generally are less intensive (i.e. fewer sessions) than therapy programs, which reduces costs. However, studies are needed to assess the average costs of preventive vs. therapeutic interventions with couples. Finally, if successful, prevention programs will decrease medical, psychological and legal costs associated with relationship distress and divorce.

RISK INDICATORS AND RISK FACTORS IN THE DEVELOPMENT OF PREVENTION PROGRAMS

There are many levels at which prevention of relationship distress can occur. One possibility is mass education through media sources. Attitudes, expectations and beliefs about relationships are reflected in and shaped by the media, including through films, newspapers, magazines, television and radio. The media can be also be used to promote healthy and realistic beliefs about relationships, as well as to model healthy ways to deal with relationship stressors. Although this strategy is used frequently in health education, little research has been conducted on the efficacy of mass education in promoting healthy relationships. Another option is to enroll the help of employers, physicians, teachers, church workers, lawyers and government workers, who are all in positions to distribute information about healthy relationships.

In contrast to the mass education approach, the approach that is the primary focus of this chapter is the educational approach in which couples are taught the skills associated with having a healthy relationship. Although mass media can impact couples in numerous ways, including demonstrating communication skills, we focus on an approach that directly teaches couples skills because much more research is available on this approach than the "mass" approach. We start this section with a review of the literature of target groups of couples with whom to potentially intervene.

Two broad approaches have been recommended in the prevention of marital distress. Coie et al. (1993) argue for the identification and modification of generic risk factors for poor mental health. In their approach, marital distress is a generic risk factor and prevention should be broadly targeted to reduce the prevalence of marital distress. In contrast, Van Widenfelt, Schaap and Hosman (1991, 1992) argue for an approach of selecting high-risk groups for marital distress. A variety of information sources can help to identify high-risk couples, such as epidemiological studies (e.g. Van Widenfelt et al., 1992) and assessment of characteristics of couples entering marital therapy (e.g. not successfully dealing with the tasks of a new life phase). A limitation of the risk factor approach is that the risk factors predictive of marital dysfunction may vary across the lifespan (Coie et al., 1993). Despite this caveat, targeting intervention or high-risk groups is probably more cost-effective than trying to deliver prevention programs universally (Lorian, Price & Eaton, 1989).

Risk Indicators, Risk Factors and Risk Groups

A number of excellent reviews analyze the variables associated with relationship distress and dissolution (Kitson & Morgan, 1990; Price-Bonham & Balswick, 1980; White, 1990). In this section, we define and give a brief overview of risk, risk indicators, and factors associated with relationship distress and dissolution. These indicators and factors can be used to identify couples at risk and to direct interventions at.

Risk refers to the statistical association between some experience, condition or behavior and the development of relationship distress and dissolution. Subgroups that are considered "at risk" have a higher prevalence of relationship distress or dissolution according to large epidemiological studies. Couples can be identified as being at risk through *risk indicators* or *risk factors*. *Risk indicators* are variables related to relationship adjustment and stability that are not modifiable, and probably are not causally related to marital distress. For example, marrying at a younger age is a risk indicator. Risk indicators cannot be targeted for change in prevention efforts, but rather they aid in identifying subgroups of the population at high risk, and are especially useful for selection and recruitment purposes.

Risk factors refer to variables that are modifiable, and any have causal influence on relationship adjustment and stability (for example, communication skills deficits are predictive of relationship distress). Risk factors are important because, being modifiable, risk factors are program targets and aid prevention program development. Risk factors, like risk indicators, characterize subgroups that have a higher prevalence of relationship distress but do not necessarily have causal impact on distress. It is only by interventions that change the risk factor, and subsequently change the occurrence of distress, that we can demonstrate a causal impact. Furthermore, single risk factors do not predict couple relationship distress or break-up, as many risk factors are involved. It can be concluded from the available knowledge base that relationship distress and dissolution are related to a complex interaction of a number of factors. As a consequence, preventive efforts need to be targeted to change multiple risk factors.

Risk Indicators for Marital Distress

Personal and familial history of divorce and relationship distress are important risk indicators of relationship distress and divorce. Large demographic studies in both the USA and The Netherlands reflect higher rates of relationship distress and/or break-up in adult offspring of divorced parents than of intact families (De Graaf, 1991; Glenn & Kramer, 1987; Kooy, 1984; Pope & Mueller, 1976). Not only is parental divorce a risk indicator, research also shows that a previous divorce of one's own is a risk indicator. Approximately 80% of divorced persons remarry (Duberman, 1975) and those second marriages have a higher and earlier chance of ending in divorce than first marriages (Martin & Bumpass, 1989). Thus, persons with a history of divorce run a higher risk of experiencing relationship distress and divorcing a second time than persons who have never experienced their own or their parents' divorce.

Another risk indicator for relationship distress and divorce is the presence of mental illness in one of the partners. In both the USA and The Netherlands, higher rates of divorce have been reported in mentally ill populations (Merikangas, 1984; NVAGG, 1988). A large number of studies over the last two decades have reported a relationship between depression and relationship distress and divorce (e.g. Barnett & Gotlib, 1988; Ruscher & Gotlib, 1988; Weissman & Paykel, 1974). Alcohol abuse has also been associated with relationship distress (Jacob, Dunne & Leonard, 1983; O'Farrell & Birchler, 1987; Schaap, Schellekens & Schippers, 1991), as well as with divorce (Reich & Thompson, 1985).

In The Netherlands, census bureau data point to a demographic pattern of higher rates of divorce for persons marrying at a young age, being married between three and ten years, having a premarital pregnancy, and having few or no children (Kooy, 1984). These indicators of high risk are similarly reported in US data by Bumpass and Sweet (1972). In contrast to US data, in which Fergusson, Horwood and Shannon (1984) report persons of lower SES to be at higher risk for divorce, Kooy (1984) reports white-collar workers in urban settings in The Netherlands to be at higher risk than those persons working and living in rural environments. This finding reflects that there may be slight differences from one country to another as to which demographic factors are most indicative of risk and therefore each country needs to examine what their own demographic risk indicators are.

Another approach of identifying couples at risk is to target efforts at couples going through an important life event or transition. Numerous studies show that relationship satisfaction decreases when couples go through the transition to parenthood (Belsky, Lang & Rovine, 1985; Cowan et al., 1985; Duncan & Markman, 1988) and second marriages have higher rates of distress and dissolution than first marriages.

In sum, a sociodemographic picture emerges from the data highlighting specific subgroups in the population as being at increased risk for relationship distress and divorce. Risk indicators can be used as a criteria to select target groups for prevention of relationship distress and divorce. For example, in the Netherlands (Van Widenfelt et al., 1991; Van Widenfelt, Hosman, Schaap & van der Staak, 1996) one research group focused on parental divorce as a risk indictor. In a similar study in Australia conducted by Halford and Behrens (1996) the following indicators were used to identify couples as at risk: (a) both partners under 21; (b) either partner previously married; or (c) divorce in family of origin. Another approach of one researcher in the USA is to focus on the transition to marriage as a critical time to intervene (Markman, Floyd, Stanley & Lewis, 1986).

Severely distressed couples are often excluded from prevention trials (e.g. Halford & Behrens, 1996; Van Widenfelt et al., 1996). Prevention efforts are intended to target non-distressed couples, and whilst the experience of distress could provide motivation for participation in a preventive program, bringing about change is more difficult once relationship distress is severe. Intervening before couples are distressed falls under primary prevention, and intervening when couples are mildly distressed is referred to as secondary prevention. Couples with a high level of relationship distress can be referred for couples therapy. Cut-off scores for inclusion and exclusion can be used with relationship satisfaction questionnaires such as the Dyadic Adjustment Scale (DAS; Spanier, 1976), Locke–Wallace (LW; Locke & Wallace, 1959) or Maudsley Marital Questionnaire (MMQ; Cobb, McDonald, Marks & Stern, 1980).

Risk Factors for Marital Distress

Across continents a series of studies evaluating the effectiveness of preventive interventions for relationship distress and dissolution are in progress (i.e. Burnett, Nordling, Brown & Baucom, 1991; Hahlweg, Thurmair, Eckert, Engel & Markman, 1992; Halford & Behrens, 1996; Markman et al., 1986, Markman, Floyd, Stanley & Storaasli, 1988; Markman, Renick, Floyd, Stanley & Clements, 1993; Markman & Hahlweg, 1993; Van Widenfelt et al., 1996). All the couples' distress prevention programs cited above have been developed from principles of cognitive–behavioral couples therapy (see Baucom & Epstein, 1990; Gottman, Notarius, Gonso & Markman, 1976; Olson, 1976; Stuart, 1980). The cognitive–behavioral approach to working with couples finds its roots in basic social learning theory (Bandura, 1977) and social exchange theory (Thibaut & Kelley, 1959) principles, advocating the notion that couples will experience relationship happiness or distress in direct proportion to the rates of positive and negative interactions in their relationship. The approach has further been supported by research findings as described in this section that happy couples report higher rates of positive exchanges and lower rates of negative exchanges than unhappy couples (Schaap, 1984). An important element in decreasing negative exchanges is helping couples decrease their reactivity during negative exchanges, through using communication skills such as emphasizing separate speaker and listener roles or helping persons reformulate negative attributions. In couples therapy the goals also usually include: increase positive interactions; effectively communicate about problems; manage and reduce conflict; have more realistic relationship expectations/beliefs; enhance sexual/sensual intimacy; discuss and clarify roles; take more individual responsibility for change; and increase awareness about, and discuss underlying issues from, the individual partners' past on family of origin that contribute to current relationship dynamics.

Interventions are also based on the assumption that couples desire and are committed to positive maintenance and change but may lack the skills to do so. It is believed that couples can learn the necessary skills by participating in an intervention, although the approach relies heavily on practicing skills outside of a structured session in their own natural setting (Notarius & Markman, 1993). The described goals and assumptions are easily translated into goals and assumptions for prevention and promotion programs (e.g. Behrens, Halford & Sanders, 1992; Markman et al., 1994; Schaap & Van Widenfelt, 1990).

The development of the Premarital Relationship Enhancement Program (PREP; Markman, Stanley & Blumberg, 1994) and PREP variants nicely exemplifies how clinical experience, as well as research on the risk factors that distinguish maritally distressed from non-distressed couples, can be used as a basis for selecting skills and program goals (Burnett et al., 1991; Hahlweg et al., 1992; Halford & Behrens, 1996; Markman et al., 1986; Van Widenfelt et al., 1996). The following is a brief overview of research on several psychological and interactional variables that distinguish distressed and non-distressed relationships that have influenced the development of these programs.

Communication variables have, across observational studies, consistently discriminated maritally distressed and non-distressed samples in several countries, including Australia (e.g. Halford, Hahlweg & Dunne, 1990), The Netherlands (e.g. Schaap, 1982), Germany (e.g. Hahlweg et al., 1979) and the USA (e.g. Margolin & Wampold, 1981). Distressed couples are described as more negative; demonstrating poorer problem-solving behavior; more coercive behavior; more defensive behavior; more criticism, sarcasm and complaining (Birchler, Weiss & Vincent, 1975; Gottman, Markman & Notarius, 1977; Halford et al., 1990; Schaap, Buunk & Kerkstra, 1988; Vincent, 1972; Vincent, Weiss & Birchler, 1975). Longitudinal studies have shown that premarital couples who show these patterns are at higher risk or break-up and distress (Markman & Hahlweg, 1993). In contrast, non-distressed couples are described as displaying more positive behavior; higher rates of problem-solving; more positive affect such as smiling, attentiveness and having a positive voice tone; higher rates of agreements and validation (Gottman, 1979; Hahlweg, Kraemer, Schindler & Revenstorf, 1980; Revenstorf, Vogel, Wegener, Hahlweg & Schindler, 1980).

Cognitive factors have also been reported to discriminate distressed and non-distressed couples. Distressed couples are more likely to have negative expectations for their relationship, to view their partners as responsible for relationship problems as well as making more global intangible attributions about their problems (Fincham, Bradbury & Scott, 1990). Non-distressed couples are reported to have more realistic beliefs about their relationships, stronger beliefs that they can work through their problems, and partners are more likely to accept responsibility for relationship issues (Fincham et al., 1990; Meeks, Arnkoff, Glass & Notarius, 1986; Notarius & Vanzetti, 1983; Vanzetti, Notarius & NeeSmith, 1992).

Finally, several studies report an association between relationship satisfaction and the quality of the sexual relationship. Distressed couples are more likely to experience a lack of intimacy, low sexual satisfaction and a higher incidence of sexual dysfunction (Appelt, 1984; Rosenzweig & Dailey, 1989).

By identifying the factors associated with relationship quality and stability in the research literature, a foundation for developing effective prevention and promotion programs can be formed. To summarize, a number of important psychological and interactional factors are found to be related to relationship satisfaction: poor communication skills; deficits in conflict management and problem-solving; unrealistic relationship beliefs; low sexual satisfaction; lack of intimacy; and low relational efficacy. These factors have a direct impact on relationship quality and thus provide a good foundation for program development. The advantage of focusing on behavioral skills and thinking patterns is that they are factors which are easier to change than other important influences such as cultural norms or family background (although bringing change about on the individual or couple level may, however, challenge the influence of cultural and familial background). Obviously, other variables related to relationship quality are also important that are not discussed in this section, such as alcohol and drug abuse, infidelity, incompatibility, physical and sexual abuse, and disagreements about gender roles (White, 1990) (see other chapters in this volume on these topics). These diverse risk factors offer a variety of possibilities for preventive efforts. It is likely that no single factor is primarily linked to relationship quality and stability. Given the array of variables to choose from in the program development phase, researchers and clinicians are faced with difficult decisions. Often their choices are founded in their own history of conducting research and clinical work. Once a researcher or clinician has chosen a population with which to intervene preventively, and reviewed the clinical and research literature, the next step is decide, given the target population, what elements the intervention should contain.

Key Elements of Prevention Programs

In this section, an overview of the main elements of PREP (Markman et al., 1994) and PREP variants (Burnett et al., 1991; Hahlweg et al., 1992; Halford & Behrens, 1996; Van Widenfelt et al., 1996) and Guerney's (1977) Relationship Enhancement (RE) program is given. Table 25.1 is a summary of these programs.

Speaker and listener skills are commonly first taught using a communication model from Gottman et al. (1976), Notarius and Markman (1993) and Guerney (1977). Emphasis is on: separating the speaker and listener role; switching speaker turns frequently; the role of filters; what are effective and ineffective ways to speak and listen. Effective listening skills include: summarizing the speaker; checking out the summary; trying to understand and see how the partner feels without having to be in agreement. Effective speaking skills include: being

Table 25.1 Elements of program

Topic	Example of session focus
Speaker and listener skills	Practice using effective communication techniques (e.g. using I statements, not blaming partner, summarizing speaker during problem discussion
Managing conflict	Identify unproductive interaction pattern (e.g. pursuit withdrawal, conflict engaging, avoidance) and plan alternative, effective strategy
Problem-solving	Identify a problem and follow steps to solve, it, including brainstorming, weighing pros and cons, and making a specific plan that can be carried out
Enhancing positives	Give homework assignment to do nice things for each other (e.g. give partner a massage, cook for partner, go to a film together)
Addressing underlying relationship themes	Use communication techniques to discuss themes such as closeness/distance, feeling loved and cared for, status/power, interest/responsiveness
Expectations/, assumptions/and beliefs	Increase awareness of and challenge unrealistic relationship beliefs, discuss expectations for the relationship
Family of origin	Use genogram to identify patterns of communication and expectations/beliefs in family of origin, identify what plays a role in own relationship: how to keep/change
Sensual/sexual intimacy	Challenge myths about sex and provide educational material, assist couple in applying communication techniques to discuss intimacy, do sensate focus task
Commitment and friendship	Provide information on types of commitment in relationships, assist couples in increasing commitment and friendship through communication
Self-regulation	Assist partners in what they can do to enhance the relationship through self-selection of relationship goals, self-monitoring, self-evaluation and self-reinforcement
Contracting	On paper, set up ground rules for relationship, include description of "high-risk" situations and what effective strategies to apply

specific; using I-statements; keeping messages brief and focused; not criticizing or blaming partner. Especially important in the speaking skills is the emphasis on taking personal responsibility (Markman et al., 1994; Schaap & Van Widenfelt, 1990).

In some programs, in addition to the basic skills of speaking and listening, couples are given extra information about managing conflict (Markman et al., 1994; Notarius, 1990; Stuart, 1980). Managing an effective level of tension is explained. Interaction patterns are described, with a focus on gender-specific patterns (e.g. male withdrawal/female pursuit; Schaap & Van Widenfelt, 1990). Ways to break unproductive cycles are discussed, and specific skills to overcome such cycles are taught.

Once communication skills are practiced, a foundation exists for learning problem-solving skills. Problem-solving is usually taught as a series of steps, including sharing complaints, brainstorming, weighing pros and cons, choosing a solution and specifying a plan that can be carried out, and finally trying out the plan and evaluating it (Markman et al., 1994; Schaap & Van Widenfelt, 1990).

In addition to developing communication skills and problem-solving skills, couples are helped to identify relationship themes which can be destructive, such as: (a) the sharing of power; (b) interest or responsiveness to the partner; and (c) being loved and cared for (see "hidden agendas" in Gottman et al., 1976). These themes are often related to the expectations, assumptions and beliefs couples bring to relationships. Unhelpful assumptions are challenged and couples are encouraged to consider and share their expectations for the relationship (Markman et al., 1994). Expectations reviewed can range from future plans about marriage and children to gender-role beliefs or practical aspects of who does which household chores.

A program element recently developed by Markman et al. (1994) focuses on relationship commitment (Stanley & Markman, 1992). Couples are given information and invited to practice the techniques of increasing commitment and friendship through communication.

Some programs attempt to address the sources of relationship beliefs and expectations, such as family-of-origin experiences. For example, McGoldrick & Gerson (1985) made use of a genogram to structure a discussion between partners about their families of origin. Couples are asked to first fill in the genogram, describing important persons and relationships between persons. Couples are then invited to look for important patterns and influences on their current relationship (Schaap & Van Widenfelt, 1990).

Sensual/sexual intimacy is also often addressed in programs. Couples are provided with education as well as assistance in talking about intimate matters. Homework assignments might include a sensate focus task to do together (Gottman et al., 1976; Markman et al., 1994) or other sexual enrichment activities as described by Spence (this volume).

Homework is stressed heavily in most programs. Couples are asked to practice newly learned skills at home. In addition to changing negative communication and interactions to more constructive positive interactions, couples are assigned homework to do some nice things together and/or for each other (see "caring days" in Stuart, 1980). Activities commonly chosen by couples include cooking a special dinner, giving and receiving massages, and going out to a film together.

Recently, Halford et al. (1994) developed a self-regulatory approach, in which each partner is stimulated to self-assess his/her contribution to relationship difficulties, self-monitor, self-select relationship goals to work on which will enhance the relationship, self-evaluate the effectiveness of his/her efforts and self-reinforce changes made. The individual partner focus differs greatly from the traditional couple focus of couple interventions.

The last session of a program is usually on engaging the skills and ground rules

(Markman et al., 1994; Notarius, 1990; Stuart, 1980). In this session, couples are assisted by a trainer to set the ground rules for their relationships, to consider the likelihood of falling into old negative patterns and to decide what to do when that happens. Both partners are encouraged to accept responsibility for maintaining change. Couples are assisted with a checklist of ground rules (Markman et al., 1994).

Commonalties and References Across Programs

One tradition in the area of relationship health promotion is that of Berney Guerney and his colleagues at Pennsylvania State University (Guerney, 1977; Guerney, Brock & Coufal, 1986). This group developed a program focused on enhancing the positive aspect of a relationship by increasing caring, giving, understanding, honesty, openness, trust, sharing, compassion and harmony in the relationship. By *learning* a set of nine skills associated with these relationship goals, they argue that couples will eliminate their pain and distress. Couples are encouraged to design the relationship they want in the above terms, and are assisted by a teacher to learn the necessary skills to achieve their goals. Guerney's Relationship Enhancement (RE) program has been evaluated in several studies and RE resulted in significantly greater gains in relationship quality and communication for participants in comparison to wait list control groups, as well as in comparison to other interventions (Guerney, 1988). This program can be called a health promotion program in our definition.

Another tradition, closely tied to a two-decade history of studying differences between distressed and non-distressed couples, is that of Markman and his colleagues at the University of Denver (e.g. Markman et al., 1994). Markman's position is that it is the negative aspects of a couple's relationship, not the positive aspects, that are of importance to focus on in interventions. Preventing the negatives (e.g. unsatisfactory conflict resolution) by teaching couples to manage negative affect and conflict, will likely lead to a more positive relationship in the future. It is the number of negatives, not the number of positives, that break couples up. Thus, couples are taught what ineffective communication is, and are helped to communicate more effectively. This program can be called a prevention program in our definition.

It is questionable whether these two approaches are as different as they may appear, and can be viewed on the same continuum. Close examination of the techniques taught in the two programs show many of the same skills are being taught (see Table 25.1). For example, what Guerney calls a positive goal: "I'd like him to spend more time talking to me" as a replacement for "I'd like him to stop being so obsessed with his work", is comparable to the interventions in the Markman program, where ineffective communication is identified and replaced with effective communication. Thus, both programs help couples reframe critical statements to positively formulated wishes. In addition to helping partners express themselves more clearly and positively, both programs also pay a great deal of attention to listening techniques of partners. Further, in both programs strategies for problem-solving are taught. In sum, couples are encouraged to accept responsibility for the quality of their relationships and are taught the skills associated with relationship health as well as the signs of relationship distress. Thus, although we label one a health promotion program and one a prevention program, the examples illustrate that the distinction between these two approaches is not always clear.

Core and Adaptable Features

In Table 25.1, 11 common program elements in prevention and promotion programs have been smmarized. When deciding on program elements, it is important to distinguish between core program features and adaptable program features (Price et al., 1989). Core features are those key elements of a program that should not be adapted or changed. In the case of PREP, a core feature would be listening skills. An adaptable feature, is something that can be modified to suit local and target group needs. We would go as far to say that adaptable features are necessary. Adapting a program is crucial for the reception of the program by the potential target group. For example, the program developers in The Netherlands had to work carefully with language and presentation of material to fit into the Dutch culture, This also meant following the daily rituals of the culture during the time the program was offered (around eight o'clock in the evening, coffee, tea and cookies are served in most households in the country). In sum, when deciding what elements to included in a prevention or promotion program, researchers should be guided by theoretical principles and prior research, and be able to in advance identify and explain the factors that are expected to influence the identified risk and protective processes (see Coie et al., 1993).

PRAGMATIC ISSUES IN PROGRAM DEVELOPMENT AND IMPLEMENTATION

Costs of preventive interventions vary and depend on a number of factors, such as the length of the program, the ratio of paraprofessionals or trainers to the number of couples, and the necessary education and training level of the trainers. Recruitment and advertising costs range from putting together a few inexpensive newspaper advertisements or distributing some pamphlets, to a full-scale community outreach strategy. Costs related to supplies (questionnaires, handouts and training manuals) are limited and space to offer training programs is usually to be found in existing institutions where other forms of treatment or courses are given, such as at university classrooms or clinics, hospitals or private practices.

The development of effective prevention programs is a very time-consuming and expensive enterprise. However, once effective programs are available, a cost-effective implementation can be expected. Preventive interventions can be supported by and given at universities, private practices, and community mental health settings. Further support can be sought by government assistance, insurance companies, churches and couples themselves.

Identifying and Overcoming Barriers in Prevention Programs

Taboos on sharing one's intimate relationship with others can serve as a barrier to participation in relationship distress prevention programs (Mace, 1987, cited in Bradbury & Fincham, 1990). Marriage and marriage-like relationships in Western culture are still viewed as private matters. Bradbury and Fincham (1990) further suggest that many hold the view that a successful marriage should come naturally to partners, without effort or help from others. Thus, seeking help is breaching privacy taboos and admitting one has failed in what is culturally viewed as a natural and simple task in life. Furthermore, in the popular media (e.g. films), happy marriage is portrayed as an easily obtained outcome of romance. For many couples, romance equals something that comes naturally spontaneously, without work. The idea that one's relationship may be happier and more romantic by working on it though a structured program is, for many, counterintuitive. Lastly, Bradbury and Fincham (1990) raise the issue that perhaps current pessimism about the institution of marriage plays a role in persons or couples resisting prevention efforts.

It is important to consider what motivates non-distressed couples to care about preventing negative outcome in the future. One motivating factor, stimulated by the media or personal experience, is the increased awareness of high divorce rates. The current awareness of divorce rates competes with current ideas of successful marriage as a byproduct of romance, perhaps motivating couples to address this gap. Further, if the long-term data from current evaluation studies reveal that individuals/couples can make a difference in their chance of working out relationship problems, and this is published in more popular magazines or TV programs, couples may be motivated to work on their relationships. Lastly, as couples are aware of programs being available in the institutions that they come into contact with (e.g. schools, day-care centers, hospitals), they may become interested in participation.

Engaging Couples in Programs

In several of the prevention programs mentioned (Halford & Behrens, 1996; Markman et al., 1986; Van Widenfelt et al., 1996), couples were recruited through the local media, including newspaper advertisements, interviews in major and local papers and magazines, radio advertisements and the distribution of posters and pamphlets. In the experience of people in Australia and The Netherlands, it was found helpful to use several of these channels. Many couples commented that they had seen the advertising for programs in several places before they responded. In Germany, the program of Hahlweg et al. (1992) was promoted by the

Catholic Church, and was listed as part of a course program available to all church members. In a new series of Denver studies, couples are being recruited from religious organizations and from healthcare organizations that serve couples having children (Stanley, Markman, St. Peters & Donglas Leber, 1995).

Once couples identify themselves as interested in prevention programs, many choose not to actually proceed. Rates of acceptance to participate and actual program completion for volunteer couples were around 39% in the USA (Markman et al., 1986), 60% in The Netherlands (Van Widenfelt et al., 1996) and about 45–50% in Australia (Halford & Behrens, 1996). The high but variable percentages of couples initially indicating interest, but subsequently not partici- pating, show that it is important to learn more about the barriers to participation. The reasons given for refusal to participation in The Netherlands were usually one of three: "Too busy", "We don't need a training," or "Too scary". Sometimes taking the opportunity to explain to an unsure couple what specifically the program entails relieves a couple of their doubts. For example, to explain that the program is not therapy, that it is very practical, and that they may stop at any time, may be helpful in reducing fears. Programs also need to be delivered in accessible formats. Researchers in Maryland and North Carolina have offered a variant of PREP in a weekend format for busy couples, attempting to accommo- date to dual income couples' tight schedules during the week (Burnett, 1993; Burnett et al., 1991). Others have suggested that self-directed programs, done by couples at home using printed and audiovisual material, may be appealing to some couples (Halford & Behrens, 1996).

For programs that are targeted at high-risk couples from disadvantaged groups, engaging couples to participate may be especially challenging. Such couples may benefit from matching recruitment and training staff on important demographic or risk-related variables. For example, if the target group is couples who have experienced parental divorce or other psychopathology in their family of origin, trainers having a similar high-risk family background who have success- fully completed the program could be used. Or, if high-risk persons are of a subculture that does not speak the dominant language very well, staff could be recruited from that subculture. Another way to reach couples that may not otherwise come into contact with or participated in a prevention program, is to work through settings that they do have contact with, such as religious organiza- tions, Primary Care facilities, or schools that their children attend. Sensitivity to gender differences in help-seeking behavior should also be taken into considera- tion when trying to engage couples. It is important to consult with persons in the population targeted on how to best reach couples in that subpopulation.

The setting for interventions is also of importance, especially in relation to accessing couples. It is important to consider where one can access couples and in what setting couples would feel comfortable participating. In Germany, Hahlweg and colleagues (1992) are evaluating a program in a church setting. In The Netherlands, few young couples at this time attend church, thus church settings were excluded. Instead, in The Netherlands and in Denver, Colorado, research- ers evaluated their program in a university setting (Markman et al., 1986; Van

Widenfelt et al., 1996). The university may for some couples to whom it is unfamiliar serve as a barrier, whereas for many others it carries the esteem that may give couples a sense of trust in the program. Other options are school settings, community centers, daycare centers and hospitals.

In addition to being sensitive to the setting in which couples feel comfortable, interventions are likely to be more effective if they are successful at taking into consideration the cultural context, the personal history and lifestage of the participants (Coie et al., 1993; Van Widenfelt et al., 1991). This "fit" between the person, environment and intervention is critical. What may be an effective approach in one culture or subculture may not be effective in another (Van Widenfelt et al., 1991). In Holland this meant, in particular, taking care in translating the material from English to Dutch. This point is crucial in effectively intervening with couples. The bottom line is: do not to create barriers between the program delivery persons and the participants. This statement is in line with what was referred to as as an "adaptable" program feature in an earlier section.

Program Implementation

The use of advance degree psychotherapists may not be necessary for prevention program delivery if participants are properly screened for relationship distress. Mental health professionals, counselors, teachers or religious figures could be trained to deliver programs. For example, in The Netherlands upper level Clinical Psychology students were used as trainers. These students had little clinical experience and were trained for approximately 60 hours. First, they were taught in a training format of a week-long intensive course, in which a major part of the training was spent in role playing. The second phase of their training was that they were carefully supervised working with a couple to implement the program. It is our experience that this is sufficient for effective program delivery.

It is essential to build in measures of quality control, starting with a solid training and a detailed manual of the protocol. Once that is established, there are several other ways quality can be controlled. It is important that trainers receive continued supervision throughout program delivery, enhanced by the use of audio- or videotapes or "live" supervision. For example in the Dutch version of PREP, quality was controlled by close supervision of each session as well as separate weekly supervision sessions. Further evaluations by both couples and trainers were conducted directly after each session, thereby providing continuous feedback. If sessions are recorded or observed, they can be rated on a set of criteria to check for adherence to the protocol. This is a common method used in therapy research that would improve prevention trials as well. Ideally, program delivery in the community should be a collaborative venture with experienced researchers/clinicians to ensure adherence to the protocol and to uphold ethical standards.

Once trainers are trained, quality control procedures put in place and couples recruited, the program can be delivered. PREP and PREP variants have usually been conducted in five or six sessions lasting, on average, about 2–2½ hours per session. Sometimes a "break" is given during the middle of the training, as in The Netherlands, extending the program length to 7 weeks in duration. Researchers in Maryland and North Carolina (Burnett et al., 1991) have managed to condense it down to a weekend and still manage positive results and in Germany, Hahlweg has successfully offered PREP over two weekends (Markman & Hahlweg, 1993). In Australia, a high-intensity version of PREP was delivered across a 6-week period with one 2½ hour session per week, as well as a low-intensity version involving two sessions in the 6-week period. More recently, researchers at New York University have been successful offering PREP on a Saturday, followed by two Thursday evenings (P. Fraenkel, personal communication, February, 1996).

The general structure of PREP sessions is to meet initially with a group of couples (ideally 4–5), where couples are provided information on the focus of the session (e.g. presentation of communication model). After a brief lecture, couples are given an exercise to practice the newly taught skills with a personal trainer (separately from the other couples). The group meets together at the end of the session to discuss the session and receive a homework assignment. Homework exercises commonly consist of having a low-intensity problem discussion applying the new skills and a "caring days" exercise. The following session usually begins with discussion of homework.

Effectiveness of Prevention Programs

Giblin, Sprenkle & Sheehan (1985) conducted a meta-analysis of 85 studies evaluating marital distress prevention programs which showed an average effect size of 0.44. This effect size is somewhat lower than that of cognitive–behavioral couples therapy (C–BCT) studies. In C–BCT studies, treated individuals did better than 83% of controls (Hahlweg & Markman, 1988), whereas according to Giblin's meta-analysis, couples participating in prevention programs only improved 67% more than controls (see Bradbury & Fincham, 1990, for a discussion of these findings). However, most of the studies included by Giblin, Sprenkle and Sheehan (1985) were very poor methodologically.

Hahlweg and Markman (1988) calculated the average effect size for a smaller, more selective, group of prevention studies (7) and found an average effect size of 0.79, indicating that the average person improved 79% more than controls. In their summary of effect sizes, Bradbury and Fincham emphasize that there is quite a range of effects of different programs that requires more analysis. For example, they point out the large difference in program effects depend on the measures used. Greater effects were found with behavioral measures than with self-report measures (0.76 and 0.35 average effect sizes, respectively.)

From the PREP and PREP variant studies mentioned in this chapter, the following conclusions can be drawn: (a) there is evidence that at least short-term changes in behavior result from prevention programs; (b) evidence for changes in relationship satisfaction in the short term appear limited, perhaps due to a ceiling effect of people being fairly happy before the intervention; (c) there is limited evidence of the long-term effectiveness of relationship distress prevention programs, with the exception of the Markman study, and this is what is required to demonstrate a prevention effect; (d) the work of Markman suggests that prevention efforts can reduce relationship distress and dissolution over the long term, but further replication is needed; and (e) it is important that future research conduct randomized controlled trials with adequate long-term follow-up to provide such replication.

The following are some addition guiding criteria for future research. A task force of the American Psychological Association, led by Richard Price, set the following as criteria for their search for effective prevention programs: (a) a clear description of the group at risk and the emotional or behavioral condition to be prevented; (b) a statement of a rationale for the intervention, including its timing, duration and sequencing; (c) a description of the actual intervention; (d) a description of the skills necessary to conduct the intervention; (e) a specification of the program steps taken to recruit intervention participants; (f) a specification of observable and measurable program objectives; (g) a description of the program evaluation, monitoring and follow-up data; (h) a description of how the program relates to community groups, organizations and agencies; (i) consideration of ethical issues; (j) the transferability of the intervention to other settings; and (k) roles of professional and non-professional caregiver resources (Price et al., 1989, p. 50). Price and his colleagues report that one of the hallmarks of effective programs is that rigorous data has been collected to document the success of the program.

Further, more studies are needed on high-risk groups and future research designs could benefit from the inclusion of normal and/or low risk controls (e.g. Halford & Behrens, 1996; Van Widenfelt et al., 1996). Designs using comparative interventions (e.g. Halford & Behrens, 1996) or attention-only controls are also needed to conclude any specific effects of the intervention (vs. a general benefit of participation in an intervention).

Randomization procedures are recommended and have been used in the studies of Markman et al. (1986) and Van Widenfelt et al. (1996) as well as Halford and Behrens (1996). There is an issue to consider on using randomization when couples are recruited to participate in a research study rather than for an intervention (e.g. Markman et al., 1986; Van Widenfelt et al., 1996) and controls are not informed of the intervention (for the purpose of lowering motivation effects in participation). The issue is whether or not control couples should be informed of the intervention. If a program's effects are known, and a group is known to be at risk, is it ethical to withhold the knowledge of an existing program?

Markman (1992) and Coie et al. (1993) argue that the long-term follow-ups of couples who have participated in programs is critical. To determine whether prevention programs prevent relationship distress and dissolution, couples need to be followed for a rather long period of time. The Denver study is the only known prevention of relationship distress and divorce study that has data on couples over a long period of time (reports published through 6-year follow-up). Given the difficulty of collecting longitudinal data, we can not afford to wait 10 years for the outcome of the couples that are now participating in programs. It is thus important to look at some of the short-term markers of program effects. For example, Markman reports that immediately after implementation of PREP, couples did not report changes in satisfaction but did show improvements in their ability to communicate effectively. However, at the 18- and 36-month follow up, differences between groups in satisfaction were evidenced with the control group showing a decline in relationship quality that was not evidenced in the intervention group. This finding indicates that perhaps satisfaction is not the only valid rating of program effects and that obtaining and measuring the goals of the programs (in this case improving communication) are also of importance. Nonetheless, short-term evaluations of benefits are likely to appear small or even nonexistent, while it is highly likely that benefits from preventive interventions increase over time (Price et al., 1989).

Lastly, the quality of measures used is of utmost importance for evaluating programs and being able to compare evaluations with existing data. It is appreciated when researchers use similar measures to facilitate the comparison of findings. The following are several commonly used instruments to measure different aspects of couple functioning: (a) the Dyadic Adjustment Scale (DAS; Spanier, 1976) to measure relationship satisfaction; (b) the Marital Agendas Protocol (MAP; Notarius & Vanzetti, 1983) for assessing relational efficacy as well as getting an inventory of problem intensity; and (c) the Conflict Tactics Scale (CTS; Straus, 1979) for assessing verbal and physical aggression. Researchers are advised to also find out what measures are validated in their own country, and try to make use of those measures.

CONCLUSION

In this chapter, we have argued for prevention of relationship distress, reviewed current risk indicators and factors for relationship distress and dissolution, briefly described a sample of program elements, shared a series of practical experiences related to program implementation, and discussed guidelines for future research.

Although setting up evaluations of prevention programs is costly, time-consuming and labor-intensive, we expect that if the programs are successful the costs are minor in comparison to the costs related to relationship problems and dissolution, including the effects on children (costs of delinquency), effects on partners (costs of mental health care and legal costs) and the financial expenses for families. We are very optimistic about achieving these goals as research and program development progresses into the next century.

REFERENCES

Albee, G.W. (1990). The futility of psychotherapy. *Journal of Mind and Behavior*. **11**, 369–384.

Appelt, H. (1984). Sexual dysfunction and partnership. In N. Jacobson & K. Hahlweg (eds), *Marital Interaction* (pp. 387–395). New York: Guilford.

Bandura, A. (1977). *Social Learning Theory*. Englewood Cliffs, NJ: Prentice Hall.

Barnett, P.A. & Gotlib, I.H. (1988). Psychosocial functioning and depression: distinguishing among antecedents, concomitants, and consequences. *Psychological Bulletin*, **104**, 97–126.

Baucom, D.H. & Epstein, N. (1990). *Cognitive–behavioral Marital Therapy*. New York: Brunner/Mazel.

Baucom, D.H., Sayers, S.L. & Sher, T.G. (1990). Supplementing behavioral marital therapy with cognitive restructuring and emotional expressiveness training: an outcome investigation. *Behavior Therapy*, **21**, 129–138.

Behrens, B.C., Halford, W.K. & Sander, M.R. (1992). Marital Preparation Program: a Leaders's Manual. Unpublished manuscript, University of Queensland, Australia.

Behrens, B.C., Sanders, M.R. & Halford, W.K. (1990). Behavioral martial therapy: an evaluation of generalization of treatment effects across high and low risk settings. *Behavior Therapy*, **21**, 423–433.

Belsky, J., Lang, M.E. & Rovine, M. (1985). Stability and change in marriage across the transition to parenthood. *Journal of Marriage and the Family*, **47**, 855–865.

Birchler, G.R., Weiss, R.L. & Vincent, J.P. (1975). Multimethod analysis of social reinforcement exchange between maritally distressed and non-distressed spouse and stranger dyads. *Journal of Personality and Social Psychology*, **31**, 342–362.

Bond, L. & Wagner, B. (1988). *Families in Transition: Primary Prevention Programs that Work*. Newbury Park: Sage.

Bradbury, T.N. & Fincham, F.D. (1990). Preventing marital dysfunction: review and analysis. In F.D. Fincham & T.N. Bradbury (eds), *The Psychology of Marriage* (pp. 375–401). New York: Guilford.

Bumpass, L. & Sweet, J.A. (1972). Differentials in marital instability: 1970. *American Sociological Review*, **37**, 754–766.

Burnett, C. (1993). Communication Skill Training for Marriage: Modification and Evaluation of the Prevention and Relationship Enhancement Program (PREP). Doctoral Dissertation, University of North Carolina: Chapel Hill.

Burnett, C., Nordling, W., Brown, R. & Baucom, D. (1991). New directions for preventive interventions with couples: the North Carolina and Maryland/DC Projects. Paper presented at Association for the Advancement of Behavior Therapy, New York City, November.

Cobb, R.L. McDonald, R., Marks, I. & Stern, R. (1980). Marital versus exposure therapy: psychological treatment of co-existing marital and phobic-obsessive problems. *Behaviour Analysis and Modification*, **4**, 3–16.

Coie, J.D., Watt, N.F., West, S.G., Hawkins, D., Asarnow, J.R., Markman, H.J., Ramey, S.L., Shure, M.B. & Long, B. (1993). The science of prevention: a conceptual framework and some directions for a national research program. *American Psychologist*, **48**, 1013–1022.

Cowan, C.P., Cowan, P.A., Heming, G., Garett, E., Coysh, W.S., Curtis-Boles, H. & Boles, A.J. (1985). Transitions to parenthood: his, hers, and theirs. *Journal of Family Issues*, **6**, 451–481.

Cowen, E.L. (1983). Primary prevention in mental health: past, presents, and future. In R.D. Felner, L.A. Jason, J.N. Moritsugu & S.S. Farber (eds), *Preventive Psychology: Theory, Research, and Practice*. New York: Pergamon.

de Leeuw, E. (1989). Health Policy. Doctoral Dissertation, Rijksuniversiteit Limburg, The Netherlands.

De Graaf, A. (1991). De invloed van echtscheiding van de ouders op demografisch gedrag van de vrouw [The impact of divorced parents on women's demographic behavior]. *Maandstatistiek van de Bevolking*, **39**, 30–38.

Duberman, L. (1975). *The Reconstituted Family: a Study of Remarried Couples and their Children*. Chicago: Nelson-Hall.

Duncan, S.W. & Markman, H.J. (1988). Intervention programs for the transition to parenthood: current status from a prevention perspective. In G.Y. Michaels & W.A. Goldberg (eds), *Transition to Parenthood: Current Theory and Research*. Cambridge: Cambridge University Press.

Fergusson, D.M., Horwood, L.J. & Shannon, F.T. (1984). A proportional hazards model of family breakdown. *Journal of Marriage and the Family*, **46**, 539–549.

Fincham, F., Bradbury, T.N. & Scott, C.K. (1990). Cognition in Marriage. In F.D. Fincham & T.N. Bradbury (eds), *The Psychology of Marriage*. New York: Guilford.

Giblin, P., Sprenkle, D.H. & Sheehan, R. (1985). Enrichment outcome research: a meta-analysis of premarital, marital and family interventions. *Jounal of Marital and Family Therapy*, **11**, 257–271.

Glenn, N.D. & Kramer, K.B. (1987). The marriages and divorces of the children of divorce. *Journal of Marriage and the Family*, **49**, 811–825.

Gottman, J., Notarius, C., Gonso, J. & Markman, H. (1976). *The Couples's Guide to Communication*. Champaign, IL: Research Press.

Gottman, J.M., Markman, H. & Notarius, C. (1977). The topography of marital conflict: a sequential analysis of verbal and non-verbal behavior. *Journal of Marriage and the Family*, **39**, 461–477.

Gottman, J. (1979). *Marital Interaction: Experimental Investigations*. New York: Academic Press.

Greenberg, L.S. & Johnson, S.M. (1988). *Emotionally Focused Couples Therapy*. New York: Guilford.

Guerney, B.J. Jr (1977). *Relationship Enhancement: Skill Training Program for Therapy Problem Prevention and Enrichment*. San Francisco: Jossey-Bass.

Guerney, B.J. Jr (1988). Family relationship enhancement: a skill training approach. In L. Bond & B. Wagner (eds), *Families in Transition: Primary Prevention Programs that Work*. Newbury Park: Sage.

Guerney, B., Brock, G. & Coufal, J. (1986). Integrating marital therapy and enrichment: the relationship enhancement approach. In N.S. Jacobson & A.S. Gurman (eds), *Clinical Handbook of Marital Therapy* (pp. 151–172). New York: Guilford.

Hahlweg, K., Helmes, B., Steffen, G., Schindler, H., Revenstorf, D. & Kunert, J. (1979). Beobachtungssystem für Partnerschaftliche Interaktion [Observational system for partner relationship interactions]. *Diagnostica*, **25**.

Hahlweg, K., Kraemer, M., Schindler, L. & Revenstorf, D. (1980). Partnerschaftsprobleme: eine empirische Analyse [Relationship problems: an empirical analysis]. *Zeitschrift für Klinische Psychologie*, **9**, 159–169.

Hahlweg, K. & Markman, H.J. (1988). Effectiveness of behavioral marital therapy: empirical status of behavioral techniques in preventing and alleviating marital distress. *Journal of Consulting and Clinical Psychology*, **56**, 440–447.

Hahlweg, K., Thurmair, F., Eckert, J., Engel, J. & Markman, H.J. (1992). *The German premarital prevention study: one-and-a-half year results*. Paper presented at 22nd Annual Convention of the Association for the Advancement of Behavior Therapy, Boston, MA, November 13–22.

Halford, W.K. (1994). Familial factors in psychiatry. *Current Opinion in Psychiatry*, **7**, 186–191.

Halford, K. & Behrens, B. (1996). Prevention of marital difficulties. In P. Cotton & H.J.

Jackson (eds), *Early Intervention and Preventive Mental Health Applications of Clinical Psychology*. Melbourne: Australian Psychological Society.

Halford, W.K., Gravestock, F., Lowe, R. & Scheldt, S. (1992). Toward a behavioral ecology of stressful marital interactions. *Behavioral Assessment*, **13**, 135–148.

Halford, W.K., Hahlweg, K. & Dunne, M. (1990). Cross-cultural study of marital communication and marital distress. *Journal of Marriage and the Family*, **52**, 487–500.

Halford, W.K., Sanders, M.R. & Behrens, B.C. (1993). A comparison of the generalization of Behavioral Marital Therapy and Enhanced Behavioral Marital Therapy. *Journal of Consulting and Clinical Psychology*, **61**, 51–60.

Halford, W.K., Sanders, M.R. & Behrens, B.C. (1994). Self-regulation in behavioral couples' therapy. *Behavior Therapy*, **25**, 431–452.

Jacob, T., Dunne, N.J. & Leonard, K. (1983). Patterns of alcohol abuse and family stability. *Alcoholism: Clinical and Experimental Research*, **7**, 382–385.

Jacobson, N. (1992). Keynote address: will the real behavioral couple therapy please stand up? Paper presented at Fourth World Congress on Behaviour Therapy, Gold Coast, Australia.

Jacobson, N.S., Schmaling, K.B. & Holtzworth-Munroe, A. (1987). Component analysis of behavioral marital therapy: two-year follow-up and prediction of relapse. *Journal of Marital and Family Therapy*, **13**, 187–195.

Kitson, G.C. & Morgan, L.A. (1990). The multiple consequences of divorce: a decade review. *Journal of Marriage and the Family*, **52**, 913–924.

Kooy, G.A. (1984). *Huwelijkswelslagen in Nederland: een vergelijking tussen 1967 en 1983* [Marital success in The Netherlands: a comparison between 1967 and 1983]. Wageningen The Netherlands.

Locke, H.J. & Wallace, K.M. (1959). Short marital adjustment and prediction tests: their reliability and validity. *Marriage and Family Living*, **21**, 251–255.

Lorion, R.P., Price, R.H. & Eaton, W.W. (1989). The prevention of child and adolescent disorders: from theory to research. In D. Shaffer, I. Philips & N.B. Enzer (eds), *Prevention of Mental Disorders, Alcohol and Other Drug Use in Children and Adolescents*. Rockville, MA: Office of Substance Abuse Prevention (OSAP).

Margolin, G. & Wampold, B.E. (1981). Sequential analysis of conflict and accord in distressed and nondistressed marital partners. *Journal of Consulting and Clinical Psychology*, **49**, 554–567.

Markman, H. (1992). Possibilities for the prevention of divorce and marital distress: an international perspective. Paper presented at World Conference on Behaviour Therapy. Gold Coast, Australia, July.

Markman, H.J., Stanley, S.M. & Blumberg, S.L. (1994). *Fighting for Your Marriage: Positive Steps for Preventing Divorce and Preserving a Lasting Love*. San Francisco, CA: Jossey-Bass.

Markman, H.J., Floyd, F.J., Stanley, S.M. & Lewis, H.C. (1986). Prevention. In N.S. Jacobson & A.S. Gurman (eds), *Clinical Handbook of Marital Therapy* (pp. 173–195). New York: Guilford.

Markman, H.J., Floyd, F., Stanley, S.M. & Storaasli, R. (1988). The prevention of marital distress: a longitudinal investigation. *Journal of Consulting and Clinical Psychology*, **56**, 210–217.

Markman, H.J. & Hahlweg, K. (1993). The prediction and prevention of marital distress: an international perspective. *Clinical Psychology Review*, **13**, 29–43.

Markman, H.J., Renick, M.J., Floyd, F.J., Stanley, S.M. & Clements, M. (1993). Preventing marital distress through communication and conflict management training: a 4- and 5-year follow-up. *Journal of Consulting and Clinical Psychology*, **61**, 70–77.

Martin, T.C. & Bumpass, L. (1989). Recent trends in marital disruption. *Demography*, **26**, 37–51.

McGoldrick, M. & Gerson, R. (1985). *Genograms in Family Assessment*. New York: W.W. Norton & Co.

Meeks, S., Arnkoff, D.B., Glass, C.R. & Notarius, C.I. (1986). Wives' employment status, hassles, communication and relational efficacy: Intra- versus extra-relationship factors and marital adjustment. *Family Relations*, **34**, 249–255.

Merikangas, K.R. (1984). Divorce and assortative mating among depressed patients. *American Journal of Psychiatry*, **39**, 1173–1180.

Notarius, C.I. & Markman, H.J. (1993). *We Can Work It Out: Making Sense of Marital Conflict*. New York: G.P. Putnam's Sons.

Notarius, C.I. & Vanzetti, N.A. (1983). The Marital Agendas Protocol. In E.E. Filsinger (ed.), *Marriage and Family Assessment: a Sourcebook for Family Therapy* (pp. 209–227). Beverly Hills, CA: Sage.

Notarius, C.I. (1990). *Marital Practicum*. Washington, DC: Departments of Psychology, Catholic University of America.

NVAGG (1988). *Nederlandse Vereniging van Ambulante Geestelijke Gezondheidszorg, Statische Zakboek* [Statistics Handbook]. Utrecht: NVAGG.

O'Farrell, T.J. & Birchler, G.R. (1987). Marital relationships of alcoholic, conflicted, and non-conflicted couples. *Journal of Marital and Family Therapy*, **13**, 259–274.

Olson, D. (1976). *Treating Relationships*. Lake Mills, Iowa: Graphics Publishing Co., Inc.

Pope, H. & Mueller, C.W. (1976). The intergenerational transmission of marital instability: comparisons by race and sex. *Journal of Social Issues*, **52**, 49–66.

Price, R.H., Cowen, E.L. Lorion, R.P. & Ramos-McKay, J. (1989). The search for effective prevention programs: what we learned along the way. *American Journal of Orthopsychiatry*, **59**, 49–58.

Price-Bonham, S. & Balswick, J. (1980). The non-institutions: divorce, desertion, and remarriage. *Journal of Marriage and the Family*, **42**, 959–972.

Reich, J. & Thompson, W.D. (1985). Marital status of schizophrenic and alcoholic patients. *Journal of Nervous and Mental Disease*, **173**, 499–502.

Revenstorf, D., Vogel, B., Wegener, C., Hahlweg, K. & Schindler, L. (1980). Escalation phenomena in interaction sequences: an empirical comparison of distressed and non-distressed couples. *Behavior Analysis and Modification*, **2**, 97–116.

Rosenzweig, J.M. & Dailey, D.M. (1989). Dyadic adjustment: sexual satisfaction in women and men as a function of psychological sex role self-perception. *Journal of Sex and Marital Therapy*, **15**, 42–56.

Ruscher, S.M. & Gotlib, I.H. (1988). Marital interaction patterns of couples with and without a depressed partner. *Behavior Therapy*, **19**, 455–470.

Schaap, C. (1982). *Communication and Adjustment in Marriage*. Lisse, The Nethelands: Swets & Zeitlinger.

Schaap, C. (1984). A comparison of the interaction of distressed and non-distressed married couples in a laboratory situation: literature survey, methodological issues, and an empirical investigation. In K. Hahlweg & N.S. Jacobson (eds), *Marital Interaction: Analysis and Modification* (pp. 133–158). New York: Guilford.

Schaap, C., Buunk, A. & Kerkstra, A. (1988). Marital conflict resolution. In M.F.P. Noller (ed.), *Perspectives on Marital Interaction*. Clevedon, UK: Multilingual Matters.

Schaap, C., Hoogduin, K., Van Widenfelt, B. & Streik, P. (1992). *Stress Management Training: Therapeut draaiboek* [Stress Management Training for Couples: therapist Manual]. Unpublished manual, University of Nijmegen, The Netherlands.

Schaap, C., Schellekens, I. & Schippers, G. (1991). Alcohol and marital interaction: the relationship between alcoholism, interaction characteristics and marital therapy. In S.M.M. Lammers, G.M. Schippers & C.P.D.R. Schaap (eds), *Contributions to the Psychology of Addiction* (pp. 65–86). Amsterdam: Swets & Zeitlinger.

Schaap, C. & Van Widenfelt, B. (1990). Prevention of Relationship Distress and Dissolution: a Practical Manual for Professionals. University of Nijmegen, The Netherlands: Unpublished Manual.

Snyder, D.K. & Wills, R.M. (1989). Behavioral versus insight-oriented marital therapy: effects on individual and interspousal functioning. *Journal of Consulting and Clinical Psychology.* **57**, 39–46.

Spanier, G.B. (1976). Measuring dyadic adjustment: new scales for asssessing the quality of marriage and similar dyads. *Journal of Marriage and the Family*, **38**, 15–28.

Stanley, S.M. & Markman, H.J. (1992). Assessing commitment in personal relationships. *Journal of Marriage and the Family*, **54**, 595–608.

Stanley, S.M., Markman, H., St. Peters, M. & Douglas Leber, B. (1995). Strengthening marriages and preventing divorce: new directions in prevention research. *Family Relations*, **44**, 392–401.

Straus, M.A. (1979). Measuring intrafamily conflict and violence: The Conflict Tactics (CT) scales. *Journal of Marriage and the Family*, **41**, 75–85.

Stuart, R.B. (1980). *Helping Couples Change.* New York: Guilford.

Thibaut, J.W. & Kelley, H.H. (1959). *The Social Psychology of Groups.* New York: Wiley.

Van Widenfelt, B., Schaap, C. & Hosman, C. (1991). Preventing marital distress in a risk group in The Netherlands. Paper presented at Association for Advancement of Behavior Therapy, New York City, November 21–24.

Van Widenfelt, B., Schaap, C. & Hosman, C. (1992). Preventing marital distress and maintaining relationship satisfaction: a program for adult children of divorce. Paper presented at Association for Advancement of Behavior Therapy, Boston, MA, November 19–22.

Van Widenfelt, B., Hosman, C., Schaap, C. & van der Staak, C. (1996). The prevention of relationship distress for couples at risk: a controlled evaluation with nine-month and two-year follow-up results. *Family Relations*, **45**, 156–165.

Vanzetti, N.A., Notarius, C.I. & NeeSmith, D. (1992). Specific and generalized expectancies in marital interaction. *Journal of Family Psychology*, **6**, 171–183.

Vincent, J.P. (1972). The Relationship of Sex, Level of Intimacy, and Level of Marital Distress to Problem-solving Behavior and Exchange of Social Reinforcement. Doctoral Dissertation, University of Oregon.

Vincent, J.P., Weiss, R.H. & Birchler, G.R. (1975). A behavioral analysis of problem solving in distressed and nondistressed married and stranger dyads. *Behavior Therapy*, **6**, 475–487.

Weissman, M.M. & Paykel, E.S. (1974). *The Depressed Woman: a Study of Social Relationships.* Chicago: University of Chicago Press.

White, L.K. (1990). Determinants of divorce: a review of research in the eigthties. *Journal of Marriage and the Family*, **52**, 904–912.

Section V

Evaluating and Improving the Effectiveness of Couples Interventions

Chapter 26

Evaluating and Improving the Efficacy of Conjoint Couple Therapy

Mark A. Whisman* and Douglas K. Snyder**
*Department of Psychology, * Yale University,
New Haven, CT, and ** Texas A & M University,
College Station, TX, USA*

Differences—eternal differences, planted by God in a single family, so that there may always be colour; sorrow perhaps, but colour in the daily gray/(E.M. Forster).

Over the past several decades, there have been widespread changes in "the" family, resulting in ever-increasing differences in what constitutes couple and familial relationships. To keep pace with these societal changes in couple relationships, there has been increasing diversification in couple therapy in terms of: (a) approaches to couple therapy (e.g. insight-oriented and experiential couple therapy); and (b) problems addressed in couple therapy (e.g. adult and child psychiatric and physical illness); and (c) expectations regarding couple therapy outcome (e.g. brief treatments, treatment accountability). Although these differences help to make the practice of couple therapy so dynamic, they also underscore the importance of evaluating and improving the outcomes of couple therapy.

In this chapter, we provide an overview and critique of methods and findings regarding the evaluation of conjoint couple therapy, with a special emphasis on evaluating mediators and moderators of change in couple therapy. In doing so, we also highlight issues and offer suggestions for improving the outcomes of couple therapy.

Clinical Handbook of Marriage and Couples Interventions. Edited by W. Kim Halford and Howard J. Markman.
© 1997 John Wiley & Sons Ltd.

EFFICACY OF COUPLE THERAPY

Although there are a number of excellent recent reviews of couple therapy outcome (e.g. Jacobson & Addis, 1993; Lebow & Gurman, 1995), one of the most comprehensive evaluations of therapy efficacy is provided by Shadish et al., (1993), who recently conducted a meta-analysis of published and unpublished family and couple therapy outcome studies. They identified 27 studies that evaluated the efficacy of couple therapy for either global relationship satisfaction (16 studies) or other specific presenting problems (11 studies). Across all 27 studies, the mean effect size (ES) was 0.60; the mean ES for the subset of 16 studies that specifically evaluated the efficacy of couple therapy on global relationship satisfaction was 0.71. In interpreting these ESs, it may be useful to bear in mind Cohen's (1988) classification of small, medium and large ESs as 0.20, 0.50, and 0.80, respectively. Thus, the ES of couple therapy falls in Cohen's medium-to-large range. Moreover, an ES of 0.60 (or 0.71 for studies specifically evaluating relationship satisfaction) (a) implies that the average couple who received therapy was better off at the end of treatment than 37% (or 76%) of control couples; (b) yields a probability of 66% (or 69%) that a randomly chosen treatment couple will have better outcome than a randomly chosen control couple (z = mean ES/$\sqrt{2}$; Smith, Glass & Miller, 1980); (c) converts to a correlation coefficient of roughly 0.29 (or 0.33; Hedges & Olkin, 1985, p. 77), so that treatment accounts for about 8% (or 11%) of outcome variance; and (d) translates into a success rate (0.50 + r/2 for the treatment group and 0.50 − r/2 for the control group; Rosenthal & Rubin, 1982) of 65% (or 67%) vs. 36% (or 34%) for control groups. Thus, results from this meta-analysis suggest that couple therapy is an effective treatment for relationship dissatisfaction and, to a slightly lesser extent, specific presenting problems. However, although outcome following couple therapy appears to be superior to no treatment, that nearly one-third of couples do not improve with treatment suggests the continued need for developing and improving effective couple therapies.

Couple therapy researchers and clinicians are often most interested in knowing the efficacy of various forms of therapy. Across all 27 trials, Shadish et al. (1993) reported that behavioral treatments (mean ES of 0.74) had larger ESs than non-behavioral treatments (mean ES of 0.51). However, studies that compared the relative effectiveness of more than one treatment yielded "non-significant effect sizes for all comparisons over many studies" (p. 998). Thus, findings suggest that there are few differences among various approaches in their observed efficacy. However, this conclusion should be tempered by the acknowledgement that there are too few direct comparisons among orientations to draw definitive conclusions regarding the relative efficacy of various forms of couple therapy.

Methodological Critique

One limitation of existing evaluations of couple therapy concerns the selection of outcome measures for evaluating the efficacy of treatment. The most common outcome measure in couple therapy is a measure of global relationship adjustment. Although beyond the scope of this chapter, commonly used measures of outcome such as the Dyadic Adjustment Scale (Spanier, 1976) have been criticized as measuring the determinants of relationship satisfaction (e.g. dyadic differences) in addition to relationship satisfaction (cf. Eddy, Heyman & Weiss, 1991); thus, there is a need for greater precision in the measurement of relationship satisfaction. In addition, although some prior studies have examined the impact of treatment on a limited number of domains besides relationship adjustment, there is a need for more comprehensive assessment of relationship functioning in future studies evaluating the efficacy of couple therapy. For example, Snyder et al. (1995) have discussed a conceptual model of couple assessment that may help aid selection of outcome measures, including assessment of: (a) cognitive; (b) affective; (c) communication and interpersonal; (d) structural and developmental; and (e) control, sanctions and related behavioral domains. Although it may be inefficient to gather outcome data on all of these domains, only some of which would be pertinent to the treatment of any given couple, selecting measures from a subset of these domains that are appropriate to the kinds of couples being treated and to the treatment setting would provide a more comprehensive evaluation of outcome than is typically provided in existing studies. Furthermore, evaluating the impact of therapy on physical and psychological health indices is important in legitimizing couple therapy as an acceptable form of treatment.

A related problem with existing outcome studies concerns the operationalization of successful treatment. That is, outcome studies most often rely exclusively on standardized self-report and observational measures of outcome, while simultaneously acknowledging that the problems that many couples present in treatment are not included in such methods. For example, a couple may seek therapy to decide whether to remain in the relationship. If they decide to separate, this may be a positive outcome for them (i.e. having resolved the issue), but would be counted as a treatment failure in an outcome study that relied exclusively on relationship status and/or satisfaction as its outcome. Because most studies rely on standardized measures of outcome, there is little available information regarding the efficacy of couple therapy on presenting problems that are not assessed under traditional methods.

One primary reason for investigators not having evaluated the impact of treatment on individualized presenting problems may be the lack of a method for operationalizing idiographic outcome. The degree to which a treatment helps couples accomplish individualized goals can, however, be evaluated with *goal attainment scaling* (GAS; Kiresuk, Smith & Cardillo, 1994). GAS is a method for quantifying treatment-induced change in any number of dimensions (goals) that are specific and unique to each individual, including the varied problems that bring couples into treatment and are major foci of treatment, but that may not be measured by standardized assessments. The GAS method involves first selecting and formulating treatment goals. The issues that will be the focus of treatment are identified, and then each problem is translated into one or more goals; clients most often actively work with therapists in this goal-setting process. The expected level of outcome is then specified for each goal, as well as the "somewhat more" and "somewhat less" than expected levels of outcome, and the "much more" and "much less" than expected levels of outcomes. Each level of outcome is assigned a value on a five-point measurement scale that ranges from -2 for much less than expected level of outcome, to $+2$ for much more than expected level of outcome. At the end of treatment (and/or at follow-up), the level of outcome is rated, and the ratings across goals can then be averaged or converted to T-scores using the tables provided by Kiresuk, Smith & Cardillo (1993) to provide a summary score for evaluating the degree to which treatment helped clients attain their own individualized goals.

To illustrate the potential use of the GAS method, consider a couple who presents with the problem of "ambivalence regarding the future of their relationship", which might include the goal of "deciding whether to stay together". The much less than expected outcome (-2) might be, "avoids discussion of and decision regarding staying together"; the somewhat less than expected outcome (-1) might be, "can state the advantages and disadvantages of staying together but unable to make a decision"; the expected level of outcome (0) might be, "made decision regarding staying together but taken no step to carry out decision"; the somewhat more than expected level of outcome $(+1)$ might be, "made decision and taken steps to carry out decision"; and the much more than expected level of outcome $(+2)$ might be, "made decision and taken steps to carry out decision and satisfied with the decision".

The GAS evaluation procedure may therefore be useful in evaluating couple therapy outcome. Aggregating GAS average or T-scores across the major presenting problems (and their related goals) for each couple would provide a summary of the success of an intervention or treatment in helping couples achieve what might possibly be quite different goals. If used in this way, inclusion of GAS would allow evaluating the relative effectiveness of an intervention (vs. no intervention or a different intervention) on the achievement of individualized goals not included in standardized assessments. Thus, in conjunction with standardized assessment methods, the GAS methodology might provide a more comprehensive evaluation of efficacy.

A third limitation of existing studies concerns the maintenance of gains following couple therapy. In Shadish et al.'s (1993) meta-analysis, only one of nine studies for which follow-up differences were computed had a follow-up period of over 1 year. Given that the relative effectiveness of treatments may differ over time (e.g. Snyder, Wills & Grady-Fletcher, 1991), increased efforts toward evaluating the long-term effects of therapy are sorely needed.

A fourth limitation of existing evaluations of couple therapy concerns statistical power for detecting relatively small treatment effects (cf. Kazdin & Bass, 1989). Specifically, Shadish et al.'s (1993) meta-analysis suggests that ESs for treatment vs. no treatment comparisons were typically in the medium-to-large range, and ESs for comparisons of alternative treatments were typically in the small-to-medium range. Based on figures provided by Cohen (1988), acceptable power (0.80) to detect large, medium and small ESs for a comparison of the means of two treatment groups (or treatment and control groups) requires 26, 64 and 393 couples per condition, respectively. Therefore, whereas sample sizes in most outcome studies are sufficient for detecting large ESs, as typically observed in comparisons between a treatment and a control condition, samples fall far below the requisite number of participants to detect small-to-medium ESs for differences of the magnitude commonly observed in between-treatment comparisons.

Therefore, greater attention is needed in maximizing power in future outcome studies. One primary method for increasing power is to increase sample size. However, as discussed by Kazdin & Bass (1989), power can also be increased by "selecting homogeneous sets of patients, ensuring the integrity of treatment, standardizing the assessment conditions, carefully choosing outcome measures, and similar practices [that] increase the power of an investigation by reducing variability in its execution" (p. 145). In addition, consideration should be given to increasing power by changing the levels of confidence adopted to protect against Type I and Type II error.

In reality, however, because the upper limits of sample sizes used in most therapy outcome research will be bound by practical considerations such as time, effort and resources, treatment differences are not likely to be detected in comparative outcome studies, even if they exist in nature. Consequently, there may be little to be gained from between-group comparative studies that have minimal chances of detecting treatment differences. Detection of significant differences between treatment approaches is even less likely as couple therapy becomes increasingly integrative. Rather, it could be argued that advances in the field of couple therapy are more likely to come from intensive analyses of why current therapies are not effective for some couples. Thus, the remainder of this chapter reviews and critiques the major findings and methods for evaluating mediators and moderators of change in couple therapy, and the implications of these findings for enhancing couple therapy outcome.

MEDIATORS OF CHANGE IN COUPLE THERAPY

One direction for improving couple therapy outcome is to identify treatment mediators (or mechanisms), which are those characteristics of the individual or couple that are changed by the treatment and which in turn produce change in outcome (e.g. relationship satisfaction). Evaluating "how" therapy works may have important implications for modifying existing treatment interventions and developing new strategies for working with couples.

Methodology Involved in the Evaluation of Treatment Mediation

As discussed elsewhere (e.g. Judd & Kenny, 1981), conventional analyses of variance strategies evaluate only the separate effects of the manipulation on the dependent variable (e.g. satisfaction) and the mechanism (e.g. communication), not the relation between mechanism and clinical outcome. Mediation can, however, be evaluated with analysis of covariance, regression (path) analysis, or maximum likelihood estimation procedures. Mediation within a given treatment is established if: (a) treatment produces significant pre- to post-treatment change in both the mediating variable and outcome variable; (b) pre- to post-treatment change in the mediator remains statistically significant when controlling for the outcome variable; and (c) pre- to post-treatment change in the outcome variable is substantially reduced when controlling for the mediating variable, with the strongest evidence for mediation being exhibited when treatment effects are reduced to zero.

This model can be extended for evaluating multiple mediators of outcome (e.g. change in communication skills and relationship cognitions) through comparing treatment effect sizes on the outcome variable or variables for one mediator (or set of mediators), controlling for some other mediator (or set of mediators). Multiple mediation is established if: (a) treatment produces significant pre- to post-treatment change in each mediating variable and the outcome variable; (b) pre- to post-treatment change for each mediating variable remains statistically significant when controlling for the outcome variable and the other mediating variable(s); and (c) each mediating variable results in an incremental decrease in pre- to post-treatment change in the outcome variable (i.e. each mediating variable reduces the amount of pre- to post-treatment change in the outcome variable).

Empirical Evaluation of Mediation in Couple Therapy

Most of the empirical evaluations that have sought to address the role of purported mediators of change in couple therapies have been conducted with behavioral interventions. As has been reviewed elsewhere (cf. Dunn & Schwebel, 1995; Hahlweg & Markman, 1988), behavior therapy consistently results in changes in observational measures of interaction patterns, which supports the first criterion for establishing that changes in communication mediate the effects of behavior therapy. There have been few studies, however, that have examined the co-variation between change in couples' interaction and change in their relationship satisfaction. Both Iverson & Baucom (1990) and Halford, Sanders & Behrens (1993) failed to find an association between changes in interaction and satisfaction. In comparison, Sayers et al. (1991) found that increases in what was labeled *constructive engagement* were associated with increases in satisfaction. Thus, there is equivocal support for co-variation between change in satisfaction and change in communication skill acquisition in behavior therapy. Finally, it should be noted that Shadish et al. (1993) found that ESs for behavioral variables were greater than ESs for global satisfaction variables for couples treated with behavior therapy, which would be consistent with the second requirement for establishing mediation; however, these findings are also consistent with the hypothesis that the larger ESs were obtained because behavioral measures were more reactive than satisfaction measures.

Several investigations have been conducted to test the role of change in cognition as a mediating factor in cognitive therapy (Emmelkamp et al., 1988a) or in cognitive restructuring components combined with behavioral interventions (Baucom & Lester, 1986; Baucom, Sayers & Sher, 1990; Halford, Sanders & Behrens, 1993). The results of these studies have generally shown that these interventions result in changes in dysfunctional cognitions, thus providing support for the first criterion of cognitive mediation. In lack of support of the cognitive mediation hypothesis, however, change in relationship satisfaction has not been found to co-vary with change in self-report measures of cognition (Emmelkamp et al., 1988b) or spouses' reports of cognition collected during problem-solving interactions (Halford, Sanders & Behrens, 1993). Consequently, as with couple interaction, lack of co-variation between change in cognition and satisfaction fails to support the hypothesis that these interventions are mediated by change in relationship cognitions.

Methodological Critique

One explanation for why investigators have failed to find support mediators of change in couple therapy concerns the issue of failure to assess relevant mediating variables (Beach & Bauserman, 1990). For example, carefully validated and widely accepted measures for assessing mediational variables in non-behavioral couple therapies are generally non-existent. Thus, a major challenge facing investigators interested in the mediation of couple therapy is the development and validation of measures for the assessment of mediational processes within alternative treatment approaches. Similarly, although cognitive therapies have included measures for the assessment of several potential mediators, there are other potential mediators that have been overlooked in prior investigations. For example, Baucom et al. (1989) have proposed five important relationship cognitive variables (i.e. selective attention, causal attributions, expectancies, assumptions, standards), each of which could be evaluated as a potential mediator of the effects of cognitive interventions. For example, although there is evidence linking causal and responsibility attributions to relationship satisfaction (as reviewed by Bradbury & Fincham, 1990) and although cognitive restructuring commonly focuses on couples' attributions (e.g. Baucom, Sayers & Sher, 1990), there has been a lack of research examining the mediating role of change in attributional style on therapy outcome.

Whereas the preceding discussion has addressed the failure to find co-variation between changes in mediating and outcome variables, prior results have also generally failed to provide supporting evidence for the specificity hypothesis of mediation (i.e. that specific treatments will have specific effects on purported mediators). For example, the results from Dunn and Schwebel's (1995) meta-analysis of couple therapy outcome research found no significant differences in promoting changes in behavior among treatment approaches; there were few studies that examined the comparative effectiveness of different therapies on affect or relationship-related cognitions. Consequently, it could be hypothesized that alternative approaches to couple therapy are mediated by a common process or common processes (principle of equifinality). Such a view of common (i.e. "non-specific") factors of change in individual therapy has been proposed to account for the lack of significant differences between alternative treatments. For example, alternative approaches to couple therapy have been hypothesized to be effective through offering alternative routes to the same ends of greater acceptance (Jacobson, 1991), greater understanding (Snyder & Wills, 1991), improved ability for handling negative affect (Markman, 1991) and, ultimately, greater satisfaction. Prior outcome studies, however, have not quantified or evaluated the potential mediating role of these proposed non-specific mediators (with the possible exception of ability for handling negative affect).

If it is indeed true that various approaches and interventions in couple therapy work through common mechanism(s), this may have important implications for improving the efficacy of couple therapy. One common strategy for enhancing couple therapy outcome in recent years has been to combine various treatment interventions (e.g. Baucom, Sayers & Sher, 1990; Halford, Sanders & Behrens, 1993). With few exceptions, the conclusions drawn from these investigations are that such combinations do not enhance efficacy. However, if it is true that interventions share a common mechanism for change, the limited success of additive studies becomes more understandable. That is, the incremental efficacy of an additive component should vary as a function of the degree of unique mediation it offers. Thus, if intervention A and intervention B share a common mechanism, then offering the two interventions for any given couple (i.e. offering "more of the same") may not be more effective than offering only one intervention. In comparison, if intervention A and intervention B improve satisfaction through different means, then the combination may indeed result in better outcome than either intervention by itself. For example, if two interventions were shown to mediate outcome through improving ability to handle conflict, then their combination may not be more effective than either intervention by itself. In comparison, if a third intervention did not affect ability to handle conflict, but did affect partners' attributional style, then combining the third intervention with either of the first two may be expected to enhance outcome. Thus, identifying which specific interventions are affecting which specific domains of relationship functioning might improve outcome through offering guidance in selecting and combining non-redundant interventions. It should be noted, however, that whereas combining two treatments that share a common mediator may not improve outcome for a *given* couple, the combination may improve outcome for a *group* of couples, if one intervention worked better (i.e. had a greater impact on the mediator) for some couples and the other intervention worked better for other couples. Elsewhere (e.g. Whisman, 1993) this effect has been discussed in terms of *moderated mediation*, which can be evaluated within a general regression model using Moderator × Mediator interaction terms.

Before leaving the topic of treatment mediation, it is important to recognize that we have been discussing mediation in terms of specific interventions, rather than entire treatment programs. As discussed in greater detail by Beach & Bauserman (1990), most treatments consist of multiple interventions that may affect a variety of mediators. Evaluating mediation for an entire treatment, therefore, may yield limited information. In comparison, repeated assessments of mediating and outcome variables are necessary to evaluate the impact of specific interventions on specific outcome variables. Furthermore, intensive analysis of specific interventions (i.e. process analysis) should improve understanding of the mediating impact of any one of these interventions. For example, Johnson & Greenberg (1988) found that session quality was mediated, in part, by the degree to which the partner assuming a blaming position reprocessed intense affective experience ("softening").

MODERATORS OF CHANGE IN COUPLE THERAPY

Besides understanding how couple therapy works, it is also important to understand for whom therapy does and does not work. Thus, there is increasing interest in investigating moderators (i.e. predictors) of outcome. Identifying moderators of outcome could target ways of improving therapy and help match couples with the treatment might work best for them.

Empirical Evaluation of Moderators of Change in Couple Therapy

Several studies have sought to identify variables associated with outcomes of couple therapy. Although a comprehensive review of these prior studies is beyond the scope of this chapter, a brief summary is provided by Snyder, Mangrum & Wills (1993), who classified predictors of couple therapy outcomes into demographic indices, measures of individual functioning, indicators or relationship functioning, and treatment characteristics. Some of the strongest relations between predictors and outcome were found for: (a) age; (b) depressive symptomatology; (c) gender roles; (d) pretreatment level of relationship distress; (e) relationship commitment; and (f) spousal affection and intimacy. In addition, Shadish et al. (1993) identified several methodological components shown to moderate outcome in their meta-analysis of treatment efficacy. Of particular interest were the findings that, for within-study between-treatment comparisons for both couple and family therapy (analyses were not conducted separately for couple therapy), "increased effect size was associated with high levels of treatment standardization, with experimenter allegiance, with a focus on present matters rather than both present and historical matters, with high levels of communication training, and with lower attrition rates" (p. 998). To the degree that these results apply specifically to couple therapy, an implication of this finding is that couple therapy outcome may be enhanced by improving standardization and focusing greater attention on present issues and communication training.

Methodological Critique

One limitation of prior studies on moderators of change has to do with the selection of potential moderating variables. Many prior studies that have evaluated characteristics associated with couple therapy outcome have examined the role of demographic characteristics or measures of individual functioning. Unfortunately, however, findings regarding such characteristics offer limited direction for improving the outcome of couple therapy, because these characteristics are not themselves directly amenable to change. For example, knowing that older couples do not respond as well as younger couples does not offer suggestions for improving therapy for older couples, because age cannot be manipulated by therapeutic intervention. In comparison, an association between outcome and characteristics that are amenable to change should offer fruitful directions for enhancing the efficacy of couple therapy. For example, one explanation for why older couples do not respond as well in behavioral couple therapy is because of more traditional gender roles regarding decision-making, which could make it more difficult for them to engage in egalitarian problem-solving. In this case, age would exert an indirect influence on outcome through gender roles which, unlike age, can be addressed (i.e. treated) prior to working on problem-solving. Therefore, future studies should seek to identify moderators of outcome that can be either directly or indirectly manipulated by treatment interventions. Alternatively, identification of moderators of outcome that cannot be directly manipulated is important if it results in modification or development of an alternative, more effective treatment (i.e. if it results in manipulation of the choice of treatment). For example, O'Leary & Turkewitz (1981) reported that age was prescriptively related to type of treatment (i.e. younger couples responded better to behavioral therapy whereas older couples responded better to communication training).

One potential moderator of couple therapy outcome that can be manipulated is *treatment delivery*. For example, outcome may vary as a function of the quality of the therapeutic alliance. Based on one popular conceptualization (Bordin, 1979), the alliance between therapist and client is achieved by agreement on the goals of treatment, perceived relevance of therapeutic tasks, and a bond appropriate to the demands of the task. Although not specifically evaluating alliance, Holtzworth-Munroe et al. (1989) found that positive outcome to behavior therapy was predicted by spouses' active and collaborative participation in therapy and therapists' ability to induce and foster such collaboration. More direct support for the importance of the alliance in couple therapy was obtained by Bourgeois, Sabourin & Wright (1990), who found that ratings of the alliance obtained at the third session were significantly related to outcome in a group couple skills-training program. If the alliance were consistently shown to moderate outcome, then couple therapy should be enhanced through improving alliance via such methods as involving couples in choosing treatment goals and making explicit what interventions are to be used to accomplish these goals.

Another aspect of treatment delivery that may moderate outcome is the inclusion of individual session in conjoint couple therapy. For example, in recent years there has been increasing interest in couple therapy as a treatment of psychiatric disorders such as depression, anxiety, and alcoholism (cf. Jacobson & Gurman, 1995). Research is needed to evaluate whether combining individual sessions with couple sessions improves outcome and if so, to determine the most effective combination and timing of individual and conjoint sessions.

A second class of potential moderators of couple therapy outcome is *relationship characteristics*. For example, there undoubtedly are particular relationship problems for which existing interventions are not efficacious. Identifying such problem areas should offer fruitful directions for the development of interventions to enhance therapy. Recently, Whisman, Dixon & Johnson (1995) conducted a national survey of practicing couple therapists to document, in part, what therapists believed were the most difficult problems to treat in couple therapy. Results showed that the most difficult problems were lack of loving feelings, alcoholism, extramarital affairs, power struggles and serious individual problems. Therapists were also asked what characteristics they believed were associated with negative outcome to couple therapy. The most common responses were one or both partners' unwillingness to change or to accept responsibility for change, and lack of commitment to the relationship or to therapy. Consequently, therapy outcome should be improved through the development of interventions that (a) target these problem areas, and (b) improve engagement and commitment. Beach & Bauserman (1990) also stressed the importance of compliance, and offered several suggestions for improving compliance based on the theories of planned behavior and attribution-efficacy model of conflict.

A second limitation of prior evaluations of moderators of couple therapy concerns the choice of statistical procedures for evaluating treatment moderation. One promising method for determining moderating effects for various approaches to therapy is the aptitude–treatment interaction (ATI) paradigm (Cronbach & Snow, 1977), developed to test whether alternative treatments have different effects as a function of individual differences. As such, this method has potential for identifying which treatment is appropriate for a given couple. As discussed in greater detail elsewhere (e.g. Cronbach & Snow, 1977; Dance & Neufeld, 1988), regression analyses can be conducted to evaluate whether a variable is related to treatment outcome in general or to outcome of a given treatment in particular. For example, to test if a predictor is differentially related to outcome following one treatment vs. another, the post-treatment outcome variable (e.g. relationship satisfaction) first would be regressed on pretreatment scores on the outcome variable (to control for the variance accounted for by pretest satisfaction), and then in subsequent steps be regressed on the predictor, the dummy code for type of treatment, and the Predictor × Treatment interaction term. A significant main effect for the predictor would indicate its association with outcome across treatments, whereas a significant interaction would indicate that the relation between predictor and outcome varies by treatment. Although well recognized by psychotherapy researchers in general, with few exceptions (e.g. Snyder, Mangrum & Wills, 1993), the ATI paradigm has been only rarely researched in couple therapy.

One potential application of ATI investigations would be to match couples to treatment interventions. It has often been proposed that the lack of significant differences among various treatment conditions is the consequence of random assignment to treatment condition, which does not take specific couples' needs into consideration. Based on this argument, treatment efficacy would be enhanced with "matching studies" in which subjects' needs are matched to appropriate treatment interventions (Jacobson, 1991). However, it has yet to be established what dimension(s) would be used to match couples to treatments (Jacobson & Addis, 1993).

One common perspective is that couples who lack certain skills should be assigned to treatments that include training in these skills. Cronbach & Snow (1977) have described this ATI model as a "compensation" model, in which the best treatment is one that remediates or compensates for couples' (skill or performance) deficits. There has been limited support, however, for the compensation model in prior ATI evaluations of psychological disorders (Dance & Neufeld, 1988). For example, according to the compensation model, treatment modalities that use cognitive techniques to overcome depression should be most efficacious for those individuals with greater cognitive dysfunction. However, as reviewed elsewhere (Whisman, 1993), results from prior investigations suggest that cognitive dysfunction is either unrelated or negatively related to outcome following cognitive therapy. Because there is limited support for the compensation model in the treatment of other disorders, it cannot be assumed that matching couples to treatments based on skills deficits would necessarily enhance outcome.

Cronbach & Snow (1977) describe an alternative model to compensation—the "capitalization" model—that could also be used to match couples with various modes of therapy. Under the capitalization model, the best treatment for a given couple is one that addresses their pre-existing skills and strengths and that builds on their prior learning history. For example, emotion-focused therapy should be most appropriate for couples who have at least a minimum amount of basic trust and intimacy in their relationship (Greenberg & Johnson, 1986); where such trust is lacking, such interventions may prove damaging to the couple (Coyne, 1986). Thus, future research is needed to test whether compensation or capitalization models best identify predictors for choosing among alternative approaches to couple therapy.

SUMMARY

There is a respectable body of empirical support for the efficacy of couple therapy, particularly as a treatment for global relationship dissatisfaction. However, empirical evaluation of "how?" and "for whom?" couple therapy works has not been as thoroughly investigated. We have argued that improving the methodology and conducting systematic evaluations of the mediators and moderators of change in couple therapy (i.e. evaluating what relationship areas are changed by couple therapy and the impact that couple differences have on the extent to which these areas are changed) should serve not only to enhance understanding of the practice of couple therapy, but should also improve the outcome of couple therapy by guiding the selection and application of specific interventions for specific couples.

Acknowledgements

Preparation of this chapter was supported by a grant from the National Alliance for Research on Schizophrenia and Depression, awarded to Mark A. Whisman.

REFERENCES

Baucom, D.H., Epstein, N., Sayers, S. & Sher, T.G. (1989). The role of cognitions in marital relationships: definitional, methodological, and conceptual issues. *Journal of Consulting and Clinical Psychology*, **57**, 31–38.

Baucom, D.H. & Lester, G.W. (1986). The usefulness of cognitive restructuring as an adjunct to behavioral marital therapy. *Behavior Therapy*, **17**, 385–403.

Baucom, D.H., Sayers, S.L. & Sher, T.G. (1990). Supplementing behavioral marital therapy with cognitive restructuring and emotional expressiveness training: an outcome investigation. *Journal of Consulting and Clinical Psychology*, **58**, 636–645.

Beach, S.R.H. & Bauserman, S.A.K. (1990). Enhancing the effectiveness of marital therapy. In F.D. Fincham & T.N. Bradbury (eds), *The Psychology of Marriage: Basic Issues and Applications* (pp. 349–374). New York: Guilford.

Bordin, E.S. (1979). The generalizability of the psychoanalytic concept of the working alliance. *Psychotherapy: Theory, Research, and Practice*, **16**, 252–260.

Bardbury, T.N & Fincham, F.D. (1990). Attributions in marriage: review and critique. *Psychological Bulletin*, **107**, 3–33.

Bourgeois, L., Sabourin, S. & Wright, J. (1990). Predictive validity of therapeutic alliance in group marital therapy. *Journal of Consulting and Clinical Psychology*, **58**, 608–613.

Cohen, J. (1988). *Statistical Power Analysis for the Behavioral Sciences*, 2nd edn. Hillsdale, NJ: Erlbaum.

Coyne, J.C. (1986). Evoked emotion in marital therapy: necessary or even useful? *Journal of Marital and Family Therapy*, **12**, 11–13.

Cronbach, L.J. & Snow, R.E. (1977). *Aptitudes and Instructional Methods*. New York: Irvington.

Dance, K.A. & Neufeld, R.W.J. (1988). Aptitude–treatment interaction research in the clinical setting: a review of attempts to dispel the "patient uniformity" myth. *Psychological Bulletin*, **104**, 192–213.

Dunn, R.L. & Schwebel, A.I. (1995). Meta-analytic review of marital therapy outcome research. *Journal of Family Psychology*, **9**, 58–68.

Eddy, J.M., Heyman, R.E. & Weiss, R.L. (1991). An empirical evaluation of the Dyadic Adjustment Scale: exploring the differences between marital "satisfaction" and "adjustment". *Behavioral Assessment*, **13**, 199–220.

Emmelkamp, P.M.G., van Linden van den Heuvell, C., Ruphan, M., Sanderman, R.,

Scholing, A. & Stroink, F. (1988a). Cognitive and behavioral interventions: a comparative evaluation with clinically distressed couples. *Journal of Family Psychology*, **1**, 365–377.

Emmelkamp, P.M.G, van Linden van den Heuvell, C., Sanderman, R. & Scholing, A. (1988b). Cognitive marital therapy: the process of change. *Journal of Family Psychology*, **1**, 385–389.

Greenberg, L.S. & Johnson, S.M. (1986). When to evoke emotion and why: process diagnosis in couples therapy. *Journal of Marital and Family Therapy*, **12**, 19–23.

Hahlweg, K. & Markman, H.J. (1989). Effectiveness of behavioral marital therapy: empirical status of behavioral techniques in preventing and alleviating marital distress. *Journal of Consulting and Clinical Psychology*, **56**, 440–447.

Halford, W.K., Sanders, M.R. & Behrens, B.C. (1993). A comparison of the generalization of behavioral marital therapy and enhanced behavioral marital therapy. *Journal of Consulting and Clinical Psychology*, **61**, 51–60.

Hedges, L.V. & Olkin, I. (1985). *Statistical Methods for Meta-analysis*. San Diego, CA: Academic Press.

Holtzworth-Munroe, A., Jacobson, N.S., DeKlyen, M. & Whisman, M.A. (1989). Relationship between behavioral marital therapy outcome and process variables. *Journal of Consulting and Clinical Psychology*, **57**, 658–662.

Iverson, A. & Baucom, D.H. (1990). Behavioral marital therapy outcomes: alternative interpretations of the data. *Behavior Therapy*, **21**, 129–138.

Jacobson, N.S. (1991). Toward enhancing the efficacy of marital therapy and marital therapy research. *Journal of Family Psychology*, **4**, 373–393.

Jacobson, N.S. & Addis, M.E. (1993). Research on couples and couple therapy: what do we know? Where are we going? *Journal of Consulting and Clinical Psychology*, **61**, 85–93.

Jacobson, N.S. & Gurman, A.S. (1995). *Clinical Handbook of Couple Therapy*. New York: Guilford.

Johnson, S.M. & Greenberg, L.S. (1988). Relating process to outcome in marital therapy. *Journal of Marital and Family Therapy*, **14**, 175–183.

Judd, C.M. & Kenny, D.A. (1981). Process analysis: estimating mediation in treatment evaluations. *Evaluation Review*, **5**, 602–619.

Kazdin, A.E. & Bass, D. (1989). Power to detect differences between alternative treatments in comparative psychotherapy outcome research. *Journal of Consulting and Clinical Psychology*, **57**, 138–147.

Kiresuk, T.J., Smith, A. & Cardillo, J.E. (1994). *Goal Attainment Scaling: Applications, Theory, and Measurement*. Hillsdale, NJ: Erlbaum.

Lebow, J.L. & Gurman, A.S. (1995). Research assessing couple and family therapy. *Annual Review of Psychology*, **46**, 27–57.

Markman, H.J. (1991). Backwards into the future of couples therapy and couples therapy research: a comment on Jacobson. *Journal of Family Psychology*, **4**, 416–425.

O'Leary, K.D. & Turkewitz, H. (1981). A comparative outcome study of behavioral marital therapy and communication therapy. *Journal of Marital and Family Therapy*, **7**, 159–169.

Rosenthal, R. & Rubin, D.B. (1982). A simple, general purpose display of magnitude of experimental effect. *Journal of Educational Psychology*, **74**, 166–169.

Sayers, S.L., Baucom, D.H., Sher, T.G., Weiss, R.L. & Heyman, R.E (1991). Constructive engagement, behavioral marital therapy, and changes in marital satisfaction. *Behavioral Assessment*, **13**, 25–49.

Shadish, W.R., Montgomery, L.M., Wilson, P., Wilson, M.R., Bright, I. & Okwumabua, T. (1993). Effects of family and marital psychotherapies: a meta-analysis. *Journal of Consulting and Clinical Psychology*, **61**, 992–1002.

Smith, M.L., Glass, G.V. & Miller, T.I. (1980). *The Benefits of Psychotherapy*. Baltimore, MD: Johns Hopkins University Press.

Snyder, D.K., Cavell, T.A., Heffer, R.W. & Mangrum, L.F. (1995). Marital and family assessment: a multifaceted, multilevel approach. In R.H. Mikesell, D.D. Lusterman & S.H. McDaniel (eds), *Integrating Family Therapy: Handbook of Family Psychology and Systems Theory* (pp. 163–182). Washington, DC: American Psychological Association.

Snyder, D.K., Mangrum, L.F. & Wills, R.M. (1993). Predicting couples' response to marital therapy: a comparison of short- and long-term predictors. *Journal of Consulting and Clinical Psychology*, **61**, 61–69.

Snyder, D.K. & Wills, R.M. (1991). Facilitating change in marital therapy and research. *Journal of Family Psychology*, **4**, 426–435.

Snyder, D.K., Wills, R.M. & Grady-Fletcher, A. (1991). Long-term effectiveness of behavioral versus insight-oriented marital therapy: a 4-year follow-up study. *Journal of Consulting and Clinical Psychology*, **59**, 138–141.

Spanier, G.B. (1976). Measuring dyadic adjustment: new scales for assessing the quality of marriage and similar dyads. *Journal of Marriage and the Family*, **38**, 15–28.

Whisman, M.A. (1993). Mediators and moderators of change in cognitive therapy of depression. *Psychological Bulletin*, **114**, 248–265.

Whisman, M.A., Dixon, A.E. & Johnson, B. (1995). Therapists' perspectives of couple problems and treatment issues in the practice of couple therapy. Manuscripts submitted for publication.

Chapter 27

A Grand Tour of Future Directions in the Study and Promotion of Healthy Relationships

Howard J. Markman*, W. Kim Halford** and Allan D. Cordova*
*Department of Psychology, University of Denver, CO; and
**Griffith University, Nathan, Queensland, Australia

Readers have now completed a grand tour of the terrain of marriage and couples interventions. When we want to recall the highlights of any significant journey we use snapshots to capture the key points of interest. In a similar vein, we present the following "snapshots" in the form of issues that we "visited" in the book. Many of these issues we need to spend some more time exploring, and we suggest directions for future work. We also describe some areas not covered in the book that we need to visit on future "trips".

COUPLES RESEARCH AND COUPLES THERAPY: SUITABLE TRAVEL COMPANIONS?

The Tension Between Research and Practice

There is a major schism between couples research and clinical practice. Couples researchers often assert that clinicians are not using empirically-based assessment and intervention programs (Markman et al., 1995). For example, researchers emphasize the need for multi-method assessments (e.g. O'Leary, 1977), but clinicians almost universally rely entirely on clinical interviews as their only

Clinical Handbook of Marriage and Couples Interventions. Edited by W. Kim Halford and Howard J. Markman.

source of assessment data (Bougher et al., 1994). On the other hand, clinicians working with couples often assert that the intervention programs tested in research often are not relevant to the complexities of clinical practice (Markman et al., 1995). For example, much couples-based clinical research is conducted with couples in which there is a conjoint commitment by the partners to therapy, and individuals with psychopathology are screened out of research studies. The realities of clinical practice are very different, with frequent presentations by either one partner alone, or with at least one partner suffering from individual problems (Halford & Bouma, this volume). The net effect is that often clinicians are sceptical about the utility of research in guiding practice (Martin, 1989).

Yet it is our experience in working with many mental health professionals that when research results are presented in a clinically relevant manner, practitioners are avid consumers of couples research. We get some of the best questions about research design and clinical practice issues in our workshops, and we are constantly pushed to make our material more user-friendly so that both clinicians and couples can benefit maximally from what we have to say.

One barrier which inhibits the impact of couples research on clinical practice is the over-reliance by researchers on publication as the means of dissemination. The use by clinicians of innovative psychological interventions like couples therapy is determined by a complex of factors. Simply publishing the result of research in scholarly journals does not lead to widespread adoption of innovative psychological interventions (Backer, Liberman & Kuehnel, 1986). Rather, innovations must be broadly consistent with the mission of target professionals and the agencies in which they work, and the procedures to be followed must be clearly explicated in an easily accessible form (e.g. published therapy manuals), if adoption is to occur. Training and supervision are needed if the innovation is to be delivered well, and often this requires a consultant who can assist professionals to adapt innovations to the needs and circumstances of particular service delivery settings.

Building on our experiences presenting research to clinicians, in this book we attempted to bridge some of the gaps between clinicians and researchers. We recruited as authors, to the degree possible, professionals who were comfortable in the worlds of both research and clinical practice. Throughout the book, our authors attempted to draw on the perceptions of both researchers and clinicians (as well as scientist–practitioners). The authors tried to translate the results of research findings into clear-cut guidelines for understanding, assessing, treating and preventing marital problems, as well as to use the wisdom from clinical experience (particularly through the use of case examples) to highlight the phenomena under investigation. We also attempted to address the complexity of many clinical presentations. For example, we included chapters on working with individual partners, the interaction of individual and couple problems, and the broader context within which couples present.

One major future direction for the field is to continue bridging between the realms of research and clinical practice. There is a need to develop opportunities for researchers and clinicians to work (and travel) together as colleagues in designing basic research and intervention studies. There are some changes needed in both research and clinical practice to promote this more effective collaboration.

Changes Needed in Research

The next time we take a journey to visit the field of couples' interactions and couples' therapy from a researcher's perspective, we hope to see progress in at least three areas.

Clinical Significance

Research on couples interventions has relied heavily on controlled trials of interventions. Typically results are presented in terms of the mean scores on standardized measures in intervention and control conditions, and the analysis focuses on the statistical significance of the difference in means scores across conditions. Whilst the controlled trial remains a powerful methodology for establishing whether interventions have an effect, in the last 10 years there has been increasing recognition that demonstrating statistically significant differences between intervention and control conditions is not very informative about the clinical significance of change resulting from interventions. Jacobson & Truax (1991) developed statistical measures of the variability and clinical significance of change resulting from interventions. There is still considerable debate as to how best to assess clinical significance of change (Speer & Greenbaum, 1995). However, these new statistics focus results on the estimation of both the proportion of presenting clients who benefit in a statistically reliable manner from intervention, and the proportion of clients who achieve clinically significant recovery from their distress. When outcome research is evaluated using indices of the variability and clinical significance of change, then the effectiveness of existing couples interventions look modest (Whisman & Snyder, this volume). By focusing research on clinical, rather that statistical, significance of change we increase the relevance of research to clinical practice.

Complicated Cases

In much of the research on couples, researchers have excluded more complex cases from their studies (e.g. screening out couples in which one partner suffers from depression, alcoholism, or drug abuse, from couples therapy outcome studies). Whilst this selectivity reduces subject variability, and enhances the detection of treatment effects, the subject selection procedures also limit the external validity of the study. In nearly 40% of couples presenting to community agencies with relationship problems the man is drinking at hazardous levels (Halford & Osgarby, 1993), and in nearly 50% of presentations the woman scores in the depressed range on the Beck Depression Inventory (Beach, Arias & O'Leary,

1986). There also are substantial correlations between couple relationship problems and adult anxiety disorders (Halford & Bouma, this volume), and between couple problems and childhood behavior problems (Sanders, Floyd & Nicholson, this volume). In other words, it is complicated cases that most clinicians see in practice. To the extent that researchers have screened out these complex cases, the research literature is limited in its clinical applicability.

Treatment Manuals

In order to conduct research studies most investigators define their interventions with treatment manuals. In order to standardize delivery and ensure that the intervention is precisely described, many treatment manuals are highly prescriptive. That is, the number of sessions, and the content and sequencing of sessions, are tightly defined. In clinical practice, no-one we know follows such a predetermined program of therapy. Experienced clinicians achieve better results for their clients when couples therapy is delivered in a clinically flexible manner than if the clinician simply follows a rigid experimental procedure (Jacobson et al., 1989). Clinical flexibility in the Jacobson study included altering the sequencing and emphasis on particular components of therapy. If we add further flexibility by varying the process and content of therapy, based on ideographic assessment and negotiation with the couple, then this might further enhance clinical outcome. (It also is feasible that too much flexibility may be unhelpful. Inexperienced therapists tend to achieve better outcomes in couples therapy when they adhere closely to detailed therapy manuals (Jacobson et al., 1989).) In essence, there is a big gap between therapy as typically implemented in outcome research and the more flexible approaches occurring in clinical practice. The flexibility probably enhances outcome, but we have little knowledge of what the experienced clinicians do that has been described as clinical flexibility.

Any successful therapy program rests on the use of the relationship between the clinician and the therapist. In the research literature there has been considerable criticism of research therapy manuals for their alleged lack of attention to these relationship factors (e.g. Jacobson, 1991). Researchers need to modify their manuals so that they reflect the important experiential and relationship-oriented factors. This will not only make the manuals potentially more accessible to the clinicians but would likely enhance the clinical significance of the programs being tested. In addition, researchers need to write manuals that are user-friendly, that appeal to clinicians so that they want to read them and use the manuals in their practices.

Changes Needed in Practice

When we make a return visit to the field of couples' interaction and therapy from a practice perspective, we also hope to see changes in the following areas of clinical practice.

Training Models

Our training models are not keeping up with the results of research or the clinical complexities of problems in the community. For example, most couples therapists trained in adult-oriented programs and have little, if any, experience with children. Yet, the majority of couples seeking help have children, and often children are integral to the presenting problem. A more family-oriented perspective needs to be taken. Other training models focus on training in systems-oriented interventions including couples and families, yet devote little time and attention to training in individual psychopathology. Once again, the clinical realities are that many couples and families do come in with individual problems. Many therapists trained in a more systems-oriented perspective lack the background needed to assess and treat individually-oriented problems. Finally, there are many people who are trained in individually-oriented therapy but receive little training in systems-oriented approaches. Despite the absence of training in family work, clinicians wind up seeing couples because relationship problems are so common among people seeking psychological services. Thus, more attention needs to be given these important, yet complicated, training issues.

One potential solution to the problems raised above, in addition to modifying training programs, is to require continuing education programs for therapists who typically see couples and families. These continuing education programs can incorporate up-to-date research findings and enable practitioners to augment the training received in their graduate programs. For example, there is remarkable variability from state to state in the USA in terms of requirements for continuing education, and we would like to see some uniform practices established.

Routine Evaluation of Outcomes for Couples-based Services

In most Western countries the services provided for couples are not evaluated in any routine or systematic manner. For example, in Australia surveys of couples who attend either couples therapy or premarital preparation programs show there is no routine, systematic evaluation of services beyond simply collecting statistics on who accesses services (Wolcott & Glezer, 1989). In Germany a recent evaluation of couple counselling services also found no routine evaluation of efficacy. When evaluation of community services for couples has been conducted there is a high level of dissatisfaction with couple therapy services (Seligman, 1995).

In mental health service delivery across different countries a variety of factors has led to increased routine evaluation of services. For example, in the USA cost-containment pressures have led to the development of managed care schemes in which development of management plans is required. Potentially this can lead to greater accountability and evaluation of services. In Australia the National Mental Health Strategy designed to improve care for people with severe metal illness has established a series of standards against which services are routinely evaluated. However, within the domain of couples work there is not the same pressure to evaluate service delivery. Hopefully, we will see the development of routine evaluation of services within the diverse systems of intervention delivery.

From Gown to Town: Travelling off the Beaten Path of Laboratory Research

The majority of intervention programs described in this book were developed and tested in university research settings. We believe that establishing the efficacy of an intervention in a university setting is only the beginning, rather than the end, of a clinical research program. Ultimately, programs must be tested in a variety of community settings and shown to impact upon the lives of couples in order to conclude that we have effective interventions. The current volume is an attempt to make the available research more accessible to practitioners. Research on how to promote the adoption of innovative couples interventions is needed.

In addition, as noted in many of the chapters, our vision for services provided to couples extends beyond mental health professionals to include clergy and family practitioners. This is particularly true of preventive interventions where the goal is to keep happy couples happy. Couples typically encounter the helping professions in the normal course of development and transition periods; these are ideal times for interventions because couples are generally more accepting of change, and more motivated to participate in intervention programs. For example, in a new study, the first author and his colleagues are assessing the extent to which we can disseminate a divorce prevention program (Prevention and Relationship Enhancement Program, PREP; Markman, Stanley & Blumberg, 1994), found to be effective in university settings, to religious organizations. We choose religious organizations because in the USA 75% of first marriages take place in religious settings, and many clergy are already committed to offering premarital counselling programs. However, traditional premarital counselling programs tend to provide information to couples, rather than teach skills. In contrast, the research-based PREP approach endeavors to help couples handle differences when they emerge. In this new study, we will assess couples in terms of relationship functioning and stability, after they have been counselled by clergy who were trained to deliver the PREP approach. They will be compared to couples who receive traditional premarital counselling, as well as to those who received the PREP program as delivered in a university-based setting.

In the future, as tests of couples' intervention programs move along the continuum from research setting to implementation in relevant community settings, and ultimately to being adopted as part of social programs and social policy, researchers will need to be making important decisions about internal vs. external validity. Issues of internal validity deal with the extent to which changes in couples' behavior can be attributed to a particular intervention. External validity refers to whether or not laboratory findings can be successfully mapped onto other settings. Our view, as the field moves forward, is that internal validity considerations are more important early in the research program, while external validity and generalization are more important later in the program.

PICTURES OF COUPLES ON THEIR JOURNEY TOGETHER

What Should Be in the Action Shot?
What Determines Couple Interaction?

Modern systems theory highlights that all systems are contained within superordinate systems, and at the same time each system is composed of subordinate systems. In order to understand the interactional processes within the couples system we need to attend both to the subordinate systems that make up the couple, and the superordinate systems that provide the context within which the couple function. Yet, many couples researchers and therapists often act as if couples interactions can adequately be understood just at the couples system level. Many of the chapters in this volume have shown how couples interaction is determined by subordinate systems, such as individual factors of personality and various forms of individual pathology. There are also a number of overlapping systems with the couple system, such as the influence that children, friends and work have on marital interaction. Thus, when we look at "pictures" of couples, we must keep in mind that the interaction we observe has multiple determinants and multiple pathways for attempts at change. It cannot be presumed that, because problems are evident at the couples level, that the couples system is the best focus for intervention.

In using a wider-angle lens through which to view couples interactions, we need to be paying attention to the backdrop of our "photographs", the superordinate systems within which the couples system exists. Several authors in this volume have spoken eloquently about how factors outside the relationship impact upon couples. Sociocultural factors both help define what are seen as the goals of a relationship and provide the social milieu within which couples adapt. For example, the adaptation to parenthood is influenced by the availability of extended family, which in turn is greatly influenced by culture. As another example, Jones & Chao (this volume) in their chapter provide an excellent example of the African-American man who feels socially invisible, and maladaptively becomes aggressive in his relationship to assert his claim on personal power.

As researchers we are intrigued by the extent to which what is known about couple functioning is generalizable outside Western, Judeo-Christian couples. The formation of long-term committed heterosexual couples seems pervasive across cultures. However, the extent to which constructs such as relationship satisfaction are meaningful in other cultures is questionable. The chapters in this book provide just one small step for the field in addressing the variations in relationships across cultures, and many giant steps in this direction are needed in the future.

Do Men and Women Photograph the Same?

Many authors in this volume have concluded that gender influences partners' interaction and relationship satisfaction in meaningful ways. To cite just one example, it has been suggested that the link between perceptions of social support from one's spouse and marital satisfaction is higher for women than for men (Acitelli & Antonucci, 1994; Julien & Markman, 1991). In other words, husbands' supportive behaviors increase wives' satisfaction to a greater extent than wives' supportive behaviors increase husbands' satisfaction. Such findings have prompted speculation that husbands may shape the trajectory and outcome of the marital relationship more than wives do (Acitelli & Antonucci, 1994). Yet other studies and analyses (Julien, Arellano & Turgeon, this volume) present a more complex picture of the way in which gender is associated with satisfaction and relationship functioning over time. In other words, while it is generally accepted that gender is probably important to consider, there is no consensus among researchers regarding precisely how, why, or if gender directly affects behavior in relationships.

Harking back to our earlier points regarding the value and need for integrating research and clinical considerations in informing relationship interventions, the field would greatly benefit from collaborative efforts among scientists and practitioners to answer fundamental questions about these issues. Are certain intervention approaches more suited for men or women? Do men and women benefit from the same therapeutic/intervention processes and characteristics? How gender-specific do interventions need to be to succeed in strengthening relationships?

Both conventional wisdom and some studies suggest that women are more likely to take advantage of services for couples than are men. For example, in a recent survey, women were twice as likely as men to endorse the need for mandatory premarital counselling or mandatory divorce counselling as a way of strengthening families (Wentz, 1996). Many interpret this as indicating that women are more dedicated or committed to relationships than men. However, it may be that men are just more likely to want to work out personal issues on their own, compared to women. One might compare this to the conventional wisdom that men are more likely to try to find destinations on their own rather than ask someone for directions as compared to women. Thus, it may be important to increase efforts to communicate to men that seeking out services for relationship problems is a sign of strength rather than weakness (just as stopping at a service station to get directions is a sign of wisdom, rather than failure). Yet in and of itself, simply telling men it is alright to seek help is unlikely to be effective.

For example, for some males, seeking the services of a professional for relationship problems connotes in-depth, soul-searching discussions in front of a stranger, an airing of the partners' collective dirty laundry. For others, the stigma lies in seeing a "shrink" of any sort ("If I'm seeing a psychologist, something awful must be wrong with me . . ."). Finally, for others—like the man who would sooner run out of gas than pull off the highway and ask for directions—getting help for relationship struggles represents defeat and weakness. We should note that it is not only possible but quite likely that *all* of these beliefs may be operating for some men (and of course, for some women, too).

Efforts should be made to educate both men and women about the benefits of psychoeducational and short-term approaches to relationship difficulties, in a style that is likely to appeal to both sexes. This would require a thoughtful approach that is mindful of the internal "baggage" partners might carry regarding what it means to seek help. Educating men and women can help to dispel misconceptions about couples interventions by specifying exactly what is involved (e.g. teaching rules and skills for communicating, enhancing the sensual/ sexual parts of one's relationship, etc.), as well as specifying what is *not* involved (e.g. "touchy-feely" group disclosures, dream analysis, etc.). Through this type of approach, men as well as women may feel more comfortable participating in couples interventions, having a clear understanding of the potential benefits of participating, and a sense of the tools they will use in achieving those gains.

THE DESTINATIONS OF COUPLES' JOURNEYS: IMPLICATIONS FOR INTERVENTION

Just as we must know our final destination when embarking on a trip, we must know the ultimate goals for couples who are journeying together. Without a destination, an itinerary is meaningless; without well-defined goals for couples, an intervention plan is purposeless. Thus, it is imperative that we consider the goals we are trying to reach and recognize those which we would like to reach but cannot at this point.

The Limits of Relationship Satisfaction

As prevention- and intervention-oriented professionals, helping couples to enhance their relationships is among our primary goals. However, focusing only on relationship satisfaction is ill-advised in creating effective intervention approaches for couples. Two main considerations limit the reliance on satisfaction as the sole, monolithic guiding principle in couples' intervention: confusion over the construct of relationship satisfaction, and the importance of assessing individual well-being.

Confusion over the Construct

Among professionals, it is not always clear what is meant by "relationship satisfaction". In part, this may be a result of the fact that clinicians rarely rely upon standardized assessment tools in determining a couple's level of relationship satisfaction (for further discussion of this issue, see "Assessing Assessment", below). Further, when such tools are utilized, there is little uniformity across clinicians in which tools are employed. Therefore, when considering satisfaction, it is important to operationalize clearly what is meant by the term. For example, one can define satisfaction in different *areas* of the relationship (e.g. sex, communication, perceived attainment of financial goals), or as a *global* feeling about the relationship and at different *times* in the relationship. The issue of timing is an especially important one, as too often psychological terms are reified and taken for immutable, easily identifiable entities.

Changes occur in relationship satisfaction over time, although the nature of these changes is debated. Researchers variously propose that satisfaction gradually increases or gradually decreases over time, while others suggest that satisfaction starts high, decreases, and then increases again (i.e. satisfaction is best described by a U-shaped curve (Anderson, Russel & Schuum, 1983; Rollins & Cannon, 1974)). The decline of relationship satisfaction in the middle period of relationships has been associated with spouses' transition to parenthood (Belsky, Lang & Huston, 1986; Cowan et al., 1985; Ruble et al., 1988) and children's transition into adolescence, although other researchers challenge this association (see Sanders et al., this volume).

Whilst the precise nature of developmental changes that occur in couples' relationships is debatable, clinical experience suggests that developmental changes are important. For example, couples have distinctive concerns and issues at various time-points throughout their relationship; the issues and concerns of newly-weds are qualitatively different from those of new parents, empty-nesters or seniors. Further, scores on satisfaction measures vary in meaning as a function of development stage. For example, a score of 110 on the widely used Dyadic Adjustment Scale for a couple planning marriage will place the couple below the 30th percentile of engaged couples, while, the same score of 110 for the same couple when married 10 years would place them in the top 40% of 10-year married couples on relationship satisfaction. Further, as noted in the Dickson chapter (this volume), elderly partners likely answer these inventories differently than younger partners.

Need to Assess Individual Well-being

The construct of relationship satisfaction also is limited by the recognition that individual partners' well-being is sometimes eclipsed by a predominant focus on the couple. Therapists can (and do) address individuals' concerns in the context of marital sessions (see discussion of the locus of couples intervention, below). Certainly, just as a relationship as a whole can be satisfied or dissatisfied, so can individual partners. Further, sometimes the needs of one partner are being met to a much greater degree than those of the other partner. In circumstances like these, a measure of global relationship satisfaction could mask the distress of a mate who is suffering in silence. Additionally, individual partners can be experiencing more severe symptoms of distress and psychopathology which, unless identified and treated, will seriously undermine any attempts to buoy a couple's sinking relationship.

Picking the Right Lens to Bring Affairs and Abuse into Focus

In this book we have featured two promising new approaches to treating affairs and spouse abuse with couple-oriented programs. As noted in the assessment section, affairs and abuse are typically not revealed by partners. Thus, therapists who want to know about the existence of affairs and abuse need to ask partners directly, either in individual interviews or in confidential self-report inventories. We recommend that couples' therapists routinely assess for affairs and abuse, and have a plan ready to implement if either abuse or an affair is revealed. Our recommendation is to use the approaches described in this book (see chapter by Glass & Wright, this volume; Heyman & Neidig, this volume).

How to respond to detected abuse is a particularly contentious issue. As Heyman & Neidig (this volume) note, little has been done to evaluate systematically different approaches to stopping abuse. One clear research funding in the area of abuse is that there are different subtypes of abuse (Holtzworth-Munroe & Stuart, 1994). We need to build on the insights offered by Straus & Gelles (1990) concerning the inherent tensions in the abuse field between advocates of individual treatment vs. couples treatment. Advocates of individual approaches are usually working with battered women in shelters or battering husbands who are in the criminal justice system, while advocates of couples-oriented approaches are basing interventions on research with community samples that reveal that both men and women are engaged in aggression (although women suffer more psychologically since they are in more danger).

Although academic and political debates regarding intervention approaches have their place, we need to redouble our efforts to develop programs to stop violence and decrease philosophical arguments in the field about which approach to use. Currently many professionals suggest that conjoint treatment is not recommended for serious violence. As reported in the Heyman & Neidig chapter (this volume), couples approaches do seem useful for mild to moderate aggression, which make up the majority of cases. However, we don't know about the efficacy of couples-oriented approaches for treating more severe violence. In fact, for some abusers, perhaps psychological interventions are not a good idea and incarceration may be the best intervention.

We strongly believe that if couples are staying together (and battered women frequently say they love their partners and do not want to leave), some form of couples work is needed, along with individual programs. Again, the point is if couples are staying together (despite our best advice to leave), it is our ethical obligation to help them work together to have a non-violent relationship—and doing this with only individual treatment is unlikely to provide the entire solution. Finally, work is needed on blending programs that use individual approaches to dealing with violent partners, with couples-oriented programs.

Is this Trip Worth It?: to Divorce or Not to Divorce?

One of the thorniest issues facing the field is the question of outcome of couples interventions. As we have been emphasizing throughout this section, we must ask, "What are the goals of couples intervention? Is it to save the marriage or is it to help couples who decide to divorce achieve a low-conflict divorce? Is it to promote marital satisfaction or individual satisfaction? What happens when the relationship improves but one spouse's level of depression increases as well?" While there are calls for assessing multiple domains of individual and couple functioning when assessing the impact of preventive and treatment interventions, there is also the issue of what defines success in relationship therapy.

This issue has become very clear in the USA with the recent release of a consumer satisfaction survey by *Consumer Reports* (Seligman, 1995). This magazine has its readers complete a survey every year, and their survey recently asked about satisfaction with psychotherapy, including marital therapy. The results were very positive in terms of the effects of psychotherapy from the consumers' point of view. However, consumers expressed less satisfaction with couples counselling than any other form of therapy. From one perspective, this makes the field of couples counselling look ineffective. However, when one thinks about the goals of couples therapy, it actually makes sense that there will be less satisfaction from the consumers' point of view. Often one, or sometimes both, partners in couples therapy are using the therapy as a way of exiting the relationship—leaving the hurt spouse on the therapist's doorstep. Some marital therapists describe how a spouse who is interested in leaving the relationship often brings in the other spouse in the hope that the therapist will help wean the more committed spouse from the marriage and ease the break-up of the relationship.

In a survey of therapists that the first author and his colleagues conducted with practitioners in Colorado in the late 1980s (Stanley, Lobitz & Markman, 1988), couples therapists were asked to indicate the percentage of couples who were significantly improved or not improved, how many of the couples seen in the practice were still together, and how many decided to end their relationship. The results indicated that about 33% of the relationships ended in separation or divorce. Interestingly, the therapists rated 80% of these relationships that ended in divorce as a successful outcome. The *Consumer Reports* survey suggests that this 80% probably did not rate the therapy as a success from their own perspective (Seligman, 1995).

Future research clearly needs to address the challenging issues involved in evaluating outcomes of couples intervention. We recommend using not only objective (e.g. communication skills) and subjective (e.g. relationship satisfaction) measures of couple functioning, but also measures of individual functioning (e.g. depression), and client and therapists' perceptions of desired goals and outcomes related to these goals. For many partners their preferred goal may be a satisfying, stable relationship, but a low-conflict separation might be preferable to an acrimonious separation.

Enhancement of Parent–Child Relationships

While we often think of our clients or research participants primarily as partners in romantic relationships, it is important to keep in mind that most of them are also parents. We know from the research (as well as personal experience) that one's functioning as a romantic partner can be greatly influenced by one's functioning as a parent, and *vice versa*. From a systemic perspective, there is a dynamic interplay between the marital dyad and the parent–child sub-system, each one affecting and being affected by the other (as well as by the myriad other subsystems that we may consider, including, for example, the sibling sub-system). Many parents experiencing marital relationship difficulties are also experiencing parent–child relationship difficulties. There has been a great deal of research on how marital conflict can "spill over" into parent–child relationships (e.g. Easterbrooks & Emde, 1988; Engfer, 1988; Erel & Burman, 1995).

In conceptualizing and designing couples' interventions, it is important to enhance parent–child relationships. One approach that is common to many couples' interventions, including the PREP program, is teaching couples to deliberately schedule in time that is uninterrupted by outside distractions (including children). We also encourage scheduling quality parent–child time, and not just for couples who are already seeing the worrisome signs of an unhappy parent–child relationship. Rather, such a preventive approach can be used to enhance an already satisfying, healthy parent–child relationship.

Enhancement of Individual Well-being

As the reader may have gathered by now, a unifying theme throughout this chapter (and throughout this book) is balancing couple- and individual-level needs. In keeping with this theme, in addition to focusing increased efforts on enhancing the quality of parent–child relationships, we also suggest that a broader goal of couples' intervention should be to deepen individuals' well-being. Declaring this as a goal has implications for interventive approaches with couples. First, it suggests that interventions will need to be geared toward helping individual partners assess the degree to which their needs are being met, both in and outside of the relationship. Within this framework, interventions may need to be broadened in scope to consider extra-relationship sources of support for partners. Setting individual well-being as a goal also implies that, in order for the couple to achieve a sense of health and well-being, the constituent partners must be independently healthy, happy and satisfied.

ASSESSING ASSESSMENT: DEVELOPING BETTER TRAVEL GUIDES

As noted in several chapters, clinicians often rely on clinical interviews as the major source of assessment data. One recent survey revealed that approximately

95% of clinicians only use clinical interviews for assessing couples (Bougher et al., 1994). In the assessment section of the book, we described other assessment tools that clinicians can easily incorporate in their practice, as well as a framework that integrates use of self-report instruments with clinical interviews. These empirically validated assessment tools not only enhance treatment planning but also can be used to evaluate treatment effectiveness. In the future we would like to see increased use of assessment instruments by clinicians and increased opportunities for practitioners actively to collaborate in the development of new and improved assessment tools.

WHERE ARE WE TAKING THE ACTION SHOTS? LOCUS OF COUPLES INTERVENTION

As noted in many chapters in the book, couples' problems do not happen in a vacuum; other levels of analysis and wider contexts need to be considered in terms of both assessing and treating relationship problems.

We need to examine adult and child problems and psychopathology that accompany marital problems, and which may be causally related or antecedents of relationship problems. At the very least, we recommend that marital researchers collect information on these other domains, even if they are not the target of the intervention or the focus of the study, so that questions can be asked concerning the co-occurrence of individual, couple and child problems. Moreover, intervention researchers should study the variety of methods practitioners employ in treating the distressed couples who have pressing individual problems. Our chapters identify how professionals can work at multiple levels ranging from the individual (Bennun, this volume), the couple (most chapters), the family (Sanders et al., this volume) and at the organizational level (e.g. Thompson, this volume). These are important preliminary steps. Nevertheless, we feel that future research should strive to capture the complexities that clinicians face each day as a result of the comorbidity of individual- and couple-level difficulties.

For example, currently, there seem to be three major therapeutic models that practitioners use to deal with the co-occurrence of individual and couple problems. First, a therapist sees couples for their relationship problems, and individual problems are handled by a different therapist. This situation often emerges when a person is in individual therapy when relationship problems arise. The therapist for the individual then recommends the couple be seen for their relationship problems with a different therapist. Under these conditions, the two therapists will usually maintain contact with each other to make certain that they are not working at cross purposes. In the second model the couple's therapist also serves as the therapist for the individual problems of one or both clients. This may raise problems of confidentiality, although many successful clinicians find that this model works for them. The third model occurs when individuals are dealt with in the context of couple therapy; at times the focus is on one individual and the partner is an active participant in the process. Links are made as to how the individual issues affect the couple and their problems and *vice versa*. Many clinicians find this model is valuable because it includes the other partner in understanding and working on solutions concerning the individual problems.

Waiting for the Perfect "Photo Opportunity": the Timing of Interventions

Developmental psychologists have long acknowledged that there are critical periods of the lifespan when psychological changes occur at a more rapid rate than at other times. Crisis intervention theorists have built on this principle by suggesting that during times of rapid change involving both predictable and unpredictable life events (e.g. planning marriage, birth of a child, illness, loss of a child, divorce), individuals, couples and families seem to be more open to interventions. Interventions delivered at these critical times have the potential to have more impact. For example, in new research the second author and his colleagues are working with women recently diagnosed with cancer, with the objective of assisting the women and their spouses/partners to work together to cope. Yet, research to date generally has neglected the issue of when interventions are delivered so that they are optimally effective. This is an important agenda for future research.

Building on the work of developmental psychologists, crisis intervention theorists also argue for delivering interventions as early in the course of the development of problems as possible. The implicit assumption is that early intervention is most effective. While certainly reasonable, this assumption generally remains untested. For example, are couples really more amenable to change during transition periods than during other periods of time? To our knowledge, there has not been a study that has tested this key assumption. Similarly, do three sessions of skill training during the transition to marriage have greater ability to prevent later problems than three sessions of skill training when a couple is on the brink of divorce?

Booster Sessions

One major finding from the work of the first author and his colleagues has been that the effects of successful interventions can attenuate over time. For example, the effects of the PREP program on satisfaction have been found to be significant in the early years of marriage, but to gradually become less marked over time (Markman et al., 1993). One possible solution to this is the use of booster sessions, sessions that review and help couples brush up on the specific skills they were originally taught.

Currently, we are beginning to explore this issue through the religious organization study described in this chapter. A subset of couples in the two PREP conditions will attend booster sessions at yearly intervals, following their initial training in PREP. Couples in the booster session condition will participate in 2-hour sessions similar in format to regular PREP sessions. Leaders will present short lecturettes reviewing major points from the program, and couples will be asked to review and practice skills learned in the session. They will review the relevance of the skills to recent life changes and problems and will practice their skills that may have begun to get "rusty".

WHAT MAKES FOR AN EFFECTIVE INTERVENTION PICTURE? THE CONTENT OF INTERVENTIONS

Revisiting the Role of Non-specific Relationship Factors

In much the same way that clinicians have widely ignored assessment tools, researchers/program developers have widely ignored non-specific relationship factors in developing and evaluating couples interventions (see Whisman & Snyder, this volume, for an exception). Rare studies that have examined the influence of such factors have shown that relationship qualities such as warmth and genuineness contribute substantially to the effectiveness of behaviorally-oriented interventions (Alexander et al., 1976).

Collaborative Set

In addition to focusing on non-specific relationship variables in the future, we want to emphasize the importance in future research of the need to engage both partners in a collaborative relationship-focused approach to couples intervention. We have noted that this is particularly difficult to do in couples therapy, where often partners tend to blame each other for the source of their relationship difficulties. On the other hand, engaging a couple in a more collaborative approach may be easier with early interventions where relationship difficulties do not currently exist, or are less severe than are typically seen in a therapeutic practice.

Engaging couples in a collaborative set is particularly difficult when the presenting problem is an individual problem, rather than a relationship problem. For example, when the couple present stating that the husband is "alcoholic", and relationship problems are evident, the therapist must work extra hard to develop a collaborative set and not focus *exclusively* on the alcohol problem (see chapters by O'Farrell & Rotunda; Halford & Bouma, both in this volume, for how to deal with this particular issue). In a similar vein, when a couple comes in with their child with a presenting problem, shifting focus to the couple and the family with the child is often a tricky clinical challenge (see chapter by Sanders, Markie-Dadds & Nicholson, this volume, on how to deal with this challenge). Further research is needed on when partners are likely to be responsive to, and benefit from, couples-focused interventions.

Focus on Skills Training

The final point we want to make about the content of couples' intervention has to do with the focus on skills training. The research seems to indicate that skills-based approaches have more positive impact on couples than any other kinds of approaches. The evidence is particularly strong in the prevention area (see chapter by Van Widenfeldt et al., this volume). However, we are much less certain about what processes mediate change. Evidence about the extent to which changes in targeted skills and cognitions mediate change in more global relationship satisfaction is at best mixed. For example, studies by Baucom and Epstein (1990) and Halford, Sanders & Behrens (1993) have found little association between these cognitive and behavioral changes and changes in broader relationship satisfaction. However, a paper by Sayers (1991) provided some evidence for covariation between communication skills, acquisition and improvements in global relationship satisfaction. This points to the need to do more research on mediators and moderators of change, as was articulately expressed in the chapter by Whisman & Snyder (this volume).

PUTTING ALL THE PICTURES TOGETHER: HOW DO WE GO ABOUT DECREASING DIVORCE RATES NOW THAT EVERYONE WANTS TO JOIN US?

There is an emerging consensus from the most liberal to the most conservative groups that satisfying marriages are good and divorce is often bad. However, there is great divergence of opinion regarding how to protect and preserve marriages. Suggestions range from requiring premarital counselling in order to get a marriage license, to toughening divorce laws, to mandating marriage counselling or parenting programs (if children are involved) before granting a divorce.

The well-intended movement to mandate premarital interventions is disturbing for a number of reasons. First, many segments of society are averse to increasing governmental intervention in family life. Mandating premarital intervention programs would be a major step in this direction. Second, mandating premarital counselling would be a bureaucratic nightmare. Premarital counselling certificates would have to be devised, and there would be endless debates concerning whose program is best, which programs qualify, etc. Third, premarital counselling has been generally housed in religious organizations; moving this service to state auspices and creating a bureaucracy around it would be contrary to most prevailing intervention principles on how to put important programs into the hands of those who need them most. Finally, there are virtually no data on the effectiveness of mandated programs; most of the data on couples' interventions are based on studies in which couples have volunteered to participate. Clearly, it would be very important to evaluate the extent to which mandated programs, if and when they were instituted, are effective over which populations, as delivered by whom, at what period of time, etc.

However, we suggest an alternative to mandating services to couples: as public policy-makers and as a society, we should make every effort to increase couples' motivation to voluntarily participate in relationship-strengthening programs. As noted in this book, there are a variety of such programs that have been successful in teaching couples skills which seem to be crucial for having successful relationships. Such an effort would require a national consensus on the importance of providing such tools to couples. Further, it would necessitate an intensive public health campaign involving a coalition of helping professions, national and local media, and politicians, working together to disseminate the information that such programs are available, and ensuring that these programs are accessible at little or no cost.

Our optimism for the potential success of such a public health campaign is fuelled from previous experiences in this area. In most Western countries, when a consensus was reached on the negative effects of smoking, massive public health campaigns were mounted and there was a dramatic decrease in smoking. Now that we have achieved some success in changing smoking habits, we would like to see attention focused on altering relationship habits. In order to achieve such goals, we must change frames of reference from a clinical perspective to a public health perspective.

A Public Health Perspective

Couples interventions vary enormously in terms of the targeting, timing and intensity of interventions. Targeting refers to which people within the population are selected for recruitment into intervention efforts. Timing refers to the point or points during the relationship life cycle at which intervention is attempted. Intensity of the intervention refers to the level of contact between the participants and the providers of the intervention.

Targeting, Timing, and Intensity of Interventions

There are four broad intervention strategies in the public health literature which guide how to address a problem of high prevalence like relationship distress: primary, secondary and tertiary prevention, and therapy. Primary prevention involves targeting all couples for intervention in an attempt to lower the total prevalence of the problem across the entire population. Secondary prevention involves targeting groups at high risk for marital problems and selectively providing them with intervention, again with the aim of reducing total prevalence of marital distress. Tertiary prevention targets couples with at least some existing difficulties, with the goal of lowering the negative impact of the problem and reducing recurrence. Therapy involves treatment of existing relationship distress.

Given the high prevalence of marital distress, it would seem that almost all couples potentially might benefit from marital distress prevention. However, the skills training approach we have been advocating currently involves four to six sessions with highly skilled trainers. Given limited resources, this approach to primary prevention may be too expensive. One possibility is to conduct primary prevention approach only using interventions which accumulate minimal costs per couple, such as mass education through media sources.

For example, as noted above, the media could be used to educate individuals about relationship-enhancing behaviors, as well as to model healthy ways of dealing with relationship conflicts and stressors. One recent example of such a campaign has been the work of Sanders and his colleagues in New Zealand, where the major television stations have joined forces with Sanders to produce a series of television shows based on his successful parenting program. Although frequently used in other preventive and health promotion efforts, there is no research on the efficacy of such an approach in promoting healthy relationships (Van Widenfelt et al., this volume).

Secondary prevention requires identification of relationships that are at high risk for subsequent marital distress. As noted earlier, certain behavioral and cognitive characteristics do define high risk (e.g. poor communication skills as assessed from behavioral coding of a conflictual discussion), but assessment of these variables is time-consuming and not suitable for a mass screening program. However, there are a number of sociodemographic variables which do identify high risk for marital distress that are easier to assess (such as parental divorce, and being under 21 when getting married) (Van Widenfelt, 1995).

Finally, tertiary prevention involves intervention with relationships that are already showing signs of distress. The earlier in the process of relationship deterioration that intervention is provided, the better the outcome is likely to be. For that reason we suggest early intervention with couples is desirable. It may be that the current mode of therapy delivery discourages some couples from seeking help. If interventions were provided which were less time-consuming and easier to access, then greater service utilization might occur. For example, there are a large number of popular books on marriage. Few of these books are based on established research findings on the determinants of marital satisfaction, and there is no evidence that any of the books actually produce change. However, this does not mean popular books cannot have any effects. In on-going work, Sanders, Markie-Dadds & Bor (1995) have shown that a popularly written book on parenting can help many parents with common childhood behavior problems. The effects of the book can be increased with access to a professional for a small number of individualized sessions, which can be provided by telephone (Sanders, Markie-Dadds & Nicholson, this volume). A similar program may be effective with couples' problems.

To date the prevention of marital distress literature has paid little attention to establishing optimum times to intervene, yet this may make a critical difference to the uptake and effects of prevention efforts (Coie et al., 1993). Couples typically progress through a series of normative transitions, such as moving in and living together, getting married, having children, children entering school, the departure of children from the family home, and retirement from paid employment. Most couples also experience other less predictable changes, such as major illness or injury, death of a close family member, unemployment, re-entry to the work force after a break away, and changes in the place of residence (Van Widenfelt et al., in press). All these transitions represent periods of change characterized by specific tasks and challenges, and research demonstrates that couples experience more difficulties and are more vulnerable to the development of distress during these critical periods (Markman et al., 1982, 1986). However, these transitional periods also represent an opportunity for positive change when the developing relationship system is adapting to transitions.

Although there is limited empirical evidence to guide our choice of optimal intervention strategies for the prevention of marital distress, a combination of primary prevention using minimal interventions and secondary prevention using brief skills-based interventions is most likely to be effective. Traditional reliance on couples therapy is ineffective, both because therapy has significant limitations in its effectiveness with severely distressed couples and because few couples elect to present for therapy. The transitions to marriage, remarriage, parenthood, retirement and adjustment to major illness all seem to be times at which couples are receptive and can benefit from preventive efforts.

AFTER THE END OF THE JOURNEY: MAKING A DIFFERENCE WITH COUPLES INTERVENTIONS

So now we end this journey through the world of couples relationships. The field of research on marriage has many gaps, and there is much more work to be done. However, looking back on all the places the journey has taken us, we are struck by how much we already know about couples relationships. One real challenge is to apply the existing knowledge to greater effect in promoting better relationships. It is our hope that many of the readers of this book will join us in this journey.

REFERENCES

Acitelli, L.K. & Antonucci, T.C. (1994). Gender differences in the link between marital support and satisfaction in older couples. *Journal of Personality and Social Psycholgy*, **67**, 688–698.

Alexander, J.F., Barton, C., Schiavo, S. & Parsons, B.V. (1976). Systems–behavioral intervention with families of delinquents: therapist characteristics, family behavior, and outcome. *Journal of Consulting and Clinical Psychology*, **44**, 656–664.

Anderson, S.A., Russell, C.S. & Schuum, W.R. (1983). Perceived marital quality and family life-cycle categories: a further analysis. *Journal of Marriage and the Family*, **45**, 127–139.

Backer, T.E., Liberman, R.P. & Kuehnel, T.G. (1986). Dissemination and adoption of innovative psychosocial interventions. *Journal of Consulting and Clinical Psychology*, **49**, 460–464.

Beach, S.H.R., Arias, I. & O'Leary, K.D. (1986). The relationship of marital satisfaction and social support to depressive symptomatology. *Journal of Psychopathology and Behavioural Assessment*, **8**, 305–316.

Belsky, J., Lang, M. & Huston, T.L. (1986). Sex typing and division of labor as determinants of marital change across the transition to parenthood. *Journal of Personality and Social Psychology*, **50**, 517–522.

Bougher, S.R., Hayes, S.F., Bubenzer, D.L. & West, J.D. (1994). Use of standardised assessment instruments by marital and family therapists: a survey. *Journal of Marital and Family Therapy*, **20**, 69–75.

Coie, J.D., Watt., N.F., West, S.G., Hawkins, J.D., Asarnow, J.A., Markman, H.J., Ramey, S.L., Shure, M.B. & Long, B. (1993). The science of prevention: a conceptual framework and some directions for a national research program. *American Psychologist*, **48**, 1013–1022.

Easterbrooks, M.A. & Emde, R.N. (1988). Marital and parent–child relationships: the role of affect in the family system. In R.A. Hinde & J. Stevenson-Hinde (eds), *Relationships Within Families: Mutual Influences* (pp. 83–103). Oxford: Clarendon.

Engfer, A. (1988). The interrelatedness of marriage and the mother–child relationship. In R.A. Hinde & J. Stevenson-Hinde (eds), *Relationships Within Families: Mutual Influences* (pp. 104–118). Oxford: Clarendon.

Erel, O. & Burman, B. (1995). The interrelatedness of marital relations and parent–child relations: a meta-analytic review. *Psychological Bulletin*, **188**, 108–132.

Halford, W.K. & Osgarby, S.M. (1993). Alcohol abuse in clients presenting with marital problems. *Journal of Family Psychology*, **6**, 1–11.

Halford, W.K., Sanders, M.R. & Behrens, B.C. (1993). Generalization of behavioural marital therapy and enhanced behavioural marital therapy. *Journal of Consulting and Clinical Psychology*, **61**, 51–60.

Holtzworth-Munroe, A. & Stuart, G.L. (1994). Typologies of male batterers: three subtypes and the differences among them. *Psychological Bulletin*, **116**, 476–497.

Jacobson, N.S. (1991). Behavioral versus insight-oriented marital therapy: labels can be misleading. *Journal of Consulting and Clinical Psychology*, **59**, 142–145.

Jacobson, N.S., Schmaling, K.B., Holzworth-Munroe, A., Katt, J.L., Wood, L.F. & Follette, V.M. (1989). Research-structured versus clinically flexible versions of social learning based marital therapy. *Behaviour Research and Therapy*, **27**, 173–180.

Jacobson, N.S. & Traux, P. (1991). Clinical significance: a statistical approach to defining meaningful change in psychotherapy research. *Journal of Consulting and Clinical Psychology*, **59**, 12–21.

Julien, D. & Markman, H.J. (1991). Social support and social networks as determinants of individual and marital outcomes. *Journal of Social and Personal Relationships*, **8**, 549–568.

Markman, H.J., Floyd, F. & Dickson-Markman, F. (1982). Toward a model of the Prediction and prevention of marital and family distress and dissolution. In S. Duck (ed.), *Personal Relationships 4:* Dissolving Personal Relationships. London: Academia Press.

Markman, H.J., Renick, M.J., Floyd, F.J., Stanley, S.M. & Lewis, H.C. (1993). Preventing marital distress through communication and conflict management training: a 4- and 5-year follow-up. *Journal of Consulting and Clinical Psychology*, **61**, 70–77.

Markman, H.J., Floyd, F.J., Stanley, S.M. & Lewis, H.C. (1986). Prevention. In N.S. Jacobson & A.S. Gurman (eds), *Clinical Handbook of Marital Therapy* (pp. 173–195). New York: Guilford.

Markman, H.J., Leber, B.D., Cordova, A.D. & St. Peters, M. (1995). Behavioral observation and family psychology—strange bedfellows or happy marriage?: Comment on Alexander et al. (1995). *Journal of Family Psychology*, **9**, 371–379.

Markman, H.J., Stanley, S. & Blumberg, S.L. (1994). *Fighting for Your Marriage*. San Francisco: Jossey Bass.

Martin, P.R. (1989). The scientist–practitioner model and clinical psychology: time for a change? *Australian Psychologist*, **24**, 71–92.

O'Leary, K.D. (ed.) (1977). *Assessment of Marital Discord: an Integration for Research and Clinical Practice*. Hillsdale, NJ: Erlbaum.

Rollins, B.C. & Cannon, K.L. (1974). Marital satisfaction over the family life cycle: a re-evaluation. *Journal of Marriage and the Family*, **36**, 271–283.

Ruble, D.N., Fleming, A.S., Hackel, L.S. & Stangor, C. (1988). Changes in the marital relationship during the transition to first time motherhood: effects of violated expectations concerning division of household labor. *Journal of Personality and Social Psychology*, **55**, 78–87.

Sanders, M.R., Markie-Dadds, C. & Bor, W. (1995). Triple P: a multi-level intervention for children at risk for disruptive behavior disorders. Paper presented to the First World Congress of Cognitive and Behaviour Therapies, Copenhagen, Denmark, July.

Seligman, M.E.P. (1995). The effectiveness of psychotherapy: the Consumer Reports study. *American Psychologist*, **50**, 965–974.

Speer, D.C. & Greenbaum, P.C. (1995). Five methods for computing significant individual client change and improvement rates: support for an individual growth curve approach. *Journal of Consulting and Clinical Psychology*, **63**, 1044–1048.

Stanley, S., Lobitz, C. & Markman, H.J. (1988). Marital therapy in Colorado. *Colorado Psychological Association Bulletin*, **May**.

Straus, M.A. & Gelles, R.J. (eds) (1990). *Physical Violence in American Families: Risk Factors and Adaptation to Violence in 8415 Families*. New Brunswick, NJ: Transaction.

Van Widenfeldt, B.M. (1995). *The Prediction and Prevention of Relationship Distress and Divorce*. Nijmegen, The Netherlands: Quickprint.

Wentz, M. (1996). Social policy issues and the family. Unpublished paper, Department of Psychology, University of Denver.

Wolcott, I. & Glazer, H. (1989). *Marriage Counselling in Australia: an Evaluation*. Melbourne: Australian Institute of Family Studies.

Index

Related titles of interest from Wiley...

Brief Therapy with Couples

An Integrative Approach

Maria Gilbert and Diana Shmukler

A concise, practical guide for couples with relationship problems, that relates therapy to the cultural, racial and religious context of relationships, as well as key issues like parenting and same-sex relationships.

Wiley Series in Brief Therapy & Counselling
0-471-96206-6   200pp   1996   Paperback

Handbook of Relational Diagnosis and Dysfunctional Family Patterns

Florence W. Kaslow

Examines the role of diagnosis in couples and family therapy, and offers clinical criteria for diagnosing a broad spectrum of relational disorders and dysfunctional relational patterns.

Wiley Series in Couples & Family Dynamics & Treatment
0-471-08078-0   592pp   1996   Hardback

Infertility

Psychological Issues and Counseling Strategies

Edited by **Sandra R. Leiblum**

Provides an overview of the causes and course of infertility, explores its psychological and relational impact, and examines alternative routes to parenthood.

Wiley Series in Couples & Family Dynamics & Treatment
0-471-12684-5 288pp 1997 Hardback

In-Laws

A Guide to Extended Family Therapy

Gloria Call Horsley

Traces the development of healthy and unhealthy in-law relationships and examines common sources of problems, including over involved in-laws, conflicting family loyalties, socio-cultural differences, illness, and financial/legal issues.

Wiley Series in Couples & Family Dynamics & Treatment
0-471-12914-3 254pp 1995 Hardback

Visit the Wiley Home Page at http://www.wiley.co.uk